1983 Commodity Year Book

EDITORIAL BOARD

Chief Editor
WALTER L. EMERY

Managing Editor
SEYMOUR GAYLINN

Associate Editors
STEPHEN W. COX

MILTON W. JILER

WILLIAM L. JILER

LUCIAN J. WEINER

PREPARED AND PUBLISHED BY

Commodity Research Bureau, Inc.
75 MONTGOMERY ST., JERSEY CITY, N.J. 07302

COPYRIGHT © 1983 BY COMMODITY RESEARCH BUREAU, INC.
All rights reserved. No part of this publication may be reproduced or transmitted in any form, or by any means, without the written permission of the publisher.
ISBN 0-910418-15-2
Library of Congress Catalog Card Number 39-11418

INTRODUCTION

The past year has witnessed some recovery from economic recession; a reduction in the rate of inflation, which at mid-year 1983 had been reflected in, but not matched by, lower interest rates; continued wide fluctuations in currency rates; and record-large supplies of some commodities, which have brought a significant reduction in 1983 intended U.S. acreage planted to some major crops through operation of the "payment-in-kind" and other acreage reduction programs. Inflationary concern remains alive, influenced by huge federal budget deficits and by the prospect that it will be difficult to further stimulate the economy without consequent inflationary pressures.

The foregoing considerations, among others, contributed to the 14 percent increase in the volume of commodities futures trading in 1982 to a record-high 112.4 million contracts.

The constantly shifting supply/demand relationships directly affecting specific commodity prices, and those broad economic and political factors which influence the underlying general commodity price trend, emphasize the importance of relating unfolding developments to past data in analysis of commodity prices. Commodity Year Book 1983 is designed to facilitate such comparisons—through the use of tables, text, and price charts—for the agricultural and industrial commodities, and financial instruments traded on futures exchanges, as well as for many other commodities.

The feature studies in Commodity Year Book 1983 are intended to help the reader to recognize and to take advantage of potentially profitable trading opportunities in these markets.

Our first feature study "Long Term Charts in Commodity Price Forecasting," written by John J. Murphy, covers an often overlooked but important phase of technical analysis. The author illustrates the maxim that "markets move in trends and trends tend to persist." His recommendation that price trend analysis should proceed from the use of long term (monthly and weekly index and specific commodity charts) to the observation of daily price charts, provides a perspective concerning price movement that is valuable not only to the commodity futures trader, but also to corporate commodity purchasing and planning departments. Mr. Murphy heads his own consulting firm, JJM Technical Advisors, which specializes in technical analysis of commodity futures markets, and also conducts courses on this subject at the New York Institute of Finance.

The impact of farm commodity programs on prices can be significant, as demonstrated by the initiation of the USDA's payment-in-kind (PIK) program covering 1983 U.S. wheat, feed grain, cotton, and rice crops. The feature study "The Agriculture and Food Act and Commodity Prices" discusses the potential impact on prices of this legislation which covers the 1982 through 1985 U.S. crops. Emphasis is placed on the influence on cash and futures prices of the price support and target programs, the reduced acreage programs, and the farmer-owned grain reserve. The author, Walter Spilka, Jr. is a grain analyst with Smith Barney, Harris Upham & Co., and was formerly a feed grain analyst with the USDA.

Option trading in T-bond, Gold and World Sugar futures on U.S. commodity exchanges was established only recently, but has considerable promise. (The current most active of these options, the Chicago Board of Trade T-bond options, started October 1, 1982.) William J. Johnson's, feature article, "Introduction to Commodity Options," discusses both the potential and the pitfalls as well as option strategies for this new, exciting trading vehicle, utilizing examples for each of these commodity option markets. Mr. Johnson is president of Reef Points, Inc. of Allentown, Pa., a consulting firm specializing in providing hedge advice to corporations, and is also a past contributor to this publication.

It may seem strange for a commodity publication to feature an article on stock indices and options. However, the distinction between the commodity and stock areas is disappearing with the advent of futures and option trading in stock indices. The very interesting study, "The Stock Index and Options Markets" by H.J. Maidenberg shows how these markets came about and how they may be used. Mr. Maidenberg is well-known as a feature writer on commodity and financial markets for the *New York Times*.

We wish to express our appreciation for the assistance provided us by governmental agencies, various trade associations and publications, and other organizations. We have attempted to list all of these institutions on page 4.

The Editorial Board
May 1983

TABLE OF CONTENTS

PAGE 4 ACKNOWLEDGMENTS
5 THE COMMODITY PRICE TREND
8 LONG TERM CHARTS IN COMMODITY PRICE FORECASTING
23 THE AGRICULTURE AND FOOD ACT AND COMMODITY PRICES
30 INTRODUCTION TO COMMODITY OPTIONS
38 THE STOCK INDEX AND OPTIONS MARKETS
45 COMMODITY FUTURES TRADING ACTIVITY

PAGE			PAGE	
48	ALCOHOL		216	MARGARINE
49	ALUMINUM		217	MEATS
53	ANTIMONY		222	MERCURY
55	APPLES		225	MILK
56	ARSENIC		228	MOLASSES
57	BARLEY		230	MOLYBDENUM
61	BAUXITE		231	NICKEL
62	BEER		232	OATS
63	BISMUTH		238	OLIVE OIL
64	BROILERS		239	ONIONS
66	BURLAP AND JUTE		241	ORANGES AND ORANGE JUICE
68	BUTTER		244	PALM OIL
70	CADMIUM		245	PAPER
71	CASTORBEANS		249	PEANUTS AND PEANUT OIL
72	CATTLE AND CALVES		254	PEPPER
79	CEMENT		256	PETROLEUM
81	CHEESE		262	PLASTICS
83	CHROMITE		264	PLATINUM & GROUP METALS
84	COAL		269	PORK BELLIES
87	COBALT		273	POTATOES
88	COCOA		278	RAPESEED
94	COCONUT OIL AND COPRA		280	RAYON AND OTHER SYNTHETIC FIBERS
96	COFFEE		283	RICE
101	COKE		287	RUBBER
103	COPPER		293	RYE
111	CORN		298	SAFFLOWER
118	CORN OIL		299	SALT
119	COTTON		300	SHEEP AND LAMBS
129	COTTONSEED AND COTTONSEED PRODUCTS		303	SILK
135	CURRENCIES		304	SILVER
138	DISTILLED SPIRITS		309	SOYBEAN MEAL
139	EGGS		313	SOYBEAN OIL
143	ELECTRIC POWER		318	SOYBEANS
145	FERTILIZERS (NITROGEN, PHOSPHATE & POTASH)		325	STOCK INDEX FUTURES (see page 38)
			326	SUGAR
148	FLAXSEED AND LINSEED OIL		335	SULFUR
154	GAS		336	SUNFLOWERSEED & OIL
157	GLASS		337	TALL OIL
158	GOLD		338	TALLOW AND GREASES
163	GRAIN SORGHUMS		340	TEA
165	HARD FIBERS		342	TIN
166	HAY		347	TITANIUM
168	HEATING OIL		349	TOBACCO
172	HIDES AND LEATHER		353	TUNG OIL
176	HOGS		354	TUNGSTEN
181	HONEY		356	TURKEYS
183	INTEREST RATES		358	TURPENTINE AND ROSIN
191	IRON AND STEEL		359	URANIUM
198	LARD		360	VANADIUM
201	LEAD		361	WHEAT AND FLOUR
206	LUMBER AND PLYWOOD		375	WOOL
213	MAGNESIUM		380	ZINC
214	MANGANESE		385	CONVERSION FACTORS

ACKNOWLEDGMENTS

The editors wish to thank the following for source material

Aluminum Association
American Bureau of Metal Statistics
American Gas Association
American Iron and Steel Institute
American Metal Market
American Paper and Pulp Association
American Petroleum Institute
Atomic Industrial Forum, Inc.
Chicago Board of Trade
Chicago Mercantile Exchange
Citrus Associates of the N.Y. Cotton Exch., Inc.
Coffee, Sugar & Cocoa Exch., Inc.
Commodity Exchange, Inc.—N.Y.
Commodity Futures Trading Commission
Edison Electric Institute
Exxon Corp.
F. W. Dodge Corp.
Federal Power Commission
Federal Reserve Board
Futures Industry Association
General Services Administration
Gill & Duffus Ltd.
Glass Container Manufacturers Institute, Inc.
Handy & Harman
International Commercial Exchange
International Cotton Advisory Committee
International Silk Association
International Monetary Market (Chicago)
Kansas City Board of Trade
Media Records, Inc.

MidAmerica Commodity Exchange
Minneapolis Grain Exchange
National Coffee Association of U.S.A., Inc.
New Orleans Commodity Exchange
New York Cotton Exchange
New York Mercantile Exchange
Newsprint Service Bureau
Nuclear Regulatory Commission
Oil World
Portland Cement Association
Rubber Manufacturers Association
Rubber Study Group
Society of the Plastics Industry, Inc.
Tanners' Council of America, Inc.
Tea Council, Inc.
Textile Economics Bureau, Inc.
Textile Organon
United Nations Organization
United States Department of Agriculture
United States Department of Commerce
United States Department of Energy
United States Department of Interior
United States Department of Labor
United States Bureau of Mines
United States Tariff Commission
United States Treasury Department
Winnipeg Commodity Exchange
Wool Services Co.
Zinc Institute, Inc.

THE COMMODITY PRICE TREND

The general commodity price level continued to decline throughout 1982. The Commodity Research Bureau Futures Price Index registered a 4-year low of 225.8 (1967=100) on October 4, 1982—33 percent below its all-time high of 337.6. The Index subsequently posted a modest recovery, helped by an easing of Federal Reserve monetary policy. It ended the year at 234.0, still 8 percent below the year-earlier level. The most significant year-to-year percentage declines were recorded by the Metals group (33 percent), the Imported group (25 percent) and the Industrials group (22 percent).

The CRB (BLS-Formula) Spot Index also trended lower in 1982, posting a 4½-year low of 225.5 on December 21 before ending the year at 227.4 percent of its 1967 base, 9 percent lower than a year earlier. The decline in the Spot Index was paced by the Raw Industrials which registered a year-to-year drop of 15 percent, whereas the Foodstuffs group, which had declined sharply in 1981, was virtually unchanged.

On an international basis, the International Monetary Fund index of spot prices, comprised of 30 basic commodities exported by primary producing countries, dropped 12 percent in 1982 to the lowest level since 1976.

Important factors which contributed to the continued downtrend in commodity prices during 1982 included the ongoing global recession, which primarily curtailed demand for industrial commodities; record-large world grain and oilseed crops and a consequent build-up of surplus stocks, especially in the United States; and topheavy supplies of cocoa, coffee, and sugar.

In the United States, the continued low rate of activity in the key interest-rate-sensitive housing and auto industries and their suppliers reduced demand for raw industrial commodities during much of 1982. Meanwhile, large supplies depressed prices for many agricultural commodities. Exports of many U.S. commodities were adversely affected by the generally strong U.S. dollar and also by reduced credit availabilities to some traditional Eastern Bloc buyers of U.S. commodities. In addition, even though declining U.S. interest rates in the second half of 1982 created a more favorable atmosphere for borrowing to finance the acquisition or carrying of inventories, the uncertain economic outlook muted borrower response.

The domestic purchasing power of the U.S. dollar, as measured by consumer prices, continued to decline throughout 1982, to 34.2 cents versus 36.7 cents a year earlier and 38.7 cents two years ago.

Approaching mid-year 1983, markets were concerned with (1) the viabiliy of the U.S. economic recovery; (2) evidence of additional cracks in the international monetary system; (3) continuing political unrest in many areas of the world; (4) the unknown side-effects of the U.S. Payment-in-Kind (PIK) program on foreign and domestic supplies of affected and related commodities—especially in the event of any serious 1983 crop problems in any important producing areas of the world and; (5) the prospect that continuing high rates of global unemployment would exacerbate the trend towards national trade protectionism.

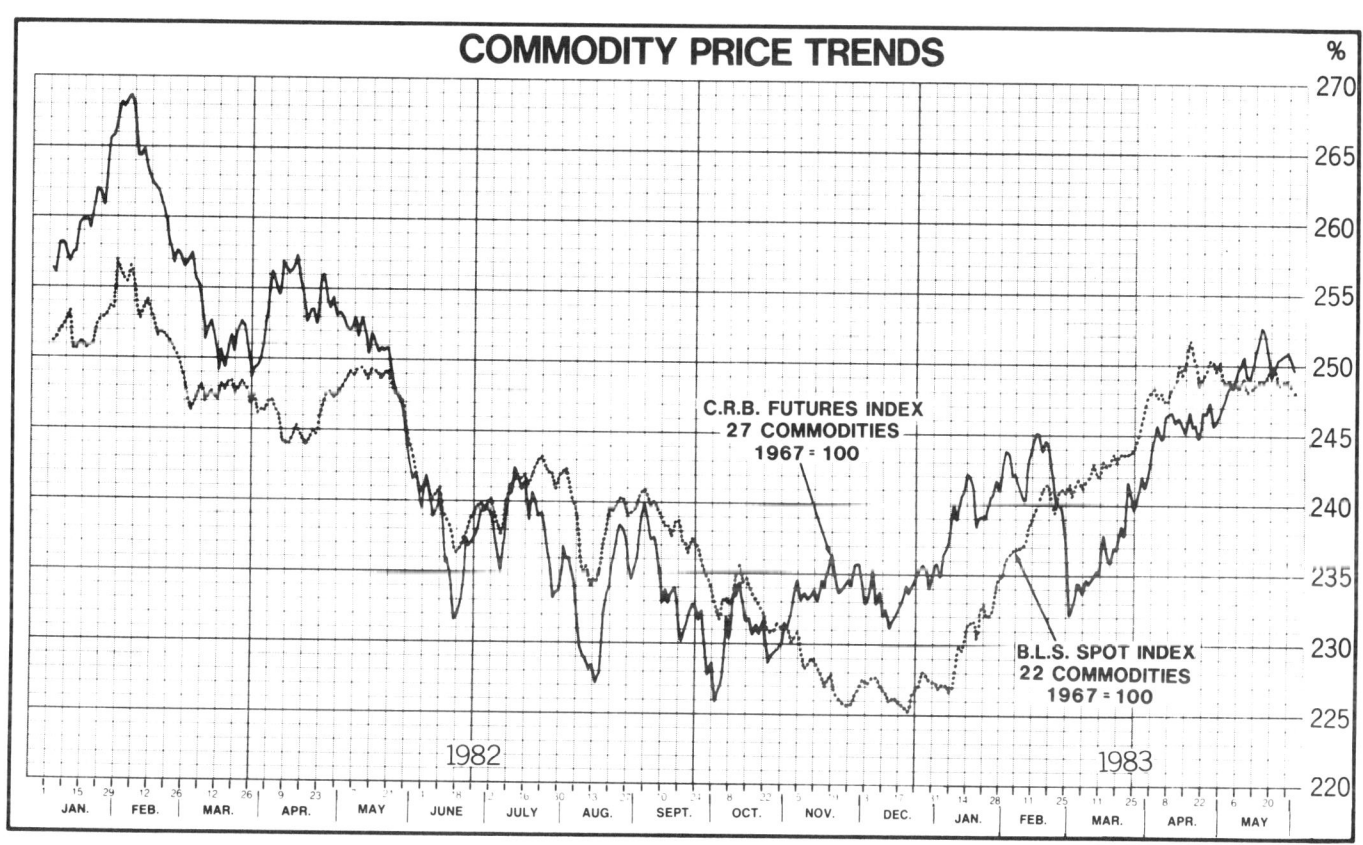

CRB Futures Price Index, Monthly High, Low & Close 1967 = 100

Year		Jan.	Feb.	Mar.	Apr.	May	June	July	Aug.	Sept.	Oct.	Nov.	Dec.	Range
1980	High	290.4	297.4	296.9	263.7	271.8	286.4	303.2	308.4	329.0	329.9	337.6	329.0	337.6
	Low	276.8	287.5	258.0	256.3	259.4	269.4	289.5	301.9	310.4	316.8	321.8	295.1	256.3
	Close	289.6	288.4	258.0	258.1	270.1	286.4	302.3	308.4	319.4	327.1	334.8	308.5	—
1981	High	314.5	306.9	298.4	300.7	290.0	286.0	279.7	279.7	276.0	274.0	269.8	264.8	314.5
	Low	299.2	296.7	287.5	287.7	280.7	263.9	266.6	268.1	266.8	266.6	260.7	250.5	250.5
	Close	300.1	296.7	298.4	289.1	287.5	263.9	279.3	269.4	268.6	268.9	262.2	254.9	—
1982	High	267.2	268.6	257.5	257.3	253.3	242.0	242.4	238.4	239.8	234.3	236.3	235.7	268.6
	Low	256.0	256.5	248.7	252.5	244.9	231.5	233.2	227.1	227.9	225.8	231.2	231.1	225.8
	Close	267.2	256.5	250.1	253.1	244.9	239.3	233.7	235.4	227.9	229.9	235.7	234.0	—
1983	High	242.7	245.1	242.1	247.3									
	Low	234.8	232.1	232.8	244.7									
	Close	242.7	232.1	242.1	246.7									

Source: Commodity Research Bureau, Inc.

T.006A

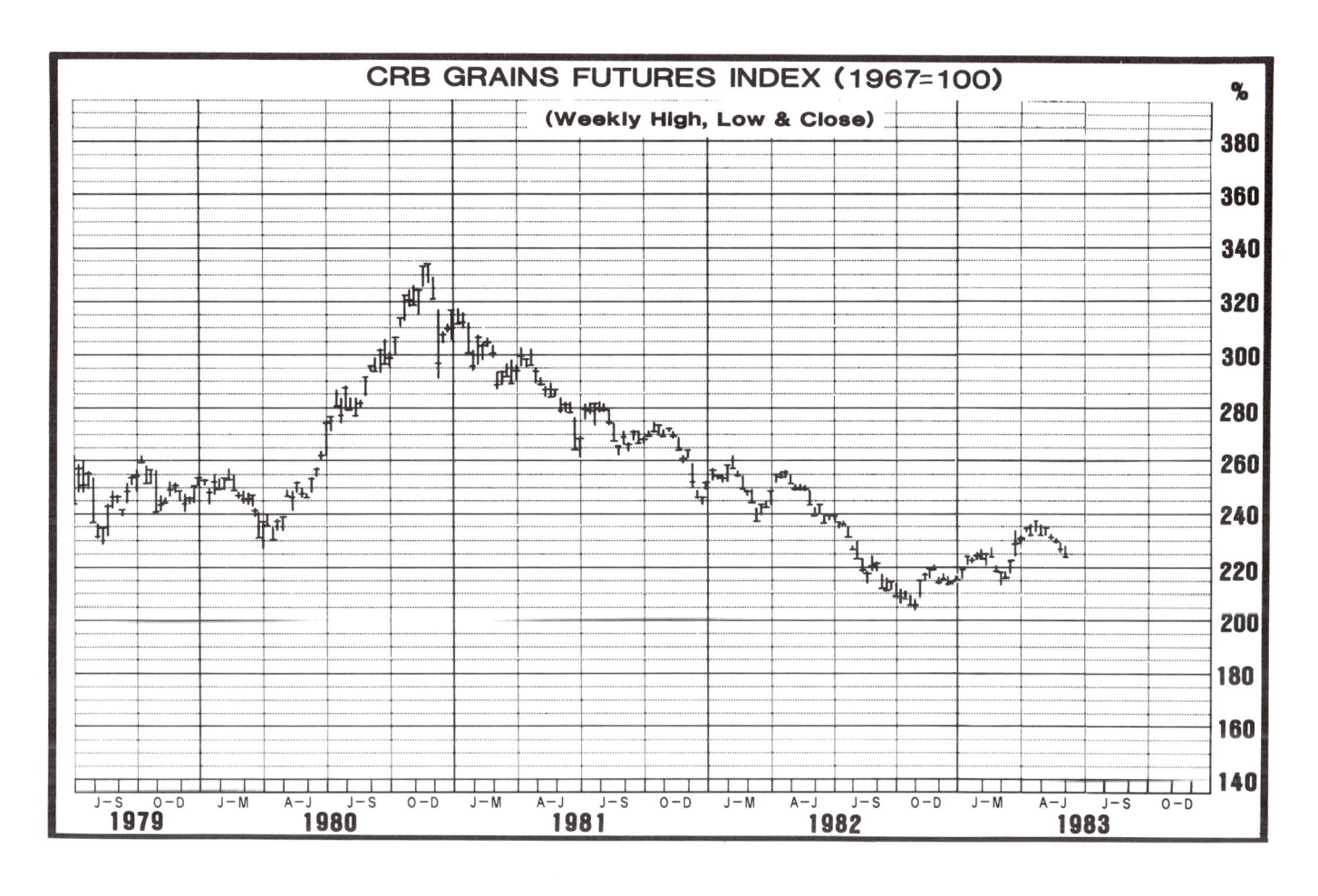

CRB GRAINS FUTURES INDEX (1967=100)
(Weekly High, Low & Close)

CRB METALS FUTURES INDEX (1967=100)
(Weekly High, Low & Close)

WILLIAM F. MAAG LIBRARY
YOUNGSTOWN STATE UNIVERSITY

LONG TERM CHARTS IN COMMODITY PRICE FORECASTING

BY JOHN J. MURPHY

Of all the charts utilized by the market technician for forecasting commodity futures markets, the most popular is the daily vertical bar chart. The daily bar chart records the high, low and settlement prices for each day's trading activity. Usually it will include volume and open interest figures. The average daily bar chart usually covers a period of only six to nine months. However, since most commodity traders and analysts tend to confine their interest to relatively short term market action, daily bar charts have gained wide acceptance as the primary working tool of the futures chartist. The relative ease in maintaining these charts and the fact that they are readily obtainable from several chart services also contribute to their popularity.

The average commodity trader's dependence on these daily charts, however, and his preoccupation with short term market behavior, cause many people to overlook a very useful and rewarding area of price charting—the use of weekly and monthly continuation charts for long range trend forecasting.

The daily bar chart covers only a relatively short period of time in the life of any market. A thorough trend analysis of a market, however, should include some consideration of how a daily market price is moving in relation to its long range trend structure. And in order to accomplish that task, long range continuation charts are the tools that must be employed. Whereas on the daily bar chart each bar represents one day's price action, on the weekly and monthly charts each price bar represents one week's and one month's price action, respectively. The purpose of weekly and monthly charts is to compress price action in such a way that the time horizon can be greatly expanded and, therefore, much longer time periods can be studied.

These long range price charts provide a perspective on market trend that is impossible to achieve with the use of daily charts alone. It should be pointed out that one of the greatest advantages of chart analysis is the application of its principles to virtually any time dimension, including long range forecasting. The idea put forward by some writers that chart analysis should be relegated to near term "timing" and that long range forecasting should be left to the traditional fundamental analysis of supply-demand information is erroneous. As the accompanying charts will amply demonstrate, most of the concepts of technical analysis, including trend analysis, support and resistance levels, trendlines and channels, percentage retracements and price patterns lend themselves quite well to the analysis of long range price movements.

Commodity Research Bureau, Inc. supplements its weekly *Commodity Chart Service* publication of daily bar charts with both weekly and monthly continuation charts. The weekly charts are published once a month and the monthly charts are issued quarterly. The weekly charts cover almost five years of price data, while the monthly charts go back more than 20 years.

Continuation Charts

The construction of continuation charts requires some explanation. The average commodity futures contract has a trading life of about a year and a half before it expires. This limited life span poses obvious problems for long range forecasting. Consider that stock market chartists, for example, do not have this problem. Stock charts are available for the entire price history of individual stocks and the stock averages. Commodity chartists, however, are faced with the problem of devising long range charts for contracts that are constantly expiring. How then are these charts constructed?

The most common solution to this problem of constructing continuation charts for any one commodity—the method of construction employed by the Commodity Research Bureau—is simply to plot the price of its nearest contract. During the final week of trading for the nearest contract, the combined high and low for it and the next nearest contract is plotted, together with the week's closing price for the new nearest contract. (For monthly charts, the high and low for the maturing futures contract to its expiration date is computed together with the subsequent high and low for the following futures contract for the remainder of the month and the highest and lowest of these combined prices are plotted.) This technique is relatively simple and solves the problem of price continuity.

It should be acknowledged, however, that this method does occasionally produce some near term distortions on the charts. Sometimes, for example, the expiring contract may be trading at a significant premium or discount to the next contract, and a sudden price drop or jump may appear on the continuation chart at the point of changeover. Another potential distortion is the extreme volatility exhibited by some "spot" contracts as they approach expiration.

Technicians have experimented with several refinements of the above technique to deal with these occasional distortions. Some, for example, will stop charting the nearest contract a month or two before it expires to avoid the volatility in the spot month. Instead of using the nearest contract, some will use the next contract or the contract with the highest open interest on the theory that the latter is actually the truest representation of market value. Continuation charts can be constructed by linking specific calendar months. For example, a November Soybean continuation chart would use only the historic data provided by each successive year's November Soybean contract. Some chartists go even further, averaging the prices of several contracts or constructing indices which attempt to smooth the changeover by making adjustments in the price premium or discount.

While some slight improvement may be achieved by the above refinements, it seems doubtful that such improvements are significant. Even with the relatively minor distortions referred to, the method of construction that links the nearest contracts is still the most commonly used, being simple to maintain and, more importantly, having been proven to be quite effective over the years. Throughout this article, this technique, as exemplified by Commodity Research Bureau publications, will be used for all of the chart examples.

It bears repeating that most of the charting techniques that are applied to daily bar charts can be applied as well to weekly and monthly charts. This claim might even be carried a step further by stating that long range trend forecasting can often be easier than short term forecasting. Two of the basic tenets of technical analysis are: (1) that markets move in trends, and (2) that trends tend to persist. One of the most striking features of long range charts is that not only are trends very clearly defined, but that long range trends often last for years; imagine making a forecast based on one of these long range trends, not being obliged to change that forecast for several years! By contrast, most technical market letters published today by the futures industry focus on the very short term and are often out of date before they reach their readers through the mail, necessitating electronic mailing and telephone hotlines to keep them current until the next letter is sent.

The persistence of long range trends raises another interesting question which should be mentioned—the question of randomness. While technical analysts do not subscribe to the theory that market action is random and unpredictable, it seems safe to observe that whatever randomness does exist in price action is probably a phenomenon of the very near term. The persistence of existing trends over long periods of time, in many cases for years, is a compelling argument against Random Walk Theory claims that prices are serially independent and that past price action has no effect on future price action.

Terminology and Techniques

Before looking at the accompanying price charts, it might be useful to briefly recap some of the technical theory and techniques utilized in the examples. To begin with, the cornerstone of the technical philosophy is that all of the relevant data that an analyst needs to forecast market direction is recorded on the price chart. Technical analysts believe that market price discounts or reflects all of the information that can ultimately affect that price. Rising prices are indicative of a bullish market psychology, while declining prices reflect a bearish psychology.

Technicians believe that the technical approach in a sense includes fundamental analysis, since the charts simply reflect the market's assessment of those fundamentals of supply and demand that cause bull and bear markets. Therefore, the chartist can conclude that, if prices are rising, demand must exceed supply and that, therefore, the fundamentals must be bullish. The chartist, then, studies market action for clues as to which way prices are most likely to move. What he is attempting to do is to spot important trends in the price data as early as possible. As mentioned earlier, prices move in trends, and these trends have a strong tendency to persist. Most technical trend-following systems do nothing more than identify existing trends in early stages of development and then take positions in the direction of that trend until some price evidence is given that the trend is ending or reversing.

Over the past 100 years, technicians have developed a terminology to describe different types of market action and a number of techniques to aid them in their forecasting. *Trend* is the general direction of the price movement. The standard definition of an *uptrend* is a series of gradually ascending peaks and troughs. A *downtrend* would be a series of descending peaks and troughs. In a sideways trend, these peaks and troughs are horizontal. Trends are usually classified as *major, intermediate* or *minor*. Major trends often last for years. These are the subject of this article.

Resistance is a price level above the market where increased selling is expected. Most often, a previous peak represents resistance. *Support* is a price level under the market where increased buying is expected. Usually, a support level is a previous reaction low. The presence of historic support and resistance levels going back for several years and their continuing ability to influence market action is probably the most striking feature of long range charts. A support or resistance level, once penetrated by a reasonable margin, becomes its opposite. In other words, once a support level is violated by a reasonable amount, it becomes a resistance level. In an uptrend, a penetrated resistance level becomes a new support level. An example of this phenomenon is seen on the Cattle chart (Figure 4) where historic resistance levels at 35¢ and 55¢ later became support levels under the market.

Trendlines work especially well on these charts. In an uptrend, for example, a basic *up trendline* is drawn under reaction lows. The uptrend is assumed to be in effect as long as that up trendline is not violated. A *down trendline* slopes down and to the right along the rally highs. Sometimes markets will form *price channels*. In a price channel, parallel trendlines are drawn over and under the price action. Figure 1 shows a ten-year price channel on the Commodity Research Bureau Futures Price Index chart.

Existing trends are often corrected by certain predictable percentages. The best-known percentage retracement is the *50 percent retracement*. In an uptrend, for example, an intermediate correction may retrace approximately 50 percent of the previous advance before resuming its major uptrend. Minimum retracements are about a third of the previous trend with two-thirds representing a maximum retracement. If a market retraces much more than two-thirds, a trend reversal is usually indicated. The two-thirds point, therefore, is especially critical. The Sugar and Gold charts in Figures 11 and 21 show examples of markets turning at about the two-thirds point.

Price patterns also appear on the long range charts, which are interpreted in the same way as on the daily charts. *Double tops and bottoms* are very prominent on these charts. A double top occurs when a market is unable to overcome a previous resistance peak and then turns down to violate the most recent reaction low. A double bottom would be just the opposite. Major double tops show up on the Copper and Corn charts in Figures 5 and 6, where the two peaks were almost seven years apart. Figure 13 shows a *head and shoulders* bottom which formed in the Wheat market from 1964 to 1972. *Triangles*, which are usually continuation patterns, but sometimes will act as reversal patterns, are very prominent. On the weekly chart of Corn in Figure 7, the 1980–1981 top is a clear *symmetrical triangle*.

Another pattern that occurs quite frequently on these charts is the *weekly or monthly reversal*. For example, on the monthly chart, a new monthly high followed by a close below the previous month's close often represents a significant turning point, especially if it occurs near a major support or resistance area. Weekly reversals are quite frequent on the weekly charts. These patterns are the equivalent of the *key reversal day* on the daily charts, except that on the long range charts these reversals carry a great deal more significance.

The best argument for using long term charts for trend analysis lies in the charts themselves. Therefore, several examples of weekly and monthly charts will be shown covering the last twenty years. It is hoped that the examples will largely speak for themselves. It is further hoped that the examples chosen will clearly demonstrate the usefulness of the charts and how well they lend themselves to trend analysis.

The Macro to Micro Approach

One final point should be made about the order in which the charts should be studied in performing a thorough trend analysis. The proper order to follow in looking at the charts is to begin with the long range and gradually work to the near term. The reason for this should be apparent as one works with the different time dimensions. If the analyst begins with only the near term picture, he is forced to constantly revise his conclusions as more price data is considered and a thorough analysis of a daily chart may have to be completely redone after looking at the long range charts. By starting with the big picture, going back as far as 20 years, all of the data to be considered are already included in the chart and a proper perspective is achieved. Once the analyst knows where the market is from a longer range perspective, he gradually "zeroes in" on the near term.

Therefore, the first chart to be considered is the 20-year monthly continuation chart. The analyst looks for the more obvious chart patterns, major trendlines, or the proximity of major support or resistance levels. He then consults the most recent five years on the weekly chart repeating the same process. Having done that, he narrows his focus to the last six to nine months of market action on the daily bar chart, thus going from the "macro" to the "micro" approach.

In stock market analysis, the starting point is always the broad market averages, such as the Dow Jones Averages or the Standard & Poor's 500 Index, in determining the general direction of the market as a whole. Then the analyst breaks the market down into the various industry groups to isolate the strongest performers. The last step is to find the best performing stocks within the best performing industry groups. Once again, the analyst begins with a very broad view and then gradually narrows his focus. This is the same process that should be followed by the futures chartist.

The first logical step in the analysis of any market is to determine the direction of the general commodity price level. This is accomplished by studying the chart of the Commodity Research Bureau Futures Price Index (Figure 1) which measures the performance of 27 commodity futures markets. There is no question that commodity prices tend to move in the same direction. It is therefore essential to determine as a starting point whether commodity prices are rising or falling.

Next, the analyst should look at the different market groups for the strongest or weakest. If the CRB Composite Index is in an uptrend or in the process of turning up, using the concept of relative strength, the analyst would normally want to concentrate his attention on those market groups that have the strongest chart patterns. For example, Figures 1 and 2 showed some chart evidence that the CRB Composite Index may have been "bottoming" in late 1982. Consulting the six group indices published by the Commodity Research Bureau, he would have observed that the strongest group late in 1982 was the metals group.

The third stage would then be to focus his attention on the strongest group, in this case the metals, to determine the best performers in that group. The answer to that question probably would have been Silver. Gold is not in the index. Therefore, during inflationary periods with the CRB Composite Index trending higher, the analyst should be concentrating his attention on the strongest acting markets in the strongest groups for buying opportunities. During deflationary periods, when the Index is trending lower, as was the case for most of 1981 and 1982, the trader should be looking to the weakest markets in the weakest groups for possible shorting opportunities.

Before even looking at the charts of the market he is interested in analyzing, therefore, the analyst should already have determined whether the commodity price level is bullish or bearish and whether the market group in which that market is included is in a bullish or bearish environment.

Putting all of this together, the correct order to follow in a thorough trend analysis should begin with the 20-year chart of the CRB Futures Price Index, then the 5-year weekly chart and then the daily chart. The next step is to consider the long range weekly and daily charts of the six CRB group indices. The final step is to study the monthly, weekly and daily charts of the individual markets in that order. In accordance with that strategy, the first chart example in Figure 1 is the 20-year monthly continuation chart of the CRB Index.

Conclusion

The techniques applied to the following examples are relatively basic and readily recognized by anyone familiar with elementary charting. It is hoped that the examples chosen, which cover a broad spectrum of commodity futures indices and markets, not only demonstrate the application of charting techniques to weekly and monthly continuation charts, but also the wisdom of consulting these long range charts.

A few final points deserve mention here. The question often raised in discussions of long range charts is whether or not historic price levels seen on the charts should be adjusted for inflation. After all, given the tremendous inflationary bias over the past 10 years, do these long range peaks and troughs have any validity if not adjusted to reflect the declining value of the dollar? This is a point of some controversy among analysts. However, it is the opinion of this author that these charts do not need to be adjusted for inflation. The reason for this statement is the belief that the markets themselves have already made that adjustment. A currency that is declining in value causes commodities quoted in that currency to increase in value. Therefore, the declining value of the dollar would contribute to rising commodity prices. There can be little doubt that much of the price increase on the long range commodity charts over the past 10 years was simply a reflection of the weaker dollar. On the other side of the coin, much of the decline in commodity prices over the past two years has been attributed to a stronger dollar.

Another way to consider this question is to realize that the tremendous price gains in commodity markets during the 1970s in fact reflected inflation at work. To suggest that commodity price levels that have doubled and tripled should then be adjusted to reflect inflation makes no sense at all.

The final point in this argument goes to the heart of the technical theory which states that price action discounts everything eventually. The market itself adjusts to periods of inflation and deflation and increases or decreases in currency values. The real answer lies in the charts themselves. The copper chart, for example, in Figure 5 shows the 1980 bull market high stopping right at the 1974 bull market high and then declining to the 1975–1977 bear market lows. Several markets have failed at historic resistance levels set several years earlier and then have declined to support levels not seen in several years. This type of action would not have happened if the chart levels needed to be adjusted for changes in the value of money.

These long range charts are not meant for trading purposes. A distinction has to be made between market analysis for forecasting purposes and for the timing of commitments. Long range charts are useful in the analytical process to help determine trend and price objectives. However, they are not suitable for the timing of entry and exit points and should not be used for that purpose. For that more sensitive task, daily charts should be utilized.

There is no reason why other charting techniques cannot be applied to weekly and monthly charts. For example, they are useful for determining long range cycles. Elliott Wave analysis can be applied as well. Examples of five–wave bull markets are seen in the corn, cotton, and wheat monthly charts. Another area where little work has been done is the application of long range moving averages to these charts. Some experimental work by the author several years ago revealed the value of 10– and 30–week moving averages applied to the weekly charts to track long range trends. These long range averages are similar to those used in stock market analysis, but they have gone largely unnoticed in futures analysis.

In conclusion, these long range charts only have to be studied in depth occasionally. Since long range price patterns change very little over the short run, a glance at the charts for perspective supplemented by an occasional in-depth analysis seems to be all that is necessary. An increased awareness of the value of these charts, when utilized in conjunction with daily bar charts, can add an entirely new dimension to standard chart analysis, and greatly improve the application of technical principles to the commodity futures markets.

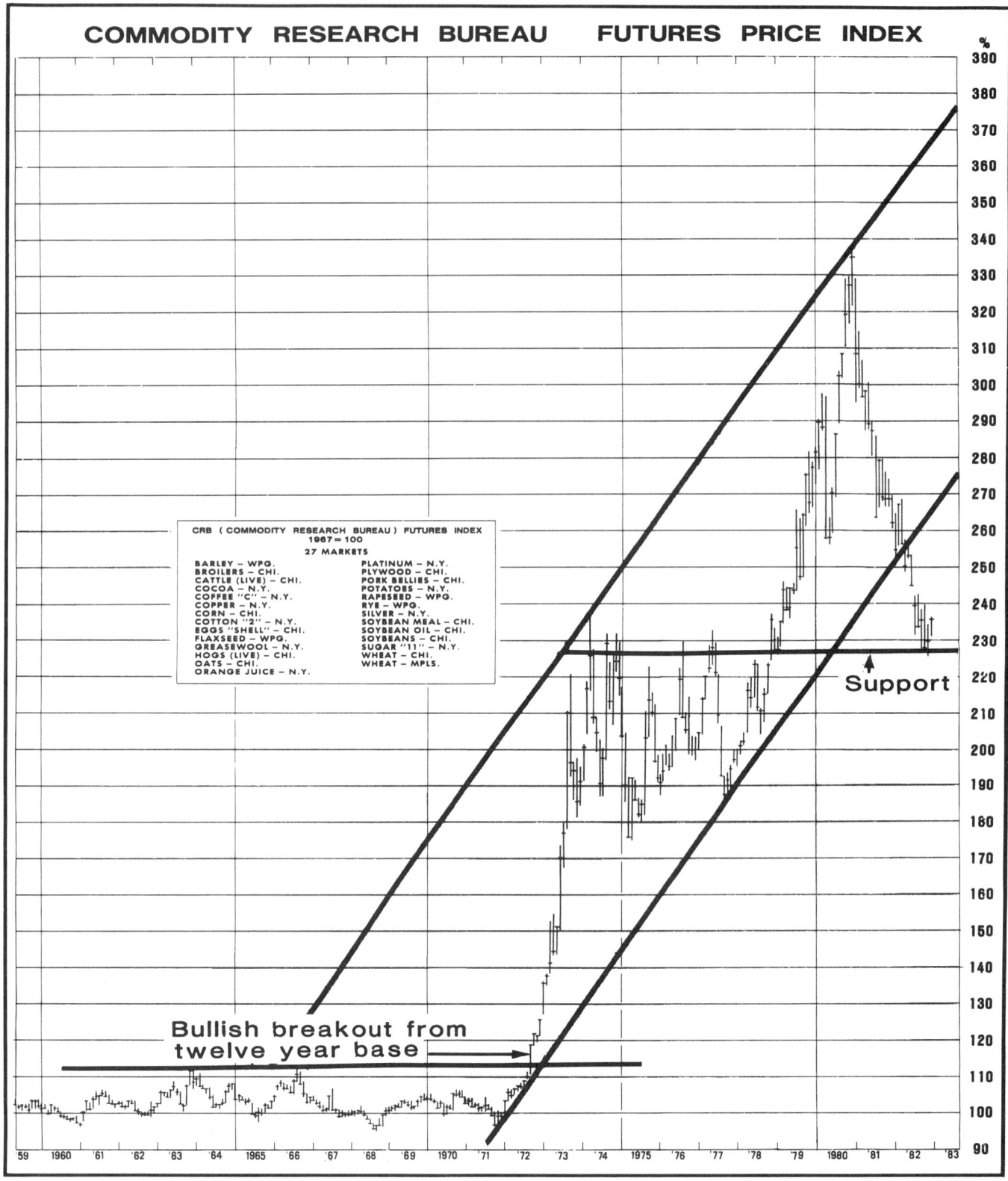

FIGURE 1: Monthly chart of the CRB Index
The monthly continuation chart of the CRB Futures Price Index shows the historic bullish breakout in 1972 from a horizontal base lasting longer than ten years. The unprecedented inflationary spiral indicated by major bull trends in most futures markets that lasted almost ten years was clearly and decisively signalled. Notice the major *up trendline* which was not broken until 1982 and the almost perfect ten year bullish *price channel*. The major two year decline is now showing signs of stabilization at the top of a major support zone in the vicinity of 230. It's also interesting that prices have retraced almost fifty percent of the entire ten year advance where support would normally be expected.

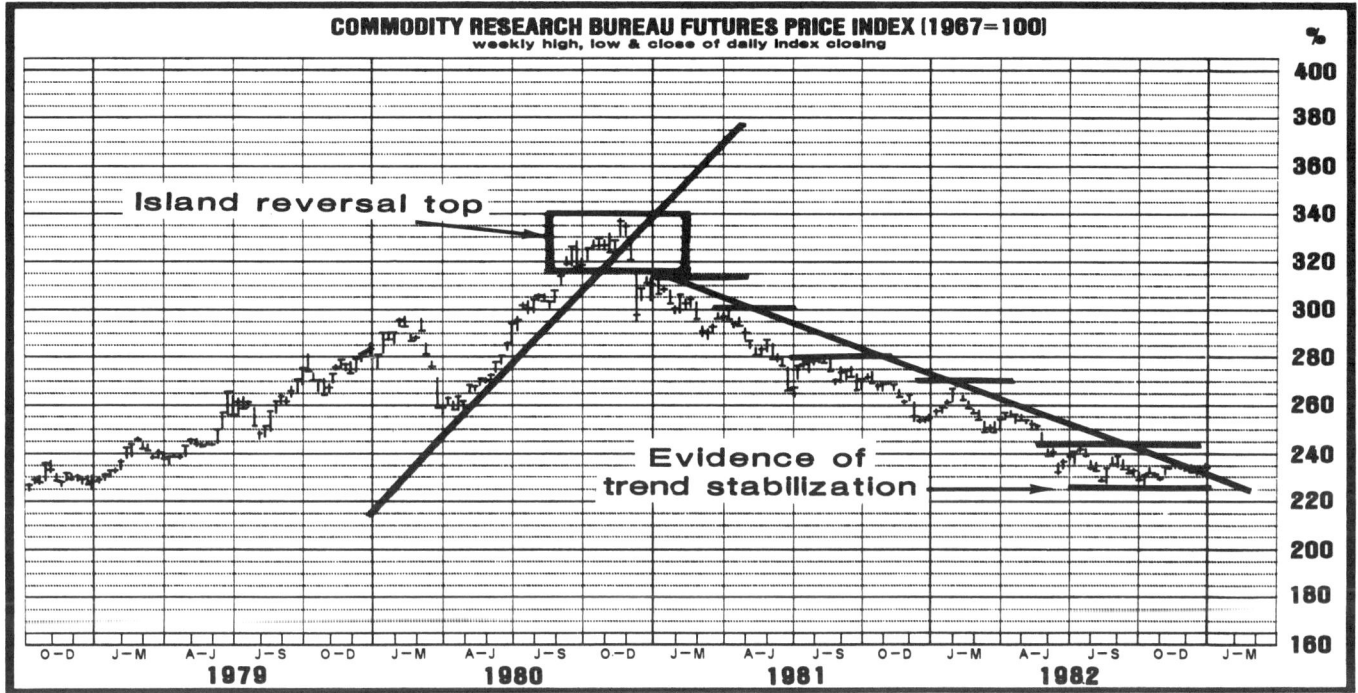

FIGURE 2: Weekly chart of the CRB Index
The monthly chart in Figure 1 showed that at the end of 1980 prices were up against the top of a ten year channel where major resistance would normally be expected. The above weekly chart shows a large *island reversal* top and the bearish pattern of descending peaks and troughs during 1981–82. The last two quarters of 1982 show stabilization and potential bottoming action in progress, suggesting a possible end to the two year decline. Figure 1 already revealed that major support could be anticipated near 230.

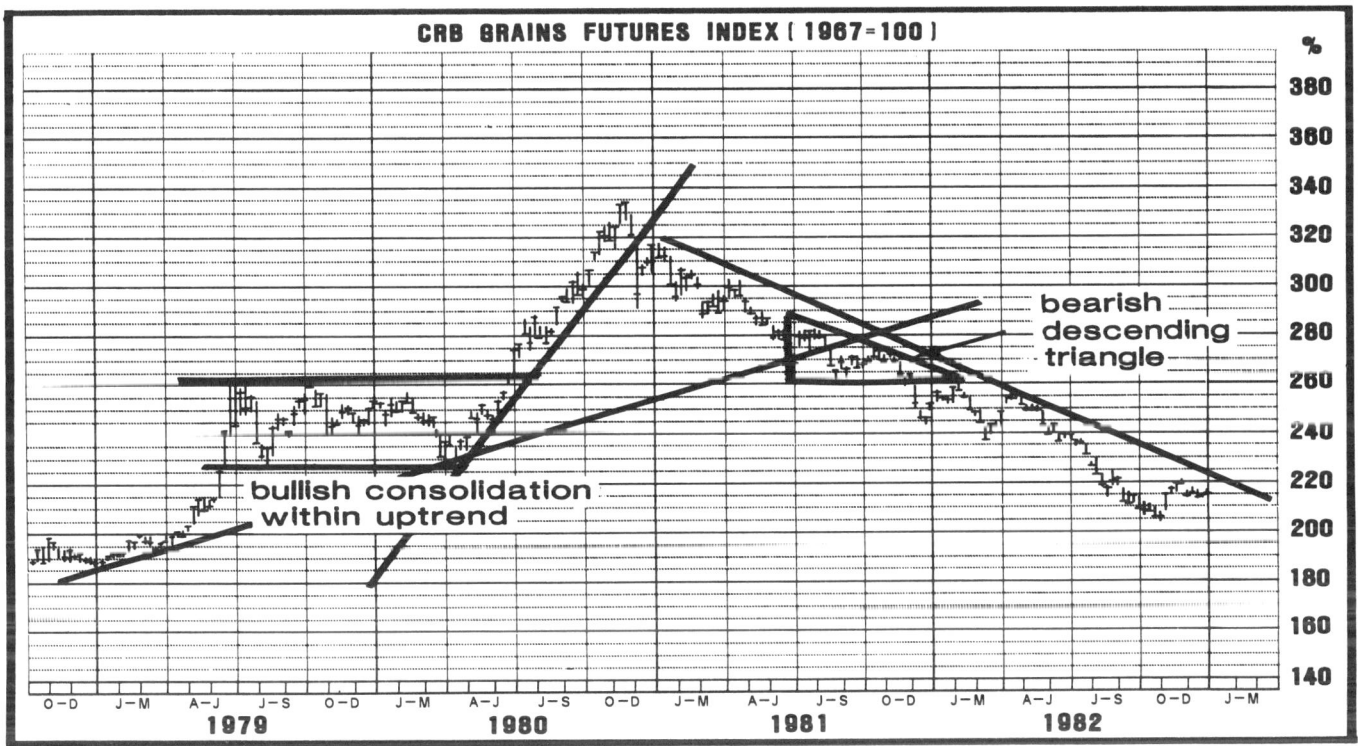

FIGURE 3: Weekly chart of CRB Grains Index
This chart illustrates how well the weekly Group Index charts lend themselves to trend analysis. Notice the bullish twelve month consolidation pattern from June 1979 to June 1980, and the major price break at the end of 1980 violating a six month up trendline. The major trend remained clearly bearish for two years. Notice the bearish *descending triangle* during the fourth quarter of 1981 and how well the major *down trendline* contained the bear market rallies.

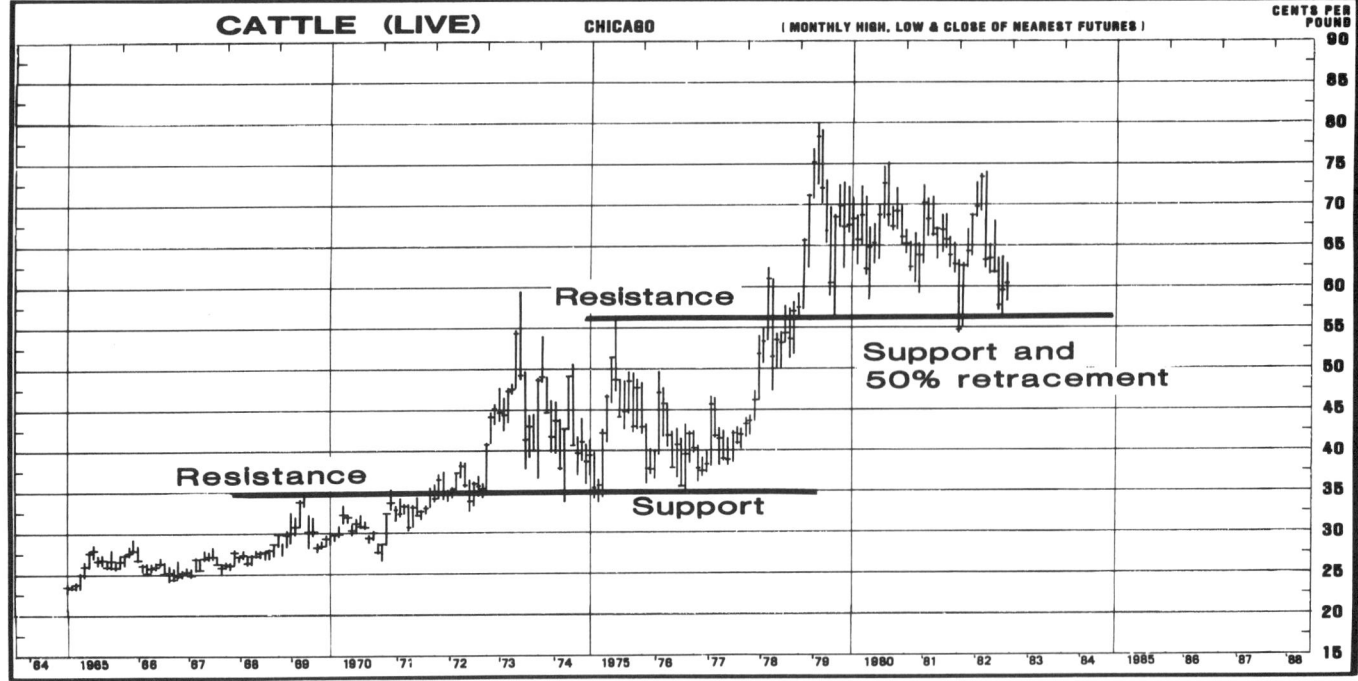

FIGURE 4: Monthly chart of Live Cattle
While the major trend is clearly up since the 1960's, notice how well the trading ranges, which lasted for several years, were contained within very orderly and predictable support and resistance areas. Major resistance at 35¢ in 1969 became a major support level for several years once it was penetrated. Major resistance in the 55–56¢ zone, once penetrated, became major support under the market beginning in 1979. Notice also that the decline from 80¢ to 55¢ is about a fifty percent retracement of the 1976–1979 advance from 35¢.

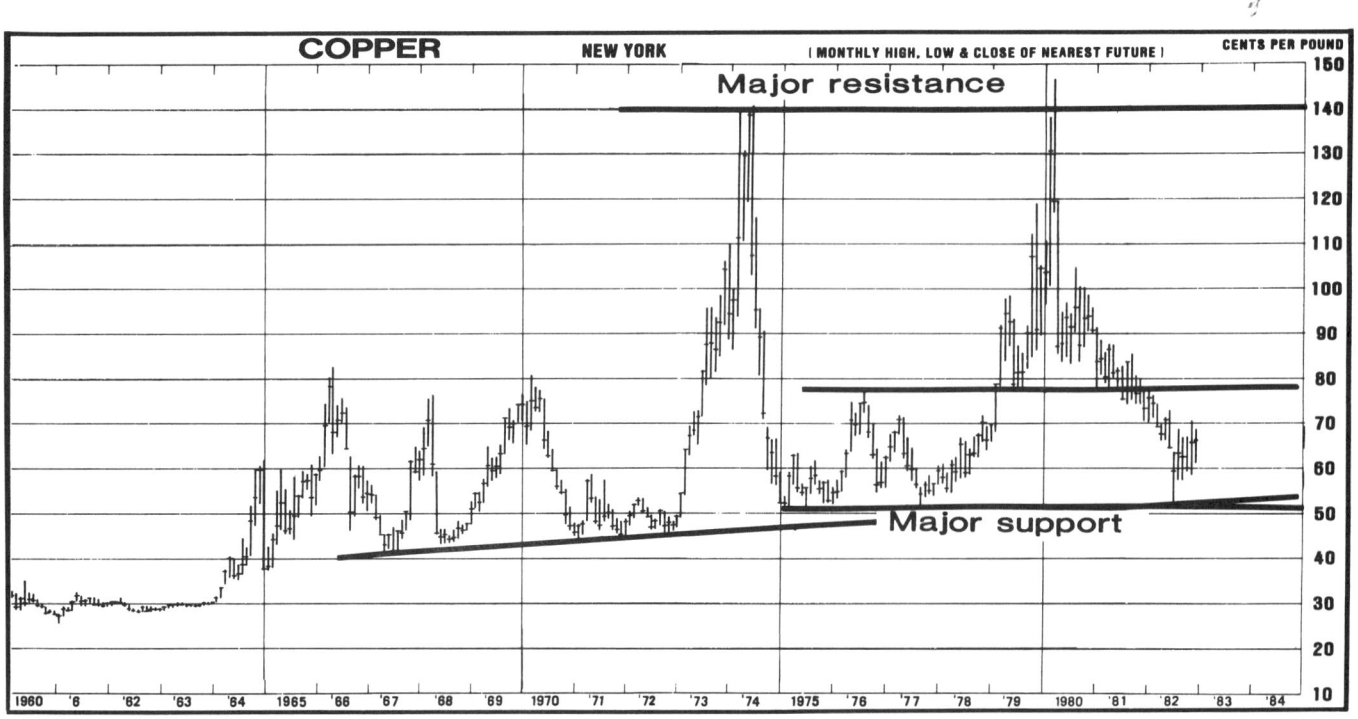

FIGURE 5: Monthly chart of Copper
This chart shows the value of knowing where historic support and resistance levels are located. In the beginning of 1980, Copper prices were setting new contract highs and looking very strong on the daily charts. Knowing that major historic resistance lay just overhead at 1.40 set by the 1974 bull market high should have made one more cautious. Note the bearish monthly reversal in 1980 forming a super *double top*. Also notice that prices declined all the way to major support near 50¢ which was defined by bear market lows from 1975 to 1977. The violation of intermediate support along the 1976 high near 78¢ signalled a decline to near 50¢. The major up trendline going back to the 1967 lows also helped contain the major bear decline.

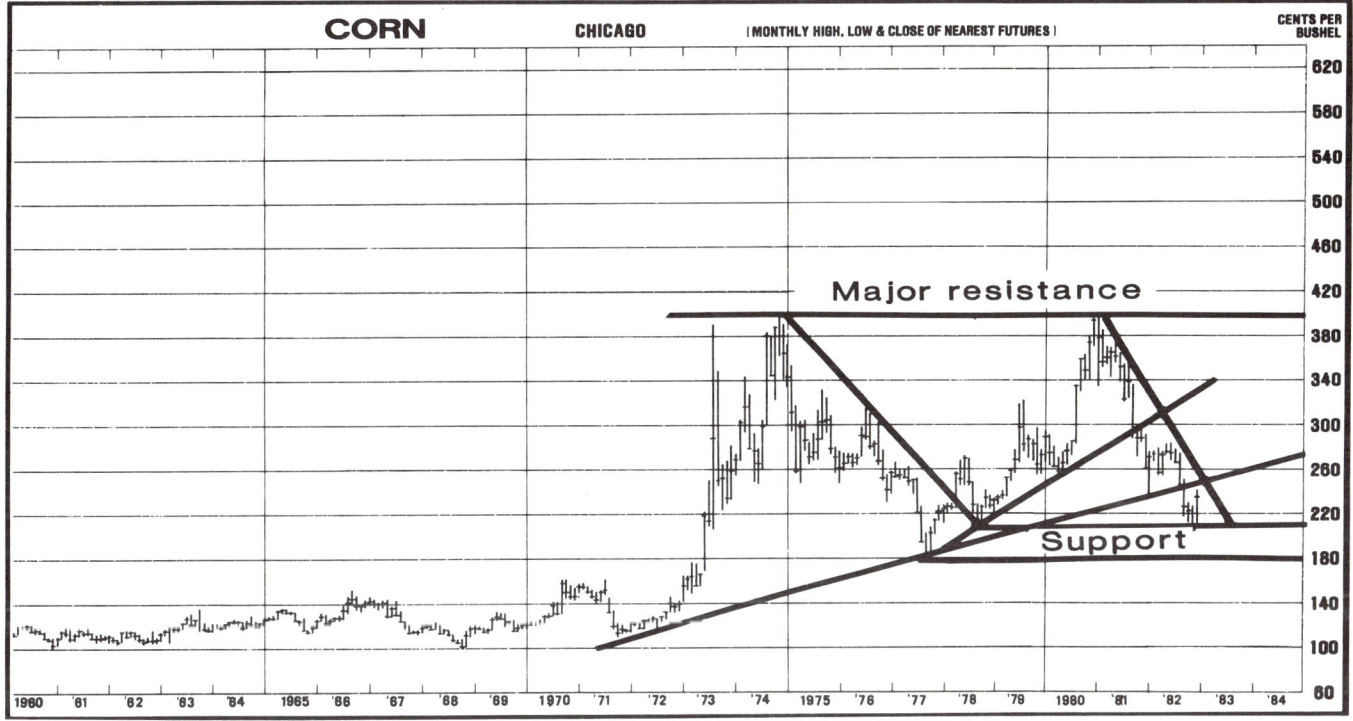

FIGURE 6: Monthly chart of Corn
Another perfect *double top* is clearly seen. The 1980 bull market high stopped right at the 1974 bull market high at $4.00. It is truly amazing to see how a previous peak established about seven years earlier still exerts such a powerful influence on market behavior. Here again, the daily charts were setting new contract highs at a time of bullish euphoria. A glance at this chart was a valuable warning that major resistance was near. Also notice how effective the major trendlines were in helping to signal major turning points. The chart shows prices bouncing off support near $2.00.

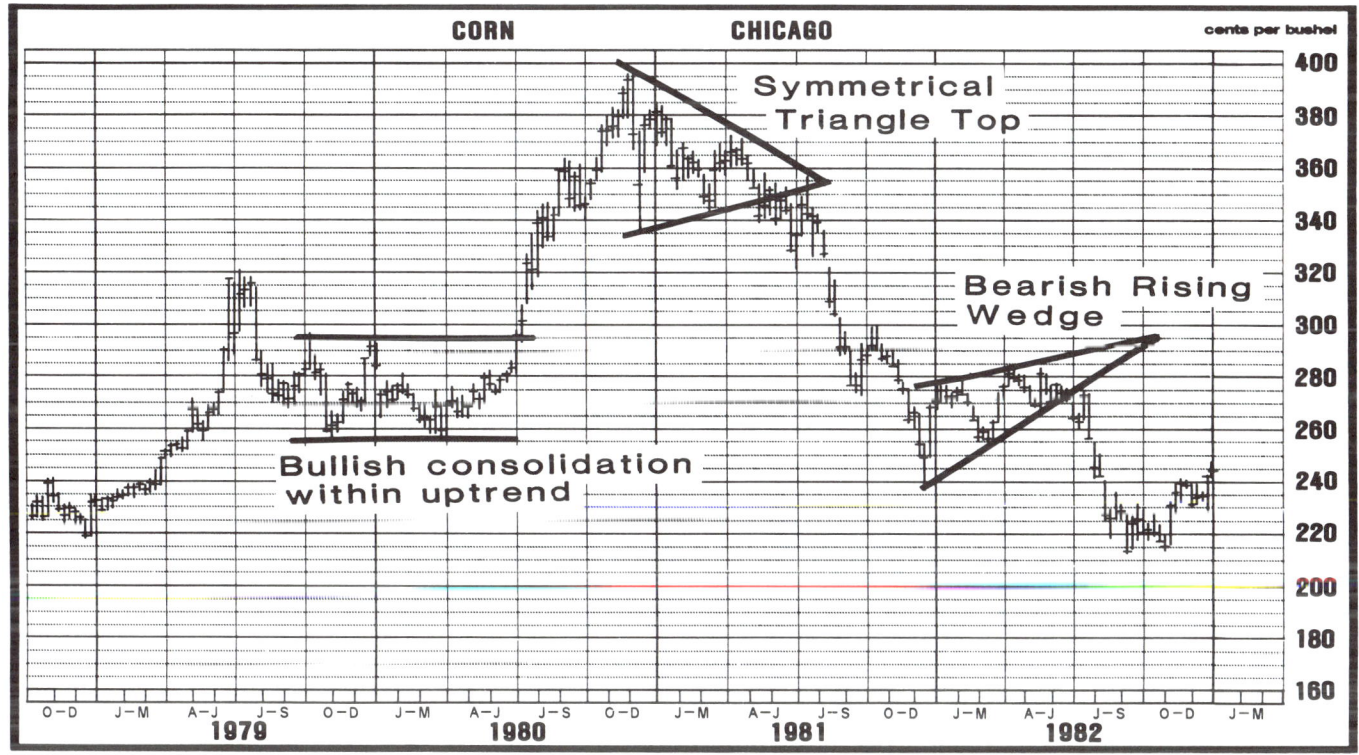

FIGURE 7: Weekly chart of Corn
A closer inspection of the 1980–1981 top shows a clear *triangular top* which gave bear signals in the second quarter of 1981. The fact that this downside reversal occurred near a major historic resistance level confirmed an unmistakable bear signal. Note the rising *wedge* during the first half of 1982. This pattern is usually a bearish continuation pattern in a downtrend and worked well in this example. Looking back to the 1979–1980 period, notice the perfect *double bottom* in a bullish consolidation pattern.

FIGURE 8: Monthly chart of Cotton
A *triple top* is clearly seen spanning a period of almost eight years with major resistance near 1.00. *Triple tops*, much rarer than *double tops*, are very potent. Even with the major bear market in effect since the beginning of 1981, however, prices have only retraced about *fifty percent* of the entire advance from 20¢ to $1.00. Note the bearish *monthly reversal* that marked the top of the market.

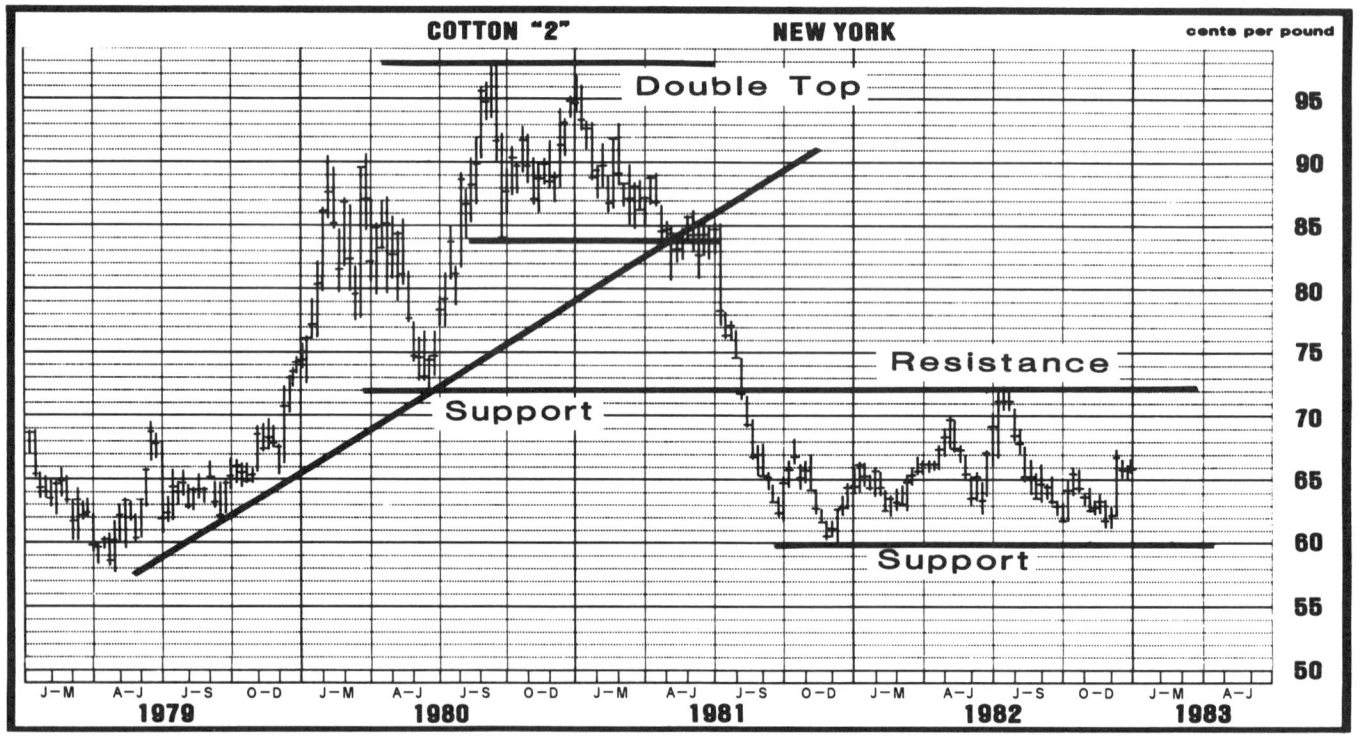

FIGURE 9: Weekly chart of Cotton
Using the weekly chart to look more closely at the 1980 top, a clear *double top* is seen. The violation of support at 8400 signalled a major bear market. Notice how support at the 1980 reaction low of 7200, once violated, became resistance and stopped the 1982 rally attempt in its tracks. Notice also the ability of the late 1982 decline to hold over support formed at the end of 1981 which may be an early indication of trend stabilization.

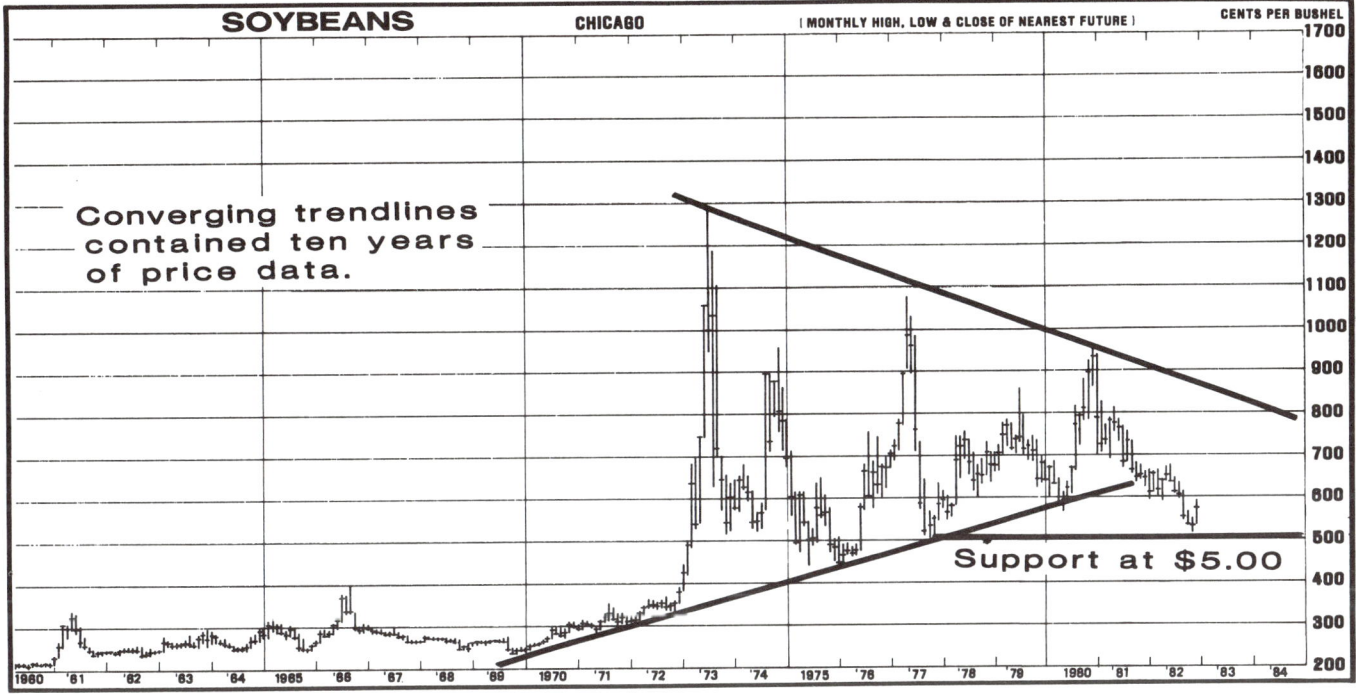

FIGURE 10: Monthly chart of Soybeans
The entire price picture since 1973 is seen resembling a huge *symmetrical triangle*. Note that these two converging trendlines contain almost ten years of price data. Prices are now testing important support near $5.00 defined by the 1977 bear market low. While there is certainly no guarantee that the market will bottom in this area, it is very clear that the market does respect these historical levels.

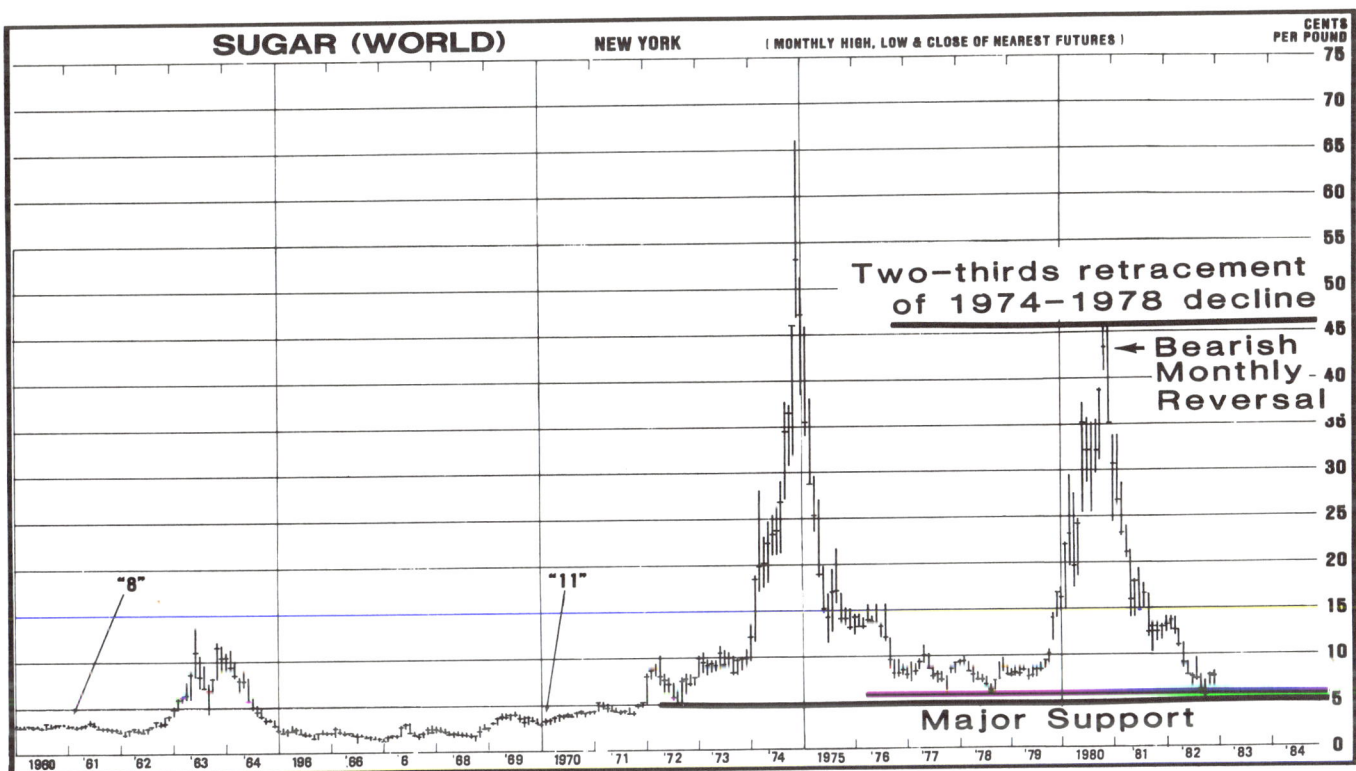

FIGURE 11: Monthly chart of Sugar
This chart places the entire 1980 bull market and the subsequent bear market in perspective. In 1980 the daily charts looked very bullish, rumors of Russian buying were rampant, and everyone was talking about a test of the 1974 high near 66¢. However, percentage retracements taken from the 1974 high at 66¢ to the 1978 low at 6¢ showed that a *two-thirds retracement* of the previous bear market would support a rally to 46¢. The two-thirds retracement is usually a very critical testing area in any trend. The bearish *monthly reversal* that took place at 46¢ was an additional warning that a major failure had occurred. Prices are now testing historic support in the 5–6¢ zone.

17

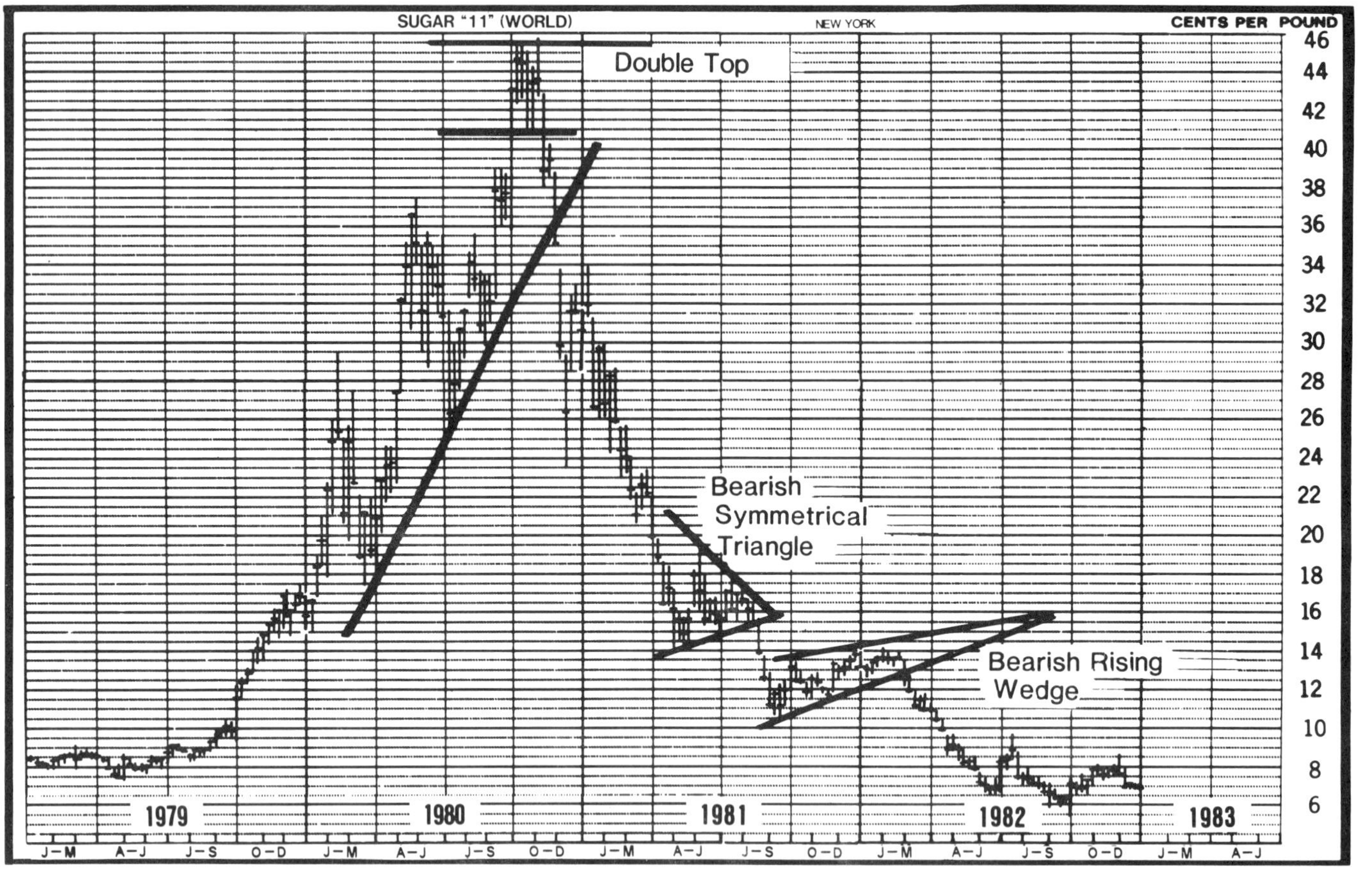

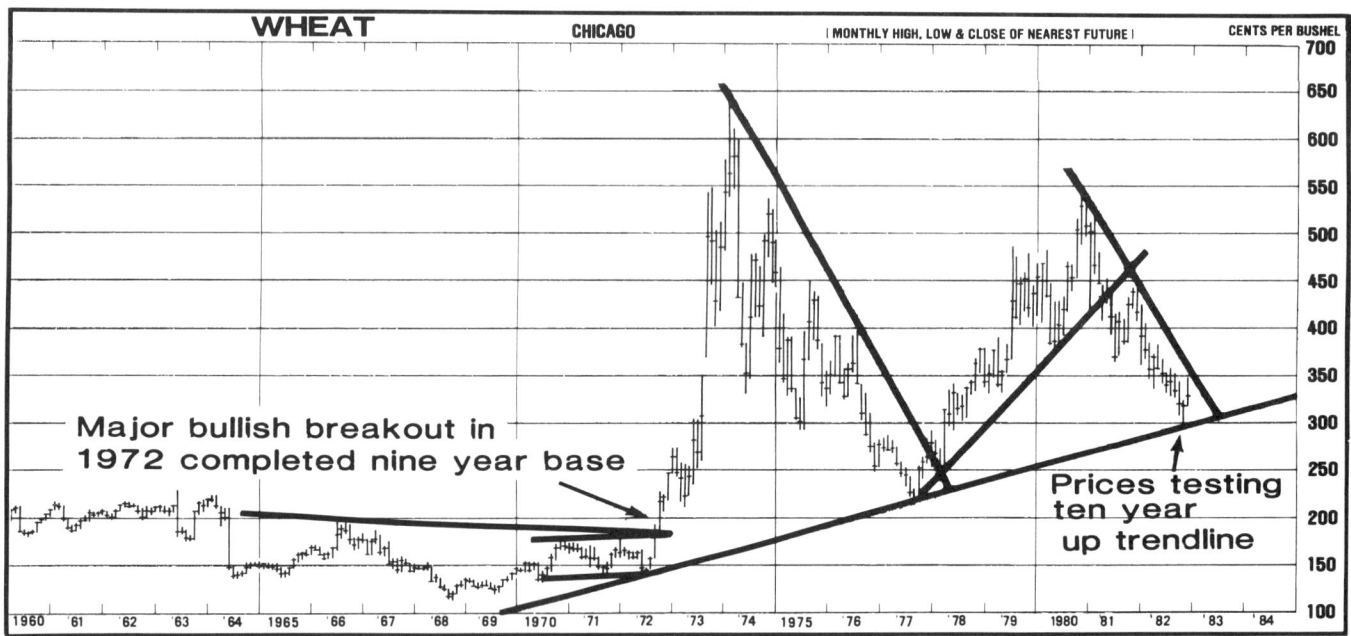

FIGURE 12: Weekly chart of Sugar
"Zeroing in" on the monthly reversal failure at 46¢ in Figure 11, the weekly chart shows a small *double top* which was completed by a close under the reaction low at 41¢. Prices then *gapped* under a major *up trendline* at the end of 1980 confirming the bearish trend reversal. Between 20¢ and 14¢ in mid-1981, a very clear *symmetrical triangle* appeared followed very shortly by a bearish rising *wedge*. These intermediate type patterns seem to appear quite frequently on the weekly charts.

FIGURE 13: Monthly chart of Wheat
The explosion of wheat prices in 1972, sparked by Russian entry into the American market, was dramatically signalled on the monthly chart. Charting theory holds that the longer a basing period takes to form, the greater the upside potential. The "basing" pattern shown on this chart, which has a strong resemblance to a *head and shoulders* bottom, began in 1964 when the "left shoulder" was formed. The middle trough, or "head," formed in 1968 and 1969, while the "right shoulder" lasted almost two years in 1971 and 1972. Therefore, the basing pattern, which was completed in 1972 by the decisive upside penetration of the "neckline," spanned eight years and indicated that an historic uptrend was being initiated. *Trendlines* worked well to help define subsequent bull and bear markets. The major bear market in wheat from the fourth quarter of 1980 to the fourth quarter of 1982 has stabilized right at a ten year *up trendline* connecting the low points of 1972 and 1977.

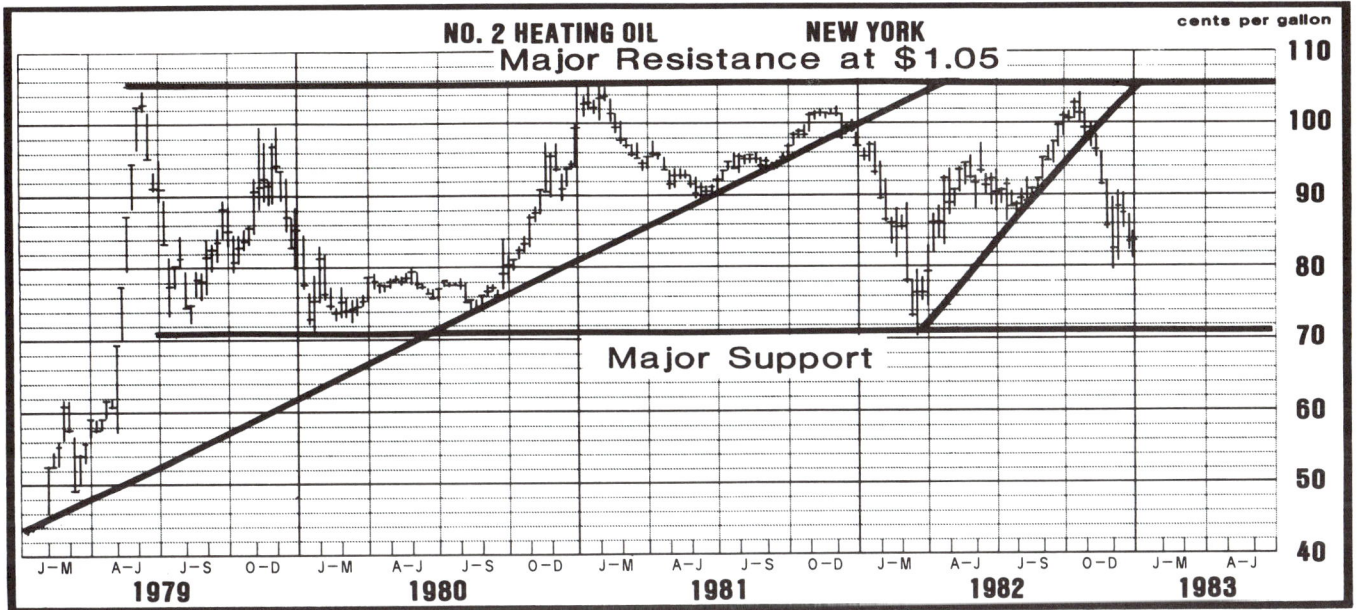

FIGURE 14: Weekly chart of Heating Oil
This chart demonstrates very graphically the importance of historic support and resistance levels, and also the need for long range perspective. Several bull and bear markets have been seen on the daily charts of Heating Oil over the past four years. This chart shows, however, that price action since mid-1979 has been nothing more than a massive *trading range* with major resistance at $1.05 and major support near 70¢. The violation of the three year *up trendline* from 1979 to 1981 signalled a major bear trend which was terminated in March of 1982 by an upside *weekly reversal* at the 1979–1980 reaction lows near 72¢. The bull market of 1982 stopped at the 1979 and 1981 bull market peaks near $1.05. None of these historic levels that have worked so well in this market could have been predicted by using the daily bar charts alone.

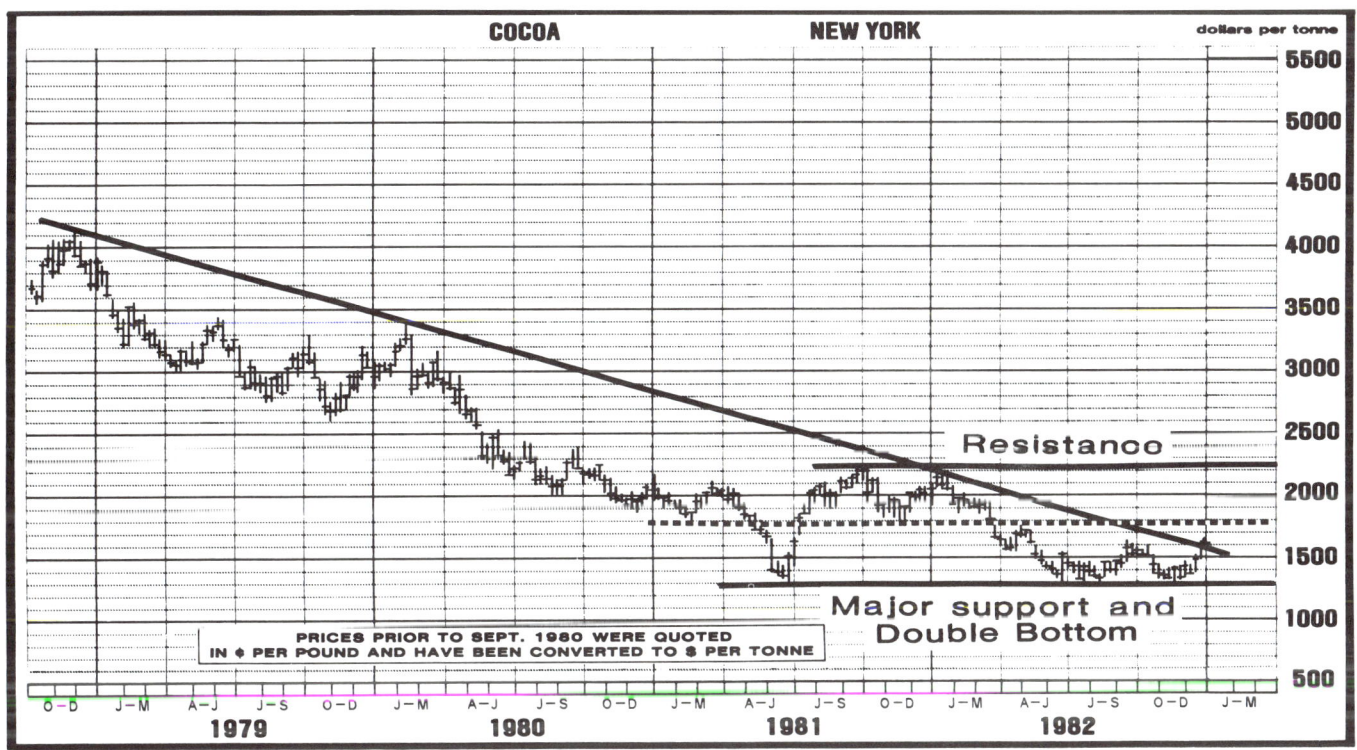

FIGURE 15: Weekly chart of Cocoa
This chart shows most of the bear market that began in 1977 and it gives an interesting perspective not seen on the daily charts. On the daily charts, prices set new contract lows in August of 1982 followed by a modest rally and then new contract lows in November. Prices then rallied sharply into 1983. The weekly chart shows a *double bottom* formed during the last six months of 1982. That *double bottom* occurred at the previous low formed the year before in mid-1981, giving it greater technical significance. Notice the four year *down trendline* connecting peaks in 1978, 1980 and 1982 which was broken with the completion of the double bottom in January 1983. Minor overhead resistance is seen near 1800 marked by reaction lows in February and November of 1981. Major resistance and a likely upside target is clearly seen at the 1981–1982 rally high near 2200.

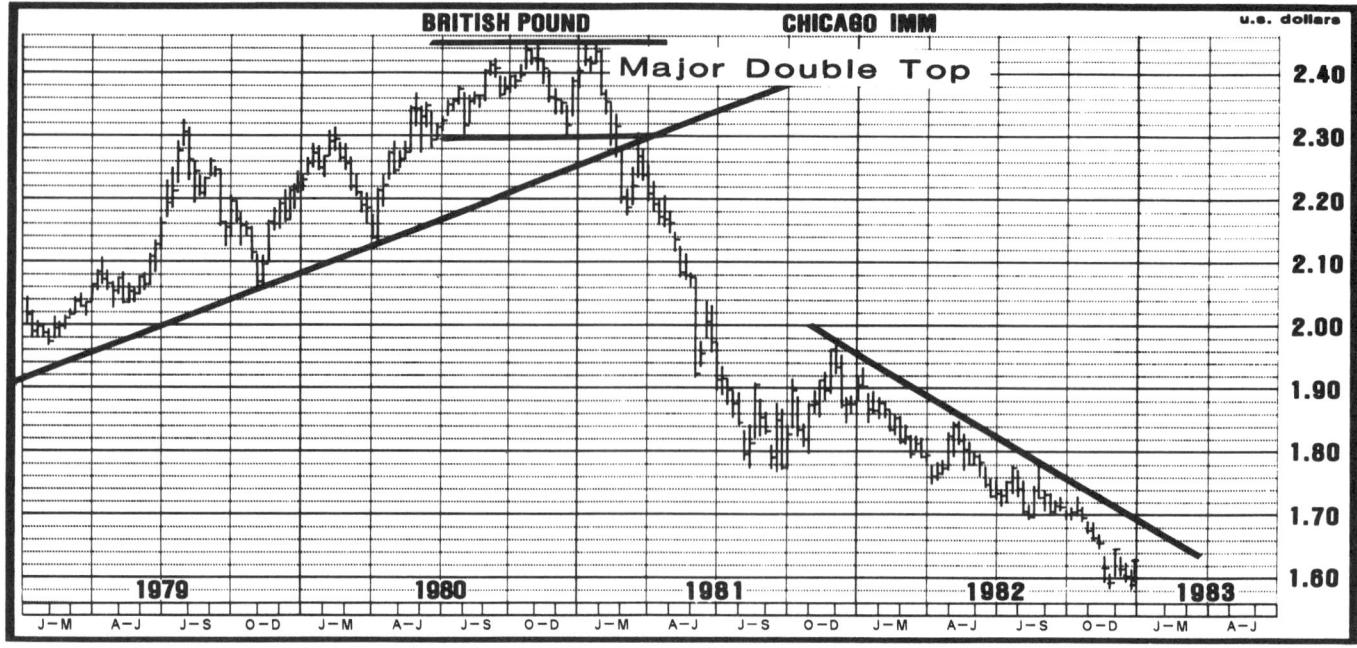

FIGURE 16: Weekly chart of the British Pound
The last two years of a bull market and the dramatic price collapse of the past two years are shown here. A clearcut *double top* was formed at the end of 1980 and the beginning of 1981 which was completed in the first quarter of 1981 with a decisive close under 2.30. The major *up trendline*, which was also penetrated, actually dates back to the second quarter of 1978 (not shown on the chart) and confirmed a major downside trend reversal. Note the return rally back to the underside of the *up trendline* after its violation. Support lines once violated become resistance lines as shown here. A *down trendline* from the end of 1981 into 1983 very nicely defined the slope of the last year's downtrend.

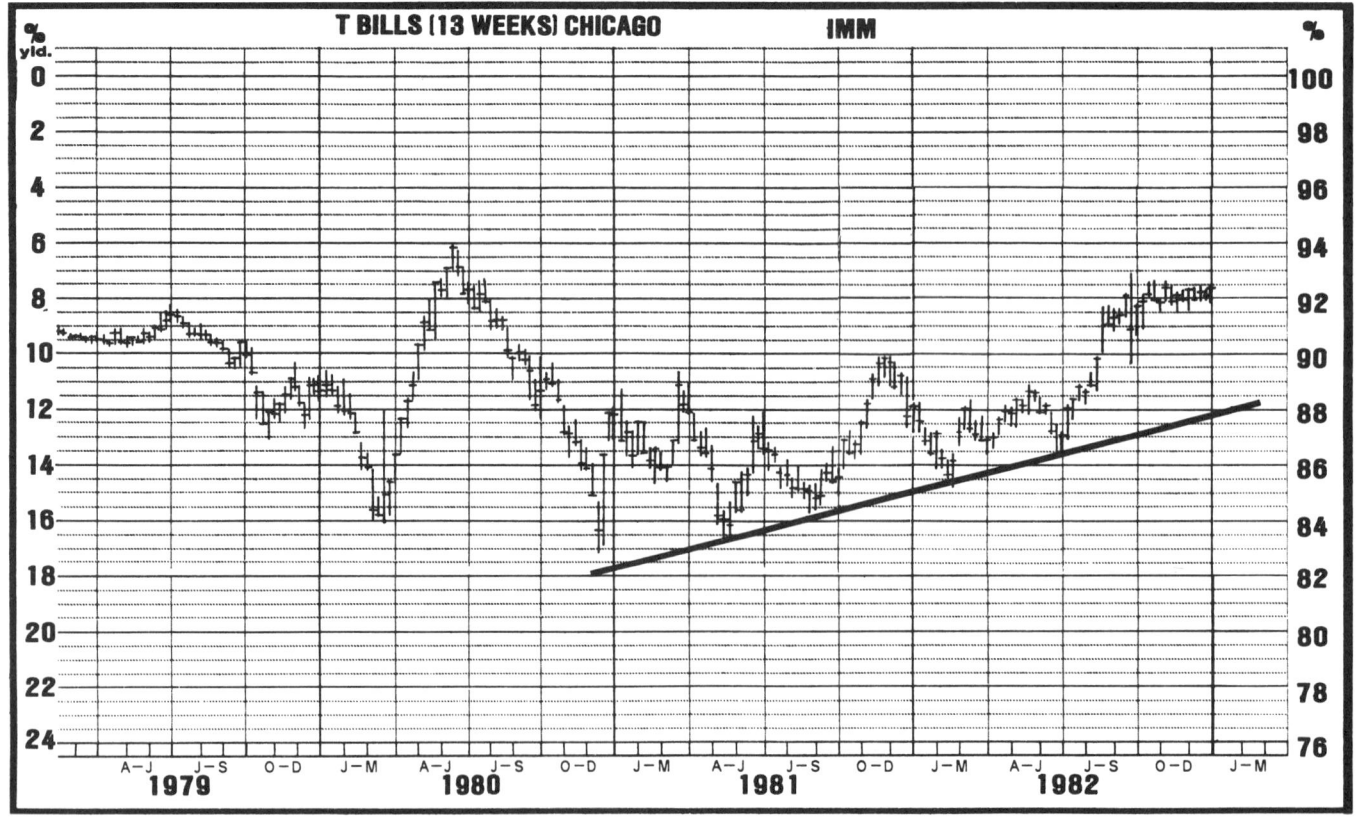

FIGURE 17: Weekly chart of Treasury Bills
The sharp rise in T-bill prices that began in July of 1982 is shown in this chart. Notice that the prelude to that advance, however, is a bullish pattern of rising bottoms that had been taking place for over a year. This chart clearly paints a much more bullish picture than the daily bar chart. Also, notice how close prices have come to the 1980 rally high at 9400.

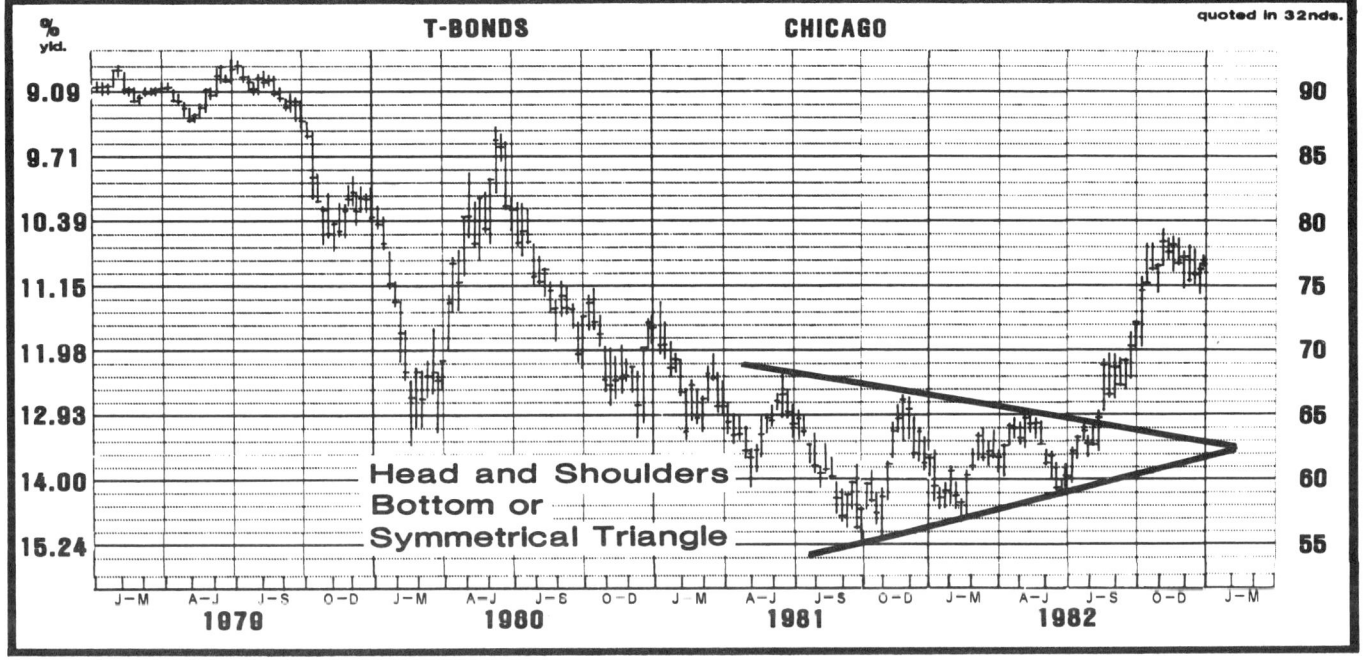

FIGURE 18: Weekly chart of Treasury Bonds
The pattern on this chart from the second quarter of 1981 through the same period in 1982 could be described as a *triangle* bottom or as a complex *head and shoulders* bottom. In either case, the breaking of the upper trendline in August of 1982 signalled a major bullish trend in the making. Notice how well the two converging trendlines confined the coiling market action for over a year.

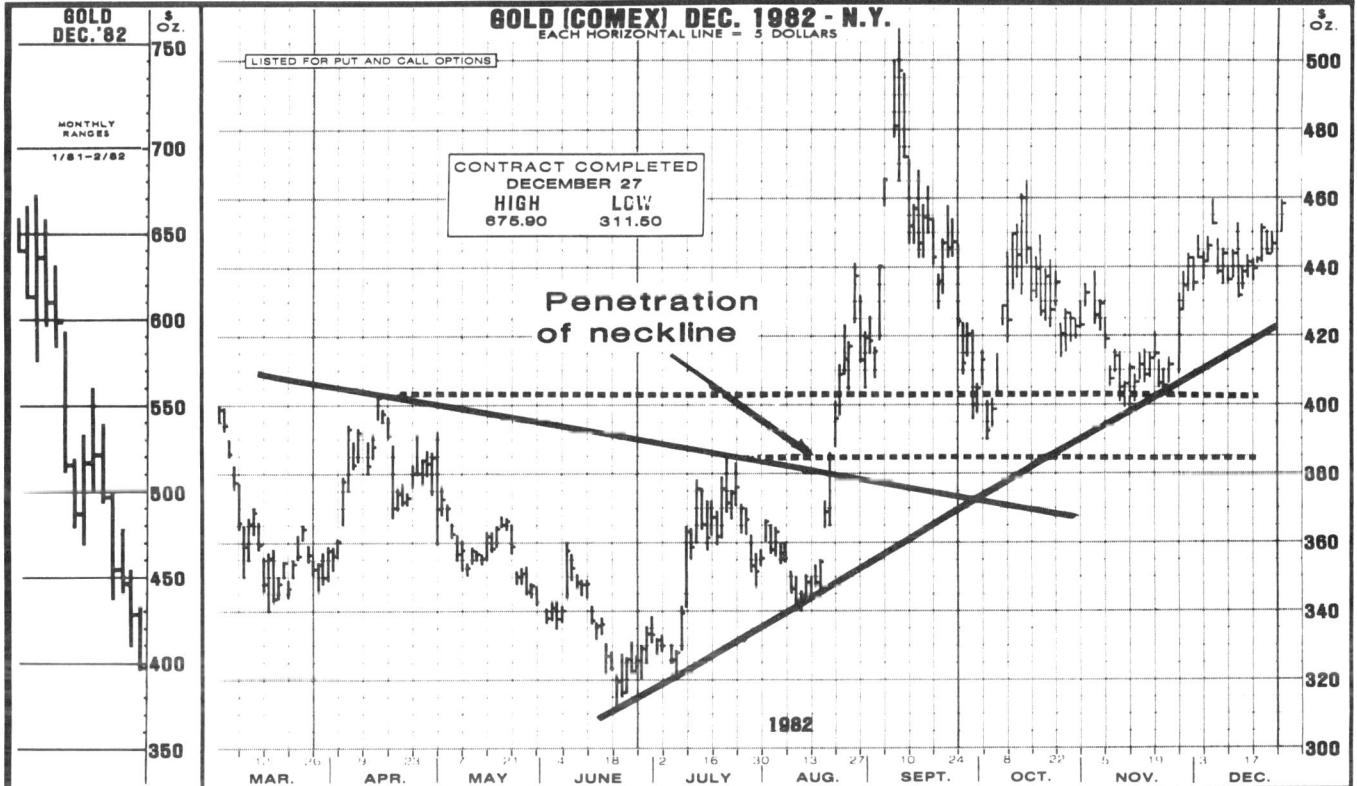

FIGURE 19: Daily chart of December 1982 (Comex) Gold
In order to demonstrate the need for long range perspective in performing a thorough trend analysis, the daily, weekly and monthly charts of the gold market will be consulted, but in the reverse order recommended earlier. The above daily chart shows a *head and shoulders* bottom from March through August with the breaking of the "neckline" in August. The consolidation period from September through December has remained above the major *up trendline* and also above the resistance peaks set in April and July.

21

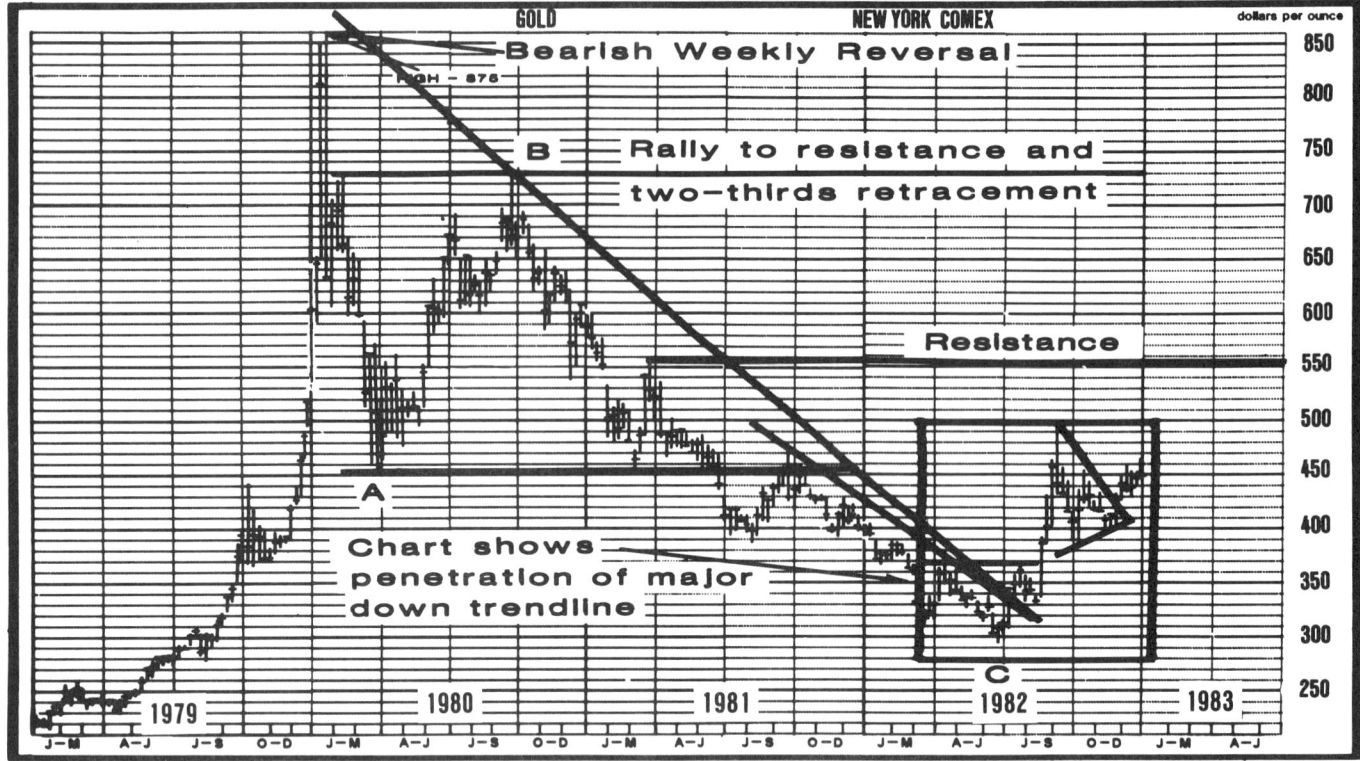

FIGURE 20: Weekly chart of Gold
This chart places the ten-month period covered in much greater perspective. The *head and shoulders* bottom in 1982 is clearly visible. The consolidation pattern between $390 and $490 looks more *triangular*. The upside penetration of the "neckline" on the *head and shoulders* bottom coincided with the breaking of two important *down trendlines*. Additional valuable information is the downside "swing objective" taken by comparing the size of the two declining waves visible on the chart. The theory of the "swing objective" says that the second major wave in a given direction will be about equal in size to the first wave in that direction. The first wave down (A) dropped from $875 to $450 for a decline of $425. The rally wave (B) retraced almost exactly two-thirds of that decline and stopped at a shelf of resistance at $725. Projecting another decline of $425 from that level to match the decline in the first wave (A), a downside target of about $300 would be expected. That is about where the decline ended.

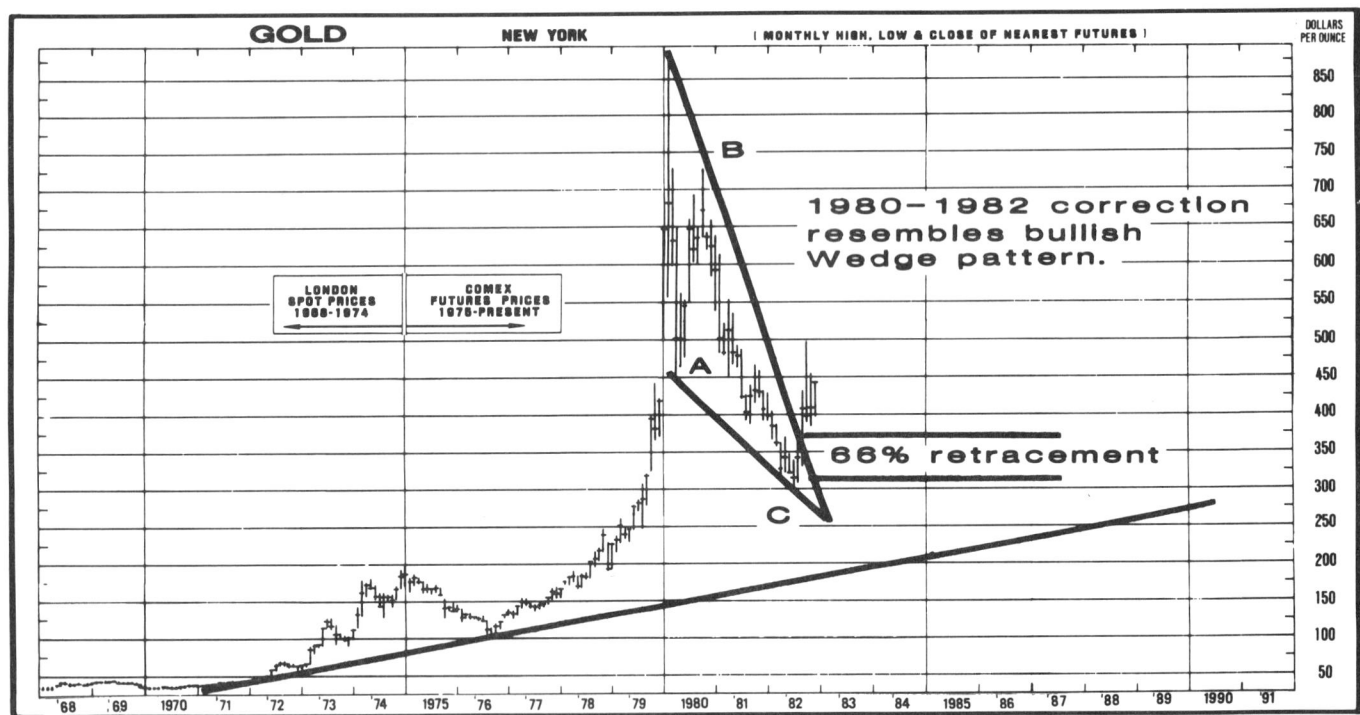

FIGURE 21: Monthly chart of Gold
This chart shows even greater perspective. The major A-B-C correction from 1980–1982 is clearly visible and the penetration of the major down trendline (B-C). The entire two-year decline resembles a bullish *wedge*, which appears to have been completed. Also the major decline from $875 to $300 retraced just over 66% of the rise from the lows registered in 1976 near $100 and in 1970 at $35. A two-thirds retracement is usually a very critical retracement level where the market must turn if existing trends are to be maintained. In this case, the actual points are $365 and $320 depending on which low is used.

THE AGRICULTURE AND FOOD ACT AND COMMODITY PRICES

BY WALTER SPILKA, JR.

The Agriculture and Food Act of 1981 provides the authority for the enactment of farm commodity programs affecting the crops of 1982 through 1985.[1] The Farm Act sets forth broad guidelines for food and agricultural policy for the next four years and provides a framework for the achievement of several goals. Among the aims of the Act are: (1) to provide minimum income and price support protection for producers; (2) to maintain a grain reserve which acts to moderate grain price volatility as well as provide food security; and (3) to assure a continuous supply of food and fiber for consumers. As the first two goals involve management of supply and price, participants in the futures markets should take more than a passing interest in the parameters involved. If the past can be used as a guide, the current legislation will have a definite impact on cash grain and fiber prices, which in turn will influence the course of futures prices. This article describes the current farm commodity programs as they pertain to the food grains, feed grains and cotton.[2] The areas examined are:

—the price support loan and target price program
—set aside, reduced acreage and paid diversion program and
—the farmer-owned grain reserve

After a description of the operation of each program, an analysis is made of the potential impact of each program on cash and futures prices.

While the 1981 Farm Act provides guidelines for commodity programs, specific operating rules are left largely to the discretion of the Secretary of Agriculture. As the economic situation in the agricultural sector changes, adjustments must be made in the programs to achieve basic goals. Often, it is these changes which exert the strongest short-term influence on prices. Therefore, a discussion of the future direction of agricultural policy also will be included.

The Changing Economic Climate

The 1981 Farm Act is a product, in part, of the economic and political climate at its passage. While the Act offers some new programs, much of its basic direction is derived from previous farm legislation. Indeed, the present Act closely resembles the Food and Agriculture Act of 1977, which defined many of the policy tools incorporated in the current legislation. Still, differences exist, partly as a result of changing economic conditions. The two most important developments over the last decade have been the almost continuous increase in production, due primarily to higher yields, and the rapid expansion of exports. Agriculture walks a tightrope, in that when usage outgrows production, stocks fall and prices rise. This was evidenced during the period of 1971–73, in corn.

During this time, exports grew sharply and corn ending stocks were reduced by over 50%, causing average season prices to increase by over 100%. Over the last few seasons, however, despite the huge growth in exports, a combination of good management, high quality inputs, favorable weather and increased plantings have led to production in excess of usage. Between 1980 and 1982, corn production increased by 26%, while usage actually grew by less than one percent. The stock buildup of over 200% caused a decline in average farm prices of over 25%. Farm income, whether measured in nominal or inflation-adjusted terms, showed a similar decline.

The basic provisions of the 1981 Farm Act provide for support of farm prices at minimum loan rates, income support based on target prices with increasing annual price adjustments and a grain reserve that accumulates stocks when prices are low and releases them at higher prices. In return for the protection offered by these measures, the Secretary of Agriculture is given the authority to require producers to reduce the amount of acreage planted.

Loan and Target Price Program

The Farm Act continues the price support loan and income support, i.e., target price, program. The Act establishes minimum loan rates through 1985, although the Secretary has the authority to adjust grain loans. A formula is used to set the loan rate for cotton. The primary purpose of the loan is to provide the producer with a source of cash at harvest so that he does not have to market his crop immediately, while also providing minimum price protection. Non-recourse commodity loans are available to eligible producers from USDA's Commodity Credit Corporation (CCC). Upon receiving the loan, the producer pledges the crop as collateral, and the amount of the loan is equal to the loan rate multiplied by the quantity put under loan. The loan period is usually nine months, although extensions have been granted.[3]

Upon maturity of the loan, the producer has two options. First, he can repay or redeem the loan and accrued interest, a course he will take if cash prices have risen enough to make loan repayment and subsequent cash sales profitable. Even if cash prices have not improved enough at loan maturity, producers' expectations of higher prices in the future will often lead them to redeem the loan and reclaim their crops. Second, the producer can forfeit the crop to the CCC, effectively removing it from the market until prices reach higher levels when the CCC can legally resell the stocks. The nonrecourse nature of the loan to the producer means that the CCC, in the event of loan forfeiture, must assume ownership of the grain or cotton.

Because of this, prices tend to be supported at the

---

[1] In this paper reference to the Agriculture and Food Act of 1981 includes the basic Act as well as subsequent legislation which provided further guidelines for farm policy affecting the crops of 1982–85.

[2] For the purposes of this paper, program crops refer to those crops having a farm program i.e., feed grains (corn, barley, sorghum and oats) food grains (wheat and rice) and cotton. Non-program crops do not have a program. Soybeans are a non-program crop though they do have a basic price support loan program.

[3] Corn and sorghum loans are available from harvest until May 31. Wheat, rice, barley and oats loans are available from harvest through March 31. Loans mature on demand but no later than the last day of the 9th calendar month following the month that the loan was made. Cotton loans are for 10 months and may be extended another 8 months whenever the spot market average price in the preceding month is 130% or less of the average for the previous 36 months. Loans are available through May 31.

23

loan rate, particularly when loans have been taken out on a large portion of the crop. Since loan rates tend to place a floor under prices, it is possible that loan rates could establish prices which exceed world price levels. In this situation, the effect would be to reduce the competitiveness of U.S. exports. The Secretary of Agriculture, therefore, has the authority to lower the loan rate for corn or wheat by no more than 10% a year if the average domestic market price is not more than 105% of the loan rate in any marketing year.

The Farm Act establishes minimum target price levels through 1985. Annual increases of between 3% and 7% are built in. Target prices for sorghum, oats and barley are set in relation to their feeding values with corn. Adjustments in target prices can be made on the basis of changing costs of production, which are measured by moving averages based on costs per acre. *Target prices are used in the calculation of deficiency or income-support payments.* Deficiency payments are made to eligible producers if, during the first 5 months of a crop's marketing year (12 calendar months for cotton), prices average below the target price. The deficiency payment rate is then determined by the difference between the target price and the higher of the average market price or the loan rate. An example of the program's implementation is the payment to 1982-crop wheat producers. The average wheat price during the June–October period was $3.34 per bushel or 21¢ per bushel below the loan rate. Deficiency payments were therefore calculated on the difference between the target price ($4.05 per bushel) and the loan rate ($3.55 per bushel), for a maximum payment of 50¢ per bushel. Total program payments were $475 million.

TABLE 1.
Corn Balance Sheet (1970–1982)

Crop Year	Beginning Stocks	Production and Imports	Domestic Use (million bu.)	Exports	Ending Stocks	Average Season Price ($/bu.)
1970	1005	4156	3977	517	667	1.33
1971	667	5647	4391	796	1127	1.08
1972	1127	5581	4742	1258	708	1.57
1973	708	5672	4653	1243	484	2.55
1974	484	4703	3677	1149	361	3.02
1975	361	5843	4093	1711	400	2.54
1976	400	6291	4121	1684	886	2.15
1977	886	6508	4334	1948	1111	2.02
1978	1111	7269	4943	2133	1304	2.25
1979	1304	7940	5194	2433	1617	2.52
1980	1617	6646	4874	2355	1034	3.11
1981	1034	8203	4984	1967	2286	2.45
1982*	2286	8398	5200	2100	3384	2.30

*USDA projections

Table 2.
Productivity Changes in Corn during 1970–82 Compared to the Base Period 1965–69

Crop Year	Yield (bu./acre)	% Change from 1965–69	Harvested Acreage (mil. acres)	% Change from 1965–69	Production (mil. bu.)	% Change from 1965–69
1965–69	78.5		56.7		4347	
1970	72.4	−8	57.4	+1	4152	−4
1971	88.1	+12	64.1	+13	5646	+30
1972	97.0	+24	57.5	+1	5580	+28
1973	91.3	+16	62.1	+10	5671	+30
1974	71.9	−8	65.4	+15	4701	+8
1975	86.4	+10	67.6	+19	5841	+34
1976	88.0	+12	71.5	+26	6289	+45
1977	90.8	+16	71.6	+26	6505	+50
1978	101.0	+29	71.9	+27	7268	+67
1979	109.7	+40	72.4	+28	7939	+83
1980	91.0	+16	73.0	+29	6645	+53
1981	109.8	+40	74.7	+32	8202	+89
1982	114.8	+46	73.2	+29	8397	+93

Loan Impact on Cash and Futures Prices

The price support loan exerts its strongest impact on price following the harvest. The effectiveness of the loan is directly related to the amount of the crop placed under loan. This will be particularly evident when cash prices are below the loan rate. The 1982 crop year provides an example of the relationship between loan eligibility and cash prices. With a reduced acreage program in effect for corn, only those producers reducing acreage by 10% would be eligible for the price support loan. Soybean producers are all eligible for the loan since they have no program requirements (such as acreage restrictions). Final season data showed that about 24% of 1982 corn acreage was enrolled in the program. With low overall grain prices, soybean producers made extensive use of the loan, and cash prices after falling under the $5.02 per bushel loan rate rose above it and remained there. Eligible corn producers also made use of the loan, but the relatively small number who were eligible for the loan was not enough to raise prices to the loan rate of $2.55 per bushel. Cash corn prices continued to remain well below the loan rate throughout the early part of the 1982/83 season.

The impact of producer use of the loan on futures prices is similar to its effect on the cash market. Nearby futures can be adjusted to a cash basis by using an historical cash-futures basis differential at harvest. During 1982, this basis was about 25¢ for both corn and soybeans. Widespread use of the loan therefore tends to support the futures price at the loan rate adjusted for the harvest basis.

Another effect of the loan is to smooth out the impact of the harvest on cash prices. By using the loan, the producer can defer cash sales and pay harvest bills with the loan. In the futures market, this type of activity would support the nearby harvest contract relative to the deferred contracts. For instance, heavy loan entries during harvest would be reflected in a narrowing of the December/September corn spread while similar activity in soybeans would be apparent in the November/September spread. As a general rule, as long as loan use remains high, the nearby contracts will strengthen relative to the deferred contracts. Some producers may also decide to take out loans after January for tax purposes, in which case the March contracts could strengthen relative to the more distant futures. It should be remembered that grain loans are for 9 months and that, at maturity, they are usually redeemed. As loans mature, the effect on cash and futures prices would be to weaken them.

Target prices are important in that they can improve the effectiveness of the farm program by inducing greater producer participation. The higher the target price, relative to the loan, the greater the potential deficiency payment and income support. If producers' price expectations are low, the target price will enhance the attractiveness of the program. Since the programs often include acreage reduction provisions, a high target price can lead to acreage and production reductions and overall higher prices. High target prices relative to loan rates and expected cash prices could indicate heavy program participation. Announcements of target prices for each program crop should be examined in light of their potential effect on program participation, which should in turn be reflected in the appropriate intercommodity price spread relationships.

The Farmer-Owned Reserve

The Food and Agriculture Act of 1977 mandated the establishment of a farmer-owned grain reserve (FOR). The 1981 Farm Act continues the FOR for feed grains and wheat. In concept the program is relatively simple. Producers who comply with basic program parameters such as acreage reduction are eligible to enter their grain in the FOR. A contract is entered into which places the grain into the reserve for three to five years in return for a loan. The grain remains in the producer's possession during the duration of the contract and is usually stored in the farmer's own bins. To facilitate the FOR, the USDA has provided financing for a storage program which has resulted in a large increase in on-farm storage capacity.

Under the 1981 Farm Act, the Secretary of Agriculture has the authority to increase loan rates, pay storage and waive interest on FOR loans in order to encourage participation in the program. The Secretary also has the authority to place an upper limit on the FOR provided it is not less than 700 million bushels of wheat and a billion bushels of feed grains. For 1982 crops, the FOR loan rate is higher than the price-support loan rate. Annual storage payments are 26.5¢ per bushel and interest on the second and third years of the FOR loan are waived. For 1983 crops, the FOR loan rate will revert to the prevailing price-support loan rate. Storage payments and the interest waiver will remain in effect. For the 1982 crops, entry into the FOR was immediate. This rule is changed for 1983 crops and FOR entry will now only be allowed after a producer has obtained the regular nine-month price support loan and it has matured. Grain remains in the FOR for the life of the contract or until the release trigger price is reached. For corn, the 1982 reserve program trigger is $3.25 per bushel while for wheat it is $4.65 per bushel. After cash prices reach the trigger, producers may repay their FOR loans and

Table 3.

Current Price Support Loan Rates and Target Prices (1982–85)

Year	Corn Loan ($/bu.)	Corn Target ($/bu.)	Wheat Loan ($/bu.)	Wheat Target ($/bu.)	Cotton Loan (¢/lb.)	Cotton Target (¢/lb.)	Rice Loan ($/cwt.)	Rice Target ($/cwt.)	Sorghum Loan ($/bu.)	Sorghum Target ($/bu.)	Barley Loan ($/bu.)	Barley Target ($/bu.)	Oats Loan ($/bu.)	Oats Target ($/bu.)
1982	2.55	2.70	3.55	4.05	57.08	71	8.00	10.85	2.42	2.60	2.08	2.60	1.31	1.50
1983	2.65	2.86	3.65	4.30	55	76	8.00	11.40	2.52	2.72	2.16	2.60	1.36	1.60
1984	2.55	3.03	3.55	4.45	55	81	8.00	11.90	NA	NA	NA	NA	NA	NA
1985	2.55	3.18	3.55	4.65	55	86	8.00	12.40	NA	NA	NA	NA	NA	NA

NA–not announced yet.
For 1984–85 these are minimum loan rates for the grains.

market their grain. If a producer thinks that prices may go even higher, he can choose to stay in the FOR. In this situation, the Secretary has the authority to stop storage payments to producers and to renew interest charges if they have been stopped. Penalties are in effect for producers who wish to leave the FOR before the trigger is reached.

Grain Reserve Impact on Cash and Futures Prices

The FOR will have a supportive influence on prices as it accumulates grain and a bearish impact during the release phase. At the harvest, when prices are low, eligible producers of the 1983 crop will be able to take out a regular price support loan and on maturity roll it over into the FOR if they choose. Prices will strengthen as grain moves into the reserve and as market stocks are gradually reduced. How much prices strengthen is a function of how much grain enters the FOR relative to the prospective carryover (ending stocks). If FOR entries are brisk but the size of the crop is large and ending stocks are projected to be more than adequate then the impact of the FOR will not be as great.

The effectiveness of the FOR in boosting prices is also related to producer eligibility and participation in the program. Producers will weigh the benefits of joining or not participating. Changes in the FOR loan rate will affect participation with higher loan rates encouraging usage of the program. Following the grain embargo of January 1980, FOR loan rates and storage payments were increased. After the initial shock of the embargo announcement, prices recovered as good use was made of the FOR; measurement of futures prices showed wheat gaining nearly 60¢ per bushel from the post-embargo lows. Corn prices rallied back to pre-embargo levels almost immediately. Since the FOR contract can be for a maximum of three to five years, interest on the loan is an important consideration. Currently (in early 1983), interest on the second and third years is waived, making the average interest rate much lower. Should the Secretary resume full interest charges, use of the FOR would become more expensive and less attractive. Finally, it is necessary to consider the other aspects of the program. To be eligible for the FOR one must comply with all program requirements, such as a set-aside. When no acreage reduction program is in effect all producers are generally eligible to use the FOR, which was the case in 1981. For the 1983 season, acreage reduction and diversion of 20% is required.

During the grain accumulation phase of the FOR, a number of price effects should be observed. Overall, the FOR will reduce free market stocks by inducing larger entries into the reserve, leading to higher prices. The prices of program crops like corn and wheat will rise relative to non-program crops like soybeans (all other effects being equal), particularly when entries are heavy and free stocks are declining. Program crops with higher levels of FOR participation should also gain price-wise on crops with lower participation rates. An example of this is usually seen in the wheat market. Hard winter and hard spring wheat producers traditionally are good participants in the government programs while soft winter wheat producers do not usually participate, since their crop is often sold right after harvest. All other effects being equal, the use of the FOR will be reflected in the intermarket commodity futures spreads as well as in the cash market relationships. Hard winter wheat, traded on the Kansas City Board of Trade, will gain on soft winter wheat, which is traded at the Chicago Board of Trade. It will be true, also, that hard spring wheat, traded at the Minneapolis Grain Exchange, will gain on Chicago's soft winter wheat.

While these relationships will be seen during the accumulation phase of the FOR, once the trigger is reached the opposite effects should be observed. Since the USDA releases national average prices daily and these are used daily to determine when the trigger is reached, they can be readily followed. After the trigger price is reached, producers may redeem their loans and market their grain as they see fit. How much prices weaken and the spreads unwind is a function of how much grain moves into market channels. The more that is marketed, the more prices can be expected to fall. A consideration to note is the time of release. Release approaching harvest is likely, since prices are then at their seasonal peak. This may cause a heavy cash movement as the next crop harvest is anticipated. Release during the winter may mean lighter cash sales as producers hold in the expectation of seasonally higher spring prices.

During the short history of the FOR, there have been a number of instances when the release trigger price has been reached. It should be noted, however, that during the previous years the FOR had a two-tiered release mechanism. As a result, the release did not operate quite like the current one-tier release price mechanism. Observation of futures price activity both before and after previous releases of the FOR confirm that the reserve did have an impact on prices. During the accumulation phase, prices strengthened as expected and then weakened after release was announced. Two examples illustrate the effect. In May 1979, wheat became eligible for release. During the accumulation phase prior to release, wheat futures strengthened by approximately 50¢ per bushel. On release, prices began to weaken. In July wheat storage payments were stopped, encouraging a further exit from the program. The immediate price effect was a decline of nearly 60¢ per bushel. (It should be noted, of course, that the harvest also exerted a strong impact on prices, and isolation of the FOR release effect is difficult.) In late January 1980, wheat again reached the release price. Prior to the release, hard winter wheat in Kansas City moved from a 20¢ per bushel discount to soft winter wheat to a premium of about 5¢ per bushel. After the release, this intermarket wheat price spread unwound and hard wheat fell back to a 10¢ per bushel discount.

Set Aside and Diversion

Historically, agricultural production adjustments often have been achieved by taking acreage out of use. The terms *set-aside*, *diversion* and *reduced acreage* all refer to methods of removing land from production. A set-aside is a method of land retirement which requires the producer to remove a given percentage of his normal crop acreage from use. Under a set-aside, the crop mix on the remaining land can change, and it is possible for program crop acreage to increase. Under paid diversion, producers receive cash payments for the idling of acreage. A reduced acreage program (RAP) is similar to a set-aside, except that the acreage reduction is specific to a given crop. The crop base against which the reduction is measured is usually the previous year's plantings or an average of previous years' plantings. The RAP is the mandatory acreage program for cotton and rice, and it may be used, as well, as an alternative to set-aside for wheat and feed grains. When the RAP is in effect, producers do not have to cross-comply, that is, participate in all programs to be eligible for any one. When a set-aside is in effect, the authority to require cross compliance is retained for wheat and feed grains. Producers who own more than one farm may be required to meet program requirements on all of their farms; that is not in effect, however, for 1983 crops.

Table 4.
Acreage Reduction Programs in Effect for 1983 Crops

Crop	Acreage Reduction Program
Corn	− 10% RAP − 10% Paid Diversion − 10%–30% PIK (optional) − 100% PIK (optional)
Wheat	− 15% RAP − 5% Paid Diversion − 10%–30% PIK (optional) − 100% PIK (optional)
Upland Cotton	− 20% RAP − 5% Paid Diversion (optional) − 10%–30% PIK (optional) − 100% PIK (optional)
Rice	− 15% RAP − 5% Paid Diversion − 10%–30% PIK (optional) − 100% PIK (optional)
Sorghum	− 10% RAP − 10% Paid Diversion − 10%–30% PIK (optional) − 100% PIK (optional)
Barley	− 10% RAP − 10% Paid Diversion
Oats	− 10% RAP − 10% Paid Diversion

Under the 1981 Farm Act, the Secretary of Agriculture has the authority to require a reduction in plantings of feed grains, wheat, rice and upland cotton, if such a reduction is necessary to bring supply into balance with usage. During the 1981 season, there was no acreage reduction, while during 1982 a reduced acreage program was in effect. For the 1983 crop, a combination RAP and paid diversion is in effect. Corn producers must reduce corn plantings by 10% and divert an additional 10% of corn acreage. For the diverted acreage, the producer receives $1.50 per bushel based on his average farm yield. Wheat producers must reduce plantings by 15% and divert 5% of acreage, for which they receive $2.70 per bushel. Cotton producers are required to reduce acreage 20% and they have the option to divert 5% additional land at a payment rate of 25¢ per pound.

All participants in the 1983 corn, sorghum, wheat, cotton and rice programs are eligible for the optional payment-in-kind program (PIK). The PIK allows program participants to further reduce acreage in return for payment in like commodities. The PIK options available are an acreage reduction of 10% to 30% above the basic program requirements—for which corn, sorghum, cotton and rice producers will receive 80% of their expected production in like payment. Wheat producers will receive 95% of their expected production since most of the crop was planted at the time of the program announcement. A second PIK option involves removal of 100% (the whole-base bid) of a farm's program crop acreage and requires the producer to submit a bid specifying how much in-kind commodity he expects to receive in return. The program is not new, having been used with some success in the early 1960's.

Impact of Reduced Acreage Programs on Cash and Futures Prices

Acreage reduction programs are supportive to both cash and futures prices. They result, normally, in curtailed production of the program crop, and the greater the amount of land removed, the stronger should be the price effect. Just as participation in the reserve supports prices of enrolled crops, relative to those not enrolled, so should participation in the reduction program. Of the three types of land retirement plans, the most likely to be effective is paid diversion, because producers are most responsive to direct cash payments. For acreage reduction of specific targeted crops, the reduced acreage program works well because it is, by definition, crop-specific. Set-asides are appropriate for the removal of given amounts of land, although the planting mix on the remaining land may result in increased plantings of program crops.

The effectiveness of the acreage reduction program in boosting prices is a function of the amount of acreage actually retired, and of production on the land remaining to be farmed. The amount of acreage idled is related directly to the degree of program participation, which, in turn, is dependent upon the appeal of the plan. The 1982-crop reduced acreage program was not effective for a number of reasons. First, the RAP only called for program crop acreage cuts of 10% with no paid diversion included. Secondly, compliance dates were in the beginning of the growing season after producers could gauge their crop prospects. Excellent weather in the Eastern Corn Belt led to heavy plantings and little use of the program. The Western Corn Belt experienced planting delays due to wet weather which led to greater participation. Expectations of better prices probably contributed to low participation also. The attractiveness of the 1983 program is enhanced by its inclusion of a combination of RAP, paid diversion (optional in cotton) and PIK option. Also, producers who enroll receive half of their diversion payment and half of their expected deficiency payment, at sign-up. This provision will increase participation. Producers will also consider other program features, such as FOR rules, loan rates and expected deficiency payments.

While initial sign-up for the program may be high and seem to indicate a successful acreage reduction, the decision to remain in the program is usually made at planting or after the crop is in the early stages of development. The producer will calculate the expected revenues and the costs incurred in producing each crop. For program crops, the benefits of participation must be included, and consideration given to the reduced revenues from less production as well as to lessened planting and harvesting expenses. The producer will then compare the profitability of producing the crops in question and will plant the most profitable. As occurred in 1982, weather can be the deciding factor, since final program compliance dates fall after planting. Initial sign-up for the 1982 RAP was encouraging, but final compliance changed markedly with the weather. In general, producers are willing to idle unproductive land but are hesitant to remove productive acreage from use. Price expectations are also a consideration. If price prospects are not good, producers will seek the income protection the program offers. Good price prospects, due perhaps to a bullish export outlook, will lead some producers to plant as much as possible. An initial indication of the success of an acreage reduction program will be contained in the USDA's June *Acreage* report of plantings. The prices of those crops which show reduced plantings will be supported. In the futures market, this will be reflected in the intercommodity as well as intermarket spreads. Also, old-crop or current-crop prices should weaken relative to new-crop prices. In corn, the relationships to observe will be the September/December and the September/March or May spreads.

One side effect of acreage reduction programs is that they generally lead to increased plantings of non-program crops. This is due, in part, to greater expected profitability in other crops at planting, weather conditions and expectations that the acreage reduction will increase the price level of all crops planted. During 1978, the set-aside in corn resulted in 3% fewer acres, while soybean acreage rose 10% and sunflower seedings increased 22%. In 1979, corn was again set-aside but acreage fell less than 1%. Soybean plantings continued to increase, rising another 11% while sunflower acreage doubled. With no reduction program in effect during 1980, corn plantings rose 3% while wheat acreage increased 13%. During the same time, soybean acreage fell 2% and sunflower acreage dropped 30%. The 1982 RAP saw corn acreage fall again while soybean acreage increased, due partly to loopholes in the program which allowed some non-program crops to be planted within the program. For the 1983 RAP, this loophole has been closed.

Table 5.
Planted Acreage of Major Crops (1970–82)

Crop Year	Corn	All Wheat	Upland Cotton	Sorghum, Oats & Barley	Soybeans	Sunflowers	Rice
1970	66.9*	48.7*	11.9	51.8*	43.1	.2	1.8
1971	74.2*	53.8*	12.3*	53.4*	43.5	.4	1.8
1972	67.1*	54.9*	13.9*	47.6*	46.9	.7	1.8
1973	72.3*	59.3*	12.4*	48.6*	56.5	.7	2.2
1974	77.9	71.0	13.6	43.3	52.5	.6	2.5
1975	78.7	74.9	9.4	43.9	54.6	.8	2.8
1976	84.6	80.4	11.6	44.1	50.3	.8	2.5
1977	84.3	75.4	13.6	45.1	59.0	2.3	2.3
1978	81.7*	66.0*	13.3*	42.6*	64.7	2.8	3.0
1979	81.4*	71.4*	13.9	37.3*	71.6	5.6	2.9
1980	84.0	80.6	14.5	37.4	70.0	3.9	3.4
1981	84.2	88.9	14.3	39.4	67.8	3.9	3.8
1982	81.9*	87.3*	11.4*	40.0*	72.2	5.0	3.3*

*Set-aside, paid diversion or RAP in effect.

A final consideration in the analysis of the effectiveness of an acreage reduction program is the issue of *slippage*. Slippage occurs when the acreage reduction program calls for a given amount of acreage to be idled but there is not a corresponding decrease in production. Slippage can occur because producers shift acreage into the program crop from a non-program crop. It can also occur through yield increases on the remaining program crop acreage. For example, a 10% reduction in corn plantings should, in theory, lead to a 10% reduction in production. In practice, such a reduction does not occur, and the actual reduction may total only 5%. Several reasons for this may be offered. First, marginal cropland is considered base acreage and will be the first to be set-aside or diverted. Yields or production on the remaining cropped acreage will therefore increase. Second, by reducing acreage, the producer has more resources available and may, therefore, intensify effort on the remaining acreage. These resources include labor, fertilizer and pesticides. Again, the result is higher yields. The current USDA policy of advance diversion and deficiency payments may well increase slippage by providing producers with additional financial resources. Analysis of acreage reduction programs between 1956–73 led USDA to determine that slippage made these programs only 50%–60% effective in reducing production.

The Commodity Credit Corporation

Any discussion of farm programs and policy would be incomplete without a description of the functions of the Commodity Credit Corporation. The CCC is a government-owned corporation, authorized to support the prices of agricultural commodities through loans, purchases, payments and other operations. The CCC borrows funds from the U.S. Treasury, and these funds provide the basic support to finance the farm programs. The interest rate on the funds borrowed is the one that accrues on price-support and FOR loans. It is adjusted monthly. In this sense, the

CCC functions as the financial arm of the USDA. The CCC has no operating personnel, and its programs are carried out by the Agricultural Stabilization and Conservation Service (ASCS).

The CCC is best known for its acquisition, carrying and disposal of agricultural products. Most prominent in its inventory are the dairy program stocks, but of importance to futures market participants is the inventory of grains. The CCC accumulates inventories in two ways: first, the commodities pledged as collateral for price-support loans are taken over (if the loans are not redeemed by loan repayment time) and become part of the CCC inventory. The CCC may also accumulate inventory through direct purchases in an attempt to support prices. This type of activity was undertaken after the 1980 grain embargo when the CCC purchased 160 million bushels of corn.

Like purchases, disposal of CCC stocks is handled by the ASCS. Under current regulations (early 1983), whenever the FOR loan program is in effect, the CCC cannot sell any of its stock of feed grains or wheat at less than 110 percent of the release trigger price. Under the 1977 Act, the CCC could not sell any of its grain stocks at less than 105 percent of the then current call price if the reserve was in effect. When the FOR is not active the minimum resale price for CCC stocks of feed grains and wheat will not be less than 115 percent of the current national average loan rate, adjusted for market differentials and reasonable carrying charges. For cotton, the CCC minimum sales price is not to be less than 115 percent of the loan rate for upland cotton with adjustments for grade, quality, location and other value factors and carrying charges.

Sales at these prices are designed to ensure that they do not interfere with commercial trade channels. Under certain circumstances, the CCC may sell part of its inventory if it is in danger of spoilage. Sales may also be authorized for special programs such as gasohol production. Disposal of stocks overseas may be authorized to help needy countries.

Future Farm Policy

The USDA has a historic mandate to use farm policy tools to bring supply and demand into balance, as well as to modify volatile prices and assure consumers of an adequate food supply. The current economic situation in the agricultural sector provides the USDA with ample opportunity to exercise this mandate. With stocks of commodities at high levels and inflation-adjusted farm prices and income reaching historic lows, different and innovative approaches to the problem may be required. The current administration has indicated it will take this approach, as demonstrated by the PIK program. The success of the 1983-crop program will, in large part, determine the program of 1984. The success of the program will be determined by how much stocks are reduced, how much cash prices recover and the improvement in farm income. Unless there is a natural reduction in supplies, for instance because of drought, it is likely the PIK program will be extended for the 1984 crop. It is also likely that the reduced acreage program will be continued and a paid diversion will be used again. Recent actions by the USDA indicate that reduced emphasis will be placed on the farmer-owned reserve program. The removal of FOR loan premiums and the nine-month loan entry rule have made the program a less attractive alternative for 1983 crops. These rules could remain in effect for 1984. A cap (limit) on the FOR also remains a possibility, although the USDA has indicated it will not cap 1983-crop entries.

Another area which will help reduce the burdensome stock situation is to stimulate the demand for exports. This is a politically sensitive issue, since the U.S. remains committed to free trade. Direct export subsidies can lead to retaliation by other producers through increased subsidies or trade restrictions on U.S. exports. The USDA has formulated a policy that reduces the cost of financing imports of U.S. commodities. The program allows importers to finance purchases through a combination of loans made at market rates of interest and interest-free loans. Initial use of this blended credit program has been termed successful. More financing has been allocated to the program and it is expected to remain a policy tool over the next few seasons. These are just some of the policy tools that may be employed to solve current farm problems. Their success could determine the shape and content of the Agriculture and Food Act of 1985.

INTRODUCTION TO COMMODITY OPTIONS

BY WILLIAM J. JOHNSON

Options are trading vehicles that assign to a buyer the financial benefits of a favorable commodity price move while at the same time assigning to the seller (writer or grantor) the financial liabilities. Naturally the seller requires compensation for accepting the risks. There are two types of commodity futures options. They are calls and puts. A call grants to its buyer the right of buying (or calling away) from the option seller a commodity futures contract at a specified price. A put grants the buyer the right to sell (or put) to the option seller a commodity contract at a specific price. The specific price at which a commodity is transferred is the strike price. The compensation received by the seller and paid by the buyer is the premium, which is the market price of the option.

As this name implies, commodity futures options provide the buyer with choices. The choices are most easily understood by the use of illustrations of both the buyers and the sellers of options.

Buyer of Call Option—Sugar

Consider a buyer of a call option of a March 1984 sugar contract with a striking price of 9¢. The buyer purchases the right to call into his futures account one March 1984 sugar contract (112,000 pounds) valued at 9¢ per pound. The price or premium for this purchase is assumed to be 1.10¢ per pound. His cost is 1.10¢ per lb. × 112,000 lbs., or $1,232 plus an assumed $50 commission. He makes money if the price of March 1984 sugar futures moves above his break-even point of 10.10¢ per lb. plus commission. (Throughout the balance of the article, commission charges are not considered in order to simplify illustrations.) If the price of March '84 sugar moves above 9¢ the option has *intrinsic value* equal to the difference figured between the strike price (9¢) and any subsequent higher price for March '84 futures. For example, if March '84 sugar advances to 9½¢ per pound, the call option holder has the right to exercise his call and establish a ½¢ per pound gain (9½¢–9¢) even though this advance does not attain his break-even level. Because this right is guaranteed, the price of the option will trade at least at that level.

There is another element of value involved in options; that is the *time value* of the option. If it is mid-December 1983, and there is 3 months left in the option, the March '84 call option with a 9¢ strike price may be trading at .75¢ per pound. Time value is calculated as the difference between the market price of the option and its intrinsic value. Assuming that March '84 futures are trading at 9½¢, the intrinsic value is .50¢ and the market value is .75¢ so the time value is .25¢ for the 3 months remaining in the option contract. (Note that the March option contract expires in February. Anyone entering into any option transaction, must know when the precise expiration date occurs.)

Let's examine more closely the above example to determine overall profitability of the option trade. The option was purchased at a premium of 1.10¢ per pound in March 1983 with a striking price of 9¢. At that time the March 1984 sugar futures contract was also trading at 9¢ so the option is regarded as *at-the-money*. In other words, the market price of the futures contract is the same as the strike price of the option. Therefore, no intrinsic value exists. The entire premium was paid to purchase one year's time during which the option buyer hopes for higher sugar prices.

TABLE 1

	Sugar Call Option Strike Price 9¢	March 1984 Futures Contract Premium Paid 1.10¢/lb.
Purchase price		
Premium		$1.10¢/lb.
Contract Size		112,000 lbs.
Total Premium		$1,232
Brokers Commission		50
Total Purchase Costs		$1,282

Date	December, 1983	February, 1984
March Sugar Price	9.50¢	9.50¢
Intrinsic Value	.50¢	.50¢
Time Value	.25¢	.0
Market Value (Per Pound)	.75¢	.50¢
Market Value (Per Contract)	$ 840	$ 560
Commission	($50)	($50)
Total Liquidated Value	$ 790	$ 510
Total Purchase Costs	$1,282	$1,282
Total Profit (Loss)	($492)	($772)

How to Read the Options Tables

"CALLS—LAST" These columns show the day's closing price or premium for call options which are rights to buy one gold futures contract. The premium is quoted in dollars per ounce of gold. To calculate the total premium of one option multiply the option's premium by 100 since there are 100 ounces to a gold contract and add the commissions which you can obtain from your broker.

Exchange on which the option is traded.

The commodity and the month which are traded on the futures market. The month is not the expiration month of the option.

Striking price is the price at which the option to buy or sell may be exercised.

The closing price for put options which are rights to sell one contract of gold options.

Estimated volume of option trades.

Actual volume traded on the previous Friday and open interest on that day. Open interest is the number of options in existence. When a buyer and a seller of the same commodity month and striking price each establish a new position in that option, the open interest increases by one.

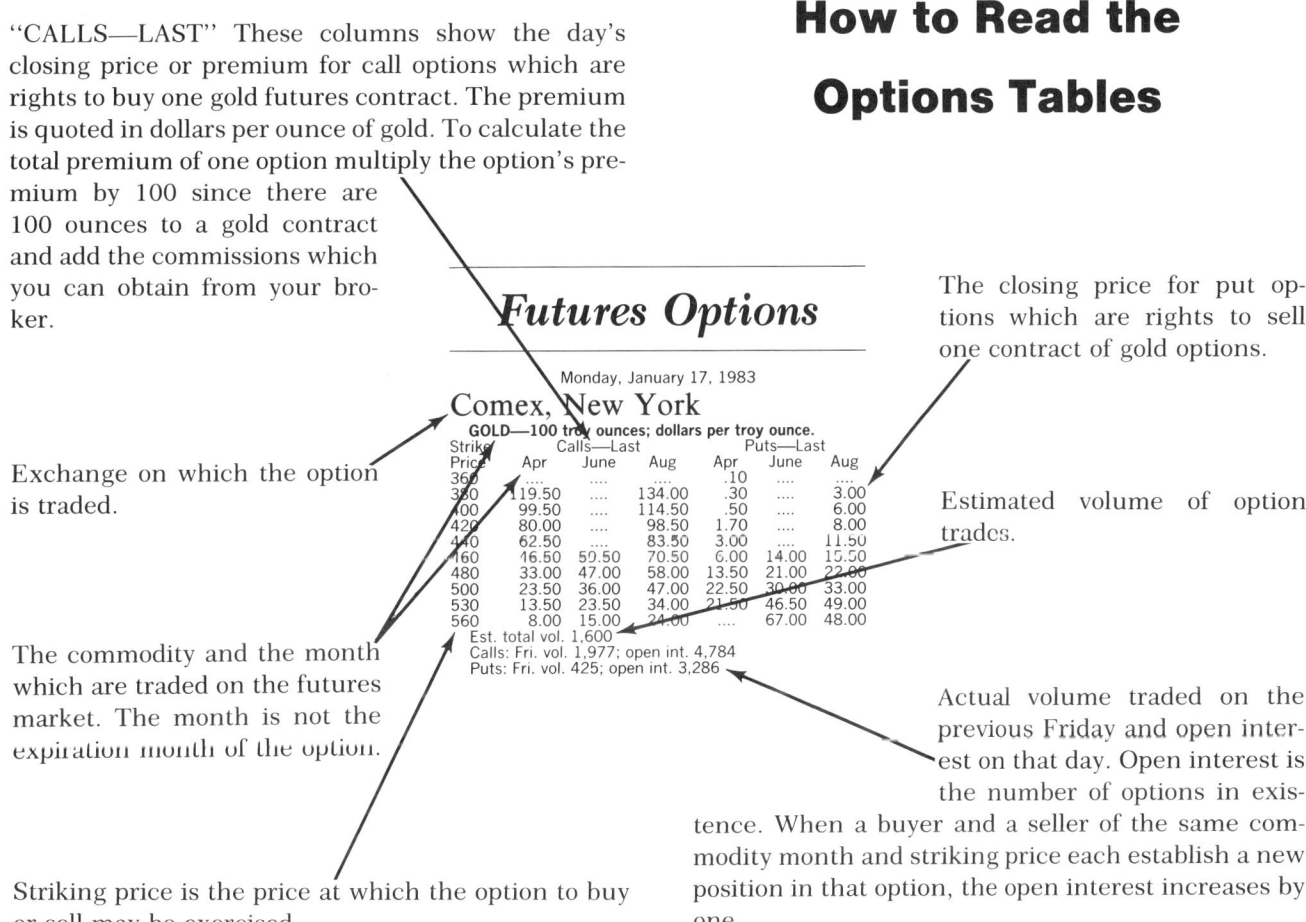

Examples:

On January 17th, the purchase of a call option on April gold with a striking price of $460 would cost the buyer $4650 (the premium of $46.50 per oz. × 100 oz.) plus the broker's commission. The buyer would hold the right to buy one contract of April gold at a price of $460 per ounce. On that day, the April gold futures were trading at $499.60 so the option had an inherent value of $39.60 per ounce or $3960 per contract.

On the same day a put option on April gold with a striking price of $460 would cost the buyer $6.00 per ounce or $600 plus a broker's commission. Since this put option gives the buyer the right to sell one contract of April gold at a price of $460 and the current price of April gold is $499.60 the put is "out-of-the-money." Note that its premium price is considerably less than the "in-the-money" call option premium with the same striking price.

Any price above 9¢ for March '84 sugar futures will contribute to the call option's intrinsic value. In this example, March '84 sugar has in fact gone up to 9.50¢ per pound. If the buyer sold in December 1983 and obtained a price of .75¢ for the option he would have lost $492 (see Table 1). If the March '84 sugar market remains at 9.50¢ until mid-February when the option expires, the 25¢ time value will be reduced to zero and the option will be worth only its intrinsic value, .50¢ per pound resulting in a total loss of $772 (see Table 1).

It is relatively easy to illustrate the break-even position of an option buyer upon expiration of the option since the time value will always be zero at that point.

Chart 1 shows the buyer reaching his break-even point of approximately 10.19¢ (including commissions) for March '84 futures at the time the option expires in February. Between 9.05¢ and 10.19¢ a loss will incur but the option has an intrinsic value which allows the option buyer to get back part of his premium. Below 9.05¢ the option holder loses all his premium. In this case there is no time value or intrinsic value. However, it is emphasized here that a call buyer cannot lose more than the premium and commission costs.

Seller of Call Option—Sugar

The option seller's situation is quite the opposite of the option buyer's situation. Having received the premium from the sale of a call option (less commission), the seller has assigned the financial gains of higher sugar prices to the buyer. Unlike the buyer, the seller has unlimited liability and in many respects has established a short position in the futures market. If prices rise, the seller is required to put up additional funds equal to the higher value of the sugar call option.

These additional funds are margin calls similar to margin calls associated with commodity futures accounts. A seller of an option can lose in excess of the entire premium price. Significantly higher sugar prices will result in significantly higher losses.

On the other hand, if sugar prices fail to rise, that is, remain stable or drop even slightly, the seller of a call option earns the total premium less the initial commission. Chart 2 shows the break-even analysis of the seller. Notice that as sugar prices increase, the seller of a call has an unlimited potential loss.

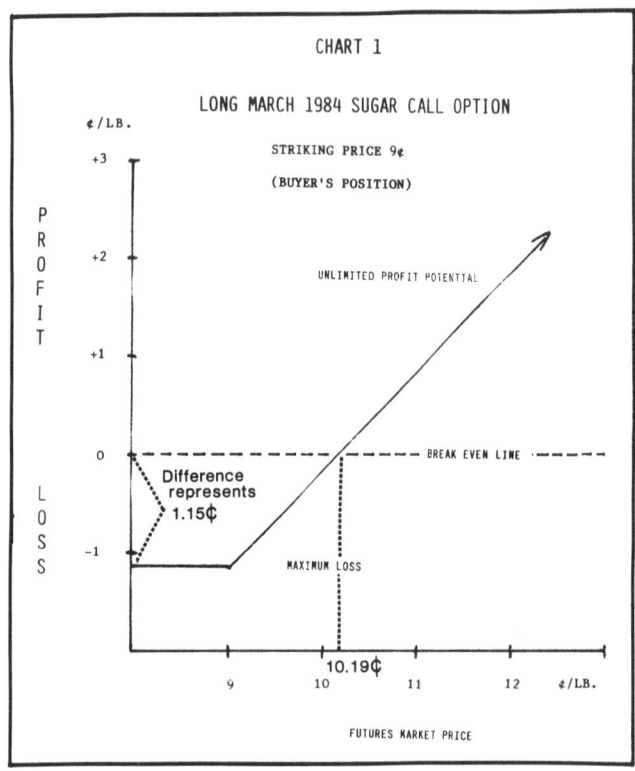

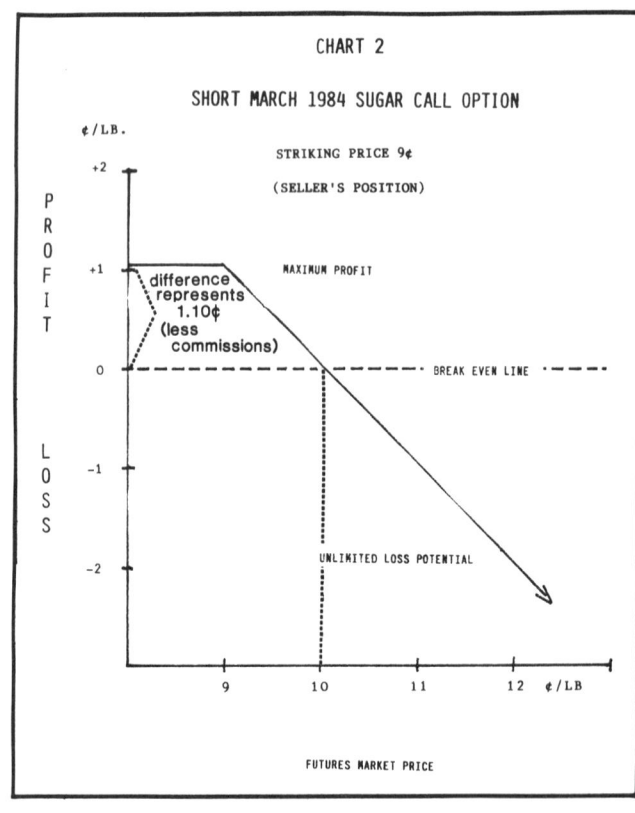

Buyer of Put Option—Treasury Bonds

Let's examine the purchase of a put option. Here the buyer purchases the right to deliver or put to another's account a commodity futures contract at a specific strike price. In this case we will examine the option on Treasury bonds (T-bonds). The buyer of a *put* holds the *right to sell* a bond futures contract at a specific strike price. If bond prices drop below that strike price the right to sell bonds at the higher price becomes the option's intrinsic value.

The following examples will deal with put options with three strike prices. These strike prices are described as being (1) *in-the-money*, that is, a commodity futures price lower than the strike price, (2) *at-the-money* where market price is equal to the strike price and (3) *out-of-the-money* where the futures market price is higher than the strike price. Bear in mind that if the discussion pertained to call options rather than put options, the market-to-strike price relationships would be reversed for in-the-money and out-of-the-money options. In addition, commissions will be ignored in this and all subsequent examples.

In order to make these comparisons let's assume that it is currently March 1983. The June 1983 Treasury bond futures contracts are trading on the Chicago Board of Trade at a price of 74-00. Table 2 lists the CBT quotes for June put options on Treasury bonds with different striking prices.

TABLE 2
June Put Options T-bonds

Strike Price	Quote (points & 64ths)
72	1–16
74	2–16
76	3–32

Chart 3 (page 34) depicts the break-even analysis for the CBT June '83 T-bond put option with the strike price of 76. Notice that the assumed 3½ point option premium would have an intrinsic value of 2 points (76-74). The 1½ point balance is its time value. *The in-the-money put option has the greatest loss potential (3½ points) and requires the smallest price move of the underlying commodity to reach the breakeven point.*

Options which are in-the-money are said to have a high *delta* which is the ratio of the move of the price of the underlying commodity to the move of the premium price of the option. The high delta simply means that the magnitude of commodity price moves and option premium price moves will be fairly close within the relevant range described as being "in the money."

The more deeply an option is in-the-money, the higher the delta. Options which are relatively close to expiration and deeply in-the-money may trade extremely close to their intrinsic value with little or no premium for its time value. Moreover, because of transaction costs, such as broker's commissions, options may trade fractionally below their intrinsic value.

Chart 4 shows the break-even analysis for this buyer of a bond put with the strike price at-the-market. Since at-the-money options hold the *greatest time value,* the passage of time will cause its premium to drop faster than options which are in-the-money or out-of-the-money. All options are known as *decaying* instruments because their time value shrinks as time passes. At-the-money options have the fastest decay rate of the time value simply because the buyer pays more for the time value of an at-the-money option.

Comparing Charts 3 and 4, it should be noted that *at-the-money options carry less potential loss and require a greater favorable price move of the underlying futures contract to break even* than an option contract which is in-the-money. These two characteristics are trade-offs to one another. They allow an option buyer to contour his trading to meet his financial situation and leverage. He can have greater maximum loss potential and a smaller distance to reach the break-even point of a trade by buying an in-the-money option. Conversely, he can reduce his maximum loss potential but have a greater distance to his break-even point by buying at-the-money options.

A buyer can also buy out-of-the-money options to reduce his maximum loss even further. As Chart 5 (page 35) points out, the Treasury bond prices must move down 3¼ points from the market price of 74 to reach the break-even point for the put with a 72 strike price and a premium of 1¼ points. This is the largest move of the 3 examples discussed. However, the maximum loss or premium paid to establish this position is only 1¼ points. Deep out-of-the-money options have the lowest delta. In other words, a greater favorable change must occur in the underlying futures contract to change the option premium.

One must be careful when treating *maximum loss potential* and risk as the same thing. An out-of-the-money option will cost the option buyer less premium. If the underlying commodity makes *a significantly* favorable price move, the option buyer will make the greatest return on his money. This means that he has the most *leverage*. Since he paid less premium for his option, his maximum potential loss is less. However, the probability of incurring his maximum loss is greater since the option is out-of-the-money. Therefore, it would be erroneous to suggest that his risk is less. More importantly a trader can purchase more out-of-the-money options for the same capital. In doing so he creates a highly leveraged speculation that assumes the underlying commodity will make a significantly favorable move. *The strategy of using out-of-the-money options increases the profit potential but also increases the risk of failure.*

Consider Chart 3 again. Ignoring brokerage commissions, a buyer can purchase a put which is 2 points in the money for 3½ points (2 points intrinsic value + 1½ points time value). Compare that situation with the one found in Chart 5. Here, an out-of-the-money option is assumed to cost only 1¼ points. The buyer can purchase almost three out-of-the-money put options for the same price as one in-the-money put option found in Chart 3. If bond prices moved down to 68, one put with a 76 strike price would have an intrinsic value of 8 points, a gain of 4½ over the purchase price of 3½.

On the other hand, three put options with a strike price of 72 would have an intrinsic value of 4 points each or a total of 12 points. Since the total purchase price of three options is 3¾ points, the gain is 8¼ points. A much greater return exists for the buyer of out-of-the-money puts when a *major* favorable price move occurs in the underlying commodity.

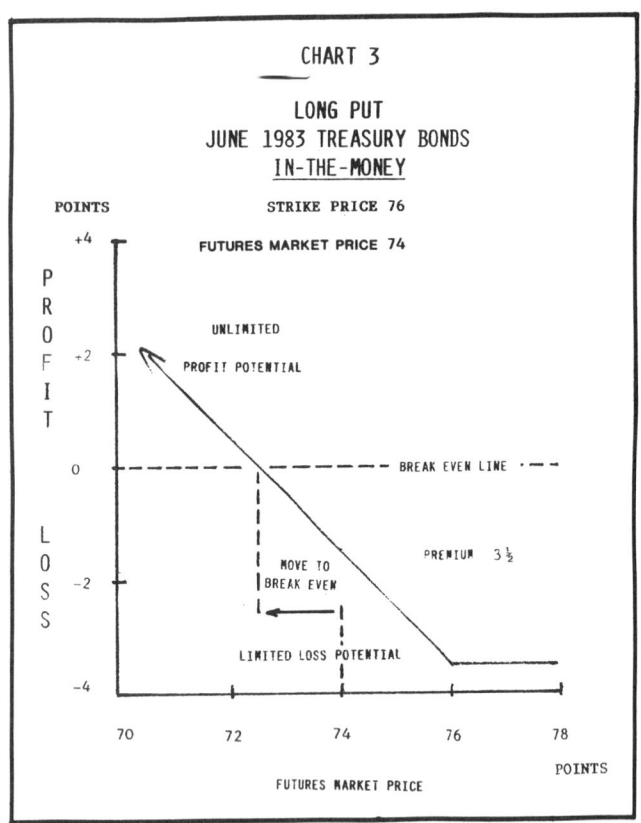
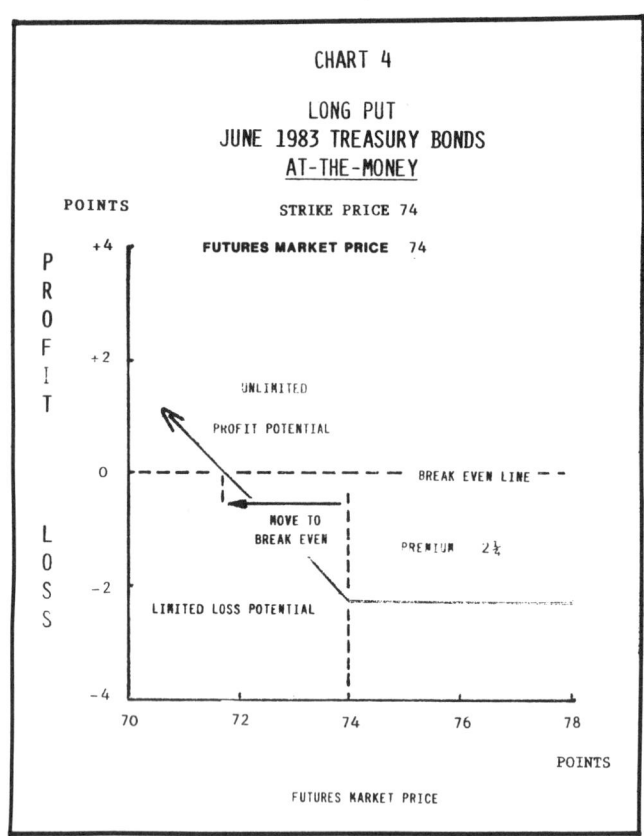

However, the risks are also major. Review the same situation if bond prices fell to 71. One long 76 put (Chart 3) would have an intrinsic value of 5 points and a gain of 1½ points on a 3½ point premium. Three 72 put options (Chart 5) would have a total intrinsic value of 3 points and a loss of ¾ point from the original purchase price of the options. Now consider the results if the market drops to 72. The 76 put holder still gains ½ point while the holder of three 72 put options loses everything.

Strategies

There are many strategies associated with options on futures contracts. Some of these strategies include spreads between two different options. Others are done in conjunction with futures contracts. The remainder of this article is designed to introduce some different trading strategies. Bear in mind that as this article is being written, commodity futures options are new financial instruments. Some of the trading ideas are merely extensions of stock options traded on the Chicago Board of Options Exchange. Others are extensions of commodity futures trading. Aggressive trading strategies often require market liquidity which has not yet developed in commodity options. Many of the discussions found in the balance of this article are theoretical and assume that option market liquidity will grow to accommodate the strategies. However, until then, strategies in options trading must consider not only the cost of commissions but also the cost of trading in illiquid markets. Consequently, these premiums will tend to have a fairly large spread between the bid and offer prices.

Selling a Covered Option

A covered position is either a call option sold where the seller is long the underlying futures contract or a put option sold where the seller is short the underlying futures contract.

The following discussion will be limited to an explanation of covered calls.

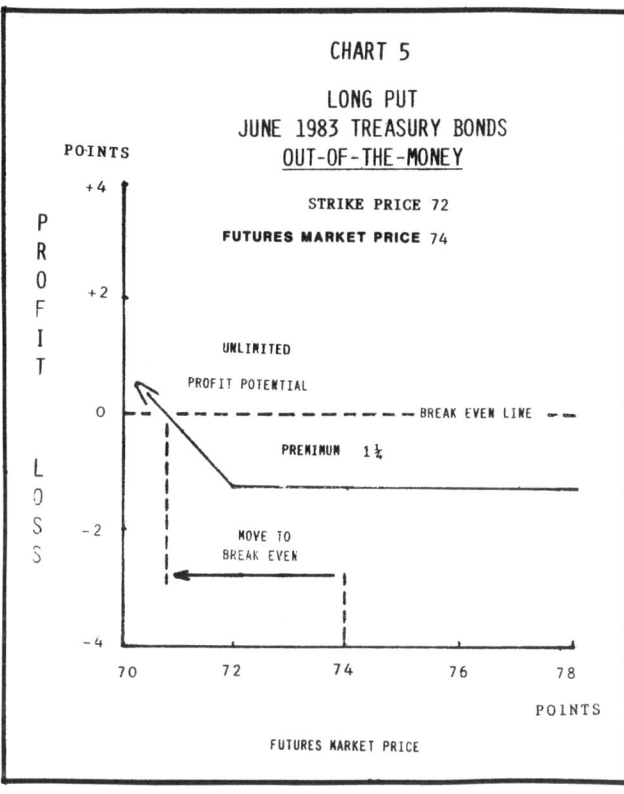

Selling covered calls is viewed by many as a means of liquidating a long commodity futures position at a slightly higher price than the current market price. The effective sales price of the commodity contract is increased by the amount of the time value of the call option. In exchange for increasing the effective sales price of the underlying commodity contract, the option seller gives up the benefits of a higher market price for his long futures position. He also is vulnerable to the loss of his commodity futures position if the futures price drops below the strike price of the option. Selling options with a greater return and loss potential or a lesser return and loss potential, is determined by the selection of the option's strike price. An in-the-money covered call increases the effective sales price of the underlying futures contract only slightly since in-the-money call options tend to lose their time value. Therefore, the return to a covered call option seller is less when he sells a deep in-the-money option. Also, the deeper a call is in-the-money, the less loss potential exists. This is the case because the premium received for deep in-the-money call options is large and represents the downside protection.

The covered call option seller is, in a sense, hedged since the losses from a downward price move in his long futures position will be offset by the gains in his short call option position.

However, if commodity market prices drop beyond the amount of the premium he received for selling the call, he is no longer hedged and losses will begin to accumulate.

At-the-money calls tend to have the greatest time value, and therefore, produce the greatest return to the seller. However, the covered call seller must carry the full financial burden inflicted by a bear market on his long futures position while foregoing all benefits of a bull market.

Out-of-the-money call options produce an interesting return. While the premiums received for selling out-of-the-money call options are small, the option seller retains part of the financial benefits of a bull market. For example, consider a participant who holds a long March sugar contract whose market price is 8½¢ per pound. If he sells a call option with a strike price of 9¢ against that position, he is selling an out-of-the-money covered call. He receives two financial benefits; (1) the premium (albeit small) and (2) a profit potential of his March sugar futures position limited to ½¢ (9¢ − 8½¢).

The direction of unlimited loss potential for the seller of a covered call is reversed when compared to that of the seller of an uncovered call. The losses will mount in a bear market in the case of selling a covered call. Lower prices would negatively affect the underlying long futures position. Considering the greater liquidity of the underlying futures position, one has to assume that trading conducted to offset unlimited potential loss would be more effectively accomplished in the futures markets than in the option markets. If prices are falling and losses are accumulating, the covered call seller can liquidate his long futures position leaving the call option uncovered.

Buying a Covered Option

A comparable trading strategy exists for the *buyer* of a covered option. Here, a buyer can retain unlimited potential profit while limiting his potential loss. For example, a trader who believes that the gold market is going up but who is reluctant to take the large risks associated with establishing an outright long futures position can buy a call option. As an alternate but equivalent strategy, he can buy a gold futures contract and a gold put option. His total risk is the option premium (adjusted for differences between the market and striking prices) and the commissions. If gold falls, the value of his put will offset losses in his futures account. Conversely, a bull market in gold will result in an unlimited potential profit in his futures account.

Spreads

There are many and varied combinations of option spreads, that is, purchases of one option and sale of another. Different spreads meet different objectives and price outlooks. Because of the off-setting nature of the purchase and sale, option spreads have a limited risk and limited potential profit. As a means of illustration, let's examine one of these spreads commonly referred to as a *bull call spread*.

Here the option trader buys a call option with a low strike price and sells another call option with a higher strike price. For example, he buys a September 1983 Treasury bond call option with a strike price 74 and sells a September 1983 Treasury bond call option with a strike price of 76. He has straddled the market price of 75. It is assumed that the premium paid for the 74 call is 3 points and the premium received for the 76 call is 2 points. It is becoming common nomenclature to refer to a call with a strike price of 74 as a "74 call."

Consider the financial results of this spread under three market conditions. First, the maximum profit when the bond price is at or above 76 for September '83 T-bond futures. Table 3 shows the profit results when the market price is at 76, 77 or 78. Notice that at consecutively higher prices above 76, the gain remains constant at one point.

TABLE 3
September 1983 T-bond Futures
Market Price Above 76

Price	76	77	78
Long 74 Call			
Sales Value	2	3	4
Purchase Price	3	3	3
Gain (Loss)	(1)	0	1
Short 76 Call			
Sales Price	2	2	2
Purchase Value	0	1	2
Gain (Loss)	2	1	0
Net Results			
Gain (Loss)	1	1	1

The second market condition occurs when the market price falls between 74 and 76. Table 4 explains the financial outcomes when the T-bond market price is at 74½, 75 or 75½ at the time of the option's expiration. Notice that as the bond market prices fall, the results of the option spread go from a profitable financial outcome, through the break-even point, to a losing position.

TABLE 4
September 1983 T-bond Futures
Market Price Between 74 & 76

Price	74½	75	75½
Long 74 Call			
Sales Value	½	1	½
Purchase Price	3	3	3
Gain (Loss)	(2½)	(2)	(1½)
Short 76 Call			
Sales Price	2	2	2
Purchase Value	0	0	0
Gain	2	2	2
Net Results			
Gain (Loss)	(½)	0	½

Third, table 5 looks at the situation when the bond market prices are below a price of 74. Here the trader loses his maximum amount of one point regardless of how low bond prices fall.

TABLE 5
September 1983 T-bond Futures
Market Price Below 74

Price	72	73	74
Long 74 Call			
Sales Value	0	0	0
Purchase Price	3	3	3
Gain (Loss)	(3)	(3)	(3)
Short 76 Call			
Sales Price	2	2	2
Purchase Value	0	0	0
Gain (Loss)	2	2	2
Net Results			
(Loss)	(1)	(1)	(1)

Chart 6 plots each of the points in the previous three tables illustrating the limited profit and loss potential of the bull call spread. It is called a bull spread because the trader makes his maximum profit if bond prices go up.

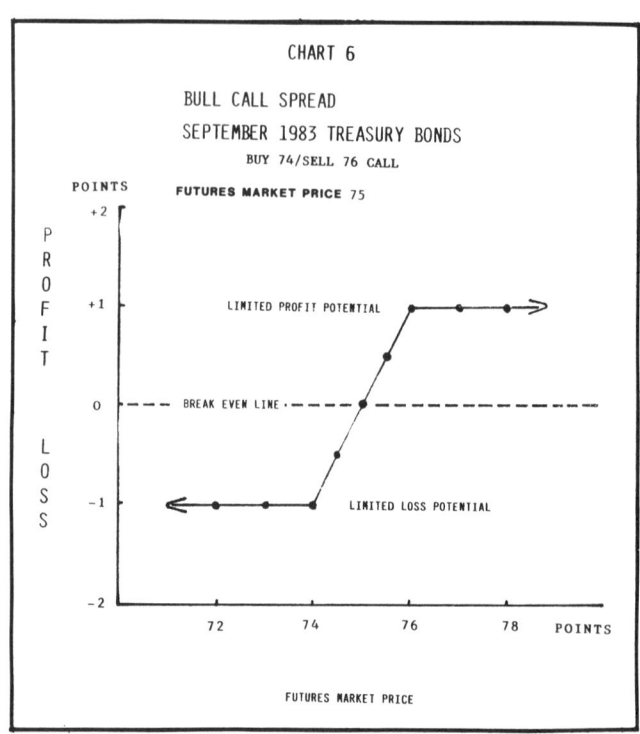

The maximum loss resulting from a bull call spread is the difference between the premium paid for the purchase of the 74 call (3 points) and the premium received for the sale of the 76 call (2 points). Therefore, the maximum potential loss (known as the debit) is 1 point. The profit potential is limited to the difference between the strike prices of the two call options (76-74) minus the debit (1 point). Hence, the maximum profit potential is also 1 point in this example.

While this example demonstrates 1 to 1 risk to reward ratio, that ratio can be altered by putting on a spread with in-the-money call options which reduce the risk to reward ratio but increases the likelihood of a gain. This is because the maximum gain occurs when both call options are in-the-money at expiration which is also the initial situation. The risk-to-reward ratio can be increased by putting on the bull call spread using two call options which are out-of-the-money. Bear in mind that while the potential profit is greater than the potential risk, the likelihood of the gain is reduced. Therefore, each risk/reward ratio has a different probability of success. Higher potential gains for each dollar exposed to loss, reduces the probability of that gain.

There are other spreads available to the option trader such as the bull put spread, bear put spread and the bear call spread. The rationale for each of these spreads is similar to that of the bull call spread just described.

Sideways Option Strategy

A trader who anticipates that a commodity futures contract will be fairly stable with prices trading in a narrow range may choose to sell out-of-the-money puts and calls.

For example, if June '83 gold futures are trading at $440 per ounce and the trader's outlook is for the market to trade between $400 and $480 through mid-May when the June option expires, he may employ a sideways options strategy. He sells a 480 call for which he is assumed to receive $11.50 per ounce and a 400 put for which he receives $9.50 per ounce. Total revenues from the sale of the put and call is $2000 on a 100 ounce gold contract. It should be clear to the reader that at expiration only one of these options will have any intrinsic value. A call at a striking price and a put at a lower striking price can never both be in-the-money. Furthermore, it is possible for both options to expire out-of-the-money resulting in the seller's maximum gain as shown in Chart 7. Notice that maximum gains are achieved if June 1983 gold futures prices fall between $400 and $480 per ounce at expiration of the options in May. If prices fall below $400 per ounce, the put begins to develop intrinsic value thus reducing the option seller's profit. Since the seller received 20 points in premium revenue, losses will not accumulate until the market drops below $380 per ounce.

Similarly, if gold rises, maximum profits will not be reduced until gold prices go above $480 per ounce and losses will not occur until the market rises above the break-even point at $500 per ounce. Below $380 and above $500 per ounce, the potential loss is unlimited.

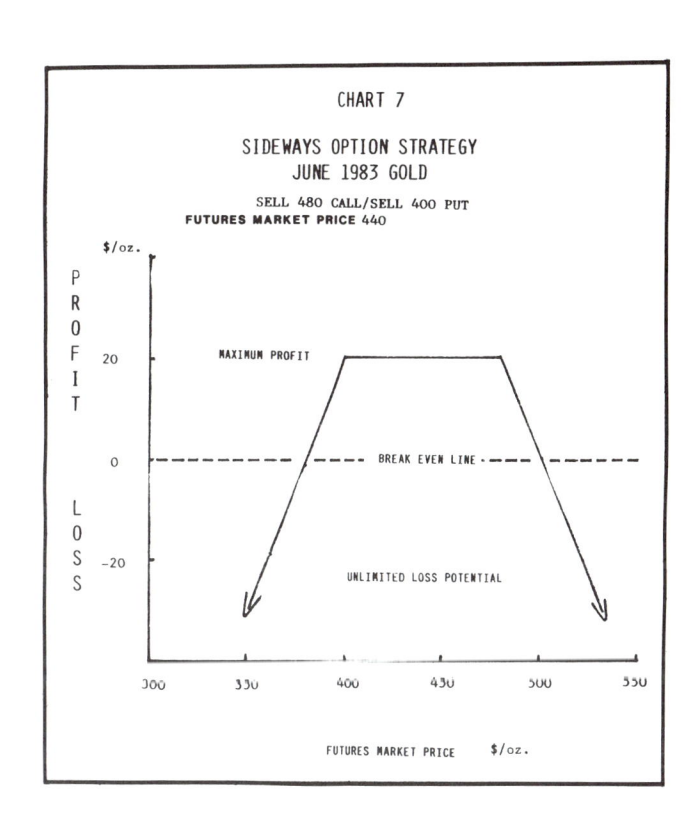

Conclusion

Several points are important to note in summarizing the recently established commodity option trading on United States commodity exchanges. Options are a way of getting involved in futures trading without undertaking the unlimited loss potential. Yet, they are a high leverage trading vehicle that can result in high profits or high losses. Because of the leverage, they must be treated with caution. Selling or writing options can have the effect of establishing a futures position with the corresponding unlimited loss potential. If you are uncomfortable with an outright futures position, you probably should not sell options.

As this article points out, there are many different ways of contouring option strategies to your financial objectives. However, this article is a mere introduction and, as such, is incomplete. Examples in this article as well as most articles on the subject show final results at the expiration date of the option. Interim market price movements may cause you to liquidate a position prematurely with less desirable results. Moreover, options on commodities are new and thus illiquid. One can not always count on receiving an expected premium in a given trade situation. Nevertheless, commodity option strategies which are well thought out and prudently applied can result in attractive profits for both the newcomer and the most experienced trader.

THE STOCK INDEX AND OPTIONS MARKETS

BY H. J. MAIDENBERG

From the moment stock index futures began trading in February 1982, commodity and equities traders knew their markets would never be the same again. Indeed, the index futures and the index options that followed also helped smash the once formidable wall that had separated the commodity and stock markets.

While the changes sparked by the index futures have far from run their course, they have provided portfolio hedgers and speculators with an extraordinary variety of tools with which to insure against adverse stock market price moves.

These include, at last count, index futures based on the Value Line, Standard & Poor's 500 and New York Stock Exchange composite indexes. Also, options on these three index futures; options settled in cash; options on a "home-made" stock index, and index futures and options on various market component averages.

Confusing? Not really. Each of these "customized" futures and options not only serves a specific purpose, but their use is probably more familiar to the average stock investor than many of the much older commodity futures.

Origin of Index and Option Markets

Before discussing the particular uses and characteristics of these instruments, it may serve to recall the developments that led to the new markets. The roots of the new index markets go back to the once common put and call trading, which still exists on an informal basis between brokers and investors.

Basically, dealers would offer investors the right, but not the obligation, to buy (call away from the owner) or sell (put to the buyer) 100 shares of a stock at a fixed price during a specified period of time. The cost, known as the premium, depended on the duration of the right (option) and the prospects that the stock would rise or fall in that period.

But the old put and call market was heavily weighted against the option buyer. Aside from the premium cost, exercising an option often required actually buying or selling the underlying stock, and paying the attendant brokerage commissions. At best it was a cumbersome affair.

It remained for the innovative commodity market to streamline the put and call business into a highly liquid, continuous two-way auction market. That happened in April 1973, when the Chicago Board of Trade opened its Chicago Board Options Exchange.

Even then the securities industry and its regulators realized that stock options could vastly transform the established securities markets, but they didn't know just how. So they limited the number of blue-chip stock options and, until a few years ago, prohibited the trading of puts. Today, the CBOE still only offers puts and calls on 120 blue chips, while the American Stock Exchange and smaller regional equities markets deal in fewer options.

Meanwhile, a revolution was sweeping the equities investment world in the aftermath of the OPEC cartel's surging energy prices. Inflation and interest rates soared and plunged twice since 1974 and promise to do so again.

As a result, investors in the past decade no longer could buy stocks and put them away for retirement or for their heirs. Gone too was the idea of living on dividend income. The object of investing now was price appreciation—more to the point, price appreciation within specific time frames, because all investments now had to be measured against the returns on such new competitive vehicles as money market funds.

The challenge was even greater for professional portfolio managers, whose institutions are responsible for hundreds of billions of dollars in pension fund, insurance, bank trust, mutual funds and other monies. With inflation, or the threat of inflation, making investments in fixed-income securities risky for the institutions, most have turned to the equities market.

Today, the institutions account for roughly 75% of the volume on the New York Stock Exchange. Equally large amounts of stocks are traded by institutions in the so-called third market in big blocks every day. Given the uncertainties of the economy and stock markets, the problems facing the institutions have grown considerably with their involvement in the equities market.

In particular, the institutions and many individual investors can only make limited use of the stock options market to hedge their holdings because they offer a relatively limited number of options, mostly the blue chips. The CBOE, for instance, trades only 120 of the Big Board's 1,520 issues.

An even greater problem is the protection of portfolios against general market declines and, in many cases, untimely advances.

The Indexes

Because market corrections often pull down prices even of profitable issues, investors are faced with the choice of holding on or selling. But the opportunity cost of holding may be high if the correction period is long. Selling may incur short-term tax liabilities. Stocks bought on margin are also vulnerable to premature selling.

Or suppose the market perks up before the investor is ready financially to buy. Chasing stocks can also be costly.

To address these problems the Kansas City Board of Trade introduced the first index futures, based on the Value Line average, in February 1982. Two months later the Chicago Mercantile Exchange followed suit with Standard & Poor's 500 index futures, and in May 1982, the Big Board's New York Futures Exchange opened its market in its parent's composite index futures.

It was not just competitive copycatting. Each index futures serves as a particular hedging or speculative instrument. The Value Line index, for example, covers the widest range of stocks, from Big Board blue chips to Amex, regional, over-the-counter, and some Canadian issues.

Value Line's index also covers 95% of the dollar volume of U.S. stocks traded and gives all its issues the same weighted value. In sum, the Value Line index reflects more of the so-called secondary issues than its rivals. Thus it suits hedgers and speculators during periods of broad-based market moves.

The S & P 500 is basically an abstract of the Big Board composite index. Its index contains 400 industrials, 20 transportation, 40 utilities, 40 financials and is heavily weighted with blue chips. The S & P 500 represents about 75% of the market value of all Big Board listed stocks.

Being the "cream" of the Big Board's 1,500 or so issues, the S & P 500 is the index used by most professional portfolio managers as a yardstick of their performance. In fact, the majority of portfolio managers tend to restrict their trading to S & P 500 issues.

The S & P 500 is similar to the Big Board's composite in that it weighs the price and number of outstanding shares against fixed base periods: an average of weekly values for 1941–43 in the case of the S & P 500 and Dec. 31, 1965 in the case of the Big Board's index.

In any case, the S & P 500 largely reflects market moves led by the blue chips and tends to be somewhat less reliable as a tracking instrument in broader-based advances or declines.

The Big Board's composite is closer to the Value Line as far as a gauge of the overall market. While it covers most of the blue chips, it also represents many issues that are traded infrequently or in such limited volume as to lessen volatility in broad market moves.

STANDARDS & POORS COMPOSITE INDEX OF 500 STOCKS 1941-43=10
(Weekly High, Low & Close)

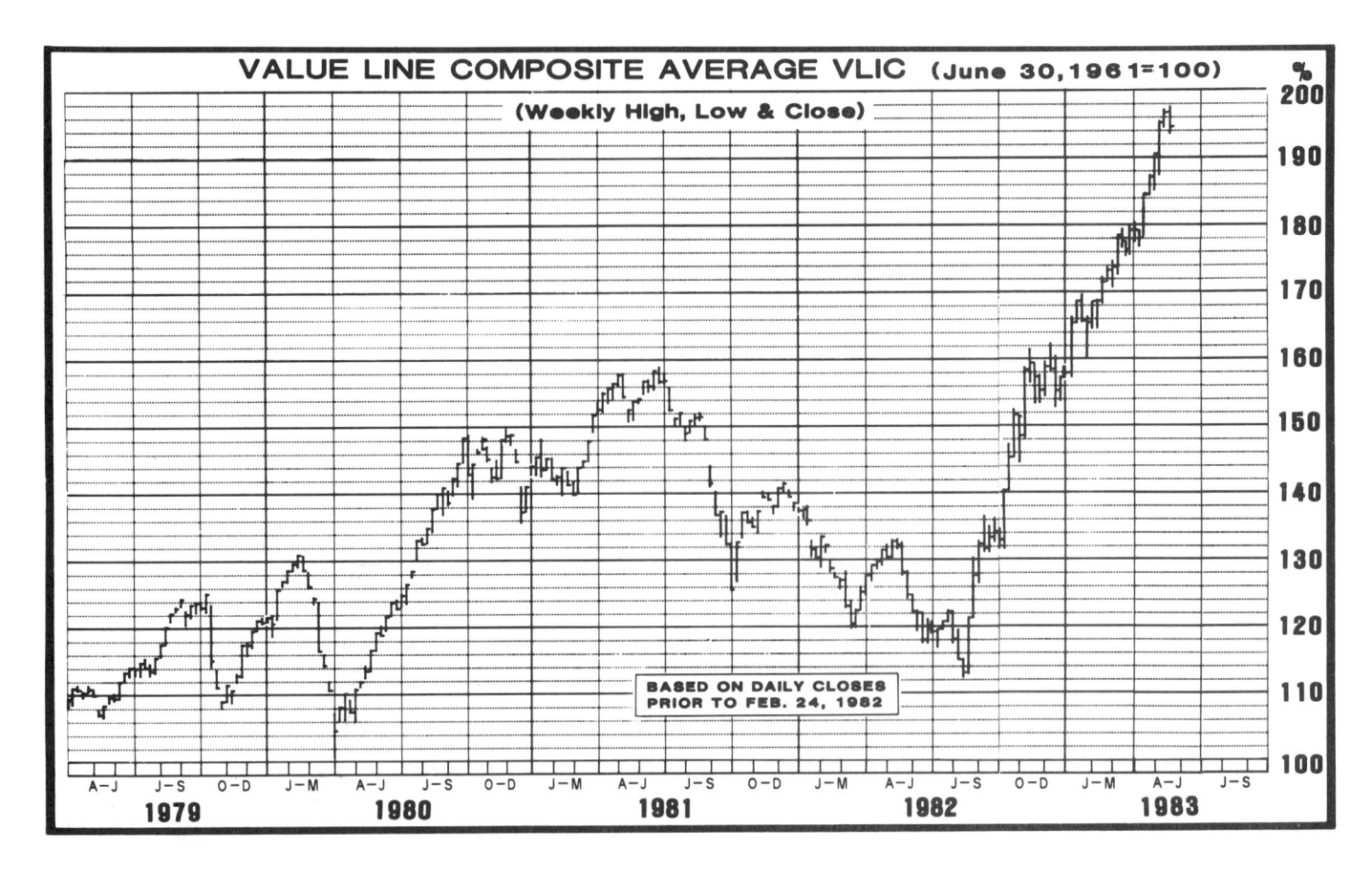

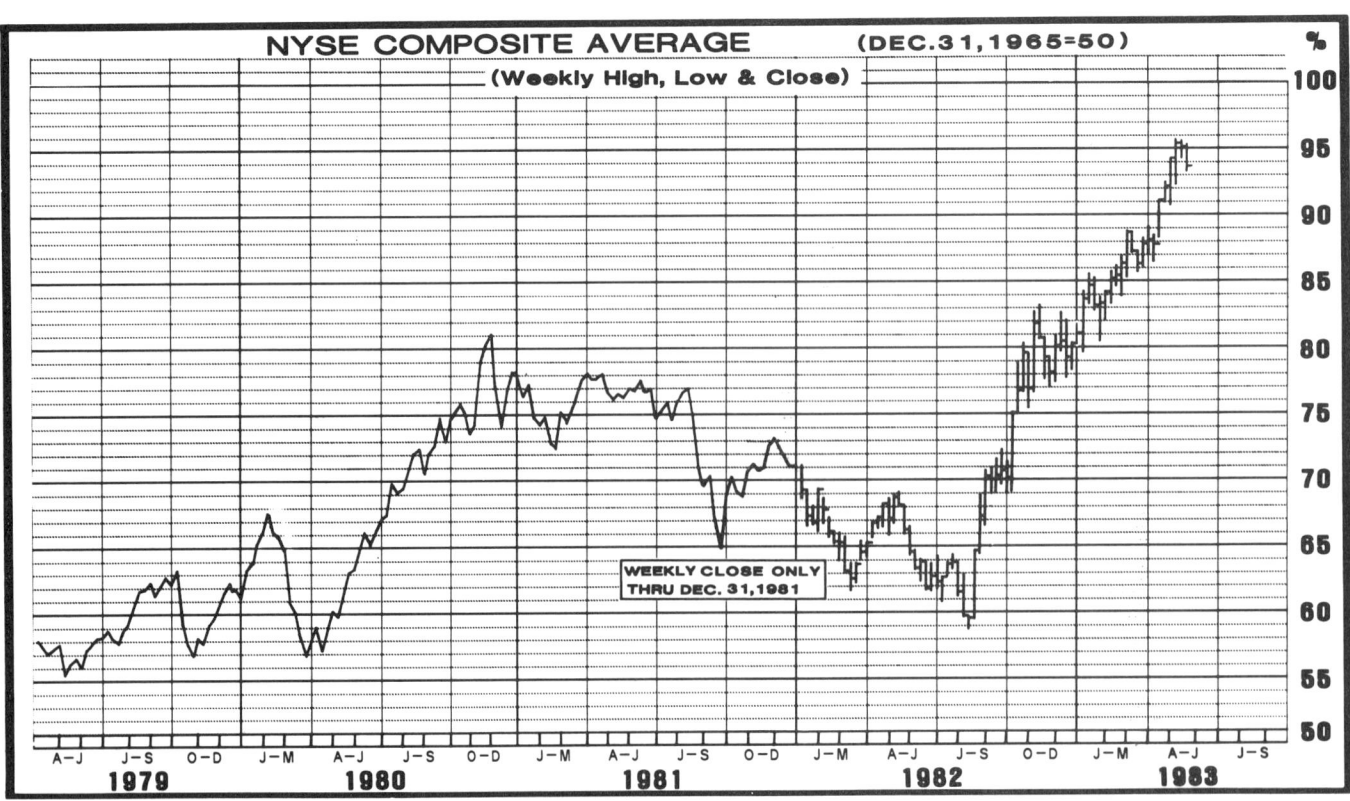

VALUE LINE COMPOSITE AVERAGE VLIC (June 30, 1961=100)
(Weekly High, Low & Close)

BASED ON DAILY CLOSES PRIOR TO FEB. 24, 1982

NYSE COMPOSITE AVERAGE (DEC. 31, 1965=50)
(Weekly High, Low & Close)

WEEKLY CLOSE ONLY THRU DEC. 31, 1981

By comparison, the most popular index, the Dow Jones Industrial average of 30 blue chips, happens to be less of a market mirror than the other indexes. Its 30 highly capitalized issues account for about 20% of the market value of all Big Board stocks.

The Chicago Board of Trade wanted to trade index futures based on the Dow Jones Industrials, but the company has refused to lend its name to a commodity product, and the exchange's efforts to pursue its plans have been thwarted by law suits.

Index Futures Trading Considerations

What the three index futures have in common is their systems of trading. Each futures contract can only be settled in cash at expiration because it would be highly inconvenient to provide the underlying issues for delivery. (This has led many in the industry to propose similar cash settlement for other commodites, such as live and feeder cattle, and live hogs, which are often also inconvenient to deliver.)

The three index futures contracts are traded in this manner: Each point is worth $5, but minimum moves are in five points. Using the S & P 500 as an example, suppose a contract closed up 1.40 at 163.30. It would mean that the contract was worth $81,650 because a contract is 500 times the index price. Thus the 1.40 price move is worth $700.

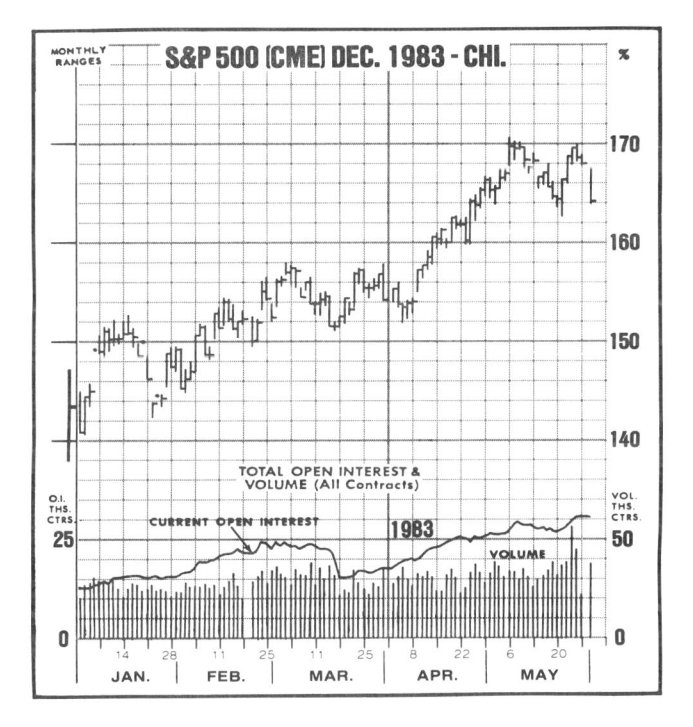

Initial cash margins run about $6,500, having been set by the three exchanges when the stock market was much lower than it is currently. Hedgers of course may put up about half the speculative margin. But the margins for speculators have raised—but not answered—a question posed by many traders: If a speculator also owns a portfolio of stocks, isn't he or she also a hedger?

One reason the question hasn't been answered is that the exchanges do not want to get involved with the Federal Reserve Board, which sets margins on equities trading, a responsibility that some officials at the Fed think should be either dropped or given over to another regulatory body.

As for the mechanics of the index futures markets, they are quite similar to those long standing in other commodities markets. Positions are marked to the market at the end of every session. Trading is done by open outcry and hand signaling.

Those hedging against a market decline would take the short side, along with speculators who expected the underlying indexes to decline. Bullish traders would take the long side.

But here again the index futures posed problems for institutional as well as individual traders. Many institutions are still inhibited by the thought of participating in futures. Because futures positions are marked to the market every trading day, hedgers and others face margin calls for cash just as other commodity traders do.

The delivery months in index futures are spaced three months apart, extending out to nine months generally. This raises the problem of coordinating portfolio trading strategies with the delivery months. As with other futures markets, there are often extraneous factors that may influence futures but not the underlying indexes.

Futures prices may be swayed either way by the personal operations of floor traders, who often trade "by the seat of their pants" in highly emotional market conditions. Hedgers, for their part, are governed by a different set of factors. These may include dividend dates that affect the values of their portfolios and, as mentioned earlier, the particular groups of stocks that are leading the market up or down at a given moment.

Because of the short statistical history of index futures, spreaders have been using a relatively simple strategy. When the blue chips were leading the recent market advance, spreaders bought the S & P 500 and sold the broader-based Value Line futures, and did the reverse when the secondary shares were thought to be leading the market.

Also, for want of a more precise "handle," the pricing of the back months in all index futures tends to be structured to reflect current interest rates.

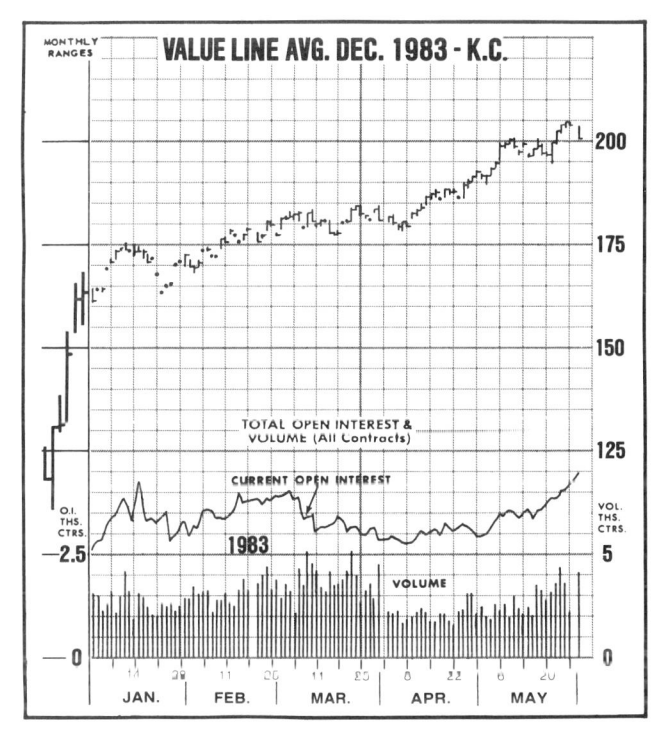

Since the Value Line index market opened, millions of dollars and countless hours have been spent by all brokerage houses and traders in trying to program their computers to find the handle. Until enough traders find what they consider to be a handle, the growth of volume and open interest is expected to be slow.

In fact, many market specialists believe that the volume and open interest of index futures would be even slower to rise if it weren't for the introduction of index options, which began late in 1982. The first three index options were based on their respective underlying futures. Being fashioned on the well-known stock options, they posed few trading problems for most investors.

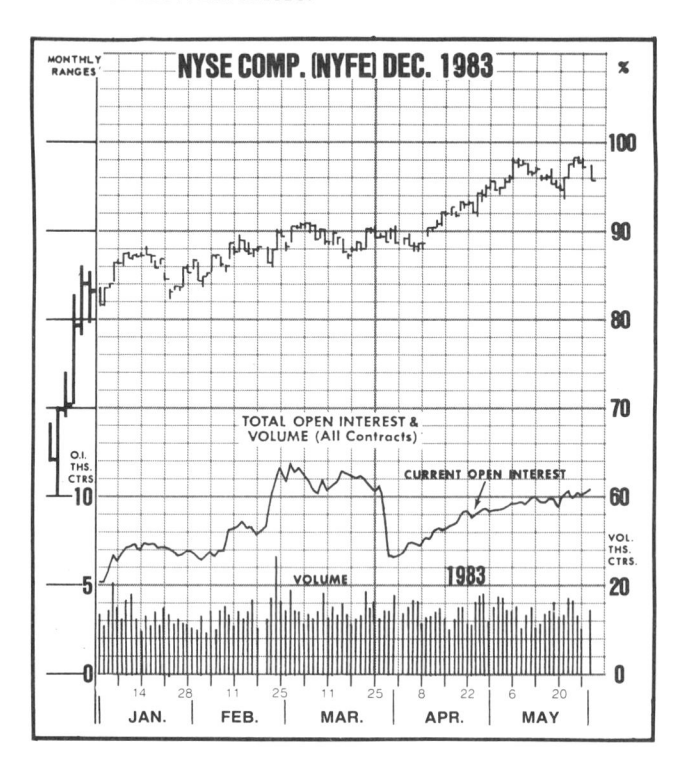

Index Options

While the trading mechanics may be familiar, the index options posed a number of problems. True, the options trader always knows the extent of the potential loss—the premium paid. Options buyers never have to face margin calls from their brokers.

But the index options predicated on underlying futures have proved burdensome to most traders, not to mention portfolio hedgers. For one, the three index options do not expire at the same time as their respective underlying futures contracts. Thus, one could have a gain on the option and a loss on the futures or vice versa.

Using a combination of index options and futures for spreading may be especially vexing. Options are not marked to the market each trading day; futures positions are. When these problems were added to the search for a trading handle, or strategy, it nearly capped the growth of both the index futures and options markets.

But the CBOE once again came to the rescue on March 11, 1983, when it opened its "home-made" options based on 100 blue chip stocks selected by the exchange. Further, the CBOE 100 is settled in cash. Because the CBOE 100 closely tracks the S & P 500 used by professional portfolio managers, hedgers found it highly effective. So did spreaders who combined CBOE 100 with the S & P 500 options or even with futures.

It was the smaller trader, however, who made CBOE 100 one of the most successful new markets in history. Within a few months, the new market's volume consisted of 45% "outside paper," which is to say that percentage came from outside traders, rather than contracts traded among floor traders. While commodity exchange floor traders provide the vital liquidity by maintaining a continuous auction, it is the public's participation as hedgers and speculators that make or break a market.

The CBOE 100 market drew the outsiders for three prime reasons. One, the new option is a fifth the size of its nearest rival, the S & P 500, which makes it less expensive to trade. This factor was indirectly acknowledged by the Kansas City Board of Trade, which plans to open a "mini" Value Line futures contract, one-fifth the size of the present futures contract.

Second, the CBOE 100 can be handled by brokers who are licensed by the Securities and Exchange Commission; its rival options (and index futures) can only be served by those registered with the Commodities Futures Trading Commission. There are currently an estimated 100,000 SEC licensed account executives, compared with about 20,000 futures commission merchants.

The third advantage is that the CBOE 100 tracks the S & P 500 because it contains most of the market movers. Small wonder that the new index options triggered an extraordinary chain of events, which began even before the market began operating.

The Kansas City Board arranged to have its Value Line options traded on the Chicago Board of Trade but activity was negligible, and trading was limited to liquidation, effective May 23, 1983.

Soon after CBOE 100 began trading, the Chicago Mercantile Exchange entered into an equally tradition-shattering accord with the Chicago Board Options Exchange to provide joint access to each other's members. As part of the deal, CBOE 100 would be renamed the S & P 100, but continue to be traded on the CBOE.

Also, Chicago Merc members would in effect have access to any other SEC-regulated CBOE index markets, while CBOE members would have the same trading privileges on CFTC regulated index markets on the Chicago Merc.

Why did the Chicago Board of Trade, the huge exchange that fathered CBOE, permit this to happen and leave itself without an index futures or options market? The fact is that the CBT and its offspring have become increasingly estranged in recent years. Probably the chief bone of contention is that while CBT members may trade on the CBOE for a few hundred dollars in fees, this access does not provide them with a separate seat. And CBOE seats are now worth more than $200,000.

By comparison, the Chicago Merc had the foresight to make seats on its International Monetary Market, Index and Options Market and other divisions separate and transferable.

In any event, the CBT plans to create its own home-made index options and possibly index futures, if the Dow Jones Company prevails in its legal actions to bar the use of its name on any commodity exchange product.

But the American Stock Exchange has already overcome this problem by opening an options market in a hand-picked 20-share index on April 29, 1983. It is called the Major Market Index and has been another roaring initial success. The MMI tracks the

Dow Industrial average and, indeed, 15 of the 20 issues in the new index options are the same as those in the popular market average.

Moreover, the MMI options are a fifth the size of the CBOE 100 and thus most affordable to small traders as well as big portfolio hedgers. The mechanics of the 20-share MMI are the same as the other index options and are also settled in cash.

The Major Market Index is also easy for the average trader to both understand and trade. To arrive at the index's value at any given time, the price of the 20 blue chips are added up and divided by 10, while the price changes are multiplied by 100.

At the close of the MMI market one day recently, the total price of the 20 stocks was $1,224.50, and the change on the day was up 1.45. Thus the index read 122.45, and the 1.45 gain was worth $145 to holders of calls as well as those who had sold puts. Those who had bought puts were down $145.

Of course, the actual profits and losses depended on the strike prices of the puts and calls when the contracts were entered into, the premiums paid and related factors.

The American Stock Exchange also plans sub-index options markets, each of which would consist of 11 financial company, transportation, aerospace and other stock sectors.

Potential Problems

Despite these innovative index futures and options and others that will undoubtedly follow, irritating problems still exist. Settling futures or options in cash is one of them. It is well known, if rarely mentioned, that futures markets do thrive on the real or perceived chance of a squeeze, a situation when, for example, the number of short contracts exceeds the available deliverable supply of a commodity.

Cash settlement is viewed by some market observers as a short step away from what one prominent lawyer termed a "homogenized, pasteurized, antiseptic electronic screen market." While this would suit hedgers who can fine tune their operations through computerized trading strategies, most small speculators would miss the volatility and with it the chance for quick and large profits.

Some fear that the institutional hedgers, once they get a handle on the index markets would soon dominate them, just as they do the Big Board. Worse, the magnitude of their operations would permit them to trade off their screens among themselves, just as the 36 primary Government securities dealers do. This would reduce the present exchanges to being residual or secondary marketplaces.

Even now large amounts of institutional stock trading is conducted among their portfolio managers off the exchange in what is termed the third market. The reason for all this concern, which is being closely monitored by the regulators in Washington, is that the securities market is far more complex and broad than any commodity futures market.

As any commodity futures trader knows, their exchanges serve as a price discovery mechanism as well as a risk transfer market. These functions have been efficiently handled for decades because the actual number of farm and industrial commodities traded is rather small. But the number of stocks is much larger and increasing rapidly. This is why subindex futures and options will be the next wave of new markets that will be opened.

Potential Benefits

But for the time being the index markets have had an enormous impact on the stock market. Many market analysts who concede they know little about index futures and options have learned that these instruments have enabled the equities market to avoid a major correction since the latest rally began in August 1982.

They know this because as the rally lengthened, against a background of a slowly recovering economy, the percentage of put options has grown much faster than the rise in the calls. This means that the index options and to a lesser extent the futures have been serving as insurance against a market decline.

This may also explain why the market forecasters whose warnings of a major correction since shortly after the rally began on Aug. 12, 1982 have been wrong so many times. While no tree or market grows to the sky, one can expect that the inevitable correction will be lessened by the insurance provided by the index markets.

Among the benefits brought to the stock market to date are several key investment tools that did not exist before February 1982. As an example, suppose a portfolio manager is faced with a market correction, the duration of which is unpredictable.

A "millenium" ago before index futures appeared, the first decision a portfolio manager would have had to make was which stocks to unload. All of XYZ Widget? Half the position? Which sectors of the market will be hit hardest? Taxable investments further complicated the decision making. Above all, the portfolio manager knew that many of his or her opposites were pondering the same questions.

Today, many if not most of these decisions can be avoided or made at a more leisurely pace by buying insurance in the form of index instruments. Thanks to the computer, almost full insurance coverage can be obtained by the hedger because of the variety of index futures and options available.

Perhaps the most dramatic benefit the new index markets will provide investors is the ability to construct "synthetic portfolios" that will obviate the need to lay out large sums for the purchase of actual stock. Using the old system of "reversals" and "conversions" that is common in the stock options market, Wall Street portfolio managers are furiously trying to employ the same strategies with index instruments. It is easy to understand why the Street is so fascinated by the prospect. In fact, many think the answer has been found.

Essentially, a reversal operation in *stock options* consists of buying calls on XYZ stock and selling puts on the same issue. This would be equivalent of owning XYZ on paper. If XYZ rises, the calls become profitable and so would the puts that were sold because chances are they would not be exercised by the buyer. A conversion is the opposite of a reversal operation.

But with *index options and futures* a reversal operation means the investor is taking a position on whether the market rises, or if a conversion is used, whether the market declines. In a limited way, these strategies are similar to the "cash and carry" operations employed in many commodities markets, whereby the investor buys the actual goods in effect and sells short more distant contracts.

This may also explain the relationship between the near delivery prices of index instruments such as futures and the back (distant) months. But interviews with scores of index market analysts have produced no instance of anyone conceding that they have found the answer. This is why the open interest in these futures markets remains heavily concentrated in the spot months.

Index options, on the other hand, are much less of a mystery to most traders. The strike prices are usually in increments of 5 points above and below the nearest at-the-money price of the option. Thus, an index option currently trading at, say, 90, would have strike prices of 80, 85, 90, 95 and 100.

The premiums, of course, would be determined by whether the option was in the money (trading above the strike price), out of the money (trading below the strike price) or at the money, as well as by the time remaining in the contract.

While the index instruments naturally rise and fall with the underlying market averages, or in the case of home-made options, the group of equities covered, dividend payment periods do affect index prices.

Professionals know that stock dividends are concentrated in the months of November, March, June and August and, as most blue-chip issues pay dividends, these contracts often trade at prices to reflect the payouts. "Haircutting" is how this factor is described, because the owners of the actual stock clip the dividends in effect from their portfolios when they price them.

Spreading Index Futures

Another practice carried over from the financial futures market is the spreading system in index futures. Between the time the recent stock market rally began in August 1982 and the following March, the biggest gainers were the secondary issues. After March, the institutions and the general public finally came into the market in large numbers.

One reason was that the big portfolio managers did not see any significant economic recovery to justify a switch from cash to invested positions. Another was that interest rates on competitive investments were still attractive until March. Most important, the flood of IRA account funds did not arrive until just before April 15, and much of these monies have since been invested in equities.

As a result, the Value Line index futures traded at significant premiums to the S & P 500 until March. The Value Line contains more secondary issues than the S & P 500 with its large number of blue chips. So, between August 1982 and the following March, spreaders bought the Value Line futures and sold the S & P 500, and then reversed the positions when the blue chips took the lead in the subsequent advance.

On March 22, the premium on the Value Line futures crested at 27.30 points over the S & P 500. A month later, the premium shrank to 26.05 points as the blue chips began to climb. Those spreaders who had sold the Value Line and bought the S & P 500 futures on March 22 (few actually did) thus had a gain of 1.25 points per spread, or $625, in that period.

But the index options market was a one-way street between August 1982 and the following May. The call buyers in that period weren't the only gainers. Traders who favored the puts, and most did, were also winners because for a modest cost they protected their portfolios during that time. Had they been frightened into taking untimely profits because of persistent rumors of an impending correction, they would have missed the substantial gains in the actual market. Thus the put options were cheap insurance indeed against being whipsawed in the stock market.

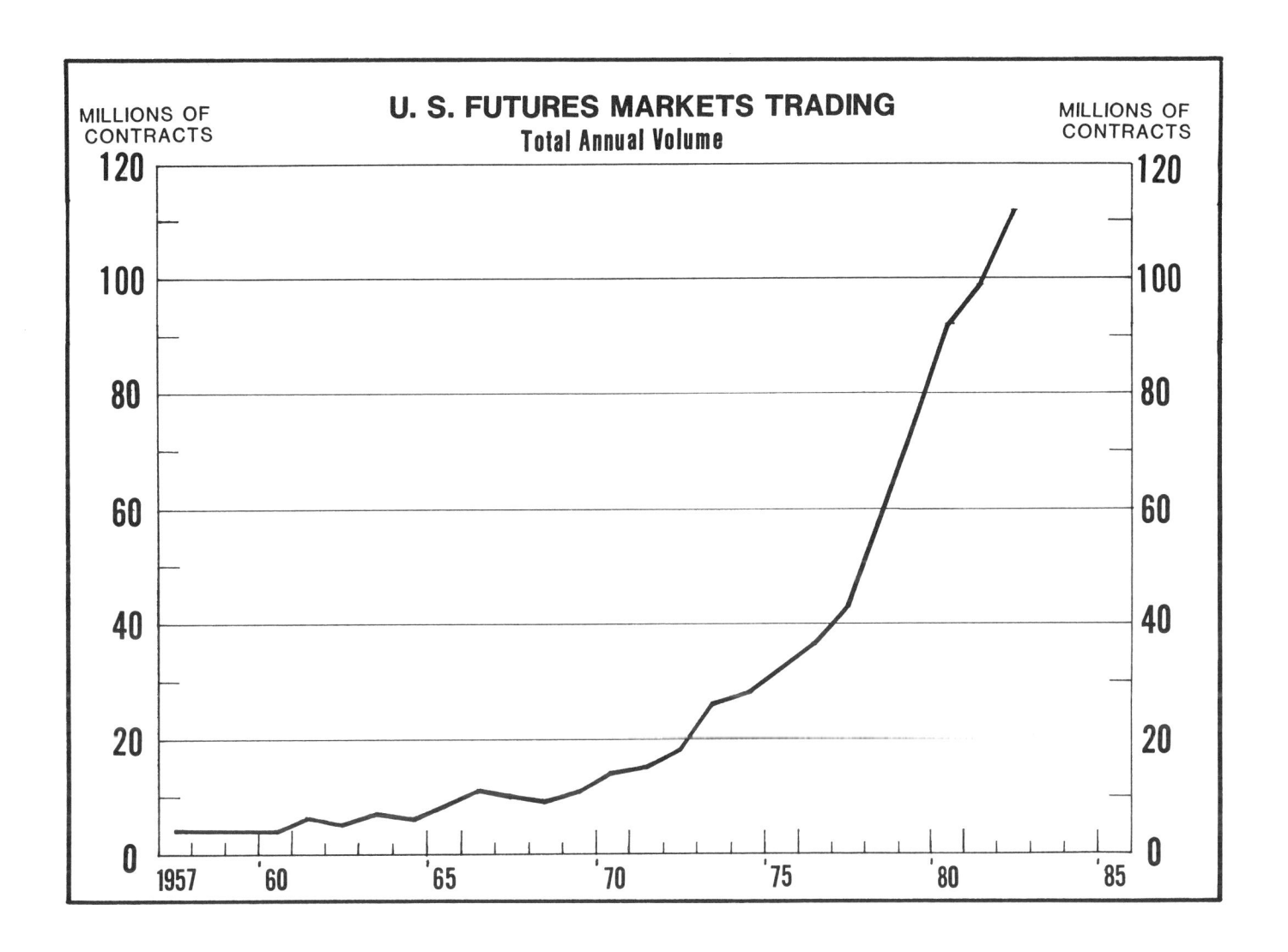

U. S. FUTURES MARKETS TRADING
Total Annual Volume

MILLIONS OF CONTRACTS

Futures Volume Highlights   1982 in Comparison with 1981

Rank	Contracts With Volume Over 100,000	1982 Contracts	%	1981 Contracts	%	Rank
1.	T Bonds, CBT	16,739,695	14.90	13,907,988	14.11	(1)
2.	Gold, COMEX	12,289,448	10.93	10,373,706	10.53	(4)
3.	Soybeans, CBT	9,165,520	8.15	10,489,932	10.65	(3)
4.	Corn, CBT	7,948,257	7.07	10,674,986	10.83	(2)
5.	T-Bills (90-day), CME	6,598,848	5.87	5,631,290	5.72	(5)
6.	Live Cattle, CME	4,440,992	3.95	4,282,293	4.35	(7)
7.	Wheat, CBT	4,031,584	3.59	4,511,934	4.58	(6)
8.	Live Hogs, CME	3,560,974	3.17	2,258,083	2.29	(13)
9.	Soybean Oil, CBT	3,049,313	2.71	3,047,490	3.09	(8)
10.	S&P 500, CME	2,935,532	2.61	—	—	
11.	Silver (5,000 oz), COMEX	2,868,639	2.55	1,240,720	1.26	(20)
12.	Pork Bellies, Fzn, CME	2,811,674	2.50	1,997,697	2.03	(14)
13.	Soybean Meal, CBT	2,784,423	2.48	3,039,633	3.09	(9)
14.	Swiss Franc, CME	2,653,332	2.36	1,518,767	1.54	(17)
15.	Copper, COMEX	2,362,625	2.10	1,647,380	1.67	(16)
16.	GNMA Mrtges, (CDR), CBT	2,055,648	1.83	2,292,882	2.33	(12)
17.	Sugar #11, CS&C	2,037,020	1.81	2,470,327	2.51	(11)
18.	Deutsche Mark, CME	1,792,901	1.60	1,654,891	1.68	(15)
19.	Japanese Yen, CME	1,762,246	1.57	960,598	.96	(23)
20.	No. 2 Heating Oil, NY, NYMEX	1,745,526	1.55	995,506	1.01	(22)

Commodity Futures Contracts Traded 1978-1982

	Contract Unit	1982	1981	1980	1979	1978
Wheat	5,000 bu	4,031,584	4,511,934	5,428,160	3,575,395	2,556,134
Corn	5,000 bu	7,948,257	10,674,986	11,946,975	8,671,719	6,127,099
Oats	5,000 bu	424,595	370,103	320,934	215,928	215,774
Soybeans	5,000 bu	9,165,520	10,489,932	11,768,197	9,114,348	8,477,277
Soybean Oil	60,000 lb	3,049,313	3,047,490	3,167,895	3,081,646	2,909,284
Soybean Meal	100 tons	2,784,423	3,039,633	3,218,690	2,647,821	2,493,086
Iced Broilers	30,000 lb	—	—	4,079	25,681	74,684
Silver	5,000 oz	77,682	214,236	341,033	2,720,589	2,657,833
Silver	1,000 oz	775,136	184,776	—	—	—
Gold	3 Kg	—	—	78	12,844	56,470
Gold	100 oz	19,515	14,749	71,401	97,509	—
Plywood	76,032 sq. ft.	100,001	144,318	169,550	146,570	261,483
Western Plywood	76,032 sq. ft.	—	30,871	—	—	—
GNMA Mrtges., CD	$100,000	—	175	12,619	77,365	6,527
GNMA Mrtges., CDR	$100,000	2,055,648	2,292,882	2,325,892	1,371,078	953,161
Com. Paper (90-day)	$1,000,000	—	49	15,996	39,702	18,767
Com. Paper (30-day)	$3,000,000	—	—	67	1,292	—
T-Notes (4-6 year)	$100,000	—	2,721	450	11,599	—
T-Notes (6½-10 year)	$100,000	881,325	—	—	—	—
T-Bonds	$100,000	16,739,695	13,907,988	6,489,555	2,059,594	555,350
Domestic CD (90-day)	$1,000,000	145,360	158,920	—	—	—
Unleaded Reg. Gasoline	1,000 brl	8,736	—	—	—	—
Chicago Board of Trade		48,206,790	49,085,763	45,281,571	33,870,680	27,362,929
Fresh Eggs	22,500 dz	18	13	2,798	21,224	72,984
Potatoes	80,000 lb	9	973	2,481	1,126	90
Live Hogs	30,000 lb	3,560,974	2,258,083	2,153,767	1,805,710	1,765,201
Pork Bellies, Fzn.	38,000 lb	2,811,674	1,997,697	2,250,945	1,514,176	1,439,651
Live Cattle	40,000 lb	4,440,992	4,282,293	5,997,047	7,214,848	5,592,364
Feeder Cattle	42,000 lb	603,769	620,885	874,313	980,619	568,728
Broilers	30,000 lb	2,118	20,048	45,237	7,794	—
Lumber	130,000 bd. ft.	516,619	635,934	838,676	649,478	560,498
Stud Lumber	100,000 bd. ft.	—	156	2,198	5,059	9,365
Plywood	152,064 sq. ft.	35	386	—	—	—
British Pound	25,000	1,321,701	1,491,102	1,263,750	513,682	240,099
Canadian Dollar	100,000	1,078,467	475,585	601,925	399,885	207,654
Deutsche Mark	125,000	1,792,901	1,654,891	922,608	450,856	400,569
Japanese Yen	12,500,000	1,762,246	960,598	575,073	329,645	361,731
Mexican Peso	1,000,000	65,036	18,905	19,301	29,982	17,844
Swiss Franc	125,000	2,653,332	1,518,767	827,884	493,944	321,451
Dutch Guilder	125,000	128	4	4	22	3,585
U.S. Silver Coins	$5,000	1	6	10	59	275
French Franc	250,000	16,474	2,080	144	406	4,449
Gold	100 oz	1,533,466	2,518,435	2,543,419	3,558,960	2,812,870
T-Bills (90-day)	$1,000,000	6,598,848	5,631,290	3,338,773	1,930,482	768,980
T-Bills (1-year)	$250,000	—	—	604	11,769	5,564
T-Notes (4-6 year)	$250,000	—	—	338	11,072	—
Domestic CD (90-day)	$1,000,000	1,556,327	423,718	—	—	—
Eurodollar	$1,000,000	323,619	15,171	—	—	—
S&P 500 Index	$500 x Index	2,935,532	—	—	—	—
Chicago Merc. Ex.		33,574,286	24,527,020	22,261,295	19,930,798	15,153,952
Wheat	5,000 bu	964,815	1,181,884	1,297,757	1,037,018	755,949
Grain Sorghum	5,000 bu	—	—	290	—	—
Value Line Index	$500 x Index	528,743	—	—	—	—
Kansas City Bd. of Tr.		1,493,558	1,181,884	1,298,047	1,037,018	755,949
Wheat	5,000 bu	346,226	357,779	333,610	328,799	284,313
Sunflower Seeds	100,000 lb	38	14,845	27,368	—	—
Minneapolis Grain Ex.		346,264	372,724	360,978	328,799	284,313
Coffee "C"	37,500 lb	556,435	515,302	906,944	449,799	163,959
Sugar #11	112,000 lb	2,037,020	2,470,327	3,576,662	1,792,723	1,016,773
Sugar #12	112,000 lb	51,093	14,333	13,839	35,474	21,875
Cocoa	30,000 lb	—	—	187,309	231,918	222,732
Cocoa	10 M tons	607,964	562,651	201,662	265	—
Coffee Sugar & Cocoa		3,252,512	3,562,613	4,886,416	2,510,179	1,425,339

	Contract Unit	1982	1981	1980	1979	1978
Wheat	1,000 bu	243,640	279,082	550,950	379,975	205,629
Corn	1,000 bu	274,324	513,953	440,615	323,808	256,022
Oats	5,000 bu	12,981	4,176	2,364	1,961	1,423
Soybeans	1,000 bu	527,411	849,169	1,052,707	964,596	994,932
Silver	1,000 oz	125,409	143,051	209,494	361,576	378,049
Gold	33.2 oz	383,499	469,460	447,494	200,359	41,939
Live Cattle	20,000 lb	107,329	119,566	186,831	208,997	54,054
Live Hogs	15,000 lb	175,624	100,139	103,181	127,674	185,927
T-Bonds	$50,000	419,277	109,944	—	—	—
T-Bills	$500,000	100,417	—	—	—	—
Refined Sugar	40,000 lb	24,000	—	—	—	—
New York Silver	1,000 oz	3,810	—	—	—	—
MidAmerica Com. Ex.		2,397,721	2,588,540	2,993,636	2,568,950	2,121,189
Copper	25,000 lb	2,362,625	1,647,380	1,848,080	2,301,033	1,408,688
Zinc	60,000 lb	0	3	28	75	677
Silver	5,000 oz	2,868,639	1,240,720	1,058,734	4,080,619	3,822,085
Gold	100 oz	12,289,448	10,373,706	8,001,410	6,541,893	3,742,378
T-Bills (90-day)	$1,000,000	0	1,052	76,081	27,860	—
T-Notes (2-year)	$100,000	0	30,188	17,653	—	—
GNMA Mrtges, CD	$100,000	—	—	7,403	873	—
Commodity Exchange		17,520,712	13,293,049	11,009,389	12,952,353	8,973,828
Cotton #2	50,000 lb	1,255,792	1,415,213	2,490,405	1,689,051	1,155,801
Orange Juice (FCOJ)	15,000 lb	207,070	387,182	162,864	186,018	285,405
Propane	100,000 gl	16,919	496	25	57	3
NY Cotton, Cit. & Pet.		1,479,781	1,802,891	2,653,294	1,875,126	1,441,209
T-Bills (90-day)	$1,000,000	—	9,766	32,452	—	—
T-Bonds	$100,000	4,464	162,942	139,410	—	—
Domestic CD (90-day)	$1,000,000	132	117,807	—	—	—
British Pound	25,000	—	37	7,352	—	—
Canadian Dollar	100,000	—	4	692	—	—
Deutsche Mark	125,000	—	3	258	—	—
Japanese Yen	12,500,000	—	13	199	—	—
Swiss Franc	125,000	—	13	3,630	—	—
NYSE Composite Index	$500 x Index	1,432,913	—	—	—	—
NYSE Financial Index	$1,000 x Index	13,933	—	—	—	—
NY Futures Exchange		1,451,442	290,585	183,993	—	—
Palladium	100 oz	63,829	40,822	62,217	46,994	45,174
Platinum	50 oz	669,024	90,493	429,708	536,124	405,748
U.S. Silver Coins	$10,000	—	41	6,808	5,462	9,887
British Pound	25,000	—	—	—	420	500
Canadian Dollar	100,000	—	—	—	3,866	181
Deutsche Mark	125,000	—	—	—	182	1,844
Japanese Yen	12,500,000	—	—	—	43	441
Swiss Franc	125,000	—	—	—	45	401
Imported Lean Beef	36,000 lb	7	7,976	24,119	16,704	5,890
Potatoes	50,000 lb	67,322	237,411	393,759	183,868	453,215
No. 2 Heating Oil, NY	1,000 brl	1,745,526	995,506	238,284	33,804	116
No. 2 Heating Oil, Gulf	1,000 brl	74	1,856	—	—	—
Leaded Reg. Gasoline, NY	1,000 brl	104,082	7,300	—	—	—
Leaded Reg. Gasoline, Gulf	1,000 brl	77	2	—	—	—
NY Mercantile Exchange		2,649,941	1,781,407	1,154,905	828,249	926,793
Rice, Milled	120,000 lb	5,262	10,249	—	—	—
Rice, Rough	200,000 lb	11,253	11,478	—	—	—
Cotton	50,000 lb	8,388	9,271	—	—	—
Soybeans	5,000 bu	1,998	4,997	—	—	—
Corn	5,000 bu	971	—	—	—	—
New Orleans Com. Ex.		27,872	35,995	—	—	—
GNMA Mrtges., CD	$100,000	—	—	4,530	52,493	16,671
T-Bills (90-day)	$1,000,000	—	—	5	4,334	—
T-Bonds	$100,000	—	—	8,050	7,492	—
Amex Commodity Ex.		—	—	12,585	64,319	16,671
Total All Contracts		112,400,879	98,522,371	92,096,109	75,966,471	58,462,172
CHANGE FROM PREVIOUS YEAR		+14%	+7%	+21.2%	+29.9%	+36.3%

Source: Futures Industry Association, Inc.

Alcohol

Salient Statistics of Alcohol in the United States   In Millions of Gallons[3]

Fiscal Year Ending Sept[6]	Ethyl Alcohol Production[5]	Tax-Paid[5] 190° & Over	Withdrawals Tax-Free For Denaturation	For Use of U.S.	Other[1]	Total	Total Withdrawn	Stocks at End of Fiscal Year	Denatured Alcohol[2] Completely Production	Specially Production	Withdrawals	Stocks Aug. 30[6]	Prod. of Refined Methanol[4] (Synthetic & Natural)
1970-1	570.0	63.3	470.6	.6	12.9	484.1	547.4	150.1	2.3	252.6	253.5	2.3	742.7
1971-2	569.0	68.0	435.4	.8	45.4	481.5	549.5	100.0	2.1	234.5	234.1	2.8	745.5
1972-3	679.7	67.8	460.9	.9	115.9	577.6	645.4	89.6	2.3	246.7	247.2	2.8	974.6
1973-4	647.4	72.4	469.7	.6	88.1	563.3	635.7	82.2	2.2	256.7	257.2	2.3	1,064
1974-5	581.0	72.7	403.3	.3	36.4	440.0	512.7	116.7	1.3	219.3	220.1	2.0	1,036
1975-6	503.4	78.5	419.3	.5	13.7	433.5	512.0	93.1	1.1	221.1	220.5	2.7	779.6
1976-7[6]	494.9	78.7	416.2	.4	14.6	431.2	509.9	79.0	1.1	223.8	224.1	2.7	940.1
1977-8	521.3	85.2	393.7	.4	15.1	409.2	494.4	76.2	1.1	221.9	222.3	2.6	971.8
1978-9	534.0		455.7	.4	17.4	473.6		61.5	1.1	221.9	222.3	2.6	970.4
1979-0								76.2	18.0	226.9	229.9	2.0	971.8
1980-1								75.4				3.5	1,077
1981-2								49.1				4.0	1,292
1982-3													1,094

[1] Represents withdrawals for hospital, scientific and educational use, for exports, etc.   [2] At denaturing plants.   [3] Ethyl alcohol in proof gallons; denatured alcohol in wine gallons.   [4] On a CALENDAR YEAR basis.   [5] Represents alcohol and spirits of 190° of proof and over.   [6] THE FISCAL YEAR PRIOR TO 1976-7 was from JULY–JUNE. Source: Alcohol and Tobacco Division
T.1

Average Wholesale Price Index of Ethyl Alcohol, in N.Y.   Dec. 1973 = 100[1]

Year	Jan.	Feb.	Mar.	Apr.	May	June	July	Aug.	Sept.	Oct.	Nov.	Dec.	Average
1970	56.5	56.5	56.5	56.5	56.5	56.5	56.5	56.5	56.5	56.5	56.5	56.5	56.5
1971	56.5	56.5	56.5	56.5	56.5	56.5	56.5	56.5	56.5	55.0	55.0	55.0	56.1
1972	55.0	55.0	55.0	55.0	55.0	55.0	55.0	55.0	55.0	55.0	55.0	55.0	55.0
1973	55.0	55.0	55.0	55.0	55.0	55.0	55.0	55.0	55.0	55.0	55.0	55.0	55.0
1974[1]	113.1	115.4	123.6	129.9	133.0	148.9	152.5	154.2	167.5	180.9	189.4	193.9	150.2
1975	201.6	206.3	219.2	219.2	217.8	218.0	216.8	214.6	215.8	217.1	218.2	216.6	215.1
1976	217.2	230.2	233.0	233.6	233.0	233.0	233.0	232.5	233.0	233.0	232.3	233.0	231.4
1977	231.6	233.0	232.3	232.3	232.3	233.0	238.8	244.9	243.6	243.1	242.5	243.9	237.6
1978	243.9	231.0	230.3	226.4	226.4	225.8	226.4	226.6	226.4	218.8	226.4	226.5	227.9
1979	234.8	239.2	239.2	243.6	248.1	249.4	260.1	265.4	277.6	284.3	291.5	292.2	260.5
1980	311.7	319.6	325.0	338.4	361.4	369.4	370.3	369.2	369.2	369.3	369.2	369.2	353.9
1981	369.2	369.2	370.3	370.3	368.5	368.5	387.3	387.3	387.3	396.8	392.0	383.3	379.2
1982	382.2	353.5	349.6	346.4	N.A.	338.7	341.1	345.2	336.6	335.5	335.9	N.A.	346.5
1983	336.4	335.2											

[1] Data prior to 1974 are for specially denatured No. 1, 190 proof, tank carlots, f.o.b. eastern works; freight prepared in CENTS PER GALLON. Source: Bureau of Labor Statistics (0614-0341.04)
T.2

U.S. Production of Ethyl Alcohol[1] & Spirits   In Millions of Tax Gallons[2]

Year	Jan.	Feb.	Mar.	Apr.	May	June	July	Aug.	Sept.	Oct.	Nov.	Dec.	Total
1970	42.2	48.5	59.8	57.7	57.8	59.2	56.9	46.9	58.3	54.8	41.4	48.3	631.5
1971	45.0	41.5	41.7	44.4	43.4	48.6	43.7	43.6	46.9	56.4	51.6	46.9	552.9
1972	38.0	43.8	46.1	43.7	52.4	56.7	64.7	57.7	64.0	59.3	51.5	53.4	621.3
1973	57.1	52.5	57.1	58.4	58.1	55.9	54.2	57.4	59.9	62.7	62.2	56.4	692.1
1974	49.9	49.9	45.3	55.5	52.8	40.8	45.3	52.4	59.5	61.0	48.6	54.8	618.2
1975	52.0	40.4	44.5	41.4	39.8	39.1	41.3	40.1	39.6	53.8	46.4	48.0	526.4
1976	41.6	36.2	44.0	39.3	36.0	37.0	45.5	46.0	43.3	39.3	42.8	47.7	498.8
1977	36.5	37.7	42.8	39.2	43.5	43.2	40.3	40.9	41.0	44.7	48.9	39.7	498.3
1978	35.8	41.1	50.4	42.2	31.3	48.7	42.5	45.4	50.5	40.3	38.0	40.7	506.9
1979	42.8	41.3	49.3	47.3	42.9	48.2	43.8	46.0	53.7	49.4	51.0	54.6	570.4
1980	57.4	52.7	54.7	54.6	54.0	45.7	52.8	46.4	57.2	64.3	47.7	53.7	643.2
1981[3]	49.2	44.3	49.3	50.9	44.0	42.2	45.3	55.8	53.1	44.0	47.8	45.4	571.2
1982[3]	42.9	39.8	48.2	37.6	41.9	52.6	51.9	44.3	53.3	61.9	61.6		

[1] At industrial alcohol plants.   [2] A "tax gallon" is the alcoholic equivalent of a U.S. gallon at 60 degrees Fahrenheit, containing 50% of ethyl alcohol by volume.   [3] Preliminary.   Source: Internal Revenue Service
T.3

Aluminum

World production of aluminum in 1982 was about 15 percent below that of 1981, according to a preliminary estimate by the U.S. Bureau of Mines. A growing portion of world primary aluminum production capacity is government-owned, and presumably economic factors have less influence on production rates than they would otherwise.

U.S. primary aluminum production dropped 27 percent in 1982. The year began with about 1.33 million tons, or 24 percent of annual capacity, shut down, and by October, 42 percent of U.S. capacity was not operating. However, at the end of December 1982 the domestic industry's operating rate had recovered to 58 percent of its annual capacity of 5,487,000 tons, and it recovered further in early 1983. Throughout most of 1982, producers closed facilities due to poor economic conditions, labor problems, and rising power costs. Secondary recovery of aluminum also declined in 1982. Recovery from new scrap was off 17 percent and old scrap (mostly recycled cans) recovery declined only 7 percent.

Total domestic apparent aluminum metal consumption decreased in 1982 due to declines in the building, transportation, and electrical industries, but these were partially offset by high demand in the container and packaging industry. Beer and soft drink cans represent the largest single market for aluminum in the United States. Packaging accounted for an estimated 39 percent of domestic consumption of aluminum in 1982, followed by transportation, 20 percent; building, 14 percent; electrical, 8 percent; consumer durables, 8 percent; and other uses, 11 percent.

U.S. imports of crude metal and alloys for consumption in 1982 decreased 6 percent from the 1981 total, but imports of plates, sheets, bars, etc. increased 50 percent from 1981 levels. Scrap imports declined 9 percent in 1982.

U.S. exports of ingots, slab, and crude metal increased 17 percent in 1982 compared to 1981 imports. However, exports of plates, sheets, bars, etc. decreased 26 percent, and exports of scrap ingot dropped 23 percent. Other scrap exports were 7 percent below the 1981 level. Total U.S. exports decreased 6 percent in 1982, according to preliminary U.S. Bureau of Mines data.

Production of domestic primary aluminum in 1982 was estimated by the Bureau of Mines to increase at a slow rate, to 3.7 million tons. Apparent consumption, including recovery from old scrap, was expected to total 4.9 million tons. From a 1978 base, apparent aluminum demand was projected to grow at a rate of about 4.5 percent a year through 1990. A greater rate of growth was expected in recovery from old scrap.

In August 1982 the Bonneville Power Administration (BPA) announced it would increase power rates to its direct service industry customers, which include the Pacific Northwest aluminum producers, by 50 percent from 17.3 mills per kilowatt hour (kwh) to 25.9 mills per kwh, effective October 1. The Northwest aluminum industry provides about one-third of the country's output of aluminum and the cost of electricity accounts for about one-third of the cost of producing aluminum, according to trade estimates. In March 1983, the BPA offered to sell surplus power (partly arising from heavy winter rains and mild weather) to Northwest aluminum firms at 11.2 mills per kwh for loads exceeding current operating levels during the sale period (March 22 to October 31, 1983).

The quoted domestic producer prices of primary aluminum held unchanged at 76 cents per pound throughout 1982. Discounting from the producer list price was heavy during 1982, but prices steadied in early 1983 as demand picked up.

Futures Market

Aluminum futures are traded on the London Metal Exchange (LME).

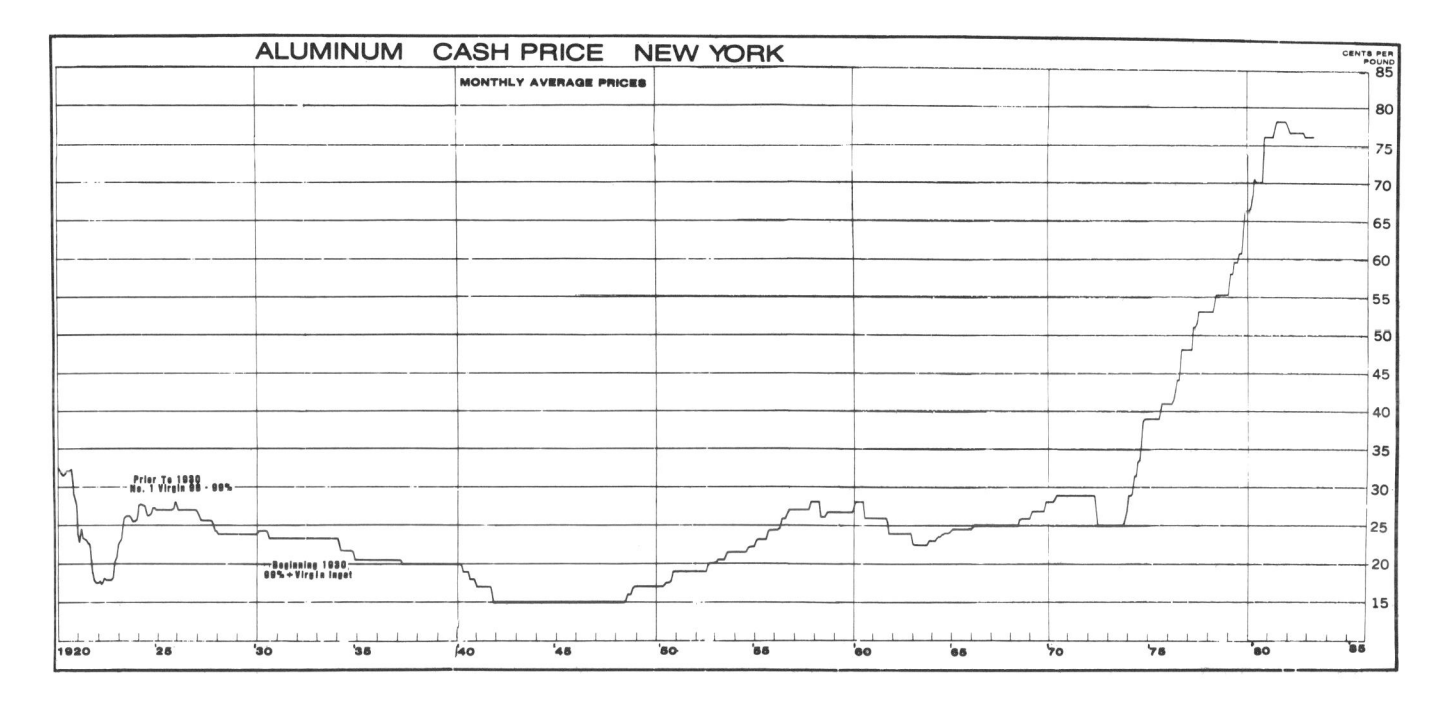

ALUMINUM

World Production of Aluminum   In Thousands of Short Tons

Year	Australia	Austria	Canada	China	France	W. Germany	Hungary	Italy	Japan	Norway	Spain	Switzerland	Cameroon	Un. Kingdom	United States	USSR	World Total
1971	247	100	1,121		423	471	74	132	984	584	139	104	56	131	3,925	1,300	11,373
1972	227	93	1,013		434	490	75	134	1,118	604	154	92	51	189	4,122	1,380	12,115
1973	228	98	1,038		396	587	75	203	1,209	684	179	94	49	277	4,529	1,500	13,364
1974	242	101	1,125	165	434	759	76	238	1,232	731	211	96	52	323	4,903	1,580	14,516
1975	236	98	978	220	422	747	77	210	1,117	656	232	87	57	340	3,879	1,690	13,387
1976	256	98	698	350	424	768	78	228	1,013	681	232	86	64	369	4,251	1,760	13,913
1977	273	101	1,073	385	440	818	79	287	1,310	686	233	88	61	386	4,539	1,810	15,189
1978	290	101	1,156	400	431	816	79	298	1,166	704	234	88	54	382	4,804	1,840	15,581
1979	298	102	948	400	435	817	79	297	1,113	727	286	91	48	396	5,023	1,930	16,061
1980[1]	334	104	1,184	400	476	806	81	321	1,203	718	426	95	48	413	5,130	1,940	17,006
1981[2]	418	104	1,238	400	480	803	82	302	849	701	437	91	50	374	4,948	1,973	16,613
1982[2]			1,190		420	780			400	700	400			250	3,600	2,100	14,200
1983																	

[1] Preliminary.   [2] Estimate.   *Source: Bureau of Mines*   T.4

Salient Statistics of Aluminum in the U.S.   In Thousands of Short Tons

Year	Net Import Reliance as a % of Apparent Consumption	Production Primary	Production Secondary	Primary Sold[1]	Recovery from Scrap Old	Recovery from Scrap New	Total Apparent Consumption	Plate Sheet Foil	Wrought Products Rolled Structural Shapes[2]	Extruded Shapes[3]	All	Castings Permanent Mold	Castings Die	Castings Sand	All	Total All Net Shipments
1975	7	3,879	980	4,806	337	899	3,907	2,332	462	821	3,713	144	433	99	688	4,401
1976	9	4,251	1,155	6,145	409	1,062	5,083	3,178	493	1,071	4,858	189	605	110	923	5,780
1977	7	4,539	1,271	6,566	531	1,074	5,492	3,423	467	1,198	5,210	220	652	113	1,004	6,214
1978	11	4,804	1,323	7,143	575	1,098	6,045	3,643	583	1,311	5,673	229	666	126	1,044	6,717
1979	4	5,023	1,401	7,051	614	1,163	5,888	3,592	618	1,263	5,615	241	635	143	1,040	6,655
1980	7[7]	5,130	1,389	6,123	680	1,058	5,065	3,346	606	1,165	5,242	193	443	121	769	6,011
1981[4]	7[7]	4,948	1,656	6,306	836	1,137	5,137	3,424	522	1,103	5,171	172	478	121	791	5,961
1982[6]	4	3,609			830	965	4,740									
1983																

[1] Or used by producers. Includes shipments to the Gov't.   [2] Also rod, bar & wire.   [3] Also rod, bar, tube, blooms & tubing.   [4] Preliminary.   [5] Consists of total shipments less shipments to other mills for further fabrication.   [6] Estimate.   [7] Net exports.   T.8

U.S. Production of Primary Aluminum (Domestic & Foreign Ores)   In Thousands of Short Tons

Year	Jan.	Feb.	Mar.	Apr.	May	June	July	Aug.	Sept.	Oct.	Nov.	Dec.	Total[1]
1974	404	376	420	410	422	405	416	411	401	417	405	416	4,903
1975	394	324	347	326	327	302	310	309	300	311	310	319	3,879
1976	322	303	326	325	350	345	365	371	366	391	387	400	4,251
1977	399	352	379	371	383	369	376	376	367	386	380	395	4,539
1978	400	367	395	387	405	395	408	410	399	416	404	418	4,804
1979[2]	418	379	419	402	423	410	428	430	419	435	423	435	5,023
1980[2]	431	406	434	421	438	425	427	426	419	437	427	439	5,130
1981[2]	445	404	448	431	441	420	426	416	393	396	364	364	4,948
1982[2]	351	311	336	319	321	300	297	287	271	275	266	275	3,609
1983													

[1] Final annual totals.   [2] Preliminary.   *Source: Bureau of Mines*   T.9

50

ALUMINUM

U.S. Aluminum Inventories, Total (Ingot, Mill Prod. & Scrap)   In Million Pounds

Year	Jan. 1	Feb. 1	Mar. 1	Apr. 1	May 1	June 1	July 1	Aug. 1	Sept. 1	Oct. 1	Nov. 1	Dec. 1
1971	4,387	4,467	4,493	4,475	4,441	4,271	4,463	4,669	4,743	4,771	4,878	4,990
1972	5,026	5,050	5,038	5,003	4,984	4,919	4,869	4,924	4,896	4,868	4,866	4,856
1973	4,861	4,840	4,764	4,697	4,623	4,559	4,609	4,576	4,545	4,504	4,422	4,375
1974	4,366	4,276	4,250	4,182	4,233	4,291	4,329	4,428	4,533	4,559	4,650	4,869
1975	5,156	5,535	5,589	5,866	5,940	6,092	6,086	6,070	6,013	6,014	5,962	6,007
1976	5,999	6,011	6,036	5,899	5,823	5,685	5,554	5,605	5,545	5,541	5,613	5,720
1977	5,701	5,854	5,893	5,666	5,597	5,553	5,470	5,620	5,662	5,628	5,707	5,742
1978	5,706	5,809	5,799	5,730	5,749	5,695	5,664	5,704	5,586	5,610	5,575	5,548
1979[1]	5,494	5,395	5,242	5,009	5,017	4,950	4,893	4,921	4,915	4,941	4,940	5,000
1980[1]	5,112	5,069	5,011	4,949	4,910	4,950	5,021	5,072	5,026	4,966	4,942	5,082
1981[1]	5,076	5,221	5,323	5,408	5,495	5,600	5,632	5,964	6,086	6,187	6,276	6,524
1982[1]	6,607	6,670	6,742	6,658	6,683	6,684	6,577	6,626	6,508	6,434	6,431	6,388
1983[1]	6,233											

[1] Preliminary.   *Source: Bureau of Mines*   T.5

Average Price of Aluminum (Virgin 99.5% Unalloyed Ingot) at N.Y.   In Cents per Pound, Carload Lots

Year	Jan.	Feb.	Mar.	Apr.	May	June	July	Aug.	Sept.	Oct.	Nov.	Dec.	Average
1975	39.00	39.00	39.00	39.00	39.00	39.00	39.00	40.42	41.00	41.00	41.00	41.00	39.79
1976	41.00	41.00	41.00	41.48	42.50	44.00	44.00	46.91	48.00	48.00	48.00	48.00	44.49
1977	48.00	48.00	48.74	51.00	51.00	51.36	52.90	53.00	53.00	53.00	53.00	53.00	51.33
1978	53.00	53.00	53.00	53.00	54.23	55.25	55.25	55.25	55.25	55.25	55.25	55.50	54.44
1979	56.64	58.00	58.00	59.50	59.50	59.50	60.75	60.75	61.18	65.82	66.25	66.25	61.01
1980	66.25	66.86	68.40	70.52	70.00	70.00	70.00	70.00	70.00	75.65	76.00	76.00	70.81
1981	76.00	76.00	76.00	76.00	76.90	78.00	78.00	78.00	78.00	78.00	78.00	77.32	77.19
1982	76.50	76.50	76.50	76.50	76.50	76.50	76.50	76.50	76.50	76.00	76.00	76.00	76.38
1983	76.00	76.00	76.00	76.00									
1984													

Sources: American Metal Market   T.11

Average Price of Cast Aluminum Scrap (Crank Cases)[1] in New York   In Cents per Pound

Year	Jan.	Feb.	Mar.	Apr.	May	June	July	Aug.	Sept.	Oct.	Nov.	Dec.	Average
1975	7.30	7.00	7.00	7.25	7.25	7.25	7.25	7.92	9.86	9.05	9.20	9.75	8.01
1976	9.75	10.17	11.90	14.09	14.10	14.00	15.50	16.45	16.74	15.02	14.50	13.60	13.81
1977	13.50	15.65	18.00	18.00	17.86	16.59	17.50	17.37	15.50	15.00	15.45	16.00	16.37
1978	16.71	18.50	19.11	22.10	22.50	22.50	22.50	22.50	22.50	22.50	22.50	22.75	21.39
1979	23.64	25.34	28.05	32.08	35.55	35.65	33.65	30.90	29.55	31.59	31.50	31.50	30.75
1980	34.36	37.90	43.85	37.47	30.52	27.00	28.18	30.52	31.00	31.00	30.08	27.50	32.45
1981	27.50	27.50	27.50	27.41	25.20	23.50	23.50	23.50	22.83	21.77	20.50	20.50	24.27
1982	20.50	20.50	19.85	19.50	19.25	16.32	16.00	16.00	16.00	16.00	14.95	14.50	17.45
1983	15.12	17.50	19.50	19.50									
1984													

[1] Dealers' buying prices.   *Source: American Metal Market*   T.12

ALUMINUM

Aluminum Products (Ingot & Mill Products) Shipments[1] in the U.S.   In Millions of Pounds

Year	Jan.	Feb.	Mar.	Apr.	May	June	July	Aug.	Sept.	Oct.	Nov.	Dec.	Total
1974	1,300	1,203	1,307	1,336	1,256	1,225	1,103	1,105	1,025	1,106	890.3	782.4	13,639
1975	769.9	735.5	675.8	736.6	747.9	832.4	825.4	866.6	899.9	921.4	824.6	968.4	9,804
1976	902.5	945.7	1,135	1,059	1,203	1,169	942.1	1,173	1,007	1,016	960.9	1,056	12,247
1977	847.2	946.8	1,417	1,161	1,142	1,189	942.8	1,046	1,023	1,019	972.5	1,102	12,831
1978	932.7	1,024	1,277	1,079	1,223	1,257	1,114	1,187	1,175	1,342	1,183	1,207	13,982
1979[2]	1,270	1,147	1,374	1,141	1,264	1,201	1,137	1,186	1,084	1,192	1,098	1,130	14,517
1980[2]	1,255	1,218	1,274	1,180	1,135	1,093	1,104	1,177	1,184	1,232	1,021	1,203	14,057
1981[2]	1,090	1,072	1,294	1,199	1,189	1,248	1,039	1,119	1,082	1,040	860	928	13,237
1982[2]	849	934	1,095	995	971	1,113	879	1,100	1,014	954	938	1,024	11,871
1983													

[1] Mill products & pig & ingot (net shipments). [2] Preliminary.   Source: *Bureau of the Census*   T.10

Aluminum Exports (Metal & Alloys, Crude) from the U.S.   In Thousands of Short Tons

Year	Jan.	Feb.	Mar.	Apr.	May	June	July	Aug.	Sept.	Oct.	Nov.	Dec.	Total
1973	12.4	11.5	10.6	12.4	11.1	10.3	14.1	16.4	29.8	31.2	47.0	22.8	229.6
1974	22.0	20.9	30.4	22.8	17.7	13.6	15.0	14.4	12.3	16.7	9.2	12.8	207.8
1975	4.8	4.9	3.6	4.5	13.4	8.6	4.8	20.9	13.7	25.2	36.8	44.9	185.8
1976	31.3	4.1	25.8	14.6	7.2	9.7	10.5	9.8	6.2	7.5	13.1	12.7	152.4
1977	9.8	10.6	8.7	12.5	4.4	6.7	7.9	9.3	9.0	2.9	8.9	7.2	97.8
1978	3.7	5.7	6.1	4.2	7.0	9.3	8.5	11.0	15.9	17.7	23.1	14.3	126.6
1979	32.4	15.4	14.8	19.4	12.0	7.7	8.3	12.2	8.4	19.2	17.2	33.6	200.6
1980	39.6	37.7	52.8	52.3	52.3	61.3	51.3	97.6	98.9	70.1	55.0	46.1	714.9
1981	59.4	23.2	32.9	48.6	29.3	23.5	29.3	16.8	9.2	24.1	23.1	24.6	344.2
1982	22.1	18.8	46.0	26.6	19.9	48.5	24.2	42.6	23.6	59.5	42.1	27.3	401.2
1983	56.1												

Source: *Bureau of the Census*   T.7

Aluminum Imports (General)—Metal & Alloys, Crude—into the U.S.   In Thousands of Short Tons

Year	Jan.	Feb.	Mar.	Apr.	May	June	July	Aug.	Sept.	Oct.	Nov.	Dec.	Total
1972	46.8	43.9	70.0	55.0	73.4	66.3	44.8	39.2	52.2	47.0	53.3	54.5	646.4
1973	58.2	38.8	50.9	43.1	44.7	50.7	34.6	36.0	33.0	46.0	35.1	36.5	507.6
1974	30.5	34.7	48.6	41.1	44.1	38.2	36.6	51.0	41.5	53.1	47.4	42.3	509.0
1975	41.9	37.4	30.7	31.5	25.5	34.9	26.7	43.5	56.4	37.8	45.3	46.3	434.1
1976	36.1	47.0	50.7	71.7	68.8	70.9	33.2	68.6	27.9	34.2	33.6	25.9	575.4
1977	15.8	48.5	68.6	59.3	59.8	74.1	67.5	75.9	42.2	49.6	54.5	57.5	670.2
1978	53.0	64.0	74.4	58.2	89.9	83.5	66.9	50.8	51.3	86.9	43.1	35.0	756.9
1979	69.6	41.0	53.9	44.3	57.8	36.0	62.6	30.8	31.9	39.4	40.8	62.6	570.6
1980	61.8	45.3	47.8	45.4	42.1	51.7	40.3	40.7	43.0	41.4	29.9	78.3	580.8
1981	55.8	55.7	75.6	50.2	67.8	55.9	63.9	67.0	60.5	55.2	41.5	49.3	710.7
1982	38.5	65.9	61.7	61.0	51.0	66.5	42.2	78.2	52.8	52.7	60.1	47.8	678.4
1983	53.1												

Source: *Bureau of the Census*   T.6

Antimony

The U.S. Bureau of Mines estimated the total world mine production of antimony during 1982 at 62,400 short tons compared with 65,246 tons during 1981. The principal world resources of antimony, which together amounted to nearly 5.6 million tons in 1982, were located in China, Bolivia, the Soviet Union, the Republic of South Africa, and in Mexico. Between 1978 and 1981, nearly 40 percent of all U.S. imports of antimony and of antimony ores and concentrates came from Bolivia, and 44 percent of the U.S. imports of antimony oxide were bought from the Republic of South Africa during the same period.

Nearly all of the U.S. production of antimony during 1982 was by two firms, one in Idaho that recovered antimony as a byproduct of complex silver-copper ores (tetrahedrite), and one in Montana producing mostly from antimony ore (stibnite). The Idaho mine was temporarily shut down in 1982 because of unprofitable silver prices. Preliminary Bureau of Mines figures indicated that the 1982 U.S. production of antimony was down nearly 15 percent from its 1981 level. This production included antimony recovered from the smelting of lead ore.

Estimated 1982 U.S. industrial consumption of primary antimony was 22 percent lower than in 1981. An estimated 55 percent of the apparent U.S. consumption of antimony was derived from old scrap. The recovery of antimony from battery-plate scrap accounted for nearly 85 percent of the secondary output, and the balance was recovered from type metal scrap, bearing metal scrap, and from miscellaneous antimony alloy scrap. Most of the recovered antimony was consumed by the battery industry in the form of antimonial lead. Changes in the types of alloys used in automotive batteries have resulted in a reduction of the amounts of antimony used as a hardener of battery grids. Antimony has been replaced by alternate metals in some original equipment starting-lighting-ignition batteries, but this decline in usage was expected to continue to be offset by an increased consumption of antimony oxide as a flame retardant. The manufacture of flame-retardant material provides the dominant market for primary antimony.

As of the end of 1982, U.S. industrial stocks of antimony were estimated to be 23 percent below the 1981 level. The domestic demand for antimony, figured from 1978 as a base, is expected to increase at an average annual rate of nearly 3.1 percent through 1990. Projections that domestic producers will supply less than 10 percent of the primary demand indicate a continuing reliance on imports of both antimony metal and concentrates. The Bureau of Mines estimated that the 1983 domestic mine production of antimony will be around 600 tons and that U.S. apparent consumption will be 34,000 tons.

The Omnibus Budget Reconciliation Act of 1981 authorized the disposal of 3,000 tons of antimony from the government stockpile at the rate of 1,000 tons per year, effective October 1, 1981.

World Mine Production of Antimony (Content of Ore)   In Short Tons

Year	Australia	Bolivia	Canada[2]	China[1]	Czechoslovakia	Italy	Morocco	Mexico[2]	Peru[5]	Turkey	South Africa	United States	USSR	Yugoslavia[4]	World Total[1]
1970	66	12,970	363	13,000	660	1,432	2,008	4,925	1,286	3,053	19,147	1,130	7,400	3,197	77,124
1971	66	12,861	162	13,000	660	1,295	2,174	3,705	757	3,124	15,704	1,025	7,600	2,207	70,653
1972	66	14,703	340	13,000	660	1,324	917	3,280	826	2,982	16,062	489	7,700	2,177	73,986
1973	66	16,461	830	13,000	770	1,497	1,364	2,632	756	3,696	17,306	545	7,800	2,265	76,920
1974	1,550	14,396	1,380	13,000	830	1,297	2,029	2,653	751	6,482	16,722	661	8,000	2,434	79,232
1975	2,431	13,136	2,020	13,000	770	1,113	1,160	3,458	305	4,010	17,553	886	8,300	2,406	77,114
1976	2,086	18,756	2,535	9,300	314	1,112	1,549	2,806	665	1,890	11,890	283	8,500	2,228	71,388
1977	2,303	18,012	3,500	11,000	330	891	1,553	2,974	903	2,118	12,715	610	8,700	2,478	74,600
1978	1,674	14,702	3,310	11,000	330	1,026	2,437	2,708	821	2,315	10,024	798	8,700	2,950	68,662
1979	1,696	14,351	3,256	11,000	450	1,047	2,175	3,166	840	2,083	12,815	722	9,000	2,245	71,384
1980[3]	1,305	17,047	2,600	11,000	452	786	606	2,399	1,157	2,153	14,413	343	9,000	2,315	71,727
1981[1]	1,323	16,861	1,600	11,000	452	772	606	1,984	1,213	2,370	10,744	646	9,000	2,205	65,246
1982[1]		16,000						2,000			9,500	550		2,000	62,400
1983															

[1] Estimate. [2] Includes antimony content of miscellaneous smelter products. [3] Preliminary. [4] Metal. [5] Recoverable.   Source: Bureau of Mines   T.13

Average Price of American Antimony R.M.M.[2] Brand (N.Y. Equivalent[1]—in Bulk)   In Cents Per Pound

Year	Jan.	Feb.	Mar.	Apr.	May	June	July	Aug.	Sept.	Oct.	Nov.	Dec.	Average
1971	98.00	98.00	82.48	81.00	70.55	70.00	60.57	59.00	59.00	59.00	59.00	59.00	71.30
1972	59.00	59.00	59.00	59.00	59.00	59.00	59.00	59.00	59.00	59.00	59.00	59.00	59.00
1973	59.00	60.26	62.00	65.14	68.00	68.00	68.00	68.00	68.00	68.00	77.00	90.00	68.45
1974	94.00	98.74	104.00	142.00	177.00	213.50	225.00	225.00	225.00	225.00	225.00	225.00	181.60
1975	213.18	199.00	199.00	199.00	188.71	160.00	160.00	160.00	160.00	160.00	160.00	160.00	176.57
1976	158.00	158.00	158.00	158.00	158.00	158.00	158.00	158.00	166.90	175.00	175.00	175.00	162.99
1977	175.00	175.00	175.00	175.00	175.00	175.00	175.00	175.00	175.00	175.00	175.00	175.00	175.00
1978	175.00	175.00	175.00	175.00	175.00	175.00	175.00	175.00	175.00	175.00	175.00	175.00	175.00
1979[2]	177.00	177.00	190.00	201.00	201.00	201.00	201.00	201.00	201.00	201.00	201.00	201.00	196.08
1980	201.00	201.00	201.00	201.00	201.00	201.00	201.00	201.00	201.00	201.00	201.00	200.00	200.92
1981	200.00	200.00	200.00	200.00	200.00	200.00	200.00	200.00	200.00	200.00	200.00	200.00	200.00
1982	200.00	200.00	200.00	200.00	200.00	200.00	200.00	200.00	200.00	200.00	200.00	200.00	200.00
1983	200.00	200.00	200.00	200.00									

[1] Of F.O.B. Laredo, Texas Base.   [2] Domestic refined in alloy beginning Jan. 1979.   Source: American Metal Market   T.14

ANTIMONY

Salient Statistics of Antimony in the United States   In Short Tons

Year	Net Import Reliance as a % of Apparent Consumption	Production (Gross Weight) Ores	Primary[2] Mine	Primary[2] Smelter	Secondary (Alloys)[2]	Imports[5] Ore Gross Weight	Imports[5] Ore Sb Content	Imports[5] Metal Gross Weight	Exports[3]	Industry Stocks, Dec. 31[2] Ores & Concentrates	Metallic	Oxide	Sulfide	Residues & Slag	Total[6]	Prod. of Antimonial Lead[2]
1970		6,681	1,381	13,381	21,424	34,415	13,820	1,290	543	2,973	1,598	2,932	39		8,847	1,184
1971		4,721	1,025	11,374	20,917	22,102	9,619	1,638	1,023	3,582	1,367	2,697	22		8,637	1,191
1972		2,072	489	13,344	22,428	33,542	17,212	2,302	121	3,562	1,332	3,179	182		8,622	1,050
1973		2,468	545	17,206	24,062	33,869	16,679	692	515	5,585	1,540	2,074	31		10,078	1,167
1974		3,217	661	16,657	23,570	31,330	14,655	2,203	871	6,275	809	3,732	35		11,694	1,097
1975	49	4,505	886	12,189	17,964	20,736	8,320	2,112	340	8,364	1,380	3,886	32		14,957	567
1976	54	1,111	283	14,618	19,799	20,945	10,023	2,083	341	7,899	1,662	4,560	31		15,070	730
1977	41	3,496	610	12,827	30,601	8,042	3,438	1,722	742	1,869	1,359	4,576	24	516	8,591	900
1978	43	4,231	798	14,110	26,456	8,672	4,495	4,127	556	1,610	1,119	4,906	19	457	8,201	783
1979	53	3,294	722	15,062	24,155	15,745	7,732	3,022	485	1,757	1,184	3,398	17	730	7,144	299
1980	48	3,041	343	16,062	19,893	11,044	5,235	2,590	453	2,743	680	3,855	13	1,116	8,411	30
1981[1]	48		646	17,761	19,856	10,813	5,168	2,631	324	2,529	916	4,707	25	864	9,158	555
1982[4]	45		480	12,333	11,361		2,770	1,899	830	1,240	539	5,003	22	155	7,009	
1983																

[1] Preliminary   [2] Antimony content.   [3] Antimony ore, metal & compounds.   [4] Estimate.   [5] Imports for consumption.   [6] Including primary antimony residues & slag.   *Source: Bureau of Mines*   T.15

Industrial Consumption of Primary Antimony in the United States   In Sort Tons (Antimony Content)

Year	Ammunition	Antimonial Lead	Sheet & Pipe	Bearing Metal & Bearings	Cable Covering	Solder	Type Metal	Total All Metal Products	Fireworks	Flame Retardant	Ceramics & Glass	Rubber Pdt's.	Non-Metal Pigments	Plastics	Total[3]	Grand Total
1970		5,246	77	481	38		220	6,574	17	1,774	1,820	519	610	1,667	7,363	13,937
1971		5,430	74	515	36		177	6,621	4	1,524	1,840	525	592	1,810	7,086	13,707
1972	64	6,149	108	559	19		142	7,382	4	2,280	1,695	587	644	2,391	8,742	16,124
1973	122	8,027	97	527	12		134	9,291	5	2,906	1,917	693	644	2,920	11,322	20,613
1974	121	7,251	69	476	16		107	8,429	11	4,383	1,384	664	460	1,431	5,229	18,041
1975	239	4,568	60	402	23	133	75	5,647	10	3,799	989	458	321	1,091	3,541	12,987
1976	63	3,861	74	405	19	188	79	4,900	12	5,552	1,260	578	415	1,277	4,885	15,337
1977	138	2,936	56	265	16	220	83	3,847	9	5,765	1,547	473	400	1,503	4,211	13,823
1978	133	2,832	39	279	21	206	81	3,736	5	5,854	1,259	254	410	1,456	3,562	13,152
1979	253	1,300	36	235	16	199	37	2,213	6	6,083	1,127	182	399	1,580	3,457	11,753
1980	362	748	29	223	31	134	21	1,650	4	5,695	1,303	325	499	1,636	3,894	11,239
1981[1]	409	1,257	36	206	24	105	19	2,145	4	6,401	782	232	341	1,551	3,046	11,592
1982[2]																9,020

[1] Preliminary.   [2] Estimate.   [3] Excludes flame-retardant.   *Source: Bureau of Mines*   T.16

Antimony Imported[3] into the U.S. & Price Ranges

Year	Antimony Ore Value Ths. $	Needle or Liquated Antimony Gross Weight Sh. Tons	Needle or Liquated Antimony Value $ Ths.	Antimony Metal Short Tons	Antimony Metal Value $Ths.	Antimony Oxide Short Tons	Antimony Oxide Value $ Ths.	Foreign Metal ¢[2] Lb.	Antim. Trioxide ¢[2] Lb.	50–55% $ Short Ton	Antimony Ore Minimum 60% $ Short Ton	65% $ Short Ton
1970	12,733	18	54	1,290	3,493	4,256	10,023	80–400	97½–170	17–40		
1971	8,787	32	47	1,638	1,914	2,791	4,317	52–95	77–100	8.64–10		
1972	9,437	78	75	2,302	2,092	5,032	5,766	53½–57	69–77	7.60–10		
1973	10,903	51	73	692	745	4,651	6,095	55–135	69–105½	7.60–18.65		
1974	20,866	86	271	2,203	7,550	6,269	15,580			17–32		
1975	14,535	74	255	2,112	5,677	9,908	12,588	130–200	165–216	25½–27½		
1976	16,911	41	129	2,083	4,986	11,611	17,029			165.26		
1977	6,832	259	580	1,722	4,536	9,641	15,150	100–155	164–180	178		
1978	6,174	60	163	4,127	7,897	10,667	18,803	105–135	164–180	175		
1979	11,860	50	255	3,022	7,011	13,679	17,921	125–160	150–180	196		
1980	11,646	34	216	2,590	7,277	12,224	15,771	145–165	150–180	200		
1981[1]	9,095	106	249	2,631	6,569	12,170	19,922	120–152	140–180	200		
1982[1]				1,899		8,659				200		

[1] Preliminary.   [2] Duty paid delivery, N.Y.   [3] Imports for consumption.   *Source: Bureau of Mines*   T.17

Apples

World Production of Apples (Dessert & Cooking) In Thousands of Metric Tons

Year	Mexico	Argentina	Australia	Spain	Belg-Lux.	Canada	France	Germany (West)	Italy	Japan	Netherlands	Turkey	United Kingdom	United States[2]	Yugoslavia	World Total
1970		424	443		252	406	1,876	1,777	2,062	1,021	450	748	491	2,902	277	14,952
1971		512	360		280	398	1,854	1,980	1,698	1,007	520	780	466	2,890	327	15,233
1972		233	456		265	393	1,719	1,239	1,873	959	400	850	350	2,668	309	13,849
1973		233	335	1,015	246	375	2,060	2,016	2,050	963	460	850	456	2,830	448	15,719
1974	213	786	368	1,038	209	406	1,610	1,281	1,886	850	385	950	340	2,964	370	14,895
1975	230	608	368	1,091	268	460	2,125	2,035	2,127	989	430	900	338	3,415	370	16,910
1976	329	576	275	1,008	241	409	1,598	1,487	2,143	879	380	1,000	388	2,936	483	15,501
1977	297	820	301	672	120	411	1,186	1,176	1,828	959	315	900	234	3,057	381	13,934
1978	313	810	258	1,015	273	452	1,768	1,783	1,874	844	510	1,000	342	3,446	381	16,589
1979	338	972	345	1,097	322	435	1,769	1,951	2,023	853	450	1,350	334	3,694	428	16,605
1980[1]	282	958	299	859	330	553	1,802	1,880	1,966	960	450	1,100	321	4,005	483	16,778
1981[3]	301	905	344	1,037	134	409	1,471	779	1,750	847	220	—	225	3,592	380	13,883
1982[3]																14,200

[1] Preliminary. [2] Commercial crop. [3] Estimate. Source: Foreign Agricultural Service, U.S.D.A.   T.18

Salient Statistics of Apples[1] in the United States

Year	Production Total	Production Having Value	Western Avg. Auction Price N.Y. $ Per Box Golden Delicious	Western Avg. Auction Price N.Y. $ Per Box Red Rome	Fresh	Canned	Dried	Frozen	Juice & Cider	Other[3]	Avg. Farm Price ¢ Per Lb.	Farm Value Million $	Foreign Trade[4] Domestic Exports Fresh	Foreign Trade[4] Domestic Exports Dried[5]	Foreign Trade[4] Imports Fresh & Dried[5]	Per Capita Consumption[5] Lbs.
1970	6,398	6,258	5.48	2.76	3,532	1,159	190	203	[6]	1,176	4.54	283.9	2.1	.2	2.1	18.3
1971	6,373	6,083	5.76	4.37	3,484	1,094	96	191	[6]	1,219	4.92	299.2	2.5	.1	1.8	16.1
1972	5,879	5,868	6.36	5.04	3,342	977	149	235	[6]	1,165	6.43	377.5	3.1	.3	2.3	17.3
1973	6,265	6,252	7.76	5.00	3,539	1,255	248	259	[6]	950	8.80	549.0	3.7	.3	1.9	14.6
1974	6,580	6,530	8.81	7.04	3,691	1,226	197	182	[6]	1,235	8.40	551.6	4.9	.2	1.6	16.0
1975	7,530	7,103	8.22	5.16	4,357	1,027	230	207	[6]	1,283	6.50	460.9	4.7	.2	2.6	17.7
1976	6,472	6,467	7.57	3.67	3,916	920	229	220	[6]	1,182	9.10	586.5	5.7	.2	2.6	18.7
1977	6,740	6,710	8.76	7.28	3,860	1,076	226	161	1,109	72	10.60	708.6	6.5	.4	2.9	17.0
1978	7,597	7,544	9.77	6.00	4,210	1,224	221	207	1,495	186	10.40	781.4	7.1	.3	3.7	15.8
1979	8,143	8,118			4,305	1,337	256	137	1,955	130	10.90	883.4	10.9	.3	3.3	17.0
1980[2]	8,828	8,810			4,942	1,202	195	168	2,139	165	8.70	761.0	12.0			17.9
1981[2]	7,754	7,740			4,434	1,009	197	173	1,792	91	11.10	822.3				20.8
1982[2]	8,210	8,000									10.60	869.5				
1983																

Utilization Millions of Pounds. Processed[5]. Foreign Trade Million Bushels.

[1] Commercial crop. [2] Preliminary. [3] Mostly crushed for vinegar. [4] Year beginning July. [5] Fresh weight basis. [6] Included in other.
Source: Statistical Reporting Service, U.S.D.A.   T.19

Wholesale Price of Apples (Delicious) in the United States   In Dollars Per Box

Year	Jan.	Feb.	Mar.	Apr.	May	June	July	Aug.	Sept.	Oct.	Nov.	Dec.	Average
1970	3.592	4.517	3.802	4.247	4.087	N.A.	N.A.	N.A.	N.A.	6.332	6.414	7.967	5.120
1971	N.A.	6.347	N.A.	6.793	6.614	6.873	N.A.	N.A.	N.A.	6.360	8.100	6.885	6.853
1972	6.045	6.393	5.956	6.164	5.903	5.748	N.A.	N.A.	N.A.	7.350	8.121	7.560	6.582
1973	7.300	6.490	7.773	8.687	8.333	10.387	N.A.	N.A.	N.A.	6.869	8.125	7.868	7.981
1974	7.110	7.370	6.066	6.650	8.500	N.A.	N.A.	N.A.	8.213	9.793	N.A.	8.320	7.753
1975	8.193	9.500	10.000	9.580	11.783	14.081	N.A.	N.A.	N.A.	7.261	7.272	7.440	9.457
1976	7.217	8.437	8.250	8.750	7.752	8.070	N.A.	N.A.	N.A.	9.610	9.008	9.785	8.542
1977	N.A.	10.900	10.030	9.794	9.725	9.935	N.A.	N.A.	N.A.	9.960	9.000	8.020	9.417
1978	11.183	11.280	11.305	N.A.	N.A.	N.A.	N.A.	N.A.	N.A.	N.A.	21.612	14.000	13.876
1979	13.500	14.000	14.000	14.500	13.500	13.750	N.A.	N.A.	N.A.	12.750	14.500	15.250	13.972
1980	15.750	15.667	16.750	16.750	16.750	19.000	N.A.	N.A.	N.A.	12.500	12.000	12.000	15.240
1981	12.000	12.250	13.500	12.583	12.875	13.500	N.A.	N.A.	N.A.	16.000	15.125	15.500	13.704
1982	15.125	16.000	16.833	15.000	N.A.	N.A.	N.A.	N.A.	N.A.	13.500	13.000	14.000	14.780
1983	13.000	13.500											
1984													

Source: Bureau of Labor Statistics (0111-0215.01)   T.20

Arsenic

World production of arsenic in 1982 was estimated by the U.S. Bureau of Mines to be about 3 percent below estimated 1981 production, with the reduction accounted for by market economy countries other than the major producers.

U.S. production of arsenic trioxide (recovered as a byproduct of copper production) and metal is small, and most domestic demands are met by imports of arsenic trioxide (there is no arsenic recovered from scrap). According to the Bureau of Mines, the U.S. supply shortage of arsenic trioxide that began in 1978 ended about the first quarter of 1982. The principal new source of U.S. supply has been low-grade trioxide from Canada, estimated around 4,000 tons in 1982, valued at about 12 cents per pound. About 2,000 tons of trioxide valued at 71 cents per pound was imported from China in 1982. Traditional important import sources are Sweden, Mexico, and France.

The two major uses for arsenic are in agricultural chemicals (herbicides and plant desiccants)-45 percent, and industrial chemicals (wood preservatives and mineral flotation reagents)-45 percent. Four major pesticide and desiccant producers and two major wood preservative producers consume 90 percent of all arsenic used. Some arsenic is used as a metal in nonferrous alloying and in compound form.

The U.S. price of imported trioxide remained unchanged in 1982. The Mexican trioxide price decreased from 78 cents to 70 cents per pound on April 1, 1982 and again to 66 cents on July 6. The domestic price of arsenic metal declined from $2.75 to $2.50 per pound in January 1982, then increased to $2.75 by July before slipping to $2.60 per pound in November.

World Production of White Arsenic (Arsenic Trioxide)   In Short Tons

Year	Portugal	Spain	Brazil	Canada	France	W. Germany	USSR	Japan	Mexico	Peru	Rep. of Korea	Sweden	Namibia[3]	World Total
1970	209	19	328	71	11,236	408	7,880	974	10,075	851	N.A.	18,078	4,478	54,607
1971	205	—	163	50	11,000	40	7,880	1,054	12,658	723	N.A.	17,600	4,080	55,453
1972	15	—	181	30	8,423	491	7,940	471	6,523	1,123	N.A.	17,857	2,612	45,666
1973	399	—	76	—	9,000	520	7,990	322	5,606	1,528	10	16,755	8,981	51,187
1974	290	—	20	—	9,000	401	8,050	213	10,477	2,175	18	16,190	7,319	54,153
1975	282	—	14	—	7,300	350	8,100	66	6,747	1,461	110	12,884	7,345	44,659
1976	306	—	0		8,023	400	8,200	66	6,062	879	1,028	7,411	5,646	38,021
1977	245		—		6,661	400	8,300	131	6,332	1,507	713	6,613	2,882	33,784
1978	279				6,500	400	8,400	100	6,884	1,386	604	6,700	2,647	33,900
1979	380				6,100	—	8,500	201	7,206	3,552	650	5,600	2,448	34,637
1980[1]	220				5,800	400	8,500	313	6,980	3,533	N.A.	4,500	1,420	31,666
1981[2]	220				5,700	400	8,500	331	7,100	3,500	N.A.	4,400	1,500	31,651
1982[2]					5,700		8,500		7,000	3,500		4,500	1,500	31,000
1983														

[1] Preliminary.   [2] Estimate.   [3] Output of Tsumeb Corp. Ltd. only.   *Source: Bureau of Mines*   T.21

Salient Statistics of White Arsenic in the U.S.   In Short Tons

Year	Trioxide (As$_2$O$_3$)	Metallic Arsenic	Arsenic Acid	Sulfide	Arsenic Compounds	Price Powdered in Barrels ¢ lb.[3]	Value of Imports Thous. $	Trioxide Domestic[4] 95% As$_2$O$_3$ ¢ lb. 12/31	Metal Domestic 99% As	Peru	Canada	France	Mexico	South Africa	Sweden	Bel-Lux.
1970	18,763					6¼–6¾	2,089			100		2,650	7,750	111	8,142	
1971	17,306					6¼–6¾	2,187			68		1,425	8,316	196	7,276	
1972	13,613	661				6¼–6¾	1,956			24		1,556	3,552	285	8,184	
1973	13,496	643			—	6¼–6¾	2,045			25		1,281	5,605	409	6,144	
1974	13,742	707			43	13	2,449			24	—	480	6,185	145	6,889	
1975	12,013	483			77	20–23	4,426	13.1	160	66	—	595	3,174	970	7,172	
1976	4,262	288			355	20–21	1,528	13.1	175	—	—	462	3,793	—	3	
1977	5,981	357	382	—	1,109	20–21	1,962	13.1	190	—	22	1,352	3,089	—	1,323	
1978	10,306	369	565	—	473	28–32	5,918	23¼	190	—	136	5,077	2,603	—	2,281	189
1979	12,325	405	176	39	1	32	7,728	24¼	190	477	277	3,242	3,125	—	5,014	184
1980	12,528	266	271	11	1	35	9,190	31¾	300	—	486	2,780	3,720	—	4,770	388
1981[2]	18,958	323	1,666	—	5	45	17,741	40	275	55	6,152	826	3,931	19	5,403	1,379
1982[1]	18,000	130				45		40	260							

[1] Estimate.   [2] Preliminary.   [3] Refined, 99%, at N.Y. docks.   [4] F.O.B. Tacoma, Wash.   *Source: Bureau of Mines*   T.22

Barley

U.S. production of barley in 1982 was a record 522 million bushels (11.4 million tonnes), 9 percent above the previous record set in 1981 and 45 percent greater than production in 1980. The record crop resulted from an all-time high yield per acre of 57.3 bushels, up 5.0 bushels from the previous record established in 1981.

Acreage harvested for grain in 1982 totaled 9.11 million, fractionally below 1981 acreage. Final compliance figures for the 1982 reduced acreage program (RAP) showed that farmers certified for compliance a total of 4.8 million acres of barley—52.97 percent of the acres enrolled or 45.95 percent of the base acreage (10.47 million acres). Acres planted for harvest on those farms complying totaled 3.5 million acres or 73.44 percent of the acres certified.

Barley disappearance for the 1982/83 U.S. marketing season (June/May) was projected at 437 million bushels, 8 percent below distribution in 1981/82. Domestic use of barley was estimated by the USDA at 392 million bushels, an increase of 16 million from the previous season. The use of barley for feed is influenced by its price relative to corn. A bushel of barley averages 14 percent lighter than a bushel of corn. Accordingly, barley costs more per pound than corn when the price of barley and corn per bushel are the same. Also, except for feeding dairy cows and wintering beef cattle, the feeding value of barley is less than that of corn on a pound-for-pound basis.

Barley exports in 1982/83 were projected to drop to 45 million bushels from 100 million in the previous season. Indicated total disappearance (domestic use and exports) for the first seven months of the 1982/83 marketing year (June–December 1982) was 252 million bushels, 31 million bushels below the comparable period of the previous season due to sharply lower exports. Ending stocks for the 1982/83 season on May 31, 1983 were forecast by the USDA at 245 million bushels, 95 million above the year-earlier level. The stocks to use ratio was estimated at 53 percent compared to 32 percent at the end of the previous season. Barley stored in all positions on January 1, 1983 totaled 419 million bushels, 26 percent larger than a year earlier. Of the January 1, 1983 total barley stocks, 70.2 million bushels were under government control—4.30 million were owned by the Commodity Credit Corporation (CCC) and 65.9 million bushels were held in the farmer-owned reserve (FOR). A year earlier, the CCC owned 3.3 million bushels and the FOR held 15.3 million, for a total under government control on January 1, 1982 of 18.6 million bushels.

U.S. Government Price Support

U.S. barley producers who participated in the 1982 acreage reduction program received 40 cents per bushel in deficiency payments, because prices for the first 5 months of the 1982/83 marketing year averaged 40 cents below the $2.60 target price for 1982.

The 1983 target price for barley remained at $2.60 per bushel, while the regular 1983 loan rate was increased to $2.16 per bushel from $2.08 in 1982.

Only producers who reduced their base acreage by 20 percent under the 1983 feed grain program (which featured a combined 10 percent acreage reduction and 10 percent paid land diversion) are eligible for program benefits, including price support loans and target price protection. The land removed from production must be devoted to conservative uses.

Producers signing up for the 1983 feed grain program could request advance payment of 50 percent (50 cents per bushel) of their diversion payment and 50 percent (7.5 cents per bushel) of their projected 1983 deficiency payment.

Futures Market

Barley futures are traded on the Winnipeg Commodity Exchange.

High, Low & Closing Prices of May Barley Futures at Winnipeg   In Canadian Dollars per Tonne

Year of Delivery		June	July	Aug.	Sept.	Oct.	Nov.	Dec.	Jan.	Feb.	Mar.	Apr.	May	Life of Delivery Range
1978	High	—	79.00	79.90	77.00	78.20	77.10	78.00	80.00	79.50	83.30	84.00	82.00	84.00
	Low	—	75.30	72.40	72.30	70.50	72.80	75.40	76.00	77.50	77.50	76.50	77.40	70.50
	Close	—	76.70	74.00	75.90	74.20	75.80	76.60	77.80	78.50	82.10	77.70	81.60	—
1979	High	—	73.80	74.00	74.80	80.20	78.50	77.40	80.00	81.90	84.00	93.20	106.40	106.40
	Low	—	72.00	71.50	70.90	74.50	74.70	75.40	76.50	78.20	80.00	82.10	93.00	70.90
	Close	—	72.00	71.80	74.50	77.50	76.60	76.50	78.40	81.10	82.50	92.60	101.30	—
1980	High	108.10	107.90	107.70	112.00	117.30	117.60	121.40	123.10	116.90	116.40	116.00	130.10	130.00
	Low	89.00	89.70	93.70	103.70	107.00	111.40	112.30	112.50	111.20	110.70	109.40	110.40	89.00
	Close	104.30	92.40	107.70	111.50	115.00	114.90	121.10	116.50	111.80	111.10	110.60	124.50	—
1981	High	131.50	139.50	139.60	143.50	150.30	165.00	166.50	162.90	156.90	153.30	153.90	153.50	166.50
	Low	121.40	126.50	130.00	137.50	137.20	149.60	141.90	150.70	151.40	145.30	146.20	145.50	121.40
	Close	128.00	138.10	139.50	141.60	149.30	164.00	160.80	150.80	151.60	146.80	153.90	145.50	—
1982	High	144.00	144.20	141.90	133.10	134.70	133.00	130.80	133.20	132.90	128.20	125.50	133.00	144.2
	Low	133.60	136.20	128.50	127.50	129.00	127.00	126.60	128.80	126.80	118.00	121.30	121.80	118.0
	Close	134.60	142.30	131.00	129.50	132.90	127.50	129.10	131.50	127.00	125.30	122.00	125.80	—
1983	High	127.90	127.50	116.80	108.70	105.00	110.50	107.10	111.30	109.50	107.50	109.20		
	Low	127.90	114.80	106.30	102.50	100.70	101.50	105.50	104.90	101.90	100.00	104.80		
	Close	127.90	115.70	107.80	104.80	101.50	105.80	106.20	108.50	103.60	106.80	107.30		

Source: Winnipeg Commodity Exchange

T.26

BARLEY

World Production of Barley In Thousands of Metric Tons

Crop Years	China	United States	Argentina	Canada	Rep. of Korea	Denmark	Morocco	France	India	Japan	USSR	W. Germany	Spain	Turkey	United King.	World Total
1970-1		9,060	367	9,050	1,974	4,813	1,477	8,126	2,716	573	31,600	4,611	3,092	3,300	7,529	119,579
1971-2		10,094	553	13,099	1,857	5,458	1,675	8,930	2,784	503	34,564	5,601	4,783	4,170	8,558	136,475
1972-3		9,220	880	11,285	1,965	5,572	1,744	10,425	2,577	325	36,800	5,817	4,358	3,725	9,238	138,500
1973-4		9,188	732	10,224	1,778	5,507	1,255	10,844	2,379	216	55,044	6,622	4,402	2,900	9,007	157,992
1974-5		6,619	430	8,802	1,388	5,967	2,387	10,037	2,371	233	54,161	7,048	5,404	3,330	9,133	159,881
1975-6		8,361	523	9,520	1,700	5,156	1,585	9,344	3,135	221	35,808	6,971	6,728	4,500	8,513	144,467
1976-7		8,099	760	10,513	1,759	4,768	2,761	8,319	3,192	210	69,539	6,487	5,473	4,900	7,648	177,987
1977-8	6,860	9,144	353	11,799	814	6,084	1,345	10,290	2,344	206	52,687	7,483	6,693	4,750	10,520	104,546
1978-9	7,000	9,776	554	10,387	1,348	6,301	2,326	11,321	2,311	326	62,077	8,608	8,608	4,750	9,850	182,600
1979-0	7,500	8,334	339	8,460	1,508	6,657	1,886	11,196	2,142	406	47,900	8,184	6,252	5,000	9,609	160,300
1980-1	7,600	7,859	217	11,259	811	6,039	2,210	11,716	1,624	375	43,400	8,826	8,561	5,200	10,323	163,200
1981-2[1]	7,400	10,436	200	13,700	771	6,257	1,039	10,231	2,242	383	37,500	8,687	4,709	5,500	10,300	156,200
1982-3[2]	7,800	11,374		14,100							43,500					163,600
1983-4																

[1] Preliminary. [2] Estimated. Source: Foreign Agricultural Service, U.S.D.A.

T.23

U.S. Barley Acreage and Prices

Year Beginning June 1	National Program	Set-aside	Planted	Harvested for Grain	Yield per Harvested Acre In Bushels	Received by Farmers[1]	Feed[2]	Malting[3]	Portland No. 2 Western	National Avg. Loan Rate	Support or Target Price	Placed Under Loan (Mil. Bu.)	Total Payments to Participants (Mil. $)
1971-2	18.0	0	11.1	10.2	45.7	.99	1.04	1.13	1.49	.81	0	88.9	0
1972-3	18.0	4.9	10.6	9.7	43.7	1.17	1.17	1.39	1.68	.86	0	41.7	107.2
1973-4	17.3	1.4	11.0	10.3	40.5	2.13	2.03	2.63	2.69	.86	1.34	15.3	77.7
1974-5	[6]	0	8.7	7.9	37.7	2.81	2.58	4.16	3.02	.90	1.13	6.9	16.0[7]
1975-6	[6]	0	9.4	8.6	44.0	2.42	2.38	3.51	2.54	.90	1.13	9.2	4.9[7]
1976-7	[6]	0	9.3	8.4	45.4	2.25	2.35	3.13	2.48	1.22	1.28	19.2	10[7]
1977-8	11.7	0	10.8	9.7	44.0	1.78	1.68	2.27	2.15	1.63	2.15	86.9	121[8]
1978-9	7.5	.8	10.0	9.2	49.2	1.92	1.80	2.38	2.10	1.63	2.25	68.0	97[9]
1979-0	7.8	.7	8.1	7.5	50.9	2.29	2.16	2.87	2.69	1.71	2.40	30	22[8]
1980-1	8.7	—	8.3	7.3	49.6	2.86	2.60	3.64	3.34	1.83	2.55	31	31[7]
1981-2[4]	10.2	—	9.7	9.2	52.3	2.45	2.21	3.06	2.87	1.95	2.60	60	63[8]
1982-3[5]	—	.4	9.6	9.1	57.3	2.10	1.72	2.50	2.44	2.08	2.60	41	60[7]
1983-4[5]			9.7							2.16			

[1] Excludes support payments. [2] Beginning June 1977, No. 2 Feed. [3] 60% to 70% plump or better. [4] Preliminary. [5] Estimate. [6] Available for total feed grains only. [7] Disaster payments. [8] Deficiency & disaster payments. [9] Deficiency, disaster & diversion payments. Source: Commodity Economic Division, U.S.D.A.

T.24

Production of Barley in the United States, by States In Millions of Bushels

Year	Arizona	California	Colorado	Idaho	Kansas	Minnesota	Oklahoma	Montana	North Dakota	Oregon	Pennsylvania	Utah	South Dakota	Washington	U.S. Total
1970	10.6	58.8	14.6	41.3	6.9	21.5	23.4	65.1	65.9	18.2	8.6	8.2	12.1	19.9	416.1
1971	8.8	53.3	13.9	41.4	7.4	40.7	15.4	58.8	99.8	18.1	9.0	8.5	19.6	27.8	462.4
1972	6.9	50.9	11.0	39.7	4.3	34.0	8.8	64.0	104.7	12.0	7.4	8.1	20.7	14.2	421.7
1973	8.3	47.9	12.3	43.5	3.0	41.1	7.3	60.0	102.5	9.2	5.7	7.7	22.1	13.5	417.4
1974	4.3	45.6	10.0	31.7	1.5	28.9	2.8	37.5	56.3	8.6	7.7	7.1	12.8	12.4	298.7
1975	4.9	60.4	12.2	37.8	1.9	30.6	2.4	50.7	79.8	8.7	6.5	8.1	16.5	20.1	379.2
1976	4.3	56.6	13.5	43.2	2.4	35.3	3.1	52.1	81.3	7.4	5.4	6.9	6.0	21.1	383.0
1977	4.2	53.2	13.6	44.2	2.8	55.1	4.2	52.2	98.7	8.9	6.3	6.2	26.9	9.5	427.8
1978	2.5	45.6	14.3	63.2	2.3	52.0	2.7	55.9	112.7	10.8	4.5	9.8	20.9	23.2	454.8
1979	3.2	47.4	18.7	54.9	2.3	40.8	2.5	40.6	75.9	8.3	4.0	10.4	20.8	17.0	382.8
1980	4.5	44.1	15.9	59.0	2.1	34.6	1.7	44.1	48.0	10.1	3.8	10.8	15.2	32.3	361.0
1981	4.1	40.3	18.6	63.1	1.7	57.7	1.6	56.8	105.6	11.7	4.1	11.1	20.1	44.1	479.3
1982[1]	6.6	38.4	17.0	74.5	2.3	51.0	1.3	76.4	108.1	14.1	3.7	13.2	23.4	49.4	522.4

[1] Preliminary, December estimate. Source: Crop Reporting Board, U.S.D.A.

T.25

BARLEY

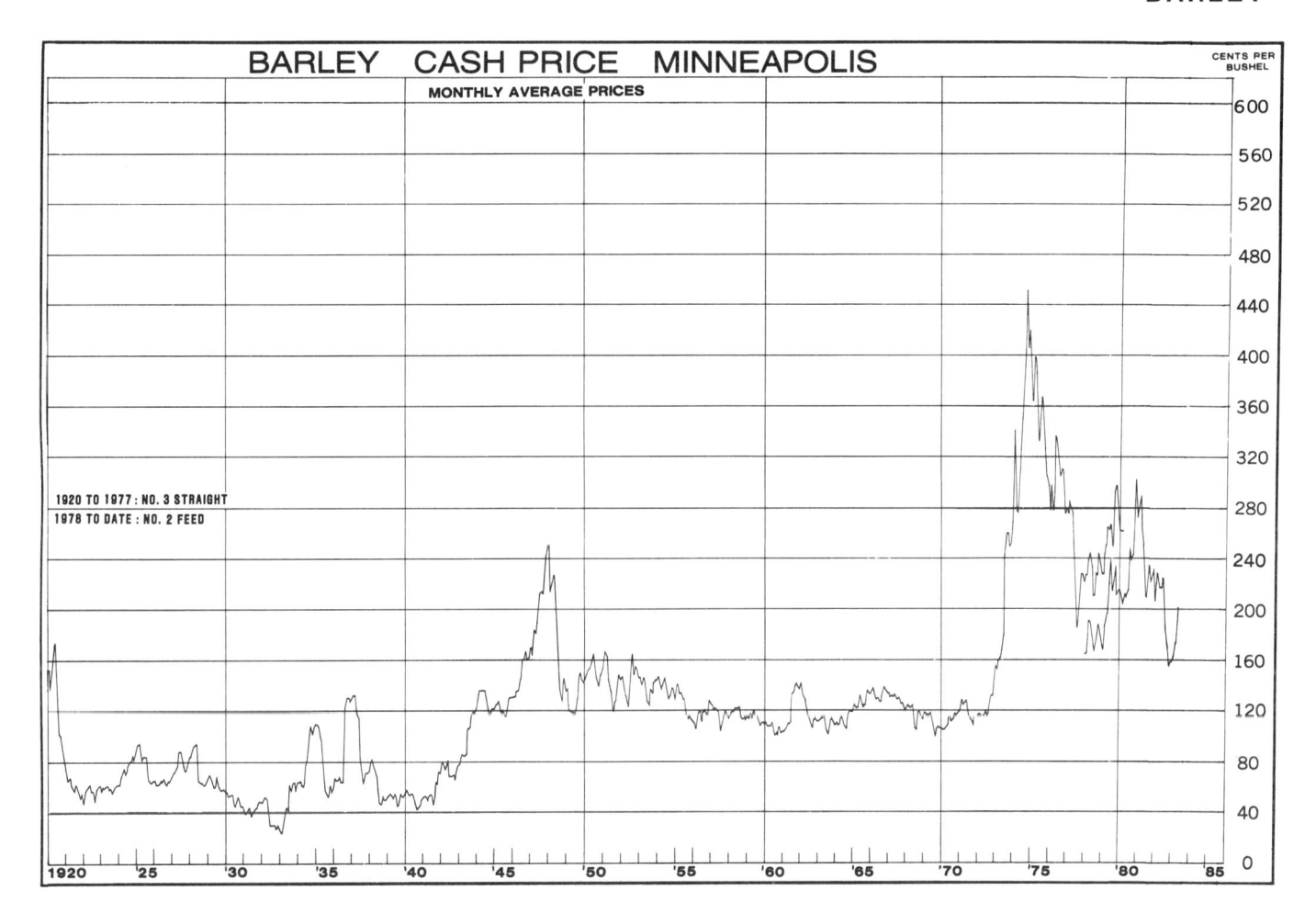

BARLEY CASH PRICE MINNEAPOLIS
MONTHLY AVERAGE PRICES
(Cents Per Bushel)

1920 to 1977: No. 3 Straight
1978 to date: No. 2 Feed

Average Cash Price of No. 2[2], Feed Barley, in Minneapolis — In Cents Per Bushel

Year	June	July	Aug.	Sept.	Oct.	Nov.	Dec.	Jan.	Feb.	Mar.	Apr.	May	Average
1971-2	108	100	95	99	104	104	104	107	107	105	106	108	104
1972-3	105	96	98	111	110	114	127	134	120	119	125	136	117
1973-4	151	167	212	212	202	180	212	234	251	232	174	210	203
1974-5	236	236	269	248	307	317	289	282	259	226	224	205	258
1975-6	167	204	277	300	283	242	223	211	226	236	239	250	238
1976-7	262	245	248	268	246	221	205	220	235	229	228	213	235
1977-8	176[2]	163	150	158	166	165	165	165	165	166	191	190	168
1978-9	184	171	168	177	181	188	179	171	169	186	189	196	180
1979-0	216	239	215	222	234	211	215	209	204	206	212	209	216
1980-1	215	248	239	243	277	303	275	281	290	263	251	239	260
1981-2[1]	209	226	235	221	226	231	206	220	227	216	216	224	221
1982-3[1]	212	185	172	169	154	158	159	163	172	173			

[1] Preliminary. [2] Prior to June 1977 prices are for No. 3 or better. *Source: Economic Research Service, U.S.D.A.* T.27

Month End Open Interest of Barley Futures at Winnipeg — In Units (20 Tonne)

Year	Jan.	Feb.	Mar.	Apr.	May	June	July	Aug.	Sept.	Oct.	Nov.	Dec.
1978	6,228	5,951	4,700	6,414	5,377	8,888	8,163	10,022	13,955	14,157	15,493	13,439
1979	16,704	18,864	18,579	23,142	17,635	23,336	26,643	25,193	24,230	20,466	22,107	21,468
1980	19,105	17,631	14,848	14,027	15,842	17,658	18,224	18,724	21,082	16,574	16,173	13,496
1981	14,560	13,335	13,836	16,380	14,252	12,968	15,101	16,620	16,086	10,971	10,591	8,832
1982	8,485	7,838	7,096	6,684	6,774	6,298	7,019	7,427	8,148	8,697	8,697	7,826
1983	9,952	10,972	9,535	10,458								

Source: Winnipeg Commodity Exchange T.28

BARLEY

Salient Statistics of Barley in the United States   In Millions of Bushels

Year & Periods Begin. June 1	Beginning Stocks	Production	Imports	Total Supply	Food	Alc. Beverages	Seed	Feed & Residual	Total	Exports	Total Disappearance	Gov't. Owned[1]	Privately Owned[2]	Total Stocks
1975-6	92.2	379.2	15.7	487.1	5.0	124.8	15.7	189.3	334.8	23.9	358.7	—	128.4	128.4
1976-7	128.4	383.0	10.8	522.2	5.0	131.5	18.2	174.9	329.6	66.2	395.8	—	126.4	126.4
1977-8	126.4	427.8	9.4	563.6	6.0	133.1	16.7	177.5	333.3	57.2	390.5	—	173.1	173.1
1978-9	173.1	454.8	10.5	638.4	6.0	147.5	13.6	217.6	384.7	25.7	410.4	2.5	225.5	228.0
1979-0	228.0	382.8	11.8	622.6	7.0	151.0	14.0	203.7	375.7	54.8	430.5	3.2	188.9	192.1
1980-1	192.1	361.0	10.2	563.3	7.0	155.3	13.2	173.8	349.3	76.7	426.0	3.4	133.9	137.3
June-Sept.	192.1	361.0	3.5	556.6	2.5	56.6	1.2	78.9	139.2	24.9	164.1	3.5	389.0	392.5
Oct.-Dec.	392.5	—	2.3	394.8	1.7	33.9	2.2	32.2	70.0	21.4	91.4	3.5	299.9	303.4
Jan.-Mar.	303.4	—	2.7	306.1	1.7	36.0	3.7	38.6	80.0	22.7	102.7	3.4	200.0	203.4
Apr.-May	203.4	—	1.7	205.1	1.1	28.8	6.1	24.1	60.1	7.7	67.8	3.4	133.9	137.3
1981-2[3]	137.3	479.3	9.6	626.2	6.9	150.9	16.3	202.3	376.4	100.1	476.5	3.3	146.4	149.7
June-Sept.	137.3	479.3	2.4	619.0	2.5	54.5	1.3	76.5	134.8	32.6	167.4	3.3	448.3	451.6
Oct.-Dec.	451.6	—	2.4	454.0	1.7	32.1	2.3	51.8	87.9	33.0	120.9	3.3	329.8	333.1
Jan.-Mar.	333.1	—	2.7	335.8	1.7	37.2	4.0	42.9	85.8	23.1	108.9	3.3	223.6	226.9
Apr.-May	226.9	—	2.1	229.0	1.0	27.1	8.7	31.1	67.6	11.4	79.3	3.3	146.4	149.7
1982-3[4]	149.7	522.4	10.0	682.1	—	177.0	—	215.1	392.1	45.0	437.1			245.0
June-Sept.	149.7	522.4	5.1	677.2	2.5	50.9	1.3	95.7	150.4	25.4	175.8	3.9	497.5	501.4
Oct.-Dec.	501.4	—	1.9	503.3	1.8	30.0	2.8	43.6	78.2	6.4	84.6	4.8	413.9	418.7
Jan.-Mar.														

[1] Uncommitted inventory.   [2] Includes quantity under loan & farmer-owned reserve.   [3] Preliminary.   [4] Estimate.   Source: *Commodity Economics Division, U.S.D.A.*
T.29

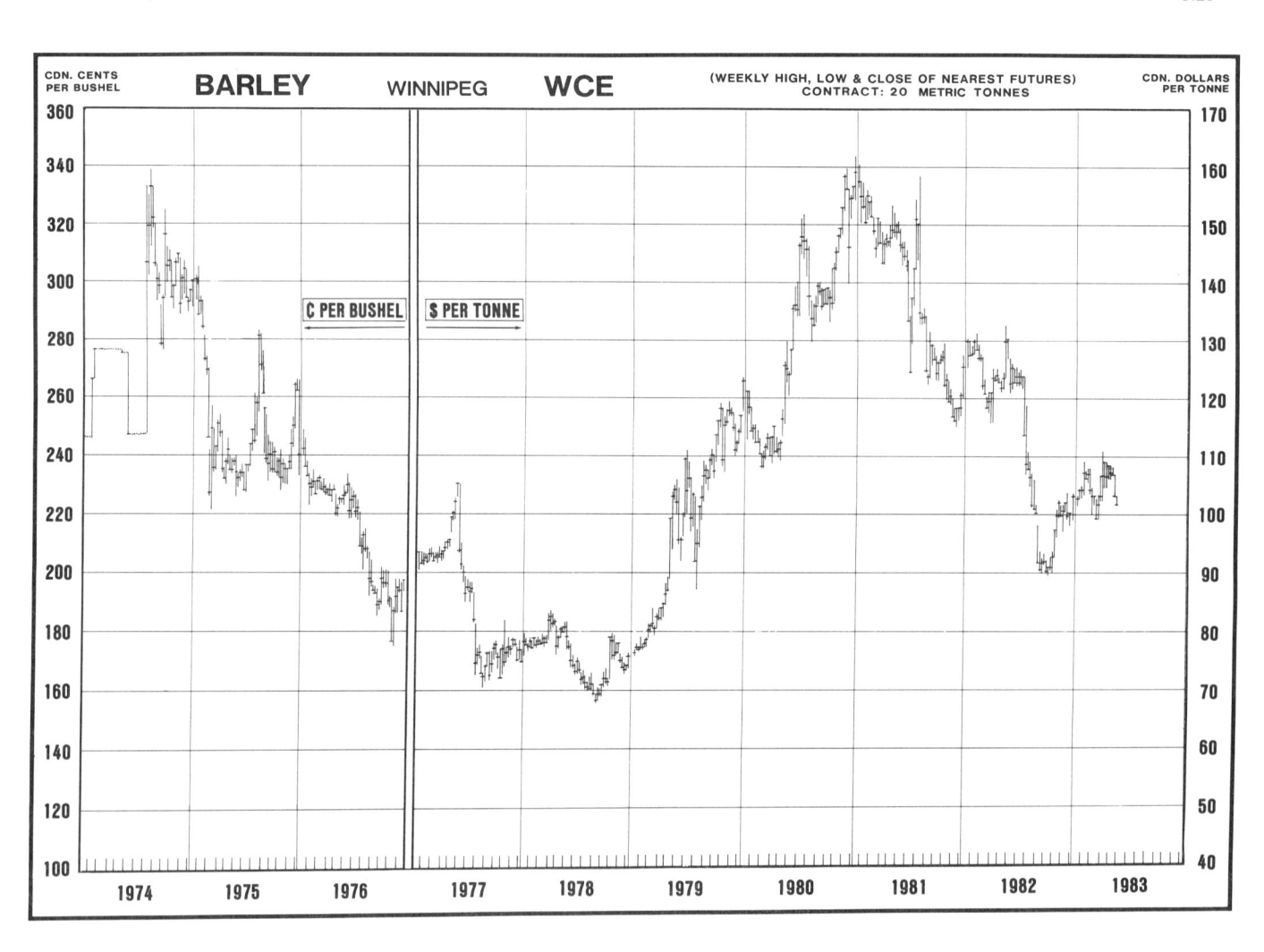

Bauxite

World bauxite reserves amounted to 40–50 billion dry tonnes in 1982. The total world mine production of bauxite during 1982 was estimated to have fallen nearly 12 percent from the 1981 level of 85.7 million dry tonnes. The three major bauxite-producing countries during 1982 were Australia, Guinea, and Jamaica, accounting for 30 percent, 13 percent, and 11 percent of world production, respectively. Of the fifteen countries that produced more than 1 million tonnes of bauxite in 1982, seven belonged to the 11-member International Bauxite Association. The exploration and development of major bauxite deposits continued in Brazil, Ghana, India, Indonesia, Saudi Arabia, and Venezuela.

U.S. domestic bauxite production during 1982 was a negligible fraction of the world total. U.S. domestic resources of bauxite were judged to be inadequate to meet long-term demand at current levels of consumption, and 95 percent of the bauxite consumed by the U.S. in 1982 was supplied from foreign sources. Imports supplied nearly a third of the U.S. consumption of alumina, an intermediate product of the aluminum production process. The amount of bauxite purchased abroad decreased only marginally during 1982, and U.S. imports of alumina were estimated to be 20 percent below the 1981 level.

U.S. bauxite mines, six companies operating from seven open pit locations, were worked at less than 50 percent of capacity during 1982, and bauxite output declined nearly 54 percent from 1981. An estimated 93 percent of all domestic and imported bauxite consumed by the U.S. during 1982 was processed into alumina by nine U.S. refineries, one of them located in the U.S. Virgin Islands. Approximately 90 percent of this alumina was further reduced to aluminum metal, and the remaining 10 percent was used to make refractories, chemicals, and abrasives and other products. Almost 4.5 tonnes of dried bauxite is required to produce 2 tonnes of alumina, and this in turn is processed into 1 tonne of aluminum metal.

Bauxite is the only raw material used in the production of commercial aluminum in the U.S. During 1982, research on processes to produce alumina from non-bauxitic materials involved experiments with clays, coal wastes, and oil shales. Substitutes for abrasives typically made from bauxite include silicon carbide, aluminum-zirconium oxide, and diamonds.

The apparent demand for bauxite, figured from a 1978 base year, was expected to increase at an annual rate below 4.5 percent through 1990, and annual U.S. mine production was expected to range up to 1.6 million dry tonnes. Preliminary estimates show 1982 U.S. industrial bauxite stocks up 2 percent from the 1981 level of 8,300 dry tonnes.

World Production of Bauxite In Thousands of Metric[4] Tons

Year	Brazil	Guyana[2]	France	Guinea	Hungary	Indonesia	Australia	Malaysia	Greece	Surinam	USSR[3]	Jamaica[3]	United States[3]	Yugoslavia	World Total
1972		3,291	3,203	2,018	2,321	1,256	14,209	1,059	2,398	7,654	4,100	12,345	1,812	2,162	64,021
1973		3,224	3,084	3,000	2,559	1,200	17,535	1,200	2,600	6,580	4,200	13,385	1,879	2,133	68,563
1974	845	3,200	2,892	7,480	2,708	1,270	19,679	933	2,739	6,600	4,200	15,086	1,949	2,333	78,362
1975	954	3,200	2,523	8,273	2,844	977	20,672	692	2,958	4,850	4,300	11,388	1,772	2,270	73,610
1976[4]	827	2,686	2,330	10,848	2,918	940	24,084	660	2,551	4,613	4,500	10,296	1,989	2,033	77,417
1977	1,120	2,731	2,059	10,841	2,949	1,301	26,086	616	2,885	4,805	4,600	11,390	2,013	2,044	81,931
1978	1,160	2,425	1,978	10,456	2,899	1,008	24,293	615	2,663	5,188	4,600	11,739	1,669	3,565	79,810
1979	2,388	2,312	1,970	13,700	2,976	1,052	27,583	387	2,812	5,010	4,600	11,618	1,821	3,012	87,777
1980[1]	4,152	2,471	1,892	10,330	2,950	1,249	27,178	920	3,286	4,696	6,400	12,054	1,559	3,138	88,786
1981[2]	5,300	1,680	1,871	12,100	2,914	1,200	25,541	701	3,300	3,728	4,600	11,664	1,510	3,249	85,729
1982[2]	5,400	1,500		10,200	3,000		23,000		3,400	2,900	4,600	8,000	700	3,300	75,800
1983															

[1] Preliminary. [2] Estimate. [3] Dry Bauxite equivalent of ore processed. [4] Data prior to 1976 are in THOUSANDS OF LONG TONS. Source: Bureau of Mines
T.30

U.S. Salient Statistics of Bauxite In Thousands of Metric[6] Tons

Year	Net Import Reliance as a % of Apparent Consumption	Av. Price F.O.B. Mine $ per Ton	Mine Production Crude	Mine Production Dried Equivalent	Value ($1,000)	Crude Ore Treated	Recovery of Processed Bauxite Recovered[1] Total	Recovery of Processed Bauxite Dried Equiv.	Dry Equivalent Imports[2]	Dry Equivalent Exports[3]	Consumption	Stocks, Dec. 31 Producers & Processors	Stocks, Dec. 31 Consumers	Stocks, Dec. 31 Govt.	Stocks, Dec. 31 Total
1972		5–15	2,200	1,812	23,238	399	210	319	12,601	29	15,375	791	2,797	16,453	20,041
1973		5–15	2,287	1,879	26,635	338	169	287	13,403	12	16,650	684	2,165	16,029	18,878
1974		5–15	2,370	1,949	25,663	348	177	279	14,976	16	16,904	534	3,982	15,152	19,669
1975[6]	91	5–15	2,199	1,801	25,083	361	182	287	11,714	20	12,587	494	5,293	15,308	21,094
1976	91	5–15	2,420	1,989	26,645	366	175	289	12,749	15	14,039	526	4,923	15,308	20,756
1977	91	5–15	2,436	2,013	27,555	419	169	294	12,989	26	14,528	685	7,264	15,087	23,036
1978	93	5–15	2,066	1,669	23,185	379	154	236	13,847	13	14,738	556	7,806	14,661	23,023
1979	93	5–15	2,186	1,821	24,875	466	235	336	13,780	15	15,697	620	7,958	14,661	23,239
1980	94	6–16	1,869	1,559	22,353	355	179	277	14,087	21	15,962	662	7,681	14,661	23,004
1981[4]	94	8–20	1,847	1,510	26,489	419	187	328	12,802	20	13,525	900	7,439	14,661	23,000
1982[5]	97	8–20	700	689					12,500	50					

[1] Calcined, or sintered. [2] Imports for consumption. "As shipped" basis. [3] Including concentrates. [4] Preliminary. [5] Estimate. [6] Data prior to 1975 are in THOUSANDS OF LONG TONS. Source: Bureau of Mines
T.31

Beer

United States Production of Beer (Fermented Malt Liquors) In Millions of Barrels (of 31 Wine Gallons[1])

Year	Jan.	Feb.	Mar.	Apr.	May	June	July	Aug.	Sept.	Oct.	Nov.	Dec.	Total
1970	9.56	9.31	11.84	12.45	12.45	13.40	12.38	11.33	11.01	10.28	9.30	9.82	133.12
1971	9.62	9.41	12.53	12.33	12.37	13.72	13.28	12.28	11.41	10.53	9.87	10.02	137.36
1972	9.96	10.38	12.62	12.53	13.25	14.21	13.18	13.06	11.41	11.24	9.93	9.59	141.34
1973	10.98	10.73	13.14	12.86	13.83	13.09	13.76	14.17	12.12	12.38	10.90	10.65	148.60
1974	12.19	10.98	13.05	13.09	14.71	15.04	15.75	14.61	12.67	12.28	10.71	11.11	156.20
1975	12.55	11.18	12.41	14.50	14.34	15.76	16.08	14.72	13.35	12.35	11.22	12.15	160.60
1976	12.44	11.89	11.86	13.69	15.18	15.76	16.54	16.10	14.31	13.42	11.29	11.19	163.66
1977	11.98	11.48	16.20	16.03	16.79	16.90	15.92	15.31	13.26	12.61	12.02	12.01	170.51
1978	12.87	12.71	15.86	15.62	16.57	16.88	16.74	17.61	14.63	14.01	12.71	12.87	179.09
1979[2]	13.83	13.57	16.89	16.34	16.97	16.77	16.94	16.76	14.70	25.28	13.14	12.18	184.19
1980[2]	14.64	14.72	16.56	16.36	17.97	17.93	18.72	17.02	16.29	14.95	13.02	13.32	194.08
1981[2]	13.31	14.58	16.72	17.68	18.87	18.63	18.80	17.72	15.72	14.61	13.12	13.93	193.69
1982[2]	15.19	15.00	17.65	17.62	18.22	18.19	17.17	19.50	15.64	15.07	13.65	13.31	196.21
1983													

[1] "Wine gallon" or "gallon" is a U.S. gallon of liquid measure equivalent to the volume of 231 cubic inches. [2] Preliminary. *Source: Internal Revenue Service*
T.32

Tax-Paid Withdrawals of Beer (Fermented Malt Liquors) in the U.S.
In Millions of Barrels (of 31 Wine Gallons[1])

Year	Jan.	Feb.	Mar.	Apr.	May	June	July	Aug.	Sept.	Oct.	Nov.	Dec.	Total
1970	8.47	8.04	10.35	10.66	11.45	11.90	11.87	10.79	10.38	9.62	8.77	9.74	121.86
1971	8.19	8.52	11.00	11.04	11.05	12.88	12.50	11.89	10.96	9.80	9.74	9.83	127.40
1972	8.62	9.09	11.69	11.09	12.41	13.12	12.22	12.89	10.89	10.61	9.92	9.27	131.81
1973	9.67	9.43	12.01	11.65	12.87	12.55	12.77	13.68	11.52	11.54	10.73	10.08	138.47
1974	10.97	9.87	11.82	11.74	13.76	13.86	14.73	13.89	12.09	11.59	10.42	10.74	145.46
1975	11.12	9.84	11.57	13.01	13.42	14.44	14.75	13.88	12.51	11.90	10.61	11.59	148.64
1976	10.86	11.00	10.99	12.91	13.59	14.16	15.01	14.86	13.44	12.22	10.52	10.83	150.39
1977	10.01	10.43	14.55	14.28	15.00	15.71	14.80	14.64	12.89	11.62	11.49	11.51	156.92
1978	10.69	11.01	14.20	13.60	14.96	15.82	15.29	16.28	13.72	12.99	12.04	11.57	162.15
1979	12.32	12.01	15.01	14.96	15.00	15.57	15.13	15.56	13.71	13.64	12.52	11.08	168.12
1980	12.54	12.49	14.08	14.33	16.19	15.81	17.08	15.35	14.51	13.53	12.51	12.38	173.37
1981	12.08	12.41	15.01	15.47	17.00	17.29	17.37	16.22	14.68	13.84	12.39	12.91	176.70
1982	11.90	12.91	15.68	15.82	16.56	17.22	16.10	16.26	14.88	13.83	13.14	12.27	176.58
1983													

[1] "Wine gallon" or "gallon" is a U.S. gallon of liquid measure equivalent to the volume of 231 cubic inches. *Source: Internal Revenue Service*
T.33

U.S. Stocks of Beer (Fermented Malt Liquors) at End of Month In Millions of Barrels (of 31 Wine Gallons[1])

Year	Jan.	Feb.	Mar.	Apr.	May	June	July	Aug.	Sept.	Oct.	Nov.	Dec.
1970	12.43	12.99	13.46	14.13	14.20	14.69	14.18	13.76	13.45	13.22	12.96	12.26
1971	12.97	13.20	13.81	14.07	14.40	14.26	14.16	13.64	13.31	13.31	12.78	12.23
1972	12.97	13.64	13.82	14.51	14.45	14.40	14.49	13.76	13.54	13.36	12.77	12.44
1973	13.07	13.70	14.01	14.43	14.48	14.20	14.30	13.81	13.58	13.52	12.93	12.76
1974	13.17	13.56	13.92	14.32	14.31	14.47	14.33	14.04	13.72	13.53	13.04	12.58
1975	13.21	13.54	13.76	14.26	14.17	14.30	14.45	14.18	13.98	13.48	13.20	12.74
1976	13.39	13.33	13.31	13.06	13.53	13.89	14.03	13.92	13.60	13.69	13.48	12.91
1977	14.01	14.17	14.58	15.03	15.57	15.37	15.13	14.45	13.58	13.53	13.02	12.42
1978	13.92	14.07	14.56	15.01	14.99	14.55	19.81	14.33	14.01	13.71	13.50	13.76
1979[2]	14.00	14.06	14.44	14.98	14.74	14.50	14.83	14.30	13.87	12.59	13.37	13.29
1980[2]	13.33	13.83	14.84	15.31	17.44	15.43	14.72	14.45	15.01	14.18	13.94	13.96
1981[2]	13.98	14.95	15.12	15.26	15.78	15.24	14.98	14.53	14.42	13.99	13.38	12.95
1982[2]	14.16	14.93	16.32	15.83	15.59	15.28	14.45	14.31	13.99	14.00	13.43	13.22
1983												

[1] "Wine gallon" or "gallon" is a U.S. gallon of liquid measure equivalent to the volume of 231 cubic inches. [2] Preliminary. *Source: Internal Revenue Service*
T.34

Bismuth

U.S. production of bismuth is insignificant and is derived from processing metallurgical products, such as lead bullion, which contain bismuth as a minor constituent. A small amount of old scrap bismuth is recycled, but most domestic needs are met by imports.

Imports of bismuth in 1982 totaled 2,026,245 pounds, 17 percent lower than the 1981 import total of 2,436,249 pounds, according to preliminary data of the U.S. Bureau of Mines. Major sources of U.S. imports of bismuth metal in 1982 were (in order of importance): Peru, Mexico, the United Kingdom, and the Federal Republic of Germany. Imports from Belgium-Luxembourg and Japan dropped sharply from the 1981 level.

The U.S. exports some bismuth, bismuth alloys, waste and scrap. In 1982, the U.S. exported a total of 52,758 pounds (gross weight), 33 percent less than in 1981. The United Kingdom replaced Canada as the most important importer in 1982. Other importers included Japan, India, and Spain. U.S. exports to France dropped sharply in 1982.

U.S. consumption of bismuth metal in 1982 was about 24 percent smaller than in 1981. The reported use of bismuth in the category of metallurgical additives registered the largest year-to-year decrease (37 percent), as demand for many capital goods items declined substantially. Bismuth metal consumed in pharmaceuticals and chemicals, which account for about 58 percent of its total use, declined 13 percent in 1982. Its use in fusible alloys—the second most important use category—declined 28 percent in 1982.

U.S. industry stocks of bismuth at the end of 1982 were estimated at 517,319 pounds, slightly larger than the 509,003 pounds on hand a year earlier.

The Bureau of Mines in an early forecast, estimated 1983 U.S. "reported" consumption of bismuth at 2.2 million pounds. The Bureau also noted that if future U.S. lead production is concentrated in the Missouri lead belt, and in areas containing no known bismuth reserves, and if production from the bismuth-bearing lead mines of the Far West continues to decline, bismuth production could also be expected to decline.

The domestic bismuth producer price remained suspended in 1982, but a major foreign producer's quoted price was $2.30 per pound throughout 1982. However, the U.S. dealer price, which started 1982 around $1.85 to $1.95 per pound, dropped to $1.35 to $1.40 by the end of the year.

World Mine Production of Bismuth   In Thousands of Pounds

Year	Romania (Ore)	Australia	Bolivia	Canada (Ore)	China (Ore)	France (Metal)	Rep. of Korea (Metal)	Yugoslavia (Metal)	Japan (Metal)	Mexico (Metal)	Peru (Metal)	Germany (Ore)	USSR (Metal)	World Total
1970	180	422	1,340	590	550	159	234	166	1,495	1,259	1,593		110	8,192
1971	180	564	1,504	271	550	170	214	202	1,790	1,257	1,415		120	8,330
1972	180	796	1,393	275	550	148	212	196	1,974	1,387	1,492		120	8,819
1973	180	1,001	1,297	71	550	126	218	121	1,900	1,290	1,262		120	8,205
1974	180	2,579	1,351	245	550	125	289	220	1,837	1,583	1,469		130	10,631
1975	180	1,861	1,348	345	550	123	249	122	1,436	1,003	1,354	23	130	8,776
1976	180	1,650	1,349	286	485	139	384	172	1,502	1,228	1,149	24	130	8,689
1977	180	2,054	1,435	363	500	115	293	163	1,538	1,607	1,420	24	140	9,872
1978	180	2,324	677	320	530	N.A.	269	29	1,375	2,156	1,347	20	150	9,412
1979	180	2,200	22	301	570	N.A.	192	50	1,010	1,662	1,162	22	160	7,573
1980[1]	180	2,000	24	328	570	N.A.	271	183	745	1,698	950	22	160	7,162
1981[2]	180	1,870	25	271	570	N.A.	220	225	990	1,390	1,200	22	165	7,159
1982[2]		1,600		200			200		900	1,300	1,200			6,700

[1] Preliminary.   [2] Estimate.   Source: Bureau of Mines   T.35

U.S. Salient Statistics of Bismuth   In Thousands of Pounds

Year	Experimental	Metallurgical Additives	Other Alloys	Fusible Alloys	Pharmaceuticals	Other Uses	Total Consumption	Consumer Stocks Dec. 31	Exports of Metal & Alloys	Peru	Mexico	Japan	Total	Price[1] $ Per Pound
1970	.1	361.5	13.0	643.7	1,183.0	8.3	2,209.6	721.7	910.3	491.1	365.0		997.9	6.00
1971	26.2	362.5	17.4	514.2	724.6	3.8	1,648.7	1,107.2	71.2	191.7	251.6		848.7	5.26
1972	1.1	550.0	18.0	754.4	983.9	8.1	2,315.5	717.5	264.3	478.9	238.7		1,562.9	3.63
1973	—	830.9	15.2	932.6	1,117.6	9.8	2,906.2	540.8	151.1	488.8	357.8		2,683.7	4.92
1974	.3	668.9	21.4	748.6	838.1	6.6	2,284.0	596.8	329.9	459.2	292.5		1,893.7	8.41
1975	.7	416.2	26.0	401.9	553.3	7.9	1,406.0	451.3	128.9	140.6	161.8		1,331.2	7.72
1976	8.8	455.9	20.3	518.6	1,391.7	15.3	2,410.6	483.8	68.5	569.1	248.1		2,328.1	7.50
1977	.6	461.6	18.6	611.2	1,274.5	13.1	2,379.6	436.1	95.3	632.4	182.2		2,013.3	6.01
1978	.6	485.3	21.8	836.0	1,149.7	18.6	2,511.9	781.9	96.3	334.7	535.3		2,657.8	3.38
1979	3.2	703.8	22.0	721.0	1,248.7	28.5	2,727.2	629.7	427.8	648.7	604.8	185.5	2,167.3	3.01
1980	1.2	467.9	26.5	650.9	1,115.6	26.7	2,288.8	674.0	128.7	619.1	860.4	138.4	2,217.4	2.64
1981[2]	.2	307.0	26.0	657.0	1,387.6	15.0	2,392.7	509.0	78.7	859.3	724.1	124.1	2,436.2	2.30
1982[3]	.2	113.1	21.4	460.8	1,204.6	10.0	1,820.1	517.3	52.8	864.1	699.5	41.4	2,026.2	2.30

[1] N.Y., average ton lots.   [2] Preliminary.   [3] Estimate.   Source: Bureau of Mines   T.36

Broilers

Projected broiler meat output from federally inspected plants during 1983 was 12.365 billion pounds, nearly 3 percent above the 1982 level of 12.032 billion. The price of broilers throughout the first half of the 1983 season was expected to average between 40 and 46 cents per pound compared with the average price of 41.5 cents during the fourth quarter of 1982.

Despite weak grain prices and reduced feeding costs during 1982, sales of whole birds were generally unprofitable, and broiler producers featured the more profitable further processed and cut-up chicken and branded whole birds and parts. Although cumulative pullet placements were expected to continue declining, the expectation of an increase in 1983 broiler production was based upon fewer excess hens and their more intensive utilization.

Early in 1983, France proposed a meeting between French, U.S. and Brazilian officials to discuss the threat of a trade war in the world poultry market, particularly over poultry exports to the Middle East. The European Community (EC) sells 55–60 percent of Middle East poultry imports compared with sales of 34–40 percent from Brazil, which subsidizes its poultry exports, and with 5–6 percent from the U.S. Agriculture Secretary Block had reportedly said that poultry might be included in a PIK-type (payment-in-kind) export subsidy program.

Futures Markets

Broiler futures are listed on the Chicago Mercantile Exchange and on the Chicago Board of Trade.

Broiler Supply and Prices in the United States

Year & Quarters	Number (Mil.)	Avg. Wt. (Lbs.)	Liveweight Pounds (Mil. Lbs.)	Certified RTC Wt. (Mil. Lbs.)	Total Production RTC[2] (Mil. Lbs.)	Per Capita Consumption (Lbs.)	Prices Farm (Cents/Lb.)	Prices City[4] (Cents/Lb.)
1976	3,253	3.81	12,408	8,987	9,067	40.4	23.1	40.2
1977	3,334	3.82	12,741	9,227	9,418	41.1	23.5	40.8
1978	3,517	3.88	13,656	9,883	10,129	43.7	26.4	44.5
1979	3,843	3.93	15,111	10,916	11,219	47.7	26.0	44.4
I	907	3.90	3,541	2,551	2,623	11.2	28.5	47.5
II	1,011	3.90	3,936	2,844	2,922	12.6	28.2	47.7
III	1,009	3.92	3,951	2,855	2,934	12.5	23.6	40.8
IV	917	4.02	3,683	2,665	2,740	11.4	23.8	41.7
1980	3,915	3.93	15,409	11,175	11,334	47.0	27.8	46.8
I	950	3.96	3,759	2,739	2,786	11.7	25.6	43.0
II	1,016	3.96	4,027	2,940	2,989	12.3	23.5	41.1
III	991	3.83	3,796	2,776	2,817	11.7	31.8	53.3
IV	932	4.00	3,729	2,720	2,742	11.3	30.5	50.0
1981[1]	4,076	4.01	16,350	11,906	11,981	48.6	28.0	46.3
I	977	4.02	3,931	2,849	2,870	11.8	30.1	49.3
II	1,069	3.98	4,259	3,096	3,115	12.5	28.1	46.7
III	1,061	3.98	4,220	3,081	3,100	12.6	28.8	47.0
IV	969	4.07	3,939	2,880	2,897	11.7	25.2	42.1
1982[1]	4,066	4.04	16,447	12,032	12,000	—	26.6	44.0
I	981	4.00	3,920	2,888	2,907	11.9	27.0	44.8
II	1,046	4.04	4,226	3,109	3,127	12.8	27.6	45.2
III	1,065	4.00	4,265	3,130	3,143		27.3	44.4
IV	974	4.14	4,036	2,905	2,923		28.5	41.5
1983[3]				2,975				42.0
I								

[1] Preliminary. [2] Total production equals fed. inspec. slaughter plus other slaughter minus cut-up & further processing condemnation. [3] Forecast. [4] 9-city weighted average. *Source: Commodity Economics Division, U.S.D.A.*

T.38

How to keep your Commodity Year Book statistics up-to-date continuously throughout the year.

To keep up-to-date statistics on the commodities in this book, you should have COMMODITY YEAR BOOK STATISTICAL ABSTRACT SERVICE. This three-times-yearly publication provides the latest available statistics for the updating of the statistical tables appearing in the COMMODITY YEAR BOOK. It is published in the Winter (Jan.), Spring (Apr.) and Fall (Oct.). Subscription price is $55 per year.

Commodity Research Bureau, Inc.
75 MONTGOMERY ST., JERSEY CITY, N.J. 07302

BROILERS

Salient Broiler Statistics in the United States

Year	Commercial[2] Production Number Millions	Live-weight Mil. Lbs.	Average Live-weight Per Bird Lb.	Farm Price ¢ Lb.	Value of Production Mil. $	Commercial Broilers	Other Chickens	Total	Storage Stocks Jan. 1	Exports & Shipments	Military	Consumption Civilian Total	Per Capita in Lbs.
1970	2,987	10,819	3.62	13.6	1,475	7,687	778	8,465	110	182	69	8,161	40.5
1971	2,945	10,818	3.67	13.8	1,487	7,724	792	8,516	163	202	75	8,253	40.5
1972	3,075	11,480	3.73	14.1	1,623	8,147	740	8,887	149	206	52	8,667	42.0
1973	3,009	11,220	3.73	24.0	2,690	8,025	736	8,761	111	203	47	8,476	40.7
1974	2,993	11,320	3.79	21.5	2,436	8,126	789	8,915	146	235	34	8,617	41.1
1975	2,950	11,096	3.76	26.3	2,915	8,127	696	8,823	175	273	39	8,572	40.6
1976	3,283	12,517	3.81	23.6	2,953	9,067	684	9,751	114	451	33	9,226	43.3
1977	3,400	12,993	3.82	23.6	3,067	9,418	700	10,118	155	481	26	9,627	44.8
1978	3,613	14,022	3.88	26.3	3,682	10,129	665	10,794	139	505	32	10,294	47.5
1979	3,951	15,519	3.93	26.0	4,031	11,219	731	11,950	102	597	33	11,280	51.6
1980	3,964	15,544	3.95	27.7	4,304	11,272	757	12,091	142	781	38	11,278	51.1
1981[1]	4,149	16,514	4.01	28.5	4,698	11,906			136				
1982[1]	4,066	16,447	4.04	26.6	4,375	12,032							
1983													

[1] Preliminary. [2] Beginning 1970 data are for the marketing year starting Dec. 1 through Nov. 30. [3] Ready-to-cook basis. *Source: Economic Research Service, U.S.D.A.*
T.39

Average Wholesale Broiler[2] Prices RTC 9-City[1] Average   In Cents Per Pound

Year	Jan.	Feb.	Mar.	Apr.	May	June	July	Aug.	Sept.	Oct.	Nov.	Dec.	Avg.	4-Region Ave. Retail Price	Hens[4] 8–16 Lbs. RTC (Chicago)[3]
1970	28.2	27.2	27.7	26.4	26.5	26.1	25.9	25.4	26.0	24.6	25.5	24.8	26.2		40.8
1971	26.1	27.1	26.7	26.4	28.2	29.1	30.0	27.6	27.0	25.4	24.4	24.1	26.8		41.0
1972	26.7	28.0	27.8	25.6	26.7	28.2	29.8	28.4	29.6	28.1	27.3	28.2	27.9		41.4
1973	32.5	36.0	40.9	44.2	41.0	41.3	47.1	60.0	48.1	39.9	34.8	36.6	41.6		59.6
1974	39.3	39.8	38.5	36.4	35.5	33.8	36.3	36.7	39.8	39.0	41.8	40.2	38.1		56.0
1975	42.8	40.9	40.2	39.8	42.3	46.9	50.9	49.6	49.6	47.2	45.6	41.7	44.8		63.3
1976	41.7	42.6	41.6	40.9	42.0	41.7	43.3	41.4	39.8	36.2	34.9	35.0	40.1		59.7
1977	38.7	41.4	42.0	41.1	41.8	42.7	43.8	41.9	40.6	38.8	36.9	35.9	40.5		53.1
1978	40.0	42.8	41.9	46.1	45.5	50.1	50.2	43.3	44.4	41.5	41.7	42.0	44.1		65.6
1979[1]	45.8	49.2	47.5	47.5	49.4	46.1	42.8	39.6	39.9	37.0	42.6	45.5	44.4		67.3
1980	45.8	42.7	40.5	38.9	41.1	43.3	52.8	52.4	54.8	51.4	49.7	48.6	46.8		62.6
1981	49.5	50.3	48.2	44.4	46.3	49.3	50.2	47.3	43.6	43.7	42.5	40.1	46.3	73.7	59.7
1982	45.2	44.5	44.8	42.6	45.8	47.0	46.1	43.4	43.6	42.3	40.3	42.0	44.0	71.6	
1983															

[1] Prices prior to 1979 are for broilers delivered at Chicago (grade A). Trucklots (U.S. & Plant). [2] Ice packed, ready-to-cook. [3] In retail stores (urban areas), whole or cut-up ready to cook. [4] Prior to 1977 prices are for frying chicken. *Source: Bureau of Labor Statistics*
T.37

How to keep your Commodity Year Book statistics up-to-date continuously throughout the year.

To keep up-to-date statistics on the commodities in this book, you should have COMMODITY YEAR BOOK STATISTICAL ABSTRACT SERVICE. This three-times-yearly publication provides the latest available statistics for the updating of the statistical tables appearing in the COMMODITY YEAR BOOK. It is published in the Winter (Jan.), Spring (Apr.) and Fall (Oct.). Subscription price is $55 per year.

Commodity Research Bureau, Inc.
75 MONTGOMERY ST., JERSEY CITY, N.J. 07302

Burlap and Jute

Production of jute and kenaf in the major producing countries of India, Bangladesh, and Thailand for the 1982/83 season (July/June) was estimated by the Foreign Agricultural Service of the USDA in late 1982 at 2,210,000 tonnes, 11 percent below estimated 1981/82 production of 2,491,100 tonnes. Production of soft fibers by the world's major producers has been trending downward since the 1978/79 season, as additional acreage has shifted from jute or kenaf to generally more remunerative crops such as rice or cassava (tapioca).

Production prospects for both India and Thailand were diminished by extremely dry weather that delayed the planting season for several weeks—a condition which was further exacerbated by the late onset of the monsoon. The dry season occurs from late November until mid-May and the rainy season from mid-May into the following November. When rains persist through the normal season, the area harvested tends to increase, and large crops may result, even though yields show little change.

Jute and kenaf production in India for the 1982/83 season was expected to total about 1,170,000 tonnes, 19 percent below estimated 1981/82 output of 1,440,000 tonnes and 1980/81 production of 1,468,800 tonnes. Indian jute and kenaf area amounted to 1,007,000 hectares in 1982/83, down from 1,299,900 hectares in 1981/82, according to USDA estimate. (One hectare equals 2.4710 acres.)

The production of jute and kenaf in Bangladesh was expected to total 840,000 tonnes in the 1982/83 season, only slightly below estimated 1981/82 production of 842,800 tonnes, but 6 percent below 1980/81 output of 896,800 tonnes. Area in jute and kenaf in 1982/83 was estimated at about 570,000 hectares, only slightly below 571,400 in the preceding season, but about 11 percent below the 1980/81 area of 634,900 hectares.

In Thailand, 1982/83 production of jute and kenaf was estimated at 200,000 tonnes, down from an estimated 208,300 tonnes in 1981/82 and 210,000 tonnes in 1980/81. The jute and kenaf area in 1982/83 was estimated at 180,000 hectares versus 189,000 in 1981/82 and 190,000 in 1980/81.

Low product prices and rising production costs continued to plague growers in all three countries. Kenaf was expected to replace cassava to an increasing degree in Thailand because of the new use for kenaf as paper pulp in the northeast. Jute accounted for only about 5.2 percent of total agricultural production in 1981, but Bangladesh depends heavily on jute for foreign exchange. In fiscal 1982, jute and jute products were expected to account for 75 percent of total projected export value.

Jute carpetbacking cloth traditionally is the dominant jute product imported into the U.S., but it must compete with synthetic substitutes. In addition, demand was adversely affected in 1982 by the acute depression in the U.S. housing construction industry.

Average Wholesale Price of Raw Jute, Bang Tossa C., Landed, at New York In Cents Per Pound

Year	Jan.	Feb.	Mar.	Apr.	May	June	July	Aug.	Sept.	Oct.	Nov.	Dec.	Average
1971	16.5	16.8	16.8	16.8	16.8	17.1	17.5	17.5	17.7	17.9	17.9	18.5	17.3
1972	N.A.	18.5	N.A.	N.A.	19.7	19.7	17.8	17.8	17.8	17.8	17.8	N.A.	18.4
1973	17.3	17.6	17.6	18.3	18.3	N.A.	18.9	18.8	18.8	18.8	18.2	18.2	18.3
1974	N.A.	N.A.	N.A.	N.A.	N.A.	19.5	19.5	21.5	N.A.	N.A.	25.8	27.8	22.8
1975	27.8	27.8	27.8	27.8	27.8	23.3	N.A.	23.3	N.A.	23.3	N.A.	20.3	25.5
1976	20.4	19.8	20.4	20.9	20.9	20.2	19.7	19.7	19.7	19.7	19.7	19.7	20.1
1977	20.2	20.2	21.4	21.4	21.4	N.A.	21.9	21.9	21.9	22.1	22.6	N.A.	21.5
1978	N.A.	N.A.	28.3	28.3	27.3	26.8	26.8	26.8	26.0	26.0	26.0	26.0	26.8
1979	26.0	26.0	26.0	25.8	26.0	26.0	25.8	N.A.	32.7	32.7	32.7	32.7	28.4
1980	N.A.	N.A.	N.A.	N.A.	N.A.	N.A.	N.A.	N.A.	29.0	28.5	29.0	29.0	28.8
1981	N.A.	27.35	27.35	N.A.	29.0	N.A.	29.0	29.0	29.0	29.0	24.0	22.55	27.30
1982	23.50	23.40	23.15	24.50	N.A.	N.A.	23.20	25.50	25.50	25.50	25.50	25.50	24.53
1983	25.50	25.50											

Source: Bureau of Labor Statistics (0155-0231.01)

BURLAP AND JUTE

Jute and Kenaf Production In Thousands of Metric Tons[3]

Crop Year	Jute Bangladesh[4]	Jute India[4]	Kenaf (Mesta) India[4]	Kenaf (Mesta) Thailand[5]	Crop Year	Jute Bangladesh[4]	Jute India[4]	Kenaf (Mesta) India[4]	Kenaf (Mesta) Thailand[5]
1970-1	2,563	1,959	498	661	1977-8	972	961	320	246
1971-2	1,702	2,256	456	820	1978-9	1,169	——1,169——		320
1972-3	2,579	1,975	461	960	1979-0	1,210	——1,553——		260
1973-4[3]	1,080	1,116	266	570	1980-1	814	——1,332——		191
1974-5	720	805	245	400	1981-2[1]	765	——1,306——		189
1975-6	782	800	265	308	1982-3[2]	762	——1,061——		181
1976-7	877	974	314	183	1983-4				

[1] Preliminary. [2] Estimate. [3] Data prior to 1973 are in MILLIONS OF POUNDS. [4] July–June year. [5] Sept.–Aug. year. Source: Foreign Agricultural Service, U.S.D.A.
T.40

Average Wholesale Price of Burlap (40 Inch—10 Oz.) at New York   In Cents Per Yard

Year	Jan.	Feb.	Mar.	Apr.	May	June	July	Aug.	Sept.	Oct.	Nov.	Dec.	Average
1971	15.4	15.5	15.3	18.3	16.9	18.1	18.4	18.4	19.0	19.3	19.4	23.2	18.1
1972	23.6	23.8	22.0	22.0	21.8	20.3	19.5	19.0	18.8	19.0	18.4	18.8	20.6
1973	18.8	18.9	19.3	20.3	19.9	19.4	19.4	19.4	18.7	18.7	20.0	20.0	19.4
1974	21.5	23.6	26.3	29.5	31.1	31.1	26.7	27.2	27.4	27.3	25.8	23.5	26.8
1975	24.0	24.1	23.8	21.1	21.5	20.6	17.9	18.2	17.6	17.1	17.4	N.A.	20.3
1976	17.2	18.1	17.9	17.4	17.0	17.2	17.4	17.2	17.0	17.4	17.8	18.0	17.5
1977	N.A.	18.3	18.3	18.0	N.A.	18.3	18.3	19.0	19.6	27.0	21.2	22.8	20.1
1978	23.2	23.4	22.6	22.9	18.4	18.5	18.0	18.0	18.0	17.3	18.0	18.0	19.7
1979	18.1	18.1	18.1	18.1	18.1	18.1	N.A.	35.4	36.7	36.0	40.3	41.5	27.1
1980	N.A.	39.8	40.0	38.5	N.A.	N.A.	N.A.	N.A.	33.5	33.5	N.A.	33.0	36.4
1981	N.A.	27.35	27.35	N.A.	29.0	N.A.	29.0	29.0	29.0	29.0	24.0	22.55	27.36
1982	23.50	23.40	23.15	24.50	N.A.	23.30	23.20	23.35	25.25	26.75	25.50	24.30	23.29
1983	22.65	24.25											

Source: Bureau of Labor Statistics (0337-0461.01)
T.42

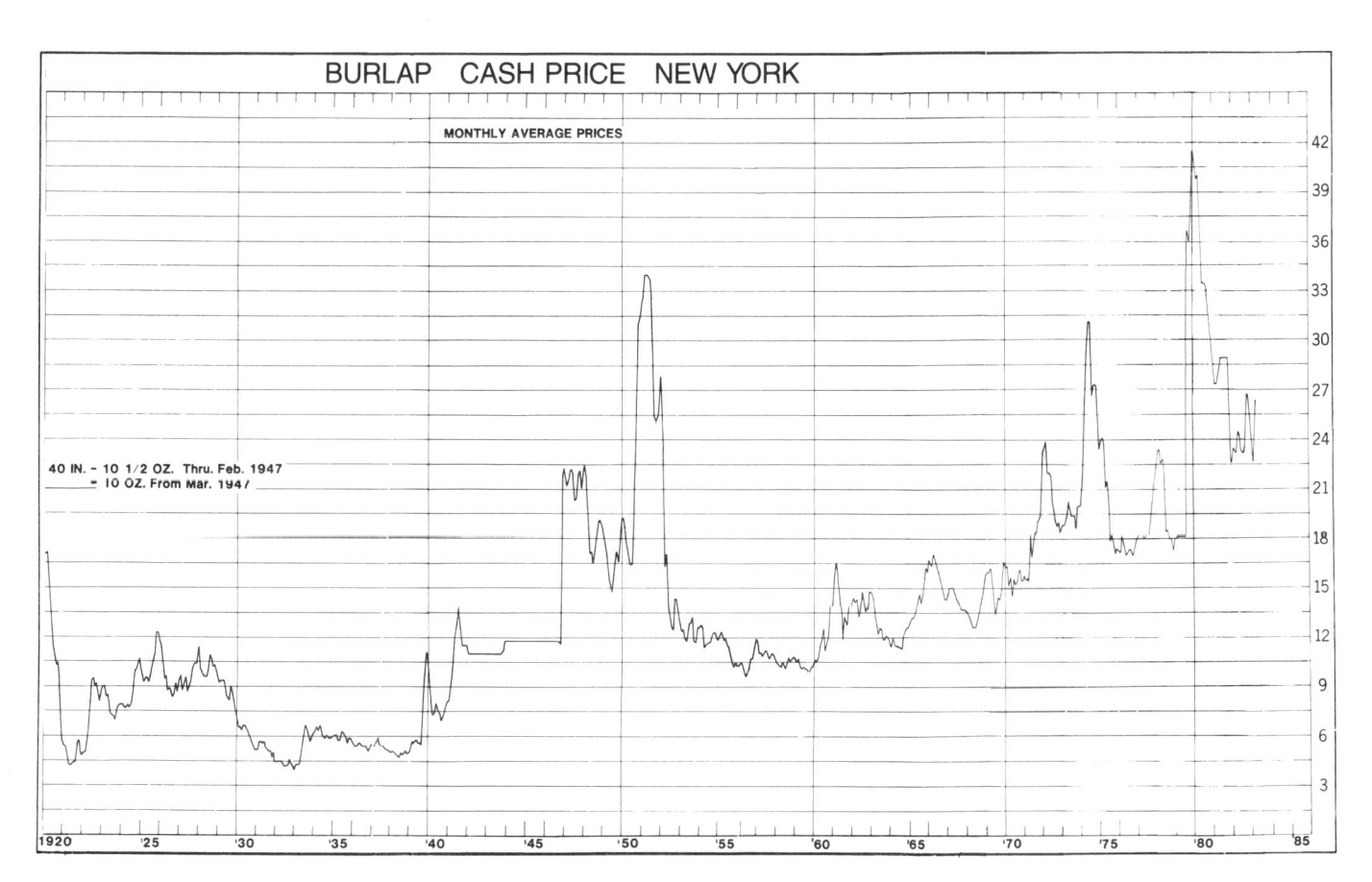

67

Butter

Preliminary estimates put the 1982 production of butter at nearly 1,258.8 million pounds, nearly 2.5 percent above the 1981 level despite a drop in production during the last quarter of 1982.

Nearly 19 percent of the net increase in milk going into manufactured products in 1982 went into butter. Analysts observed that the price of Grade B milk may have fallen below support levels since April 1980 in part because of a reduced demand for milk brought about by the relatively high cost of producing butter. For all of 1982, prices for Grade AA butter averaged nearly $2.05 per pound, up about 5.3 cents from the 1981 price level. Generally, butter prices were stable during 1982. The retail price index of butter rose by nearly 2 percent during the year. Early in 1983, the average price for Grade A butter in Chicago was about $1.47 per pound, less than 1 cent lower than its price during the comparable period of 1982. The price of butter in 1982 remained fairly steady because of ample stocks and the fact that the CCC support price for milk remained unchanged.

The commercial disappearance of butter in 1982 amounted to 898.9 million pounds, only about 4 percent above the 1981 level. The per capita civilian consumption of butter during the year was virtually unchanged. The commercial use of butter throughout most of 1982 was nearly unchanged from levels of the comparable period in 1981.

The butter removed from the commercial market by programs of the USDA during 1982 amounted to 382.3 million pounds, nearly 9 percent above the amount of butter affected by government programs in 1981. USDA purchases of butter in the first 8 months of 1982 increased by 9 percent. Purchases dropped during the June–August period as butter production declined seasonally. Purchases declined overall from a peak of 56.7 million pounds in February to 12.6 million pounds in August. The total CCC removals of butter in the October 1981–September 1982 period were projected at 380 million pounds, up 7 percent from the previous season. Government stocks of butter in early 1983 were nearly 23 percent above year-earlier levels. Some of the decline in government inventories in 1982 was due to shipments of butter to New Zealand under a 1981 purchase agreement and to the movement of butter to public schools. Approximately 95 percent of the butter remaining in inventory was government-owned. Domestic and foreign donations of 149.2 million pounds of butter, including 20 million pounds for distribution to the needy, were made in 1982. Agriculture Secretary Block announced in November 1982 that an additional 75 million pounds of butter would be distributed to the needy in 1983. The USDA established a Private Sector Inventory System designed to increase the use of surplus products by allowing private processors to produce products from bonus commodities for discount sale to eligible institutions.

International trading in butter was down in 1982, mostly due to a drop in EC exports. The Middle East and Eastern Europe, major markets for butter in 1981, took noticeably less butter in 1982. F.o.b. prices for butter in Northern Europe in the first half of 1982 were between $2,125 and $2,250 a tonne. At the end of the year, prices had dropped to between $2,000 and $2,050 a tonne.

The worldwide production of butter is expected to increase by nearly 150,000 tonnes in 1983. Production by the EC and Soviet Union is expected to account for 90,000 and 40,000 tonnes of the world output, respectively. Production by the U.S. and New Zealand is expected to change little during 1983.

In March 1982, the EC Commission announced that subsidized butter sales to the Soviet Union would be on terms similar to sales to other destinations. Formerly, EC sales of butter to the Soviet Union had been made according to a special tendering system and required approval at the Commissioner level. However, the Soviet Union did not wish to be treated differently from other EC customers, and no sales had been made under the system. Private EC exporters are now able to sell butter to all destinations and receive an export subsidy, 58 cents per pound in early 1983. Initial payments on sales of butter to the Soviet Union were to be 80 percent of the subsidy, the balance to be paid upon presentation of landing certificates.

Supply and Distribution of Butter in the United States   In Millions of Pounds

Year	Production Creamery	Production Farm	Production Total	Cold Storage Stocks[1] Jan. 1[2]	Imports	Domestic Disappearance Civilian Total	Per Capita —Lbs.—	Military	Exports & Shipments[4]	Dept. of Agr. Jan. 1 Stocks[5]	Dept. of Agr. Dec. 31 Stocks	Removed by U.S.D.A. Programs	Total Use	93 Score Wholesale Prices Calif. AA $ Lb.	Chi. AA $ Lb.
1972	1,102	—	1,102	97	2	1,017	4.9	23	54	71	96	234	1,094		
1973	919	—	919	107	56	999	4.8	9	17	96	23	98	1,025	.8397	—
1974	962	—	962	57	2	956	4.3	9	7	23	15	33	972	.8042	.6609
1975	984	—	984	49	2	1,021	4.7	9	3	15	5	63	1,024	.9729	.7941
1976	979	—	979	11	2	942	4.3	7	3	5	19	39	945	1.100	.9326
1977	1,086	—	1,086	47	2	946	4.3	5	4	19	151	222	950	1.1366	.9865
1978	994	—	994	185	2	969	4.4	3	5	151	192	112	974	1.2666	1.1058
1979	985	—	985	207	2	1,011	4.5	6	5	192	153	82	1,018	1.4327	1.2374
1980	1,145	—	1,145	176	2	1,016	4.5	4	4	153	268	257	1,021	1.6135	1.4079
1981[3]	1,228	—	1,228	303	2	1,018	4.3	4	95	268	382	352	1,115	1.6855	1.4897
1982[3]	1,259	—	1,259	429	2		4.5			382		382			
1983[3]				467											

[1] Commercial. [2] Includes stocks held by U.S.D.A. [3] Preliminary. [4] Includes U.S.D.A. shipments to Territories. [5] Includes butteroil. *Source: Department of Agriculture*

BUTTER

World (Total) Butter[1] Production   In Thousands of Metric Tons

Year	Australia	Canada	China	Argentina	Denmark	France	Ireland	W. Germany	Netherlands	N. Zealand	India	Poland	Sweden	USSR	South Africa	Un. Kingdom	United States
1975	161	129		40	139	556	86	521	204	230	451		56	1,231	26	48	445
1976	148	114	92	40	139	550	103	544	202	251	455		61	1,408	26	89	444
1977	118	113	94	30	131	551	105	535	179	263	457		61	1,500	21	134	493
1978	112	102	94	29	140	553	130	564	216	230	460	294	63	1,472	16	161	451
1979	105	106	95	32	131	596	132	568	202	255	475	293	65	1,409	18	161	447
1980	84	111	95	29	113	627	124	578	179	255	480	294	66	1,373	17	168	519
1981[2]	79	119		29	108	600	120	540	183	247	485	255	63	1,315	16	170	561
1982[3]	75	120		29	110	600	122	530	200	235	490	270	70	1,290	15	175	595

[1] Factory (including creameries and dairies) & farm.   [2] Preliminary.   [3] Forecast.   Source: *Foreign Agricultural Service, U.S.D.A.*   T.44

Production of Creamery Butter in Factories in the United States   In Millions of Pounds

Year	Jan.	Feb.	Mar.	Apr.	May	June	July	Aug.	Sept.	Oct.	Nov.	Dec.	Total
1975	100.5	90.8	98.1	103.2	101.9	88.3	69.2	57.7	58.0	68.2	64.0	83.8	983.8
1976	92.5	85.0	90.0	87.0	91.4	83.9	71.5	65.1	64.0	78.1	77.6	92.5	978.6
1977	105.5	95.4	98.4	99.9	103.2	93.0	81.8	77.8	75.0	84.5	81.5	89.5	1,086
1978	107.4	95.5	98.2	97.2	97.6	85.1	71.4	63.2	64.0	70.6	66.5	77.7	994.3
1979	98.4	86.7	89.8	92.4	99.2	83.0	72.5	64.3	60.5	78.0	75.8	84.0	984.6
1980	105.7	99.9	101.1	112.2	116.6	93.9	83.7	75.3	77.0	91.4	84.7	103.6	1,145
1981	123.1	108.4	115.5	117.3	115.5	95.9	82.7	82.3	85.2	99.5	93.4	109.5	1,228
1982[1]	127.3	115.9	123.4	———332.9———			———262.2———			———295.1———			1,257
1983[2]	133.9	120.7	126.1										

[1] Preliminary.   [2] Estimate.   Source: *Crop Reporting Board, U.S.D.A.*   T.45

Commercial Disappearance of Creamery Butter in the U.S.   In Millions of Pounds

Year	Jan.	Feb.	Mar.	Apr.	May	June	July	Aug.	Sept.	Oct.	Nov.	Dec.	Total
1975	92.9	70.4	91.4	84.9	78.1	76.6	72.7	77.9	66.5	78.6	71.4	85.1	947.7
1976	94.5	77.2	74.8	74.6	66.5	72.8	70.0	64.0	77.5	81.3	82.6	82.2	919.0
1977	71.9	53.9	83.6	65.0	56.3	44.8	71.6	72.8	89.1	81.5	74.0	94.3	859.8
1978	68.1	65.9	92.0	79.2	61.0	77.5	68.7	69.8	83.8	72.8	77.4	87.4	903.5
1979[1]	83.1	78.3	88.5	70.7	64.2	68.1	72.5	66.2	63.4	78.4	84.4	78.7	895.0
1980[1]	75.0	86.1	88.8	47.7	54.2	59.4	73.2	78.8	77.3	66.3	78.1	93.5	878.8
1981[1]	66.3	49.5	74.2	70.8	70.5	73.7	66.6	75.1	87.4	57.0	100.8	87.1	877.8
1982[1]	———213.3———			———216.5———			———222.9———			———246.1———			898.8

[1] Preliminary.   Source: *Economic Research Service, U.S.D.A.*   T.46

Cold Storage Holdings of Creamery Butter in the U.S., on First of Month   In Millions of Pounds

Year	Jan.	Feb.	Mar.	Apr.	May	June	July	Aug.	Sept.	Oct.	Nov.	Dec.
1976	10.9	9.3	16.5	31.1	44.0	69.5	80.9	83.0	82.3	68.1	60.7	47.3
1977	47.1	67.6	94.2	106.3	128.3	163.8	197.1	209.0	208.6	203.3	195.4	193.4
1978	184.9	195.7	215.9	235.8	246.2	264.6	282.0	297.7	284.6	266.7	251.8	228.9
1979	206.9	206.7	214.7	210.1	218.2	239.1	260.1	257.3	238.5	218.0	200.4	182.1
1980	177.8	191.0	205.6	217.2	238.1	281.7	295.9	308.0	306.4	302.9	301.6	302.7
1981[1]	304.6	332.1	372.3	407.4	450.4	473.6	507.5	515.5	515.6	489.5	470.0	451.1
1982[1]	429.2	430.3	440.4	447.8	—	—	541.6	—	—	510.0	—	—
1983[1]	466.8	485.4	527.9	528.1								

[1] Preliminary.   Source: *Crop Reporting Board, U.S.D.A.*   T.47

Wholesale Price of 92 Score Creamery (Grade A, Bulk) Butter at Chicago   In Cents Per Pound

Year	Jan.	Feb.	Mar.	Apr.	May	June	July	Aug.	Sept.	Oct.	Nov.	Dec.	Average
1975	66.8	68.1	68.1	69.2	69.2	69.2	76.6	83.6	87.9	93.0	97.3	103.6	79.4
1976	86.1	80.9	86.0	89.5	89.9	95.0	105.8	106.2	92.4	90.8	90.8	90.8	92.0
1977	90.8	90.8	92.7	100.1	100.7	100.7	100.7	100.7	100.7	100.7	100.9	101.5	98.4
1978	100.7	100.7	101.2	105.2	106.7	106.7	107.9	116.7	115.8	115.6	121.1	118.8	109.8
1979	111.3	111.3	114.1	120.7	121.8	121.8	122.7	128.7	127.8	128.8	130.0	130.2	122.4
1980	130.2	130.3	130.4	134.3	136.9	139.0	139.3	144.5	145.1	147.1	147.6	147.7	139.3
1981	147.2	147.2	147.2	147.2	147.3	147.5	147.9	148.0	148.5	150.6	148.9	148.1	148.0
1982	———147.6———			———147.3———			———148.0———			———147.9———			147.7

Source: *Economic Research Service, U.S.D.A.*   T.48

Cadmium

Cadmium is recovered as a by-product of smelting zinc concentrates, and is used in its metallic form for plating and alloying. Cadmium compounds are used in pigments, plastic, and batteries.

U.S. refinery production of cadmium metal (primary and secondary) in 1982 was 28 percent lower than in 1981 and fell far short of domestic demand, according to preliminary data of the U.S. Bureau of Mines. The shortfall was made up by imports and stock withdrawals. Production of sulfide was off 10 percent from the 1981 total but production of other compounds was 10 percent larger than a year earlier.

Imports of cadmium metal in 1982 dropped 25 percent from the 1981 level, with the largest losses compared to 1981 registered by Canada, Australia, Spain, and the Republic of Korea. Imports of cadmium metal from China and Peru increased in 1982.

Domestic shipments of cadmium metal in 1982 increased 42 percent, according to Bureau of Mines data, while compound shipments were about unchanged from a year earlier. The estimated consumption pattern in 1982 was: coating and plating—34 percent; pigments—27 percent; batteries—16 percent; plastics and synthetic products—15 percent; and alloys and other uses—8 percent. The use of cadmium in nickel-cadmium batteries appears to be the application with the highest growth potential. Research has provided some potential new uses for cadmium sulfide and cadmium telluride in solar photovoltaic cells. The Bureau of Mines estimates that 1983 U.S. refinery production of cadmium will be 1,300 metric tons (tonnes) and U.S. apparent consumption 4,000 tonnes.

U.S. stocks of cadmium metal held by metal producers of 655.56 tonnes December 31, 1982 were 39 percent lower than a year earlier. Stocks held by compound producers at 161.85 tonnes were sharply higher than the 44.87 tonnes on hand at the end of 1981.

The U.S. producer price of cadmium began 1982 at $1.40 per pound, but sagged to $1.00 per pound by the third quarter where it remained through the end of the year. The New York dealer price of cadmium started 1982 at $1.25 to $1.35 per pound and declined steadily to end the year at $0.65 to $0.70 per pound.

World Smelter Production of Cadmium Metal   In Metric Tons[5]

Year	Australia[3]	Belgium	Canada[3]	France	W. Germany	Italy	Japan	Mexico[3]	Norway	Poland	Un. King.	USSR	United States[4]	Zaire	World Total
1970	1,355	2,407	1,845	1,164	2,282	937	5,403	591	216	990	701	5,200	9,465	699	36,454
1971	1,234	2,088	1,568	1,276	2,162	772	5,898	424	202	880	578	5,300	7,930	578	34,014
1972	1,586	2,536	2,450	1,262	2,014	918	6,678	410	192	780	530	5,400	8,290	652	36,776
1973	1,494	2,528	3,084	1,336	2,692	876	6,988	402	194	780	692	5,500	7,502	612	37,850
1974	1,588	2,300	2,740	1,420	2,952	1,166	6,674	1,162	198	780	618	5,700	6,666	598	38,082
1975	1,210	2,094	2,628	1,004	2,244	902	5,858	1,292	104	780	606	5,800	4,386	582	33,586
1976[5]	649	1,200	1,314	532	1,275	436	2,500	710	80	750	190	2,700	2,047	266	16,998
1977	670	1,440	1,185	790	1,336	448	2,844	908	97	754	295	2,750	1,999	246	18,288
1978	747	1,164	1,265	689	1,182	378	2,531	897	120	761	291	2,800	1,653	186	17,446
1979	804	1,440	1,460	792	1,266	527	2,597	830	115	773	424	2,850	1,823	212	18,883
1980	1,012	1,527	1,033	791	1,197	568	2,173	778	130	698	375	2,850	1,578	168	18,130
1981[1]	1,050	1,070	1,274	660	1,192	600	1,977	860	115	630	278	2,900	1,603	230	17,721
1982[2]	950	800	1,200				2,500	800					1,150		17,100

[1] Preliminary.   [2] Estimate.   [3] Refined metal.   [4] Primary & secondary metal.   [5] Data prior to 1976 are in THOUSANDS OF POUNDS.   *Source: Bureau of Mines*   T.49

Salient Statistics of Cadmium in the United States   In Metric Tons[6] of Contained Cadmium

Year	Net Import Reliance as a % of Apparent Consumption	Production Primary Producers Metallic	Shipments	Value Mil. $	Cadmium Sulfide[3]	Imports (for Consumption) Metallic	Flue Dust[3]	Total	Price[5] $ per lb.	Exports Cadmium Metal, Alloys, Dross, Flue Dust	Value $ Ths.	Consumption[4]	Stocks, Dec. 31 Industry Metallic	Compounds	Distributors
1970		9,465	6,848	24.2	2,137	2,492	1,111	3,603		373	997	9,062	3,837	944	
1971		7,930	7,774	9.8	2,236	3,498	1,112	4,610	1.92	66	172	10,872	4,297	975	
1972		8,290	10,480	19.0	2,714	2,422	740	3,162	2.56	1,018	2,363	12,626	2,342	982	
1973		7,502	8,608	23.9	2,824	3,896	348	4,244	3.64	306	598	12,534	1,530	1,122	
1974		6,666	6,500	21.4	2,170	3,970	332	4,302	4.09	62	238	12,100	1,396	330	
1975[6]	41	1,990	742	4.2	895	2,375	314	2,689	3.36	180	589	3,055	1,881	121	
1976	64	2,047	2,707	10.5	729	3,094	223	3,317	2.66	229	713	5,381	1,242	148	
1977	51	1,999	1,837	7.1	639	2,332	13	2,345	2.96	107	316	3,818	1,452	72	255
1978	63	1,653	1,957	5.9	698	2,881	—	2,881	2.45	326	864	4,510	1,152	45	296
1979	64	1,823	2,468	9.5	813	813	—	2,572	2.76	211	550	5,099	517	52	327
1980	55	1,578	1,271	5.2	801	2,617	—	2,617	2.84	236	464	3,534	841	42	439
1981[2]	64	1,603	1,382	3.8	527	3,090	—	3,090	1.93	239	332	4,442	1,077	45	203
1982[1]	69	1,158	1,963			2,305	—	2,305	1.10	11		3,715	656	162	17
1983															

[1] Estimate.   [2] Preliminary.   [3] Cd content.   [4] Apparent Primary cadmium in all forms.   [5] Producer to consumer in 1 to 5 ton lots, average.   [6] Data prior to 1976 are in THOUSANDS OF POUNDS.   *Source: Bureau of Mines*   T.50

Castor Beans

Although the castor bean is planted annually, one plant is commonly harvested during two or three years, and wild plants are harvested in some cases.

Total world production of castorseed during the 1982/83 marketing season was privately estimated at nearly 825,000 tonnes compared with 892,000 tonnes the previous season. India, the major world producer, harvested 270,000 tonnes. Brazil produced the second-largest crop of 240,000 tonnes. The Indian and Brazilian harvests were down a total of 70,000 tonnes from the previous season. China, the world's third-largest producer of castorseed, increased its estimated harvest by a slim 1,000 tonnes to 130,000 tonnes.

World castor oil use declined during the 1982/83 season. Stocks at the beginning of the marketing year were estimated at 6,000 tonnes above the previous season's beginning stocks. Total world production of castor oil, projected at nearly 331,000 tonnes, was 9,000 tonnes below production during 1981/82. Disappearance, estimated at 333,000 tonnes, was 3,000 tonnes down from a year earlier. Ending stocks of the 1982/83 marketing year were projected to be 86,000 tonnes, down 3,000 tonnes from the previous season's figure. The lower demand for castor oil during recent years is an outcome of the greater substitution of synthetic oils for castor oil in industrial uses.

Early in 1983, the government of India reportedly began to allow private firms to export castor oil to any destination except Eastern Europe. Indian prices for castor oil subsequently firmed as a result of competition amongst domestic firms for the expanded world market.

World Production of Castor Beans In Thousands of Metric Tons

Crop Year	China	Brazil	Ecuador	Ethiopia	India	Romania	Iran	Israel	Mexico	Pakistan	Thailand	USSR	Rep. of So. Afr.	Sudan	World Total
1971	72	273	25	13	154	10	8	8	7	13	42	53	5	19	744
1972	66	437	22	13	175	10	7	8	7	13	42	89	5	17	943
1973	71	558	26	13	229	10	5	8	3	13	42	76	5	14	1,117
1974	67	573	16	11	229	10	4	8	4	13	32	74	5	15	1,088
1975	70	353	13	10	210	12	4	8	8	14	48	52	5	16	858
1976	70	222	10	10	143	5	4	8	6	8	43	41	5	2	614
1977-8	79	277	10	11	217	5	4	8	6	19	37	45	5	2	765
1978-9	98	388	11	11	229	6	4	8	6	19	37	43	5	9	918
1979-0	110	325	10	10	233	6	4	8	4	19	26	62	5	9	876
1980-1[1]	120	320	11	110	275	6	3	8	6	20	22	59	5	10	812
1981-2[2]															

[1] Preliminary. [2] Estimate. Source: Foreign Agricultural Service, U.S.D.A.   T.51

Salient Statistics of Castor Oil in the United States In Millions of Pounds

Year Beginning Oct. 1	Imports	Stocks Oct. 1	Total	Exports	Per Capita (in Lbs.)	Total	Paint & Varnish	Fatty Acids	Resins & Plastic	Lubricants & Oils	Other Inedible	No. 1 Braz. N.Y.[2] ¢ Lb.
1970-1	85.3	118.9	204.2	—	0.53	110.1	5	13	1	6	85	15.5
1971-2	82.5	94.0	176.5	—	0.66	137.9	30	22	13	6	67	17.2
1972-3	87.6	38.6	126.2	—	0.54	113.9	5	6	11	6	85	23.3
1973-4	123.0	12.3	135.3	—	0.55	117.1	7	3	8	6	93	52.6
1974-5[1]	86.2	18.2	104.5	—	0.41	88.6	—	—	5	6	79	44.0
1975-6[1]	116.2	15.9	132.1			92.1						31.5
1976-7[1]	117.7	44.5	162.2			106.6						33.3
1977-8[1]	264.3	31.0	295.3			104.7						43.4
1978-9[1]		17.5										41.8
1979-0[1]												44.9
1980-1[1]												34.5

[1] Preliminary. [2] Tanks, imported–calendar year. Source: Economic Research Service, U.S.D.A.   T.52

Monthly Average Wholesale Prices of Castor Oil[1] at New York In Cents per Pound

Year	Jan.	Feb.	Mar.	Apr.	May	June	July	Aug.	Sept.	Oct.	Nov.	Dec.	Average
1976	29.00	27.50	27.50	27.50	27.50	31.50	35.00	38.50	39.00	39.00	39.00	39.00	33.33
1977	39.00	39.00	40.00	40.00	45.00	45.00	45.00	45.00	45.00	46.00	46.00	46.00	43.42
1978	46.10	46.50	46.50	46.30	46.20	40.30	39.40	37.90	37.90	37.90	37.90	37.90	41.73
1979	37.90	37.90	37.80	37.80	37.80	38.40	41.30	50.90	53.10	54.10	56.00	56.00	44.92
1980	55.70	55.70	55.80	55.60	55.00	52.00	51.00	49.80	48.00	46.50	45.30	46.00	51.37
1981	46.70	45.90	45.00	45.00	44.60	44.10	43.50	44.30	43.70	43.30	43.30	43.30	44.39
1982	42.80	43.30	43.30	43.30	44.70	45.90	46.50	45.50	45.50	45.50	45.50	45.50	44.78

[1] Average wholesale, TANK CARS, IMPORTED BRAZIL. Source: Foreign Agricultural Service, U.S.D.A.   T.53

Cattle and Calves

U.S. commercial beef production during 1982 rose by only 1 percent, and cattle slaughter increased by 2 percent. The production increase was slim because average dressed weights declined by 12 pounds despite a 1 percent rise in the fed cattle proportion of the slaughter mix. All of the increase in commercial slaughter was accounted for by the larger slaughter of cows and heifers. While steer slaughter declined by close to 1 percent, cow and heifer slaughter increased nearly 12 and 4 percent respectively.

The number of replacement heifers calving and entering the cow herd declined again during 1982. The proportion of heifers entering the herd during the first half of 1982 was the smallest since 1973, and those entering during the second half of the year were the third smallest number recorded during that period. Larger numbers of heifers were slaughtered or placed in feedlots, and heifer slaughter rose more than 4 percent during 1982.

Since 1980, successively smaller calf crops and sharply increased feedlot inventories have reduced the number of cattle available for stocker operations or feedlot placement. The inventory of yearling steers and of heifers not being saved for herd replacement rose 5 and 11 percent respectively above year-earlier levels. The number of yearlings outside feedlots rose 2 percent despite larger placements because nonfed steer and heifer slaughter declined by 20 percent.

The signs of economic recovery observed during early 1983 may have indicated an end to several years of poor returns for cattle producers, but after 3 years of expansion, the latest buildup in cattle numbers ended in 1982. The U.S. cattle inventory declined to 115.2 million head on January 1, 1983 from 115.6 million a year earlier. This aggregate figure disguises the 3 percent decline in the beef breeding herd which is the base of future production. The number of heifers being saved for beef herd replacement declined by nearly 4 percent. The 1982 calf crop was estimated at 44.4 million head, the second consecutive decline. Reductions in cow herd and in replacement heifers virtually insured that the calf crop would decline again in 1983.

The projected sharply reduced slaughter of all categories of nonfed cattle during 1983 was not expected to offset the increase in fed cattle marketings. The proportion of fed cattle slaughter to total slaughter was seen as likely to increase from 69 to 72 percent, and slaughter weights were expected to rise.

Futures Markets

Live beef cattle futures and feeder cattle futures are traded on the Chicago Mercantile Exchange, and a smaller live cattle futures contract is traded on the MidAmerica Commodity Exchange in Chicago.

World Cattle and Buffalo Numbers   In Millions of Head

Year	Argentina	Australia	Brazil	Canada	China	Colombia	France	W. Germany	India	Turkey	Mexico	South Africa	USSR	Un. Kingdom	United States	World Total[1]
1971	49.8	24.4	81.1	12.2	92.6	20.5	21.7	14.0		13.9	25.1	10.0	99.2	12.4	114.6	1,245
1972	52.3	27.4	85.1	12.3	92.7	21.0	21.7	13.6		13.7	26.4	11.6	102.4	12.9	117.9	1,268
1973	54.8	29.1	86.1	12.6	92.8	22.1	22.6	13.9		14.1	26.8	11.7	104.0	13.8	121.5	1,288
1974	58.0	30.8	88.1	13.2	92.9	23.0	23.9	14.4		14.3	27.5	12.3	106.3	14.8	127.8	1,311
1975	59.6	32.8	94.0	14.0		23.0	24.3	14.4		14.4	28.7	12.3	109.1	14.8	132.0	N.A.
1976	61.5	33.4	92.0	14.0		23.8	23.6	14.5	240.5	14.8	28.9	12.8	111.0	13.9	128.0	963
1977	61.9	31.5	91.0	13.7		24.3	23.3	14.5	241.5	15.2	29.3	13.1	110.3	13.7	122.8	947
1978	61.8	29.3	89.0	12.9		25.2	23.4	14.8	242.7	15.6	29.7	13.0	112.7	13.5	116.4	941
1979	60.2	27.1	90.0	12.3		26.2	23.5	15.0	242.5	16.0	29.3	13.2	114.1	13.5	110.9	936
1980	58.9	26.2	91.0	12.4		27.2	23.6	15.1	241.0	16.6	29.5	13.6	115.1	13.3	111.2	937
1981[2]	58.8	25.2	93.0	12.5	95.0	27.8	23.6	15.1	241.5	16.9	29.6	13.2	115.1	13.1	115.1	943
1982[1]	57.8	24.5	93.0	12.5		28.7	23.5	15.0	242.0	17.2	29.9	13.5	115.8	13.0	115.9	942
1983[1]	58.2	23.0	93.0	12.5			23.6						116.0		117.1	939

[1] Estimate.   [2] Preliminary.   Source: Foreign Agricultural Service, U.S.D.A.   T.54

Commercial Slaughter of Cattle and Calves in the United States[2]   In Thousands of Head

Year	Cattle Federally Inspected	Cattle Total[2]	Calves Federally Inspected	Calves Total[2]	Total[2] Cattle and Calves	Year	Cattle Federally Inspected	Cattle Total[2]	Calves Federally Inspected	Calves Total[2]	Total[2] Cattle and Calves
1971	31,419	35,585	2,806	3,689	39,274	1977	38,717	41,856	4,696	5,517	47,373
1972	32,267	35,779	2,421	3,053	38,832	1978	36,948	39,552	3,620	4,170	43,722
1973	30,521	33,687	1,808	2,249	35,936	1979	31,504	33,678	2,499	2,824	36,502
1974	33,319	36,812	2,355	2,987	39,799	1980	31,642	33,807	2,294	2,588	36,395
1975	36,904	40,911	3,894	5,209	46,120	1981	32,819	34,953	2,478	2,798	37,751
1976	38,992	42,654	4,438	5,350	48,004	1982[1]	33,907	35,826	2,729	3,019	38,845

[1] Preliminary.   [2] Includes other wholesale and retail slaughter.   Source: Crop Reporting Board, U.S.D.A.   T.55

CATTLE AND CALVES

Cattle Supply and Distribution in the United States In Thousands of Head

Year	Cattle & Calves on Farms Jan. 1	Imports	Calves Born	Total Supply	Livestock Slaughter—Cattle and Calves Commercial Federally Inspected	Other[2]	All Commercial	Farm	Total Slaughter	Deaths on Farms	Exports	Total Disappearance
1972	117,862	1,186	47,682	166,730	34,688	4,144	38,832	503	39,335	5,126	104	44,565
1973	121,539	1,039	49,194	171,772	32,329	3,607	35,936	570	36,506	6,487	273	43,266
1974	127,778	568	50,873	179,229	35,674	4,125	39,799	729	40,528	6,110	204	46,842
1975	132,028	389	50,183	182,600	40,798	5,322	46,120	750	46,870	6,992	196	54,058
1976	127,980	984	47,385	176,348	43,430	4,574	48,004	722	48,726	5,190	205	54,121
1977	122,810	1,133	45,931	169,974	43,413	3,960	47,373	700	48,073	6,000	107	54,180
1978	116,375	1,253	43,818	161,446	40,568	3,154	43,722	550	44,272	5,680	122	50,194
1979	110,864	732	42,603	154,199	34,342	2,473	36,502	430	36,932	5,600	66	42,598
1980	111,192	681	44,998	156,871	33,936	2,458	36,395	401	36,795	5,413	66	42,274
1981	114,321	659	44,776	159,756	35,273	2,478	37,751	399	38,150	4,902	88	43,144
1982[1]	115,604	1,005	44,420	161,029	36,634	2,211	38,845	400	39,245	5,400	58	44,683
1983[1]	115,201											

[1] Preliminary. [2] Wholesale and retail. Source: Economic Research Service, U.S.D.A.   T.56

Number of Cattle & Calves on U.S. Farms & Ranches on Jan. 1, by Classes In Thousands of Head

Year	Total Cattle & Calves	Cows & Heifers That Have Calved Beef	Milk	Total	Heifers 500 lbs. & Over For Beef Cow Replacement	For Milk Cow Replacement	Other Heifers	Total	Steers 500 lbs. & Over	Bulls 500 lbs. & Over	Under 500 lbs.
1973	121,539	40,918	11,624	52,541	7,436	3,874	6,434	47,743	16,555	2,466	32,229
1974	127,788	43,008	11,286	54,293	8,226	3,942	6,821	18,988	17,802	2,645	33,942
1975	132,028	45,472	11,211	56,682	8,879	4,095	6,509	19,482	16,373	2,987	36,302
1976	127,980	43,888	11,087	54,974	7,196	3,958	7,393	18,546	17,083	2,845	34,531
1977	122,810	41,389	11,035	52,424	6,529	3,888	8,057	18,473	16,885	2,665	32,363
1978	116,375	38,809	10,939	49,748	5,845	3,896	7,970	17,710	16,779	2,544	29,595
1979	110,864	37,062	10,790	47,843	5,527	3,932	7,445	16,903	16,442	2,403	27,263
1980	111,192	37,086	10,779	47,865	5,939	4,158	7,130	17,226	16,019	2,492	27,590
1981	114,321	38,726	10,860	49,586	6,136	4,345	7,285	17,766	15,519	2,547	28,904
1982	115,601	39,319	11,012	50,331	6,615	4,532	7,181	18,328	15,501	2,618	28,827
1983[1]	115,201	38,081	11,066	49,146	6,343	4,532	7,954	18,829	16,229	2,615	28,382
1984											

[1] Preliminary. Source: Crop Reporting Board, U.S.D.A.   T.57

Number of Cattle and Calves on Feed[2] on Jan. 1 in the United States In Thousands of Head

Jan. 1	Arizona	California	Colorado	Illinois	Indiana	Iowa	Kansas	Minnesota	Missouri	Nebraska	Ohio	South Dakota	Texas	Wisconsin	Total U.S.
1970	510	1,031	795	755	349	2,213	892	589	402	1,477	318	361	1,417	146	13,190
1971	524	1,001	888	649	314	1,992	916	548	342	1,422	308	339	1,480	150	12,770
1972	539	1,045	983	662	327	2,112	1,100	537	373	1,550	320	363	1,781	144	13,912
1973	655	1,181	1,050	585	276	1,922	1,250	494	310	1,581	300	378	2,245	143	14,432
1974	609	1,209	930	530	263	1,715	1,160	464	250	1,525	280	381	2,205	136	13,642
1975	319	688	755	500	250	1,200	920	380	200	1,160	290	345	1,327	135	10,167
1976	510	960	925	630	285	1,530	1,340	430	260	1,390	320	365	1,880	168	12,940
1977	361	812	915	620	290	1,520	1,315	340	255	1,580	325	370	1,710	130	11,948
1978	422	845	1,020	650	315	1,690	1,400	400	220	1,700	295	365	1,850	130	12,811
1979	490	796	1,080	510	280	1,620	1,440	400	180	1,800	225	340	2,000	106	12,681
1980	420	764	960	460	250	1,390	1,270	390	120	1,680	180	350	1,970	112	11,713
1981	401	677	845	510	280	1,370	1,100	370	105	1,640	160	355	1,830	115	11,105
1982	330	581	750	480	240	1,130	1,110	350	90	1,640	125	335	1,660	112	10,619
1983[1]	385	581	1,020	530	275	1,210	1,320	405	100	1,880	140	345	1,920	115	12,040
1984															

[1] Preliminary. [2] Cattle & calves being fattened for slaughter market on grain or other concentrates & are expected to produce a carcass that will grade good or better. Source: Crop Reporting Board, U.S.D.A.   T.59

CATTLE AND CALVES

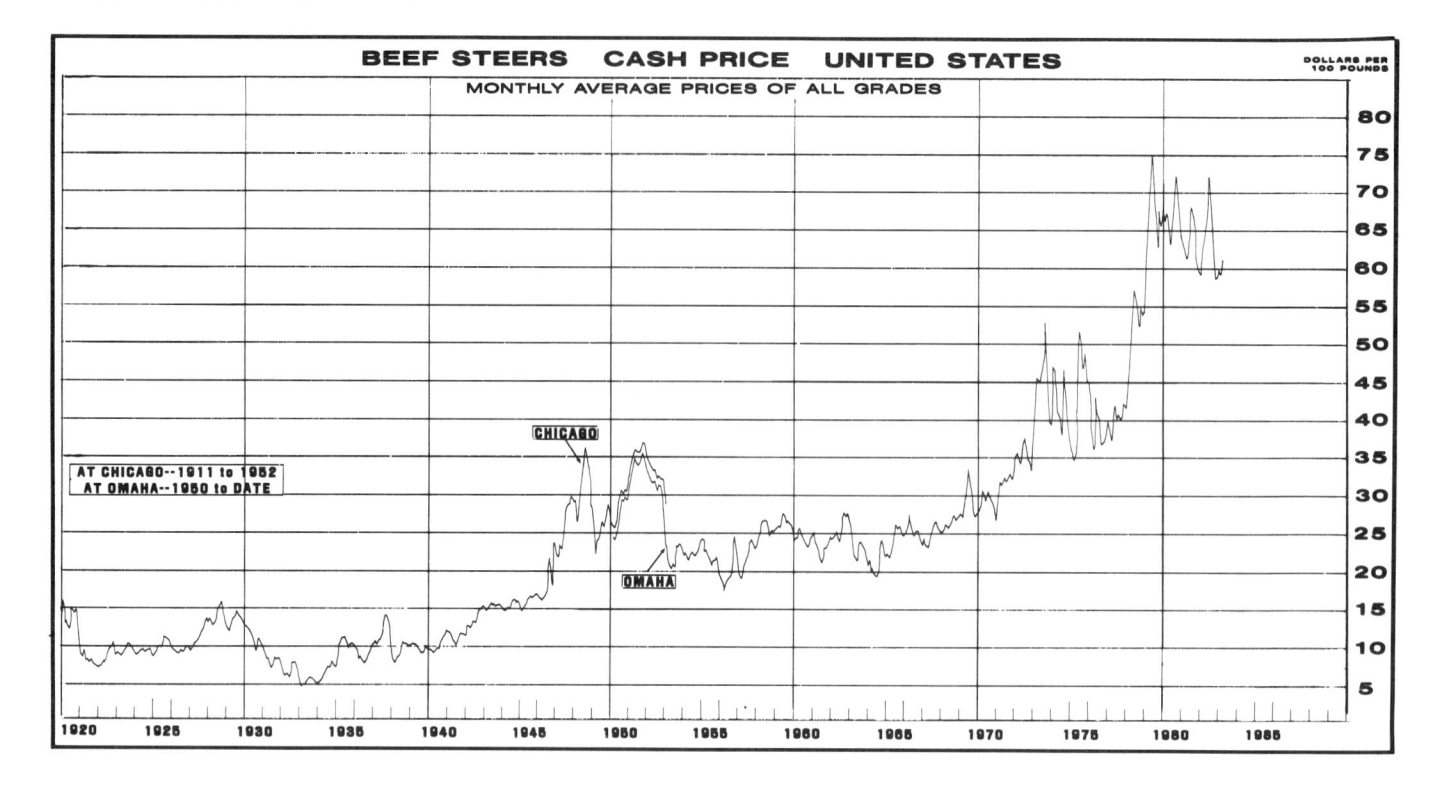

BEEF STEERS CASH PRICE UNITED STATES
MONTHLY AVERAGE PRICES OF ALL GRADES
DOLLARS PER 100 POUNDS
AT CHICAGO--1911 to 1952
AT OMAHA--1950 to DATE

Condition[1] of Pasture and Range Feed in the United States, on First of Month   In Percent of Normal

Year	Apr. 1	May 1	June 1	July 1	Aug. 1	Sept. 1	Oct. 1	Nov. 1	Dec. 1
1973	86	87	87	84	82	80	82	83	81
1974	79	81	84	82	66	71	75	70	71
1975	73	79	77	75	70	61	63	66	64
1976	73	79	77	75	70	61	63	66	64
1977	68	76	74	68	64	71	76	75	72
1978	68	75	85	85	77	75	77	73	70
1979	75	84	87	86	84	86	81	77	75
1980	76	80	81	78	60	61	63	65	63
1981	70	79	80	84	82	82	80	80	78
1982	81	79	87	90	86	82	81	80	N.A.
1983	84								

[1] Indicates current supply of feed for grazing on non-irrigated pastures & ranges relative to that expected from existing stands under very favorable weather conditions. [80 & over, good to excellent; 65–79, poor to fair; 50–64, very poor; 35–49, severe drought; under 35, extreme drought.]   *Source: Statistical Reporting Service, U.S.D.A.*   T.57A

Average Prices of Steers (Stocker & Feeder) Kansas City   In Dollars Per 100 Pounds

Year	Jan.	Feb.	Mar.	Apr.	May	June	July	Aug.	Sept.	Oct.	Nov.	Dec.	Average
1973	44.24	48.06	50.90	50.67	50.79	49.38	53.23	56.40	49.73	49.84	47.63	44.42	49.13
1974	48.70	45.30	43.65	42.49	37.24	33.16	34.44	33.26	29.80	29.80	27.97	28.05	36.49
1975	26.79	26.80	27.86	30.73	34.87	35.30	32.53	32.93	35.98	36.74	36.77	36.87	33.42
1976	36.66	36.95	38.82	43.49	42.38	40.24	37.58	37.55	34.03	36.07	35.07	35.19	37.65
1977	34.87	36.54	38.29	41.33	39.88	38.22	38.90	39.61	39.04	40.18	38.79	39.71	38.74
1978	42.85	46.89	51.39	53.81	59.85	57.42	58.67	58.22	60.23	62.06	60.75	64.19	56.16
1979	69.95	75.61	82.55	86.83	82.20	75.00	72.07	72.37	77.81	76.34	78.92	77.55	77.60
1980	76.52	78.35	72.67	66.89	65.52	68.83	69.48	71.92	71.53	71.64	70.23	70.04	71.30
1981	68.56	68.41	65.47	66.28	63.10	63.51	61.51	64.15	64.58	62.52	61.77	58.96	64.26
1982	59.22	62.37	63.96	64.72	66.07	63.70	64.17	66.42	63.55	62.21	61.24	59.17	62.79
1983	63.70	66.34											

Source: Economic Research Service, U.S.D.A.   T.61

CATTLE AND CALVES

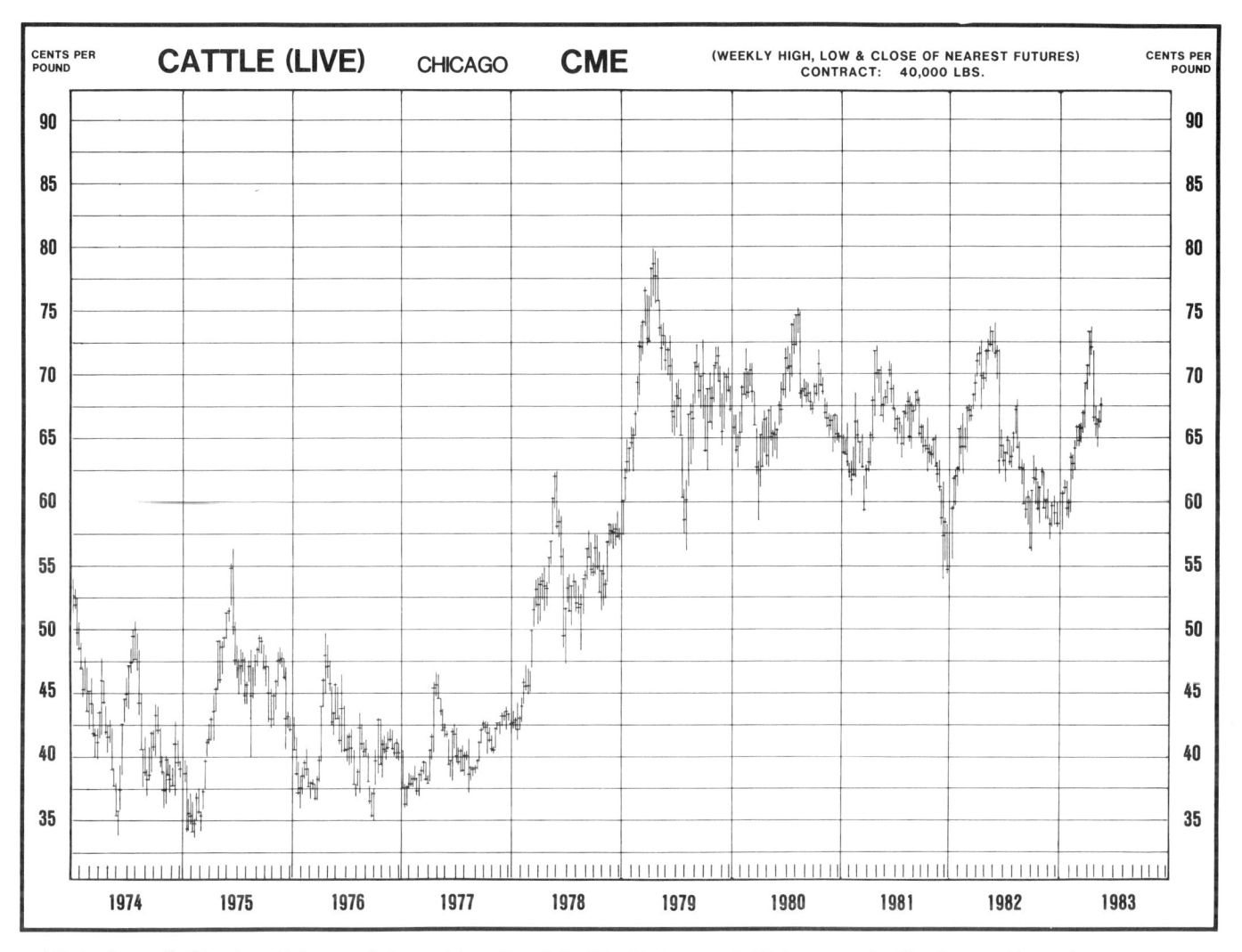

CATTLE (LIVE) CHICAGO **CME** (WEEKLY HIGH, LOW & CLOSE OF NEAREST FUTURES) CONTRACT: 40,000 LBS.

High, Low & Closing Prices of June Live Beef Cattle Futures at Chicago In Cents per Pound

Year of Delivery		Apr.	May	June	July	Aug.	Sept.	Oct.	Nov.	Dec.	Jan.	Feb.	Mar.	Apr.	May	June	Life of Delivery Range
1978	High	47.20	46.40	44.55	42.60	40.35	39.65	40.20	41.85	43.30	45.17	47.62	53.10	53.75	62.35	60.95	62.35
	Low	45.85	43.65	41.40	40.20	37.40	38.55	38.82	39.40	41.10	42.20	44.65	46.25	49.10	53.45	54.15	37.40
	Close	46.12	44.35	42.55	40.40	38.80	39.55	39.60	41.35	43.02	45.17	46.32	50.47	53.27	60.97	56.15	—
1979	High	53.65	60.27	58.75	59.57	57.85	60.60	61.90	62.25	64.50	67.90	70.50	74.22	79.75	79.12	72.97	79.75
	Low	49.90	53.65	51.10	54.40	53.45	57.05	57.25	58.25	61.20	63.00	64.65	69.52	70.75	70.10	68.05	48.60
	Close	53.60	58.35	55.70	57.60	57.07	59.62	60.25	61.30	63.55	67.67	70.20	71.35	78.35	71.97	68.15	—
1980	High	75.00	74.50	73.60	74.40	72.85	74.30	76.10	76.95	75.80	76.00	75.10	73.77	67.20	67.50	69.50	76.95
	Low	69.20	70.55	68.10	65.45	64.05	70.40	69.12	72.05	72.02	67.70	71.35	63.22	60.25	62.80	63.35	60.25
	Close	73.75	70.90	71.40	66.30	72.62	73.75	72.57	74.92	75.05	71.80	71.95	63.60	64.82	65.30	69.02	—
1981	High	—	—	—	75.25	74.92	76.00	76.60	76.50	76.35	72.65	71.42	68.55	72.40	70.72	70.97	76.60
	Low	—	—	—	70.80	71.80	72.85	72.90	73.67	69.40	68.05	66.65	63.17	70.10	66.22	67.62	63.17
	Close	—	—	—	73.95	74.87	73.55	74.37	76.07	71.32	68.72	67.77	68.55	70.17	68.17	69.35	—
1982	High	72.30	71.90	70.40	67.95	66.97	67.35	66.72	66.05	63.55	61.60	64.75	66.87	70.10	73.65	74.00	74.00
	Low	70.40	68.05	66.85	64.82	64.02	64.42	64.60	61.80	54.75	56.00	60.65	62.72	66.20	69.30	69.57	54.75
	Close	70.40	69.80	67.00	67.02	65.37	65.27	65.20	63.30	55.77	61.40	62.92	66.42	69.57	73.37	70.00	—
1983	High	—	65.50	63.30	64.55	63.72	63.25	62.50	61.80	62.00	63.90	66.47	69.77	71.15			
	Low	—	63.90	60.00	60.50	61.77	58.40	58.02	58.52	58.55	60.75	62.90	64.80	65.10			
	Close	—	64.10	62.75	62.85	62.30	59.27	59.62	60.80	61.10	62.72	65.27	69.62	66.12			
1984	High																
	Low																
	Close																

Source: Chicago Mercantile Exchange

T.62

CATTLE AND CALVES

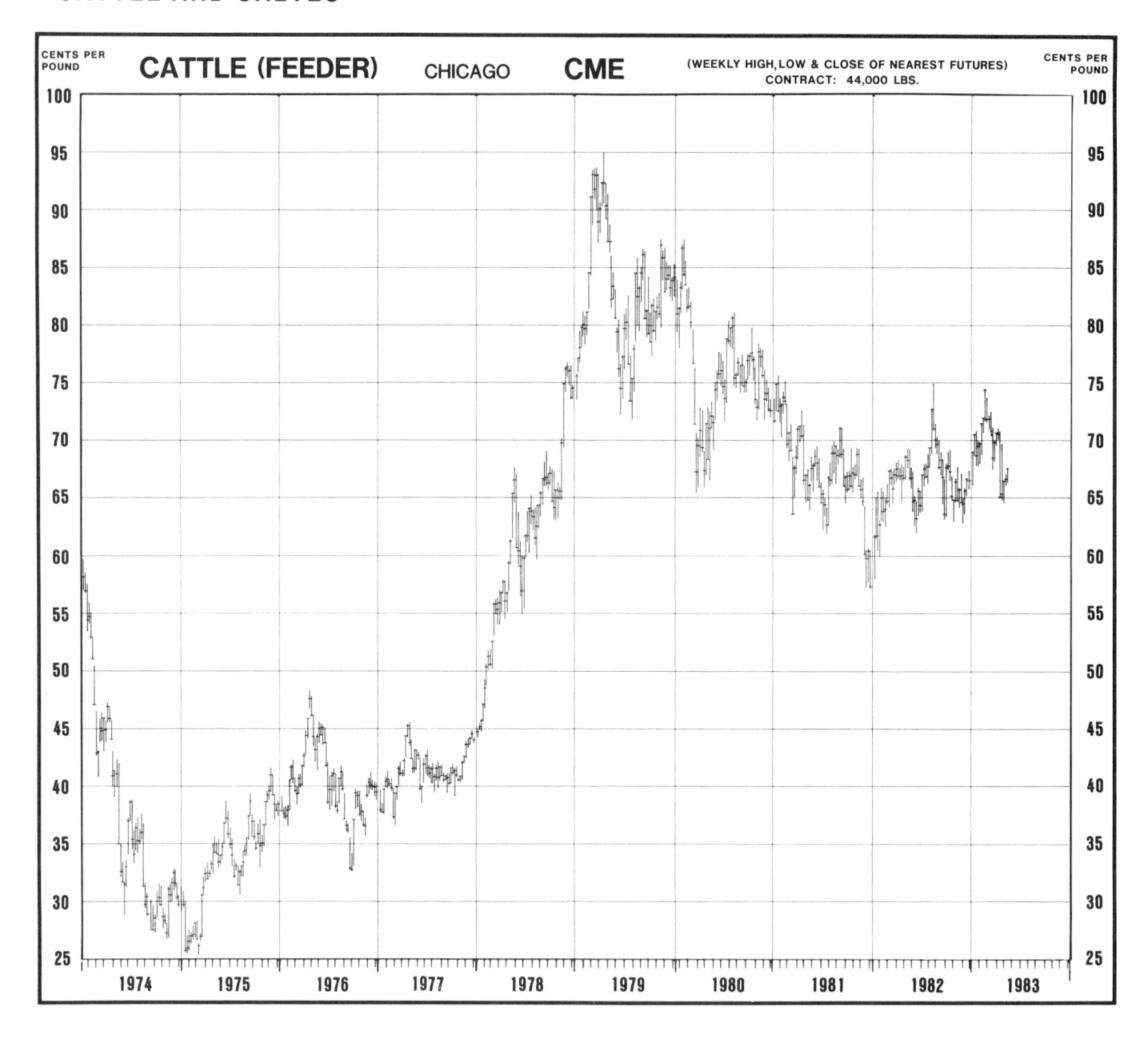

CATTLE (FEEDER) CHICAGO **CME** (WEEKLY HIGH, LOW & CLOSE OF NEAREST FUTURES) CONTRACT: 44,000 LBS. — CENTS PER POUND, 1974–1983

Cattle & Calves on U.S. Farms on January 1, by Leading States   In Thousands of Head

Jan. 1	Calif.	Colo.	Ill.	Iowa	Kans.	Minn.	Miss.	Mo.	Mont.	Nebr.	Ohio	Okla.	So. Dak.	Texas	Wis.
1972	4,662	3,610	3,400	7,773	6,757	3,998	2,322	5,238	3,165	6,780	2,113	5,441	4,408	13,464	4,241
1973	4,710	3,756	3,240	7,770	6,800	4,038	2,415	5,550	3,197	6,865	2,134	5,660	4,496	15,100	4,283
1974	5,250	3,744	3,250	7,660	6,990	4,240	2,610	6,330	3,380	7,410	2,150	6,020	5,000	16,250	4,400
1975	5,200	3,375	3,200	7,350	6,400	4,430	3,000	6,800	3,340	6,900	2,350	6,500	4,950	16,600	4,640
1976	5,000	3,250	3,400	7,500	6,450	4,430	2,723	6,600	3,150	6,550	2,305	6,400	4,500	15,600	4,550
1977	4,750	3,030	3,200	7,650	6,400	4,000	2,670	6,400	2,980	6,450	2,205	5,650	3,650	15,800	4,275
1978	4,430	3,180	2,950	7,800	6,000	3,700	2,130	6,000	2,680	6,500	2,025	5,900	3,925	14,500	4,100
1979	4,700	3,090	2,850	7,200	6,200	3,650	1,790	5,550	2,607	6,450	1,750	5,300	3,830	13,900	4,100
1980	4,550	2,975	2,700	7,150	6,200	3,750	1,810	5,400	2,645	6,400	1,825	5,500	4,010	13,200	4,280
1981	4,760	3,125	2,650	7,350	6,450	3,800	1,800	5,550	2,675	6,850	1,815	5,400	4,100	13,700	4,550
1982	5,000	3,025	2,800	6,850	6,000	3,880	1,950	5,400	2,900	7,250	1,900	5,800	3,900	13,700	4,450
1983[1]	4,900	3,040	2,800	6,450	5,750	3,610	1,800	5,500	2,990	7,200	1,900	5,350	4,060	15,000	4,400
1984															

[1] Preliminary.   *Source: Crop Reporting Board, U.S.D.A.*

T.58

76

CATTLE AND CALVES

Farm Value, Income & Wholesale Prices of Cattle & Calves

Year	United States Farm Value of All Cattle—Jan. 1 Per Head $	Total Million $	Gross Income From C. & C.[2] Million $	At Omaha Prime	Steers[3] Choice	Good	Heifers Good	Choice	Feeder Steers All Weights at K.C.	Cows, Utility Omaha	Vealers, Choice So. St. Paul	Cows, Commercial Omaha	Beef, Dressed[4] Steer, Choice	Heifer, Choice	Cow[5] Cann-ers[6]
									Dollars Per 100 Pounds						
1970	179	20,160	13,935	30.22	29.36	27.04	26.42	28.51	30.15	21.32	44.82	20.94	46.82	46.26	44.72
1971	184	21,113	15,247	33.38	32.39	29.38	28.52	31.46	32.09	21.62	46.30	21.21	52.39	51.72	45.63
1972	208	24,520	18,579	36.67	35.78	33.43	32.24	34.72	38.89	25.21	55.09	24.86	55.34	54.56	51.41
1973	252	30,584	22,814	45.61	44.54	42.01	40.43	43.11	49.13	32.82	64.08	32.90	67.41	66.44	65.78
1974	293	37,477	18,350	43.13	41.89	38.71	38.00	40.97	36.49	25.56	49.63	25.45	67.09	66.51	53.48
1975	159	21,000	17,978	41.39	44.61	39.45	37.60	43.12	33.42	21.09	40.44	21.63	73.64	71.62	43.09
1976	190	24,335	19,795		39.11	35.87	34.10	37.98	37.65	25.31	45.18	26.08	60.96	59.75	52.00
1977	206	25,249	20,708		40.38	36.70	35.20	38.96	38.75	25.32	48.19	26.11	62.66	60.94	51.55
1978	232	27,030	28,813		52.34	47.98	46.11	50.30	56.16	36.78	69.24	37.80	80.80	78.58	74.61
1979	403	44,698	35,128		67.67	63.05	61.47	65.91	77.60	50.10	91.41	50.06	101.72	100.00	100.48
1980	502	55,831	32,083		67.05	62.16	61.22	64.90	75.13	45.72	75.52	44.91	104.39	101.86	92.45
1981[1]	475	54,292	29,558		63.84	59.83	59.46	62.05	64.26	41.93	77.25	41.59	99.85	97.48	84.06
1982[1]	415	47,967			64.30	59.47			63.08	39.96	77.70	40.35	101.30		
1983[1]	406	46,749													

[1] Preliminary. [2] Excludes interfarm sales & Gov't. payments. Cash receipts from farm marketings plus value of farm home consumption. [3] Weighted average prices of beef steers, sold out of first hands for slaughter. [4] Carlots. [5] All weights. [6] And cutter. *Source: Statistical Reporting Service, U.S.D.A.*

T.60

Average Wholesale Prices of Beef Steers at Omaha, Choice (900–1100 Lbs.)   In Dollars Per 100 Pounds

Year	Jan	Feb	Mar	Apr	May	June	July	Aug.	Sept.	Oct.	Nov.	Dec.	Average
1973	40.65	43.54	45.65	45.03	45.74	46.76	47.66	52.94	45.12	41.92	40.14	39.36	44.54
1974	47.14	46.38	42.85	41.53	40.52	37.98	43.72	46.62	41.38	39.64	37.72	37.20	41.89
1975	36.34	34.74	36.08	42.80	49.48	51.82	50.21	46.80	48.91	47.90	45.23	45.01	44.61
1976	41.18	38.80	36.14	43.12	40.62	40.52	37.92	37.02	36.97	37.88	39.15	39.96	39.11
1977	38.38	37.98	37.28	40.08	41.98	40.24	40.94	40.11	40.35	42.29	41.83	43.13	40.38
1978	43.62	45.02	48.66	52.52	57.28	55.38	54.59	52.40	54.26	54.93	53.82	55.54	52.34
1979	60.35	64.88	71.04	75.00	73.99	68.53	67.06	62.74	67.84	65.81	67.00	67.78	67.75
1980	66.32	67.44	66.88	63.07	64.58	66.29	70.47	72.31	69.68	67.18	65.05	64.29	66.96
1981	63.08	61.50	61.40	64.92	66.86	68.26	67.86	66.37	65.37	61.45	59.81	59.24	63.84
1982	60.75	63.54	65.80	69.11	72.10	70.18	66.18	65.14	61.25	58.78	58.91	59.82	64.30
1983	59.33	61.20											

Source: Economic Research Service, U.S.D.A.

T.65

Month End Open Interest of Live Beef Cattle Futures at Chicago   In Contracts

Year	Jan.	Feb.	Mar.	Apr.	May	June	July	Aug.	Sept.	Oct.	Nov.	Dec.
1978	59,234	72,397	84,902	84,016	95,783	74,827	79,734	86,634	91,351	91,719	91,163	88,797
1979	97,005	96,410	84,814	75,913	65,881	60,296	57,506	59,621	75,371	55,978	64,729	62,872
1980	57,192	60,701	50,406	55,582	53,319	59,162	67,059	57,314	58,815	58,009	64,570	45,864
1981	45,325	45,425	48,336	54,045	48,667	50,162	44,597	53,142	51,267	54,025	61,763	51,226
1982	51,036	51,082	61,160	58,383	61,341	48,314	44,024	44,645	42,694	42,412	44,085	45,115
1983	49,014	56,500	59,992	59,771								

Source: Chicago Mercantile Exchange

T.64

Volume of Trading of Live Beef Cattle Futures at Chicago   In Thousands of Contracts

Year	Jan.	Feb.	Mar.	Apr.	May	June	July	Aug.	Sept.	Oct.	Nov.	Dec.	Total
1978	23.80	314.4	468.6	458.6	580.4	597.4	459.2	498.6	500.3	602.3	433.9	440.6	5,040.0
1979	534.2	526.1	660.3	697.4	720.1	586.5	554.2	683.4	553.5	674.3	554.4	470.5	7,214.8
1980	646.0	545.5	562.0	568.6	499.5	460.7	604.3	443.8	461.1	461.0	348.3	395.2	5,997.0
1981	354.8	347.8	430.7	416.4	350.0	361.0	320.8	329.3	348.9	327.7	335.3	359.7	4,282.4
1982	387.2	332.5	434.3	355.8	389.3	458.4	340.2	326.0	353.1	421.2	337.4	305.6	4,441.0
1983	370.4	332.7	455.8	489.0									

Source: Chicago Mercantile Exchange

T.63

CATTLE AND CALVES

Federally Inspected Slaughter of Cattle in the United States In Thousands of Head

Year	Jan.	Feb.	Mar.	Apr.	May	June	July	Aug.	Sept.	Oct.	Nov.	Dec.	Total
1972	2,556	2,457	2,707	2,471	2,807	2,833	2,494	2,926	2,789	2,909	2,705	2,615	32,267
1973	2,810	2,424	2,620	2,169	2,694	2,563	2,441	2,366	2,362	2,866	2,687	2,519	30,521
1974	2,794	2,303	2,621	2,643	2,793	2,621	2,821	2,876	2,787	3,230	2,929	2,902	33,319
1975	3,152	2,778	2,826	2,889	2,851	2,898	3,085	3,141	3,319	3,584	3,116	3,267	36,904
1976	3,403	3,032	3,492	3,053	2,980	3,294	3,220	3,388	3,435	3,336	3,154	3,205	38,992
1977	3,272	3,041	3,331	3,025	3,054	3,374	3,085	3,489	3,320	3,282	3,244	3,200	38,717
1978	3,238	3,047	3,243	2,969	3,215	3,052	2,869	3,247	3,027	3,180	3,029	2,834	36,948
1979	3,090	2,559	2,670	2,366	2,622	2,554	2,492	2,862	2,390	2,837	2,593	2,470	31,844
1980	2,739	2,486	2,403	2,540	2,616	2,533	2,667	2,684	2,739	3,003	2,507	2,725	31,642
1981[1]	2,803	2,483	2,726	2,625	2,593	2,770	2,765	2,772	2,846	2,939	2,668	2,829	32,819
1982[1]	———8,183———			———8,192———			———8,770———			———8,762———			33,907
1983	2,893	2,554											

[1] Preliminary. Source: Crop Reporting Board, U.S.D.A. T.66

Federally Inspected Slaughter of Calves & Vealers in the U.S. In Thousands of Head

Year	Jan.	Feb.	Mar.	Apr.	May	June	July	Aug.	Sept.	Oct.	Nov.	Dec.	Total
1972	226	217	255	185	179	166	164	208	197	211	209	202	2,421
1973	209	169	188	139	131	117	118	115	128	168	170	156	1,808
1974	181	154	180	172	167	137	164	202	212	279	251	254	2,355
1975	284	250	276	284	270	276	344	345	385	443	357	381	3,894
1976	369	327	415	353	304	339	346	373	409	394	388	420	4,438
1977	408	380	457	389	353	368	352	411	403	392	398	387	4,696
1978	368	336	386	304	288	271	261	304	275	287	274	267	3,620
1979	265	212	245	201	188	162	190	216	193	225	210	192	2,499
1980	212	187	201	185	161	154	186	182	198	229	185	214	2,294
1981[1]	215	192	213	190	159	175	204	198	228	236	217	254	2,478
1982[1]	———702———			———609———			———692———			———726———			2,729
1983[1]	221	204											

[1] Preliminary. Source: Crop Reporting Board, U.S.D.A. T.67

Average Price Received by Farmers for Beef Cattle In Dollars Per 100 Pounds

Year	Jan.	Feb.	Mar.	Apr.	May	June	July	Aug.	Sept.	Oct.	Nov.	Dec.	Average[1]
1972	31.80	32.90	32.50	32.20	33.30	34.50	34.60	33.60	34.00	34.40	33.00	34.80	33.50
1973	37.90	40.70	43.80	42.80	43.60	43.90	44.60	51.70	46.70	42.70	39.60	37.70	43.00
1974	44.20	43.60	40.70	39.20	37.30	32.60	35.30	37.00	32.60	30.60	28.20	27.70	35.80
1975	27.40	26.80	27.80	31.60	35.30	36.80	35.20	32.30	34.00	33.40	32.30	33.50	32.20
1976	32.80	33.90	33.40	38.00	37.10	36.40	33.60	33.00	32.30	32.20	31.20	32.40	33.90
1977	32.20	33.20	33.80	35.30	36.30	34.00	34.90	34.50	34.70	35.10	34.30	35.50	34.40
1978	37.70	40.50	44.00	47.20	50.50	51.10	50.10	49.30	52.20	53.20	51.90	54.60	48.50
1979	60.20	64.70	70.60	73.40	71.90	66.80	65.50	62.20	66.80	64.60	63.90	64.40	66.10
1980	63.80	67.00	64.40	60.60	60.70	61.10	63.20	64.40	63.00	62.10	60.00	59.40	62.40
1981	60.40	59.40	58.20	61.00	60.50	61.40	60.50	59.70	58.80	55.70	54.50	52.00	58.60
1982	53.50	56.30	58.60	61.70	62.60	61.10	58.80	58.10	55.60	53.80	52.60	52.50	56.70
1983[2]	54.30	57.10	59.70	61.90									

[1] Weighted average by quantities sold. [2] Preliminary. Source: Crop Reporting Board, U.S.D.A. T.68

Average Price Received by Farmers for Calves In Dollars Per 100 Pounds

Year	Jan.	Feb.	Mar.	Apr.	May	June	July	Aug.	Sept.	Oct.	Nov.	Dec.	Average[1]
1973	49.40	53.00	58.50	56.60	58.90	58.50	59.20	68.20	61.20	57.70	52.80	50.10	57.00
1974	54.10	53.30	49.60	47.40	42.70	37.40	36.00	34.30	30.10	27.70	25.70	25.00	38.60
1975	23.90	24.50	24.80	26.90	29.10	29.10	27.70	25.40	26.90	26.60	28.30	30.00	26.90
1976	30.80	33.80	34.80	38.20	38.80	37.70	34.90	34.20	32.90	33.00	32.10	32.80	34.50
1977	33.40	35.70	36.60	38.20	38.40	35.80	36.40	37.10	38.00	37.20	36.80	37.50	36.90
1978	41.00	44.90	50.00	53.70	59.50	58.70	60.10	61.90	65.70	66.40	67.20	72.10	59.10
1979	79.10	87.00	94.80	98.20	99.50	92.30	91.20	87.20	90.00	86.90	86.30	84.30	88.70
1980	86.90	90.90	82.60	75.50	75.40	76.90	75.40	75.60	74.30	73.90	72.10	70.30	76.80
1981	70.40	70.60	68.80	69.60	66.00	66.30	62.00	62.30	61.40	59.00	59.40	57.70	64.00
1982[2]	57.00	58.90	61.90	62.10	64.20	61.70	60.40	61.80	59.00	58.30	58.10	58.80	59.80
1983[2]	62.40	66.50	68.40	67.20									

[1] Weighted average by quantities sold. [2] Preliminary. Source: Crop Reporting Board, U.S.D.A. T.69

Cement

U.S. production of cement (portland, masonry, and other) in 1982 was about 12 percent smaller than in 1981, according to preliminary U.S. Bureau of Mines data. Six states accounted for 50 percent of the portland cement production; Texas, California, Pennsylvania, Missouri, Michigan, and Florida, in order of tonnage.

Total U.S. demand for cement in 1982 was at its lowest level in 20 years, primarily because of reduced industrial and commercial construction resulting from high interest rates and the generally depressed economy. Total 1982 domestic shipments of portland cement were 10 percent less than in 1981 and 27 percent below the 1973 record level. Masonry shipments were 12 percent less than in the preceding year and 42 percent below the 1973 record. Production capacity utilization declined to about 63 percent in 1982. Consumption remained near the 1981 level only in the West South Central states. Uses for domestic cement in 1982 were: ready-mixed concrete, 69 percent; concrete products such as block, pipe, and prestressed precast concrete, 12 percent; building material dealers, 6 percent; highway contractors, 4 percent; and others, 8 percent.

U.S. demand for cement is expected to increase at an average annual rate (from a 1980 base) of about 2 percent through 1990. According to a preliminary U.S. Bureau of Mines estimate, domestic production of cement in 1983 will be 70 million tons and U.S. apparent consumption 72 million tons.

The trend toward consolidation of the cement industry continued in 1982 through acquisition of companies and plants by large firms, some of which are foreign owned. To increase efficiency and economy of energy use, cement producers continued to incorporate preheaters, some with flash calciners, and dry-process kilns into new plants and modernization programs, and to convert to coal and coke as kiln fuel.

World Production of Hydraulic Cement by Selected Countries   In Millions of Short Tons

Year	Belgium	Brazil	Canada	China	France	W. Germany	India	Italy	Japan	Poland	Spain	Rep. of So. Afr.	Un. Kingdom	United States	USSR	World Total
1970	7.4	9.9	7.9	11.0	32.0	42.2	14.9	36.5	63.0	13.4	18.4	6.3	18.8	74.6	105.0	629.6
1971	7.6	10.8	9.1	25.3	31.9	45.2	16.4	35.1	65.5	14.4	18.9	6.5	19.5	80.3	110.6	679.9
1972	7.8	12.5	10.0	25.4	33.0	47.6	17.4	36.9	73.1	15.4	21.6	6.7	19.9	84.6	115.0	723.8
1973	7.8	14.8	11.1	27.6	33.9	45.2	16.5	40.0	86.1	17.1	24.7	7.6	22.0	87.6	120.7	773.8
1974	8.4	16.4	11.4	27.6	35.6	39.7	15.7	40.0	80.6	18.5	24.5	8.0	19.6	82.9	126.9	775.2
1975	7.6	19.2	11.0	33.1	32.6	36.9	17.9	37.7	72.2	20.4	26.6	7.9	18.6	69.7	134.5	774.0
1976	8.3	21.1	10.6	54.3	32.4	39.0	20.6	40.0	75.7	21.8	27.8	7.8	17.4	74.5	137.0	834.3
1977	8.6	23.3	10.6	61.3	31.8	36.8	21.0	42.1	80.6	23.5	30.9	7.2	17.0	80.1	140.1	878.6
1978	8.4	24.6	11.4	71.9	30.9	38.9	21.6	42.1	93.6	23.9	33.3	7.5	17.5	85.5	139.9	940.2
1979	8.5	27.4	13.0	81.5	31.8	40.4	20.1	43.3	96.8	21.1	30.8	7.6	17.8	85.9	135.6	959.3
1980	8.2	30.0	11.6	88.0	32.1	39.2	19.5	46.0	97.0	20.3	31.4	7.9	16.3	76.7	137.8	974.8
1981[1]	8.3	31.4	11.4	92.6	31.1	36.4	22.9	46.3	93.5	15.7	31.5	8.8	14.6	72.9	140.0	978.9
1982[2]				95.0	30.0	36.0		45.0	94.0		30.0		14.0	64.0	140.0	980.0
1983																

[1] Preliminary.   [2] Estimate.   Source: Bureau of Mines   T.70

Salient Statistics of Cement in the United States

Year	Net Import Reliance as a % of Apparent Consumption	Production Portland Million Tons	Production Others[2] Million Tons	Production Total Million Tons	Capacity Used[3] %	Shipments From Mills Total Mil. Tons	Shipments From Mills Value[4] $ Mil.	Average Value (F.O.B. Mill) $ per Ton	Stocks at Mills Dec. 31 Million Tons	Imports[5] Million Tons	Exports[5] Million Tons	Apparent Consumption Million Tons	Cement Rock Mil. Short Tons	Limestone[6] Mil. Short Tons	Clay & Shale Mil. Short Tons	Total (All) Mil. Short Tons
1970		73.2	2.9	74.3	88.4	74.6	1,336	17.91	7.6	2.5	.1	75.9	22.8	83.2	11.8	127.2
1971		77.0	3.3	78.3	87.7	80.4	1,528	19.01	6.4	3.1	.1	81.5	23.1	85.9	11.8	130.3
1972		80.7	3.8	82.6	90.6	83.3	1,724	20.69	7.0	4.9	.1	85.0	25.9	84.9	12.2	136.9
1973		83.6	1.9	85.5	83.2	88.7	1,975	22.28	5.5	6.6	.3	90.7	26.1	85.7	12.0	138.2
1974		79.5	1.4	80.9	74.8	81.0	2,151	26.54	7.5	5.7	.2	82.9	23.4	87.7	11.8	137.2
1975	4	66.8	1.3	68.1	62.9	69.1	2,159	31.25	6.9	3.6	.4	70.1	17.9	76.4	10.1	114.9
1976	5	71.2	1.8	73.0	68.4	73.7	2,510	34.07	7.2	3.1	.3	74.1	20.2	81.3	10.7	122.6
1977	6	76.3	2.3	78.6	81.6	80.2	2,932	36.54	6.0	4.0	.2	81.5	25.1	81.5	10.8	128.0
1978	7	81.4	2.6	84.0	77.5	86.6	3,544	40.94	5.3	6.6	.1	87.6	34.4	78.5	11.2	135.6
1979	11	82.1	2.4	84.5	77.1	85.7	3,992	46.55	6.6	9.4	.1	87.8	31.0	81.1	11.3	136.5
1980	6	72.2	3.0	75.2	68.9	76.2	3,886	50.98	6.8	5.2	.2	77.6	25.0	78.3	10.4	126.0
1981[1]	4	68.9	2.8	71.7	66.9	71.7	3,723	51.89	7.4	4.0	.3	73.3	26.6	73.0	9.4	120.6
1982[7]	3			63.0		64.6		52.00	7.7	2.5	.2	65.0				
1983																

[1] Preliminary.   [2] Masonry, natural & pozzolan (slag-line).   [3] At Portland-cement mills.   [4] Value received f.o.b. mill, excluding cost of containers.   [5] Hydraulic cement.   [6] Including oyster shells.   [7] Estimate.   Source: Bureau of Mines   T.71

79

CEMENT

Shipments of Finished Portland Cement from Mills in the United States   In Millions of Barrels

Year	Jan.	Feb.	Mar.	Apr.	May	June	July	Aug.	Sept.	Oct.	Nov.	Dec.	Total[1]
1970	17.1	20.2	25.7	32.9	36.4	39.7	42.3	41.6	38.2	39.1	29.9	26.4	390.5
1971	17.3	19.4	28.3	36.2	37.8	44.1	42.2	45.1	42.6	43.1	36.0	26.2	420.2
1972	22.4	23.9	32.2	34.6	42.2	45.0	42.3	50.4	44.4	46.0	33.2	24.1	440.5
1973	23.9	24.8	33.6	36.1	46.5	47.2	47.6	53.1	43.4	50.2	38.6	26.5	472.0
1974	22.2	24.6	31.8	38.6	43.1	43.4	42.7	45.2	41.6	45.5	30.7	23.2	431.9
1975	19.2	17.6	21.8	28.8	34.1	36.3	38.9	39.2	38.9	41.7	28.3	22.8	367.1
1976	17.7	20.5	28.1	33.1	34.5	39.9	38.6	41.8	38.9	37.4	31.7	23.2	385.7
1977	14.0	20.9	31.3	35.7	40.2	45.1	40.5	45.5	42.0	43.2	34.5	26.1	418.8
1978	15.3	18.5	31.5	37.2	44.9	49.8	43.8	50.3	44.6	48.5	37.9	29.0	451.3
1979	16.6	18.7	32.4	35.8	44.6	48.2	45.3	50.3	43.1	49.6	38.1	29.2	451.4
1980	22.0	22.1	26.0	33.0	36.3	39.3	39.8	39.6	40.5	43.3	31.8	28.2	404.6
1981	20.7	20.8	30.2	35.2	34.2	38.1	38.9	37.5	37.3	36.3	29.6	23.5	382.7
1982	15.1	17.8	25.7	28.2	31.0	35.4	34.5	36.0	35.4	34.1	27.4	22.7	343.5
1983	18.9												
1984													

[1] Does not necessarily agree with monthly figures. These are compiled from producers' annual reports and are final.   Source: Bureau of Mines
T.73

Index of Wholesale Price of Portland Cement[1]   Base Per Ton 1967 = 100

Year	Jan.	Feb.	Mar.	Apr.	May	June	July	Aug.	Sept.	Oct.	Nov.	Dec.	Average
1970	3.737	3.735	3.734	3.734	3.741	3.741	3.741	3.741	3.741	3.741	3.741	3.733	3.738
1971	3.983	3.963	3.957	3.958	3.958	3.958	4.059	4.088	4.092	4.092	4.094	4.094[2]	4.025
1972[1]	127.8	128.1	128.1	131.5	131.8	131.9	132.1	134.0	134.2	134.2	134.3	134.3	131.9
1973	134.4	134.4	135.3	138.4	137.6	137.6	137.9	137.9	137.9	138.2	138.3	138.3	137.2
1974	149.5	151.2	151.7	155.5	155.8	156.2	169.8	169.9	170.3	171.1	171.1	171.1	161.9
1975	187.0	189.3	189.4	191.9	193.1	193.1	195.2	195.0	196.5	196.3	196.1	196.1	193.3
1976	203.4	204.0	204.0	212.0	212.0	212.1	214.7	214.7	214.7	214.5	214.5	214.6	211.3
1977	221.1	221.4	221.4	225.4	227.8	227.8	228.8	229.0	229.0	228.9	228.7	228.7	226.5
1978	240.6	240.9	241.1	248.6	248.6	248.6	251.7	254.8	255.7	256.2	253.7	253.7	249.5
1979	275.5	278.9	280.5	283.3	283.3	283.8	285.5	285.5	285.5	285.5	285.5	286.3	283.3
1980	305.8	305.9	306.3	312.6	313.9	313.9	313.3	313.1	312.2	311.7	310.4	310.4	310.8
1981	324.3	324.2	324.3	332.4	332.3	330.9	331.5	331.5	331.9	330.2	330.2	330.2	329.5
1982	336.3	338.2	341.4	341.1	341.8	341.8	339.5	337.9	337.1	334.5	334.8	328.9	337.9
1983	324.2	327.6											
1984													

[1] Prior to 1972 prices are $ per 376 pound barrel.   [2] Price index for Dec. 1971 is 127.8.   Source: Bureau of Labor Statistics (1322-0131.99)
T.74

How to keep your Commodity Year Book statistics up-to-date continuously throughout the year.

To keep up-to-date statistics on the commodities in this book, you should have COMMODITY YEAR BOOK STATISTICAL ABSTRACT SERVICE. This three-times-yearly publication provides the latest available statistics for updating the statistical tables appearing in the COMMODITY YEAR BOOK. The ABSTRACT is published in the Winter (Jan.), Spring (Apr.) and Fall (Oct.). Subscription price is $55 per year.

Commodity Research Bureau, Inc.
75 MONTGOMERY ST., JERSEY CITY, N.J. 07302

Cheese

In 1982, the Bureau of Labor Standards index of wholesale dairy price averaged 248.9 (1967=100), an increase of nearly 1.3 percent from its 1981 average, the smallest increase since 1965. Increases in the wholesale price of cheese during 1982 just about matched this increase in the wholesale dairy price index. Early in 1983, the price of cheddar cheese (Wisconsin assembly points, 40-pound blocks) averaged $1.34 a pound, nearly 3.5 cents lower than during the comparable period in 1982, and 5.4 cents below the price two years earlier.

Cheese production rose by nearly 5 percent in 1982. Creamed cottage cheese was the only cheese product the output of which was lower than in 1981. On the other hand, the production of Italian-type cheese, figured on a percentage basis, rose by a considerable 8 percent during the year, and the overall production of non-American-type cheeses rose by 7.3 percent compared with the 0.7 percent gain recorded in 1981. American-type cheese production rose by 3.2 percent in 1982 compared with its 10 percent increase the year before. An estimated 80 percent of the net increase in milk going into manufactured products, on a milk-equivalent basis, went into the manufacture of cheese.

Uncommitted U.S. cheese stocks as of the third quarter of 1982 totaled 825.1 million pounds, up from the 554.4 million pound level of the comparable period in 1981. Stocks of American-type cheese declined by 10 percent in 1982 compared to 1981 levels. Commercial stocks of American-type cheese in the third quarter of 1982 were 56 percent of commercial disappearance compared with 70 percent a year earlier. During the same period, the usage of American-type cheese was up by 3 percent, while the usage of other types of cheese was up by 5 percent.

U.S. cheese imports rose 17 percent in 1982. Figured on a product-weight basis, 269.3 million pounds of quota and non-quota cheese were imported during 1982, 9 percent higher than the 1981 level. World cheese stocks at the end of 1983 were expected to increase slightly due to the sharp gain in U.S. government-owned inventories. Competition in world cheese markets reportedly picked up early in 1983, and traders were alert for any signs that the U.S. might be preparing to sell part of its high inventory abroad. Excepting the 9,400 metric tonnes of cheese exported to Poland in 1981 and 1982, however, no CCC stocks have been exported since the mid-1960's.

U.S. government donations of cheese totaled 316 million pounds in 1981/82, and 142 million pounds were placed in the special "cheese giveaway" program. An estimated 280 million pounds of cheese will be available to needy persons in 1983.

World Cheese (Total[1]) Production   In Millions of Metric Tons[3]

Year	Argentina	Australia	Canada	China	Czechoslovakia	Denmark	France	W. Germany	Italy	Netherlands	New Zealand	USSR	Sweden	Switzerland	United Kingdom	United States
1972	205	81	163		80	131	871	545	424	322	104	483	66	96	184	1,181
1973	206	93	165		85	124	885	558	435	333	101	536	68	97	182	1,218
1974	211	96	130		86	145	917	595	543	376	89	565	70	100	215	1,333
1975	226	99	121		90	147	943	618	529	375	89	559	81	104	239	1,275
1976	240	113	125	203	96	152	978	650	537	382	105	655	84	111	204	1,506
1977	236	104	133	208	99	172	1,023	691	553	412	81	655	87	115	207	1,523
1978	239	112	140	210	98	177	1,063	354	583	420	81	691	94	121	216	1,597
1979	239	132	167	215	99	189	1,117	387	601	432	90	701	96	125	234	1,686
1980	245	142	177	270	109	221	1,145	421	615	443	106	678	100	125	237	1,807
1981[2]	240	135	176		110	243	1,178	453	615	465	84	685	108	125	245	1,907
1982[3]	240	135	178		108	233	1,210	480	610	485	112	680	108	125	250	1,955

[1] Farm & factory production.   [2] Preliminary.   [3] Estimate.   *Source: Foreign Agricultural Service, U.S.D.A.*   T.75

Supply and Distribution of All Cheese in the United States   In Millions of Pounds

	Supply					Distribution				Domestic Disapp.		Amer. Cheese Removed
	Production		Jan. 1 Commercial Stocks	Imports[4]	Total Supply	Exports & Shipments[5]	Dept. of Agriculture				Civilian Per Capita	by U.S.D.A. Programs
Year	Whole Milk[2]	All Cheese[3]					Jan. 1 Stocks	Dec. 31 Stocks	Deliveries	Total Disap.	Military	Civilian		
1971	1,512	2,374	323	136	2,833	29	1	6		2,527	12	2,486	12.2	91
1972	1,644	2,604	301	179	3,085	30	6	—		2,759	10	2,719	13.2	30
1973	1,673	2,685	331	230	3,246	30	—	—		2,888	9	2,849	13.7	3
1974	1,859	2,937	358	316	3,611	36	—	1		3,117	10	3,044	14.4	60
1975	1,655	2,811	494	179	3,484	33	1	2		3,115	10	3,009	14.2	68
1976	2,049	3,321	369	207	3,897	35	2	2		3,366	7	3,418	15.4	38
1977	2,043	3,358	479	210	4,047	38	2	61		3,513	9	3,560	15.5	148
1978	2,074	3,519	487	242	4,248	44	61	30		3,736	11	3,791	16.5	40
1979	2,190	3,717	457	248	4,422	47	30	3		3,838	24	3,909	17.2	40
1980	2,376	3,984	513	231	4,728	46	3	190		3,975	16	4,037	17.6	350
1981[1]	2,609	4,230	691	248	5,169	45	190	249		4,111	12	4,168	18.1	563
1982[1]	2,693	4,432	976	269	5,677		249					4,250	19.6	643
1983[1]			1,064											

[1] Preliminary.   [2] Whole milk American cheddar.   [3] All types of cheese except cottage, pot and baker's cheese.   [4] Imports for consumption.   [5] Commercial.   *Source: Department of Agriculture*   T.76

CHEESE

Cheese Production in the United States   In Millions of Pounds

Year	American Whole Milk	American Part Skim	American Total	Swiss, Including Block	Brick & Munster	Limburger	Neufchatel	Cream Cheese	Italian Varieties	Blue mold	All Other Varieties	Total of All Cheese[2]	Cottage Cheese Low-Fat	Curd[4]	Creamed[5]
1973	1,673	5.1	1,678	164.2	68.8	2.6	4.2	135.5	565.3	29.8	37.4	2,685	128.0	763.0	958
1974	1,859	3.7	1,862	175.3	72.2	2.4	3.6	146.7	606.1	28.3	40.5	2,937	121.9	689.7	856
1975	1,655	5.4	1,660	173.8	71.7	1.9	5.0	155.3	671.9	28.5	43.5	2,811	129.3	701.0	862
1976	2,049	5.0	2,054	196.3	74.5	1.9	3.6	164.4	747.4	33.9	44.4	3,320	135.4	711.1	875
1977	2,043	4.1	2,046	189.3	71.3	1.7	3.3	173.1	793.5	34.8	44.4	3,358	139.0	684.5	878
1978	1,069	4.9	2,074	209.4	76.2	1.6	3.9	194.3	875.7	35.3	44.2	3,520	153.1	688.4	871
1979	2,190	4.4	2,194	213.3	78.0	1.6	5.2	207.1	929.1	34.6	54.1	3,717	158.4	668.5	840
1980	2,376	5.4	2,381	218.9	85.4	1.6	4.3	224.3	982.7	33.0	52.9	3,984	179.8	667.4	825
1981[1]	2,609	5.9	2,615	214.4	81.2	1.2	—241.3—		994.4	30.2	51.8	4,229	208.3	647.5	773
1982[3]	2,693	6.9	2,700	221.1	85.9	1.5	—262.7—		1,087.8	31.0	92.4	4,540	217.6	682.9	749

[1] Preliminary.   [2] Excludes full-skim cheddar and cottage cheese.   [3] Estimated.   [4] Includes cottage, pot, and baker's cheese with a butterfat content of less than 4%.   [5] Includes cheese with a butterfat content of 4 to 19%.   *Source: Agricultural Marketing Service, U.S.D.A.*   T.77

United States Total Cheese Production[1]   In Millions of Pounds

Year	Jan.	Feb.	Mar.	Apr.	May	June	July	Aug.	Sept.	Oct.	Nov.	Dec.	Total
1973	204.5	194.3	230.4	241.1	266.3	266.7	236.7	216.2	187.4	202.7	205.4	233.7	2,685
1974	240.7	236.6	277.2	277.8	282.7	278.4	252.4	232.9	214.5	219.2	206.4	218.4	2,937
1975	214.3	204.2	240.7	244.4	271.0	275.0	249.2	226.9	214.8	220.2	208.7	242.0	2,811
1976	245.6	236.7	278.0	293.5	314.3	322.3	294.9	283.5	261.2	254.5	255.3	280.4	3,320
1977	265.6	252.5	299.7	304.7	326.1	316.0	280.2	275.7	251.7	256.9	247.8	281.6	3,359
1978	271.1	259.9	314.4	303.7	332.9	331.9	293.6	286.5	265.0	279.3	279.7	301.4	3,519
1979	292.5	272.2	323.0	318.8	340.4	343.8	318.8	309.0	290.7	308.0	289.4	308.7	3,715
1980	312.3	303.1	339.7	336.6	360.5	359.9	332.7	317.6	317.0	332.1	317.2	354.4	3,984
1981[2]	342.8	316.5	365.4	371.2	389.8	386.3	348.9	337.6	331.1	338.5	330.5	368.6	4,229
1982[2]	347.0	325.8	376.3	——— 1,178.8 ———			——— 1,099.5 ———			——— 1,104.6 ———			4,432
1983[2]	374.9												

[1] Excludes cottage and full skim American.   [2] Preliminary.   *Source: Statistical Reporting Service, U.S.D.A.*   T.78

Wholesale Price of American Cheese, Fresh Single Daisies at Chicago   In Cents Per Pound

Year	Jan.	Feb.	Mar.	Apr.	May	June	July	Aug.	Sept.	Oct.	Nov.	Dec.	Average
1973	74.5	74.6	76.5	78.3	79.2	80.2	80.1	84.7	89.8	94.4	97.1	102.0	84.3
1974	104.8	103.9	105.9	104.8	97.9	89.2	88.8	89.8	94.5	96.5	96.2	94.6	97.3
1975	93.6	94.6	95.2	96.8	98.7	100.6	103.0	106.4	111.9	116.4	116.9	119.2	104.4
1976	118.2	108.2	113.8	116.6	114.6	115.3	120.0	125.8	118.3	114.2	114.0	114.0	116.1
1977	114.0	114.0	115.2	119.3	119.3	119.4	119.4	119.4	120.5	120.6	121.1	122.4	118.7
1978	122.9	124.1	124.6	125.9	125.9	125.9	126.0	132.1	134.0	139.4	140.0	141.0	130.1
1979	141.0	135.0	135.6	137.4	137.6	138.9	140.9	145.8	148.8	146.6	144.7	144.4	141.4
1980	146.7	147.2	150.8	153.5	154.2	154.8	155.5	157.0	161.5	165.3	164.1	164.1	156.2
1981	164.0	164.0	166.9	167.0	167.8	167.9	167.8	167.8	167.8	168.5	169.2	168.4	167.2
1982	168.4	168.4	168.4	168.4	168.4	168.4	168.4	168.4	168.3	168.6	168.6	168.6	168.4
1983	168.0	166.6											

Source: Statistical Reporting Service, U.S.D.A.   T.79

Cold Storage Holdings of All Varieties of Cheese in the U.S., on First of Month   In Millions of Pounds[2]

Year	Jan.	Feb.	Mar.	Apr.	May	June	July	Aug.	Sept.	Oct.	Nov.	Dec.
1973	331.4	324.6	321.0	302.4	303.4	330.6	374.2	392.9	395.5	382.3	371.0	356.0
1974	357.8	366.8	395.5	438.9	489.5	533.4	570.7	566.0	552.4	539.1	512.1	502.2
1975	494.0	485.9	458.5	447.5	441.0	454.8	475.1	477.6	449.7	422.2	388.3	378.5
1976	367.8	362.3	362.3	367.9	393.7	436.1	483.7	509.0	518.0	522.6	501.4	482.0
1977	478.4	485.7	471.2	485.8	510.3	557.2	583.7	592.9	592.9	553.9	502.8	479.8
1978	468.6	459.6	442.0	430.0	447.1	462.5	500.2	498.5	489.7	476.6	455.2	431.0
1979	436.4	436.6	446.2	448.6	462.2	495.3	519.9	555.3	548.5	540.6	526.9	528.2
1980	512.1	515.8	508.9	495.1	510.5	544.4	582.7	620.0	613.8	610.6	590.9	565.4
1981[1]	578.8	601.7	596.3	593.6	631.9	649.8	685.7	714.2	720.9	694.3	682.4	677.5
1982[1]	709.6	711.7	696.4	722.4	—	—	804.4	—	—	871.2	—	—
1983[1]	963.6	1,015.5	1,073.5	1,017.9	1,028.8							

[1] Preliminary.   [2] Quantities are given in "net weight."   *Source: Crop Reporting Board, U.S.D.A.*   T.80

Chromite

Chromite is the only source of commercial chromium, a highly versatile industrial and strategic metal. The U.S. continued to be one of the world's leading consumers of chromite during 1982. Most of the U.S. chromium resources is in the Stillwater Complex in Montana and in beach sands in Oregon. However, the domestic mining production of chromite is virtually nil.

World resources amount to about 36 billion short tons of shipping-grade chromite—conceivably sufficient to meet world demand for centuries. Over 99 percent of these resources are found in southern Africa; the Republic of South Africa controls nearly 26 billion tons, and Zimbabwe controls over 11 billion. Between 1978 and 1981, the U.S. imported 44 percent of its chromite and 71 percent of its ferrochromium from the Republic of South Africa. The Soviet Union supplied 18 percent of U.S. chromite imports during the same period.

Chromium is essential to the manufacture of various alloy steels and heat- and corrosion-resistant materials. Most super-alloys used in nuclear reactors, in rocket and jet engines, and in pollution control equipment are partly chromium. The U.S. demand for chromium during 1982 dropped to its lowest level in twenty years because of depressed conditions in the steel industry, the major domestic consumer of chromium. The amount of chromium used by the U.S. metallurgical industry was down by nearly 40 percent compared with 1981. It is estimated by the Bureau of Mines that the U.S. apparent consumption of chromium during 1983 will be 340,000 tons. The quoted price of chromium metal remained unchanged, between $3.75 and $4.45, during 1982.

During 1982, the Bureau of Mines conducted research of techniques for the recovery of chromium from laterites and low-grade ores. Other Bureau studies included the development of chromium-free and low-chromium alloys as substitutes for stainless steel, the reclamation of chromium from stainless steel, and the recovery of chromium from metallurgical and mining wastes. It was announced in December 1982, as an outcome of a Department of Commerce investigation of the U.S. ferroalloy industry, that the General Services Administration (GSA) would begin a program of upgrading stockpiled chromium ore into high-carbon ferrochromium. The 4 cent per pound penalty duty on high-carbon ferrochromium imported at below 38 cents per pound expired in November 1982.

U.S. industry stocks of chromite as of the end of 1982 were 459,149 short tons, 31 percent below the 663,806 short tons of total stock for the previous year.

World Mine Production of Chromite   In Thousands of Short Tons

Year	Albania	Brazil	Cuba	Finland	Greece	India	Japan	Pakistan	Philippines	Zimbabwe	Turkey	South Africa	Iran	USSR	Madagascar	World Total[1]
1971	553		22		16	288	35	27	474	600	665	1,812	194	1,980		7,093
1972	615		22		24	325	27	29	385	600	435	1,635	198	2,040		6,725
1973	674		22		20	317	26	19	640	600	481	1,818	154	2,100		7,381
1974	788	119	22	182	11	437	29	11	584	650	734	2,069	193	2,150	172	8,224
1975	859	191	35	365	39	551	26	11	573	650	790	2,288	190	2,290	214	9,136
1976	915	205	21	193	38	443	24	12	475	952	640	2,656	176	2,300	244	9,362
1977	970	342	22	443	46	389	20	9	593	746	560	3,372	257	2,400	182	10,415
1978	1,090	297	32	449	41	293	10	12	595	527	413	3,466	218	2,550	152	10,210
1979	1,120	375	31	479	49	341	13	3	613	597	500	3,634	150	2,550	141	10,676
1980	1,190	316	33	376	47	352	15	3	547	608	440	3,763	90	2,700	198	10,746
1981[2]	1,260	450	32	455	47	370	12	3	490	580	440	3,160	33	2,650	175	10,225
1982[1]				450					400	550	400	2,900				9,700

[1] Estimate.   [2] Preliminary.   *Source: Bureau of Mines*   T.81

U.S. Salient Statistics of Chromite   In Thousands of Short Tons

Year	% Net Import Reliance of Apparent Consumption	Shipments from Gov't Stockpiles	Exports	Imports (For Consumption)	Re-exports	Consumption Total	Metallurgical	Refractory	Chemical	Stocks Metallurgical	Stocks Refractory	Stocks Chemical	Total Stocks	$ Per Metric Tn. South Africa[2]
1971		268	35	1,299	145	1,093	720	193	180	667	233	119	1,019	25–27
1972		191	20	1,056	57	1,140	727	224	189	601	160	96	857	24–27
1973		285	21	931	34	1,387	920	261	206	339	154	104	597	34
1974		500	18	1,102	99	1,447	904	295	251	340	169	64	573	50
1975	91	418	139	1,252	45	881	532	183	166	701	154	97	952	35
1976	89	311	124	1,275	85	1,006	597	202	207	762	136	111	1,009	39
1977	91	517	187	1,293	61	1,000	578	208	214	900	174	264	1,338	59
1978	91	—	23	1,013	29	1,010	534	237	239	755	185	361	1,301	56
1979	90	—	27	1,024	28	1,209	774	193	242	416	161	330	907	56
1980	91	—	6	982	44	968	573	155	240	219	134	322	675	55
1981[1]	90	—	71	898	67	879	501	139	239	174	119	370	653	55
1982[3]	88	—	8	507		535	270	72	192	64	112	283	459	52

[1] Preliminary.   [2] Cr_2O_3, 44% (Transvaal).   [3] Estimate.   *Source: Bureau of Mines*   T.82

Coal

The U.S. Energy Information Administration (EIA) estimated that the 1982 U.S. production of coal was approximately 824.0 million short tons, only fractionally above the 1981 level of output. The 1982 figure included nearly 819.8 million short tons of bituminous, or soft coal, and lignite, as well as approximately 4.2 million short tons of Pennsylvania anthracite. Bituminous coal, the most common type of coal, is used for generating electricity, making coke, and for space heating. Bituminous coal has a dense, black appearance and its ignition temperature is 700–800 degrees F. Anthracite coal, mined exclusively in Pennsylvania, is a hard, jet-black material with an ignition temperature of 900 degrees F. Anthracite is also used to generate electricity and for space heating. Lignite, a brownish-black coal with a high moisture content, is used mostly to generate electricity.

Early projections of the U.S. 1982 coal output were over 7 percent above the 1981 production, which had been curtailed by a prolonged United Mine Workers' strike. These estimates evidently had not fully reckoned the sharply reduced demand for coal from the depressed industrial markets. Coal consumption by electric utilities, after having increased at an annual rate of 39 million short tons throughout the previous three years, declined 0.3 percent in the first ten months of 1982. Raw steel production in the first three quarters was down nearly 39 percent, and coal consumption by coke plants was accordingly lower by almost 29 percent than it had been during the same period in 1981. U.S. coal receipts in the first quarter of 1982, the amount of coal delivered to or purchased by end-use sectors, was lower by over 6 percent. However early-1981 receipts were high because of increased buying in anticipation of the coal miners' strike.

Preliminary projections indicated a decline of over 4 percent in the combined industrial and non-industrial U.S. demand for coal in 1982. Despite the radical drop in crude oil prices during 1982, coal remained a competitively-priced fuel, and electric utility coal consumption was projected as rising to nearly 4 percent above the 1981 level in order to accommodate an expected increased demand for electricity and to replace oil and natural gas fuels for electric power generation. An increased level of hydroelectric generation was expected to displace nearly 2 million short tons of coal in the last half of 1982, and approximately 11.1 gigawatts of coal-fired capacity was expected to come onstream during the year. U.S. coke plants were expected to use 11 percent less coal than in 1981, and the overall level of domestic coal consumption during 1982 projected to be around a 44-year low.

Private estimates put stocks of coal at U.S. mines and distributors at a record 40 million tons at the end of 1982 compared with the usual inventory of between 20 and 25 million tons. Higher inventories of coal were expected to keep 1983 U.S. production from increasing more than 1 percent above the 1982 level. The domestic consumption of coal was expected to increase by almost 5 percent during 1983.

U.S. coal exports were approximately 105 million tons in 1982, and projections of 1983 U.S. exports were nearly 12 percent lower, partly due to expectations of a generally stronger U.S. dollar.

World Production of Coal (Bituminous & Lignite)   In Millions of Metric[3] Tons

Year	Australia	E. Germany	Canada	Czechoslovakia	France	W. Germany	India	Japan	China	Poland	South Africa	Un. Kingdom	United States	U.S.S.R.	Yugoslavia
1975	104.9		27.9	126.9	22.3	229.4	108.9	20.9	495.0	233.1	74.8	139.1	648.4	688.2	
1976[3]	98.7	247.3	25.5	117.7	26.5	224.1	104.8	18.4	462.7	218.6	76.0	123.8	621.3	654.4	36.9
1977	100.2	254.1	28.5	121.2	26.1	209.5	103.9	18.3	475.4	226.9	87.1	122.1	632.8	663.3	37.3
1978	104.7	253.4	30.6	123.2	23.9	208.7	105.2	19.0	569.7	233.6	90.6	123.6	599.0	664.4	39.7
1979	106.0	256.1	33.2	124.7	21.1	216.9	106.7	17.7		239.1	105.5	122.8	708.5	657.6	42.1
1980	111.3	258.1	36.7	123.2	20.9	217.0	113.7	18.0		230.0	116.0	130.1	752.7	652.9	45.8
1981[1]	133.8	267.0	40.1	122.5	21.6	219.1	129.1	17.7		198.6	131.2	127.8	744.0	670.0	52.2
1982[2]	140	270	43	120	20	222	134	19		220	135	124.7	760	690	55

[1] Estimate.   [2] Preliminary.   [3] Data prior to 1976 are in millions of short tons.   *Sources: Bureau of Mines; United Nations.*   T.83

Salient Statistics of the Bituminous Coal Industry in the United States

Year	Underground	By Augers	By Stripping	Total Production	Total Million $	Avg. Per Ton $	Number of Mines	Thous. of Men Employed	Avg. Number of Days Worked	Net Tons Per Man	Imports	Grand Total	Canada	Europe	Asia
	(Million Net Tons)											(Thousands of Net Tons)			
1975	293	40.7	315	648	12,472	19.23	6,168	189.9	232	14.74	940	65,669	16,735	18,972	25,943
1976	295	—384—		679	13,189	19.43	6,161	202.3	232	14.46	1,203	59,406	16,497	20,026	19,271
1977	266	—425—		691	13,705	19.82	6,077	221.4	210	14.84	1,647	53,687	17,000	N.A.	N.A.
1978	242	—423—		665	14,486	21.78	6,230	242.3	166	14.68	2,953	39,848	15,239	10,449	11,344
1979[1]	320	—456—		776	18,243	23.65	5,837	224.2	227	15.33	2,059	64,809	19,158	22,744	17,608
1980[2]	337	—487—		824	21,580	24.52	5,598	224.9	225	16.32	1,194	89,947	17,039	40,414	25,481
1981[2]	320	—495—		818							1,043	110,292	17,856	56,130	31,010
1982[2]				829							742	105,297			

[1] Preliminary.   [2] Estimate.   *Source: Bureau of Mines; Dept. of Commerce*   T.84

COAL

United States Production of Coal by Principal States   In Millions of Short Tons

Year	Anthracite Pennsylvania	Alabama	Colorado	Illinois	Indiana	Kentucky	Montana	Ohio	Pennsylvania	Virginia	West Virginia	Tennessee	Wyoming	Total Bituminous	Total U.S.
1971	8.7	17.9	5.3	58.4	21.4	119.4		51.4	72.8	30.6	118.3	9.3		552.2	560.9
1972	7.1	20.8	5.5	65.5	25.9	121.2		51.0	75.9	34.0	123.7	11.3		595.4	602.5
1973	6.8	19.2	6.2	61.6	25.3	127.6		45.8	76.6	34.0	115.4	8.2		591.7	598.6
1974	6.6	19.8	6.9	58.2	23.7	137.2		45.4	80.5	34.3	102.5	7.5		603.4	610.0
1975	6.2	22.6	8.2	59.5	25.1	143.6	22.1	46.8	84.1	35.5	109.3	8.2	23.8	648.4	654.6
1976	6.2	21.5	9.4	58.2	25.4	144.0	26.2	46.6	85.8	40.0	108.8	9.3	30.9	678.7	684.9
1977	5.9	21.5	12.0	53.5	27.8	146.3	27.2	47.9	84.6	37.6	95.4	9.4	46.0	691.3	697.2
1978	5.0	20.6	13.8	48.6	24.2	135.7	26.6	41.2	81.5	31.9	85.3	10.0	58.3	665.1	670.2
1979	4.8	23.9	18.1	59.5	27.5	149.8	32.5	43.5	89.2	37.0	112.4	9.3	71.8	776.3	781.1
1980	6.1	26.4	18.8	62.5	30.9	150.1	29.9	39.4	87.1	41.0	121.6	9.9	94.9	823.6	829.7
1981[2]	5.4	24.5	19.9	51.9	29.3	157.6	33.6	37.4	78.1	42.0	112.8	10.5	103.0	818.4	823.8
1982[1]	4.2	25.2	18.2	64.3	30.3	150.1	27.9	37.1	71.9	37.2	128.8	7.6	107.9	829.2	833.4
1983															

[1] Estimate.   [2] Preliminary.   Source: Bureau of Mines   T.85

U.S. Consumption & Stocks of Bituminous Coal & Lignite   In Millions of Short Tons

Year	Electric Power Utilities	Oven Coke Plants	Steel & Rolling Mills	Other Industrials	Producers & Distrib.	Total	Electric Power Utilities	Coke Plants Beehive	Coke Plants Ovens	Steel & Rolling Mills	Other Industrials	Retail Deliveries[2]	Total
1971							326.3	1.3	81.5	5.6	68.7	11.4	494.9
1972							348.6	1.1	86.2	4.9	67.1	8.7	516.8
1973						103.1	386.9	1.3	92.3	6.4	60.8	8.2	556.9
1974						95.2	390.1	1.3	88.4	6.2	57.8	8.8	553.0
1975	109.7	8.7	— 8.5 —			126.9	403.2	1.1	82.1	2.7	59.8	7.3	557.5
1976	116.4	9.8	— 7.1 —			133.3	447.0	.9	83.4	2.7	57.8	6.9	598.8
1977	130.9	12.7	—11.0—			154.7	475.7	.6	76.7	3.2	57.1	7.0	620.5
1978	126.0	8.2	— 9.0 —			143.2	480.2	.5	70.6	—62.2—		7.9	621.3
1979	156.4	10.0	—11.6—		20.3	178.1	526.0	—77.0—		—67.1—		7.1	677.3
1980	183.0	9.1	—12.0—		24.4	228.4	569.3	—66.7—		—60.3—		6.5	702.7
1981[1]	169.8	6.5	— 9.9 —		24.1	209.4	596.8	—61.0—		—67.4—		6.9	732.2
1982[3]	174.8	9.0	— 9.4 —		33.5	226.7	620.0	—54.6—		—69.2—		8.0	745.9
1983													

[1] Preliminary.   [2] To other consumers.   [3] Estimate.   Source: Bureau of Mines   T.86

U.S. Stocks of Bituminous Coal for All Industrial & Retail Dealers, at End of Month   In Million Short Tons

Year	Jan.	Feb.	Mar.	Apr.	May	June	July	Aug.	Sept.	Oct.	Nov.	Dec.
1971	88.3	85.8	89.5	97.1	102.9	107.1	102.8	111.4	117.0	100.4	85.6	90.0
1972	92.9	93.6	97.9	103.7	110.6	114.5	109.7	112.9	114.3	118.0	119.2	116.5
1973	111.1	108.9	111.5	112.6	116.9	110.0	107.5	106.9	106.2	107.5	107.1	103.1
1974	97.8	95.8	101.6	107.2	112.9	111.9	106.2	105.5	109.2	118.7	109.2	95.2
1975	95.5	97.0	97.8	102.7	109.7	114.9	109.1	108.5	111.9	120.3	125.8	126.9
1976	119.2	119.0	123.5	128.4	136.0	140.1	129.7	123.9	129.9	133.6	135.0	133.3
1977	118.1	114.4	122.6	129.9	137.7	146.0	137.5	136.8	145.3	158.5	173.3	154.7
1978	120.2	95.0	85.3	98.3	112.4	124.7	121.3	124.3	127.4	135.3	144.8	143.2
1979[1]	131.9	125.1	130.0	137.7	147.0	150.6	144.1	148.1	153.7	167.2	176.1	178.1
1980[1]	175.8	173.1	173.0	180.3	189.9	195.1	181.7	181.3	190.0	197.3	199.6	199.1
1981[1]	193.6	192.9	202.2	181.9	162.9	153.0	149.0	151.7	159.4	169.7	177.4	179.6
1982[2]	168.4	167.4	173.6	180.8	187.2	192.7	184.2	184.4	184.0	189.0	190.6	189.1

[1] Preliminary.   [2] Estimate.   Source: Bureau of Mines   T.87

COAL

Bituminous Coal Production[1] in the United States — In Millions of Short Tons

Year	Jan.	Feb.	Mar.	Apr.	May	June	July	Aug.	Sept.	Oct.	Nov.	Dec.	Total
1976	52.6	53.8	60.9	59.1	57.9	59.7	44.3	53.6	60.6	59.0	58.8	58.4	678.7
1977	44.7	49.2	66.8	60.5	62.5	63.1	49.6	57.8	69.5	67.7	69.0	31.0	691.3
1978	23.1	23.5	38.8	59.5	68.8	65.6	53.6	64.4	57.8	69.9	69.2	59.6	655.1
1979	56.5	53.6	65.5	62.8	67.9	69.4	54.5	72.1	63.9	75.9	67.6	60.3	776.3
1980[2]	67.8	64.3	69.9	69.9	70.4	71.4	60.7	70.2	68.3	71.7	68.1	71.6	823.6
1981[2]	65.3	70.0	77.3	36.9	37.3	61.9	73.3	78.2	79.8	86.1	76.0	76.0	818.4
1982[2]	65.7	69.6	82.2	72.4	69.9	70.5	59.1	71.4	66.5	68.8	63.4	60.2	819.8

[1] Includes small amount of lignite. [2] Preliminary. Source: Bureau of Mines   T.88

Average Wholesale Price of Anthracite Coal (Chestnut—F.O.B. Mine)   Index—1967 = 100[1]

Year	Jan.	Feb.	Mar.	Apr.	May	June	July	Aug.	Sept.	Oct.	Nov.	Dec.	Average
1977	46.550	46.550	46.550	46.550	46.550	46.650	46.650	46.579	46.579	46.579	46.579	46.579	46.579
1978	46.579	46.579	46.579	46.579	—	47.192	47.192	47.498	47.542	47.537	47.530	47.675	47.135
1979[1]	46.677	47.677	47.677	407.3[1]	407.6	407.6	407.6	409.7	413.8	413.8	418.6	423.7	411.0
1980	435.6	435.7	435.7	459.7	459.7	459.7	462.1	469.8	478.2	479.6	491.1	497.9	463.7
1981[2]	508.7	542.9	542.8	545.2	552.8	572.0	589.7	597.3	619.9	629.1	642.5	643.7	582.2
1982[2]	643.7	643.7	645.5	648.1	639.0	637.5	637.5	637.4	637.4	637.4	638.0	638.0	640.3
1983[2]	636.0	635.9											

[1] Prior to Apr. 1979 data are in DOLLARS PER SHORT TON. [2] Preliminary. Source: Bureau of Labor Statistics (0511-0101.02)   T.89

Average Wholesale Price of Bituminous[1] Coal (Screenings, Industrial Use)   Index—1967 = 100

Year	Jan.	Feb.	Mar.	Apr.	May	June	July	Aug.	Sept.	Oct.	Nov.	Dec.	Average
1976	368.9	368.0	366.9	366.1	366.4	365.4	366.5	366.6	366.8	367.2	368.0	373.0	367.5
1977	375.2	376.5	377.9	379.0	386.0	389.5	392.1	393.3	394.2	397.7	400.0	401.4	388.6
1978	403.2	404.4	406.5	426.4	432.4	434.5	437.2	441.9	442.9	444.1	442.4	444.0	430.0
1979	443.8	444.2	445.5	447.4	451.2	452.4	452.0	454.6	452.8	454.9	455.6	458.7	451.1
1980	459.1	459.4	461.6	464.4	465.9	465.9	466.7	467.8	470.2	469.6	474.0	473.8	466.5
1981[2]	476.0	477.9	478.3	483.4	484.4	488.2	501.9	503.2	506.8	506.0	507.6	510.2	493.7
1982[2]	520.6	525.3	525.0	527.9	529.6	529.3	533.9	534.9	537.3	533.9	536.2	536.2	531.0
1983[2]	528.1	530.4											

[1] Prices are for Screenings, industrial use, f.o.b. mine. [2] Preliminary. Source: Bureau of Labor Statistics (0512)   T.90

Statistical Trends in the Pennsylvania Anthracite Industry

Year	Production (Millions of Net Tons) Total	By Stripping	Loaded Mech. Under.	Value of Production Million $	Avg. Value Per Net Ton	Stocks (Dec. 31) Electric Utilities	Prod. & Distrib.	Exports to: Total	Canada	France	Netherlands	Italy	Apparent Consumption (1,000 Net Tons)	Avg. No. of Men Working Daily (1,000)	Avg. Number of Days Worked	Avg. Tons Per Man Per Day
1975	6.2	2.6	.3	198.5	32.26	982	59	640	544	39	16	11	5,106	3.9	214	7.45
1976	6.2	3.0	.3	209.2	33.92	1,000	33	615	445	105	16	—	5,040	3.7	235	7.19
1977	5.9	3.1	.4	202.4	34.86	2,321		625	526	20	—	33	4,803	3.7	229	6.97
1978	5.0	3.0		177.6	35.25	2,178		869	405				3,895	3.5	223	6.51
1979[1]	4.8				41.06	3,274	559	1,233	341	162	82	19	3,238	3.1		8.21
1980[1]	6.1			259.3	42.51	4,741	432	1,795	421	266	127	19	3,671	3.6	—	8.38
1981[1]	5.4			—	—	5,000	400	2,249	361	77	22	—				

[1] Preliminary. Source: Bureau of Mines   T.91

Pennsylvania Anthracite Coal Production[1]   In Thousands of Short Tons

Year	Jan.	Feb.	Mar.	Apr.	May	June	July	Aug.	Sept.	Oct.	Nov.	Dec.	Total
1975	540	535	544	270	535	544	455	535	500	560	555	630	6,203
1976	525	440	525	520	555	610	490	590	515	490	493	475	6,228
1977	390	420	484	553	476	479	474	479	471	587	513	535	5,861
1978	350	430	525	520	540	625	555	550	560	535	530	440	6,160
1979	343	285	396	406	430	411	343	435	401	493	469	423	4,835
1980[2]	470	350	460	510	500	495	525	425	478	567	525	470	6,056
1981[2]	305	472	548	463	240	477	566	534	417	457	550	394	5,423
1982[2]	353	381	459	274	329	319	313	370	340	387	347	353	4,225

[1] Represents production in Pennsylvania only. Production outside which is small, is included in Bituminous Production series. [2] Preliminary. Source: Bureau of Mines   T.92

Cobalt

Identified world resources of cobalt amount to nearly 8 million short tons. An estimated 75 percent of these resources lie in nickel-bearing laterite deposits. The remaining amount occurs nearly equally in nickel-copper sulfide deposits hosted in mafic and ultramafic rocks and in the sedimentary copper deposits of Zaire and Zambia, the two major producers of the world's cobalt. Millions of tons of hypothetical and speculative cobalt resources are believed to exist in manganese nodules and crusts on the ocean floor. Preliminary estimates put the total world production of cobalt during 1982 at approximately 4 percent below the 1981 production of 34,179 tons. Zambia and Zaire accounted for 51 percent and 15 percent of the estimated 1982 world production respectively. A worldwide surplus of cobalt is expected to prevail through 1983, although several nickel-cobalt producers closed their mines in 1982.

The cobalt resources of the U.S. are estimated at nearly 1.0 million tons, located mostly in Minnesota. However, domestic mining of cobalt ceased in 1971 and was not expected to be resumed during 1983. Most of the U.S. resources, although large, are classified as subeconomic.

Cobalt is generally recovered as a byproduct of copper and nickel mining, and most of the environmental problems of cobalt recovery are directly associated with the mining and processing of copper and nickel ores. Most secondary cobalt is derived from recycled superalloy or cemented carbide scrap or from spent or regenerated catalysts.

The domestic demand for cobalt dropped sharply in 1982, especially for the manufacture of superalloys, cutting and wear-resistant materials, and catalysts. The spot price of cobalt fell from $13 to $4 per pound in 1982, and the major producer price of cathode cobalt dropped to $12.50 per pound early in 1982 and remained near that level for the rest of the year. The U.S. Bureau of Mines estimated that the 1983 U.S. apparent consumption would amount to around 5,500 tons. The U.S. demand for primary cobalt, figured from a 1978 base, was expected to increase at an annual rate of nearly 2.5 percent through 1990.

Preliminary Bureau of Mines estimates put 1982 U.S. stocks of cobalt at close to 4,000 short tons held by industry compared with 4,188 tons held at the end of 1981.

World Mine Production of Cobalt   In Short Tons of Contained Cobalt

Year	Australia	Zaire (Congo Repub.)	USSR	France (Metal)	Canada	Cuba	Philippines	Finland	W. Germany (Metal)	Japan (Metal)	Norway (Metal)	Morocco	Zambia	New Caledonia	World Total
1971	877	16,003	1,750	635	2,161	1,700	N.A.	1,400	662		958	1,078	2,330	N.A.	27,299
1972	849	14,453	1,800	853	1,676	1,700	N.A.	1,400	504		353	1,766	3,687	N.A.	27,376
1973	848	16,625	1,850	922	1,672	1,800	45	1,400	408		1,005	1,567	3,460	1,900	29,268
1974	1,188	19,436	1,900	848	1,724	1,800	33	1,400	392	11	1,365	1,793	2,622	2,113	34,045
1975	2,986	15,400	2,000	848	1,492	1,800	129	1,545	375	53	852	2,162	2,627	3,770	34,000
1976	600	12,100	2,000	799	1,495	1,800	542	1,409	276	568	635	1,030	2,398	90	23,609
1977	1,100	11,200	2,100	939	1,637	1,800	1,195	1,353	441	1,205	777	1,119	1,878	120	23,682
1978	1,490	14,660	2,150	998	1,360	1,610	1,313	1,336	386	2,055	575	1,250	4,124	170	29,771
1979	1,650	16,530	2,200	850	1,808	1,360	1,510	1,174	424	2,924	1,051	1,059	4,718	230	32,793
1980[2]	1,760	17,090	2,370	1,139	1,767	1,790	1,467	1,141	440	3,160	1,405	924	4,850	200	33,738
1981[1]	1,760	17,090	2,480	1,100	2,500	1,970	1,200	1,140	440	2,669	1,592	829	4,960	155	34,179
1982[1]	1,700	17,000			2,000		1,000	1,000				800	5,000	150	33,150

[1] Estimate.   [2] Preliminary.   Source: Bureau of Mines   T.93

U.S. Salient Statistics of Cobalt   In Thousands of Pounds of Contained Cobalt

Year	Net Import Reliance as a % of Apparent Consumption	Cobalt Pdt's Production	Consumer Stocks Dec. 31	Imports for Consumption	Steel Full Alloy	Stainless & Heat Resisting	Catalysts[4]	Super- Alloys	Tool Steel	Magnetic Alloys	Non ferrous Alloys	Drier in Paints, etc.[5]	Cutting & Wear Resistant Mater.	Welding & Hard Facing Rods	Total	Price $ Per Pound[3]
1971		3,220	1,411	10,912	196	50	919	1,983	318	2,278	532	2,744	1,230	246	12,500	2.2–2.45
1972		3,142	1,193	13,915	217	39	1,245	3,012	361	3,441	651	2,691	1,273	199	14,130	2.45
1973		4,119	2,451	19,238	226	32	1,793	3,282	518	4,302	789	3,569	2,511	391	18,741	2.45–3.3
1974		4,636	2,047	16,122	249	39	1,905	4,090	690	3,457	780	3,635	2,578	423	18,861	3.1–3.75
1975	98	2,960	1,801	6,608	207	32	421	1,494	233	2,024	669	1,964	1,276	298	12,787	3.75–4
1976	98	4,608	3,180	16,487	251	37	1,446	1,772	151	3,521	742	3,089	1,385	454	16,482	4–5.40
1977	97	4,563	3,738	17,548	354	72	1,285	3,097	231	3,466	624	2,883	1,256	376	16,577	5.20–6.40
1978	95	6,341	4,387	19,029	250	135	1,623	4,299	379	3,768	590	5,399	1,837	725	19,994	6.40–20
1979	94	4,212	3,390	19,998	227	137	1,882	5,276	413	3,266	392	1,791	2,123	444	17,402	20–25
1980	93	3,274	2,540	16,302	116	47	1,656	6,285	321	2,267	150	1,331	1,344	620	15,321	25
1981[1]	92	3,302	1,411	15,594	141	35	1,279	4,195	170	1,687	131	1,378	1,076	488	11,680	17.3–25
1982[2]	91		1,284	12,872	115	51	884	3,423	141	1,531	107	964	551	383	9,191	12.5–17.3
1983																

[1] Preliminary.   [2] Estimate.   [3] 97 to 99% cobalt, per contract.   [4] Prior to 1976 are for chemical & ceramics.   [5] Prior to 1979 are for salts & driers.   Source: Bureau of Mines   T.94

Cocoa

After the world output of cocoa had exceeded estimated demand in each of the preceding five years, the worldwide production of cocoa during 1982/83 (October–September) was expected to fall below the season's projected demand, resulting in a drawdown of world stocks by approximately 63,000 tonnes. The world cocoa bean crop in the 1982/83 season was forecast at 1.56 million tonnes, a 9 percent drop from the record 1981/82 harvest of 1.72 million tonnes.

Another year of poor growing conditions caused the total African harvest of cocoa beans to drop almost 13 percent below its 1981/82 level. Production by the Ivory Coast, the world's major cocoa producer, was expected to be around 370,000 tonnes, 19 percent below its record 1981/82 harvest. The 1983 mid-crop was reportedly damaged by the severe Harmattan (dry winds off the Sahara) and by brush fires. Analysts observed that a return to normal weather patterns would cause the 1983/84 Ivorian crop to soon recover given the substantial number of young trees that were not yet in production.

The Brazilian 1982/83 cocoa crop was estimated at 285,000 tonnes, including a Bahia main crop of 120,000 tonnes and a 1983 temporao crop forecast at 138,000 tonnes. This output fell 10 percent below Brazil's 1981/82 crop because of dry weather from October through December. Ghana's 1982/83 cocoa production was expected to be 16 percent below the previous poor harvest of 225,000 tonnes. A shortage of jute bags and interior logistical problems, including poor roads and damaged bridges, kept much of Ghana's harvest from reaching its ports this season. It is expected that low producer prices and a cutback in new plantings will bring further deterioration in Ghana's productivity in coming years.

World cocoa bean grindings during 1983 are expected to increase by 2 percent to a record 1.61 million tonnes. However, depressed world economic conditions resulted in an increased use of cocoa substitutes and extenders, thereby preventing a more rapid expansion of cocoa consumption. Lower domestic cocoa prices, larger-sized candy bars, and increased market featuring caused U.S. cocoa bean grindings in 1982 to rise nearly 5 percent to 199,126 tonnes.

The Executive Committee of the International Cocoa Organization (ICCO) met in early 1983 to discuss its Secretariat's 3-point price support study which involved utilizing a $75 million Brazilian bank loan to buy up to 150,000 tonnes of cocoa on a deferred payment basis. The ICCO Buffer Stock Funds manager had made no new purchases of cocoa since March 1982 when cumulative stocks amounted to 100,345 tonnes. Further discussions were scheduled throughout 1983. It was expected that ICCO negotiations of a new International Cocoa Agreement to replace the present accord due to expire September 30, 1984 would press the Ivory Coast and the U.S. to become members.

Futures Market

Cocoa Futures are actively traded on the Coffee, Sugar & Cocoa Exchange, Inc. in New York; and on the London Terminal Market.

Raw Cocoa Grindings in Selected Countries In Thousands of Metric[2] Tons

Year	Total	1st Quarter	2nd Quarter	3rd Quarter	4th Quarter	Total	1st Quarter	2nd Quarter	3rd Quarter	4th Quarter	Total	1st Quarter	2nd Quarter	3rd Quarter	4th Quarter
			France					Germany (West)					Holland		
1970	38.9	10.1	9.6	8.3	10.9	123.8	31.8	29.2	28.6	34.2	113.0	27.9	26.7	29.0	29.4
1971[2]	41.7	10.7	10.8	8.9	11.4	132.9	33.7	30.6	30.8	37.8	120.6	31.1	28.0	27.8	33.7
1972	48.0	11.0	12.2	10.1	14.7	138.8	34.4	32.6	31.6	40.2	124.4	31.9	31.1	28.5	33.1
1973	47.3	14.5	12.9	8.7	11.1	152.4	41.0	39.5	33.8	38.0	122.6	33.2	31.1	26.3	32.0
1974	36.9	11.1	9.5	7.4	9.0	138.2	37.1	31.8	30.8	38.5	114.9	33.4	28.0	23.0	30.4
1975	34.3	9.7	9.1	6.9	8.6	139.0	40.1	34.0	30.0	34.8	119.4	33.3	27.4	26.5	32.2
1976	35.7	10.1	9.5	7.2	8.8	140.6	36.2	35.2	30.6	38.6	127.3	34.6	31.8	25.9	35.1
1977	36.3	10.7	10.5	7.5	7.7	142.3	38.3	32.3	30.5	41.2	126.1	34.9	32.0	26.6	32.6
1978	40.0	10.8	10.9	7.3	10.9	143.6	39.8	34.7	30.3	38.8	125.9	34.0	31.5	26.7	33.8
1979	43.2	11.5	11.5	8.8	11.4	142.3	37.6	34.8	30.3	39.5	127.5	35.4	29.3	29.8	33.0
1980	43.1	12.5	10.9	9.1	10.7	151.2	40.2	35.4	32.9	42.6	132.6	35.1	31.4	29.5	36.7
1981	47.0	12.6	12.0	9.6	12.9	159.4	41.7	37.6	35.4	44.7	141.0	36.0	34.3	32.7	38.0
1982[1]		13.1	12.3	9.7		167.0	45.1	39.9	35.8	46.3	148.4	38.4	34.9	33.7	41.3
			Italy					United Kingdom					United States		
1970	41.7	11.5	10.4	9.6	10.3	81.1	21.0	21.0	17.7	21.4	261.3	64.2	69.0	60.9	67.2
1971[2]	39.7	9.2	9.3	10.4	10.8	84.4	20.5	20.2	18.6	25.1	279.0	65.3	67.9	66.8	78.9
1972	40.6	9.8	8.7	9.8	12.3	97.7	22.0	24.2	24.2	27.3	289.0	79.3	66.1	63.2	80.4
1973	42.9	10.8	10.9	11.4	9.8	107.0	29.1	28.2	23.9	25.8	278.5	77.9	73.4	60.7	66.5
1974	36.3	12.8	8.2	5.1	10.2	93.1	27.7	25.9	21.4	18.0	229.6	67.6	58.8	54.5	48.7
1975	29.1	8.4	6.4	5.9	8.5	72.5	20.2	18.1	15.4	18.8	207.8	43.7	51.7	53.2	59.3
1976	35.4	8.6	9.0	7.8	9.9	83.0	22.3	21.6	17.9	21.2	225.3	60.9	55.0	55.0	54.5
1977	26.4	5.9	6.9	5.3	8.3	75.3	22.0	20.5	16.4	16.4	183.7	56.5	46.9	40.9	39.4
1978	30.1	7.0	8.5	6.3	8.2	72.4	21.0	19.0	15.9	16.5	162.7	42.0	38.4	36.9	45.3
1979	33.6	6.3	10.0	6.9	10.4	60.6	17.7	15.9	12.3	14.7	160.3	40.5	41.4	41.4	37.0
1980	33.8	8.0	8.4	8.1	9.3	65.3	15.5	16.1	15.5	18.2	142.2	33.5	31.5	34.9	42.4
1981	35.1	8.6	8.1	5.8	12.6	86.0	21.4	21.3	20.2	23.1	190.2	48.4	46.0	48.8	47.1
1982[1]		9.6	10.1	6.0		88.0	25.3	21.1	19.6	22.1	199.1	47.7	50.6	50.1	50.7

[1] Preliminary. [2] Data prior to 1971 are in THOUSANDS OF LONG TONS. Source: *Gill and Duffus, Ltd.*

COCOA

World Cocoa Supply and Demand   In Thousands of Metric Tons

Crop Year[1]	Stocks Oct. 1	Net World Crop[2]	Total Availability	Seasonal Grindings	Closing Stocks	Stock Change	Crop Year[1]	Stocks Oct. 1	Net World Crop[2]	Total Availability	Seasonal Grindings	Closing Stocks	Stock Change
1970-1	500	1,484	1,984	1,399	585	+ 85	1977-8	278	1,488	1,766	1,399	367	+ 89
1971-2	585	1,567	2,152	1,536	616	+ 31	1978-9	367	1,473	1,840	1,458	382	+ 15
1972-3	616	1,383	1,999	1,583	416	−200	1979-0	382	1,606	1,988	1,486	502	+120
1973-4	416	1,434	1,850	1,512	338	− 78	1980-1	502	1,652	2,154	1,583	571	+ 69
1974-5	338	1,534	1,872	1,452	420	+ 82	1981-2[3]	571	1,684	2,255	1,572	683	+112
1975-6	420	1,497	1,917	1,523	394	− 26	1982-3[4]	683	1,524	2,207	1,602	605	− 78
1976-7	394	1,326	1,720	1,442	278	−116	1983-4[4]	605					

[1] Crop year season is OCT.–SEPT.   [2] The Net World Crop is obtained by adjusting the Gross World Crop for one per cent loss in weight.   [3] Preliminary.   [4] Forecast.   Source: Gill and Duffus, Ltd.
T.95

World Production of Cocoa Beans in Principal Producing Countries   In Thousands of Metric Tonnes

Crop Year[1]	Brazil	Colombia	Dominican Rep.	Ecuador	Equatorial Guinea[4]	Cameroon	Ghana	Ivory Coast	Mexico	Nigeria	Sao Tome & Principe	Trinidad & Tobago	Venezuela	Asia & Oceania	World Total
1970-1	182	21	25	61	30.0	111.7	392.0	180		308	10.4	4.1	18.9	44	1,499
1971-2	167	22	41	67	22	123	464	226		255	10.0	5	17	45	1,583
1972-3	162	23	28	43	10	107	418	181		241	11	5	19	40	1,397
1973-4	246	23	30	72	12	110	350	209		215	10	4	17	53	1,448
1974-5	273	25	27	78	13	118	377	242		214	7	5	19	57	1,547
1975-6	258	26	30	63	10	96	397	231		216	8	3	15	60	1,510
1976-7	234	29	30	72	6	82	320	230		165	6	4	15	60	1,339
1977-8	283	32	30	78	5	107	271	304	35	206	7	4	17	63	1,512
1978-9	314	32	34	85	8	107	265	312	36	141	8	3	15	69	1,502
1979-0	296	34	29	95	6	124	296	379	36	175	7	2	13	84	1,651
1980-1	351	36	33	85	8	120	258	412	32	155	7	3	14	97	1,683
1981-2[3]	315	39	42	88	8	120	225	456	40	181	7	3	15	112	1,723
1982-3[2]	285	40	37	85	9	120	190	370	42	165	7	3	15	123	1,563

[1] Crop years are for the 12 months October 1 to September 30.   [2] Forecast.   [3] Preliminary.   [4] Includes Fernando Po & Rio Muni.   Sources: Foreign Agricultural Service; U.S.D.A.
T.96

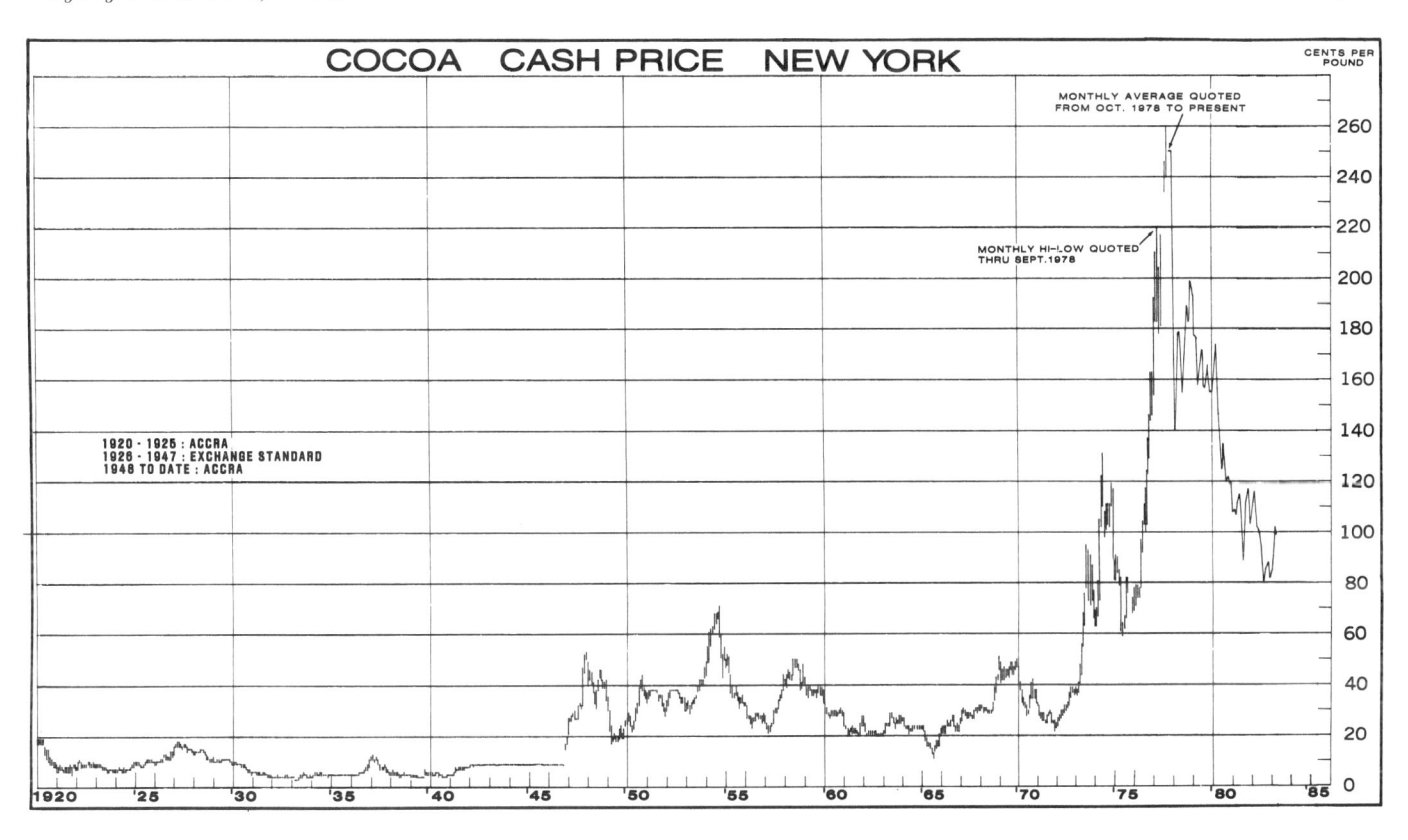

COCOA

World Absorption (Consumption) of Cocoa[2]   In Thousands of Metric Tonnes

Year	Japan	Australia	Belgium	Brazil	Canada	Colombia	France	W. Germany	Netherlands	Spain	Italy	Switzerland	USSR	United King.	United States	World Total
1972	36	16	20	90	19	36	48	144	124	31	41	18	132	98	289	1,567
1973	38	16	21	87	18	32	47	151	123	34	43	18	134	107	278	1,551
1974	30	16	22	104	16	31	37	151	115	36	36	17	143	93	230	1,489
1975	29	14	19	98	11	32	37	151	119	34	29	15	150	72	208	1,471
1976	32	16	19	116	13	31	39	153	127	38	35	16	140	83	225	1,536
1977	26	15	16	120	11	29	42	154	126	34	26	16	85	75	184	1,393
1978	21	12	15	136	11	29	44	155	126	32	30	14	90	72	163	1,417
1979	22	11	17	180	11	31	48	155	127	34	34	14	120	61	160	1,470
1980	25	11	23	200	12	31	48	158	133	34	34	17	130	65	142	1,508
1981[1]	29	12	29	195	17	35	52	167	141	36	35	18	120	85	190	1,589
1982[3]	32	10	18	170	14	35	54	175	148	37	38	18	112	88	199	1,574
1983[4]	32	10	20	175	16	35	52	170	148	38	38	18	112	90	210	1,619
1984																

[1] Preliminary.   [2] Figures represent the "absorption," "disappearance" or "grindings" of cocoa beans in each country—in other words, net imports of cocoa beans adjusted for changes in stock.   [3] Estimate.   [4] Forecast.   *Source: Gill & Duffus, Ltd.*   T.98

World Exports of Cocoa Beans by Principal Producing Countries   In Thousands of Metric Tons

Year	Brazil	Costa Rica	Dominican Repub.	Ecuador	Equatorial Guinea	Cameroon	Ghana	Malaysia	Ivory Coast	Papua New Guinea	Nigeria	Sao Tome & Principe	Trinidad & Tobago	Venezuela	Togo	Grand Total
1973	82.8	4.7	23.0	30.0	6.4	84.2	373.8	6.5	143.0	22.6	213.9	11.8	3.4	9.9	17.7	1,089
1974	129.9	4.4	26.4	68.9	9.0	88.9	313.9	9.7	205.3	34.0	197.1	9.8	3.8	11.5	15.9	1,170
1975	176.6	5.4	22.3	37.8	3.0	72.5	322.2	11.8	167.5	30.5	194.7	5.2	4.8	14.4	16.2	1,125
1976	128.8	4.2	24.5	22.2	7.0	68.6	327.6	14.8	191.4	31.3	223.0	5.6	3.0	7.6	11.8	1,115
1977	107.6	5.1	25.6	20.1	5.0	56.8	249.1	13.6	158.5	29.4	167.5	6.1	3.2	7.4	19.6	919
1978	134.1	5.8	27.6	16.2	5.0	61.6	207.0	17.6	244.0	27.1	185.9	6.1	3.2	6.4	22.8	1,015
1979	156.9	4.2	25.6	13.2	5.0	61.1	200.0	24.2	170.8	28.1	113.0	8.2	2.7	6.8	10.1	880
1980	123.6	2.2	23.4	13.7	6.0	80.5	218.6	30.3	230.9	28.8	133.9	7.6	2.1	6.5	12.1	973
1981	123.2	2.0	27.2	27.2												
1982																

[1] Preliminary.   *Source: Foreign Agricultural Service, U.S.D.A.*   T.100

Cocoa Outturns and Sales of the Bahia Crops   In Thousands of Bags of 60 Kilos

	Outturns			Cumulative Sales of Cocoa Beans (Crop Year Ending April)											
Year	Main Crop (Oct.-Apr.)	Temporao Crop (May-Sept.)	Total	Jan.	Feb.	Mar.	Apr.	May	June	July	Aug.	Sept.	Oct.	Nov.	Dec.
1972	1,791	705	2,496	3,358	3,457	3,516	3,525	536	718	1,096	1,383	1,672	1,955	2,144	2,443
1973	2,376	1,515	3,891	2,547	2,638	2,667	2,680	988	1,272	1,637	1,808	1,864	2,015	2,136	2,356
1974	1,613	2,630	4,243	2,596	2,914	3,087	3,173	1,361	1,405	1,584	1,751	2,019	2,314	2,525	2,650
1975	1,899	2,091	3,990	2,762	2,870	2,963	3,078	1,314	1,666	2,342	2,699	3,098	3,790	3,928	4,091
1976	1,497	2,102	3,599	4,308	4,407	4,443	4,530	1,906	2,480	2,646	2,868	3,083	3,197	3,349	3,460
1977	1,887	2,524	4,411	3,534	3,526	3,498	3,477	1,629	1,894	2,276	2,455	2,717	2,933	3,154	3,275
1978	1,805	3,129	4,934	3,449	3,652	3,767	3,941	1,113	1,360	1,701	2,175	2,660	3,166	3,546	3,872
1979	2,257	2,383	4,640	4,155	4,212	4,273	4,304	1,959	2,436	2,966	3,378	3,805	4,091	4,533	4,739
1980	2,658	2,892	5,550	5,008	5,145	5,206	5,387	1,306	1,646	2,257	2,791	3,390	4,093	4,361	4,605
1981[1]	1,718	3,170	4,888	4,765	4,876	4,924	5,387	1,574	1,912	2,372					
1982															

[1] Preliminary.   *Source: Gill and Duffus, Ltd.*   T.99

COCOA

Confectionery Sales by Manufacturers in the United States   In Millions of Dollars

Year	Jan.	Feb.	Mar.	Apr.	May	June	July	Aug.	Sept.	Oct.	Nov.	Dec.	Total
1973	184	172	182	154	143	135	114	183	233	227	234	180	2,141
1974	211	220	241	200	193	180	172	251	309	309	265	220	2,771
1975	246	250	221	207	202	183	168	245	300	316	251	241	2,830
1976	259	270	277	238	196	192	157	234	307	267	282	233	2,912
1977	282	342	353	265	243	237	171	268	412	348	336	330	3,587
1978	305	352	328	250	266	234	211	379	368	376	349	351	3,769
1979[1]	258	359	332	313	285	258	240	403	435	461	438	382	4,281
1980[1]	414	469	415	340	325	318	293	396	498	505	430	403	4,684
1981[1]	400	437	440	378	305	325	304	430	582	588	460	466	5,189
1982[1]	397	507	486	390	338	360	330	491	608	570	510	469	5,456

Compiled by the Department of Commerce from reports of over 200 manufacturers. The number reporting vary from month to month. Represents app. 70% of sales by all manufacturers of candy and competitive chocolate products.   [1] Preliminary.   Source: Dept. of Commerce   T.101

United States Imports of Cocoa (Includes Shells)   In Thousands of Long Tons

Year	Jan.	Feb.	Mar.	Apr.	May	June	July	Aug.	Sept.	Oct.	Nov.	Dec.	Total
1975	20.5	17.3	21.7	17.9	17.4	18.7	16.6	12.5	17.4	21.5	18.6	33.0	233.0
1976	33.9	16.4	28.8	22.4	21.4	19.5	16.3	20.9	19.6	8.2	11.6	16.5	235.4
1977	30.6	21.5	19.0	16.1	25.1	13.6	10.9	10.8	6.2	8.1	4.7	5.5	172.1
1978	19.4	20.3	27.9	20.5	16.5	12.4	16.1	14.7	7.3	15.9	18.6	20.2	209.7
1979[1]	27.3	26.7	14.6	12.8	8.8	13.7	11.8	15.7	5.7	10.1	10.0	8.0	165.2
1980[1]	11.1	9.2	8.0	19.5	15.4	12.0	16.9	9.6	8.2	9.6	9.4	19.9	148.5
1981[1]	13.5	27.8	19.2	30.4	27.1	24.1	19.3	22.0	20.3	24.1	5.8	11.5	245.0
1982[1]	10.0	29.0	17.6	15.3	16.8	11.9	13.0	20.3	14.3	14.4	14.4	17.4	194.2
1983[1]	46.0												

[1] Preliminary.   Source: Department of Commerce   T.102

Spot Cocoa Bean Prices (ACCRA) in New York   In Cents Per Pound

Year	Jan.	Feb.	Mar.	Apr.	May	June	July	Aug.	Sept.	Oct.	Nov.	Dec.	Average
1975	89.5	88.8	84.8	75.5	59.5	62.5	73.0	78.0	77.5	77.5	68.5	76.0	75.9
1976	73.5	75.5	74.0	88.3	93.5	107.5	103.5	114.5	131.3	132.5	161.5	154.3	109.2
1977	173.0	190.3	207.5	198.3	199.3	199.3	199.3	199.3	256.0	250.0	250.0	250.0	214.4
1978	165.0	140.0	178.0	179.0	170.0	155.0	161.0	175.0	189.0	183.0	199.0	196.0	174.2
1979	193.0	177.0	176.0	157.5	165.0	172.0	158.0	157.0	166.0	159.0	154.5	155.0	160.4
1980	163.8	173.5	157.0	147.0	135.0	125.3	134.5	120.0	122.0	119.0	120.0	108.0	135.4
1981	109.0	110.0	112.0	115.0	104.0	89.0	109.5	112.0	117.0	113.0	103.0	109.0	108.5
1982	116.0	107.0	102.0	99.0	94.0	80.0	83.0	86.0	87.0	88.0	82.0	85.0	92.4
1983	91.0	102.0											

Source: Bureau of Labor Statistics (0191-0221)   T.105

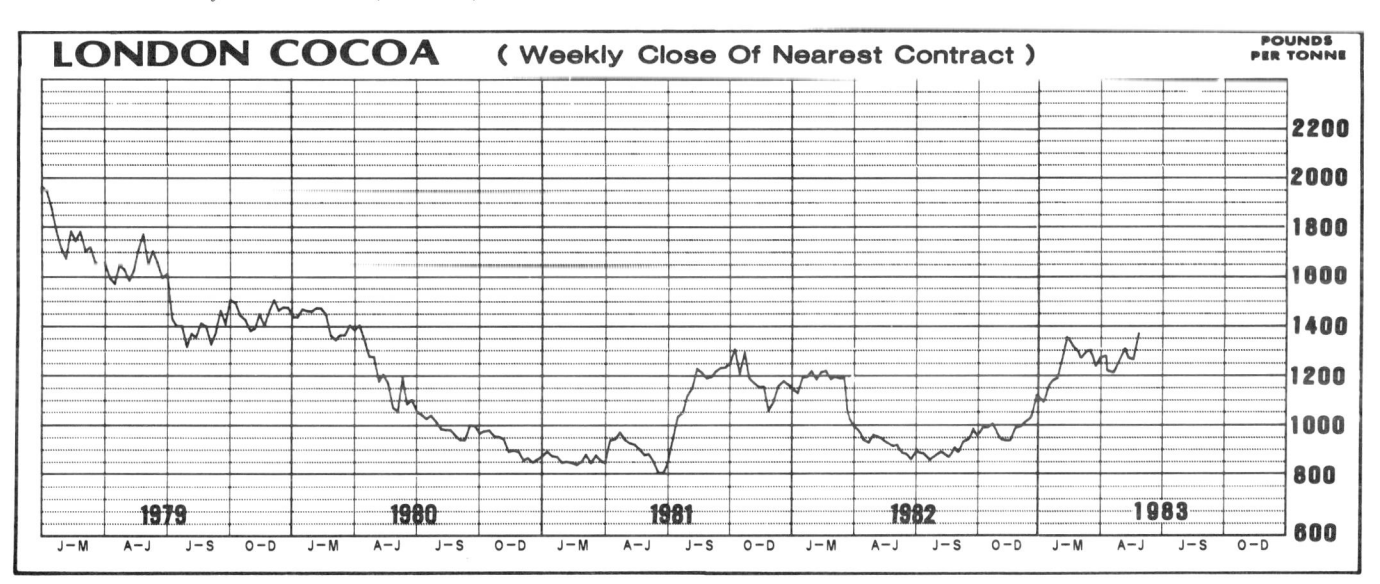

LONDON COCOA (Weekly Close Of Nearest Contract)   POUNDS PER TONNE

COCOA

Month End Open Interest of Cocoa Futures at New York   In Contracts

Year	Jan.	Feb.	Mar.	Apr.	May	June	July	Aug.	Sept.	Oct.	Nov.	Dec.
1978	10,427	9,210	7,530	6,609	6,807	6,045	6,516	5,557	7,039	7,732	7,691	8,064
1979	7,782	6,506	6,587	6,135	7,392	6,833	6,792	6,415	6,262	7,562	7,050	6,840
1980	8,314	7,723	6,744	6,639	8,114	6,682	8,900	9,529	13,548	14,282	13,210	11,978
1981	14,269	14,064	16,209	13,721	13,929	11,853	16,328	16,897	17,042	18,823	15,388	14,137
1982	14,554	14,421	15,129	14,036	15,563	14,083	15,954	14,678	16,439	18,615	17,600	19,988
1983	25,989	22,401	22,155	24,796								

Source: Coffee, Sugar & Cocoa Exch., Inc.   T.103

Volume of Trading of Cocoa Futures at New York   In Contracts

Year	Jan.	Feb.	Mar.	Apr.	May	June	July	Aug.	Sept.	Oct.	Nov.	Dec.	Total
1978	20,694	22,017	21,095	19,670	14,886	18,376	13,459	18,686	18,509	18,717	18,565	18,594	222,983
1979	19,447	17,626	16,430	14,784	21,063	23,282	18,160	21,125	16,929	25,555	22,321	15,099	232,183
1980	23,600	40,410	25,066	23,897	26,170	29,673	34,158	27,265	45,437	43,945	39,770	28,954	388,971
1981	32,916	43,352	37,056	52,875	32,691	54,479	55,525	53,557	43,764	63,751	53,674	39,011	562,651
1982	42,498	44,744	52,468	52,591	38,332	50,693	45,504	45,457	61,137	67,652	48,243	56,744	607,964
1983	88,429	97,636	82,115	91,851									

Source: Coffee, Sugar & Cocoa Exch., Inc.   T.104

Visible Stock of Cocoa in New York Warehouses[1], at End of Month   In Thousands of Bags

Year	Jan.	Feb.	Mar.	Apr.	May	June	July	Aug.	Sept.	Oct.	Nov.	Dec.
1975	9.5	9.7	6.0	7.0	23.9	21.9	11.5	3.5	.5	.1	.1	.1
1976	.1	.1	.1	.1	3.0	.7	.7	.7	.7	.7	—	2.6
1977	1.7	1.3	1.9	.9	.9	14.6	47.3	44.6	13.4	5.6	4.9	8.8
1978	5.0	9.3	24.2	19.4	24.2	29.1	38.0	17.9	12.2	16.0	19.8	28.2
1979	35.2	33.6	31.1	31.4	40.2	44.2	125.5	127.5	104.7	101.7	90.0	87.3
1980	85.3	68.2	18.0	29.4	42.8	84.3	94.8	78.3	71.6	52.7	69.5	22.7
1981	37.5	14.9	29.3	66.5	120.3	93.1	75.8	115.3	84.6	62.1	55.5	66.2
1982	33.4	61.3	66.7	57.3	99.0	98.6	115.8	137.7	108.8	97.1	96.1	68.9
1983	64.7	80.1	80.0	88.9								

[1] In licensed & unlicensed warehouses of storage companies licensed by the Coffee, Sugar & Cocoa Exch.   Source: Coffee, Sugar & Cocoa Exch., Inc.   T.106

Visible Stock of Cocoa in Philadelphia Warehouses, at End of Month   In Thousands of Bags

Year	Jan.	Feb.	Mar.	Apr.	May	June	July	Aug.	Sept.	Oct.	Nov.	Dec.
1975	22.6	19.1	16.2	23.8	42.2	26.0	24.5	15.7	16.4	9.5	13.7	20.1
1976	27.4	32.1	36.4	54.3	63.1	70.0	82.9	77.7	68.6	72.3	57.6	47.8
1977	47.8	62.2	61.2	25.5	22.5	23.4	18.2	16.3	10.6	4.1	.3	.2
1978	.2	.6	6.0	14.0	.5	.8	.8	.7	14.3	12.0	23.8	50.6
1979	60.4	77.7	107.7	114.4	110.6	101.7	100.2	124.1	132.5	106.3	81.3	86.3
1980	64.6	52.5	40.0	33.4	53.3	45.3	38.8	47.3	55.8	21.6	11.8	33.6
1981	38.1	15.5	15.4	45.7	189.7	227.4	246.6	255.8	307.5	271.9	234.6	231.3
1982	190.1	163.4	174.1	163.2	154.0	125.7	104.6	64.2	51.8	64.3	69.3	98.5
1983	123.6	192.4	281.5	356.5								

Source: Coffee, Sugar & Cocoa Exch., Inc.   T.107

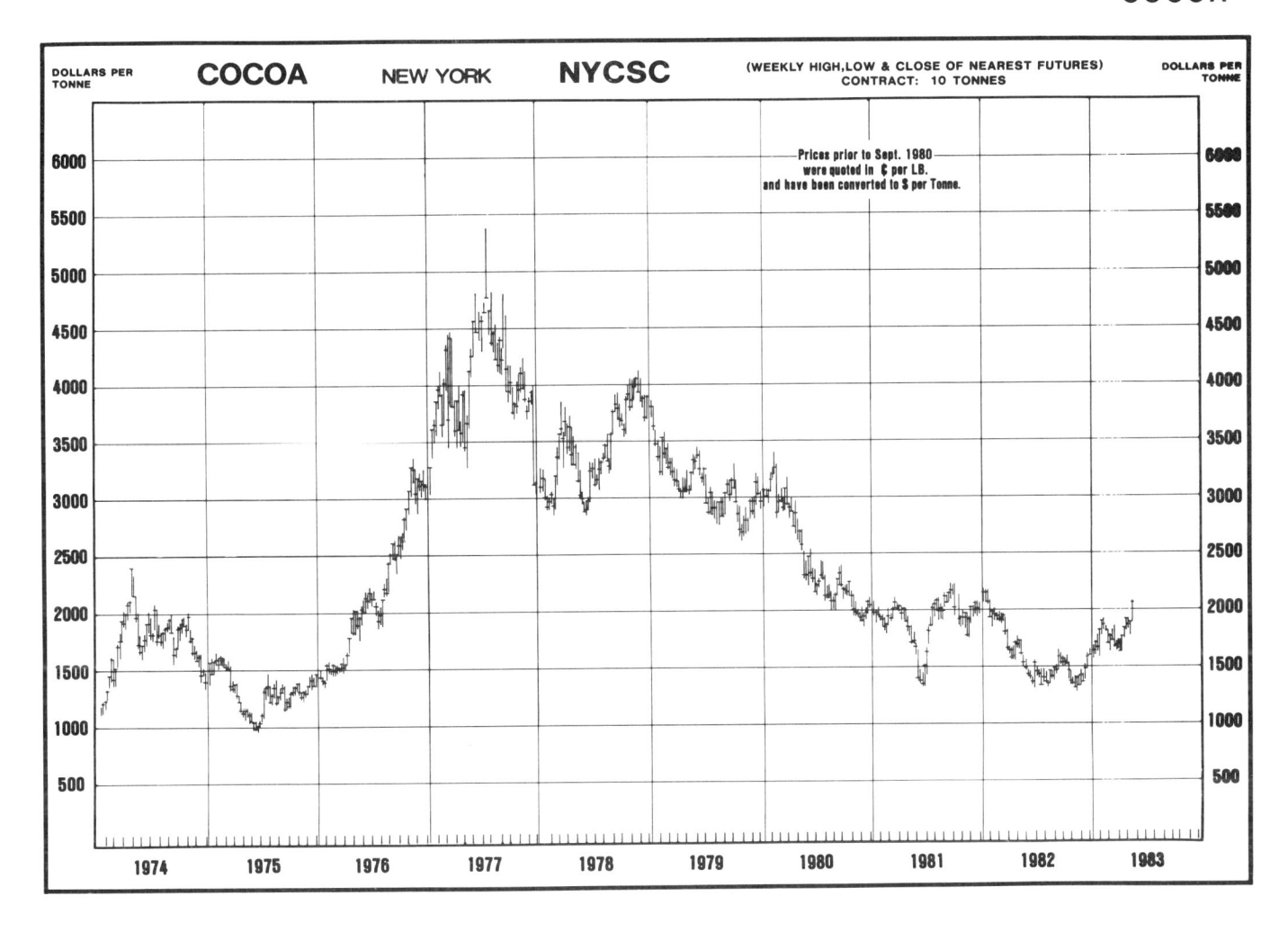

COCOA

COCOA NEW YORK **NYCSC** (WEEKLY HIGH, LOW & CLOSE OF NEAREST FUTURES) CONTRACT: 10 TONNES

Prices prior to Sept. 1980 were quoted in ¢ per LB. and have been converted to $ per Tonne.

High, Low & Closing Prices of March Cocoa Futures at New York In Dollars per Tonne[1]

Year of Delivery		Feb.	Mar.	Apr.	May	June	July	Aug.	Sept.	Oct.	Nov.	Dec.	Jan.	Feb.	Mar.	Life of Delivery Range
1978[1]	High	156.35	175.00	157.90	167.80	182.25	195.25	185.50	175.00	168.00	166.00	155.30	147.75	149.55	175.00	195.25
	Low	136.60	137.25	133.75	133.25	153.25	164.30	154.00	157.25	147.70	145.00	138.20	132.05	130.00	142.50	90.85
	Close	156.35	140.25	154.25	159.25	170.50	179.50	163.75	161.05	153.25	148.20	142.35	133.90	145.05	159.45	—
1979[1]	High	124.75	152.00	148.20	140.25	137.00	145.10	157.20	173.00	184.00	189.25	183.90	175.50	163.00	153.25	189.25
	Low	111.50	121.70	132.50	122.60	120.40	129.50	141.60	156.65	161.25	171.20	167.10	149.25	144.95	141.75	111.50
	Close	123.80	146.00	133.35	123.10	136.50	144.70	156.35	167.10	177.15	181.20	176.75	149.25	154.15	141.85	—
1980[1]	High	168.75	162.00	153.85	159.50	163.40	159.60	145.10	146.75	149.90	142.10	145.40	146.85	154.25	140.00	174.50
	Low	154.70	153.50	147.65	149.10	153.20	140.15	135.25	136.90	122.00	124.00	134.00	131.50	127.90	130.75	122.00
	Close	163.60	154.25	151.50	157.15	160.75	144.80	136.20	144.10	126.20	140.95	134.00	144.10	134.95	134.50	—
1981	High	3350	3245	3011	2830	2650	2562	2350	2454	2305	2217	2105	2084	2017	2075	3350
	Low	3085	2940	2785	2422	2385	2260	2210	2195	2121	1960	1905	1922	1795	1915	1795
	Close	3110	2960	2792	2425	2393	2275	2226	2220	2226	1965	2050	1944	1947	2025	
1982	High	2260	2300	2250	2125	1920	2215	2290	2360	2292	2065	2085	2184	2020	1965	2360
	Low	2170	2190	2081	1890	1625	1808	2160	2196	1922	1816	1910	1942	1860	1780	1780
	Close	2224	2210	2130	1935	1720	2202	2263	2283	2005	1911	2054	1942	1924	1806	—
1983	High	2145	2105	1875	1835	1663	1640	1604	1696	1669	1495	1650	1840	1919	1816	2295
	Low	2071	1840	1738	1657	1508	1485	1451	1534	1435	1383	1447	1565	1640	1688	1383
	Close	2071	1854	1802	1660	1605	1518	1527	1604	1467	1465	1603	1826	1704	1691	—
1984	High	2015	1958	1990												
	Low	1785	1790	1780												
	Close	1838	1835	1990												

[1] Prices prior to the 1981 delivery are in cents per pound. To convert to $ per tonne, multiply the ¢ per lb. by 2204.6.   Source: *Coffee, Sugar & Cocoa Exch., Inc.*

Coconut Oil and Copra

Early in 1983, the USDA estimated the 1982/83 world coconut oil production at 3.2 million tonnes, practically unchanged from the 1981/82 estimate. The world production of copra was estimated at nearly 5.0 million metric tons (tonnes), 2 percent above 1981/82. The major producers of coconut oil were the Philippines, Indonesia, and India which accounted for an estimated 48 percent, 21 percent, and 8 percent of total world production, respectively.

In September 1982 the Philippine government announced plans to redirect copra and coconut oil exports into various domestic programs in order to support coconut product prices. All intermittent or unscheduled exports of coconut oil were prohibited and the Philippine National Oil Company was directed to purchase available coconut oil for use in the government sponsored coco-diesel program. Subsequently, the number of Philippine firms exporting coconut oil dropped from thirty-one to four. All Philippine exports of copra were suspended on September 14, 1982 in order to increase the supplies of copra going to local coconut mills. Philippine copra exports throughout the first 8 months of 1982 were more than triple the 1981 level of 48,000 tons.

Coconut oil prices CIF Rotterdam averaged $422 per tonne during the first part of the 1982/83 season vs. $500 per tonne during 1981/82.

World Copra Production by Principal Countries In Thousands of Metric Tons

Year	Dom.-Rep.	Fiji	India	Indonesia	Jamaica	Malaysia	Mexico	Mozambique	Papua-New Guinea	Philippines	Solomon Isl.	Sri Lanka	Tanzania	Thailand	Vanuatu	Venezuela	Vietnam	Tons World Total
1973	15	28	345	797	13	216	118	69	125	1,808	16	100	27	38	22	19	20	3,904
1974	16	27	339	801	15	202	135	64	137	1,376	29	109	27	39	35	18	23	3,514
1975	20	26	349	947	18	234	140	63	140	2,206	25	203	27	39	27	18	23	4,636
1976	20	29	354	1,216	20	231	125	83	113	2,715	24	157	27	43	36	18	23	5,366
1977	20	30	334	1,022	21	218	120	80	139	2,449	29	73	27	39	44	19	23	5,164
1978	21	27	332	1,262	24	207	135	75	141	2,468	28	131	27	40	47	19	23	4,377
1979	21	30	317	1,296	28	213	130	60	159	1,823	34	166	27	41	45	19	23	4,835
1980	21	30	333	1,394	29	210	110	60	145	1,931	30	93	27	45	50	20	23	4,925
1981[1]	21	30	337	1,331	25	208	120	60	138	2,331	30	138	27	45	50	20	23	4,843
1982[2]	21	30	340	1,389	28	200	120	60	150	2,558	30	140	27	45	50	20	20	4,950

[1] Preliminary. [2] Forecast. Source: Foreign Agricultural Service, U.S.D.A. T.109

World Coconut Oil Exports by Principal Countries In Thousands of Metric Tons

Year	Sri Lanka (Ceylon)	Singapore[2]	Indonesia	Malaysia[2]	Philippines Registered	Sarawak[2]	Total Asia	Mozambique	Ec-10	Fiji	Papua New Guinea	Total Oceania	World Total
1972	85	15	34	21	467	2	626	6	163	15	27	53	830
1973	18	5	17	25	426	4	494	10	125	18	28	58	679
1974	22	4	0	44	432	—	502	9	78	14	27	49	643
1975	69	11	27	35	593	—	732	4	213	16	27	61	986
1976	59	10	13	34	822			9	283	14	27	59	1,270
1977	2	11	0	25	789			5	196	18	29	57	1,131
1978	28	37	2	22	990			5	165	17	29	70	1,260
1979	34	42	41	66	795			4	133	18	28	75	1,092
1980	2	35	0	65	914				114	15	33		1,208
1981	20	63	0	65	1,047				119	15	29		1,359
1982[1]	20	50		64	934				114		25		1,241
1983[3]		40		63	950						25		1,234

[1] Preliminary. [2] Net Exports. [3] Projected. Source: Foreign Agricultural Service, U.S.D.A. T.110

Supply & Distribution of Coconut Oil in the United States In Millions of Pounds

Year Begin. Oct. 1	Production From Copra	Imports[2]	Stocks Dec. 31[3]	Total Supply	Exports & Shipments	Domestic Disappearance Total	Per Capita	Total	Production of Coconut Oil (Refined) Jan.-March	April-June	July-Sept.	Oct.-Dec.
1975-6	—	1,248	107	1,355	53	1,175	5.46	716.2	146.2	169.6	186.8	213.6
1976-7	—	1,115	127	1,243	31	1,075	4.96	849.2	214.2	223.7	216.1	195.2
1977-8	—	980	137	1,117	33	939	4.30	729.4	184.5	196.7	175.6	172.6
1978-9[1]	—	967	145	1,112	8	947		768.3	187.9	207.5	196.6	176.2
1979-0[1]	—	810	157	967	30	785		595.6	183.9	137.4	143.8	129.7
1980-1[1]	—	1,122	152	1,274	38	1,032		644.7	146.1	153.4	156.0	196.1
1981-2[1]	—	960	204	1,164	28	976		700.3	193.3	175.3	171.9	159.8
1982-3[1]	—	677	160	837	19	652		665.7	162.1	162.4	168.7	172.5

[1] Preliminary. [2] Imports for consumption. [3] Includes G.S.A. stockpile & in U.S. bond. Sources: Bureau of the Census; Agricultural Marketing Service T.112

COCONUT OIL AND COPRA

Utilization of Coconut Oil in the United States   In Millions of Pounds

Year	Shortening	Margarine	Salad Oil[3]	Other	Total	Soap	Fatty Acids	Foots & Loss	Drying Oil Pdt's.	Other	Total
1975	106	20	36	249	442	163	90	34	4	—	430
1976	128	4	74	363	492	194	107	45	5	192	499
1977	78	5	42	323	383	198	116	43	5	116	495
1978[1]	75	7	29			184	128	44			
1979[2]	93	4				190					
1980[2]	103										
1981[2]	125										

[1] Preliminary.   [2] Estimate.   [3] or Cooking Oil.   Source: Economic Research Service, U.S.D.A.   T.113

U.S. Consumption of Coconut Oil in End Products   In Millions of Pounds

Year	Jan.	Feb.	Mar.	Apr.	May	June	July	Aug.	Sept.	Oct.	Nov.	Dec.	Total
1975	67.6	58.2	68.1	70.7	67.7	71.8	61.8	75.2	81.1	87.8	78.5	76.8	865.3
1976	80.3	78.4	88.1	83.3	84.9	90.3	80.2	82.6	80.8	79.2	87.1	75.1	990.3
1977	73.4	69.9	82.6	73.0	73.9	79.1	63.1	71.9	73.1	76.3	77.4	65.0	878.7
1978	69.3	71.0	81.5	88.9	87.6	76.1	73.6	79.0	72.4	84.0	75.4	55.4	914.2
1979[1]	72.7	66.3	83.3	69.1	69.8	62.0	50.4	58.5	58.0	54.4	55.3	48.5	748.4
1980[1]	55.9	49.9	59.5	55.8	58.1	56.3	56.2	51.0	62.5	66.9	63.1	58.3	693.5
1981[1]	67.7	65.0	71.1	68.3	64.0	70.4	58.0	70.4	66.7	73.2	59.8	52.2	786.8
1982[1]	63.3	59.6	61.7	58.5	64.6	64.2	62.2	63.8	66.1	60.2	70.5	60.6	755.3
1983[1]	61.3												

[1] Preliminary.   Source: Bureau of the Census   T.114

Stocks of Coconut Oil (Crude & Refined) in the United States   In Millions of Pounds

Year	Jan. 1	Feb. 1	Mar. 1	Apr. 1	May 1	June 1	July 1	Aug. 1	Sept. 1	Oct. 1	Nov. 1	Dec. 1
1976	114.1	140.6	135.4	113.6	114.1	125.3	125.6	127.3	150.3	127.4	142.4	137.9
1977	123.0	163.9	152.0	156.3	170.7	162.7	150.5	160.5	178.8	136.7	128.6	114.6
1978	133.7	146.5	176.7	173.6	166.8	140.2	146.0	132.6	130.6	144.8	115.6	112.6
1979[1]	147.2	198.4	195.7	177.2	138.6	148.3	112.5	129.9	131.6	157.0	211.5	198.4
1980[1]	217.4	222.8	177.0	164.1	163.0	154.6	132.5	152.1	176.1	152.9	190.0	210.8
1981[1]	234.6	251.6	299.0	266.4	253.7	239.1	235.2	220.9	226.7	204.3	170.1	168.7
1982[1]	173.1	153.6	186.0	160.6	153.0	170.8	194.8	184.3	166.9	159.7	144.5	144.5
1983[1]	127.2	144.0										

[1] Preliminary.   Source: Bureau of Census   T.115

Average Price of Coconut Oil (Crude)[1] at the Pacific Coast (United States)   In Cents Per Pound

Year	Jan.	Feb.	Mar.	Apr.	May	June	July	Aug.	Sept.	Oct.	Nov.	Dec.	Average
1976	16.1	16.1	17.0	17.1	17.2	18.9	22.3	21.6	23.8	23.0	23.8	26.3	20.3
1977	25.6	27.4	34.7	37.3	34.3	29.9	24.8	21.8	22.9	23.9	24.9	26.4	27.8
1978	26.4	27.1	31.9	30.5	29.9	32.4	32.9	32.3	39.2	41.6	42.6	42.6	34.1
1979	46.3	47.2	47.0	49.9	53.2	57.3	57.3	53.7	44.8	42.5	42.4	40.2	48.5
1980	40.8	40.6	37.5	34.1	29.3	29.5	30.4	29.9	29.1	27.9	29.4	27.8	32.1
1981	26.3	25.0	23.9	24.3	26.0	27.4	28.1	26.4	24.3	26.6	26.6	25.4	25.9
1982	24.8	24.8	22.9	23.0	23.3	23.1	21.1	19.3	19.8	20.0			
1983													

[1] Tank cars, f.o.b. mill. Includes 1¢ import duty.   Source: Bureau of Labor Statistics   T.116

95

Coffee

Revised USDA figures, released in March 1983, put the estimated worldwide 1982/83 coffee production at 81.2 million bags (60 kilograms each), down 1.6 percent from the December 1982 estimate, and 17 percent below the 97.8 million bags produced during the 1981/82 season. Total South American production was reduced by over 16 million bags from the previous year's level, and production in Brazil, the world's major supplier, was cut by almost a half to 17.8 million bags in the 1982/83 season. However, spokesmen for the USDA reported that the coffee trees damaged by the 1981 Brazilian frost have recovered almost all of their producing capacity, and prospects for a good 1983/84 Brazilian crop were observed. The 860,000 bag reduction in African output was attributed mostly to dry weather and brush fires in the Ivory Coast. Most of the 0.8 million bag drop in Asian coffee production in 1982/83 was accounted for by adverse weather in Indonesian growing regions.

The 1982/83 world total of exportable coffee production was 60.2 million bags compared with 76.6 million in the previous season. Exporting members of the International Coffee Organization (ICO) accounted for nearly all of total world exports during the season. Shipments by ICO exporting members to member countries in calendar 1982 amounted to 54.9 million bags compared with 52.2 million in 1981.

U.S. imports of green coffee in calendar 1982 totaled 17.4 million bags, up 5 percent from 1981 imports amounting to 16.5 million. U.S. imports of roasted coffee were about 10 percent lower than in 1981, and soluble coffee imports were down about 12 percent. The volume of green coffee roasted in the U.S. in 1982 was estimated at 17.3 million bags compared with approximately 17.6 million in 1981. Unseasonably moderate winter temperatures and an observable trend of declining coffee consumption partly accounted for the decline in roaster interest during the year. However, overall world coffee consumption was reported to be recovering slowly from the declines recorded in 1977–78, and imports of green coffee into the 14 major coffee-consuming nations rose nearly 1.5 percent through most of 1982.

Early in 1983, ICO estimates put world coffee stocks at nearly 46 million bags, an amount equivalent to world demand for roughly nine months. At the beginning of the 1982/83 season, high carryover stocks burdened the trade balances as well as the physical storage capacity of many coffee producing countries. In many cases, stocks were relieved by an ICO-member country's ability to market coffee in the Middle East and Soviet Bloc countries, which are not members of the ICO. As coffee prices settled and stocks increased throughout the year, the smuggling of ICO coffee into non-ICO ports at below-quota prices became an annoyance to the cartel. The widening spread between non-ICO prices and the higher quota prices moved ICO spokesmen to warn of the establishment of a two-tiered world coffee price structure.

In January 1983, in a move to stabilize coffee prices within established ranges, the ICO agreed on a voluntary procedure intended to monitor sales to non-ICO countries. Both producing and consuming member countries consented to provide the ICO with data that would facilitate the observation of coffee shipped to non-ICO ports, including shipment and arrival times, volume, and the countries of origin and destination. Third-quarter 1983 export quotas, effective April 1, 1983, were set at 13.2 million bags, of which 12.7 million was distributed. However, the quota was reduced by 500,000 bags in March, and a decision was scheduled for June concerning a further reduction of 250,000 bags to reflect the withdrawal of Israel and Hungary from the International Coffee Agreement. (ICA).

The U.S., the Netherlands, Spain, Belgium, Luxembourg, and Japan became ICA signatories as of March, 1983. This newest Agreement, which is to become effective September 30, 1983, was open for signature at the United Nations until June 30.

Futures Markets

Arabica coffee futures are traded on the Coffee, Sugar & Cocoa Exchange, Inc., in New York. Robusta coffee futures are traded in London.

World Green Coffee (Exportable)[3] Production   In Thousands of 60 Kilo Bags

Crop[2] Year	Angola	Brazil	Cameroon	Colombia	Costa Rica	Ethiopia	Guatemala	Indonesia	Ivory Coast	Kenya	Mexico	Salvador	Uganda	Zaire (Congo, K)	World Total
1971-2	3,300	14,850	1,220	5,750	1,190	1,490	1,845	1,320	4,400	973	1,835	2,440	2,830	1,200	53,083
1972-3	3,400	15,000	1,533	7,430	1,160	1,410	1,990	1,650	4,985	1,240	2,100	1,935	3,280	1,265	57,285
1973-4	3,095	6,370	1,213	6,250	1,400	1,005	1,925	1,795	3,219	1,073	1,690	2,203	3,078	1,184	43,674
1974-5	3,352	19,500	1,766	7,400	1,237	1,051	2,255	1,700	4,432	1,082	2,156	3,130	3,302	1,017	62,862
1975-6	1,100	15,000	1,455	7,100	1,104	1,011	1,753	2,033	5,107	1,224	2,456	2,350	2,192	922	54,307
1976-7	267	1,800	1,281	7,900	1,147	1,049	1,915	2,219	4,782	1,644	2,080	2,788	2,634	1,270	42,777
1977-8	972	10,000	1,344	9,500	1,264	1,354	2,245	2,886	3,357	1,367	2,001	2,510	1,838	954	52,571
1978-9	568	12,000	1,606	10,970	1,533	1,432	2,517	3,738	4,677	1,181	2,915	3,226	1,905	1,123	60,028
1979-0	220	14,000	1,626	10,962	1,311	1,535	2,332	3,723	3,908	1,468	2,310	3,122	2,001	1,141	62,357
1980-1	345	13,500	1,717	11,675	1,815	1,664	2,361	4,137	6,026	1,612	2,362	2,490	2,090	1,346	65,556
1981-2[1]	350	24,500	1,865	12,150	1,632	1,596	2,328	4,618	3,985	1,546	2,450	2,180	2,840	1,215	76,624
1982-3[1]	487	9,750	1,915	11,645	2,077	1,720	2,135	3,920	3,832	1,495	2,500	2,200	2,954	1,265	60,160
1983-4															

[1] Preliminary. [2] Coffee marketing year begins in July in some countries & in others about Oct. [3] Exportable production represents total harvested production minus estimated domestic consumption. Source: Foreign Agricultural Service, U.S.D.A.   T.118

COFFEE

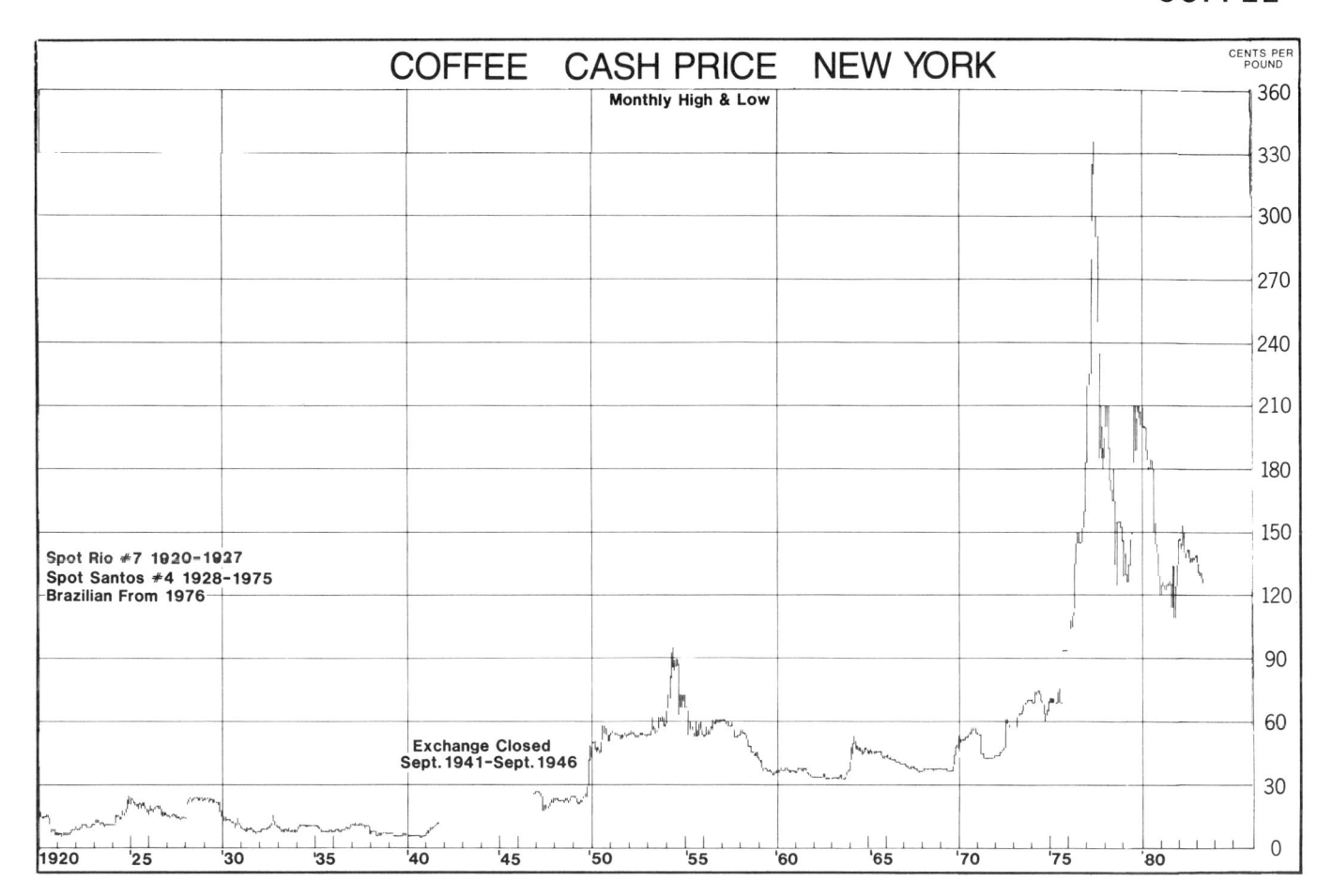

COFFEE CASH PRICE NEW YORK
Monthly High & Low

Spot Rio #7 1920-1927
Spot Santos #4 1928-1975
Brazilian From 1976

Exchange Closed Sept. 1941-Sept. 1946

Average Spot Price of Coffee (Santos No. 4) in N.Y.   In Cents Per Pound

Year	Jan.	Feb.	Mar.	Apr.	May	June	July	Aug.	Sept.	Oct.	Nov.	Dec.	Average
1970	54.8	54.8	54.3	53.8	53.8	53.8	56.8	57.0	57.8	58.8	57.5	55.0	55.7
1971	55.0	55.0	48.0	45.0	43.8	43.8	43.0	43.3	43.3	43.3	44.0	44.0	46.1
1972	N.A.	N.A.	N.A.	46.3	48.0	48.5	N.A.	62.5	59.0	48.0	56.0	57.0	54.4
1973	57.0	62.0	65.5	65.0	65.0	67.0	70.0	70.0	72.5	72.3	73.0	72.0	67.6
1974	72.0	71.0	75.0	75.5	76.5	74.0	72.0	63.0	60.0	64.0	69.0	70.0	70.2
1975	67.5	68.0	——————————————————No Quotations——————————————————										67.8
1976	————No Quote————				93.5	————No Quote————			152.0	————No Quote————			122.8
1977	——————————————————————————No Quote——————————————————————————												
1978	————————————No Quote————————————							135.0	154.0	154.0	153.0	146.0	148.4
1979	146.0	127.0	136.0	138.0	148.0	180.0	209.0	201.0	206.0	208.0	205.0	212.0	176.3
1980	189.0	213.0	205.0	208.0	218.0	211.0	195.0	206.0	206.0	210.0	210.0	208.0	206.6
1981	218.0	218.0	218.0	218.0	129.0	115.5	115.5	127.0	127.0	129.5	147.0	150.0	159.4
1982	151.0	136.0	136.0	145.0	145.0	145.0	145.0	145.0	145.0	145.0	133.0	133.0	142.0
1983	133.0	133.0											

Source: Bureau of Labor Statistics (0191-0101.01)   T.120

COFFEE

World Green Coffee (Total) Production   In Thousands of 60 Kilo Bags (132.276 Lbs. Per Bag)

Crop Year	Angola	Brazil	Cameroon	Colombia	Costa Rica	Ethiopia	Guatemala	India	Indonesia	Ivory Coast	Mexico	Salvador	Uganda	Zaire (Congo, K)	World Total
1973–4	3,200	14,500	1,260	7,800	1,570	1,700	2,200	1,535	2,750	3,285	3,300	2,378	3,100	1,317	62,459
1974–5	3,444	27,500	1,816	9,000	1,390	2,488	2,540	1,630	2,675	4,500	3,900	3,300	3,331	1,150	81,691
1975–6	1,180	23,000	1,482	8,500	1,276	2,677	2,043	1,498	3,049	5,266	3,856	2,530	2,214	1,072	73,008
1976–7	1,131	9,300	1,307	9,300	1,331	2,782	2,213	1,753	3,219	4,867	3,330	2,973	2,664	1,437	61,439
1977–8	1,047	17,500	1,371	11,050	1,449	3,143	2,550	2,147	3,911	3,393	3,401	2,700	1,868	1,129	71,374
1978–9	613	20,000	1,634	12,600	1,749	3,142	2,827	1,842	4,788	4,742	4,022	3,423	1,944	1,293	79,074
1979–0	260	22,000	1,658	12,712	1,522	3,188	2,647	2,495	4,803	3,973	3,600	3,322	2,042	1,316	82,032
1980–1	586	21,500	1,950	13,500	2,023	3,264	2,702	1,977	5,265	6,090	3,862	2,690	2,133	1,526	85,744
1981–2[1]	392	33,000	1,900	14,500	1,875	3,212	2,653	2,517	5,870	4,050	4,050	2,380	2,885	1,400	97,812
1982–3[1]	530	17,750	1,950	13,500	2,300	3,350	2,470	2,000	5,300	3,900	4,200	2,400	3,000	1,450	81,174
1983–4															

[1] Preliminary.   Source: *Foreign Agricultural Service, U.S.D.A.*   T.117

Origin of Coffee Imports (for Consumption) into the U.S.   In Thousands of 60 Kilo Bags

Year	Ethiopia	Brazil	Colombia	Costa Rica	Domin. Repub.	Peru	Ecuador	Guatemala	Indonesia	Mexico	Ivory Coast	Angola	Salvador	Venezuela	Grand Total
1970	1,071	4,717	2,497	375	352		600	716		982		1,385	539	253	19,732
1971	1,130	6,536	2,642	350	338		404	813		1,286		1,590	645	246	22,686
1972	965	6,152	2,711	294	401		490	689	744	1,070	977	1,297	391	243	20,769
1973	1,062	4,596	2,868	284	507		435	1,110	626	1,641	1,150	1,693	1,047	174	21,789
1974	505	2,725	3,090	268	381		512	1,096	942	1,324	749	2,396	1,111	246	19,245
1975	533	3,748	3,400	192	336		694	874	765	1,662	966	1,202	1,018	182	20,289
1976	703	3,092	2,688	179	551		767	749	1,082	1,869	1,330	871	1,045	288	19,788
1977	288	2,453	1,951	272	585		505	832	860	1,406	673	49	1,037	155	14,808
1978	461	2,694	2,808	334	461		1,044	942	1,177	1,390	775	304	627	239	18,133
1979	549	1,890	3,891	516	548		638	1,123	1,294	1,934	834	40	1,123	121	19,396
1980	406	3,505	3,404	298	343	565	539	1,374	1,315	1,337	438	120	1,374	35	18,153
1981	547	3,243	1,727	226	359	573	701	645	1,516	1,393	602	21	779	27	16,555
1982[1]	578	3,372	1,710	248	500	513	773	844	1,118	1,377	998	63	919	16	17,416
1983															

[1] Preliminary.   Source: *U.S. Department of Commerce*   T.122

Total Coffee Imports (for Consumption) into the U.S.   In Thousands of 60 Kilo Bags

Year	Jan.	Feb.	Mar.	Apr.	May	June	July	Aug.	Sept.	Oct.	Nov.	Dec.	Total
1970	1,783	1,841	1,716	1,639	1,644	1,891	1,550	1,616	1,355	1,713	1,597	1,382	19,727
1971	2,002	1,530	1,480	2,032	1,759	1,941	2,132	2,720	2,754	621	875	1,818	21,669
1972	2,547	2,172	1,137	1,146	1,784	1,452	1,434	1,947	2,149	2,057	1,643	1,288	20,757
1973	1,996	1,844	2,101	2,050	2,494	1,710	1,573	1,731	1,399	1,624	1,624	1,652	21,799
1974	2,182	2,022	2,457	2,264	1,873	1,529	1,499	1,152	821	740	1,159	1,550	19,248
1975	1,852	1,656	1,535	1,448	1,365	1,736	1,626	1,868	2,533	1,784	1,587	1,299	20,289
1976	1,664	1,744	2,311	1,636	1,546	1,864	1,909	1,637	956	1,013	1,649	1,858	19,788
1977	1,994	1,707	1,839	1,824	1,224	1,137	756	695	678	635	972	1,347	14,808
1978	1,682	1,575	1,707	1,557	1,345	1,249	1,316	1,124	1,337	1,901	1,689	1,651	18,133
1979	1,747	1,353	1,631	2,037	1,619	1,617	1,597	1,404	1,632	1,273	1,593	1,893	19,396
1980	2,020	1,366	1,421	1,642	1,566	1,663	1,533	1,386	1,062	1,292	1,386	1,715	18,153
1981	1,858	1,738	1,395	1,299	1,356	1,026	922	1,213	1,150	1,487	1,565	1,547	16,555
1982	1,287	1,195	1,490	1,147	1,476	1,335	1,282	1,602	1,640	2,005	1,356	1,602	17,416
1983	1,556												

Source: *U.S. Dept. of Commerce*   T.121

# COFFEE

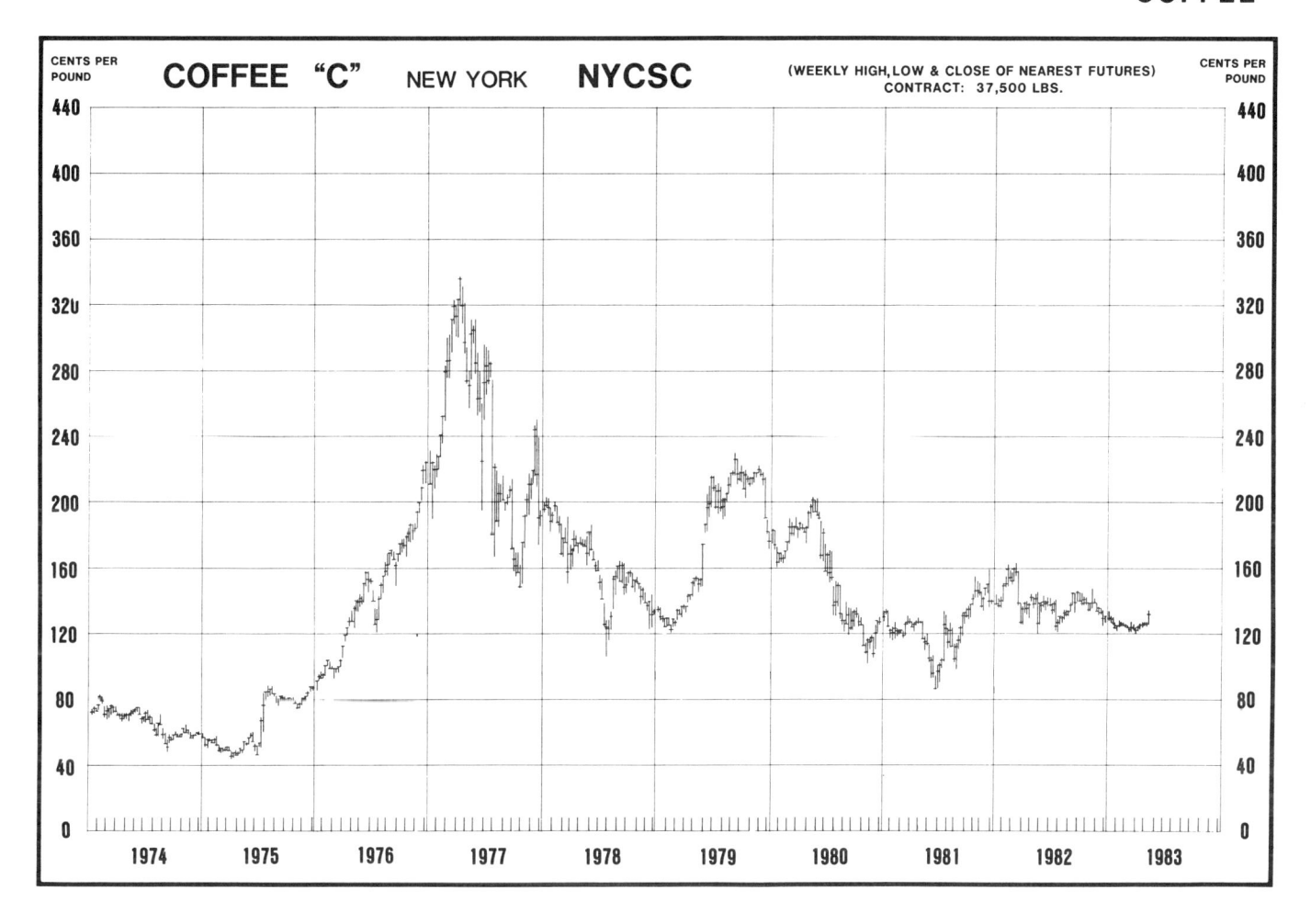

COFFEE "C" NEW YORK NYCSC (WEEKLY HIGH, LOW & CLOSE OF NEAREST FUTURES) CONTRACT: 37,500 LBS.

High, Low & Closing Prices of May Coffee Futures in New York   In Cents per Pound

Year of Delivery		Mar.	Apr.	May	June	July	Aug.	Sept.	Oct.	Nov.	Dec.	Jan.	Feb.	Mar.	Apr.	May	Life of Delivery Range
1978	High	—	314.50	294.13	255.25	201.50	185.00	171.25	150.00	161.00	175.80	190.40	179.00	173.50	183.25	179.25	314.50
	Low	—	290.75	255.90	188.00	163.00	159.00	145.50	132.00	135.00	152.00	167.00	158.80	144.50	160.25	172.00	132.00
	Close	—	292.75	261.25	194.07	179.00	164.25	147.50	147.50	158.63	174.43	170.50	159.46	168.65	174.75	179.00	—
1979	High	125.00	120.00	150.25	163.50	121.25	138.50	144.00	144.00	139.95	130.50	134.76	128.45	138.00	152.00	155.10	163.50
	Low	111.75	111.00	114.50	121.50	94.00	102.00	128.00	132.25	126.50	114.75	120.50	119.41	126.60	132.50	145.00	94.00
	Close	118.25	115.20	149.50	124.75	113.50	137.00	132.88	139.25	130.36	130.47	124.92	127.47	137.49	151.25	149.49	—
1980	High	145.00	154.86	155.00	216.49	216.35	197.00	200.00	204.75	198.00	191.50	184.00	183.50	194.75	188.00	199.00	216.49
	Low	126.49	140.50	144.05	157.00	178.29	179.25	190.35	183.50	187.00	175.00	166.91	165.50	180.75	176.50	174.75	116.00
	Close	144.99	153.50	153.00	216.49	183.90	195.09	197.25	189.31	194.08	175.96	171.00	183.26	182.25	176.60	195.25	—
1981	High	190.75	187.50	198.00	198.60	181.40	162.00	157.00	138.00	128.50	130.40	137.00	127.00	131.40	129.25	127.90	198.60
	Low	176.25	176.10	177.40	169.00	138.47	135.25	129.75	128.25	114.75	116.00	123.30	115.55	117.65	121.50	113.00	113.00
	Close	179.69	178.54	190.60	179.75	146.59	143.78	134.65	128.55	123.25	127.81	127.25	121.00	128.66	126.48	113.00	—
1982	High	126.25	124.00	123.87	111.00	126.75	120.25	123.50	130.25	138.00	133.80	137.88	147.30	149.00	143.75	144.95	149.00
	Low	120.10	117.50	111.50	80.50	81.25	98.28	96.10	123.00	124.25	122.23	128.75	137.25	124.50	129.20	135.10	80.50
	Close	122.60	122.25	112.50	87.50	121.45	98.28	123.00	129.00	126.23	133.63	137.88	141.26	128.56	141.72	138.25	—
1983	High	116.50	118.50	117.50	121.25	117.50	114.00	131.00	131.15	135.40	132.30	127.90	123.95	126.90	126.85		
	Low	114.00	107.50	109.25	113.50	103.51	107.50	111.00	124.00	126.25	121.60	120.25	118.90	120.35	120.10		
	Close	114.76	113.00	118.51	118.28	108.25	113.10	129.45	130.49	131.78	125.00	120.60	120.12	123.23	124.80		
1984	High	117.00	117.75														
	Low	109.50	113.00														
	Close	115.13	116.75														

Source: N.Y. Coffee, Sugar & Cocoa Exch., Inc.

T.125

COFFEE

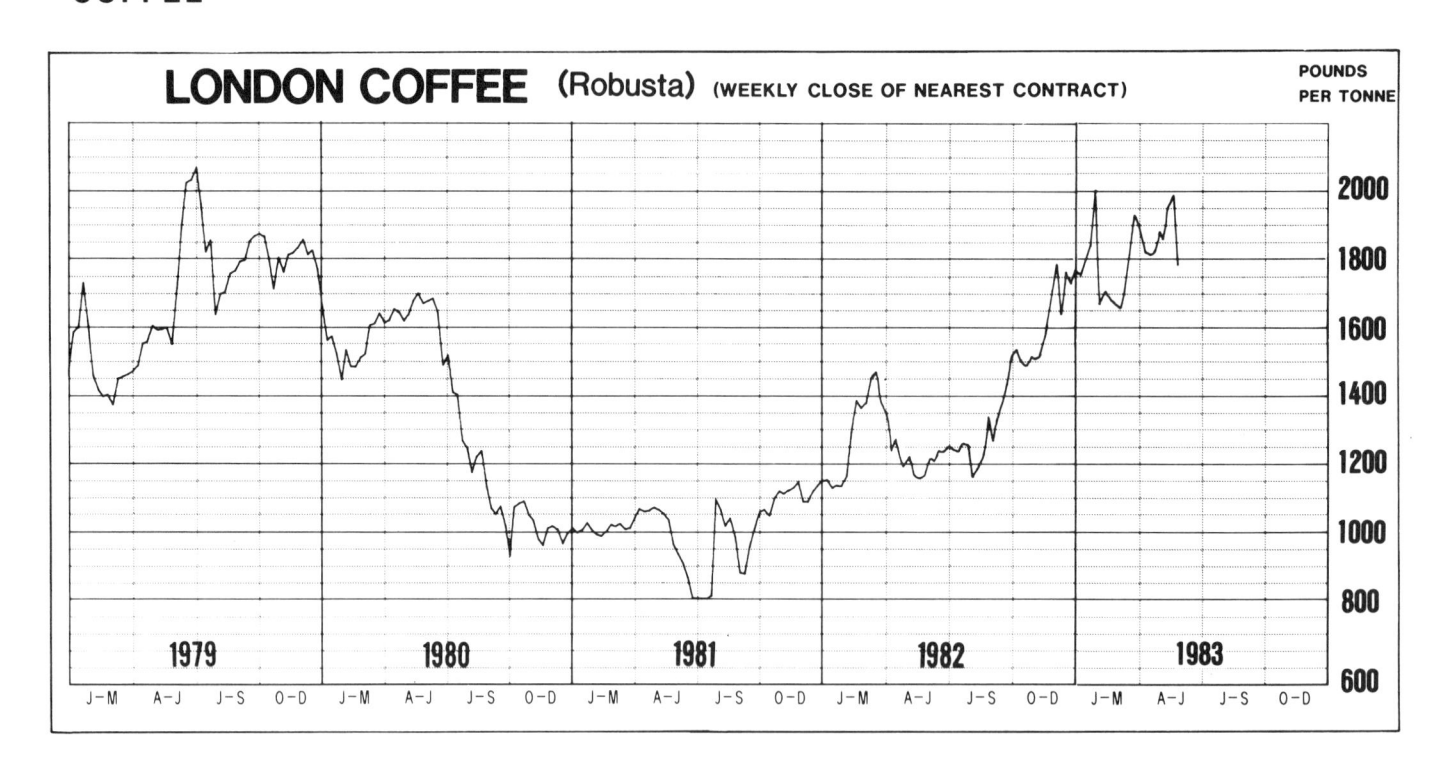

LONDON COFFEE (Robusta) (WEEKLY CLOSE OF NEAREST CONTRACT)
POUNDS PER TONNE

Month End Open Interest of Coffee Futures at New York   In Contracts

Year	Jan.	Feb.	Mar.	Apr.	May	June	July	Aug.	Sept.	Oct.	Nov.	Dec.
1978	4,413	4,191	3,942	3,661	3,733	2,952	3,152	3,926	4,004	4,767	5,951	6,581
1979	7,113	7,965	8,799	9,751	10,279	8,761	10,214	12,014	12,479	14,808	15,974	15,988
1980	13,077	13,113	12,990	11,288	16,975	15,854	13,576	10,767	11,824	11,155	9,489	8,848
1981	8,218	8,624	9,931	10,043	8,969	8,093	9,182	8,182	9,223	9,084	8,922	9,823
1982	11,236	9,647	9,249	8,753	7,949	8,358	7,791	8,393	9,677	8,876	9,152	9,273
1983	10,752	10,336	11,739	11,752								
1984												

Source: N.Y. Coffee, Sugar & Cocoa Exch., Inc.   T.124

Volume of Trading of Coffee "C" Futures at New York   In Contracts

Year	Jan.	Feb.	Mar.	Apr.	May	June	July	Aug.	Sept.	Oct.	Nov.	Dec.	Total
1978	11,125	10,341	17,202	12,049	12,194	11,112	11,346	18,526	13,526	14,615	14,589	17,334	163,959
1979	21,463	25,243	24,205	36,298	35,885	39,137	43,944	43,046	40,088	50,054	51,949	38,488	449,799
1980	70,277	77,143	112,558	93,108	145,830	87,149	80,217	66,054	69,731	37,528	35,310	32,029	906,944
1981	38,671	34,086	44,963	29,766	39,384	46,094	50,759	50,482	44,368	44,235	49,468	41,757	515,302
1982	47,560	50,976	63,168	52,708	51,062	44,428	42,779	38,457	44,583	39,967	46,247	37,500	556,435
1983	30,567	32,884	44,211	37,399									
1984													

Source: N.Y. Coffee, Sugar & Cocoa Exch., Inc.   T.123

Coke

World Production of Metallurgical Coke[1], by Specified Countries   In Millions of Short Tons

Year	Belgium	Canada	Czechoslovakia	France	W. Germany	United Kingdom	India	Italy	Japan	Netherlands	Poland	China	U.S.S.R.[2]	United States	World Total
1969	8.0	5.0	11.0	15.0	43.0	22.5	9.9	7.3	34.2	2.2	16.3	19.0	81.0	64.8	370.2
1970	7.8	5.7	11.3	15.6	44.0	22.4	9.9	7.8	41.6	2.2	15.3	20.0	83.1	66.5	386.3
1971	7.5	5.1	11.5	13.8	41.4	21.1	9.9	7.7	42.7	2.1	15.6	24.0	86.3	57.4	377.7
1972	8.0	5.2	11.8	12.7	38.0	14.8	10.0	7.8	39.8	2.2	17.5	26.5	87.9	60.5	375.4
1973	8.6	5.9	10.1	13.1	37.5	19.6	9.8	8.5	48.9	2.9	18.7	30.0	89.7	64.3	422.8
1974	8.9	6.0	10.3	12.9	38.5	17.4	9.0	9.4	50.3	3.0	18.7	30.9	91.1	61.6	424.9
1975	6.3	5.8	10.2	12.1	38.4	17.5	7.8	8.9	49.4	3.0	19.0	30.9	92.1	57.2	417.4
1976[2]	8.6	5.8	11.9	12.0	35.2	17.4	9.9	8.8	47.9	3.1	19.8	30.9	93.0	58.3	424.9
1977[3]	6.1	5.4	9.9	11.9	30.3	15.6	11.0	8.9	47.0	2.8	21.0	30.9	94.2	53.5	411.8
1978[3]														49.0	402.0
1979[3]														52.9	375.9
1980[3]														46.1	

[1] Excluding Breeze.   [2] Preliminary.   [3] Estimate.   Source: Bureau of Mines   T.126

U.S. Salient Statistics of Coke   In Thousands of Net Tons

Year	Production Total	Production Oven	Production Beehive	Producers' Stocks—Jan. 1 Oven Coke at Plants Total	Merchant	Furnace	Beehive	Exports	Imports	Exports to Canada	Exports to Mexico	Value of Coke Produced[2] Mil. $	Value of All Coal Chemical Mater. Mil. $	Value Per Ton Sold Oven Coke $	Value Per Ton Sold Beehive Coke $
1969	64,757	64,047	710	5,985	348	5,637	1	1,629	173	292.2	629.8	1,403	289	24.50	16.23
1970	66,525	65,654	871	3,120	99	3,020	1	2,478	153	347.1	376.0	1,899	293	29.97	19.89
1971	57,436	56,664	772	4,113	95	4,018	1	1,509	174	492.4	80.2	1,849	260	37.41	21.45
1972	60,507	59,853	654	3,510	134	3,376	1	1,232	185	488.0	105.2	2,080	295	40.70	22.04
1973	64,325	63,496	829	2,941	351	2,590	1	1,395	1,094	747.5	102.3	2,575	356	42.92	27.31
1974	61,581	60,737	845	1,184	71	1,113	—	1,278	3,540	709.7	158.0	4,609	653	65.74	44.02
1975	57,207	56,494	713	935	25	910	—	1,273	1,819	680.6	107.3	4,607	654	87.64	65.17
1976	58,333	57,728	605	5,001	278	4,718	—	1,315	1,311	754.4	87.7	5,021	920	94.35	72.48
1977[1]	53,509	53,060	449	6,491	314	6,173	—	1,241	1,829	634.9	49.4	4,653	883	103.27	78.87
1978[1]	49,009	48,593	355	3,534	136	6,308	—	693	5,722	299	37.4	5,635	923		
1979[1]	52,943			6,724	184	3,350	—	1,440	3,974	598	61.0	5,459	1,203		
1980[1]	46,132			5,185	595	4,590	—	2,162	659	812	75.0				
1981[1]	42,786			8,627	1,106	7,521	—	1,251	527						
1982[3]	44,000			6,724					300						
1983[3]				8,000											

[1] Preliminary.   [2] Beehive and oven, coke & breeze.   [3] Estimate.   Source: Bureau of Mines   T.127

Oven Coke Production in the United States   In Thousands of Short Tons

Year	Jan.	Feb.	Mar.	Apr.	May	June	July	Aug.	Sept.	Oct.	Nov.	Dec.	Total
1970	5,332	5,069	5,655	5,468	5,603	5,402	5,442	5,368	5,425	5,680	5,537	5,672	65,654
1971	5,647	5,054	5,752	5,621	5,693	5,268	4,816	3,455	3,976	3,961	3,220	4,200	56,664
1972	4,763	4,651	5,076	5,091	5,237	4,976	5,024	5,088	4,822	5,026	4,914	5,183	59,853
1973	5,364	4,891	5,356	5,262	5,454	5,325	5,307	5,383	5,153	5,358	5,218	5,426	63,496
1974	5,422	4,974	5,265	5,255	5,369	5,218	5,251	5,219	5,056	5,214	4,427	4,067	60,737
1975	4,924	4,750	5,324	5,030	5,052	4,765	4,532	4,427	4,250	4,527	4,365	4,549	56,494
1976	4,551	4,372	5,041	4,884	5,069	4,938	5,007	4,785	4,720	4,857	4,752	4,751	57,728
1977	4,412	4,267	4,696	4,666	4,822	4,686	4,639	4,249	4,069	4,289	4,186	4,077	53,060
1978	3,603	2,741	2,661	3,753	4,398	4,362	4,455	4,379	4,346	4,512	4,383	4,645	48,238
1979[1]	4,448	4,015	4,653	4,389	4,591	4,324	4,386	4,430	4,367	4,460	4,266	4,453	52,943
1980[1]	4,394	4,204	4,444	4,396	4,238	3,686	3,370	3,387	3,295	3,470	3,565	3,683	46,132
1981[1]	———11,382———			———9,853———			———11,175———			———10,580———			42,786
1982[1]	———8,828———			———7,507———			———6,270———						

[1] Preliminary.   Source: Bureau of Mines   T.128

COKE

U.S. Coke & Its Relationship to the Iron Industry and Coal-Chemical Production

Year	Apparent Consumption	Consumption In Iron Furnaces	All Other	Lbs. of Coke Consumed Per Net Ton of Pig Iron & Ferro-Alloys	% Yield of Coke From Coal	Lbs. of Coking Coal Consumed Per Net Ton of P. I. & F. A.	Blast Furnace Plants	Foundries	Producer & Water Gas Plants	Other Industrial Plants	Light-Oil Deriv. Mill. Gal.	Ammonium Sulfate[2] Mill. Lbs.	Crude Coal Tar Mill. Gal.	Crude Light Oil Mill. Gal.	Coke-oven Gas Billion cu. ft.
	——— 1,000 Net Tons ———						——— In Millions of Net Tons ———								
1969	66,166	60,176	5,990	1,260	69.4	1,816	61.3	3.5	—3.0—		136	1,464	769	259	962
1970	63,207	58,151	5,056	1,267	69.0	1,833	61.2	3.3	—2.3—		120	1,382	761	244	993
1971	56,689	51,498	5,191	1,261	69.0	1,827	54.0	3.3	—1.6—		95	1,154	679	202	862
1972	60,046	54,607	5,439	1,222	69.0	1,768	56.0	3.4	—1.6—		104	1,208	747	214	916
1973	65,765	60,720	5,045	1,200	68.4	1,754	61.2	3.7	—1.4—		114	1,250	732	226	995
1974	64,092	58,441	5,651	1,219	68.4	1,783	57.2	3.4	—1.2—		95	1,200	677	217	967
1975	53,687	48,817	4,870	1,222	68.4	1,786	49.6	2.6	— .9—			1,022	646	195	895
1976	56,834	51,561	5,273	1,187	68.9	1,723	52.5	3.0	—1.2—			1,044	636	198	
1977[1]	54,144	48,510	5,634	1,193	68.9	1,731	48.8	3.3	—1.5—				592	178	
1978[1]	56,984	51,286	5,662	1,439	68.6	1,667	48.1	2.6	—1.1—				541	162	
1979[1]	53,826	50,008	3,818	1,150	68.4	1,681	48.0	2.5	—1.4—				591	175	
1980[1]													534	159	

[1] Preliminary. [2] Or equivalent. Source: *Bureau of Mines* T.129

Coke (Oven-Coke) Stocks at Plants   In Thousands of Short Tons

Year	Jan. 1	Feb. 1	Mar. 1	Apr. 1	May 1	June 1	July 1	Aug. 1	Sept. 1	Oct. 1	Nov. 1	Dec. 1
1970	3,120	3,032	3,034	3,088	3,100	3,098	2,954	3,006	2,963	3,057	3,433	3,777
1971	4,113	4,241	4,054	3,842	3,599	3,343	3,153	3,401	3,818	4,070	4,143	3,596
1972	3,510	3,585	3,611	3,323	3,111	3,022	2,907	3,089	3,185	3,202	3,089	3,011
1973	2,941	2,824	2,560	2,291	2,035	1,796	1,712	1,514	1,520	1,501	1,435	1,313
1974	1,184	1,125	1,139	1,163	1,183	1,238	1,243	1,146	1,197	1,321	1,298	1,064
1975	935	1,054	1,262	1,442	1,733	2,261	2,889	3,522	3,867	3,821	4,108	4,522
1976	4,996	5,092	4,994	5,105	5,062	4,992	4,729	4,641	4,445	4,750	5,179	5,800
1977	6,487	6,950	7,231	7,283	7,038	6,736	6,468	6,516	6,281	6,192	6,554	6,526
1978	6,444	5,937	5,209	3,460	3,189	2,993	2,964	2,845	2,989	3,065	3,131	3,339
1979[1]	3,534	3,479	3,440	3,259	3,405	3,406	3,168	3,223	3,304	3,715	4,208	4,608
1980[1]	5,163	5,531	5,781	5,832	6,063	6,698	7,426	8,133	8,676	9,018	9,011	9,040
1981[1]	8,267	—	—	7,586	—	—	4,990	—	—	5,198	—	—
1982[1]	6,724	—	—	7,455	—	—	7,871	—	—	7,969	—	—
1983												

[1] Preliminary. Source: *Bureau of Mines* T.131

Index of Wholesale Price[1] of Oven Foundry Coke F.O.B. at Birmingham, Ala.   Base Per Ton 1967 = 100

Year	Jan.	Feb.	Mar.	Apr.	May	June	July	Aug.	Sept.	Oct.	Nov.	Dec.	Average
1970	37.85	37.85	37.85	41.85	41.85	41.85	41.85	41.85	41.85	48.60	48.60	48.60	42.54
1971	48.60	48.60	48.60	48.60	48.60	50.10	50.10	50.10	50.10	50.10	50.10	50.10	49.48
1972	50.10	52.35	52.35	52.35	52.35	52.35	52.35	52.35	52.35	52.35	52.35	52.35	52.16
1973	54.90	54.90	54.90	56.80	56.80	56.80	56.80	56.80	56.80	56.80	56.80	56.80	56.33
1974	59.95	59.95	63.75	73.50	80.50	80.50	80.50	91.00	95.50	100.50	100.50	100.50	82.22
1975	108.00	108.00	108.00	110.50	110.50	110.50	110.50	110.50	110.50	110.50	110.50	110.50	109.88
1976	117.00	117.00	117.00	117.00	117.00	117.00	117.00	117.00	117.00	117.00	117.00	117.00	117.00
1977	123.00	123.00	123.00	123.00	129.00	129.00	129.00	129.00	129.00	129.00	129.00	129.00	127.00
1978	134.00	134.00	134.00	134.00	139.75	139.75	139.75	139.75	139.75	139.75	139.75	139.75	137.83
1979	144.75	144.75	144.75	N.A.	N.A.	N.A.	N.A.	144.75	144.75	146.65	146.65	145.45	145.46
1980[1]	439.6	439.6	439.6	439.6	439.6	439.6	439.6	439.6	439.6	439.6	439.6	434.0	439.1
1981	434.0	434.0	434.0	434.0	478.9	478.9	478.9	478.9	478.9	478.9	478.9	478.9	463.9
1982	478.9	485.2	485.2	N.A.	485.2	454.8	467.4	465.9	465.7	463.4	463.4	463.4	470.8
1983	460.5	460.5	452.7										

[1] Prior to 1980, data are for the price of oven foundry coke, F.O.B. at Birmingham, Ala. in dollars per net ton. Source: *Bureau of Labor Statistics*
(0522-0101.99) T.130

Copper

World mine production of copper in 1982 decreased by about 5 percent, according to preliminary data of the U.S. Bureau of Mines. This substantial decrease was due to poor demand and excess supply, both of which stemmed from depressed overall economic conditions. U.S. mine production of copper in 1982 was also drastically reduced by about 28 percent from 1981's output which was the largest in 8 years. U.S. refinery production of copper was off 25 percent in 1982 from the 1981 level.

Refined copper production in the U.S. from scrap at primary plants was off 14 percent in 1982, but production from secondary plants was up 6 percent. The total amount of copper recovered as refined metal by both primary and secondary plants was seven percent below the 1981 level.

Total U.S. imports for consumption (copper content) in 1982 were 15 percent higher than in 1981, with the "Ore and concentrate" and "Blister" classes up by approximately 68 percent from 1981. Scrap was up by 4 percent, while refined was down 12 percent, and Matte was up 33 percent.

U.S. exports of refined copper in 1982 increased by 20 percent from 1981. Copper exports in the form of ore, concentrate and blister rose about 19 percent, and insulated wire and cable exports were down 27 percent. Exports of unalloyed copper scrap increased by 8 percent and alloyed copper scrap exports declined by 5 percent.

Total 1982 consumption of refined copper in the U.S. was 17½ percent below that of 1981, and consumption of purchased new and old copper-base scrap was 20 percent lower than in 1981. Refined copper consumed in mill products at wire rod mills in 1982 was 15 percent less than the amount consumed in 1981, and consumption at brass mills was about 27 percent lower than in 1981. An estimated 80 percent of net copper consumed in 1982 entered fabrication as refined metal; of this, 73 percent was estimated to have been consumed by 18 wire mills, and 24 percent by 45 brass mills. The use of copper by industry was estimated to be; electrical-54 percent; construction-20 percent; industrial machinery-13 percent; transportation-8 percent; and other uses-5 percent.

At the end of 1982, U.S. industry stocks of refined copper were larger than the previous year by almost one-third. Stocks of refined copper at wire rod mills were 13 percent above the year earlier level, while brass mill stocks were 4 percent lower than the year earlier level. Blister and copper-base scrap stocks were 16-18 percent smaller in 1982 than in 1981.

Declines in demand, production, prices and profitability caused severe problems, for the copper industry in 1982. Both housing and auto industries—the major industrial users of the metal—were highly depressed in 1982. The U.S. producer price of copper, which was quoted at 85½ cents per pound at the end of 1981, saw a steady price decline through September of 1982, hitting a low of about 71⅓ cents per pound. Prices began to pick up in October, and by the end of 1982, prices had recovered to 74½ cents per pound. Due to the depressed economy and excessive supply, domestic copper producers were forced to sell their products well below the cost of production, severely curtail production, and lay off workers. However, increases in the demand for copper, due to a rebound in the housing and auto industries, was expected to occur in 1983.

Futures Markets

Copper futures are traded on the Commodity Exchange, Inc. (COMEX) in New York and on the London Metal Exchange (LME).

World Mine Production of Copper (Content of Ore) In Thousands of Metric[5] Tons

Year	Australia	Canada[3]	Chile	China	Finland	Japan	Mexico	Peru	Zambia	Poland	Zaire	Rep. of So. Africa	Philippines	United States[3]	USSR[4]	World Total[1]
1970	173.9	672.7	783.4		34.2	131.7	67.3	242.8	754.1		425.1	164.5	176.7	1,720		6,638
1971	195.4	721.4	790.7		31.3	133.4	69.6	228.6	718.0		447.3	173.6	217.8	1,522		6,689
1972	205.9	793.3	800.0		32.1	123.6	86.8	248.0	791.1		472.0	178.5	235.6	1,665	733	7,329
1973	242.8	908.2	810.6		41.2	124.0	88.7	223.4	778.9	170.9	538.6	193.8	243.8	1,718	772	7,845
1974	277.1	905.4	994.4	110	39.9	90.5	91.1	233.2	769.4	218.3	550.5	197.4	249.1	1,597	816	8,063
1975	241.4	808.9	913.0	110	42.8	93.7	86.2	197.3	746.2	260.0	547.1	197.2	249.4	1,413	843	7,670
1976[5]	218.5	730.9	1,005	180	41.7	81.6	89.0	220.3	708.9	267.0	444.4	196.9	237.6	1,457	800	7,525
1977	221.6	759.4	1,056	195	46.7	81.4	89.7	338.1	656.0	289.3	481.6	208.3	272.8	1,364	830	7,739
1978	222.1	659.4	1,036	200	46.9	72.0	87.2	366.4	643.0	321.0	423.8	205.7	263.6	1,358	865	7,618
1979	234.6	636.4	1,061	200	41.1	59.1	107.1	390.7	588.3	325.0	400.0	190.6	298.3	1,444	885	7,674
1980	231.8	716.4	1,068	200	36.9	52.5	175.4	366.8	595.8	346.1	459.4	200.7	304.5	1,181	900	7,656
1981[2]	223.2	718.1	1,080	200	38.2	51.5	230.5	327.6	588.0	315.2	497.0	208.7	289.3	1,538	950	8,171
1982[1]	250	640	1,190				350		540	340	480		260	1,135	950	7,780
1983																

[1] Estimate. [2] Preliminary. [3] Recoverable. [4] Smelter Production. [5] Data prior to 1976 are in THOUSANDS OF SHORT TONS. Source: Bureau of Mines
T.132

COPPER

U.S. Salient Statistics of Copper   In Thousands of Metric[9] Tons

Year	New Copper Produced — From Domestic Ores — Mines	Smelters	Refineries	From Foreign Ores[2]	Total New	Secondary Recovered[7]	Imports[3] Unmanufactured	Refined	Exports Ore, Concentrate[4]	Refined[5]	Stocks—Dec. 31 At Producers	Refined	Blister & Materials in Solution	Appar. Consumption[6] Primary Copper	Primary & Old Copper[8]
1970	1,720	1,605	1,521	244	1,765	504	392	132	274	221	470	130	340	1,585	2,089
1971	1,522	1,471	1,411	181	1,592	445	359	164	263	188	378	75	303	1,623	2,068
1972	1,665	1,649	1,680	193	1,873	458	416	192	242	183	338	57	281	1,901	2,359
1973	1,718	1,705	1,698	170	1,868	486	421	203	293	189	302	37	265	1,902	2,388
1974	1,597	1,532	1,421	234	1,655	483	609	314	246	127	425	101	324	1,778	2,261
1975[9]	1,282	1,247	1,167	143	1,309	335	294	133	305	156	470	187	283	1,191	1,526
1976	1,457	1,326	1,291	106	1,396	380	485	346	218	102	463	172	291	1,656	2,036
1977	1,364	1,265	1,280	77	1,357	410	467	355	91	47	526	212	314	1,622	2,032
1978	1,358	1,270	1,327	122	1,449	502	546	415	187	92	416	153	263	1,819	2,321
1979	1,444	1,313	1,412	104	1,516	604	328	215	231	74	339	64	275	1,735	2,339
1980	1,181	994	1,122	89	1,211	613	547	427	107	14		49	272	1,638	2,251
1981[1]	1,538	1,295	1,430	114	1,544	598	430	331	160	24		151	277	1,748	2,346
1982[1]	1,135	940	1,077	148	1,225		506	258	197	31		268	233	1,324	1,800
1983															

[1] Preliminary.   [2] Also from matte, etc., refinery reports.   [3] Data are "general" imports; that is, they include copper imported for immediate consumption plus material entering country under bond.   [4] Blister (copper content)."   [5] Ingots, bars, etc.   [6] Withdrawals from total supply on domestic account.   [7] From old scrap only.   [8] Old scrap only.   [9] Data prior to 1975 are in THOUSANDS OF SHORT TONS.   Source: Bureau of Mines   T.133

Consumption of Refined Copper[2] in the United States   In Thousands of Metric[4] Tons

Year	By-Products Cathodes	Wire Bars	Ingot & Ingot Bars	Cakes & Slabs	Billets	Other	By Class of Consumer Wire Mills	Brass Mills	Chemical Plants	Secondary Smelters	Foundries	Miscellaneous	Total Consumption
1970	247.0	1,275.8	145.7	157.1	202.0	15.7	1,338.7	660.6	2.2	7.0	34.7		2,043.3
1971	309.4	1,236.9	118.3	154.8	182.3	17.7	1,324.9	655.8	1.5	6.9	30.4		2,019.5
1972	425.3	1,331.9	141.4	160.5	161.4	18.2	1,526.3	667.2	.9	10.0	34.5		2,238.9
1973	531.2	1,356.0	147.8	193.4	174.7	33.9	1,672.3	714.4	N.A.	10.6	N.A.		2,437.0
1974	579.7	1,136.7	143.1	178.0	138.6	18.1	1,474.3	670.2	.7	9.2	19.4	20.4	2,194.2
1975	527.9	722.8	72.5	97.7	75.7	4.1	1,061.3	439.0	.5	4.5	14.0	15.3	1,534.5
1976	846.0	768.0	93.5	123.8	84.0	8.6	1,346.0	574.9	.5	3.1	15.4	19.7	1,991.9
1977	965.5	861.3	90.2	115.0	103.3	11.2	1,511.2	628.6	N.A.	6.6	N.A.	N.A.	2,185.0
1978[4]	1,026.1	794.7	111.9	117.1	114.6	24.9	1,517.4	619.2	.4	7.5	12.4	32.3	2,189.3
1979	1,099.0	701.9	92.1	105.6	129.5	30.4	1,499.6	610.2	.4	6.3	11.9	30.1	2,158.4
1980	960.2	583.0	67.6	84.3	117.4	49.7	1,308.9	511.6	.3	5.0	10.9	25.3	1,862.1
1981[1]	1,198.9	489.2	66.7	121.8	101.9	46.7	1,449.6	536.2	.4	5.4	11.3	22.2	2,025.2
1982[3]	1,183.7	177.5	37.2	92.4	82.0	22.5	1,198.9	393.9		2.5			1,639.7
1983													

[1] Preliminary.   [2] Primary and secondary.   [3] Estimate.   [4] Data prior to 1978 are in THOUSANDS OF SHORT TONS.   Source: Bureau of Mines   T.134

U.S. Mine Production of Recoverable Copper, by Selected States   In Thousands of Metric[2] Tons

Year	Arizona	California	Colorado	Idaho	Michigan	Missouri	Montana	Nevada	New Mexico	Pennsylvania	Tennessee	Utah	Maine	Other States	Grand Total
1970	917.9	2.3	3.7	3.6	67.5	12.1	120.4	106.7	166.3	2.5	15.5	295.7	2.7	2.5	1,719.7
1971	820.2	.5	3.9	3.8	56.0	8.4	88.6	96.9	157.4	3.3	13.9	263.5	2.5	3.2	1,522.2
1972	908.6	.6	3.9	2.9	67.3	11.5	123.1	101.1	168.0	2.6	11.3	259.5	1.2	3.1	1,664.8
1973	927.3	.4	3.1	3.6	72.2	10.3	132.5	93.7	204.7	1.8	8.5	256.6	1.1	2.1	1,717.9
1974	858.8	.2	3.0	2.8	67.0	12.7	131.1	84.1	196.6	—	6.3	230.6	1.5	2.3	1,597.0
1975[2]	737.7	.3	3.2	2.9	66.9	12.9	79.8	73.7	132.7	—	9.1	160.7	1.8	.4	1,282.2
1976	929.3	.3	2.2	3.1	39.7	10.0	82.7	52.8	156.4	—	10.1	168.2	1.6	.2	1,456.6
1977	838.0	.2	1.7	3.7	38.4	10.6	78.2	60.8	149.4	—	5.6	176.1	1.2	.3	1,304.4
1978	891.4	N.A.	1.2	3.9	N.A.	10.8	67.3	20.5	127.8	—	11.3	186.3	—	37.1	1,357.6
1979	946.0	N.A.	.4	3.6	N.A.	13.0	69.9	N.A.	164.3	—	N.A.	193.1	—	53.3	1,443.6
1980	770.1	N.A.	.5	3.1	N.A.	13.6	37.7	N.A.	149.4	—	N.A.	157.8	—	48.9	1,181.1
1981	1,040.8	N.A.	N.A.	4.2	N.A.	8.4	62.5	N.A.	154.1	—	N.A.	211.3	—	56.8	1,538.2
1982[1]	764.4			3.2		8.1	64.1		73.9			187.7		35.0	1,137.2
1983															

[1] Preliminary.   [2] Data prior to 1975 are in THOUSANDS OF SHORT TONS.   Source: Bureau of Mines   T.135

COPPER

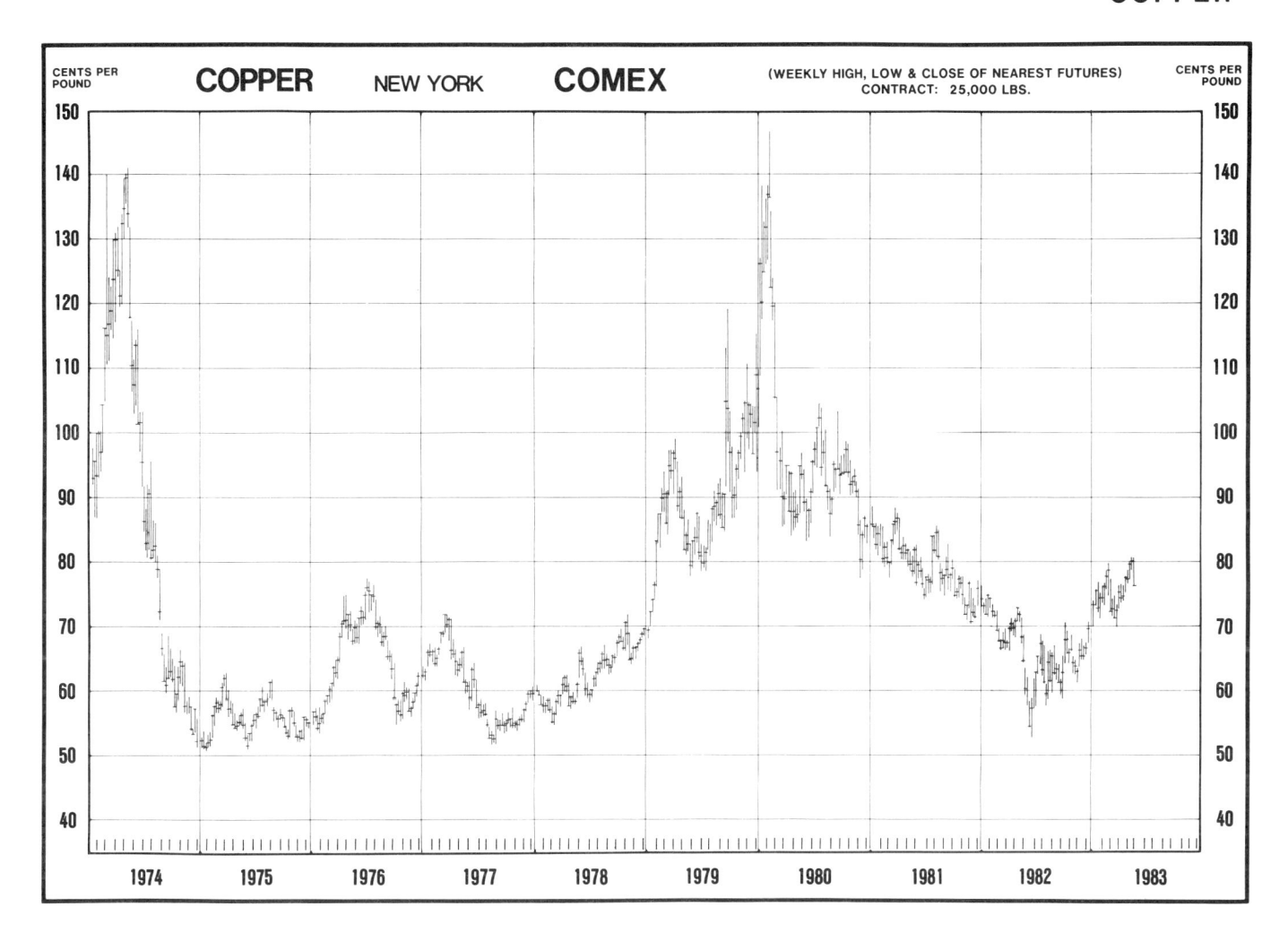

COPPER NEW YORK **COMEX** (WEEKLY HIGH, LOW & CLOSE OF NEAREST FUTURES)
CONTRACT: 25,000 LBS.

High, Low & Closing Prices of May Copper Futures on the Commodity Exch., Inc., N.Y. (COMEX) ¢ Lb.

Year of Delivery		Mar.	Apr.	May	June	July	Aug.	Sept.	Oct.	Nov.	Dec.	Jan.	Feb.	Mar.	Apr.	May	Life of Delivery Range
1978	High	75.80	76.40	71.90	68.50	63.60	59.20	59.90	60.60	58.80	62.40	62.70	59.80	62.00	62.40	64.40	76.40
	Low	75.50	67.60	63.80	61.80	59.90	55.40	56.90	56.60	56.30	58.80	58.10	56.00	55.50	57.00	57.80	55.40
	Close	75.80	68.40	64.80	64.40	59.90	57.70	58.60	57.40	58.80	61.20	59.00	56.50	60.60	59.10	64.40	—
1979	High	67.90	68.20	71.80	71.00	68.95	70.60	70.00	75.10	72.55	72.75	80.10	93.50	98.15	99.00	93.10	99.00
	Low	61.90	63.00	63.80	63.50	64.00	66.90	66.55	68.80	67.60	69.40	70.85	79.50	84.70	86.70	80.80	86.70
	Close	66.60	65.20	70.60	64.30	67.65	67.60	69.75	73.45	69.70	72.50	79.95	92.70	94.60	92.60	81.65	—
1980	High	97.60	97.50	93.10	87.85	87.35	94.50	111.90	117.05	102.50	106.50	140.80	148.40	123.30	94.90	95.50	148.40
	Low	86.70	88.70	81.90	82.00	79.75	83.70	87.20	87.50	91.50	95.00	104.20	121.00	85.20	83.80	84.80	79.75
	Close	94.85	93.10	82.95	82.75	82.80	93.40	105.80	92.60	102.50	104.75	131.60	123.00	87.10	87.90	94.60	—
1981	High	135.00	105.50	101.90	100.00	107.70	103.90	106.80	102.00	100.00	96.80	94.20	87.95	88.30	87.40	81.85	153.00
	Low	98.40	93.60	94.00	90.40	97.20	92.00	94.00	97.20	94.90	82.30	84.75	81.80	79.30	80.10	77.50	77.50
	Close	99.20	100.50	98.40	97.80	99.00	94.35	97.30	98.10	96.20	89.20	87.00	82.55	86.40	81.15	77.85	—
1982	High	100.00	99.65	96.00	94.10	92.80	95.50	87.40	84.90	81.70	80.50	77.70	76.25	71.75	71.25	72.90	115.20
	Low	92.80	94.00	91.35	86.70	85.20	85.80	79.80	79.40	74.85	74.00	73.00	71.10	66.70	66.10	66.65	66.10
	Close	98.85	95.20	93.20	86.80	93.10	87.45	82.10	81.65	77.35	77.30	76.35	71.15	67.55	70.70	66.70	—
1983	High	82.25	81.20	82.70	71.90	75.60	72.00	71.90	71.50	70.85	72.65	77.95	81.45	78.40	78.70		
	Low	77.00	76.80	73.00	62.40	65.35	63.25	62.40	62.00	64.30	67.00	71.00	75.00	70.80	73.80		
	Close	78.00	80.70	72.60	62.95	68.65	67.20	62.95	67.95	68.90	70.70	76.60	75.20	75.15	77.40		
1984	High	85.40	86.00														
	Low	78.05	81.70														
	Close	82.60	84.30														

Source: Commodity Exchange, Inc. of N.Y. (COMEX)

T.141

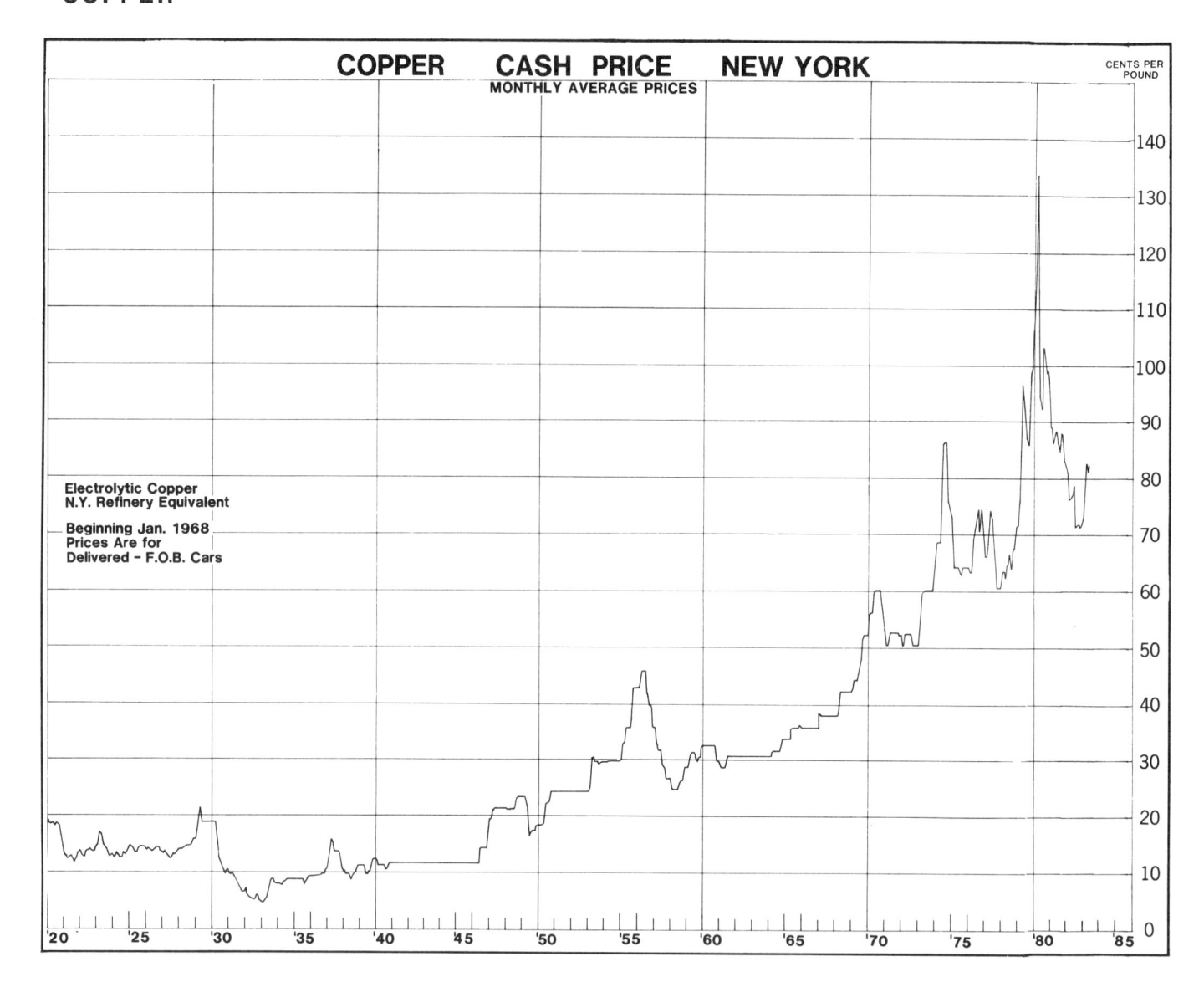

COPPER

COPPER CASH PRICE NEW YORK
MONTHLY AVERAGE PRICES — CENTS PER POUND

Electrolytic Copper
N.Y. Refinery Equivalent

Beginning Jan. 1968
Prices Are for
Delivered – F.O.B. Cars

Producers' Prices of Electrolytic (Wirebar[1]) Copper, Delivered U.S. Destinations — In Cents Per Pound

Year	Jan.	Feb.	Mar.	Apr.	May	June	July	Aug.	Sept.	Oct.	Nov.	Dec.	Average
1971	51.48	50.37	50.59	52.87	52.87	52.87	52.87	52.87	52.87	52.87	52.19	50.37	52.09
1972	50.38	50.66	52.63	52.63	52.63	52.63	52.67	50.63	50.63	50.63	50.63	50.63	51.44
1973[1]	52.41	54.55	59.85	60.13	60.13	60.13	60.13	60.13	60.13	60.13	60.13	66.56	59.53
1974	68.70	68.70	68.70	68.70	81.19	86.09	86.31	86.31	83.01	78.23	75.79	73.03	77.06
1975	68.86	64.32	64.32	64.32	64.32	63.67	63.02	64.31	64.31	64.31	64.31	64.31	64.53
1976	63.63	63.63	64.73	69.26	70.63	70.63	74.63	74.63	74.63	72.34	70.63	66.10	69.62
1977	66.13	68.63	72.54	74.41	72.77	70.13	68.10	63.89	60.63	60.63	60.63	62.11	66.72
1978	63.63	63.59	62.35	64.63	64.90	66.78	63.99	67.34	67.63	70.13	71.68	71.73	66.53
1979	76.15	89.41	94.65	98.66	91.04	87.66	86.02	89.94	95.07	98.84	98.44	106.08	92.75
1980	118.05	133.83	106.23	94.61	93.16	92.39	103.10	100.60	98.73	99.41	96.98	89.20	102.19
1981	88.64	86.07	87.32	88.44	86.33	85.68	84.71	87.98	85.63	83.28	82.09	80.94	85.59
1982	79.42	79.35	76.45	76.99	78.78	71.43	71.78	71.84	71.37	71.92	72.28	73.17	74.57
1983	79.03	82.72	81.09	82.44									
1984													

[1] Prior to Feb. 1973 prices are for delivered F.O.B. Cars.   *Source: American Metal Market*

T.136

COPPER

U.S. Imports (for Consumption[4]) of Copper (Unmanufactured), by Sources and Types   In Thousands of Metric[2] Tons

Year	Ore & Concentrates	Blister	Refined	Scrap	Australia	Canada	Mexico	W. Germany	Chile	Peru	Philippines	Yugoslavia	Zambia	Rep. of So. Afr.	Total U.S. Imports
1973	42.1	154.1	201.5	18.9	2.0	155.2	16.7	8.8	58.8	100.0	17.8	1.3	5.5	26.4	420.5
1974	53.4	207.8	313.6	31.2	2.7	151.3	16.8	8.7	131.9	108.9	14.3	15.1	2.8	38.4	608.6
1975	64.9	89.0	146.8	14.4	3.5	117.5	16.4	—	55.0	43.9	12.6	21.5	—	26.0	324.1
1976	70.7	44.5	381.5	19.7	7.0	148.0	9.1	—	102.0	40.1	15.0	45.6	128.3	4.9	534.7
1977	42.1	46.2	390.8	19.9	3.6	131.2	15.1	10.5	119.7	62.3	18.1	16.8	77.9	11.0	516.7
1978[2]	20.9	78.7	414.7	21.4	10.0	77.3	5.8	8.5	175.8	94.8	12.0	10.9	79.8	15.5	546.4
1979	22.4	68.1	215.2	22.2	2.1	89.0	8.5	6.1	116.2	52.8	15.4	3.4	15.9	2.0	328.3
1980[4]	52.4	44.5	426.9	22.8	5.4	152.4	8.3	.5	126.6	52.5	8.9	4.5	64.9	2.2	547.0
1981[1]	39.1	30.1	330.6	27.0	1.5	108.5	23.8	—	137.8	52.0	20.4	2.4	44.1	—	429.6
1982[3]	118.1	97.4	258.4	28.1											506.0
1983															

Note: Includes refined; black, blister, and converter; scrap; and copper content of ore, matte, and regulus.   [1] Preliminary.   [2] Data prior to 1978 are in THOUSANDS OF SHORT TONS.   [3] Estimate.   [4] Prior to 1980, data is for general imports.   *Source: Department of Commerce; Bureau of Mines*
T.137

United States Exports of Refined Copper[1] to Selected Countries   In Thousands of Metric[3] Tons

Year	Total U.S. Exports	United Kingdom	China Mainland	Belgium	Brazil	Canada	France	W. Germany	India	Italy	Netherlands	Taiwan	Sweden	Mexico	Japan
1972	182.7	12.1	—	3.3	16.1	18.3	25.4	28.5	.3	28.5	3.4	4.7	2.5		32.7
1973	189.4	11.7	—	4.7	21.9	12.8	23.3	17.6	—	31.5	2.9	5.8	1.2		46.3
1974	126.5	14.5	—	2.5	24.0	11.4	19.1	11.7	.1	26.5	4.4	1.1	1.4		4.0
1975	172.4	15.1	—	13.2	24.7	6.7	22.8	34.1	.1	22.2	14.9	4.0	1.0		3.0
1976	111.9	20.3	—	1.0	2.8	4.7	21.0	26.8	—	15.6	5.0	—	5.0		4.7
1977	51.5	7.3	—	3.2	.1	8.1	9.8	10.2	—	6.2	2.4	—	1.5		1.5
1978[3]	91.9	13.8	3.0	2.5	3.3	5.1	7.0	18.1	—	19.0	3.0	.9	4.2	1.0	10.0
1979	73.7	6.5	3.1	2.5	6.2	4.5	12.5	3.5	—	11.4	6.6	1.2	2.8	.5	2.0
1980	14.5	2.0	—	.6	1.5	2.9	1.9	.8	.1	1.4	.6	.3	.1	.9	.8
1981	24.4	1.3	—	—	.8	6.4	1.1	1.1	—	.7	—	—	—	7.2	3.9
1982[2]	30.6	1.3	16.1		.4	2.8	1.1	1.9		.1	3.3				.8
1983															

[1] Bars, ingots or other forms.   [2] Preliminary.   [3] Data prior to 1978 are in THOUSANDS OF SHORT TONS.   *Source: Department of Commerce*
T.138

LONDON COPPER (High Grade) (Weekly Close)   POUNDS STERLING PER TONNE

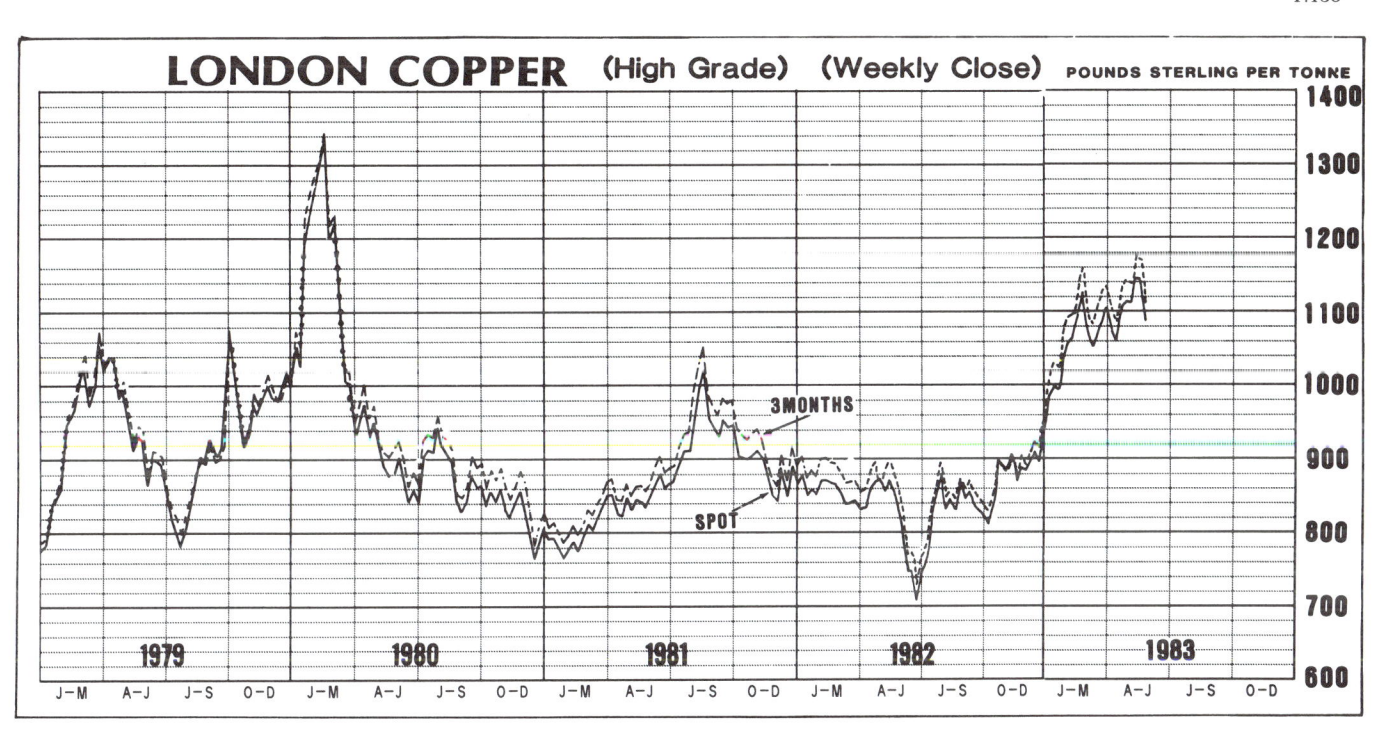

107

COPPER

Exports of Refined Copper from the United States   In Thousands of Short Tons

Year	Jan.	Feb.	Mar.	Apr.	May	June	July	Aug.	Sept.	Oct.	Nov.	Dec.	Total
1974	8.2	13.1	9.5	10.0	19.8	12.4	6.9	7.0	6.9	8.2	13.3	11.3	126.5
1975	19.7	20.8	14.3	24.9	21.3	13.5	9.8	6.7	11.5	12.5	9.0	8.4	172.4
1976	11.2	8.5	10.8	10.9	8.6	9.4	8.7	9.4	10.0	11.5	7.3	6.8	113.1
1977	3.7	1.8	3.6	5.2	5.2	5.2	5.5	1.6	4.4	4.6	5.0	6.9	52.7
1978	4.7	4.9	11.9	7.3	11.4	10.1	7.2	10.2	22.2	5.3	5.3	8.8	109.3
1979	9.8	9.4	11.6	10.0	8.9	8.7	4.8	2.9	2.9	2.7	7.3	1.5	80.5
1980	1.0	1.4	1.9	1.5	1.5	2.0	1.9	.9	.4	.5	1.0	3.4	17.4
1981	2.9	2.5	5.8	1.2	.9	3.5	1.3	1.7	3.0	.7	2.1	1.8	27.2
1982	.4	.6	.9	1.0	1.6	1.6	2.9	5.4	9.9	8.6	.8	1.1	35.0
1983	13.4												

Source: Department of Commerce   T.139

Dealers' Buying Price of No. 2 Heavy Copper Scrap at N.Y.   In Cents Per Pound

Year	Jan.	Feb.	Mar.	Apr.	May	June	July	Aug.	Sept.	Oct.	Nov.	Dec.	Average
1974	60.50	66.39	72.79	75.91	73.66	60.60	51.40	49.20	41.30	38.67	35.12	33.07	54.88
1975	31.86	30.50	33.93	33.82	31.07	29.50	32.50	36.69	38.07	37.33	36.20	35.86	33.94
1976	36.98	37.92	39.76	41.95	44.10	43.66	46.93	45.73	43.71	38.48	35.00	34.10	40.69
1977	34.00	35.73	41.50	40.63	39.62	35.91	35.00	34.04	33.00	33.00	33.00	33.00	34.23
1978	34.00	35.61	35.59	39.73	39.18	41.77	40.50	41.89	42.50	44.70	45.40	44.75	40.47
1979	47.07	58.82	65.46	68.93	63.14	59.05	57.79	58.85	62.03	62.89	62.25	65.00	60.94
1980	74.91	82.35	70.30	60.18	57.60	56.50	65.36	64.88	64.21	65.37	66.08	58.36	65.51
1981	57.60	55.50	57.14	59.50	58.20	55.32	52.68	53.50	53.00	50.16	48.08	46.00	53.89
1982	45.50	45.50	43.76	41.50	41.40	37.82	36.07	37.82	37.50	37.50	38.90	39.50	40.23
1983	42.55	46.71	51.50	51.50									

Source: American Metal Market   T.140

Month End Open Interest of Copper Futures at COMEX   In Contracts

Year	Jan.	Feb.	Mar.	Apr.	May	June	July	Aug.	Sept.	Oct.	Nov.	Dec.
1978	45,821	46,415	48,399	47,315	54,740	49,447	49,408	51,314	60,159	59,732	56,750	55,287
1979	53,776	56,481	55,719	48,857	45,572	43,992	39,372	58,966	63,825	58,451	62,659	64,363
1980	63,132	60,834	41,546	31,618	31,923	32,454	37,303	38,497	46,737	54,201	52,666	44,225
1981	47,300	47,641	48,699	49,784	52,527	52,325	54,011	54,781	57,153	58,054	52,654	52,226
1982	56,469	60,458	62,817	67,700	74,353	65,938	66,049	64,615	69,845	79,365	85,824	92,146
1983	113,044	121,875	116,706	105,451								

Source: Commodity Exchange, Inc. of N.Y. (COMEX)   T.142

Volume of Trading of Copper Futures at COMEX   In Contracts

Year	Jan.	Feb.	Mar.	Apr.	May	June	July	Aug.	Sept.	Oct.	Nov.	Dec.	Total
1978	75,219	88,765	119,423	112,834	117,745	135,363	98,274	160,456	95,360	158,815	151,284	95,150	1,408,688
1979	154,378	228,837	234,044	234,554	212,934	186,097	139,912	210,387	208,869	200,123	163,074	145,732	2,301,033
1980	243,069	205,232	185,692	121,708	102,054	130,678	148,698	125,062	169,370	132,850	127,110	156,556	7,848,080
1981	116,295	131,960	143,662	140,605	104,376	158,396	125,109	190,763	148,456	114,960	144,453	128,345	1,647,380
1982	112,118	166,562	135,434	179,854	174,157	249,276	197,828	245,973	169,909	231,771	273,546	226,257	2,332,925
1983	306,001	381,645	320,574	278,655									

Source: Commodity Exchange, Inc. of N.Y. (COMEX)   T.143

Commodity Exchange Inc. (COMEX) Warehouse Stocks of Copper   In Thousands of Short Tons

Year	Jan. 1	Feb. 1	Mar. 1	Apr. 1	May 1	June 1	July 1	Aug. 1	Sept. 1	Oct. 1	Nov. 1	Dec. 1
1975	43.2	53.6	59.0	60.8	68.3	70.6	67.6	73.4	74.8	77.7	89.7	95.9
1976	100.1	100.1	100.9	95.9	94.7	98.6	114.1	128.2	144.0	164.2	175.8	186.5
1977	201.0	204.1	211.1	214.0	214.4	211.4	211.1	205.1	201.0	200.1	195.1	189.1
1978	184.4	181.8	182.8	178.5	175.6	175.4	177.8	180.7	181.9	180.4	179.9	185.1
1979	179.2	170.8	156.4	133.6	118.3	89.9	70.7	61.5	56.8	57.0	64.9	71.3
1980	107.8	114.1	132.0	145.7	149.8	155.5	167.3	181.7	190.8	185.4	178.6	170.9
1981	179.6	179.3	179.8	173.3	182.4	175.5	170.6	168.8	167.5	171.6	173.1	171.4
1982	187.6	189.3	193.6	195.7	198.5	201.5	202.2	207.4	211.8	207.1	210.3	246.3
1983	274.4	278.5	293.6	306.1	325.9							

Source: Commodity Exchange, Inc. N.Y. (COMEX)   T.144

COPPER

Refined Copper Stocks in the U.S.A. In Thousands of Short Tons (Recoverable Copper Content)

Year	Jan. 1	Feb. 1	Mar. 1	Apr. 1	May 1	June 1	July 1	Aug. 1	Sept. 1	Oct. 1	Nov. 1	Dec. 1
1970	45.9	52.0	58.2	67.4	58.2	65.2	53.7	57.0	54.9	69.7	80.2	135.6
1971	160.6	173.3	174.5	164.3	131.3	110.4	70.4	59.9	61.0	80.8	100.8	106.7
1972	103.0	131.3	132.8	124.3	123.1	125.1	128.7	123.9	140.9	157.8	161.0	158.2
1973	157.4	142.6	140.4	126.1	97.2	95.0	82.2	72.0	71.5	63.1	55.3	36.5
1974	49.1	49.9	43.8	57.5	66.5	61.1	39.8	42.9	54.8	61.5	89.4	135.7
1975	194.9	242.7	259.2	297.8	320.6	334.6	338.2	349.5	341.8	312.3	314.9	324.6
1976	360.7	363.4	370.9	347.8	343.0	325.2	317.1	350.4	355.8	356.1	372.8	416.5
1977	473.8	469.3	487.0	472.3	442.1	447.6	435.0	408.9	370.6	409.4	418.0	456.9
1978	471.1	488.7	491.6	470.2	480.5	465.5	464.0	430.9	418.0	405.9	416.4	408.9
1979	367.0	318.4	287.5	262.1	237.4	197.8	176.0	174.6	158.0	154.6	148.6	167.3
1980	186.3	203.5	228.2	237.1	269.1	277.3	295.7	310.6	301.0	274.6	265.0	246.0
1981	253.0	261.6	249.4	236.8	245.5	243.4	264.7	276.9	276.0	275.5	281.6	301.2
1982[1]	338.6	351.9	375.9	387.3	409.8	422.5	448.1	463.7	449.9	436.2	438.2	470.8
1983[1]	484.5	489.6	501.6	508.9								
1984												

[1] Preliminary.   *Source: American Bureau of Metal Statistics, Inc.*   T.145

Refined Copper Deliveries to Fabricators Outside the U.S.A. In Thousands of Short Tons (Recoverable Copper Content)

Year	Jan.	Feb.	Mar.	Apr.	May	June	July	Aug.	Sept.	Oct.	Nov.	Dec.	Total
1970	213.0	202.4	239.8	210.6	244.5	239.1	228.7	232.9	240.2	210.9	239.8	233.2	2,735
1971	220.9	213.4	251.1	266.7	238.8	240.8	230.2	190.9	198.1	224.1	242.9	240.3	2,758
1972	227.9	230.8	236.2	226.0	244.8	249.7	220.5	214.8	268.0	222.8	242.5	266.1	2,850
1973	266.4	249.3	317.7	257.9	243.4	275.8	211.0	268.4	263.5	270.3	255.0	239.7	3,119
1974[2]	342.0	302.7	365.3	328.7	356.9	306.6	291.1	325.5	316.4	339.8	334.8	303.5	3,913
1975	287.7	315.0	330.4	288.8	301.9	304.8	231.1	232.8	250.4	274.3	269.2	303.0	3,389
1976	308.4	309.3	351.0	359.9	336.2	362.0	296.3	331.0	380.7	372.9	315.8	349.3	4,073
1977	331.6	305.6	405.0	342.6	364.9	360.0	326.5	344.9	339.8	350.7	374.0	390.8	4,236
1978	338.5	370.0	422.6	372.1	400.8	426.0	362.4	402.9	382.7	376.8	360.2	376.8	4,592
1979	424.2	395.9	460.4	342.0	349.1	383.3	376.8	357.7	408.5	390.2	377.6	386.4	4,658
1980	386.2	403.2	400.0	407.6	396.9	376.6	357.3	346.7	389.5	406.5	374.4	375.8	4,653
1981	336.8	353.7	383.2	385.4	380.8	382.7	346.0	355.9	393.4	369.5	373.9	364.5	4,426
1982[1]	373.4	380.1	423.6	387.4	348.3	365.4	341.4	342.8	354.9	343.5	331.3	301.6	4,294
1983[1]	298.9	344.9											
1984													

[1] Preliminary.   [2] New series. Not comparable prior to 1974.   *Source: American Bureau of Metal Statistics, Inc.*   T.146

Refined Copper Deliveries to Fabricators in the U.S.A. In Thousands of Short Tons (Recoverable Copper Content)

Year	Jan.	Feb.	Mar.	Apr.	May	June	July	Aug.	Sept.	Oct.	Nov.	Dec.	Total
1970	150.7	152.1	161.9	163.3	165.5	155.6	158.0	145.3	149.5	142.5	121.5	150.6	1,817
1971	156.8	151.5	164.7	170.8	190.7	193.1	71.0	97.3	126.1	139.1	157.5	141.7	1,760
1972	134.6	151.6	180.6	164.2	181.4	186.9	148.2	145.8	163.2	180.0	172.2	176.7	1,985
1973	190.6	171.2	207.4	191.9	191.7	187.5	162.3	147.3	163.6	191.5	185.5	165.4	2,155
1974	170.7	161.8	178.4	198.4	204.1	186.4	129.5	109.5	143.1	152.3	118.8	86.1	1,911
1975	99.3	84.3	94.2	95.8	115.0	118.2	110.5	127.0	137.5	131.2	117.2	115.7	1,346
1976	137.9	132.7	206.2	175.5	171.7	158.6	150.6	134.5	151.0	150.6	122.6	137.4	1,829
1977	166.6	138.2	202.0	195.6	185.3	192.4	104.5	100.6	100.5	145.7	135.9	141.0	1,808
1978	137.7	141.3	190.2	148.7	175.9	159.8	133.4	168.9	179.2	170.4	177.7	179.7	1,963
1979	191.1	174.8	193.5	182.4	204.7	192.4	166.4	179.3	157.4	190.4	161.4	156.7	2,151
1980	173.5	153.7	193.5	167.8	176.3	175.0	98.7	85.0	83.7	106.6	128.7	154.5	1,697
1981	153.0	154.2	196.5	165.1	169.1	158.8	150.6	152.7	157.5	159.5	131.6	131.2	1,880
1982[1]	134.6	112.2	131.5	114.2	121.0	111.4	106.2	110.6	131.8	113.3	78.4	119.2	1,384
1983[1]	126.2	116.3	161.9										
1984													

[1] Preliminary.   *Source: American Bureau of Metal Statistics, Inc.*   T.147

COPPER

Refined Copper Production Outside the U.S.A. In Thousands of Short Tons (Recoverable Copper Content)

Year	Jan.	Feb.	Mar.	Apr.	May	June	Refined July	Aug.	Sept.	Oct.	Nov.	Dec.	Total	Crude Primary	Secondary
1970	198.0	205.2	217.6	220.0	233.0	254.1	211.0	224.0	234.4	229.4	235.7	232.6	2,695	3,004	85.6
1971	209.2	192.7	224.7	222.4	227.1	222.3	229.9	205.1	220.1	229.9	243.9	240.5	2,668	2,948	82.3
1972	203.4	228.3	231.2	229.5	242.2	257.1	239.2	233.8	238.8	252.2	239.7	257.0	2,853	3,074	69.5
1973	220.8	205.1	260.3	238.0	241.7	236.3	254.1	261.5	234.2	275.6	251.0	265.1	2,918	3,185	89.9
1974[2]	339.3	310.0	351.5	340.0	365.6	347.4	376.2	368.5	367.6	381.4	351.5	344.5	4,244	—4,818—	
1975	323.3	299.5	348.1	336.6	330.8	314.7	303.9	305.4	318.2	338.4	311.3	335.6	3,866	—4,449—	
1976	330.3	314.3	335.3	341.0	336.7	355.1	365.3	355.7	371.7	375.2	359.3	359.2	4,199	—4,947—	
1977	358.1	352.1	380.2	363.0	383.5	386.7	361.7	379.7	372.0	367.4	388.5	393.5	4,486	—5,046—	
1978	387.3	344.0	395.9	348.7	401.9	388.1	371.9	348.4	350.0	381.9	364.5	351.5	4,434	—4,868—	
1979	359.8	347.9	360.1	336.9	345.1	364.9	358.1	377.2	366.5	400.9	388.0	382.6	4,388	—4,791—	
1980	384.2	382.8	408.4	398.3	418.7	396.8	392.2	402.9	386.1	394.4	371.8	389.9	4,727	—4,968—	
1981	359.7	347.9	393.6	390.0	388.0	391.4	377.0	377.7	378.8	379.9	366.9	393.8	4,545	—4,891—	
1982[1]	398.2	381.0	442.6	391.8	365.2	403.9	368.4	365.8	386.1	405.8	411.8	372.6	4,693	—5,065—	
1983[1]	386.8	364.9													
1984															

[1] Preliminary. [2] New series. Not comparable prior to 1974. Source: *American Bureau of Metal Statistics, Inc.* T.148

Refined Copper Production in the U.S.A. In Thousands of Short Tons (Recoverable Copper Content)

Year	Jan.	Feb.	Mar.	Apr.	May	June	Refined July	Aug.	Sept.	Oct.	Nov.	Dec.	Total	Crude Primary	Secondary
1970	172.1	164.3	178.9	161.7	184.1	154.2	161.8	150.4	152.4	162.6	175.9	185.3	2,004	1,504	180.2
1971	175.6	168.4	182.6	159.5	177.4	164.2	55.4	87.5	132.7	151.2	170.0	162.6	1,787	1,315	106.8
1972	159.5	161.0	184.7	168.2	181.1	179.3	143.5	162.6	178.4	174.2	170.8	163.5	2,027	1,517	119.8
1973	168.6	165.5	185.7	165.6	185.5	173.8	154.1	151.3	151.8	173.2	158.6	163.3	1,997	1,526	120.1
1974	157.7	135.5	164.6	163.9	157.3	140.8	101.1	87.2	130.9	177.5	171.1	153.9	1,742	1,334	104.7
1975	146.0	108.8	142.8	136.5	140.8	129.9	124.7	118.2	112.7	133.3	118.3	138.8	1,551	1,239	72.6
1976	130.3	126.6	127.7	141.1	140.8	141.6	144.0	139.0	141.1	158.1	153.3	154.0	1,698	—1,445—	
1977	140.9	140.9	162.3	150.6	166.2	152.4	52.2	46.3	124.4	120.6	137.3	113.0	1,507	—1,386—	
1978	129.0	112.5	143.2	141.0	145.3	135.1	96.1	138.9	144.9	163.4	162.4	133.3	1,645	—1,434—	
1979	135.6	135.8	152.2	149.8	154.6	149.4	132.3	144.9	137.5	148.7	170.0	155.5	1,766	—1,542—	
1980	161.0	149.5	162.3	170.4	158.7	167.2	52.4	28.7	27.3	61.0	85.8	136.9	1,361	—1,205—	
1981	133.5	116.3	152.2	155.8	135.0	158.3	131.7	124.0	140.5	127.3	124.9	147.9	1,647	—1,429—	
1982[1]	117.5	123.4	121.5	116.4	107.5	108.6	81.8	77.6	80.6	80.1	92.1	90.8	1,198	—1,026—	
1983[1]	97.3	100.6	131.9												
1984															

[1] Preliminary. Source: *American Bureau of Metal Statistics, Inc.* T.149

Refined Copper Stocks Outside the U.S.A. In Thousands of Short Tons (Recoverable Copper Content)

Year	Jan. 1	Feb. 1	Mar. 1	Apr. 1	May 1	June 1	July 1	Aug. 1	Sept. 1	Oct. 1	Nov. 1	Dec. 1
1970	234.7	235.4	245.4	233.9	255.4	259.5	291.5	280.2	284.1	279.0	307.0	305.8
1971	318.6	330.8	327.7	332.7	314.2	313.4	308.9	306.1	314.1	327.6	331.4	342.2
1972	371.8	349.0	358.1	368.2	380.1	378.2	378.8	400.9	422.4	394.2	420.1	421.8
1973	410.3	361.4	322.4	263.0	249.7	250.5	215.8	267.9	274.0	249.4	255.8	261.8
1974[2]	348.7	320.9	323.4	311.5	320.6	332.7	370.3	444.0	459.4	494.4	526.9	543.1
1975	591.2	628.8	624.5	655.8	723.1	766.0	784.7	861.5	933.4	1,007	1,072	1,108
1976	1,135	1,150	1,149	1,086	1,048	1,045	1,040	1,080	1,112	1,102	1,102	1,141
1977	1,117	1,158	1,200	1,166	1,183	1,185	1,195	1,210	1,229	1,247	1,240	1,225
1978	1,201	1,231	1,139	1,139	1,104	1,099	1,052	1,059	1,001	960.2	962.0	963.1
1979	942.2	878.2	862.4	765.1	758.8	756.7	727.2	687.1	696.6	648.2	635.4	641.3
1980	619.5	598.3	560.9	534.6	516.5	525.9	531.2	530.9	553.2	527.9	489.1	472.6
1981	476.2	485.2	471.0	463.0	458.8	449.8	446.0	454.9	454.7	433.4	419.4	403.0
1982[1]	432.5	446.3	448.4	459.6	452.0	458.7	479.3	492.0	503.6	522.7	575.1	642.9
1983[1]	699.9	760.8	765.4									
1984												

[1] Preliminary. [2] New series. Not comparable prior to 1974. Source: *American Bureau of Metal Statistics, Inc.* T.150

Corn

The 1982 U.S. corn crop was a record-large 8.40 billion bushels (213 million tonnes), 2 percent above the previous record set in 1981. Plantings of 81.9 million acres were 3 percent less than a year earlier, but excellent growing conditions throughout the season resulted in a record-high average yield of 114.8 bushels per acre. Area harvested for grain in 1982 totaled 73.2 million acres, 2 percent less than in 1981.

The total U.S. supply of corn for the 1982/83 season was also record-large, at nearly 10.7 billion bushels, primarily reflecting the virtual doubling of beginning stocks, compared with a year earlier.

Corn disappearance in the 1982/83 season was projected by the USDA to total 7.3 billion bushels, the largest since the 1979/80 season. Disappearance during the first quarter (Oct.–Dec.) of the season was slightly lower than during the same quarter of the previous season, and January 1, 1983 stocks of corn in all positions were 21 percent larger than a year earlier. As of that date, 2.36 billion bushels (28 percent) of total stocks were under Government control—398 million bushels were owned by the CCC and 1.96 billion bushels were held under the farmer-owned reserve. (About 2.1 billion bushels of the 1982 corn crop were in compliance with the feed grain program, and therefore eligible for the farmer-owned reserve (FOR) or a regular CCC loan.) Indicated disappearance of corn in the second quarter (January–March 1983) increased 12 percent from the same quarter in 1982. Of the record-high 6.36 billion bushels stored in all positions on April 1, 1983, 3.17 billion (50 percent) was under Government control, of which 472 million bushels were owned by the CCC and 2.70 billion were held under the farmer-owned reserve. In late April 1983, the USDA projected the 1982/83 season carryover at 3,384 million bushels, including 2,450 million in the farmer-owned reserve, and 474 million in CCC inventory.

The price of corn at the farm in mid-October 1982 was $2.00 per bushel and lower, compared with the regular 1982-crop loan rate of $2.55 and the 1982 FOR (farmer-owned-reserve) loan rate of $2.90. Never in the past 30 years had the cash corn price at harvest been so far under the support price. Accordingly, movement of corn under CCC loan, and particularly into the FOR, was heavy. Cash corn prices subsequently strengthened after the completion of the harvest, and no serious storage problems developed. The rapid movement of corn into the FOR also contributed considerably to the firming cash price structure. When the Payment-in-Kind (PIK) program was announced on January 11, 1983, and later when heavy producer participation in the PIK program was announced, corn prices advanced further. In the spring of 1983, the market was becoming increasingly concerned about the prices needed to bring loan and FOR corn back into the market. Corn under the 1982-crop regular loan could become available to the market at lower prices than corn in the reserve. The regular loan rate on 1982-crop corn is $2.55 per bushel, with interest accruing at about 1.9 cents per bushel per month, whereas the release price for 1982 crop FOR corn is $3.25 per bushel, and $3.15 per bushel for 1981-crop FOR corn.

According to the USDA, the 1983 U.S. corn crop could be as much as 33 percent smaller than the 1982 crop, given average weather conditions, based on indicated producer participation in the 1983 reduced acreage program, the paid land diversion program and the PIK program. On April 22, 1983, the USDA projected 1983/84 season corn supply and demand. Beginning stocks were estimated at 3,384 million bushels versus 2,286 million at the start of the 1982/83 season; production at 5,640 million versus 8,397 million; and total supply at 9,025 million versus 10,684 million. Domestic use of corn in the 1983/84 season was projected at 5,150 million bushels versus 5,300 million in 1982/83; exports at 2,100 million versus 2,000 million; total use at 7,250 million versus 7,300 million; and ending 1983/84 stocks at 1,775 million bushels versus an estimated 3,384 million for the 1982/83 season.

U.S. Government Price Support

The Secretary of Agriculture on September 23, 1982 announced the provisions for the 1983 feed grain program, including a target price of $2.86 per bushel for 1983-crop corn, up from $2.70 for the 1982 crop. The 1983-crop corn loan rate was set at $2.65 per bushel, up from $2.55 for the 1982 crop. In addition, the 1983 program featured a combined 10 percent acreage reduction and 10 percent paid land diversion. Producers who signed up for the feed grain program were eligible to request advance 1983 diversion payments equal to 50 percent of the full rate. The diversion payment rate for corn was set at $1.50 per bushel, with the advance payment equal to 75 cents per bushel. In addition, participating producers could request 50 percent of their projected 1983 deficiency payments. The estimated deficiency payment to producers for 1983-crop corn is 21 cents per bushel, with the advance payment equal to 10.5 cents per bushel. (The deficiency payment rate cannot exceed the difference between the loan rate and the target price—21 cents per bushel.) Deficiency payments of 15 cents per bushel were paid to eligible producers of 1982-crop corn. Corn harvested in 1983 is not eligible for the FOR until the regular 9-month CCC loan matures. The reserve loan rate for 1983 is the same as the regular loan.

Futures Markets

Corn futures are traded on the Chicago Board of Trade and on the Chicago MidAmerica Commodity Exchange.

CORN

World Production of Corn or Maize In Millions of Metric Tons

Crop Year	United States	Argentina	Brazil	Mexico	South Africa	France	China	India	Italy	Bulgaria	Hungary	Yugoslavia	Romania	Indonesia	USSR	World Total
1970-1	105.5	9.9	13.5	8.7	8.6	7.6	26.4	7.5	4.8	2.4	4.0	6.9	6.5	2.9	7.8	255.1
1971-2	143.3	5.9	12.9	9.1	9.4	8.8	25.3	5.1	4.5	2.5	4.7	7.4	7.9	2.6	8.6	292.1
1972-3	141.6	9.0	13.8	8.1	4.2	8.2	22.0	6.2	4.8	2.9	5.5	7.9	9.5	2.0	9.8	286.3
1973-4	143.4	9.9	15.0	9.0	11.1	10.7	28.0	5.8	5.1	2.6	5.9	8.3	7.4	2.9	13.2	314.7
1974-5	118.5	7.7	16.4	7.8	9.1	8.7	30.7	5.6	5.0	1.6	6.2	8.0	7.4	3.0	12.1	286.5
1975-6	147.3	5.9	17.9	9.2	7.3	8.2	32.0	7.0	5.3	3.0	7.1	9.4	9.2	2.6	7.3	321.6
1976-7	157.9	8.3	18.8	9.6	9.7	5.5	31.4	6.3	5.3	3.0	5.2	9.1	11.6	2.6	10.1	336.3
1977-8	161.8	9.7	13.6	9.7	10.2	8.6	49.5	5.9	6.4	2.6	6.0	9.9	10.1	3.0	11.0	364.9
1978-9	184.6	9.0	16.3	10.2	8.3	9.5	55.9	6.2	6.2	2.2	6.7	7.6	10.2	4.0	9.0	390.9
1979-0	201.7	6.4	20.2	9.2	10.8	10.4	60.0	5.6	6.2	3.2	7.3	10.1	12.4	3.6	8.4	423.7
1980-1	168.8	12.9	22.6	10.4	14.6	9.4	62.6	6.8	6.4	2.2	6.4	9.3	11.2	4.0	9.5	406.7
1981-2[1]	208.3	9.6	22.9	12.5	8.4	9.0	59.2	6.0	7.7	2.3	6.8	9.8	10.5	4.3	8.0	437.4
1982-3[2]	213.3	7.5	23.5	7.5	4.7		62.5								13.5	443.1
1983-4																

[1] Preliminary. [2] Estimated. Source: Foreign Agricultural Service, U.S.D.A.   T.151

Acreage and Supply of Corn in the United States In Millions of Bushels

Year Beginning October	Planted All Purposes	Harvested For Grain	Harvested For Silage	Harvested For Forage	Yield, Per Harv. Acre-Bus.	Carry-over, October 1 Farm	CCC Bins	Others[3]	Total	Grain Production	Imports[2]	Total (All Supply Grain)
1970-1	66.9	57.4	8.1	.7	72.4	575.6	111.3	318.3	1,005	4,152	4.0	5,161
1971-2	74.2	64.1	8.8	.7	88.1	426.7	24.5	215.5	667	5,646	1.0	6,309
1972-3	67.1	57.5	8.4	.5	97.0	751.3	26.3	348.7	1,126	5,580	1.0	6,700
1973-4	72.3	62.1	9.0	.6	91.3	404.6	20.3	283.7	709	5,671	1.0	6,380
1974-5	77.9	65.4	10.8	.6	71.9	287.6	— 195.1—		483	4,701	1.8	5,187
1975-6	78.7	67.6	9.8	.6	86.4	191.3	— 168.2—		359	5,841	1.8	6,204
1976-7	84.6	71.5	11.3	.9	88.0	229.8	— 169.4—		399	6,289	2.5	6,691
1977-8	84.3	71.6	9.3	.6	90.8	446.1	— 438.0—		884	6,505	2.6	7,394
1978-9	81.7	71.9	8.6	.4	101.0	659.3	— 444.7—		1,111	7,268	1.2	8,381
1979-0	81.4	72.4	8.0	.4	109.7	794.5	—1,103.9—		1,304	7,939	1.1	9,244
1980-1	84.0	73.0	9.2	.6	91.0	920.9	— 696.6—		1,618	6,645	1.2	8,264
1981-2	84.2	74.7	8.2	.4	109.8	490.1	— 543.8—		1,034	8,202	1.2	9,237
1982-3[1]	81.9	73.2	7.9	.3	114.8	1,356	— 929.9—		2,286	8,397	1.0	10,684
1983-4[4]	69.6									3,434		

[1] Preliminary. [2] Includes grain equivalent of cornmeal & flour. [3] Interior mills & elevators and terminal mkts. [4] Estimate. Source: Commodity Economics Division, U.S.D.A.   T.152

Corn Production Estimates and Disposition and Value in the U.S.

Crop Year	July 1	Aug. 1	Sept. 1	Oct. 1	Nov. 1	Dec. 1	Final	Farm Disposition Feed & Seed — In Millions of Bushels	Sold[1]	Season Avg. Price[1] $ Per Bu.	K.C. White No. 3 $ Per Bu.	Value of Production (Million Dollars)
1970-1	4,819,999	4,692,864	4,402,765	4,188,281	4,103,973	4,109,792	4,152,243	1,888	2,264	1.33	1.94	5,515
1971-2	—	5,345,057	5,265,641	5,399,670	5,551,769	5,540,253	5,646,260	2,447	3,200	1.08	1.26	6,101
1972-3	5,042,048	4,947,986	5,124,425	5,265,817	5,400,390	5,473,727	5,579,832	2,328	3,252	1.57	2.48	8,743
1973-4	—	5,661,379	5,768,407	5,762,927	5,678,141	5,643,256	5,670,712	2,217	3,453	2.55	3.66	14,463
1974-5	—	4,965,950	4,994,730	4,717,600	4,621,248	4,651,167	4,701,402	1,755	2,947	3.03	4.09	14,232
1975-6	6,045,621	5,849,662	5,687,248	5,737,266	5,803,596	5,766,991	5,840,757	2,117	3,712	2.54	2.92	14,818
1976-7	6,552,665	6,186,979	5,891,823	5,865,243	6,063,459	6,216,032	6,289,169	2,329	3,960	2.15	2.91	13,524
1977-8	6,330,668	6,092,054	6,229,084	6,303,034	6,366,864	6,357,424	6,505,041	2,548	3,957	2.02	3.30	13,107
1978-9	6,145,421	6,503,190	6,797,650	6,823,720	6,890,310	7,081,849	7,269,921	2,836	4,432	2.25	2.93	16,281
1979-0	6,662,681	7,108,938	7,268,175	7,390,365	7,585,535	7,763,771	7,938,819	2,976	4,963	2.52	4.70	19,904
1980-1	7,284,036	6,645,842	6,534,370	6,466,622	6,461,244	6,647,534	6,644,841	2,502	4,146	3.11	4.96	20,571
1981-2[2]	7,115,069	7,734,941	7,940,421	8,081,444	8,097,231	8,200,951	8,201,598			2.50		20,406
1982-3[2]	—	8,315,088	8,318,678	8,314,938	8,329,808	8,397,334				2.32		19,397
1983-4												

[1] Includes an allowance for unredeemed loan & purchase agreement deliveries valued at the average loan rate. [2] Preliminary. Source: Economic Research Service; Crop Reporting Board, U.S.D.A.   T.153

CORN

U.S. Corn Supply and Disappearance   In Millions of Bushels

Year & Periods Begin. Oct. 1	Beginning Stocks	Production	Imports	Total Supply	Food	Alc. Beverages	Seed	Feed	Total	Exports	Total Disappearance	Gov't. Owned[1]	Privately Owned[2]	Total
1978-9	1,111	7,268	1.2	8,381	531.2	70.0	19.5	4,323	4,944	2,133	7,077	99.7	1,204	1,304
Oct.-Dec.	1,111	7,268	.1	8,379	132.8	17.1	—	1,456	1,606	454.0	2,060	77.3	6,242	6,319
Jan.-Mar.	6,319	—	.4	6,320	116.9	16.9	3.9	1,255	1,393	426.3	1,819	98.8	4,402	4,500
Apr.-May	4,500	—	.2	4,501	90.3	13.2	11.7	711.0	826.2	387.2	1,213	100.6	3,187	3,287
June-Sept.	3,287	—	.5	3,288	191.2	22.8	3.9	900.3	1,118	865.6	1,984	99.7	1,204	1,304
1979-0	1,304	7,939	1.1	9,244	582.8	72.3	20.0	4,519	5,194	2,433	7,626	256.3	1,361	1,618
Oct.-Dec.	1,304	7,939	.3	9,243	128.2	16.3	—	1,549	1,694	662.9	2,357	99.7	6,787	6,886
Jan.-Mar.	6,886	—	.3	6,887	116.6	18.4	4.0	1,308	1,447	582.0	2,029	101.2	4,756	4,857
Apr.-May	4,857	—	.1	4,857	93.2	13.9	12.0	682.3	801.4	385.6	1,187	180.5	3,490	3,670
June-Sept.	3,670	—	.4	3,671	244.8	23.7	4.0	978.7	1,251	802.1	2,053	256.3	1,361	1,618
1980-1	1,618	6,645	1.2	8,264	641.8	73.6	20.2	4,139	4,874	2,355	7,230	237.8	796.2	1,034
Oct.-Dec.	1,618	6,645	.2	8,263	136.3	16.6	—	1,523	1,676	727.8	2,404	254.3	5,605	5,859
Jan.-Mar.	5,857	—	.3	5,859	116.3	18.6	4.0	1,100	1,239	632.9	1,872	250.0	3,737	3,987
Apr.-May	3,997	—	.1	3,987	106.7	13.8	12.2	684.7	817.4	395.7	1,213	251.6	2,523	2,774
June-Sept.	2,774	—	.6	2,775	282.5	24.6	4.0	830.9	1,142	598.8	1,741	237.8	796.2	1,034
1981-2[3]	1,034	8,202	1.2	9,237	709.4	82.7	19.4	4,173	4,984	2,355	6,951	429.0	1,984	2,286
Oct.-Dec.	1,034	8,202	.4	9,236	153.2	16.8	—	1,553	1,723	545.5	2,268	247.6	6,720	6,968
Jan.-Mar.	6,968	—	.3	6,968	128.4	20.2	3.9	1,194	1,347	489.4	1,836	261.7	4,870	5,132
Apr.-May	5,132	—	.1	5,132	119.4	15.2	12.1	672.1	818.8	409.0	1,228	269.7	3,634	3,904
June-Sept.	3,904	—	.4	3,905	308.4	30.5	3.4	753.3	1,096	523.0	1,619	302.4	1,984	2,286
1982-3[4]	2,286	8,397	1.0	10,684	—	900.0	—	4,300	5,200	2,050	7,250			3,434
Oct.-Dec.	2,286	8,397	.3	10,684	175.2	16.5	—	1,556	1,748	512.7	2,261	429.0	7,994	8,423
Jan.-Mar.														
Apr.-May														

[1] Uncommitted inventory.   [2] Includes quantity under loan & farmer-owned reserve.   [3] Preliminary.   [4] Estimate.   Source: *Commodity Economics Division, U.S.D.A.*

T.154

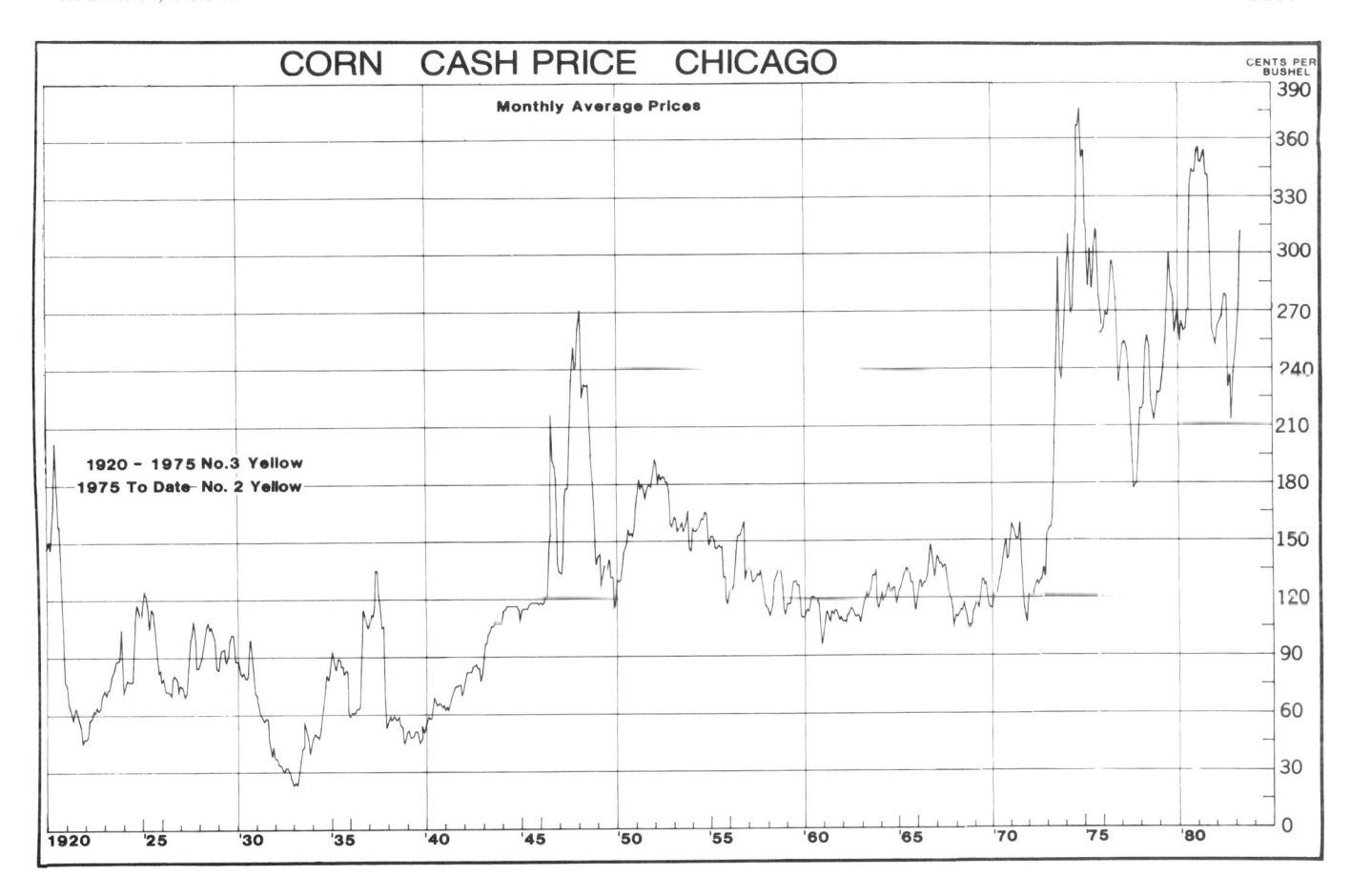

CORN   CASH PRICE   CHICAGO

Monthly Average Prices

1920 - 1975 No.3 Yellow
1975 To Date No. 2 Yellow

CENTS PER BUSHEL

CORN

Distribution of Corn in the United States   In Millions of Bushels

Year Beg. Oct.	Wet Corn Milling (Grind)	Corn Meal[4]	Corn Flour Etc.	Hominy Grits (Food)	Breakfast Foods[3]	Distilled Liquors	Fermented Malt Liquors	Fuel Alcohol	Total Shipments	Seed	Livestock Feed[5]	Exports (Incl. Grain Equiv. of Pdt's.)	Total Utilization	Domestic Disappearance
1970-1	242	24	8	17	23	24	45	0	383	17	3,581	517	4,494	3,977
1971-2	246	21	10	14	24	25	45	0	385	15	3,997	796	5,183	4,387
1972-3	284	20	12	13	24	29	45	0	427	16	4,304	1,258	5,991	4,733
1973-4	295	19	14	13	25	33	47	0	446	18	4,205	1,243	5,896	4,653
1974-5	315	18	13	10	24	16	49	0	445	18	3,226	1,149	4,826	3,677
1975-6	343	18	15	11	24	21	50	0	482	20	3,603	1,711	5,804	4,093
1976-7	362	17	17	10	25	21	53	0	505	20	3,608	1,684	5,805	4,121
1977-8	398		——121——			21	30	0	470	20	3,744	1,948	6,282	4,334
1978-9	425		——124——			21	30	0	601	19.5	4,324	2,133	7,077	4,944
1979-0[2]	455		——127——			20	31	22	655	20.0	4,519	2,433	7,626	5,194
1980-1[1]	530		——160——			20	25	60	715	20.2	4,139	2,355	7,230	4,874
1981-2[1]	570		——162——				33		792	19.4	4,173	1,967	6,951	4,984
1982-3[1]	630		——165——				35		883	17	4,300	2,050	7,250	5,200
1983-4														

[1] Preliminary. [2] Estimate. [3] Assumes sizeable quantities of corn flour are purchased by breakfast food mfg. from the dry milling industry. [4] Regular & degermed. [5] Feed & waste (residual, mostly feed). *Source: Commodity Economics Division, U.S.D.A.*   T.155

Corn (Shelled & Ear) Stocks in the United States   In Millions of Bushels

	On Farms				Off Farms				Total Stocks			
Year	Jan. 1	Apr. 1	June 1[3]	Oct. 1[2]	Jan. 1	Apr. 1	June 1[3]	Oct. 1[2]	Jan. 1	Apr. 1	June 1[3]	Oct. 1[2]
1970	3,390	2,263	1,426	576	993	768	520	430	4,383	3,031	1,945	1,005
1971	2,755	1,875	1,179	427	1,013	670	394	240	3,769	2,545	1,572	667
1972	3,551	2,483	1,589	751	1,149	869	584	375	4,700	3,381	2,173	1,126
1973	3,689	2,385	1,373	405	1,141	955	564	304	4,831	3,340	1,937	709
1974	3,357	2,012	1,063	288	1,116	850	381	195	4,473	2,861	1,443	483
1975	2,541	1,509	804	191	1,080	705	346	168	3,621	2,214	1,150	359
1976	3,196	1,920	1,290	233	1,270	913	577	166	4,467	2,833	1,867	399
1977	3,345	2,134	1,578	446	1,544	1,159	787	438	4,890	3,293	2,365	884
1978	3,824	2,517	1,849	659	1,679	1,360	989	445	5,503	3,877	2,837	1,104
1979	4,638	3,178	2,318	794	1,681	1,322	969	509	6,319	4,500	3,287	1,304
1980	5,042	3,441	2,578	921	1,844	1,416	1,093	697	5,886	4,857	3,670	1,617
1981	4,141	2,641	1,818	490	1,717	1,346	956	544	5,859	3,987	2,774	1,034
1982[1]	5,034	3,626	2,759	1,356	1,934	1,506	1,146	930	6,968	5,132	3,904	2,286
1983[1]	6,157				2,266				8,423			
1984												

[1] Preliminary. [2] Old crop only. [3] Data prior to 1976 are *as of July 1*. *Source: Crop Reporting Board, U.S.D.A.*   T.156

Production of Corn (For Grain) in the United States, by States   In Millions of Bushels

Year	Illinois	Indiana	Iowa	Kansas	Kentucky	Michigan	Minn.	Missouri	Nebraska	No. Car.	Ohio	Pa.	South Dakota	Wisconsin	Texas
1971	1,067	556.4	1,178	124.5	91.1	119.4	475.2	272.1	450.5	89.2	322.6	77.7	120.8	225.8	—
1972	1,015	507.9	1,230	130.0	83.2	142.9	455.6	227.5	534.0	102.4	284.3	64.8	154.5	203.6	—
1973	981.6	534.5	1,207	154.0	85.9	146.5	513.4	228.8	554.6	114.8	243.2	81.1	146.3	173.5	—
1974	811.8	387.6	968.0	131.9	88.2	118.5	365.8	146.3	399.0	117.8	265.5	89.1	76.9	161.2	—
1975	1,254	551.7	1,118	141.0	87.8	167.2	407.4	170.1	503.2	106.5	310.6	88.6	83.3	198.4	—
1976	1,240	693.0	1,174	171.8	138.7	153.9	330.4	173.9	518.5	150.4	393.5	103.5	37.2	151.0	186.0
1977	1,163	633.4	1,092	161.3	132.3	197.2	600.0	201.4	648.5	88.7	380.1	106.7	126.9	291.2	161.7
1978	1,240	669.6	1,478	153.0	119.9	194.4	643.8	200.1	762.8	121.6	379.1	115.9	177.6	294.0	144.0
1979	1,414	675.4	1,664	172.0	132.6	237.5	606.0	240.0	822.3	128.4	417.5	121.6	210.9	317.2	132.3
1980	1,066	602.9	1,463	110.9	103.6	247.0	610.1	109.7	603.5	103.8	440.7	96.0	121.9	348.4	117.0
1981	1,454	654.0	1,759	148.1	149.0	273.6	744.7	213.4	791.2	140.9	360.0	134.4	180.6	378.0	127.5
1982[1]	1,525	815.3	1,591	140.2	157.9	307.4	734.5	204.9	770.3	164.6	475.0	126.1	192.7	361.8	119.7
1983															

[1] Preliminary, December estimate. *Source: Crop Reporting Board, U.S.D.A.*   T.157

CORN

Average Price Received by Farmers for Corn in the U.S.   In Cents Per Bushel

Year	Oct.	Nov.	Dec.	Jan.	Feb.	Mar.	Apr.	May	June	July	Aug.	Sept.	Average[1]
1970-1	134	129	136	142	143	143	141	138	143	136	119	111	133
1971-2	100	97	108	109	109	110	113	115	113	114	115	122	108
1972-3	119	120	142	139	135	137	142	161	199	203	268	215	157
1973-4	217	218	239	259	276	268	241	245	257	291	337	330	255
1974-5	345	332	327	307	286	267	268	266	268	272	295	276	303
1975-6	262	233	237	244	248	250	246	261	274	282	264	260	254
1976-7	233	202	224	234	234	235	231	225	212	188	163	160	215
1977-8	167	188	197	200	203	215	224	229	228	216	201	198	202
1978-9	197	202	209	211	218	222	227	235	249	264	254	251	225
1979-0	241	227	238	245	239	240	236	242	249	273	292	301	252
1980-1	299	310	319	319	322	325	324	324	317	314	287	255	311
1981-2	245	234	239	254	244	246	255	260	257	250	230	215	250
1982-3	198	213	226	236	255	271	300						
1983-4													

[1] Weighted average by sales.   Source: Crop Reporting Board, U.S.D.A.   T.160

Corn Price Support Data in the United States

Year Begin. Oct. 1	National Avg. Loan Rate	Grain Reserve Loan Rate	Target Price	Placed Under Loan	Redemptions	Resealed	Total Deliveries[2]	CCC Inventory	Under CCC Loan	Farmer Owned Reserve	"Free" Stocks	Total Stocks	CCC Owned	Under CCC Loan
1970-1	135	—	—	323.3	205.8	112.3	6	105.0	237.6	0	324.1	666.7	215.4	454.2
1971-2	135	—	—	954.4	559	377	16	160.1	536.7	0	430.1	1,126.9	141.5	761.0
1972-3	141	—	—	419.7	—			79.1	89.8	0	539.0	707.9	140.5	735.0
1973-4	164	—	—	260.6	—			7.3	5.3	0	471.3	483.9	0.9	189.7
1974-5	110	—	—	76.8	77			0.3	0.6	0	360.5	361.4	6.6	48.6
1975-6	110	—	138	147.0	147			0.1	23.4	0	376.2	399.7	0.4	110.3
1976-7	150	—	157	266	267			0	148.2	0	737.7	885.9	0.1	206.3
1977-8	200	—	200	1,159	689		94	13.1	415.3	315.5	367.5	1,111.4	0.5	765.0
1978-9	200	—	210	642	585		2	99.7	115.7	549.9	538.6	1,303.9	77.3	1,038.0
1979-0	210	—	220	557	527		—	256.3	82.6	636.4	642.2	1,617.5	99.7	801.0
1980-1	225	240	235	840	742		42	237.8	100.8	185.4[4]	510.0	1,034.0	256.3	966.0
1981-2[1]	240	255	240	1,971	392		45	302.4				2,285.9	244	694
1982-3[1]	255	290	270	51	0		0						429	350
1983-4[1]	265		286											

[1] Preliminary.   [2] Includes "delivered to CCC" from original program and deliveries from reseal program and over-deliveries as determined by weight of farm-stored grain when delivered to CCC.   [3] Less than 500,000 bushels.   [4] Called Reserve Corn under extended loan.   Source: Agricultural Stabilization and Conservation Service, U.S.D.A.   T.159

Corn Under Price Support through the End of the Month (Cumulative Total from Current Season's Crop)   In Millions of Bushels

Crop Year	Sept.	Oct.	Nov.	Dec.	Jan.	Feb.	Mar.	Apr.	May	June	July	Aug.	Sept.	Total
1970-1		22.3	91.6	171.9	280.2	297.8	310.3	316.1	318.9	320.8	322.0	—	—	324.0
1971-2		60.2	313.2	585.9	833.9	881.8	907.6	918.9	923.5	937.2	950.4	—	—	952.0
1972-3		20.7	100.4	245.3	360.2	395.5	438.0	417.8	419.3	419.8	—	—	—	420.0
1973-4		13.8	100.5	183.0	244.4	253.4	257.4	259.7	260.3	260.5	—	—	—	
1974-5		9.3	24.4	49.6	69.2	69.2	71.6	75.2	76.6	76.8	—	—	—	
1975-6		18.7	52.7	112.1	137.3	142.8	145.9	146.6	147.0	147.0	147.0	—	—	
1976-7	1.5	18.5	102.6	204.8	238.0	252.8	261.1	266.4	272.5	274.5	—	—	—	
1977-8	31.31	90.3	517.8	710.0	903.2	966.9	1,007	1,018	1,032	1,041	1,045	—	—	
1978-9	9.51	57.4	303.6	458.5	583.5	605.0	616.2	627.1	629.7	637.5	639.5	639.8	—	
1979-0	2.2	17.3	106.1	206.3	347.8	409.5	461.7	488.8	539.1	545.8				
1980-1	2.3	44.6	145.0	386.0	746.7	795.2	816.0	830.6	836.0	838.1				
1981-2	13.5	81.9	418.7	1,049	1,642	1,826	1,903	1,940	1,951	1,962				
1982-3	15.5	76.2	334.5	870.2	1,369	1,505	1,551							

Source: U.S. Department of Agriculture   T.158

115

CORN

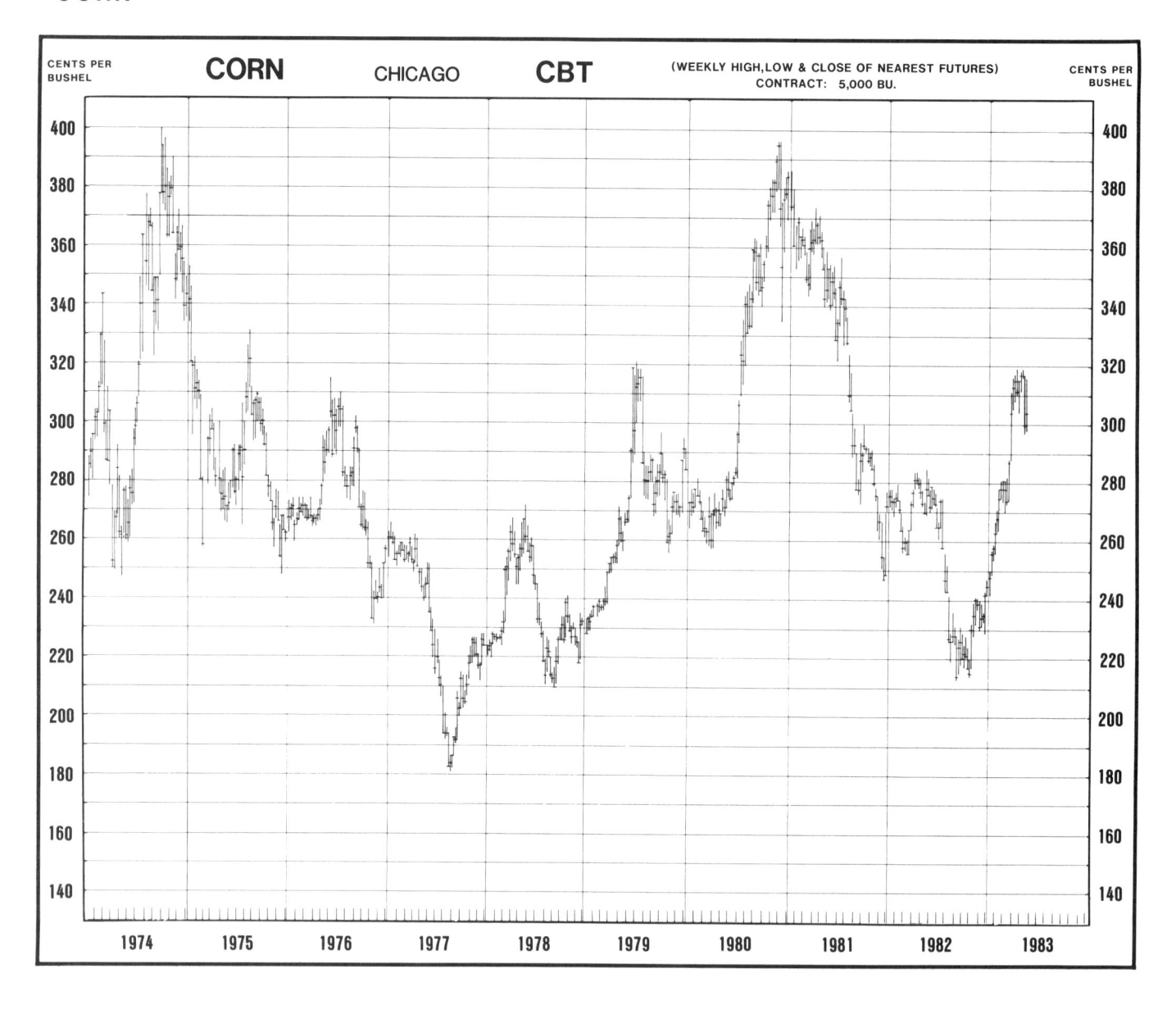

CORN CHICAGO **CBT** (WEEKLY HIGH, LOW & CLOSE OF NEAREST FUTURES) CONTRACT: 5,000 BU.

CENTS PER BUSHEL

Average Cash Price of Corn, No. 2[3] Yellow (15 Days) at Chicago — In Cents Per Bushel

Year	Oct.	Nov.	Dec.	Jan.	Feb.	Mar.	Apr.	May	June	July	Aug.	Sept.	Average[1]
1970-1	140	141	152	159	157	155	151	151	159	149	129	115	144
1971-2	110	107	121	122	121	123	126	129	127	129	130	136	118
1972-3[3]	132	133	157	158	159	159	165	201	242	252	291	247	191
1973-4	237	250	268	290	313	299	269	270	293	335	363	355	295
1974-5	374	348	347	319	296	290	296	282	289	295	312	299	312
1975-6	274	259	259	262	270	268	268	284	296	296	287	277	275
1976-7	249	233	244	253	254	252	250	241	227	205	178	180	230
1977-8	184	214	219	219	221	236	251	257	251	228	217	213	226
1978-9	222	228	227	229	235	242	253	266	283	300	282	278	254
1979-0	273	259	269	254	265	260	261	270	270	308	336	344	281
1980-1	343	343	354	356	349	348	353	347	341	341	309	272	338
1981-2[2]	261	260	252	263	263	267	278	279	277	267	241	235	262
1982-3[2]	213	238	243	253	274	299							
1983-4													

[1] Weighted average by carlot sales.   [2] Preliminary.   [3] Prices prior to 1972-3 are for NO. 3 YELLOW AT CHICAGO.   Source: *Economic Research Service, U.S.D.A.*

T.161

High, Low & Closing Prices of May Corn Futures at Chicago   In Cents per Bushel

Year of Delivery		Year Prior to Delivery Mar.	Apr.	May	June	July	Aug.	Sept.	Oct.	Nov.	Dec.	Delivery Year Jan.	Feb.	Mar.	Apr.	May	Life of Delivery Range
1978	High	279	286¾	271½	270	250¾	222¼	222½	228¾	238½	233¾	232¼	231¼	257¼	267¾	265¾	278
	Low	272½	265½	257	242¼	214	203¼	205¼	216	228	223	224½	228	228½	245	245¼	203¼
	Close	273¼	271¼	265½	243¾	214¼	205½	217	227¾	231½	226¾	229¾	228½	256¼	250¾	262¼	—
1979	High	—	271	286½	281¾	265½	249	243½	256¼	251½	247¾	244¾	250¾	252	260	270¾	286½
	Low	—	251¾	251½	263¼	246¼	230½	232¼	241½	242	237¾	236¼	242¼	242½	249¼	255½	230½
	Close	—	256	283	266½	249	236¼	243	249¾	246¼	240½	243½	246¾	251½	259¼	261¼	—
1980	High	279	287¼	295	336	341½	307½	306¼	318	307½	305½	302¾	294	280	276	277	341½
	Low	272½	275¾	279½	285½	288	283½	287¾	286	287¼	294¼	277	276	256½	257¾	265¼	256½
	Close	278½	287¼	287	319	292	303½	303¼	293¼	302½	301	287¾	276¼	258¼	265¾	271¾	—
1981	High	325	322	325	318	358	369½	379	394	418	416½	393	380	369	372½	363½	418
	Low	311	308¾	311¾	307	318¼	341½	357	358	385¼	354¼	362½	365	350¼	355½	339	307
	Close	312¾	312¾	313	318	356¾	368¾	365¼	385¾	415¾	385¼	364¾	369¾	364¾	361	341	—
1982	High	398¼	410¾	398	385¾	395½	370¾	338¼	338¼	320½	297½	287½	291	275½	283¼	277¼	410¾
	Low	385	385¼	371¼	360¾	364¼	323	310	315½	290¾	261½	277½	269¼	265¼	274	267½	265¼
	Close	397¾	390½	380¾	366	370¾	333¾	318½	318½	291	281	285½	270	274¼	276	268¾	—
1983	High	317½	322½	313½	307	294¼	281	259¼	253	258	255	278	292	315½	318¾		
	Low	310	313¼	302	291¾	274½	250¾	243½	236¼	236½	242¾	251	273	282¼	304¼		
	Close	316	313¼	303	292¾	276½	255¾	248	236¼	247¾	253	277	281½	312¾	317¼		
1984	High	325	324½														
	Low	297½	312¼														
	Close	317¾	316¼														

Source: Chicago Board of Trade T.162

Month End Open Interest of Corn Futures at Chicago   In Millions of Bushels

Year	Jan.	Feb.	Mar.	Apr.	May	June	July	Aug.	Sept.	Oct.	Nov.	Dec.
1978	657.5	705.9	754.8	673.1	784.2	569.2	552.3	544.0	632.0	758.4	667.8	644.0
1979	680.9	720.3	784.2	810.7	859.6	951.3	898.7	889.8	860.0	899.8	857.3	836.2
1980	838.9	799.0	789.8	787.7	766.7	721.6	1,048.8	1,382.4	1,398.0	1,587.9	1,575.5	1,315.0
1981	1,216.5	1,107.5	1,002.4	846.5	737.5	572.6	568.8	637.8	637.7	724.7	674.6	630.7
1982	708.0	625.6	650.0	610.0	594.5	552.6	581.8	596.6	594.7	663.5	712.1	657.8
1983	776.9	778.5	872.5	832.4								

Source: Chicago Board of Trade T.163

Volume of Trading of Corn Futures at Chicago   In Millions of Bushels

Year	Jan.	Feb.	Mar.	Apr.	May	June	July	Aug.	Sept.	Oct.	Nov.	Dec.	Total
1978	1,755	1,599	3,405	3,255	3,159	3,147	2,495	2,663	1,989	2,729	2,723	1,716	30,635
1979	1,734	2,281	2,739	3,302	3,751	5,705	5,806	3,999	3,135	4,522	3,794	2,592	43,386
1980	3,287	3,227	3,493	3,690	3,265	3,362	6,722	7,310	6,287	6,609	6,455	6,027	59,735
1981[1]	4,848	4,495	4,796	5,222	3,867	4,785	5,459	5,019	3,626	3,127	3,913	3,978	53,375
1982[1]	2,802	3,390	3,634	3,355	2,754	3,538	3,122	3,552	3,127	3,239	4,634	2,594	39,741
1983[1]	3,638	3,114	5,355	4,439									

[1] Preliminary. *Source: Chicago Board of Trade* T.164

U.S. Exports[2] of Corn (Including Seed), By Country of Destination   In Thousands of Metric Tons[3]

Yr. Begin. October	USSR	Belg. & Luxem.	Canada	Egypt	W. Germany	Greece	Israel	Italy	Japan	Mexico	Nether-lands	Nor-way	Spain	United Kingdom	Total All Exports
1973–4	129	5	51		122	35	7	85	251	48	137	3	101	38	1,226
1974–5	40	13	37		115	20	9	107	206	48	154	3	104	27	1,125
1975–6	414	35	30		172	29	11	102	228	39	163	4	86	45	1,699
1976–7	115	80	16		209	38	13	90	301	56	182	3	41	111	1,668
1977–8[3]		1,601	232	731	2,501	1,046	395	2,065	8,610		2,870	57	1,670	2,034	49,156
1978–9		2,023	364	617	1,435	1,186	258	1,503	8,979		2,193	63	1,747	1,990	53,903
1979–0		1,622	597	874	1,521	1,119	562	2,072	11,193		2,108	36	2,503	1,828	61,417
1980–1[1]		2,065	551	1,129	1,264	718	547	1,859	12,586		1,773	65	2,651	1,395	59,368
1981–2															

[1] Preliminary. [2] Exports of grain only. Does not include corn exported under the food for relief or charity program. [3] Data prior to 1977–8 are in millions of bushels. *Source: Foreign Agricultural Service, U.S.D.A.* T.165

Corn Oil

Supply & Distribution of Corn Oil   In Millions of Pounds

Year Beginning Oct.	Production	Imports	Stocks Oct. 1	Total Supply	Shortening	Margarine	Salad & Cooking Oil	Other	Total Food Uses	Foots & Loss	Other	Total Non-Food Uses	Total Domestic Disappearance	Total Exports & Shipments
1970-1	485	1	60	546	8	188	202	6	403	41	—	41	445	43
1971-2	499	—	58	557	1	190	203	10	403	35	1	36	439	49
1972-3	523	—	70	593	3	207	231	6	447	44	1	45	492	44
1973-4	528	1	57	586	6	198	198	2	404	45	1	46	450	68
1974-5	465	2	68	535	7	185	164	1	356	42	—	43	399	84
1975-6	644	1	52	697	4	212	297	1	514	44	1	45	559	98
1976-7	669	10	41	720	3	235	303	2	543	37	1	38	605	59
1977-8	695	3	46	744	4	243	288	—	510	45	1	46	580	88
1978-9	737	—	73	810		211	297						619	121
1979-0	791	—	70	861		222	317						654	141
1980-1[1]	864	—	66	930		222	360						673	181
1981-2[1]	872	—	76	948		213	385						688	206
1982-3[2]	865	—	54	919									607	272
1983-4														

[1] Preliminary.   [2] Forecast.   Source: Economic Research Service, U.S.D.A.   T.166

Crude Corn Oil Production in the United States   In Millions of Pounds

Crop Year	Oct.	Nov.	Dec.	Jan.	Feb.	Mar.	Apr.	May	June	July	Aug.	Sept.	Total
1970-1	42.0	40.1	34.7	38.0	37.3	43.7	41.4	41.0	42.7	42.4	40.1	42.0	405
1971-2	42.4	40.7	33.4	38.7	38.7	43.5	40.0	46.1	45.7	43.3	43.5	43.2	499
1972-3	44.1	40.3	40.1	42.6	41.7	46.3	40.6	47.5	45.9	45.8	44.3	43.8	523
1973-4	45.2	42.4	43.1	45.1	41.8	45.4	46.5	46.8	43.8	40.5	44.0	43.0	528
1974-5	41.2	40.1	40.1	37.0	34.6	38.6	37.6	40.6	38.9	40.5	35.2	40.3	465
1975-6	39.8	40.3	35.4	55.2	53.8	55.1	59.5	61.7	59.1	58.9	65.8	59.6	644
1976-7	62.0	50.4	51.3	48.1	49.0	59.2	55.6	58.1	57.9	64.0	59.3	53.7	668.6
1977-8	58.9	58.0	50.1	54.9	51.6	58.7	57.1	68.0	64.7	60.5	59.7	63.8	695.5
1978-9	65.4	59.8	55.8	47.6	54.9	69.4	67.4	69.7	60.6	61.5	63.9	60.3	736.3
1979-0	61.8	63.3	63.0	62.3	60.0	70.7	64.3	68.3	65.1	66.2	69.9	76.2	791.1
1980-1	80.6	68.0	59.0	65.8	63.6	76.2	69.6	74.3	76.1	76.2	76.4	77.8	863.6
1981-2[1]	81.4	69.2	66.5	56.7	64.9	76.4	71.6	77.1	73.9	76.5	79.3	78.0	871.5
1982-3[1]	79.2	72.6	78.4	79.1									
1983-4													

[1] Preliminary.   Source: Economic Research Service, U.S.D.A.   T.167

Corn Oil Spot Price, Crude, F.O.B. Midwest Mills (Tank Cars)   In Cents Per Pound

Year	Oct.	Nov.	Dec.	Jan.	Feb.	Mar.	Apr.	May	June	July	Aug.	Sept.	Average
1970-1	17.8	19.5	21.5	22.5	27.5	21.0	17.0	18.8	19.5	19.3	18.9	17.8	20.1
1971-2	17.8	19.0	18.0	18.0	17.3	17.3	17.0	17.5	16.3	15.0	14.5	15.3	16.9
1972-3	16.0	15.8	16.5	17.8	17.3	17.8	17.5	19.0	21.0	20.8	35.0	23.0	19.8
1973-4	24.0	25.5	32.0	39.0	45.0	39.5	33.0	38.5	38.0	38.0	47.5	38.0	36.5
1974-5	45.0	45.0	42.0	44.0	40.5	39.0	37.0	27.0	26.5	29.5	31.0	28.0	36.2
1975-6	29.0	28.5	28.5	32.5	28.5	26.5	23.3	19.8	22.0	26.0	23.5	27.0	26.3
1976-7	27.1	27.5	26.0	28.0	36.0	36.0	34.5	35.5	31.0	27.5	23.5	23.2	29.7
1977-8	26.5	31.5	35.0	40.0	44.0	43.0	36.5	35.3	33.0	33.3	31.5	35.5	35.4
1978-9	34.0	35.0	31.0	35.0	34.0	33.3	32.1	33.0	30.0	31.0	32.3	32.5	32.8
1979-0[1]	32.8	29.9	33.3	27.5	29.0	26.0	20.0	23.0	22.0	27.3	29.8	28.0	27.4
1980-1[1]	28.0	27.5	28.0	26.3	25.0	23.8	25.5	24.4	24.5	25.8	22.3	21.5	25.2
1981-2[1]	20.0	21.0	25.0	24.0	29.0	25.0	25.0	24.0	23.5	23.0	20.5	21.0	23.4
1982-3[1]	23.0	23.8											
1983-4													

[1] Preliminary.   Source: Economic Research Service, U.S.D.A.   T.168

Cotton

The 1982 U.S. cotton crop totaled 12.0 million bales, down 23 percent from the 1981 crop. Production consisted of 11.9 million bales of Upland cotton and 108 thousand bales of American-Pima. An estimated 9.91 million acres were harvested of the 11.5 million planted, 28 percent below acreage harvested in 1981. Abandonment was unusually heavy at 14 percent of planted acreage versus 3.4 percent in 1981. Acreage loss was particularly heavy in Texas, where hail, wind and cool temperatures in late May and early June hit the crop in the seedling stage. Nevertheless, the beltwide average yield per harvested acre was a record-high 582 pounds, compared with 543 pounds in 1981.

The 1982 U.S. Upland cotton crop averaged 34.5 thirty-seconds inches in length, according to the Cotton Division, Agricultural Marketing Service, USDA. This was the longest staple length average since records began in 1940. Strict Low Middling (Grade 41) was the predominant quality of Upland cotton ginned from the 1982 crop, accounting for about 28 percent of ginnings, the largest proportion since 1978, versus 21 percent in 1981 and 22 percent in 1980. Staples 34 and 35 (1 1/16″ and 1 3/32″) comprised the smallest proportion of ginnings (40 percent) since the crop of 1957.

U.S. cotton supply for the 1982/83 season ending July 31, 1983 totaled about 18.7 million bales, slightly more than the 1981/82 supply of 18.3 million bales, because the reduction in 1982 production was more than offset by the sharp gain in beginning stocks. U.S. cotton production in 1982 represented about 18 percent of the estimated world production of 67.6 million bales, down from 22 percent a year earlier.

U.S. mill consumption of cotton was expected to equal about 5.4 million bales in the 1982/83 season. The outlook for cotton consumption improved as the season progressed. For calendar year 1982, cotton use was 8 percent less than in 1981. In addition to the depressed economy, one of the important causes of lower mill use of cotton was the relatively large quantity of textile imports at a time of declining exports, which partially reflected the strong U.S. dollar. However, the abnormally low per capita consumption of cotton in 1982—13.5 pounds compared with 14.4 pounds in 1981—suggested that any improvement in the economy should reveal a substantial pent-up demand for cotton textiles. In addition, cotton's price was 86 percent of the polyester price in January–June 1982, and 91 percent in the July–December period. Cotton's share of the textile market tends to increase as cotton becomes relatively cheaper than polyester. As the 1982/83 season progressed, and as the economy improved, demand for a number of cotton products, including the key denim constructions, picked up. Consequently, the daily rate of mill consumption of cotton rose above year-earlier levels. The daily rate of consumption in March 1983 (21,900 bales) was the largest since October 1981 when 22,400 bales were used per day.

The U.S. cotton export prospects in the 1982/83 season were adversely affected by a number of factors, including as a major consideration, an increase in foreign supplies relative to use. China purchased virtually no U.S. cotton in 1982/83. China produced a record-large cotton crop of around 15.6 million bales and apparently drew primarily upon its own crop and large stocks to satisfy its needs. Also, China imposed a ban on the importation of U.S. cotton pending a textile agreement. Less competitive U.S. cotton prices, especially in the first half of the season, also contributed to the season's loss of market share. A 10 percent gain in the trade-weighted value of the dollar, using cotton exports as the weights, during the first 5 months of the season, was equivalent to a 10 percent rise in the foreign currency price of U.S. cotton. Both the U.S. cotton export outlook and prices improved somewhat early in 1983 as the USSR—the second largest producer and exporter in the world this season—in February and March bought upwards of 400,000 bales of U.S. cotton for early shipment, much of it being the higher quality cotton.

Some of these purchases were later cancelled, however, and exports for the season were projected at 5.4 million bales, 18 percent below the 1981/82 export total of 6.6 million bales. The Soviet Union also bought cotton from Australia, India, and Central America, with total 1982/83 imports by the USSR estimated at 600,000 bales.

The July 31, 1983 U.S. cotton carryover was expected to rise to 8.0 million bales from 6.6 million a year earlier and only 2.7 million bales two years ago, and the largest carryover since 1966/67. However, a significant portion of the ending stocks was expected to be under government control.

On March 22, 1983 the USDA reported that a huge 95 percent of the cotton base acreage had been enrolled in the 1983 cotton programs. Payment-in-kind (PIK) was the principal attraction. The base acreage on farms enrolling in PIK accounted for 76 percent of the total base. Were enrollees to remain in the program and plant all of their permitted acreage, 6.8 million acres of cotton land would be put to conservation uses. Such a diversion would reduce plantings significantly from 1982's 11.5 million acres. However, the final plantings depended on how many farmers dropped out of the program (this option was not available for PIK participants) and on how much acreage was planted by non-participants.

In late April, 1983, the USDA projected 1983 U.S. cotton production at 9.2 million bales versus 12.0 million in 1982 and total supply for the 1983/84 season at 17.2 million bales compared with 18.7 million for 1982/83. Domestic mill consumption of cotton was projected at 5.7 million bales, up from an estimated 5.4 million in 1982/83, and exports were expected to improve by about 400 thousand bales, to 6.0 million. The July 31, 1984 carryover was projected at 5.6 million bales versus an estimated 8.0 million for July 31, 1983.

U.S. Government Activities

The established 1983 target price for cotton is 76 cents per pound and the national average loan rate for 1983-crop cotton is 55 cents per pound for Strict Low Middling 1 1/16-inch cotton, 3.5 through 4.9 micronaire, at average U.S. location. Eligible producers were entitled to a deficiency payment of 13.92 cents per pound on their 1982 crop.

The 1983 Upland cotton program included a 20 percent acreage reduction program. In addition, cot-

COTTON

ton producers could place up to 5 percent of their base acreage under a paid land diversion program at a payment rate of 25 cents per pound. Participation in the diversion program was not required for program benefits. In order to encourage the idling of addition cotton acreage, the USDA on January 11, 1983 announced a payment-in-kind (PIK) program giving producers the opportunity to reduce acreage by an additional 10 to 30 percent in return for a payment in cotton (amounting to 80 percent of the farm program yield). Producers could also submit bids to take the entire cotton base out of production. The PIK entitlement does not count against the $50,000 cash payment limit from all crop programs, including both deficiency and diversion payments.

Futures Markets

Cotton futures are actively traded on the New York Cotton Exchange. A short staple contract is listed on the New Orleans Commodites Exchange.

World Production of Cotton   In Thousands of Bales[3]

Year Begin. Aug. 1	Argentina	Brazil	China	Egypt	India	Iran	Mexico	Pakistan	Israel	Sudan	Colombia	Turkey	United States	USSR	World Total
1972-3	575	3,000	9,800	2,369	5,370	965	1,780	3,237	186	920	630	2,505	13,890	11,100	63,272
1973-4	585	2,456	11,700	2,258	5,530	920	1,500	3,037	173	1,090	620	2,365	13,300	11,100	63,637
1974-5	790	2,440	11,500	2,018	5,950	1,095	2,230	2,925	230	1,015	700	2,760	11,525	12,250	64,713
1975-6	645	1,800	10,700	1,762	5,350	640	910	2,370	225	500	560	2,215	8,500	11,730	54,321
1976-7	740	2,510	10,000	1,828	4,950	720	1,045	2,006	247	735	685	2,190	10,650	12,050	57,487
1977-8	1,015	2,125	9,450	1,840	5,680	820	1,627	2,651	295	915	645	2,650	14,525	12,700	64,342
1978-9	800	2,530	10,000	2,022	6,220	610	1,570	2,183	365	640	375	2,200	10,885	12,000	59,810
1979-0	670	2,640	10,200	2,230	6,300	460	1,515	3,357	347	525	575	2,200	14,820	13,000	65,891
1980-1	385	2,825	12,500	2,440	6,000	275	1,625	3,296	360	445	535	2,300	11,200	14,062	65,455
1981-2[1]	692	2,952	13,700	2,381	6,500	325	1,443	3,492	422	721	406	2,253	15,711	13,567	71,707
1982-3[2]	623	3,250	15,400	2,050	6,400	450	860	3,700	395	900	140	2,300	12,000	13,000	68,610

[1] Preliminary.   [2] Estimate.   [3] U.S. is in running bales (500 lbs.); all others are 478 pound net weight bales.   Source: *International Cotton Advisory Committee*
T.169

Supply and Distribution of All Cotton in the United States   In Thousands of (480-Lb. Net Weight) Bales

Crop Year Beginning Aug. 1	At Mills	In Public Storage	Elsewhere	Total	CCC Held	Total Stocks	Current Crop[2] Less Ginnings	New Crop[3]	Total[4]	Imports	City Crop	Total	Mill Consumption	Exports	Total
1972-3	1,540	1,357	80	2,977	257	3,234	13,227	3	13,230	30	10	16,504	7,769	5,311	13,080
1973-4	1,500	1,881	350	3,731	198	3,929	12,608	145	12,753	48	20	16,750	7,472	6,123	13,595
1974-5	1,439	2,104	200	3,793	241	3,743	11,189	30	11,214	34	10	15,000	5,860	3,926	9,786
1975-6	1,132	4,074	275	4,511	924	5,481	8,151	47	8,198	92	5	13,776	7,250	3,311	10,561
1976-7	1,211	2,233	150	3,994	110	3,594	10,300	85	10,385	38	54	14,073	6,674	4,784	11,458
1977-8	1,054	1,791	75	2,920	316	2,920	13,933	144	14,077	5	0	17,002	6,483	5,484	11,967
1978-9	1,120	3,806	400	4,057	1,232	5,326	10,405	72	10,477	4	0	15,807	6,352	6,180	12,532
1979-0	928	2,604	250	3,145	635	3,782	14,190	200	14,390	5	0	18,177	6,506	9,229	15,735
1980-1[1]	955	1,822	250	2,485	511	3,028	10,627	44	10,671	28	1	13,898	5,891	5,926	11,817
1981-2[1]	883	1,688	25	1,943	651	2,595	15,111	40	15,151	26	0	17,772	5,264	6,567	11,830
1982-3[5]	830	5,269	300	2,640	3,759	6,399	11,650		12,000	23		18,400	5,397	5,013	10,410

[1] Preliminary.   [2] Less ginnings prior to Aug. 1.   [3] Ginnings prior to Aug. 1 end of season.   [4] Includes inseason ginnings.   [5] Estimate.   Source: *Economic Research Service, U.S.D.A.*
T.170

United States Cotton Ginnings

Ginnings to: (In Thousands of Running Bales)

Crop Year	Aug. 1	Aug. 16	Sept. 1	Sept. 16	Oct. 1	Oct. 15	Nov. 1	Nov. 14	Dec. 1	Dec. 15	Jan. 1	Jan. 16	Feb. 1	Total Crop
1972-3	40	N.A.	521	784	1,821	4,439	6,845	8,242	9,308	10,442	11,603	11,879	12,269	13,269
1973-4	3	N.A.	135	246	496	1,826	5,014	7,070	9,197	10,712	11,601	12,023	12,373	12,611
1974-5	145	N.A.	543	626	827	2,315	4,944	6,509	8,291	9,687	10,598	10,899	11,195	11,328
1975-6	30	N.A.	169	228	373	1,061	2,767	4,169	5,794	7,013	7,603	7,877	8,055	8,151
1976-7	47	N.A.	373	442	573	1,564	3,703	5,952	7,658	9,115	9,887	10,110	10,251	10,347
1977-8	86	N.A.	694	1,169	2,353	4,343	7,494	9,723	11,711	12,963	13,513	13,742	13,859	14,018
1978-9	144	N.A.	672	788	1,490	2,904	4,659	5,890	6,668	8,096	9,317	9,723	10,049	10,549
1979-0	72	N.A.	539	697	916	2,105	4,799	7,287	9,937	11,772	12,728	13,439	13,832	14,262
1980-1	200	N.A.	582	745	1,312	2,566	4,600	6,698	7,841	8,808	9,873	10,430	10,676	10,826
1981-2	44	N.A.	427	645	1,725	3,299	5,541	7,688	10,156	12,023	13,460	14,276	14,778	15,150
1982-3[1]	40	N.A.	453	579	1,531	2,660	5,290	7,214	8,866	9,640	10,580	10,980	11,299	11,528

[1] Preliminary.   Source: *Bureau of Census*
T.171

COTTON

Average Spot Cotton Prices,[2] C.I.F. Northern Europe   In Cents Per Pound (Equivalent U.S. ¢/Lb.)

Crop Year (Aug.-July)	M 1″ U.S. Orleans/ Texas	Pakistan N.T. Sind	Guate- mala	U.S. Memphis Terr. SM	Greece SM	Egypt Giza67 FG	Mexico SM	Nicara- gua SM	Syria SM	USSR Pervyi 31/32 MM	Iran	Turkey Izmir (12 MIR)	SM 1⅛″ U.S. Calif.	Uganda BP52
1970	27.46	29.60		29.68			30.71	28.45	29.26	32.47	29.20	28.35	31.32	33.15
1971	32.64	33.25		34.21			35.46	33.68	34.30	35.06	34.47	33.62	35.37	39.49
1972	34.66	32.63		36.55			37.52	35.34	37.82	37.01	37.66	37.05	37.44	39.89
1973	56.43	52.05		64.91	82.11		52.51	60.21	63.90	64.15	62.31	62.56	66.28	75.66
1974	58.91	51.52		66.69	58.66		66.16	61.06	74.06	66.71	67.60	69.54	68.17	79.84
1975	44.34	42.06		59.65	67.93		55.59	51.19	55.87	53.21	53.82	54.01	61.28	67.55
1976	77.74	N.Q.	79.14	79.88	87.24		79.26	77.12	78.15	78.11	78.50	77.68	78.98	91.73
1977	65.81	59.50	64.72	72.31	70.04		73.87	68.74	74.25	70.60	72.02	76.53	75.27	102.25
1978	63.23		75.23	72.52	83.09		72.94	70.21	72.08	72.55	75.10	73.46	77.99	N.A.
1979-80	75.36	75.41	83.63	87.49	84.00	136.37	85.86	86.13	83.50	85.89	80.77	90.25	90.69	N.A.
1980-81	89.14	84.94	93.47	101.23	83.80	137.41	94.91	92.46	101.00	92.80	N.Q.	96.65	101.85	N.A.
1981-2[1]				75.89							N.Q.			N.A.
Aug. '82	69.31	69.38	77.56	77.12	84.50	107.69	74.94	76.06	79.00	75.50	N.Q.	79.25	81.19	N.A.
Sept. '82	66.20	62.65	72.30	74.10	80.76	107.55	71.70	71.45	—	71.80		76.45	78.20	
Oct. '82	65.00	59.75	68.81	73.38	79.00	107.45	69.56	68.63	—	68.06		81.00	77.38	
Nov. '82	64.44	60.13	67.94	72.00	78.50	106.81	67.81	68.75	—	67.38		79.50	75.56	
Dec. '82	65.63	61.50	68.75	73.25	79.13	105.60	68.50	68.75	—	67.00		80.44	77.44	
Jan. '83	65.75	62.63	71.00	74.25	80.00	106.40	71.13	70.94	75.00	70.50		85.13	81.75	
Feb. '83	65.50	62.88	73.19	75.50		107.28	73.63	73.19	75.13	74.50		82.31	84.44	
Mar. '83				81.35										
Apr. '83														

[1] Preliminary.   [2] Generally for prompt shipment.   *Source: Foreign Agricultural Service, U.S.D.A.*

T.172

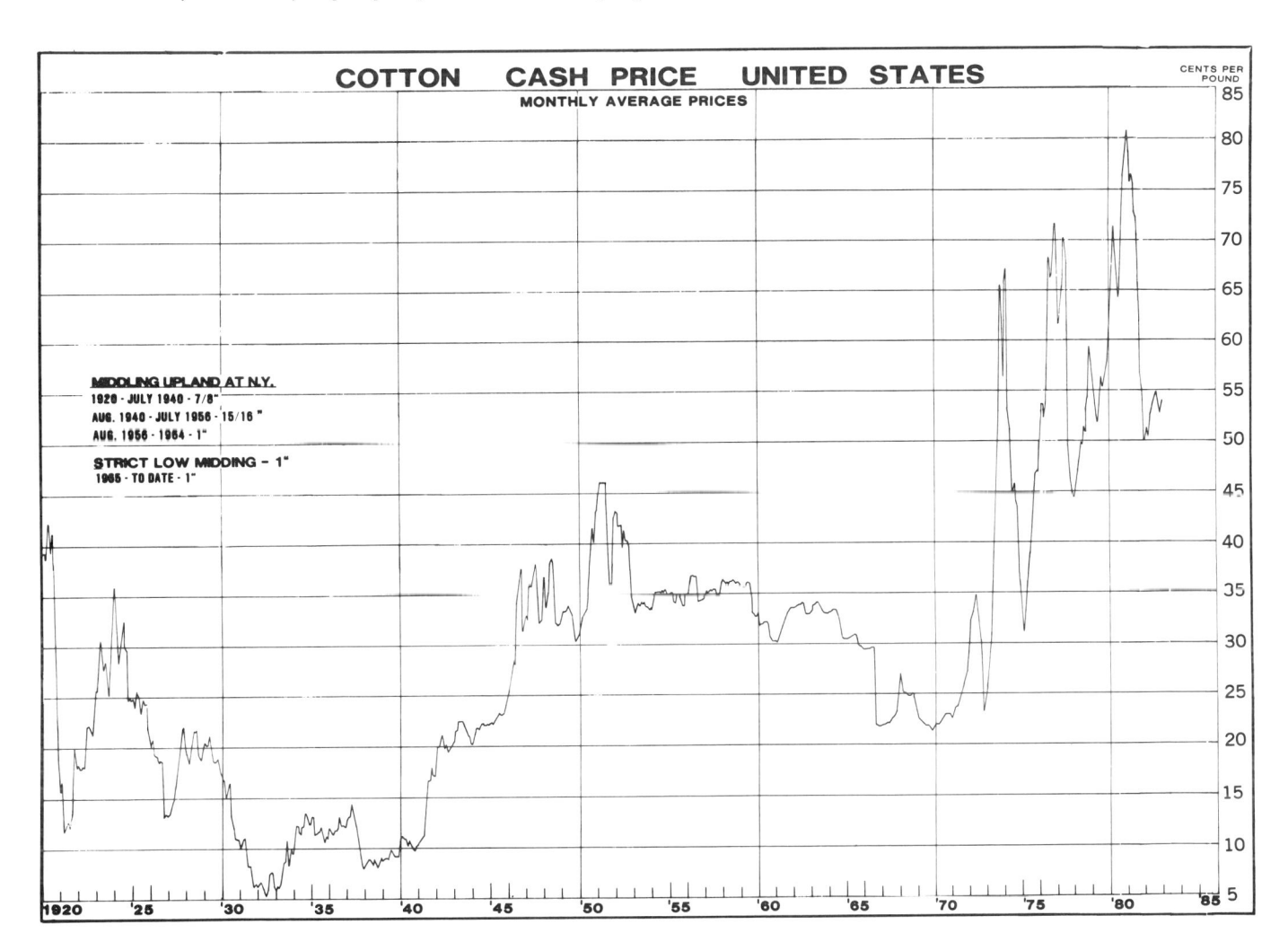

COTTON CASH PRICE UNITED STATES — MONTHLY AVERAGE PRICES (Cents Per Pound)

MIDDLING UPLAND AT N.Y.
1920 - JULY 1940 - 7/8″
AUG. 1940 - JULY 1956 - 15/16″
AUG. 1956 - 1964 - 1″
STRICT LOW MIDDING - 1″
1965 - TO DATE - 1″

COTTON

World Consumption[3] of All Cottons in Specified Countries   In Thousands of Bales (478 Pounds Net[2])

Yr. Beg. Aug. 1	Argentina	Brazil	China	East. Europe	France	W. Germany	India	Italy	Japan	Mexico	Pakistan	Un. Kingdom	United States	USSR	World Total
1970-1	492	1,380	9,300	2,707	1,095	1,078	5,200	925	3,541	675	1,985	741	8,068	8,400	56,230
1971-2	517	1,500	10,600	2,745	1,085	1,109	5,500	924	3,614	750	2,020	638	8,039	8,500	58,580
1972-3	472	1,700	11,300	2,755	1,064	1,074	5,700	862	3,724	800	2,485	650	7,800	8,500	60,358
1973-4	520	1,750	12,000	2,770	1,077	1,096	5,865	898	3,650	830	2,485	560	7,500	8,600	62,183
1974-5	515	1,900	11,800	2,700	932	962	5,785	828	2,900	820	2,020	510	5,885	8,700	58,603
1975-6	540	2,050	10,700	2,742	935	1,022	6,100	901	3,250	835	2,150	494	7,300	8,750	61,411
1976-7	540	2,100	11,400	2,752	961	966	5,500	923	3,150	760	1,800	491	6,702	8,750	60,866
1977-8	480	2,250	12,100	2,772	850	810	5,320	841	3,000	740	1,900	415	6,514	8,800	60,964
1978-9	505	2,450	12,700	2,805	825	780	5,650	979	3,300	760	1,950	449	6,374	8,900	63,247
1979-0	470	2,600	13,500	2,870	850	792	5,950	1,051	3,400	760	1,980	402	6,533	9,000	65,535
1980-1	380	2,500	15,000	2,850	770	795	6,340	956	3,270	760	2,030	221	5,916	9,100	66,149
1981-2[1]	360	2,628	15,800	2,780	746	798	5,814	897	3,250	703	2,277	215	5,292	9,400	65,725
1982-3[4]	400	2,700	16,200	2,830	743	850	5,900	850	3,300	600	2,350	210	5,400	9,500	66,544
1983-4															

[1] Preliminary. [2] Except for the U.S. which are in running bales. [3] Includes estimates for hand spinning in some countries. Excludes cotton burned or otherwise destroyed. [4] Estimate.   Source: *International Cotton Advisory Committee*   T.173

Cotton Government Loan Program in the United States

Crop Yr. Beginning Aug.	Acreage Allotments	Harvested (Thousand Acres)	Loan Rate Avg. at Spot[2] Mkts. (¢ Per Lb.)	Target Price	Gov't. Owned	Pooled	Loan	Total Stock	Loan Entries	Gov't. Purchases	Total Supply	Gov't. Cotton Released	Loan Cotton Repossessed	Total Distribution
1970-1	17,228	11,155	20.37	—	3,035	—	—	3,035	2,411	—	5,446	2,734	2,399	5,133
1971-2	11,618	11,471	19.70	—	313	—	—	313	1,250	—	1,563	288	1,006	1,294
1972-3	11,618	12,984	19.71	—	25	—	244	269	1,945	—	2,214	24	2,006	2,030
1973-4	10,118	11,970	20.65	—	1	—	183	184	1,757	—	1,941	1	1,689	1,690
1974-5	11,118	12,547	27.06	38.00	—	—	251	251	2,465	—	2,716	0	1,677	1,677
1975-6	11,091	8,796	36.12	38.00	—	—	970	970	701	—	1,671	0	1,548	1,548
1976-7	11,084	10,914	38.92	43.20	—	—	123	123	952	—	1,075	—	743	743
1977-8	11,120	13,275	44.63	47.80	—	—	332	332	4,565	—	4,897	—	3,628	3,628
1978-9	10,340	12,400	48.00	52.00	—	—	1,268	1,268	1,559	—	2,828	—	2,191	2,191
1979-0	10,749	12,831	50.23	57.70	—	—	637	637	1,757	—	2,396	—	1,853	1,853
1980-1	None	13,215	48.00	58.40	—	—	542	542	2,328	—	2,870	—	2,215	2,215
1981-2[1]	None	13,841	52.46	70.87	—	—	652	652	6,084	—	6,736	—	3,419	3,419
1982-3[1]	None	9,906	57.08	71.00	—	—	3,759	3,759	5,150	—	8,909	—	1,901	1,901
1983-4[3]	None		55.00	76.00										

Supply & Distribution of Gov't Controlled Cotton — In Thousands of Running Bales

[1] Preliminary. [2] Strict low middling, 1 1/16″ at 10 markets. [3] Estimate. [4] Early forfeitures.   Source: *Department of Agriculture*   T.174

United States Government Crop Forecasts and Actual Cotton Crops

Year	Aug. 1	Sept. 1	Oct. 1	Nov. 1	Dec. 1	Actual Crop	Aug. 1	Sept. 1	Oct. 1	Nov. 1	Dec. 1	Actual Yield
1970	11,079	10,752	10,618	10,429	10,270	10,192	470	456	450	442	441	438
1971	10,932	10,952	10,701	10,719	10,548	10,477	452	453	443	444	442	438
1972	13,343	13,582	13,670	13,955	13,469	13,704	487	494	498	504	487	507
1973	12,740	12,939	13,123	13,189	12,961	12,974	493	502	509	512	519	520
1974	12,758	13,200	12,813	12,053	11,702	11,540	470	470	470	443	443	442
1975	9,416	9,309	9,059	9,034	8,476	8,302	484	479	467	466	437	453
1976	10,734	10,375	10,251	9,891	10,264	10,581	466	451	445	435	451	465
1977	13,535	13,302	13,317	13,832	14,496	14,389	506	495	500	503	525	520
1978	11,820	11,155	10,873	10,981	10,841	10,856	462	425	429	418	421	420
1979	13,710	14,245	14,356	14,544	14,527	14,629	497	525	528	535	534	547
1980	12,812	11,689	11,589	11,224	11,125	11,122	461	421	419	408	411	404
1981	14,789	15,507	15,476	15,560	15,733	15,646	515	540	540	543	546	543
1982	11,143	11,029	11,365	11,947	12,102	12,019	563	569	587	605	613	582
1983												

Forecasts of Production (1,000 Bales of 480 Lbs.[1])   Forecasts of Yields (In Lbs. Per Harv. Acre)

[1] Net Weight bales. Data prior to 1969 are in 500-lb. gross weight bales.   Source: *Crop Reporting Board, U.S.D.A.*   T.175

COTTON

Production of Cotton (Lint) & American-Pima in the United States In Thousands of 480 Pound Net Weight Bales

Year	Alabama	Arizona	Arkansas	California	Georgia	Louisiana	Mississippi	Missouri	No. Car.	Oklahoma	So. Car.	Tennessee	Texas	New Mexico	Total Amer. Pima
1970	507	462	1,048	1,160	292	521	1,631	224	155	193	211	392	3,191		57.3
1971	640	466	1,240	1,117	374	600	1,693	401	135	177	275	528	2,579		98.1
1972	567	603	1,435	1,765	354	705	2,007	439	119	332	308	548	4,246		95.8
1973	449	611	1,041	1,749	390	521	1,816	180	164	427	290	432	4,673		78.1
1974	522	995	880	2,595	419	560	1,595	230	133	310	274	308	2,462	161	90.2
1975	312	573	687	1,954	148	346	1,040	196	46	170	98	222	2,382	72	54.5
1976	349	834	776	2,482	199	553	1,151	165	72	175	145	228	3,307	76	64.0
1977	277	1,070	1,035	2,790	82	656	1,645	235	53	436	109	255	5,465	173	112.2
1978	291	1,068	660	1,940	111	478	1,378	188	45	355	115	235	3,792	101	93.4
1979	324	1,280	606	3,408	152	690	1,437	157	43	522	116	171	5,515	104	98.6
1980	275	1,354	444	3,109	86	460	1,143	177	52	205	77	200	3,320	107	104.2
1981	422	1,556	604	3,535	159	742	1,565	168	95	440	164	315	5,645	133	79.6
1982[1]	460	1,150	530	3,050	230	870	1,760	210	100	250	155	346	2,700	80	107.6
1983															

[1] Preliminary, December estimate. Source: Crop Reporting Board, U.S.D.A. T.176

Aver. Spot Price of U.S. Cotton, 1 1/16 inches[1]—Strict Low Middling at Designated Markets In Cents Per Pound

Yr. Begin. Aug. 1	Atlanta	Augusta	Charleston	Dallas	Fresno	Galveston	Greenville	Greenwood	Houston	Little Rock	Lubbock	Memphis	Montgomery	Phoenix	Average
1970-1	23.84	24.25	—	23.29	22.91	—	24.02	23.68	23.40	23.63	23.28	23.78	23.83	22.72	23.55
1971-2	32.00	32.19	—	31.09	30.68	—	31.80	31.65	31.41	31.40	31.34	31.72	31.96	30.97	31.52
1972-3	35.04	35.02	—	31.31	32.19	—	33.38	33.37	31.38	33.75	32.40	32.45	35.30	32.33	33.14
1973-4[1]	68.63	68.63	—	63.75	71.54	—	68.06	68.06	64.57	—	61.87	68.01	68.44	66.26	67.10
1974-5	—	43.63	—	40.31	42.53	—	42.80	42.20	41.70	—	38.90	41.86	42.45	40.52	41.69
1975-6	—	60.22	—	55.84	58.72	—	59.19	58.54	57.65	—	55.06	58.48	58.93	57.20	57.99
1976-7	—	72.70	—	69.43	71.93	—	71.85	71.21	70.94	—	67.79	71.28	71.54	70.12	70.88
1977-8	—	53.81	—	50.53	56.67	—	53.33	52.75	51.58	—	50.04	52.75	53.24	52.99	52.74
1978-9	—	62.50	—	58.33	67.66	—	62.09	61.84	59.45	—	58.27	61.68	61.92	61.98	61.58
1979-0	—	73.92	—	66.91	73.76	—	73.24	72.73	—	—	66.43	72.55	72.57	71.98	71.48
1980-1	—	85.21	—	80.65	82.80	—	84.54	84.30	—	—	79.66	83.81	84.28	81.70	82.99
1981-2	—	61.87	—	58.32	61.02	—	61.57	61.34	—	—	57.96	61.00	61.34	59.93	60.48
1982-3															

[1] Prior to 1973, prices are for 1 inch middling. Source: Agricultural Marketing Service, U.S.D.A. T.177

Gross Entries of Cotton into U.S. Government Loan Program In Thousands of Running Bales

Crop Year	Aug.	Sept.	Oct.	Nov.	Dec.	Jan.	Feb.	Mar.	April	May[1]	June[1]	July[1]	Seasonal Total
1970-1	0	38	158	592	859	697	44	14	7	1	1	[2]	2,411
1971-2	37	13	38	336	285	388	124	23	1	1	2	[2]	1,250
1972-3	0	40	208	364	495	552	148	103	25	6	3	0	1,945
1973-4	0	15	137	479	589	380	96	40	12	5	4	0	1,757
1974-5	0	13	134	356	544	753	294	99	162	63	47	1	2,465
1975-6	0	1	8	80	195	298	94	15	6	5	[2]	0	701
1976-7	0	0	[2]	3	160	123	67	11	412	174	2	[2]	952
1977-8	[2]	31	214	802	1,531	1,544	310	72	30	13	18	[2]	4,564
1978-9	0	5	26	89	215	584	352	189	68	16	14	[2]	1,560
1979-0	0	[2]	23	294	319	600	316	110	51	35	8	[2]	1,759
1980-1	0	[2]	8	253	528	912	343	204	36	28	16	[2]	2,328
1981-2	0	9	132	293	1,081	2,796	1,120	473	117	39	21	2	6,083
1982-3	—	39	190	864	2,721	4,311	4,814	4,975					
1983-4													

NOTE: Seasonal totals are net, due to allowances for rejections. [1] Entries after April 30 represent late reporting. [2] Less than one thousand bales. Sources: N.Y. Cotton Exchange; Commodity Credit Corporation T.178

COTTON

U.S. Upland Cotton—Ginnings, by Staple Length   In Thousands of Bales

Crop Year	7/8" & Shorter	29/32"	15/16"	31/32"	1"	1 1/32"	1 1/16"	1 3/32"	1 1/8"	1 5/32" & Longer	Total
1970-1	37.1	350.1	1,045.8	588.1	524.4	1,016.4	3,771.7	2,001.7	612.1	107.9	10,055
1971-2	69.9	335.5	917.0	491.8	290.6	530.3	2,612.3	3,320.3	1,449.6	116.8	10,134
1972-3	11.6	156.8	802.0	1,187.7	1,145.6	1,318.4	4,694.0	2,859.1	913.9	84.5	13,174
1973-4	33.5	242.3	1,207.9	1,534.9	1,103.6	841.3	3,629.5	3,180.5	724.4	35.0	12,533
1974-5	12.3	70.3	424.0	683.8	594.4	531.7	2,543.3	4,965.9	1,316.3	97.8	11,240
1975-6	71.1	289.0	620.5	693.9	514.9	390.2	1,546.5	2,948.9	995.2	27.5	8,098
1976-7	9.2	77.4	570.3	980.2	889.7	1,060.4	2,525.5	2,952.8	1,179.9	38.7	10,284
1977-8	7.7	61.6	655.9	1,645.0	1,716.0	1,342.4	2,402.0	4,557.7	1,450.0	70.8	13,909
1978-9	9.4	89	432	877	1,335	1,090	2,497	3,113	1,017	57.8	10,459
1979-0	27.9	125.8	649.5	1,452.9	1,774.8	1,239.2	1,461.9	4,377.9	2,940.6	115.3	14,166
1980-1	58	164	452	798	1,039	903	1,670	3,317	2,321	266.5	10,722
1981-2[1]	7.3	54.7	454.5	1,474.7	1,457.3	1,048.0	2,614.7	4,113.5	2,062.1	139.2	13,426
1982-3											

[1] Preliminary.   Source: Consumer & Marketing Service, U.S.D.A.   T.179

U.S. Daily Rate of Total Cotton Mill Consumption on Cotton-System Spinning Spindles[2]   In Running Bales

Crop Yr.	Aug.	Sept.	Oct.	Nov.	Dec.	Jan.	Feb.	Mar.	Apr.	May	June	July	Average
1974-5	25,771	24,456	23,003	21,616	17,169	18,753	19,768	20,010	21,002	22,766	23,839	21,079	21,603
1975-6	25,273	26,569	27,325	27,481	24,977	28,478	29,937	28,478	27,110	27,592	27,668	22,230	26,926
1976-7	26,203	25,052	26,392	25,072	23,298	25,475	26,392	26,131	25,359	25,369	24,635	19,730	24,926
1977-8	24,687	24,230	25,590	25,235	22,476	24,629	25,042	24,790	24,213	24,173	22,984	19,169	23,935
1978-9	22,941	22,780	24,090	23,809	21,735	24,114	23,567	25,306	23,358	24,193	24,454	20,127	23,373
1979-0	23,617	24,177	25,188	24,099	21,813	24,160	25,353	25,654	24,899	24,781	23,883	18,473	28,610
1980-1	22,130	22,816	23,884	22,885	19,000	21,773	22,312	21,544	21,741	22,060	21,260	19,250	26,066
1981-2[1]	21,448	20,679	22,420	20,138	15,985	18,898	19,885	19,720	20,476	19,580	18,382	15,980	19,466
1982-3[1]	19,295	18,954	20,794	19,526	17,009	20,211	21,550						

[1] Preliminary.   [2] Not seasonally adjusted.   Source: Bureau of the Census; U.S.D.C.   T.180

Average Wholesale Price of Cotton Yarn[1] (30/1[2], Combed, Knitting) on Cones   In Cents Per Pound

Year	Jan.	Feb.	Mar.	Apr.	May	June	July	Aug.	Sept.	Oct.	Nov.	Dec.	Average
1970	102.1	102.1	101.4	100.8	100.8	100.5	100.1	100.1	100.1	100.3	100.5	101.1	100.8
1971	101.4	102.3	103.6	105.4	105.9	106.6	106.8	107.8	108.2	108.2	108.2	108.8	106.1
1972	109.6	110.7	110.7	111.5	112.1	112.3	112.3	112.1	111.7	110.7	110.3	110.5	110.5
1973[2]	85.4	86.4	88.9	91.0	97.2	100.0	98.8	106.2	108.2	108.8	112.5	116.8	100.0
1974	123.3	123.3	125.0	123.3	125.6	122.7	128.1	122.5	118.5	115.4	114.9	110.5	121.1
1975	106.3	102.9	101.4	101.4	102.7	103.9	105.1	106.3	112.5	117.1	120.5	122.0	108.5
1976	127.2	128.4	128.9	128.4	132.3	139.4	145.8	149.0	148.7	147.5	148.7	147.5	139.3
1977	145.1	144.3	146.3	147.5	148.7	147.3	146.5	142.6	156.5	153.9	153.2	153.9	148.8
1978	153.2	155.2	157.5	158.1	160.1	162.7	163.7	163.7	163.7	165.0	165.0	165.6	161.1
1979	165.6	166.3	165.6	165.6	165.9	166.9	166.9	167.3	167.9	169.9	172.8	176.3	168.1
1980	180.6	198.3	200.0	203.0	204.6	202.7	203.3	206.3	206.3	207.6	210.6	211.6	202.9
1981	212.9	214.6	214.6	212.6	211.9	211.9	210.3	207.0	203.0	199.0	196.7	192.1	207.2
1982	191.4	191.7	191.1	191.1	191.7	190.1	189.4	189.4	188.1	185.4	184.4	183.8	189.0
1983													

[1] Natural stock, f.o.b. mill.   [2] Data prior to 1973 are for 36/2.   Source: Bureau of Labor Statistics (0326-0101.05)   T.181

Cotton Cloth[1] Production in the United States   In Millions of Linear Yards

Year	First Quarter	Second Quarter	Third Quarter	Fourth Quarter	Total Year	Year	First Quarter	Second Quarter	Third Quarter	Fourth Quarter	Total Year
1970	1,656	1,561	1,468	1,562	6,246	1977	1,207	1,145	982	1,023	4,356
1971	1,607	1,608	1,405	1,527	6,149	1978	1,056	1,019	912	1,020	4,007
1972	1,530	1,475	1,277	1,384	5,616	1979[2]	1,033	1,018	931	927	3,858
1973	1,377	1,324	1,160	1,226	5,086	1980[2]	1,032	968	996	1,062	4,456
1974	1,322	1,279	1,127	985	4,714	1981[2]	971	961	942	1,002	3,913
1975	902	978	1,051	1,164	4,095	1982[2]	983	953			
1976	1,268	1,221	1,099	1,129	4,718	1983					

[1] Cotton broadwoven goods over 12 inches in width.   [2] Preliminary.   Source: Bureau of the Census   T.192

COTTON

COTTON "2" NEW YORK **NYCE** (WEEKLY HIGH, LOW & CLOSE OF NEAREST FUTURES)
CONTRACT: 50,000 LBS.
CENTS PER POUND

Month End Open Interest of Cotton Futures at New York   In Contracts

Year	Jan.	Feb.	Mar.	Apr.	May	June	July	Aug.	Sept.	Oct.	Nov.	Dec.
1978	27,493	25,289	29,942	29,780	37,143	31,736	30,252	33,901	33,574	37,272	35,537	37,283
1979	35,702	37,809	39,058	35,174	37,391	41,908	33,897	39,343	34,326	41,717	39,684	43,981
1980	54,046	57,891	44,363	38,596	31,753	27,276	39,711	46,814	49,370	45,433	40,208	38,022
1981	32,078	34,782	25,882	24,108	26,793	27,286	26,009	30,014	32,121	31,671	29,157	28,584
1982	30,296	31,740	30,230	31,422	27,665	24,675	24,978	25,052	27,047	26,070	26,949	26,581
1983	29,544	34,165	36,109	33,990								

Source: N.Y. Cotton Exchange

T.182

COTTON

Volume of Trading of Cotton Futures at New York In Contracts

Year	Jan.	Feb.	Mar.	Apr.	May	June	July	Aug.	Sept.	Oct.	Nov.	Dec.	Total
1978	75,314	76,546	92,494	75,240	96,764	117,272	64,924	98,652	94,758	120,670	146,217	96,250	1,155,101
1979	118,361	142,088	139,547	122,110	131,245	191,763	102,928	115,842	114,684	135,924	207,659	159,349	1,689,051
1980	286,058	278,901	290,133	206,682	191,067	128,393	175,619	188,542	224,323	186,615	173,081	173,133	2,523,447
1981	156,303	166,292	150,297	117,653	90,157	117,249	99,175	95,312	96,956	120,301	115,833	89,985	1,415,213
1982	100,242	104,444	103,697	106,892	95,597	151,068	116,211	99,674	101,119	94,265	98,597	83,988	1,255,202
1983	97,947	123,620	139,032	132,447									
1984													

Source: N.Y. Cotton Exchange   T.183

High, Low & Closing Prices of May Cotton Futures at New York In Cents per Pound

Year of Delivery		Mar.	Apr.	May	June	July	Aug.	Sept.	Oct.	Nov.	Dec.	Jan.	Feb.	Mar.	Apr.	May	Life of Delivery Range
1978	High	72.60	71.30	70.00	66.90	64.75	57.25	56.15	55.35	53.70	55.33	57.60	58.19	59.50	57.88	58.70	72.60
	Low	69.75	66.27	66.00	60.20	57.50	54.60	53.50	52.30	51.28	51.41	54.25	55.10	56.00	55.35	56.75	51.28
	Close	70.60	69.30	66.25	60.75	57.60	56.25	54.70	52.80	52.52	54.41	56.82	56.98	56.07	57.00	58.70	—
1979	High	63.40	63.65	67.15	66.50	66.22	69.00	69.20	75.70	75.05	73.85	70.90	68.15	64.45	61.70	62.95	75.70
	Low	61.00	61.50	63.20	63.00	63.00	65.35	66.85	68.80	70.72	68.65	65.50	63.90	59.20	57.50	59.45	54.95
	Close	62.35	63.35	65.25	64.90	66.35	68.35	69.00	73.85	73.67	69.66	65.82	64.17	59.67	61.50	60.47	—
1980	High	67.90	65.70	66.40	68.25	67.00	70.00	69.00	68.90	73.00	76.40	86.00	90.42	90.70	87.40	84.40	90.70
	Low	66.00	64.10	63.00	63.90	64.55	65.90	66.25	66.40	68.20	70.82	73.97	80.70	77.52	79.50	80.90	64.15
	Close	65.65	65.45	64.15	65.60	66.05	69.20	67.70	68.22	71.77	75.95	85.37	86.77	85.12	81.99	83.75	—
1981	High	80.60	77.60	78.42	75.00	85.70	94.50	96.87	93.50	93.12	97.67	96.50	93.70	89.80	89.20	85.20	97.67
	Low	74.50	74.30	74.92	72.80	75.50	81.65	87.00	88.20	86.70	88.40	88.35	86.00	84.75	83.75	80.65	71.00
	Close	77.00	75.05	75.00	74.80	84.80	93.92	90.40	90.20	92.08	95.60	90.90	90.14	86.12	84.00	80.45	—
1982	High	84.90	85.35	83.66	82.50	81.27	79.40	73.80	71.90	70.45	67.40	67.95	67.65	66.75	68.95	68.50	87.50
	Low	82.75	83.20	81.80	78.70	79.10	71.45	68.55	68.30	64.40	63.11	65.55	64.65	64.01	65.40	67.50	63.11
	Close	84.20	83.26	82.90	79.00	79.30	69.15	69.15	69.45	65.29	65.70	67.82	64.94	65.92	68.30	68.43	—
1983	High	74.65	76.75	76.50	77.50	77.50	74.90	72.15	69.25	68.15	68.90	68.40	71.25	76.42	75.30		
	Low	73.50	74.20	73.74	69.45	74.50	69.50	66.75	65.80	65.81	66.20	66.35	66.26	70.30	70.25		
	Close	74.53	76.40	73.30	76.60	74.66	69.90	67.25	67.42	66.62	67.41	67.33	71.20	75.32	71.08		
1984	High	74.60	75.50														
	Low	70.60	73.25														
	Close	73.80	73.80														

Source: N.Y. Cotton Exchange   T.184

Exports of American Cotton from the United States In Thousands of Running Bales

Year	Aug.	Sept.	Oct.	Nov.	Dec.	Jan.	Feb.	Mar.	Apr.	May	June	July	Total
1970-1	84	89	180	252	362	441	455	562	467	327	307	214	3,740
1971-2	162	310	195	272	417	337	402	437	275	163	147	110	3,227
1972-3	59	82	191	352	534	654	528	676	608	437	500	388	5,009
1973-4	329	266	259	257	592	545	598	778	638	561	496	426	5,745
1974-5	261	125	121	272	350	409	380	346	371	364	392	356	3,746
1975-6	325	258	226	176	237	214	141	381	302	327	315	276	3,176
1976-7	274	342	217	265	376	354	509	536	548	400	462	282	4,564
1977-8	181	200	149	333	496	521	502	704	640	510	528	456	5,218
1978-9	524	388	283	355	464	517	577	574	603	542	614	410	5,850
1979-0[1]	463	428	390	630	902	737	1,025	1,150	914	911	686	540	8,776
1980-1[1]	402	393	237	436	541	669	2,352	733	498	458	320	264	7,303
1981-2[1]	990	261	262	478	737	653	754	873	676	484	498	396	7,062
1982-3[1]	342	351	293	382	377	438							

[1] Preliminary. Source: Foreign Agricultural Service, U.S.D.A.   T.185

COTTON

Avg. Price[1] Received by Farmers for Upland Cotton in the U.S. In Cents Per Pound

Year	Aug.	Sept.	Oct.	Nov.	Dec.	Jan.	Feb.	Mar.	Apr.	May	June	July	Average[1]
1970-1	22.65	21.86	22.77	22.09	20.92	21.11	21.76	22.51	23.09	22.92	23.11	22.78	21.86
1971-2[2]	26.00	26.12	27.04	27.95	28.37	29.45	30.16	27.60	30.75	31.71	31.29	30.86	28.07
1972-3	30.67	26.69	26.67	27.45	25.21	22.39	22.78	26.38	27.06	30.25	29.52	30.38	27.30
1973-4	37.46	38.20	38.00	39.50	47.60	50.60	52.00	53.40	54.9	49.2	51.5	49.4	44.4
1974-5	53.6	54.9	51.4	50.4	43.8	37.0	32.6	33.5	35.4	36.5	38.9	40.6	42.7
1975-6	43.5	47.2	49.9	49.7	49.6	50.5	51.7	52.7	53.9	57.5	66.9	68.8	51.1
1976-7	59.7	62.4	63.2	65.9	63.7	62.7	64.8	70.1	68.3	66.8	59.8	61.7	63.8
1977-8	58.3	59.1	53.6	52.1	48.7	49.1	51.4	51.1	52.2	53.7	54.8	56.5	52.1
1978-9	57.4	56.2	59.6	61.1	59.0	57.0	55.6	53.5	54.7	56.0	58.8	61.9	58.1
1979-0	59.2	57.3	61.2	61.0	59.8	60.9	64.9	62.9	61.0	63.6	62.2	71.5	63.1
1980-1	73.7	74.0	75.3	77.6	80.9	76.6	70.8	71.9	72.7	72.5	71.2	70.4	74.4
1981-2	65.0	58.1	63.2	61.1	51.5	50.3	49.1	50.4	54.3	55.8	58.1	59.9	54.0
1982-3	52.8	55.5	59.8	59.9	57.3	56.0	56.4	59.9	58.8				
1983-4													

[1] Weighted average by sales. [2] Beginning Aug. 1971 basis for cotton prices was changed from 500 pound gross weight to a 480 pound net weight bale. *Source: Crop Reporting Board, U.S.D.A.* T.187

Consumption of American and Foreign Cotton in the United States In Thousands of Bales[1]

Year	Aug.	Sept.	Oct.	Nov.	Dec.	Jan.	Feb.	Mar.	Apr.	May	June	July	Total
1970-1	593	760	632	641	722	644	665	815	637	646	797	515	8,068
1971-2	637	771	633	642	727	632	649	808	620	627	772	493	8,010
1972-3	587	715	593	739	544	747	597	601	719	579	575	573	7,569
1973-4	567	543	706	564	509	712	592	587	679	563	546	582	7,150
1974-5	515	489	575	432	343	469	395	400	525	455	477	527	5,602
1975-6	505	531	683	550	624	570	559	712	542	552	692	445	6,965
1976-7	524	626	528	501	582	510	528	653	507	507	616	395	6,477
1977-8	494	606	512	505	562	493	501	620	484	483	575	383	6,218
1978-9[2]	459	569	482	595	435	603	468	506	584	484	489	503	6,177
1979-0[2]	472	482	630	482	436	604	507	513	622	496	478	487	6,209
1980-1[2]	443	456	597	458	475	435	446	539	435	441	531	385	5,641
1981-2[2]	429	517	448	403	400	378	398	493	410	392	460	317	5,038
1982-3[2]	386	474	416	390	425	404	431						

[1] American cotton, running bales; foreign cotton, equivalent 500 lb. bales. [2] Preliminary. *Source: Bureau of the Census* T.188

U.S. Exports of American Cotton to Countries of Destination In Thousands of Running Bales

Yr. Beg. Aug. 1	Bangladesh	Canada	Hong Kong	France	W. Germany	India	Italy	Japan	Netherlands	Spain	Sweden	United Kingdom	Rep. of Korea	China	Taiwan	World Total
1970-1	—	292	193	60	65	210	57	841	34	19	29	95	491	0	407	3,737
1971-2	—	312	48	35	77	101	121	726	30	38	11	63	489	0	288	3,229
1972-3	122	249	193	141	177	—	172	1,039	46	107	33	87	572	0	356	5,007
1973-4	98	258	356	81	101	0	124	1,312	17	35	40	57	722	0	542	5,746
1974-5	51	186	73	65	52	0	97	957	19	58	34	33	628	0	384	3,746
1975-6	142	131	126	23	11		53	646	3	17	21	10	803	0	400	3,170
1976-7	122	187	358	45	36	273	85	973	12	86	17	66	913	0	436	4,565
1977-8	42	214	479	80	65	1	77	1,028	21	64	21	59	1,172	414	490	5,219
1978-9	107	222	427	63	96	1	146	1,342	18	65	23	72	1,278	606	454	6,180
1979-0[1]		272	636	92	204	0	185	1,588	11	131	21	72	1,484	2,156	728	9,229
1980-1[1]		267	205	42	112	—	54	1,139	1	60	10	38	1,303	1,309	351	5,926
1981-2[2]																6,567
1982-3[2]																5,013

[1] Preliminary. [2] Estimate. *Source: Bureau of the Census* T.189

127

COTTON

Average Price of Strict Low Middling,[1] 1¹/₁₆″[2], Cotton at Designated U.S. Markets   ¢/Lb. (Net Weight)

Year	Aug.	Sept.	Oct.	Nov.	Dec.	Jan.	Feb.	Mar.	Apr.	May	June	July	Average
1970-1	22.99	22.98	23.00	22.82	22.58	22.81	23.22	23.56	23.79	24.46	25.07	25.31	23.55
1971-2[1]	25.99	26.52	27.03	27.41	29.55	32.35	32.82	33.14	34.30	34.75	33.43	32.13	30.78
1972-3	30.22	25.60	23.26	23.85	25.72	28.05	29.38	30.89	35.31	39.23	39.47	44.06	31.25
1973-4	53.03	65.46	63.24	56.36	65.68	67.11	57.87	53.26	51.52	45.94	44.87	45.92	55.86
1974-5[2]	50.36	47.65	44.59	39.96	36.91	36.10	36.44	37.81	40.43	41.73	42.77	45.57	41.69
1975-6	48.40	50.74	50.38	50.87	55.12	57.17	56.96	55.47	57.18	62.07	72.74	78.73	57.99
1976-7	73.25	72.26	76.98	76.53	73.10	66.95	72.15	75.75	73.67	70.65	61.08	58.18	70.88
1977-8	52.54	49.30	49.06	47.98	48.42	51.05	52.89	55.01	54.72	57.59	57.35	56.99	52.74
1978-9	59.78	60.04	64.08	65.65	64.39	61.48	60.59	58.70	58.05	60.90	63.38	61.87	61.58
1979-0	62.08	62.15	62.88	63.40	66.20	72.40	80.66	79.24	79.05	78.27	72.41	79.01	71.48
1980-1	85.60	87.51	85.78	87.05	87.23	85.11	83.30	81.52	81.15	78.46	78.12	75.08	82.99
1981-2	66.44	60.81	60.63	57.47	55.11	57.82	57.26	59.73	62.03	62.44	61.10	64.96	60.48
1982-3	60.38	58.98	58.58	58.20	59.65	60.16	61.72	66.05	65.33				
1983-4													

Note: Grade 41. [1] Prior to Aug. 1971 prices are for MIDDLING. [2] Prices prior to 1974-75 are for 1″ cotton.   *Source: Department of Agriculture*

T.190

Average Spot Cotton, 1³/₃₂″, Price at Designated U.S. Markets   In Cents Per Pound (Net Weight)

Year	Aug.	Sept.	Oct.	Nov.	Dec.	Jan.	Feb.	Mar.	Apr.	May	June	July	Average	1¹/₃₂″	1″
1970-1	25.94	25.68	25.41	25.10	24.86	25.08	25.45	25.90	26.21	26.76	27.36	27.58	25.94	24.59	24.53
1971-2[1]	28.05	28.54	29.05	29.47	31.38	34.04	34.49	34.98	37.01	38.46	36.95	35.38	33.15	31.96	31.51
1972-3	33.29	28.10	25.83	27.32	29.50	32.47	33.33	35.23	40.43	45.34	46.27	52.28	35.78	33.66	33.14
1973-4	67.14	80.71	75.50	66.91	76.82	78.28	68.76	62.58	63.59	56.48	55.40	55.50	67.31	64.59	57.66
1974-5	50.58	47.87	44.81	40.18	37.11	36.30	36.64	38.01	40.60	41.90	42.94	45.74	41.89	40.02	39.08
1975-6	48.57	50.91	50.55	51.07	55.32	57.37	57.16	55.67	57.38	62.27	72.94	78.93	58.18	56.44	54.69
1976-7	73.45	72.46	77.18	76.73	73.30	67.15	72.36	75.96	73.88	70.85	61.26	68.36	71.08	69.34	67.09
1977-8	52.72	49.48	49.24	48.16	48.65	51.28	53.12	55.24	54.95	57.82	57.58	57.22	52.96	51.27	48.26
1978-9	60.01	60.27	64.31	65.94	64.68	61.77	60.88	59.03	58.44	61.30	63.79	62.26	61.89	59.92	55.24
1979-0	62.47	62.54	63.28	63.81	66.58	72.78	81.05	79.63	79.44	78.66	72.80	79.40	71.87	69.53	63.39
1980-1	86.00	87.91	86.18	87.45	87.63	85.57	83.70	81.92	81.55	78.86	78.52	75.48	83.39	80.95	75.70
1981-2	66.84	61.22	61.08	57.91	55.52	58.24	57.70	60.12	62.41	62.82	61.48	N.A.	60.89	58.28	54.13
1982-3	60.76	59.36	58.97	58.57	60.02										
1983-4															

[1] Beginning Aug. 1971 prices are for STRICT LOW MIDDLING.   *Source: Agricultural Marketing Service, U.S.D.A.*

T.191

U.S. Exports of Cotton Cloth (Raw Cotton Equivalent)   In Thousands of Bales (Net Weight—480 Lbs.)

Year	Jan.	Feb.	Mar.	Apr.	May	June	July	Aug.	Sept.	Oct.	Nov.	Dec.	Total
1971	20.3	20.5	25.9	25.4	26.3	23.5	24.4	28.1	36.3	13.0	23.7	45.3	312.6
1972	33.8	31.6	37.7	32.2	33.8	35.8	29.7	34.2	31.3	39.0	34.0	36.0	409.2
1973	32.3	30.2	38.3	38.0	38.8	37.9	35.4	33.9	42.5	43.8	44.8	43.3	459.4
1974	44.1	43.6	52.9	51.0	51.5	51.2	44.2	36.7	39.3	41.4	39.4	36.2	531.5
1975	36.9	36.0	43.8	43.8	37.5	37.5	34.3	38.1	41.0	49.8	41.6	39.9	488.3
1976	42.8	41.6	54.6	48.0	41.1	47.8	39.0	39.0	45.8	57.5	45.6	53.2	556.0
1977	42.8	51.6	47.1	47.2	36.9	36.5	29.4	31.0	40.2	24.8	26.3	46.3	460.1
1978	32.2	35.2	37.1	35.2	34.5	33.0	31.4	35.9	37.9	44.8	50.1	50.4	457.9
1979[1]	45.6	45.4	56.7	44.1	50.5	57.0	46.2	47.1	55.8	59.0	62.3	58.1	627.7
1980[1]	50.6	54.2	52.4	45.2	42.4	47.2	34.6	44.3	48.0	42.0	38.4	40.9	540.2
1981[1]	34.8	28.2	35.8	35.7	30.9	30.8	21.7	25.9	25.8	27.5	26.6	21.9	345.6
1982[1]	18.2	18.6	20.4	20.6	24.3	24.8	22.7	15.7	18.4	20.7	18.4	16.4	239.2
1983													

[1] Preliminary.   *Source: Bureau of the Census*

T.193

Cottonseed and Products

U.S. cottonseed production for the 1982/83 season ending July 31, 1983 was estimated to be 4.78 million tons, approximately 25 percent under the 1981 figure. The average yield per acre was 0.48 ton, slightly higher than the 1981 yield. However, harvested cotton area was almost 4 million acres below the 1981 acreage because of adverse weather in Texas during the summer of 1982 and because of the 15 percent cotton acreage reduction program.

Estimates of 1983/84 cottonseed production were down sharply because of a 20 percent acreage reduction program announced for upland cotton. A producer who had signed up for this program was entitled to idle an additional 10 to 30 percent of his base cotton acreage in return for a subsidy amounting to 80 percent of his farm's established yield to be paid in kind. The program is expected to reduce total 1983/84 cottonseed supplies to 4 or 4.5 million tons from 5.6 million in the 1982/83 season.

Cottonseed crushings during the 1982/83 season were estimated at 4.1 million tons, 0.5 million under the previous season's figure. This crush was expected to produce nearly 1.3 billion pounds of oil and 1.9 million tons of meal. Total domestic 1982/83 cottonseed use, which includes exports, was estimated at 5.1 million tons versus 6.0 million the previous season, and exports were estimated at 50,000 tons versus 45,000 tons the previous season. Farm prices for cottonseed during December 1982 averaged $86 per ton, just above the year-earlier price.

Cottonseed meal supplies during 1982/83 were estimated to be 2 million tons, 12% under last season's estimate. Higher cottonseed meal prices, projected to be $160 a ton in 1983 versus a 1981/82 average $156, were attributed to higher soybean meal prices.

Cottonseed oil prices were expected to average 17.5 cents a pound during 1983 versus the 16.7 cents average during October–December 1982.

The USDA in early 1983 estimated world 1982/83 cottonseed production at 26.8 million tons, 0.4 million tons above the 1981/82 production.

Salient Statistics of Cottonseed in the United States

Year Begin. Aug.	Farm Value of Production Mil. $	Exports	Seed for Planting	Residual[2]	Crushings	Oil	Meal	Linters[5]	Hulls	Other[3]	Oil	Meal	Linters	Hulls	Total Value of Pdt's. ¢ Per Ton
		— In Thousands of Short Tons —				In Million Pounds					In Pounds				
1970-1	229.6	39	163	—	3,728	1,211	3,458	1,147	1,744	320	325	927	194	168	94.68
1971-2	240.9	3	189	70	3,960	1,275	3,588	1,145	1,956	379	322	906	182	494	89.79
1972-3	267.1	10	173	57	4,880	1,535	4,448	1,341	2,430	502	314	911	173	498	121.14
1973-4	501.2	49	198	6	4,792	1,551	4,354	1,341	2,346		324	908	175	489	186.76
1974-5	611.2	6	128	74	4,226	1,347	3,770	1,269	2,144		319	892	190	507	189.19
1975-6	312.3	61	190	367	2,952	986	2,476	847	1,546		334	891	181	523	171.66
1976-7	425.4	26	181	333	3,499	1,141	3,286	983	1,832		326	898	177	524	189.04
1977-8	388.0	41	175	454	4,313	1,386	4,166	1,174	2,152		322	918	172	500	160.89
1978-9	485.6	16	175	247	4,127	1,282	3,770	1,077	2,068						221.00
1979-0[1]	697.6	94	196	725	4,230	1,423	4,096								194.65
1980-1[4]	574.5	133	—922—		4,076	1,195	3,580								
1981-2[4]	549.0	45	—1,394—		4,575	1,565	4,420								
1982-3[4]	364.7	50	—1,008—		4,100	1,310	3,770								
1983-4															

[1] Preliminary. [2] Mainly used on farms for feed & fertilizer. [3] Including loss; and also motes, grabbots & hullfibers. [4] Forecast. [5] In THOUSANDS OF RUNNING BALES. Source: Economic Research Service, U.S.D.A.

T.195

World Production of Cottonseed   In Thousands of Metric Tons

Crop Year	Sudan	Argentina	Brazil	China[2]	Egypt	India	Mexico	Pakistan	Peru	Turkey	South Africa	USSR	United States	World Total
1970-1	472	170	994	3,300	884	1,920	631	1,105	165	640		4,365	3,690	21,324
1971-2	443	183	1,370	3,215	899	2,575	745	1,436	152	835		4,405	3,846	23,438
1972-3	351	254	1,304	2,750	895	2,247	779	1,425	135	870		4,525	4,892	23,998
1973-4	432	248	1,171	4,355	862	2,400	640	1,264	173	821		4,767	4,550	25,330
1974-5	395	349	1,034	4,185	760	2,618	989	1,285	150	956		5,212	4,091	25,745
1975-6	200	270	802	4,185	800	2,444	453	1,259	131	736		4,686	2,749	23,738
1976-7	300	364	984			2,138				768		4,888	3,764	
1977-8	357	300	977	4,100	690	2,500	590	1,151	138	920		4,693	5,009	25,004
1978-9	249	414	844	4,334	736	2,800	575	920	150	760	105	4,804	3,873	23,652
1979-0	215	330	1,076	4,414	792	2,643	560	1,436	160	750	128	4,510	5,242	25,220
1980-1[1]	264	315	1,057	5,414	896	2,700	570	1,422	160	758	121	5,082	4,056	25,642
1981-2[1]		170	1,120	5,936		2,800		1,497				5,189	5,803	28,276
1982-3[3]		290	1,156	6,800		2,700		1,586				4,695	4,334	26,824
1983-4														

[1] Preliminary. [2] Including Manchuria. [3] Estimated. Source: Foreign Agricultural Service, U.S.D.A.

T.194

129

COTTONSEED AND COTTONSEED PRODUCTS

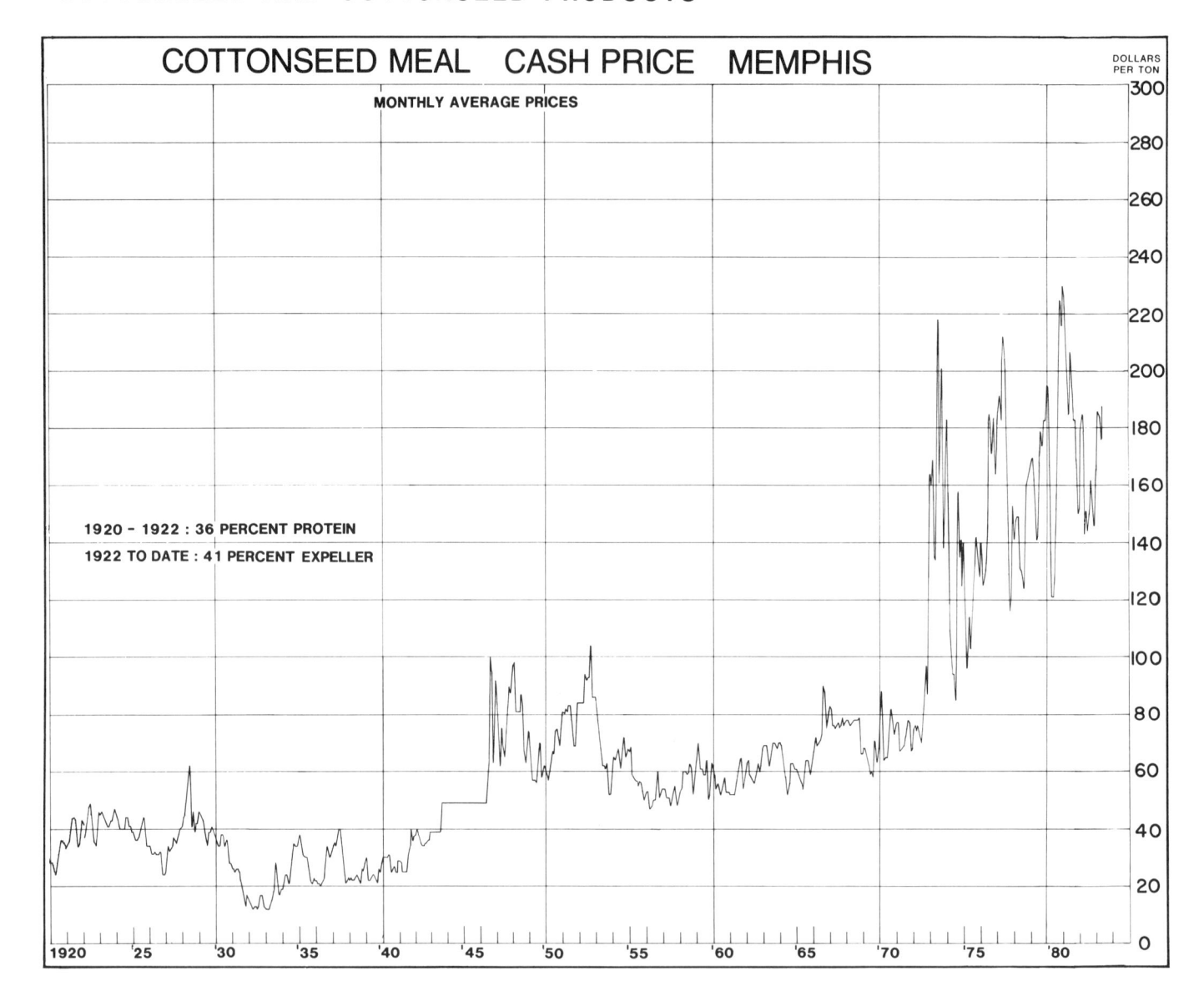

COTTONSEED MEAL   CASH PRICE   MEMPHIS   DOLLARS PER TON

MONTHLY AVERAGE PRICES

1920 - 1922 : 36 PERCENT PROTEIN
1922 TO DATE : 41 PERCENT EXPELLER

Average Wholesale Price of Cottonseed Meal (41% Protein-Expeller) at Memphis   In Dollars Per Ton

Year	Jan.	Feb.	Mar.	Apr.	May	June	July	Aug.	Sept.	Oct.	Nov.	Dec.	Average
1970	88.10	74.50	64.40	64.90	65.20	70.20	78.30	82.00	74.50	72.60	75.90	76.70	73.80
1971	77.40	73.60	66.80	68.20	68.80	71.30	74.60	78.00	76.50	66.80	67.80	74.80	72.05
1972	75.70	74.40	75.60	73.60	72.25	70.30	81.40	86.60	96.50	86.60	118.90	164.40	89.69
1973	160.30	168.75	134.75	134.20	207.80	217.50	161.20	201.25	178.75	138.00	160.60	182.50	170.47
1974	159.50	119.40	109.30	93.60	94.25	85.00	133.50	157.50	135.00	141.25	125.00	140.00	124.44
1975	121.60	100.50	95.90	114.00	105.60	116.40	123.25	131.70	141.50	131.60	127.50	139.50	119.93
1976	136.25	125.00	127.50	130.00	143.75	182.30	184.75	170.70	184.40	163.50	171.00	185.60	158.73
1977	190.00	190.60	184.50	204.40	211.90	200.00	163.10	129.00	116.25	121.25	152.60	141.25	167.07
1978	148.00	148.60	149.40	131.25	130.00	127.50	124.40	149.00	162.00	164.00	166.25	167.50	147.33
1979	169.50	161.90	156.90	141.25	143.00	171.00	178.50	173.75	183.10	183.00	183.75	195.00	170.06
1980	167.00	156.25	136.25	120.50	121.00	129.40	157.00	198.40	224.50	215.00	230.00	224.00	173.33
1981	205.60	178.75	185.00	206.90	201.75	190.00	182.50	183.10	166.50	150.00	150.60	179.00	181.64
1982	184.70	159.40	142.50	150.60	143.80	150.00	158.80	161.50	150.00	145.60	161.70	166.30	156.24
1983	185.60	183.75	175.50										
1984													

Source: Economic Research Service, U.S.D.A.

T.196

COTTONSEED AND COTTONSEED PRODUCTS

Cottonseed Crushed (Consumption) in the United States   In Thousands of Short Tons

Year	Aug.	Sept.	Oct.	Nov.	Dec.	Jan.	Feb.	Mar.	Apr.	May	June	July	Total
1970-1	84	98	417	477	471	463	439	410	311	238	186	134	3,728
1971-2	139	109	349	458	484	474	425	481	344	298	228	169	3,960
1972-3	196	175	444	529	499	528	480	522	450	426	342	290	4,880
1973-4	275	185	370	532	465	549	463	499	443	424	320	268	4,792
1974-5	235	202	385	431	441	471	434	453	356	331	261	225	4,226
1975-6	225	158	219	291	324	366	336	295	241	203	169	125	2,952
1976-7	115	91	262	403	416	422	414	407	278	266	230	194	3,499
1977-8	187	186	370	459	431	443	403	449	378	341	346	321	4,313
1978-9	312	254	348	423	392	418	404	426	355	325	255	217	4,129
1979-0[1]	258	175	304	394	379	442	388	454	374	388	359	315	4,230
1980-1[1]	330	306	365	426	400	440	378	372	314	278	248	218	4,076
1981-2[1]	191.6	186.2	323.5	455.5	473.3	478.8	446.6	482.3	424.1	426.7	357.1	329.6	4,575
1982-3[1]	290.3	285.8	391.5	481.7	423.0								
1983-4													

[1] Preliminary.   Source: Bureau of Census   T.197

Production of Cottonseed Cake and Meal in the United States   In Thousands of Short Tons

Year	Aug.	Sept.	Oct.	Nov.	Dec.	Jan.	Feb.	Mar.	Apr.	May	June	July	Total
1970-1	38.0	45.2	194.1	210.2	218.2	215.8	202.4	192.2	145.3	111.1	86.1	61.1	1,729
1971-2	66.4	50.3	161.2	208.9	219.8	212.7	191.1	216.5	155.9	132.4	101.8	76.6	1,794
1972-3	87.2	78.4	200.4	242.4	228.4	238.7	218.0	236.8	208.0	195.7	158.8	131.0	2,224
1973-4	125.6	83.1	168.6	242.4	211.4	246.7	209.0	224.1	200.3	194.0	146.7	124.6	2,177
1974-5	109.3	95.3	171.9	186.9	194.1	207.3	192.2	203.4	159.0	150.7	117.0	97.6	1,888
1975-6	100.2	70.9	100.2	127.7	141.6	158.2	150.8	133.9	107.6	91.2	76.1	56.2	1,315
1976-7	53.0	41.5	116.6	181.0	187.8	189.2	185.6	183.9	125.0	120.1	100.1	86.6	1,571
1977-8	83.2	84.0	167.9	210.2	199.4	203.2	187.9	206.6	172.5	156.6	158.7	150.1	1,980
1978-9	148.0	121.4	162.4	197.1	184.3	197.5	193.1	201.2	166.5	155.7	122.2	105.8	1,955
1979-0	119.7	79.3	145.9	183.4	173.0	201.0	178.0	204.0	168.9	181.6	167.8	148.5	1,951
1980-1[1]	152.3	144.0	170.3	202.1	191.1	204.9	176.3	173.4	145.5	130.8	114.2	104.2	1,909
1981-2[1]	88.3	88.7	152.1	220.2	219.0	226.9	206.5	220.3	195.3	195.9	164.4	150.2	2,128
1982-3[1]	129.8	129.3	173.5	219.4	198.3								
1983-4													

[1] Preliminary.   Source: Bureau of Census   T.198

U.S. Production of Crude Cottonseed Oil   In Millions of Pounds

Year	Aug.	Sept.	Oct.	Nov.	Dec.	Jan.	Feb.	Mar.	Apr.	May	June	July	Total
1970-1	26.6	30.5	134.3	153.4	152.7	151.5	141.2	134.0	103.3	78.8	61.0	43.5	1,211
1971-2	47.0	34.3	111.8	149.0	154.0	151.1	134.9	154.4	110.2	97.7	75.8	54.4	1,275
1972-3	61.2	53.4	139.3	165.5	157.3	163.3	152.0	163.4	141.8	136.3	108.4	92.9	1,304
1973-4	87.8	56.2	120.6	169.8	149.0	176.9	150.2	160.4	144.2	140.0	105.9	90.1	1,551
1974-5	78.0	66.9	122.8	138.2	139.1	147.6	137.5	143.4	111.6	105.8	84.1	72.3	1,347
1975-6	76.1	56.1	76.3	101.0	103.2	118.1	111.2	100.2	80.0	67.3	56.1	40.3	986
1976-7	38.0	28.2	80.1	129.2	135.6	135.0	134.3	134.4	91.1	89.3	78.5	67.3	1,141
1977-8	63.0	60.1	115.1	146.3	140.2	141.6	129.5	141.8	122.1	109.2	113.9	107.8	1,391
1978-9	103.5	82.0	108.8	134.0	123.5	134.4	128.0	135.3	115.0	103.7	86.3	73.8	1,328
1979-0[1]	85.5	53.5	98.6	126.5	119.9	142.8	125.7	145.1	119.8	125.5	116.8	104.2	1,363
1980-1[1]	104.9	93.1	116.4	130.6	122.3	131.7	118.9	115.4	100.8	88.7	77.4	69.6	1,270
1981-2[1]	62.1	60.9	111.2	153.5	161.8	154.1	145.6	155.9	138.4	140.1	117.5	105.9	1,507
1982-3[1]	92.0	88.8	129.8	157.3	143.7								
1983-4													

[1] Preliminary.   Source: Bureau of Census   T.199

COTTONSEED AND COTTONSEED PRODUCTS

COTTONSEED OIL CASH PRICE NEW YORK

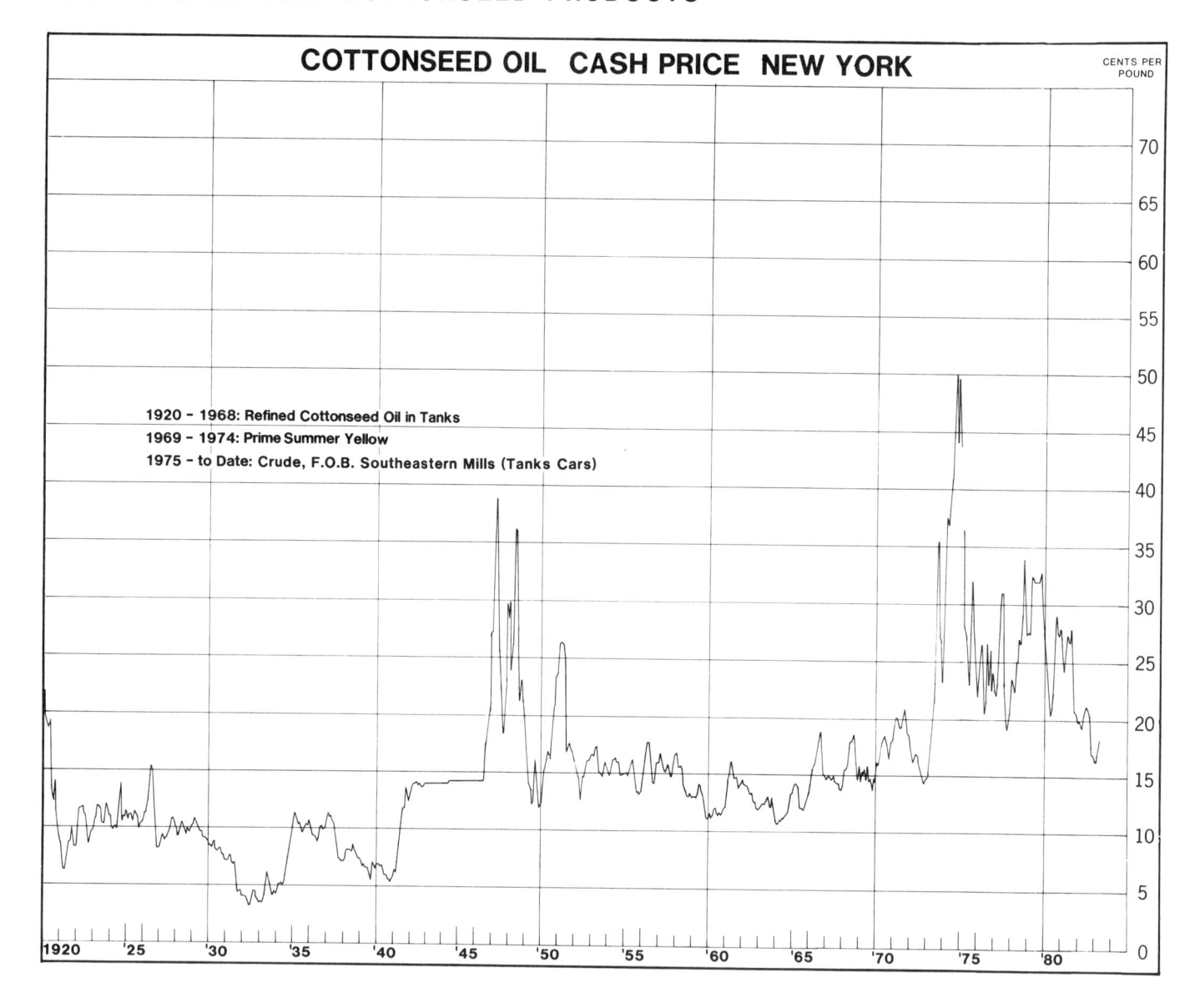

1920 - 1968: Refined Cottonseed Oil in Tanks
1969 - 1974: Prime Summer Yellow
1975 - to Date: Crude, F.O.B. Southeastern Mills (Tanks Cars)

Average Price of Crude Cottonseed Oil, F.O.B. Southeastern Mills (Tank Cars)   In Cents Per Pound

Year	Jan.	Feb.	Mar.	Apr.	May	June	July	Aug.	Sept.	Oct.	Nov.	Dec.	Average
1970	10.9	12.1	13.2	14.0	14.3	14.4	14.3	14.1	12.9	13.4	14.1	14.1	13.5
1971	14.5	16.1	16.1	15.6	15.3	15.3	15.4	16.5	16.1	14.4	13.9	13.9	15.3
1972	13.4	13.5	12.6	12.4	12.1	12.4	11.9	11.4	10.1	10.1	10.4	10.6	11.8
1973	10.6	12.9	14.6	14.6	14.6	14.6	14.6	14.6	22.5	22.0	19.0	27.0	19.8
1974	29.0	33.5	31.5	35.0	37.0	36.5	39.0	47.0	39.5	45.0	46.0	37.0	38.0
1975	36.5	32.0	28.0	27.0	23.0	23.0	29.0	32.0	28.5	26.5	23.5	22.0	27.6
1976	24.0	26.0	26.5	24.0	20.5	21.5	26.5	23.0	26.0	22.5	24.0	22.5	23.9
1977	22.0	23.0	27.0	30.0	31.0	31.0	23.0	22.0	19.0	20.0	20.5	23.5	24.3
1978	23.0	22.3	25.0	25.0	27.0	26.5	27.5	29.0	34.0	28.5	27.3	27.5	26.9
1979	27.3	32.0	32.5	32.0	32.0	32.0	32.0	32.0	32.9	29.7	27.6	26.2	30.7
1980	24.3	23.8	22.4	20.4	20.9	22.3	27.8	29.0	27.5	27.2	27.8	27.0	25.0
1981	25.3	24.2	25.3	27.3	26.7	26.6	27.9	24.6	20.7	20.5	20.4	19.8	24.1
1982	19.9	19.5	19.1	20.4	21.0	21.1	20.9	20.3	18.0	16.9	16.8	16.3	19.2
1983													
1984													

Source: Economic Research Service, U.S.D.A.

T.204

COTTONSEED AND COTTONSEED PRODUCTS

Supply & Distribution of Cottonseed Oil in the United States   In Millions of Pounds

Crop Year Beginning Oct.	Production	Imports for Consumption	Stocks Oct. 1	Total Supply	Exports	Shipments to U.S. Terr.	Domestic Disappearance	Per Capita Consumption — Lbs. —	Shortening	Margarine	Salad & Cooking Oils	Other	Total	Foots & Loss	Other	Total
1970	1,211	—	214	1,425	357.5	1.4	899	4.35	203	65	485	64	818	70	11	81
1971	1,275	—	167	1,442	421.4	1.2	815	3.91	166	64	409	80	718	79	18	91
1972	1,535	.2	204	1,739	585.9	1.9	961	4.58	192	64	567	19	841	104	16	120
1973	1,551	—	190	1,741	569.2	2.5	1,034	4.89	219	64	586	55	924	101	9	110
1974	1,347	—	135	1,482	673.2	1.1	662	3.11	164	48	349	—	560	94	7	102
1975	986	—	146	1,132	534.6	.7	439	2.04	130	49	189	—	367	65	7	72
1976	1,141	—	157	1,298	610.0	.9	535	2.47	149	47	280	—	474	51	9	60
1977[3]	1,453	—	86	1,539	758	.2	696	3.17	174	44	378	—	595	90	8	97
1978	1,282	—	85	1,367	661		620		189	42	446					
1979[1]	1,423	—	86	1,509	728		659		169	25	403					
1980[2]	1,195	—	122	1,317	710		527		189	25	460					
1981[2]	1,565	—	80	1,645	847		694		136	25	380					
1982[2]	1,310	—	104	1,414	710		624									
1983[2]			80													

[1] Preliminary.   [2] Estimate.   [3] Data prior to 1977 are for Crop Yr. beginning Aug. 1.   Source: Economic Research Service, U.S.D.A.   T.201

U.S. Exports of Cottonseed Oil to Important Countries   In Thousands of Metric Tons

Crop Year	Canada	Costa Rica	Dom. Rep.	Egypt	W. Germ.	India	Iran	Japan	Korea	Netherlands	Turkey	United Kingdom	Venezuela	Total
1976-7	4.2	0	2.0	194.8	1.7	0	20.1	20.6	.9	9.9	0	4.4	35.1	313.1
1977-8	4.2	0	7.0	192.8	2.6	0	39.7	26.6	1.1	2.1	0	1.4	43.1	344.1
1978-9	6.0	—	37.6	135.1	1.3	0	40.8	37.3	1.3	4.0	0	2.1	30.2	299.7
1979-0	5.3	1.9	28.4	157.1	—	0	—	23.0	1.9	5.2	3.0	.5	72.3	330.2
1980-1[1]	2.5	1.0	33.2	75.6	—	27.2	0	40.2	2.5	5.8	—	1.5	109.1	321.9
1981-2[1]			27.3	74.4		27.2		41.2		10.2			91.2	384.4
1982-3[1]			24.8	158.3		0		40.7		11.3			86.8	387.5
1983-4														

[1] Preliminary.   Source: Foreign Agricultural Service, U.S.D.A.   T.202A

United States Production of Refined Cottonseed Oil   In Millions of Pounds

Year	Aug.	Sept.	Oct.	Nov.	Dec.	Jan.	Feb.	Mar.	Apr.	May	June	July	Total
1970-1	27.1	27.6	71.6	116.0	116.6	108.5	108.6	119.8	77.2	80.4	73.2	44.9	972
1971-2	51.2	44.8	60.9	102.9	113.3	104.0	90.8	118.3	98.3	98.2	88.8	61.3	1,033
1972-3	74.6	41.8	95.4	121.9	140.1	124.9	135.0	140.7	128.9	126.0	99.1	76.8	1,305
1973-4	102.7	66.6	89.0	117.2	123.3	134.9	118.2	125.5	129.3	117.4	90.2	83.2	1,298
1974-5	88.5	63.5	81.8	113.0	117.2	124.4	125.5	117.0	109.0	102.5	93.0	74.0	1,209
1975-6	68.0	73.1	53.6	75.5	97.1	99.6	89.6	91.6	76.2	70.9	60.4	52.7	908
1976-7	48.5	33.4	37.7	73.0	86.2	113.9	117.0	123.7	94.5	98.0	87.5	66.6	866
1977-8	69.0	58.1	92.9	133.0	134.6	111.1	98.2	114.7	102.7	91.3	95.2	91.8	1,214
1978-9	117.5	84.7	83.7	116.0	100.4	118.8	113.1	126.4	108.2	97.9	78.7	78.7	1,224
1979-0	92.7	56.7	69.6	97.0	103.0	119.1	102.7	118.7	107.5	112.8	203.4	103.5	1,186
1980-1	96.2	94.8	94.1	119.8	125.1	131.3	99.6	102.1	113.0	82.9	79.1	73.7	1,212
1981-2[1]	56.9	53.1	84.7	129.3	144.6	110.2	121.2	135.7	124.9	128.9	121.8	104.8	1,316
1982-3[1]	91.3	76.7	91.5	127.3	124.5	119.2							
1983-4													

[1] Preliminary.   Source: Bureau of Census   T.202

133

COTTONSEED AND COTTONSEED PRODUCTS

U.S. Stocks of Cottonseed Oil (Crude & Refined) at End of Month   In Millions of Pounds

Year	Aug.	Sept.	Oct.	Nov.	Dec.	Jan.	Feb.	Mar.	Apr.	May	June	July
1970-1	158.1	121.5	140.1	163.5	184.3	202.3	224.6	246.9	265.7	279.7	224.6	167.3
1971-2	142.9	93.8	130.0	159.5	188.3	239.4	277.3	295.0	294.8	266.0	239.7	203.9
1972-3	137.9	114.2	142.5	161.5	187.4	215.3	239.0	212.7	220.6	232.5	215.8	189.9
1973-4	181.5	114.3	124.5	161.6	157.9	202.4	180.9	198.8	198.9	190.4	175.5	135.3
1974-5	121.4	109.8	123.2	166.9	177.4	197.6	210.2	188.1	208.0	173.1	164.0	146.2
1975-6	126.4	136.1	125.6	153.1	160.3	179.6	192.1	217.1	198.0	204.0	153.6	157.5
1976-7	135.9	104.9	115.5	167.2	191.6	220.7	247.0	251.4	240.3	228.1	194.9	163.2
1977-8	131.5	85.9	97.7	119.7	142.3	151.4	156.4	176.4	180.4	154.5	130.7	106.7
1978-9	102.3	84.8	101.4	123.0	127.1	152.2	152.9	141.0	143.1	141.0	139.5	116.9
1979-0	117.2	86.4	93.1	129.0	144.3	173.2	198.9	212.8	188.7	165.8	167.1	144.6
1980-1	138.6	121.9	122.5	152.8	170.1	183.5	200.1	202.4	165.9	160.1	121.7	113.0
1981-2[1]	109.4	80.0	102.5	127.2	133.2	165.7	148.2	152.0	160.1	147.8	144.5	154.1
1982-3[1]	115.2	103.6	121.1	148.8								
1983-4												

[1] Preliminary.   Source: Bureau of Census   T.203

U.S. Exports of Cottonseed Oil (Crude & Refined)   In Millions of Pounds

Year	Jan.	Feb.	Mar.	Apr.	May	June	July	Aug.	Sept.	Oct.	Nov.	Dec.	Total
1970	53.0	52.2	56.2	24.0	61.0	12.2	17.5	8.8	17.8	12.0	18.6	36.7	369.8
1971	43.5	39.2	40.3	18.2	21.4	31.7	69.8	14.3	26.2	3.1	36.3	58.5	400.7
1972	23.1	47.4	50.4	47.8	30.6	49.7	33.5	58.3	13.0	18.9	70.6	32.2	475.4
1973	57.9	56.6	78.7	40.9	63.7	55.3	39.0	23.8	43.2	22.6	24.9	38.2	545.0
1974	28.8	79.0	52.3	56.3	94.2	52.2	49.5	36.7	24.2	24.1	33.8	75.1	606.1
1975	78.4	67.3	96.6	56.8	92.6	17.8	69.7	43.7	28.9	21.3	46.7	36.7	656.5
1976	76.2	49.3	51.8	42.8	65.6	47.9	23.7	24.4	13.4	33.6	15.7	76.6	520.9
1977	50.4	80.5	104.2	72.4	23.0	58.3	57.4	52.5	65.5	35.4	64.2	67.2	731.2
1978	50.6	68.2	84.9	61.6	59.8	63.5	70.2	50.0	82.3	25.9	29.2	82.5	728.8
1979[1]	56.7	71.2	89.9	51.3	52.5	63.1	63.8	18.1	56.6	34.0	48.9	27.0	633.0
1980[1]	34.8	28.1	110.5	71.0	105.0	31.4	70.3	77.6	89.3	53.7	66.6	47.1	785.4
1981[1]	77.0	29.3	66.7	82.1	72.2	85.7	46.9	35.9	46.5	42.2	37.4	80.5	702.3
1982[1]	41.2	146.2	110.6	68.6	74.5	67.0	63.7	47.3	68.4	52.2	60.0	54.7	854.4
1983													
1984													

[1] Preliminary.   Source: Dept. of Commerce   T.205

U.S. Consumption of Cottonseed Oil in End Products[1]   In Millions of Pounds

Year	Aug.	Sept.	Oct.	Nov.	Dec.	Jan.	Feb.	Mar.	Apr.	May	June	July	Total
1970-1	63.0	65.8	77.3	79.6	76.9	67.8	73.6	69.4	56.1	61.2	70.9	50.1	811.7
1971-2	57.8	50.8	52.9	57.4	60.5	56.1	52.3	70.0	51.6	66.5	66.1	58.0	700.0
1972-3	74.9	55.0	70.1	73.1	66.8	63.7	58.4	91.8	76.7	92.2	84.1	72.3	879.1
1973-4	69.4	57.2	73.6	78.5	88.5	87.2	77.8	83.0	78.7	77.8	61.8	74.5	908.0
1974-5	57.2	52.5	58.3	62.1	61.5	60.5	57.9	58.1	56.0	66.7	53.8	56.8	698.4
1975-6	49.6	46.7	51.0	50.0	53.6	45.0	48.3	52.1	48.3	43.3	58.0	39.3	585.2
1976-7	51.2	45.0	43.7	56.6	48.0	47.9	47.8	55.7	56.7	56.1	56.2	45.9	610.8
1977-8	51.8	48.6	47.5	52.6	58.5	50.0	52.3	55.6	55.7	63.4	65.9	62.3	664.2
1978-9	60.0	57.3	55.6	64.6	54.6	55.9	57.0	60.9	48.9	64.8	45.9	41.0	666.5
1979-0	53.9	43.1	44.9	50.8	51.1	55.6	56.4	56.6	58.6	68.2	65.1	57.9	662.2
1980-1	65.5	55.6	57.5	51.8	49.5	38.0	44.5	47.1	44.2	50.6	48.0	39.0	591.3
1981-2[2]	43.4	46.5	44.8	58.6	55.0	45.7	40.3	56.8	51.7	56.0	52.5	42.2	593.5
1982-3[2]	54.1	50.4	47.3	56.1	60.0	49.8							
1983-4													

[1] Includes small amount exported but does not include imported oil.   [2] Preliminary.   Source: Bureau of the Census   T.206

134

Currencies

According to a report released in early 1983 by the Secretariat of the General Agreement on Tariffs and Trade (GATT), the world trade volume fell by 2 percent during 1982. This decline was accompanied throughout the year by a general decline in the dollar unit value of traded goods, including agricultural products, petroleum, and other primary materials, that reflected the sharp appreciation of the U.S. dollar during 1982. The dollar's rise to 6-year highs against the Deutsche mark and the Japanese yen in 1982 was attributed, for the most part, to high domestic interest rates brought about by a deflationary Federal Reserve monetary policy. The U.S. merchandise trade deficit expanded radically in the last half of 1982, and international trade analysts observed a sharp reversal of the U.S. current account surpluses in the third quarter.

During 1982, the complaints of European Community (EC) and U.S producers against each other were concerned with export subsidies, notably, U.S subsidies of agricultural exports and EC subsidies of its exports of iron and steel products. U.S. manufacturers lobbied strenuously against the encroachment of imports from Japan upon their markets, particularly the market for steel. The political pressure caused by dwindling world export markets loomed greatly behind the tendency towards monetary expansion observed in most industrial nations, including the U.S., in 1982.

Early in 1983, currencies of the European Monetary System (EMS) were realigned in order to remedy a worsening trade imbalance between France and West Germany. EC Ministers agreed to an upward revaluation of the Deutsche mark, the Dutch guilder, the Danish krone, and the Belgian and Luxembourg francs; the French franc, the Italian lira, and the Irish punt were simultaneously devalued by similar percentages. This action, which closely followed cuts in key interest rates by West Germany, Austria, Switzerland, and Holland, considerably strengthened the demand for the U.S. dollar as an investment haven. At the same time, the British pound, which is not an EMS currency, fell to record lows against the U.S. dollar as the value of Britain's North Sea oil reserves dropped amidst the world oil price war.

Depressed oil prices and inflationary policies resulted in several devaluations of the Mexican peso and severely disrupted trading in that currency during 1982. Mexico, a major oil exporter, was forced to reschedule its international debt over the next two years in order to avert a default. Similar balance-of-payment problems in smaller oil-exporting countries throughout the world prompted the International Monetary Fund (IMF) to raise its membership subscription quotas early in 1983 and to increase IMF resources available to all members by nearly $12 billion.

Analysts are expecting the industrial economies of the EC to recovery only slowly from the world depression in 1983, thus increasing the attractiveness of inflationary policies to those governments. The inflationary tendency may be less compelling in Japan if the Japanese government moves, as expected, to balance its budget. Canadian monetary policy is expected to be restrictive even as unemployment grows because of Canada's 10 percent 1982 inflation rate. The U.S. current account deficit is expected to increase by nearly $23 billion in 1983, perhaps bringing greater pressure for an easier monetary policy to bear upon the Federal Reserve.

Futures Markets

The International Monetary Market of the Chicago Mercantile Exchange lists futures contracts in the British pound, Canadian dollar, Deutsche mark, Dutch guilder, French franc, Japanese yen, Swiss franc, and Mexican peso.

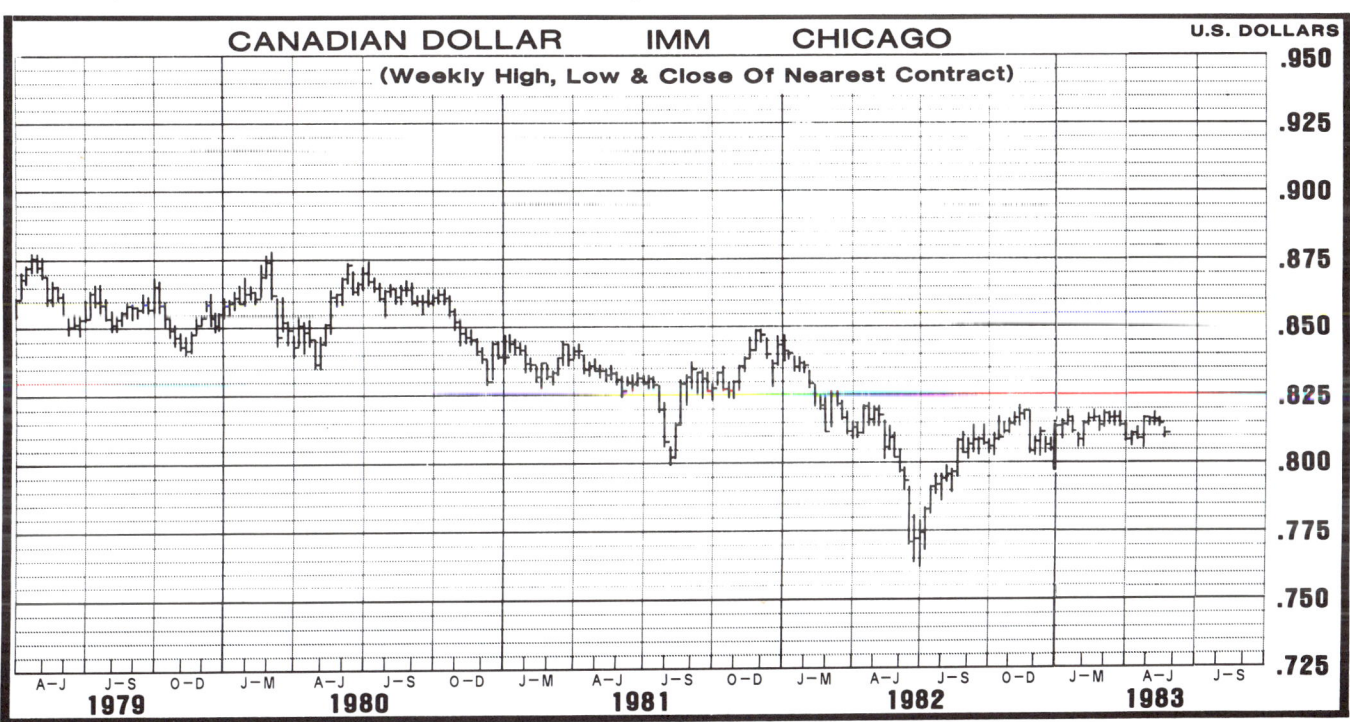

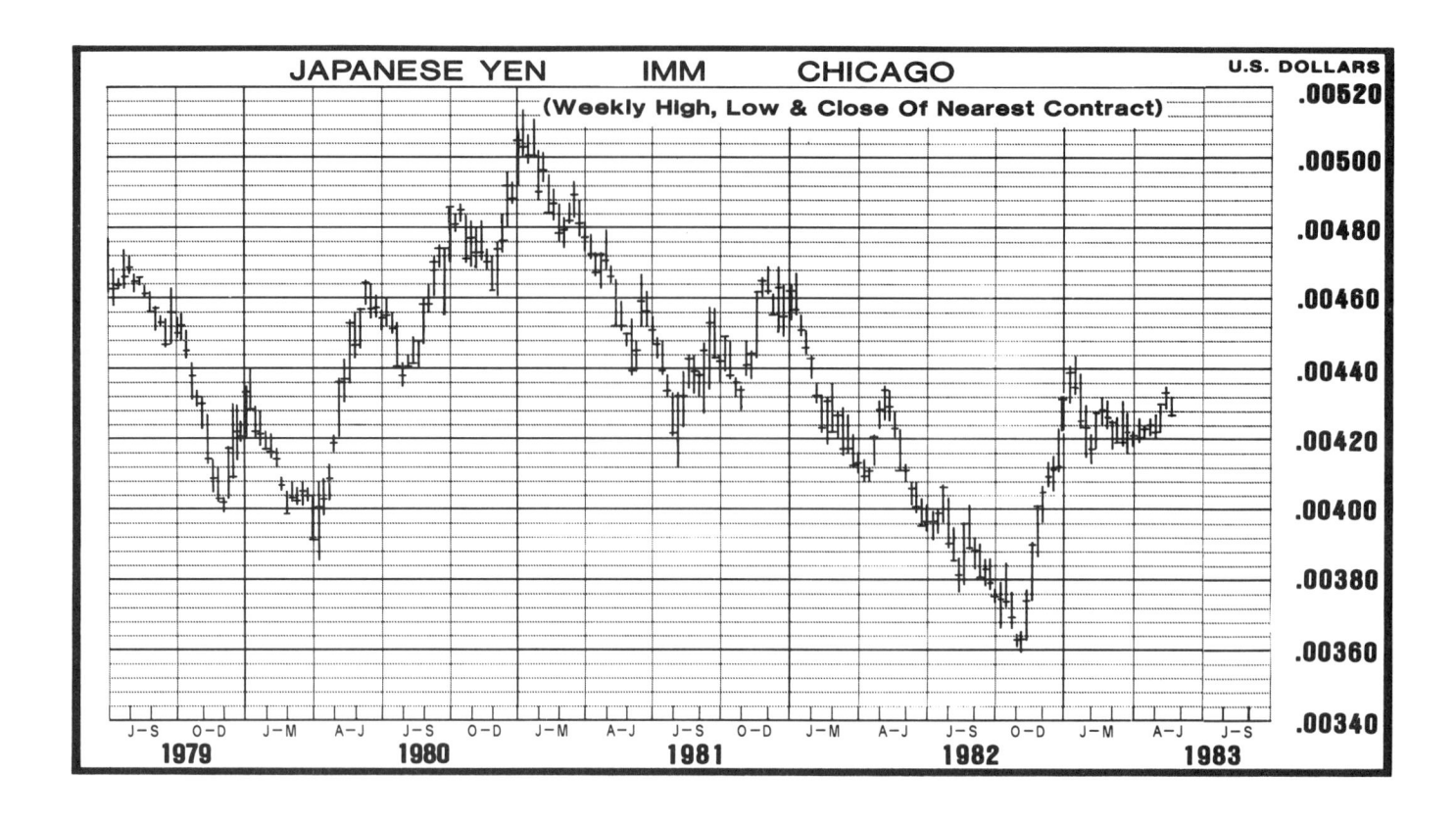

JAPANESE YEN IMM CHICAGO
(Weekly High, Low & Close Of Nearest Contract)

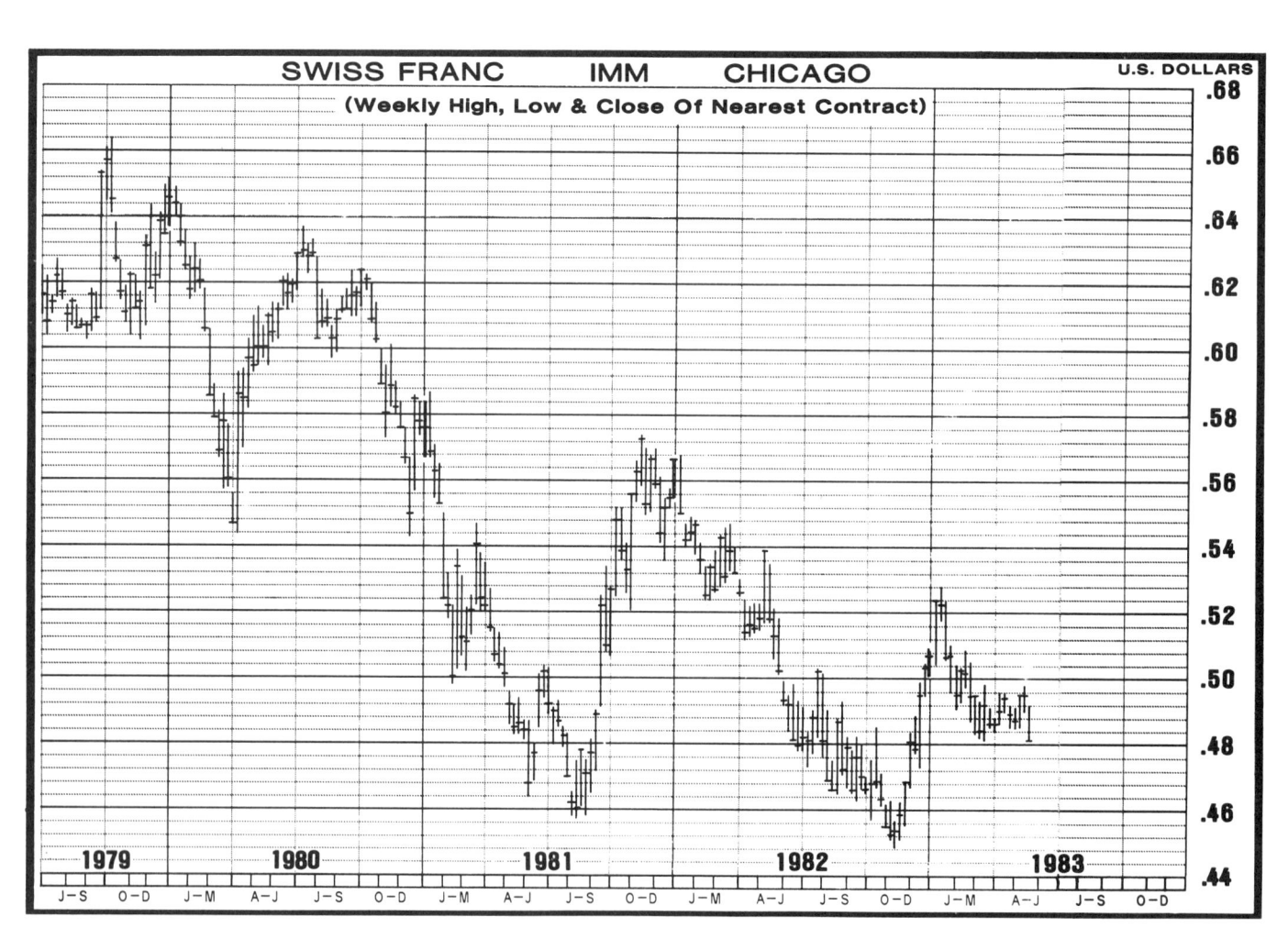

SWISS FRANC IMM CHICAGO
(Weekly High, Low & Close Of Nearest Contract)

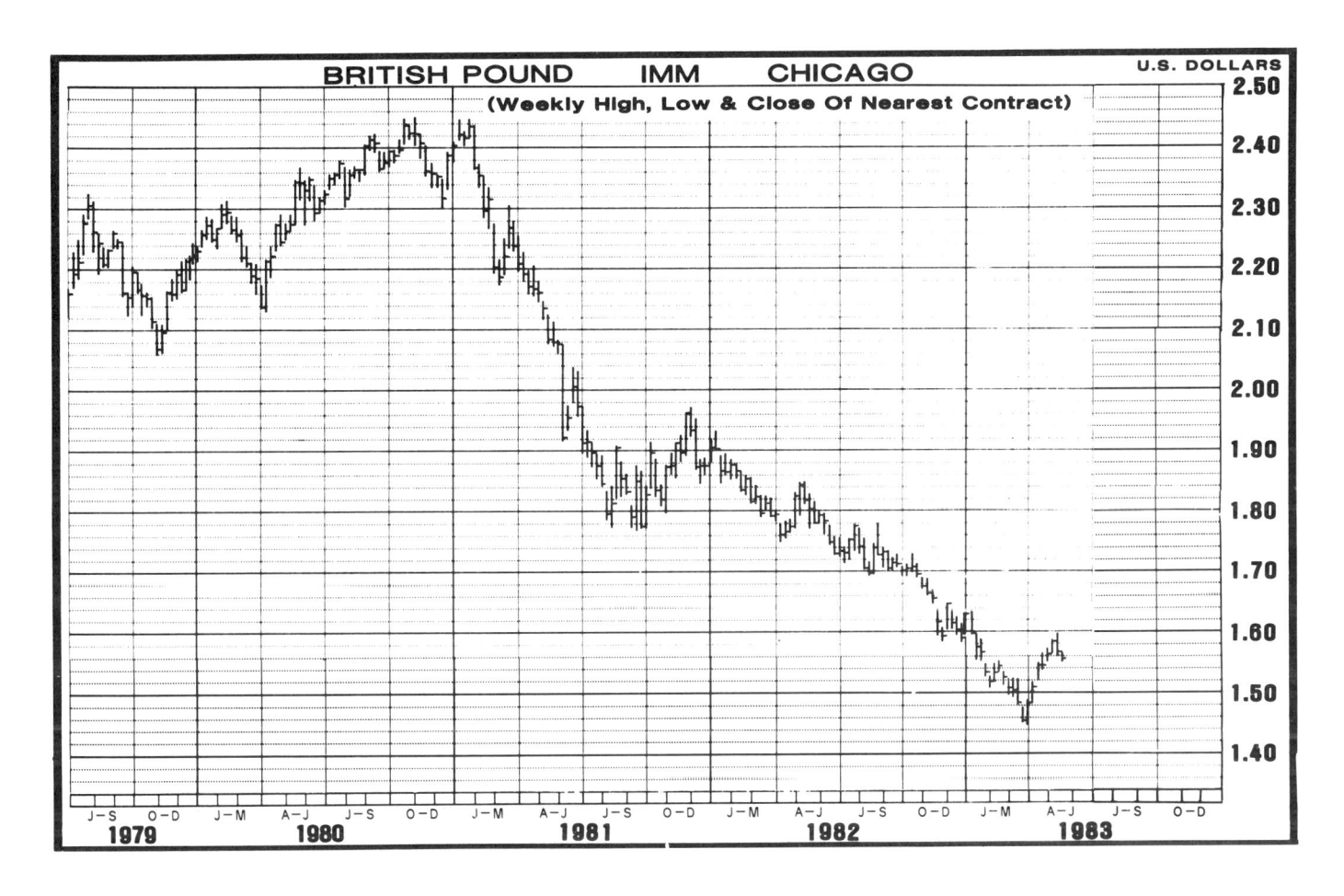

BRITISH POUND   IMM   CHICAGO
(Weekly High, Low & Close Of Nearest Contract)

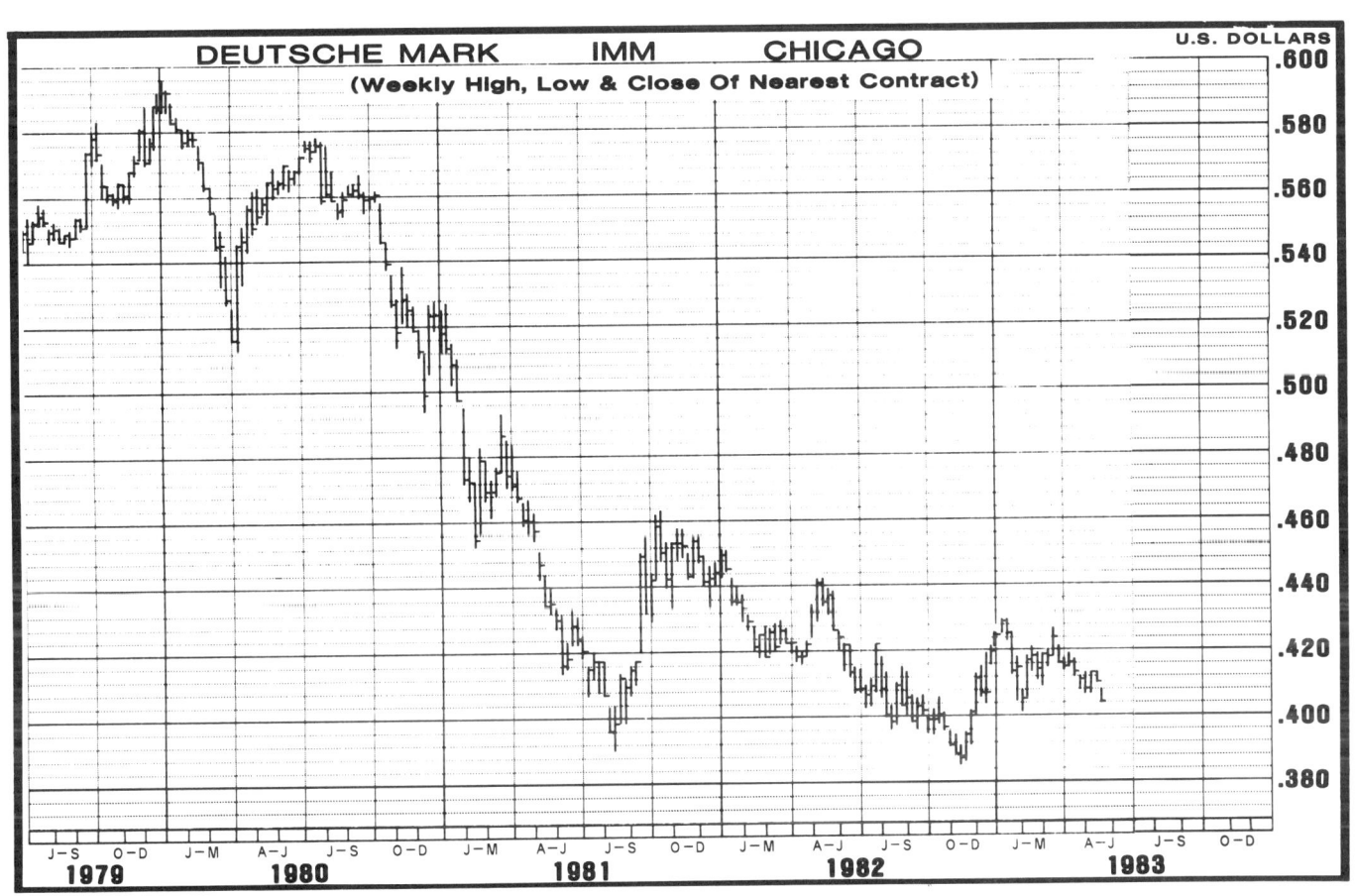

DEUTSCHE MARK   IMM   CHICAGO
(Weekly High, Low & Close Of Nearest Contract)

Distilled Spirits

Salient Statistics of Distilled Spirits in the United States In Thousands of Gallons[1]

Fiscal Year[4] Ending Sept. 30	Whiskey Production	Whiskey Tax-Paid Withdrawals	Whiskey Imports For Consumption[2]	Whiskey Stocks End of Period	Whiskey Bottled For Consumption	All Distilled Spirits Production	All Distilled Spirits Tax-Paid Withdrawals	All Distilled Spirits Imports For Consumption[2]	All Distilled Spirits Stocks End of Period	All Distilled Spirits Bottled For Consumption
1970	160,039	111,796	75,590	959,727	192,331	917,457	256,342	90,890	1,197,001	312,074
1971	127,220	111,972	89,290	960,509	186,050	759,251	256,999	102,140	1,162,398	310,056
1972	126,274	120,794	87,690	958,386	195,819	764,351	281,584	100,160	1,107,557	335,482
1973	111,974	135,937	92,300	926,112	188,245	859,152	282,840	107,280	1,060,634	336,813
1974	92,599	138,105	93,920	875,742	184,296	821,577	292,428	110,980	1,006,206	348,776
1975	49,958	136,950	94,980	779,762	181,683	717,550	295,445	113,460	950,044	356,916
1976	79,178	134,773	92,070	722,884	178,701	667,682	304,491	112,710	873,632	369,346
1977[4]	81,828	125,878	91,150	678,682	165,751	656,128	295,845	112,990	810,948	360,697
1978	71,382	125,977	101,890	624,886	175,970	676,723	321,294	128,600	759,592	396,479
1979[3]	101,260[2]	124,544	95,400	608,060	164,544	720,342	317,764	123,650	670,360	447,520[2]
1980[3]	84,310[2]		86,000	565,610				113,710	625,830	449,420[2]
1981[3]	96,660[2]		86,530	543,600				117,930	612,740	449,450[2]
1982[3]	100,000[2]		76,600	539,590				106,020	604,930	460,000[2]

[1] Production, withdrawals, and stocks are tax gallons; imports are proof gallons; consumption are wine gallons. [2] Data are for CALENDAR YEARS. [3] Preliminary. [4] Fiscal year ending JUNE 30 PRIOR TO 1977. *Sources: Internal Revenue Service; Department of Commerce* T.207

Distilled Spirits Bottled for Consumption in the U.S. In Millions of Wine Gallons[1]

Fis. Yr. End. Sept. 30[1]	Whiskey	Brandy	Rum	Gin	Cordials & Liqueurs	Vodka	Alcohol & Spirits	Other Spirits	Total
1970	192.331	11.735	2.533	35.780	20.699	47.843	.123	1.030	312.074
1971	186.050	11.913	2.864	35.042	20.555	52.407	.148	1.078	310.056
1972	195.819	13.053	3.378	38.009	23.311	60.116	.146	1.649	335.482
1973	188.245	13.908	4.693	35.890	25.095	66.494	.144	2.344	336.813
1974	184.296	13.855	5.495	37.319	28.391	75.285	.155	3.979	348.776
1975	181.683	13.483	6.791	37.169	30.416	82.159	.180	5.035	356.916
1976	178.701	14.150	8.789	39.242	34.189	88.459	.296	5.519	369.346
1977[2]	165.751	14.660	11.147	37.055	35.822	89.833	.256	6.173	360.697
1978	175.970	14.451	13.952	39.938	32.541	94.152	.214	6.620	389.654
1979	164.544	13.695	18.647	36.665	32.324	92.909	.238	6.700	377.161
1980									

[1] A "wine gallon" is a U.S. gallon of liquid measure equivalent to the volume of 231 cubic inches. [2] Fiscal year ending JUNE 30 PRIOR TO 1977. *Source: Internal Revenue Service* T.208

Grains Used in Production of Alcohol, Dist. Spirits, & Ferm. Malt Liquors in U.S. In Thousands of Bushels

Year Begin. July 1	Corn and Products Alcohol & Distilled Spirits	Corn and Products Fermented Malt Liquors[3]	Corn and Products Total	Barley and Malt Alcohol & Distilled Spirits	Barley and Malt Fermented Malt Liquors	Barley and Malt Total	Wheat Alcohol & Distilled Spirits	Wheat Fermented Malt Liquors	Wheat Total	Rye[2]	Sorghum Grains
1964-5	27,704	39,467	67,171	6,181	88,692	94,873	68	9	77	3,801	3,493
1965-6	29,830	40,688	70,518	7,064	90,340	97,404	66	8	74	4,393	3,062
1966-7	32,627	40,658	73,285	6,812	96,204	103,016			75	4,663	2,786
1967-8	33,980	40,247	74,227	7,101	97,350	104,451				4,744	2,809
1968-9	33,024	41,537	74,561	6,968	100,956	107,924				4,681	3,372
1969-0	31,202	43,121	74,333	6,669	109,512	116,181				4,279	2,963
1970-1	24,030	45,251	69,281	4,338	108,201	113,039				3,435	3,716
1971-2	24,848	45,441	70,289	4,496	113,209	117,705				3,066	4,750
1972-3	29,498	45,257	74,755	4,193	114,608	118,801					2,025
1973-4[1]	33,095	46,978	80,073	3,659	121,892	125,551					2,515
1974-5											

[1] Preliminary. [2] Used principally for distilled spirits. [3] Principally corn grits & flakes. *Source: Internal Revenue Service* T.209

138

Eggs

U.S. egg production during calendar 1982 declined 33 million dozen from the 1981 level to 5767.3 billion dozen. This decline, the second since 1976, was generally an outcome of weakened export demand and reduced per capita consumption.

The price of Grade A large eggs cartoned in New York was expected to average 62 to 66 cents per dozen throughout the first half of 1983 compared with 75 cents during the year-earlier period. Because of economic recession and the consequent drop in egg consumption, producers had been reluctant to expand their purchases of replacement pullets, and during September–November 1982, they had 1 percent fewer hens on hand than during the period a year earlier. Even so, production during 1982 was about equal to its 1981 level. The rate of lay had increased slightly because producers were slaughtering under federal inspection greater numbers of old hens that produced at the lowest rates. The proportion of hens being molted was 3.3 percent on December 1, 1982 compared with 5.5 percent on September 1, implying that more hens were in production. Because pullet replacement numbers have declined, producers are likely to molt more hens and slaughter fewer old ones. This tendency may cause the rate of lay to stabilize or to drop slightly.

In order to maintain production levels with reduced numbers of replacement pullets, egg producers are increasing the number of hens that are force molted and then kept in the flock for the duration of another laying cycle. On September 1, 1982, the proportion of the flock that had been force molted was generally 20.5 percent, sharply above the 17.6 percent record in the year-earlier period. However, producers were motivated to sell their old hens by the price weakness that appeared during November. The proportion of flocks being force molted dropped on December 1 to 18.2 percent compared with 19.1 percent on December 1, 1981. Nonetheless, these percentages were sharply improved over the 14 and 15 percent levels recorded for the same months in 1978 and 1979 respectively.

Figures issued by the Statistical Reporting Service indicated that the rate of lay in 1982 was 244 compared with 243 the previous year. Evidently, the annual rate of lay had not been affected by the proportion of force molting. The states having the largest percentage of their flocks force molted on December 1, 1982, Washington, California, and Mississippi, had annual rates of lay of 251, 241, and 230 eggs respectively. California was once again the state with the largest number of layers on hand, 34 million during 1982. Georgia was second with 22 million and Indiana moved from fifth to third place with 18 million.

U.S. exports of eggs and egg products represented only 3 percent of production during 1982 compared with 4 percent during 1981. The demand for eggs has historically been inelastic, and therefore the decline in exports that was expected to continue through mid-1983 provoked ideas of continuing weak prices. The three largest importers of U.S. eggs and egg products during October–December 1981–1982 were Japan, Mexico, and the United Arab Emirates.

Futures Market

Egg futures are presently listed (but inactive) on the Chicago Mercantile Exchange.

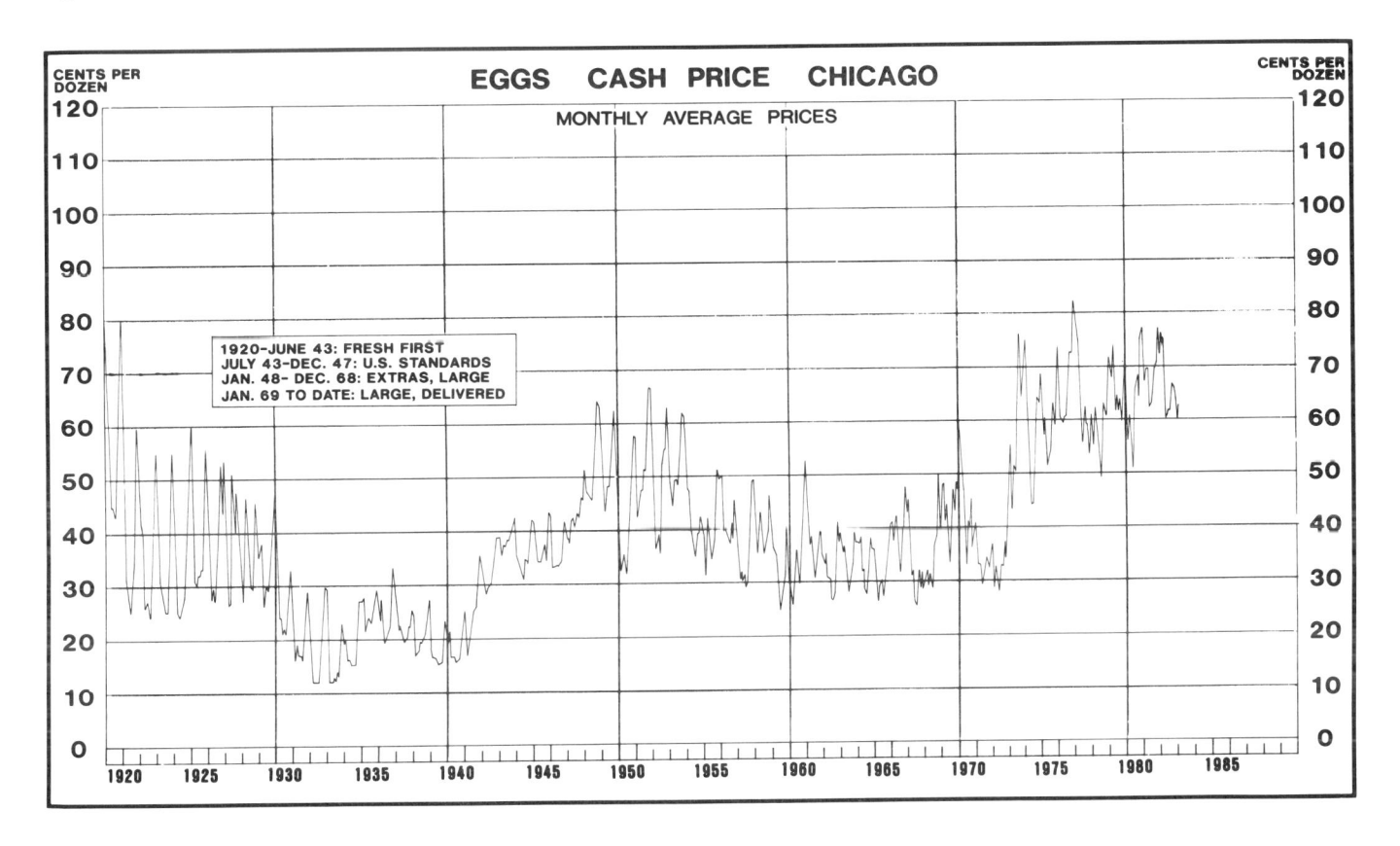

EGGS

World Production[2] of Eggs   In Billions of Eggs

Year	Argentina	Australia	Bel. & Lux.	Brazil	Canada	Israel	France	W. Germany	Italy	Japan	Netherlands	Poland	Spain	South Africa	USSR	Un. Kingdom[3]	United States
1974	3.4	3.3	3.8	6.0	5.5	1.6	12.5	15.0	11.3	30.2	4.8	7.9			55.5	14.4	65.9
1975	3.8	3.4	3.7	6.0	5.4	1.7	13.1	15.0	11.4	29.8	5.3	8.0			57.4	13.6	64.4
1976	3.7	3.2	3.5	6.1	5.2	1.8	12.9	14.4	11.5	31.0	5.6	8.0			55.6	14.0	64.8
1977	3.1	3.3	3.8	6.3	5.5	1.7	13.1	14.8	11.3	31.4	6.0	8.5	10.9	3.9	61.2	14.1	64.9
1978	3.3	3.5	3.8	6.6	5.5	1.8	13.5	14.3	11.0	32.8	7.0	8.5	10.1	3.9	64.5	14.3	67.3
1979	3.4	3.4	3.5	7.2	5.6	1.8	13.8	13.3	11.0	33.2	8.2	8.7	11.0	3.1	65.6	15.0	69.2
1980	3.4	3.4	3.3	9.6	5.9	1.6	14.5	13.7	10.7	33.3	9.0	8.8	11.6	3.1	67.8	14.0	69.7
1981[1]	3.3	3.6	3.2	9.6	6.0	1.6	15.3	13.3	11.3	33.2	9.4	8.8	11.7	3.3	70.9	13.5	69.6
1982[4]	3.3	3.5	3.2	10.0	5.9	1.6	15.6	13.5	11.5	33.2	9.6	8.0	11.7	3.4	73.2	13.5	68.9

[1] Preliminary. [2] Relates to farm production in Canada and the United States. Information for many countries is not explicit on this point. [3] Farm production, years ending May. [4] Forecast. Source: Foreign Agricultural Service, U.S.D.A.
T.210

Salient Egg Statistics in the United States

Year	Hens & Pullets On Farms Jan. 1[10] Millions	Avg.[9] Number During Year Millions	Rate of Lay Per Layer On Farms Jan. 1[2] Number	Rate of Lay Per Layer During Year[3] Number	Farm Prod. Billions	Price Per Dz.	Eggs Consumed[4] on Farms Billions	Sold Billions	Gross Income[5] Billion $	Total Egg Prod.[6] Million Dozen	Imports[7] Million Dozen	Exports[8] & Shipments Million Dozen	Used for Hatching Million Dozen	Civilian Consumption Total	Civilian Consumption Per Capita Eggs
1973	300.7	290.6	227		66.0	52.5	.63	65.41	2.89	5,502	13	49	392	5,051	291
1974	296.6	284.7	230		65.6	53.2	.58	65.04	2.91	5,461	13	57	366	5,005	286
1975	286.0	278.1	232		64.6	52.4	.54	64.09	2.82	5,382	5	62	372	4,924	280
1976	279.9	274.1	235		64.5	58.3	.50	64.01	3.13	5,377	3	65	409	4,858	274
1977	280.0	274.9	235		64.6	55.6	.48	64.13	2.99	5,407	14	91	429	4,864	272
1978	287.7	281.6	239		67.2	52.2	.46	66.68	2.92	5,607	11	120	463	5,009	278
1979	291.7	288.6	240		69.2	58.3	.45	68.76	3.36	5,777	10	104	498	5,161	278
1980	296.0	287.7	242		69.7	56.3	.45	69.23	3.27	5,807	7	162	497	5,130	273
1981[1]	294.0	287.7	243		69.8	62.3	.44	69.38	3.67	5,806	3	250	506	5,025	265
1982[1]		286.0	244		69.7	58.4	.43	69.25	3.46	5,764	1	194	503	5,044	264

[1] Preliminary. [2] Number of eggs produced during the year divided by number of hens & pullets on hand Jan. 1. [3] Number of eggs produced during the year divided by the average number of hens & pullets of laying age on hand during the year. [4] Consumed in households of farm producers. [5] Value of sales plus value of eggs consumed in households of producers. [6] Farm production, plus nonfarm output estimated at 10% of farm through 1954; thereafter, 1 percentage point less each year. [7] Shell-egg equivalent of eggs and egg products. [8] Shell eggs & shell equivalent of frozen & dried egg products. [9] Average number of layers on farms during the year. [10] Of laying age. Source: Agricultural Marketing Service, U.S.D.A.
T.211

Average Wholesale Prices of Shell Eggs (Large) Delivered, Chicago   In Cents Per Dozen

Year	Jan.	Feb.	Mar.	Apr.	May	June	July	Aug.	Sept.	Oct.	Nov.	Dec.	Average
1973	55.9	43.1	49.9	51.9	50.5	58.2	65.1	76.9	70.0	64.6	67.8	72.8	61.0
1974	75.0	69.5	62.1	54.2	44.5	44.6	50.5	57.5	64.6	63.2	63.0	68.8	59.8
1975	63.7	57.4	60.7	51.6	51.3	51.7	53.9	59.7	63.3	59.1	66.8	73.8	59.4
1976	70.9	64.2	59.5	58.6	60.7	60.9	65.4	70.6	72.8	70.6	76.7	82.3	67.8
1977	78.7	75.6	67.5	62.4	55.7	57.0	62.8	59.3	59.3	53.7	55.0	61.5	62.4
1978	55.2	62.8	62.0	57.0	52.0	49.3	61.2	61.8	63.2	60.8	67.2	71.6	60.3
1979	71.3	67.7	73.5	68.7	61.9	64.8	61.9	64.0	62.0	59.7	66.3	72.4	66.2
1980	59.9	56.3	60.6	56.8	50.8	54.6	63.2	65.9	68.8	64.3	75.7	77.3	62.8
1981	71.4	67.2	62.9	69.7	62.2	62.9	67.5	68.7	70.7	71.3	77.3	72.1	69.0
1982[1]	76.2	74.2	75.2	68.3	60.4	60.8	61.7	61.6	65.9	66.8	66.2	64.1	66.8
1983[1]	60.2	62.7											

[1] Preliminary. Source: Commodity Economics Division, U.S.D.A.
T.212

Total Egg Production in the United States   In Millions of Eggs

Year	Jan.	Feb.	Mar.	Apr.	May	June	July	Aug.	Sept.	Oct.	Nov.	Dec.	Total[2]
1977	5,447	4,917	5,546	5,361	5,478	5,213	5,310	5,369	5,318	5,592	5,534	5,803	64,602
1978	5,743	5,106	5,700	5,559	5,723	5,460	5,541	5,574	5,495	5,751	5,685	5,948	67,157
1979	5,892	5,290	5,909	5,721	5,862	5,648	5,798	5,810	5,653	5,881	5,797	6,064	69,209
1980	6,048	5,593	5,955	5,714	5,799	5,584	5,706	5,750	5,724	5,950	5,798	6,055	69,684
1981[1]	6,022	5,424	6,009	5,761	5,855	5,609	5,799	5,834	5,685	5,919	5,856	6,079	69,827
1982[1]	5,958	5,333	—17,557—			—17,231—			—17,419—			6,011	69,680
1983[1]	5,917	5,345	5,913										

[1] Preliminary. [2] Dec. 1 previous year thru Nov. 30. Source: Crop Reporting Board, U.S.D.A.
T.219

EGGS

Total Eggs—U.S. Supply and Distribution   In Millions of Dozen

Year & Quarters	Production	Imports[1]	Beginning Stocks[1]	Total Supply	Ending Stocks[1]	Exports & Shipments[1]	Eggs Used for Hatching	Military	Civilian Total	Civilian[1] Per Capita (Number)
1978 I	1,379	1.3	23.7	1,404	18.1	37.4	113.8	6.6	1,228	67.1
II	1,396	3.3	18.1	1,417	21.0	30.0	131.5	7.0	1,228	66.9
III	1,385	6.4	21.0	1,412	23.1	24.9	104.3	7.4	1,253	68.1
IV	1,449	.1	23.1	1,472	20.3	28.0	116.0	6.9	1,301	70.5
1979 I	1,424	.4	20.3	1,445	16.7	24.4	125.4	5.8	1,273	68.8
II	1,436	2.2	16.7	1,455	18.1	22.7	135.3	7.0	1,272	68.5
III	1,438	4.2	18.1	1,461	19.2	25.4	119.2	6.4	1,291	69.3
IV	1,479	2.7	19.2	1,500	18.9	31.2	117.7	6.0	1,327	71.1
1980 I	1,466	.2	18.9	1,485	18.4	35.8	127.4	6.4	1,298	69.3
II	1,425	1.6	18.4	1,445	23.2	37.3	128.7	5.7	1,250	66.6
III	1,432	1.9	23.2	1,457	23.7	39.5	119.9	6.7	1,267	67.3
IV	1,483	1.3	23.7	1,508	19.4	53.9	123.1	5.3	1,307	69.2
1981 I	1,455	− .9	19.4	1,456	17.9	56.2	128.0	5.6	1,266	67.0
II	1,463	1.3	17.9	1,462	19.6	61.7	135.2	6.1	1,259	66.5
III	1,432	2.5	19.6	1,434	19.9	57.7	123.8	6.1	1,247	65.7
IV	1,451	.5	19.9	1,453	17.5	74.0	119.4	6.6	1,254	65.9
1982[3] I	1,450	.2	17.5	1,453	14.4	55.1	126.1	6.8	1,265	66.3
II	1,451	−1.1	14.4	1,446	18.2	44.9	133.5	4.5	1,263	66.1
III	1,422	1.6	18.2	1,420	22.3	33.8	123.7	6.5	1,256	65.5
IV	1,445	.3	22.3	1,446	21.8	59.7	120.1	5.3	1,261	65.6

[1] Shell eggs & the approx. shell-egg equivalent of egg product.   [2] Less than 100,000 dozen.   [3] Forecast.
Source: Commodity Economics Division, U.S.D.A.   T.213

Shell Eggs: Civilian Per Capita Disappearance in the United States   Number of Eggs

Year	Jan.	Feb.	Mar.	Apr.	May	June	July	Aug.	Sept.	Oct.	Nov.	Dec.	Total[1]	Processed[2]	Total
1971	24.7	21.6	23.9	23.1	23.7	22.1	22.9	23.1	21.9	23.3	22.8	24.2	278	36	314
1972	24.5	22.3	24.2	22.9	22.7	21.1	22.6	22.2	21.6	22.2	21.7	23.6	272	36	308
1973	23.4	20.5	23.1	22.4	22.5	20.8	21.4	21.2	20.7	21.4	21.5	23.1	262	32	294
1974	22.8	19.8	22.2	21.0	21.2	20.2	20.7	20.9	20.3	20.9	20.6	22.1	254	34	288
1975	22.0	19.4	21.9	20.4	20.6	19.2	20.1	20.6	19.9	20.9	20.9	21.7	248	31	279
1976	21.7	19.6	20.5	19.6	20.5	19.2	20.1	20.1	19.3	20.3	19.5	20.8	241	33	274
1977	20.9	17.9	20.1	19.2	19.4	18.1	19.1	19.1	19.1	20.7	20.2	21.4	235	37	272
1978	21.1	18.6	20.8	20.0	20.3	18.8	19.7	19.8	19.7	20.9	20.7	21.9	242	36	278
1979	21.3	18.5	21.0	20.0	20.1	19.2	20.1	19.9	19.8	20.2	20.2	21.8	242	36	278
1980	21.1	19.0	20.9	19.4	19.8	18.7	19.0	19.6	19.4	19.8	20.0	20.7	237	35	272
1981	———58.7———			———58.6———			———56.5———			———58.5———			232	33	265
1982[3]	———59.1———			———57.7———			———55.7———			———56.8———			229	35	264

[1] Monthly totals do not necessarily add to yearly figures due to rounding.   [2] Liquid, frozen, & dried egg (egg solids) converted to shell egg equivalent.   [3] Preliminary.   Source: Economic Research Service, U.S.D.A.   T.214

Egg-Feed Ratio[1] in the United States

Year	Jan.	Feb.	Mar.	Apr.	May	June	July	Aug.	Sept.	Oct.	Nov.	Dec.	Average
1971	8.0	7.4	7.3	7.3	6.7	6.4	6.4	7.1	7.1	6.9	7.2	8.2	7.2
1972	7.1	7.0	7.6	6.5	6.4	6.4	7.0	6.9	7.7	6.9	8.0	8.7	7.2
1973	9.0	7.3	7.7	7.9	6.9	6.4	7.1	8.3	8.6	8.2	8.6	8.5	7.9
1974	8.8	8.4	7.5	7.0	6.2	5.8	6.2	5.7	6.7	6.5	6.6	7.2	6.9
1975	7.2	7.2	7.6	6.5	6.5	6.3	6.4	6.8	7.5	7.1	8.1	9.0	7.2
1976	8.6	8.2	7.4	7.3	7.5	6.8	6.8	7.6	7.7	7.8	8.7	9.1	7.9
1977	8.5	8.1	7.3	6.8	5.9	5.8	6.7	7.2	7.6	7.1	7.3	7.4	7.1
1978	6.7	7.5	7.4	6.7	6.3	5.6	6.4	7.0	7.3	7.0	7.5	8.0	7.0
1979	7.8	7.7	8.0	7.4	6.9	6.7	6.1	6.1	6.4	6.1	6.8	7.3	6.9
1980	6.6	5.9	6.3	6.0	5.3	5.5	5.7	6.0	6.2	5.7	6.0	6.6	6.0
1981[2]	5.9	5.7	5.7	6.0	5.2	5.2	5.5	5.8	6.4	6.5	7.2	6.7	6.0
1982[2]	6.6	6.8	7.2	7.2	5.6	5.3	5.7	5.3	6.0	6.3	6.3	6.0	6.2
1983[2]	5.7	5.8											

[1] Pounds of laying feed equivalent in value to one dozen eggs.   [2] Preliminary.   Source: Commodity Economics Division, U.S.D.A.   T.215

EGGS

Hens and Pullets of Laying Age in the U.S., First of Month   In Millions

Year	Jan. 1	Feb. 1	Mar. 1	Apr. 1	May 1	June 1	July 1	Aug. 1	Sept. 1	Oct. 1	Nov. 1	Dec. 1
1978	287.7	283.7	280.7	279.7	278.2	277.3	275.0	275.2	279.0	283.9	288.3	293.3
1979	291.7	292.1	290.2	288.6	285.5	283.4	283.7	285.1	287.2	290.2	291.7	294.5
1980	296.0	293.2	288.6	285.3	280.8	279.4	279.9	282.2	287.8	291.7	292.8	294.2
1981	294.0	291.3	291.3	285.5	283.6	282.4	280.0	283.7	283.8	286.3	289.7	293.5
1982[1]	291.7	290.1	288.1	—	—	282.5	—	—	281.5	—	—	288.9
1983	—	—	280.1									

[1] Preliminary.   Source: Crop Reporting Board, U.S.D.A.   T.216

U.S. Cold Storage Holdings of Shell Eggs, 1st of Month   In Thousands of Cases (One Case = 30 Dozen)

Year	Jan.	Feb.	Mar.	Apr.	May	June	July	Aug.	Sept.	Oct.	Nov.	Dec.
1978	39	34	27	25	36	29	26	26	48	43	23	35
1979	38	22	18	24	20	27	24	32	28	31	24	24
1980	38	47	24	22	30	47	51	39	28	39	15	19
1981[1]	31	28	18	31	31	25	41	39	20	19	21	38
1982[1]	35	26	19	39	—	—	32	—	—	29	—	—
1983[1]	35	35	25	18								

[1] Preliminary.   Source: Crop Reporting, Board U.S.D.A.   T.217

U.S. Cold Storage Holdings of Frozen Eggs, 1st of Month   In Millions of Pounds[1]

Year	Jan.	Feb.	Mar.	Apr.	May	June	July	Aug.	Sept.	Oct.	Nov.	Dec.
1977	26.1	26.9	24.9	24.6	25.3	28.0	31.4	35.1	35.4	33.7	33.4	31.2
1978	29.7	27.0	25.5	22.9	22.9	22.2	26.6	28.0	28.7	28.7	27.6	25.6
1979	25.3	25.5	24.5	21.1	21.7	21.6	22.8	25.9	24.7	24.1	25.6	23.4
1980	23.4	22.1	23.8	23.4	25.9	26.6	28.6	29.4	30.7	29.7	29.2	25.3
1981[2]	24.3	24.3	24.2	22.3	21.9	22.7	24.2	26.9	27.2	25.5	25.6	23.7
1982[2]	21.6	21.2	19.4	17.4	—	—	22.7	—	—	28.3	—	—
1983[2]	25.4	28.1	27.5	24.5								

[1] Converted on basis 39.5 pounds frozen eggs equals 1 case.   [2] Preliminary.   Source: Crop Reporting Board, U.S.D.A.   T.218

Egg-Type Chicks Hatched by Commercial Hatcheries in the United States   In Millions

Year	Jan.	Feb.	Mar.	Apr.	May	June	July	Aug.	Sept.	Oct.	Nov.	Dec.	Total
1977	40.3	40.9	51.3	55.1	52.5	44.7	37.4	37.8	37.4	37.6	34.5	32.5	501.9
1978	36.9	36.9	46.8	50.9	53.7	45.6	35.8	38.6	37.2	37.7	35.6	35.9	491.6
1979	39.9	39.5	50.1	52.4	55.9	47.8	42.8	41.9	36.6	39.5	37.5	36.4	519.0
1980	38.1	42.1	46.5	47.9	47.6	42.3	37.9	38.0	37.4	37.3	33.8	35.8	484.6
1981	37.8	36.1	44.5	48.3	46.1	40.5	32.3	33.8	32.3	35.9	33.7	33.1	454.2
1982[1]	36.0	35.5	43.8	46.2	46.5	39.0	34.6	33.4	31.8	32.3	30.2	31.0	440.2
1983[1]	33.2	32.9	39.2										

[1] Preliminary.   Source: Crop Reporting Board, U.S.D.A.   T.220

Eggs Laid Per Hundred Layers in the United States   In Number of Eggs

Year	Jan.	Feb.	Mar.	Apr.	May	June	July	Aug.	Sept.	Oct.	Nov.	Dec.	Total
1977	1,956	1,782	2,021	1,971	2,034	1,950	1,986	1,978	1,921	1,990	1,944	2,021	23,554
1978	2,009	1,808	2,035	1,993	2,061	1,979	2,016	2,012	1,954	2,011	1,955	2,033	23,867
1979	2,018	1,817	2,042	1,994	2,062	1,992	2,038	2,030	1,958	2,021	1,976	2,052	24,000
1980	2,053	1,922	2,075	2,019	2,070	1,997	2,030	2,017	1,975	2,036	1,975	2,057	24,252
1981[1]	2,052	1,858	2,081	2,015	2,062	1,990	2,051	2,053	1,991	2,049	2,006	2,083	24,291
1982[1]	2,048	1,850	—————6,159—————			—————6,111—————			—————6,105—————			2,095	22,273
1983[1]	2,085	1,899	2,127										

[1] Preliminary.   Source: Crop Reporting Board, U.S.D.A.   T.221

Electric Power

Preliminary U.S. Department of Energy figures indicated that the total U.S. production of electricity by utilities in 1982 would be little changed from the 1981 production of approximately 2.06 billion kilowatt hours. U.S. electricity generation, which had been steadily increasing throughout the past decade, tended to be limited during 1982 by economic recession and sharply reduced industrial demand.

Electric utilities consumed an estimated 24.4 quadrillion Btu of energy in 1982, 1.1 percent less than in the previous year, and 0.2 percent below the amount of energy consumed during 1980. Coal accounted for 52.0 percent of 1982 electricity production by electric utilities; natural gas, 13.7 percent; petroleum, 7.4 percent; hydro, 14.1 percent; and nuclear, 12.3 percent. Steam-driven turbine generators produce most of the electricity consumed in the U.S. Electric utilities employ two types of boilers to produce steam: conventional boilers fired by coal, oil, or natural gas, or nuclear steam supply systems which produce steam from water heated by means of nuclear fission.

Approximately 77 percent of the shipments of conventional power boilers recorded during 1982 went to U.S. electric utilities, a percentage which had changed little in the three preceding years. Shipments of turbine generator sets in 1982 were nearly 17,000 megawatts (MW) compared with the average of 24,000 MW over the preceding three years.

Electric utilities planned to install distribution-substation transformers with a total capacity of 24.0 gigavolt-amperes (GVA) during 1982, down 3 percent from the 24.8 GVA installed in 1981. Utility planners estimated that distribution substation banks could decline by 6 percent in 1983 reflecting a 22 percent drop in capacity additions equal to about 19 GVA.

World Electricity Production In Billions of KWH

Year	Australia	Brazil	Canada	Czechoslov.	France	W. Germany	Italy	Japan	Norway	Poland	Sweden	Switzerland	South Africa	Un. Kingdom	United States	USSR
1970	56.1		204.7	45.2	140.7		117.4	349.9	57.6	N.A.	60.6	33.2	50.8	249.2	1,640	740.9
1971	58.0		216.5	47.2	155.8		124.9	385.6	63.6	69.3	66.6	32.8	55.0	256.4	1,718	800.4
1972	60.9		240.2	51.4	170.9		135.3	428.5	67.6	76.5	71.7	31.3	59.1	263.6	1,853	857.4
1973	64.8		263.3	53.5	182.4		145.5	470.3	73.1	84.3	78.1	37.2	64.5	281.9	1,965	914.6
1974	69.8	72.4	280.3	56.0	188.2	311.7	148.9	459.0	76.7	91.6	75.1	37.4	70.1	273.1	1,967	975.8
1975	73.9	78.9	273.4	59.3	185.3	301.8	147.3	475.8	77.5	97.2	80.6	43.0	74.9	272.0	2,003	1,039
1976	76.6	90.0	294.0	62.7	203.1	333.6	163.5	511.8	82.1	104.1	86.4	36.2	79.4	276.9	2,123	1,111
1977	82.5	100.8	317.2	66.5	210.7	335.3	166.5	532.6	72.4	109.4	87.4	45.9	80.3	283.1	2,211	1,150
1978	88.5	112.5	335.7	69.1	226.7	353.4	175.0	564.0	81.0	115.6	90.3	42.3	84.5	287.7	2,286	1,200
1979	93.7	126.1	353.1	68.1	241.1	374.2	180.5	589.6	89.1	117.5	92.4	42.7	90.3	299.9	2,319	1,238
1980	97.9	139.3	366.7	72.6	243.3	368.8	185.7	577.5	84.1	121.9	93.4	46.6	95.0	285.0	2,356	1,295
1981[1]	103.2	142.4	377.6	74.1	260.8	368.0	181.8	583.2	92.8	115.0	100.0	48.0	97.4	277.7	2,365	1,325
1982[2]	110.0		375.0	75.0	265.0	365.0	183.0	570.0	94.0	120.0	96.5	51.0		272.3	2,350	1,320
1983																

[1] Preliminary. [2] Estimate. *Source: United Nations* T.222

Installed Capacity, Capability & Peak Load of the U.S. Electric Utility Industry In Millions of Kilowatts

Year	Total Electric Utility Industry	Hydro	Gas Turbine & Steam[2]	Internal Combustion	Investor Owned	Cooperatives	Sub-Total Gov't.	Municipal Utilities	Federal	Power Dis tricts, State Projects	Capability at Winter Peak Load	Non-Coincident Winter Peak Load	Margin of Reserve (%)	Generation	Load Factor (%)
1970	341.1	55.1	252.4	4.4	262.7	5.2	73.2	20.9	38.7	13.6	339.1	248.6	19.0	1,536	63.9
1971	367.4	55.9	259.7	4.5	286.9	5.4	75.1	21.8	39.7	13.7	366.7	261.7	20.9	1,617	63.2
1972	399.6	56.6	322.9	4.8	314.9	6.7	78.0	23.2	40.6	14.2	394.1	291.0	19.6	1,752	62.5
1973	439.9	61.8	352.1	4.9	346.5	7.3	86.1	25.0	44.5	16.6	433.2	295.1	20.8	1,869	62.0
1974	476.0	63.6	375.7	5.0	376.1	7.5	92.4	27.3	45.8	19.2	467.4	302.5	27.2	1,872	61.2
1975	508.9	65.9	397.6	5.1	399.0	9.1	100.2	28.8	50.1	21.3	492.5	331.1	34.3	1,920	61.4
1976	531.2	67.8	415.2	5.3	415.5	9.9	105.7	30.6	51.7	23.4	511.0	349.9	34.5	2,040	62.6
1977	560.4	63.8	436.4	5.3	438.4	10.9	111.1	34.3	53.2	24.6	537.6	360.2	30.2	2,132	61.4
1978	579.3	71.0	449.2	5.5	453.6	11.6	114.0	34.4	54.3	25.3	561.6	383.1	33.7	2,219	62.1
1979	598.4	75.4	463.0	5.5	464.1	13.8	120.5	34.5	58.3	27.6	554.3	368.9	36.9	2,247	64.4
1980	613.7	76.4	475.3	5.6	477.1	15.4	121.2	34.6	59.1	27.5	572.2	384.6	30.8	2,293	61.1
1981[1]	635.0	77.2	491.4	5.6	490.9	18.4	125.7	35.2	61.0	29.5	581.1	391.2	32.9	2,309	61.2
1982															

[1] Preliminary. [2] Nuclear Power for 1970–80; 6.5, 8.7, 15.3, 21.1, 31.7, 39.8, 42.8, 49.9, 53.5, 54.6; 56.5; 60.8. *Source: Federal Power Commission* T.223

ELECTRIC POWER

Available Electricity & Energy Sales in the United States   In Billions of Kilowatt Hours

Year	Generation Hydro	Steam	Nuclear	Total[5]	Other Sources[2]	Total	Total Million $	Total[4]	Residential	Inter-Departmental	Commercial & Industrial[3] Small	Large	Street & Highway	Other Public Authorities	Railways & Railroads
1970	247.5	1,256	21.8	1,532	108	1,640	22,066	1,391	447.8	4.7	312.8	572.5	11.2	37.8	4.6
1971	266.3	1,302	38.1	1,613	103	1,716	24,725	1,466	479.1	4.9	333.8	592.7	11.7	39.8	4.5
1972	272.6	1,416	54.1	1,750	105	1,854	27,921	1,578	511.4	5.1	361.9	639.5	12.2	43.2	4.4
1973	271.6	1,495	83.3	1,856	103	1,959	31,663	1,703	554.2	5.5	396.9	687.2	12.8	42.3	4.2
1974	300.9	1,446	113.7	1,866	102	1,968	39,127	1,701	555.0	5.4	392.7	689.4	13.3	40.7	4.3
1975	300.1	1,439	172.5	1,918	85	2,003	46,853	1,733	586.1	5.4	418.1	661.1	13.9	43.6	4.3
1976	283.7	1,558	191.1	2,038	87	2,125	53,463	1,850	613.1	6.4	440.6	725.2	14.4	45.6	4.3
1977	220.4	1,648	250.9	2,124	88	2,212	62,610	1,951	652.3	7.2	469.2	757.2	14.4	46.2	4.2
1978	280.4	1,645	276.4	2,206	79	2,300	69,853	2,018	679.2	7.1	480.7	782.1	14.8	49.5	4.3
1979	279.8	1,708	255.2	2,247	71	2,318	77,692	2,079	694.3	7.4	493.5	815.6	14.8	49.5	4.2
1980	276.0	1,756	251.1	2,283	68	2,351	95,462	2,126	734.4	6.4	524.1	791.8	14.8	48.3	4.3
1981[1]	260.7	1,759	272.7	2,292	70	2,362	111,584	2,154	735.7	6.6	541.4	799.9	15.0	51.1	4.1
1982[6]							120,000	2,180	770	6.9	570	770	14.9	52	4.2
1983															

[1] Preliminary. [2] Includes generation of industrial and railway electric plants. [3] The dividing point between small and large light and power is 50 kilowatts of demand. [4] Also includes interdepartmental (averages about 600 million kwh). [5] Includes internal combustion. [6] Estimate. *Sources: Federal Power Commission; Edison Electric Institute*   T.224

Electric Power Production by Electric Utilities in the U.S.[2]   In Billions of Kilowatt Hours

Year	Jan.	Feb.	Mar.	Apr.	May	June	July	Aug.	Sept.	Oct.	Nov.	Dec.	Total
1970	141.1	124.7	132.3	126.5	130.5	137.2	149.7	151.5	139.8	132.7	130.9	141.0	1,638
1971	145.6	131.3	141.4	130.7	133.7	150.5	153.9	154.2	145.9	139.5	138.9	148.0	1,714
1972	153.0	145.5	148.9	140.5	146.5	154.4	166.7	171.8	155.8	152.5	152.4	163.1	1,851
1973[2]	159.3	143.1	147.8	139.3	147.0	161.0	173.5	177.0	156.3	153.8	147.8	153.3	1,861
1974	156.9	142.4	149.9	141.9	153.4	156.0	177.9	173.8	152.2	151.9	149.8	159.5	1,867
1975	164.3	147.1	155.5	146.2	153.2	162.4	176.8	179.7	155.2	154.9	152.8	169.4	1,918
1976	178.5	156.7	164.2	153.2	157.4	173.4	186.4	186.4	165.0	163.7	169.1	183.9	2,038
1977	196.4	162.7	169.1	156.9	169.3	180.8	198.9	196.1	176.2	166.4	167.1	184.2	2,124
1978	197.3	173.7	173.2	159.7	175.2	187.4	202.6	205.6	185.6	175.6	176.3	191.7	2,204
1979[1]	209.5	186.3	183.0	169.5	178.2	186.7	202.4	204.9	180.6	179.8	177.4	188.9	2,247
1980[1]	200.0	188.7	187.5	168.6	175.7	189.4	216.1	215.4	191.5	178.5	178.6	195.4	2,286
1981[1]	205.2	179.6	185.4	172.4	177.7	202.7	220.2	210.2	186.9	181.4	175.6	195.6	2,295
1982[1]	210.1	180.3	187.7	172.6	177.3	186.2	210.2	205.7	180.7	173.0	173.4		
1983													

[1] Preliminary. [2] Data prior to 1973 are production by UTILITIES & INDUSTRIAL ESTABLISHMENTS. *Source: Federal Power Commission*   T.225

Use of Fuels for Electric Generation in the United States

Year	Consumption of Fuel Coal (Thousand Short Tons)	Fuel Oil (Thousand Barrels)[2]	Gas (Million Cubic Feet)	Total Fuel in Coal Equivalent (Thousand Short Tons)	Net Generation by Fuels[3] (Million Kw. Hr.)	Lbs. of Coal Per Kw. Hr. (Pounds)	% of Total Net Fuel Generation	Average Cost of Fuel Per Kw. Hr. (¢)	Heat Rate BTU Per Kw. Hr.	Cost Per Million BTU Consumed (¢)
1970	320,818	335,504	3,931,996	573,152	1,261,474	.909	96.4	.33	10,508	31.3
1971	327,878	396,438	3,975,972	599,766	1,307,310	.918	95.9	.40	10,536	37.5
1972	352,391	493,663	3,976,762	647,968	1,421,136	.912	95.6	.43	10,479	41.1
1973	388,190	559,842	3,640,756	688,043	1,498,958	.918	96.1	.50	10,429	48.4
1974	392,344	536,140	3,429,072	685,115	1,449,079	.946	95.6	.93	10,481	89.0
1975	406,032	506,081	3,157,591	686,236	1,441,611	.952		1.12	10,383	108.3
1976	448,431	555,583	3,080,627	740,112	1,558,951	.950		1.20	10,369	115.3
1977	477,215	623,656	3,190,571	798,425	1,648,775	.969		1.38	10,449	131.8
1978	481,624	635,829	3,188,370	811,814	1,646,163	.986		1.53	10,495	145.3
1979	527,317	523,256	3,490,517	837,371	1,708,029	.981		1.62	10,470	155.4
1980	569,453	420,214	3,681,595	916,952	1,753,749	.980		2.07	10,489	197.0
1981[1]	596,936	351,111	3,640,154	922,133	1,755,345	.992		2.42	10,506	230.2
1982										

[1] Preliminary. [2] 42-gallon barrels. [3] Excludes wood & waste fuels. *Source: Federal Power Commission*   T.226

144

Fertilizers (Nitrogen, Phosphate and Potash)

Nitrogen, phosphorous, and potassium are the primary plant nutrients produced by the fertilizer industry. Ammonia, which is made from natural gas and nitrogen, is the most widely used chemical carrier of nitrogen. Ammonia is applied in its liquid form beneath the surface of the soil, and it can be converted to solid nitrogenous fertilizers such as urea or diammonium phosphate. Phosphoric acid, which is made from phosphate rock and sulfuric acid, is the source of most of the phosphorous used in agriculture. Potassium chloride, commonly known as potash, is the major source of potassium.

The U.S. and the Soviet Union are the leading world producers of fertilizers, each country accounting for approximately 19 percent of total world production. China accounts for 10 percent of the world fertilizer output. These three countries are also among the major world consumers of fertilizers. Superior mineral resources and technology have given the U.S. an edge in the production of phosphatic fertilizer. The U.S. exports a considerable portion of its phosphorous, its nitrogen trade is in close balance, and most potash used in the U.S. is imported. On the other hand, the Soviet Union produces more of the nitrogenous fertilizers because of its large resources of natural gas, and a large portion of its nitrogen exports is sold as ammonia. China is a net importer of all three fertilizers.

Because ammonia is used in the production of almost all nitrogen fertilizer chemicals, the production of nitrogenous fertilizers can be reasonably equated to the production of ammonia. U.S. ammonia production was estimated to have reached 14.1 million tons during 1982, a positive growth rate of nearly 1.8 percent per year since 1970. However, the U.S. nitrogenous fertilizers industry was operating at about 11 percent below capacity during crop year 1982 because of low prices, heavy competition from imports, and the rising cost of natural gas. Presently, the U.S. has the capacity to produce nearly 16.2 million short tons of ammonia as a nitrogen equivalent.

On a dollar basis, U.S. production shipments of nitrogenous fertilizers in 1982 were about 7 percent below the 1981 level. The physical consumption of nitrogenous fertilizers in 1982 was estimated at 2 percent lower. Imports accounted for 15.1 percent of consumption. Since 1978, imports have averaged 16 percent of consumption, and 12 to 13 percent of U.S. supplies. The breakdown of U.S. imports of ammonia changed considerably in 1982. Because of Soviet production problems and Soviet attraction to the higher-priced European fertilizer market, the share of U.S. imports attributed to the Soviets dropped from almost 50 percent in the first half of 1981 to 35 percent in 1982. Imports from Mexico increased to 25 percent of the total, and Canada supplied 23 percent. Imports from Trinidad made up the balance.

Almost half of the U.S. facilities for the production of phosphate rock were shut down because of low demand during crop year 1982, and phosphate rock production for the year was estimated at 10 million short tons of phosphorous pentoxide. In mid-1981, the U.S. had a capacity to produce 11 million short tons of phosphorous pentoxide, and only 17 percent of this capacity was used in crop year 1982. The production of phosphoric acid in 1982 was projected at 7 million tons. Producer inventories of phosphatic fertilizers in 1982 were about 6.9 million tons, the equivalent of over four months of production. This was the highest inventory level recorded in the past ten years. The U.S. consumption of phosphatic fertilizers in 1982 was 21 percent below the 1981 level, and imports accounted for less than 2 percent of consumption.

The phosphatic materials accounting for the largest share of U.S. exports were phosphate rock, about 45 percent, and ammonium phosphate, about 30 percent. Almost all of the rest of U.S. exports were phosphoric acid and triple super phosphate. On a dollar basis, U.S. exports of phosphatic fertilizer declined about 15 percent during 1982, and imports fell by nearly 20 percent from 1981 levels. The U.S. trade balance in phosphate fertilizers has been positive throughout the past decade. The U.S. exports phosphatic fertilizers to over 60 countries, including the Soviet Union, India, Brazil, Canada, and China.

U.S. fertilizer consumption was expected to continue to decline during 1983 because of 1982 farm acreage reduction programs. Programs announced late in 1982 were expected to reduce the overall U.S. fertilizer consumption by 3 to 5 percent, and the USDA Payment-in-Kind (PIK) program was likely to reduce consumption another 4 to 7 percent. The USDA estimated that nitrogen consumption, in the absence of a PIK program, would be as much as 10.8 million tons, phosphate consumption would be 4.6 million, and potash consumption would be 5.4 million. The PIK program was expected to lower these consumption figures to 10.3 million tons, 4.5 million, and 5.2 million, respectively. The proportionate reduction of fertilizer used on PIK program crops in 1983/84 was expected to be less than the reduction of acreage because fertilizer application was likely to be increased on the acres planted. The greatest effect of the PIK program will be observed in the case of corn acreage, as corn requires large amounts of fertilizer per acre.

Farmer prices for fertilizer in late 1982/83 were projected at 1 to 5 percent below prices during the same period a year earlier, reflecting reduced demand, continued imports of nitrogen fertilizers, and above-normal producer inventories of potash. In December 1982, farm prices of major fertilizers were down an average of 5 percent from May. The greatest price weakness was observed in potash and phosphate fertilizers. Prospects for a price recovery were expected to be better for nitrogen fertilizer materials because of their higher application rates.

The dollar value of industry shipments of nitrogenous fertilizers was expected to be virtually unchanged in 1983. Inventories were expected to return to lower, more normal levels, and imports were expected to rise just slightly. The U.S. production of ammonia will probably be increased in 1983 in order to keep the value of shipments near the 1982 level. The price of U.S. ammonia is expected to move upward to equal the world price by around 1985, but a continuing cost-price squeeze will probably limit the construction of any new U.S. ammonia plants utilizing natural gas technology.

The value of phosphatic industry shipments in 1983 is not expected to show significant change from 1982 levels. Domestic consumption of phosphate fer-

FERTILIZERS (NITROGEN, PHOSPHATE AND POTASH)

tilizers could rise by 3 percent in 1983, analysts said, but the increased demand will probably be met with existing stocks. U.S. producers were able to survive the depressed prices of the past two years because of the proximity of sulfur supplies to phosphate rock resources and the proximity of seaports to phosphate producing areas. It was expected that Morocco, which owns the largest reserves of phosphate rock in the world, would become the major supplier of phosphate fertilizers to Europe. Mexico was expected to have a self-sufficient phosphate rock capacity in the next few years.

World Production of Ammonia   In Thousands of Short Tons of Contained Nitrogen

Year	Bulgaria	Canada	China	France	E. Germany	W. Germany	India	Italy	Japan	Mexico	Netherlands	Romania	Un. Kingdom	United States	USSR	Total
1976	1.0	1.4	4.5	2.0	1.2	2.1	2.1	1.3	2.5	.8	2.2	1.8	1.5	13.9	11.1	62.7
1977	1.9	1.9	6.2	2.2	1.2	2.2	2.2	1.3	2.5	.9	2.4	2.0	1.8	14.7	11.8	68.3
1978	1.9	2.1	7.4	2.2	1.3	2.2	2.4	1.6	2.7	1.4	2.4	2.5	1.8	14.2	12.5	72.6
1979	1.9	2.2	7.9	2.4	1.2	2.4	2.5	1.6	2.6	1.5	2.2	2.6	1.8	15.4	13.4	76.9
1980	1.9	2.2	8.3	2.3	1.3	2.3	2.4	1.5	2.4	1.7	2.2	2.5	1.8	16.2	13.8	78.7
1981[1]	.9	2.4	8.2	2.5	1.3	2.2	3.2	1.3	2.0	1.9	2.2	2.4	2.0	15.6	13.9	78.8
1982[2]	.9	2.4	8.2	2.5	1.3	2.2	3.3	1.3	2.1	1.9	2.2	2.4	1.9	14.5	13.9	77.6
1983																

[1] Preliminary.   [2] Estimate.   *Source: Bureau of Mines*   T.227

U.S. Salient Statistics of Nitrogen[1] (Ammonia)   In Thousands of Short Tons

Year	Net Import Reliance as a % of Appar. Con.	Production (Fixed)	Imports Fixed	Exports (Ammonia)	Apparent Consumption Fixed (Ammonia)	Apparent Consumption Elemental	Apparent Consumption Fixed	Producer Stocks Natural	Producer Stocks Fixed	Avg Price Urea F.O.B. Gulf Coast	Avg Price Urea Deliv. Corn Belt	Avg Price Fixed (Ammonia)	Ammonia F.O.B. Gulf Coast
1972		12,651			584	7,011	12,333	25	1,359			60.00	51.50
1973		12,641	271	741	588	8,229	12,720	13	713			65.00	51.50
1974		13,061	373	326	411	8,814	12,987		942			142.50	75.00
1975		13,609	662	289		9,141	13,223		1,698			190.00	
1976	1	13,856	599	361		10,463	13,939		1,850			185.00	125
1977	1	14,712	884	346		11,870	14,831		2,269			130.00	90
1978	7	14,169	1,247	434		13,707	15,270		2,044			110.00	80–84
1979	8	15,420	1,603	649		14,386	16,574		1,752			130.00	128–132
1980	9	16,244	1,921	681			17,664		2,100				120–125
1981[1]	7	15,648	1,719	506			16,384		2,384	130–135	170–180		132
1982[2]	9	14,500	1,800	700			16,000		2,000				120
1983													

[1] Elemental, Fixed, & Natural Nitrates.   [2] Estimates.   *Source: Bureau of Mines*   T.228

World Production of Phosphate Rock   In Thousands of Metric[3] Tons

Year	Brazil	China	Christmas Isl.	Israel	Jordan	Morocco	Nauru Island	Senegal	South Africa	Togo	Tunisia	United States	USSR	Vietnam	World Total
1971	220	2,400	1,092	843		13,237	2,058	1,703	1,359	1,891	3,485	38,886	20,950	300	92,508
1972	331	2,900	1,269	1,033	765	16,650	1,474	1,561	1,380	2,126	3,734	40,831	21,750	310	99,287
1973	283	3,300	1,695	860	1,191	18,824	2,561	1,931	1,505	2,527	3,829	42,137	23,400	550	108,823
1974	361	3,300	1,945	1,131	763	21,739	2,522	2,070	1,564	2,835	4,200	45,686	24,800	1,300	121,240
1975[3]	406	3,400	1,391	882	1,352	13,548	1,534	1,801	1,646	1,161	3,481	44,276	24,150	1,400	107,531
1976	490	4,000	1,033	639	1,717	15,656	755	1,799	1,731	2,008	3,301	44,671	23,900	1,500	107,594
1977	676	4,000	1,186	1,227	1,782	17,572	1,146	1,871	2,403	2,857	3,615	47,256	26,925	1,500	119,310
1978	1,096	4,500	1,386	1,725	2,303	19,713	1,999	1,759	2,699	2,827	3,712	50,037	27,712	1,800	128,620
1979	1,628	5,500	1,357	2,086	2,825	20,032	1,828	1,835	3,221	2,920	4,154	51,611	28,405	400	132,913
1980	2,472	5,500	1,638	2,307	3,911	18,824	2,087	1,632	3,282	2,933	4,582	54,415	29,450	500	138,333
1981[1]	2,637	11,500	1,336	2,290	3,523	19,696	2,000	2,017	2,910	2,244	4,596	53,624	30,950	550	145,774
1982[2]		12,000		2,600	4,300	17,200		1,000	3,250	2,000	4,500	38,000	44,000		140,000
1983															

[1] Preliminary.   [2] Estimate.   [3] Data prior to 1975 are in THOUSANDS OF SHORT TONS.   *Source: Bureau of Mines*   T.229

FERTILIZERS (NITROGEN, PHOSPHATE AND POTASH)

U.S. Salient Statistics of Phosphate Rock — In Thousands of Metric Tons

Year	Mine Production	Marketable Production	Imports for Consumption	Exports	Apparent Consumption	Stocks, Dec. 31	Price—$ Avg. Per Metric Ton (f.o.b. Plant)
1972		40,831	55	14,275	29,535	10,501	5.09
1973	126,720	38,218	59	12,585	28,328	8,482	6.24
1974	141,353	41,437	165	12,605	31,491	6,975	12.10
1975	170,077	44,276	33	11,131	31,022	9,021	25.35
1976	154,278	44,662	42	9,433	31,131	13,770	21.26
1977	166,893	47,256	158	13,230	34,365	13,682	17.39
1978	173,429	50,037	908	12,870	36,812	15,748	18.56
1979	185,757	51,611	886	14,358	39,591	14,357	20.26
1980	209,883	54,415	486	14,276	40,791	13,709	23.10
1981[1]	183,733	53,624	13	10,395	35,144	19,700	26.82
1982[2]		38,000	—	10,000	28,000	20,000	25.00
1983							

[1] Preliminary. [2] Estimate. Source: Bureau of Mines   T.230

World Production of Marketable Potash — In Thousands of Metric[3] Tons (K$_2$O Equivalent)

Year	Canada (sales)	Chile	China	Congo (Brazz.)	France	Germany East	Germany West	Israel	Italy	Spain	USSR	United States	United Kingdom	World Total
1972	3,852	28		310	1,941	2,709	2,698	618	238	703	5,989	2,659		22,060
1973	4,698	28		297	2,494	2,818	2,809	585	148	522	6,523	2,603		23,855
1974	6,041	14		318	2,508	3,157	2,888	669	169	436	7,260	2,552		26,432
1975	5,992	13	330	315	2,116	3,328	2,450	789	155	506	8,757	2,501	17	27,269
1976[3]	4,996	15	150	254	1,603	3,161	2,036	680	330	630	8,310	2,177	41	24,386
1977	5,764	11	18	136	1,580	3,229	2,341	730	224	562	8,347	2,229	81	25,252
1978	6,340	15	21	—	1,795	3,323	2,470	744	196	613	8,193	2,253	150	26,113
1979	7,074	15	16	—	1,850	3,395	2,616	737	182	668	6,635	2,225	264	25,677
1980	7,532	15	12	—	1,735	3,432	2,737	797	156	658	8,064	2,239	306	27,673
1981[1]	6,815	15	11	—	1,969	3,490	2,591	850	155	705	8,350	2,156	250	27,357
1982[2]	6,800				1,900		2,500	900	150	605		1,750	250	27,400
1983														

[1] Preliminary. [2] Estimate. [3] Data prior to 1976 are in THOUSANDS OF SHORT TONS. Source: U.S. Bureau of Mines   T.231

U.S. Salient Statistics of Potash — In Thousands of Metric[4] Tons (K$_2$O Equivalent)

Year	Net Import as % of Consum.	Production	Sales by Producers	Imports for Consumption	Exports	Apparent Consumption	Producer Stocks Dec. 31	Avg. Value Per Ton of Product—$	Average Price[3] $ Per Met. Ton
1971		2,587	2,592	2,766	564	4,794	428		34
1972		2,659	2,618	2,961	764	4,815	468		34
1973		2,603	2,865	2,587	889	5,563	206		36
1974		2,552	2,545	4,326	787	6,084	212		52
1975[4]	51	2,269	1,900	3,445	707	4,638	562		84
1976	61	2,177	2,268	4,168	857	5,578	471	48.78	73
1977	63	2,229	2,232	4,605	845	5,992	467	51.97	71
1978	64	2,253	2,307	4,707	809	6,205	414	61.38	76
1979	66	2,225	2,388	5,165	635	6,918	251	82.98	95
1980	65	2,239	2,217	4,972	840	6,349	273	89.62	130
1981[1]	65	2,156	1,908	4,796	491	6,213	520	89.12	137
1982[2]	71	1,750	1,800	4,800	350	6,000	720	85.42	80
1983									

[1] Preliminary. [2] Estimate. [3] Unit of K$_2$O, standard 60% muriate f.o.b. mine. [4] Data prior to 1975 are in THOUSANDS OF SHORT TONS. Source: Bureau of Mines   T.232

Flaxseed and Linseed Oil

In early 1983 the USDA estimated 1982 U.S. flaxseed production at 11.6 million bushels, 49 percent above the 1981 crop estimate. The 1982 acreage reduction programs for wheat and feed grains, depressed Durum wheat prices, and a relatively strong farm price for flaxseed during 1981/82 induced North Central farmers to increase planted acreage from 645,000 in 1981 to 860,000 in 1982. (Prospective plantings in 1983 were 1.0 million acres.) Generally favorable growing weather pushed 1982 yields to a record high. Flaxseed stocks as of June 1, 1982, the beginning of the 1982/83 crop season, registered an unprecedented low of 2 million bushels. Exports of flaxseed during the 1982/83 season were projected at 550,000 bushels, up from 11,000 during 1981/82. Imports during the same period were projected at a total of 1.5 million bushels, less than half the previous season's level.

The estimated 1982/83 crush of 11.5 million bushels would yield 230 million pounds of linseed oil and 215,000 tons of linseed meal. Linseed oil is primarily used in paint and varnish and resins and plastics.

Reputable trade sources estimated that the total world 1982/83 production of flaxseed was 2.84 million tonnes (approx. 111.8 million bushels) or nearly 24 percent above the previous crop. The three largest exporting countries, Canada, Argentina, and the U.S., contributed the most to the 10 percent increase in total world acreage.

Futures Market

Flaxseed futures are traded on the Winnipig Commodity Exchange.

World Production of Flaxseed   In Thousands of Metric Tons

Crop Year	Argentina	Australia	Brazil	Canada	Ethiopia	France	India	Mexico	Poland	Romania	Turkey	Uruguay	United States	USSR	World Total
1970–1	680	31	22	1,243	64	19	469	30	65	42	7	64	751	404	3,995
1971–2	316	10	12	567	70	21	474	40	75	58	7	43	462	464	2,748
1972–3	330	11	12	448	69	18	530	10	54	51	6	29	353	413	2,446
1973–4	297	14	12	493	72	18	428	11	51	45	6	26	409	507	2,393
1974–5	381	33	10	351	72	6	564	20	40	39	7	39	358	388	2,416
1975–6	377	13	8	445	75	32	598	27	36	45	8	62	395	340	2,564
1976–7	750	12	7	277	50	16	431	8	49	50	7	46	199	337	2,347
1977–8	855	35	5	650	50	44	527	18	38	50	6	40	409	300	2,941
1978–9	630	28	6	653	50	43	527	18	38	50	6	40	277	300	2,468
1979–0	600	14		572		31	535	15	52		3	31	305	250	2,687
1980–1[1]	743	14		815		42	269	10	35		3	65	201	254	2,109
1981–2[2]	600	8		468		40	474	8	45		3	21	198	165	2,107
1982–3[2]	750			747			450						296	150	2,577

[1] Preliminary.   [2] Estimate.   *Source: Foreign Agricultural Service, U.S.D.A.*   T.233

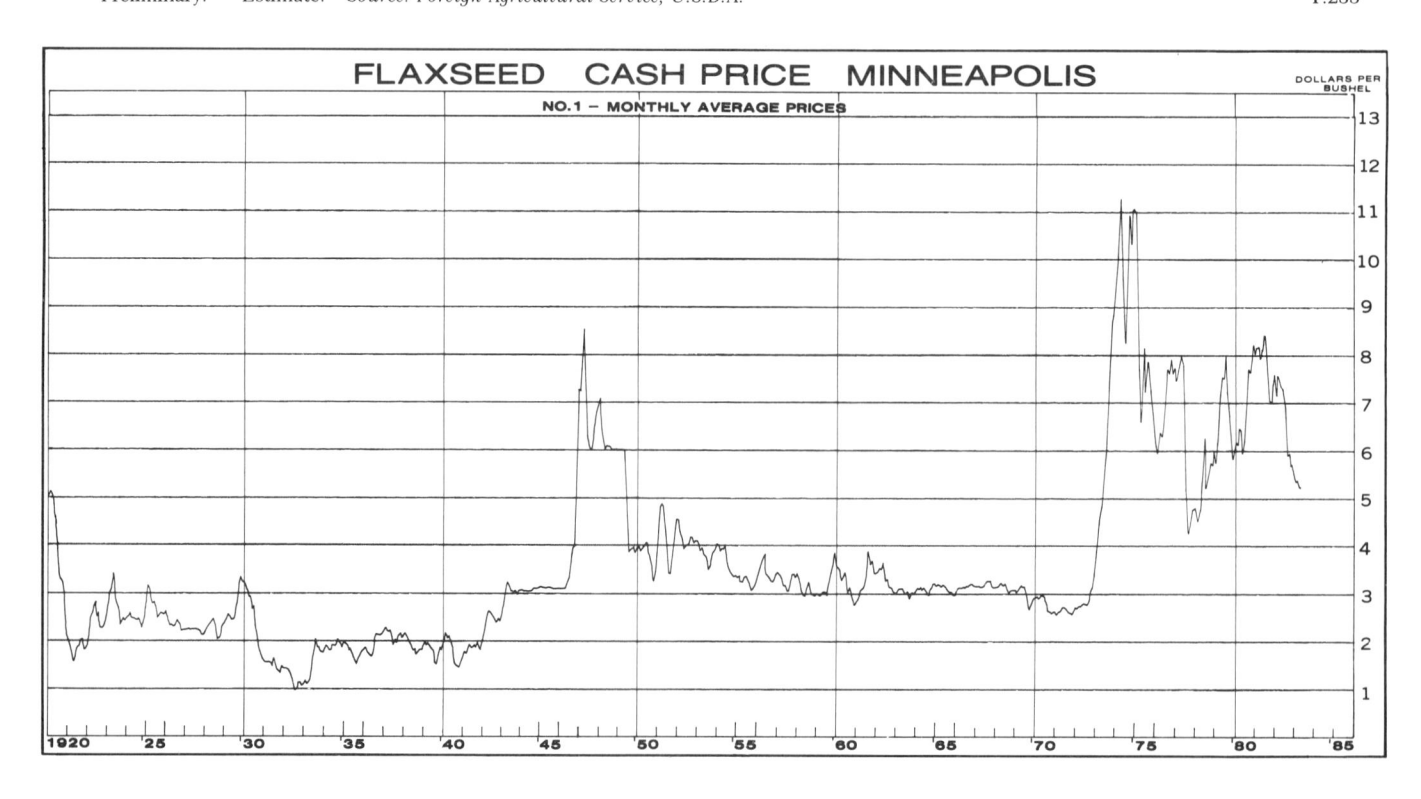

FLAXSEED CASH PRICE MINNEAPOLIS
NO. 1 – MONTHLY AVERAGE PRICES (DOLLARS PER BUSHEL)

148

FLAXSEED AND LINSEED OIL

Production of Flaxseed in the United States   In Thousands of Bushels

Year	Crop Production Estimates July 1	Aug. 1	Sept. 1	Oct. 1	Dec. 1	Arizona	California	Iowa	Minnesota	Montana	North Dakota	South Dakota	Texas	Wisconsin	U.S. Total
1970	35,401	29,146	30,065	30,877	29,970	—	78	18	4,477	253	16,440	7,025	1,125	—	29,416
1971	20,212	20,814	20,011	20,011	18,653	—	—	18	3,480	64	9,041	5,525	70	—	18,198
1972	15,488	14,240	15,051	15,300	13,909	—	—	—	1,794	104	7,320	4,500	165	—	13,883
1973	—	15,431	15,904	15,904	16,437	—	—	—	3,119	56	7,576	5,577	80	—	16,408
1974	—	13,713	14,263	14,543	13,337	—	—	—	3,163	40	6,688	3,818	374	—	14,083
1975	—	16,272	16,140	15,746	14,557	—	—	—	2,875	38	7,700	4,460	480	—	15,553
1976	—	6,776	6,967	6,951	7,356	—	—	—	1,950	50	4,000	1,380	440	—	7,580
1977	—	15,466	16,011	16,249	16,105	—	—	—	3,190	35	7,500	4,290	90	—	14,280
1978	—	11,156	11,348	11,705	10,921	—	—	—	2,201	—	4,025	2,188	200	—	8,614
1979	—	11,847	12,501	13,255	13,539	—	—	—	2,219	—	5,980	3,770	45	—	12,014
1980	—	7,060	7,700	7,940	8,128	—	—	—	1,563	—	2,900	3,445	20	—	7,928
1981	—	8,083	8,083	7,893	7,799	—	—	—	1,300	—	4,250	2,249	—	—	7,799
1982[1]		10,940	11,485	11,730	11,635	—	—	—	1,650	—	6,650	3,335	—	—	11,635
1983															

[1] Preliminary, December estimate.   Source: *Crop Reporting Board, U.S.D.A.*   T.234

U.S. Supply and Distribution of Flaxseed   In Thousands of Bushels

Year Beginning June	Supply — Stocks, June 1 Farm	Terminal	All Other	Total Stocks[4]	Imports	Production	Total Supply	Distribution Seed	Crushing	Exports	Other[2]	Total Distribution
1970-1	4,481	—17,343—		23,040	1	29,416	52,457	1,262	18,155	3,220	922	23,559
1971-2	3,174	—23,605—		28,898	74	18,198	47,170	933	21,022	910	1,102	23,967
1972-3	2,502	—17,630—		23,203	3	13,883	37,089	1,398	19,932	9,881	393	31,604
1973-4	403	— 3,103—		5,485	399	16,408	22,292	1,360	17,203	630	-953	18,240
1974-5	658	— 1,885—		4,052	130	14,083	18,265	1,231	13,386	372	245	15,234
1975-6	1,120	— 1,100—		3,031	148	15,553	18,732	1,054	11,791	953	44	13,842
1976-7	1,830	— 3,060—		4,890	2,168	7,580	14,638	1,043	10,677	196	-239	11,667
1977-8	1,070	— 1,934—		2,961	859	14,280	18,100	557	11,615	1,001	-388	12,785
1978-9	2,890	— 2,606—		5,315	1,557	8,614	15,486	724	13,009	91	-924	12,900
1979-0	977	— 1,609—		2,586	1,916	12,014	16,516	650	12,425	174	-1,751	11,498
1980-1[1]	2,681	— 2,337—		5,018	2,510	7,928	15,456	547	11,927	76	131	12,681
1981-2[3]	1,178	— 1,597—		2,775	3,502	7,799	14,076	691	11,231	11	115	12,048
1982-3[3]	1,253	— 775—		2,028	1,500	11,635	15,163	600	11,500	550		12,650
1983-4[3]				2,513								

[1] Preliminary.   [2] Other disappearance represents cleaning loss, waste, and residual.   [3] Forecasts.   [4] Estimates prior to 1975. Derived from July 1 stocks by adding June crushings & exports.   Source: *Statistical Reporting Service, U.S.D.A.*   T.235

Average Price Received by Farmers for Flaxseed in the U.S.   In Cents Per Bushel

Year	July	Aug.	Sept.	Oct.	Nov.	Dec.	Jan.	Feb.	Mar.	Apr.	May	June	Average[1]
1970-1	256	246	236	231	232	233	231	233	234	238	237	238	240
1971-2	234	234	231	225	227	237	241	242	244	249	249	250	238
1972-3	249	255	269	276	281	313	351	415	438	439	444	548	310
1973-4	572	675	729	766	810	863	936	1010	1080	927	883	776	756
1974-5	860	1080	977	1050	1060	1050	863	776	647	678	711	664	966
1975-6	755	722	682	666	560	570	537	587	574	588	554	669	657
1976-7	720	704	748	708	726	700	704	720	742	752	722	637	708
1977-8	514	415	420	456	420	432	421	407	441	485	532	589	454
1978-9	524	534	531	525	539	530	567	601	648	706	737	727	574
1979-0	690	642	634	556	544	561	551	579	585	551	604	588	597
1980-1	655	702	717	710	723	759	754	748	725	735	765	747	727
1981-2	723	708	644	621	664	684	690	691	680	669	660	665	675
1982-3	625	535	537	511	495	468	486	475	461	463			
1983-4													

[1] Season average includes an allowance for unredeemed loans.   Source: *Crop Reporting Board, U.S.D.A.*   T.236

FLAXSEED AND LINSEED OIL

Flaxseed Stocks in the United States   In Thousands of Bushels

Year	On Farms Jan. 1	Apr. 1	June 1	Oct. 1	Off Farms Jan. 1	Apr. 1	June 1	Oct. 1	Total Stocks Jan. 1	Apr. 1	June 1	Oct. 1
1975	3,946	2,668	N.A.	7,552	3,745	1,907	N.A.	6,228	7,691	4,575	3,031	13,780
1976	4,220	3,009	1,830	4,116	5,533	4,164	3,060	4,971	9,753	7,173	4,890	9,087
1977	2,853	2,070	1,070	9,292	4,375	2,879	1,934	4,307	7,228	4,949	3,004	13,599
1978	5,773	4,499	2,890	6,170	5,168	3,905	2,606	3,390	10,941	8,404	5,496	9,560
1979	3,446	2,349	977	7,449	4,027	3,039	1,609	2,999	7,473	5,388	2,586	10,448
1980	4,909	3,967	2,681	5,583	4,723	3,249	2,337	3,200	9,632	7,216	5,018	8,583
1981	3,132	2,086	1,178	4,575	3,423	2,252	1,597	1,902	6,555	4,338	2,775	6,477
1982[1]	3,232	2,035	1,253	5,650	1,864	1,521	775	1,770	5,096	3,556	2,028	7,420
1983[1]	4,306	2,891			2,151	1,798			6,457	4,689		
1984												

[1] Preliminary.   Source: Crop Reporting Board, U.S.A.   T.237

Average Price of No. 1 Flaxseed at Minneapolis   In Dollars Per Bushel

Year	Aug.	Sept.	Oct.	Nov.	Dec.	Jan.	Feb.	Mar.	Apr.	May	June	July	Average[1]
1970-1	2.65	2.64	2.60	2.62	2.63	2.58	2.62	2.63	2.71	2.72	2.70	2.68	2.66
1971-2	2.62	2.61	2.58	2.64	2.71	2.70	2.74	2.74	2.78	2.80	2.80	2.79	2.69
1972-3	2.85	3.00	3.08	3.14	3.41	3.90	4.52	4.75	4.84	5.12	5.93	6.37	3.94
1973-4	7.36	7.89	8.71	8.82	9.22	10.06	10.07	11.29	9.87	8.67	8.26	9.25	8.93
1974-5	10.92	10.33	11.04	11.08	10.97	8.76	7.70	6.60	7.39	8.15	7.23	7.88	9.12
1975-6	7.69	7.25	6.64	6.18	6.09	5.93	6.36	6.30	6.40	6.67	7.31	7.70	6.71
1976-7	7.63	7.91	7.61	7.71	7.46	7.54	7.63	7.82	7.99	7.76	6.10	5.17	7.36
1977-8	4.26	4.41	4.79	—	4.80	4.61	4.51	4.78	5.30	5.78	6.25	5.22	4.97
1978-9	5.47	5.76	5.70	5.99	5.75	6.17	6.63	7.22	7.54	7.51	7.98	7.23	6.58
1979-0	7.00	6.71	6.12	5.84	6.16	6.14	6.47	6.44	5.95	6.24	6.50	7.15	6.39
1980-1	7.70	7.65	7.82	8.23	8.04	8.17	8.19	7.93	8.11	8.42	8.06	7.85	8.01
1981-2	7.62	7.02	7.00	7.41	7.61	7.15	7.57	7.47	7.35	7.28	7.02	6.90	7.28
1982-3	5.90	5.93	5.70	5.71	5.52	5.36	5.37	5.23	5.22				
1983-4													

[1] Weighted average by carlot sales.   Source: Economic Research Service, U.S.D.A.   T.238

Supply and Distribution of Linseed Oil in the United States   In Millions of Pounds

Year Beginning June	Supply Stocks June 1	Production	Total	Exports & Shipments	Paint & Varnish	Linoleum & Oilcloth	Resins & Plastics	Other Inedible	Total	Lubricants & Similar Oils	Fatty Acids	Total	Per Capita —Lbs.—	Flaxseed (Oil Equivalent of Exports)[3]
1970-1	130	363	495	47	209	8	19	19	239	13	1	261	1.26	64
1971-2	187	428	615	66	221	7	21	16	258	13	3	274	1.31	18
1972-3	275	393	668	256	224	11	25	21	270	14	—	285	1.35	200
1973-4	127	344	471	142	205	11	21	22	248	10	—	259	1.22	13
1974-5	71	263	334	143	112	3	11	12	134	8	—	142	.66	7
1975-6	49	231	279	42	154	—	10	9	173	10	4	187	.87	19
1976-7	49	217	266	14	126		13	8	156	9	8	164	.75	4
1977-8[1]	88	232	320	25	177		23	15		7	3	225	1.03	20
1978-9[2]	70	259	329	54										
1979-0[2]	44	256	300	38										
1980-1[2]	54	251	305	51										
1981-2[2]	56	200	256											

[1] Preliminary.   [2] Estimate.   [3] Based on 20 lbs. of linseed oil per bushel of flaxseed exports.   Source: Economic Research Service, U.S.D.A.   T.239

FLAXSEED AND LINSEED OIL

Wholesale Price of Raw Linseed Oil at Minneapolis in Tank Cars   In Cents Per Pound

Year	July	Aug.	Sept.	Oct.	Nov.	Dec.	Jan.	Feb.	Mar.	Apr.	May	June	Average
1970-1	11.0	11.0	10.0	10.0	10.0	9.5	9.5	9.5	9.0	8.8	8.8	8.8	9.7
1971-2	8.8	8.8	8.8	8.8	8.8	8.8	8.8	8.8	8.8	8.8	8.8	9.5	8.9
1972-3	9.5	9.5	9.5	9.5	9.5	9.5	9.5	9.5	9.5	9.5	14.0	14.2	10.3
1973-4	15.0	N.A.	N.A.	N.A.	—	35.0	35.0	40.2	42.6	45.0	45.0	44.5	37.8
1974-5	44.0	44.0	47.0	48.5	48.5	48.5	46.2	44.0	44.0	44.0	44.0	44.0	45.6
1975-6	44.0	39.0	36.0	35.0	30.5	29.8	28.3	27.5	25.5	24.0	24.0	24.0	30.6
1976-7	25.4	27.0	27.8	30.0	30.0	30.0	30.0	30.0	28.0	28.5	28.5	28.5	28.6
1977-8	28.0	28.0	27.0	22.8	20.0	20.0	26.6	26.6	26.6	—	22.0	22.0	24.5
1978-9	22.5	24.0	24.0	24.0	24.0	24.0	24.0	24.0	24.0	24.0	30.0	30.0	24.9
1979-0	30.0	30.0	32.0	32.0	32.0	32.0	32.0	28.8	28.8	27.8	26.6	27.0	29.9
1980-1	27.0	28.6	29.0	29.2	29.0	29.8	32.8	32.0	31.3	32.0	32.6	32.8	30.5
1981-2	32.8	32.3	31.8	30.8	30.0	27.6	29.5	28.5	28.2	28.0	28.0	27.0	29.5
1982-3	27.8	26.3	26.0	24.6	25.0	25.2							
1983-4													

Source: Department of Agriculture   T.240

Linseed Oil Production (Crude, Raw)   In Millions of Pounds

Year	July	Aug.	Sept.	Oct.	Nov.	Dec.	Jan.	Feb.	Mar.	Apr.	May	June	Total
1970-1	17.5	29.1	36.2	30.7	26.8	27.5	31.9	32.4	34.9	36.7	36.8	41.4	381.9
1971-2	25.9	34.7	35.4	36.5	32.3	33.3	38.2	36.5	44.8	36.1	33.2	39.0	425.9
1972-3	33.2	40.4	41.1	34.0	35.0	28.2	31.3	25.1	26.5	28.5	30.2	39.9	393.4
1973-4	29.6	33.4	39.1	40.6	28.2	22.3	24.2	19.6	20.1	20.0	27.1	30.6	335.0
1974-5	24.8	14.6	29.2	36.5	32.2	29.8	16.5	14.2	13.9	9.5	10.9	15.2	247.3
1975-6	6.5	18.4	31.8	37.6	19.2	14.6	11.7	17.9	19.0	17.4	20.6	19.7	229.7
1976-7	21.8	16.4	21.0	20.6	12.5	22.7	19.3	14.0	14.7	13.0	20.9	21.2	216.5
1977-8	13.0	22.9	26.9	15.5	13.5	18.8	19.5	14.6	6.9	22.8	35.9	30.9	231.4
1978-9	32.4	20.3	18.4	N.A.	16.9	14.6	16.1	N.A.	23.7	28.3	26.2	26.1	223.0
1979-0	16.4	22.5	41.9	11.5	15.7	12.2	N.A.	N.A.	29.3	30.7	14.8	19.3	214.3
1980-1	14.5	19.3	N.A.	17.1	29.5	N.A.	N.A.	N.A.	N.A.	N.A.	23.3	22.7	—
1981-2[1]	24.2	30.9	38.8	N.A.	21.6								
1982-3[1]													
1983-4													

[1] Preliminary.   Source: Bureau of the Census   T.241

U.S. Linseed Oil Domestic Disappearance   In Millions of Pounds

Year	July	Aug.	Sept.	Oct.	Nov.	Dec.	Jan.	Feb.	Mar.	Apr.	May	June	Total
1970-1	18.6	18.4	16.8	15.1	14.2	12.7	13.3	15.8	18.4	19.6	19.6	22.7	205.2
1971-2	17.9	19.4	18.0	17.6	15.3	16.0	17.3	17.6	19.0	19.7	22.5	24.3	224.6
1972-3	21.9	23.2	20.9	21.7	18.5	17.1	37.8	11.2	37.0	38.6	45.9	34.7	293.4
1973-4	25.4	30.1	9.9	31.8	19.4	12.0	31.2	14.3	15.8	15.7	18.6	30.3	254.5
1974-5	.5	9.5	37.3	10.2	16.8	2.5	9.1	11.4	13.0	9.5	5.9	16.6	128.6
1975-6	12.6	22.6	20.4	22.8	8.5	12.8	22.4	15.4	15.2	9.6	23.1	15.3	187.2
1976-7	22.2	11.1	15.3	15.8	8.6	12.0	14.7	15.9	20.1	6.8	20.9	21.9	163.5
1977-8	23.9	22.9	13.7	10.9	8.9	3.8	15.4	15.8	23.9	21.2	42.5	21.5	224.7
1978-9	6.1	31.5	14.0	22.3	16.1	11.4	16.2	15.0	14.7	21.7	20.5	18.3	267.9
1979-0	18.4	19.9	15.8	24.3	14.9	11.4	11.7	12.3	14.6	17.1	11.6	12.2	184.2
1980-1	13.2	15.7	16.7	21.1	11.4	11.6	13.6	13.9	12.2	19.8	15.4	12.9	177.5
1981-2[1]	21.0	16.0	15.3	15.2	6.3	5.6	6.5	7.6	8.5	8.0	8.1	9.0	127.1
1982-3[1]	8.7	8.3	8.4	7.6	6.1	5.0	5.9						
1983-4													

[1] Preliminary.   Source: Bureau of the Census   T.242

FLAXSEED AND LINSEED OIL

High, Low & Closing Prices of May Flaxseed Futures in Winnipeg — In Dollars per Tonne

Year of Delivery		June	July	Aug.	Sept.	Oct.	Nov.	Dec.	Jan.	Feb.	Mar.	Apr.	May	Life of Delivery Range
1978	High	—	263.60	247.50	242.90	247.00	230.50	229.00	217.00	221.00	246.50	261.00	271.30	271.30
	Low	—	246.00	200.50	216.40	214.90	215.00	210.50	208.70	211.00	217.40	236.00	243.00	200.50
	Close	—	251.10	218.00	227.00	221.70	218.40	210.50	210.60	216.60	242.50	250.80	271.30	—
1979	High	246.10	243.50	255.50	262.50	285.00	284.00	288.00	325.50	385.00	357.00	344.40	346.00	385.00
	Low	243.10	233.00	234.80	249.60	256.00	260.50	271.50	284.00	326.50	332.60	321.00	313.00	233.00
	Close	243.10	243.50	251.10	256.50	279.00	273.00	284.60	325.00	351.50	343.00	322.00	336.00	—
1980	High	356.50	345.50	354.00	355.00	356.40	341.50	332.00	351.50	347.50	330.30	295.50	336.00	356.50
	Low	302.00	312.50	316.50	325.00	315.50	319.30	317.00	297.00	315.00	295.50	284.00	292.00	284.00
	Close	333.00	319.50	331.70	348.00	319.00	330.70	318.00	337.60	316.00	296.20	293.00	307.60	—
1981	High	370.50	412.70	406.00	412.70	417.50	468.90	470.50	439.10	385.80	387.30	391.40	397.00	470.50
	Low	327.50	365.00	367.00	391.50	387.00	413.00	395.70	371.00	364.00	358.00	376.30	376.70	327.50
	Close	360.60	405.50	393.00	395.80	411.90	468.00	431.10	373.00	368.20	378.40	382.70	389.50	—
1982	High	413.00	410.00	406.20	403.20	426.20	424.50	412.90	393.50	388.50	364.00	372.50	367.00	426.00
	Low	385.00	391.00	392.50	376.70	392.00	404.60	367.50	367.30	352.70	332.50	340.50	340.50	332.50
	Close	393.00	396.00	399.60	397.00	422.50	414.50	378.50	390.10	361.50	343.70	350.00	340.50	—
1983	High	385.00	374.00	369.50	369.20	332.70	325.00	318.00	304.50	304.00	299.50	294.50		
	Low	373.50	355.00	347.10	326.60	318.10	316.00	288.30	290.90	289.20	288.00	286.80		
	Close	373.50	355.10	364.50	326.60	318.30	317.70	293.50	304.00	289.30	291.00	287.00		
1984	High													
	Low													
	Close													

Source: Winnipeg Commodity Exchange

T.243

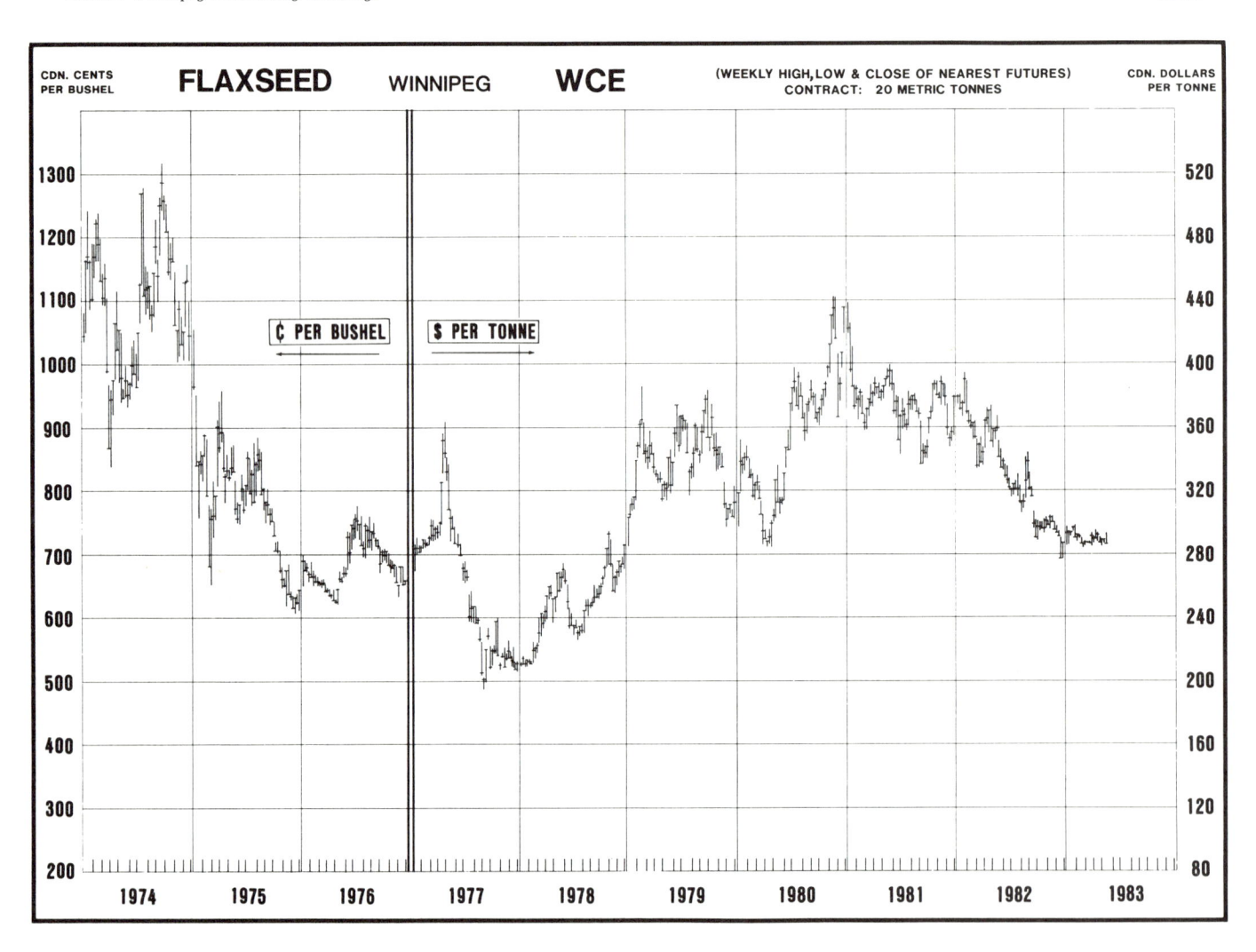

FLAXSEED — WINNIPEG — WCE
(WEEKLY HIGH, LOW & CLOSE OF NEAREST FUTURES)
CONTRACT: 20 METRIC TONNES

Weekly high/low/close bar chart of nearest flaxseed futures on the Winnipeg Commodity Exchange, 1974–1983. Left axis: Cdn. cents per bushel (200–1300); right axis: Cdn. dollars per tonne (80–520).

152

FLAXSEED AND LINSEED OIL

Month End Open Interest of Flaxseed Futures in Winnipeg In 20 Tonne Units

Year	Jan.	Feb.	Mar.	Apr.	May	June	July	Aug.	Sept.	Oct.	Nov.	Dec.
1978	3,250	3,820	4,293	5,229	5,964	5,576	4,671	5,460	5,019	5,999	5,551	5,596
1979	5,998	6,537	6,656	5,827	5,256	4,411	7,185	6,219	5,845	6,517	5,831	7,860
1980	8,319	9,117	8,790	9,210	8,059	7,460	9,606	10,414	8,728	9,656	10,455	11,786
1981	10,923	19,483	9,237	8,210	6,381	8,039	8,988	9,101	4,807	5,216	5,580	5,064
1982	6,339	7,201	7,714	7,214	4,897	4,976	4,390	6,041	6,306	5,783	6,493	4,097
1983	4,759	5,261	4,128	5,039								
1984												

Source: Winnipeg Commodity Exchange T.244

U.S. Stocks of Linseed Oil (Crude & Refined) at Factories & Warehouses In Millions of Pounds

Year	July 1	Aug. 1	Sept. 1	Oct. 1	Nov. 1	Dec. 1	Jan. 1	Feb. 1	Mar. 1	April 1	May 1	June 1
1970-1	128.7	112.8	117.1	130.0	134.9	144.9	148.5	157.5	170.5	180.7	192.8	187.2
1971-2	203.8	193.2	177.1	179.9	203.7	210.8	224.9	236.7	245.3	263.5	280.9	275.3
1972-3	276.6	263.8	253.3	259.2	258.4	246.3	253.6	225.3	224.1	177.3	153.0	127.1
1973-4	113.0	86.4	71.6	90.3	85.8	86.3	82.2	70.1	64.7	65.3	66.4	70.8
1974-5	59.2	69.4	60.2	48.2	58.9	47.6	71.5	69.2	67.0	56.0	49.8	48.6
1975-6	43.8	36.7	30.1	37.8	49.5	47.6	55.8	44.1	44.0	46.3	51.7	48.9
1976-7	47.6	42.7	48.0	53.5	58.1	59.7	70.2	89.9	87.8	82.3	88.4	88.1
1977-8	87.3	74.0	69.0	79.2	72.6	74.2	89.2	93.2	92.0	74.8	76.3	69.6
1978-9	62.6	75.6	49.9	44.8	34.4	34.8	34.9	34.8	35.5	37.4	43.6	43.9
1979-0	49.1	39.9	47.7	62.9	46.4	43.6	35.6	41.8	36.3	48.2	65.6	53.5
1980-1[1]	42.9	45.3	35.5	52.5	43.8	34.5	45.6	50.6	53.3	34.7	42.1	56.3
1981-2[1]	67.1	57.4	65.7	71.4	72.0	64.2	57.2	62.7	57.0	64.6	66.7	50.3
1982-3[1]	37.4	33.9	30.4	44.6	43.0	26.8	39.0	34.2				
1983-4												

[1] Preliminary. *Source: Bureau of the Census* T.245

Factory Shipments of Paints, Varnish and Lacquer in the U.S. In Millions of Dollars

Year	Jan.	Feb.	Mar.	Apr.	May	June	July	Aug.	Sept.	Oct.	Nov.	Dec.	Total
1970	179.0	197.6	241.2	236.0	251.8	281.1	255.8	254.7	256.4	220.6	185.9	177.0	2,737
1971	180.4	198.2	235.6	253.0	258.2	291.6	254.1	274.0	266.8	226.8	208.9	183.3	2,831
1972	209.6	226.0	261.0	252.7	285.8	292.4	257.6	286.4	269.0	254.0	224.7	190.0	3,009
1973	220.2	229.2	257.2	268.9	294.4	297.5	279.4	301.7	272.5	274.3	240.0	197.8	3,133
1974	243.8	246.3	279.5	315.9	342.3	349.5	345.5	303.8	338.8	343.2	280.4	229.9	3,672
1975	265.0	267.5	302.2	334.1	362.9	391.6	373.4	387.1	384.6	364.0	318.2	276.0	4,027
1976	305.0	353.1	396.2	419.1	434.0	477.3	423.6	455.4	420.7	355.3	357.1	322.8	4,720
1977	329.8	354.2	466.2	449.5	508.5	527.0	465.0	521.1	482.2	435.5	409.2	359.7	5,308
1978[2]	377.1	403.7	500.6	517.1	589.0	586.2	518.4	589.0	536.0	516.6	470.2	403.3	6,008
1979[1]	476.1	484.0	622.0	574.1	677.8	668.3	638.4	678.4	590.3	648.5	526.8	448.1	7,025
1980[1]	540.8	567.9	611.9	648.0	702.4	721.6	682.9	689.3	698.2	706.1	546.4	520.3	7,636
1981[1]	555.1	593.2	728.1	774.5	770.8	851.8	774.4	784.8	773.2	704.2	572.0	513.6	8,396
1982[1]	544.9	579.9	711.7	741.0	791.2	835.1	744.9	798.2	773.8	656.4	589.0	531.0	8,297
1983													

[1] Preliminary. [2] New series; not comparable with earlier data. *Source: Bureau of the Census* T.246

Gas

Early in 1983, analysts characterized as uncertain the outlook for the U.S. production and consumption of natural gas. The long-term decline in natural gas reserves was evidently being reversed, reflecting both a higher rate of discovery of new reserves as well as a decline in consumption, particularly by the industrial sector. Between 1981 and 1982, the wellhead price of natural gas rose relative to the wellhead price of crude oil. This trend was expected to persist through 1985 with the phased decontrol of natural gas prices. In the last months of 1982, however, deregulated natural gas prices weakened noticeably.

During 1982, the U.S. domestic consumption of natural gas declined by an estimated 1.8 percent compared to the 1981 level, and production declined approximately 3 percent. The slower rate of natural gas production was generally attributed to energy conservation and to economic depression. Electric utilities continued to convert gas-fired generating capacity to alternative fuels in 1982, and utility gas use in the first half of the year declined by 12 percent from usage in the first half of the previous year. The complex pricing provisions authorized by the Natural Gas Policy Act of 1978 tended to raise the price of natural gas to the consumer and thus to restrict demand. In the first five months of 1982, the average wellhead price of natural gas rose 20 percent from its level during the comparable period in 1981, and the average price of natural gas for residential heating rose 22 percent.

The U.S. consumption of natural gas is expected to increase to 20.06 quadrillion British thermal units (Btu) in 1983 from the 19.23 quadrillion Btu consumed in 1982—a 4 percent increase. The greatest component of this projected increase is likely to come from industrial production if economic recovery carries through 1983. The increase in industrial consumption of natural gas is expected to be offset somewhat as electric utilities continue to convert gas-generating capacity to alternative fuels.

Natural gas production in the U.S. is expected to increase slightly from 18.88 quadrillion Btu in 1982 to approximately 19.01 quadrillion Btu in 1983. Natural gas imports during 1983 are expected to remain unchanged, and the balance of consumption will probably be met by a drawdown of natural gas stocks.

During 1982, the production of natural gas liquids (excluding lease condensate) fell by 3.5 percent to nearly 566 million barrels. Natural gas liquids production in 1983 is projected at 577 million barrels, a 1.9 percent increase.

World Natural Gas Production (Marketed Production[3]) In Thousands of Terajoule[4]

Year	Argentina	Canada	France	Indonesia	W. Germany	Iran	Italy	Mexico	Netherlands	Poland	Romania	United Kingdom	United States	USSR	Venezuela	Australia
1970	212	2,277	243	14	460	71	465	481	1,107	183	884	398	21,921	6,990	349	
1971	228	2,499	252	101	555	299	473	479	1,536	190	892	657	22,493	7,501	368	
1972	218	2,914	260	179	637	448	501	496	2,052	206	976	939	22,532	7,818	388	
1973	238	3,119	262	248	706	702	541	542	2,495	213	980	1,018	22,648	8,346	460	
1974	256	3,046	269	273	713	786	540	561	2,957	203	1,012	1,230	21,601	9,201	476	
1975	278	3,090	260	257	639	771	514	584	3,208	211	1,042	1,274	20,109	10,206	450	
1976[4]	268	2,820	279	115	676	788	600	515	3,422	243	1,384	1,491	20,552	11,194	497	231
1977	271	2,962	299	162	673	743	524	538	3,067	249	1,465	1,536	20,717	12,102	505	264
1978	256	2,856	307	353	720	668	524	669	2,808	244	1,475	1,458	20,654	12,967	509	270
1979	303	3,041	296	482	725	700	538	803	2,936	224	1,409	1,533	21,275	14,160	600	314
1980	327	2,781	287	607	662	279	478	893	2,881	193	1,455	1,469	21,102	15,168	630	354
1981[1]	340	2,746	278	653	674	235	534	945	2,670	214		1,503	20,910	16,215	571	420
1982[2]	360	2,800	285	1,000	640		530	1,250	2,500	200		1,250	20,000	17,000	800	500

[1] Preliminary. [2] Estimate. [3] Comprises all gas collected & utilized as fuel or as a chemical industry raw material, including gas used in oilfields and/or gasfields as a fuel by producers. [4] Terajoule = 10^{12} Joule = approx. 10^9 BTU. Prior to 1976 data are in billions of cubic feet. *Source: U.S. Dept. of Energy*

T.247

GAS

Salient Statistics of Natural Gas in the United States

In Billions of Cubic Feet

Year	Marketed Production	Storage With-drawals	Imports (Consumed) (Bil. Nat. Gas Cu. Ft.)	Total Supply	Consumption	Exports	Stored	Extraction Loss	Adjustments	Total Disposition	Value At Wells[3] Million $	¢ Ths. cu. ft. At Wells	Residential	Commercial	Electric Utilities
1970	21,921	1,459	821	24,200	20,046	70	1,857		228	24,200	3,746	17.1	1.09	.82	.29
1971	22,493	1,508	935	24,935	22,677	80	1,839		339	24,935	4,085	18.2	1.15	.87	.32
1972	22,532	1,757	1,019	25,308	23,009	78	1,893		328	25,308	4,180	18.6	1.21	.92	.34
1973	22,648	1,533	1,033	25,213	22,966	77	1,974		196	25,213	4,894	21.6	1.08	.98	.35
1974	21,601	1,701	959	24,260	21,223	77	1,784	887	289	24,260	6,573	30.4	1.25	1.12	.49
1975	20,109	1,760	953	22,821	19,538	73	2,104	872	235	22,821	8,945	44.5	1.54	1.40	.77
1976	19,952	2,114	964	23,030	19,946	65	1,756	854	216	22,837	11,572	58.0	1.85	1.69	1.06
1977	20,025	1,773	1,011	22,809	19,521	56	2,307	863	41	22,786	15,834	79.0	2.26	2.10	1.33
1978	19,974	2,186	966	23,126	19,627	53	2,278	852	287	23,097	18,085	90.5	2.63	2.30	1.48
1979[1]	20,471	2,044	1,253	23,768	20,241	56	2,295	808	372	23,772	24,114	117.8	3.23	2.77	1.80
1980[2]	20,379	1,911	985	23,275	19,877	49						159	3.95		2.28
1981[2]	20,178	1,887	904	22,969	19,404	59						198	4.56		2.91
1982[2]	18,462	2,084	972	21,518	17,873	55						241	5.53		3.49
1983															

[1] Preliminary. [2] Estimate. [3] Total value of market production at the wellhead. Source: U.S. Dept. of Energy   T.248

Natural Gas Consumed[2] in the United States — In Billions of Cubic Feet

Year	Arkansas	California	Illinois	Kansas	Louisiana	Michigan	Missouri	New Mexico	New York	Ohio	Oklahoma	Pennsylvania	Texas	West Virginia	Indiana
1969	353	2,079	1,099	583	1,942	779	399	302	684	1,032	603	766	4,325	178	
1970	385	2,156	1,188	615	2,034	811	430	323	711	1,053	656	772	4,559	192	
1971	336	2,177	1,243	647	2,079	853	429	323	717	1,087	667	802	4,813	189	
1972	318	2,210	1,221	669	2,138	867	425	342	693	1,148	686	829	4,883	209	
1973	329	2,063	1,164	648	2,217	922	427	313	683	1,104	673	783	5,088	196	
1974	291	1,852	1,163	630	2,203	938	410	312	627	1,087	723	716	4,912	192	
1975	259	1,858	1,108	541	1,978	887	370	296	577	957	729	654	4,380	168	
1976	250	1,771	1,188	556	2,216	895	380	341	596	1,006	812	714	4,404	159	425
1977	230	1,772	1,167	507	2,191	741	367	230	562	847	767	668	4,143	145	398
1978	221	1,563	1,175	519	2,249	790	359	214	570	930	770	674	4,211	152	441
1979[1]	251	1,810	1,143	584	1,978	876	347	211	624	898	825	741	4,001	149	504
1980															

[1] Preliminary. [2] Includes volume of natural gas which is distributed as a component of mixed gas. Source: U.S. Dept. of Energy   T.249

United States Marketed Production[1] of Natural Gas — In Billions of Cubic Feet

Year	Arkansas	California	Kansas	Alaska	Louisiana	Mississippi	Montana	New Mexico	Ohio	Oklahoma	Pennsylvania	Texas	West Virginia	Wyoming	Michigan
1969	169	678	883	81	7,228	131	41	1,138	50	1,524	79	7,853	232	304	
1970	181	649	900	78	7,788	126	43	1,139	52	1,595	77	8,358	242	339	
1971	172	613	885	73	8,082	119	33	1,168	80	1,684	76	8,551	234	380	
1972	167	487	880	126	7,973	104	33	1,216	90	1,807	74	8,658	215	375	
1973	150	449	893	131	8,342	100	56	1,219	94	1,771	79	8,514	209	358	
1974	124	365	887	129	7,754	79	55	1,245	92	1,639	83	8,171	202	327	
1975	116	318	844	160	7,091	70	41	1,217	85	1,605	85	7,486	154	316	102
1976	110	354	829	166	7,007	71	43	1,231	89	1,727	89	7,192	153	329	119
1977	104	311	781	188	7,215	83	47	1,203	99	1,770	92	7,051	153	330	130
1978	107	311	854	203	7,476	107	47	1,174	114	1,774	98	6,548	149	357	148
1979	109	248	798	221	7,266	144	54	1,181	123	1,835	96	7,175	151	414	160
1980[2]	112	264	732	226	6,937	165	54	1,142		1,892		7,169	152	382	153
1981															

[1] Comprises gas either sold or consumed by producers, including losses in transmission, quantities added to storage and increases of gas in pipelines. [2] Preliminary. Source: U.S. Dept. of Energy   T.250

GAS

United States Recoverable Reserves and Deliveries of Natural Gas — In Billions of Cubic Feet

Year	Recoverable Reserves of Natural Gas Dec. 31[3]	Residential Deliveries	Commercial Deliveries	Field	Carbon Black	Petroleum Refineries	Used as Pipeline Fuel	Industrial	Other Consumers	Total Deliveries	Electric Utility Power[2] Plants
1969	275,109	4,728	1,955	2,212	98	998	631	6,814			3,486
1970	290,700	4,837	2,057	2,305	86	1,029	722	7,116			3,894
1971	278,806	4,972	2,173	2,297	59	1,063	743	7,373			3,993
1972	266,085	5,144	2,279	2,364	59	1,071	766	7,364			3,979
1973	249,950	4,994	2,283	2,412	50	1,074	728	7,929			3,605
1974	237,132	4,786	2,263		40	1,040	669				3,429
1975	228,200	4,924	2,268		26	946	583				3,147
1976	216,026	5,051	2,383		28	919	548	6,967	285	17,764	3,078
1977[1]	208,878	4,821	2,243		28		533	6,817	257	17,329	3,189
1978[1]	200,302	4,903	2,310				530	6,757	291	17,449	3,188
1979[4]	194,600	4,965	2,485				601	6,899	301	18,141	3,491
1980											

[1] Preliminary. [2] Figures include gas other than natural (impossible to segregate); therefore, shown separately from other consumption. [3] Estimated proved recoverable reserves. [4] Estimated. *Source: U.S. Dept. of Energy* T.251

Total Sales of All Types[2] of Gas To All Consumers in the United States — In Millions of Therms

Year	Jan.	Feb.	Mar.	Apr.	May	June	July	Aug.	Sept.	Oct.	Nov.	Dec.	Total
1969	17,844	16,400	16,368	13,753	11,240	10,089	9,882	9,545	9,466	10,306	12,899	16,105	153,897
1970	18,658	17,330	16,630	15,277	12,257	10,543	10,135	10,202	10,075	10,811	12,837	15,664	160,419
1971	18,868	18,735	17,690	15,586	13,117	11,447	10,528	10,369	10,232	11,004	13,052	16,179	166,795
1972	18,331	19,081	17,591	15,451	13,006	11,735	10,578	11,277	10,963	11,218	13,809	17,991	171,082
1973	19,094	17,528	16,453	15,001	13,321	11,438	11,048	10,690	10,631	11,365	13,067	15,163	164,799
1974	18,476	17,072	16,307	14,936	12,516	11,199	10,508	10,349	9,923	11,152	12,198	15,367	160,003
1975	17,095	16,336	15,884	14,553	11,208	9,448	9,247	9,348	9,354	10,092	11,028	15,036	148,629
1976	17,975	16,446	14,510	12,252	10,998	9,656	9,131	9,008	8,991	9,964	12,783	16,147	148,135
1977	19,019	16,827	14,257	11,684	9,748	9,045	8,758	8,665	8,607	9,767	11,535	15,498	143,409
1978[1]	17,798	18,194	15,989	12,420	10,364	9,105	8,213	8,090	8,086	9,204	11,531	15,503	144,497
1979[1]	19,251	19,238	16,305	13,563	10,746	9,394	9,037	9,209	8,913	10,389	12,534	15,870	154,404
1980[1]	18,279	19,156	17,873	13,734	10,697	9,416	8,838	8,942	8,840	10,047	12,785	16,677	155,284
1981													

[1] Preliminary. [2] Natural, Manufactured and Mixed Gas. *Source: American Gas Association* T.252

Gas Utility Sales in the United States by Types & Class of Service — In Millions of Therms

Year	Total Utility Sales	Natural	Mfg.	Mixed	No. of Cust. (Mil.)	Residential	Commercial	Industrial	Other	Residential Rev.	Commercial Rev.	Industrial Rev.	Other Rev.
1970	160,435	160,930		1,482	41.5	49,237	20,006	84,392	6,740	5,207	1,620	3,181	274
1971	166,857				42.2	50,401	21,555	86,455	8,447	5,635	1,829	3,569	324
1972	170,821				43.0	51,418	22,757	87,757	8,880	6,094	2,064	3,943	364
1973	164,799				43.7	49,936	22,808	83,708	8,347	6,247	2,172	4,197	371
1974	160,003				44.3	48,648	22,934	81,532	6,890	6,899	2,539	5,391	413
1975	148,629				44.6	49,910	23,868	68,371	6,480	8,445	3,303	6,718	608
1976	148,135				44.9	50,142	24,266	71,070	2,696	9,941	4,075	9,374	311
1977	143,409				45.7	49,463	24,094	67,107	2,746	11,541	4,980	11,385	397
1978	147,480				46.0	51,070	25,000	68,410	3,010	12,939	5,696	13,065	451
1979[1]	154,400				46.7	50,830	24,860	75,550	3,160	14,833	6,624	16,961	530
1980[2]	154,900				47.3	48,230	24,442	78,620	2,830	17,409	8,149	22,081	637
1981[2]	153,380				47.9	45,730	23,570	81,650	2,430	19,208	9,267	27,276	727
1982[2]	145,000				48.0								

[1] Preliminary. [2] Estimate. *Source: American Gas Association* T.253

Glass

Housing and automobiles are major users of flat glass, and U.S. flat glass producers in 1982 were adversely affected by the worst automobile production slump in more than two decades and by a 35-year low in new housing starts. A better picture was presented by the high level of office building construction, another major user of flat glass. However, activity in office construction was beginning to taper off because of rising vacancy rates and declining rental rates. In addition, smaller automobiles and homes results in the use of less flat glass per unit, and there is pressure to reduce glass width in automobiles in order to save weight. Nevertheless, flat glass shipments during the next five years are expected to increase at a steady compound annual rate of 5 percent.

Exports have become an increasingly important market for domestic flat glass makers, accounting for nearly 9 percent of domestic production in 1982, while imports declined to less than 4 percent of domestic consumption. Nevertheless, in 1982 flat glass exports, affected by a sluggish world economy and a strong U.S. dollar, declined an estimated 15 percent while imports rose an estimated 23 percent.

Competition has intensified in recent years due to the installation of several new float glass facilities, and many corporations have closed older plants and consolidated production in more efficient plants.

All Flat Glass Mfr.'s Shipments in the U.S., by Quarters   In Millions of Dollars

Year	1st	2nd	3rd	4th	Total	Year	1st	2nd	3rd	4th	Total
1974	146.0	149.5	135.4	112.6	543.4	1979	210.2	205.3	216.1	226.6	858.1
1975	85.7	105.2	131.1	145.9	468.0	1980[1]	220.3	191.8	211.0	248.0	868.5
1976	153.8	160.1	159.5	171.4	644.8	1981[1]	233.4	248.7	243.3	226.9	952.3
1977	165.6	182.8	192.8	198.8	739.9	1982[1]	195.0	219.1	220.5	236.8	871.3

[1] Preliminary.   Source: Bureau of Census   T.254

Index of Wholesale Price of Flat Glass (Sheet, Plate & Float)[1]   Dec. 1980 = 100

Year	Jan.	Feb.	Mar.	Apr.	May	June	July	Aug.	Sept.	Oct.	Nov.	Dec.	Average
1976	8.208	8.208	9.178	9.178	9.178	9.178	9.178	9.178	9.178	9.178	9.178	9.178	9.016
1977	9.300	9.553	9.553	9.553	9.675	9.675	9.675	9.675	9.675	10.023	10.390	10.390	9.761
1978	10.390	10.390	10.390	10.863	10.863	10.863	10.998	10.998	10.998	10.998	10.998	11.138	10.824
1979	11.138	N.A.	N.A.	N.A.	11.444	N.A.	N.A.	11.870	12.030	12.145	12.436	N.A.	11.844
1980[1]	N.A.	12.436	12.152	12.152	N.A.	12.152	12.152	12.152	12.152	N.A.	12.642	100.0	—
1981	100.7	101.0	101.7	109.6	109.6	109.7	109.7	109.7	109.7	109.9	109.9	106.6	107.3
1982	106.4	106.4	106.6	106.6	106.6	106.6	106.6	106.6	106.6	106.6	107.1	107.1	106.7
1983	110.6	110.6											

[1] Prior to December, 1980 wholesale price of WINDOW GLASS (Single B) in dollars per 50 square feet, 40 Bracket, mfg. to jobber, carlots, f.o.b. factory freight prepaid.   Source: Bureau of Labor Statistics (1311-05)   T.255

United States Production of Glass Containers   In Millions of Gross

Year	Jan.	Feb.	Mar.	Apr.	May	June	July	Aug.	Sept.	Oct.	Nov.	Dec.	Total
1974	24.4	20.8	25.1	23.4	23.1	25.3	25.0	26.0	22.8	25.7	21.6	17.1	280.4
1975	22.7	21.4	22.9	23.0	23.1	24.3	25.3	25.3	25.2	27.0	22.9	19.9	283.1
1976	23.8	24.1	26.2	24.7	26.2	26.6	25.1	28.6	24.3	27.6	24.2	21.0	302.5
1977	22.6	24.3	28.1	24.4	25.7	27.1	26.5	29.5	21.3	25.8	26.5	21.6	303.5
1978	26.0	25.4	28.9	28.8	29.2	28.8	26.9	29.4	26.2	30.0	25.7	21.4	327.6
1979	26.1	26.1	29.3	27.6	28.8	28.6	27.3	28.7	23.5	28.6	26.0	21.3	322.0
1980	27.3	28.1	28.6	27.2	26.6	27.1	27.3	28.6	27.0	29.8	25.4	21.1	328.0
1981	26.0	25.5	28.2	27.9	28.2	29.5	27.8	29.4	25.9	29.3	23.8	19.9	321.4
1982	24.4	26.1	29.2	26.7	27.3	27.9	26.0	28.0	24.7	27.7	23.4	18.0	309.4

Source: Bureau of the Census   T.256

United States Shipments (Domestic) of Glass Containers   In Millions of Gross

Year	Jan.	Feb.	Mar.	Apr.	May	June	July	Aug.	Sept.	Oct.	Nov.	Dec.	Total
1974	23.7	22.7	28.6	22.6	19.8	22.2	24.6	27.7	22.1	21.1	19.4	19.1	273.7
1975	24.2	17.9	21.3	22.6	23.8	25.4	29.5	23.8	23.5	23.9	21.0	22.2	279.0
1976	22.6	21.5	31.4	20.4	24.1	25.3	24.6	27.3	27.7	22.7	21.8	22.9	292.3
1977	22.2	22.5	34.2	21.2	23.9	26.5	24.5	35.4	23.8	21.6	23.4	25.7	304.8
1978	21.1	22.0	27.4	26.5	34.0	27.2	24.5	29.5	27.7	27.4	25.5	22.8	317.4
1979	24.6	23.0	31.0	25.2	28.1	27.1	25.6	29.4	25.1	27.6	27.0	23.3	316.0
1980	24.8	25.2	28.6	24.9	25.6	27.7	28.5	28.8	30.8	27.2	23.5	23.6	323.9
1981	23.4	23.2	29.3	27.4	26.8	30.2	29.4	27.3	26.5	25.9	24.0	23.8	319.0
1982	24.7	23.3	27.4	26.3	26.8	29.0	25.2	28.2	26.5	26.0	22.9	21.0	307.2

Source: Bureau of the Census   T.257

Gold

The continuing decline in gold prices into mid-1982 was fueled by the adverse influence on investment demand of still-high U.S. interest rates and a reduced rate of inflation, while industrial demand was curbed by the recession. Later in the year, gold prices turned firmer, influenced by the easing of Federal Reserve monetary policy, among other factors.

The price of gold (unfabricated, quoted by Engelhard Industries) began 1982 at $395 per troy ounce and subsequently declined to a 1982 low of $296.75 on June 21. Prices later advanced to a 1982 high of $481 on September 7 before dipping toward the yearend. Spot gold prices started 1983 at a price of $449.50 per ounce, and then rose to $509.25 by mid-February on fears on an imminent international banking crisis. Early in March, prices dropped to around $412.50, buffeted by a rapid deterioration in the world crude oil price structure, before rebounding to about $442 per ounce in mid-April.

World mine production of gold in 1982 totaled about 41.0 million troy ounces, according to a preliminary estimate of the U.S. Bureau of Mines, versus estimated production of 40.78 million ounces in 1981. Much of the increase in estimated production was accounted for by Canada and South Africa. In addition to mine resources, the world's above-ground stocks of gold totaled at least 2.1 billion ounces, of which 1.15 billion were official stocks of the market economy countries, 0.9 billion ounces were privately held, and 0.07 billion ounces were official stocks of centrally planned countries.

U.S. mine production of recoverable gold in 1982 dropped 11 percent from the 1981 level to 1.23 million troy ounces, influenced by a 4-month labor strike at the nation's largest gold mine, the Homestake Mine in Lead, South Dakota, and also by reduced gold prices. U.S. refinery production of gold in 1982, at 3.5 million ounces, was 9 percent below 1981 output, according to the U.S. Bureau of Mines.

Imports of gold by the U.S. for consumption (monetary gold excluded) totaled 4.92 million ounces in 1982 versus 4.65 million in 1981. U.S. exports of gold (monetary gold excluded) dropped to 2.97 million troy ounces in 1982 from 6.44 million in 1981.

Domestic consumption of gold in 1982 approximated 3.41 million ounces versus 2.79 million in 1981, according to preliminary Bureau of Mines data. The use of gold in jewelry and arts increased 35 percent from the 1981 level, and use by the dental trade was up 58 percent. The industrial use of gold was about unchanged from the 1981 level. Jewelry and arts accounted for 58 percent of estimated total domestic consumption in 1982; industrial use, 32 percent; and dental use, 10 percent.

U.S. industry stocks of gold at the end of 1982 totaled about 0.781 million troy ounces versus 0.630 million a year earlier, while futures exchange stocks totaled 2.30 million ounces vs. 2.45 million. U.S. Treasury Department stocks (including gold in the Exchange Stabilization Fund) amounted to 264.046 million ounces versus 264.116 million at the end of 1981. "Earmarked" gold held in foreign and international official accounts at the New York Federal Reserve Bank amounted to 362.009 million ounces, compared with 350.640 million at the end of 1981.

International Monetary Fund data indicated that, as of late 1982, there were no changes from a year earlier in the amounts of gold held by the governments of major countries other than slight reductions in the amounts held by the United States and Canada. There were no sales of gold bullion during 1982 by either the U.S. Treasury Department or the International Monetary Fund.

Futures Markets

The trading of gold futures options was begun on the Commodity Exchange, Inc. in October 1982 under a new pilot program approved earlier by the Commodity Futures Trading Commission. Also, in October, the London Gold Futures Market switched to a dollar-based futures contract from the original sterling-based contract. Gold futures are traded in the U.S. on the Commodity Exchange, Inc. (N.Y.), the International Monetary Market (IMM) and the MidAmerica Commodity Exchange in Chicago. Futures trading in gold is also conducted in London, Winnipeg, Hong Kong, and Tokyo.

World Production of Gold (Mine Output)   In Thousands of Fine Ounces (Troy Ounces)

Year	Australia	Zaire (Congo)	Canada	Colombia	Ghana	India	Japan	Mexico	Nicaragua	Papua N. Guinea	Philippines	Zimbabwe	South Africa	United States	USSR[1]	Total World[1]
1970	620	181	2,409	202	708	104	255	198	115		603	500	32,164	1,743	6,500	47,522
1971	672	172	2,243	189	698	119	255	151	121		637	502	31,389	1,495	6,700	46,495
1972	755	141	2,079	188	724	106	243	146	112		607	502	29,245	1,450	6,900	44,843
1973	554	134	1,954	216	723	105	188	133	85		572	800	27,495	1,176	7,100	43,297
1974	513	131	1,698	265	614	101	140	134	83		538	800	24,388	1,127	7,300	40,124
1975	527	103	1,654	309	524	91	144	145	70		503	600	22,938	1,052	7,500	38,476
1976	503	91	1,692	300	532	101	138	163	76		501	387	22,936	1,048	7,700	39,024
1977	625	80	1,734	257	481	97	149	213	66	740	559	402	22,502	1,100	7,850	38,906
1978	648	76	1,735	246	402	89	145	202	74	751	587	399	22,649	999	8,000	38,983
1979	597	70	1,644	269	362	85	128	190	61	630	535	388	22,617	964	8,160	38,769
1980[2]	544	40	1,627	510	353	79	102	196	60	452	590	368	21,669	970	8,300	39,144
1981[1]	530	70	1,513	535	330	80	99	185	50	540	670	371	21,121	1,378	8,425	40,785
1982[1]			1,800										21,200	1,400		41,000

[1] Estimated.   [2] Preliminary.   Source: U.S. Bureau of Mines

GOLD

Salient U.S. Gold Statistics In Thousands of Troy Ounces

Year	Mine Production	Value Mil. $	Refinery Prod. New (Domestic)	Refinery Prod. Secondary	Exports[2]	Imports[2] For Consumption	Stocks, Dec. 31 Treas. Dept.	Stocks, Dec. 31 Futures Exch.	Industrial	Dental	Consumption Industrial[3]	Consumption Jewelry & Arts	Total	Price $ Per Troy Oz.[4]
1970	1,743	63.4	1,750	2,780	1,074	6,652			3,984	658	1,975	3,340	5,973	36.41
1971	1,495	61.7	1,437	2,202	1,339	7,201			4,375	750	1,884	4,299	6,933	41.25
1972	1,450	85.0	1,478	2,107	1,472	6,126			4,407	750	2,191	4,344	7,285	58.60
1973	1,176	115.0	1,210	1,779	2,985	3,845			4,498	679	2,577	3,473	6,729	97.81
1974	1,127	180.0	1,021	1,926	3,963	2,651			5,670	509	1,740	2,402	4,651	161.08
1975	1,052	169.9	1,093	2,696	3,496	2,662	275	530	788	595	1,059	2,080	3,993	161.49
1976	1,048	131.3	954	2,504	3,531	2,656	275	320	928	694	1,233	2,562	4,648	125.32
1977	1,100	163.2	956	2,454	8,671	4,454	278	1,835	1,976	728	1,209	2,658	4,863	148.31
1978	999	193.3	962	3,085	5,509	4,690	276	2,752	1,672	706	1,313	2,651	4,738	193.55
1979	964	296.6	795	2,883	16,499	4,630	265	2,473	868	646	1,406	2,688	4,785	307.50
1980	970	594.1	773	3,824	6,119	4,542	264	4,998	872	341	1,287	1,505	3,215	612.56
1981[1]	1,378	633.4	801	3,055	6,437	4,652	264	2,449	630	221	1,095	1,455	2,793	459.64
1982[5]	1,227		718	2,784	2,970	4,920	264	2,303	781	349	1,092	1,963	3,412	375.80
1983														

[1] Preliminary. [2] Excludes coinage. [3] Including space & defense. [4] Engelhard selling quotations. [5] Estimate. *Source: Bureau of Mines*
T.260

GOLD CASH PRICE LONDON

WEEKLY HIGH LOW & CLOSE
(BASED ON DAILY EARLY & AFTERNOON QUOTE)

GOLD

High, Low & Closing Prices of December Gold Futures on COMEX In Dollars per Ounce

Year of Delivery		Year Prior to Deliv. Oct.	Nov.	Dec.	Jan.	Feb.	Mar.	Apr.	May	Delivery Year June	July	Aug.	Sept.	Oct.	Nov.	Dec.	Life of Delivery Range
1978	High	179.1	183.6	179.3	191.7	196.5	204.3	193.9	194.3	195.5	210.0	221.5	224.6	249.4	230.7	221.0	249.4
	Low	166.1	167.7	167.8	176.7	183.3	186.1	172.8	175.6	187.2	188.6	201.5	207.6	220.2	191.2	193.0	152.0
	Close	175.0	173.4	178.7	189.4	195.0	194.1	177.0	192.8	189.2	209.8	210.6	220.9	240.7	193.2	219.3	—
1979	High	274.6	257.0	250.8	263.0	278.0	271.6	264.1	291.6	297.6	319.5	330.0	409.0	444.5	421.0	510.0	510.0
	Low	242.0	213.1	214.0	237.2	248.5	251.5	244.0	258.9	284.4	292.4	288.0	330.5	373.0	365.0	424.0	187.6
	Close	267.0	214.9	249.8	253.2	271.6	256.6	262.4	290.7	293.5	297.3	326.7	404.5	385.7	419.1	506.3	—
1980	High	491.5	478.5	625.0	959.9	840.0	757.9	625.0	582.6	693.0	726.0	679.5	748.5	708.5	665.0	638.5	959.9
	Low	420.5	426.0	483.0	644.1	709.0	519.0	533.0	518.4	582.0	620.0	620.0	656.0	627.0	593.0	539.0	270.3
	Close	439.8	476.8	619.1	789.5	732.8	570.3	543.4	575.7	679.8	642.0	656.0	688.5	642.0	624.6	606.5	—
1981	High	814.0	779.0	753.0	690.0	585.5	605.7	585.5	549.0	523.5	453.0	463.0	482.4	469.0	436.0	428.5	981.0
	Low	733.5	695.0	640.0	551.0	538.0	497.2	512.0	502.0	445.5	417.0	405.0	428.0	426.5	392.5	394.5	392.5
	Close	750.2	738.7	680.1	563.4	536.5	562.1	529.5	518.6	449.5	423.2	443.5	443.0	431.2	408.3	393.3	—
1982	High	539.0	500.0	478.0	455.0	433.0	399.5	402.5	375.8	360.0	385.3	441.0	509.0	465.0	443.5	459.5	675.9
	Low	493.0	437.0	441.0	410.0	396.0	340.0	352.0	342.0	311.5	322.5	340.2	396.0	390.0	398.0	431.1	311.5
	Close	496.6	454.1	446.5	428.3	397.8	357.6	369.8	343.0	333.2	355.5	418.5	404.8	423.0	442.6	458.2	—
1983	High	503.0	486.0	505.5	553.0	553.5	467.5	472.0									
	Low	433.0	437.5	470.0	486.5	453.4	431.5	444.5									
	Close	465.0	486.4	489.0	551.7	453.4	442.4	453.5									

Source: Commodity Exchange, Inc. of N.Y. (COMEX) T.266

Gold Total Open Interest at New York (COMEX) & Chicago IMM In Thousands of Contracts

Year	Jan. 1	Feb. 1	Mar. 1	Apr. 1	May 1	June 1	July 1	Aug. 1	Sept. 1	Oct. 1	Nov. 1	Dec. 1	Jan. 1	Apr. 1	July 1	Oct. 1
1978	54.1	55.6	64.3	58.2	51.8	50.4	52.8	60.3	67.8	88.2	116.7	130.7	37.6	40.0	52.8	86.6
1979	183.2	165.4	173.2	160.5	165.2	160.7	143.6	177.9	176.1	171.3	176.2	197.9	99.9	68.7	74.5	61.7
1980	240.1	170.1	163.6	131.8	125.0	108.8	169.3	152.4	166.0	208.4	252.9	254.4	79.6	27.0	60.0	79.9
1981	295.5	211.4	202.5	180.8	187.9	198.6	214.7	215.9	203.1	198.6	202.6	187.3	88.6	54.8	78.5	56.5
1982	175.6	153.0	145.8	134.8	134.6	131.2	139.1	119.0	119.0	110.6	112.6	121.8	33.1	18.7	14.1	8.0
1983	127.7	120.4	123.7	91.6	105.2								7.9	5.2		
1984																

Source: Commodity Exch., Inc. of N.Y. (COMEX) & International Monetary Market of Chicago (IMM) T.261

Total Volume of Trading of Gold Futures at New York (COMEX) In Thousands of Contracts

Year	Jan.	Feb.	Mar.	Apr.	May	June	July	Aug.	Sept.	Oct.	Nov.	Dec.	Total
1978	230.6	170.9	267.7	176.6	176.6	162.5	202.6	411.4	374.4	460.6	550.6	557.9	3,742
1979	607.7	506.8	386.2	335.9	557.9	527.9	601.0	591.3	594.5	552.8	565.5	714.5	6,542
1980	829.3	378.3	560.0	316.1	391.2	652.7	747.2	460.5	839.5	863.5	938.4	1,024.7	8,001
1981	943.6	708.7	994.5	695.7	782.6	780.1	836.5	862.1	1,063.4	769.0	886.8	1,050.5	10,374
1982	922.4	669.0	1,264.7	966.3	708.7	943.3	1,153.5	1,182.7	1,224.7	1,074.1	1,044.2	1,116.6	12,124
1983	1,369.0	1,047.4	1,087.6	712.7									

Source: Commodity Exchange, Inc.—N.Y. (COMEX) T.265

GOLD

GOLD NEW YORK COMEX (WEEKLY HIGH, LOW & CLOSE OF NEAREST FUTURES)
CONTRACT: 100 TROY OZS.

Dollars per ounce

WINNIPEG QUOTED TO JAN. 27, 1975

Commodity Exchange Inc. (COMEX) Warehouse Stocks of Gold   In Thousands of Ounces

Year	Jan. 1	Feb. 1	Mar. 1	Apr. 1	May 1	June 1	July 1	Aug. 1	Sept. 1	Oct. 1	Nov. 1	Dec. 1
1975			301.6	428.7	328.1	442.3	465.8	527.0	562.6	590.6	559.2	517.1
1976	403.2	369.1	342.0	350.8	364.8	355.5	327.3	282.3	270.0	273.1	258.2	258.7
1977	291.8	364.2	359.0	379.9	409.3	454.1	466.7	522.4	601.8	601.2	946.4	1,788
1978	1,822	2,084	2,480	2,736	2,883	2,864	2,796	2,894	2,870	2,734	2,780	2,629
1979	2,604	2,566	2,540	2,501	2,286	2,443	2,700	2,480	2,509	2,512	2,281	2,277
1980	2,253	2,445	2,575	2,897	3,097	3,291	3,386	3,597	3,619	3,832	4,873	5,099
1981	4,814	4,570	4,192	3,897	3,513	3,585	3,417	3,258	2,887	2,776	2,605	2,494
1982	2,366	2,339	2,267	2,196	2,198	2,181	2,047	1,980	1,982	1,971	1,985	2,137
1983	2,247	2,621	2,754	2,645	2,636							
1984												

Source: Commodity Exchange, Inc.—N.Y.

T.263

GOLD

Monthly Average Gold Price (Unfabricated)—Engelhard Industries $ Per Troy Oz.

Year	Jan.	Feb.	Mar.	Apr.	May	June	July	Aug.	Sept.	Oct.	Nov.	Dec.	Average
1975	176.8	180.0	178.6	170.3	167.9	164.7	165.7	163.5	144.1	143.3	143.3	139.8	161.49
1976	125.3	131.7	133.1	128.4	127.4	126.2	118.0	110.1	114.7	116.6	131.4	134.4	124.77
1977	132.9	136.7	148.7	149.7	147.2	141.5	144.0	145.5	150.1	159.4	162.8	161.1	148.31
1978	173.7	178.6	184.1	175.8	176.5	184.1	189.3	206.3	212.4	227.7	206.2	208.1	193.55
1979	227.6	245.8	242.4	239.1	257.6	275.4	295.3	301.7	357.2	392.0	392.6	459.0	307.50
1980	675.4	665.3	553.6	516.8	514.0	600.7	643.3	627.5	675.8	661.2	622.4	594.9	612.56
1981	557.4	500.3	498.8	494.9	479.8	460.8	408.9	410.9	444.1	437.8	412.9	409.3	459.64
1982[2]	384.1	374.1	330.2	350.5	334.4	315.0	340.1	366.0	435.6	421.8	415.0	445.4	375.80
1983[1]	479.8	490.4	419.7	433.0									

[1] Estimate.   [2] Preliminary.   Source: U.S. Bureau of Mines   T.259

U.S. Mine Production of Recoverable Gold   In Thousands of Troy Ounces

Year	Alaska	Arizona	California	Colorado	Idaho	Montana	Nevada	New Mexico	South Dakota	Utah	Other States	Total U.S.
1970	34.8	109.9	5.0	37.1	3.1	22.5	480.1	8.7	578.7	408.0	55.3	1,743.3
1971	13.0	94.0	3.0	42.0	3.6	15.6	374.9	10.7	513.4	369.0	55.9	1,495.1
1972	8.6	103.0	3.4	61.1	2.9	23.7	419.7	14.9	407.4	362.4	41.8	1,449.9
1973	7.1	102.8	3.6	63.4	2.7	27.8	260.4	13.9	357.6	307.1	29.2	1,175.8
1974	9.1	90.6	5.0	52.1	2.9	28.3	298.8	15.4	343.7	254.9	26.0	1,126.9
1975	15.0	85.8	9.6	55.5	2.5	17.3	332.8	15.0	304.9	189.6	24.2	1,052.3
1976	22.9	102.1	10.4	50.8	2.8	24.1	288.0	15.2	318.5	187.3	26.1	1,048.0
1977	19.0	90.2	5.7	72.7	12.9	22.3	324.0	13.6	304.8	210.5	24.0	1,100.3
1978	18.7	93.0	7.5	32.1	20.5	20.0	260.9	9.9	285.5	235.9	14.6	998.8
1979	6.7	101.8	5.0	13.9	24.1	24.1	250.1	15.0	245.9	260.9	16.3	964.4
1980	12.9	79.6	4.1	39.4	[2]	48.4	278.5	15.8	267.6	179.5	40.0	969.8
1981	25.3	100.3	6.3	51.1	[2]	54.3	524.8	65.7	278.2	227.7	41.4	1,377.9
1982[1]	17.1	59.4	[2]	[2]	[2]	50.3	592.6	47.4	185.0	175.8	98.9	1,226.5
1983												

[1] Preliminary.   [2] Included in "OTHER STATES."   Source: Bureau of Mines   T.262

U.S. Monetary Stock of Gold at End of Month   In Billions of Dollars

Year	Jan.	Feb.	Mar.	Apr.	May	June	July	Aug.	Sept.	Oct.	Nov.	Dec.
1971	10.73	10.73	10.73	10.73	10.33	10.33	10.33	10.33	10.13	10.13	10.13	10.13
1972	10.13	9.59	9.59	9.59	10.41	10.41	10.41	10.41	10.41	10.41	10.41	10.41
1973	10.410	10.410	10.410	10.410	10.410	10.410	10.410	10.410	10.410	11.567	11.567	11.567
1974	11.567	11.567	11.567	11.567	11.567	11.567	11.567	11.567	11.567	11.567	11.567	11.652
1975	11.635	11.621	11.620	11.620	11.620	11.620	11.618	11.599	11.599	11.599	11.599	11.599
1976	11.599	11.599	11.599	11.598	11.598	11.598	11.598	11.598	11.598	11.598	11.598	11.598
1977	11.658	11.650	11.636	11.636	11.629	11.620	11.595	11.595	11.595	11.595	11.595	11.719
1978	11.718	11.718	11.718	11.718	11.718	11.706	11.693	11.679	11.668	11.655	11.642	11.671
1979	11.592	11.544	11.479	11.418	11.354	11.323	11.290	11.259	11.228	11.194	11.112	11.112
1980	11.172	11.172	11.172	11.172	11.172	11.172	11.172	11.172	11.168	11.163	11.162	11.160
1981	11.159	11.156	11.154	11.154	11.154	11.154	11.154	11.154	11.152	11.152	11.151	11.151
1982	11.151	11.150	11.150	11.149	11.149	11.149	11.149	11.148	11.148	11.148	11.148	11.148
1983	11.144	11.139										

Source: Federal Reserve Board   T.264

Grain Sorghums

The 1982 U.S. sorghum crop totaled 841 million bushels, 4 percent below the 1981 crop but 45 percent more than the drought-stricken 1980 crop. The 59.0 bushel yield per acre in 1982 was 5.1 bushels below the record-high yield reached in 1981. The 1982/83 season supply of sorghum, however, totaled 1,138 million bushels vs. 988 million the previous season due to the sharp increase in beginning stocks, most of which were in CCC inventory or in loans.

The USDA estimated total disappearance of sorghum during the 1982/83 season at 661 million bushels versus 691 million the previous season. Disappearance of sorghum during the October–December 1982 period totaled 345 million bushels versus 310 million for the same period in 1981, leaving 793 million on hand January 1, 1983, up 103 million from a year earlier. However, more than one-half the January 1, 1983 stocks were in CCC inventory or under loan, and the "free" stocks totaled only 345 million bushels, 100 million less than a year earlier. Stocks of sorghum in all positions on April 1, 1983 totaled 618.5 million bushels, compared with 461.9 million a year earlier. But 506.8 million bushels of the total was owned by the CCC or was in the farmer-owned grain reserve on that date compared with 254.3 million a year earlier. Ending stocks of sorghum for the 1982/83 season were forecast at 477 million bushels by the USDA, up from 297 million at the beginning of the season, but "free" stocks were expected to be exceptionally small.

During 1967–81, the sorghum price per bushel averaged 91.2 percent of the price of corn, ranging from a low of 83.9 to a high of 96.2 percent. In early 1983, the sorghum price was equal to the corn price.

In late April 1983, the USDA forecast 1983 production of sorghum at 700 million bushels and a total 1983/84 supply of 1,177 million bushels. Feed disappearance during the 1983/84 season was projected at 450 million bushels vs. an estimated 425 million for 1982/83, and exports at 250 million bushels vs. an estimated 225 million for 1982/83. Total use in the 1983/84 season was projected at 711 million bushels versus the estimated 661 million for 1982/83, and ending stocks were forecast at 466 million bushels versus estimated 1982/83 ending stocks of 477 million bushels.

U.S. Government Price Support

The target price for 1983-crop grain sorghum was set at $2.72 per bushel. The 1983-crop loan rate was set at $2.52 per bushel. Producers who reduced their base acreage by 20 percent are eligible for program benefits, including price-support loans and target-price protection. Producers who participated in the 1983 feed grain program could request advance diversion payments equal to 50 percent of the full rate. The 50 percent advance payment for sorghum producers equals 75 cents per bushel. In addition, producers could request 50 percent of their projected 1983 deficiency payments estimated at 20 cents per bushel for grain sorghum (10 cents advance payment).

Salient Statistics of Grain Sorghums in the United States

Crop Year	Acreage Planted[2] for All Purposes — 1,000 Acres —	Acreage Harv.	Production 1,000 Bushels	Yield Per Harv. Acre Bushels	Price Cents Per Bushel	Produc. Value 1,000 Dollars	Acreage Harv. 1,000 Acres	Production 1,000 Tons	Yield Per Harv. Acre Tons	For Forage Acreage Harv. 1,000 Acres	Used on Farms where Produced (In Mil. Bushels)	Sold	Mutual Security (AID) (In Ths. Metric Tons)	Total
1974-5	17,676	13,809	622,711	45.1	277	1,721,927	745	7,279	9.7	2,140	162.8	459.9	—	158
1975-6	18,104	15,403	754,354	49.0	236	1,777,100	763	7,492	9.9	1,438	174.7	579.9	148	210
1976-7	18,402	14,466	710,797	49.1	203	1,431,190	793	7,317	9.3	1,802	203.6	507.2	(610)	(657)
1977-8	16,993	13,797	780,944	56.6	182	1,411,570	839	9,184	10.9	1,556	249.3	531.6	1,306	1,834
1978-9	16,197	13,410	731,270	54.5	201	1,464,187	724	7,920	10.9	1,449	236.5	494.8	1,440	2,024
1979-0	15,277	12,901	808,862	62.7	234	1,879,823	764	9,015	11.8	1,211	260.3	548.5	1,445	2,130
1980-1	15,644	12,522	579,197	46.3	294	1,696,008	732	7,002	9.6	1,410	195.5	392.5	224	1,085
1981-2[1]	16,020	13,716	879,222	64.1	239	2,087,223	772	9,312	12.1	1,080				
1982-3[1]	16,144	14,247	841,079	59.0	222	1,856,239	581	7,167	12.3	927				
1983-4[1]	13,068													

[1] Preliminary. [2] Grain and sweet sorghums for all uses including sirup. *Source: Crop Reporting Board, U.S.D.A.* T.267

Production of All Sorghums for Grain in the United States, by States — In Thousands of Bushels

Year	Iowa	Arizona	California	Colorado	Kansas	Missouri	Nebraska	New Mexico	No. Carolina	Oklahoma	South Dakota	Texas	Arkansas
1975	1,612	8,160	14,904	7,540	144,060	28,090	104,500	15,500	4,335	19,760	6,422	374,400	9,800
1976	1,690	6,643	14,910	7,252	169,850	39,600	119,700	11,940	4,590	16,950	3,496	292,900	15,500
1977	2,368	7,200	9,636	8,153	243,000	67,890	146,970	11,760	2,664	21,470	16,807	230,400	13,104
1978	1,800	1,950	9,585	10,540	196,860	66,300	140,250	12,282	4,042	17,460	17,750	227,850	12,000
1979	1,406	1,775	10,500	12,920	246,330	59,040	151,680	13,416	3,750	23,175	15,525	243,000	10,912
1980	1,330	1,950	11,096	12,250	149,640	41,280	121,800	10,280	2,232	16,320	10,725	181,700	5,887
1981	1,600	2,158	8,880	12,775	238,520	75,200	164,800	12,240	4,134	22,050	19,565	273,420	16,986
1982[1]	650	1,092	10,010	12,920	207,700	70,470	121,910	14,570	3,710	19,890	17,250	305,250	15,780

[1] Preliminary, December estimate. *Source: Crop Reporting Board, U.S.D.A.* T.268

GRAIN SORGHUMS

U.S. Grain Sorghum Quarterly Supply and Disappearance   In Millions of Bushels

Year & Period Beginning Oct. 1	Begin. Stocks	Production	Imports	Total Supply	Food	Alc. Beverages	Seed	Feed & Resid.	Total	Exports	Total	Gov't. Owned[1]	Privately Owned[2]	Total Stocks
1979-0	159.5	808.9	[4]	968.4	6.0	4.6	2.0	484.4	497.0	324.9	821.9	43.9	102.6	146.5
Oct.-Dec.	159.5	808.9	—	968.4	1.3	1.3	—	243.6	246.5	74.2	320.7	45.3	602.4	647.7
Jan.-Mar.	647.7	—	—	647.7	1.6	1.2	.2	140.2	143.2	108.5	251.7	45.6	350.4	396.0
Apr.-May	396.0	—	—	396.0	1.4	.7	1.2	54.5	57.8	60.3	118.1	45.6	252.3	277.9
June-Sept.	277.9	—	[4]	277.9	1.4	1.4	.6	46.1	49.5	81.9	131.4	43.9	102.6	146.5
1980-1	146.5	579.2	[4]	725.7	5.0	4.3	2.0	307.1	318.4	298.7	617.1	38.2	70.4	108.6
Oct.-Dec.	146.5	579.2	[4]	725.7	1.6	1.2	—	198.2	201.0	60.3	261.3	43.7	420.7	464.4
Jan.-Mar.	464.4	—	[4]	464.4	1.6	.9	.2	63.8	66.5	84.1	150.6	43.5	270.3	313.8
Apr.-May	313.8	—	[4]	313.8	.8	.7	1.2	84.8	87.5	41.7	129.2	43.8	140.7	184.6
June-Sept.	184.5	—	[4]	184.6	1.0	1.5	.6	-39.7	-36.6	112.6	76.0	38.2	70.4	108.6
1981-2[3]	108.6	879.2	[4]	987.8	4.3	4.8	2.0	431.0	278.1	249.1	691.2	42.9	253.7	296.6
Oct.-Dec.	108.6	879.2	[4]	987.8	1.3	1.3	—	217.9	220.5	77.8	298.3	38.4	651.1	689.5
Jan.-Mar.	689.5	—	[4]	689.5	1.3	1.3	.2	150.5	153.3	74.3	227.6	38.2	423.7	461.9
Apr.-May	461.9	—	[4]	461.9	2.5	.8	1.2	57.8	60.3	21.8	82.1	40.3	339.5	379.8
June-Sept.	379.8	—	[4]	379.8	1.2	1.4	.6	4.8	8.0	75.2	83.2	42.9	253.7	296.6
1982-3[5]	296.6	841.1	[4]	1,138	—	11.0	—	334.7	345.7	245.0	590.7			547.0
Oct.-Dec.	296.6	841.1	[4]	1,138	1.4	.9	—	275.8	278.1	67.0	345.1	46.7	745.9	792.6

[1] Uncommitted inventory.   [2] Includes quantity under loan & farmer-owned reserve.   [3] Preliminary.   [4] Less than 50,000 bushels.   [5] Estimate.   Source: *Commodity Economics Division, U.S.D.A.*   T.269

U.S. Exports of Grain Sorghums, by Country of Destination   In Thousands of Metric[2] Tons

Yr. Beg. October	Poland	Belg. & Luxem.	Portugal	Spain	W. Germany	India	Venezuela	Israel	Japan	Senegal	Netherlands	Norway	Mexico	United Kingdom	Total All Exports
1975-6	22,700	18,900	6,300	3,000	3,100	19,600	16,300	25,600	88,000		13,500	4,400	1,600	700	229,000
1976-7	3,647	12,908	17,600	13,900	6	0	1,300	29,214	93,462		6,239	7,542	26,856	2,100	246,107
1977-8[2]	383.7	87.1			.2	—			633.9	2,439.8	60.6	6.7	468.0		5,422.9
1978-9	136.4	—			.8	—			689.4	1,981.1	1.2	37.8	141.5	1,124.0	5,247.1
1979-0	107.5	.3			.3	—			348.0	3,972.7	12.5	69.1	232.8	2,255.2	8,199.2
1980-1[1]	—	60.0			—	—			449.0	2,725.4	13.3	11.5	198.9	2,646.3	7,701.6

[1] Preliminary.   [2] Data prior to 1977-8 are in THOUSANDS OF BUSHELS.   Source: *Grain & Feed Division, U.S.D.A.*   T.270

Average Price of Sorghum Grain, No. 2, Yellow at Kansas City   In Dollars Per 100 Pounds (Cwt.)

Year	Oct.	Nov.	Dec.	Jan.	Feb.	Mar.	Apr.	May	June	July	Aug.	Sept.	Average
1974-5	6.32	6.10	5.36	4.95	4.55	4.48	4.64	4.60	4.53	4.82	5.13	4.66	5.01
1975-6	4.53	4.36	4.33	4.36	4.47	4.62	4.47	4.49	4.66	4.73	4.29	4.27	4.46
1976-7	3.88	3.60	3.77	3.91	3.85	3.75	3.62	3.53	3.28	3.15	2.73	2.78	3.49
1977-8	3.05	3.40	3.36	3.37	3.49	3.78	3.92	3.92	3.82	3.54	3.41	3.43	3.54
1978-9	3.61	3.67	3.64	3.71	3.73	3.77	3.81	3.92	4.41	4.89	4.44	4.34	4.00
1979-0	4.42	4.41	4.57	4.21	4.35	4.20	4.15	4.31	4.49	5.36	5.71	5.61	4.65
1980-1	5.65	5.91	5.82	5.79	5.52	5.46	5.49	5.38	5.23	5.29	4.58	4.16	5.36
1981-2[1]	4.14	4.14	4.27	4.44	4.26	4.28	4.45	4.48	4.50	4.38	4.02	4.06	4.29
1982-3[1]	38.5	4.25	4.37	4.54	4.87	5.08	5.39						

[1] Preliminary.   Source: *Economic Research Service, U.S.D.A.*   T.271

Grain Sorghum Price Support Program & Market Prices

Year Beginning October	Placed Under Price Support Loans	Purchase Agreements	Total	Redeemed by Farmers	Delivered to CCC	In Reserve Prog.	Loans Outstanding	Owned by CCC October 1	Support Loan $ Per Cwt.	Target Price	Kansas City	Fort Worth	Los Angeles	Gulf Ports
1975-6	8.8			8	0			0	1.88	2.34	4.46	4.93	5.63	4.94
1976-7	21			19	—			0	2.55	2.66	3.49	3.64	4.68	4.11
1977-8	217			133	41	1	0	0	3.39	4.07	3.54	3.88	4.82	4.16
1978-9	92			87	5	0	0	0	3.39	4.07	4.00	4.40	5.44	4.65
1979-0	64			64	0	0	0	0	3.57	4.18	4.65	4.97	6.32	5.54
1980-1[1]	32			21	1	10	—	10	3.82	4.46	5.36	5.86		6.16
1981-2[2]	277			35	7	223	12	235	4.07	4.55	4.29	4.85		4.97
1982-3[2]	44			0	0	39	5	44	4.32	4.64	4.25	4.48		4.92

[1] Preliminary.   [2] Estimate.   Source: *Economic Research Service, U.S.D.A.*   T.272

Hard Fibers

World production of hard fibers (sisal, henequen, and abaca) in 1982 was expected to be slightly lower than in the preceding year. World sisal and henequen production was forecast at 482,000 tonnes, 6 percent and 30,000 tonnes below estimated 1981 output of 512,000 tonnes. Reduced production prospects in Brazil and Tanzania more than offset increased output in Haiti, Kenya, Mozambique, and Venezuela. Tanzania's sisal industry, once a leading foreign exchange earner, continued to decline as many sisal estates were abandoned and overgrown. The outlook for near term recovery appeared limited in the absence of a massive industry rehabilitation program. Exports of raw sisal by Tanzania in 1982 were expected to total 62,000 tonnes, down from 63,000 tonnes in 1981 and 64,000 tonnes in 1980. Exports of sisal twine and cordage were projected to be down to only 20,000 tonnes in 1982, compared with 22,000 tonnes in 1981 and 25,000 tonnes in 1980. U.S. imports of raw sisal and henequen from all origins in 1981 totaled 3,524 tonnes, down 28 percent from 1980 imports.

World production of abaca in 1982 was expected to total around 77,100 tonnes, down only marginally from 1981 output of 79,800 tonnes, because of reduced production in the Philippines.

Most of the raw sisal and henequen imports into the U.S. in recent years have been used for padding and purposes other than the manufacture of twine. Imports of twine made with sisal and henequen baler and binder have declined in recent years, partly because of changes in hay harvesting methods and partly because of the increased use of domestically produced synthetic fiber twines. Much of the abaca imports reflect its use in the manufacture of specialty paper products, such as tea bags and filters.

World Production of Hard Cordage Fibers   In Thousands of Metric Tons[2]

Year	Abaca Philippines	Abaca Ecuador	Abaca Others	Abaca World Total	Sisal Tanzania	Sisal Haiti	Sisal Brazil	Sisal Angola	Sisal Madagascar	Sisal Mozambique	Sisal Kenya	Sisal World Total	Henequen Mexico	Henequen Others	Henequen World Total
1970	179.2	*Avg.*	*Avg.*	184.2	445.8	42.0	452.0	115.2	*Avg.*	63.9	96.8	1,347	307.5	*Avg.*	353.0
1971	149.0	*(1.0*	*(1.0*	155.6	399.0	28.7	463.0	143.3	*(14.0*	55.1	98.8	1,340	320.0	*(24.2*	335.5
1972	161.4	*M.T.)*	*M.T.)*	169.1	346.0	31.1	573.2	150.0	*M.T.)*	48.5	90.8	1,400	320.0	*M.T.)*	357.0
1973[2]	82.2	4.6	1.0	87.8	155.4	17.0	260.0	70.0	22.0	23.0	70.0	653.0	155.0	16.0	171.0
1974	87.0	9.5	2.0	98.5	135.4	19.0	225.0	70.0	22.6	18.8	86.0	615.1	148.7	14.6	163.3
1975	46.1	9.9	1.5	57.5	123.0	12.0	185.0	40.0	21.0	15.0	43.6	477.0	115.0	14.0	129.0
1976	72.5	13.2	1.5	87.2	119.0	5.0	165.0	25.0	18.6	19.0	33.6	422.5	116.0	14.0	130.0
1977	67.8	9.8	1.5	79.1	105.0	6.0	170.0	3.0	18.8	14.0	32.2	381.5	102.0	6.5	108.5
1978	66.0	11.2	1.5	78.7	92.0	9.0	151.0	7.0	15.9	14.0	31.5	350.4	85.0	6.6	91.6
1979	76.8	9.8	1.5	88.1	81.4	11.0	197.0	7.8	14.9	11.0	36.5	389.6	82.0	6.5	88.5
1980[1]	72.3	10.2	1.5	84.0	77.0	16.0	205.0	8.5	16.0	12.0	47.5	412.0	86.0	6.5	92.5
1981[3]	75.0	10.2	1.5	86.7	81.0	10.0	190.0	9.0	16.0	12.0	31.8	379.8	89.0	6.5	95.5
1982															

[1] Preliminary.   [2] Data prior to 1973 are in MILLIONS OF POUNDS.   [3] Estimate.   *Source: Foreign Agricultural Service, U.S.D.A.*   T.273

Imports[2] of Hard Fibers Into the U.S., by Country of Origin   In Thousands of Metric[3] Tons

Year	Abaca Philippines	Abaca Other	Abaca Ecuador	Abaca Total (All)	Henequen Mexico	Henequen Total (All)	Coir	Sisal Haiti	Sisal Brazil	Sisal Kenya	Sisal Tanzania & Uganda	Sisal Mozambique	Sisal Total (All)	Kapok Total (All)	Kapok Thailand
1970	19.0	— 1.9 —		21.2	26.8	26.8	2.8	7.0	13.8	—	9.7	—	31.8	11.5	10.6
1971	14.7	— 1.4 —		16.2	39.1	39.1	2.6	3.2	8.8	—	7.6	.3	21.8	12.2	11.2
1972	19.0	— 2.0 —		21.0	35.5	35.5	3.7	.4	6.8	—	4.5	.7	13.8	11.0	10.1
1973	17.7	— 2.9 —		20.5	17.5	17.5	5.6	3.3	7.5	—	2.1	—	14.3	13.6	13.3
1974	30.0	— 6.2 —		36.2	.6	.6	9.2	2.4	3.9	—	2.1	.1	9.6	10.1	9.8
1975	9.4	— 9.1 —		18.6			6.1	.6	5.4	—	.5	.6	8.8	6.3	6.2
1976	14.2	— 8.0 —		22.2	.3	.3	6.4	.2	7.1	—	4.0	1.6	14.5	7.5	7.5
1977[3]	14.3	—12.3—		26.7	.1	.1	8.6	—	9.1	1.3	1.0	.2	11.9	5.8	5.8
1978	13.9			22.1	.4	.4	9.7	.1	7.9	12.5	.7	0	21.5	6.3	6.2
1979	16.5	.1	8.1	24.7	.2	.2	10.5	.3	4.9	1.9	.3	.6	8.1	4.8	4.7
1980	19.1	.5	6.6	26.1	.2	.2	11.2	1.4	1.5	1.1	.6	0	4.9	3.1	2.9
1981[1]	13.3	—	7.3	20.6	.1	.1	9.2	.2	1.8	1.3	.2	—	3.5	2.4	2.3
1982															

[1] Preliminary.   [2] Imports for consumption.   [3] Data prior to 1977 are in THOUSANDS OF LONG TONS.   *Source: Dept. of Commerce*   T.274

Hay

Hay production during 1982 was a record 152 million tons, 6 percent above the 143.1 million tons harvested during 1981. Although the area harvested had increased by less than 1 percent, to 60.5 million acres from 60.2 million, the 1982 yield was a record 2.52 tons per acre, 6 percent over the 1981 yield of 2.38 million. The 1982 hay and forage production index was also a record, 118 points compared with the 1977 base of 100. This was 11 percent above the 1981 index and 20 percent above the 1980 figure. As a direct result of the record hay crop, stocks on farms were 108 million tons as of January 1, 1983, 8 percent more than in 1982, 17 percent above 1981, and only fractionally below the 1980 record. Adding carryover stocks of 25.2 million tons to the 1982 hay crop gave a total supply of 177.7 million tons available for the 1982/83 crop year from May to April. This season's supply of hay was nearly equal to the record supply of 177.9 million tons recorded during 1979/80.

Because of a greater increase in yield per acre, the production of alfalfa and alfalfa mixtures of hay increased more than the harvest of other types of hay. The increase in area harvested amounted to about a half a percent for each type of hay.

The severe winter of 1982 increased the amount of hay fed, and hay prices were firmer during the late winter and spring. Despite seasonal declines recorded since May 1982, prices have generally held above those of the previous year. The USDA estimated that the number of beef cows that had calved on farms as of July 1, 1982 was 4 percent below year-earlier levels and that the number of heifers held for herd replacement was down by 2 percent. This means that the number of roughage-consuming animal units (RCAU) available for the 1982/83 hay crop should have been lower than a year ago. The large hay stocks and the generally favorable spring grazing conditions were expected to contribute to holding down hay prices during 1983. Additional grazing or hay may become available in 1983 because of the winter wheat PIK program.

Silage production from corn declined by 2 percent during 1982, and sorghum silage dropped by 29 percent.

Salient Statistics of All Hay in the United States

Year Beginning May	Acres Harvested 1,000 Acres	Yield Per Acre Tons	Production	Carryover May 1	Disappearance	Kept on Farms	Sold	Supply Per Animal Unit In Tons	Disappearance Animal Units Fed[2] Millions	Farm Price[3] $ Per Ton	Farm Produc. Value Million $	Alfalfa Seed	Timothy Seed	Red Clover Seed
1971-2	61,355	2.10	129.1	22.2	125.8	104.1	25.1	1.66	1.38	91.1	28.10	3,335	35.00	8.05	27.50
1972-3	59,680	2.15	128.6	25.5	129.8	102.8	25.8	1.65	1.39	93.2	31.30	3,730	43.60	15.60	40.70
1973-4	61,828	2.17	134.2	24.3	133.0	107.0	27.2	1.59	1.34	99.5	41.60	5,004	86.40	31.80	61.90
1974-5	60,195	2.10	126.4	25.4	133.3	100.9	25.5	1.46	1.28	103.8	50.90	5,791	83.70	21.30	58.40
1975-6	61,353	2.16	132.4	18.5	125.4	105.6	26.6	1.54	1.28	98.2	52.20	6,458	68.60	14.80	49.50
1976-7	60,377	1.99	120.1	25.5	126.1	94.7	25.5	1.54	1.33	94.8	60.20	6,815	102.00	27.50	63.10
1977-8	60,988	2.17	132.2	19.5	127.5	105.1	27.1	1.69	1.42	89.5	53.70	6,826	108.00	50.60	73.80
1978-9	62,113	2.32	143.8	24.2	137.9	115.5	28.3	1.95	1.60	86.0	49.80	6,664	117.00	43.50	68.00
1979-0	61,666	2.40	147.8	30.1	144.6	118.8	29.0	2.03	1.65	87.5	59.50	7,363	114.00	34.30	62.60
1980-1	59,362	2.21	131.1	33.3	138.9	103.6	27.4	1.83	1.55	89.9	71.00	8,104	113.00	50.20	65.20
1981-2[1]	60,192	2.38	143.2	25.4	143.4			1.84	1.56	91.8	67.10	9,218			
1982-3[1]	60,679	2.51	152.4	25.2				1.96		90.5	68.90	9,649			
1983-4															

[1] Preliminary. [2] Roughage-consuming animal units fed annually. [3] Price of hay sold baled, for year beginning July. Source: Economic Research Service, U.S.D.A.
T.275

How to keep your Commodity Year Book statistics up-to-date continuously throughout the year.

To keep up-to-date statistics on the commodities in this book, you should have COMMODITY YEAR BOOK STATISTICAL ABSTRACT SERVICE. This three-times-yearly publication provides the latest available statistics for the updating of the statistical tables appearing in the COMMODITY YEAR BOOK. It is published in the Winter (Jan.), Spring (Apr.) and Fall (Oct.). Subscription price is $55 per year.

Commodity Research Bureau, Inc.
75 MONTGOMERY ST., JERSEY CITY, N.J. 07302

HAY

U.S. Types of Hay Production & Farm Stocks   In Millions of Short Tons

Year	Alfalfa & Mixtures	All Other	All Hay	Corn for Silage[1]	Sorghum[1] Silage	Farm Stocks Jan. 1	Farm Stocks May 1
1971	77.2	52.0	129.1	109.3	11.0	87.7	22.2
1972	78.0	50.6	128.6	109.3	9.9	89.4	25.5
1973	79.1	55.6	134.2	114.3	9.5	88.8	24.3
1974	74.7	52.5	126.4	115.7	7.3	93.2	25.4
1975	78.0	54.2	132.4	116.1	7.5	84.7	18.5
1976	69.8	50.2	120.1	118.4	7.3	86.2	25.5
1977	80.4	50.9	132.2	117.7	9.2	77.4	19.5
1978	87.3	56.5	143.8	118.1	7.9	92.1	24.2
1979	88.3	59.5	147.8	114.9	9.0	99.1	30.1
1980	79.9	51.1	131.0	111.0	7.0	108.2	33.3
1981	83.8	59.4	143.2	115.5	9.3	99.7	25.2
1982[2]	90.5	61.9	152.4	112.7	7.2	108.0	
1983							

[1] Not included in all tame hay.   [2] Preliminary.   Source: Crop Reporting Board, U.S.D.A.   T.276

Production of All Hay in the United States by Important States   In Millions of Tons

Year	Calif.	Idaho	Ill.	Iowa	Mich.	Minn.	Mo.	No. Dak.	Nebr.	N.Y.	Ohio	Pa.	So. Dak.	Wis.	Texas
1971	7.9	3.8	3.2	6.7	2.7	8.2	5.4	4.9	6.9	5.4	3.2	4.4	5.7	11.1	4.1
1972	8.2	3.7	3.4	7.0	3.1	8.2	5.5	5.1	7.1	4.5	3.1	3.8	7.3	10.2	3.9
1973	7.9	4.1	3.3	7.3	3.4	8.0	5.9	4.2	7.5	5.2	3.3	4.3	5.6	10.6	5.8
1974	7.7	4.4	3.2	6.5	3.0	7.5	5.4	4.7	6.3	5.3	3.0	4.2	5.2	10.6	5.1
1975	7.6	4.4	3.5	6.9	3.3	8.0	5.6	5.3	6.5	5.1	3.6	4.3	5.7	10.6	5.2
1976	7.6	4.2	3.5	6.7	3.1	5.8	4.9	4.0	6.0	5.4	3.6	4.1	2.8	8.1	5.4
1977	7.7	4.5	3.7	7.4	2.9	8.1	5.7	3.2	7.5	4.6	3.6	3.9	6.3	12.0	4.7
1978	7.0	4.7	3.6	8.5	3.9	8.8	6.0	6.3	7.5	5.3	3.9	4.3	8.3	11.6	5.4
1979	7.3	4.1	3.8	8.7	3.8	8.9	6.2	5.7	7.6	5.5	3.6	4.3	7.6	12.6	7.1
1980	7.7	4.4	3.6	8.0	3.8	7.1	4.5	2.5	7.1	5.8	3.6	4.2	5.4	12.5	5.5
1981	7.9	4.5	3.5	8.2	3.9	8.2	6.8	4.8	7.0	5.3	3.5	4.5	5.8	11.1	7.0
1982[1]	7.7	4.4	3.6	8.3	4.4	8.3	6.5	5.6	7.8	5.3	3.6	4.8	8.6	13.2	6.7
1983															

[1] Preliminary.   Source: Crop Reporting Board, U.S.D.A.   T.277

Average Price Received by Farmers for All Hay (Baled) on the 15th of Month   In Dollars Per Ton

Crop Year	May	June	July	Aug.	Sept.	Oct.	Nov.	Dec.	Jan.	Feb.	Mar.	Apr.	Average[1]
1971–2	25.60	24.60	24.10	24.30	24.50	24.90	25.30	26.10	29.20	29.70	29.00	28.00	28.00
1972–3	31.30	30.90	28.50	29.30	29.80	30.30	31.00	33.00	34.60	35.40	35.40	33.90	31.30
1973–4	37.50	35.20	36.30	39.00	43.10	46.20	46.80	46.00	47.10	47.10	45.40	44.40	41.60
1974–5	54.00	47.70	48.20	51.10	51.90	51.50	50.30	50.70	50.10	49.30	49.70	52.40	50.90
1975–6	56.30	53.60	51.20	51.00	50.80	50.30	50.20	51.60	52.70	54.30	54.10	54.10	52.10
1976–7	64.10	59.60	59.00	58.70	60.80	60.10	59.00	59.00	60.90	62.70	63.90	63.20	60.20
1977–8	68.10	61.30	56.80	52.50	50.00	48.20	48.40	49.50	50.50	51.80	51.40	51.40	53.70
1978–9	55.30	51.20	49.20	49.00	47.80	47.10	46.40	47.30	48.90	50.70	50.20	49.90	49.80
1979–0	65.60	58.00	56.00	57.50	59.00	60.80	58.90	60.10	59.10	60.00	57.40	60.10	59.50
1980–1	69.30	65.10	67.00	67.20	71.90	77.20	75.00	74.80	72.80	72.50	69.80	68.20	71.00
1981–2[2]	75.30	66.90	64.00	63.90	62.70	64.80	65.40	65.70	67.90	69.90	69.50	73.10	67.43
1982–3[2]	77.10	70.90	66.60	65.00	64.80	67.60	68.10	68.80	70.10	74.60			
1983–4													

[1] Weighted average by sales.   [2] Preliminary.   Source: Crop Reporting Board, U.S.D.A.   T.278

Heating Oil

Heating oil is a light fuel oil that has been distilled off during the petroleum refining process. The yield of distillate fuel per barrel of petroleum averages 20 percent. Distillate fuel oil includes products known as No. 1 and No. 2 heating oils, diesel fuels, and No. 4 fuel oil. Distillate fuels are used in the generation of electricity and steam, for space heating, and on- and off-highway diesel engine fuel (including railroad engine fuel), and distillate fuels are also used in the production of glass and ceramics.

Preliminary figures indicated that the U.S. distillate fuel oil refinery production in 1982 averaged 2.6 million barrels per day, virtually unchanged from the 1981 level. U.S. imports of distillate fuel oil averaged 96 thousand barrels per day in 1982, nearly a 45 percent drop from 1981. Average stock withdrawal during 1982 was 15 thousand barrels per day compared with 38 thousand barrels per day during the previous year. The total distillate fuel oil product supplied (disposition) in the U.S. in 1982 amounted to 2.7 million barrels per day, only fractionally greater than 1982 production, and nearly 6 percent off the total product supplied during 1981. Distillate fuel oil stocks were estimated at 181 million barrels at the end of December 1982, 5 million barrels lower than at the end of November 1982, and 11 million barrels below the stock level at the end of 1981.

During 1982, the free world consumption of petroleum products declined by about 3 percent. The corresponding decline in petroleum production by The Organization of Petroleum Exporting Countries (OPEC) surpassed the drop in worldwide consumption during the year, the balance of consumption having been supplied through increased Mexican and North Sea production. In the U.S., distillate fuel oil consumption declined by nearly 2 percent from the 1981 level because of a 7 percent drop in domestric industrial production.

In the first few months of 1983, the OPEC benchmark price of a barrel of Saudi Arabian light crude oil dropped from $34 to $29 a barrel reflecting worldwide consumer price resistance and large oil stocks as well as a developing price war with non-OPEC oil producing nations, especially the United Kingdom. In early 1983, OPEC members agreed to a production ceiling of 17.5 million barrels per day, nearly half of its peak 1979 production of 31 million barrels per day, and many analysts were saying that oil prices had found a bottom.

The drop in heating oil prices was observed to be generally less sharp than the drop in crude oil prices during 1982. The lag was attributed to refiners' attempts to recoup earlier high crude oil costs and to distributors' similar attempts to market heating oil bought at earlier, higher prices.

Futures Markets

Heating Oil futures and N.Y. Harbor Leaded Gasoline are traded on the New York Mercantile Exchange (NYMEX). Gasoil (Heating Oil) futures are traded on the International Petroleum Exchange (IPE) in London. The Chicago Board of Trade listed a Heating Oil futures contract in April 1983.

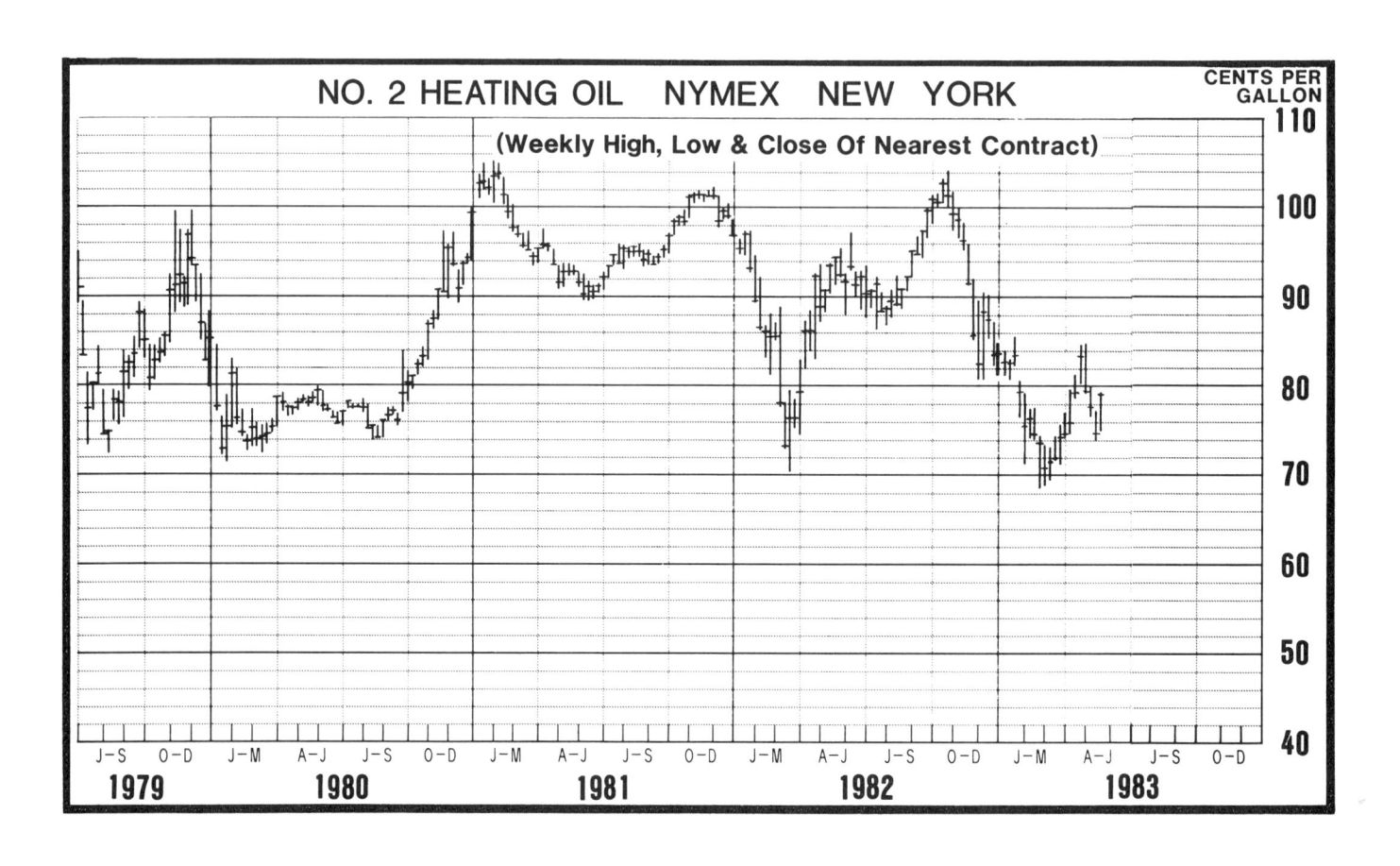

HEATING OIL

High, Low & Closing Prices of January Heating Oil Futures[1] in N.Y. In Cents per Gallon

Year of Delivery		Jan.	Feb.	Mar.	Apr.	May	Year Prior to Delivery[2] June	July	Aug.	Sept.	Oct.	Nov.	Dec.[2]	Life of Delivery Range
1980	High	—	—	69.50	70.20	102.50	106.50	91.00	88.00	94.00	95.30	102.75	99.75	106.50
	Low	—	—	59.25	69.50	90.00	91.50	74.75	78.00	83.20	83.00	92.75	82.75	59.25
	Close	—	—	69.50	70.00	102.50	92.25	80.50	85.50	89.00	95.30	97.00	82.75	—
1981	High	—	—	—	94.00	93.25	91.00	86.50	82.00	87.50	90.25	99.00	97.25	99.00
	Low	—	—	—	88.00	90.25	85.90	81.50	78.45	79.00	83.15	88.50	89.25	78.45
	Close	—	—	—	92.50	91.00	86.60	81.55	81.12	84.55	89.50	95.62	96.90	—
1982	High	—	114.00	113.10	110.70	103.40	101.10	103.75	103.05	99.35	102.35	102.85	101.75	114.00
	Low	—	113.75	109.50	101.00	100.10	97.00	99.35	98.10	96.70	99.00	101.50	96.95	96.70
	Close	—	114.50	109.50	102.00	100.95	99.90	102.35	98.19	98.89	102.06	101.78	97.10	—
1983	High	—	—	85.00	95.75	100.40	98.75	93.60	96.65	101.95	104.20	99.20	90.60	104.20
	Low	—	—	82.00	85.50	94.00	90.61	89.25	90.70	95.55	97.10	84.20	79.81	79.81
	Close	—	—	85.00	94.40	97.00	91.08	90.80	96.30	99.79	98.29	86.52	82.81	—
1984	High	—	—	75.25	84.25									
	Low	—	—	68.70	78.50									
	Close	—	—	74.60	82.49									

[1] No. 2 heating oil. [2] Contract expires the last business day of the previous calendar month quoted. *Source: N.Y. Mercantile Exchange* T.281

Month End Open Interest of Heating Oil[1] Futures in New York In Contracts

Year	Jan.	Feb.	Mar.	Apr.	May	June	July	Aug.	Sept.	Oct.	Nov.	Dec.
1978					FUTURES TRADING BEGAN NOV. 14, 1978						12	55
1979	327	200	118	299	370	485	1,165	1,280	1,894	1,952	2,221	1,973
1980	2,186	2,590	2,032	2,324	2,622	2,948	3,286	5,889	8,365	11,884	13,519	11,556
1981	11,792	12,040	13,256	14,893	17,919	16,822	19,220	28,102	36,996	35,519	33,517	31,585
1982	22,042	15,655	21,121	18,502	19,248	21,277	21,676	20,815	22,500	29,614	24,486	21,848
1983	19,642	23,307	18,980	22,868								
1984												

[1] No. 2 heating oil. *Source: N.Y. Mercantile Exchange* T.279

Volume of Trading of Heating Oil Futures[1] in New York In Contracts

Year	Jan.	Feb.	Mar.	Apr.	May	June	July	Aug.	Sept.	Oct.	Nov.	Dec.	Total
1978					FUTURES TRADING BEGAN NOV. 14, 1978						37	79	116
1979	365	515	182	369	502	1,377	2,156	2,205	2,847	5,895	9,371	8,010	33,804
1980	8,512	8,427	5,146	4,798	3,421	5,923	6,074	11,564	27,430	40,525	53,098	63,366	238,284
1981	67,368	58,514	55,299	65,350	58,933	76,580	86,394	100,102	99,790	121,455	78,972	126,749	995,532
1982	165,079	148,794	176,373	146,821	98,440	135,181	107,102	118,496	120,830	167,439	177,832	183,139	1,745,526
1983	153,864	112,649	137,237	121,300									
1984													

[1] No. 2 heating oil. *Source: N.Y. Mercantile Exchange* T.280

U.S. Gross Input to Crude Oil Distillation Units In Millions of 42-Gallon Barrels

Year	Jan.	Feb.	Mar.	Apr.	May	June	July	Aug.	Sept.	Oct.	Nov.	Dec.	Total
1970	336.9	304.8	335.9	318.4	324.0	326.2	355.5	341.7	330.3	336.6	330.6	346.7	3,968
1971	344.9	312.3	345.1	336.2	332.8	344.5	355.0	352.4	334.0	345.5	333.6	351.5	4,088
1972	353.0	329.3	351.7	335.5	355.8	355.2	368.4	369.4	363.4	368.0	355.5	375.5	4,281
1973	377.9	341.2	378.2	366.2	380.7	385.9	395.2	391.7	376.8	395.5	371.2	376.6	4,537
1974	373.2	326.5	368.7	371.6	400.4	398.8	414.1	409.1	380.0	398.3	386.0	404.9	4,632
1975	395.8	353.9	384.3	368.3	384.7	385.6	414.9	416.9	401.5	397.3	394.6	411.4	4,709
1976	403.6	388.1	412.2	396.4	413.4	427.7	446.1	446.3	425.3	428.0	437.3	457.0	5,081
1977	453.4	425.5	456.2	438.3	463.1	457.9	471.1	465.9	457.8	466.3	449.2	463.5	5,468
1978	450.1	401.4	448.3	426.6	472.4	451.5	470.5	483.8	462.2	475.9	470.6	487.6	5,501
1979	467.4	409.1	449.1	445.0	457.0	453.5	477.9	474.0	447.2	458.0	446.8	471.8	5,459
1980[1]	453.5	421.8	434.0	412.9	423.4	421.7	421.9	412.3	407.9	403.0	403.4	432.4	5,049
1981[1]	417.6	369.7	391.4	368.5	389.2	381.9	389.9	409.3	382.5	383.3	378.2	395.1	4,657
1982[1]	372.9	325.4	361.7	353.0	378.9	388.4	399.8	380.3	376.3	376.7	364.7	368.9	4,447
1983													

[1] Preliminary. *Source: Bureau of Mines* T.282

169

HEATING OIL

Average Price of Distillate (Middle) No. 2 Fuel Oil[1] Index (1967 = 100)

Year	Jan.	Feb.	Mar.	Apr.	May	June	July	Aug.	Sept.	Oct.	Nov.	Dec.	Average
1973	113.9	124.1	129.1	130.1	133.8	137.4	141.8	143.3	145.6	147.7	157.3	171.7	139.7
1974	194.8	234.1	251.8	257.9	269.2	279.7	288.9	294.8	298.8	297.9	296.0	300.1	272.0
1975	299.1	297.5	294.6	294.9	296.1	301.3	308.3	312.9	318.2	322.9	330.8	336.3	309.4
1976	336.7	339.3	335.3	331.8	328.5	329.2	332.2	336.2	338.9	341.2	344.3	349.8	337.0
1977	359.2	369.6	378.0	384.4	387.5	387.5	388.6	389.1	389.3	389.6	392.4	394.4	384.1
1978	396.7	398.6	394.8	393.3	393.3	393.3	393.2	393.6	394.0	400.0	407.6	418.0	398.0
1979	425.7	432.6	451.9	477.9	504.8	542.3	593.1	632.8	680.6	709.9	715.3	719.9	573.9
1980	739.3	793.5	837.7	858.9	964.8	860.9	870.2	875.6	873.2	868.4	873.4	891.1	850.6
1981	935.4	1,000.3	1,082.8	1,105.4	1,092.5	1,092.2	1,079.8	1,076.7	1,067.8	1,053.4	1,047.5	1,060.6	1,058.1
1982	1,067.8	1,058.2	1,029.3	953.6	928.7	974.6	1,024.0	1,022.2	1,001.7	997.7	1,040.6	1,053.6	1,012.7
1983	984.4	926.5											

[1] Barge lots, f.o.b. refinery or terminal, excluding all fees & taxes.   Source: Bureau of Labor Statistics (0573)   T.283

Average Wholesale Price of Kerosene (Light Distillate)—No. 1 Fuel Index (1967 = 100)

Year	Jan.	Feb.	Mar.	Apr.	May	June	July	Aug.	Sept.	Oct.	Nov.	Dec.	Average
1973	112.1	120.4	121.2	123.4	122.9	126.9	128.6	129.4	130.0	135.6	135.9	145.9	128.0
1974	154.3	184.8	198.7	209.4	217.6	233.2	241.7	250.2	256.8	254.7	261.4	257.9	226.7
1975	253.7	267.2	274.9	273.6	280.6	284.6	283.7	299.1	297.9	299.4	304.2	307.8	285.6
1976	310.5	316.6	313.9	311.2	306.7	303.8	305.4	309.2	311.5	316.0	320.2	323.2	312.3
1977	326.1	339.7	346.9	352.4	355.5	358.0	360.9	363.2	364.0	375.1	379.4	381.3	358.5
1978	383.0	388.2	388.4	387.9	390.7	391.4	393.1	394.4	395.8	397.6	398.4	403.0	392.7
1979	407.5	412.7	419.1	433.0	465.5	504.1	533.4	588.4	632.9	675.2	696.6	706.3	539.6
1980	733.9	776.9	834.6	862.5	870.5	878.4	892.7	903.1	903.2	896.3	896.8	911.4	863.4
1981	932.1	972.0	1,041.0	1,080.9	1,084.1	1,078.9	1,067.5	1,052.6	1,044.6	1,042.0	1,042.7	1,037.9	1,039.8
1982	1,044.3	1,034.3	1,027.9	1,009.1	975.9	974.2	984.4	983.0	976.3	969.7	984.6	991.1	996.1
1983	974.1	958.0											

Source: Bureau of Labor Statistics (0572)   T.284

Stocks of Distillate Fuel in the U.S., First of the Month In Millions of Barrels

Year	Jan.	Feb.	Mar.	Apr.	May	June	July	Aug.	Sept.	Oct.	Nov.	Dec.	Residual Fuel Oil Stocks Jan. 1	July 1
1970	171.7	130.7	111.5	101.0	102.1	115.8	137.5	163.5	188.2	205.7	216.4	218.1	58.4	46.0
1971	195.3	158.7	128.7	112.9	113.7	125.8	145.8	172.4	197.0	210.1	223.0	214.8	54.0	58.7
1972	190.6	160.1	122.2	101.8	98.3	112.9	128.8	155.6	174.7	190.3	195.6	182.6	59.7	56.1
1973	154.3	131.0	113.3	111.3	114.7	119.1	137.9	160.9	177.3	190.2	203.0	200.2	55.2	51.8
1974	196.5	181.2	149.2	128.9	125.6	141.8	160.7	182.5	198.7	208.3	209.9	212.9	53.5	57.9
1975	200.1	199.8	176.7	161.1	146.3	152.1	163.3	181.5	197.4	220.8	226.2	235.8	59.7	69.7
1976	208.8	165.5	150.5	138.3	137.3	147.1	165.1	190.9	218.0	232.3	235.6	223.7	74.1	64.3
1977	186.0	143.0	133.3	141.9	148.3	162.2	178.9	204.9	229.8	252.8	267.4	270.6	72.3	71.9
1978	250.3	213.3	165.7	137.9	136.2	144.6	157.3	180.5	200.2	220.7	233.1	233.2	90.0	72.0
1979[1]	216.5	175.7	127.1	112.7	115.0	123.1	141.4	171.3	195.4	220.3	231.1	236.6	90.0	71.9
1980[1]	228.7	212.1	191.5	177.7	177.0	183.1	195.8	213.8	226.3	232.3	225.7	223.4	95.9	87.7
1981[1]	205.4	180.0	172.6	164.7	164.7	171.9	180.2	186.7	200.3	206.8	201.2	200.0	91.5	70.1
1982[1]	190.2	166.0	146.7	127.7	108.8	114.5	124.6	148.2	158.9	161.2	170.2	185.6	78.3	60.5
1983[1]	178.6												66.2	

[1] Preliminary.   Source: Bureau of Mines   T.285

HEATING OIL

U.S. Production of Distillate Fuel Oil   In Millions of Barrels

Year	Jan.	Feb.	Mar.	Apr.	May	June	July	Aug.	Sept.	Oct.	Nov.	Dec.	Total
1976	84.8	85.9	86.6	79.7	84.9	86.6	91.8	92.4	88.4	92.9	95.4	100.9	1,070.2
1977	104.5	103.5	98.4	89.8	97.1	95.7	99.1	101.4	99.3	104.2	100.2	103.0	1,196.3
1978	95.1	82.7	93.5	88.8	100.8	93.3	96.8	102.2	95.6	102.3	101.0	104.2	1,156.1
1979[1]	93.2	80.2	92.8	88.1	95.0	94.1	102.5	103.3	101.0	100.7	97.7	99.9	1,150.8
1980[1]	93.7	80.6	79.5	73.9	76.6	79.4	74.5	82.3	78.3	77.2	81.9	88.7	974.1
1981[1]	92.6	78.7	77.0	72.5	76.1	75.0	74.5	82.3	78.3	77.2	81.9	88.7	954.9
1982[1]	81.1	68.5	71.1	70.7	81.2	81.9	84.8	78.3	79.7	88.0	85.9	82.3	953.4
1983													

[1] Preliminary.   Source: Dept. of Energy   T.286

U.S. Imports of Distillate Fuel Oil   In Millions of Barrels

Year	Jan.	Feb.	Mar.	Apr.	May	June	July	Aug.	Sept.	Oct.	Nov.	Dec.	Total
1976	5.1	6.3	4.8	2.9	3.0	4.5	3.9	4.1	4.5	4.5	4.0	6.1	53.5
1977	10.8	18.6	17.0	4.6	3.1	4.0	5.9	5.0	5.1	4.6	5.6	7.0	91.3
1978	6.1	5.9	6.0	3.0	3.9	4.4	4.6	4.4	4.9	5.5	6.7	7.9	63.3
1979[1]	7.0	5.5	5.5	4.5	5.8	5.4	6.8	6.7	3.8	6.6	7.0	7.1	70.5
1980[1]	5.5	6.4	5.5	4.4	3.9	3.2	3.6	2.4	3.0	3.6	4.0	5.2	51.9
1981[1]	8.5	9.1	4.5	3.5	5.1	6.0	5.5	4.9	3.9	3.6	3.4	2.9	61.0
1982[1]	3.0	3.6	1.5	1.8	2.3	3.0	3.8	2.4	1.8	3.0	4.2	3.4	33.8
1983													

[1] Preliminary.   Source: Dept. of Energy   T.287

U.S. Domestic Consumption of Distillate Fuel Oil   In Millions of Barrels

Year	Jan.	Feb.	Mar.	Apr.	May	June	July	Aug.	Sept.	Oct.	Nov.	Dec.	Total
1976	133.2	107.2	103.5	83.6	78.1	73.1	69.9	69.4	78.6	94.0	111.4	144.7	1,146.7
1977	158.2	131.8	106.7	88.1	86.2	83.1	79.1	81.6	81.4	94.1	102.6	130.4	1,223.3
1978	138.2	135.8	127.3	93.3	96.2	85.1	78.2	86.8	79.9	95.4	107.5	128.8	1,252.6
1979[1]	140.8	134.2	112.4	90.2	92.7	81.2	79.1	85.9	79.8	96.2	99.3	114.9	1,208.5
1980[1]	115.7	107.5	98.3	78.9	74.4	69.9	69.0	66.2	77.7	90.5	88.5	112.1	1,049.0
1981[1]	126.8	95.1	89.6	76.2	74.2	73.1	73.8	73.9	75.9	86.6	86.6	101.0	1,032.8
1982[1]	105.7	89.2	89.3	89.9	75.8	73.5	64.6	69.1	75.4	80.2	74.2	88.5	975.5
1983													

[1] Preliminary.   Source: Dept. of Energy   T.288

How to keep your Commodity Year Book statistics up-to-date continuously throughout the year.

To keep up-to-date statistics on the commodities in this book, you should have COMMODITY YEAR BOOK STATISTICAL ABSTRACT SERVICE. This three-times-yearly publication provides the latest available statistics for updating the statistical tables appearing in the COMMODITY YEAR BOOK. The ABSTRACT is published in the Winter (Jan.), Spring (Apr.) and Fall (Oct.). Subscription price is $55 per year.

Commodity Research Bureau, Inc.
75 MONTGOMERY ST., JERSEY CITY, N.J. 07302

Hides and Leather

U.S. production of cattlehides, derived from total commercial slaughter, increased about 3.5 percent in 1982 from the 1981 level, to 36.1 million. Raw calf skin production increased by about 7.4 percent in 1982. The low point in cattle slaughter during the current cycle was 33.7 million head in 1979. Increases since then have been modest compared with previous cycles, influenced by persistently high interest rates, and it is considered unlikely that slaughter levels in this cycle will reach the peak of 42.7 million reached in 1976.

U.S. cattlehide exports in 1982 totaled 22.8 million pieces, up 17 percent from the 19.5 million pieces exported in 1981. Exports represented 58 percent of hide production in 1982, up from 55 percent in 1981, vs. a record 70 percent in 1979. In 1982, Japan, the Republic of Korea, Mexico, Italy, and Taiwan were the major importers of U.S. raw and cured cattlehides. Japan and Korea alone accounted for about 50 percent of total U.S. cattlehide exports. China imported a large and increasing share of U.S. cattlehide exports in the form of partially processed "wet-blue" leather. In 1982 this quantity was estimated to have been the equivalent of more than 1.1 million cattlehides. In the first quarter of 1983, cattlehide exports totaled 5.3 million pieces vs. 5.1 million during the same quarter of 1981. (Effective April 1, 1983, sales and exports of wet blue hides were added to the USDA weekly export sales reporting program.)

Heavy Native Cow prices, f.o.b. River points, as quoted in the *Journal of Commerce*, in 1982 ranged between a high of about 50 cents per pound and a low of 41 cents, ending the year around 45½ cents per pound. Light Native Cow prices f.o.b. River points in 1982 ranged from a high of about 61 cents per pound to a low of 47 cents, ending 1982 at a price of about 55 cents per pound. Raw hides and skins are the major components of tanners' direct costs, and can be as high as 70 percent of total costs.

The sharp drop in domestic footwear production in 1982 severely affected the tanning industry even though the proportion of leather uppers in footwear production remained unchanged at 53 percent. Production of sole leather was down about 10 percent. Due to the recession and a substantial increase in leather imports, less leather was shipped to non-footwear leather products markets as well.

Domestic non-rubber footwear production in 1982 dropped about 52 million pairs to an estimated 323 million pairs. This was the largest year-to-year drop on record, and continued a downward trend that started in 1968 when production exceeded 640 million pairs. Production cuts were extremely heavy in men's footwear, down 24 percent. Manufacturers' costs were adversely influenced by high interest rates, which were reflected in an inventory decline of 7 million pairs to an estimated 34 million pairs. In contrast, footwear imports rose about 25 percent to 470 million pairs, up from 375 million in 1981. Domestic consumption of non-rubber footwear in 1982 was estimated at 774 million pairs.

In 1982, men's footwear accounted for 20 percent of the quantity and 38 percent of the value of product shipments of all non-rubber footwear. Ninety-one percent of men's footwear was made of leather. Shipments of men's footwear in 1982 declined 24 percent to 66 million pairs from 87 million pairs in 1981. Production figures for men's footwear in 1982 paralleled those for shipments, declining to an estimated 67 million pairs from 88 million in 1981. Import penetration by quantity, in the men's footwear sector in 1982 increased dramatically to an estimated 58 percent from 42 percent in 1981. In 1982, domestic production of women's footwear dropped 10 percent to 119 million pairs and shipments were off about 8 percent to an estimated 119 million pairs. About 56 percent of women's footwear was made of leather.

The quantity of leather shipped by U.S. tanners in 1982 was about 13 percent lower than in 1981, to about 16.5 million equivalent cattlehide units from 19.0 million in 1981. Included in these totals are leathers produced from hides and skins of cattle, calf, kips, goats, sheep, lambs, cabretta, and horses. Cattlehide leather represented 15.5 million units, or 82 percent of the total in 1981.

U.S. exports of semi-processed wet-blue leather increased substantially in 1982. Wet-blue has become a major item in the world leather trade because of its lower shipping costs and quality advantages compared with raw hides. China became a major importer of U.S. leathers in 1982 because of the large quantities of wet-blue leather sold to that country. Imports of leather into the U.S. increased 16 percent in 1982, following a whopping 63 percent gain in 1981.

Outlook for 1983

U.S. leather shipments were expected to decline about 2 percent in 1983 as the domestic production of leather products was expected to decline. Cattlehide exports were expected to increase, but a relatively strong U.S. dollar should continue to retard growth in leather exports, while leather imports at very competitive prices were expected to account for an even higher proportion of the domestic market for leather.

World Production of Bovine Hides and Skins In Thousands of Units of Metric Tons

Year	Argentina	Australia	Brazil	Canada	Colombia	France	Germany East	Germany West	Mexico	Italy	Poland	South Africa	Turkey	Un. Kingdom	United States	USSR
1970-4*	246.7	129.3	331.4	89.7	64.9	143.6	44.0	145.8	80.0	102.5	56.5	67.7	46.0	94.7	1,012	675.2
1975	277.4	185.5	338.0	111.7	67.2	163.3	47.3	155.5	107.7	91.4	76.1	66.9	57.0	127.4	1,199	695.3
1976	320.1	208.0	339.0	117.6	76.5	174.0	48.2	167.1	108.0	93.6	86.1	55.3	50.1	111.6	1,223	725.6
1977	339.2	219.5	375.0	115.3	73.0	162.2	49.1	161.1	114.6	95.5	80.4	58.8	52.1	102.9	1,209	735.0
1978[1]	370.8	202.1	336.0	106.1	78.2	162.8	49.7	164.5	124.0	91.9	75.9	65.1	53.4	99.0	1,134	741.0
1979[1]	355.2	174.0	330.0	94.6	81.3	163.0	50.2	170.4	122.0	91.9	77.2	69.2	53.4	95.0	964.1	760.0
1980																

* Average   [1] Preliminary.   Source: *Foreign Agricultural Service, U.S.D.A.*

T.289

HIDES AND LEATHER

Salient Statistics of Hides & Leather in the United States

Year	Federally Inspected	Uninspected[4]	Total Production	Net Exports	Total New Supply	Calf[2] Skins ¢ Lb.	Hides[3] Heavy Native Chicago	All U.S. Tanning	Cattle-Hide	All Footwear Leather Exports Ths. Sq. Ft.	Sole[5]	Upper[6]	Production[7]	Export
	\multicolumn{4}{c}{Thousands of Equivalent Hides}				\multicolumn{2}{c}{In Ths. Equiv. Hides}		\multicolumn{2}{c}{—1967 = 100—}	\multicolumn{2}{c}{—Mil. Pairs—}
1971	31,419	4,861	36,280	15,694	20,586	29.4	14.4	25,267	20,520	82,944	114.4	120.1	536	2.1
1972	32,267	4,213	36,480	17,705	18,775	56.3	29.7	24,661	20,084	117,556	157.5	125.7	527	2.3
1973	30,521	4,179	34,700	16,177	22,728	62.2	33.7	21,062	17,768	120,104	184.6	134.3	490	3.6
1974	33,319	4,381	37,700	17,924	19,776	64.4	23.0	19,998	17,084	148,565	158.8	144.0	453	4.0
1975	36,904	4,896	41,800	20,329	21,471	35.0	23.5	21,894	18,830	184,104	151.1	151.8	413	4.3
1976	38,992	4,590	43,582	24,318	19,264	75.5	33.0	23,526	20,231	203,707	197.9	163.8	423	6.0
1977	38,717	3,139	41,856	23,569	18,287	91.4	36.2	21,528	18,512	206,276	206.1	171.8	414	5.4
1978	36,948	2,604	39,552	24,101	15,451	134.6	47.2	20,199	17,371	208,799	235.2	185.3	419	6.2
1979	31,504	2,173	33,678	23,063	10,615	168.7	72.5	18,170	15,041	187,665	329.6	192.9	399	7.6
1980	31,642	2,165	33,807	18,640	15,167	109.8	44.5	17,600	14,790	192,597	283.8	211.7	396.9	9.8
1981	32,819	2,134	34,953	18,701	16,252	N.A.	43.8	19,184	15,520	192,193	306.7	214.4	375.5	9.7
1982[1]	33,906	1,920	35,826	22,553	13,273		42.3	18,229	15,115	160,000		215.9		
1983														

[1] Preliminary. [2] Packer, heavy, 9½ to 15 pounds. [3] Cents per pound. [4] Includes farm slaughter; diseased & condemned animals & hides taken off fallen animals. [5] Bends, light, f.o.b. tannery. [6] Women's Leather Upper. [7] Other than rubber. *Sources: Tanners' Council of America; Bureau of Labor Statistics; Dept. of Commerce*

T.290

U.S. Exports of Upper & Lining Leather   In Thousands of Square Feet

Year	Jan.	Feb.	Mar.	Apr.	May	June	July	Aug.	Sept.	Oct.	Nov.	Dec.	Total
1973	8,746	7,872	9,254	11,311	12,618	10,873	8,154	10,353	9,919	10,184	6,459	9,563	120,104
1974	9,984	10,163	10,407	11,917	16,191	14,674	12,800	11,699	14,108	12,831	11,032	12,759	148,565
1975	14,748	12,427	13,574	14,624	16,735	18,473	13,341	16,979	14,714	17,131	16,737	12,909	184,104
1976	14,517	17,367	18,157	19,449	21,149	18,795	14,028	12,074	18,343	14,361	15,108	18,388	203,707
1977	18,630	19,272	23,315	18,338	16,714	16,205	18,612	12,276	16,838	12,807	14,980	18,240	206,276
1978	17,364	15,308	16,408	16,720	18,899	21,427	14,160	19,726	16,224	17,438	17,947	17,176	208,799
1979[1]	13,854	16,014	18,833	16,480	15,664	18,526	13,153	15,265	14,456	13,895	16,089	15,433	187,665
1980[1]	16,769	16,873	18,710	13,024	12,652	15,483	15,481	15,215	15,818	19,051	20,880	13,641	192,597
1981[1]	19,633	14,418	19,717	17,678	18,016	18,692	13,921	10,918	15,393	12,682	19,464	11,660	192,193
1982[1]	10,849	10,343	13,696	15,534	17,449	18,610	18,486	12,065	10,417	11,842	9,726	10,786	159,804
1983[1]	11,052												
1984													

[1] Preliminary. *Source: Tanners' Council of America*

T.292

U.S. Production of Footwear (Shoes, Sandals, Slippers, Athletic, Etc.)   In Millions of Pairs

Year	Jan.	Feb.	Mar.	Apr.	May	June	July	Aug.	Sept.	Oct.	Nov.	Dec.	Total
1970	47.6	47.5	50.2	48.6	46.3	47.9	42.9	47.3	47.7	49.0	40.9	43.4	562.3
1971	44.8	44.9	50.3	46.8	44.1	46.7	37.6	46.3	45.7	45.1	40.7	42.9	535.8
1972	44.5	44.3	48.7	44.1	45.2	46.2	36.1	46.2	44.2	46.4	41.1	38.5	526.5
1973	42.9	41.9	46.8	41.9	41.7	41.7	32.1	43.7	39.2	45.2	38.5	34.2	490.0
1974	40.8	41.1	42.9	39.9	43.2	39.9	32.9	37.3	34.8	36.9	33.2	30.2	453.0
1975	32.7	31.2	31.6	32.8	32.7	34.1	32.2	36.2	37.7	42.4	34.6	35.0	413.1
1976	37.0	36.1	42.2	39.4	38.7	37.3	29.5	34.8	35.1	33.2	30.0	29.2	422.5
1977	34.8	34.5	37.6	34.3	35.5	36.9	26.9	37.5	35.6	36.4	35.9	33.2	418.1
1978	34.5	34.8	39.9	35.8	39.5	36.8	26.1	37.1	34.2	36.3	33.8	30.2	418.9
1979[1]	35.7	33.4	37.0	31.9	35.4	30.5	24.4	33.8	31.0	34.9	31.3	28.7	398.9
1980[1]	35.5	33.7	34.4	33.5	34.8	33.1	27.9	31.5	33.5	37.2	30.4	29.5	396.9
1981[1]	31.4	30.7	34.3	33.0	31.9	30.4	27.0	30.7	32.9	35.0	30.5	27.6	375.5
1982[1]	26.3	27.1	31.1	26.9	27.9	28.2	23.6	27.9	28.4	28.4	25.8	23.0	324.7
1983													

[1] Preliminary. *Source: U.S. Department of Commerce*

T.295

HIDES AND LEATHER

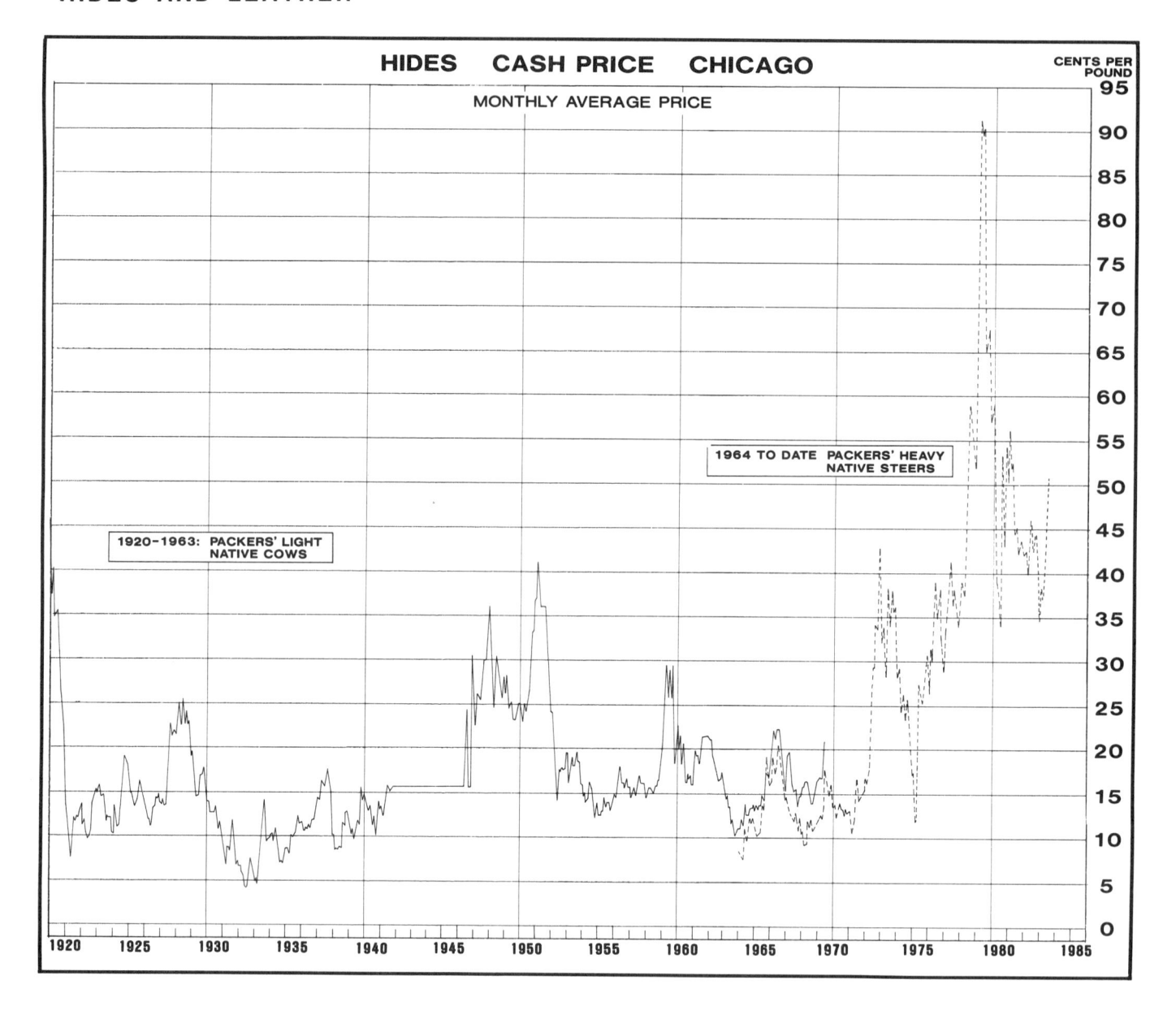

HIDES CASH PRICE CHICAGO — CENTS PER POUND

MONTHLY AVERAGE PRICE

1920-1963: PACKERS' LIGHT NATIVE COWS

1964 TO DATE PACKERS' HEAVY NATIVE STEERS

Index Price of Hides (Packer Heavy Native Steers)[1]—F.O.B. Shipping Point 1967 = 100[2]

Year	Jan.	Feb.	Mar.	Apr.	May	June	July	Aug.	Sept.	Oct.	Nov.	Dec.	Average
1970	12.3	12.8	12.8	14.1	13.4	13.4	12.3	13.5	13.0	13.1	13.1	11.0	12.9
1971	10.4	11.5	11.5	15.8	16.8	14.1	14.8	14.8	15.5	15.3	16.8	16.3	14.5
1972	17.8	19.0	23.3	25.5	28.0	29.3	29.3	34.0	33.5	40.5	43.0	32.0	29.6
1973	34.0	33.5	28.3	38.3	36.3	33.8	36.3	38.3	35.5	36.3	32.8	28.2	34.3
1974	29.3	—	24.1	26.3	26.3	23.3	25.8	25.3	24.5	17.3	17.5	14.3	23.1
1975	11.8	12.5	16.3	27.5	25.3	25.8	25.3	25.3	25.8	28.0	30.8	26.3	23.4
1976	31.5	29.8	30.0	34.9	39.0	34.8	36.3	37.3	38.3	31.8	29.0	32.3	33.8
1977	35.8	36.3	37.3	40.1	41.3	36.3	38.1	36.8	34.8	33.8	34.8	38.0	37.0
1978	38.8	37.8	37.3	41.3	41.8	45.8	47.8	53.0	59.0	57.3	54.8	51.8	47.2
1979[2]	506.4	548.4	766.9	750.1	760.2	696.3	653.0	594.6	549.2	568.9	498.5	480.1	614.4
1980	496.7	409.3	331.5	320.5	283.6	321.0	369.0	448.0	361.4	412.9	455.9	420.6	385.9
1981	375.1	344.1	356.1	405.8	385.8	364.9	351.7	373.6	344.3	347.7	347.2	343.4	361.6
1982	353.6	346.0	325.8	339.3	353.5	342.1	342.1	349.7	343.5	336.4	324.7	312.9	339.1
1983	313.9	315.0											
1984													

[1] Over 53 pounds. [2] Data prior to 1979 are in cents per pound. *Source: Bureau of Labor Statistics* (0411–0111.99)   T.296

HIDES AND LEATHER

U.S. Imports and Exports of All Cattle Hides In Thousands of Hides

Year	Imports Total	Imports From Canada	Total	Canada	France	W. Germany	Japan	Mexico	Netherlands	Poland	Spain	Romania	South Korea	Czech.	Italy
1970	385	323	15,222	761	287	714	6,206	2,046	332	152	260	449	271	499	335
1971	275	245	15,962	883	545	576	6,010	2,195	305	473	842	571	357	694	62
1972	292	283	17,578	893	753	585	7,246	1,776	299	545	758	1,201	411	852	178
1973	694	661	16,866	764	548	535	6,840	2,005	129	719	503	1,006	821	807	426
1974	520	484	18,428	790	327	396	6,642	2,500	153	639	554	1,777	1,252	638	250
1975	958	954	21,269	805	504	315	7,108	2,362	219	787	948	1,226	2,203	877	565
1976	962	958	25,270	1,057	816	518	9,356	1,708	326	389	957	1,651	3,270	678	1,561
1977	932	926	24,489	859	769	435	8,425	1,967	417	433	940	1,472	3,611	680	1,048
1978	704	694	24,791	1,093	555	379	8,797	1,938	211	349	1,019	1,942	3,720	586	1,284
1979	673	643	23,731	1,248	691	454	7,396	2,428	324	513	892	1,317	2,526	682	2,248
1980	880	859	19,512	1,046	238	206	7,476	1,972	164	522	112	1,046	2,653	318	690
1981	1,028	881	19,703	1,212	137	319	7,512	2,485	94	203	394	680	3,579	334	486
1982[3]	658	592	23,175	1,041	478	670	6,469	1,882	280	791	643	939	4,572	415	1,395
1983															

[1] Preliminary. Source: Tanners' Council of America

T.297

Average Factory Price of Footwear in the United States In Dollars Per Pair

Year	Jan.	Feb.	Mar.	Apr.	May	June	July	Aug.	Sept.	Oct.	Nov.	Dec.	Average
1970	5.11	5.18	5.36	5.20	4.97	5.02	5.10	5.23	5.15	5.09	5.11	5.54	5.17
1971	5.39	5.37	5.41	5.40	5.18	5.21	5.38	5.21	5.16	5.17	5.13	5.45	5.29
1972	5.45	5.48	5.54	5.67	5.48	5.52	5.75	5.59	5.55	5.41	5.39	6.00	5.56
1973	6.32	6.15	6.19	6.28	6.09	6.11	6.30	6.24	6.29	6.20	6.16	6.63	6.24
1974	6.84	6.67	6.81	6.76	6.91	6.86	6.99	6.90	7.20	7.25	7.31	7.63	6.99
1975	7.48	7.64	7.50	7.43	7.63	7.63	7.49	7.43	7.45	7.46	7.63	7.29	7.50
1976	8.00	7.87	8.07	8.16	8.23	8.23	8.32	8.34	8.63	8.21	8.75	8.73	8.28
1977	8.61	8.40	8.63	8.81	8.53	8.39	8.44	8.36	8.51	8.28	8.62	9.00	8.54
1978	8.50	8.39	8.76	9.35	9.51	9.37	9.41	8.66	9.40	9.37	9.61	10.31	9.20
1979	9.73	9.84	9.68	10.23	10.00	10.48	11.74	10.31	10.30	10.46	11.15	11.47	10.60
1980	11.67	11.83	11.81	12.27	12.16	11.37	11.40	11.94	11.08	11.25	11.45	11.41	11.63
1981	11.67	11.93	12.52	12.72	13.09	13.16	13.01	13.14	13.22	12.90	12.67	12.58	12.52
1982[1]	12.33	11.72	11.88	12.11	12.13	12.65	13.44	12.69	12.48	12.46	12.89	13.39	12.49
1983													

[1] Preliminary. Source: Tanners' Council of America

T.298

How to keep your Commodity Year Book statistics up-to-date continuously throughout the year.

To keep up-to-date statistics on the commodities in this book, you should have COMMODITY YEAR BOOK STATISTICAL ABSTRACT SERVICE. This three-times-yearly publication provides the latest available statistics for updating the statistical tables appearing in the COMMODITY YEAR BOOK. The ABSTRACT is published in the Winter (Jan.), Spring (Apr.) and Fall (Oct.). Subscription price is $55 per year.

Commodity Research Bureau, Inc.
75 MONTGOMERY ST., JERSEY CITY, N.J. 07302

Hogs

Commercial U.S. pork production during 1982 totaled 14.1 billion pounds, 10 percent below the year-earlier level and the lowest production recorded since 1978. The commercial hog slaughter, which was also 10 percent lower, totaled 82.2 million head. Barrows and gilts accounted for almost 94 percent of the slaughter and sows made up 5 percent.

Hog inventories continued to decline during 1982. The December 1, 1982 inventory of all hogs and pigs was 53.2 million head, down 9 percent from the figure as of that same date a year earlier. The breeding herd was down by 7 percent and the market hog inventory had declined by 10 percent. During 1982, producers added only around 3.7 million gilts to their breeding inventories compared with the 3.5 million in 1981, which was the lowest figure recorded during the past decade.

The 1982 U.S. pig crop totaled 84.1 million head, or 10 percent below a year earlier and 17 percent below the 1981 crop. As of December 1, 1982, producers indicated intentions to farrow 5.45 million sows during the December 1982–May 1983 period, 3 percent below the year-ago level. Considered with an average projected litter size of 7.31 pigs, this would indicate a spring pig crop of 39.8 million head, 3 percent, down 3 percent from a year ago. This crop would provide most of the slaughter hogs available during the second half of 1983. The June–November 1982 pig crop was estimated at 43.1 million head, 7 percent below a year ago.

In 1982, there were reportedly 483,690 hog enterprises, 17 percent fewer than a year earlier. Large operations of 500 head and more accounted for 5 percent of all operations, and these accounted for 49 percent of all hogs and pigs in 1982 compared with 46 percent during 1981 and 42 percent during 1980. Small operations, 1 to 99 head, accounted for 76 percent of all operations but for only 13 percent of the total hog inventory. Medium-sized operations of between 100 and 499 head accounted for 19 percent of the operations and 39 percent of the inventory. Over the past 12 years, each quarter's farrowings as a percentage of the breeding herd have increased, excepting the March–May period. Facilities built during the mid- and late 1970's have reduced the cold-weather death losses of baby pigs and made weather less of a factor in the selection of a farrowing time.

Hog prices were expected to average $57 to $62 per cwt. during the second half of 1983 depending upon the strength of the observed economic recovery.

Futures Markets

Live hog futures are traded on the Chicago Mercantile Exchange (30,000 lb.) and on the Mid-America Commodity Exchange (15,000 lb.)

World Hog Numbers in Specified Countries In Millions of Head

Year	Brazil	Denmark	France	W. Germany	Hungary	Italy	Japan	Mexico	Philippines	Poland	China[3]	Un. Kingdom	United States	USSR	World
1970	31.5	8.4	10.5	19.3	5.7	9.2	6.3	10.3	12.0	14.8	220.0	8.1	57.0	56.1	599.1
1971	32.1	8.7	11.6	21.0	7.3	9.0	6.9	10.0	12.5	13.9	223.0	8.5	67.3	67.5	638.4
1972	33.0	8.7	11.3	20.0	7.6	8.2	7.0	11.0	7.7	16.9	228.0	8.9	62.4	71.4	651.1
1973	34.0	8.7	11.4	20.0	6.9	8.2	7.3	9.4	8.6	19.0	231.4	8.8	59.0	66.6	651.3
1974	35.0	8.2	11.4	20.5	8.0	8.2	8.0	11.7	9.3	21.5	234.9	9.3	60.6	70.9	671.5
1975	43.5	8.1	12.0	20.2	8.3	8.8	7.7	12.1	6.6	21.7		7.9	54.7	72.3	
1976	36.0	7.6	11.5	19.8	7.0	8.9	7.5	12.0	6.5	21.6		7.7	49.3	57.9	364.1
1977	36.8	7.9	11.5	20.6	7.9	9.1	8.1	12.3	5.7	16.8		8.2	54.9	63.1	380.3
1978	37.6	8.2	11.5	21.4	7.9	9.4	8.8	12.6	6.9	20.6		7.7	56.5	70.5	402.6
1979	36.0	9.2	11.3	22.6	8.0	8.9	9.5	12.7	7.4	21.1		8.0	60.4	73.5	416.4
1980	36.5	9.5	11.4	22.4	8.4	8.8	10.0	12.8	7.9	21.0		7.8	67.4	73.9	431.3
1981[1]	35.0	9.6	12.0	22.6	8.3	8.9	10.1	15.4	8.3	18.7	305.0	7.8	64.5	73.4	425.4
1982[2]	33.5	9.8	11.8	22.3	8.3	9.0	10.0	16.5	8.8	19.0		7.9	58.7	73.3	421.4
1983[2]							10.1	15.0					52.2	76.5	416.4

[1] Preliminary. [2] Estimate. [3] Mainland. Source: *Foreign Agricultural Service, U.S.D.A.*   T.300

Hogs and Pigs on U.S. Farms on December 1 In Thousands of Head

Year	Georgia	Illinois	Indiana	Iowa	Kansas	Kentucky	Minnesota	Missouri	Nebraska	No. Carolina	Ohio	South Dakota	Tennessee	Wisconsin	Total
1970	2,065	7,630	5,129	16,110	2,202	1,680	3,752	5,120	3,691	1,985	2,838	2,009	1,395	1,932	67,285
1971	1,962	6,600	5,020	14,853	2,100	1,394	3,544	4,659	3,322	1,850	2,611	1,868	1,269	1,777	62,412
1972	1,884	6,650	4,850	14,200	2,100	1,255	3,550	4,350	3,300	1,739	2,320	1,739	1,050	1,475	59,017
1973	1,840	7,350	4,875	14,700	2,000	1,280	3,976	4,325	3,455	1,950	2,274	2,175	940	1,540	60,614
1974	1,590	6,500	4,300	13,400	1,750	1,100	3,700	3,900	3,050	1,890	1,950	1,700	880	1,400	54,693
1975	1,300	5,600	3,900	12,600	1,650	1,000	3,000	3,200	2,700	1,900	1,675	1,400	920	1,150	49,267
1976	1,600	6,400	4,000	14,200	1,850	1,080	3,600	3,750	3,100	1,940	1,900	1,500	1,010	1,250	54,934
1977	1,720	6,100	4,100	14,500	2,000	1,140	4,000	3,700	3,150	2,300	1,750	1,580	1,180	1,378	56,539
1978	1,800	6,550	4,400	15,100	2,000	1,150	4,100	4,100	3,650	2,350	1,900	1,620	1,300	1,650	60,100
1979	2,360	6,950	4,850	16,200	2,090	1,470	4,900	4,650	4,150	2,650	2,120	2,000	1,400	1,830	67,353
1980	2,300	6,600	4,600	16,100	1,900	1,220	5,100	3,980	3,900	2,460	2,150	1,860	1,140	1,680	64,512
1981	1,520	6,450	4,100	16,300	1,770	1,040	4,300	3,400	4,100	1,980	2,050	1,710	900	1,380	58,688
1982[1]	1,400	5,600	4,200	14,300	1,670	920	3,900	3,500	3,500	2,050	1,820	1,510	750	1,220	53,230

[1] Preliminary. Source: *Crop Reporting Board, U.S.D.A.*   T.301

HOGS

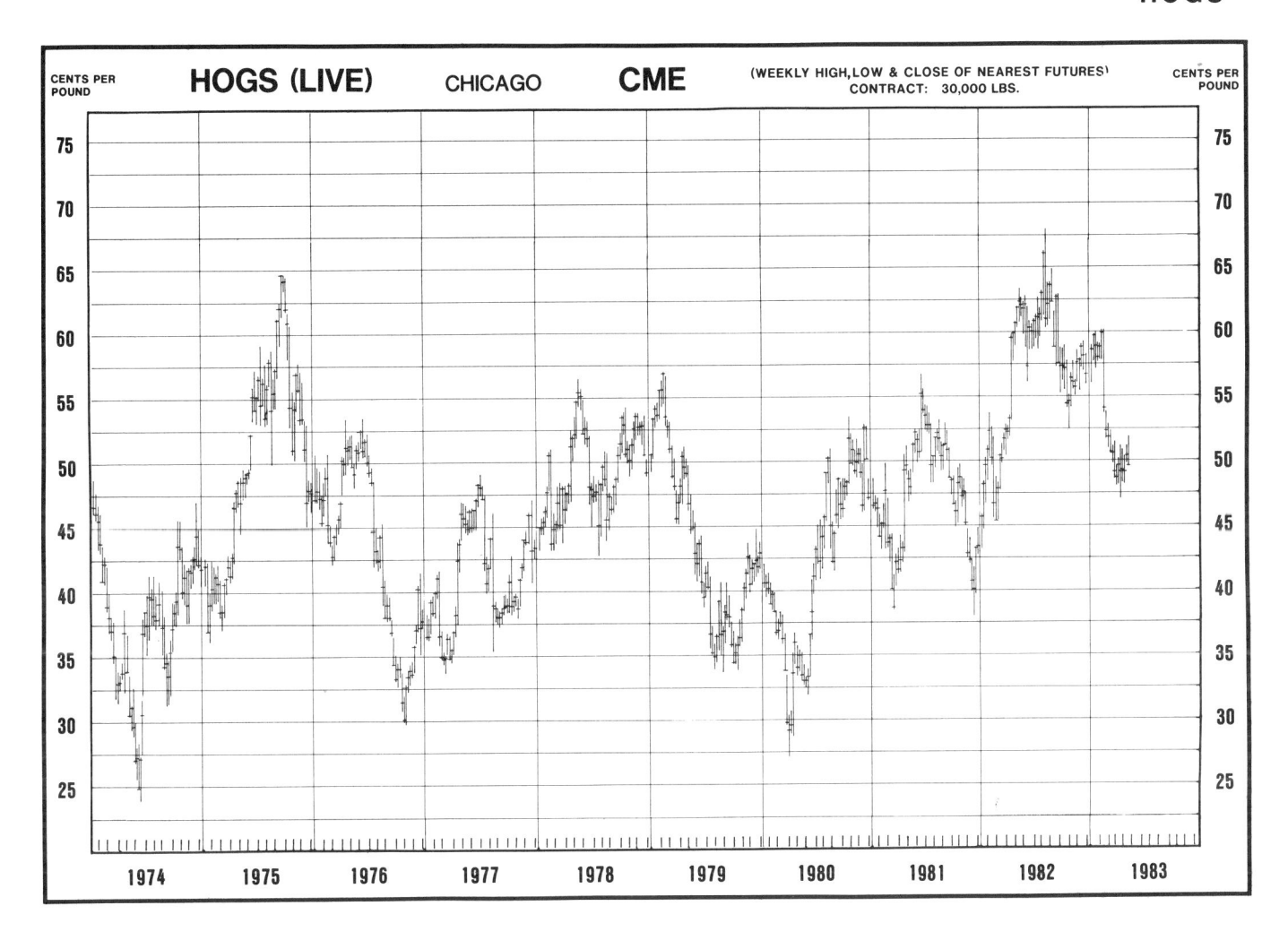

HOGS (LIVE) CHICAGO **CME** (WEEKLY HIGH, LOW & CLOSE OF NEAREST FUTURES)
CONTRACT: 30,000 LBS.

Salient Statistics of Pigs and Hogs in the U.S.

Year	Spring[2] Sows Farrowed	Spring[2] Pigs Saved	Fall[3] Sows Farrowed	Fall[3] Pigs Saved	Total Pig Crop	Value of Hogs on Farms, Dec. 1 $ Per Head	Value of Hogs on Farms, Dec. 1 Total Million $	Hog Marketings Ths. Head	Quantity Produced (Live Wt.) Mil. Lbs.	Value of Production Mil. $	Federally Inspected	Commercial Other	Commercial Total	Farm	Total
1970	7,134	52,126	6,882	49,588	101,921	23.50	1,584	86,919	21,823	4,955	78,187	7,630	85,817	1,235	87,052
1971	7,303	51,918	6,297	46,006	98,512	28.50	1,780	98,644	22,832	3,991	86,667	7,771	94,438	1,210	95,648
1972	6,512	47,523	5,967	43,053	90,828	42.00	2,477	89,555	20,919	5,245	78,759	5,948	84,707	1,158	85,865
1973	6,459	46,125	5,864	41,998	88,199	60.40	3,663	82,419	20,154	7,738	72,264	4,531	76,795	1,095	77,890
1974	6,372	44,792	5,466	38,952	83,954	44.90	2,457	85,504	19,976	6,838	77,071	4,691	81,762	1,321	83,083
1975	4,973	35,530	4,952	35,656	71,186	80.40	3,959	73,627	16,835	7,756	64,926	3,761	68,687	1,193	69,880
1976	5,777	42,177	5,850	42,218	84,395	47.00	2,583	75,747	18,160	7,856	70,454	3,330	73,784	1,175	74,959
1977	6,050	42,960	6,009	43,202	86,162	63.20	3,575	80,939	19,021	7,485	74,019	3,285	77,303	1,139	78,442
1978	6,034	42,481	6,398	46,031	88,512	83.20	5,023	81,271	19,466	9,066	74,139	3,176	77,315	1,102	78,417
1979	7,179	50,571	7,306	52,120	102,691	56.00	3,775	92,327	22,595	9,416	85,425	3,674	89,099	1,080	90,179
1980	7,229	52,286	6,829	49,256	101,542	74.70	4,821	100,388	23,352	8,847	91,882	4,192	96,074	1,100	97,174
1981	6,440	47,600	6,258	46,176	93,776	70.10	4,114	95,895	21,783	9,521	87,850	3,697	91,547	897	92,444
1982[1]	5,593	41,035	5,810	43,057	84,092	89.90	4,784	86,653	19,441	10,180	79,329	1,867	81,196	654	81,850
1983[4]	5,447	39,800													
1984															

[1] Preliminary. [2] December–May. [3] June–November. [4] Breeding intentions. *Source: Statistical Reporting Service, U.S.D.A.* T.302

177

HOGS

Federally Inspected Hog Slaughter in the United States   In Thousands of Head

Year	Jan.	Feb.	Mar.	Apr.	May	June	July	Aug.	Sept.	Oct.	Nov.	Dec.	Total
1972	6,400	6,280	7,800	6,733	6,793	6,313	5,276	6,512	6,420	7,048	6,988	6,197	78,759
1973	6,641	5,713	6,652	5,992	6,638	5,711	4,996	5,569	5,348	6,613	6,534	5,859	72,264
1974	6,804	5,584	6,568	6,867	7,077	5,894	5,722	6,363	6,523	7,023	6,402	6,243	77,071
1975	6,349	5,540	5,751	6,361	5,375	5,077	4,657	4,627	5,217	5,379	5,085	5,508	64,926
1976	5,400	4,873	6,325	5,827	5,086	5,146	4,905	5,968	6,361	6,929	7,100	6,525	70,454
1977	5,840	5,825	7,238	6,395	5,877	5,695	4,908	6,148	6,514	6,507	6,885	6,186	74,019
1978	5,969	5,840	6,795	6,213	6,298	5,778	5,402	6,227	6,203	6,576	6,737	6,101	74,139
1979	6,393	5,693	7,113	6,962	7,284	6,678	6,734	7,662	6,840	8,736	8,097	7,234	85,425
1980	8,038	7,277	7,856	8,456	8,167	7,279	6,910	6,745	7,601	8,404	7,362	7,788	91,882
1981[1]	7,768	6,873	7,988	7,993	7,004	6,682	6,540	6,580	7,320	7,872	7,309	7,923	87,850
1982[1]	6,875	6,340	7,691	—20,043—			—18,310—			—20,068—			79,328
1983[1]	6,421	5,762											

[1] Preliminary.   Source: Statistical Reporting Service, U.S.D.A.   T.305

Average Live Weight of All Hogs Slaughtered Under Federal Inspection   In Pounds Per Head

Year	Jan.	Feb.	Mar.	Apr.	May	June	July	Aug.	Sept.	Oct.	Nov.	Dec.	Average[1]
1975	242	236	236	238	240	244	241	237	238	240	246	246	240.2
1976	243	236	236	236	239	240	238	236	236	238	243	239	238.4
1977	234	233	234	236	239	241	239	237	236	239	243	239	237.4
1978	236	233	234	237	241	244	241	239	239	243	248	247	240.2
1979	241	237	238	240	243	246	246	240	240	242	245	246	242.0
1980	243	239	239	241	244	244	242	239	239	241	246	247	242.0
1981	246	242	241	242	244	245	242	239	240	243	246	247	243.0
1982[2]	243	239	239	—243—			—242—			—247—			243.0

[1] Average is weighted by Federally inspected slaughter.   [2] Preliminary.   Source: Department of Agriculture   T.311

Hog-Corn Price Ratio[1] at Omaha

Year	Jan.	Feb.	Mar.	Apr.	May	June	July	Aug.	Sept.	Oct.	Nov.	Dec.	Average
1971	11.0	13.2	11.6	11.3	11.8	12.2	13.9	15.1	16.3	17.2	16.7	16.6	13.6
1972	19.7	20.6	19.0	18.2	19.7	21.5	22.8	23.5	22.6	21.8	20.6	20.5	20.9
1973	21.5	23.3	25.4	23.4	19.5	16.9	19.0	20.8	18.4	17.8	16.9	15.7	19.5
1974	14.8	13.4	12.5	12.1	10.2	10.0	11.2	10.5	10.3	10.6	11.0	11.8	11.5
1975	12.6	14.1	14.3	14.1	16.4	17.9	19.4	18.6	20.7	21.2	19.4	18.5	17.2
1976	18.6	18.6	17.7	18.3	17.7	17.6	16.8	16.2	15.1	13.7	14.4	16.3	16.9
1977	16.4	16.8	15.9	16.0	18.8	20.7	23.8	26.4	24.6	22.6	19.2	21.4	19.8
1978	22.7	24.0	22.2	20.4	20.9	20.6	21.8	24.5	25.7	25.5	23.5	23.4	22.9
1979	24.0	25.5	22.6	19.9	18.1	16.4	14.2	15.4	16.2	14.6	15.3	16.0	18.2
1980	16.5	16.1	15.2	12.3	12.0	13.8	15.3	16.1	15.6	15.2	13.8	13.5	14.6
1981	13.0	13.3	12.4	12.3	12.9	15.2	15.9	18.1	19.8	18.7	17.5	16.8	15.5
1982[2]	18.4	20.1	19.8	19.8	21.8	22.1	23.3	27.9	28.1	27.2	22.8	23.0	22.9

[1] Ratio computed by dividing average price packer and shipper purchases of barrows and gilts by average price No. 2 yellow corn both at Omaha. This ratio represents the number of bushels of corn required to buy 100 pounds of live hogs.   [2] Preliminary.   Source: Economic Research Service, U.S.D.A.   T.304

Cold Storage Holdings of Frozen Pork[1] in the U.S. on First of Month   In Millions of Pounds

Year	Jan.	Feb.	Mar.	Apr.	May	June	July	Aug.	Sept.	Oct.	Nov.	Dec.
1971	336.1	351.1	338.8	387.0	463.6	494.8	477.3	402.3	330.0	306.9	310.4	325.3
1972	330.0	301.1	289.5	327.7	395.8	381.5	319.6	255.7	203.5	192.1	208.9	242.3
1973	214.2	203.1	201.6	239.6	248.4	258.8	252.2	200.8	179.2	196.0	223.6	277.2
1974	286.1	300.1	309.7	346.6	399.1	412.3	355.4	291.8	257.7	248.6	270.3	302.8
1975	306.7	294.4	299.6	299.3	345.1	323.6	284.3	229.7	185.9	189.5	221.9	269.3
1976	249.1	216.7	206.2	228.9	250.9	255.4	219.0	176.7	157.3	175.6	201.5	219.1
1977	212.1	197.0	203.4	224.7	264.6	269.9	227.9	178.9	145.5	158.5	166.0	208.5
1978	185.9	174.9	172.4	215.8	281.7	280.6	260.2	219.9	178.7	177.8	207.1	245.2
1979	241.8	224.5	220.4	245.6	278.3	290.2	269.9	225.1	180.2	178.4	219.1	257.2
1980	280.8	285.6	270.4	291.2	345.3	356.5	313.9	263.7	217.3	222.0	269.3	320.7
1981[2]	348.6	350.8	355.9	360.6	403.5	394.4	346.5	283.4	225.1	206.7	238.3	255.2
1982[2]	264.4	247.3	246.3	274.1	—	—	264.1	—	—	183.0	—	—
1983[2]	219.0	224.2	215.7	235.2								

[1] Excludes lard.   [2] Preliminary.   Source: Crop Reporting Board, U.S.D.A.   T.303

HOGS

Month-End Open Interest of Live Hogs Futures at Chicago In Contracts

Year	Jan.	Feb.	Mar.	Apr.	May	June	July	Aug.	Sept.	Oct.	Nov.	Dec.
1978	23,335	25,731	22,223	22,612	23,345	15,061	14,999	16,569	19,597	20,328	21,944	19,077
1979	26,338	27,694	25,613	24,204	27,004	30,108	24,544	25,730	26,155	24,313	26,317	24,966
1980	27,387	27,765	21,857	24,795	25,814	29,011	27,635	28,725	31,696	36,962	38,534	26,816
1981	21,267	21,588	20,767	28,147	31,149	26,639	19,557	20,944	23,471	21,945	22,294	17,924
1982	27,528	29,960	43,387	51,056	63,760	46,002	42,884	51,530	48,263	48,751	47,067	43,791
1983	45,184	41,338	39,469	31,915								

Source: Chicago Mercantile Exchange   T.309

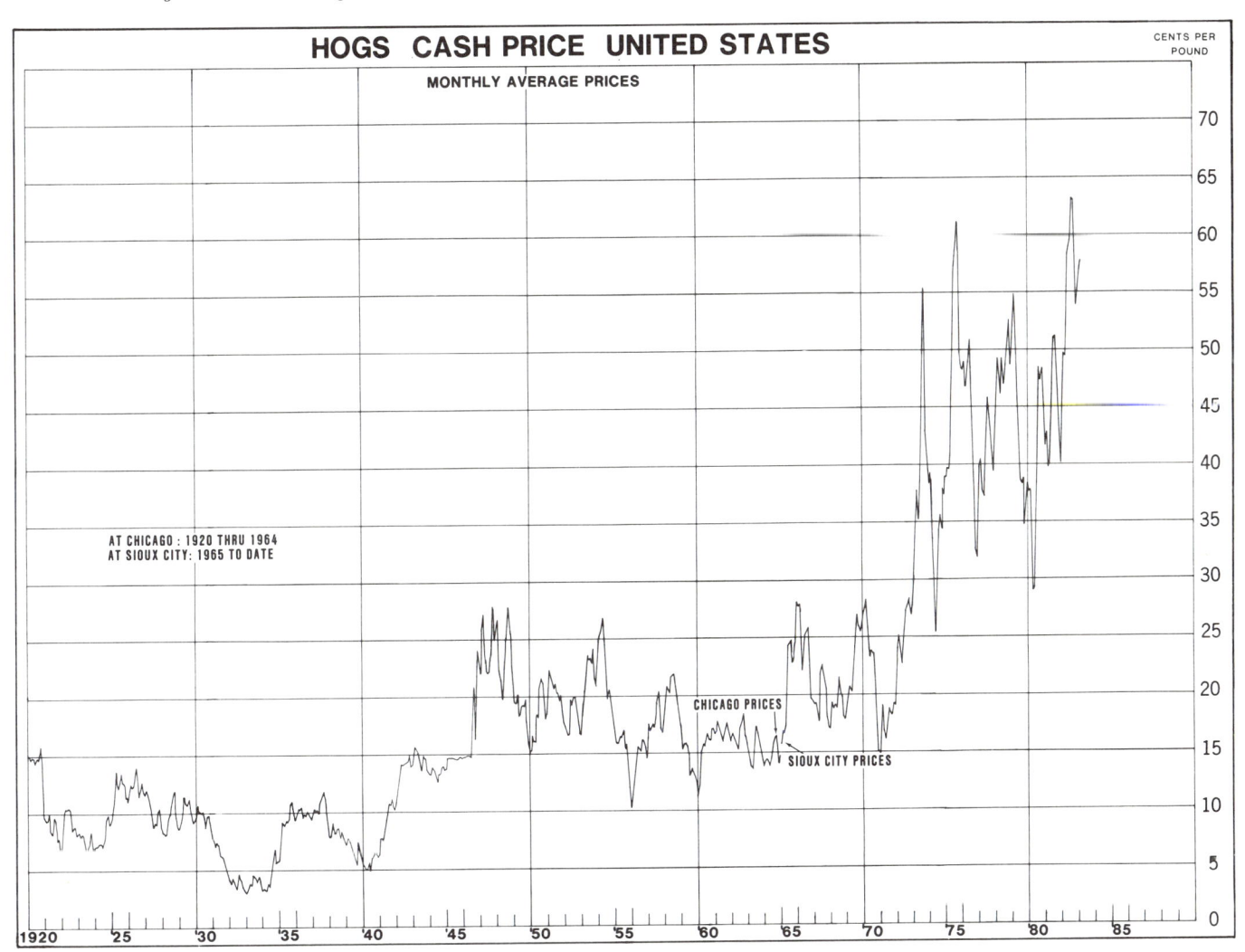

Average Wholesale Price of Hogs, Average (All Weights) at Sioux City In Dollars Per 100 Pounds

Year	Jan.	Feb.	Mar.	Apr.	May	June	July	Aug.	Sept.	Oct.	Nov.	Dec.	Average
1974	40.22	38.98	34.71	30.36	25.89	27.29	36.15	37.49	35.69	38.90	38.14	39.81	34.75
1975	38.96	39.69	39.59	40.74	46.42	51.31	57.25	58.12	61.19	58.76	49.78	48.36	48.30
1976	48.23	48.92	46.76	48.06	48.96	50.91	48.31	44.03	39.39	32.69	31.96	38.28	43.19
1977	39.65	40.40	37.61	37.20	41.94	43.89	45.76	44.34	41.39	40.97	39.44	44.13	41.12
1978	46.08	49.26	47.77	46.22	49.25	48.19	46.94	48.83	50.34	52.58	48.68	49.73	48.67
1979	52.11	54.93	49.66	45.29	43.77	39.98	38.58	38.41	38.80	34.74	36.13	38.30	42.13
1980	37.58	37.61	33.97	29.08	29.35	34.97	41.78	48.49	47.42	48.36	46.44	45.07	39.48
1981	41.67	42.78	39.88	40.15	41.96	48.78	51.01	51.14	48.89	46.15	42.10	40.17	44.29
1982	45.77	49.70	49.50	52.16	58.35	59.01	59.70	63.18	63.12	57.27	53.90	55.23	55.21
1983	57.24	57.78											

Source: Department of Agriculture   T.307

HOGS

High, Low & Closing Prices of June Live Hogs Futures at Chicago   In Cents per Pound

Year of Delivery		Apr.	May	June	July	Aug.	Sept.	Oct.	Nov.	Dec.	Jan.	Feb.	Mar.	Apr.	May	June	Life of Delivery Range
1978	High	41.52	41.30	39.00	38.10	34.60	35.85	34.87	36.80	41.10	44.17	48.75	52.25	52.95	56.27	53.75	56.27
	Low	38.05	37.80	35.60	33.85	32.70	32.95	33.40	34.75	36.00	39.95	44.20	45.50	49.90	51.12	50.10	32.70
	Close	40.55	40.10	37.90	34.20	33.10	33.72	34.75	36.55	40.95	44.17	45.75	50.85	51.85	52.90	50.57	—
1979	High	45.75	50.00	48.67	45.77	45.80	50.80	52.10	51.92	52.00	53.20	56.40	54.92	51.25	50.37	44.30	56.40
	Low	43.30	45.60	38.60	40.80	42.55	43.77	47.65	48.30	46.25	46.87	51.25	47.10	47.15	43.90	40.70	37.90
	Close	45.70	48.85	42.70	45.57	44.47	49.60	49.70	50.65	46.90	52.35	54.10	48.00	50.25	44.15	42.57	—
1980	High	44.10	44.60	45.00	44.05	43.70	46.37	43.70	46.90	45.72	46.20	43.00	42.95	36.80	35.40	40.80	46.90
	Low	42.05	39.60	38.35	38.00	37.05	40.80	37.85	41.60	42.00	41.10	40.10	33.50	31.30	32.47	31.90	31.30
	Close	43.62	39.75	42.10	38.40	43.40	41.80	42.10	42.97	43.97	43.10	41.47	34.30	34.47	33.00	39.75	—
1981	High	45.60	45.05	47.70	51.22	52.80	57.35	59.50	61.80	63.25	53.90	55.55	49.90	51.50	52.50	54.70	63.25
	Low	42.40	43.77	42.65	46.80	49.35	50.40	53.80	56.25	52.02	50.75	48.87	43.52	48.25	46.85	49.75	42.40
	Close	44.37	44.70	46.45	50.80	50.47	56.12	57.77	61.80	52.02	52.65	48.87	49.82	49.00	52.20	54.05	—
1982	High	59.90	58.70	58.90	56.60	56.10	53.80	50.60	50.47	46.60	52.65	53.05	56.45	60.00	63.32	62.75	63.32
	Low	56.40	55.82	55.50	53.20	51.05	48.10	47.57	44.65	38.75	45.35	48.35	49.82	55.10	58.85	58.15	438.75
	Close	56.55	58.65	55.50	55.80	51.12	49.00	50.02	45.85	45.67	52.32	49.95	55.47	59.92	62.12	58.82	—
1983	High	53.40	54.00	53.25	53.00	52.50	57.17	55.85	55.30	56.70	58.15	56.45	55.30	51.87			
	Low	50.60	51.15	48.00	50.10	48.90	51.12	51.65	51.45	53.30	54.60	53.55	51.15	48.25			
	Close	53.40	53.47	51.35	52.10	52.15	54.70	52.95	55.00	55.12	55.50	54.07	52.10	49.55			
1984	High	47.75															
	Low	46.75															
	Close	46.75															

Source: Chicago Mercantile Exchange   T.308

Volume of Trading of Live Hogs Futures at Chicago   In Thousands of Contracts

Year	Jan.	Feb.	Mar.	Apr.	May	June	July	Aug.	Sept.	Oct.	Nov.	Dec.	Total
1978	136.8	165.6	214.0	159.0	174.7	149.9	116.9	122.4	121.8	150.5	136.1	117.4	1,765.2
1979	143.1	137.9	185.4	132.0	145.1	160.9	144.1	164.5	151.3	154.1	162.9	124.5	1,805.7
1980	152.9	122.3	138.3	158.8	133.8	170.8	189.7	188.6	239.1	258.1	195.3	201.4	2,153.8
1981	174.8	182.0	197.5	212.0	230.7	262.9	179.8	153.9	171.9	178.6	160.2	153.7	2,258.1
1982	178.7	195.6	262.6	222.6	288.0	408.3	300.1	344.5	347.2	383.4	324.9	305.1	3,561.0
1983	291.6	254.7	213.8	230.6									

Source: Chicago Mercantile Exchange   T.310

Average Price Received by Farmers for Hogs in the U.S.   In Cents Per Pound

Year	Jan.	Feb.	Mar.	Apr.	May	June	July	Aug.	Sept.	Oct.	Nov.	Dec.	Average[1]
1974	40.10	39.30	35.00	30.60	26.30	24.20	34.30	36.00	33.70	37.10	36.80	38.40	34.30
1975	38.20	38.50	38.60	39.30	45.10	47.40	53.90	56.10	58.60	58.30	49.10	47.60	47.60
1976	47.70	48.00	45.60	47.00	47.60	49.20	47.60	42.60	39.70	32.90	31.20	36.60	43.00
1977	38.10	39.40	37.20	36.00	40.70	42.00	44.80	42.80	40.30	39.90	37.80	41.80	39.40
1978	43.90	47.40	46.40	45.00	47.90	47.60	45.40	47.40	48.00	50.80	47.30	48.00	46.60
1979	50.70	52.60	48.30	44.10	43.20	39.60	37.90	36.20	37.20	33.80	34.50	36.90	41.80
1980	36.20	36.70	33.40	28.00	28.60	33.10	41.20	46.20	46.10	47.20	45.60	43.80	38.00
1981	40.90	41.30	38.80	39.00	40.90	47.40	49.30	49.20	48.60	45.00	41.50	39.00	43.90
1982[2]	43.40	48.30	48.60	51.20	56.70	57.50	57.80	61.20	61.30	55.80	52.50	53.60	52.30
1983[2]	55.30	56.10	50.40	47.40									

[1] Weighted average by quantities sold.   [2] Preliminary.   Source: Crop Reporting Board, U.S.D.A.   T.306

Honey

The worldwide production of honey during 1982 was estimated at 902,000 tonnes, 3 percent higher than the revised figure for the 1981 production. Favorable weather as well as plentiful floral honey sources brought about increases in production in the U.S., Canada, Argentina, Brazil, and China. The production of honey in France during 1982 nearly doubled to approximately 25,000 tonnes. At the same time, drought conditions were expected to result in reduced production figures in Australia, Mexico, Italy and Spain. Cool, sunless weather over the United Kingdom during June and July reportedly hurt the production of honey in that country. Drought, in addition to over-wintering conditions and disease, has limited the output of honey from the Soviet Union throughout the past two years. However, improving weather conditions during 1982 were believed to have offset to some extent the reported decline in the Soviet Union's colony numbers. The production of honey in the Soviet Union during 1982 was nearly 180,000 tonnes, virtually unchanged from the 1981 level.

The U.S. production of honey in 1982 was estimated to have totaled 221 million pounds, nearly 19 percent above the 1981 U.S. production figure of 186 million pounds. Imports during 1982 were expected to total 92 million pounds, compared with the 1981 record production figure of 77.3 million pounds. Overall 1982 U.S. exports of honey lagged behind the exports recorded in 1981 throughout most of the year. Total exports at the end of 1982 were 9 million pounds compared with 9.2 million pounds in 1981. The domestic disppearance of honey was estimated to be approximately 242 million pounds, up from 232 million pounds in 1981.

The U.S. national average support price for 1982-crop honey was set at 60.4 cents per pound, and loan availability was for the period April 1, 1982 to January 31, 1983. The fact that the support price was higher than the market price caused approximately 87.5 million pounds of honey to placed under loan, according to reports through mid-February 1983. Nearly 39 million pounds of 1981-crop honey had been forfeited to the CCC by that date, and it was expected that an even greater quantity of 1982-crop honey would be forfeited. At the same time, given low import prices and large world honey supplies, 1983 U.S. honey imports were expected to continue at the high levels recorded during 1982.

Early in February 1983, Congress was forwarded proposed legislation that would have given the Secretary of Agriculture discretion in implementing a honey price program and in setting a price support level. The legislation would make a honey program no longer mandatory.

In April 1983, the USDA announced that honey producers would receive average loan and purchase rates of 62.2 cents per pound for their 1983 production. This price was 1.8 cents above the 1982 rate and was the minimum required under legislation. According to an administrator of the USDA Agricultural Stabilization and Conservation Service, extracted honey loan and purchase rates would range from 54.4 cents to 64.4 cents per pound depending on color and class. The rates, which applied to extracted honey in 60-pound or larger containers, were:

COLOR and/or CLASS	CENTS PER POUND
White or lighter	64.4
Extra light amber	61.4
Light amber	58.4
Other table and non-table honey	54.4

The 1983 loan rate level represented 60 pecent of the April 1983 adjusted parity price of $1.037 per pound. Loans and purchases were to be offered on 1983-crop honey in eligible containers, on or off farms. Producers were given until January 31, 1984 to request loans that would mature on April 30, 1984.

Subsidies to honey production in the European Community (EC) during 1982 were paid according to a 3-year program that began with the 1981/82 marketing year (July 1 to June 30). Subsidy payments were to be made to recognized beekeeper associations, and were intended to partially reduce the cost of sugar fed to bees and to improve honey production, technology, and marketing. Subsidy assistance was initially placed at 1 ECU (U.S. $1.13) per hive. Figured from an average yield per hive of 9.7 kilograms in France, West Germany, Italy, and the United Kingdom, a subsidy of approximately 4.7 cents per pound was paid for 1981/82 honey at the then current ECU rate. The old premiums for denaturing white sugar for feeding bees were to be eliminated in 1981, and new payments were to be broader because feed sugar grants were not to have exceeded 5 kilograms per hive. The program was expected to maintain crop yields through pollination, increase honey production and safeguard the environment, supplement farm income in important beekeeping regions, and to assist producers recovering from the effects of increased winter feed costs and the poor honey production caused by unfavorable weather.

HONEY

World Production of Honey In Thousands of Metric Tons[2]

Year	Argentina	Australia	Brazil	Canada	China (Mainland)	Ethiopia	France	W. Germany	Japan	Mexico	Poland	Spain	Turkey	United States	U.S.S.R.[3]	World Total[3]
1969	44.1	29.1		53.3	46.0	1968–	18.3	26.5	14.6	79.4	15.1	22.0	28.5	267.5	226.0	1,065
1970	55.1	49.1		51.0	36.4	72	27.6	39.7	16.4	66.1	19.8	20.3	28.2	221.8	237.0	1,053
1971	38.8	42.2		52.0	35.5	Avg.	26.5	33.1	17.0	55.1	22.8	18.1	36.0	197.4	237.0	1,030
1972	49.6	44.6		50.6	36.1	(17.5)	22.0	26.5	13.2	84.0	22.5	19.9	36.1	214.1	240.0	1,080
1973[2]	21.0	18.1		24.8	13.6	18.1	10.5	10.0	7.6	33.0	10.4	9.5	16.8	107.8	124.7	574.0
1974	27.0	21.2		20.8	50.0	18.8	9.7	16.5	7.6	42.0	10.9	9.5	17.2	84.0	79.0	597.4
1975	23.6	20.6		21.1	60.0	19.2	9.0	8.8	6.3	38.0	7.4	10.5	17.1	89.8	76.1	609.4
1976	28.0	21.4	12.0	25.4	55.0	19.4	14.5	22.0	6.1	44.0	9.6	11.0	24.1	90.0	188.0	784.2
1977	22.0	14.9	14.0	25.4	60.0	19.0	8.2	20.0	6.2	60.0	10.0	12.0	21.7	81.0	208.0	798.3
1978	35.0	18.6	16.0	30.6	75.0	20.0	9.5	15.0	8.5	54.0	12.0	11.0	21.7	104.5	179.0	827.7
1979	30.0	25.0	18.0	32.9	110.0	20.0	14.4	9.9	7.5	52.0	13.0	12.0	23.7	107.8	189.0	880.1
1980	28.0	18.0	20.0	29.2	80.0	20.5	12.0	11.0	6.2	60.0	10.0	13.0	23.0	81.6	190.0	884.3
1981[1]	34.0	21.0	24.0	32.9	115.0	21.0	10.0	13.0	8.0	62.0	10.0	13.0	23.0	81.6	193.0	884.3
1982[1]							25.0								180.0	902

[1] Preliminary. [2] Data prior to 1973 are in MILLIONS OF POUNDS. [3] New series beginning 1976. Source: *Foreign Agricultural Service, U.S.D.A.*   T.312

Salient Statistics of Honey in the United States

Year	Number of Colonies Thous.	Yield Per Colony Lbs.	Total U.S.	California	Florida	Iowa	Minnesota	So. Dak.	Texas	Wisconsin	Domestic Disapp.	Imports For Consumption	Domestic Exports	Stocks Jan. 1[2]	Farm Price of All Honey	Beeswax ¢ Lb.	All Honey
1970	4,290	51.7	221.8	15.7	25.1	12.8	19.5		10.2	12.7	234.7	8.9	8.1	50.6	17.4	60.2	17.4
1971	4,110	48.0	197.4	19.9	22.2	9.0	12.2		8.4	11.6	220.9	11.4	7.6	30.9	21.8	61.3	21.8
1972	4,085	52.8	215.6	24.5	26.6	6.9	11.8		11.4	7.7	250.1	39.0	4.1	29.8	30.2	62.1	30.2
1973	4,124	58.0	239.1	31.0	33.5	7.5	15.3		9.9	11.4	224.9	10.7	17.6	30.1	44.4	74.4	44.4
1974	4,210	44.6	187.9	23.5	16.2	6.9	9.6		10.3	7.7	212.3	26.0	4.6	37.4	51.0	114.0	51.0
1975	4,206	47.4	199.2	24.5	24.5	5.9	10.9		12.9	5.5	242.8	46.4	4.0	34.4	50.5	103.0	50.5
1976	4,269	46.4	198.0	13.7	27.4	6.6	14.3		9.4	10.3	259.1	66.5	4.7	33.2	49.9	112.0	49.9
1977	4,323	41.2	178.1	13.7	14.4	6.1	12.0		9.0	9.6	241.1	63.9	5.5	34.3	52.9	158.0	52.9
1978	4,090	56.6	231.5	31.2	23.9	4.6	13.9		8.7	6.3	276.7	56.0	8.0	30.0	54.6	174.0	54.6
1979	4,163	57.3	238.7	17.1	27.3	6.6	15.8	17.3	11.4	8.8	280.4	58.6	8.8	32.2	59.3	175.0	59.3
1980	4,141	48.2	199.8	23.2	20.3	6.3	13.7	8.1	6.9	6.0	239.2	49.0	8.5	38.0	61.5	183.0	61.5
1981[1]	4,213	44.1	185.9	9.0	24.1	3.4	8.2	9.2	11.4	4.1	232	77.3	9.2	40.5	63.2	191.0	63.2
1982[1]			221								242	92	9	48.6			

[1] Preliminary. [2] Prior to 1973, data are for producers' stocks for sale as of Dec. 15. Source: *Crop Reporting Board, U.S.D.A.*   T.313

Wholesale Price Index of Honey[1] (Extracted) at Chicago 1967 = 100

Year	Jan.	Feb.	Mar.	Apr.	May	June	July	Aug.	Sept.	Oct.	Nov.	Dec.	Average
1970	20.1	20.1	20.1	20.1	18.8	18.8	18.8	18.8	18.8	18.8	18.8	18.8	19.2
1971[2]	18.8	18.8	18.8	18.8	18.8	18.8	20.3	188.0[2]	188.0	188.0	188.0	188.0	
1972	188.0	188.0	188.0	188.0	188.0	188.0	188.0	188.0	188.0	188.0	188.0	188.0	188.0
1973	188.0	188.0	218.0	218.0	231.6	264.4	256.2	258.9	N.A.	258.9	272.5	337.9	244.8
1974	337.9	N.A.	337.9	343.3	343.3	307.9	N.A.	272.5	N.A.	272.5	343.3	343.3	322.4
1975	343.3	343.3	343.3	343.3	332.4	321.5	321.5	N.A.	248.0	N.A.	248.0	N.A.	316.1
1976	N.A.	N.A.	N.A.	223.4	231.6	224.8	N.A.	245.2	N.A.	245.2	235.4	234.3	234.3
1977	228.9	239.8	238.0	231.6	228.9	228.9	242.1	245.2	249.7	244.3	N.A.	247.3	238.6
1978	247.1	245.8	252.5	254.0	255.6	247.4	N.A.	250.5	248.7	248.4	246.4	246.5	249.4
1979	250.0	259.3	270.8	255.8	264.3	286.7	277.7	288.8	283.4	286.4	288.3	283.6	274.6
1980	286.8	289.6	287.1	272.5	284.1	283.0	277.2	283.4	284.0	285.6	285.9	288.7	284.0
1981	298.7	296.9	285.4	299.7	294.3	287.1	296.4	304.4	295.0	305.3	304.9	295.7	297.0
1982	299.7	294.3	306.6	294.3	305.2	305.2	299.7	302.2	306.3	305.2	308.8	295.7	301.9
1983	305.2	310.6	318.8										

[1] White Clover, any state of origin, in 60 lb. cans, wholesaler to baker, confectioner, or other large user. [2] Prior to Aug. 1971, data are in cents per pound. Price for Aug. 1971 was 24.0¢ lb. Source: *Bureau of Labor Statistics* (0254-0101.01)   T.314

Interest Rates

The general rate of interest is considered to be the most significant ratio generated within the financial marketplace. Roughly, the rate of interest is the premium that present money commands over money to be paid at some future date. As such, it is a paramount consideration behind decisions to invest present capital in hopes of a future return. Interest rates ultimately determine the extent of economic growth and the prices that will be bid for labor and equipment intended for future production. The relative values of currencies, as investment vehicles, are likewise affected by interest rate fluctuations.

U.S. interest rates are directly influenced by the various Federal Reserve money market operations that expand or contract the amount of funds available to the loan market. Most importantly, the Fed is empowered to finance government budget deficits by purchasing government securities, an action that pushes down short-term rates and expands the money supply. At the same time, the inflationary effect of the increased quantity of money tends to pull upward on long-term interest rates. The interest rate structure is, through this effect, sensitive to changes in the Federal deficit.

During 1982, the prime rate charged by banks on loans to their best corporate customers fell from nearly 17 percent to just above 11 percent at the end of the year. This drop reflected a loosening of the Fed's tight-money policy that had prevailed through most of 1981 when the prime rate had hovered above 20 percent. Steep U.S. interest rates brought about a contraction of domestic business and a sharply stronger dollar that drastically curtailed U.S. exports. The political pressure exerted by rising unemployment and business bankruptcies resulted in an easier Fed money policy.

The Fed implemented monetary policy in 1982 by "targeting" rates of growth for three money aggregates. M-1, the most closely observed of these, consists of currency in circulation and checking deposits. M-2 is M-1 plus savings accounts and mutual funds. M-3 is M-2 plus large time deposits and certain money market funds. In the last quarter of 1982, the Fed announced a temporary suspension of its practice of gauging money supply growth by M-1, explaining that M-1 was liable to distortion by the maturing of billions of dollars in all-savers certificates and by various newly-introduced money market savings accounts. Many analysts interpreted the announcement as an indication that the Fed would henceforth target interest rates rather than monetary reserves. A surge in M-2 growth around the same time was attributed to money market deposit accounts (MMDAs) that had no interest ceilings.

Growth targets of 4 to 8 percent for M-1, 7 to 10 percent for M-2, and 6.5 to 9.5 percent for M-3 in 1983 were said to be the sign of an easier money policy. Analysts reasoned that subsequent cuts in the Fed's discount rate, a move considered consistent with easier money, would push T-bill futures higher than T-bonds, because inflationary expectations following the cut would probably curtail the buying of long-term securities.

The fiscal 1983 (October 1982–September 1983) Federal budget assumes a 1.4 percent rate of economic growth in calendar 1983, a 5 percent inflation rate, and unemployment above 10 percent. Estimates of the fiscal 1983 Federal budget deficit average $190 billion, $186 billion for fiscal 1984.

Futures Markets

Futures in Treasury bonds, T-notes and GNMAs securities are traded on the Chicago Board of Trade. Futures in T-bill (90-day), Domestic Bank CDs, and Eurodollars are traded on the Chicago Mercantile Exchange. Smaller T-bill and T-bond futures contracts are traded on Chicago's MidAmerica Commodity Exchange. Eurodollars, Gilts, and 3-month Sterling Deposits are traded on the London International Financial Futures Exchange.

U.S. Producer Commodity Price Index (Wholesale, All Commodities)   1967 = 100

Year	Jan.	Feb.	Mar.	Apr.	May	June	July	Aug.	Sept.	Oct.	Nov.	Dec.	Average
1976	179.4	179.4	179.7	181.3	181.9	183.2	184.4	183.8	184.8	185.3	185.6	187.1	183.0
1977	188.1	190.2	192.0	194.3	195.2	194.5	194.8	194.6	195.3	196.3	197.1	198.2	194.2
1978	200.1	202.1	203.7	206.5	208.0	209.6	210.7	210.6	212.4	214.9	215.7	217.5	209.3
1979	220.8	224.1	226.7	230.0	232.0	233.5	236.9	238.3	242.0	245.6	247.2	249.7	235.6
1980	254.9	260.2	261.9	262.8	264.2	265.6	270.4	273.8	274.6	277.8	279.1	280.8	268.8
1981	284.8	287.6	290.3	293.4	294.1	294.8	296.2	296.4	295.7	296.1	295.5	295.8	293.4
1982[1]	298.3	298.6	298.0	298.0	298.6	299.3	300.4	300.2	299.5	299.9	300.4	300.6	299.3
1983[1]	300.0	301.2											

[1] Preliminary.   Source: Bureau of Labor Statistics

U.S. Consumer Price Index   (Retail Price Index for All Items: Urban Consumers) 1967 = 100

Year	Jan.	Feb.	Mar.	Apr.	May	June	July	Aug.	Sept.	Oct.	Nov.	Dec.	Average
1976	166.7	167.1	167.5	168.2	169.2	170.1	171.1	171.9	172.6	173.3	173.8	174.3	170.5
1977	175.3	177.1	178.2	179.6	180.6	181.8	182.6	183.3	184.0	184.5	185.4	186.1	181.5
1978	187.2	188.4	189.8	191.5	193.3	195.3	196.7	197.8	199.3	200.9	202.0	202.9	195.4
1979	204.7	207.1	209.1	211.5	214.1	216.6	218.9	221.1	223.4	225.4	227.5	229.9	217.4
1980	233.2	236.4	239.8	242.5	244.9	247.6	247.8	249.4	251.7	253.9	256.2	258.4	246.8
1981	260.5	263.2	265.1	266.8	269.0	271.3	274.4	276.5	279.3	279.9	280.7	281.5	272.4
1982[1]	282.5	283.4	283.1	284.3	287.1	290.6	292.2	292.8	293.3	294.1	293.6	292.4	289.1
1983[1]	293.1	293.2											

[1] Preliminary.   Source: Bureau of Labor Statistics

INTEREST RATES

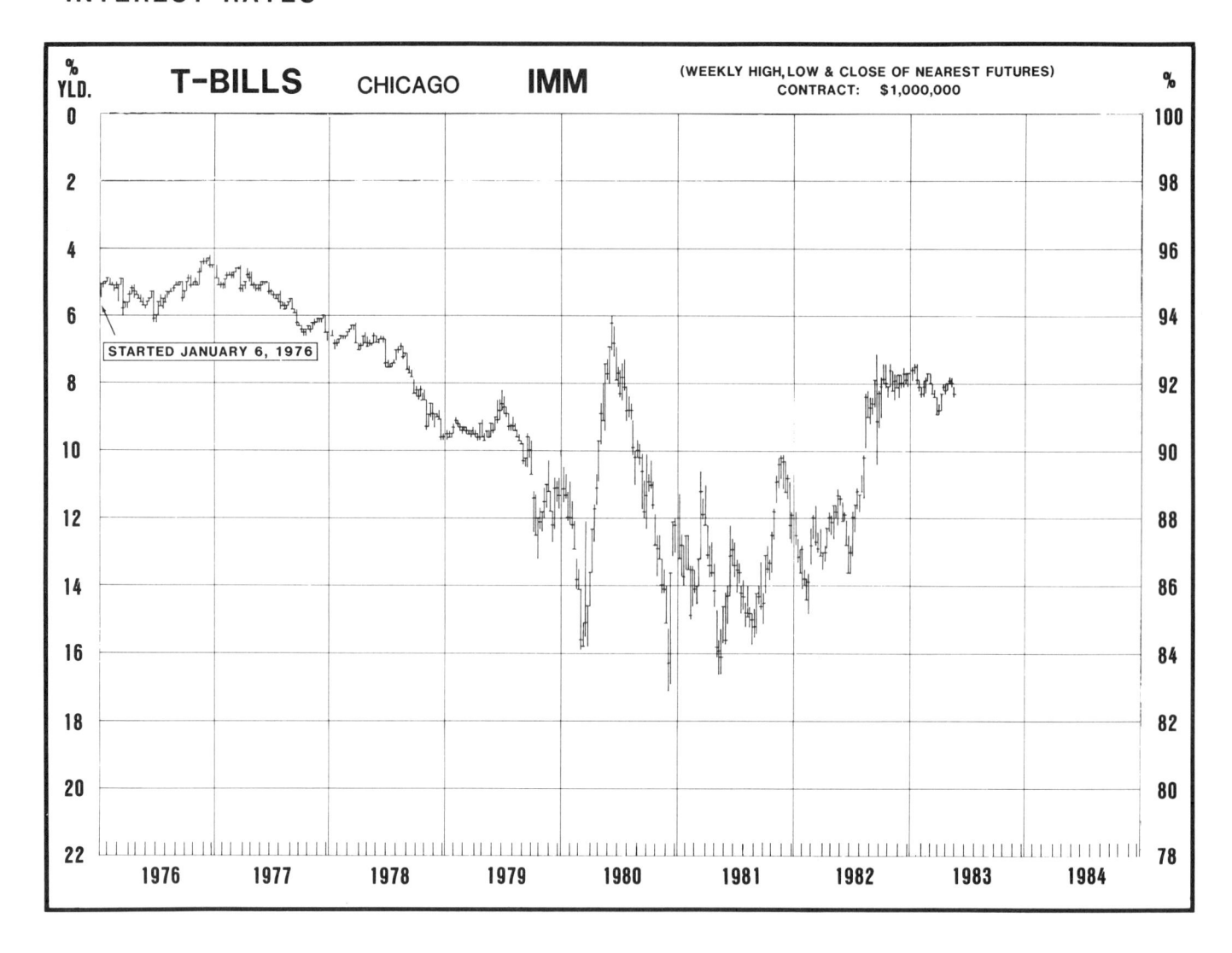

T-BILLS CHICAGO **IMM** (WEEKLY HIGH, LOW & CLOSE OF NEAREST FUTURES) CONTRACT: $1,000,000

STARTED JANUARY 6, 1976

Month–End Open Interest of 13 Wk.[1] Treasury Bills Futures in Chicago — In Thousands of Contracts

Year	Jan.	Feb.	Mar.	Apr.	May	June	July	Aug.	Sept.	Oct.	Nov.	Dec.
1978	12.5	13.7	15.6	17.6	20.3	23.7	27.7	34.4	33.9	47.9	52.6	59.2
1979	54.2	54.2	52.7	56.4	63.7	61.2	46.8	40.9	41.4	35.4	42.8	36.5
1980	30.2	25.0	28.5	28.2	24.7	25.2	22.9	23.1	21.4	24.2	39.2	42.9
1981	45.7	38.0	32.8	28.9	35.6	38.9	45.7	43.6	32.3	38.7	36.2	30.1
1982	33.9	33.0	36.5	43.9	52.5	41.4	52.2	59.6	51.1	45.8	50.1	49.0
1983	47.7	46.8	38.6	44.6								

[1] 90-day U.S. Treas. Bill.   *Source: International Monetary Market (Chicago)*   T.322

Volume of Trading of 13 Wk.[1] Treasury Bills Futures in Chicago — In Thousands of Contracts

Year	Jan.	Feb.	Mar.	Apr.	May	June	July	Aug.	Sept.	Oct.	Nov.	Dec.	Total
1978	37.9	24.7	33.6	41.9	38.9	48.4	39.9	74.1	87.2	98.6	137.0	106.8	772.0
1979	89.8	78.6	103.8	111.5	154.7	193.1	182.0	144.5	204.1	251.7	225.8	190.9	1,930.5
1980	237.5	245.4	290.3	350.1	321.2	250.7	224.4	204.9	231.1	274.3	287.7	401.1	3,338.8
1981	446.6	414.4	408.5	407.6	426.1	511.0	487.8	482.0	525.8	516.0	509.5	496.5	5,631.3
1982	503.5	465.5	638.7	529.1	595.4	546.0	615.2	738.4	628.6	521.4	442.4	374.7	6,598.8
1983	302.2	337.9	361.4	308.5									

[1] 90-day U.S. Treas. Bill.   *Source: International Monetary Market (Chicago)*   T.323

INTEREST RATES

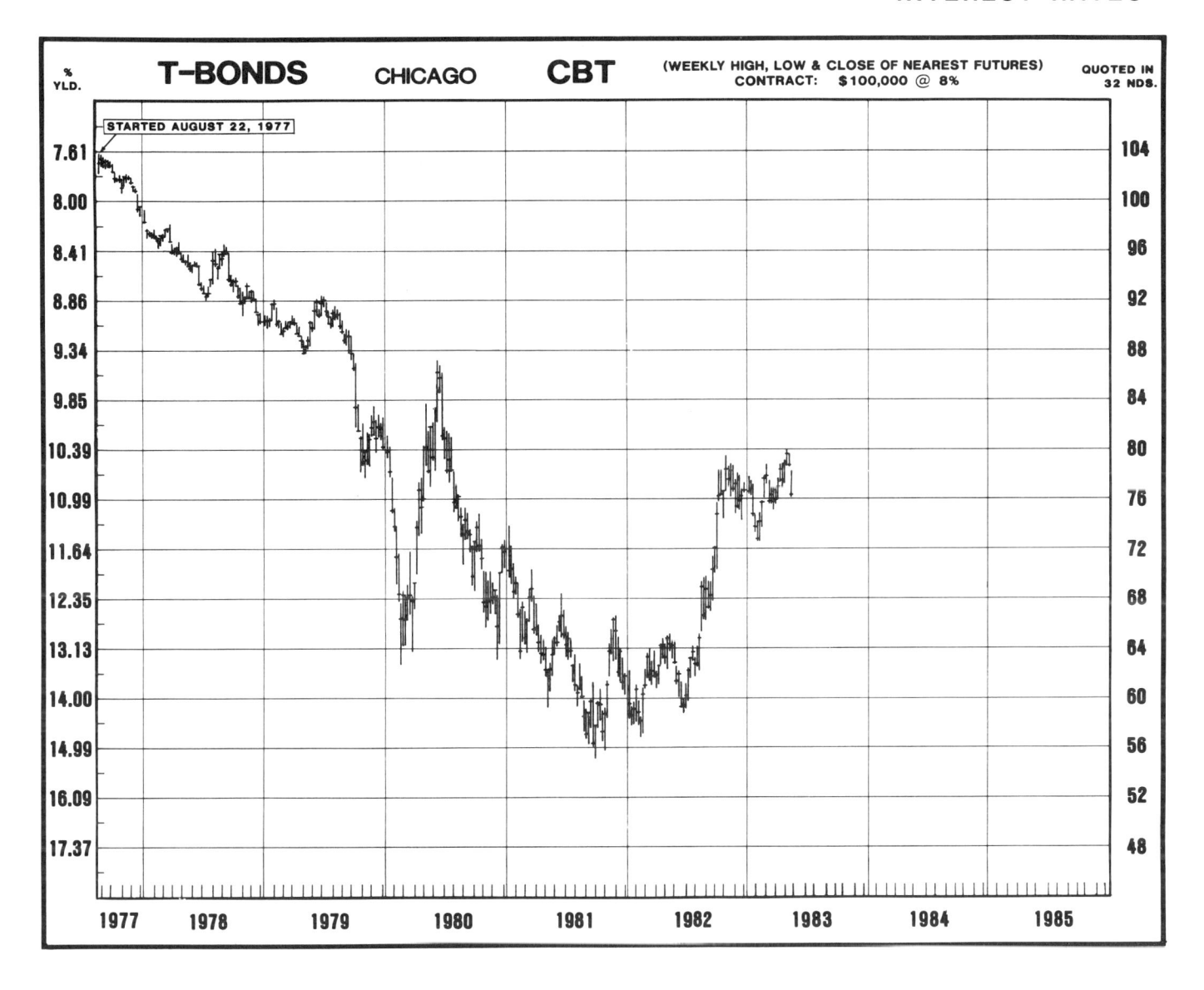

T-BONDS CHICAGO **CBT** (WEEKLY HIGH, LOW & CLOSE OF NEAREST FUTURES) CONTRACT: $100,000 @ 8% QUOTED IN 32 NDS.

Month-End Open Interest of Treasury Bond Futures in Chicago In Thousands of Contracts

Year	Jan.	Feb.	Mar.	Apr.	May	June	July	Aug.	Sept.	Oct.	Nov.	Dec.
1978	3.3	4.4	6.1	8.8	9.7	8.8	10.3	12.6	14.7	27.6	35.7	41.2
1979	41.8	45.0	45.9	46.9	53.9	61.5	63.1	65.7	65.4	65.1	74.1	90.7
1980	71.3	66.4	57.1	70.2	84.8	111.1	110.0	117.2	123.2	153.1	204.8	243.6
1981	240.7	223.6	226.1	230.4	241.3	290.9	315.1	295.4	240.5	257.7	248.7	221.7
1982	216.2	192.9	184.4	193.0	181.8	160.6	158.1	162.7	159.0	160.4	175.7	182.9
1983	177.6	142.9	147.5	142.1								

Source: Chicago Board of Trade T.317

Volume of Trading of Treasury Bond Futures in Chicago In Thousands of Contracts

Year	Jan.	Feb.	Mar.	Apr.	May	June	July	Aug.	Sept.	Oct.	Nov.	Dec.	Total
1978	11.5	10.2	14.2	19.1	23.4	33.1	37.8	62.2	60.3	87.7	95.2	98.6	555.4
1979	95.3	98.3	95.5	110.4	181.8	169.1	140.5	167.2	221.2	271.1	249.4	259.9	2,059.6
1980	311.1	332.4	349.3	423.4	520.5	608.6	502.7	516.4	501.2	691.6	722.5	1,009.8	6,489.6
1981	846.7	868.6	975.9	998.9	1,178.1	1,094.4	1,081.8	1,191.5	1,313.7	1,289.1	1,691.5	1,377.9	13,908.0
1982	1,266.4	1,306.1	1,413.9	1,259.4	1,408.2	1,254.8	1,145.5	1,669.5	1,474.4	1,644.0	1,545.2	1,352.3	16,739.7
1983	1,333.9	1,447.8	1,600.4	1,263.0									

Source: Chicago Board of Trade T.319

INTEREST RATES

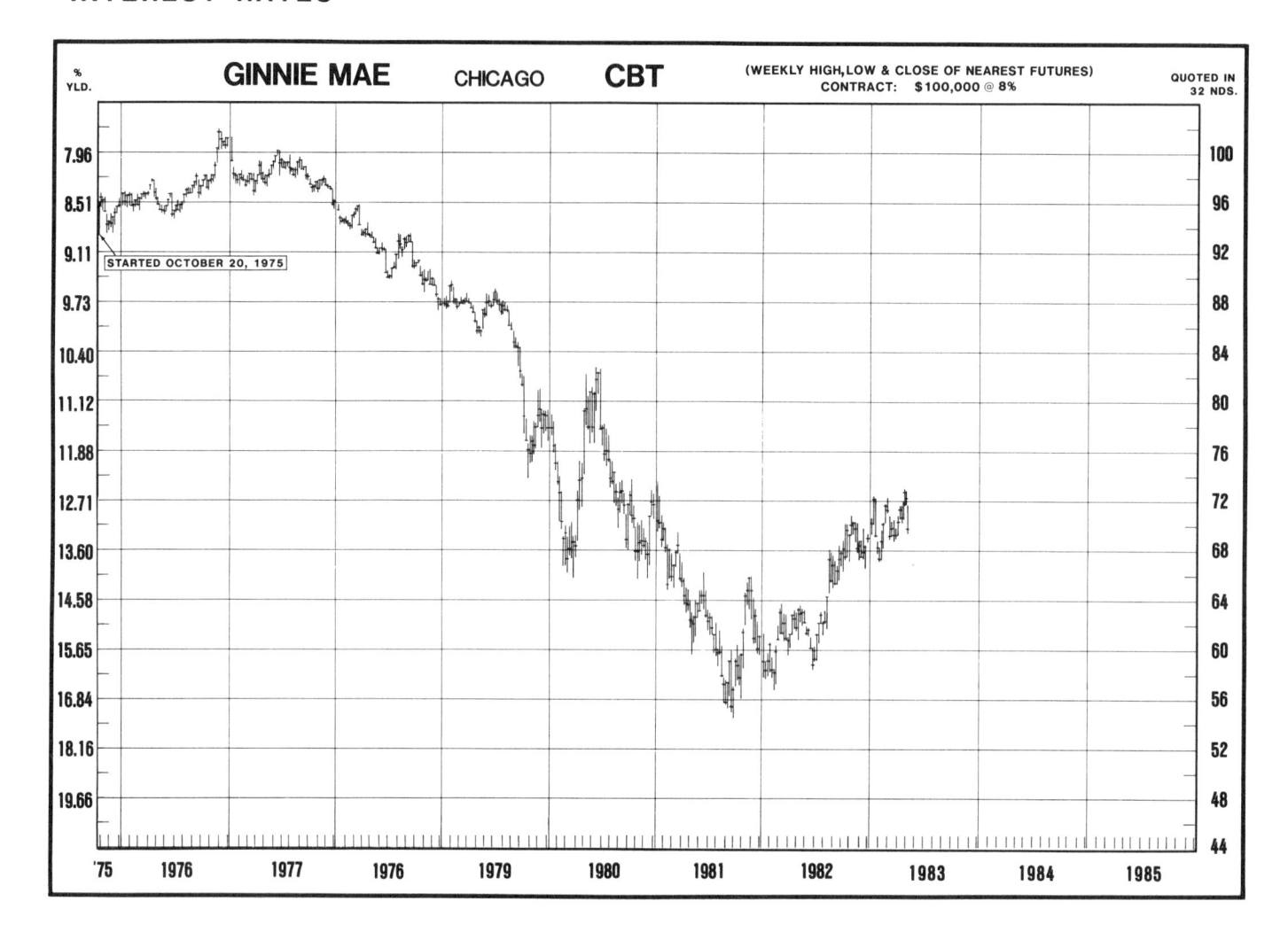

GINNIE MAE CHICAGO **CBT** (WEEKLY HIGH, LOW & CLOSE OF NEAREST FUTURES) CONTRACT: $100,000 @ 8% QUOTED IN 32 NDS.

Month-End Open Interest of GNMA (CDR) Futures in Chicago In Thousands of Contracts

Year	Jan.	Feb.	Mar.	Apr.	May	June	July	Aug.	Sept.	Oct.	Nov.	Dec.
1978	20.4	19.6	20.3	24.0	27.8	33.5	39.4	43.6	41.6	54.4	60.0	62.7
1979	62.4	63.5	62.9	62.8	68.5	73.3	70.6	75.0	77.0	71.0	76.3	89.0
1980	65.9	54.7	46.1	55.5	60.6	71.9	67.6	63.1	67.1	83.2	98.5	115.2
1981	97.0	97.1	99.8	105.7	107.5	121.0	133.9	116.6	96.5	95.2	82.7	77.2
1982	70.0	61.1	64.3	69.3	58.0	51.9	51.8	44.0	45.4	42.2	41.9	40.0
1983	34.9	35.4	45.6	41.3								

Source: Chicago Board of Trade

T.325

Volume of Trading of GNMA (CDR) Futures in Chicago In Thousands of Contracts

Year	Jan.	Feb.	Mar.	Apr.	May	June	July	Aug.	Sept.	Oct.	Nov.	Dec.	Total
1978	48.4	46.7	57.1	57.2	60.1	75.2	73.6	109.2	96.1	110.9	109.0	109.6	953.2
1979	89.8	79.8	68.1	82.0	99.8	111.8	77.0	95.3	164.9	164.9	157.9	180.4	1,371.1
1980	170.0	155.5	156.3	190.3	219.7	248.4	162.0	151.6	133.9	205.0	214.5	318.7	2,326.3
1981	179.8	159.9	186.5	202.3	228.8	188.5	162.0	156.2	189.8	194.0	242.2	202.8	2,292.9
1982	188.8	184.1	182.6	140.6	159.3	156.3	154.8	222.7		218.3	143.6	134.0	2,055.6
1983	143.5	133.8	147.7	125.3									

Source: Chicago Board of Trade

T.324

INTEREST RATES

High, Low & Closing Prices of June Treasury Bonds Futures in Chicago   In 32nds of 100%

Year of Delivery		Apr.	May	June	July	Aug.	Sept.	Oct.	Nov.	Dec.	Jan.	Feb.	Mar.	Apr.	May	June	Life of Delivery Range
1978	High	FUTURES				102-15	102-21	102-06	101-12	101-01	98-30	97-04	97-19	96-25	95-24	95-07	102-21
	Low	TRADING				101-10	101-27	100-10	99-25	98-11	96-19	95-24	95-25	95-10	94-13	94-06	94-06
	Close	BEGAN AUG. 22, 1977				102-13	102-07	100-10	100-30	99-05	97-11	96-14	95-30	95-15	94-13	94-07	—
1979	High	95-07	94-10	93-16	92-28	95-06	96-03	94-09	93-31	93-15	92-08	92-09	90-27	90-19	90-09	91-01	98-11
	Low	93-29	92-20	91-26	91-03	92-15	93-08	91-00	92-02	90-09	90-01	89-13	89-09	88-02	87-20	89-16	89-20
	Close	94-03	92-20	91-28	92-20	94-21	93-08	91-11	92-30	90-18	91-23	89-21	90-05	88-06	89-22	90-30	—
1980	High	90-31	90-18	92-13	92-12	91-18	89-18	87-13	84-14	85-00	82-24	75-07	71-24	77-27	83-20	87-07	95-31
	Low	88-24	88-08	89-24	89-27	89-09	87-05	78-11	78-15	80-20	74-07	63-15	64-30	67-12	77-00	78-09	63-15
	Close	88-27	89-31	91-27	90-20	89-11	87-21	80-12	83-01	82-29	75-04	69-00	67-27	77-02	79-14	85-25	—
1981	High	79-21	84-00	85-15	81-08	77-00	75-23	75-04	71-20	73-18	74-22	70-15	70-15	67-17	64-30	67-16	88-08
	Low	71-23	76-30	77-31	74-26	71-27	69-11	67-22	66-05	65-28	69-04	64-05	64-20	61-25	59-11	64-04	59-11
	Close	77-16	79-03	80-23	75-04	73-26	71-10	68-17	70-02	72-06	70-09	65-31	67-02	61-28	64-24	65-13	—
1982	High	68-14	67-25	69-29	66-23	64-30	62-04	61-09	66-24	66-14	62-16	62-26	64-08	64-27	65-05	62-18	74-20
	Low	64-11	62-19	65-28	62-28	59-04	56-08	56-12	58-30	60-20	58-05	57-10	60-22	61-05	62-15	59-01	56-08
	Close	64-15	67-17	65-30	63-01	59-17	57-03	59-05	65-21	62-04	61-01	61-14	61-30	63-06	62-27	59-24	—
1983	High	67-20	66-25	63-30	65-06	69 29	71-05	77-04	77-20	76-24	77-04	77-13	78-08	79-02			
	Low	63-22	64-15	60-29	61-27	63-18	67-17	70-09	73-18	73-21	72-14	71-27	74 28	75 31			
	Close	65-11	64-15	62-19	64-01	67-20	70-27	75-11	73-28	76-00	72-21	76-22	75-31	78-30			
1984	High	77-00															
	Low	74-13															
	Close	77-00															

Source: Chicago Board of Trade   T.320

High, Low & Closing Prices of June 13 Wk. Treasury Bills Futures in Chicago   In Points of 100%

Year of Delivery		Apr.	May	June	July	Aug.	Sept.	Oct.	Nov.	Dec.	Jan.	Feb.	Mar.	Apr.	May	June	Life of Delivery Range
1978	High	93.59	93.31	93.69	93.57	93.50	93.51	93.28	93.28	93.29	93.17	93.15	93.33	93.49	93.48	93.41	93.80
	Low	92.52	92.53	93.19	93.01	92.95	93.10	92.80	92.92	92.95	92.63	92.78	93.00	93.03	93.09	93.20	92.26
	Close	92.60	93.22	93.61	93.15	93.38	93.29	92.97	93.25	93.13	92.99	93.13	93.02	93.13	93.21	93.23	—
1979	High	92.12	91.87	91.90	91.81	92.11	92.12	91.55	91.08	90.83	90.74	90.88	90.72	90.87	90.84	91.45	92.83
	Low	91.76	91.62	91.49	91.51	91.62	91.40	90.50	90.39	90.14	90.16	90.35	90.43	90.31	90.30	90.50	90.14
	Close	91.76	91.68	91.55	91.75	91.93	91.51	90.58	90.62	90.22	90.65	90.47	90.51	90.50	90.60	91.06	—
1980	High	90.91	91.55	92.59	92.50	92.30	91.65	91.41	91.22	91.01	90.50	89.05	86.40	89.94	92.73	93.97	93.97
	Low	90.51	90.48	91.34	91.54	90.93	90.36	88.10	88.85	89.21	88.37	86.06	84.20	85.40	89.75	92.00	84.20
	Close	90.62	91.46	92.32	91.89	91.11	91.03	89.29	90.55	90.17	88.84	86.49	85.82	89.90	92.30	92.12	—
1981	High	90.90	92.00	92.64	92.04	91.10	89.61	89.77	88.47	88.89	89.43	89.00	89.38	88.95	85.90	86.48	92.64
	Low	87.51	90.60	91.15	90.65	88.45	87.66	87.47	87.08	85.40	87.31	86.36	86.64	85.52	83.35	84.34	83.35
	Close	90.79	91.60	91.50	90.72	89.13	88.31	87.51	87.25	88.18	88.89	87.19	88.77	85.55	85.39	85.79	—
1982	High	89.20	87.81	88.47	87.86	87.52	87.00	87.61	89.54	89.42	87.85	87.48	88.32	88.16	88.94	88.46	91.26
	Low	87.09	86.03	87.40	86.91	85.95	85.48	85.53	87.42	86.93	85.85	85.45	86.46	86.67	87.41	87.16	85.45
	Close	87.10	87.73	87.92	87.21	86.08	85.60	87.55	89.19	87.76	86.90	86.92	86.83	87.88	88.57	87.18	—
1983	High	87.37	87.82	87.56	87.93	89.12	89.66	91.19	91.43	91.94	92.26	92.40	92.28	92.04			
	Low	86.45	87.00	86.32	86.75	87.63	87.95	89.29	90.57	90.67	91.41	91.26	91.12	91.20			
	Close	87.29	87.64	86.77	87.72	88.11	89.63	90.70	90.61	91.92	91.45	92.19	91.20	91.98			
1984	High	91.23															
	Low	90.63															
	Close	91.23															

Source: International Monetary Market (Chicago)   T.321

INTEREST RATES

High, Low & Closing Prices of June GNMA (CDR) Futures in Chicago   In 32nds of 100%

Year of Delivery		Apr.	May	June	July	Aug.	Sept.	Oct.	Nov.	Dec.	Jan.	Feb.	Mar.	Apr.	May	June	Life of Delivery Range
1978	High	95-21	95-05	96-17	96-22	97-28	97-30	97-08	96-28	96-19	95-12	94-12	94-28	94-09	93-17	92-22	97-30
	Low	94-00	94-00	94-25	95-20	95-30	96-30	95-30	95-25	95-00	93-27	93-07	93-09	93-05	91-26	91-19	91-19
	Close	94-07	94-28	96-01	96-03	97-20	97-09	96-03	96-16	95-18	94-12	93-30	93-13	93-12	91-28	91-21	—
1979	High	92-15	91-18	89-23	90-08	91-31	92-16	91-13	90-29	90-17	89-16	89-22	88-20	88-09	87-16	88-19	96-20
	Low	91-12	89-10	88-06	87-31	89-24	90-11	88-26	89-15	87-21	87-17	87-12	87-19	85-27	85-14	86-23	85-14
	Close	91-15	89-10	88-07	89-31	91-14	90-24	89-00	90-02	87-30	89-04	87-26	88-00	85-31	86-28	87-20	—
1980	High	88-12	87-09	88-21	88-26	88-03	85-28	82-00	81-16	82-13	79-11	74-11	70-10	76-08	82-05	82-12	93-20
	Low	85-30	85-19	86-20	86-30	85-28	81-27	73-18	75-00	75-16	73-04	65-22	65-18	67-15	76-16	76-18	65-18
	Close	86-02	86-23	88-06	87-16	85-29	82-10	75-31	79-27	79-18	74-00	69-06	68-15	76-00	77-31	81-18	—
1981	High	77-00	82-12	82-02	77-22	74-24	73-15	73-12	70-20	73-04	74-07	70-15	69-16	67-01	64-00	65-16	91-02
	Low	69-02	76-07	76-06	72-23	69-28	68-11	67-06	66-13	65-31	69-00	65-14	65-19	61-30	59-21	63-03	58-21
	Close	76-16	77-15	77-15	73-03	71-14	70-05	67-31	69-07	71-27	70-08	66-21	66-21	62-01	63-23	63-22	—
1982	High	67-06	66-05	67-05	63-03	62-16	60-04	60-12	65-23	65-00	61-07	61-30	63-00	63-07	63-17	61-30	82-16
	Low	63-05	62-14	63-08	60-31	57-10	54-22	55-00	59-10	59-16	57-15	56-19	59-17	60-04	60-29	59-23	54-22
	Close	63-05	65-31	63-08	61-05	57-14	55-15	59-17	64-15	60-29	60-02	60-18	60-20	61-22	62-04	60-04	—
1983	High	62-15	62-23	60-15	61-27	66-12	67-11	69-10	70-00	68-21	71-19	70-27	71-10	72-00			
	Low	59-17	60-16	57-21	58-14	60-07	63-19	65-16	65-30	65-22	66-15	66-04	68-04	69-09			
	Close	61-03	60-25	59-05	60-28	63-31	66-04	68-11	66-02	68-11	66-22	70-12	69-07	71-27			
1984	High	67-25															
	Low	65-03															
	Close	67-20															

Source: Chicago Board of Trade   T.326

U.S. Industrial Production Index[1] (Seasonally Adjusted)   1967 = 100

Year	Jan.	Feb.	Mar.	Apr.	May	June	July	Aug.	Sept.	Oct.	Nov.	Dec.	Average
1973	126.3	127.8	128.5	128.5	129.6	129.9	130.4	130.4	131.1	131.4	131.6	131.3	129.8
1974	129.9	129.6	130.0	129.9	131.3	131.9	131.8	131.7	131.8	129.5	124.9	119.3	129.3
1975	115.2	112.7	111.7	112.6	113.7	116.4	118.4	121.0	122.1	122.2	123.5	124.4	117.8
1976	126.1	128.1	128.7	129.0	130.1	130.7	131.2	132.0	131.3	131.3	132.6	133.6	130.5
1977	133.7	134.5	136.3	137.1	138.0	138.9	139.0	139.3	139.6	140.1	140.3	140.5	138.2
1978	140.0	140.3	142.1	144.4	144.8	146.1	147.1	148.0	148.6	149.7	150.6	151.8	146.1
1979	152.0	152.5	153.5	151.1	152.7	153.0	153.0	152.1	152.7	152.7	152.3	152.5	152.5
1980	153.0	152.8	152.1	148.2	143.8	141.4	140.3	142.2	144.4	146.6	149.2	150.4	147.0
1981	151.4	151.8	152.1	151.9	152.7	152.9	153.9	153.6	151.6	149.1	146.3	143.4	151.0
1982[2]	140.7	142.9	141.7	140.2	139.2	138.7	138.8	138.4	137.3	135.8	134.9	135.2	138.6
1983[2]	136.9	137.3	139.7	142.6									
1984													

[1] Total Index of the Federal Reserve Index of Quantity Output.   [2] Preliminary.   Source: Federal Reserve System   T.318

How to keep your Commodity Year Book statistics up-to-date continuously throughout the year.

To keep up-to-date statistics on the commodities in this book, you should have COMMODITY YEAR BOOK STATISTICAL ABSTRACT SERVICE. This three-times-yearly publication provides the latest available statistics for the updating of the statistical tables appearing in the COMMODITY YEAR BOOK. It is published in the Winter (Jan.), Spring (Apr.) and Fall (Oct.). Subscription price is $55 per year.

Commodity Research Bureau, Inc.
75 MONTGOMERY ST., JERSEY CITY, N.J. 07302

INTEREST RATES

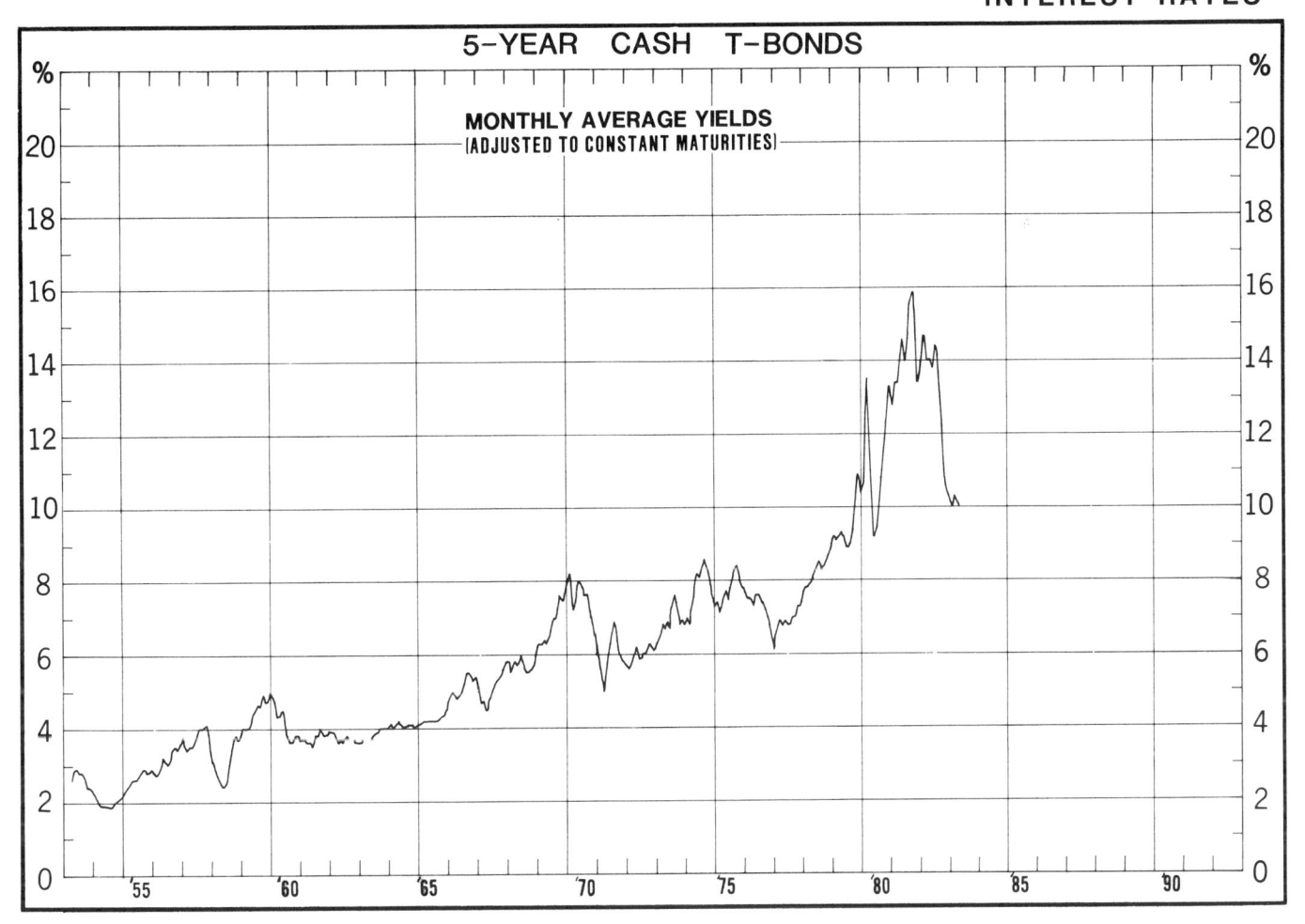

5-YEAR CASH T-BONDS
MONTHLY AVERAGE YIELDS (ADJUSTED TO CONSTANT MATURITIES)

U.S. Money Supply M1 in 1972 $ In Billions of Dollars

Year	Jan.	Feb.	Mar.	Apr.	May	June	July	Aug.	Sept.	Oct.	Nov.	Dec.	Average
1974	243.6	241.8	240.6	239.4	237.4	236.9	235.8	233.5	231.3	230.1	229.6	228.1	235.7
1975	226.6	225.4	226.1	224.6	225.7	227.3	225.5	225.8	225.5	223.7	224.1	222.3	225.2
1976	222.5	223.9	224.1	224.5	225.0	224.1	223.8	223.9	223.7	224.9	225.0	225.3	224.2
1977	221.2	220.9	221.0	221.5	221.2	220.9	221.2	221.2	221.8	222.6	222.8	223.1	221.6
1978	224.3	223.1	222.7	223.6	223.7	223.3	222.6	222.1	222.6	221.0	221.2	221.4	222.6
1979	222.4	220.8	220.6	221.9	219.6	219.7	219.3	218.3	216.8	215.0	213.4	211.9	218.3
1980	209.9	209.0	206.2	201.6	199.3	199.7	201.7	203.9	204.7	204.9	203.6	200.2	204.2
1981[1]	200.3	199.1	200.4	203.7	200.2	198.4	196.6	195.8	193.7	193.9	194.2	195.5	197.6
1982[1]	198.1	198.1	198.4	198.2	197.6	195.9	195.2	196.3	198.2	199.7	201.9	204.3	198.5
1983[1]	205.6	209.9	212.3										

[1] Preliminary.   Source: Federal Reserve System   T.327

U.S. Money Supply M2 in 1972 $ In Billions of Dollars

Year	Jan.	Feb.	Mar.	Apr.	May	June	July	Aug.	Sept.	Oct.	Nov.	Dec.	Average
1974	771.4	767.3	766.2	763.0	757.4	754.3	752.0	744.5	738.6	735.3	734.0	729.3	751.1
1975	728.1	731.3	737.5	742.8	751.0	758.1	759.2	763.2	764.1	763.5	766.8	768.0	752.8
1976	774.0	784.7	790.1	796.8	803.7	803.6	805.1	811.2	815.6	822.6	828.5	835.4	805.9
1977	840.1	841.9	845.1	848.3	852.7	853.7	856.1	859.2	861.7	865.3	866.5	868.1	854.9
1978	686.6	867.6	867.2	867.0	865.4	863.2	862.1	863.0	863.1	862.0	862.4	861.7	864.4
1979	860.7	857.4	856.8	857.0	853.9	853.2	850.7	848.9	845.5	838.7	833.0	827.7	848.6
1980	818.6	815.6	808.9	799.3	798.2	800.1	810.1	814.6	812.0	808.8	807.7	800.0	812.3
1981[1]	798.4	796.8	803.1	810.1	808.1	806.1	802.8	804.9	798.9	789.3	793.1	796.4	803.6
1982[1]	800.9	802.8	808.9	809.7	808.2	805.7	807.9	815.2	820.1	822.1	828.6	837.1	813.9
1983[1]	856.4	875.0	881.6										

[1] Preliminary.   Source: Federal Reserve System   T.328

INTEREST RATES

KEY INTEREST RATES
- Long-Term Treas. Securities
- Prime Lending Rates at Large N.Y. Banks
- Discount Rate
- Treasury Bills (90 Days)

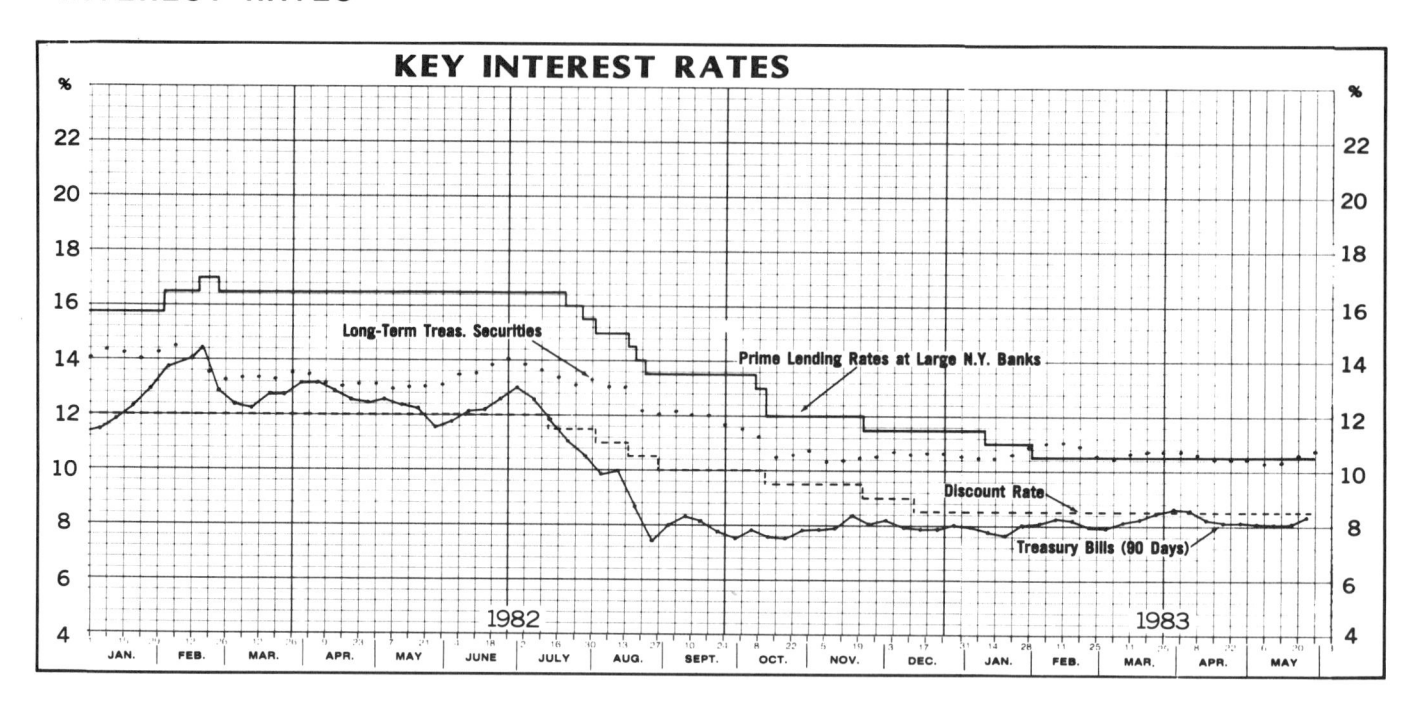

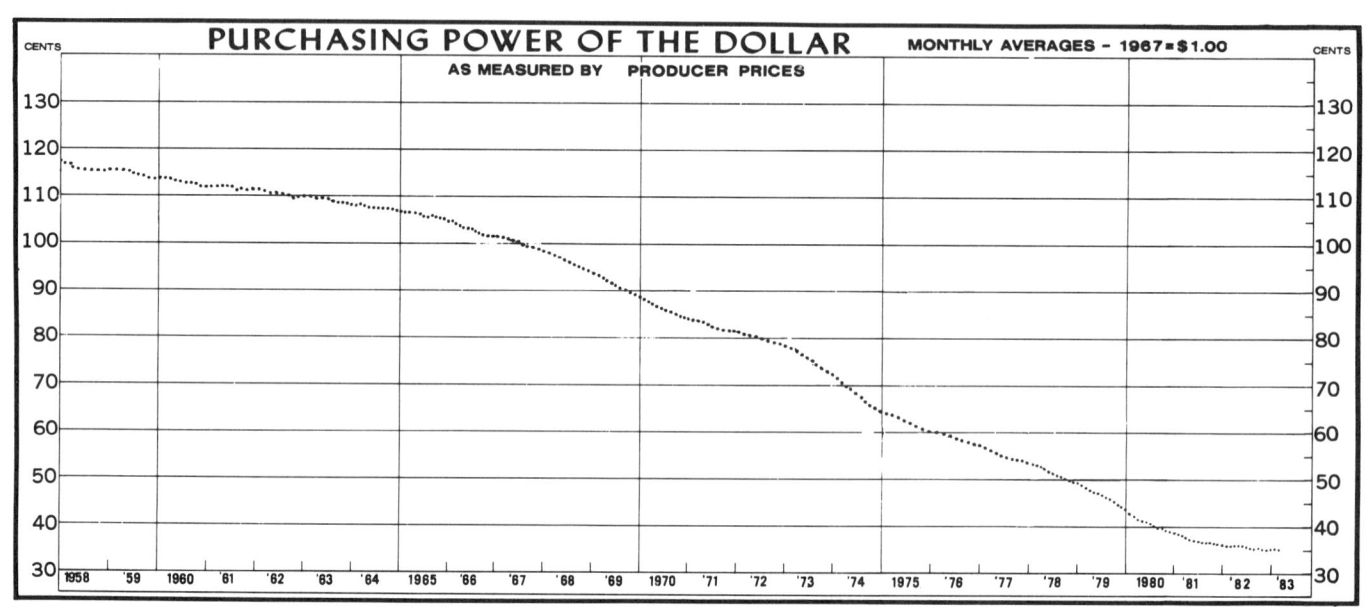

PURCHASING POWER OF THE DOLLAR — AS MEASURED BY PRODUCER PRICES — MONTHLY AVERAGES – 1967=$1.00

U.S. Gross National Product, National Income, and Personal Income   In Billions of Current Dollars[1]

Year	\multicolumn{5}{c}{Gross National Product}	\multicolumn{5}{c}{National Income}	\multicolumn{5}{c}{Personal Income}
	I	II	III	IV	Annual Total	I	II	III	IV	Annual Total	I	II	III	IV	Annual Total
1975	1,455	1,499	1,564	1,598	1,529	1,157	1,189	1,243	1,272	1,215	1,205	1,238	1,274	1,305	1,255
1976	1,672	1,699	1,729	1,773	1,718	1,346	1,364	1,389	1,418	1,379	1,349	1,374	1,404	1,438	1,391
1977	1,839	1,894	1,951	1,989	1,918	1,474	1,524	1,576	1,612	1,546	1,476	1,514	1,558	1,604	1,538
1978	2,032	2,130	2,191	2,272	2,156	1,645	1,721	1,772	1,845	1,745	1,638	1,692	1,748	1,809	1,722
1979	2,341	2,375	2,444	2,496	2,414	1,904	1,932	1,986	2,031	1,963	1,865	1,906	1,972	2,032	1,944
1980	2,572	2,565	2,637	2,731	2,626	2,089	2,070	2,122	2,205	2,121	2,088	2,115	2,182	2,256	2,160
1981[2]	2,865	2,902	2,981	3,003	2,938	2,294	2,324	2,387	2,405	2,353	2,330	2,381	2,458	2,495	2,416
1982[2]	2,996	3,045	3,088	3,108	3,059	2,397	2,425	2,456	2,472	2,437	2,511	2,553	2,593	2,624	2,570
1983															

[1] Seasonally adjusted at annual rates.   [2] Preliminary.   Source: U.S. Dept. of Commerce

T.329

Iron and Steel

Worldwide resources of iron ore are estimated to be over 800 billion long tons of crude ore containing more than 260 billion short tons of iron. The total world reserve base of crude iron ore has been estimated at nearly 263 billion long tons from which approximately 108 million short tons of iron is recoverable. Preliminary Bureau of Mines estimates indicated that the world mine production of iron ore in 1982 was nearly 8 percent below the 1981 production of 847.2 million long tons. The three major producers of iron ore during 1982 were, in order, the Soviet Union, Brazil, and Australia.

U.S. resources of iron ore are estimated at nearly 108 billion long tons of ore containing 30 billion short tons of iron. These resources are mostly the low-grade taconite-type ores of the Lake Superior district that require beneficiation and agglomeration before being suitable for commercial use. U.S. resources also include an estimated 17 billion long tons of ore from which nearly 4 billion short tons of iron is recoverable in concentrate.

Although the U.S. production of iron ore showed a slight increase near the end of 1982, the declining demand for iron and steel led to reductions of nearly 50 percent in iron ore production, trade, and consumption compared with 1981 levels. The domestic output of usable ore was at its lowest since 1938. Utilized capacity was estimated at 34 percent during the year, and more than 15,000 employees were laid off for periods from 2 to 12 months. Early in 1983, the respected trade publication *Iron Age* reported that the combined loss of the seven largest U.S. steel companies was over a billion dollars during the first three quarters of 1982. Steel employment costs at the end of 1982 were $26.29 an hour compared with $21.46 an hour a year earlier. Exports of U.S. steel during 1982 reportedly fell to the lowest level since 1958. The drop was so sharp that the relative foreign share of the U.S. steel market rose to 22 percent late in the year compared with 19 percent in 1981.

The value of the usable iron ore produced from U.S. mines during 1982 was estimated at $1.5 billion. Virtually all of the ore was concentrated prior to shipment and nearly 91 percent of the ore was pelletized. The average iron content of the usable domestic ore production was 63 percent.

Iron ore is the only source of primary iron. Small amounts of ferrous scrap may be added to blast furnace burdens, and scrap is extensively used in steelmaking and in iron and steel foundry casting. The U.S. consumption of iron ore and agglomerates during 1982 was distributed among blast furnaces (98.1 percent), steel furnaces (0.5 percent), and the manufacture of cement, heavy media materials and other products (1.4 pecent). The projected U.S. mine production of iron ore in 1983 was 50 million long tons, and the 1983 U.S. apparent consumption was expected to be 65 million long tons. Calculated from a 1980 base year, the U.S. demand for iron ore was expected to increase at an annual rate of 1.6 percent through 1990.

The U.S. Bureau of Mines and the Department of Energy, in cooperation with private firms, continued research on the gasification of coal (including subbituminous coal and lignite) and the use of the gas for the induration of pellets. Other areas of continuing research during 1982 included the beneficiation of oxidized taconite by wet high-intensity magnetic separation and flotation, direct reduction of pellets by solid fuels, reclamation of process water, vegetation of taconite tailings, and nonfreezing dust suppressants for the winter shipment of pellets. The environmental problems related to iron ore production concerned the disposal of solid wastes, the elimination of dust, and the reclamation of process water and of tailings sites.

Late in October 1982, the U.S. and the European Economic Community (EC) reached agreements to limit the steel imported to the U.S. from the EC through the end of 1985 when, under the EC State Aids Code, members are required to end subsidies to their steel industries. Under one agreement, imports in 10 major steel product categories will be limited by EC export licenses to a fixed share of the U.S. market, the shares ranging from 2.2 percent for tin plate to 21.85 percent for sheet piling and the collective share for all 10 categories to equal 5.5 percent. A second agreement would limit EC exports of pipe and tube if they exceed a market share of 5.9 percent. In return, the U.S. steel industry withdrew antidumping and countervailing duty complaints against many of the products covered in the agreements. The agreements could reduce U.S. imports of EC steel by an estimated 1 million short tons during 1983.

Through most of 1982, raw steel production was 62.2 million short tons or 39 percent below the 1981 level. Some steel mills held enough scrap inventory to last through yearend 1982 judged by the midyear melting rate. Some of the stronger scrap merchants built up large inventories or premium-grade scrap while many small tonnage processors sold scrap on an appraisal basis in order to maintain cash flow regardless of firm price levels. Scrap processors generally operated between 30 and 65 percent of capacity and idled expensive equipment. The U.S. demand for ferrous scrap is expected to increase at an average annual rate of about 1 percent through 1990 compared with a base year 1981.

U.S. stocks of iron ore at domestic furnace yards and receiving docks totaled 35.7 million tons at yearend 1982, down 7 million tons from 1981. Preliminary estimates show U.S. 1982 consumer stocks of iron and steel scrap at 7 percent under 1981

IRON AND STEEL

World Production of Raw Steel (Ingots & Castings) In Millions of Short Tons

Year	Bel-gium	Brazil	Canada	Czech.	France	W. Ger-many	Italy	Japan	Luxem-bourg	China	Po-land	Sweden	USSR	United Kingdom	United States	World Total
1970	13.9		12.3	12.7	26.2	49.6	19.0	102.9	6.0	20.0		6.1	127.7	31.2	131.5	655.2
1971	13.7		12.2	13.3	25.2	44.4	19.2	97.6	5.8	23.0		5.8	133.0	26.6	120.4	640.5
1972	16.0		13.1	14.0	26.5	48.2	21.8	106.8	6.0	25.0		5.8	138.4	27.9	133.2	692.7
1973	17.1		14.8	14.5	27.8	54.6	23.1	131.5	6.5	30.0	15.5	6.2	144.9	29.4	150.8	769.1
1974	17.9	8.3	15.0	15.0	29.8	58.7	26.2	129.1	7.1	30.0	16.0	6.6	150.1	24.7	145.7	780.4
1975	12.8	9.2	14.4	15.8	23.7	44.6	24.1	112.8	5.1	28.0	16.5	6.2	155.8	22.3	116.6	710.1
1976	13.4	10.1	14.7	16.2	25.6	46.8	25.8	118.4	5.0	22.6	17.2	5.7	159.6	24.6	128.0	742.4
1977	12.4	12.3	15.0	16.6	24.4	43.0	25.7	112.9	4.8	26.2	19.7	4.4	161.7	22.5	125.3	741.6
1978	13.9	13.3	16.4	16.9	25.2	45.5	26.8	112.6	5.3	35.0	21.2	4.8	166.9	22.4	137.0	787.2
1979	14.8	15.3	17.7	16.3	25.8	50.8	26.7	123.2	5.5	38.0	21.2	5.1	164.4	23.6	136.3	821.2
1980	13.6	16.9	17.5	16.8	25.5	48.3	29.2	122.8	5.1	40.9	21.5	4.7	163.1	12.4	111.8	787.5
1981[1]	13.5	14.6	16.3	16.8	23.4	45.9	27.1	112.1	4.2	40.0	17.3	4.2	164.2	17.2	119.9	776.4
1982[2]								110		41			163		74	706
1983																

[1] Preliminary. [2] Estimate. Source: Bureau of Mines

T.330

Salient Statistics of Steel in the United States In Millions of Short Tons

Year	Value of Exports (Million $)	Value of Imports (Million $)	Basic Oxygen	Open Hearth Acid	Open Hearth Basic	Bessemer	Electric[3]	Total Production	Stain-less	Alloy Steel[2] Other	Total Production	Shipments of Steel Products Domestic Consumption	Ex-port
1970	1,375	2,139	63.3	[5]	48.0	[5]	20.2	131.5	1.3	11.5	12.8	83.1	7.7
1971	945	2,803	63.9	[5]	35.6	[5]	20.9	120.4	1.3	12.2	13.5	83.5	3.5
1972	1,006	2,992	74.6	[5]	34.9	[5]	23.7	133.2	1.6	14.0	15.6	88.3	3.5
1973	1,581	3,045	83.3	[5]	39.8	[5]	27.8	150.8	1.9	16.2	18.1	106.4	5.0
1974	3,012	5,583	81.6	[5]	35.5	[5]	28.7	145.7	2.2	17.0	19.2	102.5	7.0
1975	2,970	4,507	71.8	[5]	22.2	[5]	22.7	116.6	1.1	15.2	16.3	76.0	4.0
1976	2,462	4,584	79.9	[5]	23.5	[5]	24.6	128.0	1.7	14.3	16.0	86.4	3.0
1977	2,284	5,936	77.4	[5]	20.0	[5]	27.9	125.3	1.9	15.3	17.2	88.0	3.1
1978	2,285	7,658	83.5	[5]	21.3	[5]	32.2	137.0	2.0	18.2	20.2	94.6	3.3
1979	2,804	7,823	83.3	[5]	19.2	[5]	33.9	136.3	2.1	18.0	20.1	98.3	2.0
1980	3,728	7,792	67.6	[5]	13.1	[5]	31.2	111.8	1.7	15.4	17.1	81.3	2.6
1981[1]	3,649	11,286	73.2	[5]	13.5	[5]	33.2	119.9	1.7	17.6	19.3	85.2	1.8
1982[4]			45.3	[5]	6.1	[5]	21.5	72.9	1.2	9.0	10.2	60.8	.8
1983													

[1] Preliminary. [2] Included under total steel production. [3] Includes crucible steels. [4] Estimate. [5] No longer published. Sources: American Iron & Steel Institute; U.S. Bureau of Mines

T.331

U.S. Production of Steel Ingots, Rate of Capability Utilization[1] In Percent[2]

Year	Jan.	Feb.	Mar.	Apr.	May	June	July	Aug.	Sept.	Oct.	Nov.	Dec.	Average
1970	104.1	107.6	110.0	108.9	107.1	108.3	99.8	99.6	102.6	99.0	95.7	96.6	103.4
1971	104.3	111.4	117.0	120.2	119.6	109.9	92.0	53.4	73.4	76.0	77.0	81.3	94.7
1972	92.6	98.7	107.3	110.8	110.5	105.0	95.7	100.4	104.4	107.9	109.0	109.9	104.5
1973	114.5	119.1	121.1	122.3	121.9	119.4	113.8	112.7	117.0	119.2	120.4	117.7	118.5
1974	117.8	118.8	118.1	119.0	118.0	116.5	112.5	109.6	113.3	116.8	111.1	101.4	114.4
1975[2]	90.4	93.8	93.4	84.9	75.9	69.6	65.1	67.3	74.7	69.0	67.4	66.2	76.2
1976	74.4	80.1	85.4	88.4	90.8	89.7	84.8	82.8	80.4	75.8	72.2	67.8	80.9
1977	66.8	72.1	81.2	83.3	88.6	84.9	76.7	77.2	77.2	77.7	75.0	74.7	78.4
1978	77.2	80.1	83.1	88.5	91.5	91.1	85.1	86.3	88.6	89.8	89.4	87.7	86.8
1979	83.5	87.9	94.5	93.4	94.8	93.7	89.9	86.0	82.8	84.4	80.6	78.0	87.2
1980	82.7	85.3	88.4	83.0	69.6	58.4	53.1	54.8	62.7	72.2	79.5	77.8	72.8
1981	79.9	83.7	88.6	87.7	86.2	81.5	77.6	77.3	75.9	68.7	62.8	58.6	78.3
1982	59.3	60.9	61.7	55.2	50.9	47.7	43.8	42.4	41.9	40.2	35.9	34.0	47.3
1983	43.4	49.0											

[1] Based on tonnage capability to produce raw steel for a full order book. [2] Data prior to 1975 are based on INDEX OF PRODUCTION 1967 = 100. Source: American Iron and Steel Institute

T.332

IRON AND STEEL

United States Production of Steel Ingots   In Thousands of Short Tons

Year	Jan.	Feb.	Mar.	Apr.	May	June	July	Aug.	Sept.	Oct.	Nov.	Dec.	Total
1970	11,243	10,498	11,886	11,386	11,574	11,323	10,781	10,765	10,726	10,699	10,008	10,438	131,514
1971	11,274	10,874	12,645	12,565	12,920	11,491	9,942	5,774	7,678	8,211	8,053	8,784	120,443
1972	10,001	9,980	11,588	11,588	11,936	10,980	10,341	10,842	10,913	11,657	11,398	11,878	133,241
1973	12,373	11,626	13,088	12,788	13,174	12,488	12,290	12,182	12,229	12,876	12,586	12,722	150,799
1974	12,726	11,598	12,758	12,442	12,752	12,185	12,155	11,837	11,849	12,617	11,615	10,960	145,720
1975	11,584	10,862	11,980	10,667	9,864	8,744	8,371	8,648	9,295	9,214	8,709	8,846	116,642
1976	9,835	9,907	11,294	11,439	12,136	11,605	11,400	11,128	10,463	10,295	9,494	9,215	128,000
1977	9,089	8,859	11,049	11,167	12,201	11,384	10,319	10,393	10,050	10,442	9,748	10,031	125,333
1978	10,301	9,643	11,083	11,528	12,320	11,861	11,388	11,550	11,467	12,105	11,654	11,812	137,031
1979[1]	11,105	10,562	12,576	12,196	12,789	12,230	11,821	11,309	10,541	10,891	9,997	9,996	136,341
1980[1]	10,701	10,332	11,439	10,658	9,226	7,501	6,796	7,019	7,767	9,442	10,057	10,180	111,835
1981[1]	10,590	10,028	11,744	11,243	11,423	10,451	10,160	10,120	9,618	9,003	7,962	7,672	120,828
1982[1]	7,737	7,178	8,049	7,006	6,678	6,050	5,719	5,538	5,299	5,262	4,546	4,456	72,903
1983[1]	5,570	5,676											

[1] Preliminary.   Source: American Iron and Steel Institute   T.333

Shipments of Steel Products[1] by Market Classifications in the United States   In Thousands of Net Tons

Year	Appliances, Utensils & Cutlery	Automotive	Containers	Construction	Contractors Prod.	Electrical Mach. & Equipment	Export	Machinery, Industrial Equip. & Tools	Oil and Gas	Rail Transportation	Steel for Converting & Processing[2]	Steel Service Center & Distributors	All Other[3]	Total Shipments
1970	2,160	14,475	7,775	9,000	4,440	2,694	5,985	5,169	1,652	3,098	3,443	17,591	13,316	90,798
1971	2,148	17,483	7,212	9,541	4,946	2,593	2,433	4,903	1,760	3,004	3,593	16,184	11,238	87,038
1972	2,362	18,217	6,616	9,299	5,055	2,824	2,555	5,396	278	2,730	4,199	18,598	13,676	91,805
1973	2,747	23,217	7,811	11,405	6,459	3,348	3,138	6,351	409	3,228	4,714	22,705	15,898	111,430
1974	2,412	18,972	8,235	12,440	6,215	3,242	3,961	6,468	521	3,414	4,486	23,206	15,900	109,472
1975	1,653	15,214	4,589	8,767	3,927	2,173	1,755	5,173	601	3,152	3,255	15,622	14,076	79,957
1976	1,961	21,334	6,914	7,406	4,543	2,670	1,838	5,188	2,652	3,027	4,141	14,662	13,111	89,447
1977	2,129	21,490	6,714	7,553	4,500	2,639	1,076	5,566	3,650	3,238	3,679	15,346	13,567	91,147
1978	2,094	21,253	6,595	9,612	3,480	2,811	1,224	5,992	4,140	3,549	4,612	17,333	15,240	97,935
1979	2,141	18,624	6,770	10,058	4,021	2,821	2,010	6,027	3,738	4,127	4,728	18,263	16,934	100,262
1980	1,726	12,156	5,549	12,149	3,362	2,441	2,597	4,566	5,368	3,178	3,881	16,174	10,706	83,853
1981	1,775	13,154	5,292	8,446	3,230	2,600	1,844	4,624	6,238	2,162	3,338	17,637	16,672	87,014
1982	1,337	9,288	4,470	6,283	2,287	2,003	832	2,584	2,745	1,020	3,222	13,067	12,429	61,567
1983														

[1] All grades including carbon, alloy & stainless steel.   [2] Net total after deducting shipments to reporting companies for conversion or resale.   [3] Includes agricultural; bolts, nuts, rivets & screws; forgings (other than automotive); shipbuilding & marine equipment; aircraft; mining, quarrying & lumbering; other domestic & commercial equipment machinery; ordnance & other direct military; & shipments of non-reporting companies.   Source: American Iron and Steel Institute   T.334

Net Shipments of Steel Products in the United States
(All Grades, Including Carbon, Alloy & Stainless Steel) In Thousands of Net Tons

Year	Cold Finished Bars	Rails & Accessories	Wire & Wire Products	Tin Mill Products	Plates	Sheets & Strip	Hot Rolled Bars	Pipe & Tubing	Shapes & Steel Piling	Reinforcing Bars	Hot Rolled Sheets	Cold Rolled Sheets	Semi-Finished	Alloy	Stainless
1970	1,490	1,590	2,998	7,243	8,065	35,101	8,107	7,778	6,060	4,891	12,319	14,250	7,387	6,944	709
1971	1,378	1,564	2,791	6,811	7,939	35,574	8,179	7,574	5,666	4,521	11,760	14,898	4,962	7,014	718
1972	1,675	1,601	2,952	6,135	7,553	39,862	9,299	7,609	5,656	4,454	14,036	16,123	4,917	7,777	855
1973	2,161	1,689	3,245	7,316	9,678	49,370	10,763	9,133	7,081	5,135	16,886	20,377	5,749	9,372	1,134
1974	2,251	1,785	3,171	7,528	10,919	44,991	11,061	9,844	7,210	5,089	15,774	18,275	5,509	10,179	1,345
1975	1,486	1,965	2,154	5,587	8,761	30,763	8,146	8,228	5,121	3,666	11,222	12,841	3,911	8,436	757
1976	1,618	2,017	2,461	6,436	7,160	42,303	8,664	6,265	4,187	3,876	15,090	18,265	4,384		
1977	1,792	1,863	2,401	6,382	7,538	41,586	9,251	7,484	4,379	4,234	14,484	17,627	4,055	8,760	1,118
1978	2,084	1,703	2,510	6,100	8,601	43,609	8,758	8,399	5,027	4,704	15,447	17,821	5,070	10,557	1,191
1979	2,245	2,026	2,449	6,310	9,035	43,507	8,493	8,242	5,596	5,303	15,995	17,284	5,496	11,023	1,361
1980	1,585	1,797	1,768	5,709	8,080	33,853	5,961	9,097	5,207	4,683	12,116	13,313	5,342	9,368	1,127
1981	1,620	1,458	1,694	4,927	7,397	36,924	6,628	10,286	4,903	4,371	13,451	14,396	5,598	10,595	1,163
1982[1]	1,015	782	1,308	4,321	4,146	7,730[2]	4,757	5,026	3,563	4,049	9,052	11,132	3,693	6,726	894
1983															

[1] Preliminary.   [2] Excludes Hot & Cold rolled sheets. Shown elsewhere.   Source: American Iron & Steel Institute   T.335

IRON AND STEEL

U.S. Foreign Trade of Iron & Steel Products In Thousands of Short Tons

Year	Steel Mill Pdts.	Other Steel Pdts.	Iron Pdts. & Ferro-alloys	Grand Total Quantity	Grand Total Mil. $	Iron & Steel Scrap	Steel Mill Pdts.	Other Steel Pdts.	Iron Pdts. & Ferro-alloys	Grand Total Quantity	Grand Total Mil. $	Iron & Steel Scrap
1975	12,012	657	1,250	13,919	5,257	305	2,953	618	575	4,146		9,608
1976	14,285	652	1,357	16,294	5,082	507	2,519	831	607	3,865		8,120
1977	19,307	985	1,366	21,658	6,839	625	1,913	765	639	3,218		6,175
1978	21,135	797	96	22,027	7,658	794	2,421	413	436	3,271	2,285	9,038
1979	17,518	787	123	18,428	7,823	760	2,818	374	208	3,400	2,804	11,054
1980	15,495	753	107	16,355	7,792	582	4,101	407	221	4,729	3,728	11,168
1981[1]	19,898	822	97	20,818	11,286	556	2,904	444	209	3,557	3,649	6,415
1982[2]				17,000		500				2,500		6,872

[1] Preliminary. [2] Estimate. *Source: U.S. Bureau of Mines; American Metal Market* T.336

Average Wholesale Prices of Iron and Steel in the U.S. In Dollars Per Net Ton

Year	Pig Iron Bessemer[2] Neville Isl., Pa.	Iron Age Composite	No. 2 F.O.B. Birmingham	Steel Billets Pitts.	No. 1 Heavy Melting Steel Scrap Pitts.	No. 1 Heavy Melting Steel Scrap Chicago	Tin Plate (¼ Lb.)	Hot Rolled Sheet[3]	Steel Bars Hot Rolled	Steel Bars Cold Finished	Structural Shapes	Carbon Steel Plates	Cold Rolled Strip	Galvanized Sheets	Wire Rods-Chi. $Gr. Ton
1973	79.82	77.12	70.03	126.00	57.61	57.29	10.00	8.40	8.38	12.00	8.50	8.50	10.55	11.03	9.15
1974	124.81	123.63	141.25	166.68	104.61	112.68	11.83	9.98	11.15	13.71	9.92	11.60	12.78	12.61	10.42
1975	181.00	187.07	181.00	195.00	72.01	71.35	14.15	11.93	11.43	15.95	12.07	13.16	15.89	15.03	12.93
1976	181.00	187.67	181.00	209.48	78.83	77.49	15.83	12.12	11.32	17.38	12.96	13.41	17.97	16.20	13.31
1977	184.03	189.57	184.33	246.15	66.42	60.21	16.0-19.1	13.75	12.68	20.15	13.85	14.64	20.33	18.05	14.56
1978	190.00	198.31	191.00	282.88	78.48	73.98	18.0-20.4	15.36	14.01	22.80	15.73	16.53	22.49	20.21	16.80
1979	190.00	203.00	191.00	302.00	100.77	96.69	19.1-23.4	17.05	16.20	25.07	17.36	18.46	24.13	22.40	17.22
1980	200.83	203.00	191.00	348.70	95.48	86.70	23.3-24.9	18.21	19.59	28.95	18.98	20.57	27.15	23.56	19.09
1981[1]	209.67	204.66	205.33	358.00	100.57	91.76	24.9-26.7	20.13	16.95	29.45	21.32	23.04	30.23	26.05	20.27
1982[4]		213.00			66.47	57.78									

[1] Preliminary. [2] Prior to 1974 prices are F.O.B. Mahoning Valley. [3] 10 gauge. [4] Estimate. *Source: American Metal Market* T.337

World Production of Pig Iron (Excludes Ferro-Alloys) In Millions of Short Tons

Year	Australia	Belgium	Canada	Czech.	France	W. Germany	India	Italy	Japan	Luxembourg	Poland	China	USSR	United Kingdom	United States	World Total
1973	8.4	14.0	10.5	9.4	21.8	40.2	8.3	11.1	99.2	5.6	8.4	31.0	104.7	18.4	101.3	552.4
1974	8.0	14.4	10.4	9.8	24.2	43.9	8.1	12.9	99.7	6.0	8.4	33.0	109.0	15.6	95.5	564.2
1975	8.2	10.0	10.1	10.2	19.3	32.9	9.1	12.5	95.8	4.3	8.4	35.0	112.4	13.3	79.7	528.3
1976	8.2	10.9	10.8	10.4	20.6	34.9	10.7	12.8	95.4	4.1	9.0	31.7	115.1	15.1	86.8	548.6
1977	7.4	9.8	10.6	10.7	19.7	31.6	10.8	12.6	94.7	3.9	10.5	27.6	117.4	13.5	81.5	537.4
1978	8.1	10.3	11.4	11.0	20.0	32.9	10.4	12.5	86.6	4.1	12.2	38.3	121.3	12.7	87.7	560.4
1979	8.6	11.9	12.0	10.5	20.9	38.4	9.7	12.5	92.4	4.2	12.1	40.5	119.3	14.2	87.0	584.4
1980	7.7	10.9	12.3	10.8	20.6	37.1	9.3	13.4	95.9	3.9	12.8	41.9	117.5	7.0	68.7	562.5
1981[1]	7.5	10.8	10.9	10.9	18.7	35.1	10.4	13.5	88.2	3.2	12.1	37.5	117.2	10.3	73.8	552.0
1982[2]									8.8			3.8	116		44	506

[1] Preliminary. [2] Estimated. *Source: Bureau of Mines* T.338

U.S. Pig Iron Production (Excluding Production of Ferro-Alloys) In Thousands of Short Tons

Year	Jan.	Feb.	Mar.	Apr.	May	June	July	Aug.	Sept.	Oct.	Nov.	Dec.	Total
1973	8,199	7,756	8,627	8,490	8,809	8,468	8,516	8,282	8,087	8,588	8,402	8,609	100,837
1974	8,563	7,804	8,386	8,233	8,387	8,185	8,337	7,872	7,713	8,187	7,250	6,731	95,670
1975	7,371	7,135	8,071	7,432	6,990	6,239	5,968	6,031	6,245	6,292	5,981	6,234	79,923
1976	6,636	6,754	7,519	7,601	8,116	7,874	7,999	7,751	6,995	6,969	6,382	6,272	86,870
1977	5,985	5,827	7,174	7,382	7,962	7,530	7,008	6,763	6,566	6,636	6,121	6,419	81,328
1978	6,390	5,971	6,894	7,189	7,936	7,754	7,637	7,518	7,391	7,809	7,533	7,658	87,679
1979	7,064	6,636	7,953	7,726	8,277	8,026	7,505	7,351	6,762	6,779	6,258	6,372	86,975
1980	6,583	6,357	7,115	6,677	5,906	4,664	4,222	4,360	4,596	5,621	6,132	6,489	68,721
1981	6,603	6,108	7,193	6,755	6,938	6,408	6,268	6,259	5,889	5,419	4,782	4,750	73,570
1982	4,489	4,169	4,622	3,967	3,904	3,595	3,516	3,277	3,160	3,077	2,648	2,712	43,136
1983	3,192	3,264											

Source: American Iron and Steel Institute T.341

IRON AND STEEL

Wholesale Price of No. 1 Heavy Melting Steel Scrap at Chicago In Dollars Per Gross Ton

Year	Jan.	Feb.	Mar.	Apr.	May	June	July	Aug.	Sept.	Oct.	Nov.	Dec.	Average
1970	40.50	48.89	45.74	39.68	42.85	43.95	40.84	40.76	45.96	41.19	34.36	35.50	41.69
1971	42.85	43.76	36.89	33.60	34.35	30.89	28.00	28.48	32.45	32.29	29.50	28.76	33.49
1972	31.50	33.58	35.89	34.50	34.50	34.55	35.50	37.50	37.50	37.50	37.50	41.23	35.94
1973	45.00	48.66	45.55	44.17	48.41	51.00	51.00	51.41	56.45	70.36	86.55	88.90	57.28
1974	87.18	114.58	125.64	132.34	100.75	115.25	137.72	119.68	113.90	114.00	107.43	83.67	112.68
1975	79.91	82.61	81.14	83.77	76.14	64.95	54.00	68.41	77.33	64.39	60.08	63.46	71.36
1976	71.67	74.90	85.04	94.96	86.45	86.86	90.67	80.95	68.90	62.00	62.00	65.14	77.46
1977	69.00	69.00	69.65	70.79	64.62	58.36	57.00	57.00	55.00	49.00	43.95	59.26	60.21
1978	71.00	71.00	71.48	76.00	70.32	72.73	76.63	74.48	69.00	69.45	79.35	86.35	73.98
1979	93.00	103.00	121.73	110.10	91.91	106.62	98.62	89.96	86.00	86.22	91.00	91.28	96.69
1980	96.14	99.00	97.00	90.54	69.62	62.24	67.45	77.95	87.24	92.22	97.29	103.68	86.70
1981	95.00	91.11	105.14	107.55	97.50	88.00	88.45	97.76	92.52	82.64	75.00	74.41	91.76
1982	83.00	78.63	69.78	63.86	58.30	51.77	49.00	51.73	48.95	47.86	45.00	45.48	57.78
1983	56.14	67.00	77.70	70.33									
1984													

Source: American Metal Market

T.339

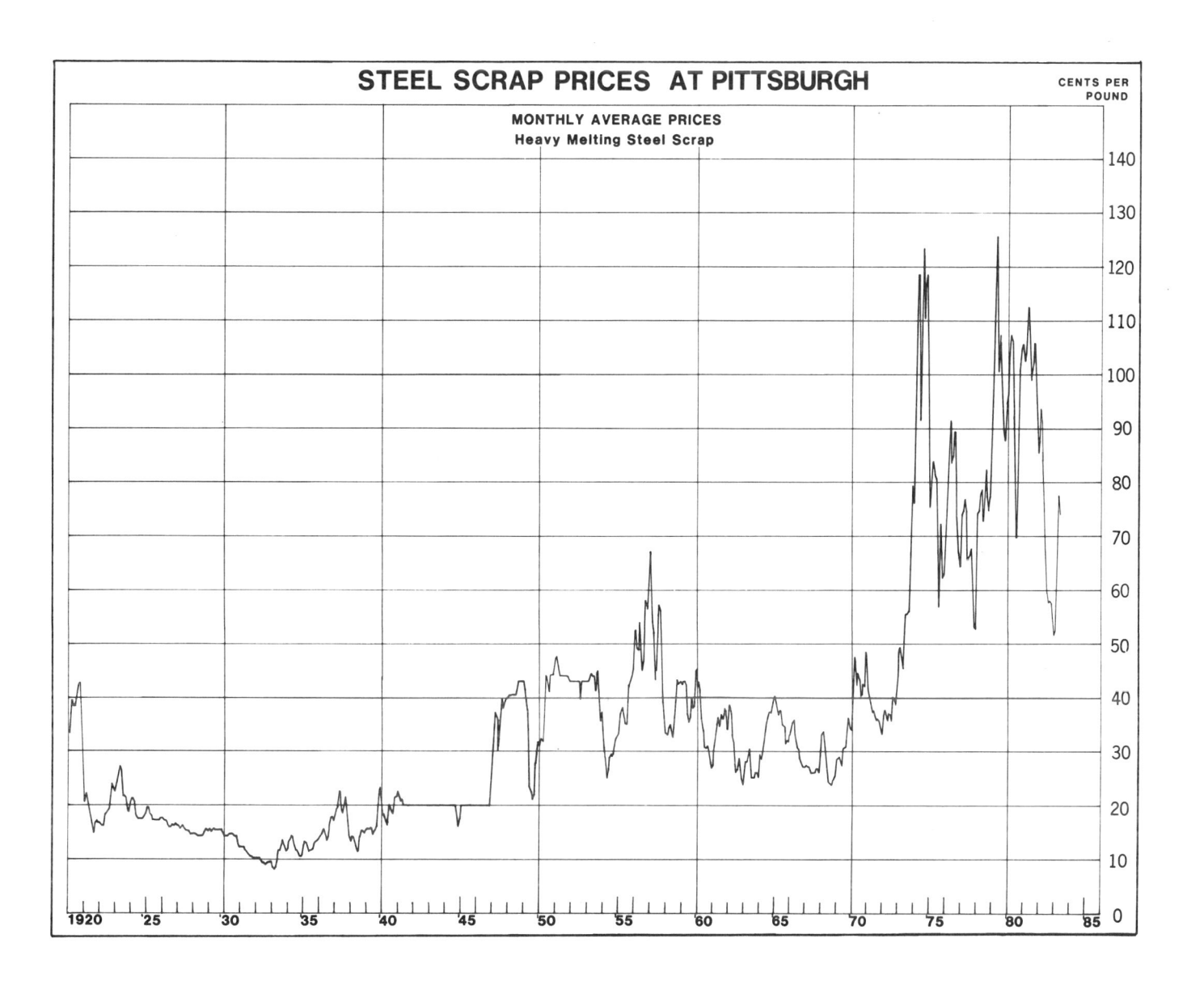

IRON AND STEEL

Consumption of Pig Iron in the U.S., by Type of Furnace or Equipment   In Thousands of Net Tons

Year	Open Hearth	Bessemer	Electric	Cupola	Air	Basic Oxygen Concentrates	Air & Other Furnaces	Direct Castings	Total
1972	22,375	3	961	2,264	139	60,233	254	3	86,226
1973	25,477	3	1,379	2,276	57	68,027	402	3	97,618
1974	22,507	3	1,220	2,123	3	66,614	632	3,697	96,792
1975	14,554	3	1,019	1,362	3	59,210	483	3,010	79,638
1976	15,410	3	638	1,197	3	66,138	406	3,255	87,045
1977	12,531	3	993	1,241	3	63,877	354	3,007	82,003
1978	13,444	3	1,440	1,056	3	69,028	398	3,055	88,420
1979	12,865	3	905	1,026	3	68,526	397	3,738	87,458
1980	8,606	3	855	698	3	56,414	299	2,182	69,053
1981[1]	8,867	3	583	685	3	62,162	254	2,489	75,040
1982[2]									45,000

[1] Preliminary. [2] Estimate. [3] Included in "Other Furnaces."   *Source: Bureau of Mines*   T.340

Salient Statistics of Ferrous Scrap & Pig Iron in the U.S.   In Millions of Short Tons

	Mfg. of Pig Iron & Steel Ingots & Castings			Iron Foundries & Misc. Users			Mfg. of Steel Castings (Scrap)	All Uses			Imports of Scrap[2]	Exports of Scrap[3]	Stocks—Dec. 31 Ferrous Scrap & Pig Iron at Consumers'		
Year	Scrap	Pig Iron	Total	Scrap	Pig Iron	Total		Ferr. Scrap	Pig Iron	Grand Total			Scrap	Pig Iron	Total Stocks
1972	73.4	84.0	157.2	17.3	2.1	19.4	2.7	93.4	89.1	182.5	.3	7.2	8.2	1.7	9.8
1973								103.6	99.8	203.4	.3	10.9	7.1	1.2	8.3
1974	81.1	92.8	173.9	21.1	3.9	25.0	3.3	105.5	96.8	202.3	.2	8.5	8.4	.8	9.2
1975	62.8	76.8	139.6	16.3	2.7	10.0	3.2	82.3	79.6	161.9	.3	9.4	8.8	1.4	10.2
1976	68.4	84.2	152.6	18.6	2.8	21.4	2.9	89.9	87.0	176.9	.5	7.9	10.0	1.5	11.5
1977	69.3	79.4	148.3	20.0	2.6	22.6	2.9	92.2	82.0	174.2	.6	5.9	9.2	1.3	10.5
1978	76.3	85.7	162.0	19.9	2.7	22.6	3.0	99.2	88.4	187.6	.8	9.0	8.3	.9	9.2
1979	77.2	84.7	161.9	18.5	2.7	21.2	3.2	98.9	87.5	186.4	.8	11.1	8.7	.9	9.6
1980	66.6	67.1	133.7	14.3	1.9	16.2	2.9	83.7	69.1	152.8	.6	11.2	8.0	.9	8.9
1981[1]	68.3	73.0	143.6	14.2	2.0	16.2	2.6	85.1	75.0	162.1	.6	6.4	8.1	.9	9.0
1982[4]	43.3	43.4	86.7	11.3	1.1	12.4	1.9	56.5	44.5	101.0	.5	6.9	6.5	.5	7.0

[1] Preliminary. [2] Including tinplate scrap. [3] Excluding tinplate circles, strips, cobbles, etc. [4] Estimate. *Source: Bureau of Mines*   T.342

Basic Pig Iron Prices at Valley Furnaces (F.O.B. Producing Point)   In Dollars Per Short[1] Ton

Year	Jan.	Feb.	Mar.	Apr.	May	June	July	Aug.	Sept.	Oct.	Nov.	Dec.	Average
1973	71.99	71.99	75.89	75.89	75.89	75.89	75.89	75.89	75.89	75.89	75.89	75.89	75.24
1974	75.89	77.44	82.81	96.00	96.00	133.80	133.80	149.88	149.88	150.63	155.75	169.40	122.61
1975	179.88	179.88	179.88	182.38	182.38	182.38	182.38	182.38	182.38	182.38	182.38	182.38	181.76
1976	182.38	182.38	182.38	182.38	182.38	182.25	—	—	—	—	182.25	182.25	182.33
1977	182.25	—	178.00	178.00	178.00	178.00	178.00	178.00	191.00	191.00	191.00	191.00	183.11
1978	191.00	191.00	191.00	191.00	191.00	191.00	191.00	203.00	203.00	203.00	203.00	203.00	196.00
1979	203.00	203.00	203.00	203.00	203.00	203.00	203.00	202.50	202.50	202.50	202.50	202.50	203.00
1980	203.00	203.00	203.00	203.00	203.00	203.00	203.00	203.00	203.00	203.00	203.00	203.00	203.00
1981	203.00	203.00	203.00	203.00	203.00	203.00	203.00	203.00	213.00	213.00	213.00	213.00	206.00
1982	213.00	213.00	213.00	213.00	213.00	213.00	213.00	213.00	213.00				
1983													

[1] Prior to May '73, prices are for long ton.   *Sources: American Metal Market; Bureau of Labor Statistics*   T.343

IRON AND STEEL

World Production of Iron Ore[3], by Specified Countries (Gross Weight) In Millions of Long Tons

Year	Australia	South Africa	Brazil	Canada	Chile	China	France	W. Germany	India	Liberia	Spain	Sweden	United Kingdom	United States	USSR[1]	Venezuela	World Total[1]
1972	62.8		41.4	39.7	8.5	59.0	53.4	4.7	34.9	22.2	6.6	32.6	8.9	75.4	204.8	18.2	766.2
1973	83.5		49.7	49.4	9.3	55.0	53.4	5.0	35.0	23.2	6.5	34.2	7.0	87.7	212.7	22.7	832.3
1974	95.4		74.3	49.2	10.1	60.0	53.4	4.4	34.9	23.4	8.1	35.6	3.5	84.4	221.3	26.0	883.8
1975	96.1		88.5	46.1	10.8	64.0	48.9	3.2	40.8	24.0	7.5	30.4	4.4	78.9	229.1	24.4	888.2
1976	91.8	15.4	92.6	54.7	9.9	59.1	44.5	2.2	43.2	20.2	8.1	29.4	4.5	80.0	237.3	18.4	885.1
1977	94.4	26.1	80.7	56.7	7.5	49.2	36.1	2.4	41.9	17.4	8.2	24.4	3.7	55.8	238.0	13.5	827.8
1978	81.8	23.8	83.6	41.1	6.7	68.9	32.9	1.6	38.2	17.7	8.4	21.1	4.2	81.6	242.4	13.3	833.9
1979	90.3	31.1	94.6	58.9	7.0	73.8	31.1	1.6	38.9	18.1	8.7	25.8	4.2	85.7	237.9	15.0	890.0
1980	94.0	25.9	112.9	48.0	8.1	73.8	28.5	1.9	40.0	17.9	9.1	26.8	.9	69.6	240.8	15.8	881.7
1981[2]	84.6	27.9	98.4	49.8	7.9	69.0	21.3	1.5	40.5	19.4	8.4	22.9	.7	73.2	238.2	15.3	847.2
1982[1]	84	26	96	35		70	20		41	18		20		36.5	236	13	776

[1] Estimate. [2] Preliminary. [3] Iron ore, iron ore concentrates and iron ore agglomerates. Source: Bureau of Mines   T.344

Salient Statistics of Iron Ore[2] in the U.S.   In Millions of Long Tons

Year	Net Import Reliance % of Apparent Consumption	Production[3] Total[3]	Lake Superior	Northeast	Southeast	West	Shipments[4]	Value Mill. $ (at Mine)	Avg. Value $ at Mine Per Ton	Stocks—Dec. 31 Mines	Consuming Plants	Lake Erie Docks	Imports	Exports	Consumption	Manganiferous Shipments[5]
1973		87.7	72.4	2.6	.3	12.0	90.7	1,163.7	12.84	10.9	46.0	3.1	43.3	2.7	146.9	.2
1974		84.4	70.7	2.4	.3	10.5	85.0	1,388.4	16.34	9.4	45.2	3.3	48.0	2.3	138.2	.2
1975	30	78.9	66.7	1.9	.1	9.6	75.7	1,620.6	21.41	12.3	52.2	4.6	46.7	2.5	114.1	.1
1976	31	80.0	67.4	2.0	.1	9.7	77.1	1,871.6	24.28	14.0	56.2	4.8	44.4	2.9	125.4	.2
1977	48	55.8	44.1	1.2	.1	9.3	54.1	1,422.7	26.32	14.8	42.3	3.0	37.9	2.1	116.0	.2
1978	29	81.6	72.7	— 8.9 —			83.2	2,401.4	28.86	12.4	39.3	3.6	33.6	4.2	124.8	.3
1979	25	85.7	77.2	— 8.6 —			86.2	2,814.4	32.64	11.3	39.0	5.4	33.8	5.1	125.4	.2
1980	25	69.6	62.3	— 7.3 —			69.6	2,544.1	36.56	11.7	35.7	6.1	25.1	5.7	98.9	.2
1981[1]	22	73.2	67.5	— 5.7 —			72.2	2,915.2	40.39	12.7	36.2	6.6	28.3	5.5	104.4	.2
1982[6]	36	36.5	31.8	— 4.7 —			36.9			12.0	29.9	6.0	14.7	4.6	55.0	

[1] Preliminary. [2] Usable; less than 5% Mn. [3] Includes by-product ore. [4] Excludes by-product ore. [5] Iron ore; 5 to 35% Mn. [6] Estimate. Source: Bureau of Mines   T.345

U.S. Imports (for Consumption) of Iron Ore from Principal Countries   In Thous. of Long Tons

Year	India	Venezuela	Australia	Brazil	Canada	Chile	South Africa	USSR	Liberia	Sweden	Peru	Norway	Total
1973	—	13,148	464	3,183	21,628	205	—	—	2,734	273	1,501	—	43,296
1974	—	15,378	638	6,572	19,702	296	1	126	2,730	335	1,810	—	48,029
1975	164	13,137	803	7,526	19,111	931	128	265	2,496	182	1,551	53	46,743
1976	130	9,001	617	5,388	24,962	608	162	44	2,153	441	716	151	44,390
1977	—	6,179	305	2,243	25,283	566	249	86	1,792	153	1,020	—	37,905
1978	—	6,083	264	3,979	19,236	390	94	—	2,170	256	818	302	33,616
1979	54	4,563	183	3,095	22,602	245	106	—	2,190	171	456	44	33,776
1980	—	3,602	—	1,995	17,311	322	6	—	1,590	33	193	—	25,058
1981[1]	—	5,071	—	1,738	18,845	342	—	—	2,160	87	78	—	28,328
1982[2]	—	1,819	—	972	9,282	47	52	—	2,399	71	35	—	14,679

[1] Preliminary. [2] Estimate. Source: Department of Commerce   T.346

Total[1] Iron Ore Stocks at End of Month in the U.S.   In Millions of Long Tons

Year	Jan.	Feb.	Mar.	Apr.	May	June	July	Aug.	Sept.	Oct.	Nov.	Dec.
1972	75.8	72.7	68.7	64.9	65.1	66.3	66.7	67.7	69.7	70.2	69.1	67.0
1973	63.2	59.6	55.3	52.4	53.5	55.3	57.0	58.5	60.3	61.6	60.7	59.5
1974	54.9	50.9	47.2	44.2	46.4	47.5	50.0	51.5	53.6	55.7	56.6	57.7
1975	56.6	54.9	52.9	52.3	56.7	57.6	61.2	63.9	66.1	66.6	67.3	68.1
1976	66.9	65.4	63.1	61.4	62.6	64.1	65.3	66.6	69.3	71.4	73.2	75.0
1977	73.5	72.2	70.1	68.5	67.7	68.5	69.7	67.2	65.9	63.5	60.7	59.4
1978	56.3	54.1	53.1	50.4	49.9	51.9	51.6	53.8	54.7	55.5	56.4	55.3
1979[2]	53.0	50.7	47.8	46.7	46.6	48.0	51.0	51.5	52.0	54.2	55.2	55.8
1980[2]	53.7	51.8	49.0	49.6	50.7	53.5	56.8	57.5	58.0	57.7	56.6	56.1
1981[2]	54.5	53.2	50.8	49.8	51.4	53.7	56.4	58.8	59.6	60.4	60.1	60.2
1982[2]	60.4	60.9	57.3	57.7	57.6	58.5	59.1	57.8	55.8	54.5	52.6	52.6

[1] All stocks at mines, furnace yards and at U.S. docks. [2] Preliminary. Source: American Iron Ore Association   T.347

Lard

Lard production in the United States in the 1982/83 season (ending September 30, 1983) was estimated by the USDA at 970 million pounds, approximately 10 percent below the previous season's output. The expected decrease in 1982/83 commercial lard production was once again a function of the continuing decline in U.S. hog slaughter, and the greatest reductions were expected to occur in the last quarter of 1982 and the first quarter of 1983. Lard yield per hog was down somewhat from the 12.5 pound level of the 1980/81 season.

Domestic disappearance of lard during 1982/83 was projected to fall below 900 million pounds. Direct lard use in the October 81–June 82 period was 44 million pounds, 11 percent above the comparable period the year before. This increase in demand for lard was attributed to a substantial decrease in the use of edible products. This pattern was expected to continue into 1983 as lard production fell and the competition from lower-priced soybean oil kept down the use of edible products.

Lard prices (loose, tanks, Chicago) fell to around 16 cents in January 1983 from 21–23 cents during most of 1982. Prospects for a price recovery in 1982/83, clouded by high world-wide stocks of fats and oils and by the record 1982 U.S. soybean crop, depended on continued reductions in hog slaughter and on the strong demand for direct use.

Supply and Distribution of Lard in the United States   In Millions of Pounds

Year	Federally Inspected	Other	Total	Farm	Total Production	Stocks Jan. 1[2]	Total Supply	Exports[3]	Shipments to U.S. Territories	Total	Short-ening	Mar-garine	Civil-ian	Mili-tary	Civilian Per Capita Lbs.
1972	1,465	77	1,541	18	1,559	100	1,659	164	25	1,418	432	128	787	1	3.8
1973	1,181	54	1,235	18	1,253	61	1,314	113	8	1,140	341	72	705	1	3.4
1974	1,289	55	1,344	22	1,366	44	1,410	161	21	1,192	317	160	681	1	3.2
1975	956	39	995	17	1,012	36	1,048	88	56	876	165	45	615	1	3.0
1976	1,010	34	1,044	17	1,061	28	1,089	181	54	819	156	37	568	1	2.7
1977	994	27	1,021	16	1,037	34	1,071	182	47	861	185	73	495	1	2.3
1978	968	23	991	15	1,006	29	1,035	120	42	966	220	68	478	1	2.2
1979[1]	1,109	32	1,141	14	1,155	44	1,199	96	42	1,126	316	76	546	1	2.5
1980[4]	1,173	30	1,203	14	1,217	50	1,267	92	38	1,024	378		540	1	2.3
1981[4]	1,131	24	1,155	12	1,167	49	1,216	—150—		950	315		572	1	2.5
1982[4]					1,011	37	1,048	—110—		870	251				

[1] Preliminary.   [2] Factory & warehouse.   [3] Includes military shipments for civilian relief abroad. Also non-food products; the bulk goes into shortening.   [4] Estimate.   Source: *Economic Research Service, U.S.D.A.*   T.348

Domestic Disappearance of Lard in the United States   In Millions of Pounds

Year	Jan.	Feb.	Mar.	Apr.	May	June	July	Aug.	Sept.	Oct.	Nov.	Dec.	Total
1973	96.4	98.3	100.9	89.4	111.7	101.8	88.5	80.4	83.7	90.3	94.3	86.2	1,122
1974	89.9	84.5	87.4	100.7	107.6	89.4	81.8	115.0	97.8	124.1	102.9	89.2	1,170
1975	98.9	61.3	90.4	81.0	78.6	59.1	65.5	65.7	55.3	68.5	69.1	65.5	859
1976	67.6	47.4	86.2	53.0	67.7	53.6	67.8	74.6	65.0	79.3	76.1	64.8	803
1977	50.5	55.0	73.3	48.3	77.0	66.9	64.3	80.8	73.0	60.1	82.7	66.4	798
1978	68.3	62.3	65.6	71.9	74.8	60.3	67.7	72.2	68.3	77.5	75.2	64.4	825
1979	70.1	62.1	76.0	78.8	84.3	88.3	78.9	97.6	88.6	103.2	94.7	86.0	1,009
1980[1]	90.4	82.0	39.1	43.0	48.2	42.8	41.8	42.0	40.5	45.0	47.0	46.9	609
1981[1]	45.5	39.1	36.8	38.4	34.2	36.7	33.2	34.6	38.8	31.5	37.8	41.5	448
1982[1]	35.3	25.4	28.6	33.4	31.2	28.1	24.2	22.2	22.4	21.6	23.3	26.3	322
1983[1]	25.3												

[1] Preliminary.   Source: *Economic Research Service, U.S.D.A.*   T.349

Average Wholesale Price of Lard—Loose, Tank Cars, Chicago   In Cents Per Pound

Year	Jan.	Feb.	Mar.	Apr.	May	June	July	Aug.	Sept.	Oct.	Nov.	Dec.	Average
1975	37.0	30.0	28.0	28.5	28.5	24.0	38.0	36.0	37.5	35.0	30.0	18.5	30.9
1976	17.0	17.4	17.0	15.8	15.6	16.0	19.0	19.3	21.0	17.8	19.0	19.1	17.8
1977	20.5	22.4	21.5	25.0	26.0	23.1	20.5	19.0	17.9	21.5	19.0	19.3	21.3
1978	19.4	20.8	23.8	25.6	22.0	22.5	23.3	22.3	26.0	24.5	24.5	23.3	23.2
1979	24.5	24.0	25.1	29.8	26.8	—	—	—	26.6	25.1	23.8	25.1	25.6
1980	22.0	21.6	19.3	19.0	18.0	17.5	17.5	22.5	23.0	21.6	23.3	23.3	20.7
1981	20.0	19.0	19.6	19.9	19.4	19.6	22.0	21.8	22.8	21.5	21.0	18.4	20.3
1982	20.0	21.5	20.0	22.0	23.0	24.6	22.6	22.8	21.3	21.0	17.3	16.5	21.1
1983	16.4	16.7	16.4	17.4									

Source: *Economic Research Service, U.S.D.A.*   T.350

LARD

United States Cold Storage Holdings of all Lard[1], on First of Month In Millions of Pounds

Year	Jan.	Feb.	Mar.	Apr.	May	June	July	Aug.	Sept.	Oct.	Nov.	Dec.
1970	70.1	64.8	61.6	67.1	75.2	65.3	64.9	66.5	54.2	59.8	59.0	74.0
1971	82.5	90.7	85.8	80.9	79.8	90.9	101.1	89.1	81.6	76.9	82.7	82.4
1972	99.9	78.1	66.1	64.3	80.7	89.6	83.2	64.1	52.3	44.0	44.0	57.5
1973	51.2	52.1	44.5	49.3	49.1	49.9	39.9	33.8	32.2	28.4	35.1	37.3
1974	43.7	56.3	45.4	53.3	55.7	55.2	50.0	54.5	50.7	47.7	37.7	33.2
1975	35.7	34.0	34.4	26.4	31.3	31.9	23.6	21.6	19.2	22.6	18.7	25.0
1976	28.3	33.5	36.1	29.3	31.9	32.0	32.2	26.9	28.4	33.6	37.5	37.4
1977	33.9	31.5	37.6	38.4	50.2	50.1	47.2	47.4	38.2	31.7	32.1	32.1
1978	28.5	30.0	29.7	33.9	35.7	35.4	36.8	32.4	29.7	35.1	29.5	32.0
1979	38.1	40.5	39.6	35.8	42.8	47.9	46.0	51.4	46.4	43.9	44.7	52.0
1980	49.9	54.4	61.3	62.5	57.9	51.7	59.1	57.1	55.0	43.5	44.6	48.7
1981	49.4	50.4	46.9	42.2	40.5	40.1	40.7	42.6	39.5	35.6	36.7	39.1
1982[2]	37.0	35.3	32.5	32.5	32.7	31.8	31.4	25.5	32.2	24.2	29.5	39.0
1983[2]	37.5	38.9										
1984												

[1] Stocks in factories & warehouses (except that in hands of retailers). [2] Preliminary. *Source: Bureau of the Census* T.351

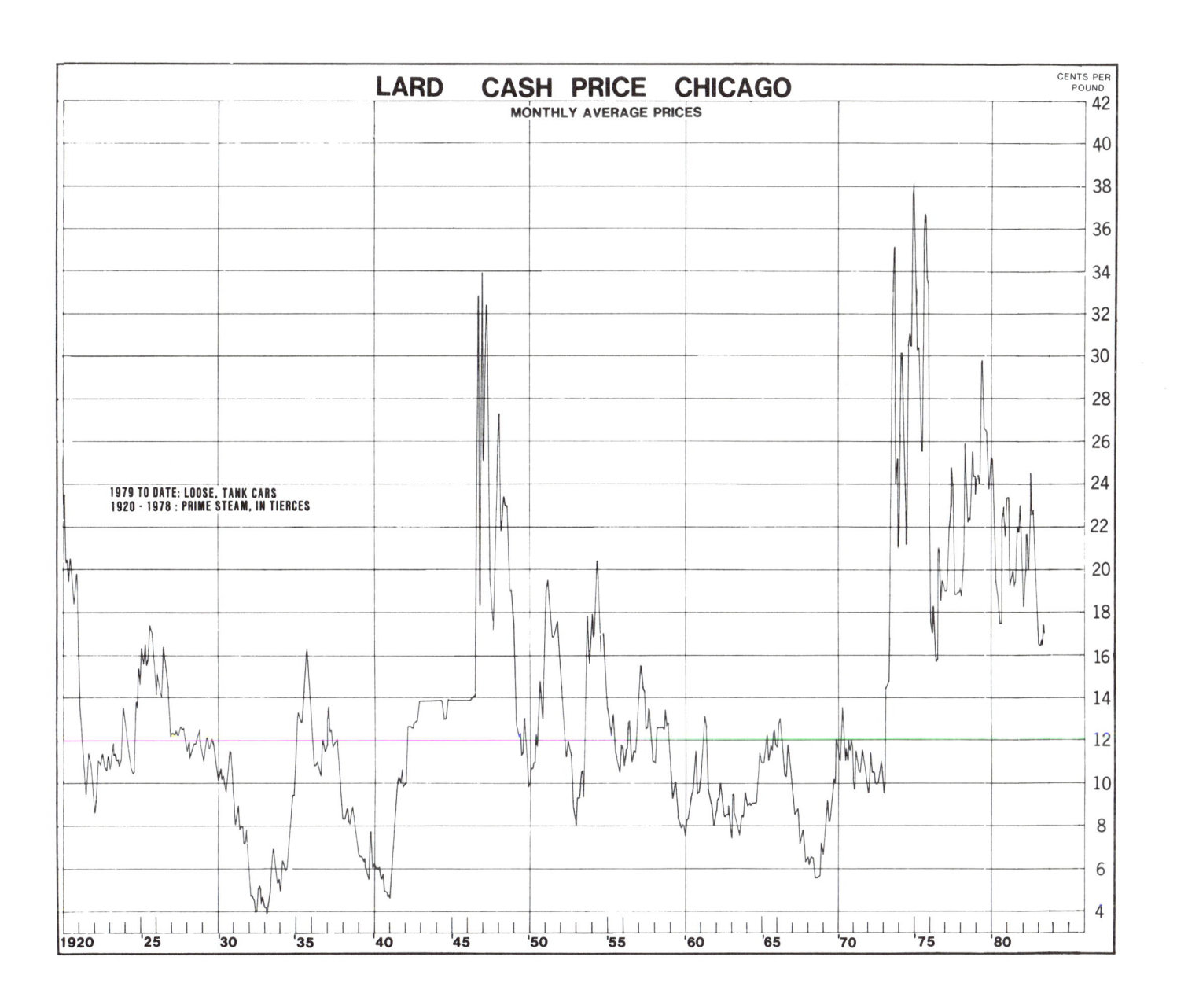

LARD CASH PRICE CHICAGO
MONTHLY AVERAGE PRICES

1979 TO DATE: LOOSE, TANK CARS
1920 - 1978: PRIME STEAM, IN TIERCES

LARD

Lard Exports[2] of the United States by Selected Country of Destination   In Thousands of Metric Tons[3]

Year	Asia	Belgium & Lux.	Canada	Belize	Bolivia	Neth. Antilles	Colombia	W. Germany	Haiti	Mexico	Ecuador	Netherlands	Poland	United Kingdom	Yugoslavia	Grand Total
1970	—	—	16.1	—		—	—	.8	1.2	44.5	—	—	—	259.3	14.3	365.9
1971	—	—	9.2	—		—	—	1.0	1.4	26.0	—	—	—	229.7	5.3	282.3
1972	—	—	11.8	—		—	—	1.2	3.2	26.3	—	—	—	116.1	—	164.4
1973	—	—	6.5	2.9	.5	.1	1.1	—	2.4	41.5	—	—	—	58.0	—	113.3
1974	—	2.0	20.1	1.9	.3	—	4.8	—	2.4	51.4	—	—	—	75.6	—	161.4
1975[3]	—	—	9.3	.9	.1	.1	—	—	.3	24.4	—	—	—	4.6	—	39.8
1976	4.3	4.1	17.0	1.4		.1	16.0	—	1.3	29.1	4.3	8.4	—	29.7	—	117.3
1977	.3	1.7	20.1	1.3	.3	.2	.1	—	1.2	31.1	25.4	12.2	3.4	19.3	—	82.6
1978	.4	—	19.4	1.4	—	.3	.2	—	.9	26.7	15.5	4.9	—	3.8	—	54.2
1979	.3	—	9.3	1.7	1.1	.4	.1	—	1.1	26.7	—	—	—	1.7	—	43.5
1980	.2	—	7.9	1.5	.3	.3	1.1	—	1.0	24.0	—	—	2.5	1.7	—	41.9
1981[1]	.1	—	9.0	1.8	2.1	.4	1.0	—	1.1	32.6	—	—	17.0	.6	—	67.9
1982																

[1] Preliminary. [2] Excludes exports for civilian relief & shipments by CARE. [3] Data prior to 1975 are in MILLIONS OF POUNDS.   *Source: Foreign Agricultural Service, U.S.D.A.*
T.352

United States Production of Lard[1] (Commercial Production[2])   In Millions of Pounds

Year	Jan.	Feb.	Mar.	Apr.	May	June	July	Aug.	Sept.	Oct.	Nov.	Dec.	Total
1970	144.1	120.7	139.4	153.0	130.0	136.5	131.5	135.4	157.6	175.5	174.2	178.1	1,776
1971	166.1	129.2	193.4	162.4	146.0	157.8	133.7	141.9	148.1	139.6	158.9	152.7	1,830
1972	123.2	105.0	148.9	131.5	138.7	130.8	101.6	120.8	108.0	122.7	130.3	103.1	1,464
1973	110.6	91.8	108.7	95.4	122.5	105.3	82.8	81.9	80.1	106.1	108.1	94.9	1,181
1974[2]	89.9	84.5	87.4	100.7	107.6	89.4	81.8	115.0	97.8	124.1	102.9	89.2	1,170
1975	103.0	87.0	94.0	96.0	86.0	74.0	68.0	67.0	75.0	78.0	83.0	84.0	995
1976	87.0	67.0	90.0	85.0	80.0	76.0	74.0	87.0	91.0	103.0	108.0	95.0	1,043
1977	73.0	65.0	100.0	85.0	85.0	85.0	73.0	86.0	89.0	93.0	102.0	85.0	1,021
1978	82.0	73.0	83.0	82.0	87.0	78.0	74.0	82.0	83.0	88.0	94.0	85.0	991
1979	83.0	69.0	86.0	91.0	102.0	95.0	95.0	104.0	92.0	117.0	112.0	95.0	1,141
1980	105.0	94.0	98.0	111.0	107.0	98.0	95.0	87.0	98.0	111.0	96.0	102.0	1,203
1981	100.0	87.0	99.0	104.0	95.0	91.0	89.0	86.0	96.0	104.0	99.0	104.0	1,155
1982[3]	88.0	77.0	94.0			257.0			234.0			261.0	1,011
1983													

[1] Includes "Rendered Pork Fat." [2] Data prior to 1974 are for FEDERALLY INSPECTED ONLY. [3] Preliminary.   *Source: Department of Agriculture*
T.354

How to keep your Commodity Year Book statistics up-to-date continuously throughout the year.

To keep up-to-date statistics on the commodities in this book, you should have COMMODITY YEAR BOOK STATISTICAL ABSTRACT SERVICE. This three-times-yearly publication provides the latest available statistics for updating the statistical tables appearing in the COMMODITY YEAR BOOK. The ABSTRACT is published in the Winter (Jan.), Spring (Apr.) and Fall (Oct.). Subscription price is $55 per year.

Commodity Research Bureau, Inc.
75 MONTGOMERY ST., JERSEY CITY, N.J. 07302

Lead

The worldwide total of subeconomic lead resources is estimated at 1.4 billion tonnes, much of it in low-tenor and unconventional deposits that will require new technological processes for development and recovery. The prospective resources of conventional lead deposits throughout the world are expected to be adequate for the satisfaction of world demand in the foreseeable future. Preliminary estimates put the 1982 world mine production of lead at nearly 3 percent above the 1981 level of 3.35 million tonnes.

U.S. producers' prices of lead fell as much as 14 cents per pound in 1982, although an increase of nearly 2 cents per pound was observed during the July period of seasonally low production. The production capacity of the U.S. lead industry was utilized to approximately 83 percent in 1982, but the secondary production sector operated at only 50 percent of capacity due to a shortage of scrap. U.S. mine production of lead in 1982 increased by 15 percent and resulted in a 70 percent increase in metal exports, much of it in the form of pigs and bars shipped to the London Metal Exchange (LME). Reported consumption was down significantly because of a declining demand for original equipment batteries by the domestic transportation industry. Stocks of lead at producer and consumer plants declined in 1982. At the end of the year, lead stocks held by primary refineries and by secondary smelters and consumers amounted to 77,375 tonnes compared with 123,216 tonnes at the end of 1981. Approximately 540,000 tonnes of lead was recovered from old scrap in 1982.

The U.S. transportation industry, which uses lead in the production of batteries and gasoline additives, accounted for nearly 75 percent of the domestic major end use of lead in 1982. Construction, paint, ammunition, and electrical consumption accounted for the next largest usage of lead. The substitution of plastics has reduced the use of lead in building construction, electrical cable covering, and in cans and containers, however. The U.S. 1983 domestic mine production of lead is expected to be 525,000 tonnes, and U.S. apparent consumption is projected at 1.1 million tonnes. The U.S. demand for lead, including secondary, was expected to increase by about 2.5 percent annually as figured from a 1978 base year.

Late in 1982, the Environmental Protection Agency (EPA) published more stringent leaded-gasoline regulations intended to reduce airborne lead by a third in the next eight years. However, the EPA decided against toughening air pollution controls for producers during the next four years.

Futures Market

Lead futures are traded on the London Metal Exchange (LME).

World Smelter (Primary & Secondary) Production of Lead[5]   In Thousands of Metric[6] Tons

Year	Australia[3]	Belgium[4]	Bulgaria	Canada[3]	China[2]	France	W. Germany	Japan	Mexico[3]	Peru[3]	Spain	United States	USSR	Yugoslavia[3]	World Total[5]
1970	388.6	98.5	108.7	204.6	110.0	132.2	124.3	230.4	165.6	79.3	83.3	666.7	485.0	107.4	3,628
1971	356.7	87.4	112.7	185.6	110.0	117.2	108.5	237.1	167.0	74.0	112.5	650.0	500.0	109.3	3,591
1972	383.7	102.3	112.4	206.0	110.0	150.1	112.4	246.1	171.8	94.3	111.1	688.6	510.0	96.4	3,745
1973	374.8	125.3	118.0	206.0	110.0	183.6	94.6	251.4	190.6	91.8	96.3	674.5	520.0	124.2	3,838
1974	371.4	109.8	124.0	139.4	110.0	174.8	128.0	251.3	220.7	88.8	87.7	673.0	525.0	125.5	3,829
1975	343.2	113.5	121.0	189.1	110.0	149.2	101.7	214.1	190.6	78.4	81.5	636.1	530.0	139.0	3,633
1976[6]	342.6	91.7	112.0	231.0	140.0	191.5	278.3	305.7	234.7	74.1	101.7	1,251	600.0	140.3	4,990
1977	337.9	73.6	120.0	240.6	150.0	144.4	373.5	305.2	216.2	79.2	118.6	1,306	610.0	145.0	5,140
1978	356.0	74.7	120.0	245.9	160.0	151.4	369.0	293.9	215.4	74.3	122.2	1,334	620.0	140.4	5,185
1979	385.1	60.7	119.0	252.4	170.0	159.9	373.3	294.2	223.0	85.1	127.0	1,377	625.0	133.6	5,370
1980	360.7	81.7	119.0	234.6	170.0	161.7	350.3	315.6	195.0	82.0	124.0	1,223	625.0	133.0	5,134
1981[1]	367.2	71.9	119.0	238.2	170.0	160.0	358.8	320.3	206.7	79.2	118.0	1,136	630.0	89.0	4,981
1982[2]	380			240					200	85		1,200		85	5,000

[1] Preliminary.   [2] Estimated.   [3] Refined & bullion.   [4] Includes scrap.   [5] Prior to 1976 data does not include secondary production.   [6] Data prior to 1976 are in THOUSANDS OF SHORT TONS.   Source: Bureau of Mines

Consumption of Lead in the United States by Products   In Thousands of Metric[5] Tons

Year	Ammunition	Bearing Metal	Building[2]	Cable Covering	Calking Lead	Casting Metals	Collapsible Tubes	Foil	Red Lead & Litharge	Solder	Storage Batteries & Oxides[4]	Chemicals Petrol. Refin.[6]	Type Metal	Brass and Bronze	Total Consumption
1973	81.5	15.7	44.7	43.0	20.1	7.2	2.9	5.0	89.6	71.8	769.4	274.4	21.9	1.7	1,541.2
1974	87.1	14.6	37.7	43.4	19.7	7.5	2.5	4.4	96.2	66.3	851.9	250.5	20.5	2.0	1,599.4
1975	75.1	12.2	39.1	22.1	14.3	7.7	2.2	3.2	65.5	57.3	699.4	208.6	16.2	2.5	1,297.1
1976	73.5	13.1	38.2	15.9	12.5	6.7	2.3	5.1	85.4	63.3	822.4	239.8	15.0	13.4	1,490.1
1977	68.4	12.0	28.4	15.1	9.6	6.0	2.1	3.6	78.1	64.3	945.9	232.9	12.6	15.7	1,582.3
1978[5]	55.8	9.5	23.1	13.9	9.9	3.6	—	91.6 —		68.4	879.3	178.3	10.8	16.5	1,432.7
1979	53.2	9.6	27.6	16.4	8.0	22.7	—	90.8 —		54.3	814.4	186.9	10.0	18.7	1,358.3
1980	48.7	7.8	28.4	13.4	5.7	19.0	—	78.4 —		41.4	645.4	127.9	9.0	14.0	1,070.3
1981[1]	49.5	6.9	28.2	12.1	5.5	18.6	—	80.2 —		29.7	770.2	111.4	7.8	13.3	1,167.1
1982[3]	43.8	5.3	12.2	14.5	2.0	8.4	—	50.7 —		19.2	522.1	119.2	5.3	8.5	1,066.2

[1] Preliminary.   [2] Chiefly pipes, traps & bends & sheet lead.   [3] Estimate.   [4] Also grids, posts, etc.   [5] Data prior to 1978 are in THOUSANDS OF SHORT TONS.   [6] Data prior to 1978 are for GASOLINE ANTI-KNOCK ADDITIVES.   Source: Bureau of Mines

LEAD

Salient Statistics of Lead in the United States   In Thousands of Metric[5] Tons

Year	Net Import Reliance as a % of Apparent Consumption	Domestic Ores[2]	Foreign Ores[2]	Total Primary	Secondary Sources	Total	Total Value of Refined Mil. $	As Refined Metal	In Antimonial Lead	In Other Alloys	Total	Total Value of Secondary Mil. $	Producers' Stocks[3]	Consumers' Stocks	New York	London
1973		567.3	107.3	674.5	—	674.5	219.8	186.1	375.8	92.4	654.3	213.2	89.8	124.1	16.29	19.47
1974		580.1	92.9	673.0	—	673.0	303.3	238.2	371.5	89.0	698.7	314.8	121.1	166.6	22.53	26.83
1975[5]	11	481.0	96.1	577.1	—	577.1	273.9	246.1	285.9	65.4	597.3	283.5	142.0	120.9	21.53	18.73
1976	15	515.8	76.5	592.3	—	592.3	301.6	282.1	310.2	66.8	659.1	335.7	110.4	117.6	23.10	20.46
1977	13	486.7	62.0	548.7	.1	548.8	371.4	303.1	383.4	71.1	757.6	512.8	91.1	121.4	30.70	28.00
1978	12	501.6	63.5	565.2	1.2	566.4	419.3	282.6	409.9	76.5	769.2	570.7	98.7	125.2	33.65	29.86
1979	5	530.0	45.6	575.6	2.9	578.5	668.0	352.2	378.8	70.3	801.4	930.0	89.3	153.2	52.64	54.52
1980	6	508.2	39.4	547.6	2.1	549.7	512.6	315.2	306.7	53.7	675.6	632.4	126.0	126.2	42.46	41.21
1981[1]	1	440.2	55.1	495.3	1.7	497.1	398.9	282.2	304.4	54.6	641.1	516.3	140.2	123.2	36.53	33.30
1982[4]	1					512.8								77.4	25.54	24.66

[1] Preliminary.   [2] And base bullion.   [3] At primary smelters & refineries.   [4] Estimates.   [5] Data prior to 1975 are in THOUSANDS OF SHORT TONS.   [6] Net exporter.   Source: Bureau of Mines
T.357

U.S. Mine Production of Recoverable Lead   In Thousands of Metric[3] Tons

Year	Arizona	California	Colorado	Idaho	Illinois	New York	Missouri	Montana	Nevada	New Mexico	Oklahoma	Utah	Virginia	Washington	Wisconsin	Total U.S.[2]
1973	.8	—	27.8	61.4	.5	2.6	484.9	.2	—	2.6	—	13.9	2.6	2.2	.8	603.0
1974	1.1	—	24.6	51.7	.5	3.1	562.1	.2	1.8	2.4	N.A.	10.5	3.1	1.3	1.3	663.9
1975[3]	.4	.1	24.6	45.7	N.A.	2.7	468.1	.2	2.7	1.8	—	11.5	2.3	N.A.	N.A.	563.8
1976	.3	.1	24.3	48.7	N.A.	2.9	454.5	.1	.5	N.A.	N.A.	14.8	1.8	N.A.	N.A.	553.0
1977	.3	—	20.9	42.9	N.A.	2.5	453.8	.1	.7	N.A.	N.A.	9.7	2.0	1.1	N.A.	537.5
1978	.4	N.A.	15.2	44.8	N.A.	1.0	461.8	.1	.7	N.A.	—	2.5	1.8	N.A.	N.A.	529.7
1979	.4	N.A.	7.6	42.6	N.A.	.5	472.1	.3	—	N.A.	—	N.A.	1.6	—	N.A.	525.6
1980	.2	N.A.	10.3	38.6	N.A.	.9	497.2	.3	—	—	—	—	1.6	N.A.	—	550.4
1981	1.0	N.A.	11.4	38.4	N.A.	1.0	389.7	.2	—	—	—	1.7	1.6	—	—	445.5
1982[1]	.3						478.0	.6								515.9

[1] Preliminary.   [2] Includes Alaska.   [3] Data prior to 1975 are in THOUSANDS OF SHORT TONS.   Source: Bureau of Mines
T.356

U.S. Foreign Trade of Lead   In Thousands of Metric[4] Tons

Year	Exports Unwrought Lead[3]	Exports Wrought Lead[5]	Exports Scrap	Exports Total	Imports Ores, Flue Dust or Fume & Mattes	Imports Base Bullion	Imports Pigs & Bars	Imports Reclaimed Scrap, Etc.	Value Million $	Ore, Flue Dust & Matte Australia	Ore, Flue Dust & Matte Peru	Ore, Flue Dust & Matte Canada	Pigs & Bars Australia	Pigs & Bars Mexico	Pigs & Bars Peru	Pigs & Bars Canada
1976	2.9	3.0	46.9	52.8	89.0	2.3	142.0	2.6	92.2	11.2	9.3	27.7	6.1	44.3	19.7	30.7
1977[4]	4.3	4.7	77.5	86.5	88.8	7.3	230.1	3.5	196.9	16.6	6.6	16.0	19.9	71.8	30.4	75.4
1978	3.2	5.1	98.6	106.9	61.9	4.3	225.4	3.3	203.0	6.5	6.3	19.6	16.3	80.2	25.7	70.4
1979	7.4	3.3	119.7	130.4	44.4	1.7	182.6	4.0	248.3	1.9	12.4	12.8	17.3	73.6	17.9	71.3
1980	156.5	8.0	119.7	284.2	29.6	.3	81.3	2.9	116.5	3.0	18.0	8.5	11.3	28.6	3.3	34.9
1981[1]	16.8	6.5	59.4	82.7	27.2	.4	100.1	2.7	110.5	2.2	14.1	23.5	10.9	33.7	2.9	50.8
1982[2]			51.8		18.9	—	94.9	4.8			7.7	14.5	4.8	7.3	23.5	8.3	49.8

[1] Preliminary.   [2] Estimates.   [3] And lead alloys.   [4] Data prior to 1977 data are in THOUSANDS OF SHORT TONS.   [5] Blocks, Pigs, etc.   Source: Bureau of Mines
T.359

U.S. Mine Production of Recoverable Lead   In Thousands of Short Tons

Year	Jan.	Feb.	Mar.	Apr.	May	June	July	Aug.	Sept.	Oct.	Nov.	Dec.	Total
1973	53.5	50.0	45.3	40.1	55.9	43.9	51.4	55.7	51.4	53.7	49.0	53.2	603.0
1974	57.1	52.8	58.0	52.3	53.3	54.9	54.8	58.7	50.0	64.9	53.2	53.9	663.9
1975	55.6	52.6	58.5	56.0	53.3	50.8	37.8	40.1	50.6	56.3	49.0	52.9	621.5
1976	50.4	52.0	57.8	50.6	51.0	50.6	48.1	51.0	49.2	49.6	49.0	50.4	609.5
1977	45.0	49.2	56.9	53.2	48.3	50.9	41.9	52.6	46.4	49.2	48.6	50.3	592.5
1978	49.8	45.0	57.1	49.4	54.3	40.1	35.5	47.6	49.5	55.5	50.0	49.1	582.9
1979[1]	47.6	44.0	42.5	37.0	41.8	42.0	41.4	48.8	34.6	50.0	46.5	43.9	525.6
1980[1]	51.6	50.4	50.0	48.1	50.0	46.3	43.5	41.7	39.3	48.5	39.6	41.2	559.5
1981[1]	42.3	40.5	43.0	26.4	27.5	17.1	31.7	31.8	47.8	47.3	39.6	41.2	445.5
1982[1]	40.5	43.5	48.7	44.3	42.1	42.6	37.0	42.9	41.7	45.0	42.1	45.4	515.9

[1] Preliminary.   Source: Bureau of Mines
T.359A

LEAD

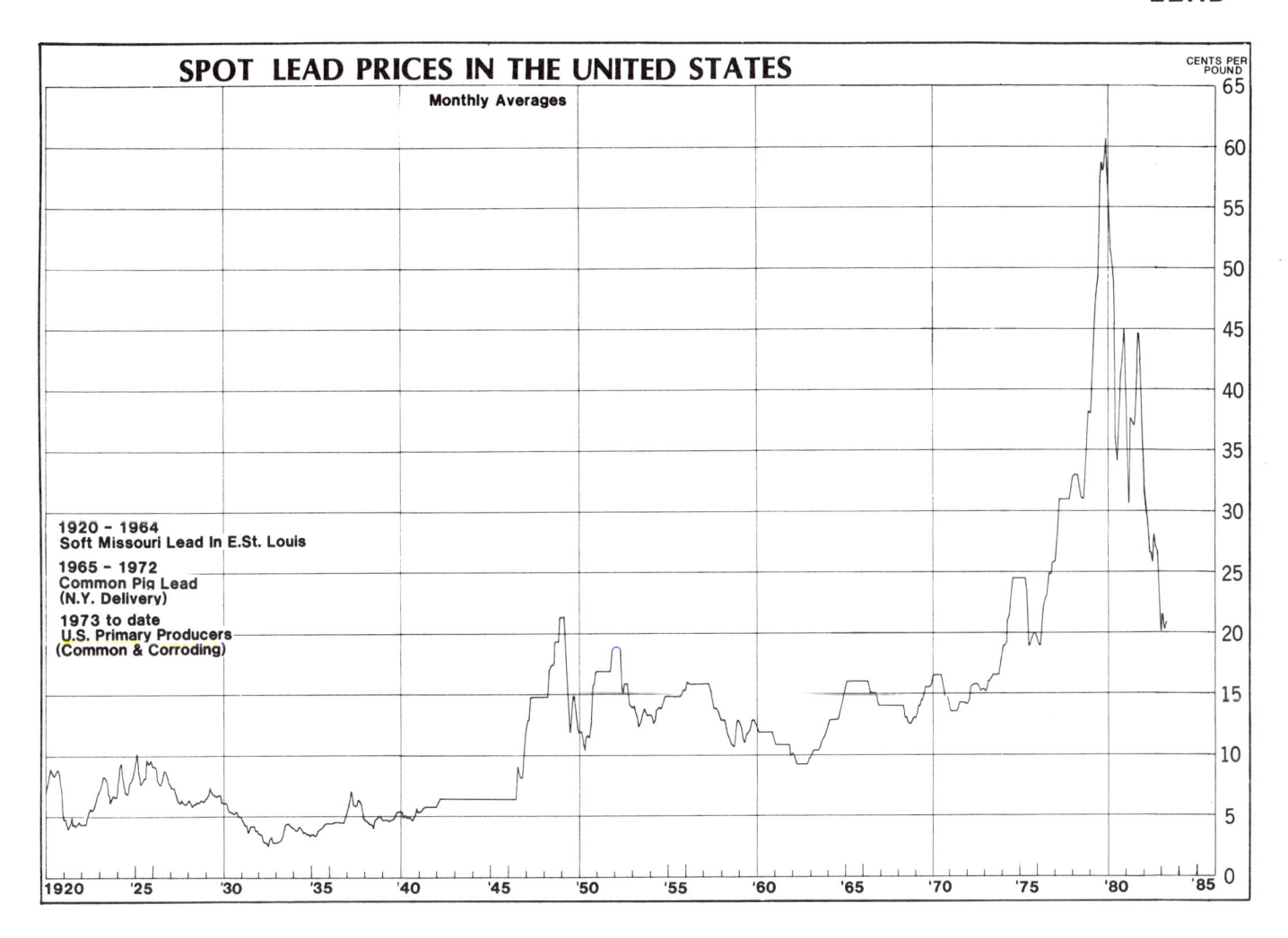

SPOT LEAD PRICES IN THE UNITED STATES
Monthly Averages
(Cents Per Pound)

1920 – 1964 Soft Missouri Lead In E.St. Louis
1965 – 1972 Common Pig Lead (N.Y. Delivery)
1973 to date U.S. Primary Producers (Common & Corroding)

Average Price of Pig Lead, U.S. Primary Producers[1] (Common Corroding) In Cents Per Pound

Year	Jan.	Feb.	Mar.	Apr.	May	June	July	Aug.	Sept.	Oct.	Nov.	Dec.	Average
1971	13.50	13.50	13.50	13.50	13.50	13.70	14.25	14.25	14.25	14.25	14.25	14.19	13.89
1972	14.15	14.63	15.50	15.63	15.75	15.75	15.75	15.71	15.50	15.21	15.25	15.25	15.34
1973	15.09	15.42	15.97	16.00	16.25	16.50	16.50	16.50	16.50	16.50	16.50	17.96	16.31
1974	18.95	19.00	19.30	21.16	21.50	23.00	24.50	24.50	24.50	24.50	24.50	24.50	23.19
1975	24.50	24.50	24.50	24.50	23.21	19.00	19.00	19.52	20.00	20.00	20.00	19.48	21.52
1976	19.00	19.00	20.30	22.00	22.90	23.00	24.26	24.75	24.75	24.77	25.71	25.75	23.02
1977	26.99	28.95	31.00	31.00	31.00	31.00	31.00	31.00	31.00	31.02	32.00	32.86	30.74
1978	33.00	33.00	33.00	33.00	31.23	31.00	31.00	32.50	34.19	36.05	38.18	38.00	33.68
1979	40.64	43.74	46.09	48.00	49.44	57.14	58.68	57.96	58.47	60.74	58.30	57.11	53.03
1980	51.06	50.00	49.52	45.34	36.00	34.19	35.95	40.95	42.43	45.00	44.06	40.43	42.91
1981	34.13	30.63	35.32	37.68	37.10	38.23	41.25	44.64	42.52	37.59	34.34	31.75	37.10
1982	29.90	28.87	27.98	26.57	26.50	25.89	27.88	27.00	26.64	23.00	21.48	20.12	26.03
1983	21.60	20.87	20.43	21.00									
1984													

[1] Prior to Nov. 1973 prices are for Common Pig (N.Y. Delivery—Carload Lots).   Source: *American Metal Market*

T.360

203

LEAD

Production[1] of Lead in the United States by Refiners   In Thousands of Short Tons

Year	Jan.	Feb.	Mar.	Apr.	May	June	July	Aug.	Sept.	Oct.	Nov.	Dec.	Total
1971	51.3	46.7	53.5	53.8	56.5	58.0	57.9	50.5	53.8	66.6	58.0	65.0	671.6
1972	62.7	59.1	63.4	42.8	66.4	58.6	60.1	62.7	56.2	61.7	62.3	58.5	714.5
1973	63.9	65.5	65.9	56.8	65.3	67.9	52.4	70.8	64.9	65.5	64.3	59.2	762.3
1974	62.5	60.3	60.2	52.8	60.2	51.8	59.6	60.6	59.7	58.2	60.7	62.6	709.2
1975	65.0	55.0	60.4	49.5	51.5	45.0	46.4	52.3	52.5	57.9	53.2	52.6	641.4
1976	57.7	56.3	56.2	58.5	61.5	54.1	52.9	57.1	50.2	53.5	49.1	51.3	658.4
1977	51.2	46.6	57.7	50.2	51.2	46.9	41.5	46.9	50.2	56.5	58.0	55.2	612.0
1978	60.0	50.1	55.3	55.5	49.1	44.8	42.5	50.4	51.5	60.9	55.1	54.2	629.2
1979	53.0	52.2	60.6	52.5	58.1	55.0	52.6	49.9	45.4	52.9	54.6	54.3	641.1
1980	56.9	49.3	54.1	47.5	47.0	47.1	52.0	48.2	50.2	52.2	48.4	53.5	606.4
1981	58.0	53.6	58.2	52.7	35.0	24.4	33.0	45.1	43.7	46.1	39.4	44.0	533.2
1982	50.3	45.2	44.0	36.1	54.3	53.0	44.2	46.4	49.2	50.6	50.8	48.6	572.6
1983	57.0	50.9	52.8	48.9									
1984													

[1] Represents refined lead produced from domestic ores by primary smelters plus small amount of secondary material passing through these smelters. Includes GSA metal purchased for remelt.   Source: American Bureau of Metal Statistics, Inc.   T.362

Shipments[1] (Domestic) of Lead in the United States by Refiners   In Thousands of Short Tons

Year	Jan.	Feb.	Mar.	Apr.	May	June	July	Aug.	Sept.	Oct.	Nov.	Dec.	Total
1971	50.5	49.0	61.0	58.0	57.6	67.5	46.8	64.1	65.1	72.6	66.9	61.1	720.1
1972	56.4	66.3	73.2	50.4	59.9	54.7	46.5	51.5	55.6	69.2	62.6	58.0	704.2
1973	70.0	69.4	68.1	64.4	67.8	70.4	62.3	69.4	69.2	75.4	72.6	54.5	823.4
1974	72.6	64.6	63.9	57.2	60.8	56.9	65.8	60.9	61.4	63.5	58.9	49.7	736.2
1975	47.2	36.7	37.3	44.2	49.7	38.2	45.4	62.5	64.9	67.6	47.0	54.1	594.9
1976	49.2	54.2	58.8	63.6	62.0	54.8	59.3	66.1	55.8	62.7	57.2	51.2	694.9
1977	57.2	56.0	62.9	53.6	50.7	51.3	42.2	47.4	51.6	54.7	55.0	55.7	638.3
1978	59.9	49.7	51.3	43.5	49.0	44.1	44.3	56.3	56.1	62.8	54.5	53.1	624.5
1979	56.7	54.7	58.9	52.2	58.5	55.2	56.1	47.0	45.9	52.9	39.7	30.8	608.6
1980	40.5	37.6	38.9	28.8	30.1	35.3	36.6	48.0	60.1	55.6	31.0	38.6	481.0
1981	31.9	42.5	51.7	48.8	41.9	33.4	34.2	51.7	55.1	35.5	28.2	24.2	479.0
1982	39.3	35.8	37.0	30.7	40.9	37.8	41.9	48.1	42.6	46.7	39.8	39.7	480.4
1983	43.7	33.9	44.4	40.3									
1984													

[1] Includes GSA metal.   Source: American Bureau of Metal Statistics, Inc.   T.363

Total Stocks of Lead[1] in the United States at Refiners, at End of Month   In Thousands of Short Tons

Year	Jan.	Feb.	Mar.	Apr.	May	June	July	Aug.	Sept.	Oct.	Nov.	Dec.
1970	30.8	33.5	36.9	47.3	53.5	63.3	79.1	87.4	86.6	90.9	93.6	98.3
1971	99.1	96.8	89.6	85.4	84.3	77.3	88.4	74.8	63.5	57.6	48.7	52.3
1972	58.3	50.4	38.0	29.1	36.3	40.6	55.6	67.7	69.3	64.0	64.4	67.3
1973	59.4	54.7	39.9	33.2	35.3	32.3	20.5	24.4	26.8	22.8	20.7	27.6
1974	40.8	35.5	35.2	28.1	21.3	19.2	18.9	21.2	21.7	20.8	25.2	38.1
1975	55.5	73.8	96.7	101.6	104.5	111.8	110.7	100.7	87.7	77.7	83.7	82.1
1976	91.5	92.8	90.6	87.8	85.3	84.6	76.7	67.7	61.7	54.3	45.6	46.0
1977	37.9	28.2	23.5	20.9	20.1	15.1	13.7	13.3	12.4	14.8	16.5	16.0
1978	16.3	16.6	20.8	32.6	32.3	33.0	31.0	24.9	20.1	18.1	18.7	19.8
1979	15.8	13.4	15.2	15.0	14.6	14.3	10.8	13.7	13.0	13.9	27.8	51.3
1980	67.8	75.0	71.6	83.8	90.8	82.7	66.3	53.8	35.2	29.2	46.5	60.9
1981	86.6	92.3	88.9	87.8	71.2	61.6	59.9	52.6	38.5	49.1	57.5	62.8
1982	65.4	67.2	65.9	60.1	65.1	73.2	70.8	64.9	71.4	72.9	78.0	79.0
1983	83.3	91.2	84.9	89.0								
1984												

[1] Stocks at own plant & elsewhere.   Source: American Bureau of Metal Statistics, Inc.   T.364

LEAD

Total[1] Lead Consumption in the United States In Thousands of Short Tons

Year	Jan.	Feb.	Mar.	Apr.	May	June	July	Aug.	Sept.	Oct.	Nov.	Dec.	Total
1972	122.3	123.7	132.3	122.4	129.0	126.7	91.4	127.4	126.0	132.2	131.4	120.5	1,485
1973	135.3	131.7	143.2	128.4	128.8	129.1	101.9	125.7	124.8	140.7	131.4	120.2	1,541
1974	141.0	129.4	130.9	126.5	142.6	121.5	112.8	144.0	143.7	156.8	136.4	113.8	1,599
1975	105.1	98.9	99.2	105.1	102.3	94.7	88.6	115.5	123.0	133.7	115.8	115.3	1,297
1976	116.3	123.3	136.1	125.7	123.4	123.3	103.4	120.7	127.4	137.4	128.0	125.2	1,490
1977	132.2	122.1	149.5	138.0	128.3	133.6	108.1	131.6	142.5	141.4	126.2	128.9	1,582
1978	122.5	115.0	125.2	122.5	117.4	121.6	99.5	125.2	124.9	140.4	130.9	123.4	1,433
1979	114.6	111.0	124.3	109.5	116.7	108.5	91.3	106.0	109.3	112.1	106.3	94.0	1,358
1980	97.3	84.9	90.0	83.8	84.1	77.2	68.2	79.5	95.6	103.0	92.5	92.0	1,070
1981	98.9	90.7	95.9	91.2	89.1	91.0	81.1	93.1	99.9	110.4	94.4	107.6	1,167
1982	93.9	84.4	90.9	88.3	82.1	84.5	73.0	90.7	87.9	95.3	83.2	83.1	1,066
1983													

[1] Represents total consumption of primary & secondary lead as metal, in chemicals, or in alloys.   Source: Bureau of Mines   T.365

U.S. Lead Recovered from Scrap (Lead Content) In Thousands of Short Tons

Year	Jan	Feb	Mar.	Apr.	May	June	July	Aug.	Sept.	Oct.	Nov.	Dec.	Total
1971	46.4	48.1	47.0	50.8	48.1	46.4	42.4	46.1	49.1	51.6	50.6	46.0	596.8
1972	45.3	41.8	54.2	51.9	55.0	50.4	48.9	49.6	51.4	49.5	51.6	45.4	616.6
1973	55.3	56.2	56.4	56.8	59.1	56.3	45.7	52.9	47.3	51.4	51.5	48.2	654.3
1974	50.3	54.8	54.9	50.9	53.7	46.4	47.0	49.2	54.3	58.4	56.4	56.8	698.7
1975	47.3	43.6	50.0	46.3	51.6	45.6	46.0	47.4	55.6	59.8	61.0	53.8	658.5
1976	52.0	55.1	64.6	57.0	53.5	57.8	49.8	57.4	56.1	58.4	64.9	57.3	726.6
1977	54.3	58.3	68.2	61.4	61.1	64.9	54.0	62.6	65.7	62.6	60.3	61.2	835.1
1978	54.7	56.4	63.7	57.8	64.3	62.1	54.1	62.6	68.5	71.2	70.1	67.6	753.1
1979[1]	54.6	60.5	65.1	64.1	62.0	65.2	51.3	58.1	58.2	65.0	60.7	54.3	801.4
1980[1]	59.2	55.4	59.6	59.1	51.2	57.1	46.0	52.2	56.0	50.2	58.1	54.9	675.6
1981[1]	46.5	43.9	43.8	42.4	44.1	46.7	46.4	49.1	52.5	50.9	52.2	48.7	641.1
1982[1]	45.5	48.2	48.0	47.6	46.1	44.8	34.4	44.2	41.9	44.6	41.9	41.5	528.8
1983													

[1] Preliminary.   Source: Bureau of Mines   T.366

205

Lumber and Plywood

Lumber products industries, including sawmills and planing mills, hardwood dimension and flooring, and structural wood members, are found in almost all of the 50 states. Nearly 80 percent of all lumber produced is softwood, and 20 percent is hardwood. The proportion of U.S. softwood lumber products produced in the Western U.S. in 1982 increased by about 5 percent to 65 percent. Southern U.S. production of softwood lumber accounted for 27 percent, compared with 30 percent the previous year. Virtually all U.S. hardwood lumber was produced in the eastern half of the U.S.

Residential construction was still the most important market for lumber products in 1982. However, the depressed level of housing construction as well as limited demand on the part of other wood-consuming industries caused 1982 lumber shipments to drop to an estimated 26.7 billion board feet, 9 percent below the 1981 level. Shipment of softwood lumber, comprising about 75 percent of total lumber shipments, were projected to be 20.8 billion board feet for 1982, and hardwood lumber shipments were expected to be around 5.9 billion board feet. Nearly all of the lumber consuming industries were operating below 1981 levels during the year because of the economic recession. Pallet production was off by 5 percent, and furniture production was 4–5 percent lower in 1982 than in the previous year. The total of U.S. lumber consumption in 1982 was estimated at 34.0 billion board feet, the lowest level recorded in several decades.

Lumber

U.S. imports of lumber have demonstrated a sensitivity to domestic residential construction levels. Because of the failure, in mid-1982, of the expected recovery in housing construction, imports of lumber during the first half of the year declined nearly 20 percent below imports during the comparable period in 1981. During the second half of 1982, lumber imports slowly trended upwards, and 1982 annualized imports were estimated at 8.7 billion board feet, a decline of nearly 7.2 percent below the 1981 level.

Canada supplied close to 96 percent of the U.S. imports of lumber during 1982. Canadian imports were comprised primarily of softwood species such as Douglas fir, pine, and cedar used mainly for construction. Relatively small quantities of hardwood such as birch, beech, and maple are imported from Canada for furniture manufacture. Lumber imports from Canada have steadily risen over the past several years to over 30 percent of the U.S. lumber consumption in 1982. Canada reportedly exported 60 percent of its logs into the U.S. compared with the 20 percent of the total U.S. log production that was shipped to Canada at the same time.

Late in 1982, the Coalition for Fair Canadian Lumber Imports, an organization of 650 U.S. companies and 9 trade associations, petitioned the U.S. government, charging that Canadian exports of lumber and softwood products into the U.S. were unfairly subsidized by the provincial governments. The Coalition, the majority of which was southern U.S. producers less directly in competition with the Canadians than are northwestern softwood producers, asked the U.S. government to impose a 65 percent duty on imported lumber which they said equalled the differences in U.S. and Canadian stumpage costs and other trade subsidies. In the U.S.—where most lumber is privately owned—producers buying lumber from the federal government are obligated to pay for the stumpage a fee which is set through competitive bidding. Canadian producers, all of whom cut timber from government forests, are charged stumpage fees that are arbitrarily allocated based on the prices of finished products. U.S. stumpage fees are generally six times Canadian fees, and the Coalition for Fair Canadian Lumber Imports argued that the lower Canadian assessment amounted to a provincial government subsidy that worked to the detriment of the U.S. lumber industry.

The U.S. Department of Commerce subsequently ruled that the wide differences between U.S. and Canadian lumber prices evidently reflected differences between the quality and availability of timber in the two countries as well as the fact that many U.S. pro-

Salient Statistics of Lumber in the United States

Year	Lumber	Pulp Products	Plywood & Veneer	Other Pdts.[2]	Total[2]	Imports	Exports	Apparent Consumption	Fuelwood Consumption	Apparent Prod. & Consum. All Pdt's.	All Eastern Hardwoods	Douglas Fir	Southern Pine	Western Hemlock	Ponderosa Pine	Maple
					In Million Cubic Feet								$ Per 1,000 Board Ft.			
1970	5,215	3,835	1,020	425	11,105	2,430	1,540	11,995	540	12,530	26.90	41.90	44.10	20.50	32.10	34.40
1971	5,385	3,560	1,175	415	11,035	2,670	1,295	12,410	500	12,910	24.60	49.10	52.20	20.60	37.60	37.80
1972	5,535	3,520	1,300	405	11,440	3,060	1,545	12,960	475	13,435	34.30	71.70	65.60	49.00	65.80	59.40
1973	5,670	3,755	1,320	405	11,925	3,150	1,755	13,320	505	13,825	44.70	138.10	93.40	99.20	92.30	71.40
1974	5,095	4,220	1,150	395	11,540	2,755	1,805	12,490	535	13,025	44.40	202.40	76.20	110.80	100.60	79.50
1975	4,980	3,485	1,165	385	10,575	2,220	1,685	11,105	570	11,675	34.00	169.50	57.00	68.80	71.20	39.60
1976	5,475	3,805	1,355	380	11,815	2,840	1,870	12,785	600	13,390	34.90	176.20	87.00	79.70	103.20	36.60
1977	5,730	3,645	1,425	385	11,960	3,310	1,795	13,475	1,030	14,505	37.90	225.90	100.30	89.30	131.40	42.10
1978	5,825	3,745	1,460	395	12,235	3,755	1,845	14,145	1,570	15,715	41.10	250.30	134.50	113.60	164.70	57.40
1979	5,680	4,110	1,370	405	12,510	3,655	2,135	14,030	2,275	16,305	46.80	394.40	155.20	200.80	239.00	33.90
1980	4,800	4,390	1,195	385	11,665	3,260	2,355	12,575	3,120	15,695	52.40	432.20	155.40	212.70	206.10	37.40
1981[1]											50.90	350.20	172.00	163.40	195.20	41.50

[1] Preliminary, subject to revision. [2] Excludes fuelwood. Includes cooperage logs, poles & piling, fence posts, etc. *Sources: National Lumber Manufacturers Ass'n.: U.S. Dept. of Commerce; Forest Service*

T.367

LUMBER AND PLYWOOD

ducers had contracted for timber as much as five years in advance of the current weak U.S. wood market. Some analysts blamed the plight of the domestic lumber industry in 1982 on U.S. monetary policy, including high interest rates and high dollar exchange rates. Between 1975 and 1981, when the fraction of U.S. lumber consumption accounted for by Canadian lumber rose nearly 12 percent, the U.S.-Canada exchange rate increased about 23 percent in favor of the U.S. dollar.

Total U.S. industry shipments of lumber in 1983 were expected to increase by 14 percent over the 1982 level, after adjustments for inflation. Shipments of softwood and hardwood lumber were forecast at 30.7 billion board feet, an increase of nearly 15 percent above the 1982 level. Improvements in the furniture industry were expected to cause the shipment of hardwood dimension and flooring to increase 4 percent over 1982 levels. Shipments of structural wood members in 1983 were expected to be up by 12 percent. Housing starts in 1983 were predicted by the National Association of Home Builders to increase to 1.55 million units from 1.08 million in 1982, with the FHA mortgage rate expected to decline from around 12 percent late in the first quarter of 1983, to around 10½ percent.

Plywood

New housing construction accounted for approximately 30 percent of the end use market for plywood during 1982, a proportion that was down from the 50 percent levels of the 1970s. The drop in softwood plywood prices accelerated in 1982 to generally 13 percent below prices in 1981. Many western softwood plywood producers were reportedly squeezed between the high-price sales contracts that they entered into with the U.S. government prior to the housing recession, and the continually declining prices for their products that were recorded during 1982. Currently, the industry is trying to develop existing markets for plywood, such as pallets and boxes, wood foundations, industrial uses and do-it-yourself kits, that may be promising alternatives to the housing construction market. Exports of U.S. plywood, especially to Europe, were expected to improve significantly during 1983.

Particleboard

Shipments of particleboard, one of the healthiest industries within the wood products sector of the economy, dropped by 19 percent during 1982. Declines in the residential and the furniture markets accounted for most of the drop. However, based on assumptions of an economic recovery, the particleboard industry was expected to grow faster than the overall wood products industry throughout the 1980s, and 1983 shipments were expected to be up 18 percent over 1982 levels. Late in 1982, the U.S. Consumer Products Safety Commission set a two-year tentative program for the evaluation of the issue of formaldehyde emission from glues used to manufacture particleboard. The issue could ultimately affect particleboard prices.

Futures Markets

Western Plywood futures are traded on the Chicago Board of Trade. Lumber futures are actively traded on the Chicago Mercantile Exchange.

United States Lumber Shipments   In Millions of Board Feet

Year	Jan.	Feb.	Mar.	Apr.	May	June	July	Aug.	Sept.	Oct.	Nov.	Dec.	Total
1973	3,153	3,102	3,474	3,386	3,351	3,264	3,044	3,402	3,096	3,312	3,008	2,623	38,353
1974	2,647	2,850	3,219	3,377	3,310	2,949	2,736	2,888	2,584	2,658	2,265	1,978	33,432
1975	2,047	2,164	2,507	2,843	2,820	2,739	2,820	2,851	3,061	3,097	2,689	2,647	31,769
1976	2,762	2,790	3,107	3,155	2,944	3,150	3,122	3,324	3,167	3,167	2,911	2,951	35,612
1977	2,683	2,873	3,362	3,364	3,314	3,387	3,077	3,358	3,296	3,269	2,859	2,983	37,899
1978	2,699	2,741	3,158	3,133	3,355	3,548	3,156	3,357	3,250	3,262	3,116	2,907	37,712
1979[1]	2,813	2,756	3,279	3,107	3,329	3,087	3,128	3,408	3,106	3,224	2,777	2,589	36,514
1980[1]	2,707	2,791	2,538	2,343	2,512	2,530	2,454	2,716	2,708	2,851	2,494	2,350	31,126
1981[1]	2,424	2,379	2,752	2,755	2,633	2,765	2,395	2,431	2,260	2,382	2,045	1,989	29,491
1982[1]	1,637	1,837	2,148	2,336	2,308	2,513	2,363	2,450	2,260	2,506	2,353	2,162	27,163

[1] Preliminary.   Source: National Lumber Manufacturers' Association

Stocks (Gross) of Lumber in the United States, Beginning of Month   In Millions of Board Feet

Year	Jan.	Feb.	Mar.	Apr.	May	June	July	Aug.	Sept.	Oct.	Nov.	Dec.
1973	4,152	3,954	3,926	3,802	3,896	3,835	3,765	3,758	3,813	3,967	4,108	4,157
1974	4,457	4,499	4,596	4,568	4,648	4,627	4,683	4,904	5,042	5,196	5,229	5,160
1975	5,134	5,137	5,123	5,064	5,000	5,052	5,124	5,101	5,165	5,090	5,140	4,982
1976	4,938	4,894	4,926	4,963	5,016	5,123	4,922	4,763	4,794	4,854	4,991	5,062
1977	5,086	5,171	5,228	5,325	5,197	5,133	4,964	4,854	4,787	4,859	4,876	4,855
1978	4,850	4,963	5,128	5,201	5,190	5,038	4,877	4,705	4,632	4,669	4,740	4,731
1979[1]	4,795	4,811	4,932	4,964	4,975	4,868	5,003	4,893	4,843	4,875	5,063	5,207
1980[1]	5,210	5,301	5,374	5,721	5,769	5,568	5,534	5,570	5,659	5,776	5,832	5,826
1981[1]	5,805	5,883	6,065	6,098	6,123	6,213	6,015	6,103	6,232	6,284	6,285	6,075
1982[1]	5,842	6,016	6,068	6,042	5,983	5,915	5,853	5,867	5,977	6,163	5,986	5,881
1983[1]	5,724											

[1] Preliminary.   Source: National Lumber Manufacturers' Association

LUMBER AND PLYWOOD

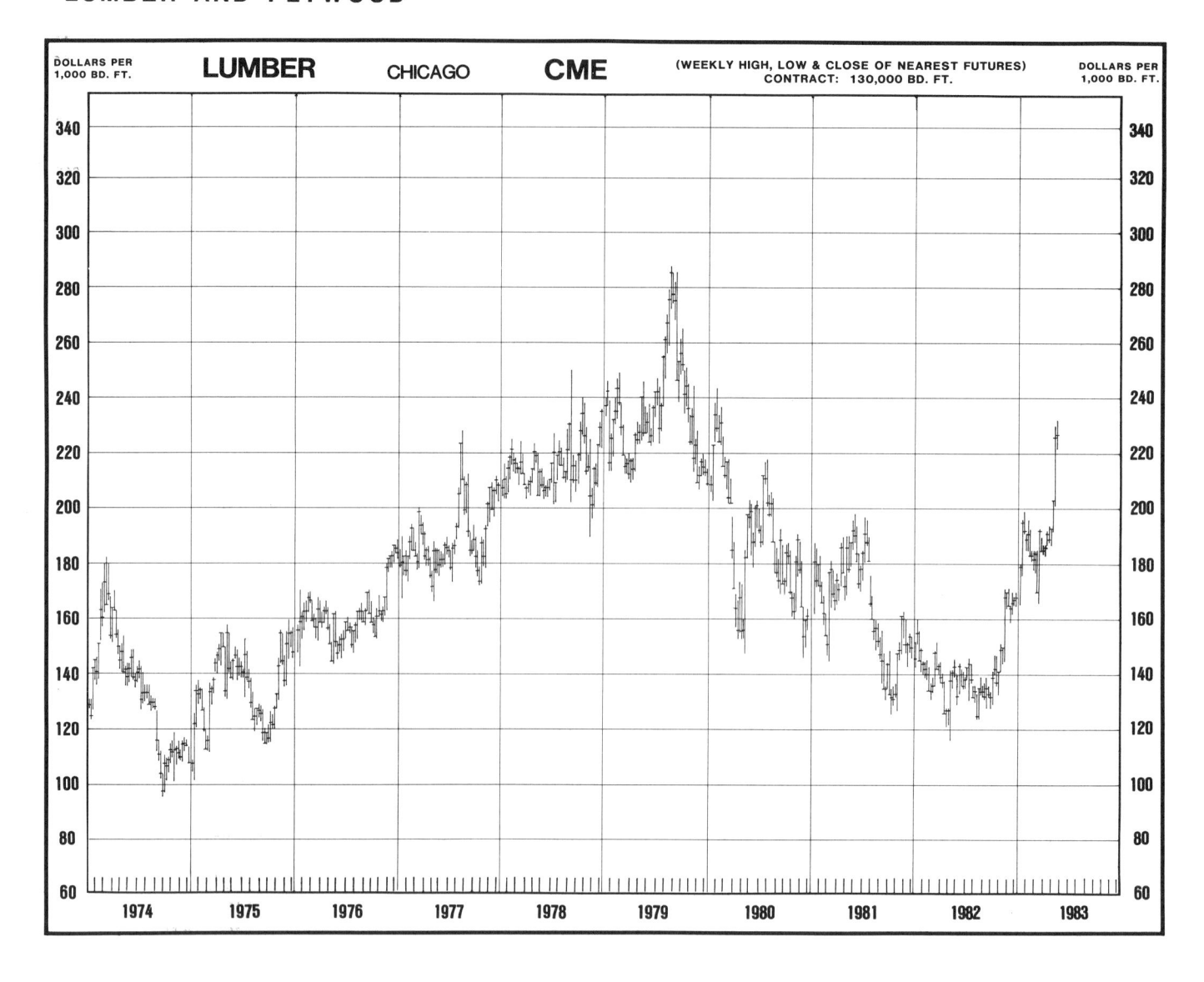

LUMBER — CHICAGO — CME (WEEKLY HIGH, LOW & CLOSE OF NEAREST FUTURES)
CONTRACT: 130,000 BD. FT.
Dollars per 1,000 BD. FT.

Month-End Open Interest of Lumber Futures at Chicago — In Contracts

Year	Jan.	Feb.	Mar.	Apr.	May	June	July	Aug.	Sept.	Oct.	Nov.	Dec.
1978	7,523	8,770	8,202	8,390	9,233	8,362	7,730	8,078	7,551	7,365	6,547	8,122
1979	8,420	9,059	7,851	7,127	8,055	7,380	8,901	11,039	10,426	10,664	10,125	10,260
1980	10,839	10,587	9,948	10,130	11,452	11,736	12,461	11,644	13,734	14,251	12,829	9,338
1981	8,882	9,053	8,029	8,102	7,639	8,161	8,554	7,586	7,690	8,809	8,808	9,067
1982	9,328	8,982	6,990	7,460	6,578	5,648	4,629	5,789	6,088	8,282	10,490	9,915
1983	10,492	10,610	10,793	11,425								

Source: Chicago Mercantile Exchange
T.370

Volume of Trading of Lumber Futures at Chicago — In Contracts

Year	Jan.	Feb.	Mar.	Apr.	May	June	July	Aug.	Sept.	Oct.	Nov.	Dec.	Total
1978	47,910	43,703	46,876	43,759	42,578	36,330	38,252	46,138	49,347	55,495	54,371	55,739	560,498
1979	60,964	57,594	52,316	43,097	46,530	50,265	56,421	62,923	56,421	71,581	63,777	39,980	649,478
1980	59,063	61,288	73,412	86,057	81,960	68,528	76,296	65,740	73,660	76,984	59,076	58,376	838,676
1981	57,173	45,937	54,295	60,517	51,007	58,879	49,427	49,428	45,592	57,021	55,044	51,614	635,934
1982	51,268	45,193	44,717	44,116	40,828	47,512	34,624	35,432	29,835	47,761	51,046	44,387	516,626
1983	54,976	56,706	51,520	48,327									

Source: Chicago Mercantile Exchange
T.371

LUMBER AND PLYWOOD

Residential Construction Contracts Awarded (All Types) in U.S.   In Millions of Dollars

Year	Jan.	Feb.	Mar.	Apr.	May	June	July	Aug.	Sept.	Oct.	Nov.	Dec.	Total
1971	1,631	1,818	2,729	3,168	3,310	3,485	3,357	3,255	3,196	3,171	3,001	2,997	34,714
1972	2,667	2,664	3,617	3,971	4,428	4,375	3,864	4,671	4,135	4,298	3,663	3,120	44,975
1973	3,195	3,277	4,643	4,512	4,754	4,612	4,224	4,233	3,638	3,673	3,299	2,341	45,696
1974	2,231	2,678	3,374	3,924	3,862	3,546	3,350	3,060	2,503	2,457	1,931	1,715	34,404
1975	1,540	1,532	2,272	2,987	3,072	3,116	3,081	2,833	2,951	3,167	2,478	2,259	31,261
1976	2,168	2,557	3,636	4,017	3,932	4,175	4,190	4,201	3,824	4,119	3,761	3,264	44,169
1977	2,967	3,519	5,328	5,503	5,803	6,043	5,703	6,198	5,641	5,534	5,359	4,340	62,017
1978	3,925	3,863	6,333	6,850	7,801	7,917	6,823	7,120	6,496	7,080	5,973	4,715	74,949
1979[1]	4,468	4,588	6,870	5,969	8,076	7,277	7,008	7,069	6,248	6,864	4,704	4,304	74,557
1980[1]	4,055	4,337	4,584	4,373	4,495	5,029	6,105	5,897	6,069	6,785	5,847	5,570	63,668
1981[1]	4,207	4,206	5,929	6,569	5,887	5,904	5,853	4,894	4,844	4,872	3,648	3,739	60,164
1982[1]	2,991	3,045	4,600	4,656	4,984	5,602	5,144	5,414	5,525	5,629	5,628	5,184	58,076
1983[1]	4,970	4,775											
1984													

[1] Preliminary.   Source: F. W. Dodge Co.   T.372

United States Imports of Sawmill Products   In Millions of Board Feet

Year	Jan.	Feb.	Mar.	Apr.	May	June	July	Aug.	Sept.	Oct.	Nov.	Dec.	Total
1970	515	423	488	535	572	562	478	540	553	533	514	422	6,095
1971	505	473	683	563	650	761	767	624	797	516	582	679	7,599
1972	757	703	768	745	889	761	888	690	820	815	886	689	9,428
1973	935	760	883	837	931	899	823	623	453	764	780	640	9,540
1974	634	547	700	721	815	765	653	541	569	530	414	361	7,249
1975	337	377	536	571	589	671	677	431	422	388	415	552	5,968
1976	477	527	627	701	669	573	890	680	781	715	759	779	8,178
1977	691	721	906	890	996	999	934	920	938	858	956	911	10,698
1978	865	840	939	915	1,173	1,117	1,194	1,119	1,014	1,091	979	954	12,199
1979	925	761	998	925	1,237	1,011	1,010	1,043	999	924	909	771	11,513
1980	727	923	896	655	730	830	876	804	863	867	892	779	9,859
1981	756	848	966	980	992	934	842	465	660	755	728	591	9,518
1982	530	585	601	792	848	888	874	888	962	758	916	781	9,421
1983	879												

Source: Department of Commerce   T.373

Lumber Production[1] in the United States   In Millions of Board Feet

Year	Jan.	Feb.	Mar.	Apr.	May	June	July	Aug.	Sept.	Oct.	Nov.	Dec.	Total
1970	2,902	2,859	3,164	3,203	3,080	2,967	3,004	3,045	3,104	3,201	2,733	2,639	34,548
1971	2,794	2,983	3,339	3,451	3,168	3,384	3,194	3,220	3,242	3,199	3,028	2,924	36,693
1972	2,832	3,076	3,383	3,272	3,420	3,301	3,102	3,417	3,303	3,528	3,193	2,664	38,044
1973	3,012	3,074	3,456	3,272	3,290	3,207	3,038	3,456	3,250	3,453	3,057	2,710	38,297
1974	2,741	2,945	3,191	3,457	3,302	3,006	2,895	3,024	2,736	2,691	2,194	1,930	34,097
1975	2,072	2,148	2,480	2,779	2,849	2,814	2,797	2,914	2,986	3,147	2,530	2,500	31,583
1976	2,821	2,804	3,144	3,209	2,960	2,949	2,963	3,265	3,226	3,305	2,972	2,921	35,760
1977	2,822	2,930	3,388	3,260	3,253	3,160	2,975	3,290	3,368	3,268	2,839	2,944	37,667
1978	2,843	2,904	3,222	3,127	3,203	3,333	2,988	3,263	3,285	3,333	3,102	2,931	37,657
1979[2]	2,877	2,877	3,306	3,119	3,219	3,143	3,018	3,355	3,131	3,412	2,914	2,631	37,061
1980[2]	2,798	2,855	2,879	2,257	2,307	2,486	2,479	2,783	2,818	2,903	2,480	2,329	31,632
1981[2]	2,523	2,542	2,818	2,780	2,651	2,588	2,483	2,554	2,307	2,379	1,831	1,765	29,592
1982[2]	1,810	1,891	2,148	2,281	2,251	2,338	2,376	2,560	2,445	2,333	2,247	2,004	26,960
1983													

[1] Adjusted with Census reports on lumber production.   [2] Preliminary.   Source: National Lumber Manufacturers' Association   T.374

LUMBER AND PLYWOOD

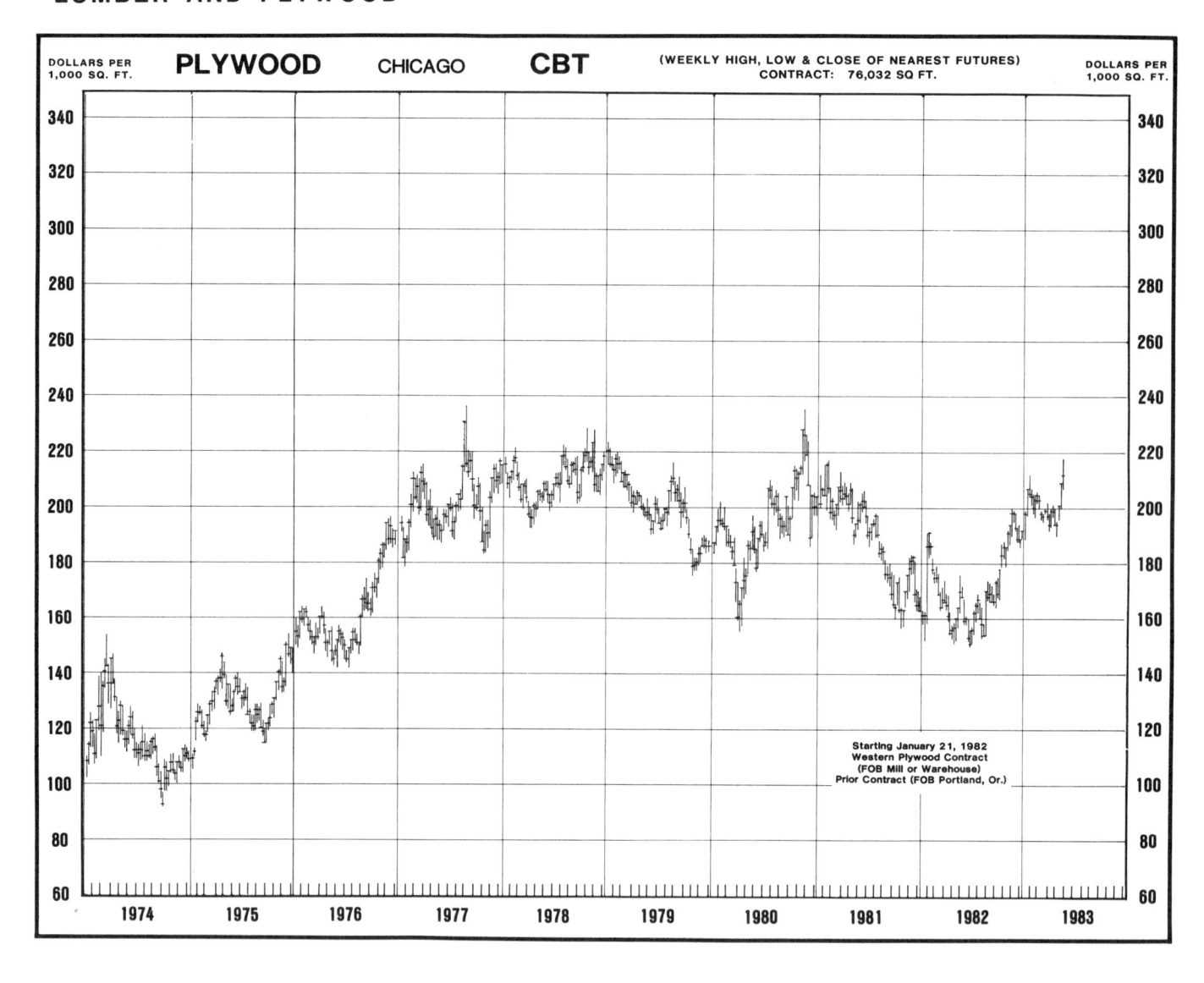

PLYWOOD CHICAGO CBT (WEEKLY HIGH, LOW & CLOSE OF NEAREST FUTURES) — CONTRACT: 76,032 SQ FT. — DOLLARS PER 1,000 SQ. FT.

Starting January 21, 1982 Western Plywood Contract (FOB Mill or Warehouse). Prior Contract (FOB Portland, Or.)

Month-End Open Interest of Plywood Futures at Chicago   In Contracts

Year	Jan.	Feb.	Mar.	Apr.	May	June	July	Aug.	Sept.	Oct.	Nov.	Dec.
1978	7,272	7,996	6,638	5,740	6,733	6,507	6,069	6,634	4,882	5,228	4,585	4,484
1979	4,364	4,430	3,284	3,621	3,932	3,637	3,584	4,181	3,711	4,048	4,422	3,742
1980	3,316	3,196	3,260	5,416	5,017	5,097	3,974	3,685	3,987	4,210	4,133	3,468
1981	3,491	4,411	4,032	4,317	4,251	4,447	4,210	3,455	3,292	3,277	3,891	4,379
1982	4,465	3,794	3,788	2,839	2,628	2,268	1,434	1,448	1,350	1,671	1,776	2,141
1983	1,921	2,089	2,309	2,481								

Source: Chicago Board of Trade   T.375

Volume of Trading of Plywood Futures at Chicago   In Contracts

Year	Jan.	Feb.	Mar.	Apr.	May	June	July	Aug.	Sept.	Oct.	Nov.	Dec.	Total
1978	29,066	30,771	25,071	24,144	21,797	19,237	18,913	18,056	16,346	24,834	17,702	15,046	261,483
1979	18,102	16,761	13,070	9,364	10,836	12,574	9,389	11,543	11,150	14,958	10,053	9,220	146,570
1980	10,605	11,908	12,452	19,084	15,266	13,393	16,903	13,384	13,185	14,191	12,859	16,310	169,550
1981	13,282	14,439	17,667	20,894	15,858	20,131	11,441	11,439	8,651	12,965	9,433	14,612	144,318
1982	9,375	15,717	11,819	13,959	6,842	10,145	5,281	6,773	4,380	5,301	4,212	6,197	99,460
1983	6,918	5,767	5,027	5,688									

Source: Chicago Board of Trade   T.376

LUMBER AND PLYWOOD

High, Low & Closing Prices of May Lumber Futures at Chicago   In Dollars per 1,000 Board Feet

Year of Delivery		Mar.	Apr.	May	June	July	Aug.	Sept.	Oct.	Nov.	Dec.	Jan.	Feb.	Mar.	Apr.	May	Life of Delivery Range
1978	High	—	—	—	211.9	212.4	202.0	201.9	206.9	208.0	216.5	218.9	223.4	219.0	214.0	222.5	223.4
	Low	—	—	—	196.5	193.8	192.0	192.8	184.5	187.0	203.9	203.0	208.5	205.2	203.2	213.1	184.5
	Close	—	—	—	210.8	198.6	199.5	198.5	190.8	207.1	214.5	209.9	212.3	207.8	213.9	214.7	—
1979	High	—	—	—	189.0	193.0	195.5	206.5	211.0	202.5	210.9	219.8	234.5	228.3	231.2	246.0	246.0
	Low	—	—	—	181.6	183.5	187.0	192.5	200.5	185.1	187.2	201.7	218.5	209.8	209.4	223.1	181.6
	Close	—	—	—	183.3	192.0	192.7	202.0	201.3	194.6	209.9	217.6	223.4	211.8	225.2	245.2	—
1980	High	—	—	—	215.0	217.0	227.0	239.5	241.0	227.5	230.2	244.4	242.2	219.3	183.0	160.0	244.4
	Low	—	—	—	208.5	211.0	214.0	222.0	197.7	201.2	216.5	215.3	215.0	181.5	153.1	146.5	146.5
	Close	—	—	—	212.7	214.6	222.7	233.5	206.3	222.8	218.4	234.1	216.3	185.5	161.5	152.2	—
1981	High	221.0	210.2	222.0	225.5	233.5	222.0	215.5	214.0	220.0	210.7	205.2	198.3	181.4	190.4	181.0	233.5
	Low	176.0	164.0	202.0	210.6	218.0	191.9	195.3	194.2	205.7	175.5	185.3	169.5	164.3	163.2	167.1	163.2
	Close	178.1	204.5	220.8	218.5	219.1	196.9	198.5	207.4	208.5	194.5	195.8	169.8	169.6	178.4	175.5	—
1982	High	—	—	—	220.3	214.3	201.5	186.0	183.0	182.8	180.0	166.5	153.1	151.9	145.2	127.5	220.3
	Low	—	—	—	204.6	199.0	183.3	160.0	157.1	162.4	163.4	147.6	142.7	137.5	120.6	115.5	115.5
	Close	—	—	—	211.0	199.3	184.0	163.2	164.8	179.2	169.1	154.0	142.9	142.4	126.8	122.6	—
1983	High	192.7	186.5	178.4	171.0	168.5	170.9	169.3	179.6	191.7	195.3	209.5	206.6	194.6	193.6		
	Low	180.0	172.0	170.0	151.5	154.8	155.2	157.6	157.9	178.6	181.1	189.8	190.7	183.8	182.7		
	Close	185.0	174.0	175.5	157.5	158.6	166.0	159.7	178.7	185.9	191.0	204.9	190.7	184.6	193.2		
1984	High	237.1	240.1														
	Low	228.8	228.6														
	Close	231.8	239.5														

Source: Chicago Mercantile Exchange   T.377

High, Low & Closing Prices of May Plywood Futures at Chicago   In Dollars per 1,000 Square Feet

Year of Delivery		Mar.	Apr.	May	June	July	Aug.	Sept.	Oct.	Nov.	Dec.	Jan.	Feb.	Mar.	Apr.	May	Life of Delivery Range
1978	High	217.5	215.5	202.9	212.5	212.5	212.8	210.5	214.8	214.0	220.0	221.9	222.5	212.0	201.8	206.1	222.5
	Low	209.5	199.0	194.0	196.0	194.0	190.0	197.5	190.9	192.6	208.1	206.0	208.1	195.5	191.5	199.2	190.0
	Close	213.5	200.0	196.1	209.5	202.5	207.8	206.0	192.4	213.3	219.5	212.0	210.5	196.8	199.0	203.3	—
1979	High	208.0	203.8	206.0	199.0	199.6	203.8	211.0	213.3	208.5	211.8	217.3	221.0	215.5	205.5	203.4	221.0
	Low	200.0	196.0	195.0	192.5	192.5	196.2	196.8	205.0	196.0	198.6	204.6	208.4	199.5	198.1	195.0	192.5
	Close	200.0	202.3	196.2	196.3	198.6	200.0	205.0	207.0	201.5	209.5	216.1	210.3	201.2	202.3	195.7	—
1980	High	205.5	208.9	206.4	204.0	202.0	201.0	201.7	203.5	192.0	197.5	206.0	203.9	194.9	182.0	193.5	208.9
	Low	203.2	203.0	201.0	198.0	195.0	195.5	194.0	181.1	183.5	189.0	188.5	188.5	165.5	155.2	170.5	155.2
	Close	203.8	206.0	204.2	201.0	198.5	197.3	199.0	184.5	190.1	193.5	200.7	191.6	172.4	171.5	192.5	—
1981	High	207.0	209.5	214.0	314.0	221.0	216.0	215.0	222.5	232.3	226.5	221.0	221.8	212.5	209.3	196.8	232.3
	Low	181.5	178.5	194.5	200.4	201.0	196.2	197.0	201.5	218.5	194.0	205.5	199.3	198.2	194.2	186.5	178.5
	Close	185.5	195.2	205.5	203.0	210.5	201.5	203.8	219.5	223.5	208.0	220.3	203.4	205.0	195.2	192.0	—
1982	High	—	240.5	239.0	240.0	228.0	224.0	220.0	212.6	214.3	214.0	190.0	180.0	183.6	169.0	164.5	240.5
	Low	—	200.0	224.0	228.0	216.0	205.0	200.0	194.0	199.2	196.8	180.0	174.0	162.5	151.0	152.1	151.0
	Close	—	231.0	239.0	232.0	218.0	210.1	200.5	200.0	213.3	199.6	180.0	175.0	165.7	156.5	164.5	—
1983	High	—	—	194.2	185.0	180.0	187.4	185.0	199.5	207.2	204.3	216.4	210.4	203.5	201.0		
	Low	—	—	191.0	168.0	170.0	167.0	177.5	178.2	196.0	194.7	197.1	201.3	192.4	189.8		
	Close	—	—	191.0	170.0	172.8	181.1	179.2	197.4	203.0	197.7	208.7	201.4	193.5	194.0		
1984	High	—	—														
	Low	—	—														
	Close	—	—														

Source: Chicago Board of Trade   T.378

LUMBER AND PLYWOOD

Average Index Price of Softwood Plywood—Western $ per Ths. Board Feet 1967 = 100

Year	Jan.	Feb.	Mar.	Apr.	May	June	July	Aug.	Sept.	Oct.	Nov.	Dec.	Average
1974	414.54	426.95	433.16	445.57	451.78	451.78	451.78	484.45	463.87	448.35	435.94	431.28	444.95
1975[1]	513.09	513.09	513.09	513.09	506.11	506.11	506.17	501.27	501.27	501.27	497.60	494.66	505.56
1976	494.90	494.90	500.54	502.99	502.99	502.99	502.99	507.89	510.34	510.34	510.34	517.69	504.91
1977	530.06	536.18	559.46	584.20	589.10	598.54	609.56	609.56	643.13	650.48	653.78	677.06	603.43
1978	710.01	741.86	740.64	779.84	795.76	812.18	812.42	812.42	852.72	852.72	869.32	874.47	804.53
1979[2]	354.3	351.7	351.5	345.6	329.8	304.1	319.1	324.3	327.6	327.4	309.4	300.4	328.8
1980	293.8	308.0	302.3	256.9	275.4	301.7	324.5	346.2	324.0	324.2	330.3	343.3	310.9
1981	326.4	330.0	323.3	332.2	319.7	329.4	322.1	311.0	301.9	283.7	286.7	296.7	313.6
1982	291.3	288.4	288.7	283.5	279.2	287.6	282.3	278.8	274.9	272.52	276.5	284.6	282.4
1983	289.3	299.7											

[1] Data prior to 1975 are for F. G., 1" × 4", R. L., dried, mixed carlot, f.o.b. mill (rail shipment) [Douglas Fir Drop Siding (C & Better)].   [2] Prior to 1979 prices are for Lumber Redwood, Boards, Clear, F.G., Dry in $ per Ths. Board Feet.   *Source: Bureau of Labor Statistics* (0831-01)   T.379

Average Index Price of Softwood Yellow Southern Pine (Dressed) Flooring[1] (C & Better)   1967 = 100[2]

Year	Jan.	Feb.	Mar.	Apr.	May	June	July	Aug.	Sept.	Oct.	Nov.	Dec.	Average
1974	321.77	321.77	329.93	346.27	346.27	347.90	352.80	352.80	352.80	352.80	341.37	341.37	342.90
1975	341.37	341.37	344.63	344.63	346.27	344.63	336.47	336.47	336.47	329.93	331.57	333.20	338.92
1976	339.73	341.37	346.27	346.27	346.27	346.27	348.55	351.17	354.43	355.09	356.07	356.07	348.96
1977	356.07	356.07	359.33	362.60	364.23	367.50	375.67	380.57	387.10	388.73	392.00	395.27	373.76
1978	400.17	403.23	406.87	405.07	409.97	409.97	413.23	419.11	421.40	424.01	424.67	426.30	413.67
1979[2]	307.0	306.4	315.7	319.0	315.8	315.2	320.7	333.7	343.6	344.4	341.1	328.2	324.2
1980	322.0	322.2	317.2	281.2	280.1	287.3	296.4	304.1	295.1	282.3	286.9	293.7	322.2
1981	291.9	292.2	294.7	308.4	313.9	309.5	297.0	291.6	279.4	273.6	267.0	279.7	291.6
1982	278.0	273.3	273.9	285.3	283.1	298.4	305.1	288.6	287.5	279.3	284.1	293.4	285.8
1983	302.6	314.8											

[1] Flooring. C and better, F. G., 1" × 4" × S/L.   [2] Prices prior to 1979 are in $ per Ths. Board Feet.   *Source: Bureau of Labor Statistics* (0811-02)   T.381

Average Index Price of Ponderosa Pine[1] Softwood Lumber—No. 2   Dec. 1980 = 100[2]

Year	Jan.	Feb.	Mar.	Apr.	May	June	July	Aug.	Sept.	Oct.	Nov.	Dec.	Average
1974	193.90	190.23	204.37	234.99	231.32	200.60	174.35	138.40	121.26	100.46	99.66	120.06	151.38
1975	126.78	132.83	150.35	154.31	173.62	170.71	145.95	141.17	131.78	128.87	127.30	—	131.97
1976	154.01	177.50	198.52	209.92	189.73	165.91	161.57	168.63	182.50	198.68	198.57	206.15	184.31
1977	227.16	232.18	245.58	251.21	239.98	216.44	219.96	232.57	236.48	235.28	215.40	226.17	231.53
1978	247.58	263.85	264.90	267.57	240.07	251.25	232.33	236.92	254.23	267.17	N.A.	317.01	237.07
1979	304.49	332.11	366.87	371.17	342.59	338.16	306.16	301.95	309.48	316.41	277.35	240.42	317.26
1980	252.62	291.36	314.97	242.34	215.48	252.06	310.05	327.35	304.06	293.25	306.22	340.83	287.55
1981[2]	102.9	102.3	103.7	107.8	111.2	110.4	106.9	103.6	100.0	93.0	90.6	93.4	102.2
1982	N.A.	95.0	97.6	99.0	97.7	97.3	98.3	95.6	91.7	87.9	N.A.	N.A.	95.7
1983	N.A.	N.A.											

[1] No. 3 1" × 12", B.L. (6' and over).   [2] Prices prior to 1981 are for Ponderosa Pine in $ per Ths. Board Feet.   *Source: Bureau of Labor Statistics* (0811-0312.99)   T.380

Average Index Price of Douglas Fir Softwood Lumber—Dimension, Construction, Dried, 2" × 4", R.L.[1]   1967 = 100[2]

Year	Jan.	Feb.	Mar.	Apr.	May	June	July	Aug.	Sept.	Oct.	Nov.	Dec.	Average
1974	159.25	163.06	181.51	186.18	179.03	167.63	162.47	152.62	146.22	135.85	139.09	133.21	158.84
1975	138.41	146.90	147.29	156.60	169.67	161.54	165.47	169.77	166.79	160.09	157.56	166.40	158.88
1976	175.43	178.29	184.90	180.05	176.06	171.45	187.49	195.59	215.08	207.79	204.02	218.77	191.24
1977	228.38	225.50	232.09	226.05	225.42	213.79	230.93	242.51	256.92	237.27	218.03	227.70	230.38
1978	238.08	241.81	246.28	238.48	238.48	245.28	245.00	272.06	274.74	266.66	271.51	262.40	253.39
1979[2]	357.2	360.1	371.0	381.1	381.8	378.3	387.4	408.4	424.0	410.4	378.7	368.8	383.9
1980	363.3	367.1	358.8	327.1	329.6	353.2	358.7	360.0	357.1	354.5	352.9	353.4	353.0
1981	347.2	330.4	321.8	332.7	328.5	333.1	320.1	318.3	296.8	277.6	268.0	267.0	311.8
1982	269.1	262.2	258.5	265.6	262.1	271.8	277.8	268.9	269.6	261.8	259.9	272.5	266.6
1983	310.0	370.0											

[1] Dried, S4S, mixed carlots, f.o.b. mill, rail shipment.   [2] Prices prior to 1979 are in $ per Ths. Board Feet.   *Source: Bureau of Labor Statistics* (0811-01)   T.382

Magnesium

Total domestic production of primary magnesium metal in 1982 was below that of 1981 according to preliminary data of the U.S. Bureau of Mines. In the third quarter of 1982, the primary magnesium metal industry was operating at about one-half of its rated production capacity as two of the small number of producing companies cut back metal production because of declining demand. Domestic magnesium metal production is derived from natural brine solutions and the mineral dolomite.

Total domestic shipments of magnesium metal in the fourth quarter of 1982 were the highest for the year. However, estimated apparent consumption for the year was nearly 7 percent lower than in 1981. The manufacture of aluminum-base alloys accounted for an estimated 55 percent of total magnesium metal consumption in 1982; wrought products and magnesium castings—17 percent; reducing agent—10 percent; cathodic protection—7 percent; manufacture of nodular cast iron—4 percent; and others—7 percent.

About 29 percent of estimated total reported metal consumption in 1982 was from old scrap.

The U.S. continued as a sizable net exporter of magnesium in 1982. Exports were about 13 percent higher than in 1981, with most of the tonnage increase accounted for by larger exports of magnesium metal and alloys in crude form and scrap. Imports of magnesium in 1982 dropped 31 percent from the previous year's total, mostly because of a sharp reduction in metallic and scrap imports.

There was no National Defense Stockpile goal or inventory for magnesium metal. Resources from which magnesium metal may be recovered are virtually unlimited and are globally widespread. In addition, aluminum and zinc may be substituted for magnesium castings and wrought products.

The quoted prices of magnesium metal and die-casting alloys remained unchanged throughout 1982 at $1.34 and $1.21 per pound, respectively.

World Production of Magnesium (Primary)   In Short Tons

Year	Canada	France	India[3]	Italy	Japan	China	Norway	Yugoslavia	USSR	Un. Kingdom[3]	United States	World Total[1]
1970	10,353	5,083		8,356	11,395	1,100	38,959		55,000	3,038	112,007	242,253
1971	7,234	7,954		8,496	10,685	1,100	39,799		57,000	3,100	123,485	255,753
1972	5,924	7,550		8,335	12,004	1,100	40,149		60,000		120,823	255,960
1973	6,840	9,511		9,850	12,349	1,100	41,360		63,000		122,431	266,441
1974	6,535	7,199		8,191	9,836	1,100	43,866		66,000		N.A.	142,727
1975	4,217	8,303		6,993	9,412	1,100	42,259		66,000		N.A.	138,284
1976	6,715	8,857	33	9,740	12,335	5,500	42,778	—	69,000	3,000	119,957	274,882
1977	8,414	9,570	—	9,663	10,379	5,500	42,070	—	72,000	3,000	125,958	283,554
1978	9,159	9,370	—	10,668	12,304	6,600	43,166	0	77,000	3,000	149,463	317,730
1979	9,937	9,968	—	9,653	12,531	6,600	48,697	0	79,000	3,000	162,464	338,850
1980[2]	10,199	10,282	—	8,693	10,199	7,700	48,943	1,100	83,000	3,000	169,477	349,593
1981[1]	9,673	9,600	—	8,500	6,247	7,700	52,910	4,600	86,000		142,887	328,117
1982[1]	8,000	9,000		8,000	6,000	7,000	50,000	4,000	86,000		125,000	303,000
1983												

[1] Estimate.   [2] Preliminary.   [3] Secondary only.   *Source: Bureau of Mines*

T.383

Salient Statistics of Magnesium in the United States   In Short Tons

Year	Primary (Ingot)	Production — Secondary New Scrap	Production — Secondary Old Scrap	Total	Exports[2]	Imports for Consumption	Stocks Dec. 31[3]	$ Price per Pound[4]	Domestic Consumption of Primary Magnesium — Castings Structural Products	Wrought	Total	Other Uses[5]	Total
1970	112,006	9,262	2,780	12,042	35,732	3,295	12,696	.35¼	10,997	12,250	23,247	70,248	93,495
1971	123,485	11,560	3,143	14,703	24,311	3,671	13,021	.36¼	8,376	10,717	19,093	73,073	92,166
1972	120,823	12,639	2,989	15,628	17,556	4,479	23,011	.37¼	10,762	12,947	23,709	79,982	103,691
1973	122,431	13,535	4,101	17,636	39,585	3,325	18,894	.37¼	12,137	12,965	25,102	90,672	115,774
1974	N.A.	9,155	5,719	14,874	46,398	5,305	23,000	41¼-.75	14,176	13,348	27,524	102,524	130,048
1975	120,203	18,090	9,783	27,873	32,591	7,903	19,664	.82	9,488	9,666	19,154	75,013	94,167
1976	119,957	19,024	11,529	30,553	13,444	14,907	17,295	.87-.92	7,051	10,241	17,292	87,161	104,453
1977	125,958	20,170	12,524	32,694	28,061	5,964	11,838	.96-.99	7,201	12,632	19,833	83,743	103,576
1978	149,463	22,135	14,093	36,228	41,807	6,668	12,583	.99-1.01	7,651	11,075	18,726	90,232	108,958
1979	162,464	23,340	13,882	37,222	54,280	4,754	13,901	1.01-1.09	7,460	11,562	19,022	89,822	108,844
1980	169,477	22,907	17,554	40,461	56,761	3,757	14,393	1.07-1.25	5,847	11,620	17,467	78,321	95,788
1981[6]	142,887	22,073	24,183	46,256	34,855	6,897	12,123	1.25-1.34	4,951	10,376	15,327	76,134	91,461
1982[1]	125,000			50,000	44,000	8,000		1.34					85,000
1983													

[1] Estimate.   [2] Metal & alloys in crude form, & scrap.   [3] Producers' & consumers' stocks of primary magnesium. Gov't. agencies continue to hold quantities of primary magnesium.   [4] Magnesium ingots (99.8%) f.o.b. Velasco, Texas.   [5] Distributive or sacrificial purposes.   [6] Preliminary.   *Source: Bureau of Mines*

T.384

Manganese

No manganese ore containing 35 percent or more manganese is produced in the U.S., and domestic needs are met almost entirely by imports. A large share of the ore is converted to ferromanganese for use in steel production, with the remainder used in the production of pig iron and dry cell batteries and for various chemical purposes. A worldwide oversupply of manganese persisted in 1982, primarily because of a large decline in world steel production.

U.S. imports of manganese ore in 1982 were 63 percent smaller than in 1981 and imports of ferromanganese were 30 percent smaller than a year earlier, according to preliminary U.S Bureau of Mines data. Major sources of ore imports were: the Republic of South Africa, Gabon and Australia. Major sources of U.S. imports of ferromanganese (mostly high-carbon) in 1982 were: the Republic of South Africa, France, Brazil, Portugal and Canada, in order of importance.

U.S. production of ferromanganese in 1982 was estimated to be about 40 percent lower than in 1981 and production of silicomanganese was estimated to be as much as 63 percent below the 1981 level.

High-carbon ferromanganese consumption in the U.S. for reported end uses in 1982 was 48 percent smaller than in 1981 and use of medium and low-carbon ferromanganese was off 45 percent from the year earlier level. Silicomanganese consumption in 1982 was off 38 percent from 1981, and manganese metal use was off 30 percent.

U.S. industry stocks of manganese ore at the end of 1982 were 24 percent below the year earlier level. Medium- and low-carbon ferromanganse and silicomanganese stocks declined 13 percent and 36 percent, respectively, and metal stocks were off 9 percent from the December 31, 1981 level. However, high-carbon ferromanganese stocks, which account for the bulk of all industry stocks, were 30 percent above the December 31, 1981 level.

As of November 30, 1982, the U.S. government stockpile consisted primarily of metallurgical ore, for which the goal was 2,700 tons and the inventory 2,409 tons—unchanged from a year earlier. In addition, the stockpile contained uncommitted inventory of 34,000 tons of natural battery ore and 961,000 tons of metallurgical ore, both nonstockpile grade. It was announced in December 1982 that the General Services Administration (GSA) would begin a program of upgrading stockpile ore into high-carbon ferromanganese (577,000 tons) and high-carbon ferrochromium (519,000 tons) over a 10-year period.

World Production of Manganese Ore In Thousands of Short Tons

Year	Hungary	Zaire (Congo)	Brazil	Chile	China	Gabon	Morocco	Ghana[3]	India	Japan	Australia	South Africa	USSR	Mexico	World Total
% Mn	30-33	30-57	38-50	33-40	20+	50-53	50-53	30-50	10-54	24-28	37-53	30-48+	35	35+	
1972		407.3	2,268	17.7	1,100	2,135	105.9	549.3	1,810	287.4	1,284	3,606	8,619	325.9	22,948
1973		368.1	1,780	15.9	1,100	2,115	161.1	350.8	1,641	208.0	1,678	4,603	9,089	401.3	23,970
1974		317.2	1,972	31.6	1,100	2,275	192.7	275.9	1,656	183.6	1,678	5,231	8,989	444.4	24,751
1975		340.1	2,377	22.1	1,100	2,475	144.3	450.6	1,738	174.1	1,714	6,359	9,324	472.3	27,175
1976	138.0	200.8	1,870	26.1	1,100	2,444	129.3	343.8	2,022	156.2	2,375	6,010	9,520	499.6	27,113
1977	132.0	42.2	1,671	19.8	1,250	2,040	125.2	321.4	2,056	139.1	1,531	5,564	9,470	536.4	25,210
1978	126.0	—	2,113	25.6	1,400	1,885	139.1	347.9	1,785	114.8	1,377	4,759	9,984	576.7	24,897
1979	91.0	—	2,490	27.5	1,650	2,535	149.6	300.0	1,935	96.9	1,872	5,713	11,292	543.1	28,908
1980[1]	97.0	18.3	2,601	30.5	1,750	2,366	144.8	278.3	1,814	87.7	2,162	6,278	10,748	492.9	29,091
1981[2]	91.0	11.0	2,090	29.8	1,760	1,640	120.0	248.0	1,650	96.1	1,554	5,555	10,360	637.5	25,985
1982[2]			1,700		1,700	1,400			1,400		1,200	4,400	10,400		23,000

[1] Preliminary. [2] Estimated. [3] Dry weight. Source: Bureau of Mines   T.385

Salient Statistics of Manganese in the United States   In Thousands of Short Tons (Gross Weight)

Year	Net Import Reliance as a % of Apparent Consumption	Manganese Ore (35% or More Mn) Alloys and Metal	Pig Iron Steel	Dry Cells, Misc.	General Imports	Consumption	Stocks, Dec. 31[2]	Ferromanganese Domes. Production	Imports for Consumption	Exports	Consumption	Manganiferous Ore[3] Production	Value Mil. $[4]	Spiegelesien Stocks Dec. 31[2]	Consumption
1972					1,620	2,331	1,795	800.7	348.5	6.8	968	147.2	1.0	13.2	19.6
1973					1,510	2,140	1,543	683.1	390.6	8.6	1,117	203.1	1.5	3.7	21.6
1974					1,225	1,880	1,841	544.4	421.2	7.0	1,115	272.9	2.3	3.1	18.1
1975	98	1,440.2	176.2	202.6	1,574	1,819	2,064	575.8	397.2	32.3	882	159.2	1.4	5.2	14.2
1976	98	1,263.5	143.8	193.6	1,317	1,601	2,256	482.7	537.4	6.8	896.8	256.6	2.3	8.1	8.4
1977	98	926.6	200.8	231.4	931	1,359	1,626	334.1	534.4	6.1	886.3	215.9	2.2	.1	6.8
1978	97	832.2	219.7	229.6	548	1,281	1,174	272.5	680.4	9.4	985.6	312.1	3.1	.1	4.0
1979	98	913.5	230.7	228.0	500	1,372	1,098	317.1	821.2	25.3	976.5	240.7	2.9	.1	3
1980	98	727.5	131.5	211.7	698	1,071	1,030	189.5	605.7	11.7	789.1	173.9	2.4	—	.3
1981[1]	98	744.8	147.8	184.0	639	1,077	1,036	192.7	671.2	14.9	820.9	175.8	2.9	—	.1
1982[5]	99				238	519	624	120.2	478.3	10.3	425.9				

[1] Preliminary. [2] Including bonded warehouses; excludes Gov't stocks; also excludes small tonnages of dealers' stocks. [3] 5 to 35% Mn. [4] Combined value for total Manganese ore & Manganiferous ores. [5] Estimate. Source: Bureau of Mines   T.386

MANGANESE

Manganese Ore (35% or More Mn) Imported[2] into the U.S.   In Thousands of Short Tons (Mn Content)

Year	Angola	Zaire	Brazil	Congo (Brazz.)	Canada	Ghana	India	Mexico	Morocco	Gabon	Australia	Turkey	South Africa	Total	Value Mill. $
1973	—	35.7	299.4	—	—	18.6	—	41.2	13.9	196.1	61.5	—	55.9	723	37.4
1974	—	25.3	222.0	—	—	4.5	—	16.4	27.5	150.1	114.0	—	32.9	593	45.1
1975	—	11.4	307.4	—	—	—	—	23.2	—	244.8	86.5	—	92.2	766	77.1
1976	—	2.9	161.1	13.3	—	—	—	18.5	18.7	256.4	117.4	—	61.0	649	73.6
1977	—	14.7	111.6	—	—	—	—	34.9	17.1	245.2	13.8	—	16.9	454	56.4
1978	—	13.2	52.1	9.5	—	—	—	18.4	14.5	127.0	32.6	—	11.0	278.2	33.6
1979	—	—	51.7	22.5	—	—	—	2.1	10.7	49.2	55.3	—	52.1	243.6	27.5
1980	—	—	33.6	—	—	—	—	18.6	5.3	79.9	106.0	—	86.4	329.8	46.4
1981	—	—	38.9	—	—	—	—	25.8	13.6	90.6	34.3	—	97.5	300.7	42.6
1982[1]			3.0		1.7			1.5	5.0	23.2	18.8		57.9	111.1	

[1] Preliminary.   [2] Imported for consumption.   Source: Dept of Commerce   T.387

United States General Imports[1] of Manganese Ore   In Thousands of Long Tons—Manganese Content

Year	Jan.	Feb.	Mar.	Apr.	May	June	July	Aug.	Sept.	Oct.	Nov.	Dec.	Total
1973	106	72	52	101	99	58	85	72	51	127	41	51	916
1974	56	41	81	27	57	76	61	50	94	92	103	112	851
1975	79	40	108	138	116	84	77	88	51	112	43	98	1,033
1976	101	39	83	68	53	161	45	134	87	75	93	114	1,053
1977	71	53	29	48	121	119	62	87	110	49	21	64	884
1978	94	50	113	50	71	55	82	42	97	62	64	63	842
1979	62	50	60	57	85	122	61	34	85	53	105	76	850
1980	199	56	54	66	97	68	54	67	60	38	57	69	795
1981	22	76	55	70	111	78	68	55	72	51	67	49	775
1982	65	49	65	55	22	58	35	33	14	25	32	15	467
1983	61												

[1] General imports of ore, concentrates manganiferous ore, manganese alloys & metals.   Source: Department of Commerce   T.388

Average Price of Ferromanganese[1] (78% Mn-F.O.B. Plant)   In Dollars Per Gross Ton—Carloads

Year	Jan.	Feb.	Mar.	Apr.	May	June	July	Aug.	Sept.	Oct.	Nov.	Dec.	Average
1973	200	200	200	200	200	200	200	200	200	200	200	200	200.00
1974	200	200	200	270	270	294¾	315	333⅓	350	350	350	440	297.76
1975	440	440	440	440	440	440	440	440	440	440	440	440	440.00
1976	432½	432½	432½	432½	432½	432½	432½	432½	432½	432½	425	417½	430.63
1977	417½	417½	417½	399½	399½	399½	399½	399½	399½	399½	399½	399½	404.00
1978	399½	399½	399½	399½	422.17	425	425	425	425	425	425	425	416.26
1979	440	440	440	465	490	490	490	490	490	493.48	510	510	479.04
1980	510	510	510	510	510	510	510	510	510	510	510	510	510.00
1981	510	510	510	510	510	510	510	510	510	510	510	510	510.00
1982	510	510											

[1] Domestic standard.   Source: American Metal Mkt.; Bureau of Labor Statistics (1016–0111.04)   T.389

Production of Ferromanganese in U.S., & Materials Used in Its Manufacture

Year	Ferromanganese Produced Short Tons	Per Cent	Manganese Contained Short Tons	Silico-Manganese Production (Gr. Wt.) Sh. Tns.	Manganese Ore Foreign	Manganese Ore Domestic	Manganese Ore Used Per Ton of Ferromanganese & Silico manganese	Ferromanganese Made
1972	800,723	78.3	627,358	153,000	1,896,483	25,620	2.0	2.3
1973	683,075	78.8	538,119	184,000	1,648,806	25,912	1.9	2.4
1974	544,361	78.0	424,405	196,000	1,348,425	55,822	1.8	2.5
1975	575,809	78.9	454,309	143,000	1,389,300	48,011	1.9	2.4
1976	482,662	79.0	381,328	129,000	1,208,336	53,632	2.0	2.5
1977	334,134	78.8	263,136	120,000	889,296	35,769	1.9	2.6
1978	272,530	80.6	219,707	142,000	740,906	90,660	1.9	
1979	317,102	80.2	254,389	165,000	785,664	125,130	1.8	
1980	189,472	79.7	150,982	188,000	691,250	34,877	1.9	
1981[1]	192,690	80.0	154,156	173,000	684,857	57,722	2.0	
1982[1]	120,000			75,000				

[1] Preliminary.   Source: Bureau of Mines   T.390

215

Margarine

Salient Statistics of Margarine in the United States   In Million Pounds (Actual Weight)

Year	Stocks Jan. 1	Production	Exports & Shipments	Domestic Disappearance[2] Total	Per Person in lbs.	Coconut Oil	Cotton seed Oil	Soybean Oil	Peanut Oil	Corn Oil	Lard & Beef Fats	Safflower Oil	All Other Edible Oil	Total Primary & Secondary Fats & Oils
1974	61	2,398	15	2,380	11.1	9	58	1,457	—	188	167	16	9	1,905
1975	64	2,399	17	2,386	11.0	20	46	1,568	1	188	52	7	38	1,917
1976	60	2,628	20	2,601	11.9	4	51	1,671	38	218	44	10	58	2,091
1977	67	2,535	20	2,502	11.4	5	44	1,585	15	243	80	8	48	2,026
1978	80	2,520	31	2,499	11.2	7	42	1,593	—	211	74	10	27	1,997
1979	70	2,553	25	2,517	11.2	4	25	1,643	—	222	86	5	12	2,016
1980	81	2,593	24	2,576	11.3		25	1,651	—	222	104			2,036
1981[1]	74	2,577	17	2,573	11.2		25	1,685		213	78			2,017
1982[1]	61				11.3									
1983[1]	62													

[1] Preliminary.   [2] Civilian & military.   Source: *Bureau of Census*   T.391

United States Production of Margarine   In Millions of Pounds

Year	Jan.	Feb.	Mar.	Apr.	May	June	July	Aug.	Sept.	Oct.	Nov.	Dec.	Total
1974	248.1	205.7	213.4	194.8	202.9	174.4	192.0	163.2	182.2	229.5	203.9	187.6	2,398
1975	211.0	201.2	198.7	181.7	183.0	180.6	173.7	178.7	216.6	212.8	219.7	241.6	2,399
1976	265.1	259.6	225.8	198.8	190.5	199.8	197.4	195.1	202.8	215.6	233.2	246.0	2,630
1977	242.3	236.5	232.7	197.3	178.8	179.8	164.8	198.2	209.1	221.8	229.0	244.7	2,535
1978	219.8	224.6	243.0	186.8	183.7	194.6	166.0	200.6	207.6	222.2	220.6	250.0	2,520
1979[1]	233.1	214.8	242.9	186.8	197.5	193.0	188.3	199.0	205.9	225.8	224.6	241.5	2,553
1980[1]	235.8	228.7	231.6	184.5	200.5	214.6	192.1	186.9	213.2	221.9	218.4	264.6	2,593
1981[1]	235.5	214.4	231.6	196.3	182.1	214.3	184.7	192.5	223.3	220.9	232.6	248.2	2,576
1982[1]	221.5	237.7	236.7	191.8	189.8	206.5	182.3	193.8	229.2	221.8	236.5	248.4	2,596
1983[1]	208.8												

[1] Preliminary.   Source: *Bureau of the Census*   T.392

Stocks[1] of Margarine in the United States   In Millions of Pounds

Year	Jan. 1	Feb. 1	Mar. 1	Apr. 1	May 1	June 1	July 1	Aug. 1	Sept. 1	Oct. 1	Nov. 1	Dec. 1
1974	61.2	55.3	63.0	74.4	75.2	80.3	77.8	70.8	69.0	71.8	74.1	70.0
1975	64.3	65.6	72.5	65.8	75.8	64.4	63.6	66.6	52.6	58.6	60.2	64.8
1976	60.1	67.0	82.1	101.1	70.2	71.4	70.8	73.6	80.0	72.4	72.2	69.8
1977	67.2	67.4	70.7	71.8	77.3	91.0	81.0	73.7	68.6	58.9	74.0	70.0
1978	79.9	61.8	70.2	59.3	72.3	63.4	68.8	67.8	60.3	66.0	69.9	58.9
1979[2]	69.5	66.8	82.1	67.5	77.3	75.2	78.3	68.7	77.1	72.7	81.6	64.9
1980[2]	80.5	71.6	80.0	73.2	69.5	62.5	74.7	78.3	60.7	66.1	80.0	71.4
1981[2]	74.2	62.2	68.3	76.8	66.1	74.2	87.0	79.8	87.7	75.4	62.5	64.2
1982[2]	61.0	62.2	66.8	64.3	60.5	67.5	65.0	59.6	68.7	68.4	80.9	83.4
1983[2]	62.1	62.7										

[1] Producers' and warehouse.   [2] Preliminary.   Source: *Bureau of the Census*   T.393

Average Wholesale Price of Margarine, Yellow, Quarters, F.O.B. Chicago[1]   In Cents per Pound

Year	Jan.	Feb.	Mar.	Apr.	May	June	July	Aug.	Sept.	Oct.	Nov.	Dec.	Average
1974	38.5	40.8	43.3	42.5	40.4	39.8	44.3	53.3	46.5	49.6	48.5	44.4	44.3
1975	41.8	41.5	39.3	41.5	39.5	39.3	39.2	38.1	36.0	34.3	33.5	31.3	37.9
1976[1]	31.0	31.0	31.0	31.0	30.7	30.0	31.8	30.0	32.0	32.0	33.0	33.0	31.4
1977	33.8	34.0	39.5	42.5	44.3	43.9	42.4	40.3	38.5	37.4	36.9	36.1	39.1
1978	36.6	36.7	41.0	43.6	42.0	40.6	37.8	37.3	41.6	41.3	40.1	39.6	39.8
1979	40.3	41.3	42.3	41.4	40.6	41.1	42.6	42.3	43.9	42.4	37.9	42.1	41.5
1980	39.8	38.3	39.0	35.6	34.8	36.1	40.3	40.0	40.3	39.3	40.3	40.2	38.7
1981	35.8	35.9	37.1	38.2	36.6	37.7	39.4	39.0	37.4	36.9	36.9	36.9	37.3
1982	37.0	37.6	38.3	39.0	40.2	40.0	39.0	38.4	38.0	38.0	38.0		
1983													

[1] Prices prior to 1976 are for WHITE (DOMESTIC VEGETABLE).   Source: *Department of Agriculture*   T.394

Meats

Soft market prices were expected to keep 1983 world red meat production below 1982 levels. The total of beef and veal, pork, and sheep and goat meat produced during 1983 was projected at 81.75 million metric tons (tonnes), 1 percent below the 1982 figure. Late 1982 forecasts of an increase in world beef production were reversed when drought conditions provoked a sharp rise in beef cattle slaughter in Mexico and Australia. Heavy cattle and calf slaughter in Poland resulted from feed shortages and from low guaranteed prices for beef. World cattle numbers at the start of 1983 were expected to be off nearly 2.5 million head. Expected reductions of the world hog inventory amounting to 9 million head were largely an outcome of feed shortages in many areas. The 1983 sheep and goat meat production was projected as nearly steady at 4.5 million tons.

Total red meat production for the U.S. in 1982 was 37.3 billion pounds compared with 38.7 billion the previous year. Beef production of 22.4 billion pounds was up nearly 1 percent from the 1981 level. Veal production of 423 million pounds was up nearly 2 percent. Pork production decreased 9 percent to 14.1 billion pounds. Lamb and mutton output increased 9 percent in 1982 to 356 million pounds.

During 1982, total per capita consumption of red meat and poultry was 2 percent below the 208 pounds (retail-weight basis) consumed during 1981. Per capita beef consumption was nearly the same as in 1981. Pork consumption dropped nearly 8 pounds, or almost 13 percent, from the 65 pounds per person consumed during 1981. Per capita meat consumption was expected to show declines again in 1983. Beef consumption was projected as being up slightly, but offset by an expected 4-pound drop in the per capita consumption of pork.

During 1982 retail prices of red meats increased because of curtailed supplies. Retail beef prices rose by 1 percent to a new high of around $2.42 per pound, and 1982 retail pork prices increased by 15 percent to $1.75 per pound. At the time, poultry prices declined by almost 2 percent as broiler stocks began to pick up thus increasing the momentum of the swing away from red meat to poultry consumption.

Declines in red meat production during 1983 are expected to result in moderately higher retail meat prices. The price of competing broiler meat is projected to remain below 1982 levels.

Early in 1983, U.S. Agriculture Secretary Block set the 1983 U.S. meat import quota trigger level at 1.231 billion pounds, 7 million pounds above estimated 1982 imports but lower than the 1982 level of 1.3 billion pounds. Imports of beef and of other meats, based upon available supply estimates, were not expected to be near the level that could invoke the import restraints authorized by the Meat Import Act of 1979.

World Total Meat[1] Production   In Millions of Metric Tons

Year	Argentina	Australia	Bel.-& Lux.	Canada	Czechoslovakia	Denmark	France	W. Germany	Japan	Italy	N. Zealand	Poland	Brazil	South Africa	Un. Kingdom	United States	U.S.S.R.
1972	2.6	2.4	.8	1.5	.7	.9	3.0	3.6	1.1	1.8	1.0	1.6	2.8	.8	2.1	16.8	10.0
1973	2.6	2.3	.9	1.5	.8	1.0	3.0	3.4	1.1	1.9	1.0	1.8	3.3	.7	2.1	15.8	9.9
1974	2.6	1.9		1.6			3.4	3.8	1.2	2.0		2.0	2.9		2.3	17.1	10.5
1975	2.8	2.4	.9	1.6	.8	1.0	3.4	3.8	1.3	1.7	1.0	2.1	3.0	.8	2.3	16.7	11.0
1976	3.2	2.7	.9	1.7	.8	1.0	3.5	3.9	1.4	1.9	1.2	2.4	3.1	.8	2.1	18.1	10.0
1977	3.3	2.0	.7	1.7	.9	1.0	3.4	3.9	1.5	2.0	1.1	2.3	3.4	.8	2.2	18.0	12.7
1978	3.5	2.8	.9	1.7	1.3	1.1	3.5	4.1	1.7	2.0	1.1	2.7	3.1	.8	2.2	17.5	13.3
1979	3.5	2.5	1.0	1.7	1.3	1.2	3.7	4.2	1.8	2.1	1.1	2.7	3.0	.9	2.2	17.1	13.2
1980	3.3	2.3	1.0	1.9	1.3	1.2	3.7	4.3	1.9	2.2	1.1	2.6	3.2	.9	2.3	17.7	12.6
1981[2]	3.4	2.2	1.0	1.9	1.3	1.2	3.8	4.3	1.9	2.2	1.1	2.1	3.3	.8	2.3	17.7	12.7
1982[3]	3.2	2.1	1.0	1.9	1.3	1.2	3.8	4.3	1.9	2.2	1.1	2.3	3.3	.8	2.3	17.5	12.8
1983																	

[1] Production of beef & veal, mutton & lamb, goat meat, & pork. Horsemeat included from 1976.   [2] Preliminary.   [3] Forecast.   *Source: Foreign Agricultural Service, U.S.D.A.*
T.395

World Per Capita Consumption of Meat[1] (Total Red Meat)   In Kilograms

Year	Argentina	Australia	Austria	Canada	Denmark	France	W. Germany	Ireland	N. Zealand	Poland	Switzerland	United Kingdom	United States	Uruguay	U.S.S.R.
1972	74	101	63	73	58	64	67	63	102	47	65	64	88	88	41
1973	79	91	63	71	53	63	65	60	104	49	66	59	81	85	40
1974	87	100	65	73	51	65	67	64	98	71	64	58	87	100	44
1975	99	109	68	73	54	66	67	67	103	73	64	58	83	100	45
1976	101.3	110.2	69.9	79.3	59.8	68.4	69.2	63.6	100.0	66.6	66.2	55.4	88.6	88.8	47.1
1977	101.2	110.1	71.1	76.8	58.7	69.4	69.6	62.4	107.2	65.5	69.5	58.1	87.2	96.8	51.0
1978	105.6	103.4	72.2	73.8	67.2	72.2	72.9	63.0	104.5	58.9	70.0	58.2	84.8	102.9	51.3
1979	103.0	88.3	73.4	71.1	66.9	74.2	74.3	64.9	100.2	57.8	70.2	59.9	81.7	81.5	51.7
1980[2]	103.3	83.8	74.3	73.6	71.0	75.1	75.7	65.9	98.1	56.6	76.8	58.2	83.9	94.0	49.8
1981[3]	103.2	77.7	74.9	72.4	72.1	74.5	75.7	65.9	97.9	48.2	77.9	56.1	80.0	95.1	47.9
1982															

[1] Summation of previous individual meat tables plus horse meat.   [2] Preliminary.   [3] Forecast.   *Source: Foreign Agricultural Service, U.S.D.A.*
T.396

MEATS

Total Red Meat Imports (Carcass Weight Equivalent[2]) of Importing Countries   In Thous. of Metric Tons

Year	Belgium & Lux.	Canada	Czecho-slovakia	France	Rep. of Korea	W. Germany	Greece	Italy	Japan	Netherlands	Spain	Switzerland	Un. Kingdom	United States	USSR
1970	79.8	169.4	108.2	331.7		375.0	114.5	427.2	252.5	88.8	108.5	55.4	1,425	1,105	105.0
1971	82.5	122.4	65.1	324.0		422.1	123.9	473.2	312.1	75.5	47.8	53.7	1,431	1,065	133.6
1972	94.5	168.3	36.8	427.2		603.8	103.1	512.9	422.1	114.5	167.6	56.7	1,524	1,212	87.9
1973	106.0	163.5	85.3	468.4		605.1	126.7	660.4	592.9	118.5	128.2	56.3	1,312	1,176	94.4
1974	87.3	130.5	41.6	422.3	1974-	563.0	34.3	550.6	394.2	105.0	25.8	33.0	1,059	981.3	455.7
1975	111.7	151.6	12.3	479.1	78	586.0	50.3	588.7	569.8	131.2	71.7	24.7	1,064	1,020	454.1
1976	120.5	249.4	22.0	482.2	(24)	614.0	95.0	593.0	692.7	150.0	101.9	26.1	1,132	1,184	274.6
1977	121.2	194.3	21.4	556.2		627.0	110.9	612.9	649.0	175.3	59.2	26.0	1,280	1,100	496.2
1978	143.9	172.9	21.0	630.4		633.0	142.0	632.1	665.4	187.5	112.3	33.8	1,276	1,296	132.0
1979	99	140	21	541	108	648	140	684	610	149	124	25	1,245	1,348	469
1980	91	112	21	594	15	700	134	722	486	167	26	23	1,122	1,210	662
1981[1]	92	113	21	583	48	670	120	685	607	157	11	25	975	1,059	696
1982[3]	98	116	21	583	48	693	112	697	560	142	11	25	1,010	1,022	780
1983															

[1] Preliminary.   [2] Excludes fat, offals & live animals.   [3] Forecast.   *Source: Foreign Agricultural Service, U.S.D.A.*   T.397

Total Red Meat Exports (Carcass Weight Equivalent[2]) of Principal Countries   In Thousands of Metric Tons

Year	Argentina	Australia	Brazil	Canada	Denmark	France	Ireland	Mexico	Netherlands	N. Zealand	Poland	United States	USSR	Uruguay	Yugoslavia
1970	859.5	786.4	145.6	94.7	613.1	157.0	230.0	61.5	485.5	710.7	175.0	51.2	75.5	162.0	119.2
1971	556.8	926.6	187.6	102.7	683.7	212.3	256.5	55.9	511.2	731.2	189.3	59.8	60.7	102.1	120.7
1972	771.0	1,137	267.7	102.6	654.8	178.7	226.9	64.1	499.7	736.9	188.7	82.9	82.0	148.4	121.4
1973	600.2	1,132	225.5	112.5	647.0	200.5	227.8	48.2	555.6	723.8	216.2	140.9	98.5	111.8	106.1
1974	357.7	6,106	154.0	81.5	690.4	337.0	300.2	27.3	589.5	620.3	153.6	109.0	79.1	123.4	59.1
1975	329.5	943.0	156.2	78.2	700.2	374.8	359.7	17.6	610.9	708.2	161.7	164.0	63.5	124.1	86.8
1976	628.6	1,129	217.0	112.2	634.1	366.8	282.9	28.5	641.0	788.6	117.7	236.4	67.6	201.8	98.5
1977	669.6	1,335	240.0	112.1	695.6	312.2	363.8	34.1	697.2	790.9	131.8	236.0	49.2	134.6	88.0
1978	823.7	1,377	178.1	117.1	753.4	267.2	359.3	46.6	751.6	724.7	141.0	256.6	38.0	118.8	113.4
1979	728	1,306	111	133	832	306	342	7	785	783	155	211	33	84	82
1980	487	1,090	170	183	849	362	440	1	843	795	141	195	30	128	98
1981[1]	506	938	286	207	872	397	327	1	951	870	50	240	30	182	62
1982[3]	499	943	331	199	880	400	338	1	965	821	40	264	30	146	85
1983															

[1] Preliminary.   [2] Excludes fat, offals & live animals.   [3] Forecast.   *Source: Foreign Agricultural Service, U.S.D.A.*   T.398

United States Exports of Livestock & Meat Products   In Thousands of Metric Trons[5]

Year	Red Meats — Beef & Veal	Pork	Lamb, Mutton & Goat	Sausage, Bol. & Frank.	Other Meats[2]	Total	Variety Meats[3]	Saus. Casings (Animal)	Lard	Tallow & Greases	Cattle Parts[4]	Cattle & Calves	Sheep & Lambs	Hogs	Horses, Mules, Etc.
1969	25.7	145.1	1.4	4.7	13.0	190.0	239.8	11.9	261.9	1,908	29.9	39.2	106.2	18.6	11.5
1970	29.3	61.2	1.1	4.1	12.0	107.7	239.5	12.3	365.9	2,261	14.4	88.0	132.9	24.8	40.7
1971	42.0	65.3	1.3	4.0	12.4	125.0	277.5	12.3	282.3	2,616	28.4	93.0	213.8	17.3	14.5
1972	52.2	99.3	1.3	4.0	12.1	168.8	254.1	13.6	164.4	2,368	27.0	103.9	159.4	12.3	21.2
1973	79.1	160.7	1.7	5.6	15.8	263.0	281.9	14.8	113.3	2,319	31.2	272.6	204.3	16.8	71.5
1974[5]	23.0	42.9	1.2	2.4	9.0	78.4	134.2	5.6	73.2	1,218	37.8	204.4	290.7	15.8	66.4
1975	20.7	91.2	1.3	2.2	5.7	121.0	133.2	5.8	39.8	916.0	13.8	195.9	339.2	16.0	36.4
1976	36.6	137.5	1.4	2.5	7.7	185.6	172.2	6.9	81.9	1,076	10.5	204.5	244.5	10.8	37.8
1977	41.5	125.2	1.8	3.4	8.2	180.0	173.1	6.9	82.6	1,319	10.5	107.0	205.1	10.2	23.0
1978	55.3	100.2	1.4	3.7	6.8	167.3	185.8	7.1	54.2	1,228	19.4	122.2	141.8	12.7	43.9
1979	57.4	97.4	.6	3.0	4.7	163.0	168.9	7.2	43.5	1,286	21.6	66.2	125.4	13.4	29.1
1980	59.5	84.2	.6	3.3	7.4	155.0	200.4	7.6	41.9	1,516	17.5	65.6	123.5	16.3	25.7
1981[1]	74.7	100.9	1.0	3.8	7.5	187.9	210.0	7.2	67.9	1,487	14.9	87.8	220.9	24.1	66.9
1982															

[1] Preliminary.   [2] Canned mainly.   [3] Beef, Pork & other byproducts.   [4] Excludes furskins.   [5] Data prior to 1974 are in MILLIONS OF POUNDS.   *Source: Foreign Agricultural Service, U.S.D.A.*   T.399

MEATS

Production and Consumption of Red Meats in the United States (*Carcass Weight*)

Year	Beef Production Mil. Lbs.	Beef Consumption Total Mil. Lbs.	Beef Consumption Per Capita Lb.	Veal Production Mil. Lbs.	Veal Consumption Total Mil. Lbs.	Veal Consumption Per Capita Lb.	Lamb & Mutton Production Mil. Lbs.	Lamb & Mutton Consumption Total Mil. Lbs.	Lamb & Mutton Consumption Per Capita Lb.	Pork (Excluding Lard) Production Mil. Lbs.	Pork Consumption Total Mil. Lbs.	Pork Consumption Per Capita Lb.	All Meats Production Mil. Lbs.	All Meats Consumption Total Mil. Lbs.	All Meats Consumption Per Capita Lb.
1970	21,652	22,926	113.5	588	581	2.9	551	657	3.3	13,426	14,661	72.6	36,217	38,825	192.3
1971	21,868	23,086	112.7	546	546	2.7	555	646	3.2	14,783	16,127	78.7	37,752	40,405	197.2
1972	22,381	23,956	115.5	458	464	2.2	543	684	3.3	13,617	14,712	70.9	36,999	39,816	191.9
1973	21,277	22,814	108.8	357	376	1.8	514	556	2.7	12,751	13,298	63.5	34,899	37,044	176.7
1974	23,138	24,488	115.7	486	493	2.3	465	482	2.3	13,805	14,493	68.5	37,894	39,956	188.8
1975	23,976	25,397	118.8	873	876	4.1	410	431	2.0	11,503	11,852	55.4	36,762	38,556	180.3
1976	25,969	27,539	127.5	853	853	4.0	371	396	1.8	12,415	12,667	58.6	39,608	41,456	191.9
1977	25,279	27,048	124.0	834	835	3.8	351	370	1.7	13,247	13,202	60.5	39,711	41,455	190.1
1978	24,242	25,998	117.9	632	645	2.9	309	343	1.6	13,393	13,293	60.3	38,576	40,279	182.7
1979	21,446	23,522	105.5	434	450	2.0	293	332	1.5	15,450	15,353	68.8	37,623	39,657	177.8
1980	21,644	23,320	103.4	400	410	1.8	318	345	1.5	16,615	16,574	73.5	38,977	40,648	180.2
1981[1]	22,389	23,756	104.3	436	438	1.9	338	360	1.6	15,875	15,927	69.9	39,037	40,481	177.8
1982[2]	22,532			447			366			14,273			37,618		

[1] Preliminary. [2] Estimate. Source: Economic Research Service, U.S.D.A.   T.400

U.S. Imports of Meats and Meat Preparations   In Millions of Pounds

Year	Jan.	Feb.	Mar.	Apr.	May	June	July	Aug.	Sept.	Oct.	Nov.	Dec.	Total
1970	173	155	175	143	112	148	171	167	167	155	134	143	1,844
1971	133	112	151	141	133	170	155	166	223	110	102	188	1,789
1972	161	140	138	159	161	152	166	216	206	202	174	138	2,012
1973	165	148	133	149	166	143	153	209	159	207	184	156	1,972
1974	171	137	168	142	126	124	102	141	130	114	134	146	1,634
1975	179	131	146	125	111	135	148	149	157	135	168	112	1,694
1976	175	117	173	158	170	187	159	151	178	170	134	94	1,868
1977	131	150	143	147	147	135	147	158	167	117	87	212	1,741
1978	138	155	183	202	181	167	161	137	182	184	201	181	2,072
1979	201	184	214	201	190	214	168	141	142	143	188	193	2,178
1980	196	152	166	134	173	154	208	170	133	207	167	191	2,052
1981	171	167	131	155	140	153	162	168	180	167	120	118	1,832
1982	127	106	160	169	167	215	158	234	246	194	124	114	2,015
1983	208												

Source: Dept. of Commerce   T.401

United States Imports of Livestock & Meat Products   In Thousands of Metric Tons[2]

Year	Red Meats Beef, Boneless	Red Meats Canned Corned	Red Meats Pork	Red Meats Lamb	Red Meats Mutton & Goat	Red Meats Total	Meat for Animal Food	Variety Meats	Byproducts Lard	Byproducts Tallow & Greases	Meat Extract	Live Animals (1,000 Head) Cattle & Calves	Sheep & Lambs	Hogs	Horses, Mules, Etc.
1969	984.6	94.7	315.5	43.9	54.2	1,653		5.6	—	12.7	.9	1,042	22.8	13.4	3.5
1970	1,083	88.5	347.6	43.5	39.5	1,810		9.8	—	8.4	1.2	1,168	11.7	67.8	3.7
1971	1,057	67.1	356.5	38.2	32.3	1,760		6.5	.5	6.1	1.2	991	5.5	77.5	3.7
1972	1,251	80.1	394.7	37.3	55.6	1,990	55.8	7.9	.3	5.7	.9	1,187	13.8	89.0	3.2
1973	1,292	69.9	398.5	27.0	13.0	1,954	41.0	7.2		15.1	1.5	1,039	9.5	87.6	3.3
1974[2]	469.0	30.4	164.2	8.1	1.8	733.6	8.3	2.7	.1	7.2	.3	568	.9	196.3	3.7
1975	533.4	24.0	148.4	11.2	.5	762.8	8.0	2.5	—	8.0	.2	389	3.5	29.8	9.2
1976	560.2	45.3	144.0	15.5	.4	838.4	3.7	2.4	—	4.8	.4	984	4.6	45.6	10.0
1977	541.0	34.1	135.3	9.5	.3	784.0	1.3	2.6	—	3.1	.3	1,133	8.5	43.0	11.3
1978	651.1	37.6	157.3	17.2	.2	931.7	1.8	2.5	.2	2.4	.5	1,253	11.2	202.4	19.0
1979	685.5	34.6	163.8	19.4	.4	978.9	1.9	4.7	—	1.1	.6	732	9.5	136.6	16.2
1980	622.6	34.5	196.6	15.0	—	923.1	3.5	4.6	—	2.2	.1	681	20.5	247.3	15.9
1981[1]	524.1	29.4	195.8	14.1	—	823.0	4.1	3.6	—	2.5	.4	659	6.9	145.7	14.2
1982															

[1] Preliminary. [2] Data prior to 1974 are in MILLIONS OF POUNDS. Source: Foreign Agricultural Service, U.S.D.A.   T.402

MEATS

U.S. Exports of Meat and Meat Preparations   In Millions of Pounds

Year	Jan.	Feb.	Mar.	Apr.	May	June	July	Aug.	Sept.	Oct.	Nov.	Dec.	Total
1970	31	32	33	37	42	41	31	43	53	49	74	51	518
1971	39	41	49	35	46	43	39	51	48	39	43	69	547
1972	40	37	44	45	64	58	48	49	47	67	57	57	614
1973	48	52	81	75	74	66	49	57	53	72	62	70	759
1974	58	51	60	56	51	54	68	64	58	77	64	54	714
1975	57	67	75	65	79	64	70	77	73	76	79	82	864
1976	85	93	114	99	119	109	90	112	110	130	117	128	1,305
1977	100	100	103	113	110	103	112	110	125	106	109	124	1,315
1978	109	101	115	108	108	99	93	119	131	124	119	111	1,338
1979	102	95	117	99	100	124	103	109	119	135	119	155	1,378
1980	101	108	144	132	139	164	145	129	136	165	144	154	1,663
1981	143	141	169	248	189	180	128	144	123	174	154	153	1,847
1982	129	147	124	131	167	147	111	108	112	133	143	115	1,566
1983	114												

Source: Dept. of Commerce

T.403

Average Wholesale Prices of Meats   In Cents Per Pound

Year	Composite Retail Price of Beef (Choice)	of Pork[4]	of Veal	of Lamb (Choice)	Steer Beef Carcass, Choice, Centr. U.S.	Fresh Beef, Steer Carcasses Choice, E. Coast	Lamb Carcasses Choice & Prime (35-45 Lb.) East Coast[5]	Pork Loins, (8-14 lbs.) N.Y.	Hams[2] Fancy Skinned, Smoked	Picnics[6] (Smoked) 4-8 Lb.[1]	Live Broilers Georgia
1970	101.7	77.4	124.3	105.5	47.33	49.0	59.13	56.86	54.2	48.40	12.3
1971	108.1	69.8	135.8	109.7	52.67	54.7	60.71	49.85	53.4	32.31	12.8
1972	118.7	82.7	153.9	118.8	55.63	57.6	65.21	64.46	62.6	40.47	13.1
1973	142.1	109.2	181.7	134.3	67.62	69.6	74.30	81.91	81.0	55.51	23.9
1974	146.3	107.8	194.1	146.4	73.12	69.1	83.33	78.56	67.8	47.95	21.1
1975	154.8	134.6	181.1	167.6	73.18	75.4	95.07	99.28	88.2	60.31	26.9
1976	148.2	134.0	173.3	185.6	61.00	64.4	102.67	97.68	85.5	61.35	24.0
1977	148.4	125.4	175.3	186.8	62.69	66.2	108.73	95.25	86.5	57.03	23.7
1978	181.9	143.6	209.5	219.6	80.43	83.9	127.20	109.15	90.0		26.0
1979	226.3	144.1	282.3	245.7	101.62	101.1	134.50	107.65	80.6		26.0
1980[3]	237.6	139.5	309.5	252.7	104.44	104.4	135.02	101.14	81.3		27.0
1981[3]	238.7	152.4	314.5	252.4	99.90	99.8	126.49	113.70	77.6		27.0
1982[3]						101.3		127.70			

[1] At NY. [2] Composite. [3] Preliminary. [4] Sold as retail cuts (ham, bacon, loin, etc.). [5] Prior to 1972—CHICAGO. [6] Prior to 1971 prices are for BACON.   Sources: Bureau of Labor Statistics; Department of Agriculture

T.404

Average Wholesale Price of Steer Beef Carcass, Choice[1], at Midwest Markets[2]   In Cents per Pound

Year	Jan.	Feb.	Mar.	Apr.	May	June	July	Aug.	Sept.	Oct.	Nov.	Dec.	Average
1970	46.89	46.74	49.34	48.78	47.18	48.02	50.26	48.86	47.38	45.91	44.86	43.79	47.33
1971	48.60	51.86	51.45	52.62	53.96	52.62	52.54	53.99	52.75	51.60	54.08	55.92	52.67
1972	57.52	57.58	54.92	53.72	56.45	59.36	58.69	54.56	53.36	52.95	51.26	57.20	55.63
1973	62.85	66.85	69.38	69.84	69.15	70.92	71.90	—	69.69	65.56	61.97	65.00	67.62
1974	75.56	75.78	67.62	65.84	66.13	62.18	84.92	77.95	79.66	75.62	72.96	73.25	73.12
1975	61.36	58.41	59.50	70.20	80.60	85.76	82.82	77.95	79.66	75.62	72.98	73.25	73.18
1976	66.68	62.22	56.97	65.85	63.56	62.45	58.20	57.05	57.24	58.36	60.85	62.52	61.00
1977	60.04	58.92	57.12	60.54	64.44	62.62	63.65	62.49	63.04	65.87	65.47	68.10	62.69
1978	68.74	71.08	74.88	81.43	88.48	85.95	84.81	79.94	81.96	82.14	80.98	84.75	80.43
1979	93.57	97.47	104.59	108.61	108.64	103.56	99.85	94.13	101.91	98.32	103.22	105.53	101.62
1980	102.26	103.70	103.15	99.41	102.00	105.18	110.11	111.96	107.97	105.49	101.44	100.57	104.40
1981	99.80	96.80	94.32	99.68	103.32	106.52	107.3	103.90	102.96	96.02	94.56	93.70	99.80
1982	97.40	101.20	103.80	109.50	115.10	111.20	102.60	100.80	95.50	96.30	92.90	92.60	101.30
1983	93.90	96.60											

[1] 500–600 pounds. [2] Prior to Oct. 1975 prices are at CHICAGO.   Source: Economic Research Service, U.S.D.A.

T.405

MEATS

Production[2] (Commercial Slaughter[4]) of All Meats[1] in the U.S. In Millions of Pounds—Carcass Weight

Year	Jan.	Feb.	Mar.	Apr.	May	June	July	Aug.	Sept.	Oct.	Nov.	Dec.	Total
1970	2,891	2,535	2,820	2,919	2,738	2,770	2,770	2,731	3,031	3,196	2,951	3,221	34,574
1971	3,076	2,663	3,233	3,074	2,940	3,104	2,879	2,966	3,116	3,027	3,072	3,062	36,209
1972	2,861	2,744	3,193	2,859	3,097	2,996	2,581	3,082	2,968	3,228	3,130	2,893	35,632
1973[4]	3,176	2,722	2,979	2,579	3,051	2,799	2,651	2,704	2,635	3,225	3,079	2,894	34,495
1974	3,255	2,661	3,098	3,149	3,266	2,945	3,026	3,132	3,074	3,471	3,155	3,088	37,323
1975	3,315	2,880	2,959	3,089	2,873	2,832	2,842	2,860	3,088	3,339	2,978	3,159	36,213
1976	3,267	2,907	3,515	3,109	2,928	3,150	3,048	3,350	3,467	3,497	3,453	3,367	39,060
1977	3,237	3,084	3,551	3,195	3,122	3,298	2,925	3,404	3,354	3,345	3,416	3,241	39,172
1978	3,215	3,045	3,342	3,079	3,269	3,081	2,883	3,274	3,139	3,355	3,345	3,094	38,119
1979	3,280	2,756	3,090	2,879	3,130	2,990	2,958	3,329	2,876	3,556	3,306	3,074	37,225
1980	3,398	3,050	3,099	3,315	3,311	3,089	3,070	3,016	3,221	3,577	3,097	3,349	38,590
1981[3]	3,417	3,014	3,389	3,299	3,071	3,118	3,041	3,044	3,247	3,433	3,185	3,417	38,675
1982[3]	3,152	2,894	3,296	——9,097——			——9,165——			——9,659——			37,266
1983[3]	3,151	2,786											

[1] Except for pork production & lard. [2] Represents the total dressed carcass weight of livestock slaughtered under Federal inspection, exclusive of meats from condemned animals. [3] Preliminary. [4] Prior to 1973 data are for INSPECTED SLAUGHTER. Source: Agricultural Marketing Service, U.S.D.A. T.406

Cold Storage Holdings of All[1] Meats in the United States, at End of Month   In Millions of Pounds

Year	Jan.	Feb.	Mar.	Apr.	May	June	July	Aug.	Sept.	Oct.	Nov.	Dec.
1970	660.1	705.9	744.0	812.9	815.8	729.6	673.1	605.7	588.1	645.8	714.6	759.3
1971	769.8	745.2	789.1	866.1	897.4	890.8	831.7	771.6	775.3	768.1	750.0	795.8
1972	745.6	707.1	732.4	819.0	797.5	710.1	638.1	598.8	594.0	641.7	702.0	670.3
1973	681.9	661.5	687.0	706.7	697.6	675.3	588.5	505.4	525.0	643.3	770.0	829.7
1974	868.9	875.4	946.4	995.9	1,011.3	913.8	796.1	725.1	692.0	715.4	754.2	803.2
1975	809.4	793.9	787.4	801.1	725.6	654.0	578.2	518.4	517.5	571.3	667.6	675.2
1976	643.4	652.8	703.1	724.3	740.9	698.1	645.4	597.6	637.7	687.8	725.9	733.3
1977	745.4	759.6	776.4	823.0	802.4	723.4	629.4	568.6	579.0	532.1	565.2	566.6
1978	559.1	571.6	658.4	753.0	759.8	720.6	644.9	581.0	598.1	639.0	715.4	723.6
1979	728.4	710.9	762.5	783.4	797.0	755.0	685.6	580.7	549.1	604.5	656.9	706.2
1980	735.3	712.6	695.4	715.5	706.5	641.8	578.6	514.3	510.0	584.2	678.6	749.6
1981[2]	790.3	782.9	775.9	817.2	795.2	716.6	628.2	538.6	508.6	546.8	552.2	578.2
1982[2]	553.4	524.2	536.0	—	—	502.2	—	—	473.9	—	—	553.8
1983[2]	573.4	571.0	581.1									
1984												

[1] Includes beef and veal, mutton and lamb, pork and products, rendered pork fat, and miscellaneous meats. Excludes lard. [2] Preliminary. Source: Crop Reporting Board, U.S.D.A. T.407

Cold Storage Holdings of Frozen Beef[1] in the United States   In Millions of Pounds

Year	Jan. 1	Feb. 1	Mar. 1	Apr. 1	May 1	June 1	July 1	Aug. 1	Sept. 1	Oct. 1	Nov. 1	Dec. 1
1970	352.9	368.3	374.3	379.6	369.1	353.1	319.3	310.3	289.1	286.9	300.7	317.9
1971	338.4	325.7	308.4	302.1	290.3	285.1	296.7	312.2	333.2	351.1	347.2	326.9
1972	366.0	338.5	308.6	286.0	283.0	276.6	255.7	260.2	283.6	297.7	326.7	351.4
1973	367.1	382.8	368.9	359.3	360.1	335.6	322.4	298.1	253.6	244.5	315.3	392.6
1974	447.8	470.5	456.1	477.1	467.4	461.3	438.0	397.5	375.2	346.8	350.4	359.8
1975	401.9	407.1	385.9	384.6	349.0	308.6	288.1	269.0	258.2	254.4	272.4	320.0
1976	349.8	342.8	355.7	390.6	390.8	399.7	395.3	382.6	362.8	382.4	405.0	429.6
1977	453.5	474.6	475.4	472.9	472.0	447.4	412.6	374.0	350.1	345.8	301.1	291.5
1978	315.6	313.1	318.4	357.2	376.0	388.2	372.3	336.5	315.7	332.2	348.4	388.2
1979	405.4	423.7	405.0	427.4	410.1	411.9	395.7	369.6	324.2	296.7	308.2	321.9
1980	350.3	367.3	357.6	335.1	296.6	277.9	256.5	242.6	228.6	219.7	243.8	279.0
1981[2]	328.2	361.3	347.8	341.5	339.8	329.1	297.5	272.9	245.5	235.4	245.3	233.6
1982[2]	256.7	249.1	223.3	211.9	—	—	189.7	—	—	247.7	—	—
1983[2]	294.4	303.1	307.0	300.1								
1984												

[1] Includes frozen beef, cured beef, and beef in process of cure. [2] Preliminary. Source: Crop Reporting Board, U.S.D.A. T.408

Mercury

World mine production of mercury during 1982 amounted to 189,500 flasks compared with 206,604 flasks mined during the previous year according to a U.S. Bureau of Mines estimate. World resources were judged to be sufficient to satisfy the world demand for mercury for the next 90 years given the 1982 production rate.

The estimated U.S. mine production of mercury during 1982 was 25,000 flasks compared with 27,904 during 1981. The bulk of the U.S. output came from a single facility in Nevada. High mining costs and the cost of environmental pollution control continued to dampen mercury consumption, especially for use in paints and in pharmaceuticals, and in agriculture and the chlor-alkali industry. No new mercury-cell chlor-alkali plants were planned during 1982, and existing plants reduced their mercury consumption by more efficient operations including the recovery and reuse of mercury previously lost in effluents.

The average New York dealer price for primary mercury early in 1983 was $396.75 per flask compared with an average $361.00 in the last half of 1982. Producers in the major exporting countries reportedly continued to restrict sales in order to keep prices firm. The U.S. Bureau of Mines estimated that 1983 apparent domestic consumption would be 50,000 flasks. The demand for mercury, figured from a 1978 base, is expected to decrease at an annual rate of less than 1 percent through 1990.

As authorized by Public Law 97-35, the General Services Administration (GSA) continued to dispose of primary mercury and mercuric oxide held in the National Defense Stockpile. In June 1982, the GSA announced that exports of primary mercury sold from the stockpile were no longer restricted but that mercuric oxide would continue to be used solely for domestic purposes. The GSA planned to continue offering for sale a maximum of 35,000 pounds of mercuric oxide on the first Wednesday of each month, the minimum acceptable bid being set at 1,000 pounds.

U.S. industry stocks of mercury on December 31, 1982 were 6.6 percent larger than a year earlier.

World Production of Mercury In Flasks of 34.5 Kilograms (76 Pounds)

Year	Yugo-slavia	Peru	Philippines	Finland	China[1]	Canada	Czechoslovakia	Turkey	Italy	Germany	Mexico	Spain	Algeria	United States	USSR[1]	World Total
1970	15,461	3,196	4,648	388	20,000	24,400		8,592	44,470	5,170	30,256	45,552		27,296	48,000	284,014
1971	16,593	3,462	5,020	502	26,000	18,500		10,460	42,613	5,564	35,390	50,831		17,883	50,000	300,634
1972	16,419	4,550	3,341	640	26,000	14,637		7,963	41,801	5,019	22,510	53,994		7,349	50,000	278,968
1973	15,606	3,581	2,169	798	26,000	12,500		7,861	33,504	3,742	21,646	62,069		2,227	52,999	270,014
1974	15,838	3,252	812	921	26,000	14,000	5,541	8,833	25,991	1,409	25,933	54,354	14,000	2,189	54,000	257,477
1975	16,941	1,530	244	97	26,000	12,000	5,900	5,421	31,677	—	14,214	44,010	28,000	7,366	55,000	252,329
1976	12,503	—	—	13	18,000	—	5,540	4,899	22,278	—	15,026	42,729	30,915	23,133	56,000	234,614
1977	3,133	—	—	630	20,000	—	5,309	4,686	406	2,872	9,660	26,851	30,429	28,244	58,000	190,736
1978	—	—	—	1,145	20,000	—	5,686	5,020	87	2,437	2,205	29,588	30,603	24,163	60,000	181,434
1979	—	—	—	1,347	20,000	—	4,960	4,786	—	2,639	1,973	33,275	14,736	29,519	61,000	174,735
1980[2]	—	—	—	2,170	20,000	—	4,612	4,437	96	1,624	4,206	49,198	24,425	30,657	62,000	203,925
1981[1]	—	—	—	2,000	20,000	—	4,600	4,400	4,000	1,200	4,000	50,000	25,000	27,904	63,000	206,604
1982[1]											4,000	45,000	23,000	25,000	57,000	189,500
1983																

[1] Estimate. [2] Preliminary. Source: Bureau of Mines

T.409

How to keep your Commodity Year Book statistics up-to-date continuously throughout the year.

To keep up-to-date statistics on the commodities in this book, you should have COMMODITY YEAR BOOK STATISTICAL ABSTRACT SERVICE. This three-times-yearly publication provides the latest available statistics for updating the statistical tables appearing in the COMMODITY YEAR BOOK. The ABSTRACT is published in the Winter (Jan.), Spring (Apr.) and Fall (Oct.). Subscription price is $55 per year.

Commodity Research Bureau, Inc.
75 MONTGOMERY ST., JERSEY CITY, N.J. 07302

MERCURY

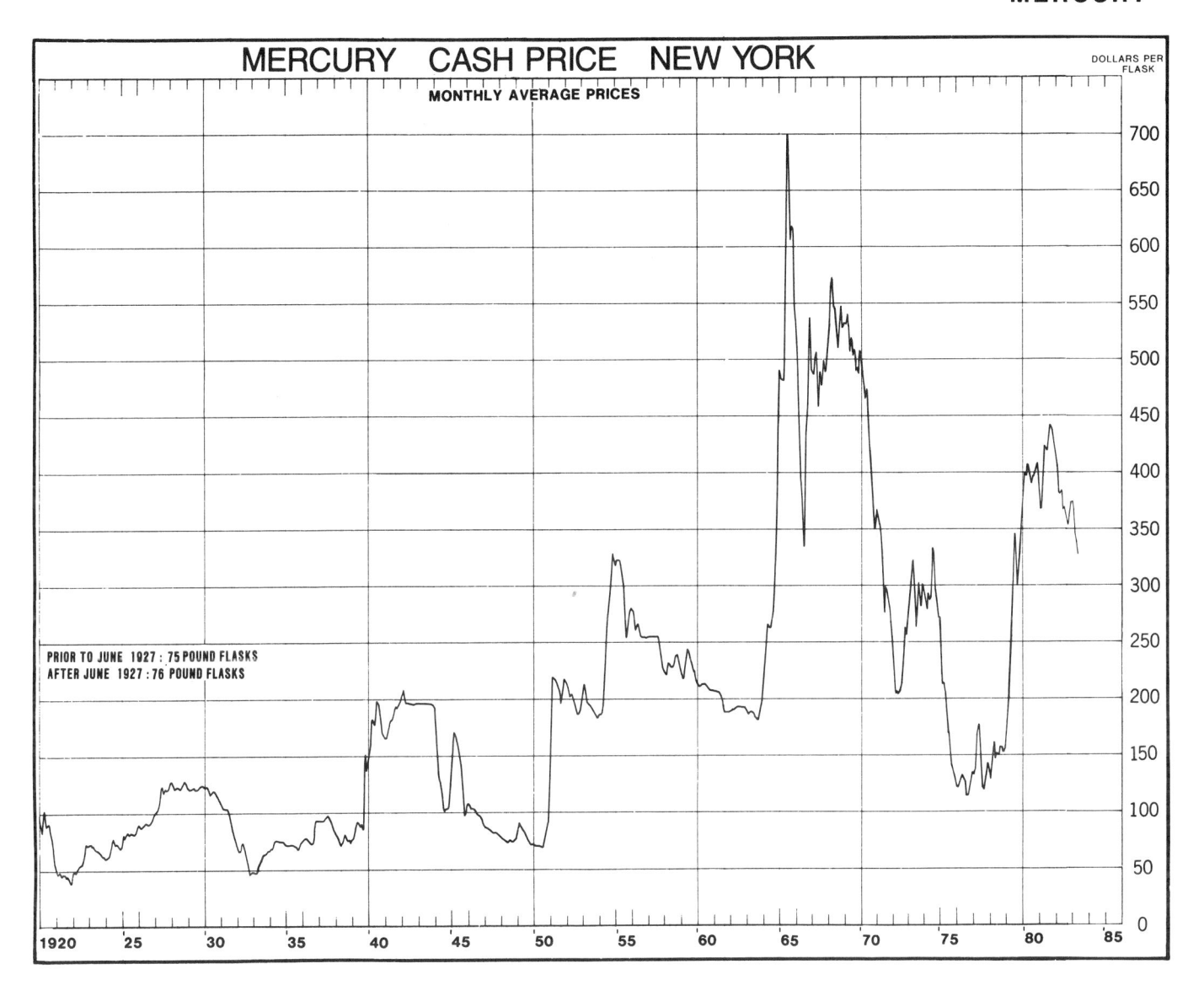

MERCURY CASH PRICE NEW YORK
MONTHLY AVERAGE PRICES
DOLLARS PER FLASK

PRIOR TO JUNE 1927: 75 POUND FLASKS
AFTER JUNE 1927: 76 POUND FLASKS

Average Price of Mercury in New York   In Dollars Per Flask of 76 Pounds

Year	Jan.	Feb.	Mar.	Apr.	May	June	July	Aug.	Sept.	Oct.	Nov.	Dec.	Average
1970	489.09	469.33	464.52	472.54	455.15	423.18	418.18	381.67	366.90	350.45	360.56	366.14	418.14
1971	357.25	353.21	340.43	323.09	301.00	275.68	299.76	295.00	288.09	280.79	269.00	252.10	302.95
1972	222.14	216.00	205.35	203.05	170.95	205.86	213.00	239.04	262.50	256.30	259.00	267.80	226.76
1973	284.59	303.10	320.13	305.81	273.49	262.50	273.95	301.83	280.79	293.45	301.83	293.83	291.27
1974	282.84	279.05	292.07	285.82	288.32	333.35	328.56	296.09	290.00	281.52	270.50	270.50	291.55
1975	223.05	212.50	212.50	202.84	170.00	170.00	149.09	141.00	137.50	131.91	130.00	121.50	166.82
1976	120.55	126.63	127.87	131.64	125.70	113.50	113.50	113.77	120.60	132.17	133.08	132.00	124.25
1977	137.02	168.03	173.50	150.38	135.79	120.68	122.26	123.54	137.57	142.76	135.80	129.12	139.70
1978	143.29	160.58	147.57	147.08	151.98	149.55	157.11	157.00	151.67	152.34	154.55	170.55	153.60
1979	190.80	202.63	224.32	255.00	300.55	343.90	322.34	300.33	313.16	324.13	328.63	362.08	288.99
1980	383.75	399.90	420.00	406.81	398.33	389.57	397.11	397.26	402.62	407.83	404.56	376.19	396.72
1981	366.00	386.79	411.18	423.41	418.50	423.07	433.75	441.14	436.55	425.91	421.84	413.07	416.77
1982	405.00	380.92	390.76	384.32	365.88	367.50	364.29	343.50	352.55	373.21	373.75	374.29	372.98
1983	366.67	346.18	338.91	327.62									
1984													

Source: American Metal Market

T.410

MERCURY

Average Price of Mercury at London   In U.S. Dollars Per Flask

Year	Jan.	Feb.	Mar.	Apr.	May	June	July	Aug.	Sept.	Oct.	Nov.	Dec.	Average
1970	494.3	460.1	464.0	464.0	439.3	414.3	413.0	370.3	355.7	346.2	359.4	358.5	411.45
1971	359.8	359.6	335.8	316.6	285.9	251.1	278.7	255.4	256.0	244.2	233.9	210.2	282.46
1972	208.1	198.8	173.4	141.4	153.3	177.4	191.1	222.5	241.1	237.8	242.8	248.5	203.01
1973	260.7	289.4	303.9	283.0	257.8	243.7	263.4	274.8	266.2	270.7	286.6	282.3	273.54
1974	266.7	269.5	270.3	268.0	274.4	315.6	304.5	274.7	272.2	259.6	245.5	194.4	267.94
1975	183.75	194.69	170.00	141.75	137.06	127.50	114.69	114.67	111.69	103.07	84.08	78.28	130.10
1976	81.38	94.51	99.06	99.63	82.00	82.50	83.25	83.25	87.75	100.23	101.67	108.38	91.07
1977	145.79	165.64	184.44	159.32	138.28	122.79	118.58	122.82	130.63	136.34	126.43	137.32	140.70
1978	131.21	130.50	130.10	132.50	131.25	124.83	127.71	128.00	127.29	126.17	137.38	151.86	131.57
1979	196.00	218.49	241.50	262.29	301.86	343.89	301.00	301.63	310.76	324.46	333.34	365.63	291.73
1980	390.06	393.33	396.56	404.39	394.17	386.88	399.33	408.11	415.00	414.72	399.31	374.94	398.07
1981	368.06	389.00	413.61	421.88	426.67	430.00	429.33	430.56	430.06	427.78	422.38	420.95	417.52
1982													

Source: U.S. Bureau of Mines   T.411

Salient Statistics of Mercury in the United States   In Flasks (76 Pounds Each)

Year	Net Import Reliance as a % of Apparent Consumption	Ore Treated (1,000 Short Tons)	Mercury Produced[2] Flasks	Pounds per Ton of Ore	Production Mine	Production Secondary	Stocks, Dec. 31 Producers	Stocks, Dec. 31 Consumers & Dealers	Total	Exports	U.S. Imports (For Consumption) Total	Canada	Italy	Mexico	Spain	Japan
1970		424.5	26,795	4.8	27,296	8,051	3,861	12,693	16,554	4,653	21,972	17,872	1,101	920	2,002	
1971		265.8	17,444	5.0	17,883	16,666	5,373	11,489	16,862	7,232	28,449	18,198	250	4,786	2,152	
1972		82.6	7,004	6.5	7,349	12,651	4,171	11,537	15,708	400	28,834	13,803	—	5,529	1,829	
1973		26.3	2,101	6.1	2,227	10,329	3,927	14,019	17,946	342	46,026	17,440	1,005	2,775	7,286	
1974		28.9	1,680	4.4	2,189	8,293	4,100	15,777	19,877	466	52,180	16,972	845	10,597	6,293	
1975	69	76.8	6,905	6.8	7,366	8,038	4,858	20,691	25,549	339	43,865	12,891	7,340	2,213	4,575	
1976	62	185.1	23,042	9.5	23,133	3,363	9,494	22,240	31,734	501	44,415	2,853	13,172	1,719	4,824	
1977	44	216.6	28,244	9.9	28,244	6,566	11,275	22,903	34,178	852	28,750	1,708	671	4,668	8,790	
1978	60	256.2	24,144	7.2	24,163	9,262	16,600	22,149	38,749	N.A.	41,693	895	5,913	813	13,923	4,428
1979	59	242.6	29,499	9.2	29,519	15,587	9,181	18,401	27,582	N.A.	26,448	3,943	4,429	403	8,507	7,960
1980	26	356.0	30,623	6.5	30,657	16,806	11,095	21,974	33,069	N.A.	9,416	843	—	989	3,352	3,813
1981[1]	44	262.4	27,888	8.1	27,909	11,244	11,783	15,556	27,339		12,408	112	—	104	4,989	2,372
1982[3]	43				26,137	4,472	14,139	15,015	29,154		8,914	6	—	180	1,403	4,344
1983																

[1] Preliminary.   [2] Excludes mercury produced from placer operation & from clean-up activity at furnaces & other plants.   [3] Estimate.   *Source: Bureau of Mines*   T.412

Mercury Consumed in the United States   In Flasks

Year	Batteries	Chlorine & Rust. Prep.	Catalysts	Dental Prep.	Electrical Lighting[3]	Electrolytic Prep.	General Lab. Use	Industrial & Control Instrum.	Paint Anti-Fouling	Paint Mildew Proofing	Wiring Devices & Switches	Meas. & Control Devices	Other	Grand Total
1970			2,238	2,286	15,952	15,011	1,806	4,832	198	10,149			5,858	61,503
1971			1,012	2,361	16,885	12,154	1,798	4,871	414	8,191			2,407	52,257
1972			800	2,983	15,553	11,519	594	6,541	32	8,190			4,258	52,907
1973			673	2,679	18,000	13,070	658	7,155	32	7,571			1,913	54,283
1974			1,298	3,024	19,678	16,897	476	6,202	6	6,807			2,452	59,479
1975			838	2,340	16,971	15,222	335	4,598	—	6,928			1,750	50,838
1976			1,264	1,990	27,498	16,054	595	5,067	—	7,845			2,909	64,870
1977			1,545	1,230	29,180	10,744	406	5,221	—	8,365			2,589	61,259
1978	13,825	11,166	N.A.	512	10,897	11,166	420	4,078		8,956	3,178	3,489	11,763	59,393
1979	7,988	12,180	548	793	7,719	12,180	410	3,602		9,979	3,213	3,603		62,205
1980	27,829	9,470	265	1,041	1,036	9,470	363	3,049		8,621	3,062	3,049		58,983
1981[1]	29,441	7,323	815	1,866	1,043	7,323	328	5,671		7,049	2,641	5,671		59,244
1982[2]	24,066	6,516		1,027			160			6,794	1,747	2,916		49,418
1983														

[1] Preliminary.   [2] Estimate.   [3] Data prior to 1980 are for Electrical Apparatus.   *Source: Bureau of Mines*   T.413

Milk

Milk production in the U.S. during 1982 totaled 135.8 billion pounds, a gain of 2.8 billion pounds (2.1 percent) over the 1981 record. The increased production was attributed to an increase in dairy cow numbers and in a larger yield per cow. Milk output per cow increased by an average 1.1 percent in 1982 compared with a 2.4 percent increase in 1981. Milk production increases were recorded in 9 of the 10 U.S. farm production regions during 1982, and production on a year-to-year basis declined in only seven states.

The average number of milk cows on farms during 1982 was nearly 1 percent higher than in 1981 compared with gains of 1 percent and 0.6 percent in 1981 and 1980, respectively. 1982 marked the first consecutive 3-year expansion in the average size of the U.S. dairy herd since World War II. The expansion of the dairy herd during 1982 was due to the relatively high number of dairy heifer calves retained in 1980 which, in turn, left a larger number of replacements available to enter the herd. The retention of a greater number of heifers in 1980 was an outcome of two support price increases and producers' expectations of higher dairy incomes. Reflecting negligible support price increases since October 1980, the Omnibus Budget Reconciliation of 1982 Act that authorized a deduction from the cash receipts of marketings, harsh late winter weather and some poor-quality roughage, a record amount of culling slowed the growth of the dairy herd in 1982.

The record dairy herd cull during 1982 partly offset the year's record replacements, and only 54,000 cows were added to the herd. An estimated 230,000 more dairy cows were sent to slaughter during 1982 than were culled during 1981.

The inventory of milk cows on farms as of January 1, 1983 was 11,066,000 head, an increase of 46,000 from the July 1, 1982 inventory, and nearly 54,000 (0.5 percent) over the previous year's number. Dairy heifers (500 pounds and over) held for herd replacement were numbered at 4.5 million head, unchanged from the previous year's number. The number of heifers was nearly 41 per 100 cows compared with the record level of 43.4 on July 1, 1982. Milk cow numbers were expected to decline during 1983, moving to below year-earlier levels by mid-year and then to nearly 100,000 head by the year's end. Cow numbers figured as a yearly average, however, were expected to be unchanged compared with 1982. The 1983 culling rate was expected to continue to be high because of the lower returns for milk brought about by the USDA's 50 cent per cwt. production assessment that went into effect on April 16, 1983. It is thought, however, that the dairy industry's commitment to their large capital investments made since 1979 will tend to slow the reduction in cow numbers, and that the expected heavy culling will again be offset by a large number of replacements. The output per cow is likely to increase by 2 percent in 1983 considering recent annual rates of yield improvement, technological factors, and expected weather conditions. The upshot of increased yields per cow and a slower reduction of cow numbers should be a 1 to 3 percent increase in the 1983 milk production compared to 1982.

During 1982, the average number of producers delivering milk to handlers regulated under Federal milk marketing orders increased by more than 1,000 to nearly 120,600. This represented the third consecutive annual increase in the number of regulated handlers. Producer deliveries to Federal order plants in 1982 totaled 91.6 billion pounds of milk, an increase of about 3 percent over the 1981 level. Milk delivered by producers to Federal order plants accounted for about 68 percent of all milk sold to plants and dealers in the country.

Deliveries of Class I milk (producer milk sold for fluid use) during 1982 rose slightly to nearly 40.8 billion pounds, even though producer deliveries used in Class I products may have dropped by 1 percent in many markets. This small change in Class I use, coupled with an increase in overall producer deliveries caused the annual Class I utilization during 1982 to drop two percentage points to 44 percent.

The Minnesota-Wisconsin (M-W) price series, generally considered to be the basic mover of class prices in Federal order markets, averaged $12.48 per cwt. in 1982, a 9 percent decline from the 1981 price. Class I prices negotiated by cooperative associations also dropped slightly during the year, and estimated average over-order payments during 1982 fell 3 cents. Due to both the drop in the Class I utilization percentage and the decline in minimum class prices, producer blend prices in Federal order markets dropped to $13.53 per cwt., 10 cents below the 1981 average. Sales of fluid milk products in Federal order marketing areas during 1982 decreased 1.3 percent from 1981—the largest year-to-year drop since 1974.

The 1982/83 marketing year support price for milk was $13.10 per cwt. for manufacturing grade milk with 3.67 percent fat. This support price, the minimum allowed under new dairy legislation in Title I of the Omnibus Budget Reconciliation Act of 1982, was in effect during 1980/81 and for most of 1981/82. The support price for milk with 3.5 percent fat was set at $12.80.

On December 1, 1982, the Secretary of Agriculture implemented a 50 cent per cwt. deduction for all milk marketed. The Secretary was authorized to collect the deduction if CCC purchases were expected to be more than 5 billion pounds of milk equivalent during the marketing year. The collected funds were to be remitted to the CCC to offset some of the costs of the dairy price support program. Parties who paid dairy farmers for their milk—usually milk handlers or dairy cooperative associations—were responsible for making the deductions and paying the CCC, as were dairy farmers who sold milk directly to consumers.

Effective April 1, 1983, the Secretary of Agriculture was empowered to provide for the deduction of an additional 50 cents per cwt. as the forecast of net marketing year purchases exceeded 7.5 billion pounds of milk equivalent, this second deduction to be refunded to producers who lowered their output by a specified amount. In his early-1983 announcement of this deduction, Secretary Block said that he would delay implementing a second Congressionally-authorized 50-cent assessment until August 1 in order to give Congress time to adopt more suitable legislation.

MILK

World Fluid Milk Production (Cow's Milk) In Millions of Metric Tons[3]

Year	Australia	Brazil	Canada	Czechoslovakia	Denmark	Finland	W. Germany	USSR	India	Netherlands	New Zealand	France	Poland	Switzerland	United Kingdom	United States
1970	17.0	17.0	18.3	10.6	10.2	7.2	48.2	181.4		18.2	13.0	60.1	'67–'71	6.9	27.3	117.0
1971	16.1	16.3	17.8	10.9	10.0	7.2	46.7	183.4		18.5	13.1	60.9	*(14.8)*	7.0	28.0	118.5
1972[3]	7.3	7.5	8.0	5.0	4.8	3.3	21.5	83.2		9.0	6.2	29.9	15.9	3.2	13.4	54.3
1973	7.3	7.2	7.7	5.3	4.7	3.2	21.3	88.3		9.4	6.0	30.4	16.6	3.3	14.3	52.4
1974	7.0	8.5	7.6	5.3	4.9	3.1	21.5	91.8		9.9	5.7	30.6	17.0	3.4	13.7	52.4
1975	6.7	8.8	7.7	5.3	4.9	3.2	21.6	90.8		10.2	5.9	30.9	16.7	3.4	13.5	52.3
1976	6.4	9.3	7.7	5.4	5.0	3.3	22.2	89.7	9.7	10.5	6.4	29.5	16.5	3.5	14.4	54.6
1977	5.9	9.5	7.7	5.5	5.1	3.2	22.5	94.9	9.8	10.6	6.6	30.2	16.9	3.5	15.2	55.7
1978	5.6	10.5	7.5	5.6	5.3	3.2	23.3	94.7	10.1	11.4	6.1	25.9	17.1	3.5	15.9	55.1
1979	5.8	10.1	7.6	5.7	5.2	3.2	23.9	93.3	12.5	11.6	6.5	26.5	16.9	3.6	15.9	56.0
1980	5.6	10.3	7.9	5.9	5.1	3.3	24.8	90.6	15.5	11.8	6.8	28.0	16.7	3.7	16.0	58.3
1981[1]	5.3	10.5	8.0	6.0	5.0	3.2	24.8	88.5	16.5	12.2	6.7	28.2	15.5	3.6	15.9	60.2
1982[2]	5.4	10.8	8.1	6.0	5.0	3.2	25.0	87.0	17.0	12.4	6.7	28.7	16.0	3.7	16.0	61.6
1983																

[1] Preliminary. [2] Estimate. [3] Data prior to 1972 are in BILLIONS OF POUNDS. *Source: Foreign Agricultural Service, U.S.D.A.*   T.414

Milk Cows & Cattle and Milk Production in the U.S.

Year	Number of Milk Cows on Farms[2] (Thousands)	Production Per Milk Cow[3] Milk Pounds	Production Per Milk Cow[3] Milk Fat	Total Milk Production[3] Quantity Billion Pounds	Total Milk Production[3] % of Fat in All Milk Produced	Milk Fat Mil. Lbs.	Milk Sold to Plants & Dealers Quantity Billion Pounds	Milk Sold to Plants & Dealers $ Per 100 Lbs.	Milk Sold Directly to Consumers Quantity Million Quarts	Milk Sold Directly to Consumers ¢ Per Quart	Milk Utilized Bill. Lbs.	Farm Value of All Milk Mill. $
1970	12,000	9,751	357	117.0	3.66	4,284	110.1	5.71	798.6	27.0	113.0	6,757
1971	11,839	10,015	367	118.6	3.66	4,344	112.2	5.87	731.2	27.9	114.8	7,035
1972	11,700	10,259	377	120.0	3.68	4,410	114.2	6.07	714.8	27.8	116.5	7,361
1973	11,413	10,119	370	115.5	3.66	4,225	109.9	7.14	706.9	31.0	112.1	8,331
1974	11,230	10,293	377	115.6	3.67	4,238	110.4	8.33	718.0	34.9	112.4	9,723
1975	11,139	10,360	381	115.4	3.68	4,240	110.5	8.75	726.8	35.4	112.3	10,199
1976	11,032	10,894	399	120.2	3.66	4,402	115.5	9.66	703.1	36.4	117.2	11,706
1977	10,945	11,206	410	122.7	3.65	4,481	118.2	9.72	695.2	36.7	119.8	12,023
1978	10,803	11,243	412	121.5	3.67	4,455	117.2	10.58	693.2	38.8	118.8	12,957
1979	10,743	11,488	421	123.4	3.66	4,518	119.4	12.00	698.8	42.3	120.9	14,949
1980	10,810	11,889	434	128.5	3.65	4,696	124.7	13.00	683.5	45.3	126.2	16,890
1981[1]	10,923	12,177	442	133.0	3.64	4,827	128.8	13.80	699.2	48.4	130.3	18,399
1982[1]	11,026	12,316		135.8				13.55				
1983												

[1] Preliminary. [2] Average number on farms during year excluding heifers not yet fresh. [3] Excludes milk sucked by calves & milk produced by cows not on farms. *Source: Crop Reporting Board, U.S.D.A.*   T.415

Utilization of Milk in the United States   In Millions of Pounds (Milk Equivalent)

Year	Butter from Whey Cream	Creamery Butter[1]	Cheese[6]	Cottage Cheese (Creamed)	Condensed Whole Milk	Evaporated Milk[5]	Dry Whole Milk Products	Frozen Dairy Products[2]	Fluid Consumption Nonfarm	Fluid Consumption Farm[5]	Fed to Calves	Other Mfg. Products[4]
1970	1,659	23,934	19,566	1,250	572	2,687	508	11,041	51,998	2,306	1,702	480
1971	1,820	23,904	20,947	1,296	537	2,702	535	10,973	51,853	2,117	1,635	705
1972	1,981	22,744	22,763	1,321	594	2,540	552	10,951	53,227	1,914	1,624	762
1973	2,054	18,609	23,605	1,138	560	2,375	577	11,070	52,413	1,766	1,584	744
1974	2,237	19,334	25,669	1,018	592	2,223	499	11,188	50,514	1,643	1,558	804
1975	2,119	19,873	23,883	1,028	686	2,020	464	11,898	51,123	1,505	1,566	672
1976	2,543	19,404	28,763	1,050	643	1,892	554	11,623	51,502	1,404	1,567	744
1977	2,543	21,853	28,865	1,056	580	1,809	514	11,707	51,380	1,295	1,541	684
1978	2,660	19,712	29,917	1,056	534	1,725	549	11,744	51,175	1,168	1,497	707
1979	2,810	19,381	31,557	1,028	568	1,752	627	11,679	51,386	1,031	1,437	1,811
1980[3]	2,998	22,826	33,925	1,016	524	1,594	607	11,926	50,933	943	1,395	1,667
1981[7]		24,500	36,500	1,000	— 2,300 —		700	12,000	50,200	902	1,420	
1982[7]		25,500	37,500	1,000	— 2,200 —		700	12,200	49,500	880		
1983												

[1] Excludes whey butter. [2] From milk and cream only. [3] Preliminary. [4] Includes dry cream, malted milk, dry part skim milk, dry ice cream mix. [5] Data includes evaporated & sweetened condensed milk. [6] American & other. [7] Estimate. *Source: Crop Reporting Board, U.S.D.A.*   T.416

MILK

Milk Production on Farms in the United States   In Millions of Pounds

Year	Jan.	Feb.	Mar.	Apr.	May	June	July	Aug.	Sept.	Oct.	Nov.	Dec.	Total
1970	9,405	8,857	10,103	10,295	11,053	10,708	10,212	9,734	9,203	9,278	8,837	9,321	117,007
1971	9,576	8,994	10,220	10,423	11,159	10,815	10,285	9,860	9,328	9,444	9,004	9,427	118,532
1972	9,728	9,391	10,452	10,566	11,268	10,946	10,442	9,978	9,431	9,437	8,911	9,362	119,904
1973	9,532	8,932	10,176	10,298	10,952	10,532	10,014	9,489	8,877	8,948	8,590	9,052	115,491
1974	9,335	8,763	9,989	10,124	10,869	10,615	10,171	9,711	9,137	9,100	8,663	9,109	115,586
1975	9,344	8,766	9,986	10,092	10,778	10,447	9,972	9,538	9,063	9,180	8,830	9,341	115,334
1976	9,600	9,290	10,281	10,464	11,110	10,806	10,444	10,129	9,607	9,626	9,231	9,681	120,269
1977	9,887	9,301	10,572	10,725	11,354	10,989	10,671	10,363	9,820	9,838	9,391	9,787	122,698
1978	9,958	9,242	10,491	10,610	11,151	10,817	10,503	10,182	9,683	9,780	9,320	9,724	121,461
1979	9,960	9,281	10,534	10,603	11,243	10,948	10,683	10,409	9,987	10,063	9,623	10,077	123,411
1980	10,320	9,972	10,945	11,024	11,697	11,335	11,075	10,792	10,353	10,461	10,055	10,494	128,525
1981[1]	10,805	10,161	11,549	11,555	12,099	11,606	11,387	11,132	10,659	10,768	10,387	10,905	133,013
1982[1]	11,116	10,391	11,728	11,650	12,248	11,825	11,648	11,375	10,960	11,055	10,645	11,154	135,795
1983[1]	11,292	10,627											

[1] Preliminary.   Source: Crop Reporting Board, U.S.D.A.   T.417

Average Price Received by U.S. Farmers for All Milk[2] (Sold to Plants)   In Dollars Per Cwt.

Year	Jan.	Feb.	Mar.	Apr.	May	June	July	Aug.	Sept.	Oct.	Nov.	Dec.	Average[1]
1970	5.59	5.58	5.61	5.82	5.93	5.93	5.69	5.64	5.61	5.68	5.75	5.84	5.71
1971	5.79	5.85	5.89	5.96	6.03	5.92	5.84	5.81	5.75	6.07	5.82	5.93	5.87
1972	5.95	6.04	6.07	6.09	6.23	6.14	6.02	6.06	5.97	6.02	6.15	6.29	6.07
1973	6.36	6.50	6.59	6.67	6.88	6.88	6.83	7.26	7.54	7.83	8.16	8.47	7.14
1974	8.89	8.92	8.96	8.84	8.26	7.69	7.75	7.75	8.08	8.35	8.49	8.27	8.33
1975	8.43	8.38	8.22	8.18	8.07	7.99	8.25	8.64	9.25	9.70	10.00	10.30	8.75
1976	10.10	9.76	9.75	9.40	9.25	9.14	9.43	9.70	9.84	9.96	9.89	9.72	9.66
1977	9.65	9.53	9.45	9.44	9.37	9.40	9.49	9.66	9.97	10.10	10.20	10.20	9.72
1978	10.20	10.20	10.20	10.10	10.10	10.00	10.10	10.50	10.90	11.30	11.60	11.80	10.60
1979[3]	11.90	11.90	11.80	11.60	11.50	11.50	11.60	12.00	12.30	12.60	12.90	12.80	12.00
1980[3]	12.80	12.80	12.80	12.70	12.60	12.50	12.60	12.80	13.20	13.70	14.00	14.10	13.00
1981[3]	14.10	14.00	13.80	13.88	13.50	13.40	13.40	13.50	13.70	14.00	14.00	14.00	13.80
1982[3]	13.90	13.80	13.60	13.40	13.20	13.10	13.20	13.20	13.50	13.80	14.00	13.90	13.55
1983[3]	13.80	13.80											

[1] Weighted average.   [2] Adjusted for seasonal variation.   [3] Preliminary.   Source: Crop Reporting Board, U.S.D.A.   T.418

Farm Price of Milk[1] Eligible for Fluid Market   In Dollars Per Hundred Pounds

Year	Jan.	Feb.	Mar.	Apr.	May	June	July	Aug.	Sept.	Oct.	Nov.	Dec.	Average
1972	6.42	6.43	6.31	6.13	6.07	5.99	6.09	6.32	6.57	6.72	7.34	7.39	6.38
1973	6.84	6.90	6.83	6.68	6.67	6.68	6.85	7.45	8.13	8.55	8.89	9.02	7.42
1974	9.09	9.13	9.19	9.16	8.68	8.10	8.00	8.11	8.40	8.67	8.83	8.63	8.66
1975	8.77	8.70	8.51	8.46	8.33	8.24	8.51	8.89	9.49	9.91	10.20	10.50	9.02
1976	10.40	10.10	10.00	9.63	9.49	9.36	9.64	9.91	10.10	10.30	10.20	9.99	9.93
1977	9.91	9.79	9.67	9.63	9.56	9.61	9.72	9.91	10.20	10.40	10.50	10.40	9.96
1978	10.50	10.50	10.40	10.30	10.30	10.20	10.30	10.70	11.00	11.50	11.80	12.00	10.80
1979	12.00	12.10	11.90	11.80	11.70	11.60	11.80	12.20	12.50	12.80	13.10	13.00	12.20
1980	13.00	13.00	12.90	12.80	12.70	12.70	12.70	13.00	13.40	13.90	14.10	14.30	13.20
1981	14.30	14.20	14.00	13.80	13.70	13.60	13.60	13.70	14.00	14.00	14.20	14.20	13.96
1982	14.10	14.00	13.80	13.60	13.40	13.30	13.30	13.40	13.70	14.00	14.10	14.10	13.73
1983	14.10	14.00											

[1] MILK, Standard Grade, 3.5% milkfat. Weighted average price per 100 pounds (f.o.b. city).   Source: Crop Reporting Board, U.S.D.A.   T.419

U.S. Milk-Feed Price Ratio[1]   In Pounds

Year	Jan.	Feb.	Mar.	Apr.	May	June	July	Aug.	Sept.	Oct.	Nov.	Dec.	Average
1978	1.50	1.52	1.51	1.47	1.49	1.43	1.45	1.54	1.59	1.64	1.62	1.63	1.53
1979	1.62	1.59	1.58	1.56	1.53	1.51	1.43	1.51	1.54	1.55	1.59	1.55	1.55
1980	1.54	1.57	1.55	1.55	1.53	1.50	1.47	1.42	1.39	1.42	1.40	1.38	1.48
1981	1.39	1.39	1.41	1.39	1.35	1.36	1.40	1.43	1.48	1.53	1.56	1.54	1.44
1982	1.55	1.54	1.52	1.50	1.46	1.46	1.47	1.49	1.56	1.61	1.62	1.60	1.53
1983	1.58	1.56											

[1] Pounds of 16% protein ration equal in value to one pound of milk.   Source: Economics & Statistics Service, U.S.D.A.   T.420

Molasses

Preliminary USDA estimates placed the 1982/83 world production of industrial molasses at approximately 34.4 million tonnes, nearly 1.3 percent below the revised 1981/82 estimate of 34.8 million. Molasses, a byproduct of sugarbeet and sugarcane processing, is used primarily as a livestock feed and in alcohol and yeast production. The lower 1982/83 molasses output was generally attributed to the smaller world sugar production expected during the season. Brazil is the world's largest producer of molasses, with an estimated 1982/83 output of 6 million tonnes. India is second with 2.8 million, and the Soviet Union is third with 2.7 million.

Total U.S. imports of molasses during calendar 1982 amounted to nearly 1.08 million tonnes, almost 4 percent above imports during 1981. At the same time, the dollar value of U.S. molasses imports in 1982 was $59.5 million compared with $112.2 million in the previous year, a decline of almost 47 percent reflecting much lower unit prices than a year ago.

New Orleans prices for mostly bulk, wholesale cane molasses were $50 per ton in January 1982. Prices gradually fell to $40 per ton by November 1982, and then rose with the overall increase in spot commodity prices to $44 per ton as of January 1983. Los Angeles prices for beet pulp molasses rose by $8 to $124 per ton between January and March 1982 before dropping sharply to the 1982 low of $112 per ton in April. As of January 1983, beet pulp molasses in Los Angeles was priced at $121 per ton.

World Production of Molasses (Industrial) In Thousands of Metric Tons

Crop Year	Argentina	Brazil	Cuba[2]	France	W. Germany	India	Italy	Mexico	Philippines	Poland	Australia	United Kingdom	United States	USSR	World Total
1973-4	638	2,069	1,312	1,200	669	2,000	250	1,240	1,000	514	599	325	1,596	2,842	26,927
1974-5	612	2,950	1,312	1,179	712	2,000	302	1,227	890	514	586	235	1,592	2,746	26,905
1975-6	557	2,400	1,364	1,013	842	1,700	330	1,227	1,050	642	620	255	1,813	2,735	27,244
1976-7	557	3,000	1,391	1,087	831	2,059	330	1,076	940	670	642	310	2,235	2,700	29,296
1977-8	599	5,400	1,436	1,050	781	2,971	340	1,340	808	656	642	100	2,195	3,242	33,530
1978-9	818	5,000	1,296	952	685	2,564	365	1,410	818	657	577	103	2,148	3,306	32,688
1979-0	789	4,800	1,185	958	653	1,582	390	1,260	818	653	598	350	2,054	3,062	30,052
1980-1[1]	654	5,400	1,111	1,013	657	2,129	410	1,141	860	430	713	360	2,012	2,669	30,907
1981-2[3]	565	4,520	1,200	1,294	836	3,400	500	1,289	885	665	719	350	2,051	2,385	34,075
1982-3[3]	541	5,073	1,050	1,250	780	3,000	370	1,280	930	636	725	400	2,010	2,530	33,925

[1] Preliminary. [2] Includes hi-test molasses. [3] Estimate. Source: Foreign Agricultural Service, U.S.D.A. T.421

Salient Statistics of Industrial Molasses in the United States In Millions of Gallons

Year	Mainland Cane	Domestic Beet	Refiners' Blackstrap	Citrus	Hydrol	Total	Imports	Total Available Supplies	Exports	Distilled Spirits	Pharmaceuticals & Other Edibles	Yeast, Citric Acid & Vinegar	Total Industrial	Livestock Feeding[2]	Total Utilization
1972	125.6	166.6	39.1	8.3	22.5	362.1	406.8	828.4	3.1	6	57	99	163	678	844
1973	112.4	158.1	44.9	9.8	23.0	348.2	403.3	797.9	4.7	13	59	100	164	641	814
1974	102.1	155.9	45.0	10.6	23.5	337.1	384.3	755.3	12.6	18	59	100	175	559	739
1975	125.4	188.2	45.0	10.2	24.5	393.3	303.3	739.6	12.6	18	59	100	175	559	739
1976	131.7	158.0	50.3	5.8	37.0	382.9	411.2	829.7	6.3	6.9	60.0	100.5	167.4	572.2	740
1977	114.3	167.1	50.7	5.2	39.7	377.0	347.6	743.9	11.2	3.5	48.2	100.9	152.6	665.8	818
1978	106.7	140.2	44.6	4.3	41.7	337.5	271.0	639.8	22.9	7.4	25.6	92.7	125.7	618.2	744
1979	107.4	164.6	39.0	3.5	40.3	354.8	231.7	624.8	20.3	8.8	19.3	77.7	105.8	519.0	624.8
1980	109.7	113.3	34.7	6.3	39.7	352.1	140.3	468.8	19.3	8.2	18.8	77.5	104.5	364.3	468.8
1981[1]	122.8	148.7	41.4	6.1	19.5	338.5	149.0	524.8	23.7	4.9	19.1	75.2	99.2	425.6	524.8

[1] Preliminary. [2] Residual. Source: Agricultural Marketing Service, U.S.D.A. T.422

U.S. Annual Average Prices of Molasses, by Types (F.O.B. Tank Car or Truck) In Dollars Per Ton[1]

Year	New Orleans	South Florida	Baltimore	Minneapolis	Omaha	Calif. Ports	Colorado	Wyo. & Montana	Ore., Utah & Idaho	Citrus Molasses Florida
1974	68.37	67.40	72.25	88.63	88.37	70.82	78.65	78.65	71.26	45.81
1975	45.32	45.63	51.37	62.75	63.81	50.03	55.80	61.81	59.70	41.97
1976	52.07	51.41	57.60	72.28	70.46	52.96	66.87	65.02	61.79	39.52
1977	40.55	42.52	47.08	54.62	58.84	42.96	41.76	45.41	55.10	50.65
1978	51.50	52.40	59.25	67.30	72.55	54.00	60.40	58.35	60.95	61.05
1979	82.95	85.50	91.20	107.90	107.75	84.05	85.30	82.65	N.A.	79.40
1980	96.50	96.80	106.75	124.45	128.85	101.70	95.60	96.55	N.A.	103.65
1981[2]	84.90	90.00	99.30	111.20	119.40	89.20	85.30	95.20	N.A.	103.10

Blackstrap columns: New Orleans, South Florida, Baltimore, Minneapolis, Omaha, Calif. Ports. Beet Molasses columns: Colorado, Wyo. & Montana, Ore., Utah & Idaho.

[1] Per ton prices are based on 171 gallons for blackstrap, beet and corn molasses and on 175 gallons for citrus molasses. Prices represent sales F.O.B. terminal to the general feed trade and do not include sales made under various pricing arrangements above or below prices generally available to the ultimate user. Ton—2,000 lbs. Gallon—U.S. gallon. Prices are not rounded off to the nearest 5 cents. [2] Preliminary. Source: *Molasses Market News, Annual Summary,* AMS, U.S.D.A. Denver Colorado, and *Molasses Market News, Weekly,* various issues T.423

MOLASSES

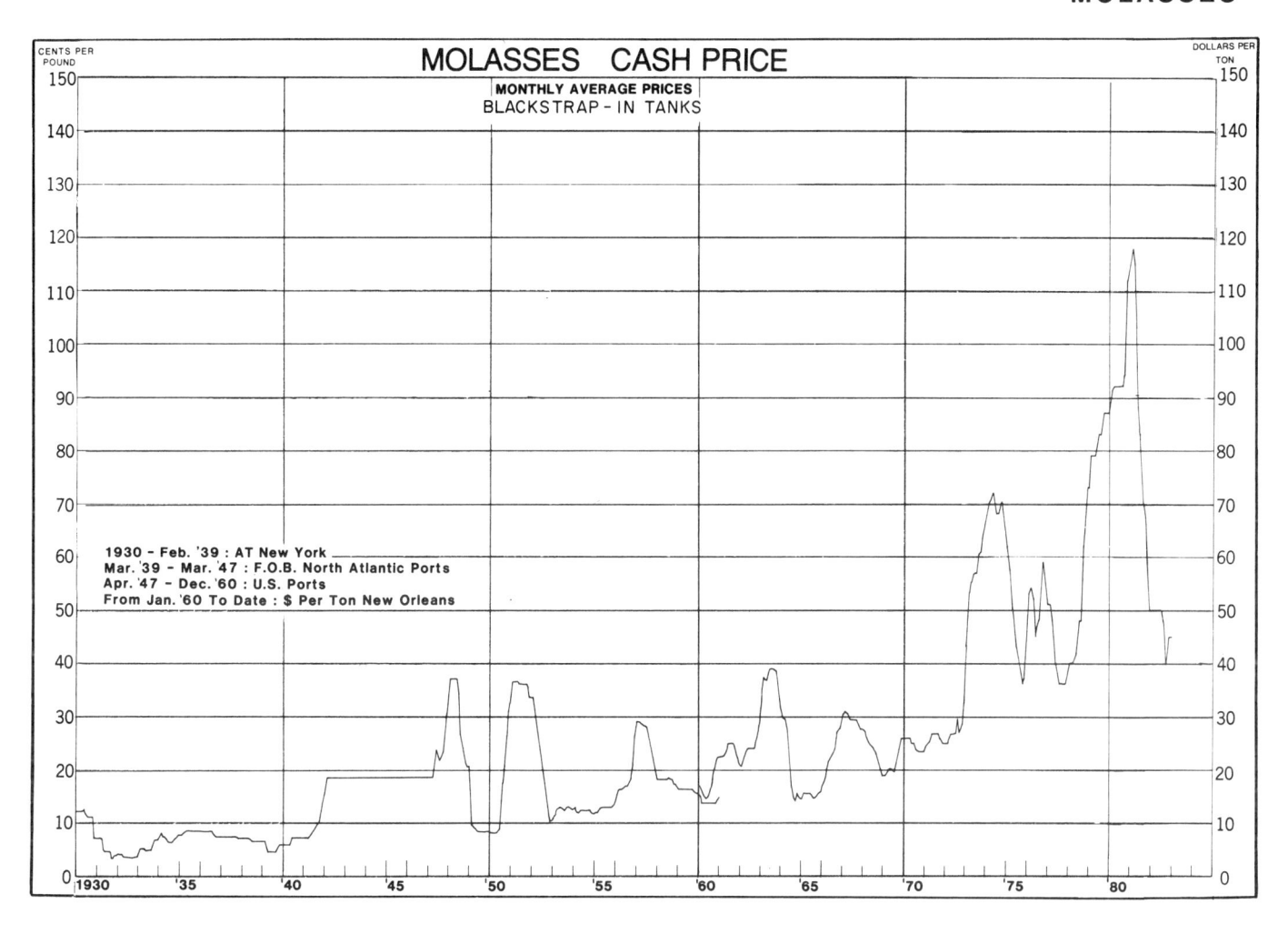

MOLASSES CASH PRICE
MONTHLY AVERAGE PRICES
BLACKSTRAP - IN TANKS

1930 - Feb. '39 : AT New York
Mar. '39 - Mar. '47 : F.O.B. North Atlantic Ports
Apr. '47 - Dec. '60 : U.S. Ports
From Jan. '60 To Date : $ Per Ton New Orleans

Wholesale Price of Blackstrap Molasses (Cane) at New Orleans In Dollars Per Ton

Year	Jan.	Feb.	Mar.	Apr.	May	June	July	Aug.	Sept.	Oct.	Nov.	Dec.	Average
1970	25.65	25.65	25.65	25.65	24.80	24.80	23.50	23.20	23.10	23.10	23.20	23.10	24.28
1971	24.20	24.60	25.00	26.50	26.50	26.50	26.50	26.50	25.60	25.20	24.80	24.80	25.56
1972	24.80	24.80	26.00	26.50	26.50	26.50	26.60	29.60	26.90	27.40	28.40	32.40	27.20
1973	43.20	48.90	53.40	55.20	56.40	57.00	57.00	60.10	60.80	64.20	65.50	67.75	57.45
1974	68.80	70.50	71.00	72.00	69.50	68.00	68.00	69.25	70.40	67.00	64.00	62.00	68.37
1975	60.00	57.75	51.30	50.00	46.00	43.00	41.00	39.00	38.00	36.00	37.00	46.00	45.42
1976	53.00	54.00	53.00	52.00	45.00	47.00	48.00	54.00	59.00	57.00	52.00	51.00	52.08
1977	51.00	51.00	48.00	42.00	40.00	38.00	36.00	36.00	36.00	36.00	36.00	38.00	40.67
1978	40.00	40.00	40.00	41.00	42.00	46.00	48.00	48.00	56.00	65.00	73.00	73.00	51.08
1979	79.00	79.00	79.00	79.00	81.00	83.00	83.00	85.00	87.00	87.00	87.00	87.00	83.00
1980	89.90	91.50	92.00	92.00	92.00	92.00	92.00	92.00	94.40	103.50	111.60	113.00	96.40
1981	116.75	118.00	115.00	103.00	95.50	88.00	83.00	71.60	67.50	58.75	52.00	50.00	76.30
1982	50.00	50.00	50.00	50.00	50.00	50.00	50.00	48.00	48.00	44.00	40.00	41.00	47.60
1983	44.00	45.00	45.00	45.00									
1984													

Source: Economics Service, U.S.D.A.

T.424

Molybdenum

An estimated 46 billion pounds of molybdenum exists in the identified world resources. Molybdenum is found as the principal metal sulfide in large low-grade porphyry molybdenum deposits and as a subsidiary metal sulfide in low-grade porphyry copper deposits.

The U.S. Bureau of Mines estimated total world mine production of molybdenum during 1982 at 27 percent below the 1981 level of 223.8 million pounds. Production in the U.S. and in Chile accounted for 40 percent and 25 percent of the worldwide output, respectively. Known resources of molybdenum are thought to be adequate for the satisfaction of world demand through the foreseeable future.

Nearly 41 percent of the worldwide resources of molybdenum are located in the U.S. The U.S. output of molybdenum from both molybdenum and copper mining operations was sharply curtailed in 1982, and mine capacity utilization at the end of the first ten months of the year was down to 45 percent. Because of depressed markets, prices for exported material dropped, and, in contrast to the market of two years earlier, merchant prices fell below the producer price level. All primary producing operations were closed down and were scheduled to remain closed through the first quarter of 1983. The Bureau of Mines estimated 1983 U.S. consumption at nearly 75 million pounds.

The apparent U.S. demand for molybdenum during 1982 was expected to decline by 46 percent compared with the 1981 level. Iron and steel producers consumed about 75 percent of the molybdenum used in the U.S. in 1982 and the two major end use applications were in the machinery and gas industries. Presently, there is little substitution for molybdenum as an alloying element in steels, cast irons, and nonferrous metals. U.S. apparent consumption during 1983 was projected at 33 million pounds, and U.S. demand, figured from a 1978 base, was projected as increasing at an annual rate of 4.2 percent through 1990.

Domestic producer molybdenum stocks in concentrate, oxide, and other product forms increased by 4 percent in 1982 to 84.0 million pounds.

World Mine Production of Molybdenum   In 1,000 Pounds (Contained Molybdenum)

Year	Canada[3]	Australia	Bulgaria	Chile	USSR	Japan	South Korea	China	Mexico	Norway	Philippines	United States	Peru	World Total
1970	33,772			12,569	17,000	582	254	3,300	311	750	71	111,352	1,338	181,429
1971	22,663			13,935	17,600	613	231	3,300	174	725	9	109,592	1,782	171,064
1972	28,493			13,045	18,100	494	111	3,300	172	562	—	112,138	1,689	178,423
1973	30,391			12,974	18,700	345	112	3,300	90	220	—	115,859	1,395	183,698
1974	30,736			21,466	19,400	235	166	3,300	95	—	—	112,011	1,434	185,568
1975	28,719	25		20,042	20,000	309	166	3,300	37	—	—	105,980	1,435	180,288
1976	32,229	0	300	24,028	20,600	485	265	3,300	35	—	—	113,233	999	195,474
1977	36,526	0	330	24,112	21,400	401	223	3,300	2	—	—	122,408	1,005	209,707
1978	30,739	—	330	29,092	21,800	271	485	4,440	24	—	121	131,843	1,607	220,712
1979	24,634	—	330	29,895	22,500	258	417	4,400	105	—	311	143,967	2,606	229,423
1980[1]	26,211	—	330	30,133	22,900	209	661	4,400	130	—	130	150,686	5,860	241,745
1981[2]	31,160	—	330	33,300	24,000	175	692	4,400	—	—	175	139,900	5,485	223,800
1982	29,000			46,000								75,000	6,000	186,000
1983														

[1] Preliminary.   [2] Estimate.   [3] Shipments.   Source: Bureau of Mines   T.425

U.S. Salient Statistics of Molybdenum   In Thous. of Pounds (of Contained Molybdenum)

| | | Concentrate | | | | | | Net Production | | | Primary Products[3] | | | |
| | | Shipments | | | | | | | | | Shipments | | | |
Year	Production	Total (Includes Exports)	Value Mill. $	For Exports	Consumption	Imports for Consumption	Stocks Dec. 31[2]	Grand Total	Molybdic Oxide[4]	Molybdenum Metal Powder	Sodium Molybdate	To Domestic Destinations	For Exports	Consumption	Producers' Stocks Dec. 31
1970	111,352	110,381	190.1	32,998	76,101	25	9,715	75,383	57,669	1,741	743	58,365	17,730	45,337	25,904
1971	109,592	97,882	164.9	31,513	66,399	854	29,077	67,016	49,918	2,418	865	52,644	14,010	40,950	31,048
1972	112,138	102,197	170.5	34,390	62,560	385	45,243	64,841	47,934	3,637	1,111	59,420	16,118	45,558	28,898
1973	115,859	135,097	217.7	48,529	82,477	458	21,998	85,046	63,280	3,631	1,538	67,365	41,322	57,049	22,387
1974	112,011	118,163	234.7	39,965	91,706	155	18,659	88,509	66,378	2,953	1,784	75,929	38,870	63,476	16,078
1975	105,980	105,170	259.3	36,618	90,046	2,567	10,680	87,501	70,143	2,953	1,069	89,789	33,084	51,743	22,863
1976	113,233	114,527	333.5	30,935	84,966	2,093	9,390	83,970	65,743	3,839	1,132	99,144	31,796	50,448	13,210
1977	122,408	124,974	450.4	29,666	91,041	1,976	9,161	90,520	68,671	4,142	1,275	100,626	33,332	54,557	10,141
1978	131,843	130,694	608.0	31,183	96,375	2,705	8,980	96,052	83,220	4,194	1,489	105,921	35,353	61,091	7,996
1979	143,967	143,504	871.1	36,405	103,152	2,329	9,520	101,752	79,035	4,946	1,541	109,419	35,773	60,388	8,502
1980	150,686	149,311	1,344	35,026	108,206	1,825	18,101	106,284	84,554	4,904	1,142	95,391	35,557	53,265	27,007
1981[1]	139,900	118,916	946	37,328	80,725	1,988	35,548	76,840	59,645	3,513	96	64,368	20,004	50,189	44,961
1982[5]	65,948	65,170		21,542	49,444		34,581	50,000	35,346	3,303	121	48,000			50,000
1983															

[1] Preliminary.   [2] At mines & at plants making molybdenum products.   [3] Comprises ferromolybdenum, molybdic oxide, & molybdenum salts & metal.   [4] Includes molybdic oxide briquets, molybdic acid, & molybdenum trioxide.   [5] Estimate.   Source: Bureau of Mines   T.426

Nickel

World resources of nickel total nearly 143 million short tons in deposits averaging approximately 1 percent nickel or greater. Worldwide deposits of lower-grade nickel are very large, and extensive resources of nickel exist in manganese nodules covering large areas of ocean floor. The 1982 world mine production of nickel was tentatively estimated by the Bureau of Mines at 576,000 tons, nearly 25 percent below the 1981 level. The major producers were Canada and the Soviet Union.

The major U.S. use of nickel during 1982 was reported in the production of stainless and alloy steel, 45 percent; nonferrous alloys, 30 percent; and in electroplating, 15 percent. Total U.S. primary nickel consumption in 1982 was 17 percent below the 1981 level. Estimates indicate that the 1983 U.S. mine production of nickel will be less than 3,000 tons, and that apparent consumption will be 175,000 tons. From a 1981 base, the U.S. demand for primary nickel is expected to grow at an annual 2.1 percent through 1990.

The U.S. consumer stocks of nickel at the end of 1982 were estimated by the Bureau of Mines to be 18 percent below the 1981 figure.

Futures Market

Nickel futures are traded on the London Metal Exchange (LME).

World Mine Production of Nickel   In Thousands of Short Tons of Contained Nickel

Year	Australia[3]	Philippines	Canada	Cuba	Finland[3]	Indonesia	Brazil	Domin. Repub.	Zimbabwe	N. Caledonia	Greece	Botswana	South Africa	USSR	United States	World Trade
1974	22.0	—	296.6	37.4	6.6	23.3	3.9	33.6	12.7	148.3	31.4		24.4	138.0	16.6	849.3
1975	40.0	10.3	367.0	40.3	6.1	21.2	3.5	29.7	11.0	146.9	31.0		22.9	168.0	17.0	890.5
1976	91.0	16.8	265.5	40.7	7.2	31.7	5.8	26.9	16.1	121.2	18.8		24.7	155.0	16.5	873.4
1977	94.7	40.5	256.3	40.5	6.7	36.5	4.7	27.4	18.4	124.9	24.9	13.3	25.1	162.0	14.3	412.9
1978	90.8	32.5	141.4	38.3	5.1	34.6	4.0	15.8	17.3	71.8	20.4	17.7	31.6	164.0	13.5	722.8
1979	76.8	36.7	139.4	35.6	6.4	34.2	3.3	27.7	16.1	88.7	22.2	17.8	33.3	166.0	15.1	748.8
1980[1]	81.9	42.2	203.7	42.1	7.2	33.6	2.8	18.0	16.6	95.5	16.8	17.0	28.3	170.0	14.7	820.9
1981[2]	81.6	40.8	176.0	44.6	7.6	28.7	2.6	21.5	12.7	82.1	17.2	18.2	29.1	174.0	12.1	772.0
1982[2]	70.0	35.0	90.0	35.0		14.0				35.0	17.0	18.0	29.0	170.0	3.2	576.0

[1] Preliminary.   [2] Estimate.   [3] Content of nickel sulfate and concentrates.   Source: Bureau of Mines   T.427

Salient Statistics of Nickel in the United States   In Short Tons

Year	Net Import Reliance as a % of Apparent Consumption	Production Primary	Production Secondary	Alloy Steels	Cast Irons	Copper Base Alloys	Magnet Alloys	Electroplating Anodes	Nickel Alloys	Stainless & Heat Resisting Steels	Super Alloys	Chemicals	Total All	Stocks, Dec. 31 At Consumers' Plants	Nickel & Pdt's Imports (Gross Weight)	Exports (Gross Weight)
1973		13,895	32,629	44.7	6.8	17.1	10.5	51.1	85.8	17.2			197,723	28,759	190,418	22,070
1974		14,093	20,930	23.3	5.3	9.3	5.3	26.2	44.1	73.8			208,409	45,291	220,655	30,442
1975	72	14,343	17,880	20.3	4.4	9.4	3.3	19.2	37.2	38.2			146,495	35,485	160,507	30,121
1976	72	13,869	13,273	19.1	4.0	7.4	5.8	28.7	32.5	48.6	9.1	2.6	162,927	31,690	188,147	47,166
1977	75	12,897	12,449	17.8	3.7	7.0	.7	21.8	31.9	53.2	11.4	2.5	155,260	18,581	194,770	39,412
1978	80	11,298	12,304	17.2	4.3	7.0	.8	27.3	39.6	60.5	15.7	1.9	180,723	20,443	234,352	36,293
1979	69	11,691	13,201	20.2	4.7	8.5	.7	28.5	41.1	69.6	17.6	1.2	196,293	19,518	177,205	50,810
1980	73	11,225	11,338	16.9	4.0	8.8	.5	18.8	27.4	54.7	19.2	1.5	156,299	15,231	189,188	56,675
1981[2]	72	10,305	N.A.	16.5	3.7	10.6	.5	22.3	10.6	50.6	13.5	2.0	144,748	22,508	200,348	46,778
1982[3]				17.5	2.5	7.6	.7	40.9	32.9	58.1	17.8	1.6	185,351	31,813	263,135	100,000

[1] Exclusive of scrap   [2] Preliminary   [3] Estimate   Source: Bureau of Mines   T.428

Average Price of Nickel (Spot Cathode Sheets—Duty Paid—F.O.B. Refinery)
In Cents Per Pound—In Carload or Truckload Lots

Year	Jan.	Feb.	Mar.	Apr.	May	June	July	Aug.	Sept.	Oct.	Nov.	Dec.	Average
1973	153.0	153.0	153.0	153.0	153.0	153.0	153.0	153.0	153.0	153.0	153.0	153.0	153.0
1974	162.0	162.0	162.0	162.0	162.0	162.0	185.0	185.0	185.0	185.0	185.0	185.0	173.5
1975	201.0	201.0	201.0	201.0	201.0	201.0	201.0	201.0	220.0	220.0	220.0	220.0	207.3
1976	220.0	220.0	220.0	220.0	220.0	220.0	220.0	220.0	220.0	241.0	241.0	241.0	225.3
1977	241.0	241.0	241.0	238.0	241.0	241.0	241.0	241.0	215.5	215.5	210.0	207.0	231.1
1978	207.0	207.0	207.0	210.0	210.0	200.0	208.0	208.0	204.0	202.5	202.5	196.5	205.2
1979	196.5	205.0	205.0	242.5	272.5	305.0	302.5	302.5	302.5	302.5	302.5	315.0	271.2
1980	325.0	325.0	350.0	350.0	350.0	350.0	350.0	350.0	305.0	305.0	305.0	305.0	345.8
1981	350.0	350.0	350.0	350.0	350.0	350.0	350.0	350.0	350.0	350.0	350.0	339.5	349.2
1982	329.0	329.0	329.0	329.0	329.0	329.0	329.0	329.0	329.0	329.0	329.0	329.0	329.0
1983	329.0												

Source: Bureau of Labor Statistics (1022-0128)   T.429

Oats

U.S. production of oats in 1982 was estimated at 617 million bushels, 21 percent larger than the 1981 crop of 509 million bushels, which was the second smallest crop since 1881. Because beginning stocks (152 million bushels) were the lowest on record for June 1, total supply for the 1982/83 season ending May 31, 1983 was only 12 percent larger than for the 1981/82 season.

Producers harvested 10.56 million acres of oats for grain in 1982, up from 9.42 million in 1981 and 8.65 million acres in 1980. Yield per harvested acre reached a record-high 58.4 bushels versus 54.1 bushels in 1981 and 53.0 bushels in 1980. Acres abandoned and used for purposes other than grain accounted for 25.7 percent of the 14.2 million planted acres compared with 31.1 percent of the 1981 crop. Seeding lagged behind normal in the major producing states due to wet conditions, and crop development was slow through the cool, wet spring. Later than normal harvesting occurred in many states because of the delayed seeding and slow growth.

Disappearance of oats for the 1982/83 season was projected by the USDA at 520 million bushels vs. 536 million in the previous season. However, disappearance during the June–December 1982 period, estimated at 297 million bushels, was 24 million bushels below disappearance during the same period in the previous season. Feed use accounts for about 85 percent of the total disappearance of oats, and use during the June–September period was relatively low, as oat prices continued high relative to corn.

Today's oat crops are superior to crops of 30 years ago, according to the USDA, with a 600 million bushel crop 30 years ago needed to equal the feed value of a 500 million bushel crop today. Oat demand is considered less price responsive than demand for corn or sorghum, partly because dairy farmers and horse owners prefer to feed oats. Most oat-deficit regions have large horse and milk cow numbers but relatively small oat production. The Lake states are the largest suppliers of oats for the Eastern deficit areas. Rolled and crimped oats are used in large amounts for dairy feed formulations in these areas. Heavy recleaned oats are fed in significant quantities to horses in the East and South.

Ending stocks of oats for the 1982/83 season were projected at 250 million bushels by the USDA in early April 1983. A carryover of this size would represent 48 percent of estimated disappearance during the 1982/83 season vs. 28 percent at the end of the 1981/82 season. Also, compliance with the acreage reduction program was low among oat producers, probably because of the strong market for oats during the 1981/82 season. Compliance with the 1982 acreage reduction program was expected to be small also, because the average farm price exceeded the regular loan rate which also discouraged movement into the CCC loan or farmer-owned grain reserve (FOR).

The USDA, in April 1983 projected 1983/84 U.S. oat supplies of 766 million bushels vs. 770 million in 1982/83, total usage of 525 million bushels vs. an estimated 250 million for 1982/83, and ending stocks on May 31, 1984 of 241 million bushels vs. projected stocks of 250 million bushels for May 31, 1983.

U.S. Government Support Program

The 1983 crop national average regular loan level for oats is $1.36 per bushel for oats grading No. 3 or better, up from $1.31 per bushel for the 1982 crop. There will be no early entry for 1983 reserve programs for feed grains. Entry will be allowed only after the 9-month regular loan matures. The 1983 loan rate for the reserve will be the same as that for regular loans. In addition, the annual storage-payment rate will remain at 20 cents per bushel for oats. In order for producers to qualify for regular and reserve loan, and target price protection in 1983, they must comply with the 10 percent acreage reduction and 10 percent paid land diversion programs. Oats are not eligible for the 1983 Payment-in-Kind (PIK) program. The target price for 1983 crop oats was set at $1.60 per bushel, up from $1.50 for the 1982 crop. The FOR release price for 1982 crop oats is $1.65 per bushel.

Futures Markets

Oat futures are traded on the Chicago Board of Trade and on the Winnipeg Commodity Exchange.

Salient Statistics of Oats in the United States & Canada

Year Begin. July	Acreage Planted[2] — 1,000 Acres —	Acreage Harvested[3]	Yield Per Harv. Acre Bushels	Farm Value of Product Mill. $	Farm Disposition Feed & Seed — Mil. Bu. —	Farm Disposition Sold	Owned By CCC July 1	Loans	Under Price Support Purch. Agree. — 1,000 Bushels —	Total	Deliveries To CCC	Nat. Avg. Sup. Rate $ Bu.	Avg. Prices No. 2 Heavy White, Portland — Dollars per Bushel —	Toledo[4]
1972–3	19,990	13,410	51.5	507	428	262	178,128			31,800	—	.54	1.02	.88
1973–4	18,605	13,770	47.9	775	404	256	104,942			10,392	—	.54	1.57	1.40
1974–5	17,013	12,608	47.6	912	389	212	24,000			3,900	—	.54	1.96	1.75
1975–6	16,486	13,038	49.0	924	395	244	5,800			3,928	—	.54	1.86	1.54
1976–7	16,734	11,834	45.7	835	350	190	—			4,631	—	.72	1.80	1.71
1977–8	17,733	13,485	55.8	823	457	295	—			82,679	100	1.03	1.44	1.36
1978–9	16,407	11,126	52.3	689	367	216	100			24,849	1,300	1.03	1.79	1.37
1979–0	13,957	9,679	54.4	714	321	205	2,400			12,000	600	1.08	1.87	1.60
1980–1	13,377	8,652	53.0	823	298	160	2,200			6,000	—	1.08	2.42	2.17
1981–2[1]	13,656	9,415	54.1							10,000	—	1.24	2.36	2.23
1982–3[1]	14,211	10,561	58.4							5,000	—	1.31	2.18	1.57
1983–4[1]	14,747											1.36		

[1] Preliminary.   [2] For all purposes.   [3] For grain.   [4] Prior to June 1981 prices are for Chicago.   *Source: Statistical Reporting Service, U.S.D.A.*
T.430

OATS

World Production of Oats   In Thousands of Metric Tons

Crop Year	United States	Canada	Argentina	Australia	Turkey	USSR	W. Germany	Spain	Netherlands	Denmark	France	Sweden	Un. King.	Poland	World Total
1972-3	10,044	4,630	566	740	396	14,100	3,909	440	144	637	3,084	1,630	1,255	3,212	51,286
1973-4	9,681	5,041	561	1,107	376	17,516	4,155	425	134	444	2,204	1,209	1,080	3,220	53,872
1974-5	8,912	3,929	327	874	380	15,257	3,482	559	163	472	2,081	1,686	950	3,244	49,320
1975-6	9,551	4,466	433	1,141	390	12,495	3,445	609	158	367	1,948	1,345	795	2,920	47,044
1976-7	7,930	4,831	530	1,073	400	18,113	2,497	505	103	256	1,402	1,251	764	2,695	48,744
1977-8	10,901	4,303	570	991	370	18,407	2,714	421	94	288	1,928	1,416	790	2,561	51,508
1978-9	8,730	3,621	676	1,763	370	18,507	4,049	553	140	206	2,203	1,550	706	2,492	51,753
1979-0	7,643	2,978	522	1,411	370	15,200	3,697	456	109	163	1,845	1,524	542	2,186	45,165
1980-1	6,652	3,028	433	1,129	355	15,544	3,250	664	94	160	1,845	1,567	605	2,250	44,250
1981-2[1]	7,375	3,570	500	1,550	340	15,200	3,200	454	115	187	1,774	1,812	635	2,768	45,657
1982-3[2]	8,695														

[1] Preliminary.   [2] Estimated.   Source: *Foreign Agricultural Service, U.S.D.A.*   T.434

United States Official Oat Crop Production Reports   In Thousands of Bushels

Year	June 1	July 1	August 1	September 1	October 1	December[1]	Final
1972	[2]	711,909	736,775	730,762	730,762	694,967	690,616
1973	[2]	716,615	707,756	702,280	702,280	663,860	659,136
1974	[2]	684,021	637,951	648,711	648,711	620,539	600,655
1975	[2]	731,431	697,834	677,754	677,754	656,862	638,960
1976	[2]	498,938	548,542	563,997	—	562,452	540,441
1977	[2]	707,074	757,589	758,669	—	747,914	752,774
1978	[2]	635,551	636,785	595,879	—	601,477	581,657
1979	[2]	509,761	530,967	531,232	—	534,386	526,551
1980	[2]	449,504	440,655	450,660	—	457,593	458,263
1981	[2]	528,118	522,408	509,457	—	508,083	509,167
1982[1]	[2]	580,288	591,478	599,008	—	616,981	

[1] Preliminary.   [2] No estimate.   Source: *Crop Reporting Board, U.S.D.A.*   T.431

Oats Under Price Support Through the End of the Month (Cumulative Total from Current Season's Crop)   In Millions of Bushels

Year	July	Aug.	Sept.	Oct.	Nov.	Dec.	Jan.	Feb.	Mar.	Apr.	May	June	Total
1971-2	1.6	18.4	46.9	61.4	66.9	70.2	76.8	78.3	79.4	80.9	81.7	81.8	81.9
1972-3	.5	5.3	18.8	25.8	28.5	29.6	31.1	31.4	31.6	31.7	31.8	31.8	31.8
1973-4	.4	4.4	7.5	8.7	9.6	10.0	10.3	10.3	10.4	10.4	10.4	10.4	10.4
1974-5	.3	1.8	2.9	3.4	3.6	3.7	3.8	3.8	3.9	3.9	3.9	3.9	3.9
1975-6	.4	1.5	2.0	3.0	3.2	3.7	3.8	3.9	3.9	3.9	3.9	3.9	3.9
1976-7	.4	1.0	1.7	2.6	3.4	4.0	4.2	4.3	4.4	4.4	4.4	4.4	4.4
1977-8	7.8	30.0	48.5	54.9	59.5	62.3	65.3	67.1	73.2	76.1	77.9	78.9	78.9
1978-9	.5	8.2	14.9	18.5	21.2	22.4	23.9	24.2	24.5	24.7	24.8	24.8	24.8
1979-0	—	2.2	5.0	7.1	8.7	9.5	10.5	11.0	11.6	12.1	12.2	12.2	12.2
1980-1	—	1.8	3.4	4.4	4.9	5.7	6.0	6.1	6.2	6.3	6.3	6.3	6.3
1981-2	.6	3.4	6.1	7.4	8.0	8.7	9.3	9.5	9.6	9.6	9.6	9.6	9.6
1982-3	.1	1.2	4.0	5.8	6.9	7.7	8.3	8.5	8.8				

Source: *U.S. Department of Agriculture*   T.432

Average Price Received by U.S. Farmers for Oats   In Cents Per Bushel

Year	July	Aug.	Sept.	Oct.	Nov.	Dec.	Jan.	Feb.	Mar.	Apr.	May	June	Average[1]
1972-3	65.5	62.3	64.5	67.1	70.0	80.6	81.1	77.6	77.1	77.4	79.6	90.4	72.5
1973-4	85.5	113	109	114	113	120	132	144	140	124	127	130	118
1974-5	137	155	157	168	170	170	162	158	146	151	154	149	153
1975-6	145	144	145	141	140	142	144	146	146	144	147	164	146
1976-7	164	148	149	146	145	151	158	163	164	164	152	129	156
1977-8	102	92.9	93.8	104	110	113	118	122	117	119	124	116	110
1978-9	108	106	106	108	115	119	122	125	127	129	129	135	120
1979-0	133	124	129	131	141	131	139	137	134	138	143	148	136
1980-1	150	153	163	165	184	192	198	201	208	205	205	199	179
1981-2	184	172	174	178	188	194	197	199	202	199	199	188	189
1982-3	157	139	135	132	140	144	146	143	148	149			

[1] Weighted average by sales.   Source: *Crop Reporting Board, U.S.D.A.*   T.433

OATS

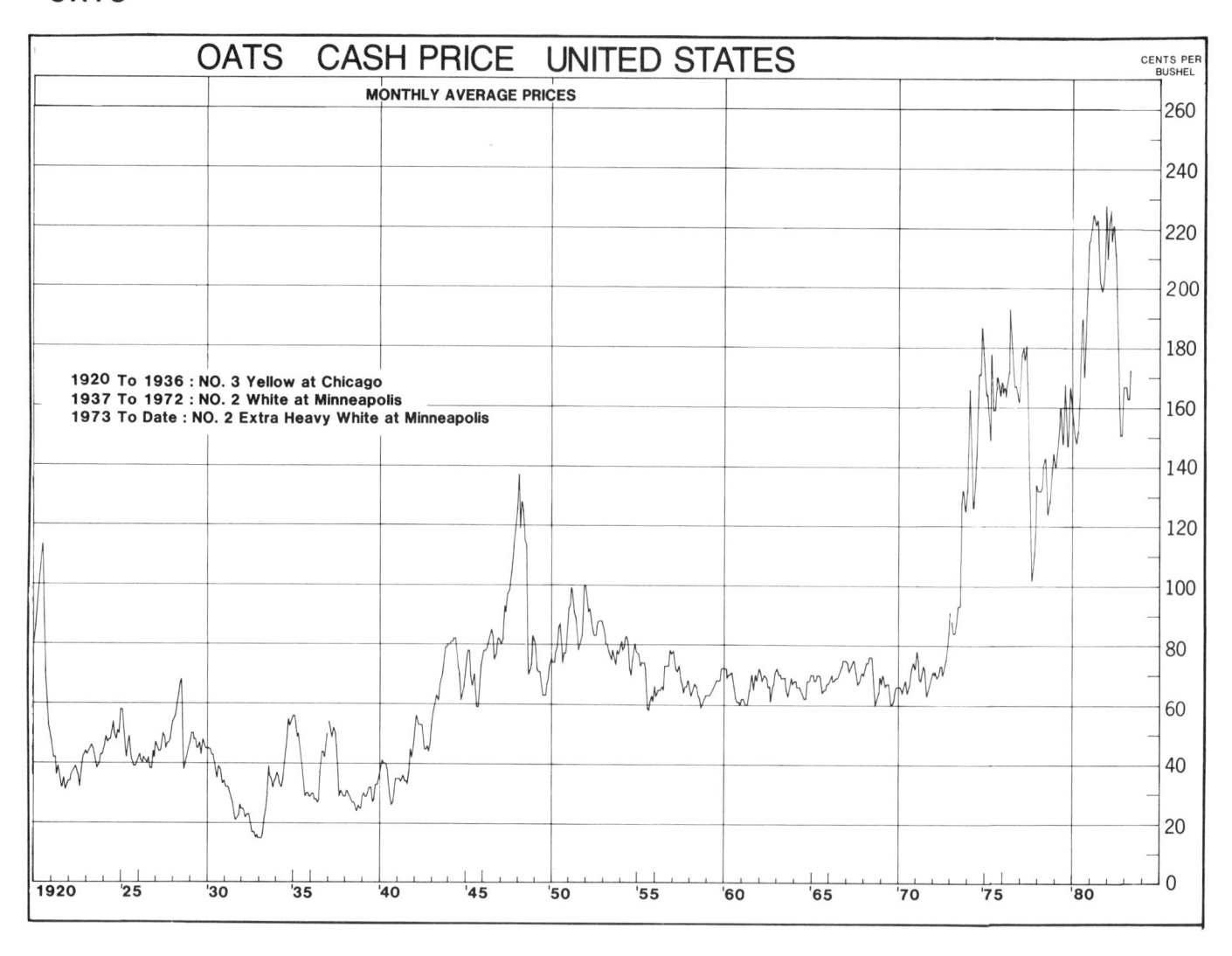

OATS CASH PRICE UNITED STATES
MONTHLY AVERAGE PRICES
(CENTS PER BUSHEL)

1920 To 1936 : NO. 3 Yellow at Chicago
1937 To 1972 : NO. 2 White at Minneapolis
1973 To Date : NO. 2 Extra Heavy White at Minneapolis

Average Cash Price[1] of No. 2 Extra Heavy White Oats[2] at Minneapolis In Cents Per Bushel

Year	July	Aug.	Sept.	Oct.	Nov.	Dec.	Jan.	Feb.	Mar.	Apr.	May	June	Average[1]
1972-3	69.0	70.0	71.0	76.0	81.0	91.0	88.0	84.0	84.0	86.0	91.0	93.0	80.0
1973-4	93.0	128	132	126	125	132	155	166	152	126	135	143	130
1974-5	163	168	171	187	180	174	164	164	149	172	178	159	168
1975-6	159	170	168	164	169	165	167	166	164	167	172	193	166
1976-7	184	167	167	166	162	167	178	180	176	181	168	138	174
1977-8	115	102	111	117	134	132	132	132	133	140	143	136	127
1978-9	124	128	136	139	147	140	147	154	160	148	155	168	143
1979-0	160	147	155	165	167	159	152	150	148	152	162	188	157
1980-1	190	170	186	196	215	216	220	225	223	221	223	218	209
1981-2	202	199	202	209	228	210	223	226	216	221	216	212	214
1982-3	187	153	151	151	167	167	167	163	163				
1983-4													

[1] Weighted average of reported daily cash sales. [2] No. 2 WHITE prior to July 1971. *Source: Department of Agriculture*

T.435

OATS

Quarterly Supply and Distribution of Oats in the United States   In Millions of Bushels

Year & Periods Begin. June 1	Beginning Stocks	Production	Imports	Total Supply	Food	Alc. Bever.	Seed	Feed	Total	Exports	Total Disap.	Gov't. Owned[2]	Privately Owned[3]	Total Stocks
1978-9	313.1	581.7	.7	895.5	41.0	—	36.1	525.7	602.8	12.7	615.5	2.7	277.3	280.0
June-Sept.	313.1	581.7	.3	895.1	14.7	—	1.8	224.8	241.3	7.9	249.2	1.5	644.4	645.9
Oct.-Dec.	645.9	—	.1	646.0	10.3	—	1.8	84.2	96.3	3.4	99.7	2.5	543.8	546.3
Jan.-Mar.	546.3	—	.2	546.5	10.7	—	7.2	146.3	164.2	.7	164.9	2.7	378.9	381.6
Apr.-May	381.6	—	.1	381.7	5.3	—	25.3	70.4	101.0	.7	101.7	2.7	277.3	280.0
1979-80	280.0	526.6	.9	807.5	40.7	—	34.6	491.7	567.0	4.1	571.1	2.7	233.7	236.4
June-Sept.	280.0	526.6	.3	806.9	14.6	—	1.7	221.6	237.9	.9	238.8	2.6	565.5	568.1
Oct.-Dec.	568.1	—	.2	568.3	10.4	—	1.7	77.5	89.6	1.9	91.5	2.6	474.2	476.8
Jan.-Mar.	476.8	—	.2	477.0	10.3	—	6.9	119.7	136.9	.5	137.4	2.7	336.9	339.6
Apr.-May	339.6	—	.2	339.8	5.4	—	24.3	72.9	102.6	.8	103.4	2.7	233.7	236.4
1980-1	236.4	458.3	1.3	696.0	41.0	—	33.0	431.8	505.8	13.3	519.1	2.5	174.4	176.9
June-Sept.	236.4	458.3	.6	695.3	15.0	—	1.8	190.0	206.8	3.9	210.7	2.7	481.9	484.6
Oct.-Dec.	484.6	—	.2	484.8	10.0	—	1.8	79.2	91.0	2.8	93.8	2.7	388.3	391.0
Jan.-Mar.	391.0	—	.3	391.3	10.0	—	7.0	115.6	132.6	2.6	135.2	2.5	253.6	256.1
Apr.-May	256.1	—	.2	256.3	6.0	—	22.4	47.0	75.4	4.0	79.4	2.5	174.4	176.9
1981-2[1]	176.9	509.2	1.6	687.7	41.2	—	35.4	452.5	529.1	6.6	535.7	.7	151.3	152.0
June-Sept.	176.9	509.2	.3	686.4	16.0	—	2.0	206.7	224.7	3.2	227.9	1.7	456.8	458.5
Oct.-Dec.	458.5	—	.2	458.7	10.0	—	2.0	80.3	92.3	1.2	93.5	1.7	363.5	365.2
Jan.-Mar.	365.2	—	.2	365.4	10.0	—	7.3	110.0	127.3	1.2	128.5	1.7	235.2	236.5
Apr.-May	236.9	—	.9	237.8	5.2	—	24.1	55.5	84.8	1.0	85.8	.7	151.3	152.0
1982-3[4]	152.0	617.0	1.0	770.0	— 75.0 —			440.0	515.0	5.0	520.0			250.0
June-Sept.	152.0	617.0	.8	769.8	16.2	—	2.0	169.0	187.2	1.3	188.5	.6	580.7	581.3
Oct.-Dec.	581.3	—	.2	581.5	10.0	—	2.0	94.9	106.9	1.0	107.9	.7	472.9	473.6
Jan.-Mar.														
Apr.-May														

[1] Preliminary.   [2] Uncommitted inventory.   [3] Includes quantity under loan & farmer-owned reserve.   [4] Estimate.   Source: Economic Research Service, U.S.D.A.

T.436

Production of Oats in the United States, by States   In Millions of Bushels

Year	Illinois	Indiana	Iowa	Michigan	Minnesota	Missouri	Nebraska	New York	No. Dakota	Ohio	Pennsylvania	So. Dakota	Texas	Wisconsin	California
1970	34.3	14.6	94.1	27.1	167.7	9.2	24.3	23.3	120.1	31.7	22.5	102.3	29.0	106.3	—
1971	34.8	18.9	91.5	19.5	177.0	11.3	26.4	20.5	113.6	36.7	20.8	128.4	6.0	95.2	—
1972	27.7	12.1	71.3	17.6	126.9	6.9	19.1	12.6	105.6	22.4	17.4	98.0	9.7	74.3	—
1973	19.8	11.8	67.0	16.5	145.4	1.4	21.1	18.5	73.8	25.9	18.4	100.6	26.7	56.2	—
1974	23.1	10.1	78.4	19.3	101.0	4.0	25.1	20.7	44.1	29.5	20.3	81.1	8.1	85.4	—
1975	24.9	12.4	75.5	20.7	104.0	3.3	28.9	20.4	56.2	30.9	19.9	98.1	19.5	74.3	—
1976	22.4	10.2	82.6	19.6	94.8	5.4	27.7	17.3	44.8	28.5	18.1	42.6	14.4	55.0	—
1977	20.7	8.0	82.4	18.7	161.8	7.3	40.6	15.4	60.0	24.8	18.6	132.3	24.0	76.1	5.3
1978	15.4	7.3	60.9	23.4	98.8	1.3	21.2	17.7	62.6	20.7	18.0	95.8	13.8	62.7	3.8
1979	15.6	6.4	63.0	18.9	84.9	2.0	21.2	18.0	37.0	20.3	18.4	94.4	16.8	55.9	4.1
1980	14.0	5.9	62.0	20.1	82.7	2.0	15.6	17.9	13.5	19.4	19.0	66.0	12.6	58.7	4.3
1981	13.5	5.5	59.5	21.1	90.1	4.6	15.4	17.9	44.2	17.0	20.0	70.5	18.9	52.6	3.6
1982[1]	11.8	6.1	56.0	28.4	107.6	3.2	24.7	18.2	62.1	23.8	19.8	133.8	10.7	48.4	2.5
1983															

[1] Preliminary, December estimate.   Source: Crop Reporting Board, U.S.D.A.

T.437

Month End Open Interest of Oats at the Chicago Board of Trade & Winnipeg Grain Exchg.

Year	Jan.	Feb.	Mar.	Apr.	May	June	July	Aug.	Sept.	Oct.	Nov.	Dec.	Mar.	June	Sept.	Dec.
1978	13.4	16.8	16.2	23.1	23.9	22.6	34.8	42.9	49.6	56.3	35.2	29.6	1,765	2,553	3,235	2,213
1979	31.1	32.8	24.4	29.8	25.4	28.8	27.0	32.2	29.2	28.6	26.2	25.8	2,515	2,778	3,085	2,635
1980	23.8	23.2	17.5	23.2	21.2	25.8	35.3	41.3	41.6	39.5	37.6	27.6	2,827	2,315	3,178	3,598
1981	36.2	36.7	27.0	25.2	27.8	29.7	25.3	23.9	29.0	45.6	42.4	34.6	3,295	2,625	2,203	1,863
1982	36.5	39.6	40.5	40.5	43.4	45.8	43.4	32.6	30.5	31.4	23.7	21.5	1,298	1,185	1,155	1,225
1983	30.8	35.8	43.3	45.1									1,202			

Chicago (In Millions of Bushels) — Winnipeg (In Contracts)

Source: Chicago Board of Trade & Winnipeg Grain Exch.

T.438

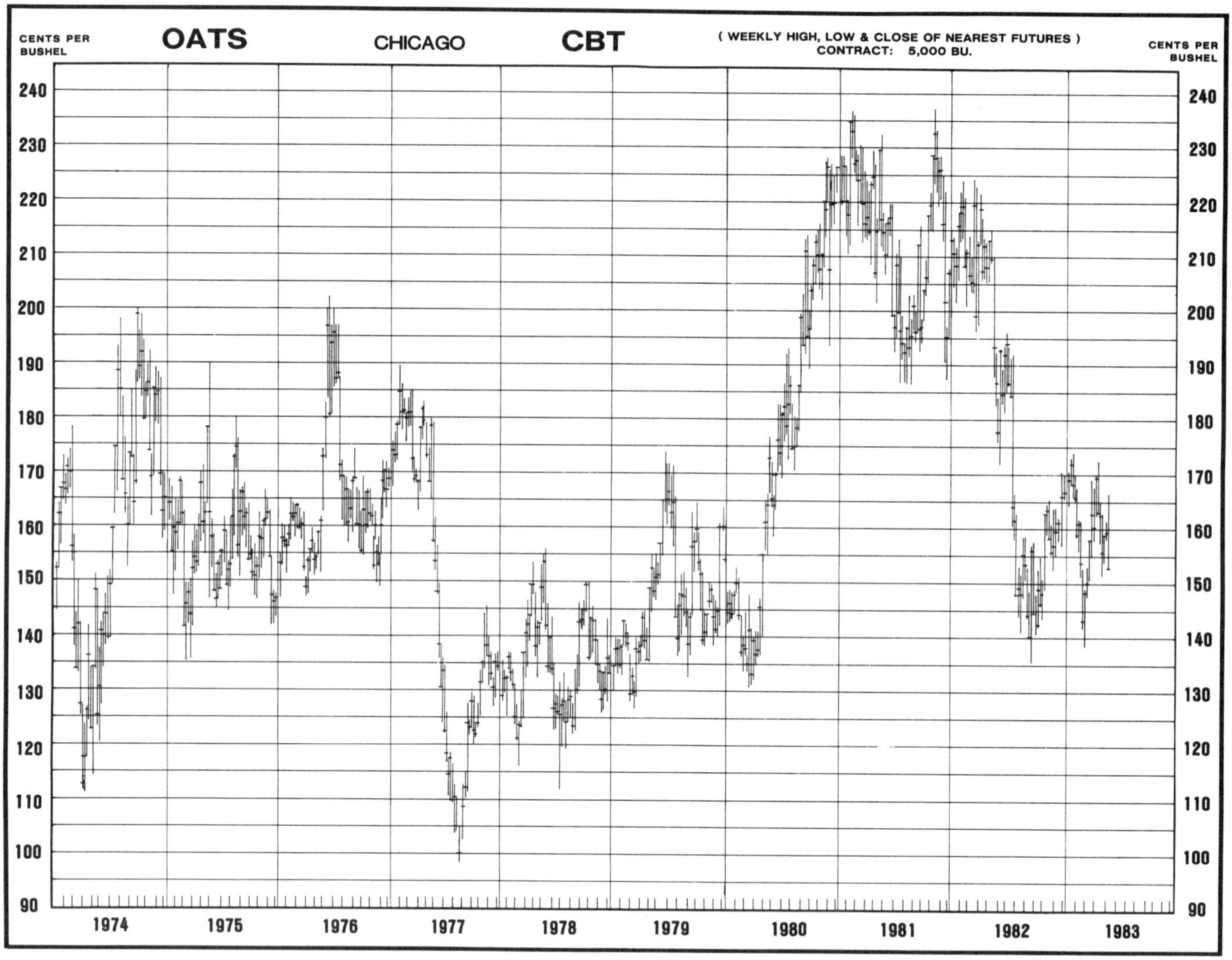

High, Low & Closing Prices of May Oats Futures at the Chicago Board of Trade In Cents per Bushel

Year of Delivery		Year Prior to Delivery								Delivery Year					Life of Delivery
		May	June	July	Aug.	Sept.	Oct.	Nov.	Dec.	Jan.	Feb.	Mar.	Apr.	May	Range
1978	High	—	—	136½	130	136¾	140	146	143	138¾	136½	146½	153¼	146½	153¼
	Low	—	—	120¾	115	127	129½	134	133	128	122	123	136	132¼	115
	Close	—	—	120¾	129½	133¼	134¾	140	138	135	122½	142	138	143	—
1979	High	172	163	154	148¼	155	162¼	158¾	152	147½	152½	142¾	144½	155	172
	Low	164	144	138	137½	144½	148½	146½	140½	137¼	137	133½	135½	138	133½
	Close	164	147¾	148½	145½	151½	155	148½	140½	142¾	137¾	137	138¼	148¾	—
1980	High	173½	196	189½	180¾	181	184½	172¼	172	169¾	162	153	147	171	196
	Low	169½	169¼	162¼	164	167	160	161	163¼	152½	144½	131	133¼	147	132
	Close	170½	184½	166	178	177¾	165¼	168	168¾	154¾	148	133¼	146½	168	—
1981	High	189	191	219½	217½	227	228	244½	244	232½	237	225¾	229½	232¼	244¼
	Low	181	179½	189	197½	207½	210	216½	210½	210½	212	206½	206	201	179½
	Close	183	189	212½	217	218	221	243½	226¾	216¼	224¼	223	213	224½	—
1982	High	231½	230	222½	217	194½	207	222½	212	209½	213¼	206	221¾	215	231½
	Low	226¼	212½	210	193	180½	185¼	197¾	177½	193¾	191½	186	202¾	200¼	177½
	Close	229¼	215	216	194½	185¾	205¾	206	200¼	207¾	199	203¼	208	207	—
1983	High	196	185	182½	177½	175	172¼	184½	179¾	181¼	175½	169	172½		
	Low	188½	173½	164	158½	163½	161	165½	172	172¼	149	151	151¾		
	Close	189	176½	167¾	171	170¼	164	177½	174½	174½	149¼	160¼	155¾		

Source: Chicago Board of Trade T.439

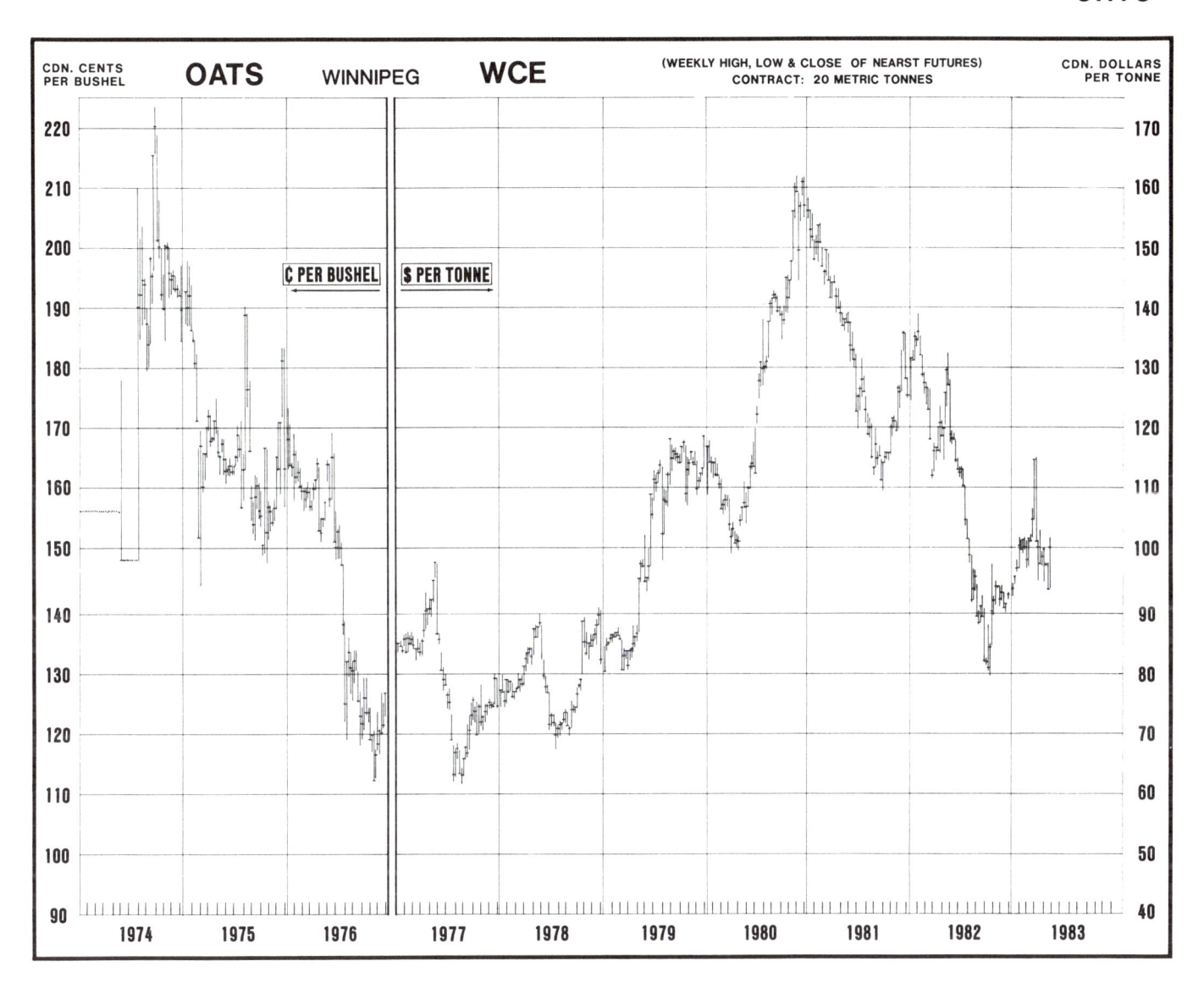

OATS

OATS WINNIPEG WCE (WEEKLY HIGH, LOW & CLOSE OF NEAREST FUTURES) CONTRACT: 20 METRIC TONNES

CDN. CENTS PER BUSHEL / CDN. DOLLARS PER TONNE

Volume of Trading in Oats Futures at Chicago Board of Trade[1]   In Millions of Bushels

Year	July	Aug.	Sept.	Oct.	Nov.	Dec.	Jan.	Feb.	Mar.	Apr.	May	June	Total
1970-1	32.6	64.8	55.1	35.4	28.1	45.3	20.6	15.9	24.7	22.6	14.3	25.5	384.9
1971-2	21.2	19.1	15.7	17.7	15.9	15.4	17.0	14.2	16.1	23.0	12.3	8.0	195.6
1972-3	19.4	22.3	19.7	12.1	16.2	39.0	28.1	30.5	26.5	30.4	73.9	123.1	441.2
1973-4	134.1	173.0	106.7	108.5	449.9	70.0	75.6[1]	86.5	96.4	83.3	91.7	80.5	1,556.2
1974-5	86.5	106.4	86.8	71.6	59.5	59.4	73.9	57.2	54.7	69.9	82.9	64.3	873.1
1975-6	71.6	74.7	62.2	53.8	56.8	50.7	37.9	41.5	39.8	25.4	44.7	82.0	641.1
1976-7	95.0	72.9	64.5	44.1	44.5	32.2	39.3	39.5	41.6	44.9	41.8	54.2	614.5
1977-8	53.8	55.3	44.6	35.0	66.1	33.8	31.4	37.7	59.7	80.2	68.8	98.5	664.9
1978-9	103.8	121.3	120.0	149.0	141.0	67.7	59.3	93.9	51.6	95.4	87.1	135.7	1,225.3
1979-0	127.8	111.6	76.1	98.6	96.0	47.1	56.9	85.3	53.8	81.1	131.5	144.8	1,110.6
1980-1	200.4	183.9	199.6	197.1	167.9	151.0	124.8	170.2	129.2	136.4	120.5	162.2	1,943.2
1981-2	125.3	134.6	117.0	144.5	264.9	221.0	166.7	184.7	204.3	223.6	196.5	247.9	2,231.0
1982-3	221.0	218.9	151.2	113.2	127.6	82.5	121.1	154.0	141.3	213.6			
1983-4													

[1] Data prior to Jan. 1974 are for ALL CONTRACT MARKETS IN THE U.S.   Source: *Chicago Board of Trade*   T.440

Olive Oil

Private reports estimated that the 1982/83 total world production of olive oil, including pressed oil and both edible and inedible residue oil, amounted to 1.9 million tonnes, an increase of nearly 31 percent from the 1981/82 production level. The three major producers of olive oil were Spain, Italy, and Greece, the outputs of which accounted for nearly 80 percent of the world production.

World stocks of olive oil at the beginning of the 1982/83 season were about 868,000 tonnes, an 18 percent decline from the previous year. Early 1983 estimates put the 1982/83 Spanish olive oil crop, the world's largest, at 582,000 tonnes, up nearly 96 percent. The Spanish government reportedly announced that it would subsidize Uteco-Jaen, the country's olive oil production cooperative, with 21.5 billion pesetas to be lent at 8 percent interest over a period of 30 years. Burdensome stocks, rising prices, and prospects of a 1983/84 bumper crop had reportedly run the cooperative into high debts. However, some analysts expected a decline in the total Mediterranean basin olive oil output in 1983/84 because of a seasonal decline in the two-year production cycle.

Early in 1983, the prospect that Spain and Portugal would enter the European Community (EC) ignited debates over a proposed fixed price ratio between olive oil and competing vegetable oils. Some EC member parliamentarians argued that the proposal would drastically increase the price of other oils, some of which were a fifth of the price of olive oil.

World Production of Olive Oil (Pressed Oil)[2]   In Thousands of Metric Tons

Crop Year[2]	Algeria	Greece	Italy	Jordan	Lebanon	Argentina	Morocco	Portugal	Spain	Syria	Tunisia	Turkey	Yugoslavia	Israel	World Total
1970-1	13	186	429	1	3	21	15	82	475	15	90	110	1	1	1,430
1971-2	23	186	616	1	11	9	68	42	341	22	167	51	1	1	1,568
1972-3	15	249	340	6	7	28	21	48	440	33	70	154	1	2	1,422
1973-4	16	192	543	—	8	22	30	42	447	14	130	53	1	—	1,520
1974-5	8	237	433	7	14	19	26	48	333	44	117	110	2	—	1,414
1975-6	18	257	633	1	5	17	38	36	455	33	180	96	4	5	1,788
1976-7	15	224	301	5	12	12	30	36	390	56	85	150	4	—	1,334
1977-8	5	234	688	2	6	14	15	30	361	38	130	60	2	4	1,594
1978-9	14	240	419	7	6	14	15	40	500	66	83	160	2	0	1,577
1979-0	10	256	475	1	3	11	30	57	433	43	85	52	3	5	1,473
1980-1[1]	18	321	686	10	7	13	15	35	446	70	120	165	2	4	1,925
1981-2[3]	10	250	463	7	4	12	18	25	297	48	85	70		2	1,303
1982-3[3]	8	260	500	8	5	11	25	40	420	40	80	160		4	1,690

[1] Preliminary. [2] Total pressed oil in marketing year ending Oct. 31; excludes sulfur oil extracted from residues. [3] Forecast. Source: Foreign Agricultural Service, U.S.D.A.

Wholesale Price of Olive Oil (Imported, Edible), in Drums at N.Y.   In Cents Per Pound

Year	Jan.	Feb.	Mar.	Apr.	May	June	July	Aug.	Sept.	Oct.	Nov.	Dec.	Average
1969	38.7	38.7	38.7	38.7	38.7	38.7	38.7	38.7	38.7	38.7	38.7	38.7	38.7
1970	38.7	38.7	40.3	40.7	40.7	40.7	40.7	40.7	39.3	39.3	39.3	39.3	40.7
1971	39.3	39.3	39.3	39.3	39.3	39.3	39.3	42.7	42.7	42.7	42.7	42.7	40.7
1972	42.7	42.7	42.7	42.7	42.7	42.7	42.7	42.7	42.7	42.7	42.7	42.7	42.7
1973	42.7	42.7	42.7	42.7	42.7	42.7	42.7	42.7	N.A.	54.5	90.0	86.7	51.3
1974	86.7	86.7	86.7	N.A.	N.A.	N.A.	N.A.	N.A.	N.A.	92.7	92.7	92.5	89.6
1975	110.7	116.7	116.7	116.7	116.7	116.7	116.7	112.0	116.7	N.A.	N.A.	N.A.	112.7
1976	103.3	103.3	103.3	103.3	103.3	103.3	103.3	103.3	86.7	86.7	86.7	86.7	97.8
1977	86.7	86.7	86.7	86.7	86.7	86.7	86.7	86.7	86.7	86.7	86.7	86.7	86.7
1978	86.7	86.7	86.7	86.7	86.7	86.7	86.7	86.3	83.3	83.3	83.3	83.3	85.4
1979	83.3	83.3	83.3	83.3	83.3	83.3	83.3	83.3	83.3	83.3	83.3	83.3	83.3
1980	62.5	78.1	83.3	83.6	85.6	87.1	85.5	86.3	87.5	86.5	87.5	87.5	83.3
1981	87.0	85.0	81.3	85.6	83.0								
1982													

Source: Economic Research Service, U.S.D.A.

Onions

Salient Statistics of Onions in the United States

Crop Year	Stocks—Jan. 1 (1,000 Cwt.) Common Storage	Cold Storage	Total Stocks	Acres Harvested Acres	Yield Per Acre Cwt.	Production 1,000 Cwt.	Price Per Cwt. Dollars	Farm Value $1,000	Domestic Exports[3] 1,000 Cwt.	Imports[3] 1,000 Cwt.	Per Capita[2] Consumption Farm Wt. (Lbs.)	Frozen
1970	4,351	185	4,536	101,000	302	30,493	3.67	98,752	1,398	500	12.2	.25
1971	5,470	180	5,650	98,800	302	29,803	3.88	105,330	1,269	590	9.8	.34
1972	4,810	170	4,980	94,470	300	28,355	6.48	167,715	1,340	1,458	9.8	.51
1973	3,961	77	4,038	104,990	283	29,689	7.57	207,226	1,773	1,079	9.2	.53
1974	4,754	81	4,835	109,730	302	33,151	4.87	147,182	1,553	909	10.5	.48
1975	5,109	80	5,189	103,080	305	31,418	9.35	266,230	3,169	696	9.5	.58
1976	4,430	89	4,519	109,520	322	35,288	6.93	217,202	3,169	1,403	10.0	.65
1977	5,156	98	5,254	108,550	319	34,583	6.76	204,313	1,941	1,345	10.0	.68
1978	5,680	63	5,743	121,920	297	36,174	7.81	251,495	2,164	1,582	10.3	.71
1979	6,556	66	6,622	123,910	312	38,602	6.98	237,432	1,851	1,304	11.2	.74
1980	7,752	99	7,851	112,960	296	33,476	11.40	346,539	2,614	1,400	9.9	.68
1981[1]	6,235	78	6,313	111,630	314	35,021	14.70	475,395			9.4	.70
1982[1]	5,560	28	5,588	124,220	333	41,337	8.45	318,500			9.6	.70
1983[1]	——Not Available——											
1984												

[1] Preliminary. [2] Onions and shallots. Includes 0.1 pounds of shallots in each year. [3] Year beginning July. Source: *Economic Research Service, U.S.D.A.*   T.443

Production of Onions in the United States   In Thousands of Hundredweight (Cwt.)

Year	Spring Texas	California	Arizona	Total (All)[2]	Summer New Mexico	Texas	California	Colorado	Idaho	Michigan	Minnesota	New York	Oregon	Total (All)	Grand Total
1970	3,300	1,888	864	2,752	328	2,872	5,874	1,711	1,978	2,208	221	4,760	2,115	21,569	30,493
1971	3,420	1,508	570	5,498	300	2,875	7,142	1,475	4,281[3]	1,674	240	4,123	[3]	21,430	29,803
1972	2,975	1,881	645	5,501	285	2,846	6,452	1,709	2,184	2,144	252	2,300	3,392	20,008	28,355
1973	3,120	1,512	768	5,400	1,073	1,820	6,384	1,392	2,475	2,046	271	2,992	3,927	24,259	29,689
1974	3,570	1,809	820	6,199	1,122	1,586	8,580	1,479	2,070	2,139	281	3,973	3,576	26,846	33,151
1975	2,975	1,587	686	5,248	1,005	1,404	9,180	1,643	2,025	1,768	165	3,443	3,567	26,170	31,418
1976	4,800	1,652	720	7,172	1,340	1,881	7,215	2,183	2,915	2,166	172	3,631	4,433	28,025	35,197
1977	2,789	1,967	616	5,372	1,040	1,870	8,453	2,040	2,412	2,095	218	4,057	4,287	29,034	34,406
1978	3,345	1,590	738	5,673	1,184	1,502	8,250	2,730	2,470	2,448	223	4,309	4,187	30,263	35,936
1979	3,504	1,904	536	5,944	960	1,520	9,504	2,535	2,295	2,686	125	4,818	4,776	32,658	38,602
1980	3,569	1,683	623	5,875	1,131	1,764	6,000	2,460	2,453	1,800	201	4,433	4,538	27,601	33,476
1981	2,700	2,160	512	5,372	1,242	1,488	7,025	2,925	2,625	2,446	199	3,933	4,460	29,649	35,021
1982	3,492	2,805	876	7,173	1,643	1,544	10,045	3,255	2,475	2,336	168	4,550	4,848	34,164	41,337
1983[1]	3,260														
1984															

[1] Preliminary. [2] Total "Spring" after 1971. Before, add "Texas" for total Spring. [3] Includes "E. Oregon." Source: *Crop Reporting Board, U.S.D.A.*   T.444

Cold Storage Stocks of Onions (Fresh) in the United States   In Thousands of Pounds

Year	Jan. 1	Feb. 1	Mar. 1	Apr. 1	May 1	June 1	July 1	Aug. 1	Sept. 1	Oct. 1	Nov. 1	Dec. 1
1970	18,467	18,797	14,872	5,541	969	2,220	1,694	722	893	5,849	13,305	15,420
1971	18,018	19,340	15,053	7,685	2,359	862	1,436	680	553	3,368	10,638	11,729
1972	17,032	16,135	13,526	8,924	1,961	1,339	416	421	666	3,118	6,848	8,911
1973	7,685	8,326	6,003	3,797	359	740	403	690	781	1,798	6,534	8,446
1974	8,061	9,510	6,617	2,952	635	870	521	315	323	3,378	6,296	8,572
1975	8,142	6,807	3,937	3,291	1,865	1,884	538	277	290	3,456	7,214	9,122
1976	8,886	7,632	5,569	2,087	2,005	2,172	4,187	2,271	2,332	837	4,563	8,586
1977	9,829	8,611	8,824	5,034	905	603	537	44	884	2,766	3,922	7,285
1978	6,336	3,981	1,744	1,360	1,127	954	538	2,159	2,607	1,535	3,656	5,201
1979	6,584	6,023	5,400	2,967	2,107	1,254	844	800	253	1,747	1,487	4,298
1980	9,913	8,446	6,430	4,070	1,124	442	1,967	954	1,298	2,089	2,265	4,901
1981[1]	7,777	6,972	4,422	3,730	1,247	591	1,828	649	143	719	665	3,219
1982[1]	3,474	3,963	3,319	1,813	—	—	275	—	—	952	—	—
1983[1]	4,183	4,379	4,116	3,017								
1984												

[1] Preliminary. Source: *Crop Reporting Board, U.S.D.A.*   T.445

ONIONS

World Production of Onions   In Thousands of Metric Tons

Year	Brazil	Egypt	India	Italy	Japan	South Korea	Mexico	Netherlands	Poland	Romania	Spain	Turkey	Yugoslavia	United States	USSR	World Total
1976	430	652	2,206	496	1,123	131	280	355	332	321	860	760	322	1,597	1,135	14,059
1977	489	723	2,164	518	1,120	159	306	590	367	358	1,195	845	375	1,561	1,016	15,336
1978	462	599	2,250	520	1,114	165	332	522	431	400	930	880	343	1,630	1,400	15,624
1979	691	560	2,100	487	1,254	393	343	457	334	380	930	1,000	293	1,462	1,400	15,732
1980[1]	685	580	2,400	478	1,112	275	315	413	350	370	921	1,100	280	1,329	1,200	15,278
1981																

[1] Preliminary.   Source: Foreign Agricultural Service, U.S.D.A.

T.446

Average Wholesale Price of Onions at Chicago[1]   In Dollars Per Hundred Pounds (Cwt)

Year	Jan.	Feb.	Mar.	Apr.	May	June	July	Aug.	Sept.	Oct.	Nov.	Dec.	Average
1970	6.81	8.69	7.77	7.04	5.89	6.40	6.94	5.60	4.43	4.53	4.02	4.62	6.06
1971	4.29	4.94	6.54	7.11	5.26	5.97	6.50	7.24	5.35	6.06	5.75	5.51	5.88
1972	6.16	6.20	5.10	5.69	6.75	8.58	12.03	11.88	9.33	7.31	9.50	8.38	8.08
1973	9.69	11.31	19.75	33.00	21.33	11.50	11.20	9.19	3.30	3.92	4.33	4.31	11.90
1974	5.03	6.05	4.16	3.79	4.03	7.81	8.63	9.83	9.19	7.80	7.04	5.97	6.61
1975	5.46	4.85	9.16	16.13	14.75	15.63	27.83	20.08	13.00	10.80	10.69	14.43	13.57
1976	15.05	11.50	9.21	12.17	13.20	12.50	8.75	8.67	8.14	7.92	7.38	8.71	10.27
1977	11.00	16.46	21.75	23.70	17.67	12.67	12.50	13.00	8.65	8.13	8.08	8.13	13.48
1978	7.47	7.44	13.08	17.25	9.67	12.92	14.56	14.25	10.50	9.58	9.56	10.56	11.40
1979	9.44	15.08	11.75	10.25	12.50	19.50	20.65	14.05	11.10	9.31	8.54	7.15	12.44
1980	7.75	7.04	6.75	9.00	20.00	20.50	14.63	13.50	13.50	12.67	11.25	14.70	12.61
1981	18.17	20.00	25.75	30.00	28.50	32.00	22.17	22.50	24.00	14.21	17.20	16.92	22.62
1982	21.44	19.79	16.88	17.00	18.25	17.92	13.25	16.00	11.25	10.00	9.50	8.29	14.96
1983	7.21	8.83	10.18										

[1] All yellow, all varieties, fair to good quality, U.S. No. 1, all sizes and field run, track and street sales.   Source: Bureau of Labor Statistics (0113–0216)

T.447

Average Price Received by Farmers for Onions in the U.S.   In Dollars Per Cwt.

Year	Jan.	Feb.	Mar.	Apr.	May	June	July	Aug.	Sept.	Oct.	Nov.	Dec.	Season Average
1970	6.36	6.95	6.82	6.41	4.71	5.15	4.98	3.88	3.29	3.10	3.04	2.94	3.67
1971	3.40	3.14	3.52	3.73	3.79	4.18	4.43	4.87	4.39	4.66	4.27	4.65	3.88
1972	4.64	4.08	3.85	4.49	5.48	6.62	8.21	8.17	6.91	6.33	6.53	6.91	6.48
1973	9.43	11.90	17.50	23.70	13.00	8.51	7.39	6.23	5.57	5.97	6.97	7.23	7.57
1974	10.40	10.50	6.30	4.85	4.79	5.24	6.07	7.11	6.34	5.39	4.57	4.27	4.87
1975	3.90	4.61	7.59	12.30	10.60	12.70	17.70	14.20	11.70	9.72	9.80	11.50	9.35
1976	11.10	8.85	6.95	7.20	6.17	5.49	5.65	5.38	5.73	5.34	5.51	6.97	6.93
1977	11.50	14.00	19.40	19.40	10.40	9.00	8.57	6.88	6.40	6.49	6.39	5.50	6.76
1978	4.95	4.76	7.79	12.10	7.50	7.64	9.85	9.14	7.13	6.44	7.05	9.53	7.81
1979	11.00	12.20	9.57	9.70	8.10	11.40	13.30	9.74	7.93	6.45	6.27	5.57	6.98
1980	4.50	4.20	5.30	6.83	9.86	10.70	9.20	10.40	11.30	10.90	11.50	14.20	11.40
1981[1]	15.40	17.20	23.50	25.40	23.00	18.10	17.70	15.40	11.50	12.80	14.80	14.60	17.45
1982[1]	18.40	18.10	13.40	12.60	13.10	9.63	11.60	13.50	8.59	6.83	6.80	6.42	11.58
1983[1]	5.29	6.02											
1984													

[1] Preliminary.   Source: Crop Reporting Board, U.S.D.A.

T.448

Oranges and Orange Juice

The 1981/82 (December/November) season Florida crop of all oranges totaled 125.8 million boxes averaging 90 pounds of oranges each. This crop was nearly 27 percent down from the 1980/81 harvest of 172.4 million because of freeze damage. Florida produced 74 million boxes of early, midseason, and Navel varieties in 1981/82 compared to 105.6 million the previous season. The Florida Valencia production amounted to 51.8 million boxes compared with 66.8 million during 1980/81.

The total pack of FCOJ in Florida during the 1981/82 season was 133 million gallons compared with 174.5 million during 1980/81. The final 1981/82 Florida FCOJ yield per box was 1.28 gallons at 42.0 degree brix versus 1.21 gallons in 1980/81.

Foreign imports of FCOJ into Florida ports during 1981/82 were 70.3 million gallons compared with 1980/81 imports of nearly 59.3 million gallons figured on a 42 degree brix basis. The U.S. Department of Commerce reported that imports of FCOJ increased sharply over the past five seasons, mainly in response to supply reductions in Florida caused by freezes in the 1976/77, 1980/81, and 1981/82 seasons. Imports of FCOJ into U.S. ports outside of Florida also increased during the season. Trade sources reported that, of approximately 374.1 million gallons (single strength) imported into the U.S. throughout 1981/82, almost 72 million were shipped to ports outside of Florida—an increase of nearly 70 percent above non-Florida FCOJ imports during 1980/81.

Most of the foreign shipments of FCOJ into the U.S. originate in Brazil. In mid-1982, the Florida citrus industry requested a hearing before the U.S. International Trade Commission (ITC) concerning Brazilian subsidies of its FCOJ exports. Subsequently, the ITC directed that importers of FCOJ from Brazil pay a provisional duty in the form of a bond amounting to 2.655 percent ad valorem, an amount equal to the Brazilian subsidy. These measures went into effect on December 17, 1982. At the end of February 1983, the U.S. Department of Commerce and Brazil agreed that Brazil would impose a tax on its FCOJ exports to the U.S. of an amount set by the Department of Commerce at nearly $36 per ton, 65 degree brix (estimated to be about 2 to 2½ cents per lb. solids), the amount of the net Brazilian subsidy. The tax was effective April 30, 1983.

The total movement of FCOJ, 42 degrees brix, during 1981/82 amounted to 230.3 million gallons compared with 240.5 million in the 1980/81 season. FCOJ stocks as of early 1983 were reported to be significantly below the year earlier level. A pickup in movement during the 1982/83 season was anticipated in light of the overall economic recovery.

The total U.S. 1982/83 orange crop was forecast at 224 million boxes, of which the Florida share was expected to be 147 million. Florida packers expected a juice yield of 1.43 gallons per box, 42 degree brix, in 1982/83.

Futures Market

Frozen concentrated orange juice (FCOJ) futures are traded on the Citrus Associates of the New York Cotton Exchange.

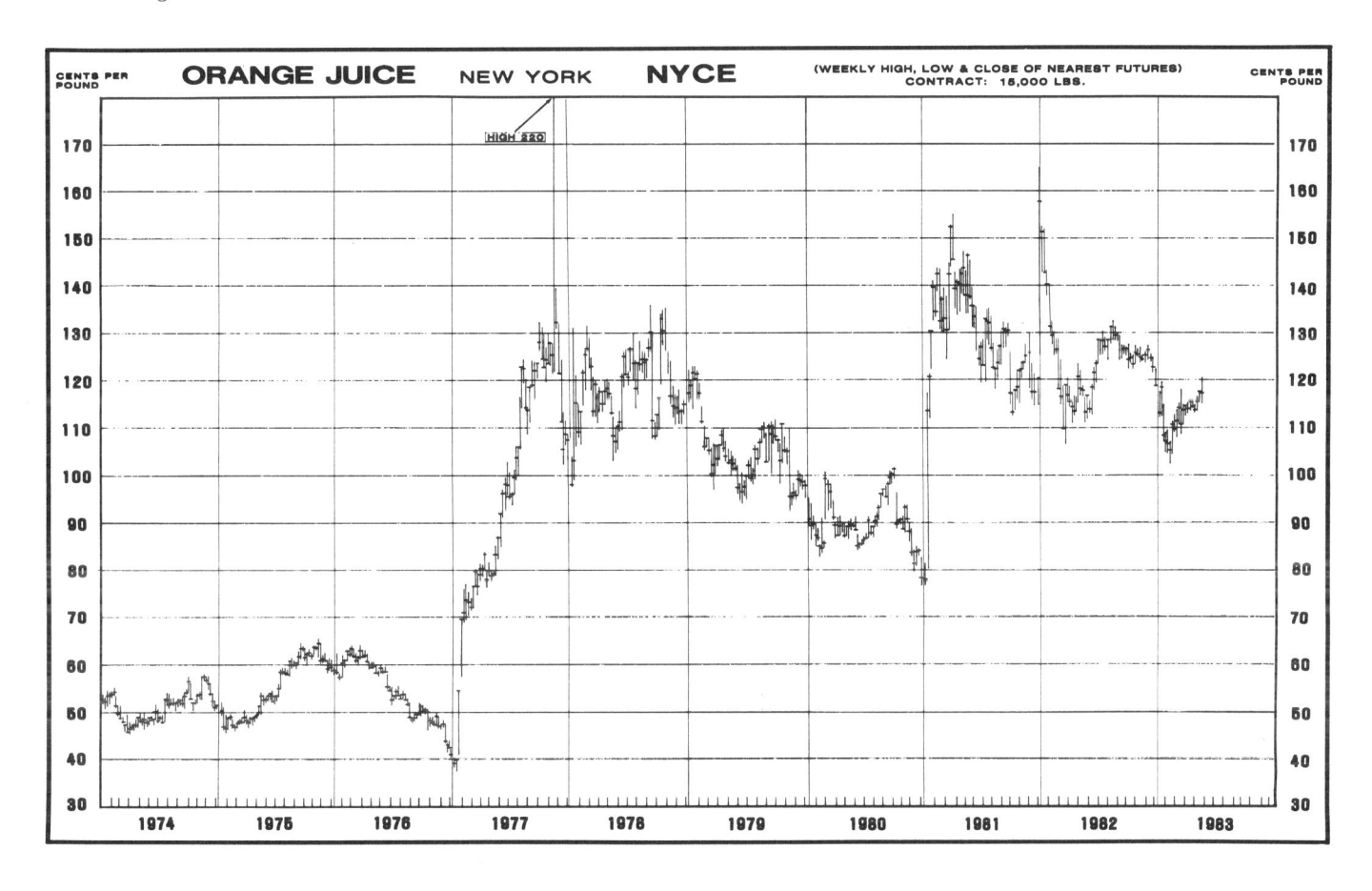

ORANGES AND ORANGE JUICE

World Production of Oranges (Including Tangarines)   In Thousands of Metric Tons

Season	Algeria	Argentina	Brazil	Australia	Greece	Israel	Italy	Japan	Mexico	Morocco	Spain	Turkey	South Africa	United States	World Total
1972-3	515	1,032	2,872	338	400	1,221	1,604	4,070	1,270	988	2,642	563	534	9,245	28,932
1973-4	520	1,063	3,782	369	422	1,233	1,891	3,864	1,089	819	2,460	554	545	8,931	29,333
1974-5	480	1,014	4,065	438	539	1,016	2,098	3,952	1,110	583	2,479	622	499	9,913	30,660
1975-6	480	958	4,065	389	567	995	1,931	4,234	905	552	2,643	645	564	10,170	30,918
1976-7	506	990	3,754	391	533	968	2,258	3,575	1,283	784	2,489	671	463	10,144	30,567
1977-8	508	990	4,321	352	455	949	1,950	4,120	750	1,070	1,914	785	600	9,268	28,479
1978-9		925	6,471	451	506	992	1,959	3,637	1,398	827	2,526	806	600	8,310	24,050
1979-0		921	9,282	448	360	943	2,104	3,945	1,810	1,024	2,597	835	565	10,734	38,502
1980-1[1]		905	9,872	381	561	810	2,055	3,229	1,720	965	2,594	862	569	9,547	36,725
1981-2[2]		820	10,853	414	729	977	2,078	3,147	1,830	966	2,475	870	577	6,977	35,446

[1] Preliminary.   [2] Estimate.   Source: Foreign Agricultural Service, U.S.D.A.   T.449

U.S. Salient Statistics of Oranges & Orange Juice

Season	Arizona	California	Florida	Texas	Total	Farm Price $ Per Box	Farm Value Million $	Carry-in	Pack	Total Supply	Total Season Movem.	Frozen Concentrates	Juice	Sections & Salads	Other Processed	Total Processed	Yield Per Box (Gall.)
1971-2	4.9	43.4	137.0	6.2	191.5	2.87	549.4					104.4	19.5	.5	7.7	132.2	1.29
1972-3	5.1	42.1	169.7	7.8	224.7	2.69	603.3					132.2	20.5	.6	8.9	162.3	1.33
1973-4	3.4	40.4	165.8	6.6	216.2	2.78	600.7					132.5	20.4	.6	7.5	161.0	1.30
1974-5	5.0	55.1	173.3	4.5	237.8	2.75	653.8					135.5	22.8	.5	7.6	166.4	1.31
1975-6	2.7	52.8	181.2	6.1	242.8	2.80	678.7	34.6	174.8	191.6	173.6	144.5	24.0	.6	7.6	176.7	1.29
1976-7	4.0	45.3	186.8	6.9	243.0	3.34	811.2	29.7	178.7	196.2	180.9	148.7	27.3	.4	8.8	185.2	1.07
1977-8	2.6	42.6	167.8	6.1	220.1	5.45	1,198.7	29.1	185.0	200.8	185.1	132.2	25.3	.4	8.1	166.0	1.23
1978-9	2.9	37.3	164.0	6.4	210.6	6.15	1,296.0	33.5	206.2	221.9	206.1	130.2	22.8	.3	6.5	159.8	1.34
1979-0	3.5	59.4	206.7	4.0	273.6	4.76	1,304.2	37.4	256.4	293.8	239.0	174.9	24.4	.3	7.0	206.6	1.34
1980-1	2.6	65.3	172.4	4.3	244.6	4.85	1,327.7	57.3	249.6	306.9	240.5	144.3	19.6	.2	6.4	171.5	1.21
1981-2[1]	3.1	43.0	125.8	5.9	177.8	5.30	1,295.3	69.0	214.9	283.9	230.3	105.1	16.3	.2	4.5	126.1	1.28
1982-3[1]	3.4	68.0	147.0	6.1	224.5	6.90	1,227.4	53.4								148.0	1.43

Production in Million Boxes. Frozen Concentrated Orange Juice—Florida in Million Gallons. Florida Crop Processed Chilled Pdt's in Million Boxes.

[1] Preliminary.   [2] Fruit ripened on trees, but destroyed prior to picking is not included.   Source: Economic Research Service, U.S.D.A. Florida Citrus Processors Assoc.   T.450

U.S. Cold Storage Stocks of Orange Juice Concentrate[2]   In Millions of Pounds (Gallon Equivalent)

Year	Jan. 1	Feb. 1	Mar. 1	Apr. 1	May 1	June 1	July 1	Aug. 1	Sept. 1	Oct. 1	Nov. 1	Dec. 1
1971	323.7	462.8	573.3	581.6	574.5	642.9	684.3	603.1	535.4	450.5	347.3	262.2
1972	289.4	391.7	484.6	540.7	578.3	688.6	764.5	748.8	646.9	528.3	437.0	343.0
1973	353.5	468.5	633.7	768.8	830.6	909.5	1,074.6	1,089.1	999.1	829.8	709.6	598.1
1974	641.9	779.1	935.9	1,025.9	1,121.4	1,239.9	1,319.7	1,228.9	1,031.7	917.8	737.4	616.9
1975	654.6	802.1	967.3	985.4	1,032.1	1,246.8	1,294.0	1,153.4	981.7	856.6	696.7	633.2
1976	756.6	943.0	1,046.9	1,016.1	1,075.8	1,203.7	1,339.9	1,229.1	1,075.4	877.1	740.3	605.2
1977	613.6	681.4	845.5	932.8	955.5	1,040.6	914.3	806.5	647.1	551.7	456.3	333.3
1978	392.8	511.5	617.1	617.3	744.4	854.7	883.1	811.6	720.2	549.6	485.4	359.8
1979	506.5	762.3	996.6	995.0	1,044.4	1,186.5	1,228.4	1,116.4	926.2	704.6	560.1	466.6
1980	559.0	827.2	1,062.5	1,124.8	1,221.4	1,429.7	1,500.3	1,369.3	1,182.4	963.7	842.7	679.5
1981[1]	722.4	907.1	1,053.2	1,180.1	1,264.4	1,502.2	1,491.3	1,307.8	1,178.8	1,022.2	892.2	759.1
1982[1]	753.1	957.0	1,172.3	1,300.7	—	—	1,406.2	—	—	846.5	—	—
1983[1]	835.9	1,028.1	1,016.2	963.4								

[1] Preliminary.   [2] Adjusted to 45° BRIX basis (10.027 lbs. per gallon).   Source: Crop Reporting Board, U.S.D.A.   T.451

Volume of Trading of Frozen Concentrated Orange Juice Futures   In Contracts

Year	Jan.	Feb.	Mar.	Apr.	May	June	July	Aug.	Sept.	Oct.	Nov.	Dec.	Total
1978	32,409	25,867	29,847	16,858	23,331	26,682	23,252	20,257	25,430	28,087	20,121	12,264	284,405
1979	25,080	17,387	15,162	11,378	11,661	15,526	14,326	16,014	15,010	15,141	12,889	15,239	184,813
1980	21,982	13,010	22,555	9,337	6,742	7,914	8,308	9,715	11,800	16,276	13,042	22,183	162,864
1981	35,041	32,755	49,107	39,785	32,611	35,459	32,944	29,979	22,927	25,435	19,747	31,392	387,182
1982	28,968	25,524	27,139	17,038	12,206	21,501	14,577	14,242	8,424	9,696	8,647	19,198	207,060
1983	28,122	20,345	11,754	6,704									

Source: Citrus Assoc. of the N.Y. Cotton Exch.   T.452

ORANGES AND ORANGE JUICE

High, Low & Closing Prices of May Orange Juice[1] Futures at New York   In Cents per Pound

Year of Delivery		Mar.	Apr.	May	June	July	Aug.	Sept.	Oct.	Nov.	Dec.	Jan.	Feb.	Mar.	Apr.	May	Life of Delivery Range
1978	High	75.30	76.00	86.00	90.10	96.00	100.00	113.25	125.25	135.00	121.90	115.50	129.00	128.65	120.25	119.90	135.00
	Low	67.55	69.50	76.00	82.60	83.80	88.80	88.60	107.50	118.60	102.40	98.00	107.60	111.40	113.55	106.65	44.50
	Close	69.80	76.00	85.95	84.40	95.65	90.50	108.75	121.60	120.50	107.50	108.60	122.65	116.50	118.20	106.65	—
1979	High	98.65	89.75	88.40	92.75	95.70	95.75	100.65	129.00	128.80	121.80	127.55	124.60	109.80	110.00	106.10	129.00
	Low	85.25	86.10	80.15	84.50	88.90	91.50	95.25	95.70	115.00	115.00	118.60	106.40	100.10	102.30	100.00	80.15
	Close	89.30	86.60	84.25	89.00	91.90	95.60	96.20	129.00	116.25	120.80	121.70	107.25	106.25	106.20	101.35	—
1980	High	104.60	104.00	102.00	101.50	102.00	109.80	109.90	111.25	100.00	102.00	100.00	91.00	101.20	91.50	89.20	111.25
	Low	94.50	96.75	97.90	92.70	95.00	102.00	101.60	97.50	95.10	97.25	87.00	83.70	88.00	86.70	86.50	83.70
	Close	98.90	100.75	101.30	95.80	102.00	108.70	109.50	98.70	98.50	97.90	89.65	86.15	88.70	88.80	87.55	—
1981	High	107.80	94.75	95.50	96.90	94.55	97.50	103.00	104.45	96.15	92.20	133.50	149.50	150.20	155.10	143.50	155.10
	Low	91.35	91.50	92.80	90.60	91.10	93.45	96.80	92.45	90.25	83.30	84.00	135.25	126.80	133.70	138.00	83.30
	Close	91.35	93.00	94.40	91.10	93.20	97.50	102.20	95.00	91.80	85.00	133.35	138.40	150.20	139.60	138.35	—
1982	High	149.50	151.50	150.95	149.40	144.75	145.90	140.00	139.50	129.30	133.50	156.90	146.40	133.00	120.50	120.00	156.90
	Low	136.00	140.25	144.80	138.75	134.00	134.00	134.25	126.00	122.30	119.00	119.50	129.00	106.75	110.90	113.50	94.00
	Close	146.45	148.45	150.70	138.75	142.90	137.25	136.95	126.10	127.70	122.55	146.20	130.30	115.10	113.30	117.70	—
1983	High	142.85	130.20	132.00	130.00	130.20	133.50	133.25	130.30	128.60	129.05	122.00	112.80	114.75	115.50		
	Low	122.00	121.95	126.05	123.80	126.50	127.60	129.00	125.55	126.00	121.25	105.70	103.10	107.30	113.10		
	Close	127.50	126.50	127.75	130.00	128.25	133.50	129.50	126.90	127.00	121.85	107.70	110.35	114.70	113.70		
1984	High	106.90	104.95														
	Low	104.00	100.50														
	Close	104.80	102.05														

[1] Frozen concentrated orange juice.   Source: Citrus Associates of the N.Y. Cotton Exch., Inc.   T.455

Month–End Open Interest of Frozen Concentrated Orange Juice Futures   In Thousands of Contracts

Year	Jan.	Feb.	Mar.	Apr.	May	June	July	Aug.	Sept.	Oct.	Nov.	Dec.
1978	8,973	10,002	10,611	11,980	12,381	12,878	11,964	13,950	12,781	12,878	9,212	9,073
1979	7,916	8,503	6,734	7,887	7,223	8,261	8,058	8,116	6,510	7,101	8,423	10,428
1980	7,612	6,501	6,126	6,390	6,210	5,923	6,186	6,920	8,046	9,063	9,239	9,582
1981	7,980	10,787	12,018	11,354	11,667	11,925	10,675	9,751	9,454	7,991	7,654	8,037
1982	9,519	8,634	6,580	6,238	6,227	5,808	6,007	6,395	5,666	5,775	7,106	9,359
1983	9,720	7,136	6,229	6,267								

Source: Citrus Assoc. of the N.Y. Cotton Exch.   T.456

Wholesale Price of Oranges (California) F.O.B. Packed Fresh   In Dollars Per Box

Year	Jan.	Feb.	Mar.	Apr.	May	June	July	Aug.	Sept.	Oct.	Nov.	Dec.	Average
1976	7.60	6.70	6.35	6.23	6.18	6.57	6.91	7.00	7.60	7.76	9.96	8.47	7.28
1977	7.00	7.50	7.28	7.38	7.11	7.88	7.70	8.78	9.10	9.70	12.70	11.30	8.62
1978	11.90	11.20	10.54	9.37	9.97	10.10	10.70	13.40	14.50	14.30	13.50	13.50	11.91
1979	13.50	12.29	13.68	13.19	13.58	15.98	13.50	12.40	12.40	11.00	11.60	10.70	12.82
1980	9.72	9.72	10.60	9.54	9.21	9.39	9.52	9.52	9.50	9.54	13.40	11.60	10.11
1981	11.00	10.90	10.20	9.78	10.00	12.10	14.10	12.80	12.60	11.70	11.50	12.70	11.62
1982	13.50	13.80	13.50	14.30	17.20	17.40	18.30	18.80	26.20	27.50	22.10	12.70	17.94
1983	11.30	10.40											

Source: Economic Research Service, U.S.D.A.   T.453

Wholesale Index Price of Frozen Orange Concentrate[1]   1967 = 100[2]

Year	Jan.	Feb.	Mar.	Apr.	May	June	July	Aug.	Sept.	Oct.	Nov.	Dec.	Average
1976	2.383	2.352	2.352	2.383	2.383	2.383	2.187	2.187	2.187	2.187	2.187	2.089	2.272
1977	2.040	2.776	2.752	2.752	2.752	2.910	2.910	3.101	3.223	3.223	3.459	3.508	2.951
1978	3.508	3.508	3.514	3.514	3.514	3.514	3.514	3.514	3.514	3.514	3.649	3.787	3.547
1979[2]	260.2	260.2	260.2	260.2	260.2	260.2	260.2	260.2	260.2	260.2	260.2	260.2	260.2
1980	260.2	260.2	260.2	254.3	254.3	249.2	249.2	249.2	249.2	249.2	236.5	236.5	250.7
1981	241.1	280.2	312.2	338.1	338.1	338.1	338.1	338.1	335.5	334.0	323.4	313.1	319.2
1982	312.9	337.7	334.5	326.5	315.4	308.4	308.7	307.1	307.8	307.7	307.5	303.2	315.5
1983	304.0	300.8											

[1] Packer to wholesale distributor, or retail chain store, f.o.b. plant.   [2] Prior to 1979 prices are in $ per dozen 6 oz. cans.   Source: Bureau of Labor Statistics (0242–0301.99)   T.454

Palm Oil

World palm oil production during 1983 was estimated by the USDA at 6.1 million tonnes, nearly 300,000 tonnes above the 1982 level. Although 1983 world production was projected to be a record high, the increase between 1982 and 1983 was the smallest recorded in the past five years. Malaysian production, which accounted for over half the world total, had increased as much as 20% in some areas after the Cameroon Weevil, imported from Africa, was introduced into crop fields with the intention of stimulating palm tree pollination. Subsequently, producers noticed evidence that weevil pollination may have "stressed" the trees, possibly limiting fruit yields and the future rate of production. Analysts said that three years may be required to assess the effect of weevil pollination. However, the initial sharp increase in Malaysian production brought about by the weevil exceeded the pickup in world use, and total world stocks of palm oil were expected to soon recover from the relatively low 1982 beginning levels.

World palm oil consumption is expected to grow in 1983 because of its more favorable price relationship this year with soybean oil and rapeseed oil. India is expected to remain the largest importer of palm oil for domestic use and the Pakistan market is growing rapidly. The Soviet Union, which uses palm oil primarily for the production of margarine, increased its imports significantly in 1982.

World Palm Oil Statistics In Thousand Metric Tons

Year	Malaysia	Colombia	China	Indonesia	Ivory Coast	Sabah	Zaire	Nigeria	Total (Prod.)	Malaysia	Indonesia	Ivory Coast	Sabah	Singapore	Zaire	Papua N. Guin.	Total (Exp.)
1974	942	51		351	140	88	174	491	2,605	870	282	102	88		66		1,461
1975	1,137	47		411	146	116	165	500	2,875	1,032	386	114	128		53		1,793
1976	1,261	40		434	151	131	155	500	3,059	1,207	406	92	128		40		1,927
1977	1,613	52	81	497	135	129	150	510	3,476	1,427	421	79	124	277	21	27	2,393
1978	1,786	51	87	525	150	146	137	515	3,713	1,514	412	82	144	299	10	28	2,481
1979	2,189	71	93	600	150	155	98	500	4,182	1,901	438	50	155	492	—	35	3,091
1980	2,576	74	100	691	160	180	93	520	4,706	2,260	455	88		679	10	38	3,755
1981[1]	3,300	88	112	800	195	203	170	535	5,784	2,785	240	80		500	5	48	3,843
1982[2]	3,500	95	115	850	200	—	165	540	6,075	3,000	250	85		520	5	50	4,081
1983																	

[1] Preliminary. [2] Projected. *Source: Economic Research Service, U.S.D.A.* T.457

Palm Oil—U.S. Supply & Distribution In Millions of Pounds

Year Begin. Oct.	Imports	Supply Stocks Oct. 1	Total Supply	Shortening	Margarine	Salad or Cooking Oil	Other	Total (Food)	Non-Food Uses	Total Disappearance	Exports (& Shipments)	Value of Imports[2]	U.S. Ports C.I.F.	Malaysia, 5% Bulk, CIF Europe
1972-3	363	93	456	299	7	9	29	344	12	356	40	9.7	12.3	13.9
1973-4	346	60	406	260	1	3	20	285	12	297	24	20.1	22.2	26.8
1974-5	757	88	845	606	16	24	37	683	9	692	27	24.2	24.7	23.9
1975-6	933	127	1,060	699	52	77	11	839	44	883	39	16.2	18.1	17.7
1976-7	661	138	813	430	48	91	11	580	30	610	58	19.8	23.8	24.0
1977-8[1]	361	131	492	253	23	50	19	346	21	367	51	26.4		
1978-9[1]	277	74	351							265	12			
1979-0[1]	212	74	280							223	21			
1980-1[1]	324	42	242	188						299	9			
1981-2[1]		58		217										
1982-3														

[1] Preliminary. [2] F.O.B. importing countries. *Source: Economic Research Service, U.S.D.A.* T.458

Average Wholesale Palm Oil Prices, CIF, Bulk, U.S. Ports In Cents Per Pound

Year	Jan.	Feb.	Mar.	Apr.	May	June	July	Aug.	Sept.	Oct.	Nov.	Dec.	Average
1974	24.9	28.0	21.2	20.4	22.6	22.8	21.4	22.9	24.0	18.6	26.3	28.8	26.9
1975	31.2	27.5	28.1	28.9	24.6	23.0	20.6	21.1	18.2	22.4	19.0	17.2	22.8
1976[1]	16.8	16.4	17.0	16.0	15.9	17.4	19.5	19.0	19.7	19.4	19.4	19.6	18.1
1977	20.5	23.0	27.1	25.5	29.5	29.6	25.0	23.3	21.6	20.2	20.4	23.9	24.3
1978	23.1	25.2	27.4	28.0	28.4	30.6	31.2	28.5	29.8	30.5	30.4	31.0	28.7
1979	31.7	32.8	31.1	31.2	31.5	32.1	33.6	31.5	30.3	29.1	29.1	30.1	31.2
1980	32.0	32.4	31.8	29.6	27.8	28.1	27.6	26.5	25.5	22.3	27.1	26.9	28.1
1981	27.5	28.3	25.5	27.5	27.6	N.A.	N.A.	25.0	24.7	N.A.	N.A.	N.A.	26.6
1982	N.A.	N.A.	24.0	23.7	24.4	22.3	18.9	18.6	19.3	18.0	19.0	20.0	20.8
1983													

[1] Prior to 1976 prices are for CONGO, TANK CARS, F.O.B. N.Y. *Source: Economic Research Service, U.S.D.A.* T.459

Paper

The U.S. production of virtually all paper and paperboard products slumped in 1982. The effect of economic depression was most severe on the production of wrapping and packaging paper and board grades that are more dependent than other grades on industrial demand. Building paper and board grades were produced at decade-low levels. Product groups such as printing and writing papers and sanitary tissues were less drastically affected. Paper mills and paperboard mills were operated between 83 and 86 percent of capacity during 1982, and price cutting and the high cost of operating at low rates cut the profits of some paper companies to 50 percent of 1981 earnings.

An estimated 2.2 million tons of paper and paperboard producing capacity was scheduled to come onstream in 1982. This newer and more cost-effective plant noticeably reduced the U.S. markets' consumption of foreign paper and paperboard products, especially from Canada. U.S. imports of paper, 90 percent of which were newsprint, accounted for at least 15 percent of the U.S. apparent consumption (production plus imports less exports). Preliminary projections indicated that U.S. imports of paper and board in 1982 were about 3.3 percent lower than in 1981. U.S. buying ahead of anticipated Canadian mill strikes and the widening U.S./Canadian dollar exchange differential kept imports from dropping as sharply as they had during the 1975 recession. Foreign producers using waste-paper as a raw material were able to compete successfully with the virgin-fiber-based U.S. products, and the dollar value of U.S. exports of paper and board fell by nearly 11 percent in 1982.

Private analysts, considering the signs of economic recovery that appeared early in 1983, projected that the productivity of the paper and board industry during 1983 would grow by nearly 4 percent, and that the upturn would be led by the production of consumer and services related paper and board products.

Shipments of (Paper Products) Shipping Containers[1]   In Millions of Square Feet Surface Area

Year	Jan.	Feb.	Mar.	Apr.	May	June	July	Aug.	Sept.	Oct.	Nov.	Dec.	Total
1970	18,246	14,428	15,516	15,589	15,081	15,108	15,926	15,406	16,527	17,194	13,878	11,964	185,864
1971	14,415	14,223	16,261	16,001	14,916	17,192	15,470	16,412	17,144	17,280	16,653	15,866	191,832
1972	15,453	16,302	18,358	16,579	17,676	18,939	15,427	15,858	21,482	19,721	18,643	17,158	211,926
1973	18,037	17,591	20,428	18,526	20,074	19,702	16,818	19,914	18,720	21,775	19,450	17,016	228,052
1974	19,784	18,480	19,729	19,658	19,842	17,979	17,826	18,807	17,169	18,592	15,576	12,630	216,072
1975	14,689	13,768	14,742	14,541	16,151	15,612	16,023	17,006	18,580	20,053	16,017	16,145	194,329
1976	17,509	16,836	19,208	18,058	17,888	19,040	17,176	18,495	18,651	18,741	17,980	16,789	216,371
1977	17,156	17,086	20,607	18,498	19,467	20,139	16,997	20,372	19,674	19,923	19,343	17,936	227,197
1978	18,075	18,711	21,804	19,482	21,772	22,060	17,601	22,301	20,531	22,608	20,354	18,599	243,898
1979[2]	20,844	19,409	22,863	20,574	21,769	20,986	19,615	22,163	20,327	23,617	20,330	18,109	250,643
1980[2]	21,935	20,452	21,466	20,636	19,150	19,115	18,456	19,345	21,054	23,229	18,849	19,313	241,377
1981[2]	21,161	20,044	21,383	21,583	19,808	20,933	20,486	20,434	21,094	21,867	18,317	17,600	246,152
1982[2]	18,961	18,638	21,218	19,941	18,720	20,071	18,610	20,414	20,657	21,604	19,043	17,540	234,846
1983[2]	19,980												

[1] Corrugated & solid fiber. [2] Preliminary. Source: *National Paperboard Association*

T.463

How to keep your Commodity Year Book statistics up-to-date continuously throughout the year.

To keep up-to-date statistics on the commodities in this book, you should have COMMODITY YEAR BOOK STATISTICAL ABSTRACT SERVICE. This three-times-yearly publication provides the latest available statistics for updating the statistical tables appearing in the COMMODITY YEAR BOOK. The ABSTRACT is published in the Winter (Jan.), Spring (Apr.) and Fall (Oct.). Subscription price is $55 per year.

Commodity Research Bureau, Inc.

75 MONTGOMERY ST., JERSEY CITY, N.J. 07302

PAPER

Salient Statistics of Newsprint in the United States and Canada   In Thousands of Metric[4] Tons

Year	Production	Exports	Canada	Finland	Italy	Norway	Sweden	U.K.	Others	Total	Consumption	Stocks, Dec. 31 At Mills	At Publishers[2]	Canada Production	Exports	Stocks At Mills
1970	3,310	141	6,320	308	—	—	7	—	—	6,635	9,727	33	749	8,607	7,876	236
1971	3,296	161	6,564	303	—	—	—	—	14	6,881	9,829	41	705	8,455	7,490	332
1972[3]	3,656	122	6,772	328	—	—	—	—	0	7,101	10,547	27	544	8,820	8,120	251
1973	3,738	107	6,855	381	—	—	—	—	0	7,236	10,794	24	603	9,140	8,340	193
1974	3,561	103	6,949	213	—	—	—	—	—	7,162	10,284	23	827	9,548	9,075	143
1975	3,691	123	5,488	33	—	—	—	—	—	5,521	9,254	21	734	7,679	6,863	95
1976	3,736	95	6,251	57	—	—	—	—	—	6,308	9,611	29	921	8,915	7,827	299
1977[4]	3,512	117	5,751	0	—	—	—	—	—	5,751	9,279	31	722	8,154	7,345	282
1978	3,418	75	6,428	0	—	—	—	—	—	6,428	9,864	20	660	8,811	7,974	184
1979	3,685	65	6,372	—	—	—	35	—	97	6,504	10,197	16	628	8,756	7,809	162
1980	4,239	159	7,127	8	9	15	54	37	13	7,279	10,089	21	732	8,625	7,642	165
1981	4,753	283	6,936	4	0	12	23	—	2	6,977	10,165	38	961	8,946	7,870	194
1982[1]	4,574	275	6,485	11	0	19	0	0	16	6,531	10,115	86	834	8,117	7,140	265
1983																

[1] Preliminary.   [2] Reporting only to A.N.P.A.; group represents about 75%.   [3] Beginning 1972 data is for 30 lb. basis.   [4] Data prior to 1977 are in THOUSANDS OF SHORT TONS.   [5] Data for imports are in thousands of short tons.   *Source: Newsprint Service Bureau, A.P.I.*   T.464

Average Price of Newsprint Rolls   Index: 1967 = 100

Year	Jan.	Feb.	Mar.	Apr.	May	June	July	Aug.	Sept.	Oct.	Nov.	Dec.	Average
1975	181.8	181.8	181.8	184.7	184.7	184.7	184.7	184.7	184.7	184.7	184.7	184.7	184.0
1976	184.7	184.7	190.1	193.1	197.9	197.9	202.7	203.3	205.3	205.3	205.3	207.6	198.2
1977	209.4	209.4	216.7	216.7	216.7	216.7	216.7	216.7	216.7	216.7	216.7	216.7	215.4
1978	216.7	216.7	216.7	228.2	228.2	228.2	228.2	230.5	230.5	230.5	230.5	230.5	226.3
1979	230.5	238.9	241.7	244.7	247.7	247.7	247.7	247.7	247.7	262.1	265.1	268.2	249.4
1980	269.4	269.4	269.4	269.4	277.6	283.7	283.7	N.A.	283.8	283.8	283.8	298.3	279.3
1981	301.9	301.9	301.9	301.9	301.9	N.A.	301.9	309.3	316.8	316.8	316.8	316.8	308.0
1982	316.8	316.8	318.1	321.1	322.4	319.4	318.4	318.4	318.4	318.4	303.7	300.7	316.1
1983	300.7	299.1											
1984													

[1] Standard rolls, contract, delivered to principal ports.   *Source: Bureau of Labor Statistics (0913–0291.99)*   T.468

Average Price of Wood Pulp, Bleached Sulphate Softwood   In Dollars Per Ton

Year	Jan.	Feb.	Mar.	Apr.	May	June	July	Aug.	Sept.	Oct.	Nov.	Dec.	Average
1975	364.13	364.13	364.13	364.13	364.13	358.11	364.13	364.13	364.13	364.13	364.13	366.50	363.83
1976	366.50	366.50	366.50	366.50	366.50	366.50	367.13	365.06	365.06	365.06	365.06	365.06	365.95
1977	360.93	364.64	364.64	364.64	368.54	368.54	368.54	368.54	357.57	354.75	N.A.	N.A.	364.13
1978	350.76	341.15	341.15	330.52	327.66	327.66	306.73	306.73	306.73	339.91	336.97	336.97	329.41
1979	345.85	346.91	358.68	363.48	363.48	373.36	377.45	383.87	383.87	413.59	413.59	413.59	377.89
1980	440.95	440.95	440.95	473.35	473.35	473.35	476.97	476.97	476.97	476.97	476.97	476.97	467.05
1981	476.97	476.97	476.97	487.64	487.54	487.54	487.54	487.54	487.54	488.07	506.75	506.75	488.15
1982	503.14	501.65	501.65	482.58	476.66	473.20	446.30	440.58	436.98	428.92	428.07	427.65	462.28
1983	N.A.												
1984													

Source: Bureau of Labor Statistics (0911–0211.09)   T.469

Index Price of Coated Printing Paper, No. 3   Dec. 1973 = 100

Year	Jan.	Feb.	Mar.	Apr.	May	June	July	Aug.	Sept.	Oct.	Nov.	Dec.	Average
1977	134.7	135.8	136.3	137.9	137.7	137.5	139.3	138.9	139.4	143.7	143.8	144.0	139.1
1978	146.1	146.3	150.0	151.7	152.5	153.8	153.8	154.9	156.3	159.7	161.2	160.6	153.9
1979	161.7	163.2	163.7	165.4	166.5	167.1	167.1	167.7	168.1	171.8	171.8	171.7	167.2
1980	170.8	175.0	176.8	178.9	178.9	178.9	179.0	179.6	179.8	179.9	182.3	183.3	178.6
1981	183.5	185.7	186.8	189.3	191.4	191.4	191.4	189.6	198.1	202.0	202.4	204.6	193.0
1982	203.8	204.9	203.8	202.7	202.7	202.7	201.4	200.0	203.3	203.0	203.5	203.5	203.0
1983	203.5	203.6											
1984													

Source: Bureau of Labor Statistics (0913–0113.99)   T.470

PAPER

U.S. Production & Consumption of Woodpulp, Pulpwood & Other Fibrous Materials in the Manufacture of Paper & Board   In Thousands of Short Tons[6]

Year	Special Alpha[2]	Sulfite Bleached	Sulfite Unbleached	Sulfate Bleached	Sulfate Semi-Bleached	Sulfate Unbleached	Soda	Ground-wood	Semi-Chemical	Defi-brated[3]	Screenings, Damaged, etc.	Total Wood Pulp	Wood Pulp[4]	Other Fibrous Materials[5]	Pulp-wood[6]
1970	1,705	1,931	413	11,348	1,906	16,217	218	4,404	3,297	—2,105—		43,546	43,192	11,423	67,562
1971	1,674	1,809	354	11,684	1,557	16,309	208	4,462	3,473	—2,372—		43,903	44,148	11,875	67,157
1972	1,656	1,827	345	12,460	1,574	17,792	184	4,639	3,786	—2,502—		46,767	47,347	12,595	71,538
1973	1,637	1,810	374	13,055	1,826	18,165	188	4,670	3,864	—2,740—		48,327	48,772	13,257	73,596
1974	1,723	1,804	405	13,705	1,672	17,635	200	4,711	3,758	—2,736—		48,349	48,341	12,936	74,327
1975	1,583	1,594	357	12,448	1,396	15,369	N.A.	4,351	3,201	—2,785—		43,084	42,431	10,992	65,421
1976	1,443	1,599	435	13,696	1,298	17,784	N.A.	4,649	3,576	—3,242—		47,421	47,541	12,616	72,011
1977	1,401	—2,012—		14,384	1,244	18,436	N.A.	4,852	3,542	—3,226—		49,132	48,477	12,929	73,935
1978	1,415	—1,643—		15,218	1,198	18,693	N.A.	4,807	3,552	—3,233—		50,020	49,614	13,305	74,170
1979	1,447	—1,814—		16,763	N.A.	19,576	N.A.	4,619	3,889	N.A.		51,177	N.A.	13,739	77,362
1980[1]	1,417	—1,910—		17,561	N.A.	19,735	N.A.	4,887	3,938	N.A.		52,055	N.A.	13,185	79,703
1981[7]	1,366	—1,812—		————39,597————				5,038	3,940			51,783		13,523	79,604

[1] Preliminary.   [2] Also includes dissolving grades.   [3] Or exploded.   [4] Does not include wood pulp consumption by plants classified outside paper & board industries.   [5] Waste paper; straw; rags; cotton fibre; manila stock; etc.   [6] Data for pulpwood expressed in thousands of cords of 128 cu. ft.—roughwood basis. Pulpwood includes slabs, chips, & millwaste.   [7] Estimate.   *Sources: Bureau of the Census; American Paper Inst.*   T.465

U.S. Foreign Trade in Pulpwood, Wood Pulp, Paper, Paper Board & Paper Products   In Thousands of Short Tons

Year	Exports Wood Chips	Wood Pulp	Waste Fibrous Mater.[3]	Paper	Paper Board	Construction P. & B.	Converted Paper & Board	Imports Pulpwood Chips	Wood Pulp	Waste Fibrous Mater.	Paper	Paper Board	Construction P. & B.	Paper & Bd. Products	Total Value of Imports Mill. $[4]
1971	1,926	2,175	419	549	2,377	65	156	1,202	3,515	113	7,268	17	293	33	1,638
1972	2,524	2,237	415	569	2,288	79	166	978	3,773	132	7,519	8	461	39	1,791
1973	3,466	2,344	683	601	2,129	98	231	1,254	3,993	133	7,928	33	452	57	2,177
1974	3,866	2,806	1,383	923	2,471	125	348	818	4,123	133	7,874	34	339	62	2,964
1975	3,177	2,565	861	947	1,808	115	301	626	3,078	134	6,118	8	176	39	2,678
1976	3,947	2,518	1,273	928	2,134	128	333	1,051	3,727	163	6,962	13	264	65	3,295
1977	4,038	2,640	1,544	724	2,210	109	342	1,386	3,864	148	7,065	28	346	201	3,568
1978	3,618	2,599	1,599	552	2,299	82	520	1,791	4,025	127	8,347	100	503	327	3,992
1979	4,499	2,935	2,233	590	2,491	80	606	1,528	4,318	123	8,372	49	470	321	4,759
1980[1]	4,478	3,806	2,664	887	3,671	78	678	1,724	4,051	121	8,008	66	358	227	5,190
1981[2]	4,000	3,678	2,200	950	3,200	120	650	1,600	4,086	118	7,700	80	370	185	5,400
1982[2]		3,395							3,894						

[1] Preliminary.   [2] Estimates.   [3] Excludes rags for paperstock.   [4] Paper base stocks, paper and manufactures.   *Source: Dept. of Commerce*   T.466

Paper and Board Production in the United States   In Thousands of Short Tons

Year	Paper News-print	Coated Printing	Publicat. & Print.[5]	Writing & Relat.	Coarse[2]	Sani-tary	All Paper Total	Paperboard Other Bleached Paperboard	Corrugating Material	Unbleac. Kraft[6]	All Paperboard Total	Wet Machine Board	Construction[3] Construction (Paper)	All Construction Total	Total All Types
1970	3,345	3,279	2,646	2,937	5,439	3,548	23,625	1,856	4,332	11,436	25,477	139	1,594	4,276	53,516
1971	3,321	3,251	2,758	2,996	5,442	3,660	23,811	1,938	4,596	11,700	26,135	138	1,837	5,001	55,086
1972	3,451	3,546	3,010	3,329	5,713	3,796	25,435	1,964	4,992	13,030	28,522	148	1,915	5,352	59,457
1973	3,459	3,814	3,116	3,817	5,694	3,726	26,483	1,971	5,285	13,139	29,267	149	1,858	5,406	61,304
1974	3,395	3,974	2,832	4,102	5,731	3,800	26,674	1,957	5,093	12,755	28,017	144	1,845	5,118	59,930
1975	3,476	3,318	2,400	3,244	4,805	3,669	23,306	1,792	4,411	11,170	24,452	115	1,616	4,648	52,521
1976	3,400	3,967	2,984	3,910	5,661	3,936	26,612	1,894	5,045	12,501	27,840	130	1,771	5,316	59,898
1977	3,525	4,215	3,316	4,170	5,930	4,045	28,096	1,968	5,485	13,241	29,006	N.A.	1,852	5,492	62,722
1978	3,489	4,513	3,507	4,277	5,778	4,036	28,506	1,634	5,792	N.A.	30,033	N.A.	1,915	5,625	64,300
1979	3,778	4,580	2,048	4,596	5,708	4,403	29,580	1,841	5,918	13,857	31,168	144	1,868	5,436	66,329
1980[1]	4,660	4,751	2,127	4,793	5,327	4,298	30,164	1,794	5,864	14,249	31,143	138	1,369	4,390	65,834
1981[1]	4,753	4,940	2,000	4,900	5,700	4,600	30,669	1,900	6,000	14,800	31,561	160	1,200	3,846	66,439
1982[4]	4,574	5,031													

[1] Preliminary.   [2] Packaging & industrial converting paper.   [3] Paper and board.   [4] Estimate.   [5] Prior to 1979 data are for Book Paper, Uncoated.   [6] Prior to 1979 data are for Linerboard.   *Source: Bureau of the Census*   T.467

PAPER

Index Price of Shipping Sack Paper[1] Dec. 1973 = 100

Year	Jan.	Feb.	Mar.	Apr.	May	June	July	Aug.	Sept.	Oct.	Nov.	Dec.	Average
1977	147.5	147.5	147.5	157.0	158.7	158.1	158.1	158.1	158.1	158.1	158.1	158.1	155.4
1978	158.1	158.1	158.1	158.1	158.1	158.1	158.1	158.7	167.7	168.2	168.2	168.2	161.5
1979	168.2	168.2	171.0	178.6	178.6	178.6	178.6	178.6	178.6	185.7	187.3	187.3	178.3
1980	176.5	183.7	188.3	195.5	195.5	195.5	192.2	194.2	194.2	194.2	N.A.	194.2	191.3
1981	203.2	213.0	217.4	221.2	224.5	224.5	224.5	224.5	224.5	224.5	223.4	219.5	220.4
1982	219.5	222.2	220.7	220.7	216.3	207.2	207.2	207.2	207.2	213.9	213.9	213.9	214.2
1983	220.7	225.4											
1984													

[1] Unbleached kraft. *Source: Bureau of Labor Statistics (0913–0304.99)*

T.471

Average Price of Boxboard[1] In Dollars Per Ton

Year	Jan.	Feb.	Mar.	Apr.	May	June	July	Aug.	Sept.	Oct.	Nov.	Dec.	Average
1975	205.27	205.27	205.27	203.62	203.63	203.63	203.63	203.63	203.63	203.63	203.63	203.63	204.04
1976	203.63	203.63	203.63	203.63	203.63	210.27	211.92	211.92	211.92	211.92	211.92	211.92	208.34
1977	211.92	211.92	211.92	211.92	211.92	216.87	216.87	216.87	216.87	216.87	218.53	218.53	215.08
1978	218.53	220.18	221.83	221.83	221.83	221.83	221.83	221.83	221.83	223.48	223.48	225.13	221.97
1979	225.13	228.43	N.A.	N.A.	311.03	311.03	320.60	322.25	322.25	328.85	328.85	335.78	303.42
1980	335.78	335.78	348.98	360.53	360.53	363.83	377.02	377.02	N.A.	390.63	390.63	393.10	366.71
1981	395.58	399.29	399.29	405.48	411.67	411.67	411.67	411.67	411.67	411.67	411.67	411.67	407.75
1982	404.86	404.86	403.62	403.62	403.62	403.62	396.20	389.40	377.85	374.55	372.90	372.90	392.33
1983	N.A.												
1984													

[1] BENDING CHIPBOARD (Folding Boxboard). *Source: Bureau of Labor Statistics (0914–0225.04)*

T.472

How to keep your Commodity Year Book statistics up-to-date continuously throughout the year.

To keep up-to-date statistics on the commodities in this book, you should have COMMODITY YEAR BOOK STATISTICAL ABSTRACT SERVICE. This three-times-yearly publication provides the latest available statistics for updating the statistical tables appearing in the COMMODITY YEAR BOOK. The ABSTRACT is published in the Winter (Jan.), Spring (Apr.) and Fall (Oct.). Subscription price is $55 per year.

Commodity Research Bureau, Inc.

75 MONTGOMERY ST., JERSEY CITY, N.J. 07302

Peanuts and Peanut Oil

Early in 1983, the USDA estimated total world production of peanuts during the 1982/83 season at 17.7 million tonnes compared with 19.6 million tonnes during the 1981/82 season. The 1982/83 world production of peanut meal was estimated to be 3.9 million tonnes compared with 4.7 million during 1981/82, and 1982/83 world peanut oil production was 2.9 million tonnes compared with 3.5 million a year earlier. The government of India, the leading exporter of peanuts, had announced that the 1982/83 Indian fiscal year (March/April) export quota for hand-picked-select peanuts would be 100,000 tons on a shelled basis. This would have been a considerable increase over the fiscal year 1982 quota of 55,000 tons. However, only 32,000 tons of peanuts were exported, all of them to the Soviet Union. Partly as a consequence of weather problems, Indian exports of hand-picked-select peanuts during the 1982/83 marketing year were estimated to be only 42,000 tons. The weakness of prices for peanuts worldwide was aggravated by South Africa's aggressive sales policies, high yields from the Sudanese rain-fed crop, and by abundant U.S. peanut stocks. China, another major exporter, which had been unwilling to sell at low prices during the fall of 1981, reportedly began to offer 40/50 peanuts at prices as low as $710 a ton CIF Europe in the second half of 1982. Brazilian exports of peanuts during 1983 were forecast at only 5,000 tons compared with the average throughout 1977–81 of 29,000 tons per year because of damaging January rains.

The 1982/83 U.S. peanut crop was forecast by the USDA to be 1.6 million tons compared with 1.8 million tons during 1981/82 and 1.04 million during 1980/81 which was the smallest U.S. peanut crop since 1964. The indicated yield per acre of 2,668 pounds was slightly under the 1981-season figure. Peanut acreage for harvest was estimated at 1.28 million, 14 percent below the previous year's acreage. The growing weather throughout calendar 1982 had been generally favorable in all areas excepting the Southwest regions. The peanut crop in the Virginia-Carolina area, compared with 1981, was down by 23 percent. The peanut crop in the Southeast was down by 11 percent, and in the Southwest it was 17 percent below the 1981/82 figure. U.S. peanut supplies during 1982/83 (August–July) were expected to total 4.2 billion pounds, or about 5 percent below the previous season's supply, because the 1982 yield of 2,703 pounds per acre, the highest ever recorded, more than offset the drop in 1982 acreage. Because of generally increased yields, as well as lower seed costs, non-land production costs were estimated to have declined slightly during 1982, and the slower rate of the increase of input prices was expected to continue through 1983.

Edible uses during 1982/83 were expected to reach the pre-1980 drought figure of more than 2 billion pounds, and it was estimated that this increase in edible demand along with the smaller crop could reduce the level of crushings by a fifth. Preliminary estimates put the 1982-season supplies of U.S. peanut oil at 40 million pounds compared with 41 million during 1981. Peanut meal supplies during recent years have totaled around 100,000 tons a year. Supplies of peanut meal, which has a crude protein range of 41 to 50 percent, are not expected to exceed current levels in the next few years.

U.S. peanut exports during 1982 continued to recover from the drought-induced 1981 shortfall by registering an increase of 37 percent. Edible peanut exports more than doubled at the same time oilstock exports declined by 48 percent. The EC, the largest buyer of U.S. shelled and unshelled peanuts, imported nearly 57,000 tonnes during the last quarter of 1982 compared with 23,000 tonnes purchased by Canada and 8,000 tonnes imported by Japan.

Government Programs

The Agriculture and Food Act of 1981 provided a poundage quota for peanuts of 1.167 million short tons in 1983, 2¾ percent below the 1982 level. The loan rate for 1982 quota peanuts remained at $550 a ton. The law stipulated that the national average support level for the 1983, 1984, and 1985 crops of quota peanuts would be the support rate for the preceding crop, adjusted to reflect increases in the national average costs of production for the preceding year, but in no event less than $550 a ton. The price support rate for 1982 additional (non-quota) peanuts was set at $200 a ton. A support level of $185 per ton was set for 1983-crop additional peanuts.

Farm prices for the 1982 crop averaged 24.9 cents a pound, 2 cents below the previous season.

Crude Peanut Oil Produced[2] in the United States   In Millions of Pounds

Year	Jan.	Feb.	Mar.	Apr.	May	June	July	Aug.	Sept.	Oct.	Nov.	Dec.	Total
1975	17.7	12.8	12.1	13.3	17.2	22.8	29.2	29.1	33.6	34.6	27.6	25.3	275.3
1976	26.6	32.6	44.3	51.1	56.9	66.5	47.6	41.5	39.0	31.5	24.6	24.5	486.6
1977	20.7	24.7	35.5	33.0	32.8	30.1	24.7	22.4	6.9	6.1	10.5	4.4	252.0
1978	9.7	9.2	11.1	18.0	18.1	18.1	10.4	16.6	7.7	10.3	6.3	9.5	145.2
1979	11.7	14.2	22.5	18.6	23.0	15.5	8.2	10.8	4.5	4.5	6.1	7.7	183.0
1980	6.2	15.1	16.7	25.9	30.7	22.9	23.5	21.2	5.9	2.1	6.3	5.9	182.4
1981[1]	6.1	6.0	10.5	17.3	19.1	19.5	13.6	9.8	5.3	9.7	12.0	12.7	141.6
1982[1]	11.3	11.1	19.4	26.3	22.3	19.0	15.0	11.8					
1983													

[1] Preliminary.   [2] Not seasonally adjusted.   *Source: Statistical Reporting Service, U.S.D.A.*

T.473

PEANUTS AND PEANUT OIL

World Production of Peanuts (in the Shell) In Thousands of Metric Tons

Crop Year	Argentina	Brazil	China[2]	Burma	India	Indonesia	Mali	Nigeria	South Africa	Senegal	Sudan	Taiwan	Thailand	United States	Zaire (Congo)	World Total
1970-1	234	928	529	2,650	6,111	402	—	780	303	545	—	122	185	1,351	180	17,431
1971-2	388	849	486	2,580	6,181	400	150	845	385	920	—	98	200	1,363	180	18,121
1972-3	252	893	390	2,450	4,092	389	100	540	197	540	568	94	203	1,485	180	15,690
1973-4	440	590	513	2,350	5,932	483	120	342	537	700	544	97	210	1,576	200	16,216
1974-5	290	453	466	2,800	5,111	512	178	460	243	900	930	94	230	1,664	230	17,384
1975-6	400	442	404	2,700	6,755	633	119	302	132	1,424	796	91	142	1,750	268	18,912
1976-7	339	514	416	2,750	5,264	568	120	310	227	1,182	748	89	142	1,701	289	17,264
1977-8	600	324	457	2,065	6,087	682	126	302	298	671	1,027	77	119	1,690	295	16,443
1978-9	372	340	384	2,377	6,208	743	107	341	179	1,053	813	92	102	1,793	295	17,664
1979-0	672	465	337	2,822	5,772	708	57	377	344	600	852	86	122	1,800	295	17,170
1980-1[1]	295	310	484	3,600	5,020	795	60	400	307	489	799	85	136	1,044	295	16,041
1981-2[3]	240	290	3,826	3,600	7,239	857		400	114	790	850	85	150	1,806	295	19,591
1982-3[3]	265	250	3,800		5,500	885			143	875	830			1,561		17,550
1983-4[3]																

[1] Preliminary. [2] Includes Manchuria. [3] Estimated. *Source: Foreign Agricultural Service, U.S.D.A.* T.474

Salient Statistics of Peanuts in the United States

Crop Year	Acreage Planted (1,000 Acres)	Acreage Harvested For Nuts (1,000 Acres)	Average Yield Per Acre In Lbs.	Production Picked and Threshed 1,000 Lbs.	Season Farm Price ¢ Lb.	Farm Value Million Dollars	Exports Unshelled (Thousand Pounds Yr. Beg. Aug.)	Exports Shelled	Imports Unshelled	Imports Shelled
1970-1	1,518	1,469	2,030	2,983,121	12.8	382,967	6,436	213,027	1,269	204
1971-2	1,529	1,455	2,066	3,005,118	13.6	408,371	35,801	403,397	1,299	859
1972-3	1,533	1,486	2,203	3,274,761	14.5	475,367	4,369	385,588	1,039	443
1973-4	1,530	1,496	2,323	3,473,837	16.2	562,460	66,094	523,986	79	444
1974-5	1,520	1,472	2,491	3,667,604	17.9	657,987	17,703	548,083	127	466
1975-6	1,532	1,500	2,564	3,846,722	19.6	754,491	22,708	318,229	207	290
1976-7	1,549	1,518	2,464	3,739,190	20.0	746,675	24,765	580,496	432	66
1977-8	1,545	1,512	2,456	3,715,055	21.0	780,869	64,284	705,032	272	148
1978-9[1]	1,541	1,509	2,619	3,952,384	21.1	833,885	94,612	745,593	53	161
1979-0[1]	1,546	1,520	2,611	3,968,485	20.6	819,276	—Not Available—			
1980-1[2]	1,521	1,399	1,645	2,301,282	25.1	578,292				
1981-2[2]	1,514	1,489	2,675	3,981,850	26.9	1,069,526				
1982-3[2]	1,299	1,273	2,703	3,441,435	24.9	855,741				
1983-4[2]	1,313									

[1] Preliminary. [2] Estimate. *Source: Economic Research Service, U.S.D.A.* T.475

Supply & Disposition (Farmers' Stock Basis) & Support Program

Crop Year Begin. Aug. 1	Production[3]	Imports	Stocks Aug. 1	Total	Exports & Shipments	Crushed for Oil	Seed, Feed & Residual	Military	Civilian	Civilian per Capita (Lbs.)	Support Price ¢ Lb.	% of Parity	Amount Put under Support Quantity Mil. Lbs.	% of Prod.	Owned by CCC July 31 Mi. Lbs.
1970-1	2,938	2	353	3,334	290	799	209	3	1,580	7.8	12.75	75	1,084	36.3	11
1971-2	3,005	2	453	3,460	552	814	79	—	1,623	7.9	13.42	75	1,238	41.2	4
1972-3	3,275	2	392	3,669	521	850	175	—	1,694	8.2	14.25	75	1,277	39.0	24
1973-4	3,474	1	429	3,904	709	683	119	—	1,840	8.8	16.42	75	1,029	29.6	0
1974-5	3,668	1	553	4,222	740	590	−54	—	1,800	8.5	18.30	75	1,072	29.2	552
1975-6	3,847	1	1,146	4,993	434	1,447	193	—	1,859	8.7	19.70	75	1,136	29.5	958
1976-7	3,739	1	1,060	4,800	783	1,108	513	—	1,789	8.4	20.70	75	854	22.8	0
1977-8	3,726	1	608	4,324	1,025	487	392	—	1,838	8.5	21.50	75	535	14.4	2
1978-9	3,952	1	581	4,534	1,141	527	284	—	1,996	9.2	21.00	67	515	12.9	—
1979-0	3,968	1	586	4,555	1,057	571	271	—	2,028	9.3	21.00	59	702	17.7	—
1980-1	2,301	401	628	3,330	503	446	321	—	1,647	9.0	22.75	57	323	14.1	—
1981-2[1]	3,982	2	413	4,403	576	574	558	—	1,933		22.75				
1982-3[2]	3,441	2	756	4,199	735	473	266	—	2,025		27.50				
1983-4[2]				700											

[1] Preliminary. [2] Estimate. [3] Production is on a net weight basis. *Source: Economic Research Service, U.S.D.A.* T.476

PEANUTS AND PEANUT OIL

U.S. Production of Peanuts (Harvested for Nuts) by States   In Millions of Pounds

Crop Year	Alabama	Arkansas	Florida	Georgia	Louisiana	Mississippi	New Mexico	No. Car.	Oklahoma	So. Car.	Tennessee	Texas	Virginia	U.S. Total
1970	315.4	—	110.0	1,125.5	—	4.4	18.3	445.9	192.0	29.6	—	429.9	312.1	2,983
1971	401.6	—	139.9	1,269.9	—	16.5	16.6	325.5	219.0	30.0	—	366.8	219.5	3,005
1972	368.4	—	137.7	1,341.4	—	16.0	20.5	370.2	242.7	31.8	—	480.5	265.7	3,275
1973	400.0	—	150.4	1,344.0	—	16.6	18.9	466.5	253.7	30.1	—	471.2	322.4	3,474
1974	474.4	—	170.5	1,661.5	—	6.0	13.0	384.3	217.7	31.0	—	413.3	295.9	3,668
1975	535.6	—	177.7	1,726.6	—	13.5	20.2	373.7	232.3	29.5	—	463.6	284.6	3,847
1976	513.6	—	165.0	1,554.3	—	12.3	21.7	440.7	246.0	24.6	—	463.6	309.0	3,739
1977	589.1	—	170.5	1,499.1	—	11.6	25.4	444.1	267.6	31.2	—	394.5	293.0	3,715
1978	551.8	—	182.1	1,725.3	—	13.1	24.1	465.4	207.0	35.7	—	436.5	311.6	3,952
1979	584.9	—	179.9	1,704.8	—	12.4	25.3	378.5	264.0	32.3	—	533.0	253.5	3,968
1980	265.0	—	143.0	994.6	—	7.5	22.4	291.3	140.2	14.3	—	293.3	129.8	2,301
1981	602.7	—	178.0	1,655.5	—	12.7	24.9	555.6	189.3	39.0	—	393.3	330.8	3,982
1982[1]	531.0		157.5	1,516.1		0	25.1	415.3	172.0	30.0		319.0	275.5	3,441
1983														

[1] Preliminary, December estimate.   *Source: Crop Reporting Board, U.S.D.A.*   T.477

Visible Supply (Stocks) of Peanuts and Products on Hand in the U.S.   In Millions of Pounds

Year Begin. Aug. 1	Farmers' Stock Peanuts[2] Virginias	Runners	Spanish	Total	Shelled Edibles Virginias	Runners	Spanish	Total	Shelled Oil Stock[3]	Total Shelled	Roasting Stock[5]	Crude Peanut Oil[4]	Peanut Cake & Meal[4]
1970-1	2.4	0	.5	2.8	105.8	65.4	67.1	238.3	12.7	251.0	16.1	8.8	7.7
1971-2	3.2	4.0	7.0	14.2	126.9	81.1	83.0	291.0	27.1	318.0	16.0	11.8	21.6
1972-3	3.4	8.2	15.7	27.4	66.9	90.7	67.0	224.5	33.8	258.3	20.9	8.5	3.0
1973-4	2.9	48.7	5.2	56.9	45.2	122.0	73.5	240.6	25.6	266.3	17.7	11.7	7.0
1974-5	3.8	30.4	4.2	38.4	87.3	209.5	62.9	359.8	16.2	375.9	15.1	10.9	6.8
1975-6	16.4	193.8	16.8	227.0	89.3	129.9	60.2	279.4	20.7	300.1	17.8	18.3	10.4
1976-7	4.0	244.0	1.9	250.0	68.5	159.9	87.2	315.7	83.2	398.8	30.6	22.9	5.9
1977-8	2.0	49.4	3.0	54.4	62.1	255.0	55.4	372.5	29.8	402.3	18.2	42.6	11.7
1978-9	8.0	20.0	.6	28.7	62.5	251.6	44.8	359.0	37.4	396.4	25.6	14.5	10.9
1979-0	7.2	5.9	.3	13.5	87.7	214.2	46.1	348.0	46.4	394.4	48.2	17.2	1.0
1980-1	8.4	44.0	11.0	63.4	67.9	265.4	38.4	401.1	29.5	401.1	30.6	21.6	8.8
1981-2	14.1	14.1	.2	28.3	56.6	181.0	30.7	268.3	10.4	278.6	14.4	15.9	7.3
1982-3[1]	24.3	60.6	0	84.9	129.0	273.3	48.2	450.4	20.6	471.0	45.2	4.3	2.3
1983-4													

[1] Preliminary. [2] Excludes stocks on farms, but includes stocks owned or held for account of C. C. C. [3] Includes ungraded or straight run peanuts. [4] Relates to peanut oil mills only. [5] Cleaned & unshelled. *Source: Agricultural Marketing Service, U.S.D.A.*   T.478

Average Price Received by Producers in U.S. for Peanuts in the Shell   In Cents Per Pound

Year	Sept.	Oct.	Nov.	Dec.	Jan.	Feb.	Mar.	Apr.	May	June	July	Aug.	Average[1]
1970-1	12.9	13.2	12.3	11.9	13.0	12.0	—	—	—	—	—	12.9	12.6
1971-2	13.5	13.8	13.6	13.9	—	—	—	—	—	—	—	13.0	13.6
1972-3	14.8	14.3	14.3	14.3	14.2	—	—	—	—	—	—	15.0	14.5
1973-4	16.1	16.4	16.1	16.5	16.6	—	—	—	—	—	—	17.7	16.2
1974-5	17.9	18.1	17.6	17.8	17.6	—	—	—	—	—	—	18.4	17.9
1975-6	19.7	19.8	19.6	18.7	—	—	—	—	—	—	—	19.1	19.6
1976-7	19.8	19.9	20.0	20.0	20.2	—	—	—	—	—	—	21.3	20.0
1977-8	20.9	20.9	20.4	20.4	21.5	—	—	—	—	—	—	21.2	21.0
1978-9	20.8	21.4	21.0	20.8	21.2	—	—	—	—	—	—	21.1	21.1
1979-0	21.4	20.3	20.3	20.6	20.4	—	—	—	—	—	—	21.0	20.6
1980-1[2]	20.7	22.0	27.1	37.1	49.2	—	—	—	—	—	—	32.6	25.1
1981-2[2]	28.6	26.5	25.7	26.8	24.9	—	—	—	—	—	—	25.3	26.9
1982-3[2]	24.9	25.2	25.2	25.5	26.6	—							
1983-4													

[1] Weighted average by sales. [2] Preliminary. *Source: Crop Reporting Board, U.S.D.A.*   T.479

PEANUTS AND PEANUT OIL

Millings and Production of Peanuts and Products in the U.S.   In Millions of Pounds

Year Begin. Aug. 1	Virginias	Runners	Spanish	Total	Virginias	Runners	Spanish	Total	Shelled Oil Stock	Total All Grades	Cleaned (In Shell)	Shelled Peanuts Crushed	Crude Peanut Oil	Peanut Cake & Meal
	Millings — Farmers' Stock Peanuts[2]				Shelled Edibles				Production					
1970-1	880.4	692.9	1,043	2,616	442.0	371.1	560.0	1,373	482.3	1,855	119.1	600.9	253.5	340.4
1971-2	675.1	1,066	909.5	2,650	303.0	565.3	517.3	1,386	518.7	1,904	121.0	612.3	260.0	334.4
1972-3	689.1	1,288	911.4	2,888	284.9	666.7	551.6	1,503	567.1	2,070	113.3	638.8	269.0	359.8
1973-4	784.2	1,398	869.1	3,051	378.2	778.4	522.0	1,679	509.3	2,188	149.5	513.6	213.9	285.0
1974-5	636.1	1,646	641.3	2,923	283.3	892.2	381.6	1,557	558.4	2,116	132.2	443.7	188.4	245.6
1975-6	663.6	2,213	584.6	3,462	283.5	966.5	340.9	1,591	914.7	2,506	154.8	1,088	476.0	601.2
1976-7	669.7	2,356	429.9	3,455	271.6	1,212	273.8	1,757	729.8	2,487	150.8	833.2	362.6	466.5
1977-8	734.0	2,246	368.7	3,349	284.2	1,383	214.8	1,882	468.8	2,350	198.1	366.2	151.0	208.1
1978-9	805.5	2,272	346.4	3,424	320.4	1,413	210.5	1,944	436.0	2,380	233.5	396.0	164.3	218.0
1979-0	682.9	2,496	323.7	3,502	254.2	1,573	176.1	2,003	487.0	2,490	183.8	429.1	179.7	236.2
1980-1	387.4	1,395	105.6	1,888	134.8	797.5	61.0	993.3	286.9	1,280	104.1	335.5	137.8	187.2
1981-2[1]	897.6	2,477	236.1	3,611	328.4	1,620	139.6	2,088	387.8	2,476	231.6	431.5	175.0	237.3
1982-3														

[1] Preliminary.   [2] For prod. of shelled edible grades, oil stock (including ungraded or straight run peanuts) and roasting stock.   Source: *Agricultural Marketing Service, U.S.D.A.*
T.480

Disappearance and Reported Uses of Peanuts and Products in the U.S.   In Millions of Pounds

Year Begin. Aug. 1	Edible Grades	Oil Stock[3]	Total All Grades	Cleaned (In Shell)	Crude Peanut Oil[4]	Cake & Meal[4]	Candy	Salted	Peanut Butter Sandwiches	Butter[5]	Other Products	Total	Oil Stock Crushed For Oil, Cake & Meal	Total All Grades
	Apparent Disappear.[2] (Milled Peanut Prod.) — Shelled Peanuts						Reported Used (Shelled Peanuts—Raw Basis) — Edible Grades Used in — Peanut							
1970-1	1,320	467.9	1,788	119.2	250.5	326.5	243.2	238.8	25.3	540.4	17.6	1,065	600.9	1,666
1971-2	1,452	512.0	1,964	116.1	263.3	353.0	246.0	241.7	25.6	556.8	17.0	1,087	612.3	1,699
1972-3	1,487	575.3	2,062	116.6	265.7	355.8	259.8	254.4	25.6	578.1	17.6	1,136	638.8	1,774
1973-4	1,559	518.8	2,078	152.1	214.7	285.1	251.5	284.3	23.9	660.0	19.3	1,239	513.6	1,753
1974-5	1,637	551.0	2,188	129.4	181.0	242.0	217.0	278.3	20.4	651.0	14.4	1,181	443.7	1,625
1975-6	1,555	852.2	2,407	142.0	471.3	605.8	239.7	301.6	21.0	648.1	16.0	1,226	1,088	2,314
1976-7	1,700	783.2	2,483	163.2	342.9	460.7	235.0	253.8	24.2	617.9	17.8	1,149	833.2	1,982
1977-8	1,895	461.2	2,356	190.6	179.1	208.9	235.2	274.2	28.2	623.8	18.7	1,180	366.2	1,546
1978-9	1,955	426.9	2,382	210.9	161.6	227.9	268.4	291.6	28.1	664.9	19.1	1,272	396.0	1,668
1979-0	1,979	503.9	2,483	201.4	175.3	228.4	258.4	284.9	30.3	700.0	19.3	1,293	429.1	1,722
1980-1	1,097	306.0	1,403	120.3	143.5	188.7	237.9	205.5	24.1	588.6	19.7	1,076	335.5	1,411
1981-2[1]	1,096	377.6	2,283	200.7	155.7	234.9	255.9	278.0	22.7	653.7	15.3	1,226	431.5	1,657
1982-3														

[1] Preliminary.   [2] Includes in transit, exports and domestic use, except for oil stock for which disappearance is assumed to equal crushings.   [3] Graded & ungraded oil stock only.   [4] Relates to peanut oil mills only.   [5] Peanuts used in peanut butter by mfrs. for own use in candy is included under peanut candy.   Source: *Statistical Reporting Service, U.S.D.A.*
T.481

World Imports of Peanut Oil (Crude & Refined) into Specified Countries   In Thousands of Metric Tons

Year	Algeria	Australia	Austria	Belgium-Lux.	Venezuela	Canada	Dominican Rep.	France	West Germany	Hong Kong	Italy	Singapore	Netherlands	Switzerland	Portugal	United Kingdom
1969	.5	4.6	6.3	17.1	—	8.4	.5	134.9	57.0	14.0		5.0	8.6	—	5.1	85.2
1970	.9	6.9	4.0	21.4	—	8.8	5.5	142.6	52.3	12.3		6.1	9.4	—	6.7	95.8
1971	0	4.7	4.4	28.5	4	5.3	17	124.0	54.7	15.0		4.8	11.1	—	3.6	67.8
1972	13	4.3	4.3	32.9	2	7.4	17	205.9	71.5	15.5		3.6	9.2	—	8.3	60.8
1973	30	2.4	4.7	32.0	15	7.4	14.1	167.3	66.3	16.2		4.0	20.0	—	5.5	74.8
1974	1	4	3	23	5	6	4	142	51	12		6	15	—	2	37
1975	0	3	3	21	32	7	4	179	38	16		1	9	—	6	29
1976	6	2	2	31	38	7	16	218	37	20	22	3	8	—	—	20
1977	5	4	2	29	64	7	15	217	37	23	31	2	8	—	—	16
1978	—	1	2	25	66	6	2	186	38	22	30	2	11	14	—	15
1979	—	2	2	35	1	5	—	221	40	25	46	2	21	20	—	15
1980[1]	—	—	3	4.2	—	5	—	247	39	29	42	3	33	20	—	17
1981																

[1] Preliminary.   Source: *Foreign Agricultural Service, U.S.D.A.*
T.482

PEANUTS AND PEANUT OIL

Production, Consumption, Stocks and Foreign Trade of Peanut Oil in the U.S. In Millions of Pounds

Year	Production Crude	Production Refined	Consumption In Refining	Consumption In End pdt's.	Stocks—Dec. 31 Crude	Stocks—Dec. 31 Refined	Imports for Consumption	Exports Crude	Exports Refined
1969	188.2	148.6	153.7	157.4	8.0	6.3	—	31.6	1.9
1970	196.5	157.6	163.3	168.0	8.7	6.6	—	24.7	7.3
1971	280.6	183.3	189.8	189.2	7.8	8.4	—	84.2	.8
1972	257.8	170.9	177.4	178.1	15.9	5.2	—	60.0	.7
1973	265.9	156.0	162.3	160.5	18.9	6.2	—	100.1	3.3
1974	185.0	128.9	134.9	130.4	16.5	7.2	1.1	45.1	.7
1975	275.3	144.9	150.8	122.7	42.6	23.1	.7	17.6	9.2
1976	486.6	259.9	267.8	249.7	192.3	17.4	1.2	9.7	95.7
1977	252.0	249.7	257.2	243.9	91.5	7.6	—	71.8	9.7
1978	145.2	171.9	178.0	169.0	7.3	4.7	—	71.7	17.2
1979[1]	183.0	130.1	134.3	120.4	22.6	7.3			
1980[1]	182.4	170.6	166.7	165.3	7.5	4.3			
1981	141.6	122.8	133.5	115.3	12.9	5.2			

[1] Preliminary.   Source: *Bureau of Census*   T.483

Utilization of Peanut Oil in the United States In Thousands of Pounds

Year Begin. Aug.	Shortening	Margarine	Cooking and Salad Oils	Other Edible	Total Food Uses	Non-Food Uses	Factory Consumption	Foots & Loss	Domestic Disappearance
1969-0	16,000	1,000	129,000	—	145,000	9,000	164,000	5,000	154,000
1970-1	16,000	—	152,000	13,000	181,000	12,000	188,000	7,000	193,000
1971-2	15,000	—	160,000	8,000	183,000	12,000	196,000	7,000	195,000
1972-3	14,000	—	122,000	11,000	147,000	11,000	156,000	6,000	159,000
1973-4	23,000	—	124,000	1,000	147,000	11,000	167,000	6,000	158,000
1974-5	13,000	—	87,000	44,000	145,000	8,000	116,000	5,000	153,000
1975-6	27,000	28,000	150,000	59,000	264,000	12,000	232,000	9,000	276,000
1976-7	29,000	27,000	143,000	26,000	225,000	8,000	218,000	6,000	232,000
1977-8[1]	20,000	—	211,000	−47,000	183,000	11,000		8,000	194,000
1978-9[2]	16,000		146,000						120,000
1979-0[2]			98,000						193,000
1980-1[2]			153,000						150,000
1981-2			100,000						

[1] Preliminary.   [2] Estimate.   Source: *Bureau of the Census*   T.484

Average Price of Domestic Crude Peanut Oil (in Tanks) F.O.B., Southeast Mills In Cents Per Pound

Year	Oct.	Nov.	Dec.	Jan.	Feb.	Mar.	Apr.	May	June	July	Aug.	Sept.	Average
1970-1	19.8	19.8	20.2	21.1	21.1	20.4	19.8	20.6	20.4	21.4	21.8	20.6	20.6
1971-2	19.8	19.9	20.4	19.3	19.0	20.1	21.6	21.3	20.6	20.9	19.9	19.3	20.2
1972-3	19.4	20.8	22.3	22.1	21.7	20.9	21.7	23.0	23.7	23.6	34.1	26.4	23.3
1973-4	28.0	28.6	37.1	42.4	48.0	49.8	48.5	49.8	50.9	49.9	50.9	49.8	44.5
1974-5	52.6	50.9	49.8	46.6	45.9	40.5	39.3	36.6	40.9	47.3	52.7	49.3	46.6
1975-6	42.2	39.3	35.3	35.4	37.8	38.9	35.4	31.0	33.5	38.3	36.4	38.0	37.1
1976-7	38.0	37.3	38.9	40.3	41.0	40.8	43.6	35.5	34.7	29.8	29.2	30.7	36.6
1977-8	34.1	33.4	42.8	47.3	44.9	41.2	46.6	48.1	47.1	44.5	44.9	48.6	43.6
1978-9[1]	45.1	49.7	46.0	51.4	47.4	37.9	40.9	41.2	36.5	39.0	37.0	35.5	42.3
1979-0	34.4	31.1	29.5	25.9	25.8	22.9	20.5	22.4	23.1	26.9	33.2	36.0	27.6
1980-1	35.8	48.7	49.1	47.7	39.3	34.1	34.0	37.1	38.0	38.1	43.2	40.3	40.5
1981-2	34.5	34.5	30.9	27.3	31.4	23.3	29.1	29.9	26.2	24.7	22.7	22.5	28.1
1982-3	22.9	25.2	26.1										
1983-4													

[1] Prices prior to 1978-9 are for REFINED in New York.   Source: *Agricultural Marketing Service, U.S.D.A.*   T.485

Pepper

Worldwide 1982 exports of black and white pepper were estimated at slightly below the record 1981 level of 132,000 tonnes. The relatively low world prices for pepper recorded during 1982 were generally attributed to continued aggressive marketing by Brazilian shippers. New York spot prices for Brazilian black pepper averaged 62.1 cents per pound during 1982 and only 54.2 cents per pound in the first quarter of 1983. Competition from Brazil reportedly caused the average price of Indonesian Lampong black pepper to fall from an average 66.3 cents per pound during 1982 to nearly 65.5 cents in the first quarter of 1983. Brazilian exports of pepper in 1982 were estimated at nearly 44,000 to 45,000 tonnes compared with the record Brazilian shipment level of 46,895 tonnes in 1981. During the first 11 months of 1982, Brazilian shipments amounted to 41,019 tonnes compared with 42,808 tonnes during the corresponding 1981 period.

Higher shipments of pepper from India during 1982 did not offset declines in exports from both Brazil and Malaysia. However, expectations of a record 1983 crop of India pepper, estimated at between 42,000 and 45,000 tonnes, led to projections of ample supplies during the year. Because of the Indian bumper crop of pepper, it was expected that India's traditional export markets, the Soviet Union and Eastern Europe, might be unable to absorb the increased supplies because of their many bilateral trade agreements with India. World pepper prices were therefore expected to continue to be weak throughout 1983 as Indian shippers competed with other origins in Western markets. India's pepper exports during 1982 were estimated to be approximately 21,000 to 22,000 tonnes vs. 18,636 tonnes in 1981.

U.S. imports of black pepper during 1982 totaled 27,811 tonnes compared with 28,563 tonnes the previous year. Brazil supplied nearly 54 percent of these imports, Indonesia supplied 42 percent, and India supplied 3 percent. U.S. imports of white pepper amounted to nearly 2,721 tonnes in 1982 compared to 2,503 tonnes in 1981. Indonesia supplied 81 percent, and Brazil supplied 16 percent. Total U.S. imports of ground black and white pepper were 82 tonnes vs. nearly 51 tonnes the previous year. Indonesian shipments accounted for nearly 37 percent of U.S. ground pepper imports. Nearly 25 percent of U.S. ground pepper imports in 1982 were shipped from Canada, and 12 percent from West Germany. U.S. 1982 imports of black pepper oleoresin totaled 146,990 kilograms, or nearly 147 tonnes, an increase of almost 40 percent. India supplied nearly 51 percent of U.S. oleoresin imports, Singapore supplied 42 percent, and Canadian shipments accounted for almost 8 percent.

During October 19–22, 1982, the tenth annual session of the International Pepper Community (IPC) met in Belem, Brazil. IPC members, Brazil, India, Indonesia, and Malaysia, agreed to revise their export floor prices upward. The new, minimum export prices for ASTA grade black pepper, c.i.f. New York, were established at 65 cents per pound for Brazil, Malaysia, and Indonesia, and at 72 cents per pound for India. Previous IPC export price levels had been set at 70 cents per pound for Brazil and Malaysia, 72 cents for Indonesia, and 73 cents per pound for India. However, because of relatively high world stocks of pepper and slack consumer demand, the IPC had difficulty enforcing sales at the higher minimum export prices. In March 1983, the IPC met in Medan, Indonesia, to discuss price support measures and the international pepper market. IPC members agreed to retain the higher prices set during the October 1982 meeting, but no new price enforcement methods were discussed.

The approximate New York spot price of Brazilian black pepper in early March 1982 was nearly 69 cents per pound, 3 cents higher than in the comparable period in 1981. But spot prices for Indonesian Lampong black pepper and Indian Malabar fell 3 cents and 1 cent, respectively in the same 1981/82 period, and the price of Brazilian white pepper fell by 2 cents per pound. By March 1983, the New York spot price of Brazilian black pepper had dropped sharply to 54 cents per pound, while prices for the other types of pepper fell 8 to 11 cents per pound.

The U.S., although it is not a pepper producer, exported 828.7 tonnes of pepper during 1982 compared with 822.2 tonnes during the previous year. Nearly 28 percent of the 1982 U.S. pepper exports were shipped to Canada, 15 percent to Saudi Arabia, and almost 13 percent to the Republic of Korea. Other important buyers of U.S. pepper shipments include, Panama, Spain, Hong Kong, and Costa Rica.

United States Imports of Pepper from Specified Countries   In Metric Tons[2]

Year	Brazil	Mexico	Sri Lanka (Ceylon)	India	Indonesia	Malaysia	Singapore	China	Total	Brazil	China	Indonesia	Malaysia	Singapore	Total
				Black Pepper								White Pepper			
1971	13,433		28.5	6,993	25,767	6,543	1,895		54,941	88.2	—	4,069	329.4	336.2	4,915
1972	8,869		—	2,753	28,911	5,088	1,778		47,440	148.8	—	4,875	158.2	210.1	5,449
1973	8,630		302	9,690	29,627	544	849		49,827	730.9	—	4,446	58.3	330.1	5,588
1974	6,914		90	16,277	19,627	5,415	1,283	—	49,781	121.4	—	5,627	189.8	155.7	6,327
1975[2]	6,436		41	6,708	4,613	4,487	773	10	23,156	170	—	1,514	63	59	1,813
1976	6,609		—	359	11,774	4,037	1,321	3	24,128	53	—	2,118	56	128	2,362
1977	5,282		157	4,890	9,466	3,140	478	—	23,540	40	—	2,765	42	63	2,920
1978	10,472		186	1,880	10,595	2,293	604	6	26,142	285	—	1,994	64	28	2,382
1979	9,704		281	627	10,898	2,644	156	61	24,482	414	10	2,159	51	94	2,756
1980	10,075		153	3,993	11,408	3,640	296	1	29,644	509	35	2,419	100	131	3,194
1981	14,716	31	295	559	12,615	273	37	21	28,563	763	1	1,561	43	75	2,503
1982[1]	14,887	10	172	848	11,620	172	63	3	27,811	423	1	2,194	—	95	2,721

[1] Preliminary.   [2] Data prior to 1975 are in THOUSANDS OF POUNDS.   *Source: Foreign Agricultural Service, U.S.D.A.*

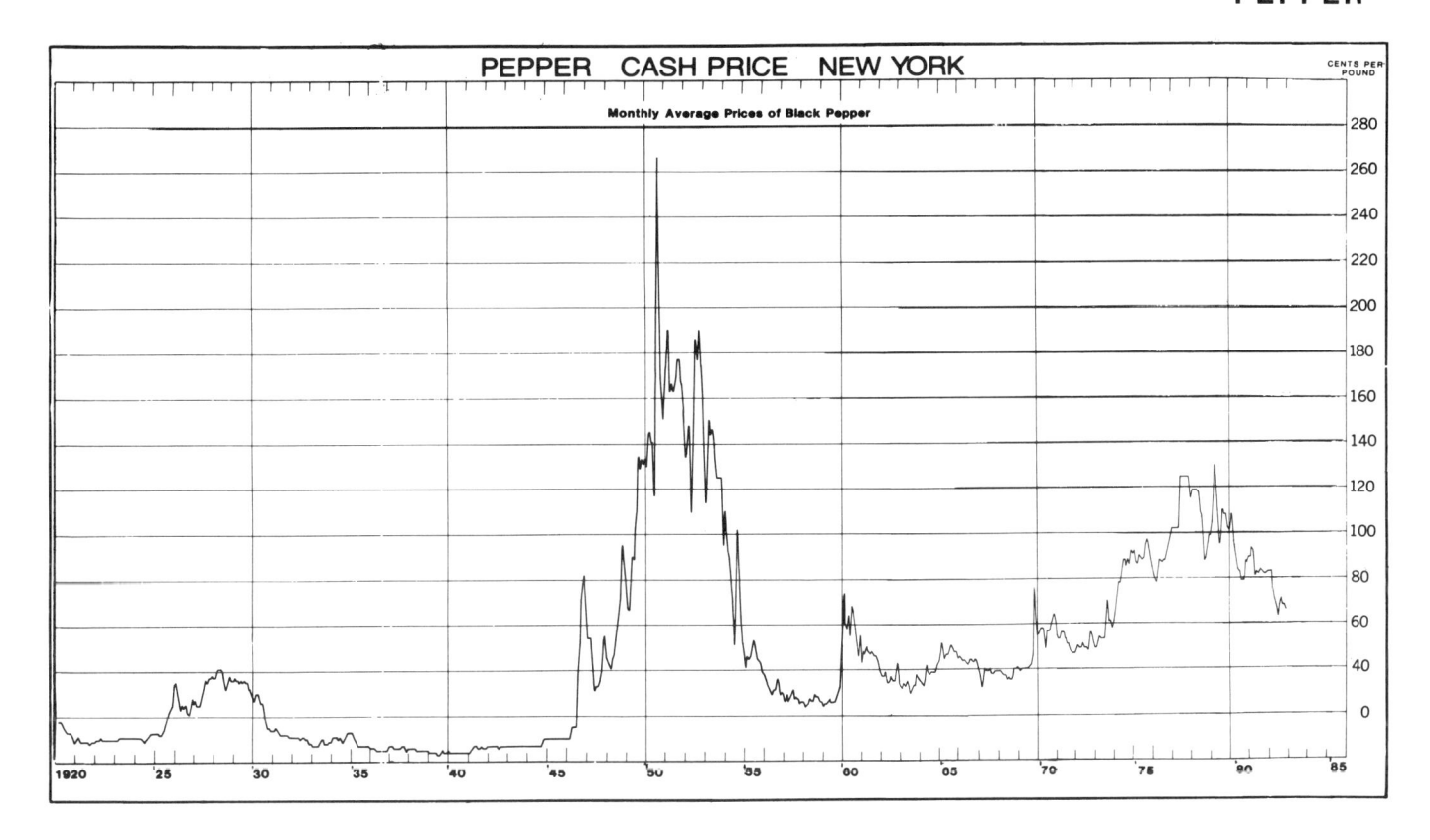

PEPPER

PEPPER CASH PRICE NEW YORK
Monthly Average Prices of Black Pepper

Average Black Pepper Prices in New York (Lampong, Whole Pepper)   In Cents Per Pound

Year	Jan.	Feb.	Mar.	Apr.	May	June	July	Aug.	Sept.	Oct.	Nov.	Dec.	Average
1971	52.5	52.5	56.0	56.0	55.0	52.5	51.0	51.0	48.0	47.0	46.5	47.0	51.3
1972	49.0	49.5	49.0	49.0	51.0	48.5	48.5	48.0	56.0	56.0	52.0	49.3	50.5
1973	49.3	52.0	54.0	53.0	52.5	53.0	65.0	70.0	61.0	61.0	57.5	61.0	57.4
1974	64.0	70.0	78.0	78.0	85.0	88.0	88.0	85.0	87.5	85.5	92.0	91.0	82.7
1975	91.5	87.0	86.0	90.0	89.0	87.5	88.5	95.0	97.0	94.0	87.5	85.0	89.8
1976	81.0	79.0	77.5	88.0	88.0	87.0	87.5	87.5	N.A.	N.A.	N.A.	102.0	86.4
1977	102.0	102.0	102.0	102.0	125.0	125.0	125.0	125.0	125.0	125.0	114.5	N.A.	115.7
1978	118.5	118.5	118.5	118.5	117.5	109.0	107.5	88.0	88.5	95.5	98.5	98.5	106.4
1979	105.0	N.A.	130.0	N.A.	N.A.	95.0	97.0	110.0	108.0	108.0	102.0	101.3	106.3
1980	108.0	101.0	96.3	93.0	87.0	84.3	82.8	79.0	79.0	88.0	86.5	89.3	89.5
1981	88.5	93.3	92.0	81.0	83.0	82.3	84.0	82.5	82.3	82.3	82.5	82.5	84.7
1982	82.5	82.5	75.0	75.0	70.0	69.0	67.0	63.0	69.0	70.5	68.5	68.3	71.7
1983	68.3	66.5											

Source: Bureau of Labor Statistics (0289–0131)   T.488

World Exports of Pepper (Black & White) by Major Producing Countries   In Metric Tons

Year	Brazil	India	Indonesia	Singapore[2]	Malagasy Rep.	Sarawak	Sri Lanka
1970	9,018	19,657	2,457		2,161	24,405	858
1971	17,235	16,901	23,566		1,284	26,914	46
1972	15,297	20,627	22,756		3,826	26,177	107
1973	13,761	27,942	25,452		3,193	22,830	518
1974	15,491	28,569	15,188		2,241	28,933	337
1975	17,944	24,399	14,525		3,461	29,815	96
1976	19,986	17,813	29,481		2,958	34,850	10
1977	17,099	25,892	30,856		3,748	26,795	635
1978	29,505	19,370	37,090	40,904	1,137	30,780	1,205
1979	25,186	20,545	24,986	38,395	N.A.	36,118	876
1980	31,964	26,795	29,345	33,233	N.A.	30,709	N.A.
1981[1]	46,895	18,636	33,996	30,098	N.A.	28,606	N.A.

[1] Preliminary.   [2] Reexports.   Source: Foreign Agricultural Service, U.S.D.A.   T.486

Petroleum

Petroleum continues to be the world's most important source of energy, even though its share of the total U.S. energy consumption has declined in recent years. Petroleum products accounted for 42 percent of the U.S. consumption of energy in 1982 compared with 47 percent in 1979—the year in which consumer resistance to sharply higher oil prices began to be reflected in slower rates of consumption. Petroleum market analysts have admitted that price-induced oil conservation was a greater than anticipated influence behind the drop in crude oil prices that took place during most of 1981 and the first half of 1982. Exploration and development efforts were redoubled in the U.S. after the oil price shock of 1979, and oil prices fell even further under the effect of the worldwide economic depression of the early '80s. The U.S. demand for crude oil imports has fallen by almost 40 percent since 1979.

In 1982, crude oil consumption in the U.S. declined for the fourth consecutive year. The U.S. demand for oil during the year was estimated at 11.9 million barrels a day, 20 percent below the peak demand level recorded in 1978, and 6.1 percent below the 1981 level.

The U.S. production of crude oil during 1982 was nearly unchanged from the 1981 production level. Crude oil production in Alaska rose by almost 6 percent, more than offsetting an estimated 0.3 percent decline in production by the 48 states. Alaska was the source of about 20 percent of the U.S. production.

Gross U.S. crude oil imports in 1982 were estimated at 3.8 million barrels per day, 12 percent under the 1981 level and 42 percent below imports in 1977. Net imports, as a percentage of U.S. crude oil use, were at their lowest level since 1972. During 1982, approximately 5 percent of U.S. crude oil imports went into the Strategic Petroleum Reserve (SPR). SPR stocks, as of July 1982, were estimated at 267 million barrels, about 40 percent of total U.S. crude oil stocks. In the first seven months of 1982, price-induced conservation by energy users, substitutions of alternative forms of energy, and product stock reductions by refiners and distributors caused a drawdown in product stocks to 782 million barrels from 890 million.

After their decontrol in January 1981, U.S. crude wellhead prices rose to nearly $35 per barrel before sinking to around $28 per barrel on the average by mid-1982. The price of U.S. crude oil imports in 1982 dropped nearly 9 percent to around $34 per barrel, and expenditures for crude oil imports fell at least 16 percent during the year. Nominal domestic prices for gasoline, middle distillates, and residual fuel oils fell by 5 to 10 percent between 1981 and 1982.

Refined petroleum product consumption in the U.S. was down 3.5 percent from 1981 levels in 1982—a weakness brought about, for the most part, by economic depression. Although the fuel efficiency of the U.S. automotive fleet improved by nearly 3 percent during the year, motor gasoline consumption did not decrease significantly in 1982, and secondary and tertiary inventories were observed to be growing in the second half of the year. Distillate fuel oil consumption fell by about 2 percent from the 1981 level because of a 7 percent decline in industrial production. The demand for residual fuel oil dropped most sharply—17 percent—because of shifts by electric utilities from residual fuel oil to coal and to increased nuclear power generation. U.S. refinery utilization rates were low in 1982 for the third straight year.

The free world consumption of petroleum in 1982 declined by close to 3 percent, continuing a trend that has been evident since the late 1970s. Reduced rates of consumption brought about a responsive drop in crude oil production since 1979 that was almost entirely absorbed by members of the Organization of Petroleum Exporting Countries (OPEC). The decline in OPEC production throughout the past three years exceeded the amount of the decrease in world consumption over the same period, and the difference was supplied principally by the increased production of both Mexican and British North Sea oil.

The complex of U.S. energy consumption in coming years is expected to include a trend towards increasing reliance on coal and nuclear energy at the expense of petroleum. Petroleum consumption in 1983 is expected to increase by less than 1 percent, to 30.72 quadrillion British thermal units (Btu). In comparison, nuclear energy consumption is expected to increase 10 percent over 1982 levels to 3.4 quadrillion Btu, and the consumption of coal is expected to increase by 4 percent to 16.6 quadrillion Btu. The use of motor gasoline is expected to remain unchanged, and the use of distillate and petroleum feedstocks (used as raw material) is expected to rise during 1983.

The production of crude oil by the U.S. is expected to fall somewhat in 1983 notwithstanding the influ-

World Production of Crude Petroleum, by Specified Countries In Thousand Barrels Per Day[3]

Year	Algeria	Canada	China	Libya	Iran	Iraq	Kuwait	Nigeria	Mexico	Indonesia	Un. King.	USSR	Saudi Arabia	United States	Venezuela	World Total
1972		561	N.A.	820	1,839	529	1,201	665	185	396		2,896	2,202	3,455	1,178	18,601
1973		648	N.A.	794	2,139	737	1,102	750	191	489		3,094	2,773	3,361	1,229	20,368
1974		617	475	555	2,198	721	930	823	238	502		3,374	3,096	3,203	1,086	20,538
1975[3]	983	1,439	1,490	1,480	5,350	2,262	2,084	1,783	705	1,307	12	9,625	7,075	8,375	2,346	52,880
1976	1,075	1,295	1,670	1,933	5,883	2,415	2,145	2,067	831	1,504	245	10,143	8,577	8,132	2,294	57,312
1977	1,152	1,320	1,874	2,063	5,663	2,348	1,969	2,085	981	1,686	768	10,682	9,245	8,245	2,238	59,685
1978	1,161	1,313	2,082	1,983	5,242	2,563	2,131	1,897	1,209	1,635	1,082	11,185	8,301	8,707	2,166	60,057
1979	1,154	1,496	2,122	2,092	3,168	3,477	2,500	2,302	1,461	1,591	1,568	11,460	9,532	8,552	2,356	62,535
1980	1,012	1,435	2,114	1,787	1,662	2,514	1,656	2,055	1,936	1,577	1,622	11,773	9,900	8,597	2,168	59,538
1981[2]	805	1,285	2,012	1,140	1,380	1,000	1,125	1,433	2,313	1,605	1,811	11,909	9,815	8,572	2,102	55,788
1982[1]	675	1,200	2,025	900	2,000	950	800	1,250	2,700	1,300	2,000	11,900	6,500	8,650	1,750	52,000

[1] Estimate. [2] Preliminary. [3] Prior to 1975, data is in millions of barrels produced. (42 gallons each.) *Source: Bureau of Mines* T.489

PETROLEUM

ence of increased exploration and reduced drillings costs that were observed during 1982. It is thought that the sharply reduced prices recorded for oil during 1982 will curtail exploration activity in 1983. Consequently, U.S. crude oil imports are expected to rise 16 percent from 1982 levels as economic recovery continues. Increased imports will probably account for 56 percent of the projected 1983 total petroleum product supply increase of 270,000 barrels per day. However, net imports are likely to represent only 7 percent of the total product supply compared with 6 percent in 1982. In 1982, residual fuel oil accounted for over 50 percent of U.S. net product imports, and thus was unusually sensitive to the sharp decline in economic activity. The business recovery projected for 1983 should therefore result in a relatively greater increase in refined product imports as compared with the increase in total product supply.

Futures Markets

Heating oil and Leaded gasoline futures (N.Y. harbor delivery) are traded on the New York Mercantile Exchange (NYMEX). Gasoil futures are traded on the International Petroleum Exchange (IPE) in London. Trading in crude petroleum futures began in early 1983 at the Chicago Board of Trade (CBOT) and at NYMEX.

Production of Major Refined Petroleum Products in Continental U.S.   In Millions of Barrels

Year	Asphalt[2]	Coke[3]	Fuel Oil Distillate	Fuel Oil Residual	Gasoline[4]	Petro-Chemical Feedstocks	Special Naphthas	Miscel. pdt's.	Total Jet Fuel	Kerosene	Liquified Gases[7] (For Fuel)	Lubricants	Road Oil	Still Gas[5]	Wax[6]
1972	155.3	119.8	963.6	292.5	2,320	124.0	32.4	16.4	310.0	80.1	84.5	65.3	7.9	171.0	6.1
1973	167.9	132.3	1,030.2	354.6	2,402	132.6	33.1	19.9	313.7	80.1	89.6	68.7	7.3	176.8	6.8
1974	164.2	123.7	974.0	390.5	2,337	134.8	33.5	25.2	305.1	56.9	81.6	70.7	7.2	175.7	6.9
1975	144.0	129.2	968.4	451.0	2,394	122.2	27.3	32.2	318.0	55.7	80.5	56.2	4.9	175.4	5.7
1976	139.7	130.1	1,070	504.0	2,517	164.4	32.6	47.2	335.8	55.7	84.2	61.8	3.2	180.7	7.0
1977	154.1	133.8	1,197	639.0	2,582	191.4	31.4	53.0	355.7	62.0	85.3	64.5	3.3	192.5	7.2
1978	172.9	134.6	1,156	608.6	2,631	223.1	36.7	47.0	353.9	56.3	87.5	69.5	3.2	200.0	6.9
1979[1]	168.8	137.3	1,151	615.6	2,515	252.1	36.6	42.7	369.2	66.8	84.7	71.0	1.6	205.1	6.9
1980[1]	141.2	135.5	974.1	578.4	2,394	254.6	36.5	38.5	365.6	50.1	87.0	65.1	2.5	190.3	6.4
1981[1]	124.2		954.9	480.3	2,351				353.5	43.6		60.6			
1982[1]	119.6		953.4	388.6	2,325				356.5	42.0		51.6			

[1] Estimated. [2] 5.5 barrels = 1 short ton. [3] 5 barrels = 1 short ton. [4] Finished. [5] 1 barrel = 3.600 cubic feet. [6] 1 barrel = 280 pounds. [7] Liquefied refinery gases. *Source: Bureau of Mines*
T.490

United States Production of Crude Petroleum   In Millions of Barrels

Year	Arkansas	California	Colorado	Illinois	Kansas	Louisiana	Michigan	Mississippi	Montana	New Mexico	Oklahoma	Alaska	Texas	Utah	Wyoming	Total U.S.
1971	18.3	358.5	27.4	39.1	78.5	935.2	11.9	64.1	34.6	118.4	213.3	79.5	1,223	23.6	148.1	3,454
1972	18.5	347.0	32.0	34.9	73.7	891.8	13.0	61.1	33.9	110.5	207.6	72.9	1,302	26.6	140.0	3,455
1973	18.0	336.1	36.6	30.7	66.2	831.5	14.6	56.1	34.6	101.0	191.2	72.3	1,295	32.7	141.9	3,361
1974	16.5	323.0	37.5	27.6	61.7	737.3	18.0	50.8	34.6	98.7	177.8	70.6	1,262	39.4	140.0	3,203
1975	16.1	322.2	38.1	26.1	59.1	650.8	24.4	46.6	32.8	95.1	163.1	69.8	1,222	42.3	135.9	3,057
1976	18.1	326.0	39.0	26.3	58.7	606.5	30.4	46.1	32.8	92.1	161.4	63.4	1,190	34.3	134.1	2,976
1977	20.2	349.7	39.4	25.7	57.5	562.9	33.0	43.0	32.7	87.1	156.4	169	1,138	32.9	111.8	2,985
1978	20.3	347.2	36.8	23.4	56.6	532.7	34.7	42.0	30.5	83.4	150.5	449	1,074	31.4	137.4	3,178
1979	18.9	352.3	32.3	21.8	57.0	489.7	34.9	37.3	30.0	79.6	143.6	511	1,018	27.7	131.9	3,121
1980[1]	18.2	356.6	29.6	22.9	60.2	467.0	32.8	36.5	29.6	75.5	152.0	592	975	25.7	129.3	3,147
1981[1]	18.4	385.0	30.3	24.9	65.8	449.3	32.7	34.0	30.8	71.6	154.1	587	945	25.8	130.6	3,129

[1] Preliminary. *Source: Bureau of Mines*
T.491

Percentage Yields of Refined Products[1] from Crude Petroleum in the United States
Computed on Total Crude Run to Stills

Year	Gasoline	Kerosene	Distillate Fuel Oil	Residual Fuel Oil	Lubricants	Jet Fuel	Coke	Asphalt	Petro-Chemical Feedstocks	Still Gas	Liquefied Gases
1971	46.2	2.1	22.0	6.6	1.6	7.4	2.6	3.8	2.7	3.8	2.9
1972	46.2	1.8	22.2	6.8	1.5	7.2	2.8	3.6	2.9	3.9	2.8
1973	45.6	1.7	22.5	7.7	1.5	6.8	2.9	3.6	2.9	3.9	2.8
1974	45.9	1.3	21.8	8.7	1.6	6.8	2.8	3.7	3.0	3.9	2.6
1975	46.5	1.2	21.3	9.9	1.2	7.0	2.8	3.2	2.7	3.9	2.4
1976[2]	45.5	1.1	21.8	10.3	1.3	6.8	2.6	2.8	3.3	3.9	2.4
1977[3]	43.4	1.3	22.6	12.5		6.6					
1978[3]	45.4	1.2	21.6	11.2		6.4					
1979[3]	43.0	1.3	21.5	11.5	1.3	6.9	2.6	3.1	4.7	3.8	2.3
1980[3]	44.5	1.0	19.7	11.7	1.3	7.4	2.7	2.9	5.1	4.0	2.4

[1] Finished products. [2] Preliminary. [3] Estimate. *Source: Bureau of Mines*
T.492

PETROLEUM

Stocks of Petroleum & Products in the United States on January 1 — In Millions of Barrels

Year	Crude Petroleum	Strategic Reserve	Total	Asphalt[2]	Coke[3]	Fuel Oil Distillate	Fuel Oil Residual	Finished Gasoline	Petro-Chemical Feedstocks	Jet Fuel	Kerosene	Liquefied Gases (For Fuel)	Lubricants	Road Oil	Wax[4]	Unfinished Oils (Net)[5]
1970	265.2		656.0	16.8	5.2	171.7	58.4	217.4	2.8	28.1	26.8	4.8	14.1	.9	1.0	97.8
1971	276.4		635.5	15.8	5.3	195.3	54.0	214.3	3.6	27.6	27.6	5.4	14.7	.6	1.0	99.0
1972	259.6		677.5	21.2	7.4	190.6	59.7	223.8	3.9	27.7	24.4	7.0	15.0	.9	1.1	100.6
1973	246.4		611.7	21.6	7.8	154.3	55.2	217.1	2.8	25.5	19.1	7.5	13.3	1.3	1.1	94.8
1974	242.5		658.8	15.0	10.0	196.5	53.5	213.4	2.4	28.5	21.0	7.4	12.2	.8	1.0	99.2
1975	265.0		695.0	21.4	5.4	200.1	59.7	221.9	3.5	29.4	15.3	5.8	16.1	1.1	1.2	106.0
1976	271.4		747.9	22.8	7.4	208.8	74.1	238.0	2.9	30.4	15.6	8.4	14.3	.6	.9	106.4
1977	285.5		707.7	19.4	10.6	186.0	72.3	234.3	4.7	32.1	12.5	6.9	12.3	.2	.7	110.5
1978[1]	347.6	7.0	841.8	18.7	10.2	250.3	89.7	260.7	3.9	34.6	18.0	7.5	12.1	.3	.6	113.2
1979[1]	376.3	67.0	784.6	20.9	11.1	216.5	90.2	240.8	4.4	33.7	14.3	7.1	12.2	.3	.8	108.7
1980[1]	339.1	91.0	778.6	18.9	5.2	228.7	95.6	239.9	4.0	38.5	15.8	6.0	12.5	.3	.7	117.7
1981[6]	357.7	107.8	788.8	18.8	4.3	205.4	91.5	264.2	5.9	42.4	11.4	6.4	13.6	.3	.5	126.5
1982[6]	598.8	230.3	712.9	19.5		190.2	78.3	205.8		40.5	11.1		14.2			176.8
1983[6]	641.6	293.8	629.3	15.9		178.6	66.2	196.7		36.8	10.4		12.5			158.0
1984																

[1] Preliminary. [2] 5.5 bbls. = 1 s. ton. [3] 5 bbls. = 1 s. ton. [4] 1 bbl. = 280 lbs. [5] And misc. products. [6] Estimate. *Source: Bureau of Mines*   T.493

Exports[2] of Petroleum and Products from the United States — In Thousands of Barrels[1]

Year	Crude	Total Refined	Finished Gasoline	Kerosene (Incl. Range Oil)	Fuel Oil Distillate	Fuel Oil Residual	Lubricants Grease	Lubricants Oil	Wax	Coke	Asphalt	Liquified Gases	Misc. Oils
1970	4,991	89,467	1,370	121	898	19,785	293	15,797	1,808	30,557	356	9,955	1,071
1971	503	81,342	1,649	181	2,761	13,217	235	15,590	1,660	27,069	306	9,390	1,028
1972	187	81,202	656	91	1,211	12,060	227	14,769	1,130	31,118	333	11,469	1,058
1973	697	83,716	1,664	85	3,231	8,507	251	12,496	965	34,976	340	9,955	1,187
1974	1,074	79,417	1,013	36	855	4,969	277	11,659	879	41,244	410	9,038	1,207
1975	2,146	74,282	850	52	267	5,342	265	8,846	607	37,253	320	9,488	1,124
1976	2,941	78,658	1,297	40	421	4,210	261	9,234	625	37,778	267	8,993	1,112
1977	18,255	70,333	725	23	519	2,305	256	9,388	734	37,393	223	6,483	1,339
1978[3]	57,728	74,329	470	40	1,202	4,634	288	9,399	543	40,438	138	7,238	171
1979[3]	85,707	86,149	155	25	1,079	3,266	279	8,275	836	53,270	181	5,414	163
1980[4]	103,908	94,289	494	32	1,238	12,232	246	8,322	736	49,872	247	7,826	210
1981[4]	83,200	133,900	700		1,900	43,200	7,000						
1982[4]	86,300	211,200											
1983													

[1] 42 gallons per barrel. [2] Includes shipments from Noncontiguous Territories. [3] Preliminary. [4] Estimate. *Source: Bureau of Mines*   T.494

Imports[2] of Petroleum & Products into the United States — In Thousands of Barrels (42 Gallons Per Barrel)

Year	Crude	Total Refined	Asphalt	Fuel Oil Distillate	Fuel Oil Residual	Finished Gasoline	Jet Fuel	Kerosene	Liquefied Pet. Gases	Lubricants	Petrochemical Feedstocks	Special Naphthas	Unfinished Oils	Wax
1970	483,293	725,508	6,201	53,826	557,845	24,320	52,696	1,451	18,921	224	5,352	2,297	39,261	117
1971	613,417	760,949	7,216	55,783	577,700	21,658	65,712	189	25,655	10	5,109	1,824	45,193	93
1972	811,135	847,046	9,263	66,449	637,401	24,787	71,174	526	32,401	669	3,178	863	45,705	335
1973	1,183,996	1,009,992	8,444	143,149	676,225	48,759	77,557	785	48,002	2,091	3,825	88	50,161	1,067
1974	1,269,155	885,200	11,252	105,579	579,157	74,402	59,396	1,744	44,971	1,786	4,364	938	44,228	956
1975	1,498,181	672,197	4,956	56,678	446,528	67,249	48,523	1,073	40,727	1,335	2,061	43	12,985	684
1976	1,935,012	705,256	3,905	53,520	517,325	47,774	27,983	3,163	47,436	1,361	1,370	45	11,735	654
1977	2,397,468	767,925	1,483	90,504	492,581	78,434	27,117	6,869	58,927	3,270	4,954	972	11,239	—
1978[1]	2,319,826	716,868	907	63,288	494,640	69,518	31,346	4,031	40,889	2,978	2,994	1,750	9,913	—
1979[1]	2,355,107	680,825	1,448	70,489	420,144	66,006	28,566	3,298	62,576	3,441	3,934	3,480	21,372	0
1980[3]	1,894,615	566,108	1,414	50,780	336,579	51,071	29,521	3,690	56,711	2,667	10,245	3,354	19,659	0
1981[3]	1,642,800	540,400		61,000	290,600									
1982[3]	1,327,100	513,100		33,800	276,700									
1983														

[1] Preliminary. [2] Includes shipments to Noncontiguous Territories. [3] Estimate. *Source: Bureau of Mines*   T.495

PETROLEUM

Crude Petroleum Refinery Operations Ratio[1]   In Percent of Capacity

Year	Jan.	Feb.	Mar.	Apr.	May	June	July	Aug.	Sept.	Oct.	Nov.	Dec.	Average
1970	93	93	93	91	86	90	87	89	89	87	89	88	90
1971	88	88	88	86	83	89	88	87	85	85	85	86	86
1972	85	85	85	84	86	89	89	89	91	89	89	91	88
1973	91	90	90	90	90	94	94	93	92	94	91	89	91
1974	84	81	82	85	89	91	91	90	86	87	87	88	87
1975	85	85	83	82	83	86	89	89	89	85	87	88	86
1976	86	88	87	86	87	93	94	91	89	86	90	91	89
1977	89	93	90	89	89	91	91	90	91	89	89	88	90
1978	85	84	85	83	89	88	88	91	90	89	91	90	88
1979	80	84	83	84	84	86	87	86	84	83	84	85	85
1980	82	81	78	76	75	77	74	73	74	71	73	76	76
1981	72	71	68	66	67	68	67	71	68	67	68	69	69
1982	66	65	65	66	68	74	75	72	74	71	71	70	70
1983													

[1] Based on the ratio of the daily average crude runs to stills to the rated capacity of refineries per day.   *Source: Bureau of Mines*   T.496

Average Price of Crude Petroleum at Wells[1]   Index (1967 = 100)

Year	Jan.	Feb.	Mar.	Apr.	May	June	July	Aug.	Sept.	Oct.	Nov.	Dec.	Average
1973	114.7	114.7	114.9	117.1	122.0	125.3	125.8	125.8	133.3	133.3	139.3	146.2	126.0
1974	178.4	201.7	201.7	201.7	201.7	201.7	224.4	225.2	225.4	236.2	231.0	223.0	211.8
1975	223.1	228.6	230.2	232.2	234.2	256.0	250.4	256.1	256.1	257.8	261.0	262.6	245.7
1976	263.3	242.3	242.5	245.0	246.0	248.1	254.3	254.3	254.3	264.4	264.4	264.4	253.6
1977	262.9	274.2	270.0	271.0	271.0	271.8	270.8	273.3	276.1	278.6	282.9	288.1	274.2
1978	288.8	289.7	293.4	294.3	295.5	298.9	301.9	302.7	305.7	307.5	310.5	312.4	300.1
1979	316.4	322.3	324.2	326.2	335.7	356.4	370.6	385.7	422.1	436.7	450.4	470.8	376.5
1980	513.6	515.1	522.8	533.9	540.1	549.0	551.4	566.8	571.3	579.6	600.6	632.8	556.4
1981	704.4	842.7	842.8	842.5	839.9	815.9	798.9	796.8	796.8	788.2	785.9	787.2	803.5
1982	787.2	770.3	744.8	717.9	717.8	718.2	718.4	718.4	718.8	735.3	734.1	720.4	733.5
1983	720.1	693.3											
1984													

[1] Buyers posted prices.   *Source: Bureau of Labor Statistics*   T.497

Average Wholesale Prices of Gasoline[1] (Regular Grade—Leaded)   Index (Feb. 1973 = 100)

Year	Jan.	Feb.	Mar.	Apr.	May	June	July	Aug.	Sept.	Oct.	Nov.	Dec.	Average
1974	136.7	147.0	161.4	172.1	177.3	188.5	196.6	196.1	197.4	196.2	186.7	184.9	178.4
1975	187.0	189.1	191.1	193.3	199.0	206.8	215.5	228.9	233.7	235.1	233.0	229.5	211.8
1976	227.3	226.4	221.7	219.1	220.6	229.2	239.4	243.2	245.0	244.7	243.8	242.2	233.6
1977	239.9	240.4	245.6	249.5	254.5	258.9	261.2	260.5	259.6	257.5	256.3	255.8	253.6
1978	255.1	252.8	252.0	253.0	255.5	260.5	266.4	271.3	275.1	278.1	277.5	282.7	265.0
1979	287.0	292.3	299.9	313.0	331.6	349.3	371.0	397.7	422.1	439.2	488.3	459.6	367.6
1980	481.1	517.5	560.4	585.4	595.5	598.6	601.1	602.9	599.6	591.5	590.8	596.1	576.7
1981	607.5	632.9	683.2	694.7	690.4	685.6	677.4	668.4	666.4	666.1	661.7	657.7	666.0
1982	651.7	642.3	621.1	578.6	555.7	582.7	628.8	636.3	628.4	617.2	611.0	600.7	613.3
1983	578.8	553.5											
1984													

[1] Excludes aviation.   *Source: Bureau of Labor Statistics (0571-02)*   T.498

PETROLEUM

Production[1] of Crude Petroleum in the United States   In Millions of Barrels of 42 Gallons

Year	Jan.	Feb.	Mar.	Apr.	May	June	July	Aug.	Sept.	Oct.	Nov.	Dec.	Total
1970	293.8	268.0	294.7	287.7	295.2	280.8	285.2	296.4	295.6	310.4	301.3	308.3	3,517
1971	299.3	272.4	302.8	293.1	299.0	288.1	293.2	291.7	274.1	284.0	274.2	282.1	3,454
1972	282.5	270.7	293.3	285.4	298.0	285.6	294.4	294.0	285.2	293.9	282.8	289.4	3,455
1973	284.5	263.1	287.4	278.8	287.1	276.4	285.7	284.2	272.0	285.9	274.8	281.0	3,361
1974	277.0	256.0	277.9	268.6	276.2	263.4	272.2	269.7	253.3	266.9	257.1	264.3	3,203
1975	262.1	240.6	263.3	253.7	259.7	252.6	258.4	255.7	248.4	258.1	248.3	255.9	3,057
1976	255.2	238.7	255.2	242.3	251.9	242.8	251.9	251.4	244.5	250.0	242.4	249.9	2,976
1977	243.5	227.9	250.8	244.3	250.3	243.1	251.2	257.5	254.4	265.8	257.4	263.1	3,009
1978	259.2	234.5	270.3	264.5	273.6	265.0	271.4	271.5	264.0	273.4	262.2	268.5	3,178
1979[2]	262.2	238.0	266.1	256.0	266.1	252.3	259.0	269.7	254.0	265.6	259.5	267.0	3,121
1980[2]	268.1	252.2	270.1	260.6	267.8	256.4	265.2	261.1	258.6	264.6	254.9	266.8	3,146
1981[2]	264.5	240.8	266.6	256.3	263.4	258.5	261.1	265.9	257.6	264.8	257.8	267.3	3,125
1982[2]	268.7	243.3	266.5	259.6	268.5	260.4	268.1	269.7	262.0	269.0	260.7	268.5	3,165
1983													

[1] Represents oil transported from producing properties, plus that remaining on properties & consumed on leases.   [2] Preliminary.   Source: Bureau of Mines
T.500

Stocks of Crude Petroleum[1] in the United States at Beginning of Month   In Millions of Barrels

Year	Jan.	Feb.	Mar.	Apr.	May	June	July	Aug.	Sept.	Oct.	Nov.	Dec.
1970	265.2	267.1	269.6	274.6	278.0	284.8	279.9	266.9	254.1	259.2	265.5	271.3
1971	276.4	269.8	266.9	267.2	271.4	284.3	279.3	273.2	272.4	269.8	265.9	265.2
1972	259.6	251.0	252.9	258.9	266.6	279.5	271.4	265.8	258.0	250.8	253.7	251.3
1973	246.4	237.5	235.4	244.1	248.8	257.9	248.9	243.7	248.3	241.3	246.3	250.0
1974	242.5	233.0	240.7	244.7	256.4	269.5	268.8	268.7	264.8	266.7	269.4	271.1
1975	265.0	270.5	276.8	280.0	281.9	281.0	276.1	264.2	256.6	259.4	269.6	271.0
1976	271.4	289.3	277.4	283.1	286.6	284.0	281.7	282.6	277.3	284.4	297.7	298.8
1977	285.5	294.1	291.5	299.5	318.9	328.8	333.7	335.3	338.9	334.1	343.2	350.3
1978	347.7	352.5	350.2	363.9	365.2	354.7	363.5	368.2	357.8	368.3	378.2	381.4
1979[2]	376.3	375.9	381.1	399.9	403.6	403.2	414.5	403.0	411.9	415.0	435.9	438.6
1980[2]	430.3	444.8	452.8	452.9	470.5	475.1	473.2	470.5	478.8	468.8	475.1	475.4
1981[2]	482.9	488.9	502.8	518.1	541.4	552.3	555.3	565.6	549.9	560.7	584.3	594.8
1982[2]	598.8	606.2	612.2	614.2	611.0	609.5	606.9	611.7	625.4	617.8	635.3	646.0
1983[2]	641.6											

[1] Total gasoline-bearing in the U.S.   [2] Preliminary.   Source: Bureau of Mines
T.501

United States Production of Gasoline[1]   In Millions of Barrels

Year	Jan.	Feb.	Mar.	Apr.	May	June	July	Aug.	Sept.	Oct.	Nov.	Dec.	Total
1970	176.5	157.0	173.4	164.3	172.5	173.8	180.6	183.0	180.8	177.7	175.6	190.2	2,105
1971	185.2	167.0	180.8	170.4	174.3	181.4	192.7	196.6	186.1	188.2	183.1	196.9	2,203
1972	192.6	175.2	184.9	176.8	188.6	189.1	206.7	206.2	199.8	204.6	194.9	200.7	2,320
1973	197.9	173.0	192.2	192.9	209.8	211.3	218.3	215.4	200.2	207.1	193.2	190.4	2,402
1974	184.2	168.2	186.5	190.5	197.7	201.4	212.2	213.0	195.6	197.8	190.1	200.1	2,338
1975	203.0	176.7	189.2	182.3	191.1	201.2	218.5	214.6	206.0	200.3	199.4	211.3	2,394
1976	201.8	188.6	201.2	197.8	211.1	220.6	223.9	223.3	207.8	208.1	209.3	223.5	2,517
1977	215.7	191.6	213.9	210.2	216.7	215.8	226.3	224.3	213.4	215.9	214.9	222.6	2,518
1978	215.8	186.5	210.1	201.2	220.1	217.8	226.6	232.7	223.4	223.6	228.7	243.9	2,631
1979[2]	226.8	195.3	207.4	204.4	211.9	211.4	219.1	215.4	200.8	202.9	201.2	218.0	2,515
1980[2]	217.5	200.2	203.5	189.5	196.6	198.1	201.7	201.4	192.4	191.2	194.9	206.9	2,394
1981[2]	208.2	176.6	193.3	184.2	190.9	187.8	200.2	206.3	198.1	200.9	198.3	206.0	2,351
1982[2]	192.3	166.3	186.8	183.7	196.8	203.9	211.3	201.0	196.6	194.6	188.9	203.1	2,325
1983													

[1] Gasoline and naphtha from crude petroleum and natural gasoline used at refineries.   [2] Preliminary.   Source: Bureau of Mines
T.502

PETROLEUM

United States Domestic Consumption of Gasoline   In Millions of Barrels

Year	Jan.	Feb.	Mar.	Apr.	May	June	July	Aug.	Sept.	Oct.	Nov.	Dec.	Total
1970	163.9	151.0	173.4	171.3	183.6	187.4	195.2	190.4	179.8	184.8	168.4	182.0	2,131
1971	164.6	154.6	182.6	187.6	184.5	195.1	201.0	197.0	183.6	188.6	184.6	189.3	2,213
1972	173.2	166.9	200.5	190.0	201.2	206.2	208.4	216.6	194.9	198.5	195.5	198.8	2,351
1973	190.9	181.5	203.2	197.5	215.7	210.3	218.9	226.9	198.7	208.6	206.0	194.5	2,453
1974	181.2	171.7	192.7	195.0	210.4	209.1	217.1	220.7	193.0	209.7	197.6	204.3	2,402
1975	193.4	171.7	197.1	202.7	214.1	213.5	219.7	218.6	203.2	211.5	192.8	212.0	2,450
1976	199.2	182.5	214.7	215.9	213.5	226.0	228.0	223.7	213.5	215.9	212.2	222.2	2,567
1977	201.4	194.1	215.3	221.5	219.1	229.3	232.3	231.4	220.8	222.1	216.8	229.5	2,634
1978	208.0	193.4	226.2	217.2	240.8	238.7	236.2	245.6	223.3	232.2	226.0	231.9	2,720
1979[1]	214.4	204.3	225.0	213.1	224.5	216.9	213.8	228.9	207.7	218.8	204.4	209.5	2,582
1980[1]	197.2	192.3	199.7	204.9	209.7	201.0	210.0	207.3	196.5	207.8	188.1	206.3	2,421
1981[1]	198.8	176.9	195.4	198.6	205.7	211.2	212.5	207.2	200.5	205.5	192.5	208.9	2,415
1982[1]	184.2	170.5	205.8	207.5	207.0	205.4	211.7	207.4	196.2	198.9	197.2	203.6	2,396
1983													

[1] Preliminary.   *Source: Bureau of Mines*   T.503

Stocks of Finished Gasoline on Hand in the United States, at End of Month   In Millions of Barrels

Year	Jan.	Feb.	Mar.	Apr.	May	June	July	Aug.	Sept.	Oct.	Nov.	Dec.
1970	231.8	238.8	240.8	235.7	226.4	214.9	201.9	196.4	199.3	194.5	204.0	214.3
1971	237.0	250.5	250.6	235.0	226.2	214.0	207.2	208.4	212.3	212.9	213.6	223.8
1972	244.6	254.8	241.2	229.5	219.2	204.3	204.7	196.8	203.7	211.7	213.2	217.1
1973	226.0	220.0	211.1	208.2	205.3	211.6	215.0	208.6	213.9	218.2	211.4	213.4
1974	221.3	223.0	223.6	226.8	221.9	220.5	222.2	222.1	230.7	224.1	221.9	221.9
1975	228.3	245.9	255.4	252.1	235.7	217.0	210.0	215.2	218.4	229.2	224.5	235.3
1976	238.0	243.4	251.8	241.9	226.6	227.5	227.7	229.4	233.2	232.6	229.1	230.5
1977	234.3	255.5	258.1	264.7	261.5	265.3	259.1	260.9	259.6	258.7	258.0	261.5
1978	260.7	275.1	273.7	262.0	251.4	235.9	222.0	219.0	211.5	219.2	216.1	223.2
1979[1]	240.8	254.4	241.9	237.9	229.7	232.0	244.1	235.2	232.3	211.0	223.3	239.9
1980[1]	264.9	277.3	285.8	275.0	266.0	267.5	263.8	262.2	261.0	249.1	259.9	213.5
1981[1]	229.5	232.3	234.5	225.2	215.0	196.3	187.7	190.6	193.2	192.9	202.9	205.8
1982[1]	216.8	216.1	201.5	182.0	176.2	180.2	185.3	187.2	193.5	194.3	191.9	196.7
1983												

[1] Preliminary.   *Source: Bureau of Mines*   T.504

U.S. Production of Residual Fuel Oil and Distillate Fuel Oils   In Millions of Barrels

Year	Jan.	Feb.	Mar.	Apr.	May	June	July	Aug.	Sept.	Oct.	Nov.	Dec.	Total
1969	97.3	91.5	99.3	90.3	88.5	90.7	93.1	90.2	88.4	90.0	93.9	101.0	1,114
1970	105.5	95.8	101.3	90.6	88.5	89.3	91.2	95.5	93.3	96.7	97.5	109.3	1,155
1971	112.2	99.4	104.5	98.9	94.1	96.8	97.8	97.1	91.0	94.5	94.5	106.0	1,187
1972	107.4	104.9	105.3	96.6	100.9	98.6	99.4	101.1	100.1	107.6	108.4	126.1	1,256
1973	128.5	111.4	112.4	101.7	108.3	112.2	112.8	113.3	110.7	120.8	119.5	133.2	1,385
1974	122.5	96.0	97.3	105.2	114.7	114.3	119.3	117.0	107.6	117.8	120.9	132.1	1,365
1975	132.3	112.9	118.8	111.9	111.1	111.8	116.1	115.9	119.0	121.2	119.4	128.3	1,420
1976	128.7	126.3	127.2	118.2	123.9	123.8	131.1	133.3	128.3	134.8	142.8	155.8	1,574
1977	163.1	158.2	151.7	140.5	149.2	147.3	152.9	152.1	151.8	158.4	151.0	160.0	1,836
1978	153.0	133.0	147.8	135.2	152.0	140.4	146.0	152.7	144.7	150.8	150.9	158.5	1,765
1979[1]	152.3	130.4	146.0	137.4	144.2	140.1	151.4	152.6	150.1	150.6	150.0	158.6	1,766
1980[1]	148.5	131.9	128.5	121.6	123.3	126.6	129.3	121.1	125.5	127.2	128.3	141.2	1,552
1981[1]	142.6	122.5	121.1	112.1	114.0	112.0	110.9	120.4	116.9	115.4	118.4	128.9	1,435
1982[1]	117.8	100.3	105.8	105.6	116.1	114.2	116.7	109.5	109.9	117.6	115.6	113.0	1,342
1983													

[1] Preliminary.   *Source: Bureau of Mines*   T.505

261

Plastics

The plastics industry, which had achieved record production and shipment levels in 1979, reported setbacks in sales and profits during 1982 even though the diversity of its products tends to give the industry a measure of stability in economic slowdowns. Housing, transportation, and construction typically account for nearly 23 percent of U.S. sales of plastics, and other markets include, in order of importance: consumer and institutional uses, electrical and electronics uses, furniture and furnishings, adhesives and inks and coatings, and industrial machinery.

U.S. product shipments of plastic materials in 1982, measured in constant dollars, were 14 percent lower than in 1981. The industry was reportedly most severely affected by the declining demand for plastics from the automobile and the housing industries. Plants were generally operated between 60 and 70 percent of capacity, and inventory liquidation reduced industry stocks to all-time low levels by the end of the year. Estimates indicated that 1982 production dropped 15 percent below the 1981 level to 34 billion pounds of plastics. Many less efficient producers operating obsolete, small reactor plants reportedly abandoned the industry, while the more successful, and generally larger, producers delayed additional plant construction and cut back expansion. The cutbacks were expected to result in tight supplies of some plastics, particularly high density polyethylene and polypropylene, throughout 1983. The domestic market for resins was adversely affected by economic depression in 1982, and the market for polyvinyl chloride (PVC) was particularly affected by the slowdown in residential construction rates and by reduced automotive demand.

Plastics producers found it impossible to maintain the price increases announced during 1982, and the prices for plastic products weakened considerably. The product price index for plastics materials increased only 1.2 percent in 1982 compared with the 3.6 percent rate of change reported in the previous year. Employment in the plastics industry was computed as having decreased at an average annual rate of 2 percent since 1978. At the same time, the average annual earnings of plastics production workers rose at a compound annual rate of 8.7 percent between 1972 and 1982.

During 1982, Congress began to review the plastic industry's record of compliance with the Clean Air Act, and amendments to the Clean Water Act were proposed as the industry argued the scientific and economic justification of environmental regulations. The measures that were scrutinized included a New York State bill proposing to study the effects of smoke and gases emitted by all classes of building construction and furnishings materials, particularly acrylonitrile-butadiene, styrene (ABS), PVC, and some engineering plastics. New York City proceeded with plans to substitute steel tubing for PVC wiring conduit in the subway system's public address network because of concerns about the toxicity of burning PVC. The rapid increase in the use of plastic pipe in building construction and in housing during 1982 raised questions of the suitability of PVC pipe for the transmission of potable water.

U.S. plastics materials shipments in 1983 were expected to increase by 6 percent over 1981 levels as measured in constant dollars, and U.S. Department of Commerce estimates indicated that the 1983 production could exceed 36 billion pounds. U.S. industry shipments throughout the 1980s, in constant dollars, are projected as increasing at a compound annual rate of 6 percent, a higher rate than is projected for most manufacturing sectors of the economy.

The so-called miscellaneous plastics products industry is a residual statistical concept that includes plastics products not consumed within the companies that produce them as well as products not reported in other industries. Miscellaneous plastics accounts for approximately half of the total U.S. consumption of plastics and resins, and the growth of these materials is primarily dependent upon growth in the automotive, construction, and packaging industries. The largest group in the miscellaneous category is unsupported film and sheeting, much of which goes into packaging products. Various analyses suggest that miscellaneous plastics products account for 80 percent of total rubber and plastics products imports. The major categories imported by the U.S. are film and sheeting, household articles, containers and packaging, and wearing apparel. The U.S. exports predominantly film and sheeting, expanded goods, laminated goods, and construction products. The foreign competition for the U.S. share of the world plastics market in coming years is expected to come mainly from Canada and the Middle East because of lower feedstock costs in those two areas.

World Production of Plastics and Resins[3] (Condensation, Polymerization, Etc.)   In Thous. of Metric Tons

Year	Australia	Austria	Czechoslovakia	France	Germany East	Germany West	Italy	Japan	Netherlands	Poland	Belgium	Hungary	USSR	United Kingdom	United States
1974	402	286	390	2,060	517	6,271	2,468	6,722	1,644	395	835	701	2,496	2,419	13,764
1975	362	304	427	1,256	605	5,046	2,052	4,373	1,350	539	660	164	2,844	2,057	10,199
1976	407	404	580	1,769	679	7,088	2,266	4,952	1,723	559	824	186	3,216	2,556	13,261
1977	480	430	738	1,834	734	6,270	2,538	4,978	1,783	583	1,471	144	3,300	2,710	11,232
1978	522	434	810	1,885	762	6,703	2,466	5,882	1,962	596	1,682	209	3,516	2,621	12,380
1979	618	437	853	2,220	779	7,255	2,562	6,964	2,012	571	1,969	289	3,504	2,647	13,866
1980	709	487	894	2,052	859	6,710	2,464	6,422	1,975	667	1,835	324	3,636	2,260	12,418
1981[1]	700	504	913	1,950	998	6,500	2,154	5,750	2,393	588	1,940	307	3,700	2,051	13,000
1982[2]	715	470	920		1,000		2,400	6,000	2,500	600	2,200	320		2,200	

[1] Preliminary.   [2] Estimate.   [3] Refers to production of thermoplastic & thermosetting resins & plastic materials obtained by chemical transformation of natural organic substances or by chemical synthesis.   Source: *United Nations*

PLASTICS

Production of Important Synthetic Plastics & Resin Materials in the U.S. In Millions of Pounds

Year	Phenolic Resins	Polyethylene & Copolymers	Polypropylene	Polystyrene & Copolymers	Polyvinyl Chloride & Copolymers	Year	Phenolic Resins	Polyethylene & Copolymers	Polypropylene	Polystyrene & Copolymers	Polyvinyl Chloride & Copolymers
1970	1,186	5,844	1,031	3,550	3,756	1977	1,797	10,100	2,706	5,203	5,267
1971	1,181	6,381	1,339	3,990	4,103	1978	1,926	11,359	3,055	5,989	5,878
1972	1,441	7,656	1,731	4,890	4,322	1979	1,779	12,408	3,824	6,327	6,211
1973	1,648	8,582	2,165	5,156	4,594	1980	1,745	11,720	3,699	5,540	5,485
1974	1,598	8,826	2,249	5,060	4,744	1981	1,688	12,604	4,008	5,915	5,618
1975	1,275	7,483	1,903	3,877	3,695	1982[1]	1,210	12,209	3,552	5,060	5,371
1976	1,305	8,775	2,551	4,743	4,545	1983					

Note: Data included in the table does not cover all Plastics production. Various types of Plastics production of lesser importance are not included because statistics are not available on a consistent basis. Also, many individual firms do not make their production figures known. [1] Preliminary. Sources: U.S. Tariff Commission, Bureau of Census

T.507

Average Wholesale Price Index of Plastic Materials in the United States (1967 = 100)

Year	Jan.	Feb.	Mar.	Apr.	May	June	July	Aug.	Sept.	Oct.	Nov.	Dec.	Average
					Plastic Resins and Materials (066)								
1979	204.2	206.3	210.9	220.6	228.5	230.1	244.5	250.1	252.0	260.0	261.4	262.5	235.9
1980	270.4	272.1	274.5	287.6	288.4	287.6	285.7	281.5	276.5	276.1	276.2	274.1	279.2
1981	274.7	276.1	279.4	285.1	287.9	290.0	295.9	297.5	296.8	299.5	293.2	294.2	289.2
1982	286.1	297.3	285.5	286.0	283.2	282.1	280.9	282.2	281.6	281.6	281.4	281.4	284.1
1983	282.8	282.3	282.8										
					PE Resin, Low, Pkg. Firm (0662-0301.99)								
1976	178.2	178.4	178.6	190.7	191.5	192.2	193.3	193.2	190.9	189.7	189.9	190.1	188.1
1977	187.7	185.2	189.5	197.7	197.1	196.9	194.8	194.8	194.0	195.2	195.6	195.2	193.6
1978	196.1	196.1	197.0	198.0	198.6	198.0	194.4	190.3	189.3	187.2	184.1	184.1	192.8
1979	186.6	186.9	186.9	203.3	210.1	213.2	225.2	225.0	225.8	243.2	247.0	249.0	216.9
1980	257.2	260.9	N.A.	275.1	270.8	264.0	259.4	254.4	249.4	249.3	251.8	250.9	258.5
1981	251.5	251.2	252.5	263.0	263.0	263.7	280.7	N.A.	279.8	279.9	N.A.	247.3	263.3
1982	207.5	208.1	209.7	224.5	202.1	197.2	184.3	185.3	184.2	183.9	184.7	184.7	196.4
1983	204.4	204.4											
					Thermoplastic Resins (0662) — Dec. 1980 = 100								
1981	100.2	101.0	102.6	104.6	105.8	106.6	109.3	110.1	109.7	110.5	107.2	107.6	106.3
1982	103.5	104.2	103.2	103.5	102.1	101.5	100.9	101.5	101.3	101.3	101.3	101.1	102.1
1983	101.8	101.7	101.9										
					Polystyrene Resin, Rubber Modified (0662-0602.99)								
1976	165.7	174.4	173.2	175.4	176.1	174.9	175.4	174.4	165.7	162.8	162.3	162.5	170.3
1977	162.5	162.1	161.6	157.1	157.2	158.8	161.9	161.7	162.8	163.2	164.4	164.6	161.5
1978	164.6	164.6	164.6	168.3	170.2	N.A.	171.6	171.6	172.7	171.7	171.7	172.1	169.4
1979	180.8	N.A.	N.A.	200.8	213.7	N.A.	220.9	236.7	272.9	272.6	273.3	274.9	238.5
1980	283.5	N.A.	278.8	291.4	291.9	293.2	288.0	287.6	282.1	286.0	287.3	289.4	
1981	290.2	294.2	291.7	299.2	299.2	305.2	303.1	N.A.	N.A.	292.6	298.9	299.7	297.4
1982	297.8	297.8	297.8	N.A.	294.2	293.9	291.2	291.2	291.2	N.A.	291.0	290.9	
1983	N.A.	N.A.											
					Thermosetting Resins (0003) — Dec. 1980 = 100								
1981	101.4	101.1	101.4	104.0	104.5	105.4	106.6	106.5	106.6	107.7	107.6	108.2	105.1
1982	108.0	107.9	108.1	108.1	108.0	108.6	108.7	108.8	108.9	108.8	108.9	109.2	108.4
1983	109.2	108.9	108.9										
					Phenolic Molding Compound (0663-0201.99)								
1976	187.9	187.9	187.9	187.9	187.9	187.9	191.2	195.2	198.6	202.0	202.0	202.0	193.2
1977	202.0	202.0	202.0	205.4	205.4	202.0	202.0	202.0	202.0	202.0	202.0	203.8	202.7
1978	202.0	194.6	195.1	195.1	195.1	195.1	195.1	195.1	192.8	184.9	185.5	185.5	193.0
1979	185.5	185.5	200.3	221.6	230.2	230.2	234.9	233.9	236.0	239.7	242.5	239.7	223.3
1980	239.7	239.7	244.3	249.9	251.3	251.3	250.4	240.2	240.2	240.2	240.2	240.2	244.0
1981	N.A.	N.A.	N.A.	N.A.	N.A.	N.A.	254.2	254.2	254.2	254.2	254.2	254.2	254.2
1982	254.2	254.2	254.2	254.2	254.6	254.6	254.6	254.5	254.5	254.5	254.5	254.5	254.4
1983	249.6	245.7	245.7										

Source: Bureau of Labor Statistics

T.508

263

Platinum-Group Metals

World production of platinum-group metals in 1982 was about 6 percent below estimated 1981 output, according to preliminary data of the U.S. Bureau of Mines. An estimated 13 percent reduction in South African production more than offset a gain in Soviet output. These two countries accounted for about 96 percent of estimated world production in 1982.

U.S. mine production of platinum-group metals is insignificant. Secondary production recovered by refineries in 1982 was 19 percent smaller than in 1981. Platinum recovery was off only 1 percent, but palladium recovery was off 37 percent.

The net U.S. import reliance on platinum-group metals in 1982 was about 85 percent of consumption vs. 83 percent in the previous year. Imports for consumption in 1982 totaled 2.49 million troy ounces, 12 percent lower than in 1981. Platinum sponge imports were 22 percent lower than in the previous year and palladium imports were off 7 percent. In December 1982, it was reported that the USSR planned to reduce sales of palladium to U.S. dealers by as much as 25 percent in 1983. Imports of platinum-group metals from the USSR are nearly all palladium and averaged 101,000 ounces quarterly in 1982. The Republic of South Africa and the USSR are the major U.S. import sources for platinum-group metals.

Consumption of platinum-group metals in the U.S. as indicated by sales to domestic industries, decreased 20 percent in 1982, to 1.5 million ounces. Platinum sales were off 18 percent and palladium sales declined 24 percent in 1982. Significant reductions in sales of platinum to the auto and petroleum industries were reported, and sales of palladium to the chemical industry and to the electrical industry also declined considerably.

In 1982, the auto industry accounted for about 33 percent of platinum-group sales; electrical, 28 percent; chemical, 15 percent; dental, 9 percent; and others, 15 percent. The auto, chemical, and petroleum refining industries used platinum-group metals primarily as catalysts. The jewelry industry accounts for a small but growing percentage of U.S. platinum use, in comparison with Japan where jewelry accounts for more than one-half (around 600 thousand ounces) of platinum's use in that country.

U.S. exports of platinum-group metals in 1982 totaled about 862 thousand ounces, and about the same amount as in 1981. The United Kingdom and Japan were the most important export destinations.

Stocks of platinum-group metals held by refiners, importers, and dealers in the U.S. on December 31, 1982 totaled 968,267 troy ounces, 2 percent more than a year earlier. However, platinum stocks were up 36 percent, to 585,870 ounces after trailing year-earlier stocks in each of the preceding three quarters, while palladium stocks dropped 31 percent to 273,421 ounces.

As of November 30, 1982, the nation's stockpile goal for platinum was 1.3 million ounces and the inventory was 440 thousand ounces. The palladium stockpile goal was 3.0 million ounces and the stockpile inventory was about 1.25 million ounces.

The producer price for platinum remained at $475 per troy ounce throughout 1982, but the dealer price dropped from a monthly average $368 in January to $272 in June before recovering to $359 in December for a 1982 average price of $327 vs. $446 per ounce in 1981. The producer price for palladium remained at $110 per ounce throughout 1982, whereas dealer prices moved erratically, advancing from $67 in January to $69 in April before dropping to $57 in June. Dealer prices increased sharply in the second half of 1982, to an average price of $90 in December, for a yearly average price of $67 per ounce vs. $95 in 1981.

Futures Market

Both platinum and palladium futures are traded on the New York Mercantile Exchange (NYMEX).

World Production of Platinum-Group Metals — In Troy Ounces

Year	Australia	Philippines	Finland	Canada	Colombia[3]	Ethiopia	Japan	South Africa	USSR	United States	Yugoslavia	World Total[1]
1971	—	2,459	600	475,169	25,610	217	8,826	1,253,200	2,300,000	18,029		4,084,110
1972	—	7,522	650	406,048	24,111	248	9,899	1,453,000	2,350,000	17,112		4,269,990
1973	975	6,656	725	354,223	26,358	235	10,197	2,362,800	2,450,000	19,980		5,232,149
1974	1,120	3,665	650	384,618	21,094	230	15,205	2,830,000	2,500,000	12,657		5,769,239
1975	1,830	1,415	600	399,218	22,114	162	19,401	2,600,000	2,650,000	18,920		5,713,660
1976	11,570	—	600	416,821	16,779	145	26,795	2,700,000	3,050,000	6,116	N.A.	6,228,826
1977	13,503		640	465,371	17,315	100	32,453	2,870,000	3,100,000	5,545	5,690	6,510,617
1978	20,653		640	346,213	13,939	123	34,397	2,860,000	3,150,000	8,246	5,979	6,440,190
1979	9,845		720	197,943	12,933	108	34,637	3,017,000	3,200,000	7,300	5,916	6,486,402
1980[2]	9,750		700	410,757	14,345	113	41,334	3,100,000	3,250,000	3,348	5,790	6,836,137
1981[1]	9,540		700	400,000	15,000	125	36,000	3,000,000	3,350,000	6,150	5,750	6,811,000
1982[1]				190,000				2,600,000	3,500,000	6,000		6,400,000
1983												

[1] Estimate. [2] Preliminary. [3] Placer platinum. *Source: Bureau of Mines*

PLATINUM-GROUP METALS

PLATINUM CASH PRICE NEW YORK
Monthly Average Prices
Dollars Per Troy Ounce

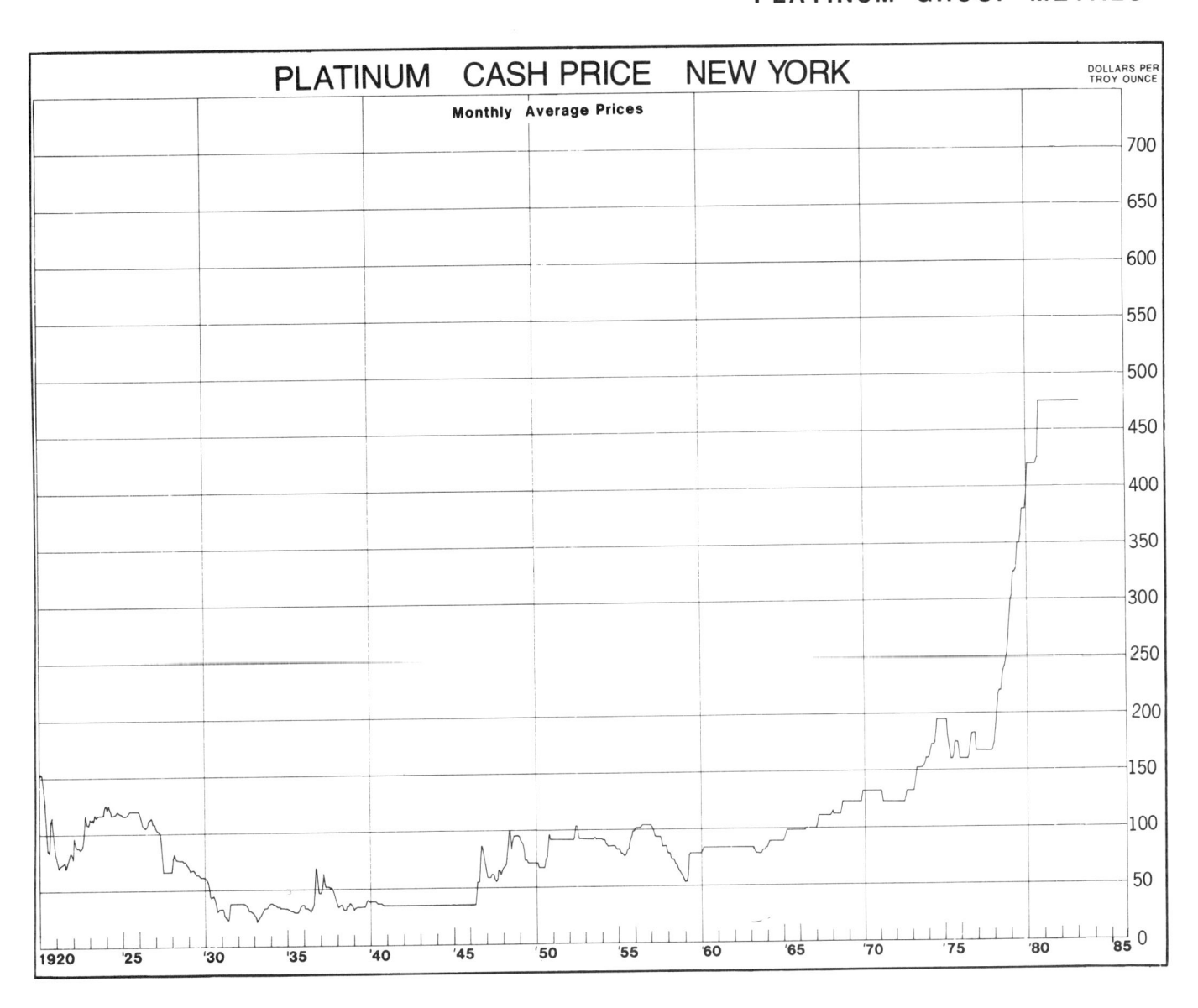

Average Price of Platinum (Producer Prices) in New York — In Dollars Per Troy Ounce

Year	Jan.	Feb.	Mar.	Apr.	May	June	July	Aug.	Sept.	Oct.	Nov.	Dec.	Average
1970	132.50	132.50	132.50	132.50	132.50	132.50	132.50	132.50	132.50	132.50	132.50	132.50	132.50
1971	129.00	122.50	122.50	122.50	122.50	122.50	122.50	122.50	122.50	122.50	122.50	122.50	123.04
1972	122.50	122.50	122.50	122.50	122.50	122.50	128.00	132.50	132.50	132.50	132.50	132.50	127.13
1973	132.50	141.97	152.50	152.50	152.50	152.50	152.50	152.50	155.24	160.50	160.50	160.50	152.18
1974	162.68	172.50	172.50	172.50	174.55	195.00	195.00	195.00	195.00	195.00	195.00	195.00	184.98
1975	195.00	180.53	175.00	163.06	160.00	160.00	162.73	175.00	175.00	172.17	160.00	160.00	169.87
1976	160.00	160.00	160.00	160.00	160.00	163.54	175.60	182.50	182.50	182.50	167.00	167.00	168.39
1977	167.00	167.00	167.00	167.00	167.00	167.00	167.00	167.00	167.00	167.00	167.65	174.81	167.71
1978	186.55	206.58	217.07	220.00	220.00	227.73	237.89	241.74	250.23	253.18	284.00	300.00	237.08
1979	303.41	325.00	325.00	327.38	350.00	350.00	350.00	357.83	380.00	380.00	380.00	393.33	351.83
1980	420.00	420.00	420.00	420.00	420.00	420.00	420.00	425.24	475.00	475.00	475.00	475.00	436.77
1981	475.00	475.00	475.00	475.00	475.00	475.00	475.00	475.00	475.00	475.00	475.00	475.00	475.00
1982	475.00	475.00	475.00	475.00	475.00	475.00	475.00	475.00	475.00	475.00	475.00	475.00	475.00
1983	475.00	475.00	475.00	475.00									

Source: American Metal Market

T.511

PLATINUM-GROUP METALS

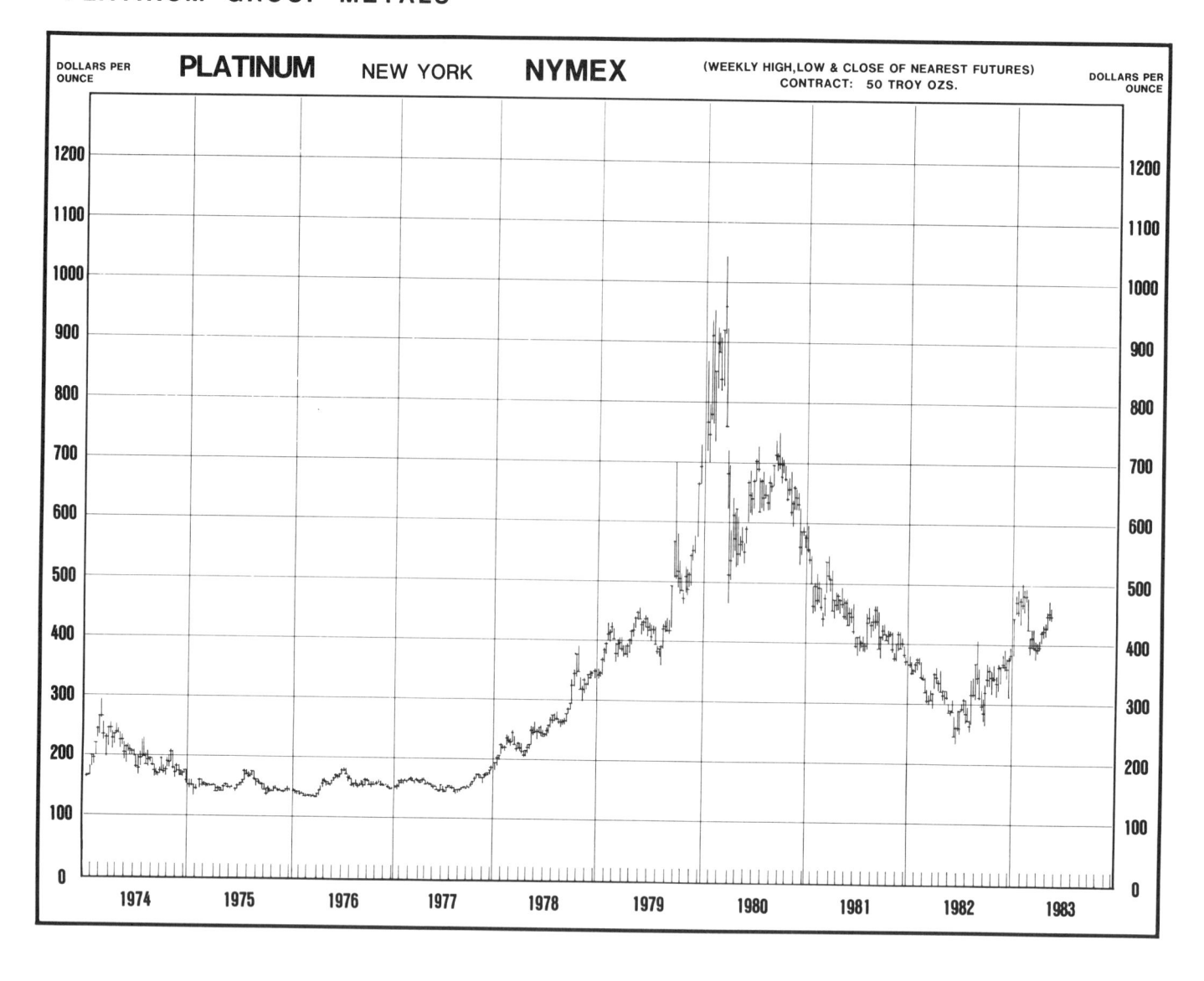

PLATINUM — NEW YORK — NYMEX (Weekly high, low & close of nearest futures) Contract: 50 Troy Ozs. Dollars per ounce.

Platinum-Group Metals Sold to Consuming Industries in the United States — In Thousands of Troy Ounces

Year	Automotive Platinum	Others[2]	Chemical Platinum	Others[2]	Electrical Platinum	Others[2]	Dental & Medical Platinum	Others[2]	Jewelry & Decorative Platinum	Others[2]	Petroleum Platinum	Others[2]	All Platinum-Group Metals Platinum	Palladium	Other[2] Metals	Total
1970			148.3	231.4	103.3	442.9	18.3	49.2	29.2	27.5	202.0	15.7	509.0	739.3	82.8	1,331.2
1971			135.1	253.8	51.9	447.6	23.1	63.1	18.6	30.6	141.8	3.5	426.7	760.1	74.5	1,261.3
1972			225.9	363.5	92.4	443.5	30.5	95.5	20.7	29.3	98.8	31.4	545.3	876.0	140.9	1,562.2
1973			239.0	334.1	117.4	551.1	27.9	136.3	22.4	38.9	123.6	20.3	658.5	1,012.5	160.9	1,833.9
1974	350.0	15.0	350.0	150.0	98.6	452.6	25.5	125.7	23.0	35.3	139.5	26.7	943.7	886.1	151.2	1,981.0
1975	273.0	97.0	148.8	166.9	73.6	153.1	17.1	115.9	22.9	29.5	108.0	5.4	698.6	541.5	68.6	1,308.7
1976	481.0	194.9	83.6	154.7	89.3	197.5	26.9	140.4	23.4	14.8	59.1	7.7	851.1	657.1	94.9	1,603.1
1977	354.3	125.9	84.4	196.6	90.2	254.5	27.1	113.9	34.7	22.1	74.8	13.6	789.8	700.5	102.0	1,592.3
1978	597.5	201.8	149.7	186.5	106.4	346.5	44.1	208.0	25.8	25.1	108.4	19.2	1,196.3	917.9	145.4	2,259.6
1979	803.2	248.3	98.6	264.9	115.8	457.4	27.1	244.9	27.7	21.6	170.0	27.9	1,408.9	1,132.6	214.5	2,756.0
1980	517.1	214.2	119.0	165.6	150.1	376.1	25.8	245.4	51.0	22.6	144.0	26.7	1,118.2	912.0	175.7	2,205.9
1981[1]	446.7	160.6	78.1	152.5	111.7	388.3	18.7	265.8	27.6	19.7	88.3	22.9	872.6	889.2	158.9	1,920.7
1982[3]													719.8	675.7	137.1	1,532.6
1983																

[1] Preliminary. [2] Palladium, iridium, osmium, rhodium, & ruthenium. [3] Estimate. *Source: Bureau of Mines*

T.512

PLATINUM–GROUP METALS

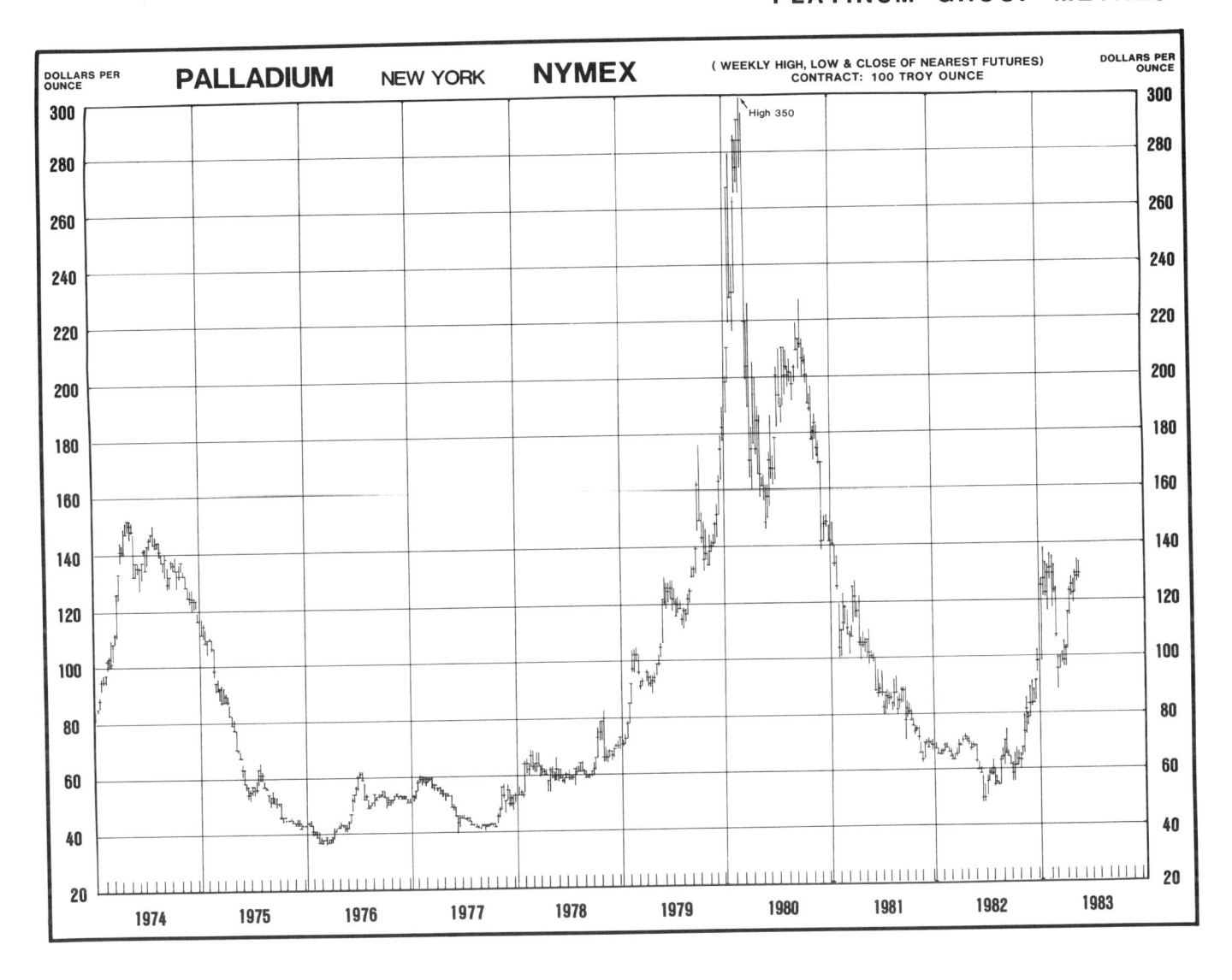

PALLADIUM   NEW YORK   NYMEX   (WEEKLY HIGH, LOW & CLOSE OF NEAREST FUTURES) CONTRACT: 100 TROY OUNCE

Salient Statistics of Platinum and Allied Metals in the U.S.   In Troy Ounces

Year	Net Import Reliance as a % of Apparent Consump.	Production Crude[5]	Refinery New Metal	Refinery Secondary Metal	Stocks as of Dec. 31[1] Platinum	Stocks Palladium	Stocks Other	Total	Imports for Consumption	Value of Imports Mil. $	Exports Platinum	Exports Other Groups[3]	Other[6]
1970		17,316	19,822	350,176	291,544	332,726	85,754	710,024	1,410,786	104.8	270,584	143,182	
1971		18,029	21,184	278,175	385,828	316,126	94,837	796,791	1,388,043	93.7	320,842	83,768	
1972		17,112	15,380	255,641	426,611	405,793	98,449	930,853	1,892,184	144.1	417,037	121,949	
1973		19,980	19,916	265,901	446,522	493,078	93,524	1,033,124	2,504,181	248.8	439,452	188,074	
1974		12,657	13,234	325,216	532,675	478,210	110,921	1,121,806	3,251,311	504.6	474,494	361,260	
1975	83	18,920	16,571	270,101	420,770	335,621	92,819	849,210	1,820,284	272.8	284,796	283,435	91,654
1976	90	6,116	7,101	215,355	536,318	459,765	89,620	1,085,703	2,667,059	291.5	138,051	186,602	186,854
1977	91	5,545	5,199	195,219	438,045	475,358	99,409	1,012,812	2,510,374	273.0	149,023	137,324	140,284
1978	90	8,246	8,303	257,191	369,823	369,937	121,651	861,411	2,921,411	450.2	166,095	356,990	179,462
1979	89	7,300	8,392	309,022	305,605	323,865	131,812	761,282	3,479,128	840.5	207,832	522,195	189,218
1980	88	3,348	2,300	330,923	502,185	353,002	118,074	973,261	3,501,782	1,177	289,454	302,457	173,053
1981[2]	83	6,150	5,607	391,637	429,830	399,083	117,856	946,769	2,849,617	800.3	391,194	258,745	212,426
1982[4]	85	6,000	6,000	320,000	585,870	273,421	108,976	968,267	2,493,706	553.9	175,805	262,764	423,576
1983													

[1] In hands of refiners, importers, & dealers.   [2] Preliminary.   [3] Palladium, rhodium, iridium, osmium, ruthenium & osmium metals & alloys.   [4] Estimate.   [5] From crude platinum placers & byproduct platinum-group metals.   [6] Ore & concentrates, waste, scrap & sweepings.   *Source: Bureau of Mines*

T.513

PLATINUM-GROUP METALS

High, Low & Closing Prices of April Platinum Futures in New York   In Dollars per Ounce

Year of Delivery		Feb.	Mar.	Apr.	May	June	July	Aug.	Sept.	Oct.	Nov.	Dec.	Jan.	Feb.	Mar.	Apr.	Life of Delivery Range
1978	High	178.4	180.3	175.0	169.7	163.2	160.3	158.3	160.8	176.3	179.2	190.0	224.8	239.5	247.2	226.0	247.2
	Low	171.0	169.0	166.2	159.6	152.5	154.5	148.5	152.8	156.4	162.3	174.3	186.6	211.6	212.0	208.9	148.5
	Close	255.0	263.0	241.5	263.5	261.3	277.4	284.3	292.5	390.0	371.6	358.0	393.0	430.5	413.2	398.0	430.5
1979	High	229.0	228.3	212.8	217.9	238.0	244.5	260.0	261.5	288.0	302.0	325.0	342.5	378.1	365.0	371.0	173.6
	Low	177.5	174.3	168.0	162.7	159.4	156.4	153.4	159.0	174.4	176.5	189.2	219.0	230.3	225.8	210.0	—
	Close	246.3	241.8	219.8	258.6	247.6	277.4	264.2	289.9	381.6	324.2	354.6	384.7	414.6	385.0	397.0	—
1980	High	438.0	421.5	409.5	458.3	446.0	429.0	434.0	573.6	608.6	550.0	715.3	974.4	960.0	1,045.0	642.0	1,045.0
	Low	388.5	370.0	369.0	402.0	410.0	382.0	368.0	417.0	468.5	467.0	537.0	715.0	827.0	465.0	525.0	270.1
	Close	423.2	390.1	409.5	451.0	426.9	388.8	428.0	573.6	485.5	546.0	692.6	832.0	920.1	560.0	602.0	—
1981	High	1,100.1	1,190.0	738.0	624.8	753.5	785.0	720.0	810.0	755.0	714.0	680.5	621.0	518.0	546.0	523.0	1,190.0
	Low	972.0	623.5	623.5	563.8	646.0	653.7	660.0	710.0	673.0	622.0	561.0	452.2	455.0	430.0	443.5	430.0
	Close	1,070.0	663.5	626.0	624.8	740.7	676.0	707.2	742.8	681.8	673.4	606.0	463.5	461.7	500.3	461.0	—
1982	High	595.0	624.7	594.5	551.0	533.0	460.6	488.5	494.0	462.5	434.5	434.0	392.5	380.0	346.5	364.0	624.7
	Low	535.7	507.0	507.0	502.0	447.0	425.5	418.7	407.0	424.0	381.0	376.0	352.5	342.0	296.5	311.5	296.5
	Close	540.2	577.1	529.9	528.0	455.5	438.7	460.7	435.4	429.8	405.0	384.1	368.2	344.3	318.3	332.2	—
1983	High	429.6	390.0	400.0	356.0	329.5	333.0	358.1	415.0	392.0	385.0	405.0	499.3	502.0	428.0	433.0	502.0
	Low	388.0	342.6	352.0	318.0	263.0	280.5	271.5	291.0	285.2	320.0	352.0	393.0	396.3	376.5	393.0	263.0
	Close	395.0	357.2	352.0	315.2	306.4	303.3	333.1	294.4	355.1	384.3	392.6	498.7	396.3	392.6	424.0	—
1984	High	526.0	461.0	459.5													
	Low	423.3	410.0	433.5													
	Close	423.3	425.6	453.4													

Source: N.Y. Mercantile Exchange   T.514

Month-End Open Interest of Platinum Futures in New York   In Contracts

Year	Jan.	Feb.	Mar.	Apr.	May	June	July	Aug.	Sept.	Oct.	Nov.	Dec.
1978	7,408	8,703	6,856	6,941	10,289	7,748	8,120	8,278	8,466	8,373	8,816	9,230
1979	8,755	9,866	9,302	9,088	8,861	9,683	10,856	9,850	8,563	7,525	7,595	8,926
1980	8,200	8,409	6,209	5,434	6,369	7,943	7,797	8,286	14,239	12,140	12,026	11,911
1981	9,410	8,946	9,441	7,709	8,130	7,891	5,520	6,446	8,421	7,055	8,601	7,839
1982	6,278	7,524	8,686	8,302	10,326	9,337	11,137	12,853	14,141	13,002	15,547	15,620
1983	19,927	23,506	15,197	15,878								
1984												

Source: N.Y. Mercantile Exchange   T.515

Volume of Trading of Platinum Futures in New York   In Thousands of Contracts

Year	Jan.	Feb.	Mar.	Apr.	May	June	July	Aug.	Sept.	Oct.	Nov.	Dec.	Total
1978	28.3	35.9	48.9	27.2	38.5	33.9	26.0	34.5	28.1	39.0	33.1	32.5	405.7
1979	43.8	45.4	43.4	42.1	45.2	50.8	47.6	56.0	48.4	35.0	38.2	40.1	536.1
1980	35.2	28.5	41.7	21.4	26.6	37.6	40.8	26.7	59.7	41.0	34.8	35.9	429.7
1981	36.5	29.7	56.1	36.7	30.8	44.7	37.9	39.1	63.9	35.4	33.2	46.6	490.5
1982	32.5	29.5	48.4	42.4	33.1	46.6	55.8	76.9	84.8	70.8	70.0	78.1	669.0
1983	126.0	117.0	107.9	71.9									
1984													

Source: N.Y. Mercantile Exchange   T.516

Average Price of Palladium (Dealer Prices)[1]   In Dollars Per Troy Ounce

Year	Jan.	Feb.	Mar.	Apr.	May	June	July	Aug.	Sept.	Oct.	Nov.	Dec.	Average
1975	124.32	105.00	93.92	90.50	73.27	57.71	55.86	58.30	50.52	47.60	44.00	44.00	70.42
1976	42.00	39.62	37.56	38.50	41.58	48.50	55.75	50.28	53.25	52.99	59.20	52.38	47.63
1977	54.06	58.10	57.82	55.20	52.97	45.18	44.90	42.36	42.20	43.07	48.83	51.97	49.72
1978	55.10	64.86	64.18	59.33	60.82	60.42	59.53	61.86	60.09	71.58	70.74	73.25	63.48
1979	76.14	103.35	95.56	93.97	105.53	124.33	121.40	117.45	136.94	143.63	141.95	163.42	118.62
1980	220.00	262.80	259.83	194.79	169.74	169.56	199.55	203.88	212.74	204.72	185.85	155.69	203.10
1981	134.38	112.18	117.82	110.42	102.90	94.76	83.61	85.86	85.50	79.08	72.13	69.51	95.68
1982[2]	67	67	67	69	68	57	57	59	64	63	74	90	67

[1] Based on wholesale quantities, prompt delivery.   [2] Estimate.   Source: American Metal Market   T.510

268

Pork Bellies

Pork bellies, the layer of meat and fat from the underside of the hog, are cured and smoked to produce bacon. A hog will yield two bellies, each weighing from about 8 to 18 pounds depending on the size of the animal when slaughtered. The bellies account for approximately 12 percent of a hog's live weight and a somewhat larger percentage of the total "cut-out" value. Profit margins for the hog producer reflect the total value of all pork products, including hams and loins as well as bacon, and even when the overall cut-out value is profitable, the price of any one of these cuts may be independently weak.

The estimated weighted-average price of retail cuts from pork throughout 1982 was slightly over $1.75 per pound compared with $1.52 in 1981. The value of the wholesale quantity equivalent to 1 pound of retail cuts was nearly $1.22 per pound in 1982, up from $1.07 in 1981. Gross farm values for pork, the market values to the producer for a quantity of live-animal equivalent to 1 pound of retail cuts, rose by almost 19 cents to just over 94 cents per pound in 1982. The net farm value of pork, not including value attributable to edible and inedible pork by-products, rose by nearly 18 cents in 1982 to 88 cents per pound.

The total farm-retail pork price spread increased by nearly 5½ cents per pound in 1982 to over 87 cents. This price included a farm-wholesale spread of nearly 34 cents, and a wholesale-retail spread of nearly 54 cents per pound. Net farm values of pork averaged 50 percent of retail prices during the year, a 4 percent increase from the 1981 proportion. Farm-wholesale price spreads for pork in 1982 declined nearly 2½ cents per pound while wholesale-retail spreads increased nearly 8 cents.

Omaha prices for No. 1 and 2 slaughter barrows and gilts, 200–230 pounds, were $56.71 per cwt. at the end of 1982 compared with $41.24 a year earlier. At the same time, 12–14 pound pork bellies averaged $74.02 per cwt., an increase of over $22.50 per cwt. over the 1981 price. The average retail price of sliced bacon in 1982 was 2.05 cents per pound compared with 1.67 cents in 1981.

U.S. commercial slaughter of hogs in 1982 dropped 10 percent from the 1981 total, to 82.2 million head, and pork production declined by the same percentage, to 15.7 billion pounds. Thus, pork belly production in 1982 was also about 10 percent smaller than a year earlier.

April 1, 1983 stocks of pork bellies in U.S. cold storage warehouses amounted to nearly 44.4 million pounds, compared with 66.1 million on the same date in 1982. The drawdown in cold storage holdings primarily reflected the reduced production of pork bellies, but the economic recovery was probably a contributing factor.

The March 1, 1983 inventory of all hogs and pigs in the 10 quarterly reporting states which account for approximately 79 percent of the total U.S. hog and pig inventory totaled 41.6 million head, up 3 percent from a year earlier. The breeding herd was 6 percent higher than a year ago, and the number of market hogs was up 2 percent. Producers indicated intentions to have 8 percent more sows farrow in March–May than a year earlier and 7 percent more in June–August. Based on these considerations, commercial pork production for all of 1983 could total 14.4 billion pounds, up 2 percent from 1982.

Futures Market

Pork belly futures are traded on the Chicago Mercantile Exchange.

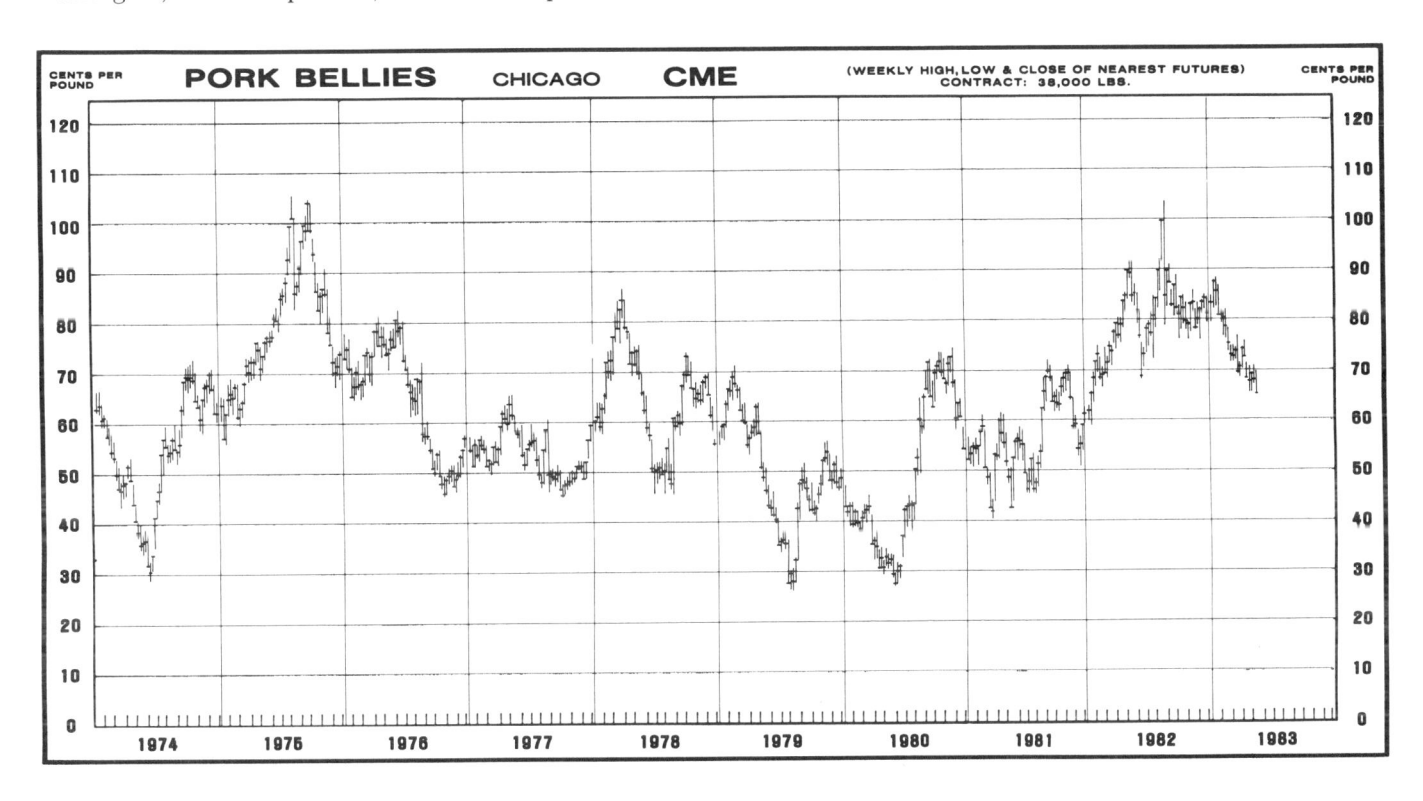

PORK BELLIES

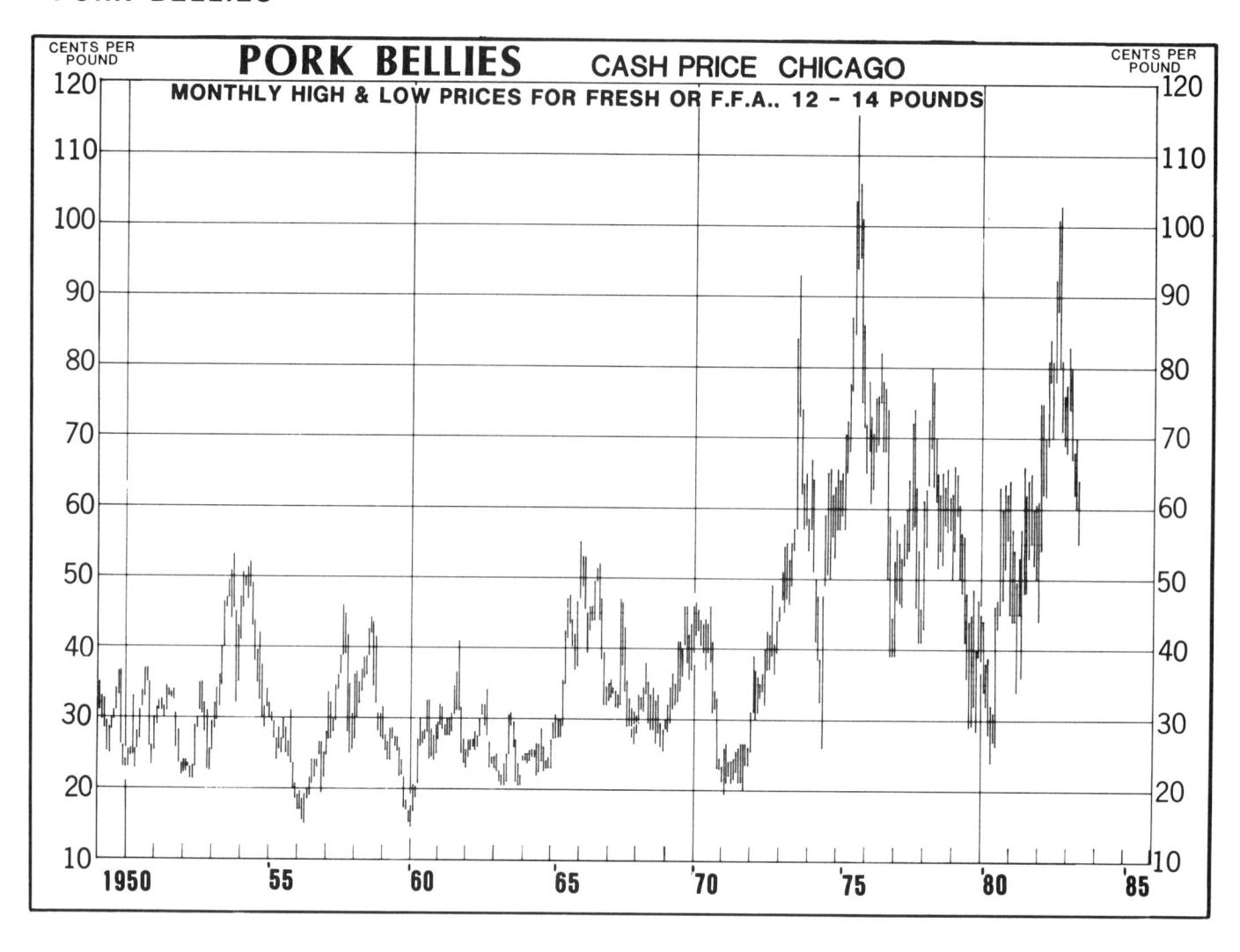

PORK BELLIES CASH PRICE CHICAGO
MONTHLY HIGH & LOW PRICES FOR FRESH OR F.F.A., 12 - 14 POUNDS
(Cents per pound, 1950–1985)

U.S. Frozen Pork Belly Storage Stocks (In Thousand Pounds, as of First of the Month)

Year	Jan.	Feb.	Mar.	Apr.	May	June	July	Aug.	Sept.	Oct.	Nov.	Dec.
1970	38,697	37,017	47,094	61,068	74,004	82,061	67,250	39,300	20,393	9,823	21,043	42,054
1971	76,437	81,561	83,004	111,579	131,262	146,093	140,778	105,015	70,504	50,654	53,057	68,004
1972	86,065	84,092	88,090	107,013	131,189	133,069	105,727	69,933	35,792	16,691	22,175	34,167
1973	39,278	32,388	30,764	46,406	50,205	54,980	48,817	26,270	10,186	9,140	15,397	31,580
1974	48,758	48,499	53,083	65,237	78,707	87,290	70,470	39,621	21,762	12,850	22,274	38,441
1975	49,514	40,374	42,846	51,771	65,645	65,470	53,389	22,995	10,057	7,418	17,645	33,532
1976	44,722	37,386	38,526	51,176	60,144	63,799	49,258	25,773	8,689	5,858	9,708	24,946
1977	42,906	38,338	36,364	52,806	69,539	80,658	62,695	29,901	9,640	5,241	4,230	20,642
1978	23,747	19,013	15,738	39,631	70,976	82,343	75,027	44,787	21,015	7,482	20,013	40,964
1979	54,367	39,432	37,172	57,744	69,689	86,065	78,935	53,373	21,800	11,077	17,739	42,156
1980	70,201	69,635	67,800	85,444	98,163	106,869	96,967	68,616	34,410	21,867	42,186	72,127
1981	97,365	90,181	94,661	104,357	125,469	132,568	117,795	72,998	36,094	16,228	18,060	35,058
1982[1]	54,639	46,167	41,855	66,061	—	—	72,593	—	—	7,558	—	—
1983[1]	31,292	33,592	33,400	44,361								
1984												

[1] Preliminary. Source: Crop Reporting Board, U.S.D.A.

T.517

PORK BELLIES

Wkly Fed. Inspected Hog Slaughter

Week Ending	1982[2]	1981	1980	1979	1978
Jan. 2	1,428	1,297	1,378		
9	1,881	1,957	1,972	1,179	1,247
16	1,656	1,885	1,762	1,625	1,473
23	1,643	1,793	1,785	1,389	1,376
30	1,623	1,816	1,777	1,345	1,261
Feb. 6	1,552	1,773	1,770	1,383	1,527
13	1,650	1,731	1,760	1,381	1,437
20	1,484	1,672	1,642	1,488	1,551
27	1,652	1,698	1,765	1,367	1,348
Mar. 6	1,698	1,757	1,806	1,533	1,424
13	1,676	1,823	1,898	1,592	1,579
20	1,663	1,826	1,885	1,663	1,508
27	1,705	1,840	1,858	1,607	1,422
Apr. 3	1,609	1,848	1,858	1,646	1,452
10	1,606	1,914	1,736	1,644	1,508
17	1,608	1,823	1,919	1,669	1,608
24	1,656	1,727	2,028	1,609	1,504
May 1	1,640	1,771	2,028	1,710	1,588
8	1,596	1,763	1,918	1,759	1,498
15	1,610	1,771	1,973	1,677	1,522
22	1,553	1,694	1,916	1,598	1,377
29	1,532	1,422	1,891	1,592	1,329
June 5	1,279	1,561	1,582	1,390	1,138
12	1,561	1,618	1,851	1,647	1,377
19	1,467	1,500	1,747	1,631	1,283
26	1,416	1,434	1,683	1,398	1,297
July 3	1,394	1,324	1,669	1,600	1,266
10	1,162	1,401	1,269	1,269	1,054
17	1,434	1,444	1,573	1,630	1,378
24	1,352	1,442	1,600	1,590	1,376
31	1,357	1,496	1,530	1,595	1,318
Aug. 7	1,398	1,539	1,574	1,638	1,337
14	1,391	1,554	1,553	1,662	1,367
21	1,424	1,576	1,611	1,692	1,329
28	1,400	1,591	1,612	1,664	1,349
Sept. 4	1,411	1,658	1,497	1,509	1,251
11	1,286	1,456	1,867	1,776	1,579
18	1,527	1,785	1,812	1,764	1,581
25	1,418	1,699	1,707	1,772	1,497
Oct. 2	1,501	1,742	1,759	1,870	1,479
9	1,482	1,769	1,791	1,950	1,533
16	1,536	1,817	1,864	1,929	1,475
23	1,599	1,786	1,861	1,909	1,478
30	1,614	1,814	1,955	2,016	1,549
Nov. 6	1,620	1,789	1,810	1,790	1,651
13	1,677	1,841	2,022	1,548	1,328
20	1,650	1,511	1,514	1,981	1,642
27	1,310	1,947	1,952	1,940	1,613
Dec. 4	1,676	1,884	1,841	1,861	1,497
11	1,523	1,884	1,841	1,861	1,497
18	1,588	1,864	1,816	1,746	1,489
25	1,278	1,223	1,191	1,277	1,149
1983[2]					
Jan. 1	1,204				
8	1,457				
15	1,564				
22	1,561				
29	1,519				
Feb. 5	1,350				
12	1,467				
19	1,491				

Weekly Pork Belly Storage Movement

Stocks[1] in Thousands of Pounds

1982[2] Week Ending	In	Out	On Hand	Net Movement	1981 Week Ending	In	Out	On Hand	Net Movement
Jan. 2	1,066	606	47,064	+ 460	Jan. 3	1,769	571	82,206	+1,198
9	575	1,449	46,190	− 874	10	1,466	1,870	81,802	− 404
16	1,374	1,260	46,304	+ 114	17	2,227	2,263	82,766	+ 474
23	527	1,457	46,480	− 930	24	1,192	3,512	79,446	−2,320
30	574	5,137	41,917	−4,563	31	1,092	4,404	76,134	−3,312
Feb. 6	223	4,901	37,239	−4,678	Feb. 7	566	2,183	74,517	−1,617
13	523	2,282	35,480	−1,759	14	1,009	1,106	74,799	− 97
20	499	1,226	34,753	− 727	21	2,536	819	76,516	+1,717
27	1,435	701	35,487	+ 734	28	3,756	829	79,443	+2,927
Mar. 6	4,754	517	39,724	+4,237	Mar. 7	3,201	235	82,409	+2,966
13	6,343	76	45,991	+6,267	14	3,047	235	85,221	+2,812
20	4,509	—	50,500	+4,509	21	2,973	383	87,811	+2,590
27	4,886	289	55,097	+4,597	28	2,465	565	89,711	+1,900
Apr. 3	3,907	314	58,690	+3,593	Apr. 4	1,548	676	90,583	+ 872
10	3,444	136	61,998	+3,308	11	4,335	391	94,527	+3,944
17	1,856	255	63,599	+1,601	18	5,779	298	100,008	+5,481
24	1,158	490	64,267	+ 668	25	5,759	466	105,301	+5,294
May 1	717	560	64,424	+ 157	May 2	5,722	475	110,548	+5,247
8	1,845	563	65,706	+1,282	9	6,131	237	116,442	+5,894
15	2,181	326	67,561	+1,855	16	4,734	274	120,992	+4,460
22	3,264	420	70,405	+2,844	23	2,010	752	122,160	+1,258
29	2,392	590	72,207	+1,802	30	500	3,146	119,514	−2,646
June 5	1,231	552	72,886	+ 679	June 6	910	2,445	117,969	−1,545
12	1,602	797	73,691	+ 805	13	160	3,377	114,752	−3,217
19	1,717	2,960	72,448	−1,243	20	391	4,459	110,684	−4,060
26	554	4,464	68,538	−3,910	27	619	4,916	106,387	−4,297
July 3	363	5,910	62,991	−5,547	July 4	128	4,840	101,675	−4,712
10	148	6,006	57,133	−5,858	11	125	7,940	93,860	−7,815
17	254	5,947	51,440	−5,693	18	417	8,503	85,774	−8,086
24	179	5,895	45,724	−5,716	25	102	11,839	74,037	−11,737
31	116	6,238	39,629	−6,095	Aug. 1	159	10,521	63,675	−10,362
Aug. 7	113	5,241	34,501	−5,128	8	824	9,026	54,973	−8,702
14	148	5,882	28,767	−5,734	15	113	8,043	47,043	−7,930
21	80	6,612	22,235	−5,532	22	114	8,251	38,906	−8,137
28	369	5,436	17,168	−5,127	29	385	8,938	30,353	−8,553
Sept. 4	761	3,320	14,609	−2,559	Sept. 5	679	4,977	26,055	−4,298
11	265	2,977	11,897	−2,712	12	155	4,527	21,683	−4,372
18	414	3,703	8,608	−3,289	19	228	3,822	18,089	−3,594
25	314	3,014	5,908	−2,700	26	257	3,810	14,536	−3,553
Oct. 2	411	1,636	4,683	−1,225	Oct. 3	258	2,261	12,533	−2,003
9	514	1,301	3,896	− 787	10	396	1,883	11,046	−1,487
16	610	1,054	3,452	− 444	17	974	948	11,072	+ 26
23	820	756	3,516	+ 64	24	2,097	483	12,686	+1,615
30	1,775	431	4,860	+1,344	31	1,385	267	13,804	+1,118
Nov. 6	1,690	140	6,410	+1,550	Nov. 7	2,286	172	15,918	+2,114
13	2,942	299	9,053	+2,643	14	2,881	514	18,285	+2,367
20	4,591	483	13,161	+4,108	21	6,005	302	23,988	+5,703
27	3,534	292	16,403	+3,242	28	4,598	185	28,401	+4,413
Dec. 4	4,208	403	20,208	+3,805	Dec. 5	6,625	322	34,704	+6,303
11	3,822	369	23,661	+3,453	12	5,632	46	40,290	+5,586
18	1,843	190	25,314	+1,653	19	4,644	37	44,897	+4,607
25	2,159	337	27,136	+1,822	26	1,707	—	46,604	+1,707
1983[2]									
Jan. 1	1,802	215	28,723	+1,581					
8	1,040	191	29,572	+ 849					
15	300	701	29,171	− 401					
22	253	778	28,646	− 525					
29	398	805	28,239	− 407					
Feb. 5	378	868	27,749	− 490					
12	200	737	27,212	− 537					
19	720	773	27,159	− 53					

[1] Total approved Chi. Merc. Exch. warehouses. [2] Preliminary. Sources: U.S. Department of Agriculture; Chicago Mercantile Exchange T.518

PORK BELLIES

High, Low & Closing Prices of May Pork Bellies Futures at Chicago   In Cents per Pound

Year of Delivery		Mar.	Apr.	May	June	July	Aug.	Sept.	Oct.	Nov.	Dec.	Jan.	Feb.	Mar.	Apr.	May	Life of Delivery Range
1978	High	56.35	60.50	59.85	53.80	54.80	49.50	49.40	48.20	52.20	57.25	62.35	74.35	86.25	84.15	75.40	86.25
	Low	53.15	54.35	52.60	46.50	46.05	43.85	44.45	44.25	46.90	48.15	56.00	62.15	71.55	69.47	67.90	43.85
	Close	55.60	56.20	53.75	52.70	46.60	47.10	44.50	46.65	46.90	57.22	61.85	71.55	84.15	73.90	69.50	—
1979	High	72.50	69.30	68.75	65.20	60.00	62.70	68.00	72.02	68.40	68.70	63.70	70.95	67.30	63.60	63.50	72.50
	Low	63.10	65.00	62.25	50.30	51.65	54.70	56.10	62.80	62.60	55.00	55.80	62.50	54.60	50.85	47.95	47.95
	Close	69.50	65.00	64.25	53.50	60.00	57.47	67.70	65.27	66.70	56.27	63.45	65.25	55.35	63.27	49.35	—
1980	High	—	56.10	55.60	51.05	49.20	49.30	52.42	50.25	57.85	54.60	53.47	44.85	46.70	38.00	34.30	57.85
	Low	—	50.25	47.90	43.10	39.35	39.10	43.40	41.65	47.60	47.92	41.55	39.65	34.77	29.45	30.40	29.45
	Close	—	56.10	47.90	43.65	41.00	48.60	45.60	48.70	50.27	49.50	43.05	42.50	36.30	30.27	31.60	—
1981	High	58.50	52.60	49.75	54.50	61.60	66.25	73.30	75.15	75.15	77.05	59.60	63.00	55.30	61.35	52.65	77.05
	Low	49.75	46.15	43.35	41.32	53.50	57.40	59.25	63.47	67.70	58.05	53.65	52.55	41.90	52.15	42.45	41.32
	Close	51.10	48.40	43.45	53.90	59.30	59.50	68.47	71.20	75.15	58.05	57.70	52.55	55.05	52.15	48.77	—
1982	High	69.15	75.50	72.70	75.90	69.40	72.10	72.50	70.22	71.40	63.75	73.55	75.80	77.85	85.10	91.50	91.50
	Low	54.50	70.15	63.00	64.10	61.75	64.12	62.70	62.95	59.25	51.90	61.12	67.55	69.00	74.75	84.15	51.90
	Close	69.15	70.15	72.70	64.10	65.15	64.95	65.15	68.85	61.05	62.70	73.55	70.37	75.15	84.92	84.95	—
1983	High	73.85	77.95	79.20	77.00	75.00	82.90	85.45	82.05	83.10	83.30	86.30	81.55	76.40	75.90		
	Low	70.20	71.65	74.00	65.25	67.25	69.02	75.37	75.80	74.25	74.35	78.15	74.25	68.50	65.60		
	Close	72.60	77.55	79.00	72.72	74.35	82.10	82.40	77.80	80.75	79.70	79.70	74.25	70.60	67.80		
1984	High	65.40	65.95														
	Low	61.25	62.80														
	Close	64.90	64.72														

Source: Chicago Mercantile Exchange

T.519

Month End Open Interest of Pork Bellies Futures at Chicago   In Contracts

Year	Jan.	Feb.	Mar.	Apr.	May	June	July	Aug.	Sept.	Oct.	Nov.	Dec.
1978	10,544	10,029	9,756	10,898	11,500	10,407	8,780	7,557	8,221	9,780	11,956	13,087
1979	10,597	10,592	9,337	10,586	14,069	23,174	25,400	22,840	22,062	21,805	25,585	27,981
1980	29,631	28,195	18,212	22,939	28,404	26,944	20,025	14,983	18,242	23,098	26,231	22,480
1981	15,687	12,471	12,821	16,714	15,825	18,911	11,550	10,058	10,424	14,088	16,425	13,643
1982	21,542	21,666	21,048	28,063	25,765	17,940	14,203	14,799	16,090	19,063	18,596	18,521
1983	19,654	16,510	17,563	16,850								
1984												

Source: Chicago Mercantile Exchange

T.520

Volume of Trading of Pork Bellies Futures at Chicago   In Contracts

Year	Jan.	Feb.	Mar.	Apr.	May	June	July	Aug.	Sept.	Oct.	Nov.	Dec.	Total
1978	137,389	132,101	150,884	134,178	166,433	126,865	113,817	92,169	83,650	109,911	100,223	92,022	1,439,651
1979	114,980	99,552	106,840	99,408	117,262	154,721	162,816	151,865	118,087	120,649	139,703	121,509	1,514,176
1980	191,920	206,539	189,881	183,876	165,844	206,669	198,256	169,404	167,355	220,435	178,821	176,622	2,250,945
1981	176,243	154,438	135,527	179,503	157,342	199,013	187,785	131,619	139,272	171,480	194,561	170,944	1,997,697
1982	196,040	216,333	263,431	265,863	301,763	248,825	217,434	229,207	188,129	224,449	227,482	232,688	2,811,674
1983	276,556	229,198	207,543	225,034									
1984													

Source: Chicago Mercantile Exchange

T.521

Potatoes

The USDA estimated the 1982 U.S. fall potato crop at 305 million cwt., 3 percent more than the 1981 crop. This made it the second largest crop in history, exceeded only by the 1978 crop. Acres harvested also increased by 3 percent to a total of 1.09 million. The 1982 U.S. average fall crop yield per acre was reduced by 1 cwt. to 277 cwt. per acre. The highest yields were recorded in Washington State (480 cwt.), a decline of 5 cwt. from 1981. Although favorable weather conditions prevailed for most U.S. potato growing regions in 1982, the Maine crop was affected by a significant shrink due to the abundance of small, rough and culled tubers.

Production in the seven Eastern states was 45 million cwt. as of October 1, down 1 million cwt. from 1981. A total of 184,500 acres were harvested, an increase of 4 percent from 1981. The average yield was estimated at 244 cwt. per acre, a decrease of 14 cwt. from 1981, and a reflection of the Maine shrink.

Fall 1982 potato production in the 9 Western potato growing states was estimated at 194 million cwt., up 4½ percent from the 185 million cwt. in 1981. The total area harvested was 597,600 acres, a 4 percent increase over 1981. Average yield per acre in 1982 was 325 cwt.—quite close to 1981's 323 cwt.

The 8 Central growing states' fall 1982 crop was estimated at 67.8 million cwt., 5 percent above the previous year's crop. In 1982, 312,400 acres were harvested vs. 293,800 in 1981. The average yield in 1982 was 217 cwt. an acre vs. 218 cwt. in 1981.

Summer potato production in 1982 was 20.6 million cwt., 3 percent above the output of 1981. Estimated area harvested totaled 95,500 acres, up 500 acres from 1981. Average yield set a record high of 216 cwt. per acre.

Producer prices for potatoes were 18 percent less than during 1981. Tablestock demand was expected to increase by approximately 3 percent from 1981. Processing demand was also expected to show a small rise from 1981 on the order of 1 percent. As of January 1, 1983, 48.7 million cwt. were used for processing, 3 thousand cwt. less than a year earlier. Large stocks on hand as of January 1 and a depressed demand help explain lower producer prices in 1982. The farm price was $3.86 per cwt. for fourth quarter 1982, compared with $4.36 in 1981. The price received by growers in January 1983 was $2.50 per cwt., down from $4.60 in January 1982.

The estimated amount of potatoes used for processing declined from the previous year's total. Frozen potato stocks on January 1, 1983 totaled 754 million pounds vs. 689 million the previous year. Of the total frozen stocks, 627 million pounds were french fries vs. 577 million a year earlier. In 1981/82, exports for dehydrated potatoes on a fresh weight basis were 5.4 million cwt., up 4 percent from last year. Exports of frozen potatoes were considerably higher than in 1981 at 3.6 million cwt., up 33%.

Potato stocks as of April 1, 1983 in 15 major fall producing states were estimated at 84.8 million cwt., 4 percent above a year ago. Estimated holdings in the 3 Eastern states totaled 9.9 million cwt., 5 percent smaller than the previous year. Stocks in Maine, at 7.9 million cwt., were down 8 percent from a year ago. In the 6 Central states, stocks were estimated at 14.1 million cwt., 8 percent above the previous year. North Dakota's stocks were 7 percent greater than a year ago, while Minnesota and Wisconsin were down 13 and up 29 percent, respectively. Holdings in the 6 Western states were estimated at 60.8 million cwt., 4 percent above April 1, 1982. Idaho's stocks were estimated at 34.5 million cwt., the same as a year earlier. Holdings in Washington were up 5 percent while Oregon was up 16%, compared with April 1, 1982.

Disappearance to April 1, 1983 totaled 209 million cwt., 2 percent above the same period a year ago.

Potatoes processed to April 1, 1983 in the 8 major processing states totaled 84.1 million cwt., 3 percent less than the same period a year earlier.

Futures Markets

Round white potato futures are traded on the New York Mercantile Exchange. Russet futures, previously listed on the Chicago Mercantile Exchange, were discontinued as of January 1983.

Salient Statistics of Potatoes in the United States

Year	Acreage Planted — 1,000 Acres	Acreage Harvested — 1,000 Acres	Yield Per Harv. Acre Cwt.	Farm Disposition Used Where Grown — Seed & Feed — Million Cwt.	Farm Disposition Shrinkage & Loss — Million Cwt.	Sold[3] Million Cwt.	Farm Price $ Cwt.	Value of Prod.[6] Million $	Value of Sales Million $	Stocks on Jan. 1[1] 1,000 Cwt.	Foreign Trade[5] Dom. Exports 1,000 Cwt.	Foreign Trade[5] Imports 1,000 Cwt.	Consumption[2] Per Capita In Lbs. Fresh	Consumption[2] Per Capita In Lbs. Processed
1972	1,301	1,256	236	7.9	20.0	268.5	3.02	896	808	148,600	4,430	759	56.6	62.2
1973	1,330	1,307	230	6.5	18.4	275.1	4.90	1,472	1,343	132,050	4,975	1,874	58.1	64.8
1974	1,422	1,392	246	6.5	32.5	303.4	4.01	1,355	1,215	131,600	4,545	1,453	47.4	65.8
1975	1,304	1,260	256	6.6	22.2	293.2	4.48	1,443	1,305	160,100	9,317	691	53.8	66.7
1976	1,407	1,371	261	6.8	26.2	324.7	3.59	1,283	1,167	156,220	11,617	806	50.5	64.6
1977	1,398	1,360	261	6.7	31.1	317.5	3.55	1,255	1,126	172,230	3,630	955	53.6	66.7
1978	1,401	1,375	267	6.3	34.4	325.6	3.38	1,224	1,097	175,300	3,025	703	51.5	69.6
1979	1,310	1,270	270	5.9	30.2	306.4	3.43	1,172	1,052	193,520	2,336	1,143	59.0	65.3
1980[1]	1,182	1,154	262	6.4	23.4	273.1	6.55	1,979	1,788	176,020			55.8	61.9
1981[1]	1,263	1,237	274	6.0	26.1	306.5	5.41	1,819	1,660	146,610			49.1	65.5
1982[1]	1,309	1,274	274				4.59	1,589		163,180				
1983[1]										173,500				

Note: 60 pounds equals one bushel. [1] Preliminary. [2] Fresh & processed. [3] For all purposes, including food, seed processing livestock feed. [4] Merchantable stocks held by growers & local dealers. [5] Year beginning July. [6] Farm weight basis. Excludes canned & frozen potatoes. Source: Economic Research Service, U.S.D.A.

T.522

POTATOES

World Production of Potatoes   In Thousands of Metric Tons

Yr. of Harvest	Austria	Canada	Czecho-slovakia	France	E. Germany	W. Germany	Italy	Japan	Nether-lands	Poland	Spain	United Kingdom	USSR	United States	World Total
1974	1,996	2,501	4,522	7,473	13,404	14,549	2,849	2,942	6,095	48,519	5,693	6,791	81,022	15,531	249,673
1975	1,579	2,111	3,565	6,865	7,673	10,853	2,900	3,261	4,743	46,429	5,338	4,551	88,703	14,617	236,123
1976	1,746	2,345	4,214	4,326	6,816	9,808	2,937	3,742	4,783	49,951	5,659	4,789	85,102	16,224	240,144
1977	1,352	2,488	3,760	7,803	10,313	11,368	3,080	3,520	5,752	41,148	5,881	6,624	83,652	16,083	242,977
1978	1,401	2,496	3,863	7,467	10,100	10,510	2,801	3,316	6,231	46,648	5,316	7,330	86,100	16,615	250,568
1979	1,494	2,760	3,725	5,900	12,243	8,716	2,957	3,381	5,937	49,600	5,400	6,485	90,956	15,536	255,134
1980	1,264	2,478	2,713	6,864	9,214	6,694	2,396	3,421	6,267	26,391	5,742	7,080	67,023	13,737	202,263
1981[1]	1,176	2,541	3,500	5,294	10,000	7,586	2,204	3,250	6,445	43,074	5,483	6,282	72,000	14,966	225,320
1982[2]		2,602						3,650		35,000			83,000	15,875	
1983															

[1] Preliminary.   [2] Estimate.   Source: Foreign Agricultural Service, U.S.D.A.   T.523

United States Potato Production by Seasonal Groups   In Millions of Hundredweight (CWT.)

Year	Winter	Spring Florida	Spring Calif.	Total Spring	Summer Va.	Summer Total	Fall Maine	Fall Wisc.	Fall Minn.	Fall No. Dak.	Fall Wash.	Fall Idaho	Fall Oregon	Total Fall	Total U.S.
1974	2.9	3.8	13.7	25.0	4.1	25.1	36.4	14.0	15.3	23.0	41.2	81.2	17.5	289.3	342.4
1975	2.9	3.5	10.5	20.0	2.4	21.0	26.8	14.9	9.7	17.6	48.3	78.5	24.4	278.4	322.0
1976	3.0	4.5	13.5	24.7	3.5	22.5	27.4	15.4	11.1	16.9	55.8	88.5	28.9	307.4	357.7
1977	2.7	4.6	11.9	22.9	3.5	22.0	28.3	18.0	13.0	21.6	50.6	88.2	25.6	307.1	355.3
1978	2.6	3.7	8.3	18.0	2.7	20.9	26.0	17.3	14.9	23.6	50.5	100.3	28.5	324.9	366.3
1979	2.4	4.4	11.1	21.3	2.6	21.8	27.7	17.0	12.9	18.2	48.5	85.1	25.3	296.9	342.5
1980	2.4	3.6	8.8	17.1	1.5	17.0	25.0	16.0	9.9	15.7	43.9	79.8	19.7	266.4	302.9
1981	2.2	5.3	10.3	20.8	2.3	20.0	26.5	18.2	13.3	20.1	52.9	84.5	21.7	295.6	338.6
1982[1]	2.3	5.4	9.6	20.6	2.2	21.5	26.5	22.6	11.5	17.3	52.8	89.9	21.1	305.0	349.3
1983[1]	2.5	4.7	8.1	17.8											

[1] Preliminary, December estimate.   Source: U.S.D.A.—Crop Reporting Board   T.524

Potato Crop Production Estimates, Stocks & Disappearance in the U.S.   In Millions of Cwt.

Year	Crop Production Estimates Total Crop Oct. 1	Nov. 1	Dec.	Fall Crop Oct. 1	Nov. 1	Dec. 1	Total Storage Stocks[2] Following Year Dec. 1	Jan. 1	Feb. 1	Mar. 1	Apr. 1	May 1	Disappearance of Previous Fall Crop Until Following Year Dec. 1	Jan. 1	Feb. 1	Mar. 1	Apr. 1
1974	337.8	339.0	340.1	286.6	287.9	287.7	183.9	160.1	131.5	103.0	75.2		97.8	122.6	152.2	181.4	200.6
1975	307.6	310.3	315.6				181.7	156.2	129.7	102.9	71.0		88.6	114.9	142.9	169.4	201.4
1976	349.9	349.3	353.4	299.8	299.2	302.8	198.6	172.2	142.0	112.8	81.1		99.1	128.3	157.8	188.0	218.4
1977	350.6	350.4	352.0	303.6	303.4	304.4	202.6	175.3	147.9	119.9	88.7		93.8	122.8	149.9	177.9	210.2
1978	353.6	357.7	360.5	312.0	316.0	318.7	219.9	193.5	163.0	132.6	99.3	64.8	94.6	122.0	153.0	185.0	218.0
1979	347.9	348.3	347.6	300.3	300.7	301.6	200.8	176.0	147.9	121.7	92.6	59.5	87.5	114.0	143.0	170.0	200.0
1980	296.9	296.9	301.0	260.7	260.7	264.6	171.7	146.6	121.6	97.3	72.5	44.4	84.1	110.0	135.0	160.0	186.0
1981[1]	329.9	329.9	333.7	287.1	287.1	290.7	192.8	163.2	137.1	111.3	81.9	50.7	93.6	121.0	149.0	175.0	204.0
1982[1]	350.0	350.0	349.3	306.9	308.9	305.0	201.8	173.5	145.0	116.5	84.8	52.9	92.3	121.0	149.0	178.0	209.0
1983																	

[1] Preliminary.   [2] Held by growers & local dealers in the fall producing areas.   Source: Crop Reporting Board, U.S.D.A.   T.525

Volume of Trading in Maine Potato Futures, on N.Y. Mercantile Exchange   In Contracts (50,000 Lbs. Per)

Year	Jan.	Feb.	Mar.	Apr.	May	June	July	Aug.	Sept.	Oct.	Nov.	Dec.	Total
1978	55,269	44,671	45,075	53,844	12,859	18,487	19,670	41,255	36,754	48,503	38,099	38,643	453,129
1979	45,986	36,632	22,321	842	1,972	3,571	10,793	8,931	12,750	15,964	12,939	11,519	184,220
1980	13,849	12,656	14,443	9,650	5,853	20,483	47,611	52,794	60,988	62,081	48,084	45,267	293,759
1981	46,231	47,793	37,909	4,585	5,606	9,095	18,019	16,271	15,888	19,478	7,910	8,626	237,411
1982	10,058	13,180	8,198	2,868	2,703	4,065	5,818	3,634	3,603	6,530	3,706	2,959	67,322
1983	3,981	4,018	5,256	442									

Source: New York Mercantile Exch.   T.526

POTATOES

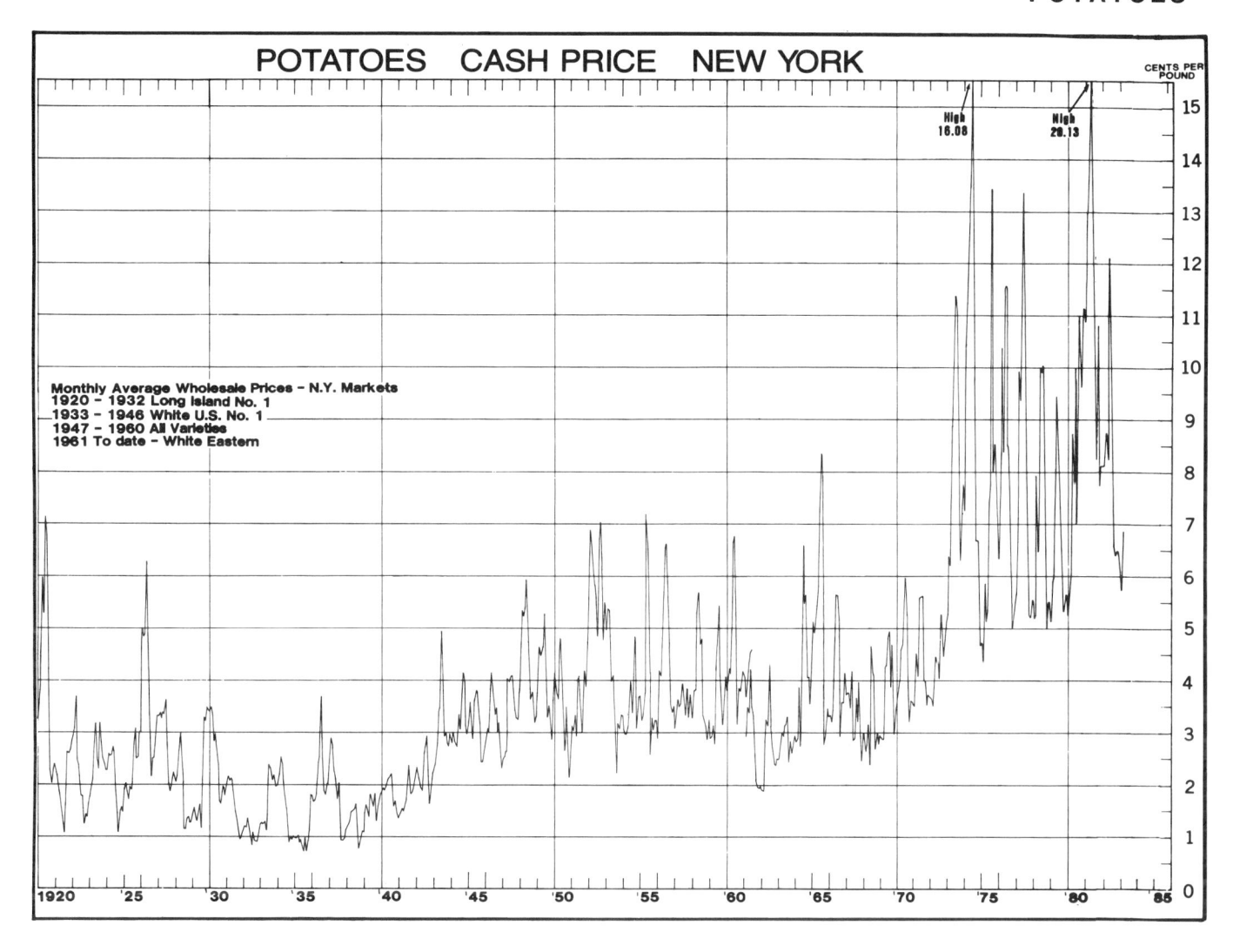

POTATOES CASH PRICE NEW YORK

Monthly Average Wholesale Prices – N.Y. Markets
1920 – 1932 Long Island No. 1
1933 – 1946 White U.S. No. 1
1947 – 1960 All Varieties
1961 To date – White Eastern

High 16.08
High 28.13

Wholesale Price of Potatoes at New York   In Dollars Per Cwt.

Year	Jan.	Feb.	Mar.	Apr.	May	June	July	Aug.	Sept.	Oct.	Nov.	Dec.	Average
WHITE, WESTERN, NEW YORK[1]													
1975	9.925	9.750	8.500	8.750	11.750	11.750	13.750	14.500	12.000	12.750	12.250	12.000	11.473
1976	11.850	12.250	12.250	12.750	12.500	12.000	10.875	9.500	N.A.	N.A.	10.000	10.250	11.423
1977	10.250	11.500	11.000	11.500	11.500	13.750	10.500	16.500	N.A.	11.000	12.250	11.000	11.886
1978	N.A.	N.A.	N.A.	N.A.	12.500	14.416	17.916	16.834	15.000	14.626	12.500	12.250	14.505
1979	12.750	17.376	16.250	11.750	12.000	13.084	7.500	6.313	6.250	6.875	6.875	9.063	10.507
1980	8.500	7.438	8.625	8.188	8.188	7.583	10.833	10.250	11.000	11.000	11.000	9.750	9.363
1981	12.375	11.875	11.000	11.000	10.250	11.000	11.417	11.750	11.000	10.000	9.750	11.500	11.076
1982	19.000	20.000	19.000	18.500	23.000	19.750	17.000	21.500	15.000	19.000	19.000	16.500	18.942
1983	N.A.	21.000											
WHITE, EASTERN, NEW YORK[2]													
1975	4.333	5.875	5.125	5.333	7.438	7.750	13.417	8.000	8.538	8.000	7.000	6.325	7.261
1976	8.375	10.375	8.375	11.467	11.583	8.500	8.063	6.250	5.000	5.250	5.500	5.683	7.868
1977	7.125	9.917	9.383	12.375	13.375	11.313	7.875	5.250	5.200	5.500	5.550	5.175	8.170
1978	5.250	7.917	6.475	8.150	10.000	9.917	10.500	6.500	5.000	5.500	5.500	5.133	7.154
1979	5.867	5.967	8.083	9.413	9.000	8.125	7.333	5.750	5.333	5.625	5.617	5.250	6.780
1980	6.000	8.500	8.717	7.750	10.000	7.000	10.500	11.000	9.625	10.625	11.125	10.875	9.310
1981	13.000	13.625	18.083	20.125	16.875	17.000	12.125	8.250	10.833	7.750	8.125	8.125	12.826
1982	8.125	8.750	8.375	8.250	12.125	11.000	9.625	6.625	6.417	6.500	6.250	6.000	8.170
1983	5.750	6.875											

[1] All varieties and types of Irish old and new stock. U.S. No. 1A, Western origin, N.Y. Market (0113–0444.01).   [2] Same. Eastern Origin (0113–0443).   *Source: Bureau of Labor Statistics*

T.527

POTATOES

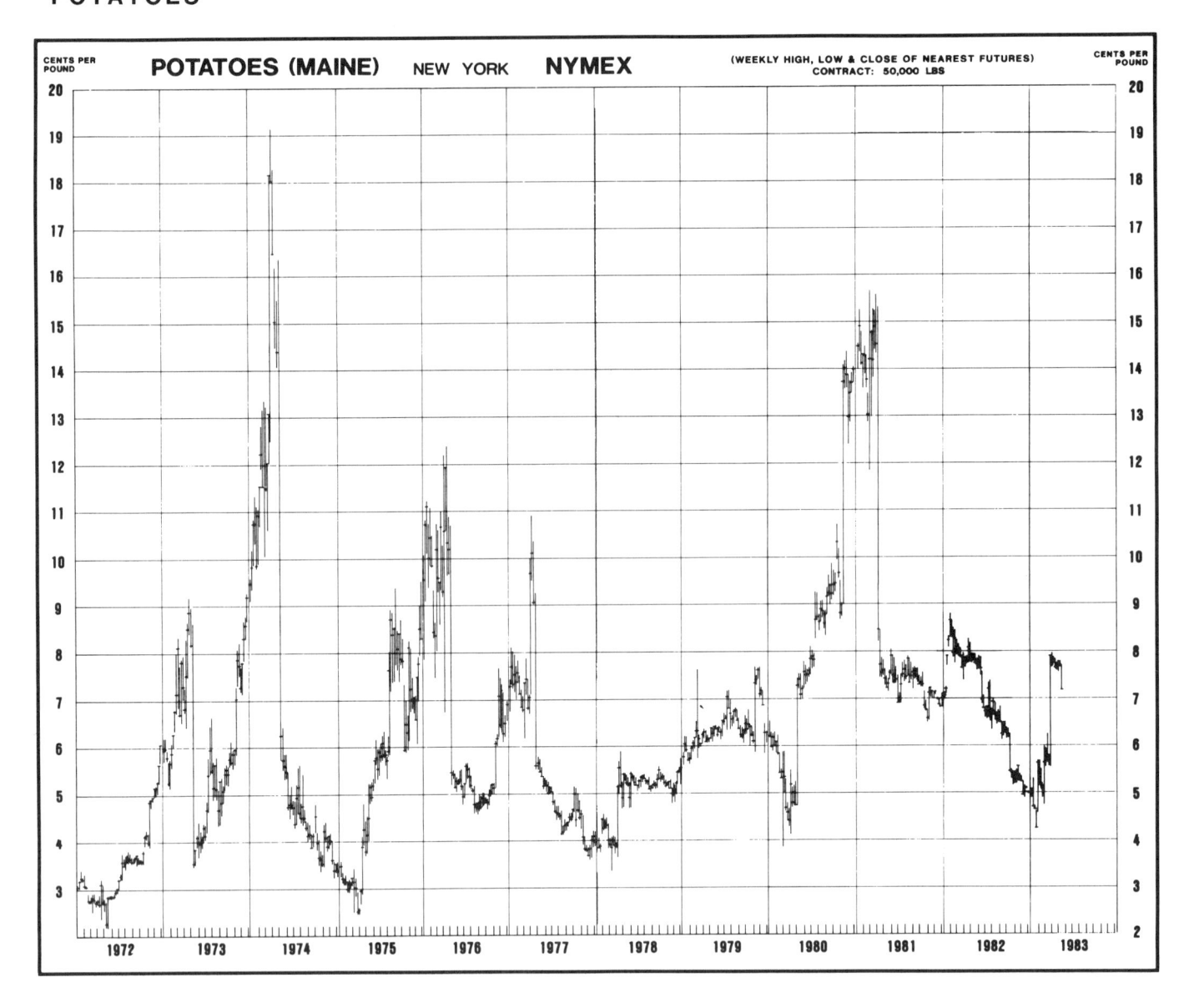

POTATOES (MAINE) NEW YORK **NYMEX** (WEEKLY HIGH, LOW & CLOSE OF NEAREST FUTURES) CONTRACT: 50,000 LBS

High, Low & Closing Prices of April[1] Potato Futures at New York — In Cents per Pound

Year of Delivery		Feb.	Mar.	Apr.	May	June	July	Aug.	Sept.	Oct.	Nov.	Dec.	Jan.	Feb.	Mar.[1]	Life of Delivery Range
1979	High	6.70	7.03	7.19	6.90	6.64	6.45	6.90	6.65	6.32	5.88	5.92	6.45	6.50	7.60	7.60
	Low	6.55	6.60	6.52	6.26	6.34	5.95	6.04	6.12	5.17	5.14	5.30	5.83	5.94	6.30	5.14
	Close	6.60	7.03	6.75	6.47	6.40	6.20	6.59	6.23	5.75	5.64	5.85	6.04	6.45	7.60[2]	—
1980	High	—	—	—	—	—	11.74	11.00	10.74	10.76	9.33	8.24	7.05	6.40	5.80	11.74
	Low	—	—	—	—	—	9.70	10.30	8.65	8.70	8.10	6.80	6.01	5.36	4.01	4.01
	Close	—	—	—	—	—	10.40	10.75	9.72	9.08	8.19	6.85	6.07	5.36	4.05	—
1981	High	—	—	—	10.10	12.22	15.62	15.47	16.06	16.70	16.74	16.98	17.75	17.40	15.51	17.75
	Low	—	—	—	8.25	9.70	11.42	13.55	14.66	14.58	14.75	14.85	15.85	13.90	12.93	8.25
	Close	—	—	—	9.96	11.91	13.73	14.72	15.38	14.77	16.58	16.73	16.79	14.14	14.44	—
1982	High	—	11.87	11.49	10.25	10.22	10.86	10.99	10.80	10.50	8.77	8.77	8.99	9.39	8.25	11.87
	Low	—	11.05	9.70	9.40	8.85	8.93	10.02	9.96	8.14	8.17	7.72	7.75	8.22	7.40	7.40
	Close	—	11.14	9.85	10.21	9.04	10.50	10.20	10.11	8.37	8.48	7.85	8.64	8.27	7.80	—
1983	High	—	—	10.74	10.65	10.20	9.75	9.13	8.72	8.49	6.90	6.83	7.41	6.69	6.23	10.74
	Low	—	—	9.71	9.85	8.52	8.44	8.49	8.20	6.20	6.10	6.28	6.37	5.82	5.46	5.46
	Close	—	—	10.50	10.01	8.74	8.73	8.70	8.25	6.25	6.56	6.57	6.50	5.82	5.87	—

[1] Contract expires the last business day of the previous month. [2] Liquidated March 8, 1979. *Source: N.Y. Mercantile Exch.*

T.528

POTATOES

Utilization of Potatoes in the United States   In Millions of Cwt.

Crop Year	Table Stock	Chips, Shoe-strings	For dehy-dration	Frozen French Fries	Other Frozen Pdt's	Canned Po-tatoes	Other Canned Pdt's[2]	Starch & Flour	Live-stock Feed	Seed	Total Sales	Used on Farms Where Grown	Total
1972-73	111.7	34.6	27.5	56.1	7.9	2.1	2.2	3.4	5.0	18.0	268.5	27.9	296.4
1973	107.6	34.5	31.4	60.3	9.6	2.7	2.5	2.7	3.7	20.1	275.1	25.0	300.0
1974	125.6	32.8	34.7	69.2	9.2	2.6	2.1	3.7	4.2	19.4	303.4	39.0	342.4
1975	114.4	34.1	33.8	70.6	9.3	1.9	2.1	2.2	4.3	20.7	293.5	28.8	322.3
1976	123.1	34.6	40.4	79.7	12.9	1.9	2.6	2.8	6.3	20.5	324.7	33.0	357.7
1977	116.6	36.9	32.8	79.9	14.6	2.8	2.5	2.4	7.4	21.0	316.8	37.8	354.6
1978	112.1	37.8	33.2	79.5	15.4	2.7	2.1	3.5	7.2	20.0	325.6[3]	40.7	366.3
1979	115.0	38.3	30.8	74.3	14.4	2.5	2.3	3.6	6.6	18.2	306.4	36.1	342.5
1980	96.8	37.9	28.2	67.2	13.7	2.1	2.0	2.2	3.9	19.2	273.1	29.8	302.9
1981[1]	110.6	38.3	30.2	79.8	16.8	2.5	1.7	2.4	3.6	20.5	306.5	32.1	338.6
1982-3													

[1] Preliminary.   [2] Hash, stews, soups.   [3] Includes 12.0 sold for livestock feed & starch under the U.S.D.A. diversion program.   Source: *Crop Reporting Board, U.S.D.A.*
T.531

U.S. Cold Storage Stocks of All Frozen Potatoes (First of Month)   In Millions of Pounds

Year	Jan.	Feb.	Mar.	Apr.	May	June	July	Aug.	Sept.	Oct.	Nov.	Dec.
1973	677.3	666.2	734.5	755.3	746.6	671.6	509.9	316.7	246.7	311.8	427.7	496.8
1974	549.3	649.7	704.9	732.6	741.0	650.7	544.0	360.3	363.0	462.7	602.4	688.4
1975	693.5	723.0	797.8	814.4	906.7	945.1	881.1	661.1	536.1	548.9	651.6	689.1
1976	683.2	689.9	744.9	787.6	791.8	794.8	756.6	606.1	508.8	562.4	666.8	745.2
1977	750.4	777.2	809.1	870.8	893.3	903.0	886.5	720.5	576.4	611.0	726.7	805.0
1978	829.8	857.8	901.2	923.7	944.4	971.6	954.8	772.6	627.2	644.9	738.4	769.8
1979	777.5	778.7	784.5	818.2	849.3	930.4	971.7	866.0	671.3	647.1	761.0	814.3
1980	812.2	835.1	868.2	906.6	908.2	958.7	964.0	814.3	598.5	626.5	754.3	813.2
1981[1]	729.9	707.5	757.8	774.4	792.6	812.4	792.7	592.2	457.9	563.9	718.4	746.9
1982[1]	688.7	703.5	783.4	846.0	—	—	939.3	—	—	626.8	—	—
1983[1]	767.3	800.1	870.9	899.8								
1984												

[1] Preliminary.   Source: *Crop Reporting Board, U.S.D.A.*
T.529

U.S. Average Price Received by Farmers for Potatoes   In Dollars Per Cwt.

Year	Jan.	Feb.	Mar.	Apr.	May	June	July	Aug.	Sept.	Oct.	Nov.	Dec.	Avg.[1]
1972	1.84	1.81	1.83	1.80	1.99	2.37	3.68	3.08	2.41	2.13	2.55	2.76	3.01
1973	3.16	3.30	3.82	4.11	4.79	6.15	7.45	4.76	3.24	2.68	3.64	3.95	4.89
1974	4.88	6.23	7.08	7.96	8.11	6.43	5.59	4.78	4.05	4.09	3.88	3.51	4.01
1975	3.36	3.15	2.79	3.23	3.56	5.33	6.58	5.06	4.04	3.63	3.84	3.92	4.48
1976	4.61	4.64	4.95	5.22	5.10	4.44	4.35	3.86	3.20	3.17	3.04	3.10	3.59
1977	3.44	3.52	3.59	3.94	4.42	4.57	5.27	4.01	3.29	3.11	3.08	3.10	3.55
1978	3.24	3.20	3.25	3.30	3.84	5.32	6.71	4.92	3.49	3.07	3.08	3.07	3.38
1979	3.09	2.77	2.94	2.82	3.08	3.00	3.41	3.61	3.23	3.14	3.35	3.51	3.43
1980	3.44	3.37	3.23	3.21	3.74	4.36	5.91	7.64	6.42	4.38	5.42	6.60	6.55
1981[2]	7.38	7.51	8.12	8.41	8.22	9.13	9.67	7.06	4.84	4.01	4.44	4.65	5.41
1982[2]	4.71	4.78	5.03	5.53	6.26	8.01	7.93	7.00	4.62	3.97	3.82	3.67	4.59
1983[2]	3.61	3.68	3.88	4.82									
1984													

[1] Annual weighted average by sales.   [2] Preliminary.   Source: *Statistical Reporting Service, U.S.D.A.*
T.530

Month End Open Interest of Potato Futures at New York   In Contracts

Year	Jan.	Feb.	Mar.	Apr.	May	June	July	Aug.	Sept.	Oct.	Nov.	Dec.
1978	20,254	13,758	15,412	5,389	8,493	9,413	10,390	11,529	12,644	12,977	11,759	11,617
1979	12,083	13,789	863	1,030	1,655	2,336	3,786	4,516	4,323	4,898	5,307	3,993
1980	4,093	4,078	3,033	1,214	3,009	7,152	12,165	15,352	18,807	17,487	16,624	11,325
1981	11,722	7,489	1,106	2,214	2,956	4,142	4,969	5,460	4,971	3,707	3,674	3,243
1982	4,129	3,353	320	1,240	1,974	2,515	2,978	3,408	3,369	2,903	3,039	3,008
1983	3,494	2,809	689	605								

Source: *N.Y. Mercantile Exchange*
T.532

Rapeseed

In early 1983, the Foreign Agricultural Service (FAS) of the USDA projected 1982/83 world production of rapeseed at 14.8 million tonnes, nearly 23 percent above the previous season's record output. Reports from key producing regions in China, the largest producer of rapeseed, raised estimates of Chinese production by 0.5 million tonnes. India's production estimates were raised by 0.4 million tonnes because of prospects that yields would improve following beneficial rains in late December and early January. This put the Indian crop at 2.7 million tonnes vs. its 1982 record of 2.6 million tonnes. Earlier USDA projections estimated the 1982/83 Canadian crop at 2.2 million tonnes, below historic levels but 23 percent above the previous season.

Within the European Community (EC), subsidy programs of intervention and target prices have so successfully increased production that the EC announced late in 1982 that, for every 50,000 tonnes of rapeseed produced over 2,150,000 tonnes in the 1982/83 season, the intervention (floor) price for 1983/84 will be reduced 1 percent up to a maximum of 5 percent. France in particular has become a net exporter of rapeseed because of these programs. Rapeseed production in the EC during 1982/83 was estimated at 2.3 million tonnes versus 2.0 million the previous season.

World rapeseed oil and meal production during 1982/83 was projected as rising about 3 percent each, to 4.7 and 7.5 million tonnes respectively. In 1982 India and Nigeria were the world's largest importers of rapeseed oil and West Germany and Denmark were the largest rapeseed meal importers. Soviet rapeseed acreage in 1982 was estimated early in 1983 to be 78,000 hectares vs. only 10,000 hectares in the late 1970s. The Soviets are increasingly using rapeseed oil for human consumption and rapeseed meal for high-protein livestock feed.

Futures Market

Rapeseed futures are traded on the Winnipeg Commodity Exchange.

World Production of Rapeseed (In Thousands of Metric Tons)

Year[2]	Canada	China	Czecho-slovakia	Den-mark	France	E. Germany	W. Germany	India	Japan	Bangla-desh	Pakistan	Poland	Sweden	Chile	World Total
1972	2,155	1,000	107.0	51	722.0	234.0	248.7	1,433	15.9	106.0	301.0	430.0	327.0	77.9	6,624
1973	1,300	1,050	117.0	92	661.0	246.0	242	1,808	13.0	98	287.0	512.0	339	35.0	7,001
1974	1,207	1,075	85	112	690	280	301	1,692	9	107	293	523	351	33	7,022
1975	1,163	1,090	115	115	532	250	194	2,300	7	110	305	726	327	55	7,989
1976	1,749			90	561							980	279		
1977	1,940	1,380		110	440			1,650			240	650	256		7,871
1978	3,497	1,868	166	91	568	301	322	1,860	5	137	243	691	330	65	10,708
1979[1]	3,414	2,402	81	148	510	195	362	1,433	5	140	300	233	297	73	10,075
1980[1]	2,483	2,384	199	290	1,091	256	380	2,247	5	140	300	566	373	75	11,380
1981[3]	1,837	4,065	150	334	990	284	360	2,363	4	130	250	496	282	12	12,305
1982[3]	2,114	5,200			1,182	285	500	2,500	4	130	275	431	305	12	14,530

[1] Preliminary. [2] Harvest generally occurs in the first half of the calendar year given in all major producing countries except Canada. [3] Estimate. Source: *Foreign Agricultural Service, U.S.D.A.*
T.533

Wholesale Price of Rapeseed Oil, Refined (Denatured), in Tanks at N.Y. In Cents Per Pound

Year	Jan.	Feb.	Mar.	Apr.	May	June	July	Aug.	Sept.	Oct.	Nov.	Dec.	Average
1972	17.5	17.5	17.5	17.5	17.5	17.5	17.5	17.5	17.5	17.5	17.5	17.5	17.5
1973	17.5	17.5	17.5	17.5	17.5	17.5	17.5	17.5	17.5	17.5	17.5	17.5	17.5
1974	17.5	18.4	21.0	21.0	30.6	45.0	45.0	59.0	46.2	47.5	45.8	59.0	36.8
1975	59.0	59.0	59.0	59.0	59.0	59.0	59.0	59.0	59.0	51.2	46.0	46.0	56.2
1976	46.0	46.0	46.0	46.0	46.0	46.0	46.0	44.2	39.0	39.0	39.0	39.0	43.5
1977	39.0	39.0	39.0	39.0	39.0	39.0	39.0	39.0	39.0	39.0	39.0	39.0	39.0
1978	39.0	39.0	39.0	39.0	39.0	39.0	39.0	39.0	39.0	39.0	39.0	39.0	39.0
1979	39.0	39.0	39.0	39.0	39.0	39.0	39.0	39.0	39.0	39.0	39.0	39.0	39.0
1980	47.0	47.0	47.0	47.0	47.0	47.0	47.0	46.0	46.0	46.0	46.0	46.0	46.6
1981	56.4	59.0	59.0	59.0	59.0	59.0	59.0	59.0	59.0	59.0	59.0	59.0	58.8
1982	57.0	55.0	56.8	57.5	56.0	56.0	56.0	56.0	55.7	55.3	55.3	55.3	56.0

Source: *Economic Research Service, U.S.D.A.*
T.534

Month-End Open Interest of Rapeseed Futures in Winnipeg In 20 Tonne Units

Year	Jan.	Feb.	Mar.	Apr.	May	June	July	Aug.	Sept.	Oct.	Nov.	Dec.
1978	9,288	11,435	11,869	11,908	14,442	14,300	17,778	20,456	17,960	18,672	16,707	15,299
1979	15,288	15,164	16,338	15,593	12,993	14,209	12,950	13,596	15,001	21,300	21,827	21,966
1980	15,718	17,516	13,392	14,285	17,722	17,254	17,126	17,108	18,827	22,036	21,911	20,504
1981	15,376	15,326	18,028	18,764	18,000	15,332	14,948	15,316	15,755	16,064	16,260	12,911
1982	13,532	14,970	9,952	12,230	15,997	11,554	12,623	16,948	13,904	15,503	17,992	20,555
1983	16,288	17,964	18,266	16,681								

Source: *Winnipeg Commodity Exchange*
T.535

RAPESEED

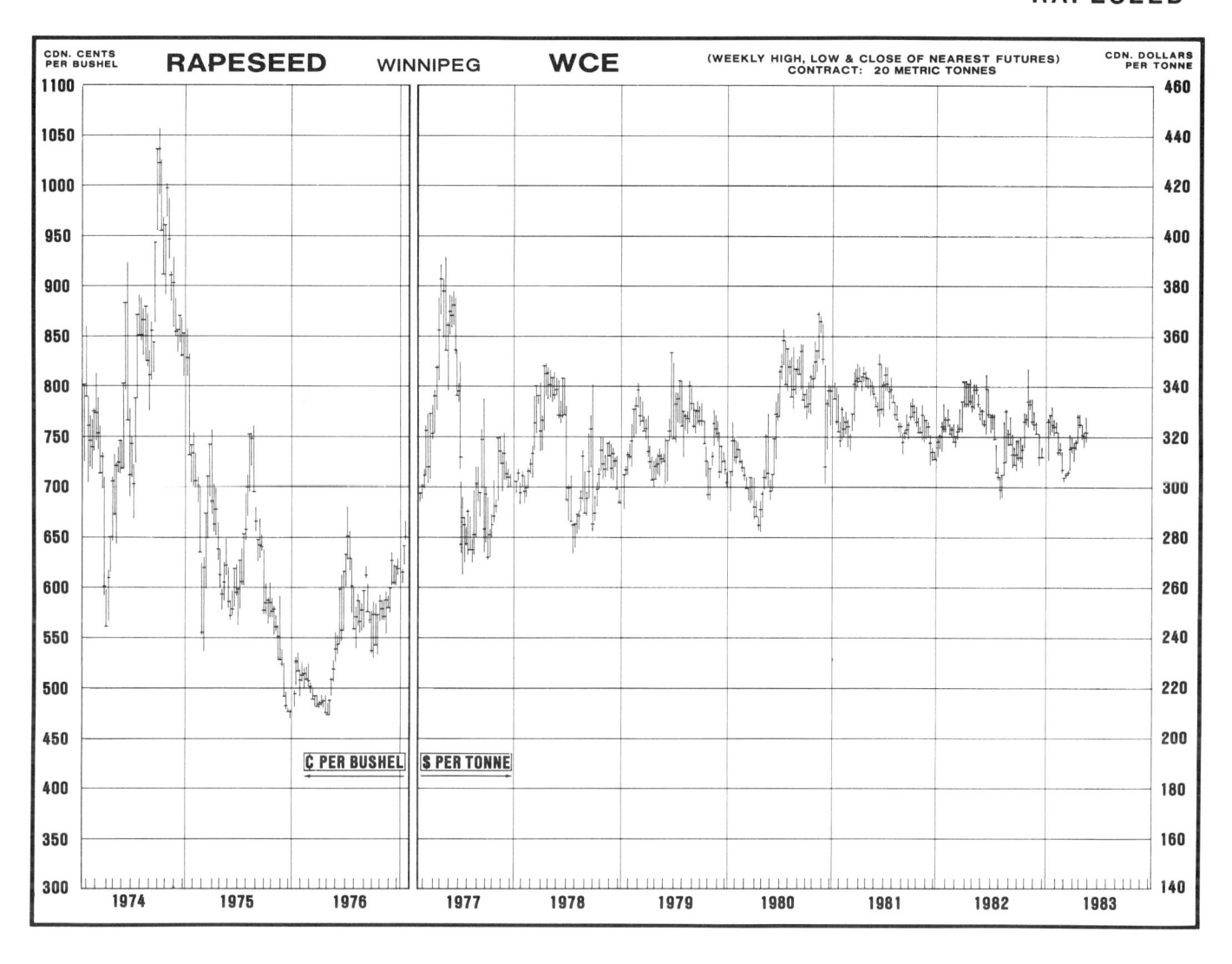

RAPESEED WINNIPEG WCE (WEEKLY HIGH, LOW & CLOSE OF NEAREST FUTURES) CONTRACT: 20 METRIC TONNES

CDN. CENTS PER BUSHEL / CDN. DOLLARS PER TONNE

High, Low & Closing Prices of June Rapeseed Futures in Winnipeg In Dollars per Tonne

Year of Delivery		Apr.	May	June	July	Aug.	Sept.	Oct.	Nov.	Dec.	Jan.	Feb	Mar	Apr	May	June	Life of Delivery Range
1978	High	—	—	—	—	259.0	268.0	272.0	297.0	302.0	294.5	306.1	338.3	351.5	348.0	345.0	351.5
	Low	—	—	—	—	253.0	243.2	244.6	270.2	285.0	279.0	287.0	303.0	316.0	334.8	313.0	243.2
	Close	—	—	—	—	253.0	257.3	272.0	288.5	288.5	287.0	301.3	323.9	346.7	340.6	313.0	—
1979	High	—	286.0	284.0	268.0	284.0	288.0	312.8	304.0	307.5	315.5	340.2	337.7	318.4	316.5	354.5	354.5
	Low	—	278.5	263.7	255.8	258.0	269.0	282.1	289.5	296.0	294.0	314.4	314.0	301.8	306.0	302.5	255.8
	Close	—	286.0	265.2	263.0	270.1	280.0	302.3	300.0	297.0	314.5	336.0	316.3	307.3	307.5	329.5	—
1980	High	301.0	315.9	354.5	351.0	340.0	339.0	340.5	339.0	331.8	342.0	330.5	319.9	295.1	331.2	326.2	354.5
	Low	295.0	299.0	315.9	319.0	321.0	326.7	314.1	320.0	318.5	301.0	318.5	291.0	282.0	287.6	299.5	282.0
	Close	299.0	315.8	329.5	325.5	337.0	335.6	324.0	330.5	319.5	324.5	319.4	291.0	289.5	299.9	317.0	—
1981	High	—	—	—	370.0	383.5	389.0	382.5	375.5	387.5	375.9	351.8	350.6	350.5	348.3	338.3	389.0
	Low	—	—	—	367.5	360.0	365.0	359.1	391.0	325.5	334.0	337.9	334.5	340.0	337.4	326.0	325.5
	Close	—	—	—	367.5	372.5	368.5	376.0	387.0	368.0	337.0	345.8	350.0	347.5	339.1	327.2	—
1982	High	—	—	—	396.0	391.0	378.3	371.8	366.5	353.0	344.0	340.8	333.5	342.8	340.8	331.7	396.0
	Low	—	—	—	384.0	375.5	355.0	358.8	341.6	334.6	331.0	328.0	319.8	327.3	329.7	321.0	319.8
	Close	—	—	—	391.0	375.5	360.3	365.4	344.8	335.1	334.5	332.7	327.0	334.1	332.7	330.0	—
1983	High	—	—	—	—	361.0	366.3	345.5	349.1	340.0	335.9	329.0	321.0	329.3			
	Low	—	—	—	—	346.0	332.0	332.6	339.6	322.3	323.1	311.5	311.8	311.0			
	Close	—	—	—	—	354.2	337.0	342.5	340.3	325.6	329.1	311.7	316.0	324.7			

Source: Winnipeg Commodity Exchange

T.536

Rayon and Other Synthetic Fibers

World Production of Rayon &/or Acetate Filament Yarn & Monofilaments In Thousands of Metric Tons[3]

Year	United States	Bel./Netherlands	Brazil	Canada	France	W. Germany	E. Germany	Un. Kingdom	Italy	Japan	India	Poland	Spain	China	USSR	World Total
1970	730.8	110.1	73.4	30.6	113.8	169.5		200.4	186.3	299.6	121.9		44.8		489.6	3,070
1971[3]	341.4	47.7	33.6	15.1	52.8	75.1	34.0	85.2	83.1	120.9	55.2	28.8	22.5	20.0	230.0	1,401
1972	296.2	47.2	36.7	15.2	49.8	70.6	32.0	67.2	67.8	119.0	61.3	29.2	21.8	22.0	245.3	1,342
1973	288.2	47.1	40.8	15.1	49.2	71.1	33.0	72.6	66.4	128.3	56.8	30.1	21.6	26.4	259.3	1,362
1974	241.9	47.9	35.9	14.6	42.1	69.4	34.0	70.1	54.2	115.6	56.9	30.5	22.0	44.5	267.0	1,302
1975	166.1	35.3	30.7	13.1	28.1	48.8	32.9	62.5	41.3	103.2	54.2	28.3	16.4	49.0	281.4	1,136
1976	160.8	39.0	34.2	5.7	24.4	66.3	36.2	70.6	46.7	109.3	60.6	28.7	15.6	55.0	286.1	1,188
1977	160.0	36.2	28.8	11.0	20.8	63.7	36.0	62.6	44.4	107.4	58.9	28.6	15.0	61.0	295.0	1,172
1978	164.6	36.0	24.1	12.3	19.3	59.7	34.0	59.7	39.3	109.8	62.4	28.0	13.8	65.0	300.0	1,167
1979	169.4	36.1	24.4	14.1	18.5	58.1	35.0	59.2	38.4	114.3	60.5	27.2	12.6	68.0	298.0	1,176
1980	161.3	37.4	26.0	14.0	16.4	65.2	36.5	36.7	36.6	119.3	57.7	25.4	12.9	75.0	305.0	1,161
1981[1]	138.6	38.6	21.0	13.5	11.0	65.0	37.2	27.0	35.1	118.7	55.9	19.5	12.6	80.0	298.0	1,103
1982[2]	103.6															
1983																

[1] Preliminary. [2] Estimate. [3] Data prior to 1971 are in MILLIONS OF POUNDS. Source: *Textile Organon* T.537

World Production of Rayon &/or Acetate Staple & Tow In Thousands of Metric Tons[3]

Year	United States	Austria	China	Czechoslovakia	France	W. Germany	E. Germany	Un. Kingdom	Italy	Japan	Poland	Spain	Sweden	India	USSR	World Total
1970	642.4	149.0		104.9	173.9	301.4		354.3	203.0	785.1	116.6	76.3	65.9	139.8	516.5	4,504
1971[3]	289.5	75.3	25.0	48.1	79.0	89.5	121.0	161.5	95.7	354.4	53.5	38.3	31.8	61.0	243.0	2,054
1972	336.2	82.6	27.4	48.9	84.5	73.0	130.0	172.8	99.7	367.9	59.7	45.7	33.3	70.7	262.4	2,217
1973	327.3	86.1	32.9	45.6	86.2	80.0	132.5	191.4	94.2	383.4	65.1	45.8	33.9	63.2	283.8	2,298
1974	301.8	88.6	55.4	50.5	83.7	80.0	132.0	147.1	85.4	328.7	66.6	46.0	32.6	77.6	301.6	2,230
1975	173.7	74.0	61.0	49.6	55.3	43.0	135.6	126.7	46.3	255.6	67.4	35.8	18.5	67.1	309.0	1,824
1976	220.6	88.9	70.0	50.3	60.3	51.0	136.8	118.6	59.8	250.3	66.9	41.0	30.4	83.7	325.8	2,022
1977	242.7	90.2	77.0	50.6	60.7	46.0	131.0	113.6	62.3	272.7	67.1	43.1	33.1	87.1	334.0	2,109
1978	245.7	96.0	80.0	49.5	55.2	49.0	129.2	124.4	46.9	279.4	65.4	46.6	36.9	92.0	335.0	2,151
1979	252.4	98.8	85.0	36.0	58.9	50.0	130.0	139.2	39.0	290.4	56.6	45.3	36.9	92.2	337.0	2,195
1980	204.3	100.6	95.0	34.9	49.6	46.0	132.0	109.3	27.5	278.0	61.0	40.1	34.9	74.7	345.0	2,081
1981[1]	210.7	101.6	105.0	36.0	42.9	50.0	128.0	102.4	24.4	273.5	44.0	37.8	34.7	94.5	345.5	2,089
1982[2]	161.5															
1983																

[1] Preliminary. [2] Estimate. [3] Data prior to 1971 are in MILLIONS OF POUNDS. Source: *Textile Organon* T.538

World[5] Production of Non-Cellulosic Man-Made Fibers (Except Olefin) In Thousands of Metric Tons[8]

Year	United States Text. Glass Fiber[1]	United States Non-Cellulose Fiber[2] Yarn[3]	United States Non-Cellulose Fiber[2] Staple[4]	United States Non-Cellulose Fiber[2] Total	Total[5]	Canada	France	W. Germany	Italy/Malta	Taiwan	Japan	Korea	Benelux	USSR	United Kingdom	World Total
1970	467.3	1,793	1,793	3,586	4,053	142.5	386.2	1,086	472.7		2,139		267.2	367.5	742.5	10,362
1971[8]	212	873.7	929.2	1,803	2,015	74.7	213.9	599.9	277.3	77.0	1,103	61.6	138.3	203.0	357.5	5,609
1972	259	1,101	1,142	2,243	2,501	75.3	237.9	639.6	291.6	102.1	1,054	81.6	149.2	238.6	373.9	6,377
1973	312	1,323	1,318	2,641	2,953	93.6	266.3	808.4	336.7	128.0	1,247	115.7	163.2	286.9	453.9	7,639
1974	310	1,352	1,233	2,585	2,894	92.0	237.7	764.9	296.7	142.8	1,126	151.7	155.3	318.5	396.1	7,487
1975	248	1,255	1,191	2,446	2,693	95.8	204.5	625.3	276.9	234.6	1,021	262.7	122.9	362.0	361.1	7,353
1976	307	1,266	1,480	2,746	3,052	96.6	248.8	759.4	376.6	272.4	1,204	309.3	146.3	400.0	414.2	8,601
1977	357	1,415	1,622	3,037	3,392	112.8	243.9	690.2	330.1	364.4	1,280	349.9	139.3	456.0	358.8	9,149
1978	419	1,467	1,751	3,218	3,637	123.1	246.4	729.4	354.4	464.2	1,376	432.5	142.7	475.0	406.4	10,034
1979	460	1,595	1,889	3,484	3,944	121.6	224.0	759.5	360.2	521.3	1,363	477.3	135.6	476.0	381.1	10,608
1980	393	1,412	1,831	3,243	3,636	122.0	192.0	720.1	354.8	557.8	1,357	536.4	104.3	550.0	287.6	10,492
1981[6]	472	1,730	1,901	3,631	4,103	109.8	201.2	752.2	435.9	587.0	1,329	610.2	105.7	563.5	248.8	10,730
1982	408	1,387	1,543	2,930	3,338											
1983																

[1] Textile glass fiber of all types, including some staple. [2] Acrylic fiber, nylon, polyester, saran, etc. [3] Includes monofilaments as well as some saran staple. [4] Includes tow, but does not include some saran staple. [5] The textile glass fiber data are included in the U.S. total & excluded from the rest of the world data. [6] Preliminary. [7] Estimate. [8] Data prior to 1971 are in MILLIONS OF POUNDS. Source: *Textile Organon* T.539

RAYON AND OTHER SYNTHETIC FIBERS

U.S. Rayon and Acetate Distribution — In Millions of Pounds

	Yarn & Monofilaments Producers' Shipments To Domestic Consumers							Staple & Tow & Fiber Fill Producers' Shipments To Domestic Consumers						
Year	Industrial	Textile	Acetate	Total	Export	Total	Import	Domestic Consump.	Rayon	Acetate	Total	Export	Total	Import	Domestic Consump.
1970	133.4	117.7	444.8	695.9	38.3	734.2	3.7	699.6	599.9	34.3	634.2	7.8	642.0	80.6	714.8
1971	164.5	132.5	432.3	729.3	33.2	762.5	5.2	734.5	643.6	26.2	669.8	3.7	673.5	81.3	751.1
1972	141.1	105.8	385.9	632.8	23.9	656.7	10.8	643.6	690.7	27.7	718.4	2.0	720.4	51.3	769.7
1973	121.8	75.8	392.3	589.9	60.7	650.6	18.1	608.0	709.5	25.0	734.5	14.7	749.2	47.4	781.9
1974	99.4	53.7	320.3	473.4	48.8	522.2	9.2	482.6	569.5	19.7	589.2	36.0	625.2	38.7	627.9
1975	——74.9——		293.7	368.6	32.9	401.5	9.2	377.8	373.4	12.0	385.4	20.2	405.6	37.9	423.3
1976	——65.1——		249.4	314.5	40.3	354.8	25.1	339.6	461.0	11.0	472.0	35.6	507.6	43.2	515.2
1977	——68.1——		259.4	327.5	25.2	352.7	23.5	351.0	444.9	8.0	452.9	62.3	515.2	57.8	510.7
1978	——63.0——		274.6	337.6	28.6	365.2	25.7	363.3	459.2	7.0	466.2	96.5	562.7	41.1	507.3
1979	——55.0——		288.4	343.4	31.8	375.2	13.3	356.7	442.4	7.0	449.4	100.1	549.5	16.5	465.9
1980	——47.5——		269.2	316.7	32.7	349.4	8.3	325.0	390.7	7.0	397.7	61.0	458.7	10.3	408.0
1981	——46.6——		226.3	272.9	34.8	307.7	10.7	283.6	396.9	4.0	400.9	59.8	460.7	16.8	417.7
1982[1]	——30.1——		169.0	199.1	29.8	228.9	8.3	207.4	293.7	1.0	294.7	66.5	361.2	13.4	308.1
1983															

[1] Preliminary. Source: Textile Organon   T.540

U.S. Domestic Shipments of Synthetic Fibers — In Millions of Pounds

	Yarn & Monofilaments Cellulosic Rayon				Non-Cellulosic			Staple & Tow Non-Cellulosic						
Year	Industrial	Textile	Acetate	Total	Nylon	Olefin[2]	Polyester & Other	Total[3]	Rayon	Nylon	Acrylic & Mod-Acrylic	Olefin & Vinyon	Polyester	Total	Textile Glass Fiber
1970	133.4	117.1	444.8	695.9	1,053	187.0	443.0	1,683	599.9	201.2	430.7	57.3	992.9	1,682	404.9
1971	164.5	132.5	432.3	729.3	1,207	246.5	646.9	2,100	643.6	330.1	463.7	58.9	1,111	1,964	466.7
1972	141.1	105.8	385.9	632.8	1,431	312.4	946.8	2,690	690.7	476.6	536.0	63.6	1,287	2,363	569.2
1973	121.8	75.8	392.3	589.9	1,545	395.4	1,334	3,274	709.5	586.8	662.0	69.3	1,530	2,848	676.0
1974	99.4	53.7	320.3	473.4	1,409	426.3	1,307	3,142	569.5	487.8	514.9	59.7	1,388	2,451	630.8
1975	——74.9——		293.7	368.6	1,290	436.1	1,489	3,215	373.4	557.9	467.3	54.7	1,474	2,554	533.5
1976	——65.1——		249.4	314.5	1,279	482.0	1,386	3,147	461.0	665.0	517.3	58.6	1,777	3,019	677.6
1977	——68.1——		259.4	327.5	1,396	539.6	1,526	3,461	444.9	791.7	619.8	81.3	1,880	3,373	791.6
1978	——63.0——		274.6	337.6	1,539	579.7	1,523	3,642	459.2	876.4	571.6	90.0	1,968	3,506	886.7
1979	——55.0——		288.4	343.4	1,631	624.2	1,525	3,798	442.4	913.2	546.6	119.3	2,134	3,714	922.6
1980	——47.5——		269.2	316.7	1,539	611.7	1,363	3,532	390.7	711.2	585.3	115.0	2,071	3,483	874.4
1981	——46.6——		226.3	272.9	1,404	628.3	1,430	3,483	396.9	696.4	494.1	132.0	2,005	3,328	982.0
1982[1]	——30.1——		169.0	199.1	1,170	577.0	1,135	2,894	293.7	674.3	457.9	138.9	1,768	3,039	875.6
1983															

[1] Preliminary. [2] Includes film fiber. [3] Includes Saran & Spandex. Source: Textile Organon   T.541

U.S. Mill Consumption of Fiber & Products & Per Capita Consumption

	Mill Consumption (Million Pounds)											Per Capita Consumption (Pounds)			
Year	Yarn & Monofilaments	Staple & Tow	Total R. & A.[2]	Noncellulosic Fiber	Textile Glass Fiber	Waste	Total Man-made	Cotton	Wool	Silk	Grand Total	Man-made	Cotton	Wool	Total
1970	699.6	714.8	1,415	3,670	404.9	138.4	5,501	3,774	273.3	1.8	9,550	27.7	19.7	1.7	49.1
1971	734.5	751.1	1,486	4,557	466.7	185.0	6,529	3,965	219.3	1.7	10,715	32.9	20.4	1.3	54.6
1972	643.6	769.7	1,414	5,568	569.2	202.1	7,566	3,850	246.9	2.1	11,665	37.5	19.9	1.3	58.7
1973	608.0	781.9	1,390	6,599	676.0	223.3	8,664	3,643	182.1	3.3	12,493	41.7	18.3	1.0	61.0
1974	482.6	627.9	1,111	5,960	630.8	198.6	7,608	3,306	116.5	2.0	11,123	35.9	16.0	.7	52.6
1975	377.8	423.3	801.1	6,081	533.5	204.6	7,417	3,069	132.0	1.0	10,618	34.7	14.9	.7	50.3
1976	339.6	515.2	854.8	6,520	677.6	223.1	8,053	3,389	145.9	2.8	11,590	37.5	16.9	.9	55.3
1977	351.0	510.7	861.7	7,228	791.6	254.6	8,888	3,170	133.9	1.6	12,193	41.1	15.8	.9	57.8
1978	363.3	507.3	870.6	7,461	886.7	210.3	9,228	3,040	141.6	2.0	12,412	42.4	15.8	1.0	59.2
1979	356.7	465.9	822.6	7,692	922.6	130.4	9,446	3,066	134.4	1.5	12,648	41.6	14.8	.9	57.3
1980	325.0	408.0	733.0	7,145	874.4	83.0	8,760	3,064	137.8	1.5	11,962	37.5	14.7	.9	53.1
1981	283.6	417.7	701.3	7,006	982.0	149.8	8,702	2,731	152.7	2.0	11,586	37.8	11.9	.7	50.4
1982[1]	207.4	308.1	515.5	6,131	875.6	132.8	7,530	2,488	129.5	2.0	10,148	32.5	10.7	.5	43.7
1983															

[1] Preliminary. [2] Rayon and acetate. Source: Textile Economics Bureau   T.542

RAYON AND OTHER SYNTHETIC FIBERS

Man-Made Fiber Production in the United States — In Millions of Pounds

Year	Rayon Yarn Indust.	Rayon Yarn Textile	Acet. Yarn	Total Yarn	Staple & Tow Rayon	Staple & Tow Acetate	Staple & Tow Total	Total	Non-Cellulosic Fiber Yarn	Non-Cellulosic Fiber Staple	Non-Cellulosic Fiber Total	Total Ray. & Acet. & Non-Cel.	Textile Glass Fiber	Total Man-made Fiber	Producers' Waste Shipments Rayon	Producers' Waste Shipments Non-Cell.
1972	146.7	105.0	401.4	653.1	713.2	28.0	741.2	1,394.3	2,773.3	2,582.4	5,355.7	6,750.0	571.6	7,321.6	38.5	202.7
1973	121.7	76.4	437.2	635.3	696.7	25.0	721.7	1,357.0	3,339.6	2,969.8	6,309.4	7,666.4	688.0	8,354.4	36.8	274.8
1974	112.9	58.9	361.6	533.4	645.4	20.0	665.4	1,198.8	3,443.0	2,780.6	6,223.6	7,422.4	682.9	8,105.3	29.9	246.4
1975	46.1	18.7	301.3	366.1	370.9	12.0	382.9	749.0	3,208.0	2,676.8	5,885.7	6,634.7	546.5	7,181.2	13.2	228.7
1976	52.3	15.3	286.9	354.5	475.4	12.0	486.4	840.9	3,306.4	3,320.2	6,626.6	7,467.5	676.0	8,143.5	14.7	262.3
1977	55.3	15.4	282.0	352.7	527.0	8.0	535.0	887.7	3,674.1	3,653.8	7,327.9	8,215.6	786.7	9,002.3	18.5	291.0
1978	47.0	15.0	300.9	362.9	534.6	7.0	541.6	904.5	3,830.3	3,952.7	7,783.0	8,687.5	923.3	9,610.8	15.7	263.9
1979	41.7	15.1	316.6	373.4	549.4	7.0	556.4	929.8	4,154.3	4,282.3	8,436.6	9,336.4	1,014.4	10,380.8	17.2	238.6
1980	32.2	15.0	308.5	355.7	443.3	7.0	450.3	806.0	3,744.3	4,148.2	7,892.5	8,698.5	867.3	9,565.8	13.5	170.2
1981	33.4	15.1	257.0	305.5	460.6	4.0	464.6	770.1	3,814.8	4,191.1	8,005.9	8,776.0	1,041.1	9,817.1	15.3	174.2
1982[1]	20.8	12.4	195.2	228.4	355.0	1.0	356.0	584.4	3,057.4	3,402.5	6,459.9	7,044.3	899.2	7,943.5	10.7	173.2
1983																

[1] Preliminary. Source: *Textile Organon* T.543

United States Imports of Man Made Fiber Manufactures — In Millions of Pounds

Year	Jan.	Feb.	Mar.	Apr.	May	June	July	Aug.	Sept.	Oct.	Nov.	Dec.	Total
1973	39.34	37.03	37.20	29.61	33.64	30.97	29.45	23.54	17.91	22.73	20.25	13.37	335.35
1974	26.30	25.10	25.76	27.12	31.12	33.45	38.37	36.53	31.53	35.88	31.03	28.49	371.25
1975	28.77	24.38	28.76	27.85	30.03	35.69	40.32	37.93	37.97	41.04	35.15	33.67	400.38
1976	36.38	29.56	36.71	35.57	38.84	47.48	54.32	46.68	41.67	36.88	40.68	34.55	479.32
1977	34.20	32.55	37.00	36.29	43.86	59.03	54.82	55.44	51.85	46.69	37.57	41.83	531.13
1978	45.54	46.68	46.34	53.87	49.74	67.70	70.41	64.90	58.31	50.47	41.08	37.54	642.59
1979	47.07	36.31	39.06	38.47	45.19	53.03	52.25	50.84	44.58	42.35	40.18	35.64	524.97
1980	36.39	39.90	39.62	37.37	46.72	55.92	57.69	50.18	52.11	49.19	40.10	35.46	540.64
1981	46.72	38.55	43.81	45.53	57.83	58.01	66.66	69.32	56.77	67.24	49.12	39.51	639.08
1982	53.18	48.07	47.74	40.14	67.85	91.93	77.34	100.05	82.75	70.14	68.76	59.16	807.10
1983													

Source: *Department of Commerce* T.544

United States Exports of Man Made Fiber Manufactures — In Millions of Pounds

Year	Jan.	Feb.	Mar.	Apr.	May	June	July	Aug.	Sept.	Oct.	Nov.	Dec.	Total
1973	37.95	41.86	43.28	48.23	48.11	46.50	45.33	38.30	56.64	54.96	52.24	55.66	569.27
1974	31.00	33.70	38.34	39.82	37.03	37.22	30.46	30.88	30.17	30.66	28.05	23.50	390.73
1975	22.84	20.83	24.50	31.56	27.85	25.73	24.67	27.07	29.20	32.31	28.62	28.55	323.73
1976	26.13	27.22	32.09	29.11	30.14	29.91	25.99	25.59	31.78	30.76	31.33	32.12	352.17
1977	27.67	30.77	34.18	32.02	31.77	31.55	29.36	27.08	35.02	25.81	27.50	34.35	367.08
1978	27.84	29.24	36.83	35.57	39.06	36.63	32.06	35.38	38.12	43.68	44.41	42.88	441.70
1979	42.86	43.91	53.20	45.03	49.28	52.81	44.92	46.69	50.61	56.16	53.00	58.12	596.58
1980	47.25	59.36	69.55	69.01	64.65	70.85	58.44	63.79	63.29	75.94	64.97	64.27	771.54
1981	53.16	53.50	67.33	64.83	58.05	58.78	47.59	49.70	48.77	50.98	46.95	38.08	637.73
1982	34.90	38.35	39.72	35.96	42.01	44.21	33.93	33.13	35.86	36.87	32.54	31.08	438.55
1983													

Source: *Department of Commerce* T.545

Rice

World rice production in the 1982/83 season was forecast by the USDA at 275 million tonnes, milled basis (408 million tons, rough basis), a decline of 1 percent from the record 1981/82 harvest. Bad weather caused the rice production of Thailand, the world's major exporter, to fall by an estimated 1 million tonnes in 1982/83 to 17.3 million. In an effort to improve its export markets, the Thai government announced that export premiums would be unchanged through June 1983. The effect of the Thai production shortfall on exports was expected to be slight. China, which accounts for three-eighths of the world's production, expected a record 1982/83 harvest, as did Indonesia, Bangladesh, Burma, and Vietnam.

The projected world consumption of a record 280 million tonnes, milled basis, is expected to draw ending stocks down to around 17 million tonnes, the lowest level in the past decade.

Rice producers in the U.S. harvested 3.25 million acres in 1982, approximately 0.5 million less than were harvested in the previous year. Large enrollments in the 1982 15-percent acreage reduction program resulted in nearly 422,000 acres being withdrawn for conservation uses. National average yields in 1982 were 4,742 pounds per acre, vs. the record 4,819 pounds per acre recorded in 1981. Because of lower acreage and yields, U.S. production of long grain rice fell by 14 percent, and medium and short grain varieties were down by 18 and 15 percent, respectively. The total U.S. rice production in 1982 was 154.2 million cwt., down 16 percent from the 1981 level.

In spite of the decreased production, U.S. 1982/83 supplies of rice reached a record 203.7 million cwt.

In March 1983, the USDA reported that rice producers enrolled about 3.41 million acres in the 1983 PIK program, and 427,726 acres in the acreage reduction and paid land diversion program. For each acre enrolled in PIK and devoted to conservation use, farmers were to receive rice equal to 80 percent of their farms' program yields times the number of PIK acres. Complying producers are eligible for a price support based on a loan rate of $8.14 per cwt., and a target price of $11.40, and to receive a cash diversion payment based on a rate of $2.70 per cwt.

U.S. food use of rice in 1982/83 was estimated at 44 million cwt., up nearly 4 percent from 1981. Rice use by U.S. brewers in 1982/83 was estimated at 13.8 million cwt., a 9 percent increase reflecting the growth in the manufacturing of beer from rice. Total domestic disappearance, including food, beer, and seed use was estimated at 61 million cwt., up only 3 percent from 1981/82.

U.S. rice exports in 1982/83 were forecast at 2.2 million tonnes, milled, compared with Thailand's 3.6 million. The U.S. share of the world rice market has been declining since 1980/81. In 1982, sales and shipments to Italy, the main European market for U.S. rice, were down sharply, and sales to Western Europe likewise trailed the 1981 level. U.S. government credits, including a blended credit agreement with Iraq and the Yemen Arab Republic, are expected to maintain U.S. rice exports to the Middle East, and, for the second consecutive year, Iraq and Saudi Arabia are expected to be the leading markets for U.S. rice. Nigeria is expected to maintain its position as the largest African market for U.S. rice despite its foreign exchange problems resulting from declining oil prices.

Futures Markets

Milled and rough rice futures are traded on the New Orleans Commodity Exchange.

World Production of Rough Rice   In Millions of Metric Tons

Crop Year	Brazil	Burma	China	Vietnam[3]	India	Japan	Indonesia	Rep. of Korea	Bangladesh	Philippines	Pakistan	Taiwan	Thailand	United States	World Total
1973-4	6.4	8.6	113.0	6.6	66.1	15.2	21.5	5.8	17.6	5.6	3.7	2.8	14.4	4.2	324.3
1974-5	7.0	8.6	120.0	11.9	59.4	15.4	22.5	6.2	17.1	5.7	3.5	3.3	14.5	5.1	330.0
1975-6	8.5	9.2	119.0	10.9	74.3	16.5	22.6	6.5	18.8	5.8	3.9	3.4	15.2	5.8	352.3
1976-7	8.0	9.3	125.5	11.5	64.2	14.7	23.3	7.2	17.7	6.5	4.0	3.6	15.8	5.3	348.2
1977-8	7.5	9.3	128.5	11.3	79.1	16.4	23.3	8.3	19.5	6.9	4.4	3.6	15.0	4.5	370.1
1978-9	7.6	10.6	136.9	10.0	80.7	15.7	25.8	8.3	19.3	7.2	4.9	3.2	17.5	6.0	386.5
1979-0	9.6	9.8	143.8	10.7	63.6	14.9	26.3	7.3	19.1	7.3	4.8	3.2	15.8	6.0	377.2
1980-1	8.6	13.3	139.9	10.0	80.5	12.2	29.7	6.2	20.8	7.3	4.7	2.8	17.4	6.6	397.6
1981-2[1]	9.5	13.6	144.0	10.5	80.5	12.8	32.8	7.0	20.5		5.1		18.8	8.3	412.5
1982-3[2]	9.0	14.0	154.0		67.6	12.8	32.8	7.2	21.2		5.1		17.3	7.0	408.1

[1] Preliminary.   [2] Estimate.   [3] Data prior to 1974-5 are for So. Vietnam   Source: Foreign Agricultural Service, U.S.D.A.   T.547

U.S. Rice (Rough) Production by Type and Variety   In Thousand Cwt.

Year	Long Grain	Medium Grain	Short Grain	Total	Year	Long Grain	Medium Grain	Short Grain	Total
1970	36,101	31,270	9,955	83,805	1977	62,206	26,272	10,745	99,223
1971	49,973	29,455	8,497	85,768	1978	84,792	36,454	11,924	133,170
1972	42,760	34,184	8,495	85,439	1979	80,692	40,421	10,834	131,947
1973	43,807	39,347	9,611	92,765	1980	86,851	51,407	7,892	146,150
1974	59,934	41,387	11,065	112,386	1981	110,426	61,497	10,819	182,742
1975	63,593	52,255	12,589	128,437	1982[1]	94,627	50,362	9,227	154,216
1976	70,051	36,792	8,805	115,648	1983				

[1] Preliminary.   Source: Crop Reporting Board, U.S.D.A.   T.548

RICE

Average Wholesale Price of Rice[1] No. 2 (Medium Grain) Southwest Louisiana In Cents Per Pound (In 100 Pound Bags)

Year	Aug.	Sept.	Oct.	Nov.	Dec.	Jan.	Feb.	Mar.	Apr.	May	June	July	Average
1970-1	8.50	8.50	8.60	8.70	8.70	8.60	8.60	8.60	8.60	8.40	8.70	8.70	8.60
1971-2	8.70	8.70	8.70	8.70	8.90	8.90	8.90	8.90	8.90	9.10	9.10	9.10	8.88
1972-3	9.10	10.00	10.50	12.50	12.50	12.90	12.90	12.90	15.30	15.30	15.30	15.30	12.88
1973-4	16.30	18.50	21.30	29.50	30.00	30.00	30.00	30.00	30.00	30.00	25.00	25.00	26.30
1974-5	23.0	20.0	18.5	20.0	20.8	20.5	21.0	20.5	20.5	18.5	19.5	19.5	20.19
1975-6	19.5	16.8	16.8	17.0	17.8	15.5	15.5	13.5	13.0	15.5	15.5	15.5	16.0
1976-7	13.5	12.5	13.0	12.3	12.3	11.3	11.8	12.1	13.3	15.6	15.5	15.3	13.2
1977-8	14.5	15.0	15.4	20.5	21.5	21.5	—	21.5	20.5	19.0	—	18.5	18.8
1978-9	17.5	14.5	14.5	14.5	14.8	14.0	14.0	14.0	16.5	16.5	16.5	16.5	15.3
1979-0	19.0	20.0	20.5	20.5	19.5	20.0	22.0	23.5	24.0	24.0	22.0	21.0	21.3
1980-1	20.5	20.5	21.0	24.5	26.5	27.0	27.0	27.5	27.5	28.0	28.0	28.0	25.5
1981-2	26.5	25.0	22.5	21.3	19.5	18.5	17.5	16.0	15.8	16.5	16.3	16.0	19.3
1982-3	16.5	16.5	16.5	15.5	18.0	17.0	16.5						
1983-4													

[1] Prior to May 1972 price is for MILLED NATO at New Orleans.   *Source: Bureau of Labor Statistics* (0213–0101)   T.549

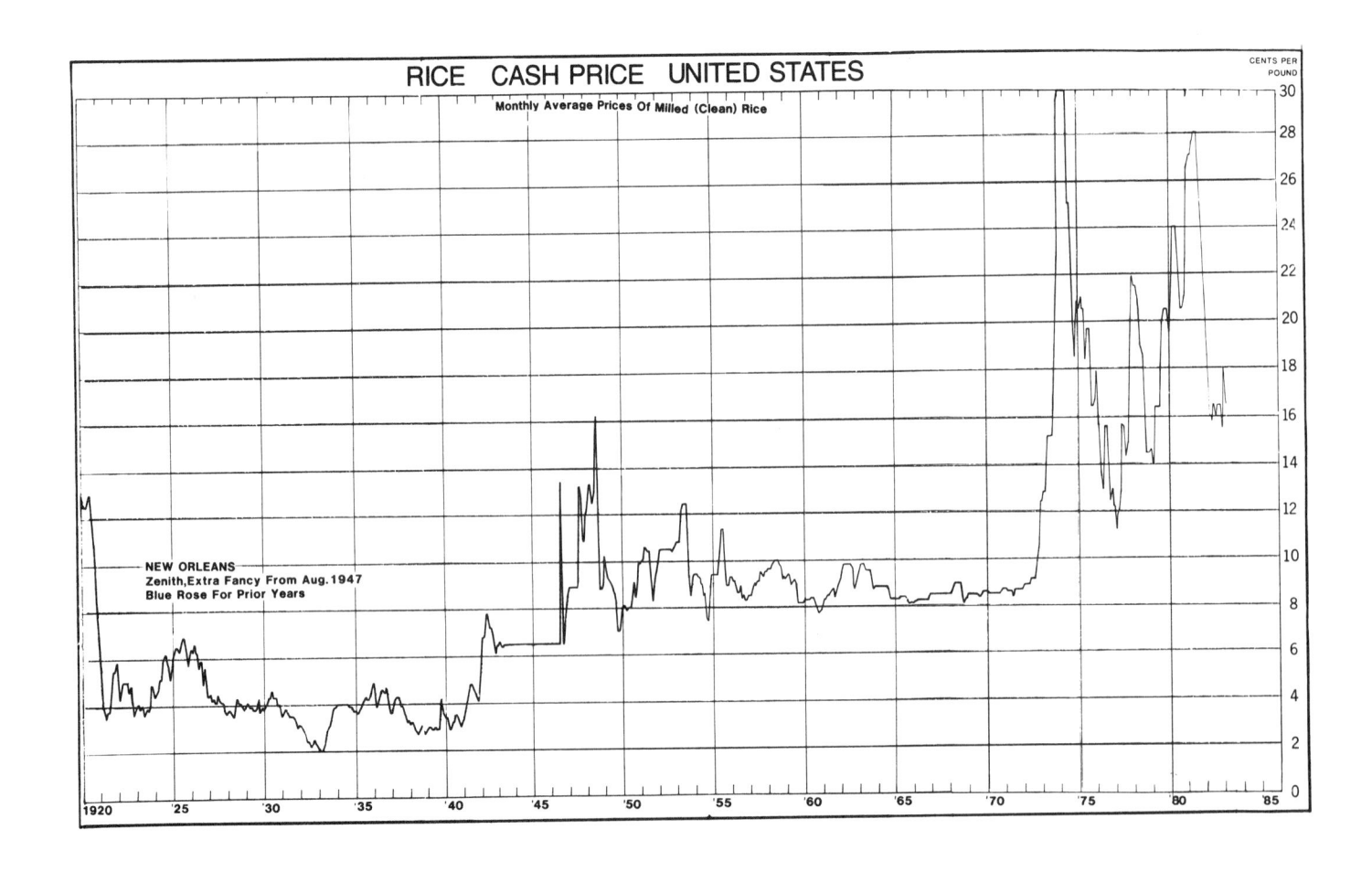

RICE

Acreage, Yield, Production, and Prices of Rice in the United States

Crop Year	Acreage Harvested (1,000 Acres) Southern States	Acreage Harvested California	Acreage Harvested United States	Yield Per Harvested Acre (In Lbs.) Southern States	Yield California	Yield United States	Production 1,000 Cwt. Southern States	Production California	Production United States	Farm Value of Production $1,000	Farm Price of Rough Rice $ Per Cwt.	Wholesale Prices ($ Per Cwt.) Milled No. 2[2]	Wholesale Prices Houston[3]
1970-1	1,484	331	1,815	4,373	5,700	4,618	64,938	18,867	83,805	433,186	5.17	8.90	10.05
1971-2	1,487	331	1,818	4,513	5,200	4,718	68,556	17,212	85,768	457,697	5.34	9.15	10.20
1972-3	1,487	331	1,818	4,415	5,700	4,700	66,571	18,868	85,439	574,907	6.73	13.55	14.45
1973-4	1,769	401	2,170	3,970	5,616	4,274	70,244	22,521	92,765	1,279,990	13.80	27.40	31.75
1974-5	2,054	477	2,531	4,252	5,290	4,440	87,165	25,221	112,386	1,261,359	11.20	19.90	22.05
1975-6	2,277	525	2,818	4,284	5,800	4,558	97,536	30,436	128,437	1,071,924	8.35	17.35	18.35
1976-7	2,081	399	2,480	4,490	5,520	4,663	93,445	22,203	115,648	811,358	7.02	14.10	14.95
1977-8	1,941	308	2,249	4,189	5,810	4,412	81,310	17,913	99,223	941,248	9.49	20.75	21.70
1978-9	2,480	490	2,970	4,358	5,220	4,484	107,592	25,578	133,170	1,087,000	8.16	16.20	18.30
1979-0	2,347	522	2,869		6,520	4,599	97,905	34,042	131,947	1,383,993	10.50	21.40	22.05
1980-1	2,747	565	3,312		6,440	4,413	109,764	36,386	146,150	1,873,007	12.80	25.55	25.55
1981-2[1]	3,199	593	3,792		6,900	4,819	141,818	40,924	182,742	1,654,413	9.05	19.30	21.15
1982-3[1]	2,717	535	3,252		6,850	4,742	117,565	36,651	154,216	1,213,679	7.87		
1983-4													

[1] Preliminary. [2] F.O.B. mills, Houston, Texas (medium grain). From 1979-80 prices are at southwest Louisiana. [3] Houston, Texas (long grain). Source: Economic Research Service, U.S.D.A.
T.550

Salient Statistics of Rice, Rough & Milled (Rough Equivalent) in the United States In Thousands of Cwt.

Year Beginning August	Supply Stocks Aug. 1	Production	Imports[2]	Total Supply	Distribution Domestic Food[3]	Industry[4]	Seed	Total	Exports	Owned By CCC Aug. 1	Under Price Support Loans	Purchase Agree.	Total	Deliveries to CCC	Support Rate $ Cwt.
1970-1	16,446	83,805	1,446	101,646	25,100	6,800	2,531	34,400	46,500	6,407	20,787	733	21,520	3,528	4.86
1971-2	18,634	85,768	1,100	105,500	25,500	7,400	2,500	35,400	56,900	9,329	31,235	107	31,342	1,214	5.07
1972-3	11,434	85,439	500	97,400	25,100	7,700	3,032	35,700	54,000	2,720	22,926	—	22,926	1	5.27
1973-4	5,139	92,765	200	98,100	26,100	8,100	3,609	37,800	49,700	148	19,146	—	19,146	—	6.07
1974-5	7,842	112,386	—	120,300	28,600	8,400	4,000	41,000	69,500	—	9,256	—	9,256	—	7.54
1975-6	7,057	128,437	—	135,500	27,700	9,100	3,500	40,300	56,500	—	21,459	1,781	23,240	19,187	8.52
1976-7	36,877	115,648	100	152,600	29,200	10,300	3,200	42,700	65,600	19,187	23,415	608	24,023	608	6.19
1977-8	40,501	99,223	100	139,800	23,500	9,900	4,300	37,700	72,800	18,307	19,541	—	19,541	—	6.19
1978-9	27,398	133,170	100	160,700	33,700	11,200	4,300	49,200	75,700	19,266	27,114	—	27,114	—	6.40
1979-0	31,618	131,947	100	163,600	33,200	11,200	4,800	49,200	82,600	9,858	25,897	—	25,897	—	6.79
1980-1	25,679	146,150	—	172,100	38,400	11,000	5,100	54,500	91,400	1,891	24,992	—	24,992	—	7.12
1981-2[1]	16,493	182,742	—	199,500	42,300	12,700	4,400	59,400	82,100	—	42,844	—	42,844	17,600	8.01
1982-3[5]	49,000	154,216	—	203,700	44,000	13,800	3,200	61,000	67,500	17,600	63,100	—	63,100	9,267	8.14
1983-4[5]	65,200														
1984-5															

[1] Preliminary. [2] Consists mostly of broken rice. [3] Includes shipments to territories and military food use. [4] Primarily for beer-production. [5] Projected. Source: Agricultural Marketing Service, U.S.D.A.
T.551

World Exports of Rice (Milled Basis), by Country of Origin In Thousands of Metric Tons

Year	Australia	Brazil	Guyana	Burma	China	Egypt (U.A.R.)	Uruguay	Pakistan	Europe	Japan	Nepal	Taiwan	Thailand	United States	World Total
1970	111	95	60	719	885	654		130				5	1,062	1,740	7,558
1971	186	129	66	800	622	515		197				34	1,576	1,415	7,695
1972	154	102	54	244	1,976	298	62	789				16	849	1,733	7,547
1973	158	33	49	133	2,096	298	65	771				49	849	1,630	7,439
1974	145	57	52	206	1,982	136	73	478				5	1,046	1,702	7,908
1975	185	3	83	288	1,440	104	91	498				—	933	2,070	7,162
1976	218	76	72	636	1,446	191	115	945			15	0	1,870	2,045	9,055
1977	260	408	67	686	1,023	223	120	757		50	105	150	2,915	2,270	10,442
1978	337	177	106	375	1,373	150	100	703		75	85	238	1,573	2,264	9,413
1979	400	—	86	590	1,053	95	115	1,366	744	564	100	409	2,696	2,267	11,590
1980	321		81	675	1,116	178	165	968	804	653	10	261	2,700	2,977	12,607
1981[1]	335		78	674	583	134	220	1,127	785	795	43	92	3,049	3,008	12,851
1982[2]	600		40	725	500	25	217	794	601	318	50	307	3,623	2,487	11,697
1983															

[1] Preliminary. [2] Estimate. Source: Foreign Agricultural Service, U.S.D.A.
T.552

RICE

U.S. Exports of Milled Rice[1] by Country of Destination In Thousands of Metric Tons[3]

Crop Year	Belg.-Lux.	South Africa	Canada	Un. Kingd.	Rep. of Korea	Nigeria	Indonesia	Italy	Bangladesh	Liberia	Saudi Arabia	Switzerland	Iraq	Iran	Total All Exports
1970-1	1970-	1,790	1,163	1970-	9,166	1970-	6,231	—		895	1,098				33,577
1971-2[3]	74	82	62	74	495	74	354	—	75	37	82	13	—	19	1,807
1972-3	Avg.	83	65	Avg.	471	Avg.	173	—	4	29	57	12	—	34	1,788
1973-4	(14.1)	86	81	(40)	121	(2)	60	—	—	28	94	14	9	42	1,608
1974-5		64	60	30	530	3	42	—	250	23	79	12	110	462	2,231
1975-6		82	71	30	129	12	—	46	245	24	117	14	81	174	1,538
1976-7		96	74	32	75	131	409	36	21	51	72	47	37	457	2,105
1977-8	19.2	71.4	73.9	12.3	—	172.0	467.3	163.2	83.6	41.3	169.7	29.4	89.9	343.7	2,270
1978-9	41.8	103.7	77.2	48.7	38.5	183.6	270.4	136.4	3.0	40.6	234.5	51.1	148.2	348.1	2,431
1979-0	85.0	105.5	77.6	30.1	574.7	137.9	225.1	42.5	—	61.9	169.5	63.3	309.6	31.1	2,706
1980-1[2]	101.6	112.4	93.3	19.3	1,057.4	283.2	138.8	11.5	—	85.1	257.0	69.5	71.4	—	3,036
1981-2[2]					234.6	152.4					189.7		198.3	85.3	3,310
1982-3															

[1] No adjustment of brown & parboiled rice has been made; treated as milled rice. [2] Preliminary. [3] Data prior to 1971-72 are in THOUSANDS OF CWT. Source: Bureau of the Census, Dept. of Commerce   T.553

Exports of Rice From the United States In Millions of Pounds[1] (Clean Basis)

Year	Aug.	Sept.	Oct.	Nov.	Dec.	Jan.	Feb.	Mar.	Apr.	May	June	July	Total
1970-1	231.4	189.0	438.1	446.8	220.5	284.0	198.7	259.5	314.6	268.5	365.4	144.3	3,361
1971-2	189.7	439.9	394.7	160.5	232.4	275.6	532.8	219.4	242.4	338.1	532.5	540.6	4,099
1972-3	360.4	241.7	313.3	443.6	407.0	339.8	300.1	478.4	423.5	271.4	159.1	204.3	3,943
1973-4	131.9	215.5	252.8	401.5	405.3	368.5	264.8	286.7	403.7	233.3	311.8	305.5	3,581
1974-5	174.4	329.0	349.8	331.9	442.0	544.9	564.4	556.2	463.9	437.0	555.4	247.7	4,996
1975-6	225.6	164.0	305.8	249.3	396.6	340.1	275.4	298.7	264.4	383.7	348.5	724.9	3,977
1976-7	396.5	319.6	308.2	405.8	574.0	233.2	312.9	487.3	262.7	529.2	380.5	497.8	4,709
1977-8	494.3	511.4	187.6	633.8	464.1	204.2	427.2	293.6	338.7	364.5	693.6	346.5	4,960
1978-9	324.8	545.1	467.0	371.0	595.8	361	416	484	498	531	334	434	5,362
1979-0	310	316	426	320	546	584	557	584	518	585	540	644	5,930
1980-1	419	577	409	474	730	533	613	809	688	794	497	371	6,914
1981-2	453	470	532	583	458	479	515	399	487	661	538	370	5,945
1982-3	809	320	431	199	307	241							
1983-4													

[1] 162 pounds rough—100 pounds clean. Source: Department of Commerce   T.554

Avg. Price Received by Farmers for Rice[1] in the U.S. In Dollars Per 100 Pounds (Cwt.)

Year	Aug.	Sept.	Oct.	Nov.	Dec.	Jan.	Feb.	Mar.	Apr.	May	June	July	Average[2]
1970-1	5.16	5.18	5.26	5.19	5.09	5.31	5.44	5.36	5.33	5.30	5.20	5.33	5.17
1971-2	5.15	5.24	5.46	5.25	5.30	5.53	5.55	5.60	5.58	5.57	5.58	5.35	5.34
1972-3	5.34	6.37	7.05	7.42	7.64	7.84	8.14	8.26	8.51	8.56	8.74	10.80	6.73
1973-4	10.90	13.30	14.80	16.70	15.50	15.80	16.90	17.20	15.90	17.20	17.50	11.90	13.80
1974-5	10.20	10.90	11.30	11.60	10.90	10.80	11.30	11.10	11.00	11.10	11.20	10.00	11.20
1975-6	9.83	9.19	8.87	8.59	8.51	7.95	7.54	6.17	7.15	7.06	6.82	7.45	8.35
1976-7	6.65	6.56	6.48	6.46	6.57	6.79	6.87	6.81	6.95	7.30	7.24	6.87	7.02
1977-8	8.02	8.12	9.13	10.20	11.00	10.70	10.70	10.70	10.80	10.10	9.58	9.49	9.49
1978-9	8.44	7.56	7.62	7.76	7.98	8.07	7.87	8.18	8.52	8.74	8.73	9.10	8.16
1979-0	10.00	9.81	10.30	9.83	8.41	9.88	11.00	11.70	11.60	11.30	10.20	10.80	10.50
1980-1	10.60	10.20	10.90	11.60	13.10	13.20	13.00	13.40	13.80	13.30	11.90	12.80	12.80
1981-2	11.80	10.70	10.20	9.86	9.34	9.34	9.46	9.46	8.54	8.55	8.54	8.25	9.05
1982-3[3]	7.19	7.60	7.63	7.78	8.06	8.05	8.26	7.99	7.80				
1983-4													

[1] Rough rice. [2] Weighted average by sales. [3] Preliminary. Source: Crop Reporting Board, U.S.D.A.   T.555

Rubber

World natural rubber production in 1982, based on International Rubber Study Group data available in late April 1983, was less than one percent below estimated 1981 production. World synthetic rubber output was projected to be about 9 percent below 1981 production. Incomplete data indicated about a 2 percent reduction in 1982 world consumption of natural rubber and an 8 percent decline in the consumption of synthetic rubber.

Natural rubber production in Peninsular Malaysia, the world's top producer, was about unchanged from 1981 output, according to that country's Statistical Department. However, exports fell to 1.34 million tonnes from 1.43 million in 1981. Stocks of rubber at the end of 1982 were reported at 258,798 tonnes versus 281,267 tonnes a year earlier.

Production of synthetic rubber in the U.S., the world's major producer, totaled 1.805 million tonnes in 1982, down sharply from 1981 production of 2.234 million tonnes. U.S. synthetic rubber consumption was off 13 percent from 1981, and year-end 1982 stocks were placed at 267,421 tonnes versus 349,087 tonnes at the end of 1981. Synthetic rubber accounted for 74 percent of total new rubber consumed in the U.S. in 1982, vs. 76 percent in 1981.

By mid-April 1983, the International Natural Rubber Organization (INRO) had made four calls for contributions (totaling 689 million Malaysian dollars) to its buffer stock operation from the 34 members of the International Natural Rubber Agreement. Buffer stock purchases were initiated by INRO in November 1981, and by early 1983 nearly 270,000 tonnes of rubber had been bought in an effort to bolster sagging prices.

The INRO 5-day moving average price (calculated on the average of prices for the previous 5 days in the four main markets, Kuala Lumpur, Singapore, London and New York) reached a record low of 168.05 Malaysian cents per kilo on January 10, 1983—the lowest level since the INRA came into provisional effect in October 1980. The level at which the INRO buffer stock manager *must buy* remained at 166 Malaysia/Singapore cents per kilo in early 1983. The *may buy* intervention price remained at 177 cents, the *may sell* price continued at 239 cents, and the upper trigger action price at which the buffer stock manager *must sell* remained at 249 cents per kilo.

A combination of buffer stock purchases, the withholding from the market of about 200,000 tonnes by Malaysia and Indonesia in the October 1982–March 1983 period, the occurrence of the "wintering" period which is associated with a seasonal decline in production, and purchases by China, the USSR, and the U.S.A., helped to lift natural rubber prices to around the "may sell" level by April 1983—the first may sell price since November 1981. The improved natural rubber prices were expected to encourage a request for an upward revision in the INRO price range.

Futures Market

Rubber futures are currently traded on the London Commodity Exchange.

World Rubber Production[1]   In Thousands of Metric Tons

Year	Sri Lanka	India	Indonesia	Malaysia	Philippines	Thailand	Liberia	Brazil	China	World Total	Canada	W. Germany	Japan	United States	United Kingdom	USSR	World Total
1973	154.7	123.2	885.8	1,542	25.9	390.0	85.5	23.4	15.0	3,403	229.8	392.9	967.5	2,607	364.4	1,350	7,760
1974	132.0	128.4	855.0	1,525	37.2	379.5	86.2	18.6	20.0	3,518	208.8	371.8	857.9	2,396	335.8	1,500	7,575
1975	148.8	136.0	822.5	1,459	52.3	355.0	82.8	19.3	25.0	3,368	173.3	315.9	788.7	1,990	260.8	1,600	6,850
1976	152.1	147.8	847.5	1,612	58.5	411.9	82.4	20.3	35.0	3,505	209.9	372.6	941.3	2,425	320.4	1,700	8,025
1977	146.2	151.6	835.0	1,588	56.3	430.9	70.0	22.6	50.0	3,715	237.9	414.3	971.0	2,660	329.2	1,800	8,615
1978	155.7	133.0	902.5	1,582	56.6	467.0	72.5	23.7	75.0	3,725	248.3	407.0	1,029	2,662	293.7	1,950	8,910
1979	152.7	147.2	905.0	1,570	63.3	531.2	75.0	25.0	97.5	3,870	282.5	418.5	1,107	2,720	277.7	2,025	9,330
1980	133.2	155.4	1,020	1,530	69.0	501.1	77.5	27.8	113.0	3,760	252.8	389.9	1,094	2,215	211.8	2,040	8,645
1981[2]	123.9	150.7	867.5	1,529	65.0	504.0	77.5	30.3	128.0	3,700	263.3	396.8	1,010	2,234	189.8	2,000	8,465
1982[3]	128	166	838	1,531	65	535	58	32	135	3,625	182	384	931	1,805	190	1,970	7,825

[1] Including rubber in the form of latex.   [2] Preliminary.   [3] Estimate.   Source: Rubber Study Group   T.556

World Consumption of Natural and Synthetic Rubber   In Thousands of Metric Tons

Year	Australia	Brazil	Canada	France	W. Germany	Japan	Un. Kingdom	United States	World Total	Canada	France	W. Germany	Japan	Un. Kingdom	United States	World Total
1973	52.1	51.2	60.4	162.3	205.6	335.0	186.5	712.0	3,403	186.2	304.7	442.6	710.0	330.6	2,440	7,575
1974	59.4	57.9	63.3	162.4	193.9	312.0	167.3	738.4	3,518	181.3	308.4	404.2	615.0	279.2	2,210	7,450
1975	49.9	58.7	72.3	156.2	197.1	285.2	170.5	666.0	3,368	179.3	277.7	359.9	584.8	266.3	1,964	7,028
1976	50.0	66.1	84.7	166.8	195.2	302.0	168.3	686.7	3,505	203.9	286.1	438.3	658.0	327.4	2,172	7,915
1977	41.4	71.4	90.4	163.6	176.5	320.0	172.4	801.8	3,715	207.1	294.9	431.2	690.0	321.0	2,645	8,615
1978	41.1	72.5	89.1	163.2	184.9	355.0	139.2	770.8	3,725	203.9	296.2	429.5	741.0	313.4	2,519	8,770
1979	45.4	75.9	93.8	177.0	184.5	390.0	137.5	740.4	3,870	232.0	317.8	447.1	830.0	301.1	2,501	9,125
1980	42.2	81.1	80.0	187.7	179.7	427.0	130.8	585.0	3,760	200.0	341.9	421.3	885.0	248.2	1,980	8,685
1981[1]	41.9	74.4	82.0	167.2	169.1	436.0	120.0	635.0	3,700	210.0	303.4	396.2	851.0	220.0	2,022	8,445
1982[2]	38	69	75	155	160	439	116	617	3,625	180	271	376	784	186	1,750	7,875

[1] Preliminary.   [2] Estimate.   Source: Rubber Study Group   T.557

RUBBER

World Stocks[1] of Natural Rubber, January 1   In Thousands of Metric Tons

		In Producing Countries							In Consuming Countries (Commercial Stocks)								
Year	Brazil	Vietnam	Sri Lanka	Indonesia	Malaysia (Peninsular)	Singapore	Thailand	Total	Australia	Canada	China	France	W. Germany	India	Japan	United Kingdom	United States	Total
1970	8.1	6.8	33.3	75.0	101.1	44.0	22.5	310.0	5.5	4.2		25.7	15.0	34.6	54.2	26.7	108.2	695.0
1971	8.4	5.4	34.6	75.0	152.5	57.3	25.0	380.0	4.9	5.2	112.5	29.6	17.5	41.6	63.4	25.9	104.2	760.0
1972	11.6	1.9	33.1	75.0	163.9	55.1	27.5	385.0	4.4	6.6	72.5	26.5	15.7	47.5	84.3	29.8	135.5	765.0
1973	8.6	2.7	29.0	75.0	195.6	52.1	27.5	415.0	3.5	6.8	60.0	27.7	11.8	56.0	64.3	27.4	118.6	695.0
1974	9.7	2.9	46.5	75.0	188.6	68.6	32.5	450.0	5.3	6.8	122.5	28.9	11.1	54.5	95.1	28.5	106.0	765.0
1975	12.9	11.5	44.7	75.0	201.1	43.4	32.5	435.0	5.7	8.5	115.0	33.4	12.7	47.8	90.8	23.0	117.9	800.0
1976	12.0	6.3	26.0	75.0	230.5	59.2	37.5	475.0	4.0	6.8	155.0	23.8	12.5	54.0	104.6	24.2	116.0	785.0
1977	11.3	4.0	33.9	75.0	239.1	38.7	56.9	495.0	4.7	8.2	125.0	24.1	12.1	60.2	94.8	31.2	138.5	805.0
1978	13.6	4.0	38.8	75.0	214.8	33.7	60.8	470.0	5.0	11.7	137.5	23.0	12.4	57.4	79.3	28.7	143.4	775.0
1979	19.1	4.0	47.4	75.0	245.5	35.8	60.3	505.0	2.7	8.3	137.5	20.1	13.7	42.9	90.7	29.0	142.3	730.0
1980	20.8	4.0	61.3	75.0	240.1	51.1	44.7	515.0	3.8	7.3	135.0	20.3	13.5	54.6	76.5	27.6	144.6	740.0
1981	20.8	4.0	58.5	75.0	250.4	46.3	61.0	530.0	3.2	6.0	150.0	19.6	13.5	40.1	106.9	21.4	126.7	785.0
1982[2]	19.6	4.0	33.7	75.0	281.3	43.8	60.0	530.0	2.7	9.9	140.0	16.8	14.5	45.9	116.9	20.0	142.4	840.0
1983[3]	18	4	13	75.0	247	27	35	555	3	7	158	13	14	57	90	20	123	880
1984																		

[1] Exclusive of "Stock Afloat" and unreported gov't. stockpiles.   [2] Preliminary.   [3] Estimate.   Source: *Rubber Study Group* (London)   T.558

Net Exports of Natural Rubber from Producing Areas   In Thousands of Metric Tons

Year	Burma	Cambodia	Sri Lanka (Ceylon)	Indonesia	Malaysia (Peninsular)	Sabah	Sarawak	Thailand	Vietnam	Zaire	Liberia	Nigeria	Other Africa	Papua New Guinea	World Total
1970	9.6	14.5	154.1	766.2	1,251	31.8	21.7	279.2	23.0	40.0	83.4	59.3	64.3	6.5	2,785
1971	11.9	.5	137.8	757.8	1,308	28.6	19.5	307.3	31.1	40.0	74.2	50.2	67.0	6.0	2,835
1972	10.0	9.3	138.3	733.9	1,285	26.3	19.9	324.4	21.8	40.0	83.3	41.2	66.8	5.9	2,810
1973	10.0	19.2	131.1	841.5	1,514	35.3	41.8	368.2	20.5	40.0	85.5	49.4	72.3	5.9	3,180
1974	10.0	26.4	127.6	794.7	1,467	31.6	32.6	365.2	23.0	26.6	86.2	60.0	59.3	5.6	3,110
1975	10.0	10.0	160.9	788.3	1,363	32.0	29.0	334.7	7.5	25.0	82.8	52.7	56.5	5.5	2,920
1976		21.0	136.9	811.5	1,504	35.8	40.3	373.0	34.0		80.7	32.5	60.0	4.6	3,165
1977		14.0	134.5	800.2	1,530	38.8	37.6	404.0	33.0		69.7	35.4	60.0	4.2	3,210
1978		16.0	138.0	863.2	1,489	36.8	39.6	441.8	35.0		71.8	29.4	57.3	4.1	3,250
1979		9.5	128.2	861.0	1,537	33.2	39.5	517.8	40.0		75.0	26.4	51.5	4.0	3,325
1980		—	120.9	976.1	1,416	30.9	35.2	456.8	35.0		76.5	14.6	60.8	4.0	3,265
1981[1]		1.0	132.5	808.7	1,402	24.5	28.0	476.0	24.0		76.9	23.6	57.8	4.5	3,095
1982[2]		1	122	770	1,320	22	16	525	24		70	20	50	5	3,000
1983															

[1] Preliminary.   [2] Estimate.   Source: *Rubber Study Group* (London)   T.559

U.S. Imports of Natural Rubber (Includes Latex & Guayule)   In Thousands of Long Tons

Year	Jan.	Feb.	Mar.	Apr.	May	June	July	Aug.	Sept.	Oct.	Nov.	Dec.	Total[1]
1970	59.0	44.1	56.8	45.7	42.1	41.6	37.8	33.7	46.6	46.7	46.9	48.9	549.9
1971	45.2	44.7	41.1	42.8	49.8	74.5	47.6	69.6	54.3	44.7	42.1	56.4	612.7
1972	57.9	51.7	64.0	47.6	49.8	36.4	38.7	50.7	39.3	54.7	55.3	56.0	602.2
1973	57.7	48.1	59.4	43.3	55.5	53.4	40.7	66.3	63.7	60.2	56.3	38.3	642.9
1974	53.2	59.1	63.4	50.2	65.3	53.2	73.5	55.0	68.3	35.1	59.8	681.3
1975	68.2	41.3	51.5	52.3	32.7	58.4	52.7	59.7	54.3	57.1	66.2	62.2	656.6
1976	66.1	55.6	72.1	69.4	46.8	65.7	58.4	40.3	67.5	50.0	52.3	68.8	712.9
1977[2]	70.2	55.6	82.3	72.2	50.0	71.2	72.9	49.3	76.3	73.2	37.4	82.0	792.4
1978[2]	46.7	45.7	71.8	83.4	76.0	54.4	47.8	71.0	77.1	54.9	46.1	71.5	746.2
1979[2]	72.8	64.2	72.8	89.9	55.0	82.0	56.2	58.3	58.9	46.1	43.6	47.9	747.7
1980[2]	76.8	56.0	74.0	38.9	55.3	44.5	38.5	31.4	55.9	31.8	50.3	45.1	598.3
1981[2]	30.1	86.6	53.4	67.6	66.4	50.5	41.6	43.4	62.8	69.4	56.23	49.13	662.4
1982[2]	50.99	59.33	45.71	53.86	56.19	63.39	38.67	54.35	40.60	54.36	51.37	49.45	618.3
1983[2]	33.01												

[1] Includes latex and guayule.   [2] Preliminary.   Source: *Department of Commerce*   T.560

288

RUBBER

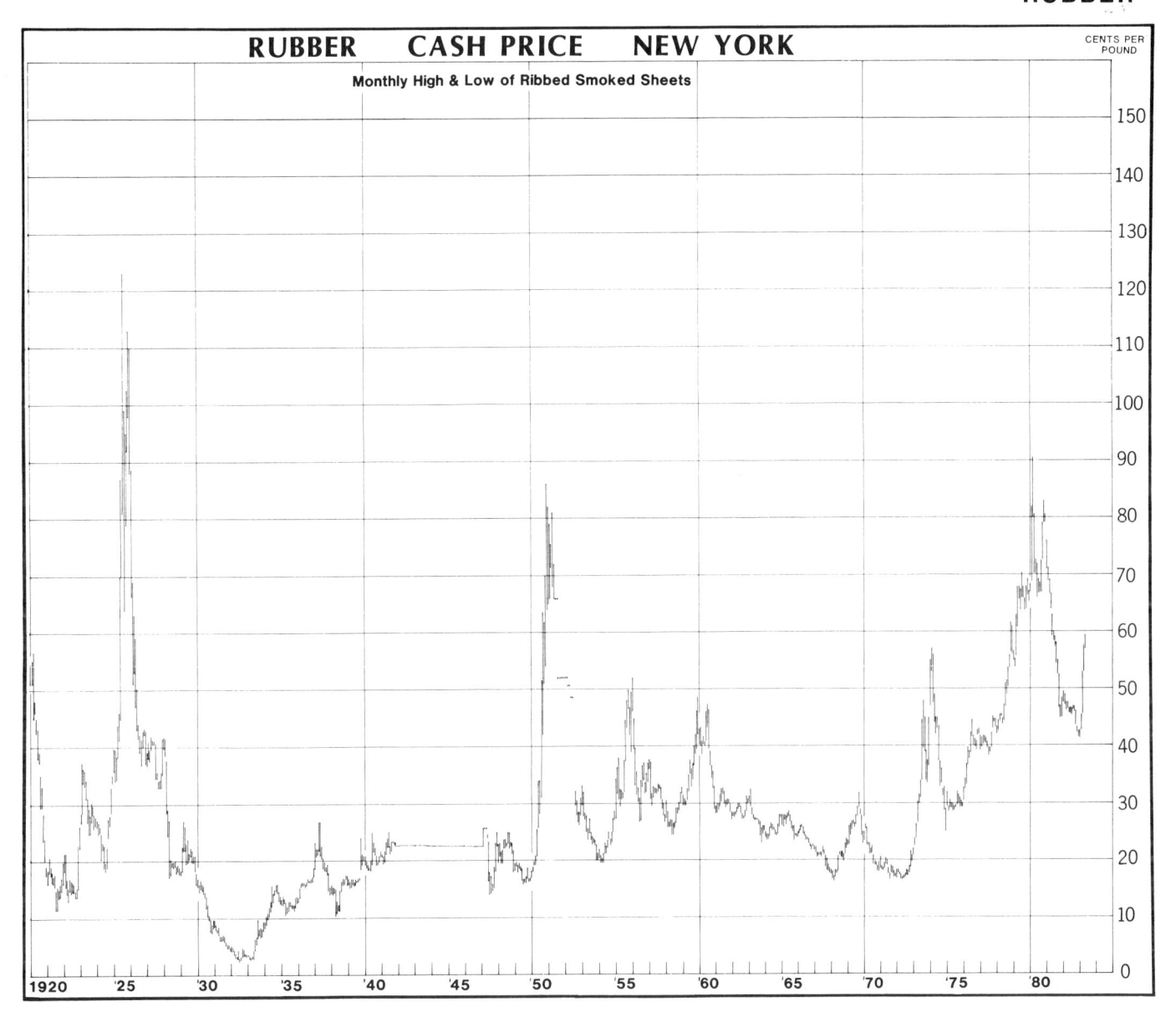

RUBBER CASH PRICE NEW YORK
Monthly High & Low of Ribbed Smoked Sheets
Cents Per Pound

Average Spot Crude Rubber Prices (Smoked Sheets[1]) in New York   In Cents Per Pound

Year	Jan.	Feb.	Mar.	Apr.	May	June	July	Aug.	Sept.	Oct.	Nov.	Dec.	Average
1970	25.5	25.1	22.3	22.1	21.8	21.6	20.0	19.5	19.1	18.3	18.4	19.3	21.8
1971	18.4	18.0	18.3	19.4	20.0	17.8	16.6	18.0	17.9	17.6	17.3	17.1	18.0
1972	18.0	17.8	17.0	16.5	16.9	17.3	17.5	17.5	18.0	19.4	20.5	21.0	18.1
1973	22.8	25.5	28.6	30.8	31.0	36.8	41.3	41.3	36.4	33.6	39.5	54.0	35.1
1974	53.8	53.8	48.8	42.8	43.8	42.0	34.3	34.8	32.0	32.0	27.5	31.5	39.8
1975	29.0	29.5	29.3	29.3	28.5	29.3	31.8	30.3	30.8	30.0	30.0	30.8	29.9
1976	33.0	35.8	37.0	38.8	40.5	44.0	40.1	40.5	39.6	42.0	43.0	40.0	39.5
1977	40.8	40.8	41.6	40.6	40.8	39.6	39.1	39.9	44.8	44.3	43.8	42.9	41.6
1978	43.0	44.6	45.5	43.9	45.0	49.0	49.4	52.0	54.4	54.3	58.1	55.8	49.6
1979	54.4	57.0	61.5	67.4	75.4	68.8	63.8	65.5	64.0	68.5	67.0	67.9	65.1
1980	73.0	86.5	73.3	72.3	69.0	68.5	67.3	68.0	72.8	79.0	—	73.0	73.0
1981	71.3	69.0	65.0	59.0	58.0	57.0	56.0	54.0	50.4	—	45.6	48.3	57.6
1982	48.8	46.5	47.0	45.3	45.3	46.1	46.5	46.8	44.5	42.6	42.1	41.8	45.3
1983	44.0	48.5											

[1] No. 1, ribbed, plantation rubber.   Source: Bureau of Labor Statistics (07–11–02.01)   T.561

RUBBER

Consumption of Natural Rubber in the United States In Thousands of Metric Tons[1]

Year	Jan.	Feb.	Mar.	Apr.	May	June	July	Aug.	Sept.	Oct.	Nov.	Dec.	Total
1970	53.0	51.0	52.9	49.8	37.8	45.8	44.4	45.0	48.3	46.7	41.5	43.2	559.3
1971	46.2	48.3	54.4	49.7	49.7	52.2	43.5	50.9	53.6	54.1	49.8	50.0	577.8
1972	55.3	52.7	59.1	51.9	56.1	53.2	40.9	55.3	54.1	58.5	52.6	52.9	640.6
1973	58.1	56.8	63.2	59.4	57.3	54.5	49.0	56.4	56.3	63.4	57.1	54.0	685.44
1974[1]	65.5	59.4	64.0	59.7	60.8	60.3	51.4	59.9	60.3	69.7	58.2	50.0	719.04
1975	61.2	53.9	52.9	56.3	58.5	58.4	49.4	54.8	61.3	62.0	47.9	53.4	669.97
1976	71.6	59.6	71.7	66.7	44.2	67.5	50.5	42.0	76.2	64.5	56.9	59.4	730.73
1977	70.2	66.8	74.5	68.5	66.8	68.2	50.4	62.8	64.6	63.6	61.3	62.5	780.13
1978	59.2	61.1	63.8	61.2	68.0	61.9	51.7	69.1	65.6	69.5	70.9	62.8	764.65
1979[2]	68.3	66.6	74.5	61.8	60.2	59.0	57.9	63.2	57.7	65.2	55.6	47.9	739.00
1980[2]	62.9	57.3	55.7	46.9	42.3	41.3	38.8	43.2	49.4	49.5	50.3	48.7	586.15
1981[2]	49.0	52.6	55.4	55.1	53.9	59.5	56.4	51.1	52.1	57.3	49.7	42.6	634.67
1982[2]	54.6	51.6	53.6	54.4	48.7	53.7	48.2	48.1	58.1	53.6	51.8	45.2	617.00
1983													

[1] Data prior to 1974 are in THOUSANDS OF LONG TONS. [2] Preliminary. *Source: Rubber Manufacturers' Association* T.562

Stocks of Natural Rubber in the United States, Beginning of Month In Thousands of Metric Tons[1]

Year	Jan.	Feb.	Mar.	Apr.	May	June	July	Aug.	Sept.	Oct.	Nov.	Dec.
1970	106.5	104.9	98.6	95.1	96.4	98.3	89.7	92.4	94.7	96.7	92.4	93.6
1971	102.6	91.4	92.9	102.7	98.6	105.9	104.9	122.0	125.6	131.4	124.9	126.4
1972	133.3	128.0	128.0	133.2	129.7	117.0	109.1	102.9	112.3	109.5	109.6	112.3
1973	116.7	122.8	116.8	120.5	117.5	122.2	115.9	113.7	117.2	128.7	122.4	122.5
1974[1]	122.4	124.0	120.1	129.5	130.3	131.0	132.6	155.4	155.2	143.0	129.9	124.5
1975	137.5	125.6	126.9	126.9	125.4	113.1	125.2	118.7	116.8	107.0	104.9	110.7
1976	105.4	99.8	158.2	127.0	140.9	104.7	102.3	106.8	92.6	104.9	64.5	71.9
1977	125.3	119.9	127.0	123.8	118.4	120.5	119.7	131.7	139.7	133.0	137.5	129.4
1978	127.6	123.3	116.4	117.1	115.6	122.8	123.4	125.4	126.1	127.7	133.5	124.0
1979[2]	125.6	121.4	115.6	116.1	136.6	130.2	137.7	146.0	144.4	135.6	135.0	124.5
1980[2]	132.1	131.4	135.3	141.4	152.4	145.7	144.4	149.9	138.5	132.9	129.5	123.1
1981[2]	126.7	128.0	125.4	122.8	127.6	124.1	119.5	113.5	111.2	114.4	123.0	130.5
1982[2]	142.4	138.4	138.0	134.4	67.0	126.3	121.9	62.1	115.3	105.7	110.6	113.7
1983[2]	123.3											

[1] Data prior to 1974 are in THOUSANDS OF LONG TONS. [2] Preliminary. *Source: Rubber Manufacturers' Association* T.563

Stocks of Synthetic Rubber in the United States, Beginning of Month In Thousands of Metric Tons[1]

Year	Jan.	Feb.	Mar.	Apr.	May	June	July	Aug.	Sept.	Oct.	Nov.	Dec.
1970	411.0	434.4	436.7	433.3	422.4	457.5	455.5	464.7	479.4	481.8	488.3	499.3
1971	514.8	526.3	517.1	497.6	491.2	501.8	487.8	505.3	483.9	468.3	462.1	480.3
1972	488.2	487.4	478.7	480.1	492.7	491.3	485.1	519.2	512.6	515.5	504.4	495.7
1973	495.7	471.9	473.1	454.8	461.6	469.4	469.9	499.3	501.6	511.2	500.9	494.7
1974[1]	521.0	508.9	507.4	489.4	478.1	503.1	505.6	567.6	583.5	569.1	560.3	585.7
1975	618.7	596.0	590.2	479.3	426.6	424.7	408.2	390.8	378.9	368.0	358.9	365.3
1976	369.9	405.1	406.4	386.7	416.4	453.9	472.7	499.1	513.6	475.5	464.7	449.0
1977	458.1	441.4	431.8	407.6	412.9	409.3	402.2	430.4	430.3	422.3	424.5	424.0
1978	426.8	441.0	427.9	434.5	446.9	441.4	433.1	456.5	445.1	435.8	425.3	419.9
1979[2]	424.1	407.1	400.0	393.6	398.9	391.5	401.3	411.3	402.2	402.8	389.9	402.1
1980[2]	402.9	439.9	436.2	427.6	452.2	445.1	429.2	391.2	372.3	339.7	325.4	328.9
1981[2]	341.8	364.5	354.6	347.0	365.9	368.3	359.8	369.4	353.4	333.5	352.6	364.4
1982[2]	349.0	340.4	340.4	356.3	376.9	375.6	374.7	357.9	345.5	310.3	327.6	306.0
1983[2]	267.4											

[1] Data prior to 1974 are in THOUSANDS OF LONG TONS. [2] Preliminary. *Source: Department of Commerce* T.564

RUBBER

Production of Synthetic Rubber in the United States   In Thousands of Metric Tons[1]

Year	Jan.	Feb.	Mar.	Apr.	May	June	July	Aug.	Sept.	Oct.	Nov.	Dec.	Total
1970	193.1	178.9	186.8	178.8	182.4	179.8	181.5	187.3	182.9	185.0	179.4	181.1	2,197
1971	183.6	166.5	181.8	184.1	196.5	182.1	187.5	187.0	187.0	193.8	194.9	196.1	2,241
1972	200.0	193.0	210.1	208.7	210.7	191.0	195.5	202.7	200.4	211.6	201.7	199.1	2,417
1973	216.1	208.0	216.6	223.1	221.2	199.9	210.0	220.4	210.7	227.5	212.6	219.4	2,585
1974[1]	226.1	212.0	229.5	224.1	225.7	212.5	206.0	211.3	208.2	205.1	185.9	154.8	2,498
1975	155.9	136.7	137.1	138.7	153.6	149.8	144.9	172.7	182.0	194.3	185.7	189.2	1,938
1976	191.5	193.1	210.5	204.2	191.4	176.3	156.7	160.7	192.7	209.5	206.3	210.9	2,304
1977	204.0	193.0	213.1	204.8	211.5	201.8	191.3	198.8	201.7	205.6	195.4	196.6	2,418
1978	198.2	193.8	210.3	214.9	211.2	194.4	195.9	205.7	207.4	212.3	212.1	219.1	2,475
1979[2]	207.9	200.8	232.1	216.7	223.3	210.7	202.9	202.8	210.0	213.8	206.0	207.6	2,535
1980[2]	195.6	194.7	206.8	192.4	159.6	129.6	110.3	123.7	149.8	174.6	178.5	193.7	2,015
1981[2]	193.5	169.7	200.4	180.9	175.9	158.2	161.5	159.7	168.9	170.0	157.7	125.5	2,021
1982[2]	140.49	145.76	170.32	154.86	155.44	139.71	117.46	124.91	127.19	135.18	108.11	103.79	1,632
1983													

[1] Data prior to 1974 are in THOUSANDS OF LONG TONS.   [2] Preliminary.   *Source: Department of Commerce*   T.565

Consumption of Synthetic Rubber in the United States   In Thousands of Metric Tons[1]

Year	Jan.	Feb.	Mar.	Apr.	May	June	July	Aug.	Sept.	Oct.	Nov.	Dec.	Total
1970	175.8	170.8	181.5	173.1	131.8	158.8	152.9	154.9	160.4	163.9	144.4	149.6	1,918
1971	163.7	163.5	187.8	174.0	174.2	184.5	152.1	176.7	186.1	190.3	173.3	178.7	2,093
1972	182.2	186.8	201.4	189.7	197.0	197.7	152.1	191.9	195.3	210.2	194.0	193.5	2,292
1973	206.5	199.8	220.6	199.0	197.7	196.1	180.3	197.8	197.4	219.7	196.9	189.0	2,401
1974[1]	222.6	203.5	220.0	208.1	204.1	199.4	177.4	204.0	198.6	213.6	174.5	148.8	2,356
1975	178.4	162.4	143.3	167.5	165.7	170.1	154.3	171.5	183.2	201.2	157.7	167.0	2,022
1976	183.8	195.0	221.9	169.6	151.5	146.7	118.2	142.5	220.2	213.3	211.9	200.6	2,175
1977	217.6	203.6	232.6	203.1	218.8	208.6	161.1	209.8	209.0	205.7	190.9	203.4	2,464
1978	193.7	193.2	206.2	197.5	212.7	194.7	170.6	213.9	211.7	220.3	212.1	209.8	2,436
1979[2]	226.0	201.4	224.4	201.5	212.0	179.6	176.5	202.3	187.9	202.8	174.5	163.3	2,340
1980[2]	170.8	176.1	191.1	148.9	135.7	120.1	131.0	133.7	166.0	167.9	157.7	155.1	1,854
1981[2]	153.0	166.7	194.0	144.9	167.1	154.1	144.7	165.0	156.7	163.8	141.1	131.9	1,890
1982[2]	143.1	138.9	149.9	134.6	133.1	132.2	106.5	135.2	151.8	118.4	129.8	141.5	1,625
1983													

[1] Data prior to 1974 are in THOUSANDS OF LONG TONS.   [2] Preliminary.   *Source: Department of Commerce*   T.566

Exports of Synthetic Rubber from the United States   In Thousands of Long Tons

Year	Jan.	Feb.	Mar.	Apr.	May	June	July	Aug.	Sept.	Oct.	Nov.	Dec.	Total
1970	23.4	23.7	22.3	26.1	25.3	27.3	23.2	23.3	22.1	24.1	24.5	26.2	290.1
1971	19.8	23.3	27.3	24.4	25.9	20.8	24.4	29.4	35.0	14.2	9.8	15.5	269.8
1972	26.8	26.7	20.0	16.8	20.0	18.1	20.1	22.1	16.5	24.0	21.9	24.0	257.1
1973	23.65	22.21	22.99	22.37	24.18	23.58	20.86	18.97	29.34	25.01	21.60	21.10	275.84
1974	22.41	20.55	27.76	27.50	26.01	21.06	21.08	25.78	21.05	18.00	19.13	16.80	267.12
1975	14.52	17.05	15.06	17.17	15.69	16.78	16.24	18.36	19.28	20.64	21.15	22.57	214.50
1976	21.24	22.55	25.15	21.38	22.55	22.48	24.75	22.70	20.59	21.59	19.86	21.13	267.99
1977	19.11	20.97	24.34	21.48	22.06	20.78	24.72	14.86	26.15	14.59	13.80	17.13	239.98
1978	16.94	18.86	22.55	19.48	24.90	22.28	19.35	20.04	20.77	22.22	23.81	23.77	254.96
1979	23.62	22.29	27.74	29.43	28.74	34.61	34.51	39.37	34.90	38.61	36.53	34.76	385.11
1980	31.46	34.48	41.98	41.68	46.88	37.33	36.54	30.46	25.51	33.45	30.72	32.31	422.78
1981	31.21	31.65	38.73	31.77	32.00	28.55	26.27	21.97	24.40	23.94	22.49	21.65	334.63
1982	27.76	23.46	31.18	26.53	24.73	25.23	20.40	22.04	22.83	21.13	20.47	18.86	284.62
1983	20.24												

Source: Department of Commerce   T.567

RUBBER

Production of Auto. Pneumatic Casings[2] & Motor Vehicle Registrations in the U.S.   In Ths. of Casings

Year	Jan.	Feb.	Mar.	Apr.	May	June	July	Aug.	Sept.	Oct.	Nov.	Dec.	Total	Regis.[1] (Dec. 31)
1970	18,174	17,522	17,606	17,216	12,642	15,658	15,466	14,657	15,885	15,938	14,560	15,079	190,403	108.3
1971	16,790	17,678	19,693	17,987	18,036	18,911	15,954	17,640	19,204	19,454	17,447	17,584	216,361	113.0
1972	19,064	19,132	20,584	19,005	19,725	20,270	14,765	18,608	19,352	20,999	18,721	19,387	229,611	118.8
1973	21,001	19,993	22,229	19,193	18,693	17,752	14,287	17,325	17,727	19,841	18,035	17,343	223,418	125.7
1974	20,366	19,349	20,497	18,334	18,379	17,830	14,484	17,454	17,426	19,737	15,245	12,294	211,390	130.0
1975	14,753	13,184	12,107	15,222	15,677	16,678	14,531	16,413	17,878	18,821	15,212	16,215	186,705	133.0
1976	17,598	18,200	20,552	16,085	9,856	10,453	8,025	8,954	18,096	21,113	18,827	20,194	187,953	138.5
1977	20,638	20,094	22,640	20,087	19,512	20,734	15,050	19,495	19,321	18,926	17,716	17,425	231,638	143.8
1978	18,290	18,319	18,987	18,828	19,148	18,946	15,108	19,245	19,155	20,497	18,299	18,869	223,406	148.8
1979[3]	20,352	19,592	21,807	18,609	18,544	15,603	14,904	16,911	15,985	17,775	14,480	12,340	206,687	154.1
1980[3]	15,188	15,059	15,082	13,678	11,370	10,716	10,206	12,057	13,911	15,790	12,861	13,346	159,263	155.9
1981[3]	15,463	15,641	16,834	15,466	15,151	15,406	14,277	14,902	15,851	16,534	13,750	11,855	181,762	159.8
1982[3]	14,866	15,387	17,051	15,077	14,856	15,669	12,293	14,835	15,528	15,381	13,585	13,972	178,500	
1983[3]														
1984														

[1] Registrations, in millions, of all privately & publicly owned vehicles (except military). [2] Passenger cars, buses, trucks & motorcycle tires. [3] Preliminary. *Sources: Rubber Manufacturers' Association; Motor Vehicle Mfg. Association*
T.568

Stocks of Auto. Pneumatic Casings & Passenger[1] Car Registrations in the U.S.   In Ths. of Casings

Year	Jan. 1	Feb. 1	Mar. 1	Apr. 1	May 1	June 1	July 1	Aug. 1	Sept. 1	Oct. 1	Nov. 1	Dec. 1	Regis.[1] (Dec. 31)
1970	49,152	53,750	57,105	56,400	54,620	49,670	45,196	46,055	45,758	45,758	45,586	48,111	89.2
1971	50,175	52,894	56,462	57,656	54,436	53,454	50,821	50,397	50,401	49,396	50,083	51,015	92.8
1972	54,982	59,380	62,689	63,234	60,896	59,753	58,836	57,836	56,895	54,965	55,769	56,319	97.1
1973	60,255	63,646	66,419	66,700	62,872	60,485	56,834	52,341	50,392	47,775	45,636	46,472	102.0
1974	50,275	53,308	57,056	60,553	59,020	58,995	56,322	53,469	53,260	51,645	50,851	53,321	104.9
1975	55,242	58,758	60,970	57,721	54,082	52,037	49,803	46,990	47,405	45,711	46,002	47,569	106.7
1976	50,020	53,172	55,395	54,837	49,125	40,259	32,405	25,581	21,285	24,594	27,581	30,200	110.2
1977	34,768	39,010	43,212	45,616	45,832	46,231	44,887	43,460	45,229	44,542	43,841	45,176	113.7
1978	47,181	51,523	54,621	51,986	50,006	49,277	46,293	44,280	44,057	41,796	40,135	40,394	116.6
1979[2]	43,472	47,212	51,284	52,223	53,540	53,033	46,362	49,397	48,422	46,002	44,357	44,546	120.2
1980[2]	44,873	46,760	49,993	50,471	49,220	46,972	42,817	40,079	37,057	33,730	32,112	32,363	121.7
1981[2]	33,298	40,188	43,258	43,686	42,393	43,480	38,570	37,116	36,709	36,088	36,556	41,112	124.3
1982[2]	40,863	42,904	46,254	47,817	46,583	45,337	43,475	40,763	40,192	38,685	38,116	38,436	
1983[2]	39,955												
1984													

[1] Registrations, in millions, of privately and publicly owned passenger cars (except military). [2] Preliminary. *Sources: Rubber Manufacturers' Association; Motor Vehicle Mfg. Association*
T.569

How to keep your Commodity Year Book statistics up-to-date continuously throughout the year.

To keep up-to-date statistics on the commodities in this book, you should have COMMODITY YEAR BOOK STATISTICAL ABSTRACT SERVICE. This three-times-yearly publication provides the latest available statistics for updating the statistical tables appearing in the COMMODITY YEAR BOOK. The ABSTRACT is published in the Winter (Jan.), Spring (Apr.) and Fall (Oct.). Subscription price is $55 per year.

Commodity Research Bureau, Inc.
75 MONTGOMERY ST., JERSEY CITY, N.J. 07302

Rye

The 1982/83 (June/May) U.S. rye season started with stocks of only 3.1 million bushels, the lowest in recent years. With U.S. supplies very short and high-priced (over $4.00 per bushel), record purchases of Canadian rye were needed to satisfy early-season U.S. demand. However, the 1982 U.S. rye crop increased 11 percent from the previous year to 20.8 million bushels. An increase in yield to a record-high 29.1 bushels per acre from 26.7 bushels in 1981 accounted for most of the additional production in 1982 as acreage harvested increased only 1.2 percent.

The 1982/83 U.S. rye supply increased to 25.9 million bushels from 23.4 million in 1981/82, as the increase in production more than offset the smaller beginning stocks than in the previous season.

Disappearance of U.S. rye during June–December 1982 was only slightly less than for the same period in 1981. An increase in feed use nearly offset a sharp drop in exports. However, January 1, 1983 stocks were 38 percent larger than a year earlier reflecting the larger supply of rye. The USDA projected a sharp gain to 7.1 million bushels in 1982/83 ending stocks on May 31, 1983, primarily because of the larger supply and a sharp drop in projected exports for the full season.

U.S. acreage seeded to rye for all purposes in the fall of 1982 for harvest in 1983 amounted to 2.67 million acres, 2 percent above seeding to the 1982 crop. However, production prospects for 1983 were expected to be influenced considerably by the 40 percent increase in planted acreage in the major rye-producing states of the North Central area (Minnesota, North Dakota and South Dakota). These states usually harvest around 85 percent of their rye area for grain compared with less than 20 percent for most other regions where rye is often consumed as livestock forage.

U.S. Government Price Support

The loan rate for 1983 crop rye is $2.25 per bushel, up $0.08 from the 1982 loan rate. Rye is not eligible for entry into the Grain Reserve or for target price protection.

Futures Market

Rye futures are traded on the Winnipeg Commodity Exchange.

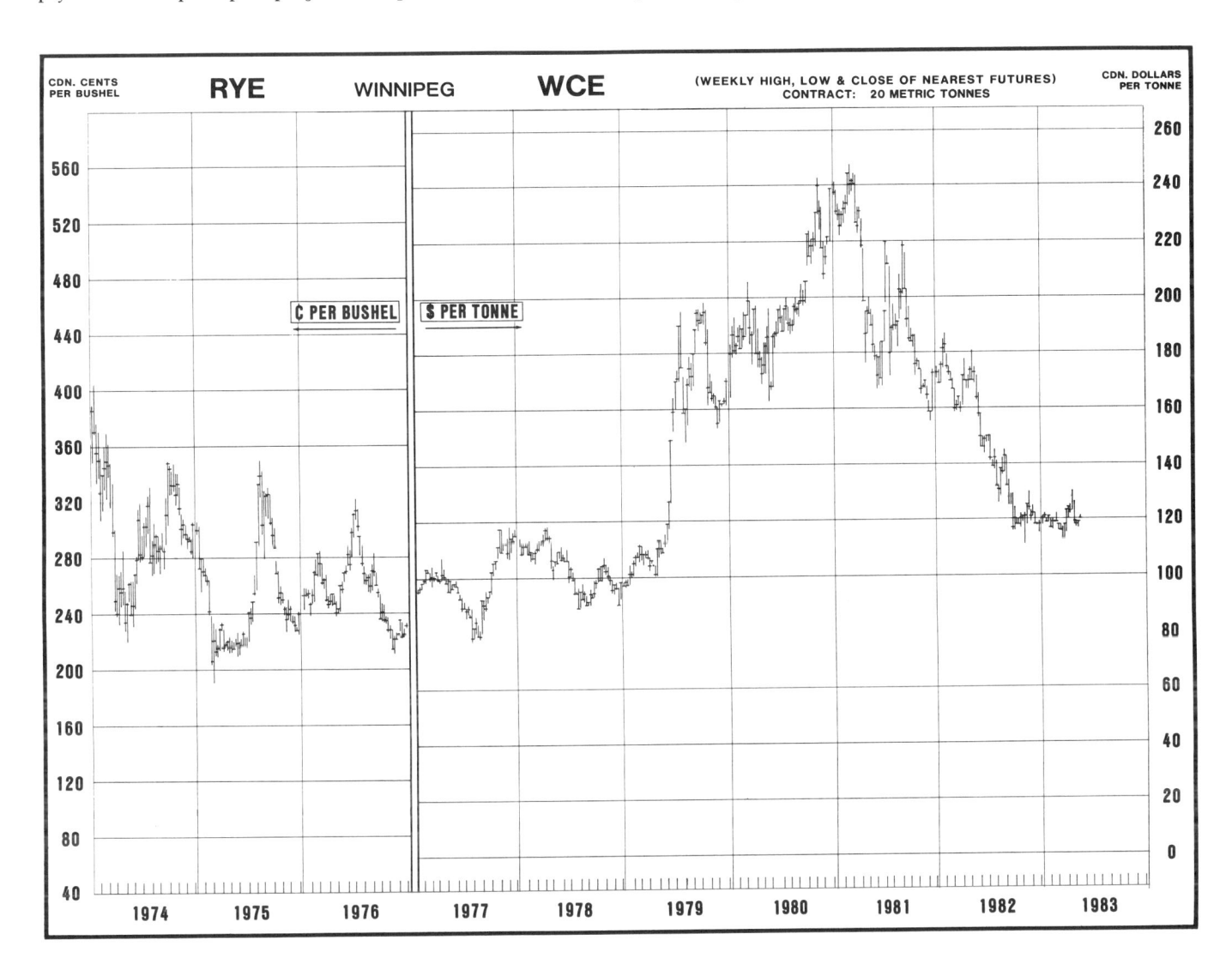

RYE

World Production of Rye   In Thousands of Metric Tons

Crop Year	Argentina	Austria	Canada	Czechoslovakia	Denmark	France	Germany West	Germany East	Hungary	Netherlands	Poland	Spain	Turkey	USSR	United States	World Total
1970-1	181	363	570	454	134	306	2,701	1,483	155	172	5,433	256	680	10,800	936	25,596
1971-2	256	448	557	619	150	308	3,188	1,754	182	209	7,827	269	900	10,600	1,252	29,605
1972-3	500	402	344	633	155	350	2,954	1,947	171	151	8,149	263	755	9,600	741	28,212
1973-4	613	400	363	688	140	327	2,693	1,699	175	105	8,268	252	690	10,759	660	28,859
1974-5	306	415	480	671	168	315	2,559	1,949	175	78	7,881	254	560	15,218	483	32,629
1975-6	273	347	523	530	163	292	2,126	1,563	147	63	6,270	241	750	9,064	457	23,702
1976-7	330	410	440	561	214	284	2,100	1,455	156	65	6,922	214	740	13,991	381	29,397
1977-8	170	351	392	540	320	375	2,546	1,500	142	74	6,257	205	690	8,471	462	23,440
1978-9	210	410	605	625	315	435	2,548	1,895	136	68	7,434	251	620	13,603	665	30,698
1979-0	202	278	525	486	257	355	2,189	1,830	92	49	5,201	221	620	8,100	569	21,727
1980-1[1]	155	383	448	575	199	408	2,184	1,917	130	39	6,564	292	525	10,205	419	25,283
1981-2[2]	200	330	964	500	213	342	1,794	1,820	129	29	6,789	216	500	9,500	473	24,528
1982-3																

[1] Preliminary.   [2] Estimate.   Source: Foreign Agricultural Service, U.S.D.A.   T.570

Salient Statistics of Rye in the United States

Year Begin. June 1	Stocks, June 1 Privately Owned[2]	Gov't.[3]	Total Stocks	Production	Imports	Total Supply	Food	Alc. Beverages	Seed	Feed[5]	Total	Exports	Total Disappearance	Planted	Harvested for Grain — Mil. Acres	Yield Per Harvested Acre Bushels
1970-1			21,880	36,840	1,047	59,767	5,430	3,522	6,873	11,407	27,232	3,204	30,436	4,196	1,427	25.8
1971-2			29,331	49,223	241	78,795	5,195	3,005	5,262	16,276	29,738	2,177	31,915	4,842	1,751	28.1
1972-3			46,880	28,256	154	75,290	5,122	3,038	5,321	16,458	29,939	6,535	36,474	3,458	1,050	26.9
1973-4			38,816	24,677	1	63,494	6,250	2,547	4,967	8,042	21,806	27,513	49,319	3,380	955	25.8
1974-5	14,175	—	14,175	17,506	277	31,958	5,459	1,386	4,215	7,811	18,871	6,465	25,336	2,828	784	22.3
1975-6	6,622	—	6,622	15,924	944	23,524	4,172	2,060	4,217	7,554	18,003	1,117	19,120	2,829	728	21.9
1976-7	4,404	—	4,404	14,891	248	19,500	3,696	1,930	4,217	5,304	15,147	38	15,100	2,652	719	20.7
1977-8	4,418	—	4,418	16,543	127	21,100	3,648	1,875	4,806	7,000	17,100	24	17,100	2,652	677	24.4
1978-9	4,137	—	4,137	24,065	145	28,200	3,690	2,369	4,600	8,100	18,800	400	19,200	2,865	926	26.0
1979-0	8,973	—	8,973	22,389	7	31,369	3,523	2,116	4,034	7,082	16,755	2,422	19,177	2,921	869	25.8
1980-1	12,000	192	12,192	16,483	10	28,685	3,515	2,050	4,150	7,331	17,046	7,494	24,540	2,537	675	24.4
1981-2[1]	4,000	145	4,145	18,822	432	23,399	3,458	2,242	4,160	8,915	18,775	1,529	20,304	2,613	706	26.7
1982-3[4]			3,095	20,817	2,000	25,900	3,500	2,100	4,200	8,500	18,300	500	18,800	2,621	715	29.1
1983-4[4]				7,100										2,665		

[1] Preliminary.   [2] Includes total loans.   [3] Uncommitted, gov't only.   [4] Forecast.   [5] Residual; approximates total feed use.   Source: Economics Service, U.S.D.A.   T.571

Production of Rye in the United States   In Thousands of Bushels

Year	Illinois	Indiana	Kansas	Michigan	Minnesota	Georgia	Nebraska	No. Dakota	Ohio	Oklahoma	Oregon	So. Dakota	Virginia	Texas	Wisconsin	So. Carolina
1969	576	525	1,121	1,120	2,268	1,692	2,565	5,175	403	980	390	7,128	442	722	280	
1970	529	485	1,892	1,134	2,850	1,656	4,750	5,249	336	936	250	8,768	486	566	253	
1971	529	432	2,640	850	5,404	1,955	5,880	9,750	396	780	260	12,320	475	378	288	
1972	529	300	500	806	2,990	1,500	1,440	4,615	256	1,260	200	9,108	408	630	210	
1973	462	299	735	675	3,150	1,425	1,300	3,039	232	1,333	168	7,480	322	648	189	
1974	361	216	266	450	1,550	1,900	900	2,650	180	595	184	4,278	324	300	240	
1975	374	234	168	456	2,225	1,350	855	2,975	210	570	192	2,346	230	760	315	
1976	315	230	136	468	2,048	2,090	765	2,831	210	608	168	1,485	264	378	252	
1977	330	260	180	456	2,436	1,995	1,050	2,080	248	646	125	3,480	350	400	364	640
1978	368	175	315	600	2,352	2,530	760	5,400	186	570	168	6,200	425	406	357	836
1979	391	208	504	625	2,275	2,310	770	4,200	155	910	144	5,700	384	513	368	609
1980	368	182	210	504	1,900	1,995	666	1,470	231	816	150	4,030	325	494	368	616
1981	336	234	252	532	2,883	2,730	924	2,560	150	680	150	3,220	364	475	408	726
1982[1]	299	260	240	638	3,300	1,470	1,107	3,400	155	874	155	4,680	364	504	248	621
1983																

[1] Preliminary, December estimate.   Source: Crop Reporting Board, U.S.D.A.   T.572

RYE

U.S. Rye Crop Production Reports and CCC Operations   In Thousands of Bushels

Year Begin. June 1	Official Crop Reports July 1	Aug. 1	Dec. 1	Final	National Average Support Rate $ Per Bushel	% of Parity	Placed Under Loan	Direct Purchases	Total	Delivered to CCC	Ending Carryover[1]	CCC Uncommitted	Privately Owned[3] Under Loan[4]	Other
1970-1	35,745	36,186	38,552	36,840	1.02	68	10,880	1,288	12,168	11,246	29,331	16,889	4,250	8,192
1971-2	51,179	52,306	50,935	49,223	.89	57	18,958	1,238	20,196	11,500	46,880	28,073	12,715	6,092
1972-3	30,798	31,315	29,536	28,256	.89	56	6,695	195	6,890	1,500	38,816	—	8,788	30,028
1973-4	24,865	25,506	26,398	24,677	.89	51	443	2	445	—	14,175	—	80	14,095
1974-5	22,020	19,616	19,293	17,506	.89	46	196	—	196	—	6,622	—	30	6,592
1975-6	18,830	18,551	17,875	15,958	.89	39	87	—	87	—	4,403	—	47	4,468
1976-7	16,957	17,382	16,667	14,951	1.20	48		—	100	—	4,414	—	—	
1977-8	17,787	18,242	16,998	17,312	1.70	61		—	900	—	4,418	—	—	
1978-9	28,518	28,567	26,160	26,160	1.70	56		—	3,000	—	4,137	—	—	
1979-0[2]	23,638	23,736	24,549	22,389	1.79	49			2,000	—	8,973	—	—	
1980-1[2]	15,784	16,189	16,265	16,483	1.91	51			450	—	12,192	—	—	
1981-2[2]	16,743	17,083	18,621	18,822	2.04						4,145			
1982-3[2]	20,119	19,924	20,817		2.17						3,095			
1983-4					2.25						7,100			

[1] Old-crop rye under loan at end of crop year.   [2] Preliminary.   [3] Derived by subtracting CCC stocks & loans outstanding from ending carryover.   [4] Includes previous crops under reseal.   Source: Economic Research Service, U.S.D.A.   T.573

High, Low & Closing Prices of May Rye Futures in Winnipeg   In Dollars per Tonne

Year of Delivery		June	July	Aug.	Sept.	Oct.	Nov.	Dec.	Jan.	Feb.	Mar.	Apr.	May	Life of Delivery Range
1978	High	—	—	91.50	99.00	112.20	117.00	119.00	113.50	112.80	114.80	118.00	109.00	119.00
	Low	—	—	82.30	90.00	96.80	105.90	109.50	107.50	104.50	107.90	103.30	98.50	82.30
	Close	—	—	89.90	97.20	111.20	111.00	114.50	108.00	107.90	113.00	105.50	108.50	—
1979	High	—	101.90	98.00	105.20	112.40	111.00	104.00	104.20	109.40	110.50	106.90	113.00	113.00
	Low	—	94.80	92.20	93.30	100.70	101.40	96.00	96.20	100.10	105.00	99.90	100.90	92.20
	Close	—	97.00	94.50	100.30	108.60	102.20	97.80	100.50	108.50	106.70	101.50	112.10	—
1980	High	154.00	188.00	167.50	189.40	191.00	181.00	175.00	192.50	195.00	205.50	196.50	195.50	205.50
	Low	117.50	148.50	139.50	159.40	171.50	170.50	160.80	163.50	182.00	176.00	173.80	168.50	117.50
	Close	143.50	158.00	159.40	184.00	181.50	172.10	169.40	183.00	186.00	187.60	178.50	195.50	—
1981	High	193.50	205.90	194.50	205.70	231.00	250.50	244.00	242.00	244.50	242.50	232.50	199.50	250.50
	Low	170.50	189.00	182.10	192.00	201.80	228.00	216.50	223.00	225.50	223.40	176.00	186.70	170.50
	Close	192.90	194.00	194.20	203.00	230.00	242.80	237.00	225.50	244.50	230.20	189.50	194.00	—
1982	High	167.00	181.50	215.90	233.50	218.00	195.60	187.00	185.20	187.30	171.00	178.00	180.90	233.50
	Low	151.20	154.90	183.50	211.20	193.00	181.50	169.80	168.70	169.50	158.50	160.00	163.40	151.20
	Close	151.20	181.50	215.90	217.70	194.20	183.40	171.00	182.00	169.50	160.30	170.00	165.50	—
1983	High	162.00	162.00	152.50	150.50	139.50	140.20	133.00	126.30	123.20	123.00	130.00		
	Low	162.00	152.00	138.00	133.80	128.00	129.00	121.00	119.80	116.40	115.30	118.10		
	Close	162.00	152.50	145.00	133.80	128.20	130.20	121.00	123.10	120.50	122.70	118.70		
1984	High													
	Low													
	Close													

Source: Winnipeg Commodity Exchange   T.576

How to keep your Commodity Year Book statistics up-to-date continuously throughout the year.

To keep up-to-date statistics on the commodities in this book, you should have COMMODITY YEAR BOOK STATISTICAL ABSTRACT SERVICE. This three-times-yearly publication provides the latest available statistics for the updating of the statistical tables appearing in the COMMODITY YEAR BOOK. It is published in the Winter (Jan.), Spring (Apr.) and Fall (Oct.). Subscription price is $55 per year.

Commodity Research Bureau, Inc.
75 MONTGOMERY ST., JERSEY CITY, N.J. 07302

RYE

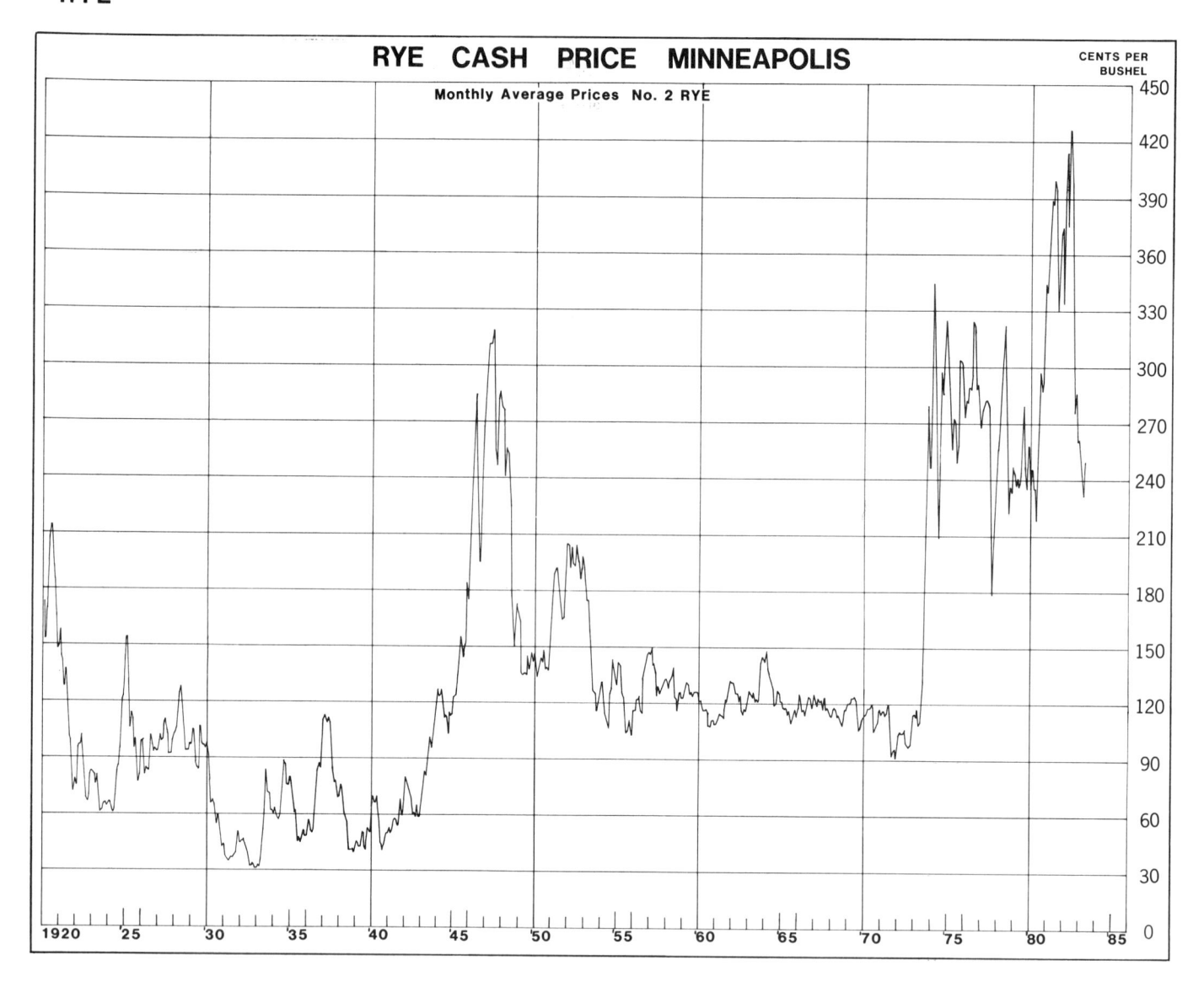

RYE CASH PRICE MINNEAPOLIS
Monthly Average Prices No. 2 RYE

Average Price of Cash Rye No. 2 at Minneapolis   In Cents per Bushel

Year	July	Aug.	Sept.	Oct.	Nov.	Dec.	Jan.	Feb.	Mar.	Apr.	May	June	Average
1970-1	107	105	108	109	114	114	116	116	114	115	120	115	113
1971-2	100	92	95	96	91	99	103	105	104	104	106	99	100
1972-3	98	97	98	105	114	115	113	117	109	110	123	132	111
1973-4	160	217	279	265	246	286	344	338	316	221	209	257	262
1974-5	297	289	307	325	319	305	293	280	256	272	270	249	288
1975-6	258	304	303	301	286	273	282	281	289	288	296	324	284
1976-7	322	288	290	277	268	270	277	280	282	282	279	253	287
1977-8	194	179	206	228	246	256	269	282	294	305	322	293	253
1978-9	259	222	236	233	247	244	237	241	236	238	244	273	244
1979-0	279	247	235	257	249	235	245	235	235	218	244	266	247
1980-1	297	287	292	307	344	340	352	363	389	387	396	394	346
1981-2	352	330	356	371	374	334	394	414	375	426	410	397	378
1982-3	342	276	286	260	261	256	251	246	231				
1983-4													

Source: Economic Research Service, U.S.D.A.

T.575

RYE

United States Rye Quarterly Supply and Disappearance In Millions of Bushels

Periods Begin. June 1	Beginning Stocks	Production	Imports	Total Supply	Food	Alc. Beverages	Seed	Feed[2]	Total	Exports	Total Disappearance	Gov't. Owned	Privately Owned	Total Stocks
1978-9	4.0	24.1	.1	28.2	3.7	2.4	4.6	8.1	18.8	.4	19.2	—	9.0	9.0
June-Sept.	4.0	24.1	.1	28.2	1.1	.5	2.3	1.8	5.7	[3]	5.7	—	22.5	22.5
Oct.-Dec.	22.5	—	—	22.5	1.1	.6	2.1	3.5	7.3	[3]	7.3	—	15.2	15.2
Jan.-Mar.	15.2	—	[3]	15.2	1.0	.7	.2	1.6	3.5	[3]	3.5	—	11.7	11.7
Apr.-May	11.7	—	[3]	11.7	.5	.6	—	1.2	2.3	.4	2.7	—	9.0	9.0
1979-0	9.0	22.4	[3]	31.4	3.5	2.1	4.0	7.1	16.7	2.4	19.2	.2	12.0	12.2
June-Sept.	9.0	22.4	[3]	31.4	1.2	.6	2.0	2.2	6.0	.6	6.6	.2	24.6	24.8
Oct.-Dec.	24.8	—	[3]	24.8	.9	.4	1.8	2.4	5.5	1.6	7.1	.2	17.5	17.7
Jan.-Mar.	17.7	—	[3]	17.7	.9	.6	.2	1.0	2.7	[3]	2.7	.2	14.8	15.0
Apr.-May	15.0	—	[3]	15.0	.5	.5	[3]	1.5	2.6	.2	2.8	.2	12.0	12.2
1980-81	12.2	16.5	[3]	28.7	3.5	2.1	4.2	7.3	17.0	7.5	24.5	.1	4.0	4.1
June-Sept.	12.2	16.5	[3]	28.7	1.2	.4	2.1	3.4	7.0	3.2	10.2	.2	18.3	18.5
Oct.-Dec.	18.5	—	[3]	18.5	1.0	.5	1.9	2.7	6.0	3.1	9.2	.3	9.0	9.3
Jan.-Mar.	9.3	—	[3]	9.4	.8	.7	.2	[3]	1.8	.7	2.5	.3	6.6	6.9
Apr.-May	6.9	—	[3]	6.9	.6	.5	[3]	1.2	2.3	.4	2.7	.1	4.0	4.1
1981-2[1]	4.1	18.8	[3]	23.4	3.5	2.2	4.2	8.9	18.8	1.5	20.3			4.0
June-Sept.	4.1	18.8	[3]	23.0	1.2	.4	2.1	4.7	8.4	[3]	8.4	.1	14.4	14.6
Oct.-Dec.	14.6	—	.1	14.6	.9	.6	1.9	1.9	5.3	1.4	6.7	.1	7.7	7.9
Jan.-Mar.	7.9	—	.3	8.0	.9	.8	.2	.2	2.1	.1	2.2			5.8
Apr.-May	5.8	—	.4	6.1	.5	.4	[3]	2.1	3.0	[3]	3.0			3.1
1982-3[4]	3.1	20.8	2.0	25.9	3.5	2.1	4.2	8.5	18.3	.5	18.8			
June-Sept.	3.1	20.8	.8	24.7	1.2	.5	2.1	4.4	8.2	.1	8.3			16.5
Oct.-Dec.	16.5	—	1.0	17.5	.9	.7	1.9	3.2	6.6	[3]	6.6			10.9
Jan.-Mar.	10.9													
Apr.-May														

[1] Preliminary. [2] Residual. [3] Less than 50,000 bushels. [4] Estimate. Source: Economics Service, U.S.D.A.

Rye Under Price Support Through the End of the Month (Cumulative Total from Current Season's Crop) In Thousands of Bushels

Year	July	Aug.	Sept.	Oct.	Nov.	Dec.	Jan.	Feb.	Mar.	Apr.	May	June	Total
1969-0	—	1,422	3,486	4,469	4,718	4,920	5,903	6,085	6,293	6,415	6,418	6,419	6,417
1970-1	681	3,584	6,394	7,609	8,080	8,432	9,910	10,226	10,669	10,877	10,884	10,883	10,887
1971-2	323	5,828	11,156	13,332	14,357	15,035	17,175	17,779	18,442	18,930	18,949	18,955	18,960
1972-3	50	2,091	4,309	5,393	5,760	5,918	6,288	6,381	6,546	6,696	6,699	6,699	6,700
1973-4	44	253	331	367	407	427	442	442	442	442	442	442	450
1974-5	39	178	190	193	194	194	196	196	196	196	196	196	196
1975-6	8	59	59	63	64	85	87	87	87	87	87	87	87
1976-7	10	21	58	66	91	105	110	123	146	144	144	144	144
1977-8	74	250	647	719	769	800	858	887	917	914	913	913	913
1978-9	114	1,467	2,064	2,325	2,537	2,626	2,818	2,857	3,001	3,031	3,036	3,050	3,050
1979-0	5	338	765	1,106	1,313	1,397	1,592	1,653	1,790	1,882	1,900	1,905	1,905
1980-1	—	97	240	297	348	384	396	399	402	406	406	406	
1981-2	36	264	359	398	424	439	448	456	456	456	456	456	
1982-3	7	344	771	1,008	1,096	1,193	1,324	1,369	1,588				

Source: U.S. Department of Agriculture

Month End Open Interest of Rye Futures in Winnipeg In 20 Tonne Units

Year	Jan.	Feb.	Mar.	Apr.	May	June	July	Aug.	Sept.	Oct.	Nov.	Dec.
1978	2,062	2,242	2,428	2,600	2,306	2,414	2,757	2,969	2,646	2,951	2,598	2,206
1979	2,556	3,238	3,494	3,042	3,372	5,617	6,332	5,988	6,872	6,293	5,751	4,808
1980	4,648	5,028	5,379	6,172	3,313	5,229	5,348	4,839	5,814	6,106	4,250	3,428
1981	3,876	4,811	3,704	3,640	2,948	3,368	5,028	6,440	5,251	2,516	4,404	3,828
1982	3,739	3,622	3,219	3,583	4,426	3,008	2,268	4,286	5,250	4.052	3,773	3,244
1983	3,227	3,628	3,097	4,625								
1984												

Source: Winnipeg Commodity Exchange

Safflower Oil

Safflower Oil Supply & Distribution in the U.S.   In Million Pounds

Crop Year Begin. Oct. 1	Stocks Oct. 1	Supply Production	Total	Exports	Distribution Domestic Disapp.	Total	Salad & Cooking Oils	Margarine	Shortening	Other Edible	Paint & Varnish	Other Inedible	Loss	Total
1970	19	120	149	20	100	120	12	22	1.2	4	8.3	7.1	.7	49.3
1971	29	140	169	40	90	130	11	19		3				
1972	39	150	189	40	118	158	22	20		2				
1973	31	100	131	25	98	123	29	32		1				
1974	8	115	123	25	75	100	17	16		10				
1975	25	100	125	25	75	100	22	7		—				
1976[1]	44	75	119	15	70	85	22	10		—				
1977[1]	25	119	120	25	74	99		8						
1978[1]	41	126	141	25	85	110		10						
1979[1]	31	139	131	25	75	100		5						
1980[1]		70												
1981[1]		68												

[1] Preliminary.   [2] Data are for calendar year shown.   *Sources: Bureau of Census; Economic Research Service, U.S.D.A.*

T.579

Safflower Oil Wholesale Price Tanks (Non-break), New York   In Cents per Pound

Year	Jan.	Feb.	Mar.	Apr.	May	June	July	Aug.	Sept.	Oct.	Nov.	Dec.	Average
1970	15.6	15.6	16.3	16.5	16.5	16.5	16.5	16.5	16.5	16.5	16.5	16.5	16.3
1971	17.7	18.4	18.4	18.4	18.4	18.4	18.4	18.4	18.4	18.4	18.4	18.4	18.3
1972	18.4	18.4	18.4	18.4	18.4	18.4	18.7	19.6	19.6	19.6	19.6	19.6	18.9
1973	19.6	19.6	19.6	19.6	19.6	19.6	19.6	19.6	19.6	19.6	19.6	19.6	19.6
1974	19.6	19.6	19.6	19.6	19.6	19.6	19.6	19.6	19.6	55.0	55.0	55.0	28.4
1975	65.5	69.0	69.0	69.0	69.0	69.0	69.0	69.0	69.0	52.8	47.0	52.0	64.1
1976	52.0	52.0	52.0	52.0	52.0	52.0	52.0	47.0	41.0	41.0	41.0	41.0	46.2
1977	41.5	41.5	41.5	41.5	41.5	41.5	41.5	41.5	41.5	41.5	41.5	41.5	41.5
1978	41.0	41.0	41.0	41.0	41.0	41.5	41.5	41.5	41.5	41.5	41.5	41.5	41.4
1979	41.0	41.0	41.5	41.5	41.5	41.5	41.5	—	—	—	—	—	41.3
1980	46.5	46.5	46.5	46.5	46.5	46.5	46.5	46.0	46.0	46.0	46.0	46.0	46.3
1981	46.0	46.0	46.0	46.0	46.5	46.5	46.5	46.5	72.5	72.5	72.5	72.5	55.0
1982	72.5	72.5	72.5	72.5	72.5	72.5	72.5	72.5	72.5	72.5	72.5	72.5	72.5
1983													

Source: Economic Research Service, U.S.D.A.

T.580

How to keep your Commodity Year Book statistics up-to-date continuously throughout the year.

To keep up-to-date statistics on the commodities in this book, you should have COMMODITY YEAR BOOK STATISTICAL ABSTRACT SERVICE. This three-times-yearly publication provides the latest available statistics for updating the statistical tables appearing in the COMMODITY YEAR BOOK. The ABSTRACT is published in the Winter (Jan.), Spring (Apr.) and Fall (Oct.). Subscription price is $55 per year.

Commodity Research Bureau, Inc.
75 MONTGOMERY ST., JERSEY CITY, N.J. 07302

Salt

The quantity of salt sold or used by U.S. producers in 1982 decreased slightly compared to 1981, according to preliminary data of the U.S. Bureau of Mines. The chemical industry continued as the largest consumer. But its share of the market declined to about 58 percent in 1982 from 61 percent in 1981. The manufacture of chlorine and caustic soda, which accounts for most of the salt used by the chemical industry, decreased about 15 percent in 1982. The demand for chlorine through its derivatives such as vinyl chloride monomer and polyvinyl chloride, whose major markets are the auto and residential construction industries, was expected to improve in 1983.

Salt used for highway de-icing accounted for approximately 17 percent of the domestic salt demand in 1982. The percentage of salt sold or used by type was salt in brine, 52 percent; rock salt, 34 percent; vacuum and open-pan evaporated salt, 8 percent; and solar evaporated salt, 6 percent.

According to the Bureau of Mines, 1983 domestic mine production of salt is estimated at 41 million tons and U.S. apparent consumption at 42 million tons.

World Production of All Salt   In Thousands of Short Tons

Year	Brazil	Canada	China	France	W. Germany	India	Italy	Japan	Netherlands	Poland	Spain	United Kingdom	United States	USSR	World Total
1973	2,044	5,565	22,000	7,023	11,245	7,566	5,370	1,119	3,355	3,393	2,421	9,390	43,940	13,450	170,483
1974	1,711	6,004	28,000	6,913	12,479	5,812	5,395	1,229	3,734	5,171	2,488	9,282	46,565	13,780	183,236
1975	2,365	5,330	33,000	6,104	10,269	5,353	4,863	1,115	2,965	3,885	3,453	8,410	41,057	15,100	178,207
1976	2,726	6,607	22,046	6,491	12,475	5,070	4,423	1,125	3,336	4,209	3,481	8,825	44,218	15,650	177,105
1977	3,058	6,657	18,850	6,367	13,583	5,877	5,092	1,164	3,429	4,803	3,428	9,041	43,439	15,760	173,107
1978	3,637	7,112	21,528	6,926	13,953	7,385	5,436	1,183	3,240	4,843	3,714	8,058	42,896	15,980	189,105
1979	3,918	7,585	16,281	8,882	16,633	7,755	6,249	1,202	4,355	4,882	3,800	8,619	45,820	15,760	191,345
1980[1]	4,230	7,748	19,048	7,830	14,300	8,006	5,806	1,215	3,818	4,998	3,867	7,888	40,378	16,000	185,788
1981[2]	4,415	8,030	20,200	7,315	13,515	8,004	5,400	1,100	3,860	3,735	3,975	7,505	38,915	16,000	183,106
1982[2]		7,900	20,000	7,300	14,000	8,000	5,700			3,600		7,500	38,700	16,000	182,000

[1] Preliminary.   [2] Estimate.   *Source: Bureau of Mines*   T.581

Salient Statistics of the Salt Industry in the United States   In Thousands of Short Tons

Year	Net Import Reliance as a % of Apparent Consumption	Evaporated (Mfg.) Bulk Open Pans or Grainers	Vacuum Pans	Solar	Pressed Blocks	Total Evaporated	Rock Salt Bulk	Pressed Block	Total Salt Rock	Salt in Brine	Total Salt	Value[3] Million $	Imports for Consumption	Exports Total	To Canada	Apparent Consumption
1972		388	3,287	1,799	376	5,850	14,369	66	14,434	24,737	45,022	296.8	3,463	869	627	47,616
1973		525	2,984	1,924	451	5,884	12,275	72	12,347	25,680	43,910	306.1	3,207	609	561	46,508
1974		540	3,032	1,910	440	5,922	14,753	82	14,835	25,779	46,536	360.8	3,358	521	464	49,373
1975	4	526	2,801	1,583	436	5,345	14,200	84	14,283	21,401	41,030	368.1	3,215	1,332	1,315	42,913
1976	7	536	2,908	1,752	412	5,607	15,592	76	15,668	22,917	44,191	431.0	4,352	1,007	958	47,536
1977	8	—3,481—		1,808	388	5,677	14,893	65	14,958	22,777	43,412	451.6	4,529	1,008	963	46,933
1978	10	—3,463—		2,001	381	5,845	14,630	58	14,688	22,336	42,869	499.3	5,380	776	750	47,473
1979	10	—3,726—		2,104	391	6,221	14,827	64	14,891	24,681	45,793	538.4	5,275	697	681	50,371
1980	7	—3,587—		2,334	393	6,314	11,742	65	11,806	22,231	40,352	656.2	5,263	831	800	44,784
1981[1]	8	—3,500—		2,298	404	6,201	11,809	62	11,871	20,835	38,907	636.3	4,974	1,043	1,011	42,180
1982[2]	8										38,700		4,100	750		42,050

[1] Preliminary.   [2] Estimate.   [3] Values are f.o.b. mine or refinery & do not include cost of cooperage or containers.   *Source: Bureau of Mines*   T.582

Salt Sold or Used by Producers in the U.S. by Classes & Consumers or Uses   In Thousands of Short Tons

Year	Chlorine Caustic Soda, Ash	Flour Processors	Textile & Dyeing	Meat Packers, Tanners, Etc.[2]	Canning	Baking	U.S. Govt.	Feed Dealers	Feed Mixers	Rubber	Oil	Paper & Pulp	Metals	Water Softener Mfg.[3]	Grocery Stores	Flour Proc.	Highway Use
1972	26,517		207	619	228	117		1,386	577	173	202	201	227	698	1,258		9,255
1973	27,374		201	577	238	122	102	1,370	713	166	215	209	228	687	1,292	85	6,079
1974	27,643		205	591	241	118	90	1,512	471	157	242	165	252	835	1,252	85	7,757
1975	23,444	101	180	579	259	125	119	1,310	552	127	261	172	265	586	991	101	7,680
1976	25,008	98	204	578	257	126	74	1,332	593	108	312	213	342	580	998	98	8,930
1977	24,142	95	196	569	255	112	72	1,269	556	125	361	222	351	650	1,043	95	8,678
1978	23,735	91	182	540	254	111	86	1,197	654	96	451	221	346	764	1,057	91	8,487
1979	26,200	95	188	546	280	119	78	1,194	723	99	550	194	356	810	1,140	95	8,742
1980	23,941	92	177	546	287	113	121	1,172	662	95	709	230	272	686	995	92	6,389
1981[1]	21,893	83	220	450	230	109	127	1,144	644	102	837	247	294	703	1,017	83	6,676

[1] Preliminary.   [2] Also casing mfg.   [3] Also service companies.   *Source: Bureau of Mines*   T.583

Sheep and Lambs

The January 1, 1983 U.S. sheep and lambs inventory amounted to 11.9 million head, 8 percent below the 1982 figure. The inventory recorded 1.64 million sheep and lambs on feed in the 24 major feeding states, 5 percent above year-earlier levels. The stock sheep inventory was 10.3 million head, or 10 percent below 1982 and the lowest number since estimates were begun in 1867. The 1982 lamb crop of 8.5 million head was 4 percent below the year-earlier figure, and the lambing rate of ewes 1 year old and older was 97 compared with 101 in 1981 and 97 in 1980.

The commercial slaughter of sheep and lambs during 1982 amounted to 6.4 million head, up 7 percent from 1981. Higher dressed weights pushed 1982 commercial production up 9 percent to a total of 356 million pounds.

The cutback in numbers of sheep and lambs was a direct function of deteriorating producer profit margins since 1979. In 1982, farm prices for lambs averaged $54.52 per cwt., a dollar below the 1981 price. Price for mature sheep averaged $20.19 per cwt., 10 percent under a year earlier. These were the lowest prices recorded since 1977. At the same time, production operations decreased in only 13 of the 41 states for which data was collected by the USDA. An operation, by definition, has one or more sheep on hand during the year. Small sheep herds are kept on many farms to utilize forages on small uncultivated acreages and crops residues which may not be readily marketable.

World Sheep Numbers in Specified Countries   In Millions of Head

Year	India	Argentina	Australia	Brazil	Peru	Iran	New Zealand	Spain[2]	Turkey	United Kingdom	United States	South Africa	Uruguay	USSR	China[4]	World[5]
1970		42.5	180.1	25.7	17.1	32.0	60.3	18.7	36.4	19.2	20.4	34.1	19.8	130.7	70.6	1,040
1971		39.0	177.8	25.0	16.9	32.0	58.9	18.4	36.5	18.5	19.7	31.6	18.5	138.1	71.0	1,038
1972	1972–	40.0	162.9	25.5	12.5	32.0	60.9	17.9	36.8	18.7	18.7	30.2	16.3	139.9	71.3	1,022
1973	76	41.0	140.0	26.0	13.0	34.0	56.7	17.2	38.8	19.6	17.7	33.3	17.0	139.1	71.6	1,009
1974	Avg.	41.0	145.2	26.5	13.5	35.0	55.9	16.3	40.1	20.2	16.4	33.6	15.1	142.6	71.9	1,022
1975	(40.0)	38.5	151.7	25.0	15.3	36.5	55.3	16.3	40.5	20.2	14.5	31.6	14.9	145.3		
1976		35.0	148.6	17.3	15.0	33.5	56.4	15.7	41.4	19.5	13.3	31.8	15.7	141.4		718
1977	40.4	35.2	135.4	17.2	14.5	33.0	59.1	14.5	41.5	19.9	12.8	32.6	16.6	139.8		690
1978	40.7	34.2	131.4	17.2	14.0	33.0	62.2	14.5	42.7	20.5	12.4	32.6	18.9	141.0		695
1979	41.0	32.8	134.2	17.8	14.0	32.5	63.5	13.8	43.9	21.7	12.4	32.5	20.7	142.6		708
1980	41.0	32.0	136.0	18.0	13.5	32.0	68.8	14.2	46.0	21.7	12.4	34.9	23.3	143.6		724
1981[1]	41.5	30.0	134.4	18.0	13.5		71.2	14.7	48.6	21.7	12.9	33.8	24.1	141.6	187.0	726
1982[3]	42.0	30.0	135.4	18.0	13.0		72.0	14.7	50.0	22.1	13.1	34.2	23.4	141.6		730
1983																

[1] Preliminary. [2] One year old & older. [3] Estimate. [4] Mainland. [5] From 1976 to date equals total of selected countries. *Source: Foreign Agricultural Service, U.S.D.A.*

T.584

Salient Statistics of Sheep & Lambs in the United States

Year	On Hand Jan. 1 Mil. Head	Lambs Saved Mil. Head	In Shipments Ths. Head	Marketings[2] Ths. Head	Slaughter Farm Ths. Head	Slaughter Total[4] Ths. Head	Production Mil. Lbs.	Marketings[2] Mil. Lbs.	Value of Production	Cash Receipts[3]	Value of Home Consumption	Gross Income	Farm Value (1/1) All	Farm Value (1/1) $ per Head
1970	20.4	13.5	4,032	14,823	249	10,801	1,099	1,436	260.4	333.7	5.7	339.4	512.7	25.10
1971	19.7	13.0	4,004	14,829	236	10,965	1,071	1,447	250.2	323.0	5.4	328.4	465.4	23.60
1972	18.7	12.6	3,976	14,553	224	10,525	1,004	1,411	271.4	353.8	5.7	359.5	428.9	22.90
1973	17.7	11.5	3,275	13,077	302	9,799	896	1,278	293.7	389.6	6.9	396.5	470.8	26.70
1974	16.4	10.5	2,629	12,060	217	9,064	807	1,178	272.0	368.7	7.9	376.6	534.8	32.80
1975	14.5	9.9	2,349	10,851	212	8,047	785	1,077	303.3	385.8	8.5	394.3	442.5	30.50
1976	13.3	8.9	2,469	9,615	202	6,911	733	970	315.6	393.1	9.2	402.3	496.3	37.30
1977	12.8	8.6	2,148	8,811	198	6,555	706	883	320.3	386.4	9.9	396.2	540.2	42.50
1978	12.3	7.9	2,148	7,968	174	5,543	688	838	381.6	452.9	11.2	464.2	641.5	51.60
1979	12.4	8.0	2,136	7,678	172	5,189	709	812	410.1	474.2	11.7	485.9	891.0	72.10
1980	12.7	8.3	2,216	8,112	165	5,579	744	852	401.5	469.7	11.6	481.3	992.1	78.20
1981	12.9	8.8	1,862	8,597	189	6,007	770	884	358.5	415.7	12.4	428.1	903.3	69.80
1982[1]	13.0	8.5	2,120	9,589	194	6,500	774	1,033	351.2	447.4	13.0	460.3	737.8	56.90
1983[1]	11.9												615.7	51.70
1984														

[1] Preliminary. [2] Excludes interfarm sales. [3] Includes receipts from marketings & from sales of farm slaughter meats. [4] Includes all commercial & farm. *Source: Crop Reporting Board, U.S.D.A.*

T.585

SHEEP AND LAMBS

Sheep and Lambs on Farms in the United States, January 1   In Thousands of Head

Year	Minne-sota	Cali-fornia	Colorado	Idaho	Missouri	Mon-tana	New Mexico	Ohio	South Dakota	Texas	Utah	Wyo-ming	Iowa	Total[2]	Total[1] Stock
1970	554	1,317	1,263	785	288	1,180	834	728	1,155	3,708	1,053	1,853	869	20,423	17,411
1971	504	1,264	1,274	828	251	1,067	742	687	1,201	3,789	1,009	1,829	765	19,731	16,946
1972	467	1,113	1,220	728	230	1,000	714	672	1,181	3,524	976	1,735	735	18,739	15,835
1973	445	1,071	1,204	707	215	955	743	623	1,161	3,214	905	1,678	660	17,641	14,852
1974	415	1,132	1,140	684	224	794	672	582	976	3,090	772	1,505	531	16,310	13,744
1975	390	1,070	990	595	194	770	575	517	792	2,688	697	1,350	460	14,515	12,436
1976	315	1,052	920	536	168	635	590	500	686	2,600	590	1,265	385	13,311	11,427
1977	275	1,113	830	503	134	570	560	445	659	2,520	580	1,206	388	12,766	11,035
1978	255	1,115	810	536	131	530	571	370	704	2,460	491	1,115	370	12,348	10,725
1979	255	1,150	795	466	126	475	604	350	740	2,415	486	1,080	380	12,365	10,786
1980	264	1,175	870	468	123	574	660	320	783	2,400	625	1,050	408	12,687	11,065
1981	295	1,205	810	512	138	595	650	310	780	2,360	650	1,110	437	12,936	11,287
1982	335	1,210	710	498	133	616	615	313	750	2,400	636	1,130	485	12,966	11,402
1983[3]	300	1,115	750	429	116	560	610	275	680	2,225	565	1,060	457	11,904	10,263
1984															

[1] Stock sheep & lambs; does not include sheep & lambs on feed for market.   [2] Includes sheep & lambs on feed for market and stock sheep & lambs.   [3] Preliminary.   Source: Crop Reporting Board, U.S.D.A.   T.586

Average Wholesale Price of Lambs at Omaha   In Dollars Per 100 Pounds

Year	Jan.	Feb.	Mar.	Apr.	May	June	July	Aug.	Sept.	Oct.	Nov.	Dec.	Average
1970	28.88	28.75	28.75	26.00	29.00	29.50	28.38	27.12	26.75	26.75	25.38	23.88	27.43
1971	24.00	25.12	26.88	30.25	31.12	31.25	28.88	27.75	27.50	25.88	24.75	25.75	27.43
1972	27.88	28.38	29.38	31.00	33.75	34.00	32.88	31.25	30.00	26.75	27.00	29.25	30.13
1973	33.62	39.25	40.75	34.25	36.25	38.00	39.25	41.50	33.38	31.75	34.75	37.50	36.69
1974	38.38	40.00	37.50	39.50	47.25	46.25	41.25	39.00	36.12	35.88	37.50	38.50	39.76
1975	37.50	40.50	43.00	47.88	50.75	46.12	45.00	41.00	44.12	44.00	45.00	48.13	44.42
1976	49.33	47.75	53.50	60.75	63.88	50.50	45.75	38.88	40.00	39.75	39.00	45.00	47.84
1977	49.00	50.25	51.50	56.75	56.25	53.00	50.75	51.87	55.75	56.88	50.00	58.50	53.38
1978	64.00	68.00	69.38	64.80	71.00	59.50	60.00	59.25	62.50	60.00	59.50	64.00	63.49
1979[1]	73.75	71.25	61.25	70.50	70.75	65.00	61.52	60.62	67.01	65.91	65.00	67.75	66.58
1980[1]	66.00	63.00	61.38	59.50	62.75	64.00	67.50	68.25	65.75	62.00	55.67	53.13	59.81
1981[1]	46.50	54.50	55.25	59.25	65.00	66.25	59.00	53.75	50.25	51.00	45.27	45.10	52.23
1982[1]	49.75	51.50	59.00	59.50	66.25	60.50	57.25	50.50	50.00	48.25	46.75	48.50	53.98
1983[1]	53.50	58.50											

[1] Preliminary.   Source: Economic Research Service, U.S.D.A.   T.587

Federally Inspected Slaughter of Sheep & Lambs in the United States   In Thousands of Head

Year	Jan.	Feb.	Mar.	Apr.	May	June	July	Aug.	Sept.	Oct.	Nov.	Dec.	Total
1970	855	742	859	903	795	841	829	789	897	917	735	847	10,009
1971	903	806	920	899	772	827	815	812	919	919	818	846	10,256
1972	847	801	903	786	803	807	737	840	866	937	828	751	9,905
1973	835	700	710	690	858	727	807	844	789	915	747	612	9,234
1974	749	612	772	782	670	581	713	777	842	851	612	595	8,556
1975	663	570	648	627	616	614	635	621	758	701	515	584	7,552
1976	582	513	570	561	429	502	525	563	622	556	517	534	6,474
1977	498	461	579	539	474	550	468	553	568	525	477	441	6,133
1978	425	390	487	430	451	441	406	438	435	457	413	396	5,169
1979	391	354	431	425	421	371	384	415	410	455	386	389	4,833
1980	448	419	470	466	454	400	420	427	466	510	415	468	5,363
1981	489	426	489	512	425	440	439	467	546	558	476	522	5,789
1982	510	490	570	——1,493——			——1,577——			——1,634——			6,273
1983	509	457											

Source: Economic Research Service, U.S.D.A.   T.588

SHEEP AND LAMBS

Cold Storage Holdings of Lamb and Mutton, on 1st of Month   In Thousands of Pounds

Year	Jan.	Feb.	Mar.	Apr.	May	June	July	Aug.	Sept.	Oct.	Nov.	Dec.
1970	16,134	17,074	18,064	21,794	20,919	18,808	20,032	23,093	22,834	20,738	21,028	19,653
1971	19,336	20,526	19,653	20,403	20,221	22,506	22,848	21,292	19,391	20,719	20,059	18,626
1972	19,260	16,355	12,836	12,238	15,205	19,916	19,277	21,272	21,220	19,171	18,226	17,200
1973	15,704	14,258	11,847	10,920	13,210	15,644	16,004	14,451	12,739	13,083	15,517	14,691
1974	15,034	12,465	13,018	13,749	14,149	16,820	15,909	15,977	15,333	14,198	14,894	14,169
1975	13,690	12,154	11,221	9,254	9,963	8,819	7,388	9,089	10,107	10,749	10,765	11,543
1976	11,785	10,808	11,123	9,244	9,626	10,935	12,261	14,461	15,152	16,958	15,678	16,552
1977	14,535	14,131	13,884	11,813	12,771	14,583	14,381	13,848	13,567	11,630	10,097	9,356
1978	10,096	9,261	8,628	7,947	9,176	10,149	10,011	11,891	11,259	11,323	12,200	11,804
1979	11,716	10,965	10,827	12,022	12,072	12,897	11,483	11,943	11,763	10,951	11,697	11,071
1980	10,751	10,302	9,464	7,945	8,475	8,995	10,229	10,263	8,880	8,336	8,165	9,779
1981[1]	9,142	8,997	7,843	7,823	10,196	10,403	12,297	12,564	13,694	13,311	12,676	11,362
1982[1]	10,540	9,569	8,449	8,783	—	—	8,266	—	—	8,571	—	—
1983[1]	8,653	7,682	7,673	8,205								
1984												

[1] Preliminary.   Source: Crop Reporting Board, U.S.D.A.   T.589

Average Price Received by Farmers for Sheep in the U.S.   In Dollars per 100 Pounds

Year	Jan.	Feb.	Mar.	Apr.	May	June	July	Aug.	Sept.	Oct.	Nov.	Dec.	Average[1]
1970	7.95	8.22	8.45	8.11	8.07	8.04	7.99	7.43	7.16	7.09	6.97	6.67	7.68
1971	6.90	7.03	7.34	7.08	6.87	6.50	6.23	6.78	6.39	6.05	6.13	6.22	6.63
1972	6.17	6.69	7.12	6.74	7.08	6.92	7.08	7.32	7.33	7.31	7.78	8.35	7.16
1973	9.36	10.80	12.10	12.10	11.40	12.00	12.40	15.70	13.50	13.30	13.00	14.20	12.50
1974	14.70	15.80	15.10	13.60	12.20	10.60	10.50	10.90	9.80	8.20	8.10	8.90	11.50
1975	9.85	10.30	10.60	11.70	11.60	11.30	11.80	10.80	11.30	10.80	10.80	11.80	11.10
1976	12.60	12.80	13.90	15.30	14.70	12.80	13.40	12.90	12.90	11.90	11.50	13.00	13.10
1977	13.80	13.90	15.40	14.40	13.00	12.00	12.30	12.40	13.40	13.20	14.10	14.60	13.50
1978	16.50	18.40	19.70	19.50	19.20	19.30	19.40	20.80	24.40	24.90	24.70	25.50	21.80
1979	26.20	26.30	28.10	31.00	27.90	24.00	25.10	24.30	26.50	27.20	26.30	25.00	26.30
1980	27.40	30.50	26.90	21.90	21.70	20.30	17.80	19.40	21.40	18.90	19.90	20.80	21.10
1981	27.40	29.00	26.10	23.40	19.50	20.30	23.00	20.40	20.30	19.70	19.10	19.20	21.20
1982[2]	25.10	21.30	27.20	22.20	21.00	22.00	21.00	18.60	16.50	15.20	15.30	16.80	19.50
1983[2]	21.30	21.90	20.80	20.00									
1984													

[1] Weighted average by quantities sold.   [2] Preliminary.   Source: Crop Reporting Board, U.S.D.A.   T.590

Average Price Received by Farmers for Lambs in the U.S.   In Dollars per 100 Pounds

Year	Jan.	Feb.	Mar.	Apr.	May	June	July	Aug.	Sept.	Oct.	Nov.	Dec.	Average[1]
1970	28.10	27.90	27.50	26.30	26.80	27.20	27.00	26.70	26.20	26.10	25.20	23.40	26.50
1971	23.10	23.90	25.50	26.70	27.10	28.10	27.10	27.40	25.90	25.40	25.20	25.40	25.90
1972	26.90	28.20	28.70	28.60	30.40	30.70	31.40	30.20	29.10	28.20	27.60	28.70	29.10
1973	32.60	35.30	39.20	35.10	33.60	36.20	35.40	41.80	33.10	32.50	33.80	35.40	35.30
1974	39.30	39.20	36.00	37.40	41.20	42.70	37.90	37.50	33.20	33.20	35.20	36.10	37.40
1975	36.80	37.90	39.80	43.00	45.70	44.80	43.10	39.90	40.50	42.60	44.20	46.30	42.10
1976	47.90	47.20	50.20	54.90	60.10	51.10	46.80	41.50	41.80	42.60	41.90	44.70	47.60
1977	48.30	49.60	49.10	50.80	55.00	50.90	50.60	49.10	51.30	52.60	52.40	56.90	51.30
1978	60.70	63.20	67.10	63.90	66.50	61.80	58.80	58.50	63.70	62.50	61.40	65.70	62.80
1979	74.10	69.90	64.90	70.40	69.70	66.40	64.00	61.40	66.70	65.70	64.90	66.90	66.70
1980	66.40	64.40	67.10	59.20	60.30	64.60	65.30	65.80	66.70	64.30	59.90	58.40	63.60
1981	54.10	55.40	56.50	58.80	63.10	65.00	59.50	56.20	50.40	50.60	47.40	47.50	54.90
1982[2]	50.40	53.30	60.30	61.50	63.50	57.80	56.30	52.90	50.90	49.10	47.70	50.90	53.10
1983[3]	55.50	60.30	63.20	60.50									
1984													

[1] Weighted average by quantities sold.   [2] Preliminary.   Source: Crop Reporting Board, U.S.D.A.   T.591

Silk

Salient Statistics of Silk in the United States

Year	World Production (Raw) Million Lbs.	Total Imports	Brazil	United Kingdom	Hong Kong	India	Italy	Japan	Switzerland	China	Korea	U.S. Silk Imports² Raw —Mil. Lbs.—	Waste	Total Mil. Pounds	Per Capita Pounds
						Thousands of Pounds									
1970	90	1,846	141	2	—	—	911	416	—	—	355	.8	.9	1.8	.10
1971	90	1,702	38	—	—	—	345	1,154	—	—	74	.3	1.4	1.7	.10
1972	93	2,139	76	—	—	—	227	1,339	—	—	106	.6	1.6	2.1	—
1973	95	3,342	79	13	—	—	472	2,197	—	—	15	.6	2.8	3.3	—
1974	99	2,593	145	0	—	—	397	1,476	—	—	107	.4	2.2	2.6	—
1975	104	968	176	1	—	—	0	386	—	353	0	.6	.4	1.0	—
1976	106	2,653	247	1	—	—	98	1,727	—	457	—	.7	1.9	2.8	—
1977	108	1,621	106	0	—	—	0	1,230	—	268	0	.4	1.2	1.6	—
1978	112	1,989	182	0	—	107	1	918	—	607	119	.7	1.3	2.0	—
1979	121	1,565	193	—	—	—	—	602	—	747	—	.8	.8	1.5	—
1980	123	1,053	139	—	5	—	—	108	—	713	71	.5	.6	1.5	—
1981[3]	126	1,983	176	—	29	—	223	175	—	1,280	0	.8	1.2	2.0	—
1982[4]														2.0	

[1] In skeins, wild or tussah, cocoons, and waste. [2] Imports for consumption. [3] Preliminary. [4] Estimate. *Sources: Department of Commerce; Textile Organon*

T.592

Raw Silk Deliveries in the U.S. In Bales (132 Lbs.—60 Kilos)

Year	Jan.	Feb.	Mar.	Apr.	May	June	July	Aug.	Sept.	Oct.	Nov.	Dec.	Total
1970	1,209	882	1,046	931	730	406	458	344	390	310	232	141	7,079
1971	247	205	187	277	228	129	192	241	247	355	165	253	2,726
1972	233	184	308	198	141	195	182	445	529	209	229	313	3,166
1973[1]	556	355	450	499	393	119	577	214	71	93	105	246	3,678
1974	124	305	233	277	175	288	269	139	97	302	151	96	2,456
1975	190	188	410	393	394	219	380	219	505	585	225	641	4,349
1976	925	469	689	362	251	579	337	358	422	268	222	159	5,041
1977	352	239	242	212	254	259	322	311	370	424	322	433	3,740
1978	321	394	424	382	397	299	316	341	401	280	468	214	4,237
1979	501	302	687	353	471	418	407	756	492	490	368	518	5,763
1980	312	644	422	507	366	285	257	332	342	365	265	323	4,420
1981	471	380	471	446	322	529	300	259	348	414	487	611	5,038
1982	450	489	662	398	234	369	495	403	364	226	514	317	4,921
1983													

[1] Includes re-exports from 1973. *Source: International Silk Association*

T.593

How to keep your Commodity Year Book statistics up-to-date continuously throughout the year.

To keep up-to-date statistics on the commodities in this book, you should have COMMODITY YEAR BOOK STATISTICAL ABSTRACT SERVICE. This three-times-yearly publication provides the latest available statistics for updating the statistical tables appearing in the COMMODITY YEAR BOOK. The ABSTRACT is published in the Winter (Jan.), Spring (Apr.) and Fall (Oct.). Subscription price is $55 per year.

Commodity Research Bureau, Inc.
75 MONTGOMERY ST., JERSEY CITY, N.J. 07302

Silver

World mine production of silver in 1982 was slightly below 1981 output, according to preliminary data of the U.S. Bureau of Mines. U.S. mine production of recoverable silver in 1982 was 14 percent below the 1981 level, due in part to low silver prices early in the year which forced extended shutdowns at a number of mines, and to lower production of by-product silver from copper mining.

U.S. refinery production of silver in 1982 totaled 108.96 million troy ounces, 17 percent lower than production in 1981, according to preliminary Bureau of Mines data. Refinery production from domestic and foreign concentrates and ores (mostly domestic) totaled 44.15 million ounces, off 6 percent. Output from old scrap dropped 30 percent, to 27.16 million ounces and production from new scrap declined 16 percent, to 37.65 million ounces.

Imports of silver into the U.S. for consumption, mostly bullion, increased 25 percent, to 117.46 million troy ounces. Canada accounted for the largest share of U.S. imports (32 percent), followed by Mexico (22 percent), Peru (15 percent), and the United Kingdom (11 percent). U.S. exports of silver in 1982 declined 9 percent. Canada, the United Kingdom and Japan accounted for most of the exports.

Net U.S. industrial consumption of silver in 1982 increased 4 percent to 121.67 million ounces. Preliminary Bureau of Mines data indicated that consumption of photographic materials increased slightly from the 1981 level and accounted for 43 percent of net industrial consumption. The use of silver in contacts and conductors increased nearly 10 percent, to 28.93 million ounces, representing 24 percent of consumption. Other end-use categories approximated the following percentages of net industrial consumption: brazing alloys and solder, 6.5 percent; jewelry, 5.8 percent; sterling ware, 5.4 percent; batteries, 3.7 percent; miscellaneous—including silver-bearing copper, silver-bearing lead anodes, ceramic paints, etc.—3.7 percent; catalysts, 1.9 percent; dental and medical supplies, 1.4 percent; electroplated ware, 2.8 percent; and coins, medallions and commemorative objects, 1.3 percent. In addition, coinage used 1.85 million ounces of silver in 1982 versus only 0.18 million ounces in 1981.

Industry stocks of silver (held by refiners, fabricators, and dealers) on December 31, 1982 totaled about 20.73 million ounces, slightly above holdings of 20.69 million a year earlier. Commodity Exchange, Inc. licensed warehouse stocks of silver were 90.66 million ounces at the end of 1982 versus 77.64 million at the end of 1981, and Chicago Board of Trade licensed warehouse stocks were 15.52 million ounces, down from 18.88 million a year ago. The U.S. strategic stockpile held 137.5 million ounces of silver, of which 103.1 million were authorized for disposal as of November 30, 1982.

Public Law 97-114, the Defense Appropriations Act of 1982, halted sales of silver from the National Defense Stockpile authorized by Public Law 97-35 until a new study could be performed to determine the amount of silver needed for defense purposes and the best method of disposing of any excess. Silver sales remained suspended throughout 1982 into the second quarter of 1983.

The Bureau of Mines estimated 1983 U.S. mine production of silver at 38 million ounces and U.S. apparent consumption at 144 million ounces. Demand for silver is expected to increase at an annual rate of about 2.9 percent through 1990 from a 1978 base.

U.S. (N.Y.) silver prices, as quoted by Handy & Harman, trended lower in the first half of 1982, from around $8.32 per troy ounce on January 6 to a 1982 low of $4.88 on June 21. Subsequently, prices increased, reaching a 1982 high of $11.21 on December 29. The average daily price in 1982 declined to $8.00 per ounce from $10.52 in 1981.

Futures Markets

Silver futures are traded on the Commodity Exchange, Inc. in New York, and the Chicago Board of Trade and MidAmerica Commodity Exchange, both in Chicago. Trading in silver futures is also conducted on the London Metal Exchange and on the Winnipeg Commodity Exchange.

World Production of Silver, by Selected Countries   In Millions of Fine Ounces (Troy Ounces)

Year	Poland	Argentina	Australia	Zaire (Congo)	Bolivia[1]	Canada	Morocco	W. Germany	Honduras	USSR[2]	Japan	Mexico	Peru	United States	Yugoslavia	World Total[2]
1971		3.18	21.70	1.47	5.37	46.02	2.94	1.80	3.64	39.0	11.29	36.66	38.40	41.56	3.35	294.7
1972		3.27	21.89	2.08	5.58	44.79	3.38	1.74	3.60	40.0	10.05	37.48	40.19	37.23	3.58	301.5
1973		2.44	22.42	2.00	5.80	47.49	3.38	1.45	3.15	41.0	8.55	38.79	42.02	37.83	4.30	307.9
1974	5.8	3.10	21.54	1.65	5.39	42.81	3.06	1.24	3.66	42.0	7.31	37.55	34.89	33.76	4.70	292.2
1975	13.2	2.28	23.35	2.29	5.47	39.70	3.04	1.08	3.80	43.0	8.73	38.03	37.53	34.94	5.41	303.0
1976	17.8	2.25	25.03	2.47	5.34	41.20	2.05	1.03	3.18	44.0	9.30	42.64	35.58	34.33	4.63	316.4
1977[1]	20.7	2.45	27.53	2.73	5.81	42.24	2.82	1.06	2.82	45.0	9.60	47.03	39.73	38.17	4.68	331.3
1978	21.9	2.16	26.12	4.39	6.29	40.73	3.13	.80	2.79	46.0	9.66	50.78	37.02	39.39	5.13	345.4
1979	22.6	2.21	26.76	3.89	5.74	36.87	3.28	1.04	2.43	46.0	8.68	49.41	39.25	37.90	5.21	344.6
1980	24.7	2.31	25.38	2.73	6.10	33.34	3.15	1.04	1.77	46.0	8.93	47.34	42.99	32.33	4.79	339.8
1981[3]	22.7	2.30	25.00	2.10	6.60	38.7	2.50	1.04	2.40	46.5	8.98	53.20	46.94	40.69	4.44	366.1
1982[2]						41						55	48	36		364

[1] Exports.   [2] Estimate.   [3] Preliminary.   *Source: Bureau of Mines*

SILVER

Average Price of Silver in New York In Cents per Troy Ounce (.999 Fine)

Year	Jan.	Feb.	Mar.	Apr.	May	June	July	Aug.	Sept.	Oct.	Nov.	Dec.	Average
1970	187.7	189.6	188.9	185.3	167.0	163.9	168.7	179.8	180.2	174.6	176.0	163.5	177.1
1971	164.0	160.0	166.9	172.6	166.7	160.8	158.1	158.7	142.1	133.6	132.0	139.4	154.6
1972	147.3	150.4	153.6	157.2	158.3	156.9	173.6	184.6	177.7	181.1	183.3	197.6	168.5
1973	201.7	223.6	230.9	220.7	240.1	262.1	270.6	263.7	267.5	288.6	286.0	313.7	256.0
1974	363.7	535.9	532.6	503.6	543.2	489.6	441.6	443.1	404.9	483.0	469.4	439.1	470.8
1975	419.3	437.0	434.5	420.9	453.8	448.9	470.5	492.5	451.6	432.9	433.2	408.5	442.0
1976	406.3	408.6	418.9	435.1	448.9	481.2	478.0	423.7	429.5	422.5	437.3	434.7	435.4
1977	440.9	452.7	484.2	477.7	469.2	444.3	449.8	444.4	453.9	476.3	482.8	470.6	462.3
1978	493.4	493.6	526.8	511.6	512.0	531.6	533.1	549.5	557.5	591.8	586.5	593.0	540.0
1979	625.5	741.7	745.4	749.3	836.6	853.8	913.5	933.4	1,395.9	1,678.1	1,655.3	2,179.3	1,109.0
1980	3,827.2	3,508.5	2,413.3	1,384.1	1,253.3	1,574.8	1,606.0	1,589.7	2,014.4	2,018.1	1,864.8	1,639.3	2,063.3
1981	1,475.2	1,306.5	1,236.9	1,091.7	1,084.8	1,000.1	863.1	892.3	1,003.6	925.1	854.7	843.2	1,048.1
1982	803.1	826.8	721.3	731.1	667.4	557.8	649.7	713.6	872.5	946.8	991.8	1,058.6	795.0
1983	1,239.6	1,396.4	1,061.9	1,169.4									

Source: Handy & Harman

T.595

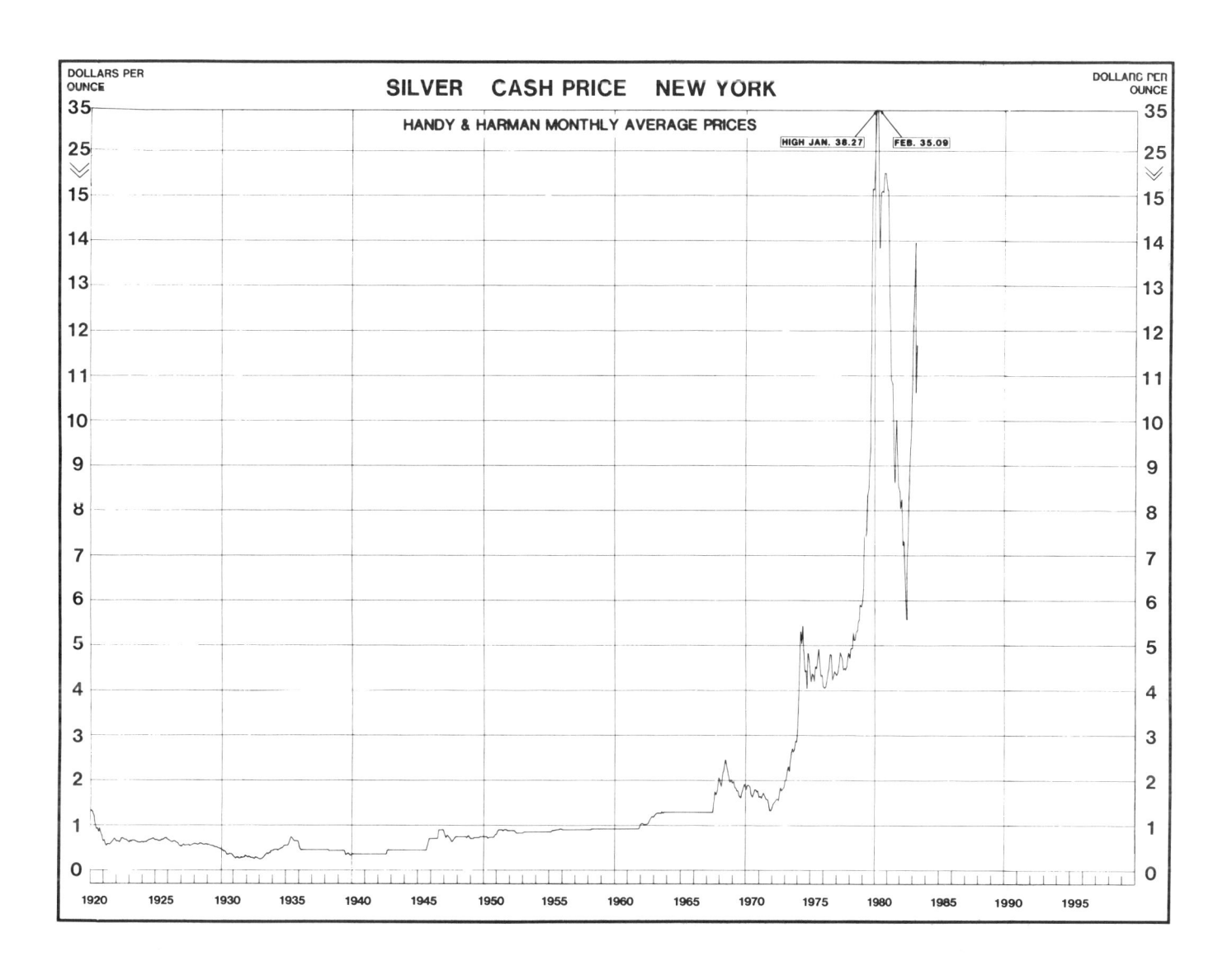

SILVER

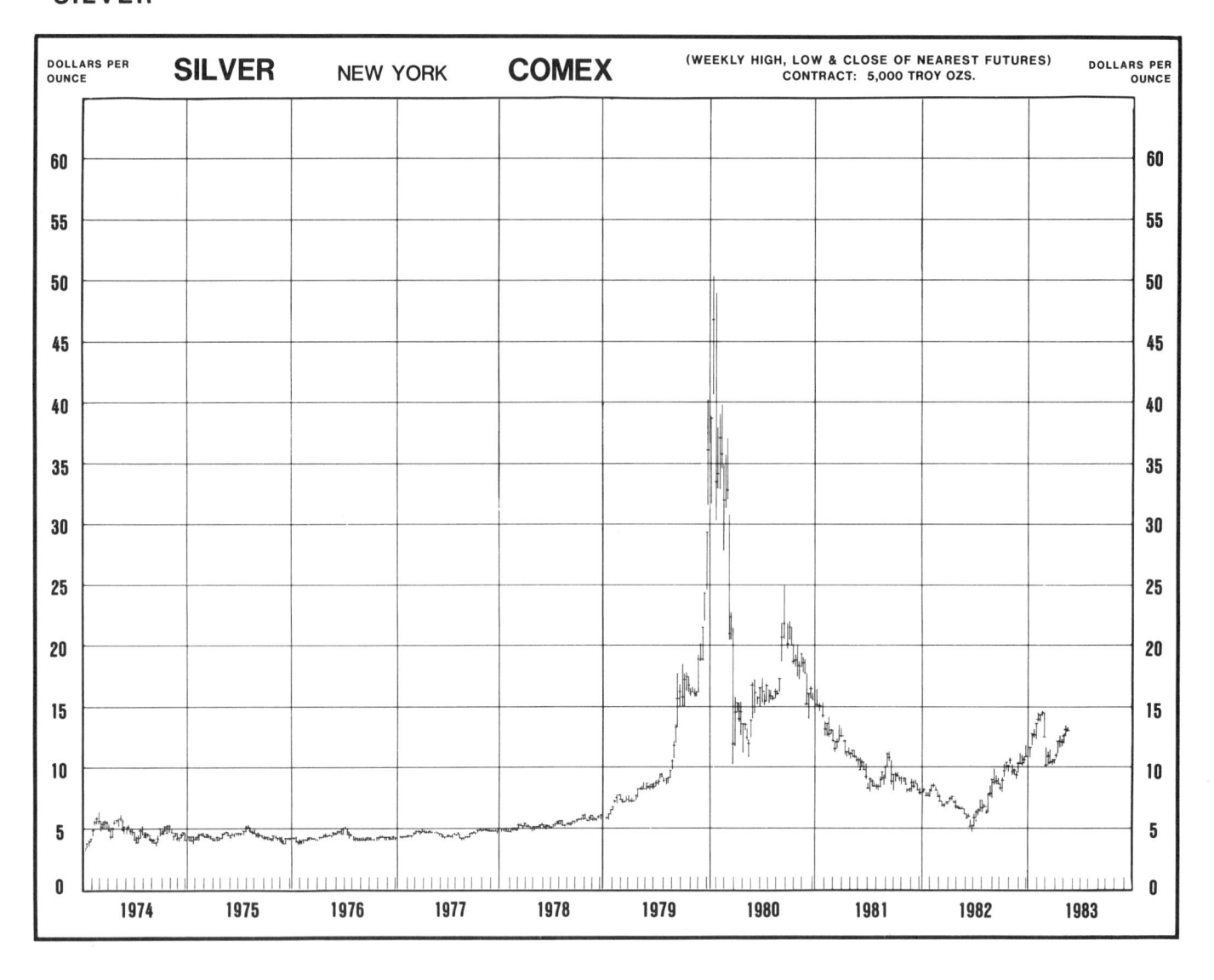

SILVER NEW YORK **COMEX** (WEEKLY HIGH, LOW & CLOSE OF NEAREST FUTURES) CONTRACT: 5,000 TROY OZS.

Highest and Lowest Prices of December Silver Futures at New York (Comex)   In Dollars per Ounce

Year of Delivery		Yr. Prior to Delivery Oct.	Nov.	Dec.	Jan.	Feb.	Mar.	Apr.	May	Delivery Year June	July	Aug.	Sept.	Oct.	Nov.	Dec.	Life of Delivery Range
1978	High	5.292	5.377	5.166	5.425	5.43	5.877	5.752	5.668	5.718	5.823	5.863	5.795	6.40	6.11	6.02	6.400
	Low	5.022	5.01	4.95	5.16	5.135	5.25	5.10	5.174	5.392	5.325	5.43	5.506	5.71	5.645	5.80	4.715
	Close	5.251	5.134	5.143	5.33	5.29	5.775	5.219	5.621	5.40	5.817	5.597	5.715	6.215	6.00	5.986	—
1979	High	6.94	6.558	6.538	7.16	8.405	8.23	8.363	9.36	9.235	9.975	10.935	16.90	18.13	19.40	25.75	25.750
	Low	6.296	6.205	6.26	6.36	6.99	7.453	7.625	8.31	8.64	8.842	8.985	11.15	15.91	15.85	18.65	5.585
	Close	6.758	6.465	6.514	7.089	8.14	7.839	8.363	9.091	8.96	9.293	10.86	16.80	16.79	18.82	25.50	—
1980	High	19.55	20.528	30.91	44.37	42.15	39.78	20.27	14.75	20.20	20.09	17.14	24.18	22.28	20.32	19.02	44.370
	Low	16.79	17.54	20.705	31.91	35.20	21.27	13.86	11.45	16.975	17.57	15.90	16.67	18.54	17.58	13.37	7.564
	Close	18.395	20.528	30.91	37.645	38.64	21.27	13.86	14.53	19.24	17.84	16.84	21.25	19.10	18.59	16.61	—
1981	High	26.00	23.525	22.615	18.80	15.90	14.67	13.58	12.70	11.84	9.78	10.26	11.80	10.05	9.41	9.05	43.750
	Low	22.12	20.875	17.19	14.60	13.75	12.80	11.90	11.21	9.08	8.77	8.73	8.49	9.00	7.87	7.98	7.970
	Close	22.54	22.015	18.19	15.165	13.72	13.135	12.205	11.685	9.18	9.032	9.72	9.38	9.25	8.205	7.985	—
1982	High	11.45	10.70	10.15	9.49	9.86	8.82	8.39	7.54	6.68	7.72	8.66	9.975	10.07	11.01	11.18	17.975
	Low	10.509	9.11	9.04	8.73	8.65	7.60	7.35	6.67	5.11	5.80	6.32	7.70	8.02	8.95	10.02	5.11
	Close	10.68	9.28	9.185	9.182	8.622	7.87	7.47	6.675	6.406	6.965	8.04	8.24	10.09	10.09	11.14	—
1983	High	11.55	11.90	12.35	15.238	16.07	12.18	13.38									
	ow	9.00	9.90	11.07	11.84	12.666	10.71	11.44									
	Close	10.94	11.09	11.91	15.238	12.666	11.382	12.715									

Source: Commodity Exchange Inc., of N.Y. (COMEX)

T.596

306

SILVER

World[2] Silver Consumption   In Millions of Troy Ounces

				Industrial Uses								Coinage					
Year	Canada	France	W. Germany	India	Italy	Japan	Un. Kingdom	United States	World Total	Canada	France	W. Germany	Austria	Mexico	United States	World Total	World Total
1970	6.0	15.5	48.2	16.0	32.0	46.0	25.0	128.4	338.9	—	3.7	7.3	4.1		.7	26.9	365.8
1971	6.0	15.6	59.9	16.0	30.5	46.5	25.0	129.1	351.4	.2	.4	19.2	3.2		2.5	28.3	379.7
1972	7.4	16.5	60.0	13.0	32.0	54.3	27.0	151.7	388.9	.1	.3	22.6	5.8		2.3	38.4	427.3
1973	8.6	14.3	64.7	13.0	41.5	69.0	31.0	195.9	477.8	1.4	.1	9.5	6.6		.9	29.2	507.0
1974	9.6	15.5	59.9	15.0	38.6	46.5	25.0	177.0	409.4	8.9	.1	8.8	5.6		1.0	27.9	436.9
1975	10.6	21.2	38.9	13.0	28.9	46.4	28.0	157.7	376.8	10.4	5.2	4.3	13.4	—	2.7	38.8	415.6
1976	9.5	19.0	50.8	18.0	32.1	60.7	28.0	170.5	437.5	8.4	6.7	2.9	6.9	—	1.3	29.7	467.2
1977	8.8	20.6	59.5	17.6	33.8	63.2	32.2	153.6	433.6	.3	6.9	2.6	3.0	4.2	.4	23.4	457.0
1978	9.0	22.2	47.2	20.0	41.8	64.8	29.0	160.2	442.6	.3	11.1	3.6	4.5	6.3	.1	36.3	478.9
1979	8.1	21.5	37.1	19.0	33.0	68.7	26.5	157.2	419.8	.3	7.7	3.7	5.0	5.0	.1	27.8	447.6
1980	8.7	20.2	29.1	19.0	24.5	61.7	20.5	124.7	349.9	.2	—	—	4.3	6.1	.1	13.7	363.6
1981	8.5	20.6	28.0	19.0	24.7	59.8	18.5	116.6	344.1	.2	—	—	3.0	—	—	9.0	353.1
1982[1]	9.0	18.6	33.6	22.5	23.0	60.1	20.0	122.3	357.2	.3	—	—	4.0	—	1.5	11.8	369.0
1983																	

[1] Preliminary.   [2] Non-communist areas only.   Source: Handy & Harman   T.597

U.S. Consumption of Silver, by End Use   In Thousands of Troy Ounces

						Electrical & Electronic Products							Total Net		
Year	Bearings	Brazing Alloys & Solders	Catalysts	Dental & Medical	Electroplated Ware	Batteries	Contacts & Conductors	Jewelry	Mirrors	Photographic Materials	Sterling Ware	Coins, Medallions[2]	Industrial Consumption	Coinage	Total Consumption
1970	383	14,035	1,999	1,804	11,437	6,342	25,183	5,119	1,386	38,044	19,115	3,556	128,404	709	129,113
1971	355	12,085	1,730	1,485	10,909	5,631	27,954	3,447	1,112	36,073	22,729	5,636	129,146	2,474	131,620
1972	344	12,214	3,430	1,991	12,716	6,044	36,434	4,870	1,225	38,251	27,163	6,381	151,063	2,284	153,347
1973	375	17,736	5,988	3,022	14,542	4,155	40,209	5,778	2,579	51,979	40,100	9,477	195,941	920	196,861
1974	416	14,514	7,293	2,401	13,179	4,195	31,218	5,235	3,947	49,579	22,147	22,272	177,015	1,017	178,031
1975	458	13,582	8,785	1,503	8,717	4,253	27,211	12,734	3,150	46,074	23,717	7,186	157,650	2,740	160,390
1976	273	11,198	12,267	1,942	9,534	3,490	32,329	10,995	4,622	55,350	19,815	8,240	170,559	1,315	171,874
1977	523	12,362	8,883	2,232	6,844	5,783	31,316	8,059	2,131	53,679	16,690	4,252	153,613	91	153,704
1978	373	10,987	8,197	2,033	7,274	6,029	30,756	6,766	1,862	64,299	17,908	2,727	160,165	45	160,210
1979	332	10,912	5,637	2,295	8,065	4,583	33,506	5,358	1,850	65,978	13,088	4,676	157,258	168	157,426
1980	649	8,508	3,035	2,212	4,350	5,976	27,796	5,893	672	49,825	9,082	4,693	124,694	72	124,766
1981[1]	248	7,718	3,830	1,709	3,904	3,803	26,411	5,368	581	51,025	4,407	2,622	116,621	179	116,800
1982[3]	228	7,884	2,416	1,716	3,444	4,488	28,932	7,064	968	51,764	6,654	1,547	121,671	1,846	123,517
1983															

[1] Preliminary.   [2] Includes commemorative objects.   [3] Estimate.   Source: Bureau of Mines   T.598

U.S. Mine Production of Recoverable Silver   In Thousands of Troy Ounces

Year	Arizona	California	Colorado	Idaho	Michigan	Missouri	Montana	Nevada	New Mexico	New York	Tennessee	So. Dakota	Utah	Other States	Total
1970	7,330	451	2,933	19,115	892	1,817	4,304	718	782	24	95	120	6,030	393	45,006
1971	6,170	444	3,390	19,140	670	1,661	2,748	601	782	18	131	107	5,294		41,564
1972	6,653	176	3,664	14,251	785	1,972	3,325	595	1,017	25	83	100	4,300		37,233
1973	7,199	56	3,942	13,620	850	2,058	4,350	624	1,111	54	73	72	3,619	197	37,827
1974	6,356	42	2,784	12,436	643	2,387	3,512	872	1,195	64	20	62	3,208	171	33,762
1975	6,286	80	3,366	13,868	632	2,525	2,617	1,600	702	56	54	68	2,822	104	34,938
1976	7,015	57	4,083	11,501	311	2,277	3,279	784	892	49	78	58	3,134	146	34,328
1977	6,828	58	4,663	15,292	335	2,363	3,367	738	918	56	60	69	3,283	125	38,166
1978	6,638	58	4,217	18,379	N.A.	2,056	2,918	804	895	21	N.A.	53	2,885	457	39,385
1979	7,479	64	2,809	17,144	N.A.	2,201	3,302	560	N.A.	11	N.A.	58	2,454	1,812	37,896
1980	6,268	49	2,987	13,695	N.A.	2,357	2,024	940	N.A.	21	N.A.	51	2,203	1,725	32,329
1981[1]	8,055	53	3,009	16,547	N.A.	1,837	2,989	3,039	1,632	29	N.A.	56	2,883	480	40,685
1982[2]	6,162	N.A.	2,012	14,746	N.A.	2,213	6,134	242	N.A.	N.A.	N.A.	26	2,352	1,255	35,142
1983															

[1] Preliminary.   [2] Forecast.   Source: Bureau of Mines   T.599

SILVER

Month-End Total Open Interest of Silver Futures at New York (COMEX) & Chicago In Thousands of Contracts

Year	Jan. 1	Feb. 1	Mar. 1	Apr. 1	May 1	June 1	July 1	Aug. 1	Sept. 1	Oct. 1	Nov. 1	Dec. 1	Jan. 1	Apr. 1	July 1	Oct. 1
				At New York (COMEX)										At Chicago (1,000 oz.[1])		
1975	123.9	95.2	84.5	88.4	74.7	85.6	84.6	88.9	118.1	140.5	176.5	214.5	118.1	62.2	99.6	124.2
1976	250.3	197.6	176.4	176.7	169.0	168.1	138.4	130.7	138.1	155.7	208.6	287.2	169.8	88.4	121.6	127.5
1977	398.1	338.0	309.5	282.2	234.6	205.8	156.1	130.1	135.6	181.7	211.3	241.7	186.0	156.8	183.5	211.6
1978	287.8	245.4	242.4	226.0	217.8	208.6	196.2	212.6	214.4	239.1	277.5	304.8	275.9	240.2	230.0	235.4
1979	299.5	242.9	218.7	203.5	185.7	170.0	153.3	154.5	156.2	167.3	144.3	133.4	252.8	180.5	166.6	156.7
1980	123.6	77.7	63.4	48.5	27.1	23.8	22.9	25.1	24.5	29.8	35.0	36.0	88.9	23.6	22.9	24.0
1981	32.0	27.6	24.3	25.7	26.1	28.8	29.4	31.0	31.0	29.9	32.3	27.5	28.0	21.2	29.8	16.3
1982	27.6	27.5	25.0	29.3	28.3	27.0	27.3	29.0	27.2	24.6	30.0	31.0	7.1	8.6	7.0	12.5
1983	33.9	44.6	54.3	45.9	50.1								19.4	32.6		

[1] 1,000 oz. Contract from Jan. 1982. Prior data is for 5,000 oz. Contract. Source: Commodity Exchange of N.Y. (COMEX) & Chicago Board of Trade

T.601

Volume of Trading in Silver Futures at New York (COMEX) In Thousands of Contracts

Year	Jan.	Feb.	Mar.	Apr.	May	June	July	Aug.	Sept.	Oct.	Nov.	Dec.	Total
1978	330.0	270.7	391.0	287.5	244.9	247.2	254.1	316.2	192.0	469.0	438.0	381.4	3,822
1979	460.0	388.3	304.6	367.3	545.3	480.5	383.9	404.1	283.1	191.7	178.6	111.1	4,081
1980	167.7	76.2	143.5	94.0	46.6	63.3	45.6	41.8	100.9	92.9	97.1	90.6	1,059
1981	70.7	71.0	74.9	72.6	58.0	97.4	77.4	116.0	171.9	121.4	136.6	172.8	1,241
1982	112.8	193.9	211.5	192.9	99.7	217.4	263.1	317.2	258.0	288.9	350.6	372.8	2,827
1983	502.7	601.4	446.6	452.9									

Source: Commodity Exchange of N.Y. (COMEX)

T.602

Commodity Exchange, Inc. (COMEX) Warehouse Stocks of Silver In Millions of Ounces

Year	Jan. 1	Feb. 1	Mar. 1	Apr. 1	May 1	June 1	July 1	Aug. 1	Sept. 1	Oct. 1	Nov. 1	Dec. 1
1974	63.9	63.9	60.6	64.3	69.8	74.9	76.8	72.3	69.6	68.2	68.4	69.6
1975	68.0	69.5	72.6	70.5	73.7	77.2	78.3	80.9	80.2	82.7	82.4	81.7
1976	86.3	84.1	82.8	79.3	77.3	71.8	65.3	58.0	54.6	50.0	49.3	52.3
1977	54.8	56.5	57.2	63.3	65.6	67.0	69.4	70.6	65.2	64.9	60.2	64.5
1978	68.7	70.0	72.3	74.2	73.4	70.8	72.8	73.6	72.4	66.7	64.3	63.0
1979	58.2	52.0	51.8	49.2	50.3	55.5	54.1	48.9	47.3	51.8	60.3	70.2
1980	74.8	76.0	77.8	83.1	84.2	82.3	82.0	81.7	82.6	82.2	87.1	86.1
1981	86.9	86.8	85.4	84.6	85.7	85.1	86.6	85.4	78.8	78.1	76.0	77.3
1982	77.6	76.3	78.5	77.1	79.9	78.0	72.4	66.2	60.0	60.7	59.2	80.6
1983	91.2	90.9	106.4	96.8	91.3							

Source: Commodity Exchange, Inc.—New York

T.600

United States Production[1] of Refined Silver from All Sources In Thousands of Troy Ounces

Year	Jan.	Feb.	Mar.	Apr.	May	June	July	Aug.	Sept.	Oct.	Nov.	Dec.	Total
1973		55,975			12,406	12,633	11,650	13,841	12,235	15,535	13,541	13,949	161,765
1974	14,476	13,483	17,322	17,147	19,300	18,550	9,679	12,455	14,050	14,019	16,148	19,890	186,519
1975	16,815	14,623	14,619	13,693	12,281	12,267	12,090	12,996	13,222	13,832	12,372	14,251	161,568
1976	9,369	11,558	14,260	14,155	10,952	12,633	8,771	10,342	12,598	13,998	16,018	18,378	154,230
1977	13,196	10,114	13,173	13,335	13,260	14,100	5,781	7,840	10,412	13,643	13,002	14,966	143,125
1978	10,694	12,699	12,503	10,871	12,196	12,000	10,186	12,214	10,727	12,666	11,526	12,721	141,003
1979	10,592	10,888	13,070	11,451	11,938	11,600	12,433	9,837	9,118	12,476	12,221	17,008	155,723
1980	18,088	17,548	17,673	16,941	10,400	14,800	6,676	11,583	10,785	10,603	10,578	14,553	166,326
1981	12,889	12,000	11,352	11,889	10,402	11,500	10,433	10,114	10,533	9,954	8,105	11,589	130,783
1982	9,043	8,407	10,300	8,856	9,095	8,840	7,781	8,518	7,872	8,307	9,607	11,655	108,252
1983	9,121	8,533											

[1] Output of commercial bars .999 fine, including U.S. Mint purchases of crude. Production is from both foreign and domestic silver. Sources: American Bureau of Metal Statistics; The Silver Institute, Inc.

T.603

Soybean Meal

Total U.S. soybean meal supplies during 1982/83, including beginning stocks and production, were projected to be 26.8 million short tons compared with 24.8 million during the 1981/82 season. Domestic use was forecast at 18.5 million tons, more than 4 percent above the previous season's total. U.S. exports of soybean meal were projected at 8.05 million tons, 16.5 percent above the 1981/82 level.

The projections of an increase in domestic soybean meal use were based upon higher livestock feeding rates especially for hogs which had become more profitable to feed. Early in 1983, the hog/meal price ratio was over 6.3, quite a bit higher than last season's average of 5.7. It was expected that more soymeal would be fed to broilers during 1982/83 as poultry production was expanded by nearly 2 percent and as the broiler/meal price ratio increased. Attractive feeding margins are usually a sign of an upturn in livestock feeding, and an attractive hog/corn ratio of 23 to 1 was expected to enhance the overall demand for feed. However, the USDA Hogs and Pigs report showed total inventories down 9 percent as of December 1. The breeding hog inventory also registered a decline, and farrowing intentions for the December–May period were 3 percent below the year-earlier figure. Farmers remained reluctant to expand operations because of high real interest rates and adverse balance sheets.

The European Community (EC) was the key market for U.S. exports of soybean meal during 1982/83. Because of slight increases in expected livestock production and a lower soybean meal/corn price ratio, EC meal consumption was projected as increasing nearly 10 percent this season. The EC market took over 60 percent of U.S. soybean meal imports during 1981/82. Soybean meal exports from Brazil were expected to remain nearly unchanged from the previous season thus allowing the U.S. to increase its share of the world market. The total world use of soybean meal was forecast at 26 million short tons during 1982/83 (October–September), 6 percent above the 1981/82 level.

Soybean meal prices in the 1982/83 season were expected by the USDA to average $165 to $185 a ton. This range represented an increase from the fall 1982 forecast, but its midpoint was nonetheless below the previous season's average of $182.50 a ton.

Futures Markets

Soybean meal futures are traded on the Chicago Board of Trade and on the London Commodity Exchange.

Supply and Distribution of Soybean Meal in the United States — In Thousands of Short Tons

Year Begin. Oct.	For Stocks Oct. 1	Production Total	Production For Animal Feed	Production For Edible Protein Pdt's.	Supply Total	(Domestic) Feed[2]	Exports	Shipments to U.S. Terr.	Distribution Total	Price Per Ton Bulk, Decatur 44% Protein	Price Per Ton 49–50% Protein
1970-1	137	18,035			18,172	13,406	4,559	61	18,126	78.51	84.33
1971-2	146	17,024			17,170	13,110	3,805	63	16,978	90.20	98.20
1972-3	192	16,709			16,900	11,920	4,745	52	16,717	228.99	253.42
1973-4	183	19,674	N.A.	N.A.	19,858	13,766	5,548	36	19,350	146.35	160.57
1974-5	507	16,701	16,437	265	17,209	12,501	4,299	50	16,850	130.86	141.26
1975-6	358	20,754	20,395	359	21,112	15,552	5,145	61	20,758	147.77	157.68
1976-7	355	18,488	18,101	388	18,843	14,001	4,559	55	18,615	199.80	218.73
1977-8	228	22,557	21,405	410	22,785	16,462	6,080	61	22,542	163.56	179.45
1978-9	243	24,354	23,205	368	24,597	17,720	6,610	47	24,330	190.06	206.30
1979-0	267	27,105	25,930	297	27,372	19,214	7,932	60	27,146	181.91	195.55
1980-1	226	24,312	23,232	286	24,538	17,591	6,784	—	24,375	218.18	235.13
1981-2[1]	163	24,634	23,500	308	24,797	17,714	6,908	—	24,622	182.52	196.63
1982-3[3]	175	26,635			26,810	18,500	8,050	—	26,550	165–185	
1983-4[3]	260										

[1] Preliminary. [2] Includes small quantities used for industrial purposes, estimated at 30,000 tons annually. [3] Estimate. Source: Economic Research Service, U.S.D.A.

T.606

U.S. Exports of Soybean Cake & Meal by Country of Destination — In Thousands of Metric Tons[2]

Yr. Beg. Oct. 1	Belg.-Lux.	Japan	Canada	Denmark	France	W. Germany	Spain	Ireland	Italy	Netherlands	Philippines	Poland	United Kingdom	Yugoslavia	Grand Total
1970-1	308.8	32.8	242.1	85.6	712.1	987.4		36.5	330.8	675.4	53.8	112.3	100.1	186.8	4,559
1971-2	328.4	24.5	204.5	95.5	610.3	705.0		72.4	295.6	482.8	58.0	65.8	58.3	116.2	3,805
1972-3	179.8	287.0	199.2	114.3	678.5	987.7	140.0	76.3	445.0	248.4	14.2	337.0	48.5	152.2	4,745
1973-4	204.7	137.2	289.8	56.6	866.6	1,192	96.0	53.3	631.6	313.3	49.9	287.6	60.2	316.4	5,548
1974-5	243.8	.1	224.5	17.6	786.7	995.4	69.0	37.3	422.2	428.7	12.6	220.6	91.4	—	4,299
1975-6[2]	238.2	120.1	277.8	35.1	761.9	1,008	347.3	49.1	421.4	102.5	.1	360.8	54.5	183.5	4,667
1976-7	83.4	217.5	256.4	36.8	131.0	953.1	143.3	36.1	428.8	565.8	—	256.9	46.7	95.2	4,117
1977-8	37.0	271.3	339.5	26.1	146.6	1,004	237.3	83.6	741.6	654.7	21.0	493.3	65.0	113.1	5,515
1978-9	3.8	204.5	416.0	65.6	355.1	717.6	253.5	117.9	691.1	748.1	—	243.0	66.8	57.9	5,998
1979-0	13.3	210.0	355.9	48.5	270.2	1,013	58.0	74.1	855.7	1,490	41.1	400.0	69.0	152.9	7,196
1980-1[1]	48.9	153.7	331.2	.1	8.0	710.3	21.6	.5	684.3	1,502	—	312.3	56.9	191.4	6,140
1981-2															

[1] Preliminary. [2] Data prior to 1975-6 are in THS. OF SHORT TONS. Source: The Bureau of the Census, U.S.D. of Commerce

T.607

SOYBEAN MEAL

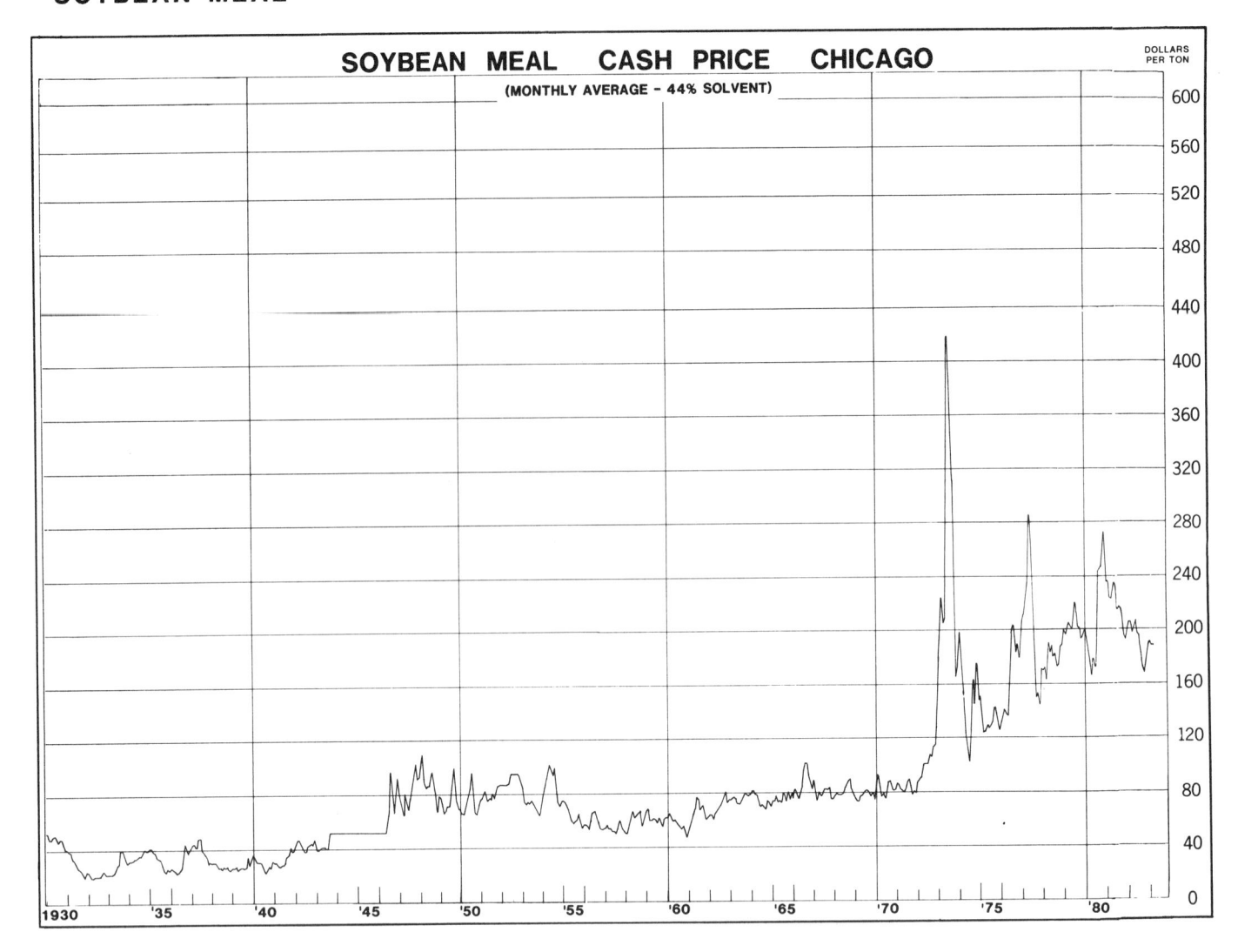

SOYBEAN MEAL CASH PRICE CHICAGO
(MONTHLY AVERAGE – 44% SOLVENT)

DOLLARS PER TON

Average Price of Soybean Meal (44% Protein) at Chicago   In Dollars per Ton (Bagged)

Year	Jan.	Feb.	Mar.	Apr.	May	June	July	Aug.	Sept.	Oct.	Nov.	Dec.	Average
1970	92.50	90.25	76.80	79.60	76.20	79.90	88.10	89.20	86.00	82.40	83.20	87.40	84.35
1971	85.60	82.60	82.40	80.25	84.25	87.50	90.25	84.75	79.25	80.75	79.80	86.60	83.67
1972	88.60	91.00	97.00	100.60	101.40	101.20	107.50	107.10	113.90	114.90	129.40	180.60	111.09
1973	195.00	225.30	206.50	209.80	321.20	418.90	317.80	291.60	214.70	166.20	173.80	198.80	244.97
1974	178.80	166.80	154.20	124.30	116.30	107.10	145.80	164.00	146.00	176.00	148.80	151.20	148.28
1975	137.00	125.00	125.60	129.90	128.30	129.20	132.30	143.40	143.00	135.30	126.90	134.60	132.54
1976	137.75	141.75	137.50	136.60	162.10	198.10	204.10	183.50	189.60	179.80	191.40	207.80	172.42
1977	217.20	221.20	236.40	285.80	268.40	235.50	172.50	150.90	154.25	145.40	172.30	170.70	202.55
1978	173.10	164.00	190.50	184.10	188.50	180.80	183.10	174.10	175.40	188.40	188.70	200.40	182.59
1979	196.50	202.40	306.20	202.80	199.70	221.40	213.60	201.00	200.70	193.50	195.20	200.10	202.76
1980	192.40	186.50	176.90	166.60	178.90	173.40	200.40	220.10	247.20	259.10	274.10	236.40	209.33
1981	236.20	225.30	223.40	235.10	234.10	214.20	217.40	215.50	203.30	194.25	191.75	201.00	215.96
1982	204.50	204.50	197.10	203.75	205.90	197.10	195.40	182.40	172.40	168.00	184.30	189.50	192.07
1983	190.75	188.10	188.30										

Source: Consumer Marketing Service, U.S.D.A.

T.608

SOYBEAN MEAL

Production & Foreign Trade of Soybean Cake & Meal in the U.S. In Thousands of Short Tons

Crop Year	Oct.	Nov.	Dec.	Jan.	Feb.	Mar.	Production April	May	June	July	Aug.	Sept.	Total	Soybeans (Meal Equivalent of Exports)[2]
1972-3	1,562	1,661	1,618	1,656	1,523	1,507	1,364	1,449	1,226	1,043	1,116	984	16,709	11,208
1973-4	1,465	1,688	1,704	1,757	1,658	1,786	1,647	1,694	1,630	1,704	1,654	1,288	19,674	13,170
1974-5	1,467	1,458	1,427	1,484	1,282	1,436	1,368	1,245	1,256	1,408	1,533	1,338	16,702	10,024
1975-6	1,701	1,697	1,808	1,748	1,617	1,820	1,830	1,891	1,772	1,670	1,556	1,645	20,754	13,316
1976-7	1,747	1,763	1,741	1,725	1,709	1,771	1,596	1,454	1,340	1,211	1,187	1,243	18,488	13,200
1977-8	1,781	2,017	2,044	2,007	1,778	2,050	1,903	1,959	1,725	1,681	1,758	1,695	21,629	16,895
1978-9	2,052	2,069	2,222	2,095	1,892	2,052	1,921	1,999	1,910	1,836	1,759	1,766	23,573	17,681
1979-0	2,214	2,359	2,431	2,477	2,319	2,379	2,129	2,167	1,922	1,990	1,945	1,896	26,227	21,118
1980-1	2,253	2,291	2,179	2,133	1,838	2,074	1,976	1,896	1,709	1,681	1,726	1,763	23,518	
1981-2[1]	2,502	2,326	2,451	2,266	2,077	2,050	1,931	2,066	1,844	1,684	1,620	1,819	24,634	
1982-3[1]	2,386	2,581	2,678											

[1] Preliminary. [2] Calculated at 47.5 lbs of meal per bushel. *Sources: Economic Research Service, U.S.D.A.; Bureau of Census.* T.609

Month End Open Interest of Soybean Meal Futures at the Chicago Board of Trade In Contracts

Year	Jan.	Feb.	Mar.	Apr.	May	June	July	Aug.	Sept.	Oct.	Nov.	Dec.
1978	30,042	34,991	42,325	40,969	50,633	50,628	52,895	56,288	52,315	60,233	63,302	61,014
1979	48,076	54,316	54,873	48,923	49,678	56,627	47,847	47,804	49,348	56,178	52,426	50,072
1980	49,490	53,379	51,143	47,016	46,603	47,769	50,797	61,261	66,805	82,421	84,051	64,965
1981	53,077	50,584	47,002	51,831	45,160	50,909	45,901	48,379	48,152	47,619	48,140	38,804
1982	41,034	39,700	43,830	45,035	45,481	45,877	47,094	50,823	46,833	44,740	47,300	46,016
1983	50,744	44,808	52,979	46,653								

Source: Chicago Board of Trade T.610

Volume of Trading of Soybean Meal Futures at the Chicago Board of Trade In Thousands of Contracts

Year	Jan.	Feb.	Mar.	Apr.	May	June	July	Aug.	Sept.	Oct.	Nov.	Dec.	Total
1978	173.1	123.6	275.5	213.6	190.2	224.5	191.3	207.3	162.2	257.3	260.2	214.2	2,493
1979	204.7	244.5	290.3	219.4	211.2	382.2	257.9	182.6	186.3	219.6	183.3	146.8	2,648
1980	172.6	159.2	152.1	183.0	159.1	183.9	370.8	281.5	371.9	413.6	369.3	401.7	3,219
1981	261.9	203.1	220.9	254.3	218.4	294.8	301.8	241.3	276.3	219.0	242.8	304.4	3,040
1982	219.6	238.1	258.6	279.7	197.3	244.0	229.9	225.1	198.8	244.0	233.4	218.9	2,784
1983	269.2	248.0	252.7	272.9									

Source: Chicago Board of Trade T.611

High, Low & Closing Prices of May Soybean Meal Futures on the Chicago Board of Trade $ per Ton

Year of Delivery		Mar.	Apr.	May	June	July	Aug.	Sept.	Oct.	Nov.	Dec.	Jan.	Feb.	Mar.	Apr.	May	Life of Delivery Range
1978	High	207.0	209.0	207.5	216.5	181.0	161.5	161.8	162.3	181.0	170.5	169.2	158.5	194.5	186.0	182.3	216.5
	Low	188.5	185.0	190.0	183.0	158.0	143.6	143.5	147.5	161.0	158.6	153.2	152.1	155.0	169.1	172.3	143.5
	Close	196.0	195.0	203.5	189.0	158.0	147.8	151.3	162.1	163.1	166.7	153.6	154.1	178.7	176.0	179.0	—
1979	High	—	180.0	182.0	181.0	172.0	178.5	183.0	202.0	197.0	193.9	195.5	209.5	205.5	202.7	194.0	209.5
	Low	—	168.0	167.0	168.0	165.0	165.1	172.5	179.0	170.7	184.0	184.5	190.5	193.7	186.5	185.8	165.0
	Close	—	169.0	181.2	173.2	167.7	175.8	178.5	197.0	187.0	188.3	192.2	203.2	202.2	186.9	188.9	—
1980	High	—	201.0	204.0	233.0	221.0	205.5	211.3	213.0	204.5	201.2	197.5	193.0	182.0	169.0	173.0	233.0
	Low	—	195.7	197.5	202.0	196.0	194.5	197.5	188.5	189.3	189.6	179.9	179.0	160.7	158.1	163.3	158.1
	Close	—	200.0	203.7	202.5	198.7	203.0	207.0	192.7	199.9	189.7	190.3	179.4	161.4	163.9	168.0	—
1981	High	206.5	200.5	201.0	205.0	238.0	242.5	265.0	299.0	300.5	294.8	259.5	232.5	224.0	231.7	230.2	300.5
	Low	193.0	191.0	191.5	190.3	205.0	217.0	241.0	244.3	275.0	227.0	213.5	214.5	205.2	216.9	214.0	190.3
	Close	195.2	195.5	192.0	205.0	229.6	242.5	251.7	290.2	292.7	249.0	220.7	215.2	220.8	226.9	214.0	—
1982	High	—	261.5	252.0	242.0	241.0	230.0	218.0	210.5	206.5	203.5	197.0	197.7	188.5	196.0	196.5	261.5
	Low	—	248.5	234.5	221.0	223.0	207.0	203.5	201.8	194.1	181.5	187.8	182.7	178.4	186.2	188.0	181.5
	Close	—	249.5	239.0	225.0	231.5	209.0	206.5	203.5	197.3	188.3	195.9	186.1	187.7	190.9	189.0	—
1983	High	—	215.0	210.0	205.5	199.0	195.5	176.0	169.0	180.5	178.5	186.0	186.1	192.8	193.3		
	Low	—	203.0	201.5	197.0	189.5	171.0	165.3	160.3	166.5	171.3	174.1	170.6	172.5	183.3		
	Close	—	209.5	201.5	197.7	192.0	174.0	166.5	166.0	178.0	175.2	185.6	171.4	189.7	189.4		
1984	High	219.5	217.5														
	Low	213.5	207.5														
	Close	215.2	211.5														

Source: Chicago Board of Trade T.612

311

SOYBEAN MEAL

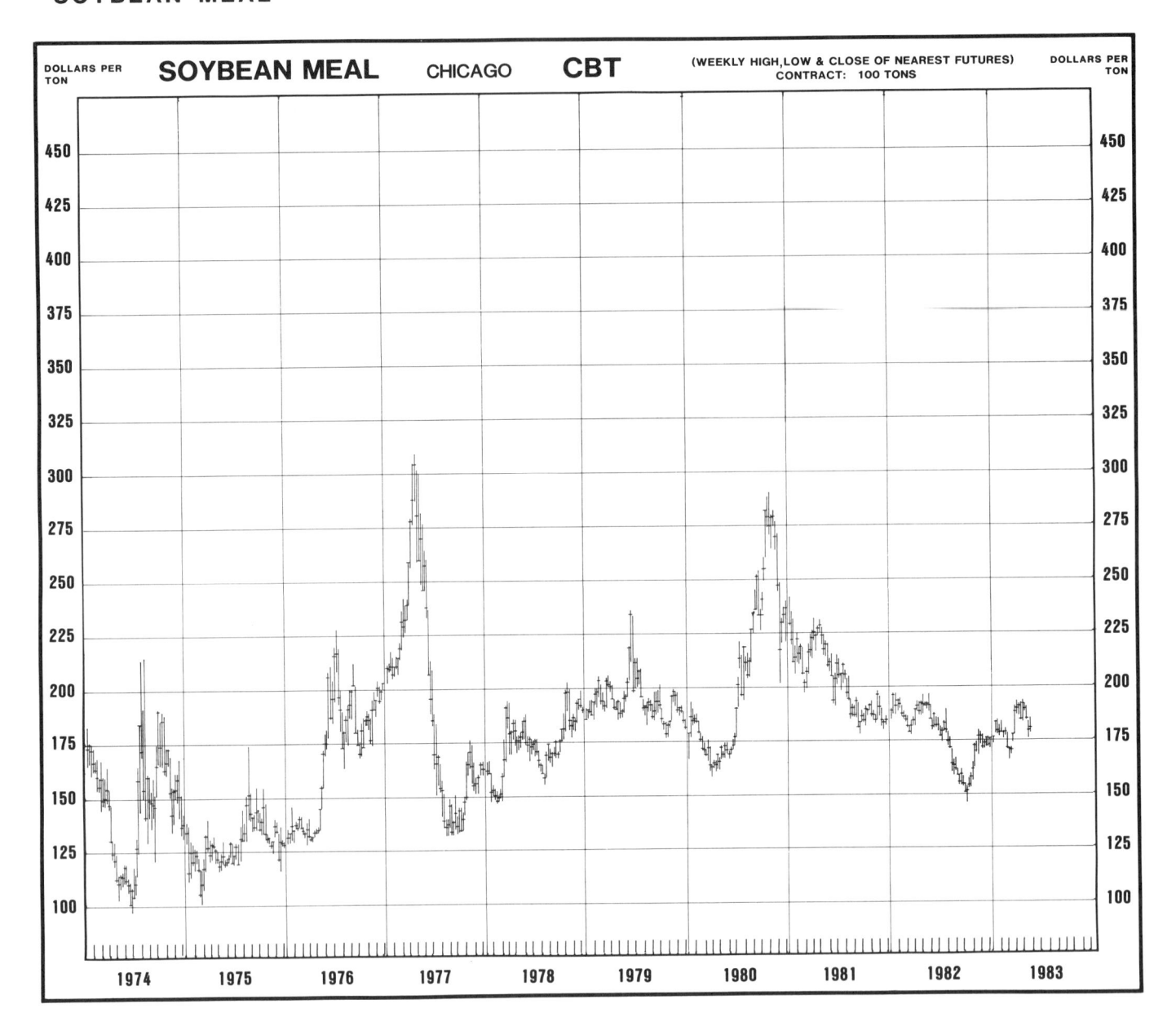

SOYBEAN MEAL CHICAGO **CBT** (WEEKLY HIGH, LOW & CLOSE OF NEAREST FUTURES) CONTRACT: 100 TONS

Stocks (at Oil Mills) of Soybean Cake & Meal in the United States   In Thousands of Short Tons

Year	Oct. 1	Nov. 1	Dec. 1	Jan. 1	Feb. 1	Mar. 1	April 1	May 1	June 1	July 1	Aug. 1	Sept. 1
1970–1	137.0	168.8	182.7	129.7	185.5	189.3	153.2	168.1	219.3	169.1	215.0	215.4
1971–2	145.8	205.2	192.8	144.3	153.9	135.5	160.5	218.0	186.7	189.1	243.2	221.6
1972–3	191.7	185.7	170.7	217.9	193.3	210.0	206.3	213.5	203.4	204.5	214.4	212.8
1973–4	183.2	234.3	242.2	284.6	249.0	281.1	361.6	348.0	427.9	514.3	475.9	535.4
1974–5	507.3	508.2	563.7	529.0	541.0	540.0	556.7	470.5	448.1	421.7	394.8	404.5
1975–6	358.3	396.1	441.4	371.4	378.1	419.5	358.3	358.8	462.8	369.8	406.9	350.5
1976–7	354.9	423.5	427.7	353.9	384.7	429.9	412.6	449.0	408.3	390.7	399.0	270.4
1977–8	228.3	270.0	239.8	245.1	251.7	239.7	227.3	308.2	263.3	191.1	262.6	234.1
1978–9	242.9	210.4	178.2	260.5	215.1	198.4	210.4	231.6	207.4	205.3	232.2	140.3
1979–0	224.3	204.1	164.2	207.7	158.7	160.6	219.1	193.9	265.0	262.0	232.4	225.1
1980–1	189.7	211.1	350.0	221.8	209.7	214.4	232.2	184.4	254.0	209.7	156.1	199.7
1981–2[1]	233.8	309.2	314.8	279.4	315.7	324.9	190.3	172.1	309.3	224.9	209.1	189.7
1982–3[1]	175.2	342.8	349.6	331.6								

[1] Preliminary.   Sources: *Economic Research Service, U.S.D.A.; Bureau of the Census*

T.613

Soybean Oil

Early in 1983, the USDA estimated 1982/83 total world production of soybean oil at 13.8 million tonnes. Of the three major producing countries, the U.S. accounted for nearly 39 percent of the total, Brazil—18 percent, and the European Community (EC)—nearly 15 percent.

The domestic demand for soybean oil during 1982/83 was expected to continue strong, resulting in a record usage figure of 9.75 billion pounds, nearly 3 percent above the 1981/82 figure. During October–August 1981/82, the soybean oil used in baking and frying fats amounted to 2.74 billion pounds compared with 2.68 billion for all of 1980/81. The portion of this usage attributed to soybean oil was 67 percent, almost 4 percent higher than the 1980/81 figure. The total use of baking and frying fats was higher as well. Low soybean oil prices relative to lard and to edible tallow was the most effective influence behind the rise in soybean oil use.

Soybean oil exports from the U.S. during 1982/83 were projected by the USDA to be about 2.15 billion pounds, only marginally higher than the year-earlier figure. The USDA estimated that nearly a third of U.S. soybean oil exports in 1981/82 went to Pakistan and that virtually all of these sales were funded under government programs.

Soybean oil stocks were expected to be worked down somewhat during 1982/83 both in the U.S. and abroad. U.S. 1982/83 ending stocks of soybean oil were forecast at 1.13 billion pounds compared with 1.15 billion during the previous season and with 1.74 billion pounds two years before. The expected drawdown in stocks, which had built up during the previous season partly as a by-product of increased crushing for meal, was attributed to prospects for an improvement of the overall world economy and to the consequent increased demand for vegetable oils, especially on the part of the Soviet Union and third-world countries. Early in 1983, American soybean producers began to lobby Congress in behalf of a PIK-type subsidy measure that would make payments in kind to exporters of soybeans and soybean products. The lobby effort was expressly concerned with the high level of U.S. soybean oil stocks, and analysts estimated that the subsidy measure could generate sales of nearly 940,000 tonnes of soybean oil, including an estimated 500,000 tonnes to India.

Prices during the 1982/83 season were forecast at between 16 and 20 cents per pound, most likely in the upper end of that range, compared with the 19 cents per pound average during 1981/82.

Futures Markets

Soybean oil futures are traded on the Chicago Board of Trade and the London Commodity Exchange.

Production, Consumption, Stocks and Foreign Trade of Soybean Oil in the U.S. — In Millions of Pounds

Year	Production Crude	Production Refined	Consumption In Refining	Consumption In End Pdt's.	Stocks December 31 Crude	Stocks December 31 Refined	Imports for Consumption	Exports Crude	Exports Refined
1970	8,086	6,276	6,523	6,322	450.7	304.9	—	1,119.4	367.6
1971	8,082	6,298	6,551	6,323	447.6	354.6	—	1,288.6	427.5
1972	8,084	6,521	7,032	6,827	581.5	315.0	—	841.6	452.1
1973	7,540	6,509	7,046	6,831	411.7	278.8	—	723.9	243.8
1974	8,705	6,812	7,000	7,039	375.6	299.4	.1	1,607	
1975	7,861	6,423	6,686	6,830	495.3	304.6	—	758	
1976	9,640	7,185	7,476	7,577	1,141	347.1	—	901.7	77.3
1977	8,836	7,790	8,092	7,451	524.0	340.0	.2	1,427.3	81.3
1978	10,625	8,618	8,955	8,175	623.1	347.5	—	1,560.8	77.8
1979	11,504	9,110	9,456	8,656	656.6	373.5	—	2,371	
1980	12,097	8,982	9,300	8,585	1,369.6	368.2	—	2,315	
1981[1]	11,301	9,461	9,817	9,024	1,680.2	343.6	—	1,698	
1982[1]	11,183	9,671	10,042	9,307	1,241.1	345.6			

[1] Preliminary. Source: Bureau of Census

T.614

U.S. Exports of Soybean Oil,[1] by Country of Destination — In Thousands of Metric Tons[3]

Yr. Beg. Oct. 1	Australia	Colombia	Canada	Chile	Ecuador	France	Haiti	Peru	India	Israel	Mexico	Morocco	Pakistan	Panama	Egypt	Grand Total
1970-1		17	50	58			26	111	284	41	1	90	278			1,742
1971-2		15	43	2			27	84	144	44	—	122	142			1,398
1972-3		7	38	2	30		21	92	95	51	33	7	130	11	2	1,066
1973-4		24	73	69	29		16	135	94	21	135	43	197	39	3	1,435
1974-5		18	44	6	28		26	56	8	15	119	5	26	24	8	1,028
1975-6[3]	13.1	14.2	31.8	1.0	19.5	—	14.3	14.5	15.8	9.9	3.1	4.9	150.8	13.2	.5	443
1976-7	20.1	27.3	26.0	12.0	16.2	—	17.2	57.3	252.2	3.1	15.4	3.0	119.2	12.5	1.4	702
1977-8	21.0	44.1	27.7	22.0	26.0	5.0	13.8	68.6	247.7	6.3	29.6	5.6	95.8	8.3	6.1	933
1978-9	16.2	84.1	20.9	22.8	22.4	3.6	17.2	29.4	181.1	9.8	5.1	6.0	163.3	19.0	13.9	1,059
1979-0	16.4	82.6	14.8	13.2	35.3	2.9	22.8	36.2	427.7	9.6	31.4	2.3	147.4	17.9	6.0	1,220
1980-1[2]	16.5	60.3	7.8	22.8	38.6	0	22.4	41.2	61.8	5.2	21.6	5.0	125.7	14.7	3.4	739
1981-2[2]																1,000

[1] Crude & refined oil combined as such. [2] Preliminary. [3] Data prior to 1975-6 are in MILLIONS OF POUNDS. Source: The Bureau of the Census, U.S.D. of Commerce.

T.615

SOYBEAN OIL

U.S. Stocks of Soybean Oil (Crude & Refined) at Factory & Warehouses   In Millions of Pounds

Year	Oct. 1	Nov. 1	Dec. 1	Jan. 1	Feb. 1	Mar. 1	April 1	May 1	June 1	July 1	Aug. 1	Sept. 1
1970-1	543.4	562.3	717.6	755.7	751.7	787.8	756.0	765.8	757.9	719.0	745.3	819.2
1971-2	772.6	725.9	808.6	802.2	782.8	847.1	881.2	952.6	944.9	829.6	854.1	841.6
1972-3	785.2	806.2	839.1	896.5	948.6	966.5	920.6	1,005	778.3	822.7	748.8	620.0
1973-4	515.5	531.6	599.9	690.5	623.3	642.5	626.0	726.3	765.1	708.6	702.7	777.1
1974-5	793.6	734.7	681.5	673.6	689.6	633.8	647.4	662.2	606.7	528.6	544.3	567.1
1975-6	560.5	568.0	657.7	799.9	844.8	913.3	946.0	1,061	1,109	1,275	1,230	1,295
1976-7	1,251	1,351	1,432	1,488	1,606	1,616	1,493	1,485	1,361	1,174	1,037	942.5
1977-8	771.1	756.4	771.1	864.0	913.8	856.5	803.8	822.2	828.7	834.4	820.8	777.5
1978-9	728.6	813.4	837.1	970.6	932.2	942.8	1,004	987.3	1,043	922.9	915.4	815.1
1979-0[1]	775.8	819.8	867.3	1,030	1,155	1,205	1,176	1,184	1,145	1,226	1,305	1,263
1980-1[1]	1,210	1,374	1,677	1,738	1,900	1,976	2,017	2,119	2,166	2,139	2,024	1,783
1981-2[1]	1,736	1,790	1,884	2,024	2,160	2,141	2,141	2,112	2,018	1,889	1,647	1,397
1982-3[1]	1,103	1,208	1,298									
1983-4												

[1] Preliminary.   Source: Bureau of the Census   T.616

U.S. Production of Refined Soybean Oil   In Millions of Pounds

Year	Oct.	Nov.	Dec.	Jan.	Feb.	Mar.	Apr.	May	June	July	Aug.	Sept.	Total
1970-1	534.5	514.5	538.8	543.5	511.1	557.9	495.0	506.7	526.7	482.9	532.8	568.6	6,313
1971-2	534.5	504.2	534.1	529.7	527.5	564.2	537.9	562.6	537.0	484.7	557.9	530.3	6,364
1972-3	562.9	565.4	560.7	574.6	522.9	579.4	514.7	542.1	516.6	433.2	544.8	504.6	6,373
1973-4	577.1	601.6	597.3	666.4	596.0	616.1	575.0	581.8	542.4	560.5	583.9	510.8	7,009
1974-5	585.0	511.4	482.1	515.0	468.6	497.1	497.0	467.9	489.6	509.3	550.9	538.3	6,112
1975-6	666.9	617.3	605.0	611.9	558.7	646.5	606.6	624.2	627.1	584.7	607.9	568.1	7,325
1976-7	575.4	596.3	578.0	564.4	578.4	710.9	636.9	651.6	589.3	563.9	661.0	623.8	7,330
1977-8	700.1	764.2	745.0	705.6	653.2	801.4	738.0	732.1	649.9	636.8	725.3	679.9	8,532
1978-9[1]	782.8	747.7	765.7	753.3	681.7	768.9	760.1	835.4	742.8	748.3	762.8	693.0	9,043
1979-0[1]	805.9	797.6	760.3	801.9	760.5	767.7	687.1	712.8	669.0	720.3	760.7	764.5	9,038
1980-1[1]	784.1	760.5	763.1	741.6	706.3	833.9	741.2	754.9	812.9	765.4	813.3	812.1	9,289
1981-2[1]	833.6	840.9	805.2	768.7	767.6	866.4	754.5	817.3	866.3	775.4	811.7	794.0	9,702
1982-3[1]	824.6	827.8	795.1	785.7									
1983-4													

[1] Preliminary.   Source: Bureau of the Census   T.617

U.S. Production of Crude Soybean Oil   In Millions of Pounds

Year	Oct.	Nov.	Dec.	Jan.	Feb.	Mar.	Apr.	May	June	July	Aug.	Sept.	Total
1970-1	729.8	705.6	727.7	724.8	653.2	695.9	695.7	696.4	670.9	674.9	692.2	597.5	8,265
1971-2	645.2	644.2	690.6	689.9	658.9	706.4	646.7	698.8	635.4	648.6	645.7	581.0	7,891
1972-3	713.3	742.4	716.6	723.5	676.8	680.8	618.3	655.8	553.1	470.1	510.5	439.8	7,501
1973-4	676.8	764.9	769.8	797.7	751.5	809.0	750.8	777.8	756.7	788.3	759.0	592.3	8,995
1974-5	672.9	627.5	621.4	651.6	555.9	632.4	600.9	557.6	557.8	623.9	674.5	599.8	7,376
1975-6	783.9	776.7	846.7	807.4	757.6	852.4	846.1	869.8	813.9	788.7	720.5	766.1	9,630
1976-7	807.4	804.0	805.7	786.7	791.2	823.7	747.3	682.4	631.1	566.6	553.6	578.2	8,578
1977-8	821.9	922.3	931.5	911.9	809.5	943.3	866.9	908.2	795.1	777.9	815.8	783.3	10,287
1978-9[1]	984.3	974.8	1,050	989.1	902.3	982.2	939.6	964.7	930.5	899.9	856.7	849.9	11,324
1979-0[1]	1,020	1,068	1,102	1,115	1,065	1,098	993.7	1,010	901.6	927.8	913.8	890.1	12,105
1980-1[1]	1,080	1,078	1,024	1,011	887.8	991.3	954.2	914.9	830.7	815.8	827.2	855.6	11,271
1981-2[1]	1,125	1,018	1,070	995.6	917.7	912.1	866.8	930.2	828.4	765.6	732.0	818.3	10,979
1982-3[1]	1,079	1,145	1,198										
1983-4													

[1] Preliminary.   Source: Bureau of the Census   T.618

SOYBEAN OIL

U.S. Exports of Soybean Oil (Crude & Refined)   In Millions of Pounds

Year	Jan.	Feb.	Mar.	Apr.	May	June	July	Aug.	Sept.	Oct.	Nov.	Dec.	Total
1970	62.7	46.2	151.7	73.8	81.1	197.8	136.0	126.7	165.2	103.9	52.7	174.6	1,372
1971	112.0	109.3	156.0	168.0	191.8	140.9	189.0	78.1	122.2	143.0	43.5	153.8	1,612
1972	157.8	71.3	59.3	69.3	89.0	263.3	94.1	57.5	68.3	58.4	109.7	50.7	1,149
1973	52.7	120.9	132.3	49.3	111.8	90.3	81.5	37.0	45.2	12.9	31.7	108.6	874.3
1974	122.2	120.2	98.3	146.0	96.9	226.6	239.0	84.1	83.2	85.9	111.1	193.0	1,067
1975	129.0	71.6	116.1	57.6	72.9	55.7	65.3	13.1	13.5	43.8	78.9	40.4	758.0
1976	32.6	120.2	89.6	55.5	160.9	74.4	77.6	41.8	151.5	100.8	107.7	75.8	1,088
1977	103.7	92.3	236.4	103.3	209.4	159.9	154.2	72.0	66.0	108.8	185.5	175.3	1,667
1978	113.1	141.8	252.6	218.9	176.4	147.2	165.5	108.8	193.4	96.8	154.8	175.4	1,945
1979	219.1	249.8	199.0	185.6	107.3	299.0	166.2	187.4	159.1	127.8	208.5	261.9	2,371
1980	173.4	250.0	325.4	269.6	327.3	194.6	109.7	175.7	171.2	112.5	84.7	120.5	2,315
1981[1]	116.0	113.8	202.8	76.1	109.6	108.8	93.1	291.7	97.9	187.2	146.6	184.3	1,698
1982[1]	43.9	176.7	126.5	148.5	103.3	208.0	270.2	237.4	244.1	181.1	174.9	142.0	2,057

[1] Preliminary.   Source: Dept. of Commerce

T.619

Average Prices of Crude Domestic Soybean Oil (in Tank Cars) F.O.B. Decatur   In Cents per Pound

Year	Oct.	Nov.	Dec.	Jan.	Feb.	Mar.	Apr.	May	June	July	Aug.	Sept.	Average
1970-1	14.0	13.9	12.4	12.3	12.1	12.2	11.2	11.4	12.8	14.5	14.5	12.8	12.8
1971-2	13.2	12.5	11.7	10.9	11.0	11.7	11.9	11.4	10.7	10.3	10.1	9.8	11.3
1972-3	9.6	9.6	9.7	10.1	13.0	13.9	15.0	17.1	19.3	22.4	33.5	24.3	16.5
1973-4	23.1	20.4	26.0	28.6	36.4	30.2	28.2	29.4	31.6	40.5	43.3	40.7	31.5
1974-5	42.3	40.4	38.0	33.6	29.4	29.1	28.2	23.6	23.3	27.5	28.5	24.4	30.7
1975-6	21.4	18.9	16.8	16.2	16.3	16.6	16.3	15.8	17.6	20.9	20.4	22.5	18.3
1976-7	20.7	21.8	21.0	20.9	22.4	26.5	29.6	31.3	28.3	23.8	21.1	19.2	23.9
1977-8	18.8	21.0	22.6	20.9	21.6	26.6	26.8	28.8	26.9	25.9	26.3	27.8	24.5
1978-9	26.7	23.7	25.8	25.8	27.3	26.9	26.7	27.8	27.4	29.1	29.2	30.0	27.2
1979-0	27.9	27.8	26.2	23.6	23.4	22.1	20.3	20.8	21.6	26.2	25.9	26.1	24.3
1980-1	25.1	26.7	23.7	23.0	22.0	23.1	23.4	21.6	21.3	22.8	20.8	19.4	22.7
1981-2	19.7	19.9	18.9	18.4	18.2	18.5	19.7	20.6	19.4	19.0	17.9	17.4	19.0
1982-3	17.4	17.6	16.6										

Source: Bureau of Labor Statistics

T.620

Soybean Oil Consumption in End Products in the U.S.   In Millions of Pounds

Year	Jan.	Feb.	Mar.	Apr.	May	June	July	Aug.	Sept.	Oct.	Nov.	Dec.	Total
1970	531.0	523.3	554.7	526.1	491.0	549.5	488.3	513.7	524.3	548.2	519.9	552.3	6,322
1971	534.7	505.8	535.0	497.9	505.6	556.3	497.3	537.3	554.0	522.0	522.2	554.8	6,323
1972	557.4	535.3	592.2	553.5	589.0	572.6	506.5	578.4	562.8	594.7	590.7	594.1	6,827
1973	595.8	546.3	599.0	529.6	592.5	542.6	471.7	580.8	530.3	621.0	629.2	591.9	6,831
1974	673.7	599.8	644.9	583.4	585.0	571.3	597.0	569.2	524.4	621.8	552.1	516.4	7,039
1975	553.4	521.2	528.2	540.3	527.4	531.3	555.3	562.8	604.8	672.0	609.2	624.4	6,830
1976	658.0	617.6	687.3	623.4	625.9	634.6	626.8	635.1	623.7	621.3	609.1	613.8	7,577
1977	571.5	591.2	694.5	597.1	611.0	553.8	517.9	629.8	621.5	658.6	682.3	721.9	7,451
1978	664.1	648.8	771.7	686.5	662.4	640.5	596.2	699.8	672.5	715.9	709.3	707.5	8,175
1979[1]	695.1	636.2	755.3	682.4	775.0	701.6	711.4	744.8	700.9	781.4	742.2	730.1	8,656
1980[1]	750.7	719.4	762.9	671.6	693.6	683.7	671.2	754.5	737.1	719.6	682.6	738.8	8,585
1981[1]	697.8	680.8	775.1	722.3	728.7	774.1	763.1	755.2	796.4	796.8	783.5	749.4	9,024
1982[1]	739.9	737.7	809.7	715.3	761.0	834.6	775.2	811.9	820.5	799.9	763.1	733.2	9,302
1983[1]	769.6												

[1] Preliminary.   Source: Bureau of the Census

T.624

Month-End Open Interest of Soybean Oil Futures of the Chicago Board of Trade   In Contracts

Year	Jan.	Feb.	Mar.	Apr.	May	June	July	Aug.	Sept.	Oct.	Nov.	Dec.
1978	40,175	44,145	49,994	49,592	55,292	52,682	52,230	49,553	50,322	60,842	57,363	54,133
1979	50,713	57,729	57,893	55,657	57,820	64,671	58,852	58,258	60,854	67,778	65,893	64,374
1980	62,515	63,472	59,707	52,805	61,089	65,949	64,710	63,908	66,723	75,815	91,407	71,527
1981	58,671	65,580	57,956	67,241	56,968	63,400	54,007	56,847	49,411	50,786	54,232	48,295
1982	53,029	53,375	49,824	53,395	57,366	58,151	56,863	50,574	44,091	41,930	45,976	50,290
1983	49,329	49,360	57,446	59,894								

Source: Chicago Board of Trade

T.625

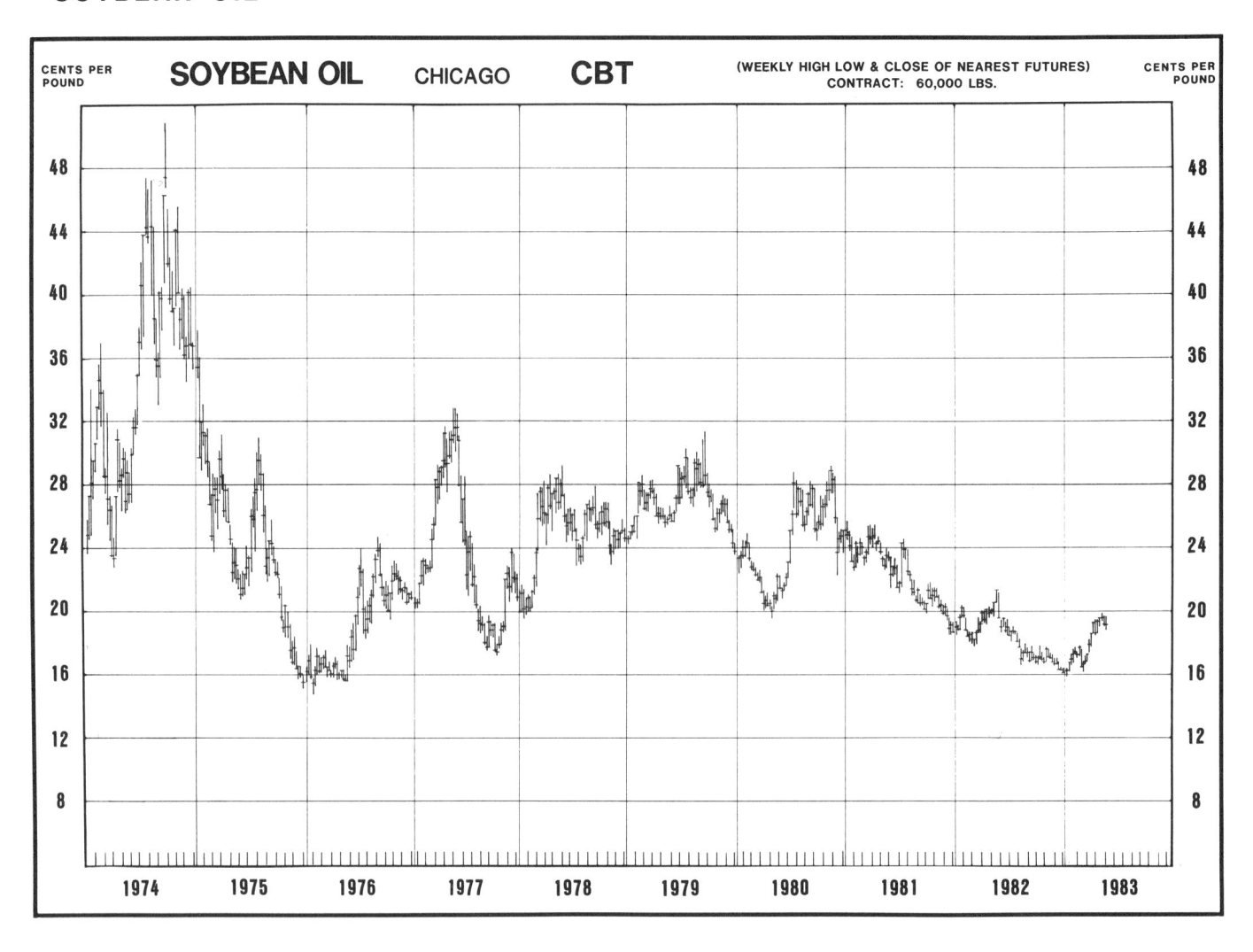

SOYBEAN OIL

SOYBEAN OIL CHICAGO **CBT** (WEEKLY HIGH LOW & CLOSE OF NEAREST FUTURES) CONTRACT: 60,000 LBS. — CENTS PER POUND

High, Low & Closing Prices of May Soybean Oil Futures on the Chicago Board of Trade ¢ per lb.

Year of Delivery		Mar.	Apr.	May	June	July	Aug.	Sept.	Oct.	Nov.	Dec.	Jan.	Feb.	Mar.	Apr.	May	Life of Delivery Range
1978	High	26.20	27.35	27.90	28.35	23.32	20.95	20.39	20.10	21.75	22.40	21.88	22.15	28.25	28.65	28.80	28.80
	Low	24.50	25.20	25.60	22.90	20.35	18.35	18.05	18.00	18.65	20.40	19.82	20.02	22.25	24.15	26.30	18.00
	Close	26.00	26.55	27.90	24.32	20.70	18.50	19.82	18.92	20.45	21.05	20.36	22.13	26.15	27.47	27.97	—
1979	High	22.13	23.70	25.12	24.95	22.45	24.05	25.15	26.35	25.80	25.70	25.97	28.85	28.30	27.85	26.45	28.85
	Low	21.40	20.90	21.50	21.35	20.95	21.10	23.10	23.92	23.55	23.92	24.28	25.31	26.35	25.50	25.27	20.90
	Close	21.75	21.58	25.00	22.30	22.13	22.90	24.10	25.90	24.65	24.67	25.37	27.53	27.57	26.00	25.85	—
1980	High	25.70	25.74	26.45	29.20	28.45	27.35	28.25	27.25	26.50	26.15	24.80	25.37	23.54	21.19	21.20	29.20
	Low	24.70	24.55	25.25	25.95	25.80	25.35	25.55	25.05	25.16	24.60	23.45	23.21	20.72	19.53	19.75	19.53
	Close	25.25	25.37	26.22	26.60	26.05	26.40	26.68	25.58	25.88	24.62	24.63	23.32	20.74	19.86	20.90	—
1981	High	26.15	24.00	24.05	25.65	29.40	28.55	29.70	29.20	31.45	30.75	27.35	25.55	25.40	25.51	24.05	31.45
	Low	23.60	22.35	22.35	22.80	25.45	26.50	26.80	26.81	28.25	24.25	23.40	23.60	23.50	23.60	22.61	22.35
	Close	23.60	22.37	23.38	25.62	28.30	28.05	27.21	28.28	30.70	26.00	23.57	24.84	25.15	23.84	22.85	—
1982	High	28.60	29.02	28.10	26.50	27.90	25.90	24.50	24.25	23.25	21.85	21.01	21.08	19.45	20.25	20.90	29.02
	Low	27.13	27.75	26.30	24.70	24.85	23.50	22.52	22.45	21.20	19.65	19.70	18.72	18.26	18.88	19.70	18.26
	Close	28.60	27.75	26.35	25.02	25.90	23.60	22.87	23.00	21.21	19.76	20.88	19.13	18.88	19.83	20.72	—
1983	High	—	—	22.90	21.65	20.42	19.90	19.35	18.60	18.40	17.75	17.96	18.30	18.59	19.64		
	Low	—	—	21.66	20.30	19.73	18.15	18.00	17.50	17.25	16.91	16.61	16.65	16.80	18.54		
	Close	—	—	21.66	20.32	19.73	18.85	18.00	17.60	17.48	16.91	17.91	16.74	18.56	19.61		
1984	High	—	21.60														
	Low	—	20.75														
	Close	—	21.53														

Source: Chicago Board of Trade

T.622

SOYBEAN OIL

Supply & Distribution of Soybean Oil in the U.S.   In Millions of Pounds

Year Begin. Oct.	Production	Stocks Oct. 1	Exports & Shipments	Total	Shortening	Margarine	Cooking & Salad Oils	Other Edible	Total Food	Paint & Varnish	Resins & Plastics	Fatty Acids	Other Inedible	Foots & Loss	Total Non-Food
1970-1	8,265	543	1,782	6,253	2,077	1,381	2,288	34	5,780	82	65	3	56	267	472
1971-2	7,892	773	1,440	6,440	2,089	1,413	2,469	48	6,009	81	55	6	38	251	431
1972-3	7,501	785	1,086	6,685	2,230	1,491	2,469	39	6,229	81	57	9	40	270	456
1973-4	8,995	516	1,461	7,256	2,321	1,513	2,884	30	6,748	91	77	12	48	280	508
1974-5	7,375	794	1,090	6,518	1,882	1,486	2,680	22	6,070	82	58	16	31	260	448
1975-6	9,630	561	1,035	7,906	2,416	1,691	3,274	24	7,405	94	96	23	25	294	501
1976-7	8,578	1,251	1,607	7,454	2,189	1,568	3,165	25	6,947	85	83	26	36	278	507
1977-8	10,288	771	2,137	8,273	2,279	1,585	3,325	29	7,621	87	79	42	33	308	549
1978-9	11,323	729	2,411	8,942	2,480	1,593	3,825								
1979-0	12,105	776	2,741	8,981	2,680	1,643	4,060								
1980-1[1]	11,270	1,210	1,631	9,113	2,660	1,651	4,041								
1981-2[2]	10,979	1,736	2,077	9,535	2,767	1,685	4,308								
1982-3[2]	11,990	1,103	2,075	9,803											
1983-4[2]		1,215													

[1] Preliminary.   [2] Forecast.   Source: Economic Research Service, U.S.D.A.   T.623

Volume of Trading of Soybean Oil Futures at the Chicago Board of Trade   In Thousands of Contracts

Year	Jan.	Feb.	Mar.	Apr.	May	June	July	Aug.	Sept.	Oct.	Nov.	Dec.	Total
1978	209.5	183.4	312.7	266.8	258.1	278.6	215.2	236.3	204.3	285.4	257.3	201.7	2,909
1979	215.0	291.5	233.8	254.4	212.3	321.7	313.0	252.5	262.0	311.6	222.3	191.6	3,082
1980	200.7	210.3	177.1	185.0	198.2	216.9	361.8	284.8	329.9	332.6	327.0	343.7	3,168
1981	243.8	231.1	237.9	254.0	221.7	274.8	355.1	233.7	240.2	235.0	228.1	292.1	3,047
1982	219.1	245.6	239.8	272.2	277.7	270.7	264.5	294.9	260.5	195.4	307.4	221.6	3,049
1983	273.6	244.1	264.4	273.2									

Source: Chicago Board of Trade   T.626

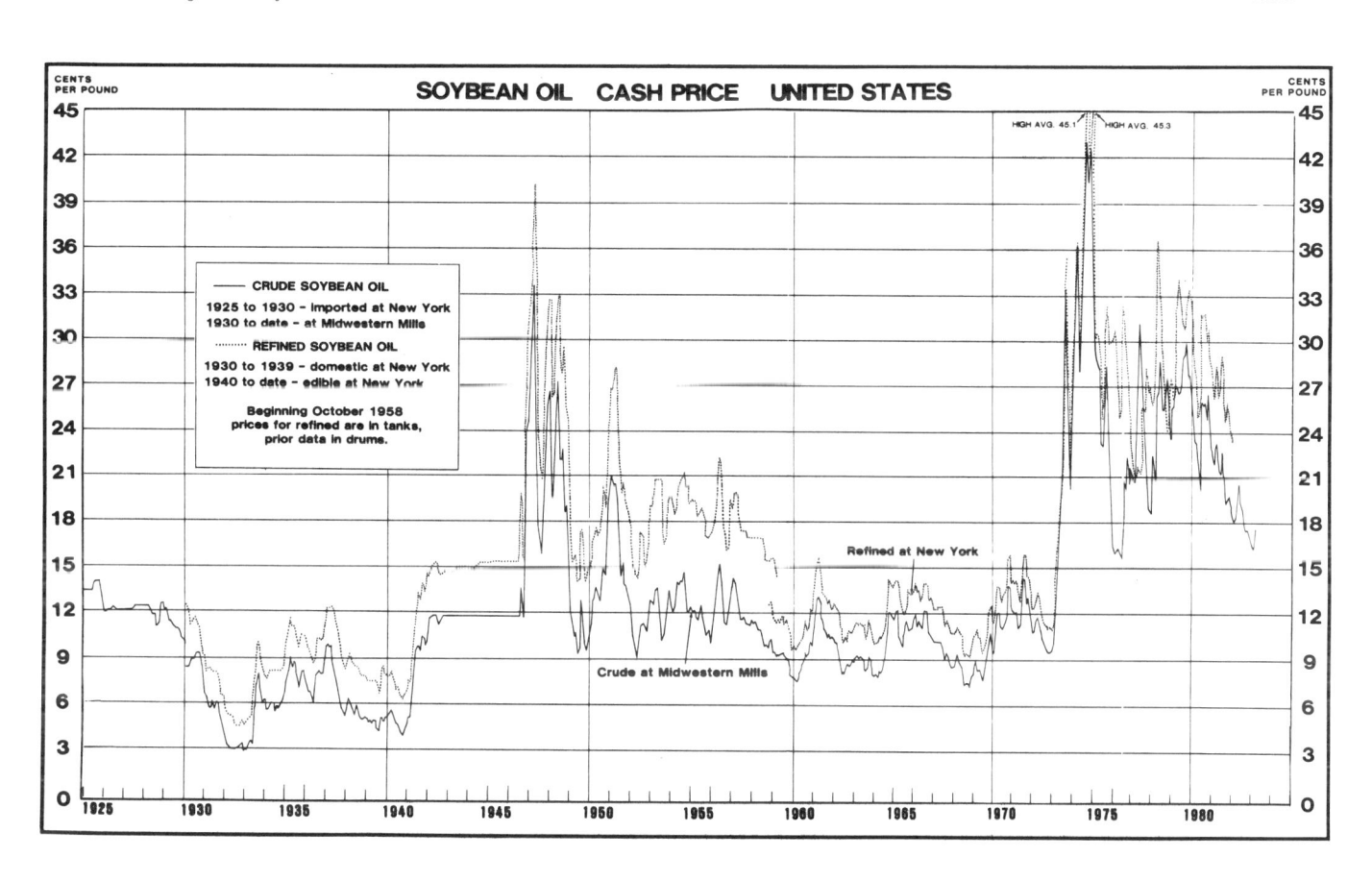

Soybeans

World soybean production during 1982/83 was forecast by the USDA at 96.8 million metric tons (tonnes), 10.6 million above the previous season's figure. The increase in U.S. soybean production accounted for 71 percent of the increase, and production increases in the major growing countries, Brazil, Argentina, and the People's Republic of China, made up a combined 23 percent of the world increase.

Although the world market for soybeans was expected to expand slightly during 1982/83, the U.S. share of that market was projected as dropping from more than 88 percent during 1981/82 to about 84% during 1982/83. This projection was based upon expectations of a 47 percent increase in Argentine exports and a 25 percent rise in Brazilian exports. The European Community (EC), the major importer of U.S. soybeans, remained the most promising market for U.S. production during 1982/83. As a result of EC pricing policies for grains, the price of soybean meal relative to other feeds was highly favorable. EC purchases of U.S. soybeans were expected to reach the same level as in 1981/82. Japan, the second largest importer of U.S. soybeans, commonly taking 20 percent of U.S. sales, was expected to increase its purchases only marginally. The world soybean crush was forecast at 79 million tonnes during 1982/83, a 6 percent increase from year-earlier levels. However, higher soybean usage was not expected to offset increases in world production, and 1982/83 season world ending stocks were projected at 27 percent above the previous season's figure.

U.S. soybean production during 1982/83 was estimated by the USDA to be 2.28 billion bushels, compared with 2 billion during the previous season. This output, added to an estimated 266 million bushel carryover, amounted to a record estimated soybean supply of 2.54 billion bushels which exceeds the previous record of 2.44 billion set during 1979/80. The large 1982/83 crop was the outcome of a 4.4 million acre increase in acreage over 1981/82 and of a record yield of 32.2 bushels per acre, nearly 2.1 bushels greater than the previous year's average. The 1982/83 soybean acreage increased because many farmers participating in the 10 percent feed grain acreage reduction program planted less than 90 percent of their corn acreage base. Often the difference between actual corn acreage and 90 percent of the base was planted to soybeans. Heavy rain in the Western Corn Belt delayed corn planting in May and part of the intended corn acreage was eventually planted to soybeans. In the Southeast and the Delta States, double cropping of soybeans and wheat continued. Double-cropped soybean acreage during 1982/83 was nearly 60 percent above the 1981/82 level to about 8 million acres.

Soybean prices were expected to recover from the season's lows because of the consequent stronger prices for corn even though the PIK program was expected to have little direct effect on soybean acreage. However, some analysts thought that U.S. soybean acreage could fall by 1 to 3 million acres during 1983/84 because of generally low prices during 1982/83.

Domestic processors were expected to crush 1.12 billion bushels during 1982/83, about 9 percent above the previous season's depressed levels. Large soybean supplies and an increase in demand for soybean meal were the main reasons for expectations that the season's gross crushing margin—the value of oil and meal less the season-average farm price for soybeans—might be as high as 50¢ a bushel.

U.S. 1982/83 ending stocks of soybeans were forecast at 390 million bushels, well above the August 31, 1982 carryover of 266 million bushels and the 1980/81 ending stocks of 318 million bushels. These high stocks were expected to keep prices relatively weak compared with recent years.

U.S. Government Support Program

The national average loan rate for 1983 crop soybeans was established by the USDA at $5.02 per bushel (No. 1 grade; 12.8–13.0 percent moisture) unchanged from 1982. Loans mature nine months after the date of loan approval (producers with 1981 crop soybean loans that matured at the end of January 1983 or later had the option of extending their loans an additional six months).

Futures Markets

Soybean futures in the U.S. are currently traded on the Chicago Board of Trade and on the Mid-America Commodity Exchange in Chicago.

World Production of Soybeans   In Thousands of Metric Tons

Year of Harvest[3]	Argentina	Brazil	Canada	China	Colombia	Indonesia	Japan	Korea, South	Mexico	Romania	Paraguay	Thailand	United States	USSR	World Total
1972	78	3,666	375	6,500	122	516	127	224	375	186		80	34,581	258	47,646
1973	496	7,876	397	10,000	114	541	118	246	510	244		115	42,117	424	63,912
1974	485	9,892	301	9,500	114	589	133	319	420	298		114	33,102	360	56,513
1975	695	10,810	367	10,000	169	590	126	311	625	213		121	42,113	780	67,914
1976	1,400	12,200	250	9,000	75	590	126	311	280	213	333	121	35,042	480	59,288
1977	2,700	9,534	527	7,300	135	523	111	319	470	191	333	90	47,947	540	72,157
1978	3,700	10,240	516	7,565	137	680	190	293	330	230	549	100	50,898	634	77,266
1979	3,600	15,156	671	7,460	146	642	192	257	680	383	575	102	61,722	467	93,717
1980	3,500	15,200	713	7,940	155	650	174	216	280	448	600	105	48,772	525	80,800
1981[1]	4,000	12,835	607	9,330	89	660	212	330	680	268	600	110	54,435	450	86,269
1982[3]	3,400	14,900	833	8,700	110	665	213	330	730	350	600	110	61,969	460	95,222

[1] Preliminary.   [2] Projected.   [3] Split year includes Northern Hemisphere crops harvested in the late months of the first year shown combined with Southern Hemisphere crops harvested in the early months of the following year.   *Source: Foreign Agricultural Service, U.S.D.A.*   T.627

SOYBEANS

U.S. Soybean Price Support Program & Official Crop Production Reports   In Millions of Bushels

Year	Quantity Put Under Support	Deliveries to C.C.C.	Sept. 1 Stocks Total	Sept. 1 Stocks Gov't. Owned	National Avg. Support % of Parity	National Avg. Support $ Per Bu.	August 1	September 1	October 1	November 1	December 1	Final
1970	146.4	2	229.8	196.9	60	2.25	1,113,566	1,133,193	1,134,595	1,134,151	1,135,769	1,127,100
1971	168.2	2	98.8	11.4	56	2.25	1,235,451	1,186,301	1,175,447	1,200,201	1,169,361	1,176,101
1972	90.6	2	72.0	1.5	54	2.25	1,269,616	1,286,015	1,317,090	1,350,517	1,276,290	1,270,608
1973	124.2	2	59.6	—	45	2.25	1,539,771	1,598,746	1,588,361	1,574,586	1,566,518	1,547,543
1974	34.6	—	170.8	—	37	2.25	1,314,232	1,315,792	1,262,352	1,243,912	1,233,425	1,216,287
1975	—	—	188.2	.4	—None—		1,457,672	1,442,422	1,473,782	1,519,882	1,521,370	1,548,344
1976	22.5	—	244.9	—	34	2.50	1,344,343	1,274,263	1,249,713	1,252,148	1,287,560	1,288,608
1977	97.5	—	102.9	—	46	3.50	1,602,065	1,644,220	1,647,315	1,682,705	1,761,755	1,767,267
1978	64.2	—	161.0	—	51	4.50	1,765,024	1,772,364	1,792,064	1,810,389	1,870,181	1,868,754
1979	120.0	—	174.1	—	45	4.50	2,129,254	2,174,179	2,213,289	2,235,869	2,267,647	2,267,901
1980	—	—	358.8	—	38	5.02	1,880,342	1,831,172	1,757,272	1,774,742	1,817,097	1,792,062
1981[1]	—	—	318.3	—		5.02	2,017,468	2,089,418	2,106,568	2,076,998	2,030,452	2,000,145
1982[1]			266.2			5.02	2,293,420	2,313,880	2,300,345	2,299,520	2,276,976	
1983[1]			390			5.02						

[1] Preliminary.   [2] Less than 50,000 bushels.   Source: Crop Reporting Board, U.S.D.A.   T.628

Soybean Stocks in the United States   In Thousands of Bushels

Year	On Farms Jan. 1	On Farms April 1	On Farms June 1[2]	On Farms Sept. 1	Off Farms Jan. 1	Off Farms April 1	Off Farms June 1[2]	Off Farms Sept. 1	Total Stocks Jan. 1	Total Stocks April 1	Total Stocks June 1[2]	Total Stocks Sept. 1
1970	372,069	209,236	78,711	40,580	683,425	525,001	324,676	189,256	1,055,494	734,237	403,387	229,836
1971	391,960	246,491	90,595	20,554	553,012	369,063	190,832	78,225	944,972	615,554	281,427	98,779
1972	397,605	218,609	58,438	11,779	491,387	333,677	174,394	60,183	888,992	552,286	232,832	71,962
1973	429,071	145,333	33,855	9,415	437,924	358,372	145,352	50,222	866,995	503,705	179,207	59,637
1974	608,160	331,885	151,104	64,545	552,756	405,943	190,865	106,337	1,160,916	737,828	341,969	170,882
1975	483,869	331,241	165,324	75,114	505,392	323,317	191,704	109,922	989,261	654,558	357,028	185,036
1976	590,466	411,366	253,963	86,150	665,689	456,283	300,938	158,781	1,256,155	867,649	554,901	244,931
1977	473,120	227,723	92,374	32,748	559,045	390,214	243,335	70,168	1,032,165	617,937	335,709	102,916
1978	672,861	393,684	207,102	59,000	652,400	455,448	298,815	102,044	1,325,261	849,132	505,917	161,044
1979	699,556	412,570	241,255	61,509	692,534	467,646	284,850	112,579	1,392,090	880,216	526,105	174,088
1980	892,934	602,779	396,650	128,888	877,896	580,322	378,152	229,880	1,770,830	1,183,101	774,802	358,768
1981	730,157	533,082	362,266	159,029	790,300	496,619	317,156	159,276	1,520,457	1,029,701	679,422	318,305
1982[1]	888,184	581,276	360,237	129,602	743,188	459,361	291,921	136,571	1,631,372	1,040,637	652,158	266,173
1983[1]	1,074,278	695,003			752,223	501,674			1,826,501	1,196,677		
1984												

[1] Preliminary.   [2] Data prior to 1976 are AS OF JULY 1.   Source: Crop Reporting Board, U.S.D.A.   T.629

U.S. Commercial Stocks of Soybeans on the First of the Month   In Millions of Bushels

Year	Jan.	Feb.	Mar.	Apr.	May	June	July	Aug.	Sept.	Oct.	Nov.	Dec.
1970	79.4	84.8	82.5	82.3	72.4	59.0	43.8	8.7	34.3	17.8	30.1	40.7
1971	47.2	51.4	54.4	57.1	54.2	41.6	35.0	36.5	17.3	12.1	48.5	48.8
1972	41.8	37.7	41.1	49.0	48.4	36.1	27.1	18.8	13.6	7.0	25.0	32.0
1973	39.1	32.0	56.8	59.7	48.9	31.8	22.8	16.6	12.1	10.5	30.4	35.6
1974	33.6	32.0	35.3	36.2	27.3	21.2	21.2	20.3	18.0	14.3	51.6	55.4
1975	48.1	43.3	40.5	31.1	18.0	12.8	16.6	13.0	12.6	14.2	60.2	62.5
1976	52.0	55.7	57.1	51.7	42.5	37.0	32.5	30.4	21.3	27.9	54.4	52.2
1977	46.8	49.5	51.1	52.3	55.4	50.0	38.7	19.6	8.5	10.9	43.6	50.9
1978	46.2	44.3	41.8	49.1	47.9	42.7	30.6	23.0	10.7	13.0	58.3	63.2
1979	60.9	57.6	62.0	60.8	52.5	40.7	37.6	31.2	19.3	11.5	77.6	84.9
1980	76.5	71.5	73.2	72.3	56.5	52.6	53.2	51.8	44.8	51.5	80.6	79.5
1981	73.1	71.1	69.0	53.1	45.3	35.7	24.7	19.0	11.2	12.6	40.7	51.7
1982	50.6	50.4	41.1	39.9	34.7	67.4	21.5	18.4	11.5	12.8	43.9	53.5
1983	53.6	58.2	57.5	55.7	55.9							
1984												

Source: Foreign Agricultural Service, U.S.D.A.   T.630

SOYBEANS

Salient Statistics of Soybeans in the United States

Crop Year	Planted Alone — 1,000 Acres	Acreage Harvested — 1,000 Acres	Yield Per Acre (Bus.)	Farm Price ($ Bu.)	Farm Value (Million Dollars)	Pounds Per Bushel Crushed Yield of Oil	Pounds Per Bushel Crushed Yield of Meal	U.S. Exports Grand Total	Bel.-Luxem.	Den-mark	Can-ada	W. Ger-many	Japan	Nether-lands	Tai-wan	U.S.S.R.
1970-1	43,802	42,249	26.7	2.85	3,215	10.83	47.39	433.8	13.2	21.4	42.2	53.0	102.8	57.9	19.6	—
1971-2	43,472	42,705	27.5	3.03	3,560	10.98	47.43	416.8	5.7	16.2	31.3	52.0	107.4	64.1	23.9	0
1972-3	46,885	45,683	27.8	4.37	5,550	10.59	47.04	479.4	8.2	17.4	22.1	54.7	121.0	84.3	19.6	31.5
1973-4	56,675	55,667	27.8	5.68	8,790	10.76	47.18	539.1	13.2	12.5	37.9	72.9	98.8	101.1	20.5	.7
1974-5	53,507	51,341	23.7	6.64	8,079	10.51	47.48	420.7	5.6	5.9	26.9	51.0	96.9	77.7	24.4	0
1975-6	54,550	53,617	28.9	4.92	7,622	10.94	47.27	555.1	17.7	15.1	28.0	45.6	118.1	130.5	32.8	11.4
1976-7	50,226	49,401	26.1	6.81	8,776	11.09	47.81	15,351	411	306	462	1,520	3,219	3,007	697	825
1977-8	58,760	57,830	30.6	5.88	10,383	10.89	47.34	19,061	475	423	264	1,521	3,636	4,086	854	744
1978-9	64,708	63,663	29.4	6.66	12,450	11.07	47.63	20,117	420	341	352	1,486	3,865	4,012	1,271	1,178
1979-0	71,632	70,566	32.1	6.28	14,250	10.76	48.01	23,818	584	342	392	1,318	3,868	6,035	780	813
1980-1[1]	70,037	67,856	26.4	7.57	13,560	11.09	47.93	19,712	670	156	345	1,791	3,816	3,839	1,063	—
1981-2[1]	67,810	66,368	30.1	6.04	12,071			24,766								
1982-3[1]	72,162	70,783	32.2	5.48	12,480			24,902								
1983-4[1]																

[1] Preliminary. [2] Data prior to 1976-7 are in MILLIONS OF BUSHELS. Source: Crop Reporting Board, U.S.D.A. T.631

Supply and Distribution of Soybeans in the United States — In Millions of Bushels

Crop Year Begin. Sept. 1	Farms	CCC	Mills, Elevators[2]	Total	Production	Total Supply	Crushings	Exports	Seed	Feed	Residual	Total Distribution
1970-1	40.6	8.7	180.5	229.8	1,127.1	1,356.9	760.1	433.8	48.1	1.1	15.1	1,258.2
1971-2	20.6	—	78.2	98.8	1,176.1	1,274.9	720.5	416.8	51.0	1.1	13.5	1,202.9
1972-3	11.8	0	60.2	72.0	1,270.6	1,342.6	721.8	479.4	60.8	1.1	19.8	1,282.9
1973-4	9.4	0	50.2	59.6	1,547.5	1,607.1	821.3	539.1	56.1	1.2	18.7	1,436.4
1974-5	64.5	0	106.3	170.9	1,216.3	1,387.2	701.3	420.7	57.2	1.0	21.7	1,198.9
1975-6	75.1	0	109.9	188.2	1,548.3	1,736.5	865.1	555.1	53.5	1.2	15.7	1,490.6
1976-7	86.2	0	158.8	244.9	1,288.6	1,533.5	790.2	564.1	61.0	1.0	13.3	1,429.6
1977-8	32.7	0	70.2	102.9	1,767.3	1,870.2	926.7	700.5	68.0	1.0	13.0	1,703.6
1978-9	59.0	0	102.0	161.0	1,868.8	2,029.8	1,018	739.0	75.0	1.0	23.0	1,856.0
1979-0	61.5	0	112.6	174.1	2,267.9	2,442.0	1,123	875.0	67.0	1.0	17.0	2,083.0
1980-1	128.9	0	229.9	358.8	1,792.1	2,350.0	1,020	724.0	——66——		23.0	1,833.0
1981-2[1]	159.0	0	159.3	318.3	2,000.1	2,318.4	1,030	929.0	——70——		23.0	2,052.0
1982-3[3]	129.6	0	136.6	266.2	2,277.0	2,543.2	1,115	950.0	——70——		17.0	2,153.0
1983-4[3]					390							

[1] Preliminary. [2] Also warehouses. [3] Estimates. Source: Economic Research Service, U.S.D.A. T.632

Production of Soybeans for Beans in the U.S., by Selected States — In Millions of Bushels

Year	Ark.	So. Car.	Ill.	Ind.	Iowa	La.	Mich.	Minn.	Miss.	Mo.	N. Car.	Ohio	Tenn.	Nebr.	Ky.
1970	99.0	20.2	210.8	101.6	184.6	40.5	13.3	78.8	58.1	88.4	20.8	72.7	26.5	17.9	14.3
1971	92.5	23.0	236.0	111.4	178.8	39.5	10.3	63.9	56.6	97.3	23.8	80.3	31.7	15.2	20.8
1972	81.0	20.0	259.4	108.8	216.0	38.3	13.6	90.3	48.0	108.9	29.1	79.8	28.6	23.0	23.6
1973	116.3	23.0	281.3	135.1	263.5	34.8	16.6	127.3	60.5	126.9	34.8	89.8	36.9	36.3	26.0
1974	81.7	24.0	202.6	97.3	199.1	44.0	13.2	84.0	46.3	93.5	30.5	79.8	31.9	28.2	25.0
1975	117.5	30.4	299.5	121.6	237.0	48.0	15.9	98.6	70.2	113.6	33.4	102.3	46.3	32.4	29.7
1976	82.1	21.4	249.5	111.5	200.0	63.0	11.6	66.4	71.5	84.0	24.6	95.0	40.5	19.6	28.9
1977	105.8	26.7	336.3	144.3	251.3	63.0	21.6	133.8	78.5	148.8	29.0	120.0	52.2	40.7	40.9
1978	115.2	32.3	309.5	144.2	283.1	76.0	21.6	146.2	81.7	155.0	40.3	127.7	56.9	42.5	40.8
1979	144.2	39.8	379.1	159.1	306.4	93.8	30.3	162.6	118.9	183.6	45.8	144.8	70.7	54.7	54.0
1980	65.3	20.8	309.9	157.7	318.4	67.0	30.4	149.9	61.6	135.5	34.7	135.4	45.9	53.1	36.0
1981	99.0	31.0	351.5	151.8	326.0	64.2	29.1	139.2	75.6	155.6	46.3	99.8	61.1	78.7	47.9
1982[1]	109.2	40.7	367.0	183.2	320.6	76.7	32.2	174.6	93.6	184.3	52.5	138.0	63.5	82.8	53.1
1983															

[1] Preliminary. Source: Crop Reporting Board, U.S.D.A. T.633

High, Low & Closing Prices of May Soybean Futures at the Chicago Board of Trade In Cents per Bushel

Year of Delivery		Year Prior to Delivery										Delivery Year					Life of Delivery
		Mar.	Apr.	May	June	July	Aug.	Sept.	Oct.	Nov.	Dec.	Jan.	Feb.	Mar.	Apr.	May	Range
1979	High	648	659	695	691	639	673½	697	753	736	727	733	797	785	755½	738½	797
	Low	614½	608½	619	620¼	606	606	646½	674	669	681	685	714	738	714	705¼	606
	Close	632	625½	690¼	645¼	625½	657	672¼	736½	697½	700¾	718¾	766	771¼	717	723½	—
1980	High	744½	747	760	859	823	773	790	788	739½	726½	704	710½	669½	611	624	859
	Low	735	719½	734	749	730½	720	729½	695	702	686½	653	656½	582½	569½	589½	569½
	Close	737½	739¾	756	764	738¾	757¾	762½	709¾	723¼	687¼	695½	657½	583	594½	612	—
1981	High	741½	713½	710	750	859	855½	933	997½	1,006	1,001	882	798½	788½	812½	785	1,006
	Low	696½	681	684	680	744	783	842	847½	937	765½	735	754½	719½	757½	733	680
	Close	699	692	695¾	750	822	854½	873¼	966½	997½	843½	751½	761	783½	778½	741	—
1982	High	894	922	883	832½	853½	807	751	739	721	696¼	677	683	642	670¾	669½	922½
	Low	859	872	820	772	787	722	703½	705	670	619	637	617½	605½	639½	647	605
	Close	888½	873	829	788½	812½	730	715¼	714¼	678¼	641¼	674½	632¾	640	651¾	666	—
1983	High	713	729½	723½	704½	678½	664½	611½	588	607¾	595½	620	622	643¾	655½		
	Low	667½	698	687½	670	651	593½	572½	558½	570½	576¼	577	572½	577½	620¼		
	Close	696	716½	687½	671	654¾	601	574¼	568¼	594	581¾	618½	575½	637	640¼		
1984	High	718	732														
	Low	645	695½														
	Close	714	719														

Source: Chicago Board of Trade T.634

Soybean Stocks at U.S. Mills on First of Month in Thousands of Short Tons[1]

Crop Year	Sept.	Oct.	Nov.	Dec.	Jan.	Feb.	Mar.	Apr.	May	June	July	Aug.
1972-3	38.1	12.3	91.3	111.1	117.4	136.6	133.3	124.0	107.9	88.5	68.2	58.5
1973-4	30.7	13.5	89.5	125.8	115.8	119.0	123.0	112.3	95.5	81.5	66.5	57.0
1974-5	41.6	23.0	93.9	123.0	102.5	83.2	79.2	65.3	55.4	44.3	37.7	35.4
1975-6	27.4	26.8	116.6	137.2	131.5	121.1	109.8	101.3	92.8	79.4	80.5	66.3
1976-7	48.7	63.0	127.5	159.8	154.2	147.5	146.5	140.3	126.8	108.6	83.4	50.9
1977-8[1]	23.4	20.3	3,045[1]	3,716	3,390	2,832	2,620	3,085	2,705	2,291	1,724	1,339
1978-9	1,136	957	4,153	4,480	3,820	3,371	3,722	3,626	2,902	2,133	2,190	1,668
1979-0	1,124	1,176	4,996	5,536	4,899	4,363	3,931	3,559	2,874	2,392	2,272	2,218
1980-1	1,706	2,412	4,981	5,159	4,162	3,777	3,162	2,917	2,533	2,035	1,475	1,316
1981-2	1,002	946	3,173	4,055	3,436	2,993	2,539	2,376	2,167	1,824	1,536	1,308
1982-3	919	870	3,426	4,366	3,752	3,510						
1983-4												

[1] Data prior to Nov. 1977 are in MILLIONS OF BUSHELS. *Sources: Economic Research Service, U.S.D.A.; Bureau of the Census* T.635

Soybean Exports from the United States In Millions of Bushels

Year	Sept.	Oct.	Nov.	Dec.	Jan.	Feb.	Mar.	Apr.	May	June	July	Aug.	Total
1971-2	29.2	29.4	47.4	50.3	42.4	35.5	31.3	37.3	31.7	31.1	26.3	24.9	416.8
1972-3	15.0	54.3	61.2	49.7	47.1	54.7	59.1	45.5	41.0	26.5	14.2	11.0	479.4
1973-4	7.5	46.6	74.4	58.0	48.3	56.4	57.9	62.0	43.5	36.1	27.1	21.2	539.1
1974-5	22.9	32.2	63.2	41.4	50.0	33.3	38.4	35.8	25.1	14.0	31.0	33.4	420.7
1975-6	24.3	62.7	61.5	49.6	51.8	52.2	52.3	50.5	49.5	47.2	29.2	24.3	555.1
1976-7	22.2	60.1	67.4	56.7	50.9	59.9	58.4	57.0	55.1	31.0	27.2	18.1	564.1
1977-8	15.0	77.6	87.7	57.0	52.6	54.4	66.6	72.7	79.3	63.4	34.7	39.3	700.5
1978-9	38.0	87.6	101.7	70.6	77.0	53.2	83.5	67.7	46.8	40.9	32.7	39.7	739.2
1979-0	40.9	88.9	118.1	78.3	85.8	73.0	69.4	81.3	74.2	58.7	49.1	57.7	875.2
1980-1[1]	41.4	60.3	75.0	74.5	71.7	55.5	103.2	60.0	69.6	41.8	29.6	41.8	724.3
1981-2[1]	50.9	100.8	103.7	73.6	84.3	89.4	79.0	85.7	90.6	59.8	53.8	57.5	929.1
1982-3[1]	58.0	94.4	93.6	90.1									
1983-4													

[1] Preliminary. *Source: Bureau of the Census* T.636

SOYBEANS

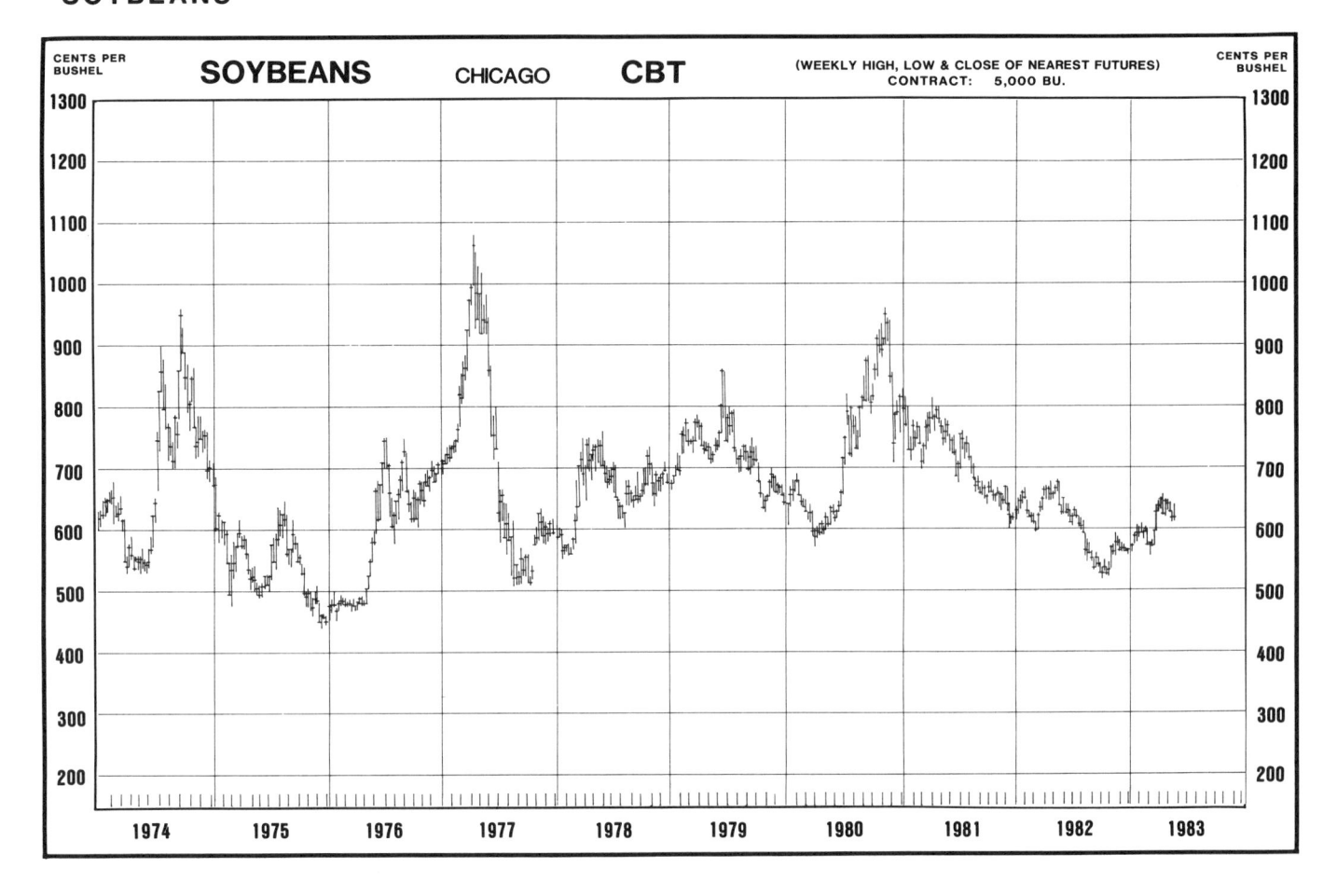

SOYBEANS CHICAGO **CBT** (WEEKLY HIGH, LOW & CLOSE OF NEAREST FUTURES) CONTRACT: 5,000 BU.

Month End Open Interest of Soybean Futures at Chicago Board of Trade — In Millions of Bushels

Year	Jan.	Feb.	Mar.	Apr.	May	June	July	Aug.	Sept.	Oct.	Nov.	Dec.
1978	470.3	438.0	499.4	483.9	553.5	491.8	452.8	485.8	562.2	726.6	720.1	775.1
1979	613.9	719.0	642.0	576.1	562.2	584.4	514.4	477.1	534.9	564.7	630.4	704.3
1980	533.2	540.0	502.2	449.6	513.5	615.0	703.5	784.4	880.4	1,069.6	1,102.7	1,056.4
1981	645.7	586.9	565.0	551.4	523.3	513.6	470.3	455.7	449.1	523.2	491.4	426.6
1982	400.8	391.6	435.2	422.1	399.1	377.0	400.2	353.7	357.7	422.9	433.3	424.7
1983	465.3	413.9	485.7	507.5								

Source: Chicago Board of Trade

T.642

Volume of Trading in Soybean Futures at the Chicago Board of Trade[1] — In Millions of Bushels

Year	Jan.	Feb.	Mar.	Apr.	May	June	July	Aug.	Sept.	Oct.	Nov.	Dec.	Total
1972	1,441	1,371	2,133	2,086	1,732	1,543	1,398	1,665	1,150	1,559	2,039	2,100	20,217
1973	2,150	1,344	1,387	1,241	1,345	871	757	879	577	992	1,178	993	13,712
1974	1,229	1,045	1,224	1,187	1,234	1,194	1,103	1,122	885	1,368	892	1,173	13,564
1975	1,409	1,204	1,473	1,497	1,481	1,400	2,117	1,893	1,621	2,204	1,759	1,508	19,567
1976	1,533	1,298	1,215	1,456	2,410	3,414	2,638	2,333	2,480	3,023	2,893	2,678	27,371
1977	3,483	2,564	5,062	4,707	3,550	4,012	2,468	2,312	2,378	2,734	3,897	2,813	39,981
1978	2,978	2,224	5,057	4,121	3,820	3,742	2,662	2,965	2,561	4,754	3,992	3,511	42,386
1979	3,701	5,038	4,123	3,856	3,686	5,485	4,184	2,843	2,920	3,946	3,115	2,674	45,572
1980	3,222	2,916	2,808	3,035	2,911	3,602	6,803	5,226	6,562	7,706	7,025	7,024	58,841
1981[2]	5,808	4,074	4,796	4,585	3,917	4,737	4,821	3,897	3,626	4,087	3,765	4,337	52,450
1982[2]	3,120	3,497	4,478	4,484	3,517	4,245	4,017	3,822	3,197	4,014	4,282	3,198	45,828
1983[2]	3,942	3,820	4,247	4,373									

[1] Trading on this market represents approximately 98% to 99% of all trading in Soybeans. [2] Preliminary. *Source: Commodity Futures Trading Commission*

T.638

SOYBEANS

Soybeans Under Price Support Through the End of the Month (Cumulative Total from Current Season's Crop) In Thousands of Bushels

Year	Sept.	Oct.	Nov.	Dec.	Jan.	Feb.	Mar.	Apr.	May	June	July	Aug.	Total
1970-1	128	23,449	64,494	114,092	140,103	143,355	145,300	146,127	146,406	146,463	146,462	146,462	147,000
1971-2	992	41,831	101,163	140,421	163,979	167,187	168,044	168,221	168,271	168,297	—	—	168,278
1972-3	58	21,067	56,609	75,190	86,803	89,338	90,368	90,546	90,561	90,560	—	—	
1973-4	171	11,009	75,213	101,310	120,240	122,752	123,613	124,067	124,170	124,188	—	—	
1974-5	121	3,868	13,186	19,410	22,426	23,275	23,828	34,217	34,543	34,574	—	—	
1975-6	——————————————————————No Program——————————————————————
1976-7	270	3,398	8,471	13,398	14,966	15,253	15,433	22,450	22,491	22,491	—	—	
1977-8	360	13,135	47,879	68,269	89,128	93,293	96,234	96,808	97,048	97,146	—	—	
1978-9	0	6,403	31,008	43,015	58,278	61,489	62,365	63,146	63,508	65,087	—	—	
1979-0	11	9,507	39,559	67,372	101,052	106,135	113,638	119,860	121,684	122,013	—	—	
1980-1	22	11,705	28,541	67,744	100,809	116,167	125,480	130,236	132,346	133,160	—	—	
1981-2	1,044	26,019	81,377	138,202	191,386	208,285	216,412	219,743	144,165	221,303			
1982-3	861	50,145	203,031	311,105	363,696	382,536	391,432						
1983-4													

Source: U.S. Department of Agriculture   T.639

Soybean Receipts at Primary Markets in the United States In Thousands of Bushels

Year	Jan.	Feb.	Mar.	Apr.	May	June	July	Aug.	Sept.	Oct.	Nov.	Dec.	Total
1969	2,651	3,776	3,622	3,808	3,671	4,366	5,859	6,988	9,633	36,390	22,796	8,058	111,618
1970	5,876	8,481	8,786	10,648	7,516	12,056	15,063	9,417	7,017	24,277	20,112	14,120	143,369
1971	6,672	6,048	8,164	5,508	6,116	13,053	12,438	6,075	5,237	29,273	13,580	2,358	114,972
1972	2,565	3,904	5,111	3,516	2,023	2,426	2,729	3,859	1,297	17,623	11,080	12,886	69,019
1973	13,106	8,779	6,776	4,267	5,717	3,331	3,354	2,059	1,077	14,946	13,330	3,976	80,718
1974	4,596	5,647	5,712	5,051	5,224	3,964	7,159	4,557	2,348	18,486	7,795	3,070	74,065
1975	1,969	1,390	1,865	1,823	1,843	2,665	4,505	3,066	2,131	25,944	5,988	2,049	55,238
1976	2,449	2,337	3,002	2,146	2,228	3,715	3,640	1,280	3,374	13,927	4,533	1,933	44,564
1977	3,335	3,337	4,736	4,075	6,824	781	152	1,980	1,208	11,960	7,986	4,023	50,397
1978	2,575	1,933	3,346	4,494	7,588	3,986	1,780	3,803	2,856	17,056	8,468	2,353	60,238
1979	2,718	4,007	2,938	2,916	2,669	3,545	2,370	2,034	2,375	20,795	9,360	3,138	58,965
1980	2,994	4,404	3,445	5,987	7,339	11,406	6,950	4,524	8,222	31,589	9,752	3,849	100,461
1981	4,419	3,395	3,485	4,986	3,918	4,616	3,573	3,735	7,694	21,027	13,882	5,596	80,236
1982													

Source: Chicago Board of Trade   T.640

Soybeans Crushed (Factory Consumption) in the U.S. In Millions of Bushels—One Bushel = 60 Pounds

Year	Sept.	Oct.	Nov.	Dec.	Jan.	Feb.	Mar.	Apr.	May	June	July	Aug.	Total
1970-1	53.3	66.8	65.9	68.1	67.7	60.1	63.6	63.8	63.8	61.1	62.4	63.6	760.1
1971-2	54.5	59.5	59.8	64.0	63.9	60.2	63.9	58.5	63.0	57.1	58.2	57.9	720.5
1972-3	52.2	66.8	70.7	69.2	70.6	64.8	64.4	58.2	61.7	52.2	44.5	46.5	721.8
1973-4	41.4	62.8	71.8	72.8	74.7	70.4	75.8	69.6	71.7	69.4	72.2	68.8	821.3
1974-5	53.6	61.6	60.8	60.2	63.1	54.1	61.0	57.5	53.0	53.1	59.2	64.0	701.3
1975-6	58.5	71.4	71.1	77.8	74.9	69.3	77.9	77.2	79.6	74.6	70.6	64.2	865.1
1976-7	68.8	72.9	73.4	72.7	72.2	71.6	74.4	67.1	61.2	56.2	50.6	49.1	790.2
1977-8	51.9	75.8	85.3	86.6	85.3	75.4	86.5	80.1	82.7	72.4	70.8	73.9	926.7
1978-9	71.4	89.3	89.6	96.4	90.6	81.5	89.0	83.3	86.9	82.8	80.6	76.4	1,018
1979-0	75.9	95.8	101.4	104.4	106.6	100.0	102.2	92.0	93.8	82.7	84.9	83.7	1,123
1980-1[1]	81.0	97.8	98.5	94.1	92.2	79.6	88.7	85.4	82.3	73.4	72.3	74.6	1,020
1981-2[1]	75.4	104.5	97.6	102.5	94.9	86.7	85.1	81.0	86.6	77.1	70.6	67.8	1,030
1982-3[1]	76.0	100.2	108.1	111.8									
1983-4													

[1] Preliminary. *Source: Bureau of the Census*   T.641

SOYBEANS

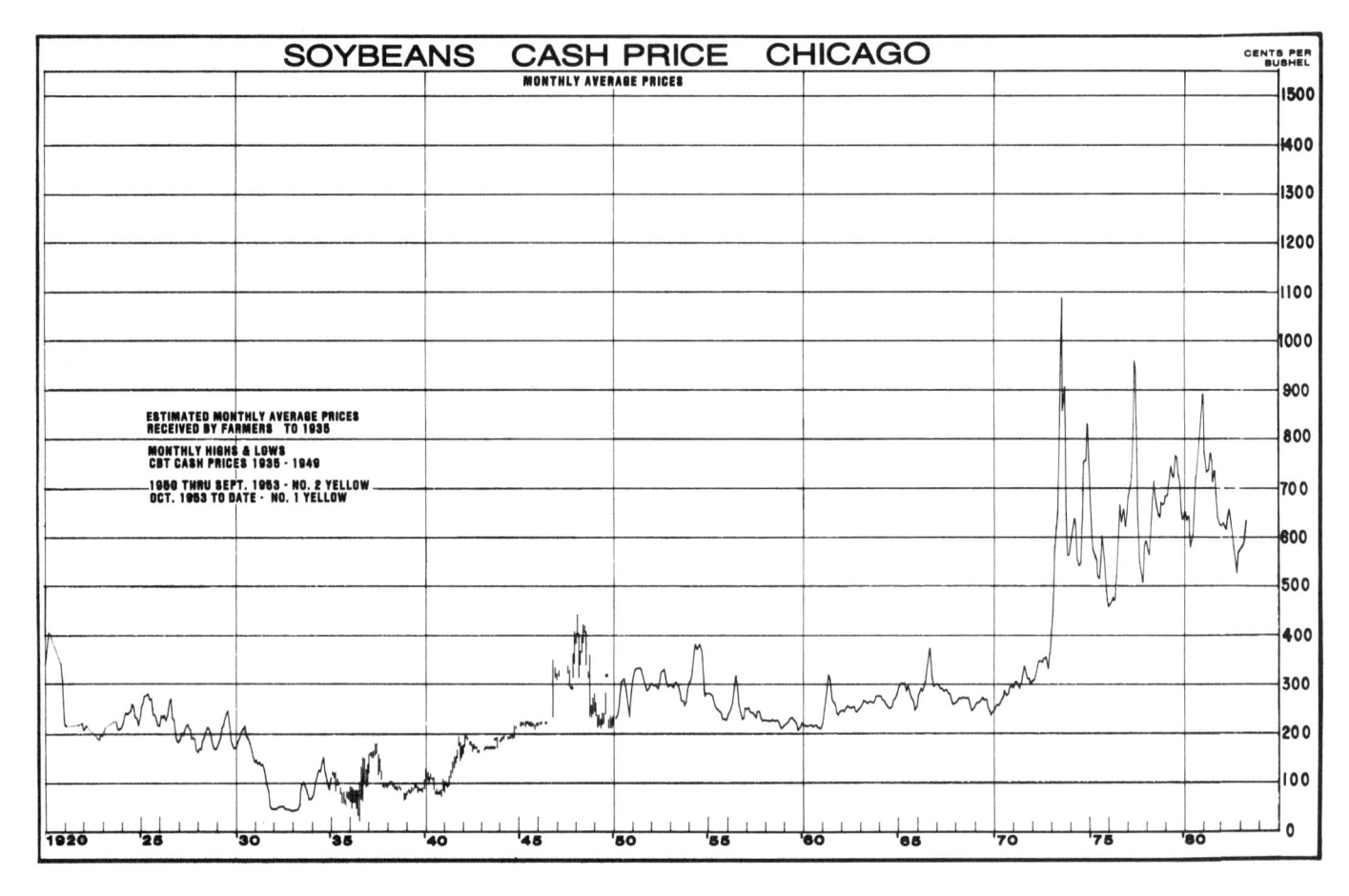

SOYBEANS CASH PRICE CHICAGO
Monthly Average Prices

Estimated monthly average prices received by farmers to 1935
Monthly highs & lows CBT cash prices 1935-1949
1950 thru Sept. 1963 - No. 2 Yellow
Oct. 1963 to date - No. 1 Yellow

Average Cash Price of No. 1 Yellow Soybeans at Illinois Processor[1]   In Cents per Bushel

Year	Oct.	Nov.	Dec.	Jan.	Feb.	Mar.	Apr.	May	June	July	Aug.	Sept.	Average
1970-1	295	300	293	303	306	304	291	303	321	338	329	312	308
1971-2	312	300	308	309	318	337	349	349	347	351	355	348	324
1972-3	333	364	413	446	580	624	652	894	1087	847	900	610	622
1973-4	562	557	592	617	635	629	559	547	551	711	776	764	612
1974-5[1]	830	754	723	638	569	560	555	523	516	560	602	557	632
1975-6	501	471	460	466	477	471	475	523	623	666	631	659	526
1976-7	622	655	686	706	726	825	960	942	825	640	549	516	721
1977-8	507	584	594	573	565	658	681	701	676	662	647	642	624
1978-9	672	668	681	689	728	745	727	721	768	764	728	704	716
1979-0	656	652	653	636	642	607	580	604	610	722	745	813	660
1980-1	827	891	773	757	734	737	772	758	713	736	694	644	753
1981-2	630	628	623	630	624	616	642	656	631	620	573	540	618
1982-3	526	570	573	581	586	598							

[1] Prior to Oct. 1974, prices are at Chicago.   *Source: Consumer & Marketing Service, U.S.D.A.*   T.643

Average Price Received by Farmers for Soybeans in the U.S.   In Cents Per Bushel

Year	Sept.	Oct.	Nov.	Dec.	Jan.	Feb.	Mar.	Apr.	May	June	July	Aug.	Average
1975-76	532	492	445	428	446	450	446	452	487	616	673	607	492
1976-77	665	590	611	656	681	706	783	905	924	813	652	548	681
1977-78	517	528	561	568	575	553	620	649	477	669	640	621	588
1978-79	620	626	641	649	658	699	716	706	706	736	736	707	666
1979-80	681	635	630	627	639	620	594	563	576	591	675	718	628
1980-81	759	768	818	780	780	750	759	760	740	705	713	671	761
1981-82	621	606	603	600	613	604	604	617	627	612	599	559	605
1982-83	522	506	534	546	556	566	582	604					

Source: Crop Reporting Board   T.637

Stock Index Futures (*See feature article on page 38*)

Futures trading in stock indexes was initiated in February 1982, and met with immediate favorable response by both speculators attempting to profit from fluctuations in overall stock prices and those traders or institutions who were interested primarily in hedging stock portfolios.

The volume of contracts traded in the Standard & Poor's (S&P) Composite Index of 500 Stocks ranked No. 10 of all futures contracts traded in 1982. The New York Stock Exchange (NYSE) Index ranked 24th and the Value Line (VLIC) Composite Average was in 34th place in 1982.

Futures Markets

Value Line Index futures are traded at the Kansas City Board of Trade. S&P 500 Index futures are traded at the Chicago Mercantile Exchange. Futures in the New York Stock Exchange Composite Index are traded at the New York Futures Exchange.

High, Low & Closing Prices of the December S&P 500 Stock Futures — Index at the Chi. IOM

Year of Delivery		Yr. Prior to Del. Dec.	Jan.	Feb.	Mar.	Apr.	May	June	July	Aug.	Sept.	Oct.	Nov.	Dec.	Life of Delivery Range
1982	High	Futures Trading				124.20	121.90	113.85	115.90	120.30	127.65	143.00	146.80	145.70	146.80
	Low	Began				117.80	111.80	104.35	106.80	101.40	116.95	118.55	131.40	134.75	101.40
	Close	April 21, 1982				120.60	112.05	111.85	107.90	119.45	119.35	134.55	138.65	135.30	—
1983	High	147.20	152.60	156.50	158.00	166.70									
	Low	138.00	140.60	144.75	151.10	151.90									
	Close	143.00	149.20	152.40	154.05	166.40									

High, Low & Closing Prices of the December NYSE Composite Stock Futures — Index at New York

Year of Delivery		Yr. Prior to Delivery Nov.	Dec.	Jan.	Feb.	Mar.	Apr.	May	June	July	Aug.	Sept	Oct	Nov	Dec.	Life of Delivery Range
1982	High		Futures Trading					70.55	65.35	66.85	69.10	73.50	82.10	84.45	83.95	84.45
	Low		Began					64.65	60.20	61.45	58.10	67.20	68.15	76.10	77.70	58.10
	Close		May 6, 1982					64.60	64.30	62.05	68.45	68.45	77.55	81.65	81.30	—
1983	High	85.70	85.35	88.20	90.25	91.00	95.90									
	Low	78.80	80.20	81.50	83.80	87.00	87.65									
	Close	84.00	83.30	86.70	88.05	88.65	95.75									

High, Low & Closing Prices of the December Value Line Stock Futures — Index at the K.C. Board of Trade

Year of Delivery		Yr. Prior to Delivery Nov.	Dec.	Jan.	Feb.	Mar.	Apr.	May	June	July	Aug.	Sept.	Oct.	Nov.	Dec.	Life of Delivery Range
1982	High		Futures Trading	137.00	132.50	136.00	134.70	123.50	124.25	130.65	137.65	154.70	164.95	164.70	164.95
	Low		Began	129.90	117.00	125.30	122.10	112.70	115.20	109.90	127.40	128.50	146.80	151.90	109.90
	Close		Feb. 24, 1982	130.10	125.20	133.60	122.65	119.35	116.55	130.00	129.40	147.00	159.15	158.94	—
1983	High	165.65	168.50	175.50	181.00	184.25	192.80									
	Low	150.30	155.55	160.80	168.10	177.20	178.20									
	Close	161.55	163.20	172.65	177.20	180.60	192.60									

Month End Open Interest of S&P 500 Futures — Index at Chicago IOM in Contracts

Year	Jan.	Feb.	Mar.	Apr.	May	June	July	Aug.	Sept.	Oct.	Nov.	Dec.
1982	—	—	—	1,613	6,780	9,603	15,482	13,840	12,901	12,625	16,601	11,681
1983	15,748	22,841	17,766	25,556								

Month End Open Interest of NYSE Composite Futures — Index at New York in Contracts

Year	Jan.	Feb.	Mar.	Apr.	May	June	July	Aug.	Sept.	Oct.	Nov.	Dec.
1982	—	—	—	—	4,024	4,384	4,646	4,690	5,722	5,459	7,753	5,273
1983	6,841	10,781	6,583	9,120								

Month End Open Interest of KC Value Line Futures — Index at Kansas City in Contracts

Year	Jan.	Feb.	Mar.	Apr.	May	June	July	Aug.	Sept.	Oct.	Nov.	Dec.
1982	—	1,402	3,679	3,176	3,803	4,250	5,065	5,858	3,456	3,235	3,094	2,777
1983	3,292	3,942	2,879	2,948								

Sugar

Preliminary USDA forecasts placed the 1982/83 world sugar production at 98.5 million tonnes, raw value (107 pounds, raw value, equals 100 pounds refined). This output was down only 1.5 million tonnes from the record 1981/82 production of 100 million. Improved production was expected from several countries. Poland's production was expected to be up over 220,000 tonnes from initial estimates, and West German sugar production was expected to be 160,000 tonnes greater in 1982/83 because of increased beet yields and sugar content. However, production estimates were down for Indonesia, Pakistan, and South Africa, and, as of early 1983, analysts were uncertain of the extent to which world supplies would be affected by inordinately heavy rains in Mexico and Cuba.

The 1982/83 world sugar use was estimated at 92 million tonnes, raw value, up 2.8 percent from the previous season, but notably short of the estimated world output. Reductions in retail prices were observed to have stimulated consumer demand in Asia, particularly in India. However, the world economic recession, artificially high domestic prices, and market inroads by alternative sweeteners, kept potential demand from rising to absorb the world's vast surplus stocks of sugar. For example, the world consumption of high fructose corn sirup (HFCS), a major competitor with sugar, rose from less than 500,000 tonnes in 1975 to 4 million tonnes in 1982, and the consumption of this alternative sweetener was expected to continue to grow in 1983. Global sugar stocks were estimated to have reached 42 million tonnes by the end of the 1982/83 season, nearly 45 percent of estimated annual world usage.

In mid-January 1983, the price of raw sugar on the U.S. market exceeded 21 cents per pound for the first time since the market stabilization price of 20.73 cents per pound became effective in October 1982. Domestic prices c.i.f. New York, duty/fee-paid, averaged 21.2 cents in January 1983, 3 cents above the January 1982 price, and up from 20.8 cents in December 1982. The price rise may have been partly brought about by reduced imports from countries that expected a reinstatement of the Generalized System of Preferences (GSP) status early in 1983. GSP status would have allowed exporting nations to ship sugar free of duty (around 2.81 cents per pound of raw sugar) into the U.S. Part of the increase in U.S. sugar prices was attributed to an unexpected strength in domestic demand during fourth-quarter 1982. Domestic raw sugar prices averaged 19.9 cents per pound in calendar 1982, virtually unchanged from 1981, but far under the 30.1 cents recorded in 1980. The differential between the U.S. raw sugar price and the world residual price (f.o.b. Caribbean, Contract No. 11) widened from 2.8 cents per pound in 1981 to 11.5 cents in 1982.

The USDA January 1983 Crop Production report estimated the 1982/83 U.S. sugar production at 5.61 million tons, 10 percent under the previous season. Beet sugar output, amounting to 2.74 million tons, was off by 19 percent. Acreage planted to beets was reduced by 15 percent, and sugar yield per acre of beets dropped to 2.65 tons from 2.76, an improved rate of sucrose recovery partially offsetting the 1.8 ton decrease in average beet yields. U.S. cane sugar production was estimated at 2.88 million tons, up nearly 2 percent from the previous season. Higher cane crop yields offset a 3 percent reduction in acreage.

The 1982/83 U.S. cane crop for processing was 27.7 million tons, 6 percent above the 1981/82 level. The 1982/83 U.S. sugar beet crop amounted to 21.3 million tons, a 23 percent drop from 1981/82. Harvested acreage was off 16 percent, and the 1982/83 yield average was down 1.8 tons to 20.6 tons per acre.

The harvest of U.S. seed cane in 1982/83 declined by 6 percent. Assuming a 1983/84 cane acreage unchanged from 1982/83, an average 37.18 tons of sugarcane per acre, and 10.54 percent sucrose recovery, the decline in seed cane indicates that the U.S. 1983/84 output of cane sugar could fall by 200,000 tons. The U.S. acreage planted to sugarbeets is expected to increase by 4 percent to 1.1 million acres, and the U.S. beet sugar output is expected to rise slightly to 2.8 million tons, raw basis. Currently, sugarbeet growers are paid on sugar content and/or recoverable sugar, and there is an increasing incentive for growers to plant beets that produce as much as 2 tons per acre less but have 1 to 2 percent higher sugar content. On the other hand, sugarcane breeders tend to emphasize the development of seed varieties with increased tonnage per acre.

U.S. sugar stocks in 1982 fell nearly 550,000 tons below 1981, but ending stocks as a portion of total use fell only 1.3 percent. Calendar 1982 deliveries of sugar for U.S. consumption were estimated at 9.3 million tons, down 4.4 percent from 1981, and total caloric sweetener use in calendar 1982 was estimated at 14.5 million tons, up slightly from 1981. In March 1983, a large cola company announced plans to permit up to 75 percent HFCS in its fountain sirup, and analysts estimated that similar plans by competing cola companies could lead to the replacement of as much as 400,000 metric tons of sugar per year. The soft drink industry accounted for a fifth of total U.S. sugar shipments in 1982.

A loan program for sugar processors, effective as of October 1, 1982, covered 1982-crop refined beet sugar, raw cane sugar, cane sirup, and edible molasses processed between April 1, 1982 and June 30, 1983. Processors were eligible for loans on raw cane and refined beet sugar at national average prices of 17 and 20.15 cents per pound, respectively. As of February 16, 1983, 797 million lbs. of 1982-crop cane sugar was placed under loan, 91 million of which had been redeemed. The comparable figures for beet sugar were 2,055 million lbs. under loan and 895 million redeemed.

Negotiations for a new International Sugar Agreement (ISA) were scheduled in 1983. The present ISA expires at the end of 1984. The cooperation of the EC, which is not a member of the ISA, but has contributed significantly to world output, was considered essential to the success of any new accord.

Futures Markets

Both world (No. 11) and domestic (No. 12) sugar futures are traded on the Coffee, Sugar, and Cocoa Exchange, Inc., in New York. World raw sugar futures are actively traded on the London United Terminal Sugar Market. A white sugar futures contract is traded in Paris.

SUGAR

World Production of Sugar (Centrifugal Sugar—Raw Value)   In Thousands of Metric Tons

Crop Year	Australia Cane	Brazil Cane	China (Mainland)	Cuba Cane	Hawaii Cane	India Cane	Indonesia Cane	Philippines Cane	Poland Beet	W. Germany	United States Beet	United States Cane	USSR Beet	Mexico	France	World Total All
1973-4	2,592	6,959	2,065[3]	5,800	944	4,949	950	2,643	1,817	2,500	2,918	1,253	9,568	2,805	3,255	80,488
1974-5	2,927	7,400	2,400	6,300	1,004	5,794	1,000	2,466	1,557	2,438	2,645	1,334	7,730	2,696	2,948	78,620
1975-6	2,988	6,200	2,311	6,200	953	5,464	1,030	2,875	1,860	2,540	3,646	1,657	7,700	2,698	3,239	81,679
1976-7	3,405	7,500	2,153	6,100	938	6,043	1,068	2,753	1,801	2,734	3,534	1,519	7,350	2,696	2,974	86,263
1977-8	3,322	8,863	2,450	7,200	934	8,201	1,125	2,397	1,819	3,076	2,820	1,497	8,825	3,029	4,268	92,454
1978-9	2,978	7,740	2,558	7,500	962	7,071	1,372	2,347	1,763	2,997	2,984	1,436	9,300	3,058	4,000	91,264
1979-0	2,967	6,990	2,507	6,500	928	5,170	1,331	2,325	1,582	3,095	2,612	1,488	7,800	2,763	4,257	84,560
1980-1	3,389	8,508	3,000	7,542	951	6,542	1,265	2,373	1,134	2,988	2,857	1,547	7,196	2,518	4,195	88,265
1981-2[2]	3,586	8,346	3,400	8,207	853	9,729	1,465	2,503	1,873	3,688	2,985	1,619	6,400	2,842	5,481	99,981
1982-3[1]	3,600	9,400	3,665	7,900	907	8,409	1,600	2,450	1,759	3,400	2,531	1,718	7,300	2,700	4,780	98,458
1983-4																

[1] Estimated.   [2] Preliminary.   [3] Average 1969/70–1973/4.   Source: Foreign Agricultural Service, U.S.D.A.   T.644

United States Sugar (Cane & Beet) Supply and Utilization   In Thousands of Short Tons (Raw Value)

Year	Production Cane	Production Beet	Production Total	Offshore Receipts Foreign	Offshore Receipts Territories	Offshore Receipts Total	Beginning Stocks	Total Supply	Total Use	Exports	Net Changes in Invisible Stocks	Residual	Livestock Feed & Alcohol	Domestic Disappearance Military & Civilian Total	Per Capita
1972	2,481	3,534	6,015	5,459	149	5,608	2,823	14,446	11,623	50	-21	45	62	11,487	102.3
1973	2,708	3,353	6,061	5,329	79	5,408	2,823	14,292	11,646	26	91	69	31	11,429	100.8
1974	2,441	3,221	5,662	5,770	157	5,927	2,646	14,235	11,381	72	305	51	8	10,945	95.6
1975	2,827	3,473	6,300	3,882	96	3,978	2,854	13,132	10,276	216	-277	29	6	10,302	89.1
1976	2,795	4,003	6,798	4,658	203	4,861	2,856	14,515	11,017	76	-24	72	—	10,893	93.4
1977	2,666	3,423	6,089	6,138	102	6,240	3,498	15,827	11,336	22	201	14	—	11,099	94.2
1978	2,535	3,067	5,602	4,683	52	4,735	4,491	14,828	11,074	16	57	108	4	10,899	91.4
1979	2,727	3,066	5,793	5,027	47	5,074	3,754	14,621	10,920	18	43	103	—	10,756	89.3
1980	2,684	3,052	5,736	4,495	178	4,673	3,701	14,110	11,028	650	111	78	—	10,189	83.6
1981[1]	3,043	3,183	6,206	5,025	48	5,073	3,082	14,381	10,921	1,048	50	53	—	9,769	79.5
1982[2]	2,765	3,217	5,738	2,964	80	3,044	3,461	12,487	9,575	65	108	60	—	9,342	75.3
1983															

[1] Preliminary.   [2] Estimate.   Source: Agricultural Marketing Service, U.S.D.A.   T.645

Sugar Cane for Sugar & Seed and Production of Cane Sugar and Molasses in the United States

Year	Acreage Harvested 1,000 Acres	Yield of Cane per Acre Tons	Production for Sugar 1,000 Tons	Production for Seed 1,000 Tons	Production Total 1,000 Tons	Farm Price $ per Ton	Farm Value of Cane used for Sugar 1,000 Dollars	Farm Value of Cane used for Sugar & Seed 1,000 Dollars	Sugar Production Raw Value Total 1,000 Tons	Sugar Production Raw Value Per Ton of Cane Lbs.	Refined Basis 1,000 Tons	Molasses Made Blackstrap (80° Brix) 1,000 Gallons	Molasses Made Edible 1,000 Gallons	Molasses Made Total 1,000 Gallons
1972	702	40.4	27,239	1,093	28,332	12.64	201,639	211,724	2,740	201	2,561	178,263	2,290	180,553
1973	741	34.9	24,924	903	25,827	21.97	319,503	333,061	2,549	205	2,383	164,001	1,926	167,486
1974	734	33.8	23,721	1,091	25,140	49.64	1,166,809	1,221,232	2,512	212	2,347	152,682	1,550	156,355
1975	774	36.6	27,306	1,038	28,344	19.60	586,622	607,895	2,934	214	2,743	177,428	2,114	178,988
1976	747	37.6	26,919	1,201	28,120	13.70	408,403	425,342	2,724	202	2,545	179,180	2,574	180,730
1977	759	35.3	25,730	1,100	26,830	18.50	454,217	474,257	2,684	209	2,508		2,538	164,894
1978	744	35.0	24,821	1,176	25,997	19.40	483,905	507,069	2,612	210	2,441		2,750	161,810
1979	733	36.2	25,410	1,122	26,532	26.00	661,212	690,544	2,700	213	2,524		2,900	164,581
1980	733	36.8	25,582	1,381	26,963	38.50	984,559	1,035,990	2,728	199	2,550		1,900	163,341
1981[1]	755	36.3	26,165	1,243	27,408	24.90	650,721	681,983	2,833		2,647			182,656
1982[1]	731	39.5	27,707	1,168	28,875				2,878		2,689			171,181
1983														

[1] Preliminary.   Source: Statistical Reporting Service, U.S.D.A.   T.646

327

SUGAR

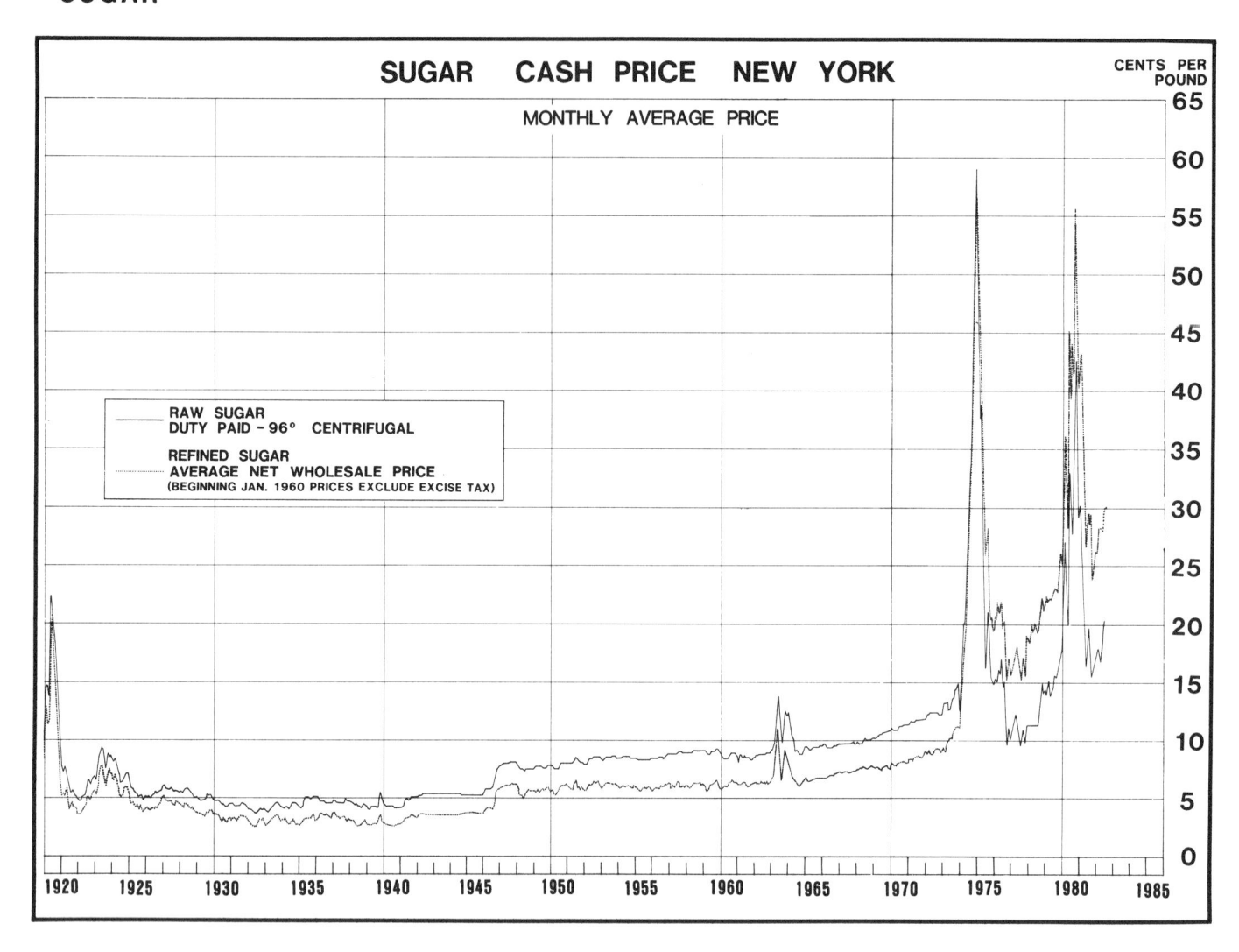

SUGAR CASH PRICE NEW YORK
MONTHLY AVERAGE PRICE
Cents per Pound

- RAW SUGAR DUTY PAID – 96° CENTRIFUGAL
- REFINED SUGAR AVERAGE NET WHOLESALE PRICE (BEGINNING JAN. 1960 PRICES EXCLUDE EXCISE TAX)

Raw Sugar N.Y. Spot Price (C.I.F., Duty/Fee Paid, Contract #12)   In Cents per Pound

Year	Jan.	Feb.	Mar.	Apr.	May	June	July	Aug.	Sept.	Oct.	Nov.	Dec.	Average
1972	9.10	9.02	9.16	8.89	8.76	8.77	9.17	9.33	9.39	9.32	9.03	9.19	9.09
1973	9.38	9.14	9.45	9.65	10.06	10.25	10.25	10.75	10.97	11.15	11.10	11.34	10.29
1974	12.63	17.09	18.11	19.25	23.05	26.30	28.35	32.60	33.71	38.83	57.30	46.74	29.50
1975	37.5	38.8	30.0	28.2	19.5	14.8	19.4	22.5	17.5	15.2	15.5	15.6	22.9
1976	15.4	15.0	16.4	15.6	16.7	14.4	15.0	11.9	9.5	11.2	10.6	10.2	13.5
1977	10.5	11.3	11.7	12.4	11.2	10.0	9.5	11.0	10.8	9.8	11.4	11.4	10.9
1978	11.4	11.4	11.4	11.4	11.4	11.4	11.4	13.5	14.4	15.0	14.2	14.5	14.3
1979	13.8	15.0	15.3	13.9	14.1	14.6	15.7	15.4	15.7	15.9	16.2	18.0	15.3
1980[1]	19.66	24.69	21.18	22.67	31.89	32.10	28.75	33.14	36.03	41.70	39.28	30.29	30.12
1981	29.57	26.07	23.81	19.91	17.43	18.95	19.10	17.42	15.49	15.66	16.28	17.07	19.73
1982	18.16	17.77	17.13	17.89	19.57	21.03	22.15	22.45	20.88	20.44	20.79	20.83	19.92
1983	21.23	21.76	21.86										

[1] Prices prior to 1980 are for raw cane (96°), duty paid C.I.F. New York.   *Sources: Economic Research Service, U.S.D.A.; N.Y. Coffee & Sugar Exchange*

T.648

SUGAR

Sugar, Refined—Deliveries by Type of Product of Buyer in the U.S. In Thousands of Cwt.

Year	Bakery & Allied Pdts.[2]	Beverages	Confectionery[3]	Hotels, Restaurants[4]	Ice Cream & Dairy Products	Jams, Jellies, Preserves[5]	Multiple & Other Food Uses	Non-Food Uses	Retail Grocers[6]	Wholesale Grocers[7]	All Other[8]	Total Deliveries	In Consumer Size Pckgs.	To Industrial Users
1971	27,125	47,287	21,046	1,588	11,125	20,575	9,917	1,861	26,580	43,197	1,903	212,204	52,199	138,935
1972	28,987	48,740	21,139	1,693	11,985	19,739	10,158	1,811	26,324	42,057	1,757	214,390	51,136	65,807
1973	29,074	49,387	20,704	1,879	11,901	20,496	10,040	2,221	26,325	41,269	2,125	215,420	50,603	68,338
1974	28,856	46,992	20,374	1,811	11,404	18,981	10,278	2,557	27,072	40,043	2,421	210,788	51,617	66,396
1975	23,757	40,390	15,334	1,423	9,755	14,045	9,359	1,679	24,626	37,089	1,640	185,453	48,188	59,299
1976	24,571	43,263	17,332	1,275	10,353	13,644	9,793	1,954	25,404	40,684	2,595	200,868	48,790	64,455
1977	26,641	47,918	18,391	1,391	10,914	14,201	14,458	2,048	25,235	40,668	2,901	207,046	49,196	70,600
1978[1]	25,657	51,540	17,895	2,078	10,380	13,444	8,142	3,167	23,363	39,259	3,140	200,540	45,342	67,352
1979[1]	24,718	47,069	17,621	2,038	9,198	12,887	9,294	2,463	24,284	39,624	3,358	198,689	49,192	67,156
1980[1]	25,956	42,429	18,122	1,913	8,738	10,330	11,396	2,342	23,009	36,847	8,466	189,548	46,941	65,439
1981[1]	25,587	36,584	19,265	1,791	9,020	9,480	11,422	2,507	23,044	39,600	3,599	181,896	48,497	64,606
1982														

[1] Preliminary. [2] Cereals and cereal products. [3] And related products. [4] And institutions. [5] Canned, bottled & frozen foods. [6] Chain stores, supermarkets. [7] Jobbers, sugar dealers. [8] Including Gov't. agencies. *Source: Stat. Rep. Serv., U.S.D.A.* T.649

World Stocks of Centrifugal Sugar as of Sept. 1 In Thousands Metric Tons[2] (Raw Value)

Sugar-Making Season	Australia	Brazil	France	W. Germany	India	Italy	Japan	Mexico	Netherlands	Philippines	Sweden	Iran	United Kingdom	Ins. Areas	Total
1971-2	475	1,430	1,021	861	1,554	263	493	486	43	251	86	550	543	1,450	12,190
1972-3	279	1,377	1,080	941	659	287	591	334	72	62	160	578	841	1,204	11,136
1973-4[3]	253	1,249	980	854	598	260	536	303	65	56	145	524	763	1,092	10,101
1974-5	408	791	143	757	657	357	259	327	50	152	157	385	629	1,135	8,368
1975-6	155	1,591	269	137	843	500	267	547	96	405	139	191	208	2,444	9,902
1976-7	328	1,746	174	165	737	337	98	642	139	744	138	207	139	2,399	10,574
1977-8	534	1,286	706	202	732	562	104	198	199	1,607	127	304	253	2,718	12,820
1978-9	383	1,516	947	305	1,448	859	350	134	207	1,290	140	364	234	3,375	15,843
1979-0	687	3,008	962	537	1,934	758	421	138	222	1,214	108	354	455	3,549	19,122
1980-1	555	1,937	899	535	386	833	497	192	196	727	93	469	524	2,903	14,344
1981-2[1]	517	1,937	683	244	699	821	196	220	175	446	76	569	460	2,491	12,770
1982-3															

[1] Preliminary. [2] Data prior to 1973-74 are in THOUSANDS OF SHORT TONS. *Source: Foreign Agricultural Service, U.S.D.A.* T.650

U.S. Sugar Beets, Beet Sugar, Pulp, & Molasses Produced from Sugar Beets & Raw Sugar Spot Prices

Year of Harvest	Acreage Planted 1,000 Acres	Acreage Harv. 1,000 Acres	Yield Per Har. Acre Tons	Production 1,000 Tons	Price[1] Dollars	Farm Value $1,000	Sugar Production Refined Basis 1,000 Sh. Tons	Equivalent "Raw Value"[2] 1,000 Sh. Tons	Intern.[4] Agreem. Cents Per Lb.	Cof., Sugar Exch. World Cents Per Lb.	N.Y. Duty Paid Cents Per Lb.	Sugar Act Beet Payments $ Per Ton
1973	1,280	1,218	20.1	24,499	29.60	725,661	2,990	3,200	9.45	9.61	10.29	2.08
1974	1,252	1,213	18.2	22,123	46.80	1,035,567	2,725	2,916	29.66	29.99	29.50	2.06
1975	1,595	1,517	19.6	29,704	27.60	820,743	3,756	4,019	20.37	20.49	22.47	
1976	1,525	1,479	19.9	29,386	21.00	616,813	3,640	3,895	11.51	11.58	13.31	
1977	1,273	1,216	20.6	25,007	24.20	604,399	2,905	3,108	8.10	8.11	11.00	
1978	1,305	1,269	20.3	25,788	25.20	649,846	3,074	3,289	7.81	7.82	13.93	
1979	1,161	1,120	19.6	21,996	33.90	745,273	2,691	2,879	9.65	9.66	15.56	
1980	1,231	1,190	19.8	23,502	47.20	1,108,974	2,943	3,149	28.66	29.02	30.11	
1981	1,252	1,228	22.4	27,538	29.20	803,569	3,166	3,388	16.89	16.93	19.73	
1982[3]	1,060	1,032	20.6	21,272			2,556	2,735	8.40	8.42	19.92	
1983[3]	1,105											

[1] Includes support payments, but excludes Sugar beet payments. [2] Refined sugar multiplied by factor of 1.07. [3] Preliminary. [4] International Sugar Agreement, World Price. *Source: Statistical Reporting Service, U.S.D.A.* T.647

SUGAR

United States Production & Imports of Edible Sirups   In Thousands of Gallons

			Production[2] Sirups							Imports		
Year	Corn	Cane	Sorghum	Maple	Refiners'	Edible Molasses	Honey	Total	Maple Sirup	Edib. Molas. & Cane Sirup	Honey	Shipm. From Terr.	Total
1970	292,000	—	—	1,110	1,695	2,121	18,726	315,652	956	2,052	749	—	3,757
1971	304,000	—	—	962	1,883	2,517	16,708	326,070	577	2,333	967	—	3,877
1972	387,880	—	—	1,099	2,077	2,290	18,210	411,556	710	1,623	3,291	—	5,624
1973	451,264	—	—	857	2,309	1,926	20,193	476,549	803	2,857	900	—	4,560
1974	498,313	—	—	1,087	2,564	1,559	15,866	519,389	801	2,469	2,196	—	5,466
1975	561,215	—	—	1,207	2,482	2,114	16,823	583,841	607	2,483	3,917	—	7,007
1976	615,498	—	—	927	2,403	2,574	16,756	638,158	886	3,188	5,608	—	9,682
1977	695,196	—	—	1,221	2,197	2,538	15,076	716,228	867	1,773	5,396	—	8,036
1978	751,809	—	—	1,154	2,571	2,750	19,466	777,750	811	2,077	4,727	—	7,615
1979	845,741	—	—	1,219	2,524	2,900	20,160	872,544	857	2,944	4,948	—	8,749
1980	941,056	—	—	973	1,983	1,900	16,871	962,783	855	3,422	4,143	—	8,420
1981[1]	1,073,933	—	—	1,410	1,446	1,982	15,703	1,094,474	1,046	2,040	6,530	—	9,616
1982													

[1] Preliminary. [2] Production of cane sirup, sorghum sirup, & edible molasses is of the fall of the preceding year.   Source: Agricultural Marketing Service, U.S.D.A.   T.652

U.S. Exports & Domestic Consumption of Edible Sirups, Corn Sugar & Sugar   In Thousands of Gallons

	Exports			Indicated Domestic Consumption Sirups					Per Capita Consumption in Pounds			Sugar		Total Sugar Consumption Mil. Tons
Year	Corn Sirup	Honey	Total	Corn	Maple	Cane & Refin. & Edib. Mol.	Honey	Total	Corn Sweetners[2]	Corn Sugar	Saccharin	U.S. Grown	Cane	Total	
1970	1,324	689	2,013	290,676	2,066	5,981	18,717	317,510	19.3	5.0	5.8	56.3	70.4	101.7	11.2
1971	1,324	639	1,964	302,676	1,539	6,870	17,035	328,120	20.8	5.0	5.1	53.5	71.5	102.1	11.3
1972	1,205	346	1,551	386,675	1,809	6,061	21,155	415,700	21.1	4.8	5.1	55.6	72.0	102.3	11.5
1973	1,377	1,485	2,861	449,887	1,660	7,170	19,609	478,326	23.4	5.2	5.1	54.9	70.6	100.8	11.4
1974	1,736	386	2,122	496,577	1,888	6,631	17,676	522,772	25.1	5.3	5.9	46.6	69.8	95.6	10.9
1975	1,070	337	1,407	560,145	1,814	7,079	20,403	588,441	27.5	5.5	6.2	54.7	59.0	89.1	10.3
1976	1,674	396	2,070	613,824	1,813	8,165	21,968	645,770	29.7	5.5	6.1	54.4	61.4	93.4	10.9
1977	1,543	466	2,009	693,653	2,088	6,508	20,006	722,255	31.2	5.5	6.6	52.7	64.4	94.2	11.1
1978	1,694	679	2,373	750,115	1,965	7,398	23,514	782,992	33.7	5.5	6.9	50.3	64.0	91.4	10.9
1979	1,207	747	1,954	844,534	2,076	8,368	24,361	879,339	36.8	5.5	7.0	47.6	62.8	89.3	10.8
1980	3,498	722	4,220	937,558	1,828	7,620	20,292	967,298	40.3	5.5	7.1	51.2	56.8	83.6	10.2
1981[1]	2,926	777	3,703	1,071,009	2,456	5,468	21,456	1,100,389	44.6		7.1	50.0	53.9	79.5	9.8
1982[1]									48.2					75.3	9.3
1983															

[1] Preliminary. [2] Corn Syrup & Dextrose.   Source: Agricultural Marketing Service, U.S.D.A.   T.653

Sugar Deliveries and Stocks in the United States   In Thousands of Short Tons, Raw Value

	Deliveries by Primary Distributors							Stocks (January 1)					
Year	Cane[1] Sugar Refineries	Beet Sugar Factories	Importers of Direct Consumption Sugar	Cane Sugar Mills[1]	Total	Sales of Refined Sugar For Export	Total Domestic Consumption[2]	Cane Sugar Refineries	Beet Sugar Factories	Importers of Direct Consumption	Refiners' Raws	Mainland Cane Mills	Total
1970	7,158	3,336	144	57	10,695	66	11,163	251	1,321	9	695	412	2,799
1971	7,306	3,213	111	51	10,681	89	11,345	237	1,266	4	804	376	2,792
1972	7,326	3,281	87	70	10,764	50	11,487	255	1,258	1	785	116	2,710
1973	7,334	3,282	75	81	10,772	26	11,429	233	1,280	3	972	100	2,583
1974	7,590	2,826	56	54	10,526	28	10,946	257	1,130	1	998	412	2,799
1975	6,237	3,068	83	65	9,453	147	9,304	295	1,314	1	886	211	2,799
1976	6,534	3,572	76	15	10,197	68	10,895	250	1,490	0	428	458	2,731
1977	7,026	3,280	172	17	10,495	35	11,248	279	1,661	0	776	509	3,341
1978	6,987	2,989	180	18	10,174	48	10,889	334	1,691	91	1,678	556	4,349
1979	6,985	2,982	84	18	10,069	73	10,756	286	1,560	0	964	641	3,450
1980	7,104	2,777	7	45	9,933	689	10,189	257	1,205	0	541	1,068	3,071
1981[3]	7,183	2,983	17	24	10,207	1,191	9,769	315	1,286	0	691	658	2,950
1982[3]							9,342	273	1,277	0	844	931	3,344
1983[3]								266	1,285	0	510	679	2,741

[1] Sugar for direct consumption only. [2] Includes deliveries for U.S. military forces at home and abroad. [3] Preliminary.   Source: Department of Agriculture   T.654

SUGAR

Centrifugal Sugar (Raw Value) Imported into Selected Countries In Thousands of Metric Tons

Year	Algeria	Canada	Chile	France	W. Germany	Israel	Japan	Malaysia	Morocco	Nigeria	Iran	Un. Kingdom	China	United States	USSR	World Total[2]
1970	207	949	100	60	193	118	2,600	380	273			1,839	530	4,711	3,005	21,372
1971	261	899	195	108	177	139	2,427	330	246			2,134	464	4,821	1,536	20,708
1972	230	908	233	128	125	161	2,777	356	222		170	2,163	749	4,719	1,924	20,981
1973	278	965	297	100	140	80	2,372	351	278		297	2,050	736	4,781	2,631	22,231
1974	277	901	174	158	100	157	2,771	352	278		226	2,269	411	5,238	1,856	21,860
1975	360	998	178	182	196	150	2,473	345	268		626	2,346	241	3,490	3,327	20,508
1976	354	895	98	136	169	131	2,439	336	263		626	2,101	638	4,136	3,760	22,593
1977	431	1,064	342	110	108	153	2,708	336	389	329	277	1,870	1,676	5,290	4,776	25,949
1978	437	1,030	317	117	152	195	2,284	398	294	595	875	1,689	1,438	3,616	3,993	23,843
1979	482	1,009	285	103	146	256	2,605	427	279	530	746	1,424	985	4,437	4,080	24,895
1980[1]	569	859	433	69	150	179	2,265	508	332	709	785	1,404	946	3,802	4,981	26,640
1981																

[1] Preliminary. [2] Excludes U.S. trade with Territories. Source: *Foreign Agricultural Service, U.S.D.A.* T.655

Centrifugal Sugar (Raw Value) Exported from Selected Countries In Thousands of Metric Tons

Year	Australia	Brazil	Czechoslovakia	Cuba	Dom. Republic	France	Thailand	Mauritius	Peru	Philippines	South Africa	Taiwan	Un. Kingdom	USSR	World Total[2]
1970	1,389	1,126	350	6,906	793	900	*1968–72*	575	435	1,237	790	410	203	1,517	22,064
1971	1,762	1,191	350	5,511	1,011	1,168	*(133)*	489	432	1,422	828	523	284	1,401	21,455
1972	2,010	2,054	229	4,140	1,099	1,425	419	670	481	1,240	1,168	489	330	64	21,714
1973	2,086	2,820	225	4,797	1,031	1,653	276	701	407	1,474	892	487	299	46	22,839
1974	1,759	2,357	189	5,491	1,055	1,202	444	726	462	1,542	779	553	328	103	23,160
1975	1,969	1,746	227	5,744	975	994	595	498	422	972	809	409	385	59	21,112
1976	2,016	1,252	71	5,764	977	1,422	1,124	584	284	1,467	860	519	285	79	22,818
1977	2,558	2,518	171	6,238	1,101	1,816	1,657	637	434	2,443	1,384	599	178	87	28,271
1978	2,482	2,005	306	7,231	901	2,357	1,040	579	275	1,142	719	365	93	174	26,088
1979	1,842	1,860	280	7,269	986	2,347	1,190	612	187	1,150	724	424	76	244	26,117
1980[1]	2,410	2,604	186	6,191	794	2,750	460	655	53	1,793	784	0	100	164	26,428
1981															

[1] Preliminary. [2] Excludes U.S. trade with Territories. Source: *Agricultural Marketing Service, U.S.D.A.* T.656

Spot Raw Sugar International Sugar Agreement World Price[1] In Cents per Pound

Year	Jan.	Feb.	Mar.	Apr.	May	June	July	Aug.	Sept.	Oct.	Nov.	Dec.	Average
1970	11.1	10.9	10.9	10.9	10.9	11.3	11.3	11.3	11.4	11.4	11.4	11.4	11.2
1971	11.4	11.4	11.7	11.6	11.6	11.6	11.8	11.8	11.8	11.8	11.8	11.8	11.7
1972	11.8	12.2	12.2	12.4	12.4	12.4	12.4	12.4	12.4	12.4	12.2	12.2	12.3
1973	12.2	13.2	13.2	13.3	12.7	12.7	13.2	13.7	13.7	14.1	15.0	12.8	13.3
1974	14.3	16.1	20.0	20.0	24.8	28.5	31.9	33.8	39.5	40.8	54.9	59.2	32.0
1975	51.8	47.9	41.0	36.1	31.9	25.9	26.8	28.3	23.2	20.5	20.7	19.4	31.1
1976	20.9	20.3	22.1	21.0	22.2	19.7	20.4	17.1	15.2	17.2	16.0	15.6	19.0
1977	16.0	16.7	17.1	18.1	17.2	15.7	15.1	17.2	16.5	15.5	19.1	18.5	16.9
1978	18.7	20.1	19.3	20.1	20.0	19.8	19.1	20.5	21.3	22.3	21.4	22.0	20.4
1979[1]	7.57	8.23	8.46	7.82	7.85	8.14	8.52	8.85	9.90	11.94	13.68	14.93	9.65
1980	17.16	22.69	19.64	21.24	30.94	30.80	27.70	31.77	34.89	40.53	37.81	28.79	28.66
1981	27.78	24.09	21.81	17.83	15.06	16.38	16.34	14.76	11.65	12.04	11.97	12.98	16.89
1982	12.90	13.07	11.26	9.58	8.11	6.84	7.80	6.77	5.76	5.93	6.52	6.31	8.40
1983[2]	6.03	6.43	6.20	6.71									

[1] Prices prior to 1979 are for refined cane at N.Y. (excluding excise tax). [2] Preliminary. Source: *Sugar Division, Commodity Stabilization Service* T.657

SUGAR

Average Refined Cane Sugar[1] (Wholesale)—Northeast   In Cents per Pound

Year	Jan.	Feb.	Mar.	Apr.	May	June	July	Aug.	Sept.	Oct.	Nov.	Dec.	Average
1973	13.15	13.18	12.94	13.30	13.55	13.96	14.05	14.50	14.80	14.95	15.13	15.33	14.07
1974	15.65	18.49	20.90	23.78	27.61	31.04	32.50	36.83	40.74	43.59	60.69	60.41	34.35
1975	52.95	48.96	40.50	37.01	32.23	25.57	26.89	27.05	23.30	21.15	20.84	20.53	31.42
1976	21.31	20.86	22.20	21.41	21.87	20.22	20.46	17.04	15.85	16.90	16.28	15.97	19.20
1977	16.70	16.94	17.45	18.52	17.52	16.40	16.13	17.38	16.57	16.35	18.50	18.88	17.28
1978	19.85	20.54	20.03	20.18	20.31	20.13	19.90	20.70	21.83	22.65	22.05	22.27	20.87
1979	22.27	22.44	22.54	22.35	22.53	22.71	22.96	23.79	23.50	23.34	23.48	26.47	23.20
1980	27.51	35.00	29.48	31.55	41.96	43.53	39.92	44.15	48.05	55.06	52.84	42.86	40.99
1981	41.80	37.47	35.51	31.42	27.90	29.74	29.96	28.79	25.08	25.99	27.10	27.40	30.68
1982	27.5	27.8	26.9	27.7	29.3	30.7	32.0	32.5	31.9	30.9	30.7	31.0	29.9
1983	31.3												

[1] These are f.o.b. basis prices in 100-lb. paper bags, not delivered prices. To obtain delivered prices, add freight "prepays" & deduct discounts & allowances.   Source: Economies & Statistics Service, U.S.D.A.   T.658

United States Deliveries[1] of All Sugar by Primary Distributors   In Thousands of Short Tons, Raw Value

Year	Jan.	Feb.	Mar.	Apr.	May	June	July	Aug.	Sept.	Oct.	Nov.	Dec.	Total
1970	827	795	944	880	948	1,049	1,023	1,089	1,093	932	833	1,048	11,459
1971	727	718	1,026	860	894	1,087	1,034	1,121	1,123	947	903	997	11,439
1972	823	727	1,058	811	978	1,096	1,001	1,167	1,106	865	855	1,039	11,528
1973	787	740	1,058	892	988	1,063	1,027	1,203	1,026	942	890	919	11,538
1974	959	867	924	901	1,040	990	1,060	1,135	1,003	1,045	879	469	11,273
1975	514	552	693	832	870	961	1,205	1,005	936	916	767	877	10,127
1976	769	778	980	881	928	997	983	1,038	1,055	858	827	828	10,924
1977	832	764	1,024	898	878	1,030	976	1,130	1,005	914	958	833	11,242
1978	766	775	930	864	891	1,033	905	1,122	1,020	894	853	840	10,892
1979	838	774	964	811	893	947	923	1,103	860	924	879	840	10,756
1980	794	848	866	772	943	882	910	904	909	825	717	818	10,189
1981[2]	700	678	839	787	818	917	880	857	989	786	768	748	9,769
1982[2]	641	649	790	708	742	972	—2,597—			—2,244—			9,342
1983													

[1] Includes for domestic consumption and for export.   [2] Preliminary.   Source: Department of Agriculture   T.659

Month-End Open Interest of World Sugar (#11) Futures at New York   In Contracts

Year	Jan.	Feb.	Mar.	Apr.	May	June	July	Aug.	Sept.	Oct.	Nov.	Dec.
1978	41,918	32,736	30,260	31,558	34,902	34,186	35,419	34,381	30,702	31,290	30,439	31,498
1979	35,004	34,529	36,200	31,824	36,521	39,646	44,938	58,184	61,442	73,701	87,182	92,007
1980	103,041	87,843	68,667	61,126	69,666	68,554	68,996	70,993	71,316	79,313	76,754	64,740
1981	61,522	57,087	59,025	54,898	62,330	61,022	66,730	64,604	52,740	60,761	66,399	72,326
1982	76,623	60,990	65,457	57,719	61,332	51,267	54,706	51,737	42,363	50,682	61,916	64,406
1983	78,889	76,429	83,851	88,011								
1984												

Source: Coffee, Sugar & Cocoa Exch., Inc., N.Y.   T.660

SUGAR

SUGAR "11" (WORLD) NEW YORK NYCSC (WEEKLY HIGH, LOW & CLOSE OF NEAREST FUTURES) CONTRACT: 112,000 LBS.

Volume of Trading of World Sugar (#11) Futures at New York   In Contracts

Year	Jan.	Feb.	Mar.	Apr.	May	June	July	Aug.	Sept.	Oct.	Nov.	Dec.	Total
1978	61,854	70,103	86,634	79,359	65,623	98,323	75,940	116,271	115,808	99,632	75,243	71,983	1,016,773
1979	72,961	107,951	76,267	82,804	64,224	132,200	121,474	142,006	192,220	255,858	278,458	256,919	1,783,342
1980	381,805	354,441	338,118	245,233	309,417	277,846	271,884	279,149	317,170	295,673	250,627	255,379	3,576,702
1981	233,217	237,286	212,519	240,420	212,708	241,736	192,142	203,404	247,160	138,529	137,768	183,438	2,470,327
1982	166,913	209,386	199,263	217,689	138,377	177,657	176,641	144,980	151,639	140,262	160,656	154,657	2,037,020
1983	207,678	249,392	198,034	261,939									

Source: *Coffee, Sugar & Cocoa Exch., Inc., N.Y.*

T.661

SUGAR

High, Low & Closing Prices of March World Sugar (#11) At New York In Cents per Pound

Year of Delivery		Dec.	Jan.	Feb.	Mar.	Apr.	May	June	July	Aug.	Sept.	Oct.	Nov.	Dec.	Jan.	Feb.	Life of Delivery Range
1979	High	11.03	11.03	10.67	10.18	9.53	9.11	8.95	7.70	8.14	9.38	9.88	9.38	9.04	8.58	8.74	11.03
	Low	10.56	10.56	10.10	8.64	8.78	8.32	7.72	6.55	6.89	8.22	8.70	8.37	8.27	7.91	7.94	6.55
	Close	10.90	10.68	10.13	9.43	9.04	8.72	7.75	6.90	8.11	9.23	9.42	8.48	8.43	8.22	8.12	—
1980	High	10.27	9.94	10.30	10.15	9.74	9.72	10.14	10.58	10.91	12.10	14.64	16.91	17.40	22.05	29.45	29.45
	Low	9.76	9.44	9.71	9.55	9.12	9.20	9.29	9.74	9.94	10.50	11.56	14.16	14.85	15.10	19.75	9.12
	Close	9.86	9.75	10.09	9.74	9.45	9.38	9.96	10.07	10.69	11.56	14.08	16.86	16.31	22.01	23.20	—
1981	High	17.06	22.42	28.50	30.08	28.00	39.45	39.38	38.35	37.30	42.20	45.05	45.75	33.75	33.85	28.60	45.75
	Low	15.50	15.56	22.35	21.70	22.60	28.00	33.30	28.17	32.40	33.90	40.85	35.05	24.50	26.15	23.00	13.75
	Close	16.41	22.38	27.37	23.53	27.20	37.94	38.34	32.25	35.07	41.16	43.34	35.11	30.58	26.79	23.25	—
1982	High	28.20	27.68	26.18	22.20	20.30	17.85	19.00	17.95	16.80	13.60	13.36	13.28	14.06	14.10	13.98	36.60
	Low	23.75	23.85	22.10	19.35	16.65	15.40	16.05	15.85	13.25	11.75	11.50	11.67	12.52	12.64	12.23	11.50
	Close	25.68	24.50	22.13	20.08	17.43	17.85	16.05	16.98	13.26	13.11	12.52	13.01	13.18	13.58	12.63	—
1983	High	15.15	15.25	15.05	13.68	12.51	10.50	9.35	10.74	8.97	8.22	7.85	8.33	8.28	6.84	7.34	15.25
	Low	13.98	14.03	13.49	12.18	10.28	9.24	8.28	8.37	7.83	7.05	6.60	7.27	6.80	6.05	6.08	6.05
	Close	14.71	14.90	13.65	12.49	10.52	9.25	9.33	8.78	7.96	7.11	7.84	8.32	6.85	6.20	6.28	—
1984	High	9.95	8.92	9.45	9.00	9.77											
	Low	8.75	8.48	8.11	8.08	8.72											
	Close	8.98	8.62	8.17	9.00	9.64											

Source: Coffee, Sugar & Cocoa Exch., Inc., N.Y.

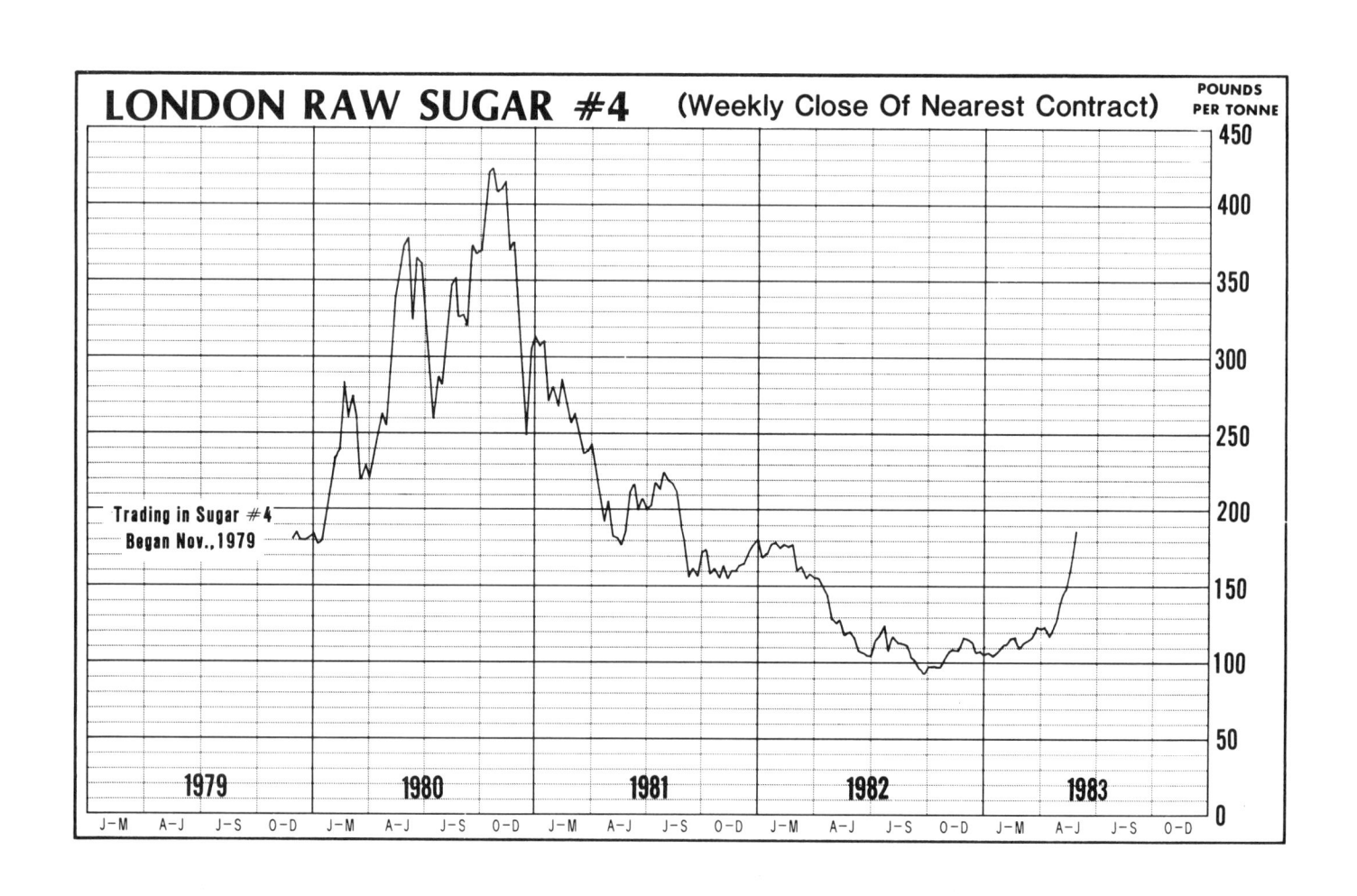

T.662

Sulfur

World resources of elemental sulfur and sulfur associated with natural gas, petroleum, tar sands, and metal sulfides amounted to about 5 billion tons in 1982. The sulfur found in gypsum and anhydrite is virtually limitless, but it is as yet uneconomical to recover. Preliminary Bureau of Mines estimates put the total world production of sulfur during 1982 at nearly 52,000 tonnes, 3 percent below the 1981 level.

The U.S. is the major world producer of sulfur, and domestic U.S. resources made up about one-fifth of the world total during 1982. Agricultural chemicals and fertilizers accounted for 52 percent of domestic demand in 1982, and chemicals and petroleum refining accounted for 22 percent. There are no satisfactory substitutes for sulfur at either present or anticipated prices.

Preliminary estimates of 1982 yearend U.S. producer stocks of sulfur totaled 4,300 tonnes, 18 percent above the 1981 level.

World Production of Elemental Sulfur (Native & Other Elemental [All Forms])   In Thous of Metric[4] Tons

Year	Argentina	Spain	Chile	China	France[3]	W. Germany	Canada	Italy	Japan	Mexico	Poland	USSR	Israel	Turkey	United States	World Total
1973	35	1,207	30	N.A.	1,826	538	7,998	1,151	2,723	1,646	3,741	7,520	10	66	10,921	47,437
1974	47	1,393	55	N.A.	2,068	1,284	7,772	776	2,765	2,312	4,326	7,770	8	98	11,419	50,345
1975	32	1,349	47	N.A.	1,962	1,262	7,417	692	2,450	2,181	5,001	7,854	10	90	11,259	49,397
1976[4]	39	1,180	48	1,350	1,968	1,363	7,261	612	2,649	2,225	5,210	9,140	10	128	10,879	50,908
1977	47	1,235	61	1,752	2,217	1,602	7,483	666	2,825	1,936	5,150	9,740	10	118	10,727	52,341
1978	38	1,176	52	2,155	2,221	1,601	7,247	684	2,728	1,918	5,421	10,550	10	122	11,175	53,687
1979	20	1,224	104	2,282	2,284	1,650	7,027	571	2,891	2,125	5,195	10,550	10	114	12,101	54,745
1980	N.A.	1,236	121	2,300	2,213	1,775	7,405	604	2,784	2,252	5,535	11,000	10	121	11,866	56,635
1981[1]	N.A.	1,210	125	2,300	2,100	1,750	6,850	550	2,700	2,225	5,072	11,215	10	119	12,145	53,800
1982[2]		1,200			2,000	1,800	6,800	500	2,800	2,200					10,100	52,000

[1] Preliminary.   [2] Estimate.   [3] Content of ore.   [4] Data prior to 1976 are in THOUSANDS OF LONG TONS.   Source: Bureau of Mines   T.663

Salient Statistics of Sulfur in the United States   In Thousands of Metric[6] Tons of Sulfur Content

Year	Frasch-Process Total	Louisiana	Texas	Recovered Elemental Brimstone	Pyrites (Includ. Coal Brasses)	By-product Sulfuric Acid[3]	Other Sulf. Acid Compounds	Production (All Forms)	Imports—Pyrites & Sulfur	Producers' Stocks Dec. 31[4]	Exports (Sulfur)	Apparent Consumption (All Forms)	Value $ Metric Ton Elem. Sulfur F.O.B. Mine/Plant
1972	7,290	3,534	3,755	1,950	283	546	149	10,218	1,188	3,796	1,852	9,854	17.03
1973	7,605	3,311	4,294	2,416	212	600	88	10,921	1,222	3,927	1,776	10,235	17.84
1974	7,901	3,308	4,593	2,632	162	654	70	11,419	2,150	3,957	2,663	10,818	28.88
1975[6]	7,327	3,119	4,208	3,017	241	779	76	11,440	1,927	5,208	1,316	10,773	45.63
1976	6,365	2,527	3,838	3,188	291	957	78	10,879	1,755	5,652	1,217	10,941	45.72
1977	5,915	2,461	3,454	3,624	169	960	59	10,727	2,009	5,557	1,088	11,657	44.38
1978	5,648	1,928	3,720	4,062	301	1,103	61	11,175	2,177	5,345	827	12,600	45.17
1979	6,357	2,460	3,897	4,070	400	1,167	107	12,101	2,494	4,239	1,963	13,739	55.75
1980	6,390	2,309	4,081	4,073	322	1,003	78	11,866	2,523	3,094	1,673	13,659	89.06
1981[1]	6,348	2,440	3,908	4,259	307	1,159	72	12,145	2,522	3,634	1,392	12,785	111.48
1982[5]	4,210			4,386	—	1,200	—	10,100	1,905	4,240	961	10,400	114.50

[1] Preliminary.   [2] Or sulfur ore.   [3] Basis 100%—produced at Cu, Zn, & Pb plants.   [4] Frasch & recovered sulfur.   [5] Estimates.   [6] Data prior to 1975 are in THOUSANDS OF LONG TONS.   Source: Bureau of Mines   T.664

Sulfur Consumption & Foreign Trade of the United States   In Thousands of Metric[5] Tons

Year	Net Import Reliance as a % of Apparent Consumption	Native Sulfur (Frasch)	Recovered Sulfur Sales	Total Pyrites	Smelter Acid Prod.	Other Prod.[2]	Total	Imports of Recovered Sulfur	Sales to Consumers of Native Sulfur	Imports of Native Sulfur	Exports Quantity	Exports Value Ths. $	Imports Quantity	Imports Value Ths. $
1973		5,964	2,451	212	600	88	10,235	920	7,438	302	1,776	35,791	1,222	14,871
1974		6,251	2,547	162	654	70	10,818	1,196	7,898	954	2,663	97,345	2,150	51,124
1975[3]		5,841	2,929	241	779	76	10,773	945	6,175	982	1,316	71,801	1,927	70,848
1976	—	5,480	3,196	291	957	78	10,941	1,012	5,954	743	1,217	63,584	1,755	59,494
1977	6	5,723	3,627	169	960	59	11,657	1,228	6,030	781	1,088	52,111	2,009	65,154
1978	12	5,902	4,088	301	1,103	61	12,600	1,185	5,736	993	827	34,667	2,177	75,671
1979	11	6,773	4,108	400	1,167	107	13,739	1,265	7,507	1,229	1,963	142,966	2,494	94,147
1980	14	6,717	4,115	322	1,003	78	13,659	1,533	7,400	990	1,673	185,866	2,523	138,852
1981[1]	5	5,374	4,207	307	1,159	72	12,785	1,666	5,910	856	1,392	187,407	2,522	209,766
1982[4]	3						10,400				961	122,143	1,905	164,885

[1] Preliminary.   [2] Includes hydrogen sulfide, liquid sulfur dioxide.   [3] Crude sulfur equivalent.   [4] Estimate.   [5] Data prior to 1975 are in THOUSANDS OF LONG TONS.   Source: Bureau of Mines   T.665

Sunflowerseed and Oil

World sunflowerseed production was forecast by the USDA at 16.4 million metric tons (tonnes) in 1982/83, 12 percent below the year-earlier levels. Drought in major producing regions of China accounted for the slight decrease in early-1983 world crop projections. An increase in the Soviet sunflower crop late in 1982 was more than offset by reductions in the U.S. crop.

The USDA estimated 1982 U.S. sunflower production at 2.66 million tonnes, up 27 percent from the previous year. During the spring of 1982, acreage reduction programs for wheat and cotton were the most important cause of the 1.1 million acre increase in sunflower plantings. The 1983 PIK program for corn, wheat, sorghum, rice, and cotton had no corresponding effect on 1983 sunflower acreage because PIK land taken out of production was restricted to conservation uses. Early indications showed 1983 sunflower acreage slightly below the 1982 level.

U.S. exports during 1982/83 were estimated at 1.5 million tonnes, or slightly below the previous season. The projected decline in U.S. exports were attributed to a more than 13 percent increase in world sunflowerseed supplies.

Domestic sunflowerseed crushings in 1982/83 were expected to reach 600,000 tons, an increase of over 50 percent from the previous year. This pickup in crush activity was partly because of the operation of two new large-capacity crushing plants in North Dakota. It was thought that the 1982/83 crush would yield around 235,000 tonnes of sunflower oil. The USDA projected 1982/83 U.S. exports of sunflower oil to be even with the 1981/82 level of 103,000 tons. Exports of domestic sunflower oil have been particularly influenced by the price and the availability of cottonseed oil. A lower cottonseed availability in the United States will tend to help sunflower oil find markets in a number of foreign countries that are major users of cottonseed oil. The Soviet Union, which had been the largest market for U.S. sunflower oil during 1981/82, had taken no U.S. oil during the first two months of 1983.

Futures Market

Sunflowerseed futures are listed but inactive on the Minneapolis Grain Exchange.

Sunflowerseed Statistics in the United States

Crop Year	Acres Harvested In Ths.	Yield per Harv. Acre Pounds	Farm Price $ Metric Ton	Value of Production Mil. $	Production	Imports	Stocks Sept. 1	Total	Crushings	Exports	Non-Oil Usage	Seed	Residual	Total
1975-6	709	1,109	238	85.0	544	2	33	546	180	273	91	2	-82	546
1976-7	810	1,058	243	94.2	499	2		501	35	337	103	3	11	478
1977-8	2,205	1,252	224	280.4	1,330	3	23	1,356	219	942	113	5	175	1,279
1978-9	2,798	1,365	236	409.9	1,823	7	77	1,907	292	1,366	150	9		1,817
1979-0	5,410	1,349	200	660.0	3,409	10	90	3,509	547	1,820	——162——			2,529
1980-1	3,683	1,016	245	410.4	1,697	28	980	2,758	780	1,505	——167——			2,452
1981-2[1]	3,611	1,177	238	524.5	2,035	32	304	2,434	374	1,555	——180——			2,109
1982-3[1]	4,924	1,156	191		2,581	24	325	3,010	600	1,500	——195——			2,295

In Thousands of Metric Tons

[1] Preliminary. Source, Economic Research Service, U.S.D.A. T.666

Sunflowerseed Oil Statistics in the United States — In Millions of Pounds

Crop Year Begin. Oct.	Stocks Oct. 1	Production	Total	Exports & Shipments	Domestic Disappearance	Total	Price $ per Metric Ton (Crude Mpls.)
1975-6	—	72	72	48	16	64	—
1976-7	8	14	22	15	7	22	243
1977-8	—	86	86	34	49	83	
1978-9	3	115	118	41	70	111	728
1979-0	7	224	231	86	72	158	573
1980-1	73	298	371	301	29	330	594
1981-2[1]	41	137	178	103	63	166	549
1982-3[2]	12	235	247	100	102	202	485
1983-4[2]	45						

[1] Preliminary. [2] Estimate. Source: Economic Research Service, U.S.D.A. T.667

World Production of Sunflowerseed — In Thousands of Metric Tons

Crop Year	Argentina	Australia	Bulgaria	Canada	China	France	Hungary	Romania	South Africa	Spain	Turkey	United States	USSR	Yugoslavia	World Total
1977-8	1,600	158	423	81	200	69	211	807	444	388	455	1,330	5,904	479	12,877
1978-9	1,430	186	369	120	279	76	223	816	312	470	485	1,823	5,333	539	12,814
1979-0	1,650	142	415	218	340	159	417	888	328	504	550	3,409	5,414	525	15,328
1980-1	1,260	139	378	166	910	222	454	817	517	670	630	1,750	4,618	302	13,259
1981-2[1]	1,810	120	448	165	1,332	397	621	806	260	405	575	2,035	4,678	327	14,573
1982-3[2]	2,100	146	450	94	1,100	590	550	650	500	750	650	2,581	5,300	227	16,158

[1] Preliminary. [2] Estimate. Source: Foreign Agricultural Service, U.S.D.A. T.668

Tall Oil

Tall Oil—Supply & Distribution in the U.S.   In Millions of Pounds

Year Beginning Oct. 1[3]	Supply (Crude) Production	Stocks Oct. 1[4]	Total Supply	Exports	To U.S. Territ.	Soap	Paint & Varnish	Linoleum & Oilcloth	Resins & Plastics	Other Drying Oils	Lubricants & Similar Oils	Fatty Acids	Other	Total Nonfood Products
1970	1,271	140	1,411	145	.2	3	42	—	—	32	8	1,023	41	1,118
1971	1,299	148	1,447	165	.1	3	46	—	—	28	8	1,033	41	1,132
1972	1,326	150	1,476	173	.2	3	45	—	—	—	9	1,062	43	1,163
1973	1,235	139	1,374	219	.3	3	42	—	—	—	8	967	42	1,062
1974	1,054	93	1,147	120	.1	2	33	—	—	—	7	783	33	858
1975-6[1]	1,176	169	1,345	233	1.6	3	39	—	—	—	7	861	42	953
1976-7[1]	1,181	148	1,329	176		7								1,015
1977-8[2]	350	169	519	168		3								230
1978-9[2]	1,267	150	1,417	107		3	8		5			1,141	96	1,254
1979-0[2]	1,353	155	1,508			3	11		10		6	1,208	74	1,312
1980-1[2]	1,336	137	1,573			4	11		15		5	1,206	94	1,334
1981-2[2]	1,190	151	1,341			3	16		17		4	1,096	48	1,185
1982-3														

[1] Preliminary. [2] Estimated. [3] Data prior to 1970 are for the CALENDAR YEAR. [4] Prior to 1970 data are for JAN. 1. Source: *Agricultural Marketing Service, U.S.D.A.*

T.669

U.S. Tall Oil Consumption in Selected Products[2]   In Millions of Pounds

Year	Jan.	Feb.	Mar.	Apr.	May	June	July	Aug.	Sept.	Oct.	Nov.	Dec.	Total
1970	106.9	83.1	94.8	100.8	101.5	89.7	76.1	101.1	96.2	100.4	93.3	81.7	1,126
1971	102.2	88.3	82.0	93.0	90.8	106.2	92.3	90.9	96.6	88.2	107.7	72.6	1,111
1972	95.8	92.8	105.4	91.9	95.6	92.8	88.7	104.4	95.8	102.4	88.9	74.0	1,129
1973	102.0	77.2	106.2	96.6	107.6	87.0	105.4	115.3	100.2	103.6	104.6	81.0	1,187
1974	98.6	77.5	90.5	86.8	92.9	81.4	90.5	84.0	70.6	83.1	82.5	84.0	1,022
1975	62.5	85.4	31.9	55.1	63.3	78.1	62.4	80.3	89.5	77.6	68.2	71.2	825
1976	65.7	91.0	87.2	70.4	101.5	82.8	69.4	98.9	68.6	80.8	79.4	79.5	975
1977[2]	81	88	103	97	99	95	87	97	85	110	100	91	1,134
1978	85	103	105	108	117	112	95	107	100	100	100	94	1,226
1979	97	102	111	119	125	123	90	85	107	117	105	103	1,284
1980	97	114	113	125	111	118	95	104	111	116	113	104	1,321
1981[1]	110	110	107	110	128	124	97	112	104	104	108	83	1,203
1982[1]	95	107	122	105	97	96	85	96	88	94	84	67	1,136
1983													

[1] Preliminary. [2] Prior to 1977, data is for Domestic Disappearance. Source: *Statistical Reporting Service, U.S.D.A.*

T.670

U.S. Average Wholesale Price of Tall Oil, Crude (Tanks-Works)   In Cents per Pound

Year	Jan.	Feb.	Mar.	Apr.	May	June	July	Aug.	Sept.	Oct.	Nov.	Dec.	Average
1968	3.4	3.4	3.4	3.4	3.4	3.4	3.4	3.4	3.4	3.4	3.4	3.4	3.4
1969	3.4	3.4	3.4	3.4	3.4	3.4	3.4	3.4	3.4	3.4	3.4	3.4	3.4
1970	3.4	3.4	3.4	3.4	3.5	3.5	3.5	3.5	3.5	3.5	3.5	3.5	3.5
1971	3.8	3.8	3.8	3.8	3.8	3.8	3.8	3.8	3.8	3.8	3.8	3.8	3.8
1972	3.8	3.8	3.8	3.8	3.8	3.8	3.8	3.8	3.8	3.8	4.1	4.3	3.8
1973	4.3	4.3	4.3	4.3	4.3	4.3	4.3	4.3	4.3	4.3	4.3	4.3	4.2
1974	4.3	4.3	4.3	5.6	6.3	6.3	7.5	7.8	9.0	11.4	11.3	11.3	7.4
1975	13.4	13.4	10.9	9.0	8.3	7.3	6.0	5.8	5.8	5.8	5.9	6.0	8.1
1976	6.1	6.3	6.3	5.8	5.8	5.8	5.5	5.5	5.5	6.0	6.0	6.0	5.9
1977	6.6	6.6	6.6	7.0	7.0	7.0	7.0	7.1	7.1	7.1	7.1	7.2	7.0
1978	7.4	7.5	7.5	7.8	7.8	7.8	7.8	7.5	7.5	7.5	7.5	7.6	7.6
1979	7.8	7.8	7.8	7.8	7.8	7.8	7.8	7.8	7.8	7.8	7.8	7.8	7.8
1980	7.8	7.8	7.8	7.8	7.8	7.8	7.8						
1981													

Source: *Economic Research Service, U.S.D.A.*

T.671

Tallow and Greases

Production of edible tallow during the 1982/83 season was projected by the USDA at 1,130 million pounds, with beef production up slightly. During the first two months of the season, edible tallow production had run about unchanged from the previous season's level. Apparently, the rapid rise in edible tallow production in recent years, an outcome of the conversion of meat-packing plants to the boxed beef method of operation, has ceased, and the influence of this production technique may no longer be a factor in increasing tallow production. The level of subsequent tallow production will likely be most affected by the number of cattle slaughtered under Federal inspection and by the yield of edible tallow per head. Production of edible tallow remained above lard output during the 1981/82 season.

During the first 2 months of the 1982/83 season, domestic disappearance of edible tallow continued to be characterized by an increase in the direct use of edible tallow alongside of a decline in the consumption of edible products. Direct use was 30 million pounds above the previous season's figure and the consumption of edible products was 15 million pounds below the corresponding year-earlier figure. Exports of edible tallow during the first three months of the 1982/83 season continued falling, to 5 million pounds versus 29 million a year earlier. The drop in exports was attributed to competition from lower-priced palm and soybean oils. During the 1981/82 season, the number one purchaser of U.S. edible tallow and greases was Egypt, followed by the Netherlands, Pakistan, Japan, Mexico, and the Republic of Korea. Total exports during the 1982/83 season were expected to run about even with the last season's figure of 3 billion pounds.

Hog slaughter during 1982/83 was expected to fall 9 percent accompanied by a rise of less than 1 percent in beef slaughter and a rise of 2% in broiler slaughter. Consequently, the production of inedible tallow and grease was expected to fall to 5,950 million pounds compared with 6,042 million during 1981/82. The decline in the domestic use of inedible tallow and grease during the first two months of the 1982/83 season was directly related to the reduced consumption of soap and of fatty acids due to depressed business activity. However, the use of inedible tallow and greases in feed, the largest domestic use, is continuing to expand and is expected to eventually offset losses in the fatty acid market. Exports of inedible tallow and grease for all of 1982/83 were projected by the USDA at 2,975 million pounds, down more than 100 million pounds from the previous season.

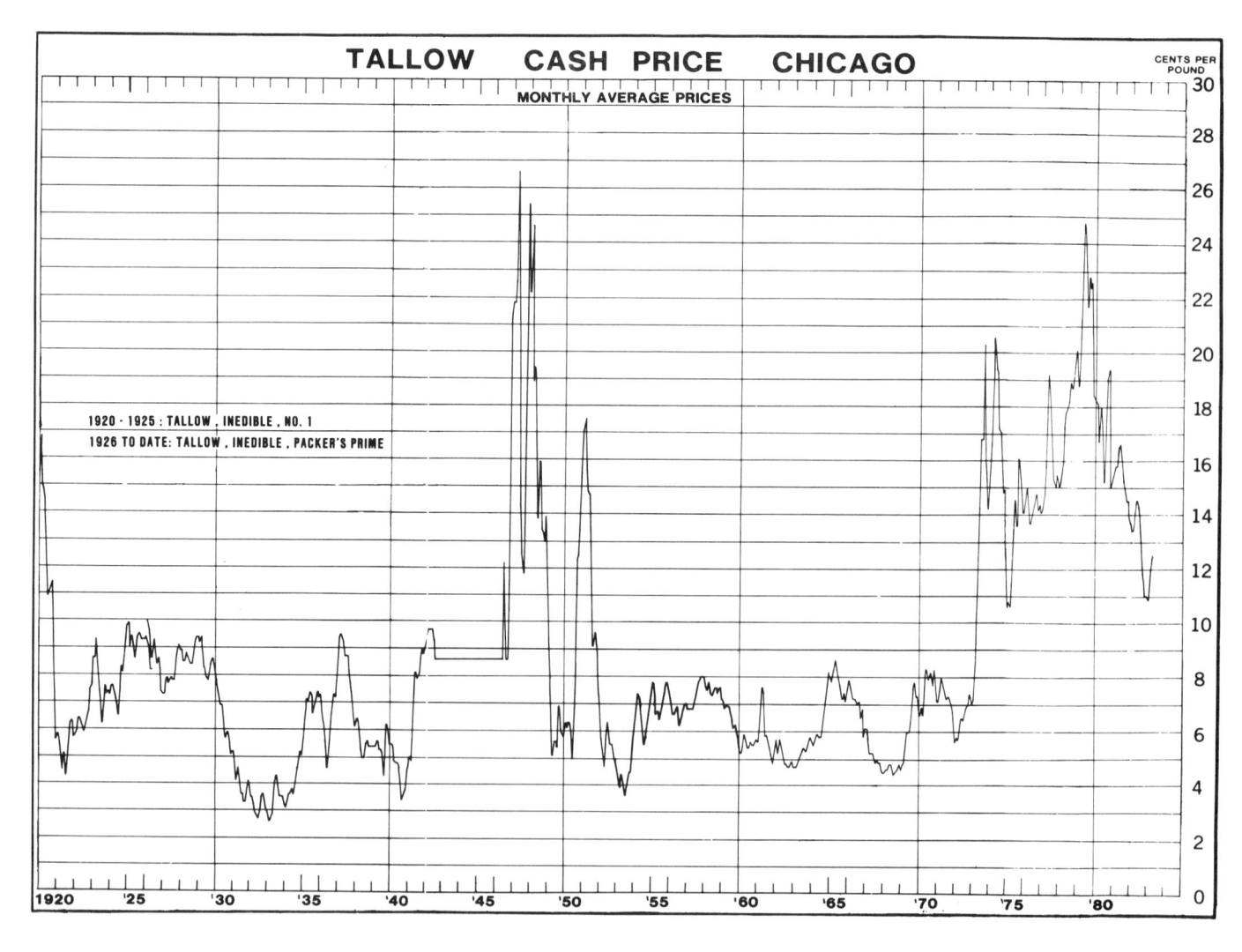

TALLOW AND GREASES

World Production of Tallow and Greases (Edible and Inedible)   In Thousands of Metric Tons

Year	Argentina	Australia	Brazil	Canada	Colombia	USSR	France	W. Germany	Italy	Mexico	Netherlands	New Zealand	United Kingdom	United States	Eastern Europe	World Total
1970	281	335	172	180	23	298	145	128	70	22	75	97	147	2,478	103	4,856
1971	214	385	167	200	23	305	145	161	75	21	79	97	147	2,499	101	4,935
1972	234	373	184	204	21	310	150	135	80	21	78	100	138	2,440	102	4,878
1973	230	319	198	204	18	318	157	140	85	25	78	80	104	2,591	115	4,991
1974	231	347	189	200	19	343	179	162	90	27	91	84	120	2,768	128	5,334
1975	261	368	198	199	22	346	195	166	90	29	83	122	135	2,344	138	5,072
1976	301	370	203	216	23	342	205	181	95	29	81	134	145	2,817	136	5,647
1977	312	400	233	217	22	333	230	186	100	31	83	120	152	2,770	131	5,675
1978	342	397	214	270	23	343	232	205	95	33	88	98	153	2,638	135	5,644
1979	331	334	200	203	26	345	243	221	100	32	90	112	188	3,058	137	5,993
1980[1]	308	309	200	204	29	340	220	235	105	33	94	118	235	3,157	132	6,114
1981[1]																6,218
1982[1]																6,137

[1] Preliminary.   Source: Foreign Agricultural Service, U.S.D.A.   T.672

Salient Statistics of Tallow and Greases (Inedible) in the United States   In Millions of Pounds

	Supply				Exports & Shipments	Utilization in Nonfood Products						Wholesale Prices, ¢ Per Lb.			
Year	Apparent Production[2]	Imports	Stocks Jan 1	Total		Soap	Animal Feed	Fatty Acids	Lubricants & Oils	Other	Total[3]	Edible (Loose) Chicago	Inedible Chicago No. 1	Bleachable Fancy	N.Y. Special, Tanks
1970	4,905	7	348	5,260	2,242	602	1,098	585	96	240	2,622	11.2	7.1	8.1	7.6
1971	5,210	5	396	5,611	2,607	588	1,143	585	81	226	2,623	10.8	6.6	7.7	7.1
1972	5,078	2	380	5,460	2,357	640	1,116	698	83	206	2,762	10.1	6.0	7.0	6.1
1973	4,843	10	341	5,194	2,299	566	1,077	899	111	270	2,540	18.4	12.4	14.9	7.2
1974	5,664	12	356	6,032	2,623	632	962	750	92	207	3,029	26.8	15.2	18.2	N.A.
1975	4,801	15	380	5,196	2,011	662	1,287	698	115	149	2,908	24.3	12.0	14.2	
1976	5,774	9	277	6,060	2,337	764	1,396	817	142	164	3,367	16.5	13.2	15.0	
1977	5,981	4	355	6,340	2,893	737	1,397	764	128	158	3,099	21.2	13.6	17.1	
1978	5,871	3	344	6,218	2,698	695	——2,489——				3,184	22.8	16.0	19.8	
1979[1]	5,956	3	347	6,306	2,795	663	——2,454——				3,117	26.2	18.8		
1980[4]	6,110		422		3,254	617	1,308	813	69	177	2,984	21.6	14.3		
1981[4]	6,042		451								2,894	31.1	15.3		
1982[4]			399												

[1] Preliminary.   [2] Apparent production based on reported factory production, net foreign trade, & change in stocks. Reported factory production excludes that from small rendering plants.   [3] Includes small amounts used in drying-oil products in some years.   [4] Estimate.   Sources: Economic Research Service, U.S.D.A.; Bureau of Labor Statistics   T.673

Average Wholesale Price of Tallow, Inedible, Packers (Prime), C.A.F. Chicago   In Cents per Pound

Year	Jan.	Feb.	Mar.	Apr.	May	June	July	Aug.	Sept.	Oct.	Nov.	Dec.	Average
1970	6.9	6.6	7.4	8.1	8.3	7.9	8.1	8.2	7.7	8.3	8.0	7.2	7.7
1971	7.1	7.6	8.0	7.8	7.6	7.4	7.2	7.3	7.2	7.0	6.7	5.6	7.2
1972	5.8	5.7	5.8	6.5	6.5	6.4	6.6	6.9	7.0	7.4	7.2	7.0	6.6
1973	7.2	8.6	10.1	11.8	14.3	16.8	16.8	20.3	15.9	14.6	14.2	15.4	13.8
1974	16.6	19.4	20.5	19.4	19.3	17.2	17.1	17.0	14.8	14.9	14.3	10.8	16.8
1975	10.6	10.8	10.6	12.2	13.6	14.6	13.6	16.1	15.9	14.9	14.5	14.1	13.5
1976	14.1	14.4	15.0	13.7	13.9	14.2	14.8	14.2	14.4	14.1	14.1	14.3	14.3
1977	14.7	14.9	15.9	17.6	19.2	17.6	16.9	15.3	15.0	15.5	15.3	15.0	16.1
1978	15.4	16.0	17.3	17.8	17.9	18.2	18.9	18.7	19.5	19.8	20.1	18.8	18.4
1979	19.8	20.8	22.9	24.8	24.1	21.7	22.8	22.4	22.6	20.9	18.4	18.2	21.6
1980	18.1	16.7	17.5	18.0	16.8	15.2	16.8	19.0	19.4	17.5	20.4	19.0	17.9
1981	15.8	15.8	16.0	16.5	15.6	16.0	15.2	15.0	14.5	14.5	13.9	13.6	13.6
1982	13.4	13.4	14.1	14.4	14.5	14.3	13.6	12.0	11.4	11.0	11.0	10.8	12.8
1983													

Source: Economic Research Service, U.S.D.A.   T.674

Tea

Tea production in selected producing countries in 1982 was estimated by the Foreign Agricultural Service of the USDA in early April 1983 at 1.895 million tonnes, 3.6 percent above the 1.829 million tonnes produced in 1981. India remained the world's largest tea producer (567,000 tonnes) as output recovered somewhat from the prolonged dry weather in both northern and southern Indian producing areas in late 1981 and early 1982. Production in China, the second largest producer, increased to 381,000 tonnes in 1982, 11 percent above the 1981 level and 50 percent larger than in 1976. Severe drought in key Sri Lanka producing areas from November 1981 through March 1982 reduced 1982 tea production in that country to 188,000 tonnes, 10 percent below the excellent 1981 crop for this third largest tea producer. Tea production in Japan was slightly above the 1981 level at 105,000 tonnes.

Total 1982 tea production in Asia was estimated at 1.387 million tonnes, compared with 1.378 million in 1981. Production in Africa totaled 212,000 tonnes, up from 201,000 in 1981. Favorable weather resulted in higher production in Kenya, the principal producer, and in record production for Malawi. Estimated production of tea in the USSR in 1982 was 135,000 tonnes versus 134,000 in 1981, while estimated production in Turkey increased sharply, to 90,000 tonnes from 43,000 in 1981.

Imports of tea (crude or prepared) into the United States in 1982 totaled 82,833 tonnes, 4 percent less than the 86,299 tonnes imported in 1981.

In the United States, iced tea accounts for over 80 percent of the market. Coffee is the major competitor of tea in the hot beverage market, while soft drinks offer the greatest competition for iced tea.

Salient Statistics of Tea in the United States In Millions of Pounds

Year	Brazil	Argentina	Sri Lanka (Ceylon)	China	India	Indonesia	Japan	Kenya[2]	Mozambique	Netherlands	Malawi	Taiwan	Total	Total Supply	Military	Civilian	Per Capita per Lb.
1970			46.1		15.8	21.4	2.8	15.2	2.4	6.3	5.1	5.3	137.2	192	3	146	.72
1971			54.8		22.8	25.4	2.6	21.4	3.9	8.7	7.4	8.0	175.4	217	2	158	.77
1972			42.9		16.8	21.7	3.9	14.6	4.6	7.6	6.9	8.2	151.5	207	3	160	.77
1973[3]		1.1	19.7	.6	8.2	13.3	2.1	8.4	3.1	5.1	2.7	3.2	78.9	216	2	165	.79
1974		1.8	19.6	1.2	7.5	13.3	1.9	7.9	3.1	6.4	3.2	3.3	80.9				.80
1975		1.8	18.3	2.0	6.8	12.9	1.7	8.4	2.7	2.4	2.2	4.0	72.3				.80
1976		2.1	21.1	3.0	8.0	11.6	3.2	10.7	2.0	1.3	4.1	4.8	82.2				.81
1977		4.9	16.6	4.2	12.3	14.7	3.4	9.5	2.3	3.0	5.6	5.7	92.1				.90
1978	2.0	6.7	14.0	2.9	1.7	10.7	3.2	8.2	1.4	4.1	4.2	3.0	68.8				.70
1979	3.5	7.0	14.7	6.5	5.9	11.2	2.9	9.4	2.4	4.7	2.5	2.3	79.2				.70
1980	2.8	10.3	12.2	8.0	4.2	13.9	2.5	6.8	5.0	5.9	2.1	3.1	83.8				.68
1981[1]	3.5	10.0	13.0	7.1	4.7	14.7	2.5	5.5	4.2	7.7	2.4	4.2	86.3				
1982																	

[1] Preliminary. [2] Imports prior to 1973 are in MILLIONS OF POUNDS. Sources: Statistical Reporting Service, U.S.D.A.; Bureau of Census

N.Y. Wholesale Price of Tea (Black)[1] In Cents per Pound

Year	Jan.	Feb.	Mar.	Apr.	May	June	July	Aug.	Sept.	Oct.	Nov.	Dec.	Average
1970	43.9	44.2	44.6	44.8	45.3	45.4	45.8	47.1	47.8	47.5	45.9	47.7	45.8
1971	48.1	47.8	48.8	48.1	48.3	47.7	48.1	48.1	49.7	49.5	49.6	50.7	48.7
1972	50.3	50.8	53.0	53.5	53.5	52.1	51.0	49.1	49.6	49.5	47.8	47.6	50.7
1973	46.8	47.9	48.6	48.8	48.9	48.2	48.7	48.8	48.0	48.0	48.0	48.3	48.3
1974	49.1	50.4	58.2	62.7	62.3	64.7	63.8	64.9	64.4	65.3	66.9	71.4	62.0
1975	71.3	73.9	75.5	72.1	69.4	68.7	65.3	65.0	63.6	65.4	65.9	66.4	68.5
1976	66.1	66.7	67.3	67.1	68.2	71.4	75.9	82.4	81.7	81.3	80.3	82.5	74.2
1977	N.A.	99.9	136.8	211.4	191.6	157.9	144.2	136.0	129.4	116.1	116.8	112.1	141.1
1978	109.9	122.1	121.5	115.1	110.4	109.4	109.6	108.8	107.4	110.3	110.5	106.6	118.8
1979	108.9	107.0	105.3	102.1	99.9	96.4	97.5	97.8	102.0	105.9	103.3	101.8	102.3
1980	103.9	108.9	110.3	110.0	109.3	106.3	106.6	107.1	107.8	N.A.	104.6	103.6	107.1
1981	103.3	107.3	108.4	108.9	106.8	106.3	104.3	103.7	100.4	99.3	99.6	99.5	104.0
1982	96.7	98.3	99.6	97.8	98.3	99.8	101.0	101.9	104.3	106.2	107.0	107.6	101.5
1983	111.7	112.8	112.6										

[1] Medium broken grade from Ceylon & India; ex-dock or ex-warehouse. Source: Bureau of Labor Statistics (0191–0331.02)

TEA

World Tea Production, in Major Producing Countries In Thousands of Metric Tons

Year	Argentina	China	Sri Lanka (Ceylon)	India	Indonesia	Iran	Japan	Kenya	Malawi	Mozambique	Bangladesh	Taiwan	Turkey	Uganda	USSR	World Total
1970	18.5	N.A.	212.2	418.5	44.0	16.0	91.2	41.1	18.7	17.0	31.4	27.6	33.4	18.2	66.8	1,098
1971	25.0	N.A.	217.8	435.5	48.2	24.0	92.9	36.3	18.6	16.5	12.5	27.0	33.6	18.0	68.6	1,123
1972	24.0	N.A.	213.5	456.0	49.8	22.0	94.8	53.3	20.7	18.7	23.8	26.2	46.5	23.4	71.3	1,197
1973	23.1	N.A.	211.3	472.0	54.5	23.0	101.0	56.6	23.6	18.8	27.6	28.6	43.2	20.4	74.8	1,236
1974	26.0	N.A.	204.0	492.1	51.7	25.0	95.2	53.4	23.3	17.6	32.2	24.2	42.8	21.7	80.8	1,245
1975	29.0	N.A.	213.7	487.1	56.8	23.0	105.4	56.7	26.2	13.1	29.0	26.1	55.6	18.4	86.3	1,284
1976	33.0	N.A.	196.6	511.8	61.1	22.0	100.1	62.0	28.3	13.8	33.3	24.8	59.5	15.4	92.0	1,316
1977	21.6	252.0	208.6	556.3	64.3	24.0	102.3	86.3	31.7	17.0	38.0	26.3	84.1	15.2	106.4	1,709
1978	26.3	268.0	199.0	563.8	73.2	23.0	104.7	93.4	31.7	18.1	38.0	25.9	86.5	10.9	111.2	1,755
1979	32.1	277.0	206.4	551.9	73.3	21.0	98.0	93.3	32.6	19.7	35.9	27.1	102.0	1.8	117.6	1,782
1980[1]	34.0	304.0	191.4	575.9	72.2	20.0	102.3	89.9	29.9	19.0	39.9	24.5	95.9	1.5	129.8	1,816
1981[2]	25.0	343	210.1	561	78.9	20.0	102	90.9	32.0	22	41.1	26.0	43	1.2	134	1,829
1982[2]		381	188	567			105	96	38	20			90		135	1,895
1983																

[1] Preliminary. [2] Estimate. Source: *Foreign Agricultural Service, U.S.D.A.*

T.677

World Tea Exports from Producing Countries In Thousands of Metric Tons

Year	Sri Lanka (Ceylon)	China	India	Indonesia	Japan	Malaysia	Bangladesh	Taiwan	Total Asia	Kenya	Mozambique	Total Malawi	Africa	Argentina	Grand Total
1969	201.4	32.4	168.7	27.1	1.6	1.5	—	21.3	463.4	33.8	15.4	17.3	98.8	14.6	579.8
1970	208.3	30.0	200.2	36.9	1.6	1.3	—	20.4	509.4	36.1	16.7	17.7	103.5	19.1	636.3
1971	200.8	41.0	204.4	40.2	1.5	1.0	—	22.8	531.7	34.3	17.5	18.2	105.6	22.4	665.5
1972	190.1	42.0	209.8	38.5	1.9	.8	13.2	21.3	535.8	47.4	18.4	19.9	129.3	18.9	688.7
1973	205.5	50.2	188.2	35.6	2.2	.6	20.3	21.1	547.0	51.5	17.9	22.1	137.4	18.0	709.0
1974	185.1	63.6	205.9	50.2	1.8	.6	21.2	17.2	563.6	49.6	17.2	23.8	134.3	24.1	728.3
1975	212.4	61.3	219.4	46.0	2.2	.5	24.1	20.1	592.3	52.6	12.2	24.2	132.6	17.4	747.5
1976	199.7	61.2	237.3	47.5	3.2	.5	30.7	21.1	608.7	59.3	12.9	29.6	142.2	25.1	782.7
1977	185.5	81.8	229.6	51.3	3.5	.5	26.0	20.8	611.1	70.2	12.9	29.9	158.6	26.9	803.1
1978	192.6	86.9	176.1	56.2	3.4	.6	30.9	20.4	576.7	85.0	16.7	30.6	178.1	31.0	795.1
1979	187.5	106.8	199.6	53.6	3.1	.6	31.9	19.3	616.0	94.0	18.2	31.0	180.1	29.6	834.6
1980[1]	184.7	106.0	224.5	74.1	2.7	.6	31.0	18.2	656.0	74.8	18.0	31.3	157.2	32.7	855.6
1981															

[1] Preliminary. Source: *Foreign Agricultural Service, U.S.D.A.*

T.678

United States Imports of Tea In Thousands of Pounds

Year	Jan.	Feb.	Mar.	Apr.	May	June	July	Aug.	Sept.	Oct.	Nov.	Dec.	Total
1970	10,826	10,264	15,285	12,767	11,503	10,972	8,940	8,778	10,805	11,971	10,409	12,682	135,202
1971	13,226	12,360	15,073	18,078	15,128	16,529	20,150	25,141	19,427	4,631	3,828	11,862	175,432
1972	12,914	16,907	10,276	10,165	12,885	16,563	10,835	11,581	12,830	14,348	11,460	10,731	151,495
1973	15,481	14,295	15,399	14,107	17,423	12,425	13,660	12,614	12,527	16,878	16,506	11,997	173,314
1974	11,675	14,974	16,583	17,177	18,122	17,489	21,788	16,432	13,954	10,460	7,735	11,844	178,326
1975	14,297	12,200	15,486	13,648	14,694	12,170	9,915	11,276	12,404	17,594	13,940	11,843	159,287
1976	11,842	12,309	15,779	15,805	13,053	13,893	14,259	15,051	19,224	15,683	16,133	18,273	181,304
1977	16,059	15,064	22,389	23,302	27,345	22,335	22,252	15,932	9,994	9,702	7,213	10,924	203,012
1978	9,023	12,791	18,648	15,450	17,523	8,286	13,141	13,788	9,390	12,502	8,877	12,332	151,751
1979	14,797	10,568	15,584	13,822	13,556	14,352	13,361	14,809	15,841	16,992	15,432	15,578	174,690
1980	18,749	17,562	17,456	18,501	15,871	16,460	14,099	11,883	11,870	14,271	12,126	15,936	184,786
1981	12,891	18,354	14,696	19,220	18,990	17,736	14,586	19,128	13,205	15,855	13,473	12,121	190,254
1982	15,055	15,464	13,787	13,176	16,518	14,309	14,286	15,598	17,425	16,207	18,222	12,567	182,613
1983	13,748												

Source: *Department of Commerce*

T.679

Tin

U.S. production of primary tin is negligible, and since the U.S. is the world's largest consumer of both primary and secondary tin virtually all primary tin must be imported. The largest use of tin is in metal containers fabricated from tinplate.

U.S. imports of tin metal for consumption in 1982 were 39 percent lower than in 1981, but imports of concentrates increased sharply, according to preliminary U.S. Bureau of Mines data. The major suppliers of U.S. tin metal imports in 1982 were Thailand, Indonesia, Bolivia, China, Brazil, and Malaysia. The major supplier of concentrates was Peru.

Primary tin use in 1982 was 4 percent lower than in 1981 while secondary tin consumption was up 4 percent, according to preliminary Bureau of Mines data. The major uses for tin in 1982 were in cans and containers—an estimated 25 percent of total use vs. 20 percent in 1981; electrical—17 percent; construction—13 percent; transportation—13 percent; and other uses—32 percent. Although total U.S. consumption of tin in 1982 was off only slightly from the 1981 level, reported consumption by finished products showed a 33 percent drop, according to Bureau of Mines data. Reduced usage occurred in bronze and brass products, babbitt, solder, and tinplate.

The General Services Administration (GSA) continued its fixed price program for selling Government stockpile tin during 1982, despite opposition from producer countries in the International Tin Council (ITC). Since the daily sales program began on December 1, 1980, a total of more than 10,000 metric tons (tonnes) of tin has been sold. As of November 30, 1982, the U.S. stockpile held 193,581 tonnes of pig tin, with 25,332 tonnes authorized for disposal.

During the first half of 1982, negotiations were conducted for the Sixth International Tin Agreement (ITA). Despite many conflicts between producer and consumer countries, the Sixth ITA entered into force on July 1, 1982, with substantially fewer members than in the prior pact. The United States did not join. During the last 2 quarters the ITC imposed a reduction of 36 percent on exports from the level of the same period in 1981 on member countries. This was an attempt to balance world tin supply and demand.

Tin prices declined sharply in the first half of 1982 and rose somewhat during the last half of the year; ending the year substantially lower than at the start of 1982. The massive price support buying that began in mid-1981 continued through early 1982, and contributed to a higher than expected market price during that period in view of the slackened demand. There was a large worldwide excess of supply relative to demand, primarily due to sharply reduced demand.

Meanwhile, notwithstanding severe International Tin Council export controls, the ITC buffer stock manager was forced to buy continued sizable amounts of tin at the International Tin Agreement (ITA) floor price of 29.15 ringgits per kilo in Penang ($5.79 per pound) into early 1983. However, it was expected that the combination of export controls with the hoped for improvement in world demand for tinplate in 1983 would provide a modest price recovery.

Futures Market

Tin futures trade on the London Metal Exch.

United States Tin Stocks (Pig—Industrial) In Metric[1] Tons

Year	Jan. 1	Feb. 1	Mar. 1	Apr. 1	May 1	June 1	July 1	Aug. 1	Sept. 1	Oct. 1	Nov. 1	Dec. 1
1973[1]	11,757	10,435	9,023	9,764	9,419	8,286	9,175	9,038	10,795	9,300	9,002	9,495
1974	10,124	9,078	8,829	9,978	10,069	10,331	9,983	9,307	10,669	9,800	9,998	10,369
1975	10,420	11,873	13,117	10,333	10,986	11,240	11,049	9,164	9,133	9,249	9,883	8,840
1976	9,642	9,395	8,624	9,189	7,855	6,963	8,375	9,623	8,749	7,871	7,929	7,213
1977	7,282	8,032	7,883	5,874	6,157	5,644	4,720	6,305	5,557	5,378	9,124	7,272
1978	8,441	7,626	6,628	6,291	7,785	8,139	7,846	7,817	7,260	5,774	4,975	5,666
1979	5,040	4,594	4,254	5,891	6,097	5,938	6,317	6,270	6,096	5,058	4,901	4,244
1980	4,238	7,720	6,882	7,527	5,443	7,263	6,592	6,544	6,051	5,180	5,208	5,086
1981	5,504	5,968	5,745	5,229	5,745	5,978	6,227	6,465	5,663	5,710	5,325	5,563
1982	5,988	3,872	3,490	3,829	5,222	4,953	4,653	3,888	2,910	2,940	2,770	3,437
1983	3,242											

[1] Data prior to 1973 are in LONG TONS. Source: Bureau of Mines

United States Tin (Pig) Consumption (Total) In Metric Tons

Year	Jan.	Feb.	Mar.	Apr.	May	June	July	Aug.	Sept.	Oct.	Nov.	Dec.	Total
1974	6,757	5,995	6,259	6,533	6,386	6,061	4,689	5,431	5,614	6,147	4,166	4,283	65,781
1975	3,871	4,847	4,841	5,055	4,394	4,308	3,810	4,298	4,521	4,755	4,410	4,618	55,800
1976	5,170	4,930	5,825	5,415	5,490	5,965	5,240	5,380	5,680	6,395	5,950	5,700	62,828
1977	5,600	5,500	6,800	5,800	5,800	6,000	5,200	5,800	5,900	5,400	5,000	5,100	68,000
1978	5,400	5,000	5,500	5,200	5,700	5,400	4,600	5,200	5,200	5,300	5,400	4,900	63,100
1979	5,400	5,500	6,400	5,400	5,400	5,300	4,900	4,900	5,000	5,500	5,000	4,600	62,465
1980	5,500	5,300	5,750	5,300	4,600	4,100	3,700	3,900	4,150	4,300	4,050	3,750	56,362
1981	4,300	4,400	4,100	4,600	4,400	4,350	3,900	4,200	3,950	3,900	3,400	2,950	54,373
1982	3,400	3,300	3,750	5,100	5,000	5,100	4,900	4,700	4,700	4,600	4,500	4,400	53,450

TIN

World Mine Production of Tin (Content of Ore) In Thousands of Metric[4] Tons

Year	Australia	Bolivia[1]	Brazil	USSR	China[3]	Zaire (Congo)	Indonesia	Japan	Malaysia	Nigeria	Rwanda	South Africa	Thailand	United Kingdom	World Total
1970	8.7	28.9	3.6	27.0	20.0	6.4	18.8	.8	72.6	7.8	1.3	2.0	21.4	1.7	228.5
1971	9.9	29.5	2.1	28.0	20.0	6.4	19.4	.8	74.3	7.2	1.3	2.0	21.3	1.8	231.4
1972	11.8	31.0	3.7	28.5	20.0	5.9	21.0	.9	75.6	6.6	1.3	2.1	21.7	3.3	240.3
1973[4]	10.8	30.3	5.4	29.0	20.0	5.4	22.3	.8	72.3	5.8	1.3	2.7	20.9	3.8	237.8
1974	10.5	29.5	4.4	29.5	20.0	4.7	25.0	.5	68.1	5.5	1.3	2.5	20.3	3.8	232.9
1975	9.6	24.3	5.0	30.0	22.0	4.6	25.3	.7	64.4	4.7	1.4	2.6	16.4	4.1	222.3
1976	10.6	30.3	5.4	31.0	11.0	3.8	23.4	.6	63.4	3.7	1.6	2.8	20.5	3.3	218.4
1977	10.6	33.7	6.3	33.0	13.0	5.1	25.9	.6	58.7	3.3	1.6	2.9	24.2	4.1	230.7
1978	11.9	30.9	6.3	34.0	14.0	4.4	27.4	.6	62.7	2.9	1.5	2.9	30.2	3.1	241.1
1979	12.6	27.6	7.0	35.0	14.0	3.9	29.4	.7	63.0	2.8	1.9	2.7	34.0	2.7	245.9
1980	10.8	27.3	6.9	36.0	14.6	3.0	32.5	.5	61.4	2.5	2.1	2.9	33.7	3.3	246.5
1981[2]	12.0	29.8	9.0	36.0	15.0	2.2	34.9	.6	59.9	2.5	1.8	2.8	32.0	3.9	252.5
1982[3]	12	26	10	37	15	2	32		55	2			30	3	238
1983															

[1] Exports. [2] Preliminary. [3] Estimate. [4] Data prior to 1973 are in LONG TONS. Source: Bureau of Mines   T.682

World Smelter Production of Tin In Thousands of Metric[3] Tons

Year	United States[1]	Australia	Belgium	Bolivia	Brazil	Zaire (Congo)	Malaysia	China	W. Germany	Japan	Nigeria	Indonesia	Portugal	USSR	Un. Kingdom	Total
1970	N.A.	5.1	4.2		3.2	1.4	90.0	20.0	1.2	1.4	7.9	5.1	.4	27.0	21.7	223.7
1971	4.0	6.2	3.9		3.4	1.3	85.7	20.0	1.2	1.3	7.2	9.1	.5	28.0	22.8	232.0
1972	4.2	6.9	3.9		3.5	1.4	89.6	20.0	.8	1.3	6.6	11.8	.6	28.5	21.0	236.3
1973[3]	4.9	6.9	3.7		3.8	1.0	82.5	20.0	1.0	1.4	6.0	14.6	.5	29.0	20.4	233.9
1974	6.1	6.7	3.4	7.1	4.9	1.0	83.1	20.0	1.4	1.3	5.6	15.1	.5	29.5	20.4	236.2
1975	6.5	5.3	4.6	7.5	5.4	.6	83.1	22.0	1.3	1.2	4.7	17.8	.4	30.0	11.5	227.9
1976	5.7	5.6	4.1	9.8	6.4	.5	77.3	11.0	1.4	1.1	3.7	23.3	.3	31.0	11.2	224.1
1977	6.7	5.6	3.5	13.0	7.4	.8	66.3	13.0	3.9	1.3	3.3	24.0	1.0	33.0	10.5	228.5
1978	5.9	5.1	3.3	16.3	9.3	.5	72.0	14.0	4.8	1.1	3.0	25.8	.9	34.0	8.4	244.1
1979	4.6	5.4	2.2	15.0	10.1	.5	73.1	14.0	4.1	1.3	2.9	27.8	1.1	35.0	8.0	249.2
1980	3.0	4.8	3.0	18.2	18.6	.5	71.3	14.6	2.3	1.3	2.7	30.5	.9	36.0	5.8	250.1
1981[2]	2.0	4.2	2.5	20.0	7.6	.6	68.5	15.0	1.8	1.3	2.7	32.0	1.0	36.0	3.4	242.1
1982																

[1] Imports into the U.S. of tin concentrates (tin content). [2] Preliminary. [3] Data prior to 1973 are in LONG TONS. Source: Bureau of Mines
T.683

Tin Foreign Trade of the United States In Metric[5] Tons

| | | Concentrates[3] (Ore) | | | Imports (For Consumption) | | | | | | | | | | |
| | | | | | Total | | | Bars, Blocks, Pigs, etc.[4] (Metal) | | | | | | | |
Year	Exports (Metal[2])	Total All Ore	Bolivia	Peru	Total All Metal	Thailand	Belgium	Indonesia	Malaysia	Australia	Singapore	United Kingdom	Bolivia	Brazil	China	Nigeria
1970	4,452	4,467	4,467	—	50,554	15,395	11	—	31,819	—	—	412	—	—	—	481
1971	2,262	3,060	3,010	—	46,940	13,861	16	—	27,745	—	—	621	864	—	—	306
1972	1,134	4,216	4,216	—	52,451	11,727	71	1,997	32,645	—	—	471	1,104	—	—	184
1973	3,406	4,798	4,782	—	45,845	7,964	118	2,829	28,255	—	—	888	832	—	—	105
1974	8,415	5,877	5,877	—	39,602	5,766	10	4,121	20,668	—	—	1,834	1,135	—	—	521
1975[5]	3,596	6,415	6,415	—	44,366	7,305	—	4,302	23,542	—	46	444	147	—	—	58
1976	2,338	5,733	5,733	—	45,055	6,885	—	4,972	26,981	—	15	284	1,978	—	—	—
1977	5,480	6,724	6,667	—	47,774	7,780	—	5,294	27,084	—	207	513	3,358	2,380	381	2
1978	4,692	3,873	3,541	—	46,776	6,865	155	5,664	23,928	—	230	468	5,768	1,810	1,571	—
1979	3,417	4,529	3,745	—	48,355	10,440	100	5,429	23,448	—	1,070	550	5,387	933	185	—
1980	4,294	840	528	—	45,982	12,414	190	6,477	15,548	145	864	416	5,597	2,031	858	770
1981[1]	6,080	232	—	232	45,874	11,967	—	7,096	13,163	552	656	46	8,277	1,129	2,032	520
1982[6]	9,079	1,960	191	1,417	27,939	9,116	10	5,744	2,364	334	600	55	4,340	2,409	2,632	124
1983																

[1] Preliminary. [2] Pigs, bars, etc.; includes re-exports. [3] Tin content. [4] Also grain, or granulated. [5] Data prior to 1975 are in LONG TONS. [6] Estimate. Source: Department of Commerce
T.684

TIN

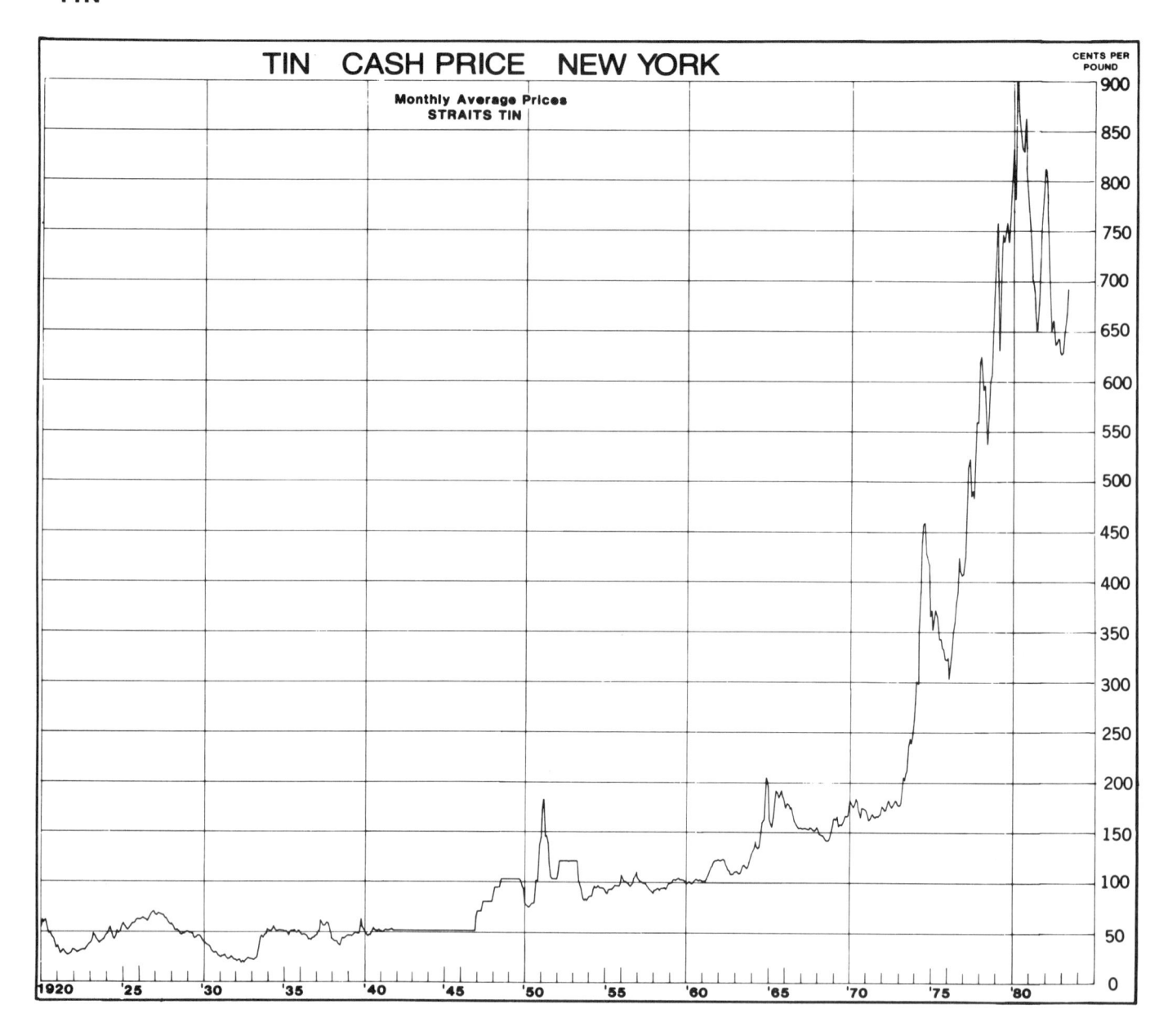

TIN CASH PRICE NEW YORK
Monthly Average Prices — STRAITS TIN
(Cents per Pound)

Average Price of Straits Tin (Alloyer Price[1]) in New York — In Cents per Pound

Year	Jan.	Feb.	Mar.	Apr.	May	June	July	Aug.	Sept.	Oct.	Nov.	Dec.	Average
1970	179.17	174.91	177.12	183.87	180.54	170.23	164.77	174.51	174.74	173.65	172.25	163.85	174.13
1971	161.64	162.85	167.01	168.88	166.02	164.48	166.44	166.07	167.29	167.70	175.39	174.36	167.34
1972	171.31	172.00	179.81	181.98	177.92	175.03	176.61	179.12	181.99	180.40	177.21	176.25	177.47
1973	179.05	192.00	205.90	202.44	209.11	212.27	237.55	243.45	239.50	245.91	262.44	300.99	227.48
1974	298.14	351.54	389.43	440.77	456.88	458.50	426.61	422.99	415.92	365.33	370.96	351.87	395.75
1975	363.76	372.03	366.04	354.10	342.54	342.48	333.32	331.85	322.77	321.95	324.03	303.02	339.83
1976[1]	312.39	326.00	349.07	358.80	377.00	390.30	424.27	411.27	405.40	406.77	414.84	423.25	383.34
1977	470.54	514.16	522.97	485.28	491.93	482.15	518.71	559.51	558.47	619.25	626.16	613.36	538.76
1978	591.19	595.93	557.48	537.85	570.58	600.95	606.21	641.80	679.66	739.69	758.84	695.86	631.34
1979	684.56	724.57	746.14	740.06	745.18	760.14	712.31	739.93	762.03	785.54	801.23	830.88	756.87
1980	836.46	866.39	900.23	872.21	861.84	845.19	836.95	834.61	861.92	832.92	788.67	751.36	840.73
1981	739.94	705.76	691.70	677.38	652.07	652.77	680.22	746.06	777.36	798.70	813.00	801.59	728.05
1982	787.41	749.93	669.51	649.58	662.35	643.00	638.00	636.33	644.33	627.94	627.93	630.18	663.88
1983	648.90	653.89	669.18	692.29									

[1] Prices prior to 1976 are for PROMPT DELIVERY. Source: American Metal Market

T.685

TIN

U.S. Consumption of Primary and Secondary Tin   In Metric[3] Tons

Year	Net Import Reliance as a % of Apparent Consumption	Industry Stocks Jan. 1	Net Receipts Primary	Net Receipts Secondary	Net Receipts Scrap	Net Receipts Total	Available Supply	Industry Stocks Dec. 31	Total Processed	Consumed in Mfg. Pdt's.
1970		23,441	52,096	2,502	19,748	74,346	97,787	21,505	76,622	73,837
1971[3]		21,505	52,557	2,531	16,439	71,527	93,032	18,855	74,177	71,073
1972		18,855	55,958	2,842	14,115	72,915	91,770	18,787	72,983	70,312
1973		18,787	60,125	4,089	13,915	78,129	96,916	18,534	78,382	75,838
1974		18,534	55,382	2,285	12,296	69,963	88,497	21,051	62,269	65,780
1975	84	21,051	42,430	2,699	10,568	55,697	76,748	19,510	57,238	55,800
1976	85	19,510	49,995	2,019	10,189	62,203	81,713	16,894	64,819	62,928
1977	82	16,894	48,215	4,025	10,604	62,844	79,738	16,858	62,880	60,732
1978	79	16,858	46,821	2,541	10,499	59,861	76,719	13,584	63,135	61,531
1979	80	13,584	50,126	2,636	10,659	63,421	77,005	12,938	64,067	62,465
1980	79	12,938	43,545	2,461	7,709	53,715	66,653	9,456	57,197	56,362
1981[1]	77	9,456	41,162	5,692	8,050	54,904	64,360	9,261	55,099	54,373
1982[2]	72	9,261						1,766		53,500
1983[2]		1,766								

[1] Preliminary. [2] Estimated. [3] Data prior to 1971 are in LONG TONS.   *Source: Bureau of Mines*   T.686

Secondary Tin Recovered in the United States   In Metric[4] Tons

Year	Tinplate Scrap Treated (Ths. Tons)	Tin Recovered As Metal	Tin Recovered In Compounds[2]	Total	Weight of Tin Compounds Produced	Avg. Quantity of Tin Recov. Per Ton of Tin-Scrap (Kilog.[5])	Tin Metal	Bronze & Brass	Solder	Type Metal	Babbitt	Anti-Monial Lead	Chemical Compounds	Misc.[3]	Grand Total
1970	771.4	1,988	620	2,608	1,076	7.57	2,574	9,277	4,898	1,517	683	351	700	1	20,001
1971	742.3	1,786	583	2,369	1,105	7.15	2,324	8,934	5,482	1,202	899	631	612	12	20,096
1972	715.0	1,494	672	2,166	1,284	6.79	2,199	9,354	5,213	1,232	854	604	716	8	20,180
1973	764.2	1,416	677	2,093	1,450	6.13	2,012	9,487	5,488	1,052	751	948	727	12	20,477
1974[4]	717.8	1,449	585	2,034	1,085	2.83	2,021	8,963	5,319	987	570	729	599	12	19,200
1975	651.2	1,146	670	1,816	1,344	2.79	1,741	7,144	4,414	877	569	442	670	12	15,869
1976	685.5	1,195	424	1,619	1,348	2.36	1,467	8,319	4,513	668	495	548	424	12	16,446
1977	667.4	1,376	365	1,741	1,516	2.61	1,668	10,397	4,094	708	694	565	365	12	18,503
1978	714.9	1,324	463	1,787	1,803	2.50	1,565	12,419	4,363	1,038	521	712	463	19	21,100
1979	841.4	1,536	433	1,969	1,256	2.34	1,767	12,090	5,282	584	441	867	433	29	21,493
1980	766.9	1,457	321	1,778	1,533	2.32	1,703	10,402	4,423	525	378	856	321	30	18,638
1981[1]	668.0	1,328	265	1,593	1,220	2.38	1,587	8,894	3,035	576	261	791	265	29	15,438
1982[6]															14,000

[1] Preliminary. [2] Tin content. [3] Includes foil, cable lead & terne metal. [4] Data prior to 1974 are in LONG TONS. [5] Data prior to 1974 are in POUNDS. [6] Estimate. *Source: Bureau of Mines*   T.687

How to keep your Commodity Year Book statistics up-to-date continuously throughout the year.

To keep up-to-date statistics on the commodities in this book, you should have COMMODITY YEAR BOOK STATISTICAL ABSTRACT SERVICE. This three-times-yearly publication provides the latest available statistics for the updating of the statistical tables appearing in the COMMODITY YEAR BOOK. It is published in the Winter (Jan.), Spring (Apr.) and Fall (Oct.). Subscription price is $55 per year.

Commodity Research Bureau, Inc.
75 MONTGOMERY ST., JERSEY CITY, N.J. 07302

TIN

Consumption of Tin in the United States by Finished Products   In Metric[5] Tons of Contained Tin

Year	Tin-plate[2]	Solder	Babbitt	Bronze & Brass	Collap. Tubes & Foil	Tinning	Chemicals[3]	Tin Powder	Type Metal	Bar Tin & Anodes	White Metal	Total Primary	Total Secondary
1970	25,127	20,184	3,241	13,666	860	2,143	3,125	1,059	1,109	1,052	1,274	52,957	20,880
1971	23,669	19,759	3,164	11,023	733	2,294	3,640	1,533	820	842	1,447	51,980	17,970
1972	21,070	21,961	3,135	9,722	806	2,540	4,030	1,150	840	896	1,717	53,501	15,700
1973	21,267	24,727	3,475	9,976	1,002	2,585	4,828	1,459	640	705	2,103	58,142	16,498
1974[5]	22,686	15,586	3,306	9,508	968	2,563	4,942	1,331	344	812	2,005	52,439	13,341
1975	18,869	15,075	2,605	7,555	538	1,896	3,998	850	265	637	2,217	43,620	12,180
1976	20,766	17,728	2,423	7,656	694	2,308	5,621	1,208	216	758	2,347	51,767	11,161
1977	18,539	17,315	2,093	8,606	787	2,323	5,727	1,287	202	578	1,655	47,596	13,136
1978	17,280	17,770	2,346	9,048	673	2,431	4,557	1,360	171	424	1,484	48,403	13,128
1979	17,929	18,022	2,243	8,690	686	2,584	4,797	1,435	140	567	1,258	49,496	12,969
1980	16,346	15,618	2,380	7,478	526	2,577	N.A.	1,109	N.A.	486	914	44,342	12,020
1981[1]	13,306	15,799	3,844	7,041	561	2,491	4,417	983	52	455	1,201	40,229	14,144
1982[4]	10,867	10,546	1,026	3,535		1,200		890		397	435	38,700	14,750
1983													

[1] Preliminary.   [2] Includes small quantity of secondary pig tin and tin acquired in chemicals.   [3] Including tin oxide.   [4] Estimated.   [5] Data prior to 1974 are in LONG TONS.   Source: Bureau of Mines

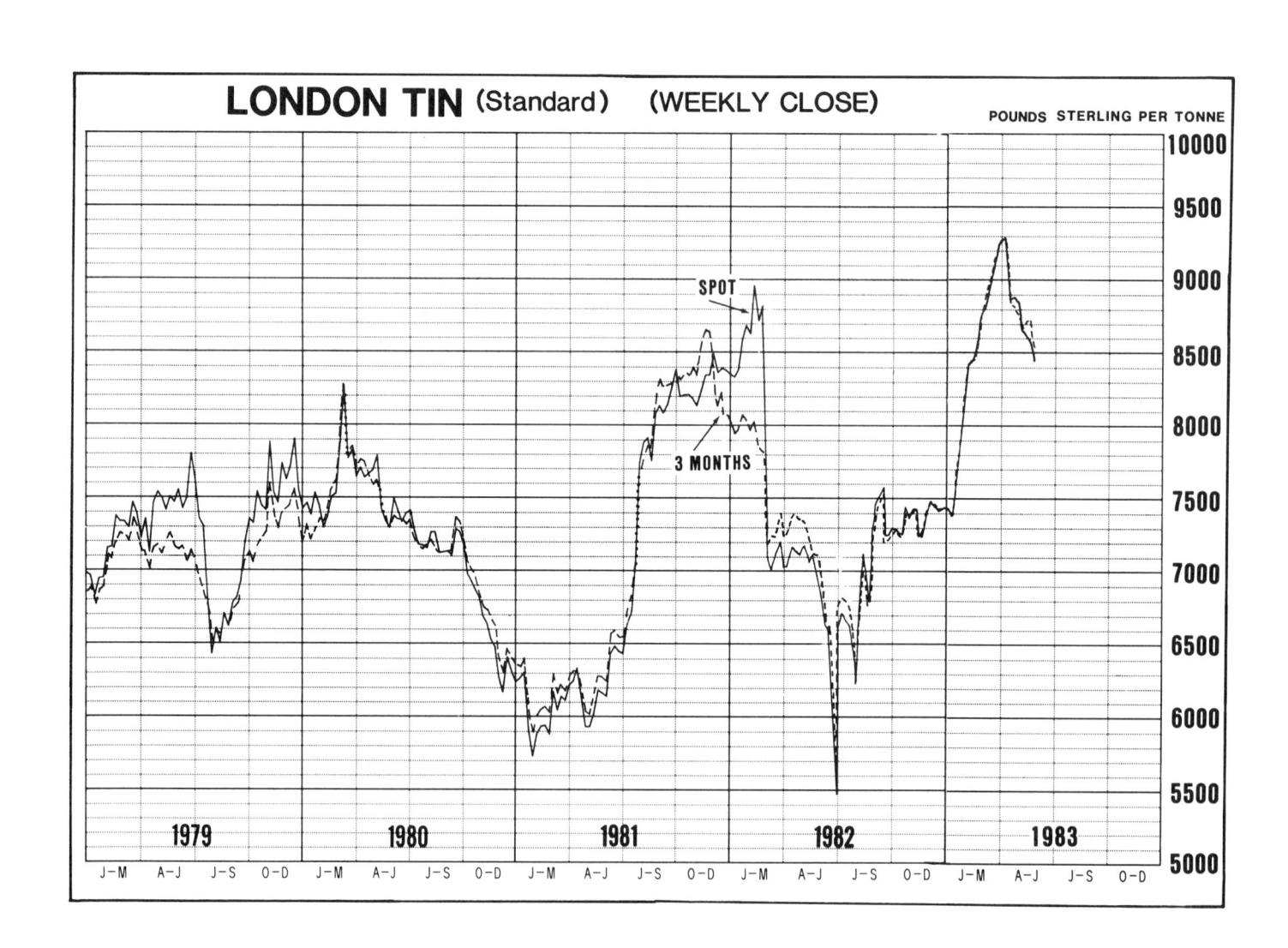

T.688

Titanium

Calculated titanium sponge metal production in 1982 was more than 30 percent lower than in 1981, based on preliminary U.S. Bureau of Mines data. Overall utilization of the 33,000 ton-per-year U.S. production capacity was estimated to be only about 35 percent. Estimated ingot production in 1982 was off 45 percent from the year earlier total.

U.S. imports of rutile, the source of titanium for sponge production, declined 14 percent in 1982. The major sources of rutile imports were Australia and Sierra Leone. Synthetic rutile imports, mostly from Australia, declined 41 percent in 1982. U.S. imports of ilmenite, the source of titanium for pigment production, increased 48 percent in 1982. Australia accounted for virtually all of the ilmenite imports. Titanium slag imports, mostly from Canada, were 8 percent lower than in 1981. Imports of titanium pigments in 1982 increased by some 7 percent.

U.S. titanium dioxide pigment production in 1982 declined 15 percent from the 1981 level, imports for consumption were up 11 percent, exports were up 9 percent, stocks dropped 20 percent and apparent consumption was off 8 percent from the 1981 level, according to U.S. Bureau of Mines data.

Estimated U.S. consumption of sponge metal during 1982 decreased 45 percent and net shipments of mill products fell 39 percent. Scrap consumption decreased 42 percent. The weak picture in the U.S. titanium industry in 1982 reflected inventory liquidation, a reduction in U.S. commercial aircraft production, low chemical capital spending, and increasing weakness in electric power plant production (especially nuclear), according to trade reports. The outlook for improvement in 1983 and beyond appears to be dependent on developments in the aerospace industry, which accounts for an estimated 60 percent of U.S. consumption of titanium metals and alloys in jet engines, airframes and space and missile applications. The rate of growth in still small but growing industrial applications is expected to be a factor. There was some belief that titanium demand could increase somewhat in the second half of 1983 due to rising defense-related activity, but that the commercial aircraft market would continue depressed throughout 1983.

Total U.S. industry stocks of titanium metal at the end of December 1982 were only 5 percent smaller than a year earlier. Stocks of ingots were 31 percent lower than on December 31, 1981 and sponge metal stocks were off 10 percent. However, stocks of scrap were up nearly 6 percent. U.S. government stocks of sponge metal were unchanged from a year earlier at 32,331 tons, which included 21,465 tons of stockpile grade and 10,866 tons of nonstockpile grade material. The stockpile goal was 195,000 tons, as of November 30, 1982.

The Bureau of Mines, in a preliminary report, estimated 1983 U.S. production of titanium sponge at 18,000 tons, apparent consumption of sponge at 20,000 tons, production of titanium dioxide pigment at 685,000 tons, and apparent consumption of pigment at 780,000 tons.

World Production of Titanium Ilmenite Concentrates[2]   In Thousands of Short Tons

Year	Australia (Shipments)	Canada[2]	Sri Lanka (Ceylon)	Finland	India	Japan[3]	Malaysia (Exports)	Norway	Brazil	USSR	China	South Africa	United States[4]	World Total[2]
1972	791.6	920.4	90.9	164.8	100.4	6.0[5]	170.1	670.7	4.2	—	—	—	681.7	3,626
1973	792.7	942.7	103.0	175.3	85.1	7.1[5]	204.3	829.9	4.6	—	—	—	776.0	3,925
1974	916.6	931.2	93.9	167.6	146.0	4.9	169.2	934.9	7.4	338.0	—	—	744.6	3,519
1975	1,111	826.6	70.6	135.1	90.0	4.9	123.7	580.5	5.1	360.0	—	—	717.3	4,026
1976	1,071	897.4	61.5	135.1	90.0	3.8	198.4	845.1	16.1	420.0	—	—	652.4	4,391
1977	1,139	763.2	37.6	137.5	151.4	1.4	169.4	913.3	14.6	440.0	—	—	638.5	4,418
1978	1,383	937.0	36.4	145.4	178.1	.2	205.9	845.5	22.1	450.0	N.A.	100	598.8	4,912
1979	1,302	525.8	61.0	131.9	161.9	.2	220.3	903.7	25.0	450.0	N.A.	316	639.3	4,762
1980	1,443	964.2	37.4	175.3	185.1	—	208.5	912.5	18.6	460.0	N.A.	379	548.9	5,362
1981[1]	1,474	840.0	88.2	175.0	208.1	—	160.0	724.9	19.0	470.0	150	408	509.3	5,227
1982[6]	1,340	720		160	175		135	620		470	150	420	260	4,540
1983														

[1] Preliminary.   [2] Includes Ti slag containing approx. 70% TiO$_2$.   [3] Represents titanium slag.   [4] Includes a mixed product containing ilmenite, leucoxene, & rutile.   [5] Includes slag & concentrate.   [6] Estimate.   Source: Bureau of Mines   T.692

Average Prices in the United States

Year	Titanium Ilmenite—54% TiO$_2$ F.O.B. Atlantic Seaboard—$ per Long Ton	Titanium Rutile F.O.B. Atlantic & Great Lakes Ports, Last Quarter (Spot) $ per Short Ton	Synthetic F.O.B. Mobile, Ala.	Titanium Metal Sponge, Yearend $ per Pound	Titanium Dioxide Pigments ($ per Lb.) Anatase	Titanium Dioxide Rutile, Yearend $ per Pound
1975	55	710		2.70	0.385	0.435
1976	55	510		2.70	0.410	0.465
1977	55	360		2.98	0.435	0.485
1978	50	340		3.28	0.460	0.510
1979	50	390		3.98	0.530	0.590
1980	55	440	310	7.02	0.570	0.630
1981	70	460	340	7.65	0.690	0.750
1982[1]	70	460	340	5.55	0.690	0.750
1983						

[1] Preliminary.   Source: U.S. Bureau of Mines   T.690

TITANIUM

World Production of Titanium Rutile Concentrates   In Short Tons

Year	South Africa	Australia	USSR	Egypt	Brazil	Sierra Leone	India	Sri Lanka (Ceylon)	United States	World Total
1970	—	405,156	—	—	258	48,593	2,400	3,100	N.A.	459,507
1971	—	404,233	—	—	129	13,153	3,210	3,100	N.A.	423,825
1972	—	345,176	—	—	454	—	3,379	2,371	N.A.	351,380
1973	—	358,914	—	—	46	—	3,748	2,482	9,255	374,445
1974	—	351,308	30,000	—	161	—	6,400	3,450	6,446	397,765
1975	—	383,990	30,000	—	115	—	4,000	3,427	11,000	421,532
1976	—	429,625	10,000	—	56	—	4,000	1,145	N.A.	444,826
1977	5,000	358,561	10,000	—	141	—	6,053	1,078	N.A.	380,833
1978	20,000	283,376	10,000	—	402	—	6,239	12,673	N.A.	332,690
1979	46,000	302,621	10,000	—	484	11,000	5,445	16,176	N.A.	391,726
1980	53,000	323,801	10,000	—	472	52,356	5,908	14,097	N.A.	459,634
1981[1]	55,000	252,706	10,000	—	440	55,992	9,647	14,662	N.A.	398,447
1982[2]	55,000	250,000				55,000	9,000	15,000	N.A.	390,000

[1] Preliminary.   [2] Estimate.   Source: Bureau of Mines   T.691

World Production of Titanium Sponge Metal & U.S. Consumption of Titanium Concentrates
In Short Tons

| | Production of Titanium Sponge Metal[1] ||||| U.S. Consumption of Titanium Concentrates, by Products ||||||||
| | ||||| Ilmenite (TiO$_2$ Content) ||| Rutile (TiO$_2$ Content) |||||
Year	Central Economy Countries	Other Mkt. Econ. Count.	Japan	United States	Total	Pigments	Misc.	Total	Ceramics	Welding Rod Coatings	Alloys & Carbine	Pigments	Misc.	Total
1972		2,500	5,133	12,000	—	453,248	8,174	461,422	N.A.	10,392	N.A.	199,894	21,945	232,231
1973		2,500	6,100	17,000	—	470,087	9,144	479,231	N.A.	10,059	N.A.	221,658	31,648	263,365
1974		2,500	9,825	20,000	—	492,206	9,070	501,276	N.A.	11,181	N.A.	228,507	38,032	277,720
1975		2,500	8,358	18,000	—	424,302	8,107	432,409	—	9,782	—	181,128	28,013	218,923
1976		2,100	6,995	14,000	—	490,845	7,168	498,013	—	7,736	—	194,950	20,926	223,612
1977	39,000	2,400	7,049	N.A.	—	514,429	6,765	521,194	—	8,184	—	136,191	29,465	173,840
1978	39,000	2,400	10,115	N.A.	—	467,410	8,038	475,448	—	8,427	N.A.	195,431	41,326	245,184
1979	43,000	2,600	14,000	N.A.	—	475,342	11,886	478,228	—	9,947	N.A.	230,776	52,189	292,912
1980	45,000	2,600	21,257	N.A.	—	502,108	11,207	513,315	—	6,876	N.A.	211,599	59,407	277,882
1981[3]	42,000	2,600	27,500	26,419	100,519	501,301	9,721	511,022		6,944		192,779	66,873	266,596
1982[2]	42,000	2,600	18,000	18,400	82,500									

[1] Unconsolidated metal in various forms.   [2] Estimated.   [3] Preliminary.   Source: Bureau of Mines   T.689

Salient Statistics of Titanium[4] in the United States   In Short Tons

| | Ilmenite |||| Titanium Slag ||| Rutile ||| Exports of Titanium Products ||||
Year	Production (Gross Wt.)	Shipments (TiO$_2$)	Imports[3]	Stocks Dec. 31 (TiO$_2$)	Consumption (TiO$_2$)	Imports[3]	Stocks (TiO$_2$)	Imports[3]	Stocks Dec. 31 (TiO$_2$)	Ores & Concentrates	Scrap	Dioxide & Pigments	Ingots, Billets, Etc.
1970	867,955	487,298	96,123	458,046	91,639	134,996	81,761	243,259	227,689	1,058	2,902	26,194	1,740
1971	683,075	388,802	28,093	383,113	101,751	152,661	76,741	227,784	225,925	1,760	1,711	26,759	430
1972	677,944	417,553	14,836	314,584	187,608	298,259	100,746	220,533	150,801	1,802	3,510	10,335	562
1973	776,013	458,541	69,691	329,477	199,287	237,248	78,650	226,860	139,641	1,494	4,142	20,769	745
1974	744,571	434,605	82,448	325,918	182,257	236,272	40,836	246,489	101,394	3,264	4,730	30,379	1,719
1975	717,281	404,269	122,010	378,181	104,585	212,682	62,130	224,499	131,742	3,147	4,326	15,807	1,900
1976	652,404	374,989	168,402	429,801	144,506	171,624	70,242	281,712	143,243	4,802	6,144	20,580	1,065
1977	638,503	331,139	334,990	494,658	106,201	150,564	44,464	123,800	136,935	22,679	3,394	16,336	1,050
1978	589,751	352,842	308,671	510,430	91,490	149,172	75,097	289,617	172,685	N.A.	5,453	39,341	1,340
1979	639,292	389,535	184,478	462,415	106,201	111,210	56,917	283,479	119,947	9,903	4,967	51,456	1,984
1980	548,882	358,181	357,488	584,280	91,490	194,994	127,981	281,605	147,670	17,830	3,300	45,795	3,278
1981[1]	509,342	310,854	236,217	516,135	106,346	268,825	150,706	202,373	159,687	7,297	3,280	62,432	4,203
1982[2]	260,000		348,366		247,845		163,325			22,000	4,286	66,900	2,196

[1] Preliminary.   [2] Estimate.   [3] For consumption.   [4] Natural & synthetic.   Source: Bureau of Mines   T.693

Tobacco

The 1982 global production of tobacco was projected at 14.5 billion pounds, 11 percent over the total 1981 world production.

Preliminary estimates indicated that U.S. tobacco production in 1982 was nearly 6 percent below its 1981 level. Total acreage planted to tobacco was 9 percent lower and was the lowest acreage recorded since 1979. The average yield for all tobacco crops was 2 percent above the 1981 average. U.S. tobacco use during the 1982/83 season was expected to fall short of production, and, consequently, 1983 summer ending stocks could be as much as 6 percent higher than the 3.6 billion pounds of tobacco carried into 1983. Domestic tobacco supplies for 1982/83 were 3 percent above those of last season despite the smaller crop, and beginning stocks were 8 percent larger.

Although U.S. carryover stocks of flue-cured tobacco were 7 percent larger at the beginning of 1982/83, the smaller crop resulted in a flue-cured supply of 3.13 billion pounds, slightly below year-earlier levels. Harvested acreage of flue-cured tobacco was down 14 percent from 1981, and the yield was 4 percent lower. A downturn in both U.S. exports and domestic use during the 1982/83 marketing year was expected to result in a total disappearance of flue-cured tobacco below the previous year's level. Carryover stocks as of mid-1983 were expected to rise, loan holdings being likely to account for most of the increase. The price of flue-cured tobacco in 1982 was up nearly 7 percent from 1981, about half of the price gain recorded a year earlier.

Reduced demand for cigarettes caused a 3 percent reduction in the domestic use of burley tobacco during 1982/83. The estimated supply of burley, including marketings plus carryover, was a record 1.86 million pounds, nearly 8 percent above the 1981/82 level. The record burley crop, estimated at 789 million pounds, was expected to increase carryover at the end of the third quarter of 1983. Sales of burley tobacco at the end of 1982 totaled 597 million pounds (gross) and averaged $1.80 per pound.

As of January 1, 1983 the 1982/83 carryover of Maryland tobacco was estimated to be 3 million pounds above the year earlier. The 1982/83 crop was projected at 36 million pounds, a 20 percent reduction from the previous season. The total supply of 1982/83 Maryland tobacco was 83 million pounds, 1.5 million above 1981/82.

The quality of fire-cured tobacco was lower in 1982/83 and prices were down 7 to 18 cents a pound. The 1982/83 fire-cured crop was estimated at 47 million pounds, a 26 percent increase that raises the total 1982/83 supply of fire-cured types to 119 million pounds. The supply of dark air-cured and sun-cured tobacco for 1982/83 was estimated at 58.4 million pounds, 4 million above the previous season.

Domestic Use

U.S. smokers consumed an estimated 633 billion cigarettes during 1982, a 1 percent decline from the 1981 consumption. The total estimated domestic output of cigarettes during 1982 was 698.0 billion, a drop of nearly 5 percent due to falling sales and a sharp rise in prices. The domestic consumption of large cigars (including cigarillos) was down by 7 percent during 1982 and falling sales were expected to continue throughout 1983. The production of chewing tobacco and of snuff during 1982 were estimated to be up 1 percent and 7 percent respectively.

Foreign Trade

Preliminary estimates placed total 1982 U.S. exports of unmanufactured tobacco between 550 and 575 million pounds compared with 584 million during 1981. West Germany and Japan continued to be the major customers for U.S. tobacco, but Europe took less U.S. tobacco during 1982 and Asian markets increased their purchases. During most of 1982, U.S. exports of flue-cured and Maryland tobacco declined while exports of burley and many sun- and fire-cured types rose. Calendar 1983 exports were expected to fall from the 1982 level because of a stronger dollar and large overseas production. U.S. stocks of foreign-grown cigarette and smoking tobacco rose nearly 17 percent during most of 1982.

U.S. Government Programs

In November 1982, the USDA announced a national flue-cured tobacco marketing quota of 910 million pounds for 1983, a 10 percent reduction. After adjustment for shortfalls and for excesses in individual 1982 marketings, the 1983 effective quota is around 895 million pounds, 8 percent lower than in 1982 and the lowest quota on record. USDA estimates indicated that a crop close to the quota level would, when added to the prospective carryover, result in a 1983/84 supply only a little smaller than in 1982/83. As a condition for price supports on 1983 flue-cured tobacco, producers were obligated to contribute 7 cents a pound to a no-net-cost tobacco fund on all flue-cured tobacco sold. The contribution of 3 cents a pound in 1982 was thought to be insufficient to cover expected losses from the disposition of the 1981/82 crop.

Burley poundage legislation requires that the national burley quota be neither less than 95 percent of estimated disappearance during a given marketing year nor less than 95 percent of the previous year's quota. The basic allotment for the 1982/83 burley crop was set at 680 million pounds. Because of declining cigarette demand and exports, disappearance was expected to be down slightly during 1982/83, and marketings were expected to fall short of the effective quota.

TOBACCO

World Production of Leaf Tobacco   In Thousands of Metric Tons[5] (Farm Sales–Weight[3])

Year	United States	Brazil	Canada	China	USSR	France	Greece	India	Indonesia	Italy	Japan	Pakistan[4]	Philippines	Turkey	World Total[1]
1970	1,911	432	222	1,700	569	106	200	743	240	173	332	360	218	330	10,021
1971	1,712	432	225	1,781	604	96	184	798	173	166	328	336	155	383	9,865
1972	1,754	421	187	1,852	516	109	188	924	165	176	318	192	107	401	10,155
1973	1,744	399	257	2,103	672	112	202	821	287	207	347	139	168	334	10,670
1974[5]	906.1	225.5	116.5	983.8	313.0	51.7	81.1	462.1	78.3	92.7	151.3	64.6	88.4	203.5	5,185
1975	994.0	285.6	106.1	959.8	298.0	56.3	118.2	394.8	82.2	113.4	165.7	78.0	66.3	208.6	5,369
1976	971.0	276.1	81.5	1,370	318.0	61.4	140.0	349.8	88.4	108.6	176.2	60.7	89.0	324.0	6,038
1977	870.0	310.0	104.3	1,389	307.0	43.6	118.9	418.8	83.7	109.7	173.2	72.6	84.3	248.0	5,892
1978	919.8	330.0	115.6	1,452	282.0	50.5	130.3	493.6	82.5	109.7	172.0	76.3	79.2	292.6	6,097
1979	693.3	401.0	78.9	941.4	301.0	50.6	127.2	453.8	141.2	136.6	153.3	69.9	85.3	214.3	5,701
1980	809.7	350.0	107.9	898.0	289.0	46.5	116.8	438.5	117.6	125.5	141.4	71.0	75.5	228.3	5,259
1981[2]	935.5	314.0	112.1	1,250	285.0	42.8	118.4	455.6	119.7	129.0	137.7	67.1	81.3	180.0	5,654
1982[1]	872.9	339.0	119.3	1,250	304.0	41.2	113.1	445.0	115.0	132.5	136.2	70.5	82.7	210.0	5,682
1983															

[1] Estimated. [2] Preliminary. [3] Farm–Sales–weight is about 10% above dry weight which is normally reported in trade statistics. [4] Bangladesh (Formerly East Paskistan) excluded from 1972 to date. [5] Data prior to 1974 are in MILLIONS OF POUNDS. Source: Foreign Agricultural Service, U.S.D.A.

T.694

Production and Consumption of Tobacco Products in the United States

	Production								Consumption[3] Per Capita[4]					
	Chewing Tobacco				Cigarettes	Cigars[2]	Smoking Tobacco	Snuff	Cigars[2]	Cigarettes	Cigars[2]	Cigarettes	Smoking Tobacco	Total Pdt.'s
Year	Plug	Twist	Fine-cut	Loose-leaf	Total	Billion		Million Lbs.		Number		Pounds			
	Million Pounds														
1970	22.0	2.4	4.8	39.5	68.7	583.2	7.09	69.4	26.5	125.3	3,985	2.08	7.77	1.15	9.68
1971	20.6	2.4	5.1	43.2	71.4	576.4	6.71	60.5	26.4	119.2	4,037	1.94	7.75	1.06	9.52
1972	19.6	2.2	5.2	45.6	72.6	599.1	6.03	55.9	25.5	108.9	4,043	1.74	7.95	1.00	9.65
1973	18.6	2.2	5.7	47.6	74.0	644.2	5.66	53.0	25.3	102.4	4,148	1.61	7.92	.88	9.53
1974	18.0	2.2	6.2	52.9	79.2	635.0	5.28	49.0	25.0	91.9	4,141	1.47	7.90	.87	9.40
1975	18.1	2.3	7.3	53.7	81.5	651.2	4.52	46.2	24.4	82.4	4,123	1.32	7.73	.76	9.14
1976	16.7	2.3	8.4	56.3	83.7	693.4	4.18	44.6	24.8	75.0	4,092	1.20	7.35	.75	8.69
1977	16.4	2.2	10.1	61.3	90.0	665.9	3.93	40.7	24.6	67.9	4,051	1.13	7.21	.65	8.49
1978	15.9	2.1	12.0	64.6	94.6	695.9	3.80	36.4	25.1	63.4	3,967	1.05	6.89	.60	8.10
1979	15.3	2.0	13.3	71.7	102.3	704.4	3.60	32.8	23.7	56.0	3,861	.92	7.00	.51	8.12
1980	17.3	1.9	14.7	72.1	106.0	714.1	3.45	32.2	24.3	51.1	3,851	.84	6.79	.48	7.98
1981	17.9	1.8	15.2	70.3	90.0[5]	736.5	3.43	30.3	42.5[5]	48.9	3,840	.81	6.54	.46	7.61
1982[1]	15.7	1.7	[5]	73.0	90.4[5]	694.2	3.20	28.3	43.8[5]	45.3	3,746	.74	6.38	.42	7.38
1983															

[1] Preliminary. [2] Large cigars & cigarillos. [3] Consumption of tax-paid tobacco products; Represents unstemmed equivalent of tobacco used in the manufacture of these products. [4] 18 years old & over. [5] New classifications. Sources: Bureau of the Census; Internal Revenue Service

T.695

Production of Tobacco in the United States   In Millions of Pounds

Year	Conn.	Florida	Georgia	Indiana	Kentucky	Maryland	Massachusetts	North Car.	Ohio	Pa.	South Car.	Tenn.	Virginia	Wisconsin	W. Virg.
1970	8.7	28.9	133.3	14.6	411.9	29.4	3.6	815.5	20.8	30.1	141.1	114.3	125.8	18.4	3.3
1971	7.6	25.6	115.1	12.1	356.3	28.1	2.9	727.1	17.5	24.5	133.2	105.6	118.4	22.5	2.0
1972	5.6	23.5	115.2	15.5	446.7	23.8	1.9	680.4	22.5	18.2	131.1	124.7	112.1	18.7	3.3
1973	6.8	24.0	97.9	10.6	320.9	31.5	2.0	811.9	15.9	22.1	132.7	101.3	138.1	19.0	2.8
1974	7.9	27.8	161.4	16.7	452.0	30.2	2.4	789.2	23.1	26.0	172.0	110.9	141.6	18.5	2.9
1975	6.4	29.6	151.0	17.0	456.7	21.9	2.0	957.0	23.7	19.8	189.0	134.6	142.1	20.8	3.1
1976	7.2	30.8	123.8	18.2	497.4	29.9	1.8	902.9	23.3	23.6	153.4	139.7	153.9	20.2	3.2
1977	5.6	24.8	134.9	16.6	452.0	30.1	1.9	744.5	22.7	26.2	138.7	136.7	143.0	24.4	3.2
1978	5.0	22.1	125.7	15.5	469.7	30.6	1.5	849.7	22.5	25.2	150.5	142.1	135.2	20.3	2.7
1979	4.9	23.2	101.0	11.9	343.1	22.0	1.5	621.4	14.1	17.7	117.7	104.8	109.6	25.1	1.7
1980	5.3	20.4	110.6	16.8	420.7	25.3	1.9	762.4	20.0	24.7	125.5	111.9	106.9	26.0	1.8
1981	5.6	22.8	121.0	18.8	509.6	33.0	2.0	795.9	22.9	27.3	149.6	161.5	157.8	26.4	2.4
1982[1]	3.8	20.1	105.5	22.1	573.7	37.5	.8	693.3	30.1	25.4	124.2	172.5	123.9	19.7	3.1
1983															

[1] Preliminary, December estimate.   Source: Crop Reporting Board, U.S.D.A.

T.696

TOBACCO

U.S. Salient Statistics for Flue-Cured Tobacco (Types 11-14)

Crop Year	Acres Harvested 1,000	Yield Acre 100 Lbs.	Production	Stocks, July 1	Total Supply	Exports	Dom. Disappearance	Total Disappearance	Farm Price ¢ Lb.	Crop Value Mil. $	Parity Price[2]	Price Support Level ¢ Lb.	Placed Under Gov't. Loan Mil. Lb.	Under Loan July 1
1970-71	584.1	20.4	1,178	1,972	3,151	534	640	1,174	72.0	848	96.3	66.6	144.2	744.9
1971	525.8	20.5	1,076	1,976	3,053	480	663	1,143	77.2	832	101.0	69.4	55.7	761.9
1972	513.6	19.7	1,022	1,910	2,932	519	664	1,183	85.3	864	106.0	72.7	24.3	617.8
1973	575.1	20.1	1,159	1,749	2,908	598	703	1,301	88.1	1,019	123.0	76.6	30.7	402.3
1974	616.3	20.1	1,245	1,607	2,852	548	652	1,201	105.0	1,307	136.0	83.3	23.0	276.7
1975	717.2	19.7	1,415	1,652	3,067	523	671	1,193	99.8	1,442	150.0	93.2	259.0	179.9
1976	666.6	19.7	1,316	1,898	3,214	514	634	1,148	110.4	1,453	155.0	106.0	277.3	359.2
1977	589.3	19.2	1,124	2,075	3,199	539	608	1,147	117.6	1,329	162.0	113.8	195.6	556.9
1978	602.1	20.5	1,206	2,052	3,258	599	584	1,183	135.0	1,663	176.0	121.0	64.1	534.0
1979	502.8	18.8	946	2,075	3,021	520	563	1,083	140.0	1,324	203.0	129.3	72.0	564.0
1980	555.1	19.6	1,086	1,965	3,052	509	530	1,039	144.5	1,569	222.0	141.5	137.2	554.4
1981	540.6	21.6	1,144	2,013	3,157	523	489	1,012	166.4	1,947		158.7	105.9	595.8
1982[1]	472.3	21.2	994	2,145	3,139	480	450	930	178.6	1,775		169.9	259.9	518.7
1983-4[3]	429.5	20.0	897	2,209	3,106									700.0

[1] Preliminary. [2] As of applicable date when support level was computed. [3] Estimate. Source: Agricultural Marketing Service, U.S.D.A. T.697

U.S. Salient Statistics for Burley Tobacco (Type 31)

Crop Year	Acres Harvested 1,000	Yield Per Acre 100 Lbs.	Production	Stocks, Oct. 1	Total Supply	Exports	Dom. Disappearance	Total Disappearance	Farm Price ¢ Lb.	Crop Value Mil. $	Parity Price[2]	Support Level ¢ Lb.	Placed Under Gov't. Loan Mil. Lb.	Under Loan on Oct. 1
1970	216.4	25.9	561	1,343	1,903	54	503	557	72.2	405	101.0	68.6	47.7	454.8
1971	213.5	22.1	473	1,346	1,818	55	515	570	80.9	382	104.5	71.5	.2	468.4
1972	235.6	25.5	590	1,249	1,839	75	535	610	79.2	476	111.0	74.9	22.9	327.6
1973	222.1	20.3	461	1,229	1,691	87	533	619	92.9	418	129.0	78.9	.7	276.7
1974	260.7	23.5	610	1,071	1,681	68	519	587	113.7	694	147.0	85.8	2.8	139.2
1975	282.2	22.7	638	1,094	1,733	92	510	603	105.5	673	158.0	96.1	50.7	12.0
1976	285.8	23.8	664	1,160	1,824	117	490	606	114.2	775	160.0	109.3	46.6	44.8
1977	268.6	23.0	613	1,217	1,830	117	495	611	120.0	741	166.0	117.3	57.0	54.9
1978	261.4	24.0	618	1,218	1,836	121	503	624	131.2	822	184.0	124.7	67.7	113.5
1979	238.1	18.7	446	1,212	1,658	133	499	632	145.2	700	210.0	133.3	7.3	155.4
1980	276.6	20.3	558	1,026	1,583	106	478	583	165.9	930	236.0	145.9	.0	66.3
1981	331.2	22.0	726	1,000	1,726	141	464	605	180.7	1,318		163.6	.8	0
1982[1]	337.7	23.7	773	1,121	1,894	155	450	605	180.6	1,396		175.1	268.4	.7
1983-4[3]	302.0	21.6	680	1,289	1,969									266.0

[1] Preliminary. [2] As of applicable date when support level was computed. [3] Estimate. Source: Agricultural Marketing Service, U.S.D.A. T.698

Exports[1] of Tobacco from the United States   In Millions of Pounds

Year	Jan.	Feb.	Mar.	Apr.	May	June	July	Aug.	Sept.	Oct.	Nov.	Dec.	Total
1970	20.5	28.2	41.1	38.3	39.9	42.3	34.7	29.6	46.8	53.7	72.8	62.5	510.3
1971	39.3	32.3	52.4	44.5	47.4	39.8	35.4	41.8	76.8	3.5	2.4	59.6	474.2
1972	95.4	87.0	28.6	17.9	42.7	33.3	39.2	40.5	48.3	54.1	63.1	56.2	606.2
1973	43.1	45.3	45.6	43.6	46.2	45.3	40.1	40.6	54.6	70.2	81.9	56.6	613.0
1974	53.5	47.6	39.1	52.7	57.7	62.8	45.2	47.6	40.0	64.1	73.0	68.3	651.4
1975	57.1	33.5	52.5	46.7	44.2	32.1	23.2	39.5	44.9	52.7	73.9	62.9	563.0
1976	93.2	52.0	47.1	43.5	29.7	26.0	23.9	34.7	48.2	52.9	51.3	75.6	578.0
1977	76.8	53.0	54.7	31.3	38.0	41.5	49.7	47.5	66.3	17.9	49.5	102.4	628.6
1978	52.5	55.6	73.2	40.9	32.3	29.2	42.7	52.3	41.3	85.8	95.8	86.3	687.8
1979[2]	35.6	50.1	57.1	51.8	42.2	25.3	38.0	29.5	30.1	41.6	78.9	81.5	561.8
1980[2]	28.0	52.5	80.1	54.6	53.2	43.0	40.9	25.8	32.3	47.6	64.4	66.6	591.5
1981[2]	44.8	32.8	53.7	49.4	44.6	40.1	31.3	27.4	45.5	63.2	86.8	55.6	575.3
1982[2]	31.7	39.4	49.9	41.8	54.0	37.2	23.9	30.2	24.8	74.5	92.2	50.5	550.0
1983[2]	24.2												

[1] Represents unmanufactured tobacco, including stems, trimmings and scrap. [2] Preliminary. Source: Department of Commerce T.699

TOBACCO

Salient Statistics of Tobacco in the United States

Year	Acres Harvested 1,000 Acres	Yield Per Acre Lbs.	Production Million Lbs.	Farm Price ¢ Lb.	Farm Value Mil. $	Tobacco (July–June) Exports[2] Mil. Lbs.	Imports[3] Mil. Lbs.	Cigarettes Millions	U.S. Exports of Cigars & Cheroots Millions	Chewing Tobacco & Snuff Metric Tons[6]	Smoking Tobacco[7] Metric Tons[6]	Stocks of Leaf Tobacco[4] All Types Jan. 1 Billion Pounds	April 1	July 1	Oct. 1
1970	898	2,122	1,906	72.9	1,389	554.7	223.9	29,163	54	64	25,022	4,940	4,822	4,439	4,650
1971	838	2,035	1,705	78.6	1,340	524.2	259.1	31,812	53	39	32,086	5,006	4,763	4,371	4,474
1972	842	2,076	1,749	83.0	1,451	569.1	250.3	34,602	75	42	30,425	4,828	4,531	4,186	4,405
1973	887	1,965	1,742	90.0	1,572	657.4	294.2	41,543	107	93	27,084	4,700	4,459	4,039	4,196
1974	963	2,067	1,990	108.6	2,160	604.0	322.4	46,901	86	121	39,848	4,409	4,215	3,762	4,123
1975	1,087	2,008	2,182	102.6	2,239	588.2	313.3	49,935	92	32	8,703	4,457	4,310	3,946	4,282
1976	1,047	2,041	2,137	112.5	2,404	581.8	293.7	61,370	124	34	6,680	4,738	4,568	4,166	4,608
1977	966	1,982	1,914	118.6	2,268	617.0	335.7	66,845	107	43	4,844	4,798	4,797	4,431	4,710
1978	964	2,101	2,025	132.4	2,679	671.9	359.7	74,359	166	47	1,578	5,008	4,781	4,451	4,728
1979	827	1,845	1,527	141.1	2,154	617.4	398.1	79,717	177	43	10,634	5,071	4,914	4,518	4,740
1980	920.5	1,940	1,786	152.3	2,720	553.4	439.8	82,000	200	124	3,250	4,974	4,608	4,284	4,548
1981[1]	976.0	2,114	2,064	170.6	3,518	584.7	384.9	82,600	181			4,850	4,617	4,285	4,697
1982[1]	903.5	2,171	1,962	179.2	3,473	575.0	375.0	73,600	181			5,080	4,983	4,675	5,034
1983[1]	820.4[5]											5,371			
1984															

[1] Preliminary. [2] Domestic. [3] For consumption. [4] Owned by dealer & mfgrs., converted to a farm-sales weight equivalent. [5] Farmers' intentions to plant, MARCH 1. [6] Data prior to 1975 are in THOUSANDS OF POUNDS. [7] In packages & in bulk. *Source: Agricultural Marketing Service, U.S.D.A.*

T.700

Tobacco Production in the U.S., by Types   In Million Pounds (Farm–Sales Weight)

Types	11–14	31	32	21	22–23	35–36	37	41	42–44	72	51–52	54–55	61
1970	1,193	561	29.4	6.2	30.9	15.4	1.1	30.6	2.9	.2	2.9	18.4	14.9
1971	1,078	473	28.1	5.9	37.6	15.7	1.1	24.5	3.8	.2	2.8	22.5	12.4
1972	1,012	601	23.8	4.7	37.5	15.5	.8	18.2	4.2	.1	2.5	18.7	9.7
1973	1,157	450	31.5	5.7	27.7	12.4	.9	22.1	3.1	.2	2.7	19.0	9.8
1974	1,241	613	30.2	5.9	26.0	11.6	.9	26.0	3.1	.1	2.5	18.5	11.0
1975	1,415	639	21.9	4.9	32.6	14.0	.7	19.8	3.0	.1	2.4	20.8	7.7
1976	1,316	679	29.9	5.3	33.2	15.1	.8	23.6	2.8	.1	2.4	20.2	7.2
1977	1,130	617	30.1	7.2	45.2	20.4	.8	26.2	3.6	.1	2.5	24.4	5.3
1978	1,232	626	30.6	6.8	51.4	22.2	.9	25.2	3.0	.1	2.6	20.3	3.8
1979	946	446	22.0	5.4	39.6	16.1	.6	17.7	2.0	.1	2.4	25.1	4.0
1980	1,086	561	26.2	3.6	32.7	16.2	.4	24.7	2.4	.1	2.6	26.0	4.5
1981	1,170	730	46.4	5.2	32.4	15.6	.7	27.3	2.4	.1	3.5	26.4	4.1
1982[1]	1,001	801	37.6	5.5	43.6	18.6	.7	25.4	3.5		3.1	19.7	1.6
1983													

[1] Preliminary. *Source: Crop Reporting Board, U.S.D.A.*

T.701

U.S. Exports of Unmanufactured Tobacco   In Millions of Pounds (Declared Weight)

Year	Australia	Belg.-Luxem.	Denmark	France	W. Germany	Thailand	Ireland	Japan	Netherlands	Norway	Italy	Sweden	Switzerland	United Kingdom	Total U.S. Exports
1970	10.2	12.4	18.1	9.0	92.6	20.1	10.2	58.6	26.6	8.1	3.1	19.5	24.7	95.5	510.4
1971	10.9	15.6	16.7	10.1	100.0	18.9	9.0	18.6	28.1	4.3	16.4	14.7	18.2	89.8	473.3
1972	14.8	12.9	20.8	7.7	99.3	30.5	14.3	87.3	22.4	7.0	23.1	20.5	23.5	115.1	606.1
1973	13.9	16.7	37.0	6.6	99.9	8.6	8.9	79.0	31.6	5.7	21.8	17.1	31.4	119.7	612.5
1974	18.7	14.4	12.6	8.2	97.1	20.6	10.2	109.6	31.0	5.4	24.3	14.5	21.3	94.3	651.4
1975	15.5	8.1	16.4	9.5	91.0	18.7	8.2	81.5	29.9	5.6	31.5	15.3	25.9	78.5	563.0
1976	10.3	7.5	9.0	8.3	73.7	21.8	7.7	132.7	24.7	5.5	33.2	14.1	24.4	71.8	578.1
1977	14.2	10.4	16.9	6.3	78.9	16.0	5.4	135.4	30.5	6.0	40.6	11.8	28.8	46.8	628.6
1978	12.4	16.9	27.1	9.8	53.2	18.2	5.3	102.3	34.2	4.2	41.0	17.5	26.2	148.8	700.0
1979	12.4	5.4	16.4	11.5	67.7	18.8	6.9	95.9	29.3	5.7	34.8	13.7	19.3	68.2	567.4
1980	13.4	7.9	17.5	4.5	100.7	22.6	3.6	82.1	44.9	6.8	30.7	15.4	20.1	32.5	598.7
1981	12.6	9.5	11.1	6.1	83.2	18.4	3.9	117.0	28.6	4.2	26.5	9.9	22.2	39.4	584.5
1982[1]	10.1	15.2	16.8	5.3	68.2	27.7	4.7	110.3	25.1	3.6	28.1	8.7	26.7	30.7	572.0
1983															

[1] Preliminary. *Source: Bureau of the Census*

T.702

Tung Oil

Tung oil is produced from a tree crop and its production in recent years appears to have shown little overall variation worldwide. The People's Republic of China is, by far, the world's largest producer of tung oil, accounting for around 75 percent of estimated world production. Argentina and Paraguay account for an average 11 percent and 9 percent of estimated world production, respectively. These three countries are also the major exporters of tung oil.

Japan appears to have overtaken the United States as the world's largest importer of tung oil in recent years. U.S. imports of tung oil in 1982 declined 4 percent to 6,531 tonnes from 6,819 tonnes in 1981. U.S. imports of tung oil in 1980 amounted to 7,366 tonnes. Other major importers are the Soviet Union, Poland, and West Germany.

Supply and Distribution of Tung Oil in the United States   In Thousands of Pounds

Year	Stocks Jan. 1	Production	Imports	Exports[2]	Total Supply	Appar. Disappearance	Factory Consumption Total	Paint & Varnish	Linol. & Oilcloth	Printing Ink	Other	Resins & Plastics	Drying Oil Ind.	Oil Acquired By CCC
1970	54,902	4,000	18,151	2,110	74,943	28,233	28,400	20,000	[4]	[4]	[4]	3,900	28,000	5,700
1971	47,710	100	22,239	1,962	68,087	23,282	27,200	17,100				3,700	23,000	3,800
1972	44,703	2,250	21,597	1,257	67,273	33,307	31,800	18,100				3,800	31,000	100
1973	33,986	500	21,796	1,955	54,327	28,589	31,000	20,000				4,000	28,000	2,300
1974	25,738	—	21,037	700	46,075	34,858	34,000	24,000				2,000	35,000	—
1975	11,217	—	30,063	1,700	39,580	33,228	43,000	26,000				4,000	33,000	—
1976[1]	6,352	—	34,509	1,600	39,261	36,961	25,000						35,000	—
1977[1]	2,300	—	18,821	1,200	19,900	16,900	20,100						19,000	
1978[3]	3,000		17,912				16,900	7,200			2,600	3,700		
1979[3]	1,200		20,038				15,700	10,400			2,300	3,000		
1980[3]	3,500		16,239				16,600	8,300			4,600	3,700		
1981[3]	2,800						14,600	5,800			5,600	3,200		
1982[3]	2,200													

[1] Preliminary. [2] Also including re-exports. [3] Estimate. [4] Included in misc. to avoid disclosure of figures for individual companies. Source: Economic Research Service, U.S.D.A.   T.703

Average Price of Tung Oil[1] (Imported-Drums) F.O.B. New York   In Cents per Pound

Year	Jan.	Feb.	Mar.	Apr.	May	June	July	Aug.	Sept.	Oct.	Nov.	Dec.	Average
1970	24.0	23.9	25.4	26.0	26.0	26.0	26.0	26.0	26.0	26.0	26.0	26.0	25.6
1971	26.0	26.0	26.0	26.0	26.0	24.0	18.0	16.1	15.5	15.5	15.5	15.5	20.8
1972	15.5	15.5	15.5	15.5	15.5	15.5	15.5	15.5	15.5	15.5	15.5	15.5	15.5
1973	15.5	15.5	15.5	15.5	17.1	20.0	N.A.	N.A.	31.0	31.2	33.8	35.0	23.0
1974	35.0	36.0	39.0	39.0	38.3	35.5	35.5	35.5	35.0	35.2	38.9	41.0	37.0
1975	41.0	41.0	41.0	41.0	41.0	41.0	41.0	35.4	32.2	33.0	33.0	33.0	37.8
1976	33.0	33.2	34.0	34.0	33.8	37.0	54.0	65.0	65.0	65.0	65.0	65.0	48.7
1977	65.5	72.7	97.0	142.4	147.0	147.0	128.2	100.0	100.0	100.0	100.0	100.0	108.3
1978	100.0	100.0	100.0	100.0	100.0	100.0	100.0	87.5	87.5	87.5	68.5	66.4	91.5
1979	68.9	68.9	67.9	69.0	69.0	69.0	69.0	69.0	62.5	55.0	51.0	51.0	64.2
1980	51.0	55.1	55.8	53.0	51.1	48.3	45.2	43.7	46.6	56.5	65.5	67.2	53.3
1981	69.6	68.0	64.0	60.3	62.9	64.5	64.0	64.0	62.1	60.3	58.5	58.5	63.1
1982	61.4	69.5	68.2	66.5	68.3	69.4	66.9	63.5	60.6	60.5	60.5	60.5	64.7
1983													

[1] Carlots, imported, f.o.b. New York.   Source: Economic Research Service, U.S.D.A.   T.704

How to keep your Commodity Year Book statistics up-to-date continuously throughout the year.

To keep up-to-date statistics on the commodities in this book, you should have COMMODITY YEAR BOOK STATISTICAL ABSTRACT SERVICE. This three-times yearly publication provides the latest available statistics for the updating of the statistical tables appearing in the COMMODITY YEAR BOOK. It is published in the Winter (Jan.), Spring (Apr.) and Fall (Oct.). Subscription price is $55 per year.

Commodity Research Bureau, Inc.
75 MONTGOMERY ST., JERSEY CITY, N.J. 07302

Tungsten

Estimated world production and consumption of tungsten (in concentrate) each decreased 12 percent in 1982 compared with 1981 as demand for tungsten in mill products and cemented carbides dropped substantially, according to preliminary data of the U.S. Bureau of Mines.

U.S. production of ammonium paratungstate (APT), an intermediate product of tungsten concentrate containing 89 percent tungsten, was 45 percent lower in 1982 than in the preceding year. Consumption of APT, including tungsten oxide, was 36 percent lower than in 1981 and APT stocks at the end of 1982 were 7 percent higher than a year earlier.

The reported consumption of tungsten concentrate in 1982 was 54 percent below that of a year earlier, while imports for consumption were off 34 percent and ending stocks rose by 88 percent. However, reported scrap consumption increased by 17 percent in 1982, according to the Bureau of Mines.

Net U.S. production of intermediate products (tungsten metal powder, tungsten carbide powder, chemicals, and other products) in 1982 was 35 percent below the 1981 level. Reported consumption of intermediate products dropped 54 percent in 1982, but ending stocks were about unchanged from a year earlier.

U.S. tungsten concentrate production in August 1982 declined to its lowest level in 23 years because of low market prices and reduced tungsten carbide demand, driving unemployment in the tungsten mining industry to over 50 percent of the work force. Carbides account for around 50 percent of tungsten consumption in the U.S., and mining and drilling tools for oil, gas and coal account for an estimated 35 percent of this share of the market. The demand outlook for tungsten carbide cutting tools in 1983 was expected to reflect improvement in the U.S. economy.

The U.S. Bureau of Mines estimated that domestic mine production of tungsten in 1983 would total 3.5 million pounds, and U.S. apparent consumption would be 16 million pounds. More than 90 percent of the world's estimated tungsten resources are located outside the United States, with almost 55 percent located in China. The U.S. relies on imports for close to 50 percent of its apparent consumption. Major import sources in the 1978–81 period were Canada, 21 percent; Bolivia, 19 percent; China, 14 percent; others, 39 percent.

The General Services Administration (GSA) continued to offer excess tungsten concentrate for sale at a rate of 9 million pounds per year through September 1982 and at a rate of 6 million pounds for the rest of the year. From bids opened on February 10, 1983, the GSA sold 41,493 pounds of nonstockpile-grade tungsten in concentrate from excess Government stocks to Norore Corp. for export at a price of $71.99/stu WO_3. There were no bids for the February 22 GSA offering of 300,000 pounds of excess tungsten in concentrate.

The average weighted price of tungsten $US/stu, which was $117.07 in late February 1982, as indicated by information from the International Tungsten Indicator, dropped to $83.69 by late December 1982 and declined further to $71.47 in late January 1983 before steadying.

World Concentrate Production of Tungsten   In Thousand Pounds of Contained Tungsten (60% WO_3 Basis)

Year	Japan	Argentina	Australia	Bolivia	Brazil	Burma	China	Rep. of Korea	Canada	Portugal	Spain	Thailand	USSR	United States	World Total
1970	1,882	317	2,800	4,068	2,549	487	13,200	4,564	2,956	2,390	899	1,565	14,800	9,625	71,360
1971	1,609	304	3,184	4,608	2,989	842	15,400	4,784	3,667	2,176	897	5,527	15,400	6,900	78,055
1972	1,980	348	3,487	4,954	2,515	1,213	16,500	3,966	3,527	3,093	798	7,370	15,900	8,150	84,952
1973	2,072	183	2,917	4,264	2,194	1,133	17,600	4,504	3,680	3,336	690	5,295	16,300	7,575	83,612
1974	1,786	207	3,128	4,471	2,189	750	18,700	5,046	2,822	3,236	765	4,497	16,800	7,381	82,832
1975	1,693	190	4,145	5,661	2,496	1,091	19,800	5,298	2,584	3,139	774	3,609	17,200	5,588	84,508
1976	1,795	137	4,385	7,015	2,209	608	12,600	5,703	3,792	2,776	725	4,519	17,600	5,830	83,883
1977	1,702	154	5,198	5,355	2,672	613	19,800	5,809	3,995	2,216	677	4,859	18,100	6,008	90,541
1978	1,709	214	5,968	5,373	2,568	1,038	25,400	5,910	5,046	2,433	789	7,026	18,700	6,896	102,742
1979	1,645	130	7,039	5,445	2,595	1,526	28,900	5,981	5,726	3,036	868	4,026	19,200	6,643	107,287
1980	1,473	77	7,881	5,873	2,504	1,814	33,100	6,034	7,010	3,457	983	3,560	19,200	6,072	114,059
1981[1]	1,470	111	7,315	6,031	2,646	1,796	29,800	5,824	4,393	3,090	750	2,870	19,500	7,815	107,574
1982[2]			5,100	5,100	2,600	1,500	25,000	5,000	6,600	3,000		2,200	19,500	3,200	94,200
1983															

[1] Preliminary.   [2] Estimate.   *Source: Bureau of Mines*

T.706

TUNGSTEN

Salient Statistics of Tungsten in the U.S.   In Thousands of Pounds of Contained Tungsten

Year	Net Import Reliance as a % of Apparent Consumption	Production[1]	Shipments from Mines[1]	Total Consumption	Tool	Stainless & Heat Assisting	Alloy Steel[3]	Superalloys	Cutting & Wear Resistant Materials	Pdt's. Made from Metal Powder	Miscellaneous	Chemicals & Ceramic	Exports	Consumers & Dealers	Producers[1]
1970		9,625	9,312	16,700	1,475	N.A.	185	N.A.	7,028	3,306	—	N.A.	19,470	1,467	787
1971		6,900	6,827	11,622	1,420	187	149	209	5,082	2,044	—	381	2,006	2,657	863
1972		8,150	7,045	14,107	1,451	173	157	429	6,657	2,525	—	179	95	2,229	1,966
1973	66	7,575	7,059	15,386	2,015	211	353	606	10,000	2,660	—	444	90	1,446	225
1974	68	7,381	7,836	16,298	2,045	258	641	607	12,239	2,673	—	159	1,187	1,565	529
1975	55	5,588	5,490	14,012	892	158	139	379	8,355	1,490	—	310	1,316	1,958	531
1976	53	5,830	5,869	16,107	1,133	126	244	435	10,402	2,432	—	704	1,729	1,002	150
1977	52	6,008	6,022	17,100	1,124	175	262	527	10,880	2,482	—	275	1,283	826	124
1978	56	6,896	6,901	18,806	1,385	236	152	641	11,550	2,725	—	393	1,853	1,424	87
1979	58	6,643	6,646	21,589	1,554	305	173	596	12,969	3,348	—	506	1,929	1,538	84
1980	53	6,072	6,036	20,432	1,300	200	100	1,500	9,000	3,250	—	1,000	2,029	1,325	106
1981[2]	50	7,948	7,815	21,692	947	101	66	439	13,732	3,855	706	849	175	1,480	239
1982[4]	48		3,200	9,927	400	51	15	314	3,904	3,355	257	714	672	2,782	100
1983															

[1] Primary concentrates.   [2] Preliminary.   [3] Other than tool.   [4] Estimate.   *Source: Bureau of Mines*   T.707

U.S. Imports[1] of Tungsten Ores and Concentrates and Ferrotungsten   In Thousands of Pounds (Tungsten Content)

Year	Australia	Bolivia	Brazil	Canada	Rep. of Korea	Mexico	Portugal	Spain	Thailand	Peru	Total 1,000 Pounds	Value Mil. $	Austria	France	West Germany	Total 1,000 Lbs.
1970	—	—	—	1,234	—	12	—	—		38	1,284	3.2	0	0	0	0
1971	58	—	—	203	—	81	—	—		76	418	1.0	0	0	0	30
1972	392	780	124	1,634	370	90	9	—	883	814	5,739	12.1	25	10	88	814
1973	320	2,183	465	3,311	548	348	176	79	954	1,039	10,834	23.7	333	26	157	1,107
1974	87	2,065	266	1,633	364	336	1,635	95	1,527	1,375	11,096	40.7	235	112	—	808
1975	390	787	187	1,600	513	419	197	14	629	866	6,570	31.7	132	34	18	418
1976	172	580	2	1,343	202	417	420	21	588	863	5,301	28.3	260	246	53	844
1977	128	1,580	108	2,046	69	647	199	—	518	626	6,919	55.9	282	—	18	505
1978	211	2,012	2	3,030	230	850	—	—	840	180	9,138	67.7	241	110	63	575
1979	398	2,980	26	3,127	84	607	195	20	1,246	810	11,352	84.7	104	83	25	570
1980	235	2,794	63	2,914	19	515	576	94	1,046	526	11,372	87.1	68	10	17	446
1981[2]	304	2,511	444	2,005	156	616	1,028	49	706	652	11,752	91.2	92	17	26	325
1982[3]	92	1,418	561	2,794	925	545	622	—	295	252	11,844					
1983																

[1] Imports for consumption.   [2] Preliminary.   [3] Estimate.   *Source: Bureau of Mines*   T.708

Tungsten Prices   In U.S. Dollars

Year	U.S.[1] Markets	European Markets	Total (Mil. $)	Avg. per Unit of WO₃	Avg. per Lb. of Tungsten	Year	U.S.[1] Markets	European[1] Markets	Total (Mil. $)	Avg. per Unit of WO₃	Avg. per Lb. of Tungsten
1972			18.1	40.77	2.56	1978	128.19	130.43	56.7	130.29	8.22
1973			19.2	43.04	2.71	1979	127.31	125.95	55.8	133.13	8.40
1974			67.4	76.70	4.77	1980	131.07	120.87	50.6	132.00	8.38
1975			29.1	84.05	5.30	1981	130.25	129.16	62.2	126.29	7.96
1976	—	103.68	37.3	100.70	6.35	1982[3]	98.00	96.00			
1977	148.88	155.03	55.1	145.03	9.15	1983					

[1] Conc., Stu WO₃, Average (a short ton unit [stu] of tungsten trioxide [WO₃] contains 15,862 pounds of tungsten).   [2] Values apply to finished concentrate & are in some instances f.o.b. custom mill.   [3] Preliminary.   *Source: Bureau of Mines*   T.709

Turkeys

The 1982 U.S. turkey crop amounted to nearly 165 million head, a 3 percent decrease from the 1981 record level of 171 million. The number of heavy breed turkeys raised was down 1 percent from 1981 to 157 million head. Light breeds totaled nearly 8.16 million head, 30 percent below the previous year's level. Turkey breeder hens totaled 3.43 million on December 1, 1982, 2 percent below their number a year earlier. Heavy breed hens totaled 3.28 million head, also down 2 percent from the 1981 figure. Light breed hens totaled 150,000, a decline of 15 percent from 1981. The hatch of 12.5 million turkey poults in December 1982 was 4 percent higher than in 1981. The hatch of heavy breeds was 6 percent higher, and the hatch of light breeds was off 24 percent.

Turkey growers in the 20 major producing states had announced intentions of raising 165 million turkeys during 1983, up 3 percent from the intentions reported to the Crop Reporting Board during 1982. The 2 percent drop in the inventory of breeder hens indicates that egg supplies could be too tight to meet these intentions. The 18.0 million turkey eggs in incubators as of January 1, 1983 had increased 2 percent from the 17.6 million of a year earlier. Eggs set for heavy breed turkeys were 3 percent higher, but the light breed set was 10 percent below the January 1, 1982 figure. North Carolina held its place as the largest turkey-producing state during 1982, with 27 million head raised. Minnesota was second with 26 million, and California was third with 20 million.

The increased level of hatchery activity for first-half 1983 marketings was an outcome of good grain crops and resulting large feed supplies and of generally favorable prices during 1982. Turkey producers began making a profit in June 1982 based on estimated wholesale costs and returns, and this condition continued through November. However, the ongoing high rates of unemployment and relatively low prices for competing meats dampened consumer demand and resulted in an overall decline in turkey prices since the Thanksgiving season. The farm-retailer price spread averaged 20.4 cents per pound during 1982 compared with 23.0 in 1981. Despite a sharp drop in turkey prices in December, the price of young hen turkeys, 8 to 16 pounds, in New York, averaged 64 cents per pound throughout the fourth quarter of 1982, 9 cents above the year-earlier price. Unless turkey prices improve or the economy generally recovers during 1983, the percentage increase in the number of poults hatched is expected to decrease as producers enter the main hatching months for second-half output. It was expected that weak prices for turkeys during the first few months of 1983 could bring about a level of second-half output about equal to a year earlier.

The per capita consumption of turkey during the fourth quarter of 1982 was about 7 percent below the 1981 level. Despite the reduction in retail movement compared with the year before, lowered production caused the 1982 cold storage stocks of frozen turkeys to fall 32 million pounds under the 1981 level of 238 million. Year-end stocks around 200 million pounds are considered to be a normal maintainence level, and stocks at this level would have little effect on prices. Turkey prices were weak during December and January, indicating that stocks were high, and stocks were estimated to be adequate to meet first-half 1983 consumption. It was thought that a slowdown in hatchery activity could cause 1983 stocks to be increased earlier than normally in order to assure supplies for fourth-quarter consumption.

Overseas demand for whole and cut-up turkeys was generally weak during 1982. Turkey exports were 16 percent below 1981 levels and were expected to continue weak throughout the first half of 1983, depending upon the quickness of the observed recovery of the world economy. Turkey prices during the first half of 1983 were expected to average 52 to 57 cents per pound, 5 cents below prices of a year earlier. U.S. turkey exports during the fourth quarter of 1982 amounted to 13.7 million pounds, nearly 55 percent below exports during the same quarter in 1981. The Federal Republic of Germany purchased 17 percent of U.S. exports. Venezuela, whose imports of U.S. turkey increased during the period, purchased 15 percent, and Egypt purchased 9 percent.

Salient Statistics of Turkeys in the U.S.

Year	Breeder Hens on Farms—Dec. 1 Number In Millions	$ Value Per Head	Raised	(Liveweight) Produced Million Lbs.	Price ¢ Lb.	Gross Income Million $	Production	Commercial Storage Jan. 1	Exports & Shipments	Military	Civilian Total	Per Capita Lb.	Production Costs Liveweight Feed	Total	Wholesale Ready-to-Cook Total Costs	3-City Composite Price
1970	3.4	5.82	116.1	2,198	22.6	498	1,729	192	43	49	1,610	8.0				
1971	3.4	6.18	119.7	2,256	22.1	500	1,772	219	27	41	1,700	8.3				
1972	3.3	6.46	128.7	2,424	22.2	537	1,909	223	42	42	1,840	8.9	13.5	20.5	34.1	35.8
1973	3.6	9.47	132.2	2,452	38.2	936	1,933	208	54	31	1,775	8.5	25.6	33.1	50.6	64.2
1974	2.9	9.81	131.9	2,437	28.0	683	1,921	281	43	14	1,870	8.9	22.5	30.7	48.8	45.6
1975	3.1	10.81	124.2	2,277	34.8	793	1,803	275	53	19	1,811	8.6	22.1	30.7	49.4	55.1
1976	3.1	11.12	140.0	2,605	31.7	825	2,059	195	71	18	1,961	9.2	22.4	31.4	50.9	51.0
1977	3.0	11.32	136.4	2,562	35.5	910	2,023	203	56	11	1,992	9.3	22.6	31.6	51.4	56.2
1978	3.4	12.53	138.9	2,653	43.6	1,157	2,098	168	57	15	2,019	9.2	22.1	31.7	51.7	68.8
1979	3.7	13.58	156.5	2,958	41.4	1,226	2,343	175	57	19	2,204	9.9	25.3	35.8	58.2	67.0
1980	3.7	14.11	164.9	3,069	41.3	1,268	2,425	240	81	16	2,370	10.5	26.1	37.1	61.0	66.0
1981[1]	3.5	15.35	159.9	3,263	38.4	1,247	2,574	198	68	15	2,450	10.7	30.2	41.2	66.1	64.0
1982[2]	3.4	14.60	164.7	3,176	37.2	1,254	2,518	238	65	12	2,500	10.9	24.5	36.3	60.1	63.6

[1] Preliminary. [2] Estimate. *Source: Economic Research Service, U.S.D.A.* T.710

TURKEYS

Turkey Per Capita Consumption in the U.S. by Quarters In Pounds

Year	First	Second	Third	Fourth	Total	Year	First	Second	Third	Fourth	Total
1971	1.0	1.2	2.1	4.1	8.4	1977	1.3	1.5	2.3	4.2	9.3
1972	1.1	1.3	2.2	4.4	9.0	1978	1.3	1.7	2.2	4.0	9.2
1973	1.2	1.3	2.1	3.9	8.5	1979	1.5	1.9	2.3	4.2	9.9
1974	1.2	1.6	2.0	4.1	8.9	1980	1.8	2.0	2.7	4.0	10.5
1975	1.1	1.4	2.0	4.1	8.6	1981	1.6	1.9	2.5	4.6	10.7
1976	1.2	1.5	2.1	4.4	9.2	1982[1]	1.8	2.1			

[1] Preliminary. Source: *Economic Research Service, U.S.D.A.* T.711

Certified Federally Inspected Turkey Slaughter in the U.S. In Millions of Lbs.

Year	Jan.	Feb.	Mar.	Apr.	May	June	July	Aug.	Sept.	Oct.	Nov.	Dec.	Total
1970	40.5	22.2	22.1	27.6	44.9	109.5	172.1	212.0	244.6	276.9	244.9	149.2	1,567
1971	49.9	31.5	42.7	47.7	63.1	127.7	177.1	221.2	235.8	256.0	242.9	146.1	1,642
1972	57.6	45.2	45.8	44.3	74.6	149.0	186.9	254.6	241.7	282.7	261.3	152.7	1,797
1973	69.7	41.6	45.3	55.8	84.2	142.9	185.0	234.1	212.3	272.6	269.9	174.6	1,788
1974	97.3	59.8	58.9	80.1	113.2	159.7	213.1	237.2	220.2	261.1	215.2	119.9	1,836
1975	64.9	47.1	54.4	68.7	81.9	138.4	193.2	203.3	229.0	257.5	220.2	157.5	1,716
1976	76.3	61.7	68.6	79.9	106.5	182.2	213.9	243.8	252.8	256.6	261.5	146.4	1,950
1977	70.5	58.7	80.3	78.9	110.0	176.5	189.6	244.4	238.2	250.3	246.8	148.2	1,892
1978	81.8	59.7	86.3	80.8	129.3	189.5	199.9	248.8	230.9	271.2	248.9	156.3	1,983
1979	99.3	77.2	95.0	112.3	157.3	195.9	219.2	267.7	233.0	297.5	261.9	165.5	2,182
1980		378.6			528.3			711.6			713.9		2,232
1981		398.1			553.2			785.2			772.6		2,509
1982		410.4			527.9			761.5			758.1		2,458

Source: *Economic Research Service, U.S.D.A.* T.714

Storage Stocks of Turkeys (Frozen) in the United States In Millions of Pounds

Year	Jan. 1	Feb. 1	Mar. 1	Apr. 1	May 1	June 1	July 1	Aug. 1	Sept. 1	Oct. 1	Nov. 1	Dec. 1
1971	218.9	207.1	177.3	146.0	119.4	111.5	140.3	202.8	307.6	389.0	475.2	308.7
1972	223.1	208.0	178.5	144.5	121.3	111.1	143.4	213.2	314.0	408.5	472.9	297.3
1973	208.1	188.4	152.6	115.4	91.3	88.1	137.1	199.4	261.2	350.7	450.5	321.1
1974	281.0	274.0	250.5	235.9	225.0	227.4	265.8	335.8	431.8	528.7	554.6	372.0
1975	275.0	267.1	239.9	207.3	180.2	162.7	193.2	248.6	328.6	409.8	472.4	286.2
1976	195.2	186.8	160.7	140.7	114.5	120.8	177.3	261.8	370.3	459.7	512.3	298.8
1977	203.4	190.3	167.8	142.3	130.3	138.2	201.4	253.6	329.9	409.3	444.5	269.4
1978	167.9	168.2	136.6	113.0	101.1	103.9	152.8	213.6	301.2	373.3	425.4	236.2
1979	175.1	170.7	154.7	135.7	128.0	153.1	200.9	272.5	382.5	432.3	445.5	281.2
1980	240.0	246.8	225.0	208.9	206.6	233.8	286.6	325.8	384.0	398.8	420.2	257.6
1981[1]	198.0	208.3	207.9	220.7	228.7	255.8	327.3	400.8	466.0	532.1	)28.1	305.1
1982[1]	238.4	236.9	236.4	232.8	—	—	292.0	—	—	435.8	—	—
1983[1]	203.9	193.8	187.7	182.8								

[1] Preliminary. Source: *Crop Reporting Board, U.S.D.A.* T.712

Wholesale Price of Turkeys[3] (Hens; 8–16 lbs.) N.Y. In Cents per Pound

Year	Jan.	Feb.	Mar.	Apr.	May	June	July	Aug.	Sept.	Oct.	Nov.	Dec.	Avg.	Yearly Avg. Hens (12–14 lbs.)	Farm Price[2]
1971	43.5	43.3	41.7	32.7	40.4	40.5	41.4	42.5	42.5	41.2	42.3	43.8	41.4	39.6	21.9
1972	43.8	43.6	34.1	43.4	42.6	42.1	40.3	39.1	38.5	38.9	41.1	42.1	40.8	38.5	22.1
1973	45.1	48.6	56.0	57.7	60.6	67.9	69.4	81.1	86.0	84.2	80.2	71.2	67.3	62.2	34.8
1974	60.7	54.2	51.9	45.3	48.4	52.5	52.8	55.8	55.7	54.4	56.3	58.8	53.9	51.7	28.8
1975	59.0	56.7	55.9	52.0	52.6	56.5	59.5	61.8	64.3	66.8	69.9	70.0	60.3	57.0	34.8
1976	69.0	69.0	69.9	70.0	70.6	71.0	71.0	71.0	71.0	71.0	72.8	73.0	70.8	52.4	31.7
1977	72.5	70.2	68.8	68.8	69.0	70.1	72.1	73.2	73.6	74.6	75.5	78.2	72.2	57.3	35.5
1978	78.5	78.5	78.9	79.0	82.2	86.1	86.8	87.0	87.0	89.1	91.6	90.7	84.6	70.3	43.6
1979	91.0	90.8	90.0	89.5	90.9	91.0	91.0	91.5	91.4	93.1	94.5	92.9	91.5	72.1	41.9
1980[1]	62.3	57.8	56.8	54.1	53.3	55.5	63.3	67.2	74.5	77.0	75.0	67.0	63.6	67.8	40.0
1981	59.4	60.7	63.8	61.2	63.5	66.2	66.8	61.8	59.5	56.4	57.3	51.7	60.7	64.7	38.4
1982	53.6	55.8	56.0	55.8	58.8	61.8	64.1	64.1	68.0	69.6	67.2	54.2	60.8		37.2

[1] Prior to 1980 prices are for frozen eviscerated tom turkeys (N.Y.C.); heaviest weights. [2] Live turkeys. [3] Ready-to-cook. Source: *Economic Research Service, U.S.D.A.* T.713

Turpentine and Rosin

U.S. Production of Gum Turpentine and Miscellaneous Naval Stores   In Barrels of 50 Gallons

Crop Year— April 1 to March 31	Exports of Pine Oil	Gum Turpentine Florida	Gum Turpentine Georgia	Gum Turpentine Other States	Gum Turpentine Total	Stocks of Pine Oil (Mar. 31)	Pine Oil (All Sources[3])	Other Steam Distilled Terpenes	Stocks of Other Steam Distil. Terp. (Mar. 31)
1976-7[1]	69,310				17,420	32,830	190,060	45,220	21,860
1977-8[1]	71,250				14,530	26,730	189,780	46,430	19,580
1978-9[1]	103,370				9,740	11,840	192,680	52,880	7,500
1979-0[2]	193,340				6,740	17,460	192,700	59,070	10,040
1980-1[2]	N.A.				6,260	——No Longer Available——			

[1] Preliminary. [2] Forecast. [3] Includes production from imported pine wood extract. Source: Crop Reporting Board, U.S.D.A.   T.715

Supply and Distribution of Turpentine in the United States   In Thousands of Barrels (50 Gallon Barrels)

Crop Year Beginning April 1	April 1 Carryover Gum	April 1 Carryover Wood	April 1 Carryover Total	Production Gum	Production Wood	Production Total	Imports For Consumption	Available Supply Gum	Available Supply Wood	Available Supply Total	Exports	App. Consumption Gum	App. Consumption Wood	App. Consumption Total
1976-7	9.6	104.0	113.6	17.4	464.8	482.2	16.3	42.7	569.4	612.1	20.3	33.3	430.8	464.1
1977-8	7.4	120.4	127.8	14.5	462.6	477.1	7.9	29.4	583.5	612.9	19.4	23.7	478.8	502.6
1978-9	4.8	86.1	90.9	9.7	498.0	507.7	7.1	21.0	584.7	605.7	15.3	17.2	498.6	515.8
1979-0[1]	3.3	71.3	74.6	6.7	521.1	527.8	7.9	17.8	592.5	610.3	13.5	14.0	509.5	523.5
1980-1[2]	3.2	70.1	73.3				12.7				23.1			
1981-2	——————————————— No Longer Available ———————————————													

[1] Preliminary. [2] Estimate. Source: Crop Reporting Board, U.S.D.A.   T.716

United States Industrial Consumption of Rosin and Turpentine, by Industries

Beginning April 1	Rosin[1] (Drums of 520 Lbs. Net[2]) Chemicals & Rubber	Ester Gum & Synthetic Resins	Paint, Varnish & Lacquer	Paper & Paper Size	Other Industries	Total	Turpentine (Barrels of 50 Gallons) Chemicals & Rubber	Paint, Varnish & Lacquer	Other Industries	Total
1976-7	445,870	283,060	22,260	370,370	81,220	1,202,70	476,160	740	3,690	480,590
1977-8	376,040	241,940	22,260	357,560	75,750	1,073,550	464,150	1,020	8,110	473,280
1978-9	362,100	233,130	19,440	463,610	89,540	1,167,820	496,840	650	7,780	505,270
1979-0[3]	353,650	268,020	21,660	352,510	68,690	1,064,530	497,720	410	6,180	504,310
1980-1	——————————————— No Longer Available ———————————————									

[1] Includes B-wood resin. [2] Gum rosin in drums of 517 lbs. [3] Preliminary. Source: Crop Reporting Board, U.S.D.A.   T.717

Supply and Distribution of Rosin in the United States   In Thousands of Drums (520-lb. Net Weight Drums)

Crop Year Beginning April 1	April 1 Carryover Gum	April 1 Carryover Wood	April 1 Carryover Total	Production Gum	Production Wood	Production Total	Imports For Consumption	Available Supply Gum	Available Supply Wood	Available Supply Total	Exports	Apparent Consumption Gum	Apparent Consumption Wood	Apparent Consumption Total
1976-7	60	173	232	61	1,296	1,357	25	135	1,480	1,615	280	85	1,069	1,154
1977-8	36	145	181	51	1,250	1,301	31	114	1,399	1,513	215	79	987	1,066
1978-9	21	211	232	35	1,304	1,339	55	97	1,528	1,626	328	59	1,023	1,032
1979-0[1]	20	195	215	24	1,339	1,363	52	93	1,538	1,631	396	56	1,041	1,097
1980-1[2]	19	119	138				39				383			
1981-2	——————————————— No Longer Available ———————————————													

[1] Preliminary. [2] Estimate. Source: Crop Reporting Board, U.S.D.A.   T.718

U.S. Market Prices & Value of Gum Naval Stores   In Dollars

Crop Yr. Beg. April	Avg. Price Received By Producers[1]	Market Price Turpentine, Per Gallon	Market Price Rosin, Per 100 Lbs.	Market Value of Production Turpentine —Thousand Dollars—	Market Value of Production Rosin —Thousand Dollars—	Crop Yr. Beg. April	Avg. Price Received by Producers[1]	Market Price Turpentine, Per Gallon	Market Price Rosin, Per 100 Lbs.	Market Value of Production Turpentine —Thousand Dollars—	Market Value of Production Rosin —Thousand Dollars—
1969-0	36.57	1.138	11.80	1,991	7,244	1975-6	59.59	1.585	25.15	1,640	9,338
1970-1	47.37	1.200	15.03	1,550	6,818	1976-7	59.46	1.427	24.46	1,278	7,971
1971-2	51.14	1.200	16.93	1,702	6,210	1977-8	65.46	1.425	25.35	1,035	6,702
1972-3	55.17	1.046	18.89	1,389	8,694	1978-9	67.82	1.610	27.54	784	4,925
1973-4	60.97	.806	22.72	863	8,737	1979-0	82.19	2.036	35.05	686	4,385
1974-5	84.36	1.389	35.92	1,084	10,106	1980-1	——— No Longer Available ———				

[1] Per standard barrel for commercial crude gum delivered at central stills. Source: Economic Research Service, U.S.D.A.   T.719

Uranium

Trade analysts estimated that the worldwide uranium production capacity, given current rates of consumption and steady economic growth, will be sufficient to satisfy anticipated world demand throughout the remainder of this century. Non-Communist countries reportedly produce close to 110 million pounds of uranium per year and consume about 60 million pounds. Australia owns nearly a fifth of the world's low-cost, high-grade uranium reserves. The world's largest uranium deposit, amounting to nearly 172,000 tons of uranium oxide, is located in Australia's Northern Territory. One ton of some Australian ores will reportedly yield 47 pounds of uranium oxide while most deposits are considered good if they yield 10 pounds to the ton.

Uranium prices had been steadily dropping from mid-1978 peaks because of stepped-up production and the cancellation of construction plans for some new nuclear power plants. U.S. demand for uranium was weak during 1982, and many uranium mines were shut down as a result. Late in the year, domestic uranium prices rose by 50 cents a pound. Much of the increased demand for uranium was the outcome of falling interest rates and prices, and some analysts observed buying in anticipation of a proposed embargo that would have limited U.S. imports of uranium. Almost all of the increased demand was reportedly from utilities supplementing inventories that were not scheduled for utilization until the latter 1980s. This behavior indicated that domestic uranium consumers expect uranium prices to continue to rise throughout the decade. U.S. imports of uranium, estimated to be about 10 percent less than domestic needs figured at current rates of consumption, are nevertheless expected to increase sharply in coming years.

Near the end of 1982, U.S. nuclear power plants had generated a total of 23.2 billion net kilowatt-hours (kWh) of electricity, equal to a daily output of 774.5 thousand net kWh. This amounted to nearly a 2 percent increase over nuclear-generated electrical output in the comparable period a year earlier. Nuclear power supplied almost 13.4 percent of the electricity generated by domestic utilities—the highest proportion of electricity demand met by nuclear energy to date.

U.S. manufacturers reportedly received no new orders for nuclear steam supply systems during 1982, and no domestic electric companies were expected to place new equipment orders until the late 1980's. Mexico, Taiwan, and Korea had been considered likely prospects for new equipment orders in 1982, but trade analysts subsequently revised their expectations of these new orders to 1983 at the earliest. Nuclear steam supply system completions in 1983 were expected to reach a total capacity of approximately 144 million pounds of steam per hour, 12 percent below the 1982 capacity level. These completions are expected to reach a higher number than usual as the nuclear industry complies more and more closely with operational changes that the federal government has mandated since the Three Mile Island accident in 1979.

Public trading in the spot market for tri-uranium oct-oxide, or "yellowcake," was initiated in mid-October 1982.

Free-World Production of Uranium Oxide (U$_3$O$_8$) Concentrate — In Thousands of Short Tons

Year	Argentina	Australia	Canada	Spain	Namibia	Gabon	France	Portugal	Niger	Malagasy Rep.	Sweden	South Africa	United States	World Total
1969	.1	.3	3.9	.1		.5	1.8	.1	—	—	.1	4.0	12.3	23.1
1970	.1	.3	4.1	.1		.4	1.9	.1	.1	—	.1	4.1	12.9	24.2
1971	.1	—	4.1	.1		.6	1.9	.1	.5	—	.1	4.2	12.3	23.9
1972	.1	—	4.9	.2		.6	1.9	.1	1.0	—	.1	4.0	12.9	25.6
1973	.1	—	4.8	.1		.8	2.0	.1	1.2	—	.1	3.4	13.2	25.5
1974	[1]	—	4.8	.1		1.0	2.1	.1	1.5		.1	3.5	11.5	24.6
1975	[1]	—	6.1	.1		1.2	2.2	.1	1.8		.1	3.2	11.6	26.7
1976	[1]	.5	6.7	.2	.8	1.2	2.3	.1	1.9		.1	3.6	12.75	30.1
1977		1.0	7.0	.2	1.5	1.2	2.4		2.1			4.0	14.94	33.8
1978													18.49	43.0
1979													18.73	50.0
1980													21.85	
1981[2]													19.24	
1982														

[1] Less than 50 tons. [2] Preliminary. Source: Bureau of Mines, Dept. of Energy T.720

U.S. Salient Statistics of Uranium (Depleted) — Nonenergy Data in Short Tons

Year	Production	Imports[3]	Exports	Apparent Consumption (Nonenergy)	Price, Derby Metal $ Per Lb.
1976	17,591	188	341	1,700	2.00
1977	18,822	453	273	2,000	2.50
1978	15,763	373	590	2,200	2.50
1979[2]	15,116	852	1,531	2,500	3.25
1980[1]	18,000	1,000	7,000	3,500	4.50
1981					

[1] Estimate. [2] Preliminary. [3] For consumption. Source: U.S. Bureau of Mines, Dept. of Energy T.721

Vanadium

World resources of vanadium were estimated to have exceeded 140 billion pounds in 1982. Vanadium is found in deposits of titaniferous magnetite, phosphate rock, and uraniferous sandstones and siltstones where it makes up less than 2 percent of the host rock. Significant amounts of vanadium are present in bauxite and carboniferous materials including oil, coal, oil shale, and tar sands. Because vanadium is generally recovered as a byproduct or coproduct, proven world resources are only a part of potential available supplies.

The total world mine production of vanadium during 1982 was estimated by the U.S. Bureau of Mines at 72.7 million pounds, nearly 7 percent below the 1981 figure of 77.9 million. The Republic of South Africa and the Soviet Union produced 34 percent and 30 percent of the world total vanadium output, respectively. Between 1978 and 1981, sales from the Republic of South Africa accounted for 58 percent of U.S. imports of vanadium. The U.S. produced about 8 percent less vanadium in 1982 compared with the previous year according to preliminary Bureau of Mines data. Although U.S. domestic resources were estimated to be adequate to supply then-current needs, a substantial part of the U.S. demand for vanadium was met by foreign material because of price advantages favoring imports.

Figured from a 1981 base, the U.S. demand for vanadium was expected to increase at an annual rate of 3 percent through 1990. The U.S. consumption of vanadium had dropped sharply during 1982 because of reduced steel production. The U.S. Bureau of Mines estimated that the 1983 domestic mine production of vanadium would be 11 million pounds on a recoverable basis and that U.S. apparent consumption would amount to 16 million pounds.

The chief domestic use of vanadium during 1982 was as an alloying agent for iron and steel. It was important in the production of titanium alloys, and as a catalyst for the production of sulphuric acid. Steels containing various combinations of other alloying metals can be substituted for steel containing vanadium. Columbium, molybdenum, manganese, titanium, and tungsten are all to some degree interchangeable with vanadium, and platinum may substitute for vanadium compounds as a catalyst in some chemical processes.

Throughout 1982 the Bureau of Mines investigated roasting techniques for recovering vanadium from phosphate beneficiation tailings. The Bureau also continued to research the extraction of vanadium from low-grade uranium ores found on the Colorado Plateau and in Wyoming. The U.S. Environmental Agency published regulations in 1982 that specifically dealt with the mining of vanadium ores and uranium-radium-vanadium ores, by limiting the concentration of uranium in mine drainage.

U.S. consumer stocks of vanadium at the end of 1982 were estimated to be only 50 percent of holdings a year earlier.

World Production of Vanadium from Ores and Concentrates In Short Tons (of Contained Vanadium)

Year	USSR	Chile	China	Finland	Australia	Norway	South West Africa[1]	South Africa	United States[1]	Other[4]	World Total
1973	4,246	1,060		1,388	—	820	715	9,047	4,377		21,653
1974	3,230	640		1,635	—	500	903	8,984	4,870		20,762
1975	8,800	660		1,405	—	510	619	11,734	4,743		28,471
1976	8,800	1,199	N.A.	1,598	—	580	771	10,885	7,376		31,209
1977	9,500	950	N.A.	2,055	—	590	826	12,388	6,504	912	33,725
1978	10,000	760	2,200	3,092	—	510	485	12,400	4,272	1,697	35,416
1979	10,000	510	4,000	3,051	—	630	—	13,600	5,520	2,337	39,648
1980	10,500	300	5,000	3,135	—	540	—	14,000	4,806	2,295	40,576
1981[2]	10,500	140	5,000	3,432	95	540	—	14,100	5,126	2,700	41,633
1982[3]	11,000		5,000	3,050				12,500	4,700		36,350

[1] Recoverable vanadium. [2] Preliminary. [3] Estimate. [4] Production from petroleum residues, ashes, & spent catalysts. Mainly in Japan & the United States. Source: Bureau of Mines T.722

Salient Statistics of Vanadium in the United States In Short Tons of Contained Vanadium

Year	Vanadium in Ores & Concentrates — Mine Production	Recoverable Vanadium	Prod. of Vanad. Pentoxide (V$_2$O$_5$)	Consumer Stocks Dec. 31	Tool Steel	Cast Irons	High Strength Low All.	Nonferrous Alloys	Chemicals	Carbon	Full Alloy	Total	$ Per Lb. Van. Pentoxide[3]	General Imports[5]	Exports Ore & Concentrates[4]	Ferro-Vanadium (Gross Weight)
1973	4,117	4,377	8,683	1,291	997	56	2,252	527	163	687	1,544	6,393	1.50	2,600	232	1,416
1974	5,240	4,870	9,583	1,984	936	52	2,398	722	255	900	1,744	7,200	2.12	2,485	203	1,335
1975	5,213	4,743	8,674	1,141	413	59	2,004	425	239	931	1,307	5,501	2.76	2,895	215	1,018
1976	8,076	7,376	11,063	1,080	565	61	1,636	313	212	516	1,311	4,720	2.90	2,998	99	1,210
1977	7,565	6,504	9,297	845	549	35	1,800	323	110	688	1,419	5,261	2.90	2,812	192	658
1978	4,446	4,272	9,290	974	858	59	2,440	467	123	1,051	1,506	6,630	3.17	2,234	1,721	1,309
1979	5,841	5,520	10,279	976	852	62	2,410	563	81	1,096	1,522	6,719	3.39	2,442	1,047	880
1980	5,832	4,806	9,829	879	653	54	1,986	728	59	1,114	1,420	6,139	3.54	1,786	960	803
1981[1]	5,852	5,126	11,367	683	584	42	2,123	852	56	1,278	1,832	6,863	3.52	2,435	463	435
1982[6]		4,700		608	490	39	2,256	965	36	1,323	1,557	6,795	3.50	1,300	2,000	653

[1] Preliminary. [2] Represent about 90% of the total consumption. [3] Dealer export. [4] Also includes fused vanadium oxide. [5] Ores, slags, residues. [6] Estimate. Source: Bureau of Mines T.723

Wheat and Flour

World wheat production in the 1982/83 season was estimated by the USDA at a record-large 473 million tonnes, 5 percent above the previous record output of 448 million tonnes in 1981/82. Although the Southern Hemisphere harvest was slightly smaller than in the preceding season, output in the Northern Hemisphere was record-large. All major wheat exporting nations, except Australia, whose crop was hit by drought, harvested their largest crops ever, and importing nations produced about 7 percent more than in the preceding season.

World utilization of wheat in 1982/83 was projected by the USDA to increase to around 458 million tonnes from nearly 440 million in the previous season. Ending stocks were projected to increase to about 98 million tonnes from 83 million a year earlier. World stocks of wheat were projected to amount to 21.6 percent of utilization compared to 19.1 percent the previous year—the highest ratio of stocks to use since 23.8 percent in 1978/79. (Stocks data are based on an aggregate of differing local marketing years and should not be construed as representing world stock levels at a fixed point in time.)

Global wheat trade during 1982/83 (July/June basis) was expected to be slightly below the record 101.9 million tonnes estimated for the 1981/82 season. Export patterns were changing, with Canada, the European Community (EC), and Argentina expanding their share of the market to account for an estimated 45 percent of world exports compared with less than 38 percent in the previous season. The U.S. share of the world export market was expected to decline almost 8 percentage points from the record 49 percent in 1981/82—mainly because of reduced sales to the USSR and China. Recent political and economic tensions between the United States and those countries apparently prompted them to take advantage of record supplies from other exporters.

In the United States, the combined production of winter, other spring and durum wheat in 1982 was estimated at a record-high 2,810 million bushels, up fractionally from the previous record high set in 1981. The 1982/83 season's supply of all wheat totaled 3,977 million bushels, exceeding the record-large 3,791 million in the previous season. Total domestic use of wheat was estimated at 870 million bushels versus 854 million in the preceding season. Exports were projected at 1,525 million bushels, off 14 percent from the 1,773 million bushels exported in 1981/82. Ending stocks on May 31, 1983 were expected to total 1,549 million bushels versus 1,164 million a year earlier.

U.S. wheat stocks, amounting to 1,860 million bushels in all positions on April 1, 1983, were record-high for the date. However, 68 percent of the April 1 stocks were under government control versus 47 percent a year earlier. In addition, the USDA projected that of the estimated 1,549 million bushel carryover on May 31, 1983, 1,050 million would be in the farmer-owned reserve (FOR) and 180 million in the CCC inventory. Thus, "free" stocks would amount to only 319 million bushels versus 410 million bushels a year earlier.

U.S. wheat export activity in the first half of the 1982/83 season was adversely affected by the world economic recession, the strength of the U.S. dollar, foreign exchange constraints in some importing countries, and increased production by most major wheat exporters. In a continuing effort to counter slow export demand, the "blended credit" export program was expanded. This program combines the amount of money authorized for interest-free direct credit with government-guaranteed private credit to produce interest rates below commercial levels. Also, the USDA announced that CCC stocks of wheat would be used to enable U.S. flour exporters to sell 1 million tonnes (50 million bushels grain equivalent) of U.S. flour to Egypt at prices competitive with other commercial flour sold to that country.

U.S. farm prices of wheat for the first 7 months of the 1982/83 marketing year averaged around $3.40 per bushel, 15 cents below the national average loan rate. Although prices subsequently improved somewhat, it was considered possible that 1982/83 would be the first season since 1968/69 with a season price below the loan value. Important factors contributing to low wheat prices were the reduced exports of Hard Red Winter (HRW) wheat to the USSR, perennially the largest buyer of HRW wheat, and the sharp reduction in shipments of Soft Red Winter (SRW) wheat to China, the largest buyer of SRW wheat.

The 1983-crop acreage reduction and paid land diversion programs were announced in advance of planting time for winter wheat producers. However, the January-announced payment-in-kind (PIK) program was announced too late to affect plantings to this class of wheat, and those producers had to plow-down, graze, or hay part of their growing crop in order to participate in the PIK program.

U.S. Government Support Program

The target price for 1983-crop wheat was set at $4.30 per bushel. The 1983-crop regular loan rate was established at $3.65 per bushel versus $3.55 for the 1982 crop. Entry of wheat in the farmer-owned reserve is permitted only after the 9-month regular loan period, and the reserve loan rate is the same as the regular loan—$3.65 per bushel. Producers entering wheat in the reserve program receive 26½ cents per bushel first year storage payment in advance. Producers who complied with the 1982 acreage reduction program received 50 cents per bushel deficiency payment.

Provisions of the 1983 acreage reduction program were expanded to encourage greater producer participation than in 1982 when 42 percent of the 90.7 million wheat acreage base was in compliance. The program is a combination 15 percent acreage reduction plus a 5 percent paid land diversion, totaling a 20 percent reduction of acreage for harvest from the farm's established acreage base. Also, participating farmers could request in advance 50 percent of the full diversion payment of $2.70 per bushel and 50 percent of the projected deficiency payment for the 1983 marketing year. The advance deficiency pay-

WHEAT AND FLOUR

ment would equal 32.5 cents per bushel.

Under the payment-in-kind (PIK) program, producers who reduced acreage beyond that in the 15 percent acreage reduction and 5 percent paid land diversion program were to receive an amount of wheat representing a percentage (95 percent) of their base program yield per acre. To provide producers with marketing flexibility, the CCC would pay storage at an annual rate of 26.5 cents per bushel from when the PIK grain is received by the participating farmer until disposition, but not for more than 5 months.

Futures Markets

Wheat futures in the U.S. are traded on the Chicago Board of Trade, the Kansas City Board of Trade, the Minneapolis Grain Exchange, and the Mid-America Commodity Exchange in Chicago.

World Production of Wheat   In Thousands of Metric Tons

Crop Year	Argentina	Australia	Canada	China	France	W. Germany	India	Italy	Pakistan	Spain	Turkey	Un. Kingdom	USSR	United States	World Total[1]
1972-3	6,800	6,510	14,514	26,000	18,123	6,410	26,410	9,423	6,889	4,562	9,500	4,761	85,993	42,046	331,056
1973-4	6,560	12,094	16,459	28,000	17,792	7,134	24,735	8,900	7,800	3,915	8,000	5,003	109,784	46,407	371,600
1974-5	5,970	11,357	13,295	37,000	19,142	7,761	22,072	9,697	7,800	4,534	8,300	6,130	83,849	48,797	356,410
1975-6	8,570	12,024	17,078	40,000	15,013	7,014	24,104	9,610	7,673	4,302	11,500	4,488	66,224	58,078	350,057
1976-7	11,000	11,700	23,587	50,500	16,150	6,702	28,846	9,528	8,691	4,436	13,000	4,740	96,882	58,500	421,200
1977-8	5,700	9,400	19,900	41,000	17,046	7,126	29,032	6,650	9,100	3,988	13,500	5,267	92,200	55,700	384,200
1978-9	8,100	18,100	21,100	53,800	21,056	8,118	31,700	9,191	8,400	4,795	13,300	6,615	120,800	48,300	446,800
1979-0	8,100	16,200	17,200	62,700	19,544	8,061	35,500	8,980	9,900	4,082	13,000	7,169	90,200	58,080	423,300
1980-1	7,800	10,900	19,200	55,200	23,683	8,156	31,800	9,150	10,900	5,901	13,000	8,470	98,200	64,618	441,100
1981-2[2]	8,100	16,300	24,800	59,600	22,857	8,314	36,300	8,827	11,500	3,356	13,200	8,409	80,000	76,169	448,200
1982-3[1]	14,000	8,700	27,600	63,000			37,800		11,200		13,800		86,000	76,441	472,900

[1] Estimated. [2] Preliminary. *Source: Foreign Agricultural Service, U.S.D.A.*   T.724

Wheat Supply and Distribution in Canada, Australia and Argentina   In Millions of Metric Tons

	Canada (Yr. Beg. Aug. 1)					Australia (Yr. Beg. Dec. 1)					Argentina (Yr. Beg. Dec. 1)				
	Supply			Disappearance		Supply			Disappearance		Supply			Disappearance	
Crop Year	Stocks Aug. 1	New Crop	Total Supply	Domestic	Exports[1]	Stocks Dec. 1	New Crop	Total Supply	Domestic	Exports[1]	Stocks Dec. 1	New Crop	Total Supply	Domestic	Exports[1]
1973-4	9.9	16.2	26.1	4.6	11.4	.6	12.0	12.6	3.5	7.0	.3	6.6	6.9	4.2	1.6
1974-5	10.1	13.3	23.4	4.6	1.07	2.0	11.4	13.4	3.1	8.6	1.0	6.0	7.0	4.5	1.8
1975-6	8.0	17.1	25.1	4.6	12.3	1.7	12.0	13.7	2.3	8.7	.7	8.6	9.3	5.4	3.2
1976-7	8.2	23.6	31.8	5.0	13.4	2.7	11.7	14.4	2.8	9.5	.7	11.0	11.7	4.2	5.9
1977-8	13.3	19.9	33.2	5.1	16.0	2.1	9.4	11.5	2.2	8.4	1.6	5.7	7.3	4.3	1.8
1978-9	12.1	21.1	33.2	5.3	13.5	.8	18.1	18.9	2.6	6.7	1.2	8.1	9.3	4.1	3.3
1979-0	14.9	17.2	32.1	5.5	15.0	4.6	16.2	20.8	3.3	14.9	1.1	8.1	9.2	4.0	4.8
1980-1	10.7	19.2	29.9	5.0	17.0	4.4	10.9	15.3	3.6	10.6	.4	7.8	8.2	3.9	3.9
1981-2[2]	8.6	24.8	33.4	5.2	17.8	2.1	16.3	18.4	3.6	11.0	.4	8.1	8.5	4.1	4.3
1982-3[3]	9.7	27.6	37.3	5.2	20.5	3.0	8.5	11.5	3.6	7.5	.7	14.0	14.8	4.2	8.0
1983-4[3]	11.7					.9					.5				

[1] Including flour. [2] Preliminary. [3] Forecast. *Source: Foreign Agricultural Service, U.S.D.A.*   T.725

Seeded Acreage, Yield and Production of All Wheat in the United States

	Seeded Acreage—1,000,000 Acres					Yield Per Harvested Acre—In Bushels					Production—1,000,000 Bushels				
Year	Winter	All Spring	Not Durum	Durum	All	Winter	All Spring	Not Durum	Durum	All	Winter	All Spring	Not Durum	Durum	All
1973	43.5	15.8	12.8	3.0	59.3	33.0	28.1	28.3	27.2	31.6	1,278.2	432.6	354.1	78.5	1,710.8
1974	52.0	19.0	14.8	4.2	71.0	29.4	21.9	22.4	19.8	27.3	1,375.5	406.4	325.1	81.2	1,781.9
1975	56.0	18.9	14.1	4.8	74.8	32.0	26.7	26.8	26.4	30.6	1,642.9	484.1	360.7	123.4	2,126.9
1976	57.8	22.5	17.8	4.7	80.4	31.5	27.3	26.8	29.4	30.3	1,564.1	584.6	449.7	134.9	2,148.8
1977	56.5	18.8	15.8	3.2	75.4	31.6	28.0	28.4	26.4	30.7	1,540.4	505.1	425.1	80.0	2,045.5
1978	47.5	18.4	14.3	4.1	66.0	31.8	29.7	30.0	33.1	31.4	1,222.4	553.1	419.8	133.3	1,775.5
1979	51.8	19.6	15.6	4.0	71.4	36.9		28.2	27.1	34.2	1,601.2	532.9	426.2	106.7	2,134.1
1980	57.6	23.0	17.5	5.5	80.6	36.8		25.3	22.4	33.4	1,895.4	478.9	370.5	108.4	2,374.3
1981	66.0	23.0	17.1	5.9	88.9	35.9		30.7	32.3	34.5	2,103.5	695.2	509.3	185.9	2,798.7
1982[1]	66.4	20.9	16.6	4.4	87.3	36.1		34.0	35.0	35.6	2,108.2	700.5	553.0	147.5	2,808.7
1983[2]	63.0														

[1] Preliminary. [2] Estimate. *Source: Crop Reporting Board, U.S.D.A.*   T.726

WHEAT AND FLOUR

Stocks, Production, and Exports of Wheat, by Classes — In Millions of Bushels

Year Beginning June[5]	Hard Spring June 1[6] Stocks	Hard Spring Production	Hard Spring Exports[2]	Durum[3] June 1[6] Stocks	Durum Production	Durum Exports[2]	Hard Winter June 1[6] Stocks	Hard Winter Production	Hard Winter Exports[2]	Soft Red Winter June 1[6] Stocks	Soft Red Winter Production	Soft Red Winter Exports[2]	White June 1[6] Stocks	White Production	White Exports[2]
1970-1	178	198	113	80	53	39	574	755	450	23	174	26	30	171	110
1971-2	146	366	104	58	92	44	492	747	337	15	212	43	20	201	104
1972-3	275	276	198	69	73	65	471	761	704	18	226	68	30	209	151
1973-4	212	328	245	45	79	45	287	957	775	25	159	27	30	182	125
1974-5	87	293	130	33	81	47	170	883	510	23	273	136	27	252	195
1975-6	104	327	160	26	123	52	225	1,058	581	37	326	165	43	288	215
1976-7	116	411	124	53	135	41	379	976	418	57	336	181	60	284	186
1977-8	250	399	156	92	80	62	606	997	535	72	349	197	93	221	174
1978-9	335	380	232	67	133	72	632	830	610	71	189	95	73	244	185
1979-0	320	363	217	86	106	83	423	1,089	725	27	317	154	68	259	196
1980-1	285	312	188	61	108	59	440	1,181	701	40	435	299	76	338	267
1981-2[1]	257	468	206	60	186	82	541	1,117	755	38	676	460	93	355	270
1982-3[4]	348	500	240	108	148	65	539	1,255	705	60	610	390	109	296	200
1983-4															

[1] Preliminary. [2] Includes flour made from U.S. wheat & shipments to territories. [3] Includes "Red Durum." [4] Estimate. [5] Data prior to 1973-4 are for YEAR BEGINNING JULY. [6] Data prior to 1973-4 are as of JULY 1. Source: Economic Research Service, U.S.D.A. T.727

Salient Statistics of Wheat in the United States

Crop Year	Acreage Harvested Winter (1,000 Acres)	Spring	All	Avg.—All Yield Per Acre In Bushels	Farm Disposition Used for Seed	Fed to Livestock	Sold (Million Bushels)	Value of Production Ths. $	Foreign Trade[5] Domestic Exports[2]	Imports[3] —Million Bushels—	Export Value of U.S. Wheat & Pdt's. Mil $	Per Capita[1] Consumption Flour	Cereal —In Pounds—
1970-1	32,702	10,862	43,564	31.0	35.4	59.9	1,256	1,803,241	693.8	1.5	965	111	2.9
1971-2	32,370	15,315	47,685	33.9	37.3	71.8	1,510	2,167,797	590.2	1.1	1,225	111	2.9
1972-3	34,859	12,444	47,303	32.7	38.0	47.0	1,461	2,706,121	1,127.5	1.3	1,071	110	2.9
1973-4	38,747	15,401	54,148	31.6	48.4	28.1	1,634	6,744,631	1,106.7	2.6	2,387	114	2.9
1974-5	46,778	18,590	65,368	27.3	— 87.5 —		1,695	7,287,261	1,018	3.4	4,738	112	2.9
1975-6	51,376	18,084	69,391	30.6	— 94.8 —		2,032	7,549,829	1,173	2.4	5,001	116	2.9
1976-7	49,578	21,311	70,771	30.3	—104.8—		2,044	5,867,836	950	2.7	4,976	120	2.9
1977-8	48,772	17,797	66,461	30.7	—117.4—		1,928	4,764,557	1,124	1.9	3,054	117	2.9
1978-9	38,491	18,004	56,495	31.4	— 83.2 —		1,692	5,280,634	1,194	1.9	4,139	117	2.9
1979-0[4]	43,427	19,027	62,454	34.2	— 87.6 —		2,046	8,070,378	1,375	2.1	4,862	120	2.9
1980-1[4]	51,494	19,490	70,984	33.4	—104.2—		2,266	9,277,608	1,514	2.5		120	2.9
1981-2[4]	58,647	22,359	81,013	34.5				10,224,661	1,773	2.8			
1982-3[4]	58,347	20,466	78,841	35.6				9,516,018	1,600	4.0			
1983-4													

[1] Civilian only. [2] Includes flour milled from imported wheat. [3] Total wheat, flour & other products. [4] Preliminary. [5] Year beginning June. Source: Economic Research Service, U.S.D.A. T.728

Wheat Under Price Support Through the End of the Month (Cumulative Total from Current Season's Crop) In Millions of Bushels

Year	July	Aug.	Sept.	Oct.	Nov.	Dec.	Jan.	Feb.	Mar.	Apr.	May	June	Total
1970-1	126.4	160.3	193.8	213.0	221.0	226.4	240.9	244.3	247.8	251.5	253.7	254.2	254.2
1971-2	77.2	134.3	252.2	318.2	342.5	359.3	408.9	420.1	427.9	434.3	437.4	438.0	438.1
1972-3	59.4	78.3	103.7	121.9	130.3	135.1	140.5	141.8	142.6	142.9	143.0	143.0	143.0
1973-4	32.2	42.2	50.9	55.0	58.1	59.7	59.9	59.9	59.9	59.9	59.9	59.9	59.9
1974-5	14.2	22.2	28.8	31.3	31.8	33.8	35.6	36.1	36.3	36.4	36.4	36.5	36.5
1975-6	12.5	16.4	18.8	23.8	26.4	39.3	45.8	46.8	47.4	47.8	47.8	47.8	47.8
1976-7	8.3	22.0	44.0	82.2	148.1	226.1	278.7	300.7	341.5	363.1	424.7	468.3	468.3
1977-8	186.9	327.2	406.7	438.7	462.8	478.7	509.2	523.6	556.4	572.6	579.5	582.1	582.1
1978-9	53.0	105.7	154.6	183.1	202.5	213.4	237.5	242.8	251.0	254.0	254.3	255.0	255.0
1979-0	6.5	30.1	55.6	82.8	103.3	115.5	138.2	145.4	161.0	176.4	179.4	180.5	180.5
1980-1	35.7	56.6	99.2	126.5	142.2	183.3	228.6	261.0	297.4	328.0	328.0	329.4	329.4
1981-2	84.6	164.4	254.8	296.1	314.1	344.7	392.3	411.7	427.4	443.3	444.5	445.8	
1982-3	106.7	206.5	335.2	414.0	467.2	501.1	579.1	606.1	629.4				
1983-4													

Source: Economic Research Service, U.S.D.A. T.729

WHEAT AND FLOUR

U.S. Wheat Foreign Trade and Domestic Disappearance   In Millions of Bushels

Year Begin. June	Imports (Grain Only) June-Sept.	Oct.-Dec.	Jan.-Mar.	Apr.-May	Total	Exports (Grain Only) June-Sept.	Oct.-Dec.	Jan.-Mar.	Apr.-May	Total	Domestic Disappearance June-Sept.	Oct.-Dec.	Jan.-Mar.	Apr.-May	Total
1970-1	.7	.2	.3	.3	1.5	222	212	180	128	741	324	167	170	110	772
1971-2	.4	.2	.3	.2	1.0	216	130	147	117	610	352	196	190	111	849
1972-3	.4	.3	.4	.2	1.3	289	288	310	248	1,135	370	184	162	82	798
1973-4	.5	.3	.3	1.5	2.6	526	341	232	119	1,217	331	183	149	91	754
1974-5	2.1	.6	.4	.2	3.3	330	283	255	150	1,019	232	172	191	78	672
1975-6	.7	.7	.3	.6	2.4	428	344	247	154	1,173	245	156	202	119	722
1976-7	.9	.4	.3	1.1	2.7	399	220	179	152	950	226	187	214	127	754
1977-8	.8	.4	.4	.3	1.9	382	225	279	238	1,124	373	183	189	114	859
1978-9	.6	.5	.5	.3	1.9	493	309	225	168	1,194	327	195	177	138	837
1979-0	.7	.5	.5	.4	2.1	511	388	283	194	1,375	277	167	209	130	783
1980-1	.8	.6	.7	.4	2.5	518	371	400	220	1,510	286	198	175	117	776
1981-2[1]	.7	.8	.8	.5	2.8	622	428	441	282	1,773	431	130	181	111	854
1982-3[1]	1.2	3.0				546	315				441	153			
1983-4															

[1] Preliminary.   Source: Crop Reporting Board, U.S.D.A.

T.730

Wheat Stocks in the United States   In Millions of Bushels

Year	On Farms Jan. 1	Apr. 1	June 1[2]	Oct. 1	Off Farms Jan. 1	Apr. 1	June 1[2]	Oct. 1	Total Stocks Jan. 1	Apr. 1	June 1[2]	Oct. 1
1970	609.4	456.5	307.1	663.7	923.4	740.7	577.8	1,124.8	1,532.8	1,197.2	884.9	1,788.5
1971	526.1	381.1	240.3	826.9	883.9	679.4	491.2	1,046.9	1,410.0	1,060.4	731.5	1,873.8
1972	694.5	525.7	355.1	730.2	853.1	685.0	508.2	1,140.7	1,547.6	1,210.7	863.3	1,870.9
1973	510.2	316.1	133.9	608.5	888.8	611.3	304.6	843.1	1,399.0	927.3	438.5	1,451.6
1974	364.4	181.7	89.5	680.5	564.0	366.4	158.2	881.7	928.3	548.1	247.7	1,562.1
1975	446.3	274.1	132.7	755.5	661.2	388.0	194.3	1,129.0	1,107.5	662.1	327.0	1,884.5
1976	547.6	342.6	235.5	833.3	838.0	594.2	429.8	1,354.9	1,385.7	936.8	665.3	2,188.2
1977	665.4	511.0	426.3	1,035.1	1,116.4	878.5	685.9	1,365.3	1,781.8	1,389.5	1,112.2	2,400.4
1978	831.3	639.9	492.9	1,033.7	1,162.5	887.8	683.8	1,104.2	1,993.8	1,527.7	1,176.7	2,137.9
1979	814.4	633.3	484.3	1,030.1	816.4	596.2	439.8	1,240.7	1,630.8	1,229.4	924.1	2,270.8
1980	773.9	569.6	376.5	974.7	942.2	655.5	525.5	1,497.6	1,716.2	1,225.1	902.0	2,472.3
1981	753.4	538.9	414.3	1,206.2	1,149.7	789.8	574.5	1,529.0	1,903.2	1,328.6	988.8	2,735.2
1982[1]	955.6	748.4	581.0	1,421.0	1,222.4	808.7	582.9	1,566.0	2,178.0	1,557.1	1,163.9	2,987.1
1983[1]	1,166.1	884.4			1,354.5	984.4			2,520.5	1,868.9		
1984												

[1] Preliminary.   [2] Data prior to 1976 are *as of July 1*.   Source: *Crop Reporting Board, U.S.D.A.*

T.731

United States Wheat and Wheat Flour Imports and Exports   In Thousands of Bushels

Year Beginning June	Imports — Wheat Suitable for Milling	Unfit for Human Consumption	Flour	Other Pdt's.[2] (Wheat Equivalent)	Total	Exports — Public Law 480 Sales for Foreign Currency[3]	Long-Term $ & Conver. for Cur. Credit Sales	Gov't. to Gov't. Donations[4]	Donations Thru Voluntary Relief Agencies	Barter for Strategic Materials	Mutual Security (A.I.D.)[5]	Total Specified Gov't. Programs
1970-71	397	265	90	723	1,475	46,970	143,267	30,477	11,381	—	966	233,061
1971-72	101	82	89	781	1,053	22,686	153,382	37,858	13,006	—	754	227,686
1972-73	29	52	90	1,131	1,302	—	90,576	35,954	12,603	—	−86	139,047
1973-74	1,262	70	178	1,113	2,623	—	26,355	10,891	8,502	—	11,074	56,822
1974-75	1,734	109	387	1,134	3,364	—	102,269	6,705	7,873	—	—	116,847
1975-76	631	344	92	1,307	2,374	—	105,861	2,734	7,046	—	8,348	123,989
1976-77	1,298	20	32	1,381	2,731	—	133,504	8,887	17,842	—	15,836	158,277
1977-78	424	2	20	1,475	1,921	—	119,225	6,313	11,487	—	12,520	149,545
1978-79	18	15	45	1,772	1,850	—	126,819	5,968	9,808	—	243	142,838
1979-80	155	50	62	1,869	2,136	—	107,283	8,724	7,064	—	2,147	125,218
1980-81[1]	128	58	200	2,148	2,534	—	98,799	9,145	6,484	—	153	114,581
1981-82[1]					2,800							

[1] Preliminary.   [2] Includes macaroni, semolina & similar pdt's.   [3] Authorized by title, I, P.L. 480.   [4] Author, by title II, P.L. 480.   [5] Foreign Assist. Act of 1961.   Source: *Economic Research Service, U.S.D.A.*

T.732

WHEAT AND FLOUR

Comparative Average Cash Wheat Prices   In Dollars per Bushel

Crop Year— June to May[3]	Received by U.S. Farmers	No. 2 Soft Red Winter Chicago	No. 1 Hard Red Ordin. Prot. Kansas City	No. 2 Soft Red Winter St. Louis	No. 1 Hard Winter Denver	Minneapolis No. 1 Dark Northern Spring	Minneapolis No. 2 Hard Amber Durum	No. 1 Soft Portland Oregon	No. 2 Western White Pacific N.W.	No. 2 White Soft Toledo	Export Prices ($ per Metric Ton) Gulf No. 1 H.R. Winter Ports	Gulf No. 1 Soft Red Win.	Portland No. 2 White West.
1972–3	1.76	2.23	2.33	2.24	1.92	2.21	2.17	2.47	2.48	2.28			
1973–4	3.95	4.93	4.51	4.61	4.00	4.73	6.76	4.81	4.81	4.80	4.85		
1974–5	4.09	4.09	4.20	4.03	3.76	4.96	6.44	4.37	4.55	3.89	4.46		5.05
1975–6[3]	3.56	3.54	3.74	3.46	3.33	3.74	5.16	3.88	3.95	3.36	4.05		4.47
1976–7	2.73	2.81	2.88	2.78	2.38	2.96	3.30	3.10	3.16	2.75	115		116
1977–8	2.33	2.56	2.72	2.54	2.16	2.66	3.37	3.09	3.15	2.48	110		116
1978–9	2.97	3.57	3.38	3.43	2.77	3.17	3.66	3.73	3.80	3.54	135		140
1979–0	3.78	4.24	4.25	4.10	3.54	4.16	5.09	4.22	4.38	4.06	171	164	161
1980–1[1]	3.91	4.33	4.45	4.39		4.46	6.81	4.36		4.07	178	171	166
1981–2[1]	3.65	3.74	4.27	3.66		4.17	4.61	4.20		3.70	171	144	158
1982–3													

[1] Preliminary.   [2] Estimate.   [3] Data prior to 1975–6 are for crop year July to June.   *Source: Economic Research Service, U.S.D.A.*   T.733

Production of Winter Wheat in the United States   In Millions of Bushels

Year	Colorado	Idaho	Illinois	Indiana	Kansas	Michigan	Missouri	Montana	Nebraska	Ohio	Oklahoma	Oregon	Pa.	Texas	Wash.	Total U.S.
1972	51.6	34.7	54.0	39.6	314.9	21.4	36.1	48.3	92.8	46.3	89.7	35.2	8.6	44.0	119.5	1,186.5
1973	63.2	32.8	39.0	24.6	384.8	19.9	25.5	55.1	93.8	25.6	157.8	33.6	7.4	98.6	74.2	1,278.2
1974	71.9	39.8	51.9	46.9	319.0	34.0	38.0	78.2	98.6	59.5	134.4	47.3	11.5	52.8	110.4	1,375.5
1975	55.6	36.1	67.5	61.6	350.9	34.2	48.5	105.0	98.2	70.6	160.8	54.1	10.1	131.1	137.0	1,642.9
1976	51.6	39.2	72.2	54.0	339.0	33.1	58.1	98.6	94.4	64.0	151.2	56.1	9.0	103.4	132.7	1,564.1
1977	56.1	32.4	67.5	55.8	344.9	33.0	68.6	81.2	103.3	72.4	175.5	45.2	8.9	117.5	95.2	1,540.4
1978	57.3	41.8	33.4	28.9	300.0	16.4	28.6	83.7	81.6	42.1	145.8	47.3	7.1	54.0	117.0	1,222.4
1979	67.6	35.7	53.8	44.4	410.4	31.6	70.4	57.4	86.7	63.4	216.6	48.0	7.3	138.0	94.6	1,601.2
1980	107.2	51.9	75.4	53.9	420.0	35.2	89.0	54.8	108.3	67.1	195.0	72.0	9.3	130.0	143.0	1,895.4
1981	83.9	55.7	92.5	62.1	305.0	41.5	115.5	89.3	104.4	72.6	172.8	73.2	9.7	183.4	161.3	2,103.5
1982[1]	84.0	52.4	67.5	46.4	462.0	24.6	75.8	80.6	101.5	55.0	227.7	60.5	8.2	144.0	125.4	2,108.2
1983																

[1] Preliminary, December estimate.   *Source: Crop Reporting Board, U.S.D.A.*   T.734

Production of All Spring Wheat in the United States   In Millions of Bushels

Year	Durum Wheat Arizona	California	Minnesota	Montana	North Dakota	South Dakota	Total Durum	Other Spring Wheat Colorado	Idaho	Minnesota	Montana	North Dakota	Oregon	South Dakota	Utah	Washington	Total U.S.
1973			2.1	4.0	69.6	2.7	78.5	.5	15.6	74.9	37.6	169.7	2.4	36.1	1.4	15.0	354.1
1974			2.4	5.1	70.8	2.9	81.2	.7	22.1	77.4	36.9	136.5	5.4	29.9	1.7	13.2	325.1
1975			2.8	10.1	104.9	4.4	123.4	.7	24.0	83.7	40.8	156.3	4.0	35.1	1.5	10.9	360.7
1976	23.9		2.7	8.6	90.5	1.6	134.9	1.6	29.2	123.5	60.2	193.6	4.2	20.5	1.3	11.3	449.7
1977	6.1		2.8	4.8	60.5	3.3	80.0	1.1	18.4	125.6	44.9	167.0	2.4	51.7	.6	6.1	425.1
1978	6.4		3.8	8.7	102.1	3.8	133.3	2.0	33.6	87.8	53.7	180.1	4.6	44.0	1.4	11.2	419.8
1979	5.3		2.8	6.8	84.5	3.6	106.7	2.6	38.4	85.8	52.3	165.1	9.3	46.0	1.6	23.4	426.2
1980	12.4	7.8	3.4	7.6	73.2	4.1	108.4	3.1	44.2	96.9	57.4	105.5	5.4	37.4	1.4	17.2	370.5
1981	18.3	14.7	5.4	11.0	130.8	5.8	185.9	4.0	34.1	134.0	72.5	197.4	4.2	52.8	1.4	7.0	509.3
1982[1]	7.0	11.6	3.0	10.2	112.3	3.5	147.5	3.5	41.8	120.8	92.8	213.9	4.0	58.8	1.7	13.4	553.0
1983																	

[1] Preliminary, December estimate.   *Source: Crop Reporting Board, U.S.D.A.*   T.735

WHEAT AND FLOUR

United States Official Winter Wheat Crop Production Reports   In Thousands of Bushels

Crop Year	Previous December	April 1	May 1	June 1	July 1	August 1	Sept. 1	Current December	Final
1973-4	1,277,848	—	1,281,999	1,315,672	1,319,702	1,293,053	1,291,463	1,269,653	1,278,220
1974-5	1,513,462	—	1,612,106	1,531,355	1,402,445	1,393,460	1,390,800	1,391,303	1,375,526
1975-6	1,599,527	—	1,619,776	1,618,598	1,636,524	1,634,227	1,650,037	1,651,209	1,642,900
1976-7	1,495,869	—	1,458,996	—	1,530,124	1,542,660	1,542,330	1,566,074	1,564,118
1977-8	1,438,015	—	1,477,455	—	1,539,029	1,526,029	1,528,844	1,526,713	1,540,419
1978-9	1,321,068	—	1,284,375	—	1,801,705	1,248,405	1,243,685	1,248,272	1,222,446
1979-0	1,441,306	—	1,390,848	—	1,560,768	1,602,901	1,595,591	1,608,897	1,601,234
1980-1	1,567,817	—	1,711,010	1,757,170	2,317,068	2,234,951	2,353,641	1,891,251	1,895,383
1981-2	1,977,079	—	2,078,137	—	2,092,692	2,064,845	2,059,205	2,098,719	2,103,538
1982-3	2,128,133	—	2,063,336	—	2,124,854	2,095,554	2,106,149	2,108,246	
1983-4	—	—	1,893,241						

Source: Crop Reporting Board, U.S.D.A.   T.736

Supply and Distribution of Wheat in the United States   In Millions of Bushels

Crop Yr. Beginning June	On Farms	Mills, Elevators[3]	C.C.C.	Total Stocks	Production	Imports[4]	Total Supply	Food	Seed	Industry	Residual[5]	(On Farms Where Grown)	Total Dom. Disap.	Exports[4]	Total Disappearance
1970-1	307.1	576.6	1.2	982.6	1,351.5	1.5	2,336	517.2	62.1	.1	192.6	(62.0)	772.0	740.8	1,513
1971-2	240.3	489.4	1.8	822.8	1,618.6	1.1	2,442	523.7	63.2	.1	262.3	(71.7)	849.3	609.7	1,459
1972-3	355.1	506.3	1.8	983.4	1,546.2	1.3	2,531	531.8	67.4	.1	199.5	(47.0)	798.8	1,135.0	1,934
1973-4	133.9	302.8	1.8	597.1	1,710.8	2.6	2,311	544.3	84.1	—	125.1	(31.5)	753.5	1,217.0	1,971
1974-5	89.5	157.9	.3	340.1	1,781.9	3.4	2,125	545.0	92.0	—	—— 34.9 ——		671.9	1,018.5	1,690
1975-6	132.7	194.3	—	435.0	2,126.9	2.4	2,564	588.6	99.0	.1	—— 38.2 ——		725.8	1,172.9	1,899
1976-7	235.5	429.8	—	665.3	2,148.8	2.7	2,817	588.0	92.0	.1	—— 74.4 ——		754.4	949.5	1,704
1977-8	426.3	685.9	—	1,113.2	2,045.5	1.9	3,161	586.5	100.0	.1	——192.5——		859.0	1,123.9	1,983
1978-9	492.9	683.8	—	1,176.7	1,775.5	1.9	2,955	592.4	87.0	.1	——157.6——		837.0	1,194.1	2,031
1979-0	484.3	439.8	—	924.1	2,134.1	2.1	3,060	596.1	101.0	—	—— 86.0 ——		783.1	1,375.2	2,158
1980-1	376.5	525.5	—	902.0	2,374.3	2.5	3,279	610.5	114.0	—	—— 51.7 ——		776.2	1,513.8	2,290
1981-2[1]	414.3	574.5	—	988.8	2,798.7	2.8	3,790	600.1	112.0	—	——141.4——		853.5	1,772.9	2,626
1982-3[2]	581.0	582.0	—	1,163.9	2,808.7	4	3,977	610	100	—	——165 ——		875	1,600	2,475
1983-4															

[1] Preliminary. [2] Estimated. [3] Also warehouses and all off-farm storage not otherwise designated, including flour mills. [4] Imports & exports are for wheat, including flour & other products in terms of wheat. [5] Approximate feed use.   Source: Economic Research Service, U.S.D.A.   T.737

Exports of Wheat (Only) from the United States   In Millions of Bushels

Year	July	Aug.	Sept.	Oct.	Nov.	Dec.	Jan.	Feb.	Mar.	Apr.	May	June	Total
1970-1	47.9	56.3	49.9	69.0	60.3	61.6	59.3	46.7	59.9	50.7	66.7	43.4	671.7
1971-2	47.4	38.3	59.4	31.7	39.5	45.2	36.5	45.6	49.8	47.3	59.6	66.9	567.2
1972-3	58.8	68.1	69.0	82.6	83.5	107.3	101.9	92.9	98.7	108.3	128.8	126.1	1,127.0
1973-4	115.2	149.1	131.6	122.1	120.5	89.5	83.1	72.8	63.9	55.7	55.0	56.9	1,115.4
1974-5	82.8	91.6	86.0	91.3	98.3	82.3	108.4	71.3	65.2	77.0	65.3	77.2	996.7
1975-6	99.7	111.2	125.5	123.6	117.8	92.3	91.6	72.4	76.4	76.8	67.8	66.7	1,121.8
1976-7	85.4	113.0	109.9	98.7	53.3	56.9	49.0	57.7	50.7	68.1	66.4	75.6	884.7
1977-8	82.8	93.4	108.5	68.3	56.7	86.7	64.6	94.5	103.3	101.8	118.8	108.8	1,088.2
1978-9	106.1	131.9	118.3	113.0	92.3	90.0	70.4	67.1	75.5	77.0	76.8	102.2	1,120.6
1979-0	133.3	117.8	129.6	149.0	108.9	114.9	82.7	89.5	94.7	98.3	88.6	96.2	1,305.5
1980-1	123.6	139.6	136.0	116.2	112.2	131.9	129.9	124.4	128.8	127.7	76.0	124.5	1,470.8
1981-2	138.1	145.4	194.1	156.9	127.5	137.4	124.2	138.7	159.1	147.4	114.8	155.7	1,739.3
1982-3	117.9	124.0	130.8	98.5	94.1	88.5	143.1						
1983-4													

Source: Department of Commerce   T.738

WHEAT AND FLOUR

United States Wheat Quarterly Supply and Disappearance In Millions of Bushels

Year & Begin. June 1	Beginning Stocks	Production	Imports[2]	Total Supply	Food	Alc. Beverages	Seed	Feed[3]	Total	Exports[2]	Total Disappearance	Gov't Owned[4]	Privately Owned[5]	Total Stocks
1976-7	666	2,149	2.7	2,817	588.0	.1	92.0	74.3	754.4	949.5	1,704	—	1,113	1,113
June-Sept.	665	2,149	.9	2,815	200.4	6	32.0	-6.3	226.1	398.8	624.9	—	2,190	2,190
Oct.-Dec.	2,190	—	.4	2,191	152.5	6	34.0	.4	186.9	220.3	407.2	—	1,784	1,784
Jan.-Mar.	1,784	—	.3	1,784	147.3	6	1.0	65.9	214.2	178.8	393.0	—	1,391	1,391
Apr.-May	1,391	—	1.1	1,392	87.8	6	25.0	14.3	127.2	151.6	278.8	—	1,113	1,113
1977-8	1,113	2,046	1.9	3,161	586.5	.1	80.0	192.5	859.0	1,124	1,983	45.7	1,132	1,178
June-Sept.	1,113	2,046	.8	3,160	193.3	6	32.0	148.1	373.4	381.7	775.1	8.2	2,396	2,405
Oct.-Dec.	2,405	—	.4	2,405	153.5	6	23.0	6.0	182.5	225.4	407.9	31.8	1,965	1,997
Jan.-Mar.	1,997	—	.4	1,997	145.5	6	1.0	42.4	188.9	278.6	467.5	44.8	1,485	1,530
Apr.-May	1,530	—	.3	1,530	94.2	6	24.0	-4.0	114.2	238.2	352.4	45.7	1,132	1,178
1978-9	1,178	1,776	1.9	2,955	592.4	.1	87.0	157.6	837.1	1,194	2,031	50.2	873.9	924.1
June-Sept.	1,178	1,776	.6	2,954	191.7	6	27.0	108.0	326.7	493.3	820.0	48.9	2,085	2,134
Oct.-Dec.	2,134	—	.5	2,134	153.8	6	34.0	7.0	194.8	308.8	503.6	49.5	1,581	1,631
Jan.-Mar.	1,631	—	.5	1,631	147.8	6	1.0	28.6	177.4	224.5	401.9	49.5	1,180	1,229
Apr. May	1,229	—	.3	1,230	99.1	.1	25.0	14.0	138.1	167.5	305.6	50.2	873.9	924.1
1979-0	924.1	2,134	2.1	3,060	596.1	—	101.0	86.0	783.1	1,375	2,158	141.7	760.3	902.0
June-Sept.	824.1	2,134	.7	3,059	198.5	6	33.0	45.6	277.1	511.0	788.1	49.9	2,221	2,271
Oct.-Dec.	2,271	—	.5	2,271	157.9	6	37.0	-27.7	167.2	387.9	555.1	49.6	1,667	1,716
Jan.-Mar.	1,716	—	.5	1,717	145.1	6	1.0	62.8	208.9	282.7	491.6	63.3	1,162	1,225
Apr.-May	1,225	—	.4	1,226	94.6	.1	30.0	5.3	129.9	193.6	323.5	141.7	760.3	902.0
1980-1	902.0	2,374	2.5	3,279	610.5	—	114.0	51.7	776.2	1,514	2,290	199.7	789.1	988.8
June-Sept.	902.0	2,374	.8	3,277	197.2	6	38.0	51.2	286.4	518.4	804.8	202.1	2,270	2,472
Oct.-Dec.	2,472	—	.6	2,473	167.1	6	44.0	-12.8	198.3	371.4	569.7	203.5	1,700	1,903
Jan.-Mar.	1,903	—	.7	1,904	150.1	6	1.0	23.7	174.8	400.4	575.2	203.2	1,125	1,329
Apr.-May	1,329	—	.4	1,329	96.1	6	31.0	-10.4	116.7	223.6	340.3	199.7	789.1	988.8
1981-2[1]	988.8	2,799	2.8	3,790	600.1	6	112.0	141.4	853.5	1,773	2,626	190.3	973.6	1,164
June-Sept.	988.8	2,799	.7	3,788	202.5	6	37.0	191.7	431.2	621.8	1,053	191.3	2,544	2,735
Oct.-Dec.	2,735	—	.8	2,736	158.6	6	46.0	-74.3	130.3	427.7	558.0	188.7	1,989	2,178
Jan.-Mar.	2,178	—	.8	2,179	151.7	6	1.0	28.0	180.7	441.0	621.7	189.1	1,368	1,557
Apr.-May	1,557	—	.5	1,558	87.3	6	28.0	-4.0	111.3	282.4	393.7	190.3	973.6	1,164
1982-3[7]	1,164	2,809	4.0	3,977	610	6	100	165	875	1,600	2,475			1,502
June-Sept.	1,164	2,809	1.2	3,974	206.4	6	37.0	197.6	441.0	545.7	986.7	190.6	2,797	2,987
Oct.-Dec.	2,987	—	3.0	2,990	150.0	6	41.0	-37.7	153.3	315.4	468.7	179.0	2,342	2,521
Jan.-Mar.	2,521	—												
Apr.-May														

[1] Preliminary. [2] Imports & exports include flour and other products expressed in wheat equivalent. [3] Residual. [4] Uncommitted, Gov't. only. [5] Includes total loans. [6] Less than 50,000 bushels. [7] Projected. *Source: Economics Research Service, U.S.D.A.* T.740

Wheat Government Loan Program Data in the United States Loan Rates (Cents Per Bushel)

Crop Year Beginning June	Total Support Rate	National Avg.[1]	Target Rate	Corn Belt (Soft Red Winter)	Central & So. Plains (Hard Winter)	Pacific North-West (White)	Placed Under Loan	Direct Purchases	Total	Delivered to CCC	Ending Carryover	CCC Uncommitted	Current Crop	Previous	Sealed Under Bond	Other
1970-1	200	125	75	159	147	146	254.2	—	254.2	5.2	822.8	352.6	47.6	191.7	8	222.9
1971-2	179	125	54	162	149	147	438.1	22.5	460.6	35.1	983.4	355.1	180.6	198.6	13	236.1
1972-3	172	125	47	163	150	148	143.0	24.1	167.1	24.1	597.1	6.3	23.9	101.8	11	454.1
1973-4	146	125	21	131	124	125	59.9	—	59.9	—	340.1	.6	.4	.1	—	339.0
1974-5	205	137	68	139	139	141	36.5	.8	37.3	0	435.0	—	4.3	—	—	430.7
1975-6	205	137		138	138	142	47.8	3.7	51.5	0	665.3	—	21.4	—	—	665.3
1976-7	230	225		227	225	232	498.8			480	1,113					1,113.2
1977-8	247	225	290	226	219	231	590.8			2.2	1,178					1,132.1
1978-9	340	235	340	234	228	241	255.1			—	924.1					873.9
1979-0	340	250	340	248	243	257	180.5			—	902.0					760.3
1980-1[2]	363	300	363	300	294	308	329.4			—	988.8					789.1
1981-2[3]	381	320	381	320	313	329	445.8			10.9	1,164					973.6
1982-3[3]	405	355	405	356	336	365	501.1			—						
1983-4[3]		365	430													

[1] The national average loan rate at the farm as a percentage of the parity-priced wheat at the beginning of the marketing year. [2] Preliminary. [3] Estimate. *Source: Agricultural Marketing Service, U.S.D.A.* T.741

WHEAT AND FLOUR

Average Price of No. 1 Hard Winter (Ordinary Protein) Wheat, at Kansas City In Cents per Bushel

Year	July	Aug.	Sept.	Oct.	Nov.	Dec.	Jan.	Feb.	Mar.	Apr.	May	June	Average
1970-1	138	147	159	158	159	159	158	158	155	156	161	163	156
1971-2	154	154	153	156	156	158	158	157	158	161	162	152	157
1972-3	158	182	210	215	225	262	267	248	242	251	263	269	233
1973-4	290	467	501	467	478	522	568	582	501	407	359	405	462
1974-5	436	433	435	494	488	466	415	393	369	366	334	323	413
1975-6	361	412	421	409	371	350	357	381	381	361	357	375	374
1976-7	363	321	301	277	262	264	270	273	263	252	236	231	288
1977-8	235	231	247	256	281	280	282	284	307	321	312	312	272
1978-9	314	314	324	342	348	339	342	350	352	353	364	417	338
1979-0	434	412	426	439	453	451	433	432	407	390	410	407	425
1980-1	421	431	445	470	489	454	460	447	435	448	436	424	445
1981-2	425	414	419	431	446	435	433	426	425	428	422	406	427
1982-3	374	370	375	361	386	398	400	408	418				
1983-4													

Source: Agricultural Marketing Service, U.S.D.A. T.739

Average Price of No. 1 Dark Northern Spring Wheat at Minneapolis (14%[1] Protein) In Cents per Bushel

Year	July	Aug.	Sept.	Oct.	Nov.	Dec.	Jan.	Feb.	Mar.	Apr.	May	June	Average
1970-1	190	187	192	196	197	190	190	187	182	183	182	180	188
1971-2	173	166	172	177	172	172	174	169	170	173	176	170	172
1972-3	174	196	209	214	222	242	242	229	233	239	257	280	228
1973-4	307	450	480	450	448	498	552	583	533	441	423	507	473
1974-5	536	507	520	563	562	538	480	449	453	456	443	430	494
1975-6	469	490	512	503	474	446	454	470	466	448	465	475	469
1976-7	444	379	356	341	330	314	313	315	313	309	291	271	348
1977-8[1]	254	248	275	287	296	292	294	290	303	323	327	321	288
1978-9	311	313	326	341	347	332	330	336	342	345	373	432	335
1979-0	442	419	429	445	429	417	407	408	402	396	431	433	421
1980-1	469	455	456	482	495	477	481	478	467	480	477	456	471
1981-2	450	425	423	429	438	422	428	421	416	425	420	413	429
1982-3	416	396	402	400	408	396	393	392	408				
1983-4													

[1] Prior to 1977-8, prices are for 15% protein. Source: Agricultural Marketing Service, U.S.D.A. T.742

Average Price[1] Received by Farmers for Wheat in the U.S. In Cents per Bushel

Year	July	Aug.	Sept.	Oct.	Nov.	Dec.	Jan.	Feb.	Mar.	Apr.	May	June	Average[2]
1970-1	123	131	141	143	145	141	140	141	139	140	143	146	133
1971-2	134	128	126	130	131	134	133	134	134	136	138	133	131
1972-3	132	151	173	189	197	238	238	197	206	215	215	243	176
1973-4	247	445	462	422	420	478	529	552	496	398	352	357	396
1974-5	404	424	432	485	487	465	411	395	365	369	347	292	404
1975-6	333	389	411	402	358	341	343	366	365	350	343	346	355
1976-7	333	297	288	259	246	239	243	247	243	237	219	203	273
1977-8	204	213	216	230	246	247	253	259	267	282	282	281	233
1978-9	281	288	292	299	304	301	299	299	297	301	320	372	298
1979-0	389	374	387	398	394	381	374	378	364	358	369	369	382
1980-1	381	394	399	419	432	422	421	417	409	407	395	370	396
1981-2	362	362	365	377	385	380	378	370	367	368	364	339	368
1982-3	326	334	338	343	348	351	357	359	366	378			
1983-4													

[1] Weighted average by sales. [2] Includes an allowance for unredeemed loans at average loan values. Source: Statistical Reporting Service, U.S.D.A. T.743

WHEAT AND FLOUR

United States Grindings of Wheat by Mills   In Millions of Bushels (of 60 Pounds Each)

Year	July	Aug.	Sept.	Oct.	Nov.	Dec.	Jan.	Feb.	Mar.	Apr.	May	June	Total
1970-1	44.7	47.4	49.4	51.7	46.2	46.1	46.4	44.0	46.7	43.5	45.0	46.7	557.8
1971-2	45.2	49.4	49.3	48.2	44.5	46.3	45.9	44.5	46.9	43.8	46.9	47.2	558.1
1972-3	44.2	47.5	47.7	50.1	46.8	46.4	47.5	44.5	46.8	42.8	45.8	43.8	553.9
1973-4	44.7	48.9	48.1	49.3	46.3	46.9	48.9	45.0	46.1	41.4	42.2	41.6	549.4
1974-5	42.2	45.6	47.0	51.5	47.0	44.3	43.9	39.7	42.8	46.4	45.7	44.4	540.5
1975-6	47.4	49.0	51.2	54.1	45.2	46.0	50.0	47.3	51.7	49.9	49.5	50.4	575.2
1976-7	52.1	57.8	55.3	54.2	50.3	49.7	50.9	50.8	57.6	49.2	49.7	49.1	591.7
1977-8	46.1	54.8	52.2	52.4	53.2	52.1	48.4	48.9	54.8	50.5	53.6	51.5	606.9
1978-9[1]	49.7	56.1	50.5	55.3	52.9	48.9	50.9	48.2	52.5	50.2	55.1	50.3	620.6
1979-0[1]	59.0	58.9	52.4	58.9	55.7	50.6	55.0	50.4	49.1	47.2	49.8	47.8	634.8
1980-1[1]	51.8	53.0	54.8	58.4	54.6	56.9	57.5	51.1	55.3	53.4	52.2	52.6	651.5
1981-2[1]	51.2	53.3	54.6	55.6	51.0	50.2	53.7	52.8	56.7	50.3	49.0	50.2	628.6
1982-3[1]	52.3	55.8	54.3	56.3	53.8	54.8							
1983-4													

[1] Preliminary.   Source: *Bureau of the Census*   T.744

Commercial Stocks of Domestic Wheat[1] in the United States, at First of Month   In Millions of Bushels

Year	July	Aug.	Sept.	Oct.	Nov.	Dec.	Jan.	Feb.	Mar.	Apr.	May	June
1970-1	215.0	205.6	289.0	302.6	302.6	285.6	253.0	241.8	215.9	184.8	176.1	151.4
1971-2	159.9	195.1	209.6	223.5	211.9	205.0	194.8	179.9	170.3	218.8	181.3	175.2
1972-3	206.5	268.1	324.2	372.3	356.0	323.1	297.2	267.7	241.2	212.9	174.2	124.1
1973-4	149.8	196.9	215.2	208.2	185.1	158.8	146.6	141.4	128.4	117.2	97.6	85.4
1974-5	162.9	253.1	217.4	267.5	276.3	256.6	217.8	179.3	149.5	126.6	105.3	83.0
1975-6	172.5	313.9	380.2	415.8	398.0	338.1	274.7	238.8	220.1	209.0	179.6	168.7
1976-7	291.9	420.3	461.6	504.9	477.5	432.3	416.5	388.2	370.0	350.4	332.7	320.6
1977-8	383.9	469.3	526.5	509.0	488.0	460.2	418.6	385.4	355.8	321.5	281.9	240.5
1978-9	250.9	305.6	319.9	318.9	272.0	246.9	223.1	199.1	181.1	166.6	144.7	131.0
1979-0	197.0	326.8	360.0	371.4	338.2	302.9	274.5	259.0	253.4	228.1	200.3	184.2
1980-1	283.9	432.6	502.4	505.9	490.5	458.1	412.2	347.9	299.4	243.4	194.9	194.4
1981-2	312.2	427.0	472.0	487.4	476.9	425.8	395.6	352.4	285.1	254.3	218.2	204.9
1982-3	256.8	401.4	471.5	500.7	493.9	454.2	442.5	404.9	360.4	333.8	300.9	
1983-4												

[1] Domestic wheat in store in public and private elevators in 39 markets and wheat afloat in vessels or barges at lake and seaboard ports, the first Saturday of the month.   Source: *Department of Agriculture*   T.746

Commercial Stocks of Canadian Wheat[1] in Canada, at First of Month   In Thousands of Metric Tons[2]

Year	July	Aug.	Sept.	Oct.	Nov.	Dec.	Jan.	Feb.	Mar.	Apr.	May	June
1970-1	401.8	437.2	402.8	411.9	379.5	364.4	371.1	359.7	353.8	347.2	330.5	310.0
1971-2	334.4	304.6	311.2	316.4	312.1	296.0	306.6	302.5	290.8	275.7	265.2	255.0
1972-3	287.2	276.2	290.4	277.4	293.8	292.6	291.5	285.7	264.2	218.7	214.0	178.1
1973-4	172.8	205.1	192.3	208.2	213.3	198.7	185.6	177.9	194.0	197.7	181.5	171.6
1974-5	211.0	241.9	217.1	222.4	203.9	204.0	202.8	199.3	192.0	198.3	167.7	151.9
1975-6	163.3	190.7	183.0	207.2	219.6	220.8	217.2	209.9	203.1	187.3	178.0	151.5
1976-7	153.6	183.5	185.6	222.8	223.9	244.2	253.0	236.7	233.7	220.5	208.5	189.8
1977-8[2]	4,905	4,985	5,477	6,263	6,358	5,948	5,645	5,108	5,159	5,194	4,987	4,711
1978-9	5,612	6,251	6,045	5,596	5,131	5,034	5,113	4,799	4,799	4,894	4,637	4,147
1979-0	4,810	5,149	5,581	5,990	5,992	5,754	6,172	6,069	5,731	5,260	4,620	4,539
1980-1	4,210	5,659	4,963	4,997	5,137	5,338	5,292	5,234	5,288	5,130	4,719	3,939
1981-2	4,311	5,697	5,742	5,924	5,082	5,829	6,131	5,526	5,953	5,718	4,820	4,294
1982-3	4,952	5,107	4,756	6,976	7,262	6,360	6,715	6,765	6,199	5,797	5,540	
1983-4												

[1] Canadian wheat in Canada exclusive of farm stocks, first Wednesday of month.   [2] Data prior to July 1977 are in millions of bushels.   Source: *Board of Grain Commissioners of Canada*   T.747

WHEAT AND FLOUR

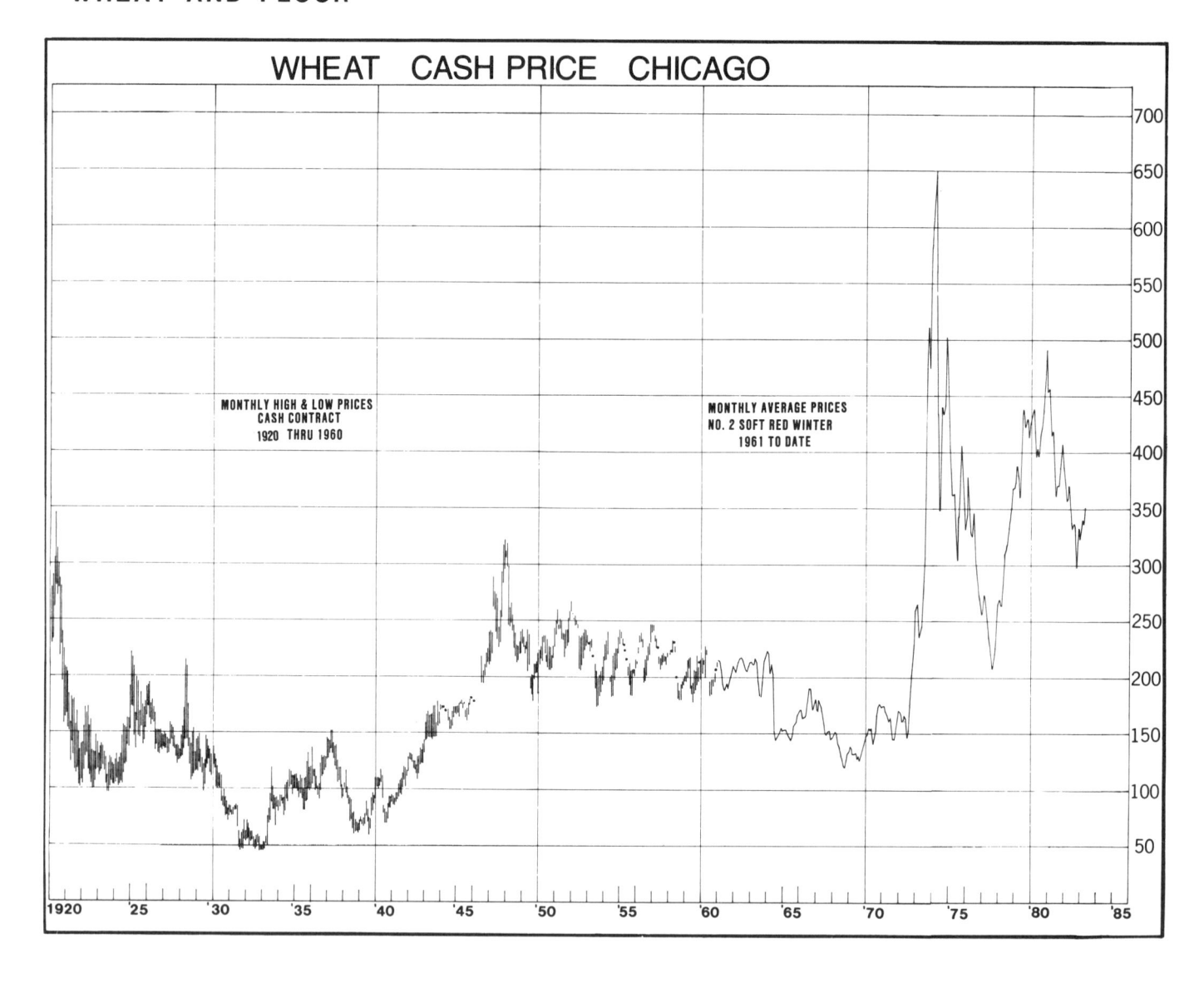

WHEAT CASH PRICE CHICAGO

MONTHLY HIGH & LOW PRICES
CASH CONTRACT
1920 THRU 1960

MONTHLY AVERAGE PRICES
NO. 2 SOFT RED WINTER
1961 TO DATE

Average Price of No. 2 Soft Red Winter (30 Days) Wheat at Chicago   In Dollars per Bushel

Year	June	July	Aug.	Sept.	Oct.	Nov.	Dec.	Jan.	Feb.	Mar.	Apr.	May	Average
1970–1	1.41	1.45	1.52	1.67	1.74	1.77	1.74	1.75	1.74	1.70	1.67	1.61	1.67
1971–2	1.64	1.54	1.45	1.45	1.53	1.60	1.71	1.69	1.61	1.62	1.66	1.63	1.58
1972–3	1.46	1.53	1.76	2.02	2.11	2.28	2.60	2.65	2.47	2.37	2.45	2.71	2.31
1973–4	2.82	3.08	4.75	5.11	4.75	5.47	5.84	6.30	6.50	5.59	4.33	3.48	4.93
1974–5	3.91	4.40	4.34	4.41	5.03	4.86	4.69	4.02	3.84	3.62	3.63	3.25	4.09
1975–6	3.03	3.42	3.82	4.06	3.84	3.49	3.32	3.45	3.78	3.66	3.34	3.30	3.54
1976–7	3.47	3.37	3.01	2.89	2.72	2.60	2.66	2.73	2.74	2.63	2.53	2.35	2.81
1977–8	2.29	2.20	2.08	2.20	2.27	2.59	2.65	2.69	2.64	2.82	3.11	3.14	2.56
1978–9	3.18	3.22	3.32	3.42	3.51	3.68	3.68	3.73	3.88	3.79	3.60	3.86	3.57
1979–0	4.36	4.39	4.23	4.28	4.30	4.13	4.26	4.36	4.39	4.18	3.96	4.04	4.24
1980–1	3.96	4.17	4.21	4.38	4.70	4.92	4.54	4.57	4.34	4.15	4.18	3.80	4.33
1981–2	3.60	3.70	3.70	3.87	3.97	4.08	3.86	3.77	3.57	3.59	3.70	3.43	3.74
1982–3	3.31	3.36	3.35	3.18	2.98	3.33	3.23	3.32	3.40	3.36			
1983–4													

Source: Agricultural Marketing Service, Grain Division, U.S.D.A.   T.745

WHEAT AND FLOUR

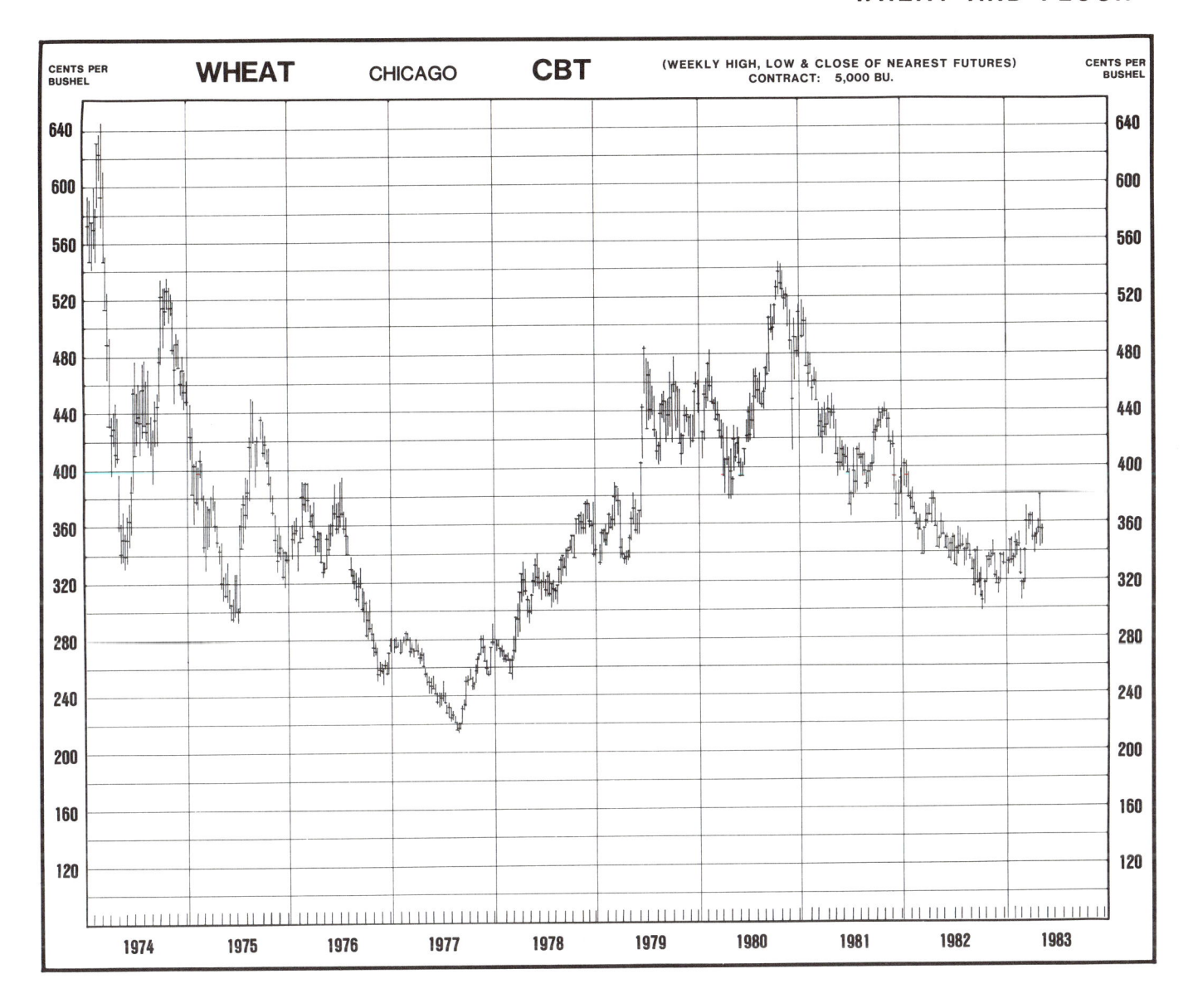

WHEAT CHICAGO **CBT** (WEEKLY HIGH, LOW & CLOSE OF NEAREST FUTURES) CONTRACT: 5,000 BU.
CENTS PER BUSHEL

Open Interest of All Wheat Futures Contracts at Chicago,[1] K.C. & Mpls. In Millions of Bushels

Year	Jan.	Feb.	Mar.	April	May	June	July	Aug.	Sept.	Oct.	Nov.	Dec.	Kansas City[3] Jan. 1	July 1	Minn.[2] Jan. 1
1970	91.7	93.5	81.2	76.9	66.5	69.5	93.1	90.4	96.8	98.0	88.6	85.5	34.0	34.3	8.8
1971	86.0	74.6	62.1	61.3	58.7	73.1	80.6	81.1	81.6	79.6	83.9	66.3	32.5	28.7	6.8
1972	61.8	66.2	53.1	52.6	50.3	60.0	77.6	100.1	98.6	109.2	112.3	95.2	21.2	26.9	5.9
1973	115.3	114.5	107.1	125.8	119.8	110.0	92.9	90.3	98.2	108.2	114.5	134.4	77.8	46.1	32.4
1974	154.1	161.5	154.8	144.8	136.9	136.4	147.4	147.5	153.0	164.5	150.6	150.0	53.2	48.0	30.3
1975	149.3	149.9	137.4	143.0	133.8	139.7	188.6	199.7	224.7	222.5	199.9	181.4	55.1	61.0	31.7
1976	165.8	206.7	202.9	171.2	183.5	226.4	237.2	227.2	233.8	270.2	260.5	229.4	102.5	120.6	27.4
1977	220.0	238.0	203.0	196.6	183.0	200.1	207.6	208.1	240.9	248.2	236.9	245.1	107.4	81.6	27.4
1978	229.4	200.7	180.6	164.9	193.2	163.1	190.0	240.9	255.9	241.7	240.4	186.4	102.7	84.8	25.9
1979	195.0	195.1	173.5	187.2	176.0	250.2	258.6	302.6	319.7	284.1	287.5	286.9	84.7	120.1	35.3
1980	279.5	266.6	222.5	214.2	213.5	270.0	345.4	345.7	376.3	442.9	420.1	350.5	121.0	92.0	31.5
1981	291.1	236.5	211.7	209.8	243.0	283.1	324.4	329.5	337.3	384.7	368.7	312.9	142.6	80.7	28.7
1982	335.9	274.7	244.5	234.9	253.2	235.5	277.6	254.8	238.9	218.7	186.8	182.3	137.0	97.7	28.7
1983	193.9	155.5	194.9	172.2									118.5		21.3

[1] Chicago Board of Trade. [2] Minneapolis Grain Exchange. [3] Kansas City Board of Trade. *Source: Commodity Futures Trading Commission*
T.748

WHEAT AND FLOUR

Volume of Trading in Wheat Futures at Chicago Board of Trade In Millions of Bushels

Year	July	Aug.	Sept.	Oct.	Nov.	Dec.	Jan.	Feb.	Mar.	Apr.	May	June	Total
1970-1	458.3	534.0	491.1	377.4	343.0	293.3	230.2	247.6	230.7	338.2	267.1	424.1	4,235
1971-2	421.1	371.0	328.9	330.4	322.3	338.7	273.3	244.2	233.0	242.1	197.2	233.1	3,535
1972-3	516.77	1,065	981.7	809.6	774.7	835.4	767.3	810.6	782.5	725.5	927.6	765.1	9,764
1973-4[1]	898.0	758.8	1,018	1,087	1,131	1,130	1,153[1]	970.6	1,137	922.4	864.0	1,026	12,096
1974-5	1,285	1,049	907	1,154	810	653	902	731	768	637	682	858	10,436
1975-6	1,520	1,313	1,062	1,159	960	721	848	1,399	1,472	1,288	1,121	1,758	14,621
1976-7	1,796	1,228	1,876	1,180	1,005	601	577	810	888	693	597	846	12,097
1977-8	824	62	777	740	982	747	694	713	1,130	1,179	1,063	1,122	10,594
1978-9	1,133	1,312	1,034	1,260	1,272	878	889	843	805	660	1,092	1,878	13,056
1979-0	1,932	1,806	1,642	2,714	1,858	1,551	2,064	2,216	1,897	2,091	2,054	2,011	23,836
1980-1	3,336	1,949	2,551	2,720	2,190	2,060	1,855	1,509	1,735	1,334	1,412	2,130	24,781
1981-2	2,368	2,055	1,833	1,821	2,340	2,122	1,600	1,621	1,780	1,683	1,517	1,815	22,555
1982-3	2,103	1,988	1,758	1,338	1,848	1,108	1,406	1,586	1,838	1,374			

[1] Data prior to Jan. 1973 are for ALL "CONTRACT" MARKETS IN THE U.S. Source: *Commodity Futures Trading Commission; Chicago Board of Trade*

T.749

High, Low & Closing Prices of May Wheat Futures on the Chicago Board of Trade In Cents per Bushel

Year of Delivery		Apr.	May	June	July	Aug.	Sept.	Oct.	Nov.	Dec.	Jan.	Feb.	Mar.	April	May	Life of Delivery Range
1978	High	316	295	282½	274¼	252½	270¾	277½	297	293	287¾	276	314¼	335	326	335
	Low	294½	271½	263¼	245¼	238¾	241½	258	272½	267	272	259¼	261¼	296	291½	238¾
	Close	294½	275½	274¼	248¾	242¼	267¾	274	280	284¾	272¾	260¾	313½	309	325¾	
1979	High	349	351	341½	337	327¼	335¼	355½	356	356	340	355½	361	354½	382½	382½
	Low	316	310½	316	308¼	297½	320	329¼	334½	328¾	323	328	335½	332	352½	297½
	Close	322	342½	320¼	314¾	323	332¾	351¼	354¾	333½	331¼	353¼	339¾	353¾	358¾	—
1980	High	371	398	514	486	475	481	500	469½	474¾	474	491	458½	429	428½	514
	Low	344½	366½	390	406½	411	430½	436	433	443	415¾	447	383	376½	383	344½
	Close	368½	390¾	451	415	464½	474¼	450¾	462¼	462¼	473½	447¼	383½	385½	414	—
1981	High	477	490	482½	503½	506	541½	570½	563½	553½	526	487	451	451	439½	570½
	Low	440½	451	444	462½	482½	502	517	541¼	455½	465	455	418½	426	393	393
	Close	450	453½	470	500¾	502¼	531	554¼	553¼	510¼	471¼	457½	433¾	433¾	398	—
1982	High	526	510	489	491	484½	465	476½	478½	453½	412	400½	375½	382½	360	526
	Low	500	479	447	455	446½	447	455	444½	384	382	360½	345	357	342	342
	Close	506	487	454	476	449½	458	474¼	447¾	400¾	391¾	366¾	370¼	357	354	—
1983	High	444¼	434½	411	403½	399	390½	354¼	368¼	355	356¾	363½	370½	366¼		
	Low	423	406¼	388½	381	374	343¼	327¼	338½	333¼	330½	318½	322¼	338¼		
	Close	431	406¼	395	392	383¼	349½	337¾	353¾	338½	351½	321½	360¼	351¼		

Source: *Chicago Board of Trade*

T.750

Wheat and Flour—Price Relationships at Milling Centers (In Dollars)

	At Kansas City					At Minneapolis				
			Wholesale Price of					Wholesale Price of		
Crop Year (June-May[5])	Cost of Wheat to Produce 100 lb. Flour[1]	Bakery Flour Per 100 lb.[2]	By-Products Obtained 100 lb. Flour[3]	Total Products Actual	Over Cost of Wheat	Cost of Wheat to Produce 100 lb. Flour[1]	Bakery Flour Per 100 lb.[2]	By-Products Obtained 100 lb. Flour[3]	Total Products Actual	Over Cost of Wheat
1973-4[5]	10.58	10.36	1.60	11.96	1.38	10.48	10.67	1.56	12.23	1.75
1974-5	10.43	10.07	1.61	11.68	1.25	11.04	11.28	1.58	12.86	1.82
1975-6	9.43	9.23	1.56	10.79	1.36	10.04	10.39	1.51	11.90	1.86
1976-7	7.06	7.02	1.66	8.68	1.62	7.46	8.12	1.70	9.82	2.36
1977-8	6.56	6.76	1.26	8.02	1.46	6.73	7.49	1.20	8.69	1.96
1978-9	7.85	7.89	1.47	9.36	1.51	7.76	8.22	1.34	9.56	1.80
1979-0	9.85	10.02	1.70	11.72	1.87	9.73	10.26	1.51	11.77	2.04
1980-1	10.30	10.38	1.99	12.37	2.07	10.95	11.00	1.78	12.78	1.83
1981-2[4]	9.81	10.37	1.57	11.94	2.13	9.80	10.67	1.41	12.08	2.28
June-Sept. '81	9.69	10.33	1.55	11.88	2.19	10.08	10.82	1.49	12.31	2.23
Oct.-Dec. '81	9.93	10.13	1.79	11.92	1.99	9.84	10.52	1.43	11.95	2.11
Jan.-Mar. '82	9.85	10.66	1.41	12.07	2.22	9.63	10.82	1.23	12.05	2.42
Apr.-May '82	9.76	10.38	1.52	11.90	2.14	9.64	10.54	1.48	12.02	2.38
June-Sept. '82	9.24	10.14	1.39	11.53	2.29	9.31	10.43	1.25	11.68	2.37
Oct.-Dec. '82	9.22	10.06	1.58	11.64	2.42	9.22	10.43	1.29	11.72	2.50

[1] Cost of 2.28 bushels. [2] Quoted as 95% patent at K.C. & standard patent at Minn., bulk basis. [3] Assumes 50–50 millfeed distribution between bran & shorts or middlings, bulk basis. [4] Preliminary. [5] Data prior to 1973-4 are for July–June crop year. Source: *Economic Research Service, U.S.D.A.*

T.751

WHEAT AND FLOUR

World Wheat Flour Production In Thousands of Metric Tons

Year	Argentina	Australia[2]	Canada	Spain	India[3]	Mexico	Israel	Japan	W. Germany	Egypt	Poland	South Africa	United Kingdom	United States	Yugoslavia
1970	2,352	1,284	1,812	3,192	2,220	1,332	329	3,396	2,412	N.A.		728	3,756	11,508	2,172
1971	2,388	1,308	1,776	2,976	2,520	1,382	360	3,468	3,436	1,920		715	3,780	11,352	2,280
1972	2,424	1,200	1,788	3,060	2,832	1,488	372	3,588	2,316	2,172		756	3,696	11,364	2,268
1973	2,304	1,092	1,728	2,904	1,932	1,560	420	3,576	2,376	2,340		806	3,768	11,304	2,292
1974	2,388	1,140	1,692	2,808	1,752	1,608	396	3,732	2,364	2,592	2,220	917	3,756	10,980	2,388
1975	2,484	1,260	1,788	3,000	1,680	1,584	456	3,996	3,060	2,736	2,292	919	3,888	11,208	2,316
1976	2,532	1,236	1,933	2,952	1,666	1,716	444	4,008	3,252	2,880	2,462	950	3,960	11,772	2,424
1977	2,616	1,176	1,872	2,976	2,136	1,680	468	3,960	3,264	3,240	2,262	917	3,900	11,856	2,388
1978	2,592	1,092	1,951	2,504	2,227	1,752	492	4,044	3,336	3,480	2,324	940	3,852	12,612	2,388
1979	2,556	1,080	1,978	2,600	1,636	1,920	480	4,176	3,456	3,492	2,440	901	3,780	12,876	2,400
1980	2,494	1,084	1,930	2,429	2,614	2,158	455	4,152	3,652	3,188	2,522	890	3,696	12,822	2,404
1981[1]	2,545	1,134	1,900		2,412	2,286	463	4,201	3,612	3,512		718	3,611	12,600	2,330
1982[4]	2,700	1,150	1,750		2,600	2,400	480	4,250	3,450	3,400		710	3,500	12,550	2,500
1983															

[1] Preliminary. [2] Twelve months ending June 30 of the year stated. [3] Represents 60 percent of the total production. [4] Estimate. Source: United Nations
T.752

Supply and Distribution of Wheat Flour in the United States In Thousands of Cwt.

Year	Wheat Ground 1,000 Bu.	Milfeed Production 1,000 Tons	Flour Production[1]	Flour and Product Imports[2]	Total Supply	Exports Flour	Exports Products[2]	Domestic Disappearance	Total Population July 1 Millions	Per Capita Disappearance Pounds
1970	563,714	4,409	253,094	325	253,419	26,054	14	227,351	204.9	111
1971	555,092	4,279	249,810	341	250,151	20,685	15	229,451	207.1	111
1972	557,801	4,303	250,441	477	250,918	20,335	19	230,564	208.8	110
1973	567,287	4,395	254,661	550	255,211	16,107	26	239,078	210.4	114
1974	562,962	4,483	251,097	665	251,762	14,453	33	237,276	211.9	112
1975	582,675	4,701	258,985	621	259,606	12,364	22	247,220	213.6	116
1976	618,284	4,920	275,077	604	275,681	16,064	44	259,573	215.2	121
1977	618,125	4,787	275,784	604	276,388	22,053	37	254,298	216.9	117
1978	621,321	4,860	277,950	773	278,723	22,170	43	256,510	222.6	117
1979	636,375	4,945	284,051	823	284,874	20,927	86	263,861	225.1	117
1980	628,499	4,867	282,655	905	283,560	17,378	54	266,128	227.7	117
1981[3]	637,973	5,044	285,579	1,159	286,738	18,809	84	267,845	229.8	117
1982										

[1] Commercial production of wheat flour, whole wheat, industrial and durum flour and farina reported by Bureau of Census. Production prior to 1970 includes estimate for non-commercial wheat milled. [2] Imports and exports of macaroni products (flour equivalent). [3] Preliminary. Source: Economics & Statistics Service, U.S.D.A.
T.753

United States Wheat Flour Production In Millions of Sacks (100 Pounds Each)

Year	July	Aug.	Sept.	Oct.	Nov.	Dec.	Jan.	Feb.	Mar.	Apr.	May	June	Total
1970-1	20.0	21.2	22.2	23.4	20.7	20.8	20.9	19.8	21.0	19.7	20.2	21.0	250.9
1971-2	20.2	22.2	22.1	21.7	20.1	21.0	20.7	20.0	21.1	19.7	21.1	21.1	251.0
1972-3	19.8	21.3	21.3	22.5	21.1	20.8	21.3	20.0	21.1	19.3	20.6	19.8	248.9
1973-4	20.1	21.9	21.6	22.0	20.7	21.0	22.1	20.1	20.8	18.5	18.9	18.6	246.3
1974-5	18.7	20.3	20.8	22.8	20.0	19.7	19.5	17.7	19.1	20.6	20.4	19.6	240.1
1975-6	21.2	21.7	22.7	24.1	20.1	20.5	22.3	21.1	23.1	22.4	22.1	22.3	263.6
1976-7	23.1	25.7	24.6	24.1	22.3	22.1	22.6	22.7	25.8	21.9	22.1	21.8	278.8
1977-8	20.6	24.4	23.4	23.4	23.8	23.4	21.8	21.8	24.3	22.6	24.1	23.1	276.7
1978-9	22.3	25.1	22.5	24.8	23.7	21.9	22.8	21.5	23.5	22.3	24.6	22.5	277.5
1979-0[1]	23.5	26.3	23.3	26.1	24.8	22.7	24.6	22.6	22.2	21.2	22.8	21.4	281.5
1980-1[1]	23.1	24.0	24.8	26.3	24.4	25.2	25.9	22.8	25.0	24.0	23.4	23.5	292.4
1981-2[1]	23.3	23.7	24.2	24.7	22.8	22.3	24.0	23.6	25.3	22.5	21.9	22.5	280.8
1982-3[1]	23.2	24.7	24.2	25.0	23.9	24.5							
1983-4													

[1] Preliminary. Source: Bureau of the Census
T.754

WHEAT AND FLOUR

Stocks of Wheat Flour Held by Mills in the United States   In Thousands of Sacks (100 Pounds)

Year	Jan. 1	April 1	July 1	Oct. 1	Year	Jan. 1	April 1	July 1	Oct. 1
1970	4,595	4,237	4,227	4,438	1977	1,334	4,248	4,167	3,537
1971	4,329	4,732	4,586	4,861	1978	4,160	4,096	3,459	3,342
1972	4,362	4,542	4,379	4,886	1979[1]	3,214	3,477	3,895	3,813
1973	4,746	5,581	5,393	4,174	1980[1]	3,975	3,323	4,268	3,716
1974	5,505	5,297	3,748	3,885	1981[1]	3,842	3,897	3,895	4,222
1975	4,499	4,755	4,434	4,140	1982[1]	3,460	3,384	3,744	3,563
1976	3,907	4,510	3,923	3,621	1983[1]	4,276			

[1] Preliminary.   Source: Department of Commerce   T.755

United States Wheat Flour Exports   In Thousands of 100 Pound Sacks

Year	July	Aug.	Sept.	Oct.	Nov.	Dec.	Jan.	Feb.	Mar.	Apr.	May	June	Total
1970-1	863	1,164	1,074	2,438	1,537	2,104	1,134	1,528	1,188	1,282	1,536	2,841	18,689
1971-2	1,627	1,374	1,178	982	908	1,060	1,318	1,472	1,169	757	2,300	2,494	16,639
1972-3	1,381	930	965	1,049	1,665	1,049	1,553	611	1,626	1,134	977	993	13,933
1973-4	1,352	1,596	1,607	483	612	912	914	1,015	904	832	957	858	12,042
1974-5	784	797	699	816	929	1,058	820	715	577	516	1,718	1,119	10,548
1975-6	1,084	999	753	735	588	555	423	379	525	1,149	1,789	2,184	11,163
1976-7	1,294	2,083	2,449	997	447	188	1,218	2,334	2,519	3,272	1,857	1,248	12,483
1977-8	1,194	1,146	730	473	766	1,237	723	1,539	1,774	2,554	2,297	2,694	17,127
1978-9[1]	1,674	2,145	1,963	1,505	357	486	382	1,165	1,163	752	2,689	1,727	16,008
1979-0[1]	1,669	2,489	2,218	1,223	842	1,971	1,018	1,300	2,713	867	918	1,606	18,833
1980-1[1]	894	2,137	1,396	1,034	522	609	980	1,896	2,241	2,932	1,724	2,350	18,715
1981-2[1]	987	1,420	724	284	117	184	605	2,165	2,336	2,858	1,760	944	14,384
1982-3[1]	352	1,196	698	593	824	185	1,587						

[1] Preliminary.   Source: Department of Commerce   T.756

Average Wholesale Price of Wheat Flour (Spring[1]), at Minneapolis   In Dollars per Hundred Pounds (Bulk)

Year	July	Aug.	Sept.	Oct.	Nov.	Dec.	Jan.	Feb.	Mar.	Apr.	May	June	Average
1970-1	6.13	6.13	6.28	6.41	6.41	6.36	6.35	6.31	6.25	6.24	6.23	6.20	6.28
1971-2	6.11	6.06	5.98	6.00	6.01	6.00	6.00	5.99	5.91	5.91	5.93	5.95	5.99
1972-3	6.025	6.525	6.888	6.850	6.938	7.625	7.613	7.138	7.263	7.325	7.313	7.875	7.11
1973-4	7.738	10.280	10.600	9.913	10.225	11.525	12.975	13.313	12.700	10.188	9.838	10.963	10.85
1974-5	12.013	11.513	11.425	12.600	12.938	12.175	11.488	11.025	10.388	10.363	9.863	9.550	11.28
1975-6	10.213	10.513	11.238	11.163	10.675	10.150	10.150	10.213	10.713	10.250	10.075	10.350	10.48
1976-7	10.288	9.438	8.500	8.375	7.913	7.838	7.750	7.863	7.725	7.125	6.925	6.500	8.015
1977-8	6.588	6.688	7.025	7.188	7.338	7.200	7.588	7.325	7.650	8.638	8.388	8.100	7.746
1978-9	8.250	7.938	7.825	7.900	8.400	8.138	7.813	8.038	8.313	8.300	9.013	9.288	8.268
1979-0	10.638	10.513	10.463	10.563	10.713	10.438	10.088	10.413	10.113	9.688	10.375	10.338	10.362
1980-1	11.025	10.963	10.975	11.113	11.138	—	11.050	11.113	10.975	11.100	11.075	11.125	11.059
1981-2	10.813	10.750	10.588	10.525	10.675	10.338	10.763	10.950	10.738	10.538	10.550	10.500	10.644
1982-3	10.538	10.188	10.475	10.388	10.463	10.450	10.163	10.300					

[1] Standard patent.   Source: Bureau of Labor Statistics (0212-0103)   T.758

Average Wholesale Price of Wheat Flour (Winter, Hard—95% Patent) at Kansas City $ Per Cwt.

Year	July	Aug.	Sept.	Oct.	Nov.	Dec.	Jan.	Feb.	Mar.	Apr.	May	June	Average
1970-1	5.53	5.53	5.71	5.71	5.65	5.59	5.59	5.61	5.50	5.49	5.50	5.59	5.58
1971-2	5.48	5.31	5.28	5.33	5.34	5.35	5.34	5.34	5.31	5.34	5.34	5.34	5.34
1972-3	5.463	6.163	6.363	6.413	6.500	7.500	7.375	6.813	6.875	7.163	7.038	7.738	6.78
1973-4	7.538	9.388	10.463	9.863	10.113	11.075	12.913	13.150	12.488	9.738	9.188	9.688	10.47
1974-5	10.725	10.150	10.325	11.363	11.775	11.200	10.438	9.938	9.125	8.975	8.550	8.088	10.050
1975-6	8.938	9.363	10.213	10.113	9.650	8.988	8.963	9.350	9.563	9.063	8.713	8.838	10.160
1976-7	N.A.	8.075	7.613	7.375	6.938	6.838	6.763	6.813	6.525	6.200	5.838	5.575	6.778
1977-8	5.850	5.913	6.088	6.325	6.575	6.488	6.988	6.675	6.963	8.250	7.463	7.225	6.734
1978-9	7.600	7.575	7.550	7.600	7.925	7.788	7.550	7.775	8.175	8.125	8.800	9.075	7.962
1979-0	10.388	10.088	10.075	10.100	10.600	10.463	10.000	10.263	9.813	9.488	10.013	9.838	10.094
1980-1	10.000	10.113	10.475	10.600	10.675	N.A.	10.663	10.400	10.275	10.525	10.313	10.525	10.415
1981-2	10.275	10.300	10.200	10.025	10.313	N.A.	10.638	10.700	10.638	10.425	NA	NA	10.390
1982-3	NA	NA	NA	NA	NA	NA	10.200						

Source: Bureau of Labor Statistics (0212-0102.01)   T.757

Wool

The worldwide production of wool in the 1982/83 season was estimated at 3.58 billion pounds, clean, only fractionally below the 1981/82 output. The world clip was only slightly above the level of the previous season. Economic recession dampened the demand for wool in the major wool consuming countries during 1982. The 1982/83 world carryin of 364 million pounds, the highest in five years, was partly the result of the purchasing of wool by government marketing authorities in order to maintain prices. Nearly two-thirds of the world carryin stocks of wool was held by wool marketing authorities in Australia, New Zealand, and South Africa.

Revised forecasts estimated the 1982/83 Australian wool production at 1.53 million pounds, clean, nearly 3 percent below the 1981/82 output because of the worst Australian drought in history. Australian sheep numbers in the spring of 1983 were expected to be 3 percent below the year-earlier figure, and the clip was expected to be at least 5 percent smaller. The average 1982/83 Australian wool price, as measured by a weighted-average index across 11 wool categories, was expected to be about 440, 2 percent above the 1981/82 average. The Australian Wool Corporation purchased nearly one-third of the wool offered for sale in the first half of the season in order to keep prices above the 422 floor, and Corporation stocks were almost doubled to 1.1 million bales. Australian prices, which rose to 438 early in 1983 because of buying from Eastern Europe, the EC and China, were expected to strengthen further throughout the year. Early in 1983, the Australian floor price for wool at auction was raised by 7.5 percent following a 10 percent devaluation of the Australian dollar.

Notwithstanding the good lambing season in New Zealand, the major source of crossbred and carpet wools, the clip rose only 2 percent, to 816 million pounds, because of an extended winter drought. New Zealand wool prices, as measured by the New Zealand market indicator, dropped nearly 11 percent in the last quarter of 1982. Nearly one-third of that loss was recovered early in 1983 because of buying interest from European, Chinese, and Japanese importers. The New Zealand Wool Board, which had allowed its stocks to flow freely onto the world market, was able to reduce its inventory by 8 percent from the season's opening level.

South African wool stocks increased by 76 percent during 1982. Dry weather was expected to keep South African wool production at 1981/82 levels. Wool production in the Soviet Union, the world's largest sheep-raising country, is expected to increase slightly in 1983 because of slightly reduced slaughterings. Both sheep numbers and wool production were expected to increase in China, Pakistan, and Uruguay during the year. The merino share of the 1982/83 world clip was 1 percent below the previous season's level because of the reduced Australian production. The share of the world 1982/83 clip attributed to the coarser grades were: crossbred, 34 percent, and carpet wools, 27 percent, both unchanged from 1981/82.

The U.S. mill consumption of raw wool during 1982 was nearly 114.8 million pounds, clean, 17 percent below the 1981 level. The mill demand for the finer grades of wool continued to be strong throughout the year. The amount of raw wool used for carpet manufacture was 9.8 million pounds, 10 percent below the previous year, and wool use for apparel was 105 million pounds, down 18 percent. Nearly 60 percent of the raw wool used for apparel in both the woolen and the worsted systems was 60's and finer during both 1981 and 1982.

The total U.S. production of wool during 1982 was estimated at 58.6 million pounds, clean, compared with 58.8 million in 1981. Early in 1983, the U.S. inventory of stock sheep was estimated to be at its lowest level since 1867, and the 1983 U.S. production of wool was expected to be down to 53 million pounds, clean. Depressed consumer demand was expected to limit the U.S. 1983 mill consumption of wool to about 112 million pounds.

U.S. imports of raw wool were 61.4 million pounds, clean, in 1982, down nearly 17 percent from 1981 imports. Duty-free imports amounted to 21.4 million pounds, 71 percent of which came from New Zealand. Australia supplied 62 percent of the 40 million pounds of U.S. dutiable imports of wool. Mostly because of the sharp drop in wool prices in 1982, U.S. exports of raw wool were 1.35 million pounds, clean, nearly 4 times the average of the previous four years. Shipments to France accounted for 36 percent of U.S. exports, thus making France the largest customer for U.S. wool during the year.

In December 1982, the USDA Agricultural Stabilization and Conservation Service announced that the support price for 1983 marketings would be $1.53 a pound, shorn wool. The Service said that pulled wool would continue to be supported at a level comparable to the support price for shorn wool through payments on unshorn lambs.

Futures Markets

Greasy merino wool futures are traded on the Sydney Futures Exchange, and New Zealand crossbred wool futures are traded in London.

WOOL

World Production of Wool[3]   In Thousands of Metric Tons (Greasy Basis)

Year	Brazil	Argentina	Australia	China	France	Morocco	India	N. Zealand	Spain	Turkey	South Africa	Un. Kingdom	United States	Uruguay	USSR	World[1] Total
1970	40.6	199.8	885.4	86.4	20.3	15.5	36.0	333.9	33.8	47.5	126.8	47.2	85.0	80.0	418.9	2,663
1971	34.4	188.8	880.4	88.6	21.0	13.5	37.0	322.3	32.1	47.5	121.2	44.5	81.9	62.0	428.8	2,606
1972	37.1	177.0	735.2	90.3	21.2	20.0	30.8	308.8	31.7	50.3	114.7	46.7	79.6	61.0	420.0	2,413
1973	36.5	179.2	700.9		21.4	23.0	30.1	284.8	31.8	47.3	113.3	49.4	72.0	53.0	433.0	2,355
1974	34.4	183.4	793.5		21.7	19.0	30.5	294.1	34.0	52.4	114.6	49.9	64.7	55.0	461.0	2,495
1975	31.3	190.2	757.4		21.9	20.0	31.0	311.8	29.0	53.0	114.3	50.3	58.6	60.0	463.0	2,481
1976	30.3	176.3	702.7	61.0	22.0	21.0	32.0	302.5	28.6	53.9	110.5	49.9	53.8	60.4	432.0	2,457
1977	26.9	172.0	677.4	61.0	22.4	20.0	33.1	310.8	28.0	54.1	113.4	48.0	49.9	62.2	455.0	2,465
1978	28.0	170.8	709.2	61.0	22.6	12.0	34.2	310.8	29.0	56.7	113.4	49.2	46.2	65.8	460.0	2,433
1979	31	166	709	153	26	21	35	357	29	59	110	48	48	72	412	2,553
1980[2]	35	163	700	176	27	22	35	381	28	61	112	50	49	79	443	2,641
1981[1]	33	163	711	180	27	22	35	385	21	62	112	42	50	79	454	2,653
1982																

[1] Estimated.   [2] Preliminary.   [3] Includes shorn, pulled, & wool exported on skins.   Source: *Foreign Agricultural Service, U.S.D.A.*   T.760

World Consumption of Wool   In Millions of Pounds (Clean Basis)

Year	Argentina	Australia	Belgium	Canada	France	W. Germany	Italy	Japan	Netherlands	New Zealand	South Africa	United Kingdom	United States[3]	Uruguay	Soviet Bloc	World Total
1970	60	81	89	11	275	150	204	403	18	24	27	337	240	48		3,308
1971	74	77	67	10	318	163	195	402	19	28	26	311	191	45		3,263
1972	80	75	68		322	170	227	400	19			336	219			3,480
1973	67	62	51		259	119	202	411	14			301	151		1,037	3,180
1974	71	47	45		231	85	189	258	12			248	93		1,102	2,861
1975	70	48	54		236	120	196	294	12			244	110		1,099	3,032
1976[1]	71	61	70		276	145	262	346	14			264	122		1,070	3,293
1977[2]	81	57	68		259	134	251	291				250	108		1,116	3,176
1978[2]													115			
1979[2]													117			
1980[2]													123			
1981[2]													138			
1982[2]													115			

[1] Preliminary.   [2] Estimate.   [3] Consumption on woolen & worsted systems only.   Sources: *Bureau of the Census; Commonwealth Economic Committee*   T.761

Wool: Mill Consumption, by Grades in the U.S. Scoured Basis   In Millions of Pounds

	Apparel Wool[1]							
	Woolen System			Worsted System				
Year	60's & Finer	50's Up to 60's	Total[4]	60's & Finer	Coarser Than 60's	Total	All Total	Carpet Wool[2]
1971	14.8	21.7	40.4	37.7	38.1	75.8	116.2	75.2
1972	19.9	26.7	50.2	54.6	37.4	92.0	142.2	76.4
1973	13.6	24.7	41.7	40.2	28.0	68.2	109.9	41.4
1974	10.9	18.9	33.0	23.8	18.0	41.8	74.9	18.6
1975	15.7	25.3	41.0	34.1	19.0	53.1	94.1	15.9
1976	20.6	29.2	49.8	34.9	21.9	56.8	106.6	15.1
1977	22.3	26.3	48.6	27.6	19.3	46.9	95.5	12.5
1978	24.4	28.6	53.0	32.7	16.5	49.2	102.3	13.0
1979	29.0	28.3	57.4	27.2	21.9	49.2	106.5	10.5
1980	28.2	28.8	57.0	35.5	20.9	56.4	113.4	10.0
1981[3]	35.2	29.3	64.5	41.2	22.0	63.3	127.8	10.9
1982[3]							105.0	9.8
1983								

[1] Domestic & Duty-Paid Foreign.   [2] Duty-Free Foreign.   [3] Preliminary.   [4] Includes 48's & coarser prior to 1975.   Source: *Economic Research Service, U.S.D.A.*   T.762

WOOL

Wool Goods[1] Production in the United States   In Millions of Square Yards

Year	First Quarter	Second Quarter	Third Quarter	Fourth Quarter	Total Year	Year	First Quarter	Second Quarter	Third Quarter	Fourth Quarter	Total Year
1970	58.1	54.2	35.4	30.9	178.6	1977	26.2	26.7	23.3	25.4	101.6
1971	37.0	32.6	22.7	21.1	113.3	1978	28.2	31.2	27.3	30.0	116.6
1972	25.3	27.7	22.2	26.6	101.8	1979[2]	33.5	31.3	26.5	28.2	117.4
1973	28.4	29.6	23.7	19.3	101.1	1980[2]	33.6	33.9	43.7	40.0	158.3
1974	23.6	22.7	17.6	17.1	81.0	1981[2]	53.7	56.5	36.4	33.1	165.0
1975	17.3	19.4	20.4	21.7	78.9	1982[2]	38.1	36.1			
1976	26.0	26.4	22.9	21.9	97.3	1983					

[1] Woolen and worsted woven goods, except woven felts.   [2] Preliminary.   Source: Bureau of Census   T.763

United States Imports[1] of Unmanufactured Wool (Clean Yield)   In Millions of Pounds

Year	Jan.	Feb.	Mar.	Apr.	May	June	July	Aug.	Sept.	Oct.	Nov.	Dec.	Total
1970	12.9	15.7	18.0	12.3	11.3	17.0	13.7	14.7	11.2	8.4	6.9	10.9	153.1
1971	12.0	9.4	11.2	11.1	11.5	10.4	13.8	17.0	13.3	5.3	1.0	10.7	126.0
1972	7.1	10.5	7.2	11.8	8.6	6.3	9.9	10.7	6.2	5.8	6.7	5.7	96.6
1973	7.7	7.2	5.7	5.6	6.4	6.8	5.4	4.7	2.5	2.8	2.0	1.9	57.9
1974	1.6	3.0	2.5	2.5	3.1	3.2	2.4	2.9	1.8	1.7	1.0	1.3	26.9
1975	2.2	1.4	1.7	2.1	2.2	2.9	2.4	2.4	2.9	4.9	4.0	4.4	33.6
1976	5.8	5.3	5.6	5.9	4.7	3.9	4.8	5.7	4.6	4.0	3.3	4.4	58.0
1977	5.2	5.0	4.7	5.1	7.4	7.4	4.0	4.7	2.4	2.2	1.8	3.0	53.0
1978	3.7	3.2	4.1	4.9	4.0	3.8	4.7	5.4	3.4	4.0	4.8	4.0	50.4
1979	4.5	3.4	4.2	3.9	4.3	3.1	4.1	3.3	2.6	2.0	3.5	3.5	42.3
1980	6.1	4.9	5.1	4.6	5.7	4.5	5.3	4.8	4.1	3.9	3.6	4.0	56.5
1981	6.9	7.7	6.6	7.5	8.6	4.9	6.5	5.3	3.7	6.0	5.1	5.3	75.3
1982	8.0	6.3	6.6	4.9	6.0	6.6	4.0	4.2	4.7	2.9	3.6	3.7	61.4
1983													

[1] Data are imports for consumption.   Source: Department of Commerce   T.764

Price Received by Farmers for Shorn[2] Wool in the U.S.   In Cents per Pound

Year	Jan.	Feb.	Mar.	Apr.	May	June	July	Aug.	Sept.	Oct.	Nov.	Dec.	Average[1]
1970	35.6	35.7	36.5	37.5	36.6	37.5	37.1	34.2	31.6	32.5	31.7	28.2	35.5
1971	25.3	24.6	23.3	22.9	21.2	21.3	18.7	17.9	18.9	17.0	17.9	16.8	19.4
1972	17.7	19.6	24.2	29.1	34.5	39.4	39.2	38.4	35.8	50.9	52.5	49.3	35.0
1973	78.0	77.3	90.4	86.1	82.3	84.5	83.0	78.8	83.7	74.3	70.1	70.6	82.7
1974	78.4	70.0	66.1	62.5	60.6	59.7	61.1	52.5	48.7	49.6	45.8	43.5	59.1
1975	40.9	33.7	36.7	43.6	48.0	46.7	48.0	46.2	44.8	52.8	47.4	49.0	44.7
1976	50.7	58.4	59.5	64.4	65.1	68.1	68.3	67.0	68.2	70.8	71.2	69.5	65.7
1977	72.9	72.5	72.4	72.5	71.9	73.7	72.3	70.4	66.4	71.3	70.6	69.3	72.0
1978	72.6	68.9	71.2	73.7	73.9	76.2	74.8	74.6	72.7	77.1	81.2	73.6	74.5
1979	78.7	77.3	79.5	86.9	88.0	89.4	87.7	81.8	84.9	87.5	89.0	86.5	86.3
1980	82.1	86.8	93.5	92.2	86.6	86.5	85.8	85.5	84.7	89.4	92.1	90.9	88.1
1981	84.6	88.3	91.8	101.0	99.8	101.0	94.4	84.8	84.3	87.3	91.1	84.2	94.5
1982[3]	80.4	80.4	83.4	83.6	88.5	79.6	74.5	68.3	66.7	59.2	61.6	57.1	70.0
1983[3]	52.3	57.7	58.4	67.4									
1984													

[1] Weighted average.   [2] Grease basis.   [3] Preliminary.   Source: Crop Reporting Board, U.S.D.A.   T.765

WOOL

Salient Statistics of Wool in the United States

Year	Sheep & Lambs Shorn[2] Ths.	Weight per Fleece Lbs.	Shorn Wool Production Ths. Lbs.	Price per Lb.	Value of Production Mil. $	Pulled Wool Production Avg. Weight per Skin Lbs.	Pulled Wool Total	Total Wool Production[4]	Apparel Wool (Clean Content) Domestic Prod.	Exports Domestic Wool	Imports for Consumption[4]	Total New Supply[3]	Carpet Wool Imports for Cons.	Mill Consumption Apparel	Mill Consumption Carpet
											Thousand Pounds				
1970	19,163	8.43	161,587	35.4	57.2	3.40	15,200	176,787	88,158	200	79,810	167,768	73,325	163,652	76,609
1971	19,036	8.41	160,156	19.6	31.4	3.46	12,000	172,156	85,142	6,318	42,682	121,506	83,893	116,310	75,151
1972	18,770	8.44	158,506	35.0	55.5	3.40	9,700	168,206	90,762	11,224	24,790	104,328	71,849	142,233	76,368
1973	17,425	8.25	143,738	82.7	118.8	3.49	8,000	151,738	81,726	3,726	19,587	97,601	40,694	109,872	41,394
1974	15,956	8.23	131,382	59.2	77.8	3.31	5,700	137,082	73,525	4,271	11,800	81,053	15,147	74,856	18,595
1975	14,403	8.30	119,535	44.7	53.5	3.33	5,300	124,835	67,488	7,674	16,605	76,419	17,021	94,117	15,908
1976	13,669	8.11	110,817	65.7	73.1	3.32	4,000	114,817	62,197	1,130	38,387	99,454	19,076	106,629	15,117
1977	13,270	8.11	107,159	72.0	77.1	3.28	1,700	108,859	58,455	385	36,303	94,373	22,655	95,485	12,526
1978	12,609	8.08	101,874	74.5	75.9	3.16	1,000	102,874	55,082	425	27,000	81,657	23,404	102,246	13,009
1979	13,068	8.02	104,860	86.3	90.5	3.20	900	105,760	56,022	313	20,283	75,992	22,047	106,533	10,513
1980	13,255	7.95	105,367	88.1	92.8	3.08	1,050	106,417	56,444	304	30,491	86,631	25,992	113,423	10,020
1981[1]	13,477	8.14	109,689	94.4	103.6		1,150	110,903	58,800	300	48,106	106,876	26,146	127,752	10,896
1982[1]	13,138	7.99	104,966	68.4	71.8				58,600	1,400	39,989	97,189	21,433	105,009	9,825
1983															

[1] Preliminary. [2] Includes sheep shorn at commercial feeding yards. [3] Production minus exports plus imports; stocks not taken into consideration. [4] Apparel wool includes all dutiable wool; carpet wool includes all duty-free wool. *Sources: Economics Service, U.S.D.A.; Dept. of Commerce*

T.766

Consumption of Apparel Wool in the United States (Clean Basis)   In Millions of Pounds (Clean Basis)

Year	Jan.	Feb.	Mar.	Apr.	May	June	July	Aug.	Sept.	Oct.	Nov.	Dec.	Total
1970	16.0	15.6	18.8	15.6	14.1	16.3	9.8	10.8	13.3	10.7	10.8	12.0	163.7
1971	10.2	9.5	13.0	9.4	9.7	12.1	7.3	8.0	10.7	8.8	7.7	9.8	116.2
1972	9.5	10.4	14.6	11.8	12.6	15.5	9.0	12.6	13.6	10.9	12.5	9.2	142.2
1973	12.6	9.9	9.6	10.9	9.8	9.4	8.5	8.4	7.7	10.0	6.8	6.2	109.9
1974	7.8	6.3	6.4	7.2	6.6	6.5	5.5	6.1	5.6	6.9	5.5	4.6	74.9
1975	6.5	5.8	6.5	8.4	7.8	7.6	8.1	8.1	8.1	10.3	7.8	9.3	94.1
1976	8.9	8.7	12.0	9.1	8.8	11.1	7.3	7.6	9.3	7.9	6.9	9.0	106.7
1977	8.2	8.3	10.0	7.9	7.7	9.5	5.2	7.4	8.6	7.7	7.0	7.9	95.5
1978	7.7	8.2	10.5	8.8	9.2	10.3	7.0	8.4	9.4	8.1	8.1	7.5	102.2
1979[1]	10.1	8.2	8.9	10.0	8.5	7.8	7.5	7.6	6.7	9.9	8.5	8.4	106.5
1980[1]	11.3	10.2	9.8	11.4	9.2	8.3	7.5	8.4	7.7	10.9	9.0	10.0	113.4
1981[1]	10.2	11.0	12.9	10.8	10.2	12.8	8.4	10.1	11.4	9.4	9.4	11.2	127.8
1982[1]	9.4	9.6	12.8	9.0	8.2	9.4	5.9	8.0	8.3	7.1	7.7	9.4	105.0
1983													

[1] Preliminary. *Source: Bureau of the Census*

T.767

Average Wool Prices[1]—Australian—64's, Type 62, Duty Paid—U.S. Mills   In Cents per Pound

Year	Jan.	Feb.	Mar.	Apr.	May	June	July	Aug.	Sept.	Oct.	Nov.	Dec.	Average
1975	199.0	204.0	209.0	211.2	219.6	209.0	206.8	204.3	198.5	197.3	206.0	205.0	205.8
1976	205.5	206.0	—	—	212.4	213.5	213.5	216.5	224.2	232.5	224.0	227.3	217.5
1977	229.0	227.3	227.6	228.3	228.0	226.3	227.0	224.0	227.0	227.0	230.5	226.5	227.4
1978	228	230	231	232	233	236	236	236	236	236	236	236	234
1979	237	249	265	273	278	282	283	283	293	309	290	280	277
1980	292	310	306	299	310	321	311	306	311	306	320	321	309
1981	319	312	307	314	316	319	323	320	316	316	317	312	316
1982	301	303	313	323	336	321	304	294	287	276	269	267	299
1983	279												
1984													

[1] Raw, clean basis. *Source: U.S. Dept. of Agriculture*

T.768

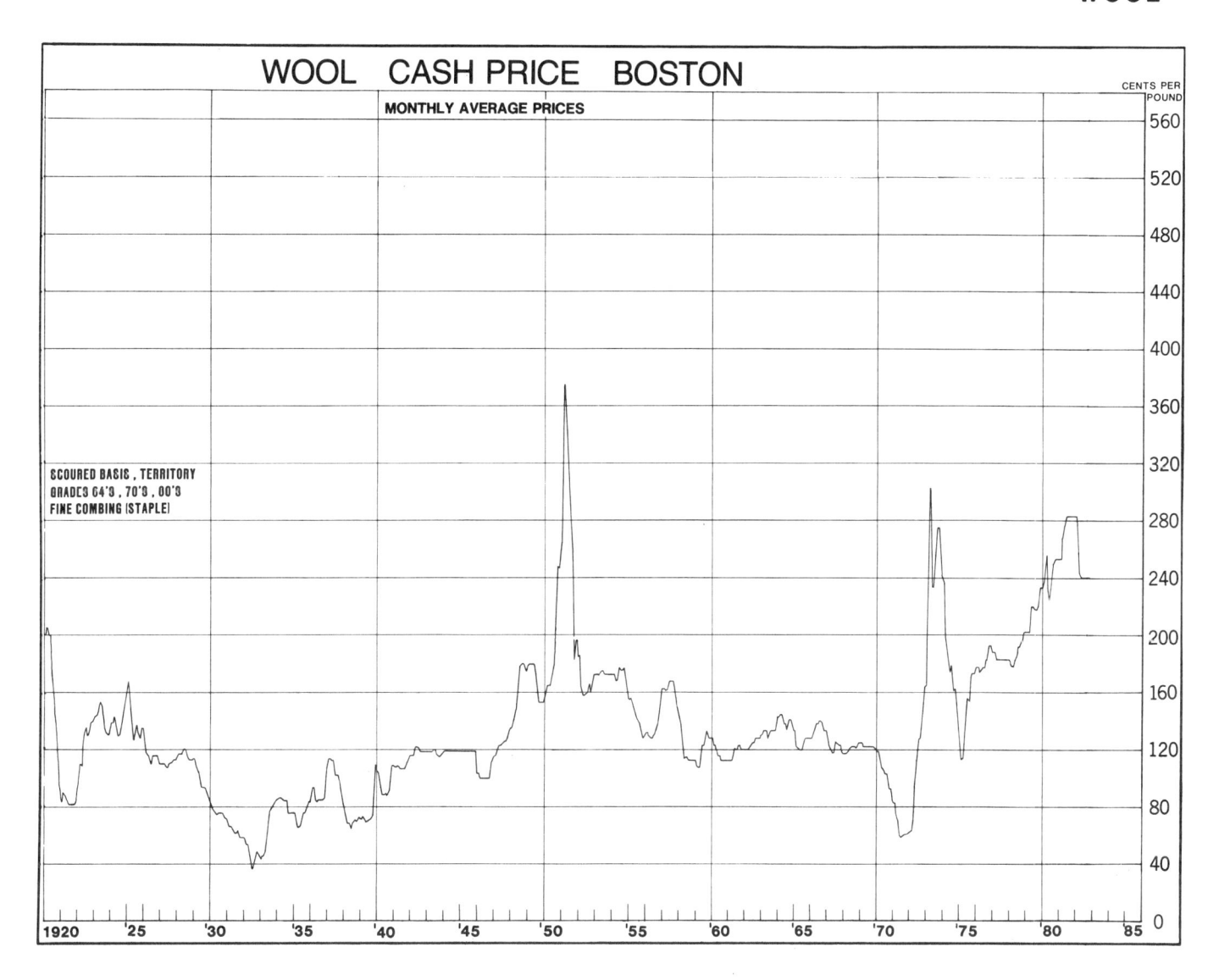

WOOL

WOOL CASH PRICE BOSTON
MONTHLY AVERAGE PRICES

Scoured basis, Territory grades 64's, 70's, 80's fine combing (staple)

Average Wool Prices—Domestic[1]—Graded Territory, 64's, Staple 2¾" & Up—U.S. Mills ¢ Lb.

Year	Jan.	Feb.	Mar.	Apr.	May	June	July	Aug.	Sept.	Oct.	Nov.	Dec.	Average
1970	118.5	118.5	111.0	108.1	107.0	105.5	102.5	102.5	95.3	92.5	92.5	85.0	102.4
1971	82.5	82.5	75.7	70.8	63.0	59.7	59.0	59.5	61.0	61.0	60.5	61.5	66.4
1972	62.5	64.0	70.8	94.4	113.0	120.0	127.0	127.5	135.0	145.5	163.5	165.0	115.7
1973	188.0	232.5	302.5	233.8	233.5	257.5	260.0	275.0	275.0	263.0	241.9	237.5	250.0
1974	236.0	222.5	197.5	185.0	174.0	178.8	188.5	161.2	162.5	156.5	141.2	130.8	176.0
1975	116.2	112.5	113.8	134.0	150.6	155.6	153.8	171.2	172.5	172.5	172.5	177.5	150.2
1976	177.5	177.5	173.5	176.2	177.5	177.5	182.5	182.5	187.5	192.5	192.5	187.5	182.1
1977	187.5	187.5	182.5	182.5	182.5	182.5	182.5	182.5	182.5	182.5	182.5	182.0	183.3
1978	182	178	178	181	184	192	192	192	195	197	202	202	190
1979	202	202	206	220	220	218	218	218	220	230	233	233	218
1980	238	253	256	231	225	233	245	251	253	253	253	253	245
1981	253	268	274	278	278	283	283	283	283	283	283	283	278
1982	275	263	244	240	240	240	240	240	240				
1983													

[1] Raw, shorn, clean basis. *Source: U.S. Dept. of Agriculture*

T.769

Zinc

The total world identified resources of zinc are estimated at nearly 1.8 billion tonnes. According to preliminary data released by the International Lead and Zinc Study Group, the mine production of zinc in non-Communist countries during 1982 increased to 4.697 million tonnes from 4.456 million tonnes in 1981—the highest production since 1977. The three largest producers of mined zinc were Canada, whose output accounted for approximately 19 percent of the 1982 world total, Australia, and Peru. Zinc is mined using underground methods. Tailings and mine water can present disposal problems, but the tailings are often sold as crushed rock or as agricultural limestone.

The largest decline in the consumption of refined zinc in 1982 was recorded in the U.S. Mine production was off because of mine shutdowns, but no strikes were reported in 1982 and the opening of two new zinc mines minimized the production loss relative to that of 1981. By the end of 1982, primary smelters were being operated at about 50 percent of capacity. The production of secondary slab zinc increased slightly. The total U.S. consumption of slab zinc decreased, however, partially due to reductions in the manufacture of automobiles and in residential and commercial construction. The domestic consumption of rolled zinc increased in 1982 because of production of the zinc penny.

U.S. imports of zinc during 1982 decreased as overall demand was reduced. Exports of concentrate from the U.S. increased sharply as a reflection of a greater availability of domestic material and of higher world concentrate prices, particularly in Europe. U.S. stocks of zinc decreased throughout 1982 from 195,354 tonnes to an estimated 138,634 tonnes, a drop of nearly 29 percent, and price discounting from list prices was reportedly widespread throughout the year.

Based on the price of zinc metal, the value of the U.S. 1982 mine production was nearly $255 million. The production of 75,000 tonnes of secondary slab zinc accounted for 10 percent of slab zinc consumption. Nearly 30,000 tonnes of zinc dust and 35,000 tonnes of zinc oxide were produced from scrap zinc. Construction materials accounted for 40 percent of the U.S. zinc consumption in 1982. Transportation equipment accounted for 20 percent; machinery, 12 percent; electrical equipment and chemicals, 15 percent. Galvanizing and zinc-base alloys accounted for a combined 75 percent of the direct zinc consumption. Estimates place the U.S. 1983 mine production of recoverable zinc at 315,000 tonnes and the U.S. apparent consumption at 1 million tonnes. The domestic demand for zinc is expected to increase annually by 1.1 percent through 1990.

Aluminum and magnesium are primary substitutes for zinc in diecasting. Plastic coatings, paints, electroplated cadmium, and special zinc-aluminum coatings can replace zinc to some extent as corrosion protection material, and aluminum alloys can replace brass. Aluminum, magnesium, titanium, and zirconium can be substituted for zinc in the production of chemical and pigments.

"Undiscovered" world zinc resources, including hypothetical and speculative reserves, are estimated to be between 2.5 and 3 billion tonnes.

Futures Market

Zinc futures are traded on the London Metal Exchange (LME).

Salient Statistics of Zinc in the United States — In Thousands of Metric[7] Tons

Year	Net Import Reliance as a % of Apparent Consumption	Production of Slab Zinc — Primary Domestic	Production of Slab Zinc — Primary Foreign	Production of Slab Zinc — Total	Value Mil. $[6]	Redistilled Secondary	Total Production	Dec. 31 Stocks at Producer Plants	Dec. 31 Stocks at Consumer Plants	Gov't. Stockpile	Consumption Zinc Slab	Ores[2]	Base Scrap[2] Zinc[3]	Base Scrap[2] Copper	Aluminum[4]	Total
1970		404.0	473.9	877.8	164	77.2	955.0	124.2	92.7	216.9	1,187.0	124.8	93.5	160.0	6.4	1,572
1971		403.8	362.7	766.4	162	80.9	847.0	48.6	91.5	140.1	1,254.1	119.3	104.0	166.5	6.9	1,651
1972		401.0	232.2	633.2	170	73.7	707.0	30.1	125.0	949.6	1,418.3	118.3	93.0	191.3	7.9	1,844
1973	64	399.1	184.4	583.5	198	83.2	667.0	25.9	114.3	677.0	1,503.9	129.7	90.5	192.0	7.6	1,932
1974	59	347.0	208.2	555.2	359	78.5	634.0	39.7	211.2	391.6	1,287.7	127.1	87.7	162.5	8.0	1,673
1975[7]	61	279.4	118.0	397.4	366	52.5	449.9	67.7	97.3	349.9	839.4	75.1	177.8	106.3	.5	1,117
1976	59	346.4	106.1	452.6	359	62.2	514.7	88.0	109.9	349.4	1,028.9	91.8	138.4	139.2	.5	1,394
1977	57	322.2	86.2	408.4	309	45.9	454.3	83.8	86.5	347.8	999.5	86.5	139.6	139.6	.6	1,368
1978	66	267.4	139.3	406.7	207	34.8	441.5	37.9	99.3	345.5	1,050.6	90.0	73.2	141.5	.5	1,442
1979	63	255.3	217.1	472.5	220	53.2	525.7	59.1	92.6	345.7	1,000.6	79.7	146.7	166.4	.9	1,394
1980	60	231.9	108.6	340.5	262	29.4	369.9	22.6	69.6	342.4	811.1	59.0	133.0	138.2	1.1	1,142
1981[1]	64	256.9	86.7	343.7	307	49.3	393.0	44.7	81.9	340.6	834.2	60.3	149.3	138.7	.7	1,184
1982[5]	53			215			254.3	30.0	62.0		697.4	53.1	69.7	138.4	.8	959.4
1983																

[1] Preliminary. [2] Recoverable zinc content. [3] Excludes redistilled slab & zinc produced by remelting. [4] Aluminum & magnesium-base scrap. [5] Estimate. [6] Domestic ores (recoverable content). [7] Data prior to 1975 are in THOUSANDS OF SHORT TONS. Source: Bureau of Mines
T.770

ZINC

World Smelter Production of Zinc In Thousands of Metric[4] Tons

Year	Australia	Belgium	Canada	France	W. Germany	Italy	Japan	Mexico	Norway	Peru	Poland	Spain	USSR	Un. Kingdom[3]	United States	World Total
1970	287.3	265.9	460.7	246.6	114.3	156.6	745.4	88.9	68.0	75.7	230.4		672.0	161.6	877.8	5,321
1971	285.2	234.5	410.0	241.0	121.7	153.1	789.7	85.8	69.0	63.0	242.5	94.4	717.0	128.4	766.4	5,229
1972	325.2	286.3	524.9	288.3	235.5	171.8	887.7	92.4	80.9	74.0	251.3	109.9	717.0	81.4	633.2	5,656
1973	330.1	309.8	587.0	285.9	283.3	200.6	929.2	78.7	89.2	76.8	259.0	118.0	740.0	92.4	583.5	5,877
1974	305.2	318.3	469.9	305.0	441.0	216.5	936.9	150.9	79.8	78.7	257.0	143.3	750.0	93.0	555.2	6,183
1975	213.1	235.0	470.6	164.9	302.4	198.1	769.7	169.7	67.1	69.7	267.9	147.0	760.0	58.9	438.1	5,526
1976[4]	249.2	241.2	472.3	233.3	304.8	191.2	776.0	175.2	64.4	64.7	237.0	161.1	800.0	41.6	514.7	5,675
1977	256.4	258.2	494.9	238.3	354.8	169.4	805.0	174.4	69.8	66.9	228.0	156.6	815.0	81.5	454.3	5,812
1978	294.8	241.5	495.4	231.2	306.8	177.6	792.7	173.1	71.6	62.9	222.0	177.0	850.0	73.6	441.5	5,884
1979	310.1	265.8	580.4	249.0	355.5	202.8	816.4	161.7	77.8	68.2	209.0	182.7	850.0	76.7	525.7	6,269
1980	306.0	249.2	591.6	252.8	370.6	206.4	785.1	143.9	79.4	63.8	215.3	151.8	865.0	86.7	369.9	6,057
1981[1]	300.9	257.4	618.6	271.8	366.6	180.9	720.1	126.5	80.3	125.0	167.1	184.0	870.0	81.7	393.0	6,140
1982[2]	320		650					130			140				254.0	6,300
1983																

[1] Preliminary. [2] Estimated. [3] Some secondary metal included. [4] Data prior to 1976 are in THOUSANDS OF SHORT TONS. Source: Bureau of Mines T.771

U.S. Mine Production of Recoverable Zinc In Thousands of Metric[3] Tons

Year	Arizona	Colorado	Idaho	Illinois	Missouri	Montana	Pennsylvania	New Mexico	New York	New Jersey	Tennessee	Utah	Virginia	Washington	Wisconsin	Total U.S.
1970	9.6	56.7	41.1	16.8	50.7	1.5	29.6	16.6	58.6	28.7	118.3	34.7	18.1	12.0	20.6	534.1
1971	7.8	61.2	45.1	12.7	48.2	.4	27.4	14.0	63.4	30.0	119.3	25.7	16.8	5.8	10.6	502.5
1972	10.1	63.8	38.6	11.4	61.9	—	18.3	12.7	60.7	38.1	101.7	21.9	16.8	6.5	6.9	478.3
1973	8.4	58.3	46.1	5.3	82.4	.1	18.9	12.3	81.4	38.0	64.2	16.8	16.7	6.4	8.7	478.9
1974	9.7	49.5	39.5	4.1	92.0	.1	20.3	13.8	93.1	32.8	85.7	12.6	17.2	6.9	8.7	499.9
1975[3]	7.9	44.0	37.1	N.A.	67.9	.1	19.1	10.0	69.5	28.2	75.6	17.8	13.7	N.A.	N.A.	425.8
1976	8.6	45.9	42.3	N.A.	75.8	.1	20.2	N.A.	66.8	30.6	74.9	20.4	10.2	N.A.	N.A.	439.5
1977	4.0	36.5	28.1	N.A.	74.1	.1	20.7	N.A.	64.3	30.4	82.0	16.1	12.0	5.1	N.A.	407.9
1978	N.A.	22.2	32.4	N.A.	59.0	.1	19.1	N.A.	26.5	28.9	87.9	3.5	11.0	N.A.	N.A.	302.7
1979	N.A.	9.9	29.7	N.A.	61.7	.1	21.4	N.A.	12.1	31.1	85.0	N.A.	11.4	—	N.A.	267.3
1980	N.A.	13.8	27.7	N.A.	65.2	.1	22.6	N.A.	33.6	28.9	111.8	N.A.	12.0	—	—	317.1
1981[1]	.1	N.A.	N.A.	N.A.	52.9	N.A.	24.7	N.A.	36.9	16.2	117.7	1.6	9.7	—	—	312.4
1982[2]					63.8		24.8				120.7	17.0				303.1
1983																

[1] Preliminary. [2] Estimated. [3] Data prior to 1975 are in THOUSANDS OF SHORT TONS. Source: Bureau of Mines T.772

Consumption of Slab Zinc in the United States, by Industries and Grades In Thousands of Metric[4] Tons

		By Industries							By Grades					
Year	Total	Galvanizers	Brass Products	Zinc-Base Alloy[2]	Rolled Zinc	Oxide Zinc	Light-Metal Alloys	Other	Special High Grade	High Grade	Intermediate	Brass Special	Prime Western	Remelt
1970	1,187.0	474.2	127.7	463.6	41.1	43.8	—36.4—		647.6	126.0	10.0	92.5	309.9	.9
1971	1,254.1	474.8	150.5	516.1	38.9	40.0	—33.8—		683.7	133.1	10.0	102.5	328.0	1.8
1972	1,418.3	518.2	192.1	579.8	45.2	52.0	—31.0—		684.7	147.1	19.0	129.9	397.2	.7
1973	1,503.9	563.8	197.7	598.7	40.8	61.7	—2.93—		739.4	167.5	37.4	132.1	426.6	.9
1974	1,287.7	523.3	181.6	440.3	39.4	65.4	—37.8—		572.9	153.1	26.3	122.1	412.1	1.2
1975[4]	839.4	341.9	104.6	303.2	24.8	35.4	5.3	24.3	397.5	75.7	12.9	71.8	280.9	.7
1976	1,028.9	392.9	150.8	387.4	27.1	35.4	5.2	30.1	500.1	101.1	21.0	94.8	310.7	1.2
1977	999.5	396.4	128.3	367.1	27.4	38.5	5.6	36.1	492.6	91.0	19.7	101.2	293.7	1.2
1978	1,050.6	454.0	141.5	354.1	24.9	37.2	11.0	27.8	491.3	109.7	21.8	98.4	327.7	1.7
1979	1,000.6	452.8	141.4	314.1	22.0	35.5	12.9	21.9	443.1	108.6	22.5	86.8	336.8	2.8
1980	811.1	379.2	98.8	254.2	21.1	27.0	11.1	19.6	354.3	76.2	—88.8—		290.3	1.6
1981[3]	834.2	411.0	113.0	243.4	23.2	19.0	8.2	16.5	361.5	97.6	—98.5—		275.3	1.2
1982[1]	697.4	310.2	73.3	163.9	37.2	17.7	—13.0—							
1983														

[1] Estimated. [2] Die Casters. [3] Preliminary. [4] Data prior to 1975 are in THOUSANDS OF SHORT TONS. Source: Bureau of Mines T.773

ZINC

Zinc Foreign Trade of the United States   In Metric[4] Tons

Year	Ores[1]	Imported for Consumption — Blocks, Pigs, Slabs	Zinc Fume	Waste & Scrap	Dross, & Skimmings	Dust, Powder & Flakes	Total Value Thous. $	Zinc Ore & Manufactures Exported — Blocks, Pigs, Anodes, etc. Unwrought	Unwrought Alloys	Wrought & Alloys Sheets, Plates & Strips	Angles Bars, Rods, etc.	Waste & Scrap	Dust (Blue Powder)	Zinc Ore & Concentrates
1973	154,174	590,751	17,953	1,544	2,328	4,873	304,871	10,574	14,566	2,480	4,503	6,366	666	
1974	133,733	543,806	18,235	2,418	3,863	9,131	479,357	18,865	19,062	3,487	9,591	10,936	1,152	
1975	428,544	374,922	33,327	1,418	3,158	5,739	399,857	2,730	6,897	1,628	11,466	4,448	603	
1976	155,803	695,131	6,927	1,803	12,445	6,009	546,239	1,593	3,513	2,271	7,727	8,171	774	
1977[4]	109,277	503,621	233	9,188	11,739	6,702	411,414	215	899	2,432	4,677	7,445	928	N.A.
1978	106,315	622,470	60	3,310	7,436	8,978	434,376	723	554	2,262	860	14,986	1,803	10,973
1979	87,499	524,130	28	3,259	4,454	3,586	434,677	279	366	1,824	1,451	28,149	966	20,095
1980	182,370	410,163	25	3,470	4,062	3,928	401,134	302	485	2,103	804	29,542	4,512	54,457
1981[2]	245,710	612,007	184	5,782	7,629	7,993	676,299	323	378	1,500	1,160	30,046	5,003	54,232
1982[3]	66,809	456,233	11	2,653	7,104	5,864		341				16,992	2,068	77,288
1983														

[1] Zinc content.   [2] Preliminary.   [3] Estimate.   [4] Data prior to 1977 are in SHORT TONS.   Source: Bureau of Mines   T.774

U.S. Mine Production of Recoverable Zinc   In Thousands of Metric Tons

Year	Jan.	Feb.	Mar.	Apr.	May	June	July	Aug.	Sept.	Oct.	Nov.	Dec.	Total
1980	28.3	26.5	28.2	26.9	25.5	27.1	24.6	25.2	24.1	28.2	24.0	24.5	334.9
1981	24.6	24.8	27.6	25.5	24.8	23.1	23.6	24.6	28.3	28.0	25.4	23.4	312.4
1982	24.2	24.7	25.3	23.4	25.6	27.0	21.3	27.4	25.7	27.8	25.9	23.3	303.1
1983													

Source: Bureau of Mines

U.S. Consumption of Slab Zinc by Fabricators   In Thousands of Metric Tons

Year	Jan.	Feb.	Mar.	Apr.	May	June	July	Aug.	Sept.	Oct.	Nov.	Dec.	Total
1980	80.4	80.3	82.8	74.1	61.0	55.5	46.8	58.2	66.7	74.6	72.3	70.5	811.1
1981	74.5	73.6	77.3	74.3	73.6	77.2	64.4	72.4	70.2	66.2	59.8	52.0	834.2
1982	55.1	55.3	60.0	57.8	58.8	65.8	56.3	60.7	61.4	60.8	53.7	50.8	697.4
1983													

Source: Bureau of Mines

How to keep your Commodity Year Book statistics up-to-date continuously throughout the year.

To keep up-to-date statistics on the commodities in this book, you should have COMMODITY YEAR BOOK STATISTICAL ABSTRACT SERVICE. This three-times-yearly publication provides the latest available statistics for updating the statistical tables appearing in the COMMODITY YEAR BOOK. The ABSTRACT is published in the Winter (Jan.), Spring (Apr.) and Fall (Oct.). Subscription price is $55 per year.

Commodity Research Bureau, Inc.
75 MONTGOMERY ST., JERSEY CITY, N.J. 07302

ZINC

Stocks of Slab Zinc[1] (at Smelter) in the United States, at End of Month — In Thousands of Short Tons

Year	Jan.	Feb.	Mar.	Apr.	May	June	July	Aug.	Sept.	Oct.	Nov.	Dec.
1972	50.5	37.8	29.4	23.4	21.2	21.3	26.7	23.5	28.0	31.2	32.3	31.8
1973	32.7	31.3	30.4	28.1	24.6	22.2	25.1	27.4	32.3	31.6	29.7	29.3
1974	29.8	25.1	22.9	18.8	17.6	19.1	19.6	18.1	20.3	22.3	30.9	42.9
1975	64.4	86.0	108.0	115.7	116.0	108.6	90.5	73.5	61.0	54.0	60.7	67.4
1976	73.4	74.6	67.5	68.0	67.6	69.3	73.0	64.6	59.1	72.6	82.7	88.8
1977	90.5	84.2	58.9	67.9	78.9	77.3	74.9	64.7	59.7	60.3	65.3	65.8
1978	64.3	62.8	56.9	50.0	40.9	32.5	31.8	27.4	30.1	26.9	32.9	38.4
1979	39.9	38.0	37.5	44.5	46.7	45.1	51.8	58.1	57.5	56.3	66.0	61.5
1980	47.5	34.0	31.9	31.4	36.9	42.8	42.1	35.4	30.1	23.4	20.6	20.6
1981	18.4	18.8	20.9	17.6	17.2	17.9	20.9	22.9	21.5	27.0	34.9	38.1
1982	40.4	45.4	46.1	44.0	39.0	30.8	22.6	16.5	17.6	22.0	23.7	27.1
1983	24.2	24.4	21.4	19.8								
1984												

[1] Figures include zinc produced from foreign ores as well as domestic ores. Source: American Bureau of Metal Statistics, Inc. T.777

Smelter Production of Slab Zinc[1] in the United States (Includes GSA Metal) — In Thousands of Short Tons

Year	Jan.	Feb.	Mar.	Apr.	May	June	July	Aug.	Sept.	Oct.	Nov.	Dec.	Total
1973	61.8	56.1	63.1	60.5	59.6	52.6	55.1	55.3	56.9	57.0	54.6	55.3	687.9
1974	50.4	48.8	52.1	47.7	51.5	48.4	49.2	44.7	46.2	49.9	51.5	49.8	590.2
1975	52.1	45.0	45.1	42.7	34.1	29.7	26.9	28.0	32.2	33.5	35.7	40.9	445.9
1976	45.8	45.3	47.2	46.5	47.5	45.3	45.0	39.9	40.6	46.6	41.2	45.1	536.0
1977	45.6	39.6	43.6	42.9	37.2	31.9	26.8	25.4	26.0	34.2	40.0	40.9	434.1
1978	39.2	33.0	30.4	33.5	35.7	34.5	34.5	37.6	37.3	44.2	42.4	42.6	444.8
1979	45.7	46.1	52.9	51.1	49.9	43.0	44.0	42.0	39.8	46.0	43.4	33.5	537.4
1980	30.5	30.6	34.8	32.1	31.9	28.5	20.8	26.7	28.6	31.0	29.9	33.2	358.6
1981	33.4	31.5	34.5	34.1	32.2	30.8	33.0	33.5	29.4	29.8	29.3	25.3	376.8
1982	26.7	23.8	23.6	21.3	23.7	23.7	20.6	22.4	26.5	27.3	20.6	19.9	280.3
1983	20.0	22.8	25.0	24.7									
1984													

[1] Smelter & refinery production from domestic & foreign ores. Source: American Bureau of Metal Statistics, Inc. T.775

Domestic Shipments of Slab Zinc[1] in the United States — In Thousands of Short Tons

Year	Jan.	Feb.	Mar.	Apr.	May	June	July	Aug.	Sept.	Oct.	Nov.	Dec.	Total
1972	67.1	73.5	74.0	68.0	75.5	74.4	63.2	71.4	56.6	65.7	65.0	60.2	814.6
1973	63.6	62.5	67.0	64.8	65.2	58.3	59.2	59.8	55.6	57.8	59.1	53.7	726.5
1974	50.1	57.7	58.3	60.2	63.1	54.0	56.8	55.6	52.0	52.7	45.1	38.3	643.9
1975	30.8	29.6	29.1	36.2	33.8	37.1	44.9	45.0	44.8	40.4	29.0	34.2	421.7
1976	39.8	44.1	54.3	46.0	47.9	43.6	41.2	48.3	46.1	33.0	31.2	39.0	514.6
1977	44.0	45.9	68.9	33.8	26.2	33.5	29.2	35.6	31.0	33.5	35.0	40.4	457.1
1978	40.7	34.5	36.3	40.3	44.8	42.9	35.1	42.0	34.7	47.3	36.4	37.1	472.2
1979	44.2	47.9	53.5	44.1	47.7	44.5	37.4	35.7	40.3	47.3	33.7	37.9	514.3
1980	44.5	44.2	36.8	32.7	26.4	22.6	21.5	33.4	34.0	37.6	32.7	33.3	399.6
1981	35.6	31.1	32.3	37.4	32.6	30.2	30.0	31.5	30.8	24.3	21.4	22.0	359.2
1982	24.4	18.8	22.9	23.4	28.7	31.9	28.7	28.6	25.4	23.0	18.9	16.5	291.3
1983	22.9	22.6	28.0	26.3									
1984													

[1] Does not include export shipments & Gov't. account shipments. Source: American Bureau of Metal Statistics, Inc. T.776

ZINC

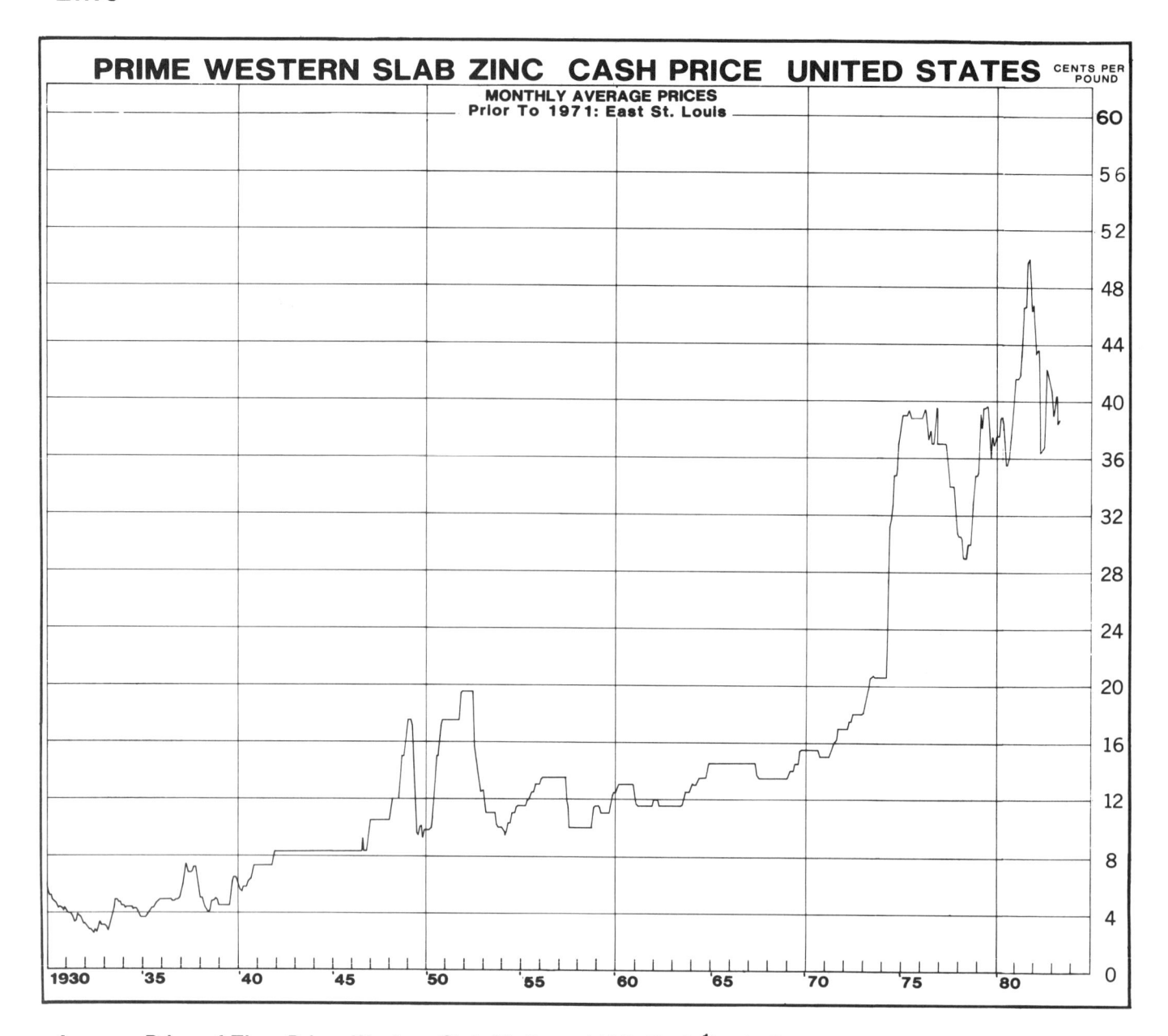

PRIME WESTERN SLAB ZINC CASH PRICE UNITED STATES
MONTHLY AVERAGE PRICES
Prior To 1971: East St. Louis — Cents Per Pound

Average Price of Zinc, Prime Western Slab (Delivered U.S. Basis[1]) In Cents per Pound

Year	Jan.	Feb.	Mar.	Apr.	May	June	July	Aug.	Sept.	Oct.	Nov.	Dec.	Average
1970	15.50	15.50	15.50	15.50	15.50	15.50	15.50	15.33	15.00	15.00	15.00	15.00	15.32
1971[1]	15.00	15.00	15.16	15.50	15.81	16.00	16.21	17.00	17.00	17.00	17.00	17.00	16.14
1972	17.00	17.00	17.26	17.50	17.89	18.00	18.00	18.00	18.00	18.00	18.00	18.09	17.73
1973	18.58	19.25	19.83	20.46	20.63	20.70	20.63	20.63	20.63	20.63	20.63	27.46	20.84
1974	31.18	31.75	32.70	34.75	34.75	35.25	36.97	38.00	38.95	39.00	39.00	39.00	35.94
1975	39.25	39.07	38.75	38.75	38.75	38.75	38.75	38.75	38.75	39.66	38.75	38.75	38.89
1976	37.26	37.00	37.00	37.00	37.00	37.00	37.00	38.75	39.50	37.00	37.00	37.00	37.38
1977	37.00	37.00	37.00	37.00	35.64	34.00	34.00	34.00	34.00	31.74	30.66	30.50	35.21
1978	30.50	30.26	29.00	29.00	29.00	29.95	30.00	31.92	32.75	33.66	34.75	34.75	31.30
1979	35.00	36.90	38.09	39.50	39.50	39.55	39.63	36.82	36.03	37.50	36.88	37.50	37.74
1980	37.50	38.70	38.92	38.50	37.50	36.55	35.50	35.98	37.46	38.48	39.69	41.63	38.03
1981	41.63	41.63	42.13	43.73	46.55	46.63	46.67	49.74	49.88	46.41	46.75	43.65	45.45
1982	43.31	43.56	43.56	36.39	36.64	36.69	38.86	40.00	42.21	42.50	40.80	38.99	39.95
1983	40.20	40.35	38.38	38.73									
1984													

[1] Prior to 1971, prices are for delivered E. St. Louis.   Source: American Metal Market

T.778

Conversion Factors

The following equivalents are among those most commonly used in international agricultural trade:

METRIC EQUIVALENTS

1 hectare	(ha)	equals	2.471	acres
1 liter	(l)	equals	1.0567	liquid quarts
1 kilogram	(kg)	equals	2.204622	pounds
1 tonne	(1,000 kgs)	equals	2,204.622	pounds

1 metric ton equals:
  2204.622 lbs.
  22.046 hundredweight
  10 quintals

Bushel weights:
  Wheat & soybeans = 60 lbs.
  Corn, sorghum & rye = 56 lbs.
  Barley (grain) = 48 lbs.; Barley (malt) = 34 lbs.
  Oats = 32 lbs.; Rapeseed = 50 lbs.

Bushels to metric tons:
  Wheat & soybeans = bushels × .027216
  Barley = bushels × .021772
  Corn, sorghum, rye = bushels × .025400
  Oats = bushels × .014515

One metric ton (tonne) 1,000 kilograms =
  36.7437 bushels wheat or soybeans
  29.3679 bushels corn, sorghum, rye, flaxseed
  45.9296 bushels barley
  68.8944 bushels oats
  44.092 rapeseed
  22.046 cwt. rice

Area:
  1 Acre = .404694 hectares
  1 Hectare = 2.4710 acres

Yields:
  Wheat = bushels per acre × 0.6725 = quintals per hectare
  Rye, corn = bushels per acre × 0.6277 = quintals per hectare
  Barley = bushels per acre × 0.5380 = quintals per hectare
  Oats = bushels per acre × 0.3587 = quintals per hectare

Commodity	Unit	Approximate net Weight U.S. (pounds)	Metric (kilograms)
Apples	Northwest box[1]	44	20
Barley	Bushel	48	21.8
Butter	Box	64	29
Castor Beans	Bushel	41	18.6
Castor Oil	Gallon	8[2]	3.6
Corn (shelled)	Bushel	56	25.4
Corn Oil	Gallon	7.7[2]	3.5
Cotton	Net Bale	480[3]	218
Cottonseed	Bushel	32[4]	14.5
Cottonseed Oil	Gallon	7.7[2]	3.5
Eggs (average size)	Case of 30 dozen	47	21.3
Flaxseed	Bushel	56	25.4
Flour (various)	Bag	100	45.4
Honey	Gallon	11.84	5.4
Linseed Oil	Gallon	7.7[2]	3.5
Milk	Gallon	8.6	3.9
Molasses (inedible)	Gallon	11.74	5.3
Oats	Bushel	32	14.5
Olives	Lug[5]	25–30	11.3–13.6
Olive Oil	Gallon	7.6[2]	3.5
Onions (dry)	Sack	50	22.7
Oranges (Fla. & Tex.)	Box[6]	90	40.8
Palm Oil	Gallon	7.7[2]	3.5
Peanuts (unshelled, Runners, Southeastern)	Bushel	21	9.5
Peanut Oil	Gallon	7.7[2]	3.5
Potatoes	Bag	50	22.7
Rapeseed	Bushel	50 and 60	22.7–27.2
Rice (rough)	Bushel	45	20.4
Rosin	Drum, net	520	236
Rye	Bushel	56	25.4
Sorghum Grain	Bushel	56	25.4
Soybeans	Bushel	60	27.2
Soybean Oil	Gallon	7.7[2]	3.5
Sugarcane: sirup	Gallon	11.45	5.2
Sunflower Seed	Bushel	24 and 32	10.9–14.5
Tobacco (flue-cured)	Hogshead	950	431

[1] Approximate inside dimensions 10½ × 11½ × 18″.
[2] Commonly used in trade. Actual weights vary according to temperature conditions.
[3] Estimated at 478 lbs. prior to 1946. Actual bale weights vary considerably.
[4] Average weight in most states.
[5] Approximate inside dimensions 5¾ × 13½ × 16⅛″.
[6] Approxmiate inside dimensions 12 × 12 × 24″.

TECHNIQUES OF A PROFESSIONAL COMMODITY CHART ANALYST

by Arthur Sklarew

The secrets of how a 30-year "pro" uses price charts (and other simple technical indicators) to trade more profitably.

What a serious student can learn from more than three decades of poring over commodity price charts can be yours in this exciting new book. You'll see just how uncanny are the author's innovative "Rule of Seven" and "17-35" measurements for projecting price moves... find out how *curved* trend channels can be effectively used... learn how to keep and use a simple but unique 5-day net-change oscillator that raises the "caution" flag when a price move is "pooping out."

There are 76 different chart illustrations in the book, which not only include the author's unique formations, but all the classic chart patterns as well. He describes head & shoulders, tops and bottoms, triangles, diamonds, flags, etc., and tells us which formations are most effective based on his practical experience.

This is really more than a book about chart analysis. Mr. Sklarew, unwittingly or not, imparts to the reader some of the intuitive feel he has developed for price-chart action over the past 30 years. That's one reason why it should appeal to the neophyte as well as the experienced chartist. Another reason is the absence of complicated procedures or mathematical formulas. All you need to work Mr. Sklarew's "magic" is a pencil, some chart paper, and the daily prices from the local newspaper. Each concept is fully but simply explained, and there's hardly a page without a price chart, graph, or other helpful illustrative example.

Even if you consider yourself basically a fundamental trader, you should benefit greatly from the skill you will acquire in using simple price-chart analysis to improve the *timing* of your trades. If you are already a died-in-the-wool chartist, you should find this book fascinating.

$18.95 PER COPY
From the publishers

Commodity Research Bureau, Inc.
75 MONTGOMERY ST., JERSEY CITY, N.J. 07302

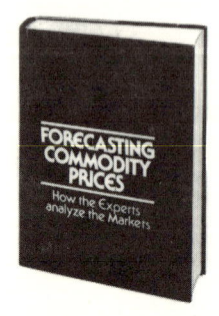

The Priceless Collection of Special Studies for Analyzing Commodity Futures Markets.

FORECASTING COMMODITY PRICES
How the Experts analyze the Markets

• FORECASTING COMMODITY PRICES is a collection of special studies, which identify and evaluate the special market factors that are specifically important for forecasting prices in specific commodity markets. A separate exclusive study, prepared by a highly qualified expert, is devoted to each of 20 different markets.

The authors explain how and why some markets are influenced primarily by changes in the supply outlook while others may be more responsive to changing patterns of demand. Some markets are highly geared to changes in weather. Certain specific commodities are "inflation oriented" and respond quickly to currency fears, while others appear to ignore inflation developments.

For each different commodity study there is a separate collection of price charts showing daily fluctuations in recent years. You can ascertain which markets are prone to follow definite trends—up or down—for weeks or months, and which markets have more random price movements. The charts also will help you identify the seasonal price movements as they occur in different markets, as well as other special price characteristics.

The original versions of the studies appeared in previously published Commodity Year Books. They were selected for this anthology because of their specific value as aids in forecasting prices.

We think this anthology is one of the most important books published by Commodity Research Bureau. The authors are experts; some have spent a lifetime in their respective fields.

$19.95 PER COPY
From the publisher

Commodity Research Bureau, Inc.
75 MONTGOMERY ST., JERSEY CITY, N.J. 07302

Now more than ever...
The Essential "Working Tool" for Commodity Price Projection
Commodity Chart Service

This comprehensive weekly service provides up-to-date price charts plus technical interpretation of chart patterns.

MORE THAN 200 DIFFERENT CHARTS EVERY FRIDAY

HERE'S WHAT YOU GET EVERY WEEK

1. Thorough coverage for every active futures market

a. *Daily Action Futures Prices Charts* — For each actively traded commodity contract you get a separate chart showing daily high, low and close, brought up-to-date after the market closes on Friday (and mailed to you the same day). Each issue contains approximately 240 of these price charts.

b. Charts of 10- and 40 day weighted moving averages and exclusive momentum oscillators for 26 major commodities, to help you identify price trends, trend changes, and comparative market strength and weakness.

c. *Seasonal Open Interest Charted* — Average open interest of previous six-year period is plotted right on the current chart of open interest and volume. Unusual build-ups or declines in open interest can be spotted at a glance (approx. 40 charts).

d. *Cash Prices Charted* — Cash, or "actuals" prices of individual commodities are charted on the same page as the futures contracts, for easy comparison (approx. 20 charts).

2. Chart Interpretation — A full page of technical comment describing significant chart formations as they develop for specific commodities. Other technical factors are also carefully analyzed, such as volume and open interest changes and their effect on future price movements. When appropriate, computer analysis is also discussed.

3. Overseas Markets — Selected charts covering aluminum, cocoa, coffee, copper, gas oil, lead, nickel, rubber, silver, sugar, tin and zinc futures at London. Also includes London spot gold.

4. Commodity Indices — Charts showing the movements of important commodity price indices.

5. Special Commodity Straddle Charts — Charts of price relationships between selected individual commodity futures disclose potentially profitable straddle.

6. Computer Trend Analyzer — An important trend indicator, based on mathematical calculations. Serves as a valuable check on other methods of analysis.

7. Commitments of Traders — Conveniently shows the net long or short positions of the three major market interests. These open interest configurations can often point out the direction of future price moves.

PLUS

Long-Term Charts — Monthly charts, which show futures price movements for 20 years or more in most cases, are sent quarterly.

Weekly Charts — Showing the weekly high, low and close for each commodity (nearest futures). These charts, which cover periods of about 4½ years, are issued approximately every 6 weeks.

Lifetime Ring Binder — Each subscriber gets a durable ring binder for the preservation of his chart collection.

WHY THE SERVICE IS A "MUST" FOR THE COMMODITY TRADES AND SPECULATORS

The rapidly broadening demand for practical charts as "working tools" has been stimulated by repeated demonstrations of their usefulness. Today, most of the important trading interests in commodities utilize various charts, either as visual aids for keeping abreast of the markets, or for forecasting trends, estimating objectives, determination of "stop-loss" points, etc.

For most traders, the maintenance of a complete set of essential charts is very time-consuming and often difficult. As a subscriber of CCS, the charts are continuously available to you for use in your own office or home. You can make your own notations and trend lines and other markings without fear of destroying their value, because each Friday night we send you new charts, brought up-to-date.

SUBSCRIPTION RATES

Subscription rates to COMMODITY CHART SERVICE are: $100 for three months; or $175 for six months; or $295 for a full year. (Postage additional — billed to subscribers at cost.)

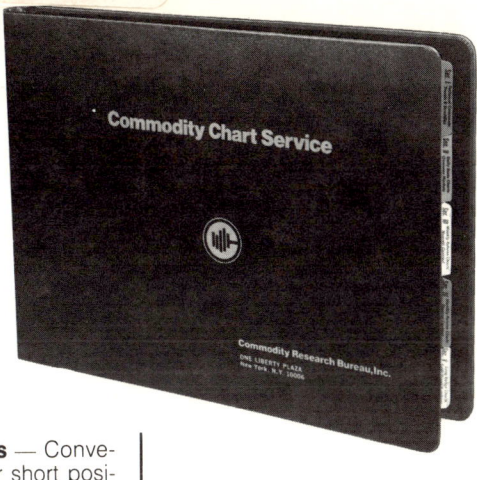

Brochure available on request

Commodity Research Bureau, Inc.
75 Montgomery St., Jersey City, N.J. 07302

FUTURES MARKETS COVERED EACH WEEK

Aluminum	London
Barley	Winnipeg
Cattle (Live)	Chicago
Cattle (Feeder)	Chicago
Certificates of Deposit	Chicago
Cocoa	N.Y., London
Coffee	N.Y., London
Copper	N.Y., London
Corn	Chicago
Cotton	New York
Currencies	Chicago
Eurodollar	Chicago
Flaxseed	Winnipeg
Gasoline	New York, London
Ginnie Maes	Chicago
Gold	N.Y., Chicago
Heating Oil #2	New York
Hogs (Live)	Chicago
Lead	London
Nickel	London
Lumber	Chicago
Oats	Chicago
Orange Juice	New York
Palladium	New York
Platinum	New York
Plywood	Chicago
Pork Bellies	Chicago
Rapeseed	Winnipeg
Rubber	London
Rye	Winnipeg
Silver	Chic., N.Y., London
Soybeans	Chicago
Soybean Meal	Chicago
Soybean Oil	Chicago
Stock Index Futures	N.Y., Chic., K.C.
Sugar "11"	New York
Sugar	London
Tin	London
T-Bills	Chicago
Treasury Bonds	Chicago
Wheat	Chic., K.C., Mpls.
Zinc	London

Now... you can keep your

COMMODITY YEAR BOOK

information up-to-date throughout the year with the

STATISTICAL ABSTRACT SERVICE

As the major commodity reference annual, COMMODITY YEAR BOOK has for many years enjoyed a world-wide reputation as the best single source of needed commodity information. For those who regularly require more frequently updated information, Commodity Research Bureau, Inc. now publishes the COMMODITY YEAR BOOK STATISTICAL ABSTRACT SERVICE.

A three-times-yearly publication, it presents the latest information available to update the wealth of data presented in the *Year Book*. The *Abstract* is compiled and edited by the staff of Commodity Research Bureau, Inc. It is published at end-of-month in the Winter (Jan.), Spring (Apr.) and Fall (Oct.). Each issue consists of three sections.

SECTION I contains approximately 400 statistical tables — updated in each issue — corresponding to the *monthly tables* found in *Commodity Year Book*. Each table shows you the latest statistical data available, plus the data for at least one preceding year. Commodities are listed alphabetically. Within each commodity section, tables are arranged to follow the *Year Book* format.

SECTION II presents all *annual tables* in which there have been significant statistical changes since the publication of *Commodity Year Book*. Each table in this section also shows the most recent statistical data available, plus the data for at least one preceding year. Commodities are listed alphabetically. Within each commodity section, tables are arranged to follow the *Year Book* format.

SECTION III contains charts of cash prices for approximately 35 selected commodities. These charts are plotted on a monthly basis and cover about 10 years of activity. They too, are updated for each issue of the *Abstract*.

The total subscription price for this wealth of factual data, in statistical and chart form, is only $55.00 per year.

Commodity Research Bureau, Inc.
75 MONTGOMERY ST., JERSEY CITY, N.J. 07302